THE
LAW OF
SUCCESS

IN SIXTEEN LESSONS

Teaching, for the First Time in the History of the World, the True Philosophy upon which all Personal Success is Built.

••◖▸◌◂◗••

BY

NAPOLEON HILL

••◖▸◌◂◗••

1969

PUBLISHED BY

SUCCESS UNLIMITED INC.

6355 BROADWAY

CHICAGO, ILLINOIS 60660

SUCCESS UNLIMITED EDITION
SUCCESS UNLIMITED INC.
PUBLISHERS OF PERSONAL DEVELOPMENT MATERIALS
6355 BROADWAY
CHICAGO, ILLINOIS 60660

Printed in the U.S.A.

PREFACE TO THIRD EDITION

In presenting this new Third Edition of the LAW OF SUCCESS philosophy to the world, the publishers may be pardoned a few words of justifiable pride in the good the books are accomplishing. It is always helpful to new readers to derive encouragement and inspiration from what others have achieved, and to know of the causes and progress that have become history in the unfolding of any great movement that has lent itself to the betterment of men and women of the present generation.

As to what others have done, and the place occupied by these lessons in our national life of today, the following from a former President of the United States is weighty: "The business and industrial interests of the country owe Napoleon Hill (author of the LAW OF SUCCESS) a debt of gratitude. His influence is a perfect antidote for radicalism and Bolshevism." And a physician states: "The author has accumulated epoch-making material for the enlightenment of mankind, and I predict the Law of Success course will run into many editions and serve to nourish the minds of remote and unborn posterity. There is nothing else like this course in existence. I know that it will be a priceless treasure to all who will take advantage of its teachings."

The LAW OF SUCCESS lessons in the form in which you now receive them, have come a long way from the first edition in a few small paper pamphlets. Today, greatly enlarged over the first edition, and in handy, durable text-books, the Philosophy has risen to dominant importance in shaping not only the affairs and careers of men of great influence—but has also led to actual change in existing business and social standards.

The LAW OF SUCCESS has "travelled around the world." It has been called for in all parts of the globe. Large quantities of the sets have been taken by executives and business concerns for distribution; there have been inquiries for as high as ten thousand sets at a time. Such results mean but one thing—*the lessons are UNUSUAL.*

So, you are about to start upon the course of reading and instruction which by rights should be called *"THE MAGIC LAWS OF SUCCESS."* No man or woman with an ounce of ambition, can pass through the lessons that follow and not be a changed person. Changed for the better! No one but who will emerge from these absorbing pages with a stronger grasp on his or her future—a surer understanding of what he or she CAN DO and has all along been able to do, but didn't THINK he or she could. You are one of these people and these books are for you.

The volumes are full of priceless secrets, startling truths, unexpected revelations about YOUR POSSI-BILITIES TODAY. Every word sinks deep; the lessons are written in simple, straight-shot, strong, man-to-man language that you can't get away from or misunderstand. There is page upon page of rich surprises for the man or woman who needs help and inspiration—something substantial upon which to build life anew!

And so we deliver the LAW OF SUCCESS Philosophy to you with the sincere hope and belief that both good fortune and boundless benefit will become yours as a result of this study.

THE PUBLISHERS.

TRIBUTES TO "LAW OF SUCCESS"
From Great American Leaders

The publishers feel that you will realize more keenly the enormous value of these lessons—if you first read a few tributes from great leaders in Finance, Science, Invention, and Political Life.

Supreme Court of the United States
Washington, D. C.

MY DEAR MR. HILL: I have now had an opportunity to finish reading your Law of Success textbooks, and I wish to express my appreciation of the splendid work you have done in this philosophy. It would be helpful if every politician in the country would assimilate and apply the 17 principles upon which the Law of Success is based. It contains some very fine material which every leader in every walk of life should understand.

(Former President of the United States.)

WM. H. TAFT
(Former Chief Justice)

Laboratory of
Thomas A. Edison

MY DEAR MR. HILL: Allow me to express my appreciation of the compliment you have paid me in sending me the original manuscript of Law of Success. I can see you have spent a great deal of time and thought in its preparation. Your philosophy is sound and you are to be congratulated for sticking to your work over so long a period of years. Your students . . . will be amply rewarded for their labor.

(The world's greatest inventor)

THOS. A. EDISON

PUBLIC LEDGER
Philadelphia

DEAR MR. HILL: Thank you for your Law of Success. It is great stuff; I shall finish reading it. I would like to reprint that story "What I would do if I had a Million Dollars," in the Business Section of the Public Ledger, if you will give me your permission.

CYRUS H. K. CURTIS
(Publisher of *Saturday Evening Post, Ladies Home Journal*, etc.)

KING OF THE 5 AND 10 CENT STORES

"By applying many of the 17 fundamentals of the Law of Success philosophy we have built a great chain of successful stores. I presume it would be no exaggeration of fact if I said that the Woolworth Building might properly be called a monument to the soundness of these principles."

F. W. WOOLWORTH

A GREAT STEAMSHIP MAGNATE

"I feel greatly indebted for the privilege of reading your Law of Success. If I had had this philosophy fifty years ago, I suppose I could have accomplished all that I have done in less than half the time. I sincerely hope the world will discover and reward you."

ROBERT DOLLAR

FAMOUS AMERICAN LABOR LEADER

"Mastery of the Law of Success philosophy is the equivalent of an insurance policy against failure."

SAMUEL GOMPERS

A FORMER PRESIDENT OF THE UNITED STATES

"May I not congratulate you on your persistence. Any man who devotes that much time . . . must of necessity make discoveries of great value to others. I am deeply impressed by your interpretation of the 'Master Mind' principles which you have so clearly described."

WOODROW WILSON

A MERCHANT PRINCE

"I know that your 17 fundamentals of success are sound because I have been applying them in my business for more than 30 years."

JOHN WANAMAKER

WORLD'S LARGEST MAKER OF CAMERAS

"I know that you are doing a world of good with your Law of Success. I would not care to set a monetary value on this training because it brings to the student qualities which cannot be measured by money, alone."

GEORGE EASTMAN

A NATIONALLY KNOWN BUSINESS CHIEF

"Whatever success I may have attained I owe, entirely, to the application of your 17 fundamental principles of the Law of Success. I believe I have the honor of being your first student."

WM. WRIGLEY, JR.

Dedicated to

ANDREW CARNEGIE

who suggested the writing of the course, and to

HENRY FORD

whose astounding achievements form the foundation for practically all of the Sixteen Lessons of the course, and to

EDWIN C. BARNES

a business associate of Thomas A. Edison, whose close personal friendship over a period of more than fifteen years served to help the author "carry on" in the face of a great variety of adversities and much temporary defeat met with in organizing the course.

W HO said it could not be done? And what great victories has he to his credit which qualify h i m to judge others accurately?

—*Napoleon Hill.*

A PERSONAL STATEMENT BY THE AUTHOR

Some thirty years ago a young clergyman by the name of Gunsaulus announced in the newspapers of Chicago that he would preach a sermon the following Sunday morning entitled:

"WHAT I WOULD DO IF I HAD A MILLION DOLLARS!"

The announcement caught the eye of Philip D. Armour, the wealthy packing-house king, who decided to hear the sermon.

In his sermon Dr. Gunsaulus pictured a great school of technology where young men and young women could be taught how to succeed in life by developing the ability to THINK in practical rather than in theoretical terms; where they would be taught to "learn by doing." "If I had a million dollars," said the young preacher, "I would start such a school."

After the sermon was over Mr. Armour walked down the aisle to the pulpit, introduced himself, and said, "Young man, I believe you could do all you said you could, and if you will come down to my office tomorrow morning I will give you the million dollars you need."

There is always plenty of capital for those who can create practical plans for using it.

That was the beginning of the Armour Institute of Technology, one of the very practical schools of the country. The school was born in the "imagination" of a young man who never would have been heard of outside of the community in which he preached had it not been for the "imagination," plus the capital, of Philip D. Armour.

Every great railroad, and every outstanding financial institution and every mammoth business enterprise, and every great invention, began in the imagination of some one person.

F. W. Woolworth created the Five and Ten Cent

Store Plan in his "imagination" before it became a reality and made him a multimillionaire.

Thomas A. Edison created the talking machine and the moving picture machine and the incandescent electric light bulb and scores of other useful inventions, in his own "imagination," before they became a reality.

During the Chicago fire scores of merchants whose stores went up in smoke stood near the smoldering embers of their former places of business, grieving over their loss. Many of them decided to go away into other cities and start over again. In the group was Marshall Field, who saw, in his own "imagination," the world's greatest retail store, standing on the selfsame spot where his former store had stood, which was then but a ruined mass of smoking timbers. That store became a reality.

Fortunate is the young man or young woman who learns, early in life, to use imagination, and doubly so in this age of greater opportunity.

Imagination is a faculty of the mind which can be cultivated, developed, extended and broadened by use. If this were not true, this course on the Fifteen Laws of Success never would have been created, because it was first conceived in the author's "imagination," from the mere seed of an idea which was sown by a chance remark of the late Andrew Carnegie.

Wherever you are, whoever you are, whatever you may be following as an occupation, there is room for you to make yourself more useful, and in that manner more productive, by developing and using your "imagination."

Success in this world is always a matter of individual effort, yet you will only be deceiving yourself if you believe that you can succeed without the co-operation of other people. Success is a matter of individual effort only to the extent that each person must decide, in his or her own mind, what is wanted. This involves the use of "imagination." From this point on, achiev-

ing success is a matter of skillfully and tactfully inducing others to co-operate.

Before you can secure co-operation from others;
nay, before you have the right to ask for or expect
co-operation from other people, you must first show a
willingness to co-operate with them. For this reason
the eighth lesson of this course, THE HABIT OF DO-
ING MORE THAN PAID FOR, is one which should
have your serious and thoughtful attention. The law
upon which this lesson is based, would, of itself, practically insure success to all who practice it in all they
do.

In the back pages of this Introduction you will observe a Personal Analysis Chart in which ten well
known men have been analyzed for your study and
comparison. Observe this chart carefully and note the
"danger points" which mean failure to those who do
not observe these signals. Of the ten men analyzed
eight are known to be successful, while two may be
considered failures. Study, carefully, the reason why
these two men failed.

Then, study yourself. In the two columns which
have been left blank for that purpose, give yourself a
rating on each of the Fifteen Laws of Success at the
beginning of this course; at the end of the course rate
yourself again and observe the improvements you have
made.

The purpose of the Law of Success course is to enable you to find out how you may become more capable
in your chosen field of work. To this end you will
be analyzed and all of your qualities classified so you
may organize them and make the best possible use of
them.

You may not like the work in which you are now
engaged.

There are two ways of getting out of that work.
One way is to take but little interest in what you are
doing, aiming merely to do enough with which to "get

by." Very soon you will find a way out, because the demand for your services will cease.

The other and better way is by making yourself so useful and efficient in what you are now doing that you will attract the favorable attention of those who have the power to promote you into more responsible work that is more to your liking.

It is your privilege to take your choice as to which way you will proceed.

Again you are reminded of the importance of Lesson Nine of this course, through the aid of which you may avail yourself of this "better way" of promoting yourself.

Thousands of people walked over the great Calumet Copper Mine without discovering it. Just one lone man used his "imagination," dug down into the earth a few feet, investigated, and discovered the richest copper deposit on earth.

You and every other person walk, at one time or another, over your "Calumet Mine." Discovery is a matter of investigation and use of "imagination." This course on the Fifteen Laws of Success may lead the way to your "Calumet," and you may be surprised when you discover that you were standing right over this rich mine, in the work in which you are now engaged. In his lecture on "Acres of Diamonds," Russell Conwell tells us that we need not seek opportunity in the distance; that we may find it right where we stand! THIS IS A TRUTH WELL WORTH REMEMBERING!

NAPOLEON HILL,
Author of the Law of Success.

The Author's Acknowledgment of Help Rendered Him in the Writing of This Course

This course is the result of careful analysis of the life-work of over one hundred men and women who have achieved unusual success in their respective callings.

The author of the course has been more than twenty years in gathering, classifying, testing and organizing the Fifteen Laws upon which the course is based. In his labor he has received valuable assistance either in person or by studying the life-work of the following men:

Henry Ford	Edward Bok
Thomas A. Edison	Cyrus H. K. Curtis
Harvey S. Firestone	George W. Perkins
John D. Rockefeller	Henry L. Doherty
Charles M. Schwab	George S. Parker
Woodrow Wilson	Dr. C. O. Henry
Darwin P. Kingsley	General Rufus A. Ayers
Wm. Wrigley, Jr.	Judge Elbert H. Gary
A. D. Lasker	William Howard Taft
E. A. Filene	Dr. Elmer Gates
James J. Hill	John W. Davis

The Law of Success

Captain George M. Alexander (To whom the author was formerly an assistant)
Hugh Chalmers
Dr. E. W. Strickler
Edwin C. Barnes
Robert L. Taylor (Fiddling Bob)
George Eastman
E. M. Statler
Andrew Carnegie
John Wanamaker
Marshall Field

Samuel Gompers
F. W. Woolworth
Judge Daniel T. Wright (One of the author's law instructors)
Elbert Hubbard
Luther Burbank
O. H. Harriman
John Burroughs
E. H. Harriman
Charles P. Steinmetz
Frank Vanderlip
Theodore Roosevelt
Wm. H. French

Dr. Alexander Graham Bell (To whom the author owes credit for most of Lesson One).

Of the men named, perhaps Henry Ford and Andrew Carnegie should be acknowledged as having contributed most toward the building of this course, for the reason that it was Andrew Carnegie who first suggested the writing of the course and Henry Ford whose life-work supplied much of the material out of which the course was developed.

Some of these men are now deceased, but to those who are still living the author wishes to make here grateful acknowledgment of the service they have rendered, without which this course never could have been written.

The author has studied the majority of these men at close range, in person. With many of them he enjoys, or did enjoy before their death, the privilege of

Acknowledgment

close personal friendship which enabled him to gather from their philosophy facts that would not have been available under other conditions.

The author is grateful for having enjoyed the privilege of enlisting the services of the most powerful men on earth, in the building of the Law of Success course. That privilege has been remuneration enough for the work done, if nothing more were ever received for it.

These men have been the back-bone and the foundation and the skeleton of American business, finance, industry and statesmanship.

The Law of Success course epitomizes the philosophy and the rules of procedure which made each of these men a great power in his chosen field of endeavor. It has been the author's intention to present the course in the plainest and most simple terms available, so it could be mastered by very young men and young women, of the high-school age.

With the exception of the psychological law referred to in Lesson One as the "Master Mind," the author lays no claim to having created anything basically new in this course. What he has done, however, has been to organize old truths and known laws into PRACTICAL, USABLE FORM, where they may be properly interpreted and applied by the workaday man whose needs call for a philosophy of simplicity.

In passing upon the merits of the Law of Success Judge Elbert H. Gary said: "Two outstanding features connected with the philosophy impress me most. One is the simplicity with which it has been presented, and the other is the fact that its soundness is so obvious to all that it will be immediately accepted."

The student of this course is warned against passing

judgment upon it before having read the entire sixteen lessons. This especially applies to this Introduction, in which it has been necessary to include brief reference to subjects of a more or less technical and scientific nature. The reason for this will be obvious after the student has read the entire sixteen lessons.

The student who takes up this course with an open mind, and sees to it that his or her mind remains "open" until the last lesson shall have been read, will be richly rewarded with a broader and more accurate view of life as a whole.

Contents of This Introductory Lesson

1. POWER—what it is and how to create and use it.
2. CO-OPERATION—the psychology of co-operative effort and how to use it constructively.
3. THE MASTER MIND—how it is created through harmony of purpose and effort, between two or more people.
4. HENRY FORD, THOMAS A. EDISON and HARVEY S. FIRESTONE—the secret of their power and wealth.
5. THE "BIG SIX"—how they made the law of the "Master Mind" yield them a profit of more than $25,000,000.00 a year.
6. IMAGINATION—how to stimulate it so that it will create practical plans and new ideas.
7. TELEPATHY—how thought passes from one mind to another through the ether. Every brain both a broadcasting and a receiving station for thought.
8. HOW SALESMEN and PUBLIC SPEAKERS "sense" or "tune in" on the thoughts of their audiences.
9. VIBRATION—described by Dr. Alexander Graham Bell, inventor of the Long Distance Telephone.
10. AIR and ETHER—how they carry vibrations.
11. HOW and WHY ideas "flash" into the mind from unknown sources.

12. HISTORY of the Law of Success Philosophy, covering a period of over twenty-five years of scientific research and experimentation.
13. JUDGE ELBERT H. GARY reads, approves and adopts the Law of Success course.
14. ANDREW CARNEGIE responsible for beginning of Law of Success course.
15. LAW OF SUCCESS TRAINING—helps group of salespeople earn $1,000,000.00.
16. SO-CALLED "SPIRITUALISM" explained.
17. ORGANIZED EFFORT the source of all power.
18. HOW TO ANALYZE yourself.
19. HOW A SMALL FORTUNE was made from an old, worked-out, worthless (?) farm.
20. THERE'S A GOLD MINE in your present occupation if you will follow directions and dig for it.
21. THERE'S PLENTY OF READY CAPITAL for development of any practical idea or plan you may create.
22. SOME REASONS why people fail.
23. WHY HENRY FORD is the most powerful man on earth, and how others may use the principles which give him his power.
24. WHY SOME PEOPLE antagonize others without knowing it.
25. THE EFFECT of sexual contact as a mind stimulant and health builder.
26. WHAT happens in the religious orgy known as the "revival."
27. WHAT we have learned from "Nature's Bible."
28. CHEMISTRY of the mind; how it will make or destroy you.

Introduction

TIME is a Master Worker that heals the wounds of temporary defeat, and equalizes the inequalities and rights the wrongs of the world. There is nothing "Impossible" with time!

THE LAW OF SUCCESS

Lesson One

THE MASTER MIND

"You Can Do It if You Believe You Can!"

THIS is a course on the fundamentals of Success.

Success is very largely a matter of adjusting one's self to the ever-varying and changing environments of life, in a spirit of harmony and poise. Harmony is based upon understanding of the forces constituting one's environment; therefore, this course is in reality a blueprint that may be followed straight to success, because it helps the student to interpret, understand and make the most of these environmental forces of life.

Before you begin reading the Law of Success lessons you should know something of the history of the course. You should know exactly what the course promises to those who follow it until they have assimilated the laws and principles upon which it is based. You should know its limitations as well as its possibilities as an aid in your fight for a place in the world.

From the viewpoint of entertainment the Law of Success course would be a poor second for most any of the monthly periodicals of the "Snappy Story" variety which may be found upon the news stands of today.

The course has been created for the serious-minded person who devotes at least a portion of his or her time to the business of succeeding in life. The author of the Law of Success course has not intended to compete with those who write purely for the purpose of entertaining.

The author's aim, in preparing this course, has been of a two-fold nature, namely, first—to help the earnest student find out what are his or her weaknesses, and, secondly—to help create a DEFINITE PLAN for bridging those weaknesses.

The most successful men and women on earth have had to correct certain weak spots in their personalities before they began to succeed. The most outstanding of these weaknesses which stand between men and women and success are INTOLERANCE, CU-PIDITY, GREED, JEALOUSY, SUSPICION, RE-VENGE, EGOTISM, CONCEIT, THE TENDENCY TO REAP WHERE THEY HAVE NOT SOWN, and the HABIT OF SPENDING MORE THAN THEY EARN.

All of these common enemies of mankind, and many more not here mentioned, are covered by the Law of Success course in such a manner that any person of reasonable intelligence may master them with but little effort or inconvenience.

You should know, at the very outset, that the Law of Success course has long since passed through the experimental state; that it already has to its credit a record of achievement that is worthy of serious thought and analysis. You should know, also, that the Law of Success course has been examined and endorsed by some of the most practical minds of this generation.

The Law of Success course was first used as a lecture, and was delivered by its author in practically every city and in many of the smaller localities, throughout the United States, over a period of more than seven years. Perhaps you were one of the many hundreds of thousands of people who heard this lecture.

During these lectures the author had assistants located in the audiences for the purpose of interpreting the reaction of those who heard the lecture, and in this manner he learned exactly what effect it had upon people. As a result of this study and analysis many changes were made.

The first big victory was gained for the Law of Success philosophy when it was used by the author as the basis of a course with which 3,000 men and women were trained as a sales army. The majority of these people were without previous experience, of any sort, in the field of selling. Through this training they were enabled to earn more than One Million Dollars ($1,000,000.00) for themselves and paid the author $30,000.00 for his services, covering a period of approximately six months.

The individuals and small groups of salespeople who have found success through the aid of this course are too numerous to be mentioned in this Introduction, but the number is large and the benefits they derived from the course were definite.

The Law of Success philosophy was brought to the

attention of the late Don R. Mellett, former publisher
of the Canton (Ohio) Daily News, who formed a partnership with the author of the course and was preparing to resign as publisher of the Canton Daily
News and take up the business management of the
author's affairs when he was assassinated on July
16, 1926.

Prior to his death Mr. Mellett had made arrangements with Judge Elbert H. Gary, who was then
Chairman of the Board of the United States Steel
Corporation, to present the Law of Success course to
every employee of the Steel Corporation, at a total
cost of something like $150,000.00. This plan was
halted because of Judge Gary's death, but it proves
that the author of the Law of Success has produced
an educational plan of an enduring nature. Judge
Gary was eminently prepared to judge the value of
such a course, and the fact that he analyzed the Law
of Success philosophy and was preparing to invest the
huge sum of $150,000.00 in it is proof of the sound-
ness of all that is said in behalf of the course.

You will observe, in this General Introduction to
the course, a few technical terms which may not be
plain to you. Do not allow this to bother you. Make
no attempt at first reading to understand these terms.
They will be plain to you after you read the remainder
of the course. This entire Introduction is intended
only as a background for the other fifteen lessons
of the course, and you should read it as such. You
will not be examined on this Introduction, but you
should read it many times, as you will get from it
at each reading a thought or an idea which you did
not get on previous readings.

In this Introduction you will find a description of a newly discovered law of psychology which is the very foundation stone of all outstanding personal achievements. This law has been referred to by the author as the "Master Mind," meaning a mind that is developed through the harmonious co-operation of two or more people who ally themselves for the purpose of accomplishing any given task.

If you are engaged in the business of selling you may profitably experiment with this law of the "Master Mind" in your daily work. It has been found that a group of six or seven salespeople may use the law so effectively that their sales may be increased to unbelievable proportions.

Life Insurance is supposed to be the hardest thing on earth to sell. This ought not to be true, with an established necessity such as life insurance, but it is. Despite this fact, a small group of men working for the Prudential Life Insurance Company, whose sales are mostly small policies, formed a little friendly group for the purpose of experimenting with the law of the "Master Mind," with the result that every man in the group wrote more insurance during the first three months of the experiment than he had ever written in an entire year before.

What may be accomplished through the aid of this principle, by any small group of intelligent life-insurance salesmen who have learned how to apply the law of the "Master Mind" will stagger the imagination of the most highly optimistic and imaginative person.

The same may be said of other groups of salespeople who are engaged in selling merchandise and other

No MAN HAS A
CHANCE TO EN-
JOY PERMANENT
SUCCESS UNTIL HE
BEGINS TO LOOK IN
A MIRROR FOR THE
REAL CAUSE OF
ALL HIS MISTAKES.
—*Napoleon Hill.*

more tangible forms of service than life insurance. Bear this in mind as you read this Introduction to the Law of Success course and it is not unreasonable to expect that this Introduction, alone, may give you sufficient understanding of the law to change the entire course of your life.

It is the personalities back of a business which determine the measure of success the business will enjoy. Modify those personalities so they are more pleasing and more attractive to the patrons of the business and the business will thrive. In any of the great cities of the United States one may purchase merchandise of similar nature and price in scores of stores, yet you will find there is always one outstanding store which does more business than any of the others, and the reason for this is that back of that store is a man, or men, who has attended to the personalities of those who come in contact with the public. People buy personalities as much as merchandise, and it is a question if they are not influenced more by the personalities with which they come in contact than they are by the merchandise.

Life insurance has been reduced to such a scientific basis that the cost of insurance does not vary to any great extent, regardless of the company from which one purchases it, yet out of the hundreds of life insurance companies doing business less than a dozen companies do the bulk of the business of the United States.

Why? Personalities! Ninety-nine people out of every hundred who purchase life insurance policies do not know what is in their policies and, what seems more startling, do not seem to care. What they really purchase is the pleasing personality of some man or woman who knows the value of cultivating such a personality.

Your business in life, or at least the most important part of it, is to achieve success. Success, within the meaning of that term as covered by this course on the Fifteen Laws of Success, is "the attainment of your Definite Chief Aim without violating the rights of other people." Regardless of what your major aim in life may be, you will attain it with much less difficulty after you learn how to cultivate a pleasing personality and after you have learned the delicate art of allying yourself with others in a given undertaking without friction or envy.

One of the greatest problems of life, if not, in fact, the greatest, is that of learning the art of harmonious negotiation with others. This course was created for the purpose of teaching people how to negotiate their way through life with harmony and poise, free from the destructive effects of disagreement and friction which bring millions of people to misery, want and failure every year.

With this statement of the purpose of the course you should be able to approach the lessons with the feeling that a complete transformation is about to take place in your personality.

You cannot enjoy outstanding success in life without power, and *you can never enjoy power without sufficient personality to influence other people to co-operate with you in a spirit of harmony.* This course shows you step by step how to develop such a personality.

Lesson by lesson, the following is a statement of

that which you may expect to receive from the Fifteen Laws of Success:

I. A DEFINITE CHIEF AIM will teach you how to save the wasted effort which the majority of people expend in trying to find their life-work. This lesson will show you how to do away forever with aimlessness and fix your heart and hand upon some definite, well conceived purpose as a life-work.

II. SELF-CONFIDENCE will help you master the six basic fears with which every person is cursed—the fear of Poverty, the fear of Ill Health, the fear of Old Age, the fear of Criticism, the fear of Loss of Love of Someone and the fear of Death. It will teach you the difference between egotism and real self-confidence which is based upon definite, usable knowledge.

III. HABIT OF SAVING will teach you how to distribute your income systematically so that a definite percentage of it will steadily accumulate, thus forming one of the greatest known sources of personal power. No one may succeed in life without saving money. There is no exception to this rule, and no one may escape it.

IV. INITIATIVE AND LEADERSHIP will show you how to become a leader instead of a follower in your chosen field of endeavor. It will develop in you the instinct for leadership which will cause you gradually to gravitate to the top in all undertakings in which you participate.

V. IMAGINATION will stimulate your mind so that you will conceive new ideas and develop new plans which will help you in attaining the object of your Definite Chief Aim. This lesson will teach you how to "build new houses out of old stones," so to speak. It will show you how to create new ideas out of old, well known concepts, and how to put old ideas to *new uses*. This one lesson, alone, is the equivalent of a very practical course in salesmanship, and it is sure to prove a veritable gold mine of knowledge to the person who is in earnest.

VI. ENTHUSIASM will enable you to "saturate" all with whom you come in contact with interest in you and in your ideas. Enthusiasm is the foundation of a Pleasing Personality, and you must have such a personality in order to influence others to co-operate with you.

VII. SELF-CONTROL is the "balance wheel" with which you control your enthusiasm and direct it where you wish it to carry you. This lesson will teach you, in a most practical manner, to become "the master of your fate, the Captain of your Soul."

VIII. THE HABIT OF DOING MORE THAN PAID FOR is one of the most important lessons of the Law of Success course. It will teach you how to take advantage of the Law of Increasing Returns, which will eventually insure you a return in money far out of proportion to the service you render. No one may become a real leader in any walk of life without practicing the habit of doing more work and better work than that for which he is paid.

IX. PLEASING PERSONALITY is the "fulcrum" on which you must place the "crow-bar" of your efforts, and when so placed, with intelligence, it will enable you to remove mountains of obstacles. This one lesson, alone, has made scores of Master Salesmen. It has developed leaders over night. It will teach you how to transform your personality so that you may adapt yourself to any environment, or to any other personality, in such a manner that you may easily dominate.

X. ACCURATE THINKING is one of the important foundation stones of all enduring success. This lesson teaches you how to separate "facts" from mere "information." It teaches you how to organize known facts into two classes: the "important" and the "unimportant." It teaches you how to determine what is an "important" fact. It teaches you how to build definite working plans, in the pursuit of any calling, out of FACTS.

XI. CONCENTRATION teaches you how to focus your attention upon one subject at a time until you have worked out practical plans for mastering that subject. It will teach you how to ally yourself with others in such a manner that you may have the use of their entire knowledge to back you up in your own plans and purposes. It will give you a practical working knowledge of the forces around you, and show you how to

If you must slander someone don't speak it—but write it—write it in the sand, near the water's edge!

—*Napoleon Hill.*

harness and use these forces in furthering your
own interests.

XII. CO-OPERATION will teach you the value of
team-work in all you do. In this lesson you
will be taught how to apply the law of the
"Master Mind" described in this Introduction
and in Lesson Two of this course. This lesson
will show you how to co-ordinate your own efforts with those of others, in such a manner that
friction, jealousy, strife, envy and cupidity will
be eliminated. You will learn how to make use
of all that other people have learned about the
work in which you are engaged.

XIII. PROFITING BY FAILURE will teach you
how to make stepping stones out of all of your
past and future mistakes and failures. It will
teach you the difference between "failure" and
"temporary defeat," a difference which is very
great and very important. It will teach you
how to profit by your own failures and by the
failures of other people.

XIV. TOLERANCE will teach you how to avoid the
disastrous effects of racial and religious prejudices which mean defeat for millions of people
who permit themselves to become entangled in
foolish argument over these subjects, thereby
poisoning their own minds and closing the door,
to reason and investigation. This lesson is
the twin sister of the one on ACCURATE
THOUGHT, for the reason that no one may
become an Accurate Thinker without practicing
tolerance. Intolerance closes the book of
Knowledge and writes on the cover, "Finis!

I have learned it all!" Intolerance makes enemies of those who should be friends. It
destroys opportunity and fills the mind with
doubt, mistrust and prejudice.

XV. PRACTICING THE GOLDEN RULE will
teach you how to make use of this great universal law of human conduct in such a manner
that you may easily get harmonious co-operation from any individual or group of individuals. Lack of understanding of the law upon
which the Golden Rule philosophy is based is
one of the major causes of failure of millions
of people who remain in misery, poverty and
want all their lives. This lesson has nothing
whatsoever to do with religion in any form,
nor with sectarianism, nor have any of the other
lessons of this course on the Law of Success.

When you have mastered these Fifteen Laws and
made them your own, as you may do within a period
of from fifteen to thirty weeks, you will be ready to
develop sufficient personal power to insure the attainment of your Definite Chief Aim.

The purpose of these Fifteen Laws is to develop
or help you organize all the knowledge you have, and
all you acquire in the future, so you may turn this
knowledge into POWER.

You should read the Law of Success course with a
note-book by your side, for you will observe that ideas
will begin to "flash" into your mind as you read, as
to ways and means of using these laws in advancing
your own interests.

You should also begin teaching these laws to those

in whom you are most interested, as it is a well known fact that the more one tries to teach a subject the more he learns about that subject. A man who has a family of young boys and girls may so indelibly fix these Fifteen Laws of Success in their minds that this teaching will change the entire course of their lives. The man with a family should interest his wife in studying this course with him, for reasons which will be plain before you complete reading this Introduction.

POWER is one of the three basic objects of human endeavor.

POWER is of two classes—that which is developed through co-ordination of natural physical laws, and that which is developed by organizing and classifying KNOWLEDGE.

POWER growing out of organized knowledge is the more important because it places in man's possession a tool with which he may transform, redirect and to some extent harness and use the other form of power.

The object of this reading course is to mark the route by which the student may safely travel in gathering such facts as he may wish to weave into his fabric of KNOWLEDGE.

There are two major methods of gathering knowledge, namely, by studying, classifying and assimilating facts which have been organized by other people, and through one's own process of gathering, organizing and classifying facts, generally called "personal experience."

This lesson deals mainly with the ways and means of studying the facts and data gathered and classified by other people.

.   .   .   .

The state of advancement known as "civilization" is but the measure of knowledge which the race has accumulated. This knowledge is of two classes— mental and physical.

Among the useful knowledge organized by man, he has discovered and catalogued the eighty-odd physical elements of which all material forms in the universe consist.

By study and analysis and accurate measurements man has discovered the "bigness" of the material side of the universe as represented by planets, suns and stars, some of which are known to be over ten million times as large as the little earth on which he lives.

On the other hand, man has discovered the "little-ness" of the physical forms which constitute the universe by reducing the eighty-odd physical elements to molecules, atoms, and, finally, to the smallest particle, the electron. An electron cannot be seen; it is but a center of force consisting of a positive or a negative. The electron is the beginning of everything of a physical nature.

MOLECULES, ATOMS AND ELECTRONS: To understand both the detail and the perspective of the process through which knowledge is gathered, organized and classified, it seems essential for the student to begin with the smallest and simplest particles of physical matter, because these are the A B C's with which Nature has constructed the entire frame-work of the physical portion of the universe.

The molecule consists of atoms, which are said to be little invisible particles of matter revolving continuously with the speed of lightning, on exactly the same principle that the earth revolves around the sun.

These little particles of matter known as atoms, which revolve in one continuous circuit, in the molecule, are said to be made up of electrons, the smallest particles of physical matter. As already stated, the electron is nothing but two forms of force. The electron is uniform, of but one class, size and nature; thus in a grain of sand or a drop of water the entire principle upon which the whole universe operates is duplicated.

How marvelous! How stupendous! You may gather some slight idea of the magnitude of it all the next time you eat a meal, by remembering that every article of food you eat, the plate on which you eat it, the tableware and the table itself are, in final analysis, but a collection of ELECTRONS.

In the world of physical matter, whether one is looking at the largest star that floats through the heavens or the smallest grain of sand to be found on earth, the object under observation is but an organized collection of molecules, atoms and electrons revolving around one another at inconceivable speed.

Every particle of physical matter is in a continuous state of highly agitated motion. Nothing is ever still, although nearly all physical matter may appear, to the physical eye, to be motionless. There is no "solid" physical matter. The hardest piece of steel is but an organized mass of revolving molecules, atoms and electrons. Moreover, the electrons in a piece of steel are of the same nature, and move at the same rate of speed as the electrons in gold, silver, brass or pewter.

The eighty-odd forms of physical matter appear to be different from one another, and they are different,

Don't be afraid of a little opposition. Remember that the "Kite" of Success generally rises AGAINST the wind of Adversity—not with it!

because they are made up of different combinations of atoms (although the electrons in these atoms are always the same, except that some electrons are positive and some are negative, meaning that some carry a positive charge of electrification while others carry a negative charge).

Through the science of chemistry, matter may be broken up into atoms which are, within themselves, unchangeable. The eighty-odd elements are created through and by reason of combining and changing of the positions of the atoms. To illustrate the modus operandi of chemistry through which this change of atomic position is wrought, in terms of modern science:

"Add four electrons (two positive and two negative) to the hydrogen atom, and you have the element lithium; knock out of the lithium atom (composed of three positive and three negative electrons) one positive and one negative electron, and you have one atom of helium (composed of two positive and two negative electrons)."

Thus it may be seen that the eighty-odd physical elements of the universe differ from one another only in the number of electrons composing their atoms, and the number and arrangement of those atoms in the molecules of each element.

As an illustration, an atom of mercury contains eighty positive charges (electrons) in its nucleus, and eighty negative outlying charges (electrons). If the chemist were to expel two of its positive electrons it would instantly become the metal known as platinum. If the chemist could then go a step further and take from it a negative ("planetary") electron, the mercury atom would then have lost two positive electrons and one negative; that is, one positive charge on the whole; hence it would retain seventy-nine positive charges in the nucleus and seventy-nine outlying negative electrons, thereby becoming GOLD!

The formula through which this electronic change might be produced has been the object of diligent search by the alchemists all down the ages, and by the modern chemists of today.

It is a fact known to every chemist that literally tens of thousands of synthetic substances may be composed out of only four kinds of atoms, viz.: hydrogen, oxygen, nitrogen and carbon.

"Differences in the number of electrons in atoms confer upon them qualitative (chemical) differences, though all atoms of any one element are chemically alike. Differences in the number and spacial arrangement of these atoms (in groups of molecules) constitute both physical and chemical differences in substances, *i.e.*, in compounds. Quite different substances are produced by combinations of precisely the same kinds of atoms, but in different proportions.

"Take from a molecule of certain substances one single atom, and they may be changed from a compound necessary to life and growth into a deadly poison. Phosphorus is an element, and thus contains but one kind of atoms; but some phosphorus is yellow and some is red, varying with the spacial distribution of the atoms in the molecules composing the phosphorus."

It may be stated as a literal truth that the atom is the universal particle with which Nature builds all material forms, from a grain of sand to the largest star that floats through space. The atom is Nature's "building block" out of which she erects an oak tree or a pine, a rock of sandstone or granite, a mouse or an elephant.

Some of the ablest thinkers have reasoned that the earth on which we live, and every material particle on the earth, began with two atoms which attached themselves to each other, and through hundreds of millions of years of flight through space, kept contacting and accumulating other atoms until, step by step, the earth was formed. This, they point out, would account for the various and differing strata of the earth's substances, such as the coal beds, the iron ore deposits, the gold and silver deposits, the copper deposits, etc.

They reason that, as the earth whirled through space, it contacted groups of various kinds of nebulæ, or atoms, which it promptly appropriated, through the law of magnetic attraction. There is much to be seen, in the earth's surface composition, to support this theory, although there may be no positive evidence of its soundness.

These facts concerning the smallest analyzable particles of matter have been briefly referred to as a starting point from which we shall undertake to ascertain how to develop and apply the law of POWER.

It has been noticed that all matter is in a constant state of vibration or motion; that the molecule is made up of rapidly moving particles called atoms, which, in turn, are made up of rapidly moving particles called electrons.

THE VIBRATING FLUID OF MATTER: In every particle of matter there is an invisible "fluid" or force which causes the atoms to circle around one an-other at an inconceivable rate of speed.

This "fluid" is a form of energy which has never been analyzed. Thus far it has baffled the entire scientific world. By many scientists it is believed to be the same energy as that which we call electricity. Others prefer to call it vibration. It is believed by some investigators that the rate of speed with which this force (call it whatever you will) moves deter-mines to a large extent the nature of the outward visible appearance of the physical objects of the universe.

One rate of vibration of this "fluid energy" causes what is known as sound. The human ear can detect only the sound which is produced through from 32,000 to 38,000 vibrations per second.

As the rate of vibrations per second increases above that which we call sound they begin to manifest them-selves in the form of heat. Heat begins with about 1,500,000 vibrations per second.

Still higher up the scale vibrations begin to register in the form of light. 3,000,000 vibrations per second create violet light. Above this number vibration sheds ultra-violet rays (which are invisible to the naked eye) and other invisible radiations.

And, still higher up the scale—just how high no one at present seems to know—vibrations create the power with which man THINKS.

It is the belief of the author that the "fluid" portion of all vibration, out of which grow all known forms of energy, is universal in nature; that the "fluid" portion of sound is the same as the "fluid" portion of light, the difference in effect between sound and light being only a difference in rate of vibration, also that the "fluid" portion of thought is exactly the same as that in sound, heat and light, excepting the number of vibrations per second.

Just as there is but one form of physical matter, of which the earth and all the other planets—suns and stars—are composed—the electron—so is there but one form of "fluid" energy, which causes all matter to remain in a constant state of rapid motion.

AIR AND ETHER: The vast space between the suns, moons, stars and other planets of the universe is filled with a form of energy known as ether. It is this author's belief that the "fluid" energy which keeps all particles of matter in motion is the same as the universal "fluid" known as ether which fills all the space of the universe. Within a certain distance of the earth's surface, estimated by some to be about fifty miles, there exists what is called air, which is a gaseous substance composed of oxygen and nitrogen. Air is a conductor of sound vibrations, but a non-conductor of light and the higher vibrations, which are carried by the ether. The ether is a conductor of all vibrations from sound to thought.

Air is a localized substance which performs, in the main, the service of feeding all animal and plant life with oxygen and nitrogen, without which neither could exist. Nitrogen is one of the chief necessities of plant life and oxygen one of the mainstays of animal life. Near the top of very high mountains the air becomes very light, because it contains but little nitrogen, which is the reason why plant life cannot exist there. On the other hand, the "light" air found in high altitudes

Render more service than that for which you are paid and you will soon be paid for more than you render. The law of "Increasing Returns" takes care of this.

consists largely of oxygen, which is the chief reason why tubercular patients are sent to high altitudes.

. . . .

Even this brief statement concerning molecules, atoms, electrons, air, ether and the like, may be heavy reading to the student, but, as will be seen shortly, this introduction plays an essential part as the founda- tion of this lesson.

Do not become discouraged if the description of this foundation appears to have none of the thrilling ef- fects of a modern tale of fiction. You are seriously engaged in finding out what are your available powers and how to organize and apply these powers. To complete this discovery successfully you must combine determination, persistency and a well defined DESIRE to gather and organize knowledge.

. . . .

The late Dr. Alexander Graham Bell, inventor of the long distance telephone and one of the accepted authorities on the subject of vibration, is here intro- duced in support of this author's theories concerning the subject of vibration:

"Suppose you have the power to make an iron rod vibrate with any desired frequency in a dark room. At first, when vibrating slowly, its movement will be indicated by only one sense, that of touch. As soon as the vibrations increase, a low sound will emanate from it and it will appeal to two senses.

"At about 32,000 vibrations to the second the sound will be loud and shrill, but at 40,000 vibrations it will be silent and the movements of the rod will not be perceived by touch. Its movements will be perceived by no ordinary human sense.

"From this point up to about 1,500,000 vibrations per second, we have no sense that can appreciate any effect of the intervening vibrations. After that stage is reached, movement is indicated first by the sense of temperature and then, when the rod becomes red hot, by the sense of sight. At 3,000,000 it sheds violet light. Above that it sheds ultra-violet rays and other invisible radiations, some of which can be perceived by instruments and employed by us.

"Now it has occurred to me that there must be a great deal to be learned about the effect of those vibrations in the great gap where the ordinary human senses are unable to hear, see or feel the movement. The power to send wireless messages by ether vibrations lies in that gap, but the gap is so great that it seems there must be much more. You must make machines practically to supply new senses, as the wireless instruments do.

"Can it be said, when you think of that great gap, that there are not many forms of vibrations that may give us results as wonderful as, or even more wonderful than, the wireless waves? It seems to me that in this gap lie the vibrations which we have assumed to be given off by our brains and nerve cells when we think. But then, again, they may be higher up, in the scale beyond the vibrations that produce the ultra-violet rays. [AUTHOR'S NOTE: The last sentence suggests the theory held by this author.]

"Do we need a wire to carry these vibrations? Will they not pass through the ether without a wire, just as the wireless waves do? How will they be perceived by the recipient? Will he hear a series of signals or will he find that another man's thoughts have entered into his brain?

"We may indulge in some speculations based on what we know of the wireless waves, which, as I have said, are all we can recognize of a vast series of vibrations which theoretically must exist. If the thought waves are similar to the wireless waves, they must pass from the brain and flow endlessly around the world and the universe. The body and the skull and other solid obstacles would form no obstruction to their passage, as they pass through the ether which surrounds the molecules of every substance, no matter how solid and dense.

"You ask if there would not be constant interference and confusion if other people's thoughts were flowing through our brains and setting up thoughts in them that did not originate with ourselves?

"How do you know that other men's thoughts are not interfering with yours now? I have noticed a good many phenomena of mind disturbances that I have never been able to explain. For instance, there is the inspiration or the discouragement that a speaker feels in addressing an audience. I have experienced this many times in my life and have never been able to define exactly the physical causes of it.

"Many recent scientific discoveries, in my opinion, point to a day not far distant perhaps, when men will read one another's thoughts, when thoughts will be conveyed directly from brain to brain without intervention of speech, writing or any of the present known methods of communication.

"It is not unreasonable to look forward to a time

when we shall see without eyes, hear without ears and talk without tongues.

"Briefly, the hypothesis that mind can communicate directly with mind rests on the theory that thought or vital force is a form of electrical disturbance, that it can be taken up by induction and transmitted to a distance either through a wire or simply through the all-pervading ether, as in the case of wireless telegraph waves.

"There are many analogies which suggest that thought is of the nature of an electrical disturbance. A nerve, which is of the same substance as the brain, is an excellent conductor of the electric current. When we first passed an electrical current through the nerves of a dead man we were shocked and amazed to see him sit up and move. The electrified nerves produced contraction of the muscles very much as in life.

"The nerves appear to act upon the muscles very much as the electric current acts upon an electromagnet. The current magnetizes a bar of iron placed at right angles to it, and the nerves produce, through the intangible current of vital force that flows through them, contraction of the muscular fibers that are arranged at right angles to them.

"It would be possible to cite many reasons why thought and vital force may be regarded as of the same nature as electricity. The electric current is held to be a wave motion of the ether, the hypothetical substance that fills all space and pervades all substances. We believe that there must be ether because without it the electric current could not pass through a vacuum, or sunlight through space. It is reasonable to believe that only a wave motion of a similar character can produce the phenomena of thought and vital force. We may assume that the brain cells act as a battery and that the current produced flows along the nerves.

"But does it end there? Does it not pass out of the body in waves which flow around the world unperceived by our senses, just as the wireless waves passed unperceived before Hertz and others discovered their existence?"

EVERY MIND BOTH A BROADCASTING AND A RECEIVING STATION: This author has proved, times too numerous to enumerate, to his own satisfaction at least, that every human brain is both a broadcasting and a receiving station for vibrations of thought frequency.

If this theory should turn out to be a fact, and methods of reasonable control should be established, imagine the part it would play in the gathering, classifying and organizing of knowledge. The possibility, much less the probability, of such a reality, staggers the mind of man!

Thomas Paine was one of the great minds of the American Revolutionary Period. To him more, perhaps, than to any other one person, we owe both the beginning and the happy ending of the Revolution, for it was his keen mind that both helped in drawing up the Declaration of Independence and in persuading the signers of that document to translate it into terms of reality.

In speaking of the source of his great storehouse of knowledge, Paine thus described it:

"Any person, who has made observations on the

Every failure is a bless-
ing in disguise, providing
it teaches some needed
lesson one could not have
learned without it. Most
so-called Failures a r e
only temporary defeats.

state of progress of the human mind, by observing his own, cannot but have observed that there are two distinct classes of what are called Thoughts: those that we produce in ourselves by reflection and the act of thinking, and those that bolt into the mind of their own accord. I have always made it a rule to treat these voluntary visitors with civility, taking care to examine, as well as I was able, if they were worth entertaining; and it is from them I have acquired almost all the knowledge that I have. As to the learning that any person gains from school education, it serves only like a small capital, to put him in the way of beginning learning for himself afterwards. Every person of learning is finally his own teacher, the reason for which is, that principles cannot be impressed upon the memory; their place of mental residence is the understanding, and they are never so lasting as when they begin by conception."

In the foregoing words Paine, the great American patriot and philosopher, described an experience which at one time or another is the experience of every person. Who is there so unfortunate as not to have received positive evidence that thoughts and even complete ideas will "pop" into the mind from outside sources?

What means of conveyance is there for such visitors except the ether? Ether fills the boundless space of the universe. It is the medium of conveyance for all known forms of vibration such as sound, light and heat. Why should it not be, also, the medium of conveyance of the vibration of Thought?

Every mind, or brain, is directly connected with every other brain by means of the ether. Every thought released by any brain may be instantly picked up and interpreted by all other brains that are "en rapport" with the sending brain. This author is as sure of this fact as he is that the chemical formula H_2O will produce water. Imagine, if you can, what a part this principle plays in every walk of life.

Nor is the probability of ether being a conveyor of thought from mind to mind the most astounding of its performances. It is the belief of this author that every thought vibration released by any brain is picked up by the ether and kept in motion in circuitous wave lengths corresponding in length to the intensity of the energy used in their release; that these vibrations remain in motion forever; that they are one of the two sources from which thoughts which "pop" into one's mind emanate, the other source being direct and immediate contact through the ether with the brain releasing the thought vibration.

Thus it will be seen that if this theory is a fact the boundless space of the whole universe is now and will continue to become literally a mental library wherein may be found all the thoughts released by mankind.

The author is here laying the foundation for one of the most important hypotheses enumerated in the lesson Self-confidence, a fact which the student should keep in mind as he approaches that lesson.

This is a lesson on Organized Knowledge. Most of the useful knowledge to which the human race has become heir has been preserved and accurately recorded in Nature's Bible. By turning back the pages of this unalterable Bible man has read the story of the terrific struggle through and out of which the present civilization has grown. The pages of this Bible are made up of the physical elements of which this earth and the other planets consist, and of the ether which fills all space.

By turning back the pages written on stone and covered near the surface of this earth on which he lives, man has uncovered the bones, skeletons, footprints and other unmistakable evidence of the history of animal life on this earth, planted there for his enlightenment and guidance by the hand of Mother Nature throughout unbelievable periods of time. The evidence is plain and unmistakable. The great stone pages of Nature's Bible found on this earth and the endless pages of that Bible represented by the ether wherein all past human thought has been recorded, constitute an authentic source of communication between the Creator and man. This Bible was begun before man had reached the thinking stage; indeed, before man had reached the amœba (one-cell animal) stage of development.

This Bible is above and beyond the power of man to alter. Moreover, it tells its story not in the ancient dead languages or hieroglyphics of half savage races, but in universal language which all who have eyes may read. Nature's Bible, from which we have derived all the knowledge that is worth knowing, is one that no man may alter or in any manner tamper with.

The most marvelous discovery yet made by man is that of the recently discovered radio principle, which operates through the aid of ether, an important portion of Nature's Bible. Imagine the ether picking up the ordinary vibration of sound, and transforming that vibration from audio-frequency into radio-frequency, carrying it to a properly attuned receiving station and there transforming it back into its original form of audio-frequency, all in the flash of a second. It should surprise no one that such a force could gather up the vibration of thought and keep that vibration in motion forever.

The established and known fact of instantaneous transmission of sound, through the agency of the ether, by means of the modern radio apparatus, removes the theory of transmission of thought vibration from mind to mind from the possible to the probable.

THE MASTER MIND: We come, now, to the next step in the description of the ways and means by which one may gather, classify and organize useful knowledge, through harmonious alliance of two or more minds, out of which grows a Master Mind.

The term "Master Mind" is abstract, and has no counterpart in the field of known facts, except to a small number of people who have made a careful study of the effect of one mind upon other minds.

This author has searched in vain through all the textbooks and essays available on the subject of the human mind, but nowhere has been found even the slightest reference to the principle here described as the "Master Mind." The term first came to the attention of the author through an interview with Andrew Carnegie, in the manner described in Lesson Two.

CHEMISTRY OF THE MIND: It is this author's belief that the mind is made up of the same universal "fluid" energy as that which constitutes the ether which fills the universe. It is a fact as well known to the layman as to the man of scientific investigation, that some minds clash the moment they come in contact with each other, while other minds show a natural affinity for each other. Between the two extremes of natural antagonism and natural affinity growing out of the meeting or contacting of minds there is a wide range of possibility for varying reactions of mind upon mind.

Some minds are so naturally adapted to each other that "love at first sight" is the inevitable outcome of the contact. Who has not known of such an experience? In other cases minds are so antagonistic that violent mutual dislike shows itself at first meeting. These results occur without a word being spoken, and without the slightest signs of any of the usual causes for love and hate acting as a stimulus.

It is quite probable that the "mind" is made up of a fluid or substance or energy, call it what you will, similar to (if not in fact the same substance as) the ether. When two minds come close enough to each other to form a contact, the mixing of the units of this "mind stuff" (let us call it the electrons of the ether) sets up a chemical reaction and starts vibrations which affect the two individuals pleasantly or unpleasantly.

The effect of the meeting of two minds is obvious to even the most casual observer. Every effect must have a cause! What could be more reasonable than to suspect that the cause of the change in mental attitude between two minds which have just come in close contact is none other than the disturbance of the electrons or units of each mind in the process of rearranging themselves in the new field created by the contact?

TO BELIEVE IN THE HEROIC MAKES HEROES.

—*Disraeli.*

For the purpose of establishing this lesson upon a sound foundation we have gone a long way toward success by admitting that the meeting or coming in close contact of two minds sets up in each of those minds a certain noticeable "effect" or state of mind quite different from the one existing immediately prior to the contact. While it is desirable it is not essential to know what is the "cause" of this reaction of mind upon mind. That the reaction takes place, in every instance, is a known fact which gives us a starting point from which we may show what is meant by the term "Master Mind."

A Master Mind may be created through the bringing together or blending, in a spirit of perfect harmony, of two or more minds. Out of this harmonious blending the chemistry of the mind creates a third mind which may be appropriated and used by one or all of the individual minds. This Master Mind will remain available as long as the friendly, harmonious alliance between the individual minds exists. It will disintegrate and all evidence of its former existence will disappear the moment the friendly alliance is broken.

This principle of mind chemistry is the basis and cause for practically all the so-called "soul-mate" and "eternal triangle" cases, so many of which unfortunately find their way into the divorce courts and meet with popular ridicule from ignorant and uneducated people who manufacture vulgarity and scandal out of one of the greatest of Nature's laws.

The entire civilized world knows that the first two or three years of association after marriage are often marked by much disagreement, of a more or less petty nature. These are the years of "adjustment." If the marriage survives them it is more than apt to become a permanent alliance. These facts no experienced married person will deny. Again we see the "effect" without understanding the "cause."

While there are other contributing causes, yet, in the main, lack of harmony during these early years of marriage is due to the slowness of the chemistry of the minds in blending harmoniously. Stated differently, the electrons or units of the energy called the mind are often neither extremely friendly nor antagonistic upon first contact; but, through constant association they gradually adapt themselves in harmony, except in rare cases where association has the opposite effect of leading, eventually, to open hostility between these units.

It is a well known fact that after a man and a woman have lived together for ten to fifteen years they become practically indispensable to each other, even though there may not be the slightest evidence of the state of mind called love. Moreover, this association and relationship sexually not only develops a natural affinity between the two minds, but it actually causes the two people to take on a similar facial expression and to resemble each other closely in many other marked ways. Any competent analyst of human nature can easily go into a crowd of strange people and pick out the wife after having been introduced to her husband. The expression of the eyes, the contour of the faces and the tone of the voices of people who have long been associated in marriage, become similar to a marked degree.

So marked is the effect of the chemistry of the human mind that any experienced public speaker may

quickly interpret the manner in which his statements
are accepted by his audience. Antagonism in the mind
of but one person in an audience of one thousand may
be readily detected by the speaker who has learned
how to "feel" and register the effects of antagonism.
Moreover, the public speaker can make these interpretations without observing or in any manner being influenced by the expression on the faces of those in his
audience. On account of this fact an audience may
cause a speaker to rise to great heights of oratory, or
heckle him into failure, without making a sound or
denoting a single expression of satisfaction or dissatisfaction through the features of the face.

All "Master Salesmen" know the moment the "psychological time for closing" has arrived; not by what
the prospective buyer says, but from the effect of the
chemistry of his mind as interpreted or "felt" by the
salesman. Words often belie the intentions of those
speaking them but a correct interpretation of the
chemistry of the mind leaves no loophole for such a
possibility. Every able salesman knows that the majority of buyers have the habit of affecting a negative
attitude almost to the very climax of a sale.

Every able lawyer has developed a sixth sense
whereby he is enabled to "feel" his way through the
most artfully selected words of the clever witness who
is lying, and correctly interpret that which is in the
witness's mind, through the chemistry of the mind.
Many lawyers have developed this ability without
knowing the real source of it; they possess the technique without the scientific understanding upon which
it is based. Many salesmen have done the same thing.

One who is gifted in the art of correctly interpreting

the chemistry of the minds of others may, figuratively speaking, walk in at the front door of the mansion of a given mind and leisurely explore the entire building, noting all its details, walking out again with a complete picture of the interior of the building, without the owner of the building so much as knowing that he has entertained a visitor. It will be observed, in the lesson Accurate Thinking, that this principle may be put to a very practical use (having reference to the principle of the chemistry of the mind). The principle is referred to merely as an approach to the major principles of this lesson.

Enough has already been stated to introduce the principle of mind chemistry, and to prove, with the aid of the student's own every-day experiences and casual observations that the moment two minds come within close range of each other a noticeable mental change takes place in both, sometimes registering in the nature of antagonism and at other times registering in the nature of friendliness. Every mind has what might be termed an electric field. The nature of this field varies, depending upon the "mood" of the individual mind back of it, and upon the nature of the chemistry of the mind creating the "field."

It is believed by this author that the normal or natural condition of the chemistry of any individual mind is the result of his physical heredity plus the nature of thoughts which have dominated that mind; that every mind is continuously changing to the extent that the individual's philosophy and general habits of thought change the chemistry of his or her mind. These principles the author BELIEVES to be true. That any individual may voluntarily change the chemistry of his or her mind so that it will either attract or repel all with whom it comes in contact is a KNOWN FACT! Stated in another manner, any person may assume a mental attitude which will attract and please others or repel and antagonize them, and this without the aid of words or facial expression or other form of bodily movement or demeanor.

Go back, now, to the definition of a "Master Mind" —a mind which grows out of the blending and co-ordination of two or more minds, IN A SPIRIT OF PERFECT HARMONY, and you will catch the full significance of the word "harmony" as it is here used. Two minds will not blend nor can they be co-ordinated unless the element of perfect harmony is present, wherein lies the secret of success or failure of practically all business and social partnerships.

Every sales manager and every military commander and every leader in any other walk of life understands the necessity of an "esprit de corps"—a spirit of common understanding and co-operation—in the attainment of success. This mass spirit of harmony of purpose is obtained through discipline, voluntary or forced, of such a nature that the individual minds become blended into a "Master Mind," by which is meant that the chemistry of the individual minds is modified in such a manner that these minds blend and function as one.

The methods through which this blending process takes place are as numerous as the individuals engaged in the various forms of leadership. Every leader has his or her own method of co-ordinating the minds of the followers. One will use force. Another uses per-

IF YOU DO NOT BE-
LIEVE IN CO-OP-
ERATION, LOOK
WHAT HAPPENS TO
A WAGON THAT
LOSES A WHEEL.

suasion. One will play upon the fear of penalties while another plays upon rewards, in order to reduce the individual minds of a given group of people to where they may be blended into a mass mind. The student will not have to search deeply into history of statesmanship, politics, business or finance, to discover the technique employed by the leaders in these fields in the process of blending the minds of individuals into a mass mind.

The really great leaders of the world, however, have been provided by Nature with a combination of mind chemistry favorable as a nucleus of attraction for other minds. Napoleon was a notable example of a man possessing the magnetic type of mind which had a very decided tendency to attract all minds with which it came in contact. Soldiers followed Napoleon to certain death without flinching, because of the impelling or attracting nature of his personality, and that personality was nothing more nor less than the chemistry of his mind.

No group of minds can be blended into a Master Mind if one of the individuals of that group possesses one of these extremely negative, repellent minds. The negative and positive minds will not blend in the sense here described as a Master Mind. Lack of knowledge of this fact has brought many an otherwise able leader to defeat.

Any able leader who understands this principle of mind chemistry may temporarily blend the minds of practically any group of people, so that it will represent a mass mind, but the composition will disintegrate almost the very moment the leader's presence is removed from the group. The most successful life-insurance sales organizations and other sales forces meet once a week, or more often, for the purpose of— OF WHAT?

FOR THE PURPOSE OF MERGING THE IN-DIVIDUAL MINDS INTO A MASTER MIND WHICH WILL, FOR A LIMITED NUMBER OF DAYS, SERVE AS A STIMULUS TO THE IN-DIVIDUAL MINDS!

It may be, and generally is, true that the leaders of these groups do not understand what actually takes place in these meetings, which are usually called "pep meetings." The routine of such meetings is usually given over to talks by the leader and other members of the group, and occasionally from someone outside of the group, meanwhile the minds of the individuals are contacting and recharging one another.

The brain of a human being may be compared to an electric battery in that it will become exhausted or run down, causing the owner of it to feel despondent, discouraged and lacking in "pep." Who is so fortunate as never to have had such a feeling? The human brain, when in this depleted condition, must be re-charged, and the manner in which this is done is through contact with a more vital mind or minds. The great leaders understand the necessity of this "re-charging" process, and, moreover, they understand how to accomplish this result. THIS KNOWLEDGE IS THE MAIN FEATURE WHICH DISTIN-GUISHES A LEADER FROM A FOLLOWER!

Fortunate is the person who understands this prin-ciple sufficiently well to keep his or her brain vitalized or "recharged" by periodically contacting it with a more vital mind. Sexual contact is one of the most effective of the stimuli through which a mind may be recharged, providing the contact is intelligently made, between man and woman who have genuine affection for each other. Any other sort of sexual relationship is a devitalizer of the mind. Any competent practitioner of Psycho-therapeutics can "recharge" a brain within a few minutes.

Before passing away from the brief reference made to sexual contact as a means of revitalizing a depleted mind it seems appropriate to call attention to the fact that all of the great leaders, in whatever walks of life they have arisen, have been and are people of highly sexed natures. (The word "sex" is not an indecent word. You'll find it in all the dictionaries.)

There is a growing tendency upon the part of the best informed physicians and other health practitioners, to accept the theory that all diseases begin when the brain of the individual is in a depleted or devitalized state. Stated in another way, it is a known fact that a person who has a perfectly vitalized brain is practically, if not entirely, immune from all manner of disease.

Every intelligent health practitioner, of whatever school or type, knows that "Nature" or the mind cures disease in every instance where a cure is effected. Medicines, faith, laying on of hands, chiropractic, osteopathy and all other forms of outside stimulant are nothing more than artificial aids to NATURE, or, to state it correctly, mere methods of setting the chemistry of the mind into motion to the end that it readjusts the cells and tissues of the body, revitalizes the brain and otherwise causes the human machine to function normally.

The most orthodox practitioner will admit the truth of this statement.

What, then, may be the possibilities of the future developments in the field of mind chemistry?

Through the principle of harmonious blending of minds perfect health may be enjoyed. Through the aid of this same principle sufficient power may be developed to solve the problem of economic pressure which constantly presses upon every individual.

We may judge the future possibilities of mind chemistry by taking inventory of its past achievements, keeping in mind the fact that these achievements have been largely the result of accidental discovery and of chance groupings of minds. We are approaching the time when the professorate of the universities will teach mind chemistry the same as other subjects are now taught. Meanwhile, study and experimentation in connection with this subject open vistas of possibility for the individual student.

.   .   .   .

MIND CHEMISTRY AND ECONOMIC POWER: That mind chemistry may be appropriately applied to the workaday affairs of the economic and commercial world is a demonstrable fact.

Through the blending of two or more minds, in a spirit of PERFECT HARMONY, the principle of mind chemistry may be made to develop sufficient power to enable the individuals whose minds have been thus blended to perform seemingly superhuman feats. Power is the force with which man achieves success in any undertaking. Power, in unlimited quantities, may be enjoyed by any group of men, or men and women, who possess the wisdom with which to submerge their own personalities and their own immediate individual interests, through the blending of their minds in a spirit of perfect harmony.

Observe, profitably, the frequency with which the word "harmony" appears throughout this Introduction! There can be no development of a "Master Mind" where this element of PERFECT HARMONY does not exist. The individual units of the mind will not blend with the individual units of another mind UNTIL THE TWO MINDS HAVE BEEN AROUSED AND WARMED, AS IT WERE, WITH A SPIRIT OF PERFECT HARMONY OF PURPOSE. The moment two minds begin to take divergent roads of interest the individual units of each mind separate, and the third element, known as a "MASTER MIND," which grew out of the friendly or harmonious alliance, will disintegrate.

We come, now, to the study of some well known men who have accumulated great power (also great fortunes) through the application of mind chemistry.

Let us begin our study with three men who are known to be men of great achievement in their respective fields of economic, business and professional endeavor.

Their names are Henry Ford, Thomas A. Edison and Harvey S. Firestone.

Of the three Henry Ford is, by far, the most POWERFUL, having reference to economic and financial power. Mr. Ford is the most powerful man now living on earth. Many who have studied Mr. Ford believe him to be the most powerful man who ever

COURAGE IS THE STANDING ARMY OF THE SOUL WHICH KEEPS IT FROM CONQUEST, PILLAGE AND SLAVERY.

—*Henry van Dyke.*

lived. As far as is known Mr. Ford is the only man now living, or who ever lived, with sufficient power to outwit the money trust of the United States. Mr. Ford gathers millions of dollars with as great ease as a child fills its bucket with sand when playing on the beach. It has been said, by those who were in position to know, that Mr. Ford, if he needed it, could send out the call for money and gather in a billion dollars (a thousand million dollars) and have it available for use within one week. No one who knows of Ford's achievements doubts this. Those who know him well know that he could do it with no more effort than the average man expends in raising the money with which to pay a month's house rent. He could get this money, if he needed it, through the intelligent application of the principles on which this course is based.

While Mr. Ford's new automobile was in the process of perfection, in 1927, it is said that he received advance orders, with cash payments, for more than 375,000 cars. At an estimated price of $600.00 per car this would amount to $225,000,000.00 which he received before a single car was delivered. Such is the power of confidence in Ford's ability.

Mr. Edison, as everyone knows, is a philosopher, scientist and inventor. He is, perhaps, the keenest Bible student on earth; a student of Nature's Bible, however, and not of the myriads of man-made Bibles. Mr. Edison has such a keen insight into Mother Nature's Bible that he has harnessed and combined, for the good of mankind, more of Nature's laws than any other person now living or who ever lived. It was he who brought together the point of a needle and a piece of revolving wax, in such a way that the vibration of the human voice may be recorded and reproduced through the modern talking machine.

(And it may be Edison who will eventually enable man to pick up and correctly interpret the vibrations of thought which are now recorded in the boundless universe of ether, just as he has enabled man to record and reproduce the spoken word.)

It was Edison who first harnessed the lightning and made it serve as a light for man's use, through the aid of the incandescent electric light bulb.

It was Edison who gave the world the modern moving picture.

These are but a few of his outstanding achievements. These modern "miracles" which he has performed (not by trickery, under the sham pretense of superhuman power, but in the very midst of the bright light of science) transcend all of the so-called "miracles" described in the man-made books of fiction.

Mr. Firestone is the moving spirit in the great Firestone Tire industry, in Akron, Ohio. His industrial achievements are so well known wherever automobiles are used that no special comment on them seems necessary.

All three of these men began their careers, business and professional, without capital and with but little schooling of that type usually referred to as "education."

All three men are now well educated. All three are wealthy. All three are powerful. Now let us inquire into the source of their wealth and power. Thus far we have been dealing only with effect; the true philosopher wishes to understand the *cause* of a given effect.

It is a matter of general knowledge that Mr. Ford, Mr. Edison and Mr. Firestone are close personal friends, and have been so for many years; that in former years they were in the habit of going away to the woods once a year for a period of rest, meditation and recuperation.

But it is not generally known—it is a grave doubt if these three men themselves know it—that there exists between the three men a bond of harmony which has caused their minds to become blended into a "Master Mind" which is the real source of the power of each. This mass mind, growing out of the co-ordination of the individual minds of Ford, Edison and Firestone, has enabled these men to "tune in" on forces (and sources of knowledge) with which most men are to no extent familiar.

If the student doubts either the principle or the effects here described, let him remember that more than half the theory here set forth is a known fact. For example, it is known that these three men have great power. It is known that they are wealthy. It is known that they began without capital and with but little schooling. It is known that they form periodic mind contacts. It is known that they are harmonious and friendly. It is known that their achievements are so outstanding as to make it impossible to compare these achievements with those of other men in their respective fields of activity.

All these "effects" are known to practically every school-boy in the civilized world, therefore there can be no dispute as far as effects are concerned.

Of one fact connected with the *cause* of the achieve ments of Edison, Ford and Firestone we may be sure, namely, that these achievements were in no way based upon trickery, deceit, the "supernatural" or so-called "revelations" or any other form of unnatural law. These men do not possess a stock of legerdemain. They work with natural laws; laws which, for the most part, are well known to all economists and leaders in the field of science, with the possible exception of the law upon which chemistry of the mind is based. As yet chemistry of the mind is not sufficiently developed to be classed, by scientific men, in their catalogue of known laws.

A "Master Mind" may be created by any group of people who will co-ordinate their minds, in a spirit of perfect harmony. The group may consist of any number from two upward. Best results appear available from the blending of six or seven minds.

It has been suggested that Jesus Christ discovered how to make use of the principle of mind chemistry, and that His seemingly miraculous performances grew out of the power He developed through the blending of the minds of His twelve disciples. It has been pointed out that when one of the disciples (Judas Iscariot) broke faith the "Master Mind" immediately disintegrated and Jesus met with the supreme catastrophe of His life.

When two or more people harmonize their minds and produce the effect known as a "Master Mind," each person in the group becomes vested with the power to contact with and gather knowledge through the "subconscious" minds of all the other members of the group. This power becomes immediately noticeable, having the effect of stimulating the mind to a higher rate of vibration, and otherwise evidencing itself in the

form of a more vivid imagination and the consciousness of what appears to be a sixth sense. It is
through this sixth sense that new ideas will "flash" into
the mind. These ideas take on the nature and form of
the subject dominating the mind of the individual. If
the entire group has met for the purpose of discussing
a given subject, ideas concerning that subject will
come pouring into the minds of all present, as if an
outside influence were dictating them. The minds of
those participating in the "Master Mind" become as
magnets, attracting ideas and thought stimuli of the
most highly organized and practical nature, from—no
one knows where!

The process of mind-blending here described as a
"Master Mind" may be likened to the act of one who
connects many electric batteries to a single transmission wire, thereby "stepping up" the power flowing
over that line. Each battery added increases the
power passing over that line by the amount of energy
the battery carries. Just so in the case of blending
individual minds into a "Master Mind." Each mind,
through the principle of mind chemistry, stimulates
all the other minds in the group, until the mind energy
thus becomes so great that it penetrates to and connects with the universal energy known as ether, which,
in turn, touches every atom of the entire universe.

The modern radio apparatus substantiates, to a considerable extent, the theory here expounded. Powerful
sending or broadcasting stations must be erected
through which the vibration of sound is "stepped up"
before it can be picked up by the much higher vibrating energy of the ether and carried in all directions.
A "Master Mind" made up of many individual minds,

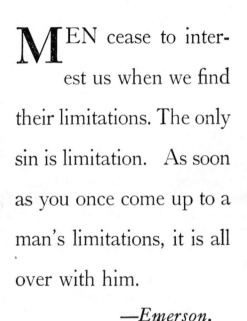

MEN cease to interest us when we find their limitations. The only sin is limitation. As soon as you once come up to a man's limitations, it is all over with him.

—*Emerson.*

so blended that they produce a strong vibrating energy, constitutes almost an exact counterpart of the radio broadcasting station.

Every public speaker has felt the influence of mind chemistry, for it is a well known fact that as soon as the individual minds of an audience become "en rapport" (attuned to the rate of vibration of the mind of the speaker) with the speaker, there is a noticeable increase of enthusiasm in the speaker's mind, and he often rises to heights of oratory which surprise all, including himself.

The first five to ten minutes of the average speech are devoted to what is known as "warming up." By this is meant the process through which the minds of the speaker and his audience are becoming blended in a spirit of PERFECT HARMONY.

Every speaker knows what happens when this state of "perfect harmony" fails to materialize upon part of his audience.

The seemingly supernatural phenomena occurring in spiritualistic meetings are the result of the reaction, upon one another, of the minds in the group. These phenomena seldom begin to manifest themselves under ten to twenty minutes after the group is formed, for the reason that this is about the time required for the minds in the group to become harmonized or blended.

The "messages" received by members of a spiritualistic group probably come from one of two sources, or from both, namely:

First: From the vast storehouse of the subconscious mind of some member of the group; or

Second: From the universal storehouse of the ether,

in which, it is more than probable, all thought vibration is preserved.

Neither any known natural law nor human reason supports the theory of communication with individuals who have died.

It is a known fact that any individual may explore the store of knowledge in another's mind, through this principle of mind chemistry, and it seems reasonable to suppose that this power may be extended to include contact with whatever vibrations are available in the ether, if there are any.

The theory that all the higher and more refined vibrations, such as those growing out of thought, are preserved in the ether grows out of the known fact that neither matter nor energy (the two known elements of the universe) may be either created or destroyed. It is reasonable to suppose that all vibrations which have been "stepped up" sufficiently to be picked up and absorbed in the ether, will go on forever. The lower vibrations, which do not blend with or otherwise contact the ether, probably live a natural life and die out.

All the so-called geniuses probably gained their reputations because, by mere chance or otherwise, they formed alliances with other minds which enabled them to "step up" their own mind vibrations to where they were enabled to contact the vast Temple of Knowledge recorded and filed in the ether of the universe. All of the great geniuses, as far as this author has been enabled to gather the facts, were highly sexed people. The fact that sexual contact is the greatest known mind stimulant lends color to the theory herein described.

Inquiring further into the source of economic power, as manifested by the achievements of men in the field of business, let us study the case of the Chicago group known as the "Big Six," consisting of Wm. Wrigley, Jr., who owns the chewing gum business bearing his name, and whose individual income is said to be more than Fifteen Million Dollars a year; John R. Thompson, who operates the chain of lunch rooms bearing his name; Mr. Lasker, who owns the Lord & Thomas Advertising Agency; Mr. McCullough, who owns the Parmalee Express Company, the largest transfer business in America; and Mr. Ritchie and Mr. Hertz, who own the Yellow Taxicab business.

A reliable financial reporting company has estimated the yearly income of these six men at upwards of Twenty-five Million Dollars ($25,000,000.00), or an average of more than Four Million Dollars a year per man.

Analysis of the entire group of six men discloses the fact that not one of them had any special educational advantages; that all began without capital or extensive credit; that their financial achievement has been due to their own individual plans, and not to any fortunate turn of the wheel of chance.

Many years ago these six men formed a friendly alliance, meeting at stated periods for the purpose of assisting one another with ideas and suggestions in their various and sundry lines of business endeavor.

With the exception of Hertz and Ritchie none of the six men were in any manner associated in a legal partnership. These meetings were strictly for the purpose of co-operating on the give and take basis of assisting one another with ideas and suggestions, and occasionally by endorsing notes and other securities to assist some member of the group who had met with an emergency making such help necessary.

It is said that each of the individuals belonging to this Big Six group is a millionaire many times over. As a rule there is nothing worthy of special comment on behalf of a man who does nothing more than accumulate a few million dollars. However, there is something connected with the financial success of this particular group of men that is well worth comment, study, analysis and even emulation, and that "something" is the fact that they have learned how to coordinate their individual minds by blending them in a spirit of perfect harmony, thereby creating a "Master Mind" that unlocks, to each individual of the group, doors which are closed to most of the human race.

The United States Steel Corporation is one of the strongest and most powerful industrial organizations in the world. The Idea out of which this great industrial giant grew was born in the mind of Elbert H. Gary, a more or less commonplace small-town lawyer who was born and reared in a small Illinois town near Chicago.

Mr. Gary surrounded himself with a group of men whose minds he successfully blended in a spirit of perfect harmony, thereby creating the "Master Mind" which is the moving spirit of the great United States Steel Corporation.

Search where you will, wherever you find an outstanding success in business, finance, industry or in any of the professions, you may be sure that back of the success is some individual who has applied the principle of mind chemistry, out of which a "Master

Mind" has been created. These outstanding successes often appear to be the handiwork of but one person, but search closely and the other individuals whose minds have been co-ordinated with his own may be found. Remember that two or more persons may operate the principle of mind chemistry so as to create a "Master Mind."

POWER (man-power) is ORGANIZED KNOWL-EDGE, EXPRESSED THROUGH INTELLIGENT EFFORTS!

No effort can be said to be ORGANIZED unless the individuals engaged in the effort co-ordinate their knowledge and energy in a spirit of perfect harmony. Lack of such harmonious co-ordination of effort is the main cause of practically every business failure.

An interesting experiment was conducted by this author, in collaboration with the students of a well known college. Each student was requested to write an essay on "How and Why Henry Ford Became Wealthy."

Each student was required to describe, as a part of his or her essay, what was believed to be the nature of Ford's real assets, of what these assets consisted in detail.

The majority of the students gathered financial statements and inventories of the Ford assets and used these as the basis of their estimates of Ford's wealth.

Included in these "sources of Ford's wealth" were such as cash in banks, raw and finished materials in stock, real estate and buildings, good-will, estimated at from ten to twenty-five per cent of the value of the material assets.

YOU cannot become a power in your community nor achieve enduring success in any worthy undertaking until you become big enough to blame yourself for your own mistakes and reverses.

One student out of the entire group of several hundred answered as follows:

"Henry Ford's assets consist, in the main, of two items, viz.: (1) Working capital and raw and finished materials; (2) The knowledge, gained from experience, of Henry Ford, himself, and the co-operation of a well trained organization which understands how to apply this knowledge to best advantage from the Ford viewpoint. It is impossible to estimate, with anything approximating correctness, the actual dollars and cents value of either of these two groups of assets, but it is my opinion that their relative values are:

"The organized knowledge of the Ford Organ-
    ization 75%
The value of cash and physical assets of every
    nature, including raw and finished materials 25%"

This author is of the opinion that this statement was not compiled by the young man whose name was signed to it, without the assistance of some very analytical and experienced mind or minds.

Unquestionably the biggest asset that Henry Ford has is his own brain. Next to this would come the brains of his immediate circle of associates, for it has been through co-ordination of these that the physical assets which he controls were accumulated.

Destroy every plant the Ford Motor Company owns: every piece of machinery; every atom of raw or finished material, every finished automobile, and every dollar on deposit in any bank, and Ford would still be the most powerful man, economically, on earth. The brains which have built the Ford business could duplicate it again in short order. Capital is always available, in unlimited quantities, to such brains as Ford's.

Ford is the most powerful man on earth (economically) because he has the keenest and most practical conception of the principle of ORGANIZED KNOWLEDGE of any man on earth, as far as this author has the means of knowing.

Despite Ford's great power and financial success, it may be that he has blundered often in the application of the principles through which he accumulated this power. There is but little doubt that Ford's methods of mind co-ordination have often been crude; they must needs have been in the earlier days of this experience, before he gained the wisdom of application that would naturally go with maturity of years.

Neither can there be much doubt that Ford's application of the principle of mind chemistry was, at least at the start, the result of a chance alliance with other minds, particularly the mind of Edison. It is more than probable that Mr. Ford's remarkable insight into the laws of nature was first begun as the result of his friendly alliance with his own wife long before he ever met either Mr. Edison or Mr. Firestone. Many a man who never knows the real source of his success is made by his wife, through application of the "Master Mind" principle. Mrs. Ford is a most remarkably intelligent woman, and this author has reason to believe that it was her mind, blended with Mr. Ford's, which gave him his first real start toward power.

It may be mentioned, without in any way depriving Ford of any honor or glory, that in his earlier days of experience he had to combat the powerful enemies of illiteracy and ignorance to a greater extent than did either Edison or Firestone, both of whom were gifted by natural heredity with a most fortunate aptitude for acquiring and applying knowledge. Ford had to hew this talent out of the rough, raw timbers of his hereditary estate.

Within an inconceivably short period of time Ford has mastered three of the most stubborn enemies of mankind and transformed them into assets constituting the very foundation of his success.

These enemies are: Ignorance, illiteracy and poverty!

Any man who can stay the hand of these three savage forces, much less harness and use them to good account, is well worth close study by the less fortunate individuals.

.   .   .   .

This is an age of INDUSTRIAL POWER in which we are living!

The source of all this POWER is ORGANIZED EFFORT. Not only has the management of industrial enterprises efficiently organized individual workers, but, in many instances, mergers of industry have been effected in such a manner and to the end that these combinations (as in the case of the United States Steel Corporation, for example) have accumulated practically unlimited power.

One may hardly glance at the news of a day's events without seeing a report of some business, industrial or financial merger, bringing under one management enormous resources and thus creating great power.

One day it is a group of banks; another day it is

a chain of railroads; the next day it is a combination of steel plants, all merging for the purpose of developing power through highly organized and co-ordinated effort.

Knowledge, general in nature and unorganized, is not POWER; it is only potential power—the material out of which real power may be developed. Any modern library contains an unorganized record of all the knowledge of value to which the present stage of civilization is heir, but this knowledge is not power because it is not organized.

Every form of energy and every species of animal or plant life, to survive, must be organized. The oversized animals whose bones have filled Nature's bone-yard through extinction have left mute but certain evidence that non-organization means annihilation.

From the electron—the smallest particle of matter —to the largest star in the universe: these and every material thing in between these two extremes offer proof positive that one of Nature's first laws is that of ORGANIZATION. Fortunate is the individual who recognizes the importance of this law and makes it his business to familiarize himself with the various ways in which the law may be applied to advantage.

The astute business man has not only recognized the importance of the law of organized effort, but he has made this law the warp and the woof of his POWER.

Without any knowledge, whatsoever, of the principle of mind chemistry, or that such a principle exists, many men have accumulated great power by merely organizing the knowledge they possessed. The majority of all who have discovered the principle of mind chemistry and developed that principle into a "MASTER MIND" have stumbled upon this knowledge by the merest of accident; often failing to recognize the real nature of their discovery or to understand the source of their power.

This author is of the opinion that all living persons who at the present time are consciously making use of the principle of mind chemistry in developing power through the blending of minds, may be counted on the fingers of the two hands, with, perhaps, several fingers left to spare.

If this estimate is even approximately true the student will readily see that there is but slight danger of the field of mind chemistry practice becoming overcrowded.

It is a well known fact that one of the most difficult tasks that any business man must perform is that of inducing those who are associated with him to coordinate their efforts in a spirit of harmony. To induce continuous co-operation between a group of workers, in any undertaking, is next to impossible. Only the most efficient leaders can accomplish this highly desired object, but once in a great while such a leader will rise above the horizon in the field of industry, business or finance, and then the world hears of a Henry Ford, Thomas A. Edison, John D. Rockefeller, Sr., E. H. Harriman or James J. Hill.

Power and success are practically synonomous terms!

One grows out of the other; therefore, any person who has the knowledge and the ability to develop power, through the principle of harmonious co-ordi-

NEVER, in the history of the world, has there been such abundant opportunity as there is now for the person who is willing to serve before trying to collect.

nation of effort between individual minds, or in any
other manner, may be successful in any reasonable
undertaking that is possible of successful termination.

.   .   .   .

It must not be assumed that a "Master Mind" will
immediately spring, mushroom fashion, out of every
group of minds which make pretense of co-ordination
in a spirit of HARMONY!

Harmony, in the real sense of meaning of the word,
is as rare among groups of people as is genuine Christianity among those who proclaim themselves Christians.

Harmony is the nucleus around which the state of
mind known as "Master Mind" must be developed.
Without this element of harmony there can be no
"Master Mind," a truth which cannot be repeated too
often.

Woodrow Wilson had in mind the development of a
"Master Mind," to be composed of groups of minds
representing the civilized nations of the world, in his
proposal for establishing the League of Nations. Wilson's conception was the most far-reaching humani-
tarian idea ever created in the mind of man, because
it dealt with a principle which embraces sufficient
power to establish a real Brotherhood of Man on earth.
The League of Nations, or some similar blending of
international minds, in a spirit of harmony, is sure to
become a reality.

The time when such unity of minds will take place
will be measured largely by the time required for the
great universities and NON-SECTARIAN institutions
of learning to supplant ignorance and superstition with

understanding and wisdom.   This time is rapidly approaching.

THE PSYCHOLOGY OF THE REVIVAL MEETING: The old religious orgy known as the "revival" offers a favorable opportunity to study the principle of mind chemistry known as "Master Mind."

It will be observed that music plays no small part in bringing about the harmony essential to the blending of a group of minds in a revival meeting.   Without music the revival meeting would be a tame affair.

During revival services the leader of the meeting has no difficulty in creating harmony in the minds of his devotees, but it is a well known fact that this state of harmony lasts no longer than the presence of the leader, after which the "Master Mind" he has temporarily created disintegrates.

By arousing the emotional nature of his followers the revivalist has no difficulty, under the proper stage setting and with the embellishment of the right sort of music, in creating a "Master Mind" which becomes noticeable to all who come in contact with it.   The very air becomes charged with a positive, pleasing influence which changes the entire chemistry of all minds present.

The revivalist calls this energy "the Spirit of the Lord."

This author, through experiments conducted with a group of scientific investigators and laymen (who were unaware of the nature of the experiment), has created the same state of mind and the same positive atmosphere without calling it the Spirit of the Lord.

On many occasions this author has witnessed the

creation of the same positive atmosphere in a group of men and women engaged in the business of salesmanship, without calling it the Spirit of the Lord.

The author helped conduct a school of salesmanship for Harrison Parker, founder of the Co-operative Society, of Chicago, and, by the use of the same principle of mind chemistry which the revivalist calls the Spirit of the Lord, so transformed the nature of a group of 3,000 men and women (all of whom were without former sales experience) that they sold more than $10,000,000.00 worth of securities in less than nine months, and earned more than $1,000,000 for themselves.

It was found that the average person who joined this school would reach the zenith of his or her selling power within one week, after which it was necessary to revitalize the individual's brain through a group sales meeting. These sales meetings were conducted on very much the same order as are the modern revival meetings of the religionist, with much the same stage equipment, including music and "high-powered" speakers who exhorted the salespeople in very much the same manner as does the modern religious revivalist.

Call it religion, psychology, mind chemistry or anything you please (they are all based upon the same principle), but there is nothing more certain than the fact that wherever a group of minds are brought into contact, in a spirit of PERFECT HARMONY, each mind in the group becomes immediately supplemented and re-enforced by a noticeable energy called a "Master Mind."

For all this writer professes to know this uncharted energy may be the Spirit of the Lord, but it operates just as favorably when called by any other name.

The human brain and nervous system constitute a piece of intricate machinery which but few, if any, understand. When controlled and properly directed this piece of machinery can be made to perform wonders of achievement and if not controlled it will perform wonders fantastic and phantom-like in nature, as may be seen by examining the inmates of any insane asylum.

The human brain has direct connection with a continuous influx of energy from which man derives his power to think. The brain receives this energy, mixes it with the energy created by the food taken into the body, and distributes it to every portion of the body, through the aid of the blood and the nervous system. It thus becomes what we call life.

From what source this outside energy comes no one seems to know; all we know about it is that we must have it or die. It seems reasonable to suppose that this energy is none other than that which we call ether, and that it flows into the body along with the oxygen from the air, as we breathe.

Every normal human body possesses a first-class chemical laboratory and a stock of chemicals sufficient to carry on the business of breaking up, assimilating and properly mixing and compounding the food we take into the body, preparatory to distributing it to wherever it is needed as a body builder.

Ample tests have been made, both with man and beast, to prove that the energy known as the mind plays an important part in this chemical operation of compounding and transforming food into the required substances to build and keep the body in repair.

It is known that worry, excitement or fear will interfere with the digestive process, and in extreme cases stop this process altogether, resulting in illness or death. It is obvious, then, that the mind enters into the chemistry of food digestion and distribution.

It is believed by many eminent authorities, although it may never have been scientifically proved, that the energy known as mind or thought may become contaminated with negative or "unsociable" units to such an extent that the whole nervous system is thrown out of working order, digestion is interfered with and various and sundry forms of disease will manifest themselves. Financial difficulties and unrequited love affairs head the list of causes of such mind disturbances.

A negative environment such as that existing where some member of the family is constantly "nagging," will interfere with the chemistry of the mind to such an extent that the individual will lose ambition and gradually sink into oblivion. It is because of this fact that the old saying that a man's wife may either "make" or "break" him is literally true. In a subsequent lesson a whole chapter on this subject is addressed to the wives of men.

Any high-school student knows that certain food combinations will, if taken into the stomach, result in indigestion, violent pain and even death. Good health depends, in part at least, upon a food combination that "harmonizes." But harmony of food combinations is not sufficient to insure good health; there must be harmony, also, between the units of energy known as the mind.

A man is half whipped the minute he begins to feel sorry for himself, or to spin an alibi with which he would explain away his defects.

"Harmony" seems to be one of Nature's laws, without which there can be no such thing as ORGANIZED ENERGY, or life in any form whatsoever.

The health of the body as well as the mind is literally built around, out of and upon the principle of HARMONY! The energy known as life begins to disintegrate and death approaches when the organs of the body stop working in harmony.

The moment harmony ceases at the source of any form of organized energy (power) the units of that energy are thrown into a chaotic state of disorder and the power is rendered neutral or passive.

Harmony is also the nucleus around which the principle of mind chemistry known as a "Master Mind" develops power. Destroy this harmony and you destroy the power growing out of the co-ordinated effort of a group of individual minds.

This truth has been stated, re-stated and presented in every manner which the author could conceive, with unending repetition, for the reason that unless the student grasps this principle and learns to apply it this lesson is useless.

Success in life, no matter what one may call success, is very largely a matter of adaptation to environment in such a manner that there is harmony between the individual and his environment. The palace of a king becomes as a hovel of a peasant if harmony does not abound within its walls. Conversely stated, the hut of a peasant may be made to yield more happiness than that of the mansion of the rich man, if harmony obtains in the former and not in the latter.

Without perfect harmony the science of astronomy would be as useless as the "bones of a saint," because the stars and planets would clash with one another, and all would be in a state of chaos and disorder.

Without the law of harmony an acorn might grow into a heterogeneous tree consisting of the wood of the oak, poplar, maple and what not.

Without the law of harmony the blood might deposit the food which grows finger nails on the scalp where hair is supposed to grow, and thus create a horny growth which might easily be mistaken, by the superstitious, to signify man's relationship to a certain imaginary gentleman with horns, often referred to by the more primitive type.

Without the law of harmony there can be no organization of knowledge, for what, may one ask, is organized knowledge except the harmony of facts and truths and natural laws?

The moment discord begins to creep in at the front door harmony edges out at the back door, so to speak, whether the application is made to a business partnership or the orderly movement of the planets of the heavens.

If the student gathers the impression that the author is laying undue stress upon the importance of HARMONY, let it be remembered that lack of harmony is the first, and often the last and only, cause of FAILURE!

There can be no poetry nor music nor oratory worthy of notice without the presence of harmony.

Good architecture is largely a matter of harmony. Without harmony a house is nothing but a mass of building material, more or less a monstrosity.

Sound business management plants the very sinews of its existence in harmony.

Every well dressed man or woman is a living picture and a moving example of harmony.

With all these workaday illustrations of the important part which harmony plays in the affairs of the world—nay, in the operation of the entire universe—how could any intelligent person leave harmony out of his "Definite Aim" in life? As well have no "definite aim" as to omit harmony as the chief stone of its foundation.

.   .   .   .

The human body is a complex organization of organs, glands, blood vessels, nerves, brain cells, muscles, etc. The mind energy which stimulates to action and co-ordinates the efforts of the component parts of the body is also a plurality of ever-varying and changing energies. From birth until death there is continuous struggle, often assuming the nature of open combat, between the forces of the mind. For example, the life-long struggle between the motivating forces and desires of the human mind, which takes place between the impulses of right and wrong, is well known to everyone.

Every human being possesses at least two distinct mind powers or personalities, and as many as six distinct personalities have been discovered in one person. One of man's most delicate tasks is that of harmonizing these mind forces so that they may be organized and directed toward the orderly attainment of a given objective. Without this element of harmony no individual can become an accurate thinker.

It is no wonder that leaders in business and industrial enterprises, as well as those in politics and other fields of endeavor, find it so difficult to organize groups of people so they will function in the attainment of a given objective, without friction. Each individual human being possesses forces, within himself, which are hard to harmonize, even when he is placed in the environment most favorable to harmony. If the chemistry of the individual's mind is such that the units of his mind cannot be easily harmonized, think how much more difficult it must be to harmonize a group of minds so they will function as one, in an orderly manner, through what is known as a "Master Mind."

The leader who successfully develops and directs the energies of a "Master Mind" must possess tact, patience, persistence, self-confidence, intimate knowledge of mind chemistry and the ability to adapt himself (in a state of perfect poise and harmony) to quickly changing circumstances, without showing the least sign of annoyance.

How many are there who can measure up to this requirement?

The successful leader must possess the ability to change the color of his mind, chameleon-like, to fit every circumstance that arises in connection with the object of his leadership. Moreover, he must possess the ability to change from one mood to another without showing the slightest signs of anger or lack of self-control. The successful leader must understand the Fifteen Laws of Success and be able to put into practice any combination of these Fifteen Laws whenever occasion demands.

Without this ability no leader can be powerful, and without power no leader can long endure.

THE MEANING OF EDUCATION: There has long been a general misconception of the meaning of the word "educate." The dictionaries have not aided in the elimination of this misunderstanding, because they have defined the word "educate" as an act of imparting knowledge.

The word educate has its roots in the Latin word *educo*, which means to develop FROM WITHIN; to educe; to draw out; to grow through the law of USE.

Nature hates idleness in all its forms. She gives continuous life only to those elements which are in use. Tie up an arm, or any other portion of the body, taking it out of use, and the idle part will soon atrophy and become lifeless. Reverse the order, give an arm more than normal use, such as that engaged in by the blacksmith who wields a heavy hammer all day long, and that arm (developed from within) grows strong.

Power grows out of ORGANIZED KNOWLEDGE, but, mind you, it "grows out of it" through application and use!

A man may become a walking encyclopædia of knowledge without possessing any power of value. This knowledge becomes power only to the extent that it is organized, classified and put into action. Some of the best educated men the world has known possessed much less general knowledge than some who have been known as fools, the difference between the two being that the former put what knowledge they possessed into use while the latter made no such application.

An "educated" person is one who knows how to acquire everything he needs in the attainment of his main purpose in life, without violating the rights of

SEEK the counsel of men who will tell you the truth about yourself, even if it hurts you to hear it. Mere commendation will not bring the improvement you need.

his fellow men. It might be a surprise to many so-called men of "learning" to know that they come nowhere near qualification as men of "education." It might also be a great surprise to many who believe they suffer from lack of "learning" to know that they are well "educated."

The successful lawyer is not necessarily the one who memorizes the greatest number of principles of law. On the contrary, the successful lawyer is the one who knows where to find a principle of law, plus a variety of opinions supporting that principle which fit the immediate needs of a given case.

In other words, the successful lawyer is he who knows where to find the law he wants when he needs it.

This principle applies, with equal force, to the affairs of industry and business.

Henry Ford had but little elementary schooling, yet he is one of the best "educated" men in the world because he has acquired the ability so to combine natural and economic laws, to say nothing of the minds of men, that he has the power to get anything of a material nature he wants.

Some years ago during the world war Mr. Ford brought suit against the Chicago Tribune, charging that newspaper with libelous publication of statements concerning him, one of which was the statement that Ford was an "ignoramus," an ignorant pacifist, etc.

When the suit came up for trial the attorneys for the Tribune undertook to prove, by Ford himself, that their statement was true; that he was ignorant, and with this object in view they catechized and cross-examined him on all manner of subjects.

One question they asked was:

"How many soldiers did the British send over to subdue the rebellion in the Colonies in 1776?"

With a dry grin on his face Ford nonchalantly replied:

"I do not know just how many, but I have heard that it was a lot more than ever went back."

Loud laughter from Court, jury, court-room spectators, and even from the frustrated lawyer who had asked the question.

This line of interrogation was continued for an hour or more, Ford keeping perfectly calm the meanwhile. Finally, however, he had permitted the "smart Aleck" lawyers to play with him until he was tired of it, and in reply to a question which was particularly obnoxious and insulting, Ford straightened himself up, pointed his finger at the questioning lawyer and replied:

"If I should really wish to answer the foolish question you have just asked, or any of the others you have been asking, let me remind you that I have a row of electric push-buttons hanging over my desk and by placing my finger on the right button I could call in men who could give me the correct answer to all the questions you have asked and to many that you have not the intelligence either to ask or answer. Now, will you kindly tell me why I should bother about filling my mind with a lot of useless details in order to answer every fool question that anyone may ask, when I have able men all about me who can supply me with all the facts I want when I call for them?"

This answer is quoted from memory, but it substantially relates Ford's answer.

There was silence in the court-room. The question-

ing attorney's under jaw dropped down, his eyes
opened widely; the judge leaned forward from the
bench and gazed in Mr. Ford's direction; many of the
jury awoke and looked around as if they had heard
an explosion (which they actually had).

A prominent clergyman who was present in the
court-room at the time said, later, that the scene reminded him of that which must have existed when
Jesus Christ was on trial before Pontius Pilate, just
after He had given His famous reply to Pilate's question, "What is truth?"

In the vernacular of the day, Ford's reply knocked
the questioner cold.

Up to the time of that reply the lawyer had been
enjoying considerable fun at what he believed to be
Ford's expense, by adroitly displaying his (the lawyer's) sample case of general knowledge and comparing it with what he inferred to be Ford's ignorance
as to many events and subjects.

But that answer spoiled the lawyer's fun!

It also proved once more (to all who had the intelligence to accept the proof) that true education
means mind development; not merely the gathering
and classifying of knowledge.

Ford could not, in all probability, have named the
capitals of all the States of the United States, but he
could have and in fact had gathered the "capital" with
which to "turn many wheels" within every State in
the Union.

Education—let us not forget this—consists of the
power with which to get everything one needs when
he needs it, without violating the rights of his fellow
men. Ford comes well within that definition, and for

the reason which the author has here tried to make plain, by relating the foregoing incident connected with the simple Ford philosophy.

There are many men of "learning" who could easily entangle Ford, theoretically, with a maze of questions none of which he, personally, could answer. But Ford could turn right around and wage a battle in industry or finance that would exterminate those same men, with all of their knowledge and all of their wisdom.

Ford could not go into his chemical laboratory and separate water into its component atoms of hydrogen and oxygen and then re-combine these atoms in their former order, but he knows how to surround himself with chemists who can do this for him if he wants it done. The man who can intelligently use the knowledge possessed by another is as much or more a man of education as the person who merely has the knowledge but does not know what to do with it.

The president of a well known college inherited a large tract of very poor land. This land had no timber of commercial value, no minerals or other valuable appurtenances, therefore it was nothing but a source of expense to him, for he had to pay taxes on it. The State built a highway through the land. An "uneducated" man who was driving his automobile over this road observed that this poor land was on top of a mountain which commanded a wonderful view for many miles in all directions. He (the ignorant one) also observed that the land was covered with a growth of small pines and other saplings. He bought fifty acres of the land for $10.00 an acre. Near the public highway he built a unique log house to which he attached a large dining room. Near the house he put in a gasoline filling station.   He built a dozen single-room log houses along the road, these he rented out to tourists at $3.00 a night, each.   The dining room, gasoline filling station and log houses brought him a net income of $15,000.00 the first year.   The next year he extended his plan by adding fifty more log houses, of three rooms each, which he now rents out as summer country homes to people in a near-by city, at a rental of $150.00 each for the season.

The building material cost him nothing, for it grew on his land in abundance (that same land which the college president believed to be worthless).

Moreover, the unique and unusual appearance of the log bungalows served as an advertisement of the plan, whereas many would have considered it a real calamity had they been compelled to build out of such crude materials.

Less than five miles from the location of these log houses this same man purchased an old worked-out farm of 150 acres, for $25.00 an acre, a price which the seller believed to be extremely high.

By building a dam, one hundred feet in length, the purchaser of this old farm turned a stream of water into a lake that covered fifteen acres of the land, stocked the lake with fish, then sold the farm off in building lots to people who wanted summering places around the lake.   The total profit realized from this simple transaction was more than $25,000.00, and the time required for its consummation was one summer.

Yet this man of vision and imagination was not "educated" in the orthodox meaning of that term.

Let us keep in mind the fact that it is through these

WHEN you lose your sense of humor, get a job running an elevator, because your life will be a series of UPS and DOWNS, anyway.

simple illustrations of the use of organized knowledge that one may become educated and powerful.

In speaking of the transaction here related, the college president who sold the fifty acres of worthless (?) land for $500.00 said:

"Just think of it! That man, whom most of us might call ignorant, mixed his ignorance with fifty acres of worthless land and made the combination yield more yearly than I earn from five years of application of so-called education."

.   .   .   .

There is an opportunity, if not scores of them, in every State in America, to make use of the idea here described. From now on make it your business to study the lay of all land you see that is similar to that described in this lesson, and you may find a suitable place for developing a similar money-making enterprise. The idea is particularly adaptable in localities where bathing beaches are few, as people naturally like such conveniences.

The automobile has caused a great system of public highways to be built throughout the United States. On practically every one of these highways there is a suitable spot for a "Cabin City" for tourists which can be turned into a regular money-making mint by the man with the IMAGINATION and SELF-CONFI-DENCE to do it.

There are opportunities to make money all around you. This course was designed to help you "see" these opportunities, and to inform you how to make the most of them after you discover them.

WHO CAN PROFIT MOST BY THE LAW OF SUCCESS PHILOSOPHY?

RAILROAD OFFICIALS who want a better spirit of co-operation between their trainmen and the public they serve.

SALARIED PEOPLE who wish to increase their earning power and market their services to better advantage.

SALESPEOPLE who wish to become masters in their chosen field. The Law of Success philosophy covers every known law of selling, and includes many features not included in any other course.

INDUSTRIAL PLANT MANAGERS who understand the value of greater harmony among their employees.

RAILROAD EMPLOYEES who wish to establish records of efficiency which will lead to more responsible positions, with greater pay.

MERCHANTS who wish to extend their business by adding new customers. The Law of Success philosophy will help any merchant increase his business by teaching him how to make a walking advertisement of every customer who comes into his store.

AUTOMOBILE AGENTS who wish to increase the selling power of their salesmen. A large part of the Law of Success course was developed from the life-work and experience of the greatest automobile salesman living, and it is therefore of unusual help to the Sales Manager who is directing the efforts of Automobile Salesmen.

LIFE INSURANCE AGENTS who wish to add new

policy-holders and increase the insurance on present policy-holders. One Life Insurance Salesman, in Ohio, sold a Fifty Thousand Dollar policy to one of the officials of the Central Steel Company, as the result of but one reading of the lesson on "Profiting by Failures." This same salesman has become one of the star men of the New York Life Insurance Company's staff, as the result of his training in the Fifteen Laws of Success.

SCHOOL TEACHERS who wish to advance to the top in their present occupation, or who are looking for an opportunity to enter the more profitable field of business as a life-work.

STUDENTS, both College and High School, who are undecided as to what field of endeavor they wish to enter as a life-work. The Law of Success course covers a complete Personal Analysis service which helps the student of the philosophy to determine the work for which he or she is best fitted.

BANKERS who wish to extend their business through better and more courteous methods of serving their clients.

BANK CLERKS who are ambitious to prepare themselves for executive positions in the field of banking, or in some commercial or industrial field.

PHYSICIANS and DENTISTS who wish to extend their practice without violating the ethics of their profession by direct advertising. A prominent physician has said that the Law of Success course is worth $1,000.00 to any professional man or woman whose professional ethics prevent direct advertising.

PROMOTERS who wish to develop new and heretofore unworked combinations in business or industry.

The principle described in this Introductory Lesson is said to have made a small fortune for a man who used it as the basis of a real estate promotion.

REAL ESTATE MEN who wish new methods for promoting sales. This Introductory Lesson contains a description of an entirely new real-estate promotion plan which is sure to make fortunes for many who will put it to use. This plan may be put into operation in practically every State. Moreover, it may be employed by men who never promoted an enterprise.

FARMERS who wish to discover new methods of marketing their products so as to give them greater net returns, and those who own lands suitable for subdivision promotion under the plan referred to at the end of this Introductory Lesson. Thousands of farmers have "gold mines" in the land they own which is not suitable for cultivation, which could be used for recreation and resort purposes, on a highly profitable basis.

STENOGRAPHERS and BOOKKEEPERS who are looking for a practical plan to promote themselves into higher and better paying positions. The Law of Success course is said to be the best course ever written on the subject of marketing personal services.

PRINTERS who want a larger volume of business and more efficient production as the result of better co-operation among their own employees.

DAY LABORERS who have the ambition to advance into more responsible positions, in work that has greater responsibilities and consequently offers more pay.

LAWYERS who wish to extend their clientele through dignified, ethical methods which will bring them to the attention, in a favorable way, of a greater number of people who need legal services.

BUSINESS EXECUTIVES who wish to expand their present business, or who wish to handle their present volume with less expense, as the result of greater co-operation between their employees.

LAUNDRY OWNERS who wish to extend their business by teaching their drivers how to serve more courteously and efficiently.

LIFE INSURANCE GENERAL AGENTS who wish bigger and more efficient sales organizations.

CHAIN STORE MANAGERS who want a greater volume of business as the result of more efficient individual sales efforts.

MARRIED PEOPLE who are unhappy, and therefore unsuccessful, because of lack of harmony and co-operation in the home.

To all described in the foregoing classification the Law of Success philosophy offers both DEFINITE and SPEEDY aid.

AN AIM IN LIFE IS THE ONLY FOR-
TUNE WORTH FIND-
ING; AND IT IS NOT
TO BE FOUND IN
FOREIGN LANDS,
BUT IN THE HEART
ITSELF.

—*Robert Louis Stevenson.*

SUMMARY OF INTRODUCTORY LESSON

The purpose of this summary is to aid the student in mastering the central idea around which the lesson has been developed. This idea is represented by the term "Master Mind" which has been described in great detail throughout the lesson.

All new ideas, and especially those of an abstract nature, find lodgment in the human mind only after much repetition, a well known truth which accounts for the re-statement, in this summary, of the principle known as the "Master Mind."

A "Master Mind" may be developed by a friendly alliance, in a spirit of harmony of purpose, between two or more minds.

This is an appropriate place at which to explain that out of every alliance of minds, whether in a spirit of harmony or not, there is developed another mind which affects all participating in the alliance. No two or more minds ever met without creating, out of the contact, another mind, but not always is this invisible creation a "Master Mind."

There may be, and altogether too often there is, developed out of the meeting of two or more minds a negative power which is just the opposite to a "Master Mind."

There are certain minds which, as has already been stated throughout this lesson, cannot be made to blend in a spirit of harmony. This principle has its comparable analogy in chemistry, reference to which may enable the student to grasp more clearly the principle here referred to.

For example, the chemical formula H_2O (meaning the combining of two atoms of hydrogen with one atom of oxygen) changes these two elements into water. One atom of hydrogen and one atom of oxygen will not produce water; moreover, they cannot be made to associate themselves in harmony!

There are many known elements which, when combined, are immediately transformed from harmless into deadly poisonous substances. Stated differently, many well known poisonous elements are neutralized and rendered harmless when combined with certain other elements.

Just as the combining of certain elements changes their entire nature, the combining of certain minds changes the nature of those minds, producing either a certain degree of what has been called a "Master Mind," or its opposite, which is highly destructive.

Any man who has found his mother-in-law to be incompatible has experienced the negative application of the principle known as a "Master Mind." For some reason as yet unknown to investigators in the field of mind behavior, the majority of mothers-in-law appear to affect their daughters' husbands in a highly negative manner, the meeting of their minds with those of their sons-in-law creating a highly antagonistic influence instead of a "Master Mind."

This fact is too well known as a truth to make extended comment necessary.

Some minds will not be harmonized and cannot be blended into a "Master Mind," a fact which all leaders of men will do well to remember. It is the leader's responsibility so to group his men that those who have been placed at the most strategic points in his organization are made up of individuals whose minds CAN and WILL BE blended in a spirit of friendliness and harmony.

Ability so to group men is the chief outstanding quality of leadership. In Lesson Two of this course the student will discover that this ability was the main source of both the power and fortune accumulated by the late Andrew Carnegie.

Knowing nothing whatsoever of the technical end of the steel business, Carnegie so combined and grouped the men of which his "Master Mind" was composed that he built the most successful steel industry known to the world during his life-time.

Henry Ford's gigantic success may be traced to the successful application of this selfsame principle. With all the self-reliance a man could have, Ford, nevertheless, did not depend upon himself for the knowledge necessary in the successful development of his industries.

Like Carnegie, he surrounded himself with men who supplied the knowledge which he, himself, did not and could not possess.

Moreover, Ford picked men who could and did harmonize in group effort.

The most effective alliances, which have resulted in the creation of the principle known as the "Master Mind," have been those developed out of the blending of the minds of men and women. The reason for this is the fact that the minds of male and female will more readily blend in harmony than will the minds of males. Also, the added stimulus of sexual contact often enters into the development of a "Master Mind" between a man and a woman.

It is a well known fact that the male of the species is keener and more alert for "the chase," let the goal or object of the chase be what it may, when inspired and urged on by a female.

This human trait begins to manifest itself in the male at the age of puberty, and continues throughout his life. The first evidence of it may be observed in athletics, where boys are playing before an audience made up of females.

Remove the women from the audience and the game known as football would soon become a very tame affair. A boy will throw himself into a football game with almost superhuman effort when he knows that the girl of his choice is observing him from the grandstand.

And that same boy will throw himself into the game of accumulating money with the same enthusiasm when inspired and urged on by the woman of his choice; especially if that woman knows how to stimulate his mind with her own, through the law of the "Master Mind."

On the other hand, that same woman may, through a negative application of the law of the "Master Mind" (nagging, jealousy, selfishness, greed, vanity), drag this man down to sure defeat!

The late Elbert Hubbard understood the principle here described so well that when he discovered that the incompatibility between himself and his first wife was dragging him down to sure defeat he ran the gamut of public opinion by divorcing her and marrying the woman who is said to have been the main source of his inspiration.

Not every man would have had the courage to defy

public opinion, as Hubbard did, but who is wise enough to say that his action was not for the best interest of all concerned?

A man's chief business in life is to succeed!

The road to success may be, and generally is, obstructed by many influences which must be removed before the goal can be reached. One of the most detrimental of these obstacles is that of unfortunate alliance with minds which do not harmonize. In such cases the alliance must be broken or the end is sure to be defeat and failure.

The man who has mastered the six basic fears, one of which is the Fear of Criticism, will have no hesitancy in taking what may seem to the more convention-bound type of mind to be drastic action when he finds himself circumscribed and bound down by antagonistic alliances, no matter of what nature or with whom they may be.

It is a million times better to meet and face criticism than to be dragged down to failure and oblivion on account of alliances which are not harmonious, whether the alliances be of a business or social nature.

To be perfectly frank, the author is here justifying divorce, when the conditions surrounding marriage are such that harmony cannot prevail. This is not intended to convey the belief that lack of harmony may not be removed through other methods than that of divorce; for there are instances where the cause of antagonism may be removed and harmony established without taking the extreme step of divorce.

While it is true that some minds will not blend in a spirit of harmony, and cannot be forced or induced to do so, because of the chemical nature of the in-

IF you cannot do great things yourself, remember that you may do small things in a great way.

dividuals' brains, DO NOT BE TOO READY TO CHARGE THE OTHER PARTY TO YOUR ALLIANCE WITH ALL THE RESPONSIBILITY OF LACK OF HARMONY—REMEMBER, *THE TROUBLE MAY BE WITH YOUR OWN BRAIN!*

Remember, also, that a mind which cannot and will not harmonize with one person or persons may harmonize perfectly with other types of minds. Discovery of this truth has resulted in radical changes in methods of employing men. It is no longer customary to discharge a man because he does not fit in the position for which he was originally hired. The discriminating leader endeavors to place such a man in some other position, where, it has been proved more than once, misfits may become valuable men.

The student of this course should be sure that the principle described as the "Master Mind" is thoroughly understood before proceeding with the remaining lessons of the course. The reason for this is the fact that practically the entire course is closely associated with this law of mind operation.

If you are not sure that you understand this law, analyze the record of any man who has accumulated a great fortune, and you will find that they have either consciously, or unconsciously employed the "Master Mind" principle.

You cannot spend too much time in serious thought and contemplation in connection with the law of the "Master Mind," for the reason that when you have mastered this law and have learned how to apply it new worlds of opportunity will open to you.

This Introductory Lesson, while not really intended as a separate lesson of the Law of Success course, contains sufficient data to enable the student who has an aptitude for selling to become a Master Salesman.

Any sales organization may make effective use of the law of the "Master Mind" by grouping the salesmen in groups of two or more people who will ally themselves in a spirit of friendly co-operation and apply this law as suggested in this lesson.

An agent for a well known make of automobile, who employs twelve salesmen, has grouped his organization in six groups of two men each, with the object of applying the law of the "Master Mind," with the result that all the salesmen have established new high sales records.

This same organization has created what it calls the "One-A-Week Club," meaning that each man belonging to the Club has averaged the sale of one car a week since the Club was organized.

The results of this effort have been surprising to all!

Each man belonging to the Club was provided with a list of 100 prospective purchasers of automobiles. Each salesman sends one postal card a week to each of his 100 prospective purchasers, and makes personal calls on at least ten of these each day.

Each postal card is confined to the description of but one advantage of the automobile the salesman is selling, and asks for a personal interview.

Interviews have increased rapidly, as have, also, sales!

The agent who employs these salesmen has offered an extra cash bonus to each salesman who earns the right to membership in the "One-A-Week Club" by averaging one car a week.

The plan has injected new vitality into the entire organization. Moreover, the results of the plan are showing in the weekly sales record of each salesman.

A similar plan could be adopted very effectively by Life Insurance Agencies. Any enterprising General Agent might easily double or even triple the volume of his business, with the same number of salesmen, through the use of this plan.

Practically no changes whatsoever would need to be made in the method of use of the plan. The Club might be called the "Policy-A-Week Club," meaning that each member pledged himself to sell at least one policy, of an agreed minimum amount, each week.

The student of this course who has mastered the second lesson, and understands how to apply the fundamentals of that lesson (A Definite Chief Aim) will be able to make much more effective use of the plan here described.

It is not suggested or intended that any student shall undertake to apply the principles of this lesson, which is merely an Introductory Lesson, until he has mastered at least the next five lessons of the Law of Success course.

The main purpose of this Introductory Lesson is to state some of the principles upon which the course is founded. These principles are more accurately described, and the student is taught in a very definite manner how to apply them, in the individual lessons of the course.

The automobile sales organization referred to in this summary meets at luncheon once a week. One hour and a half is devoted to luncheon and to the discussion of ways and means of applying the principles of this course. This gives each man an opportunity to profit by the ideas of all the other members of the or‑ ganization.

Two tables are set for the luncheon.

At one table all who have earned the right to mem‑ bership in the One-A-Week Club are seated. At the other table, which is serviced with tinware instead of china, all who did not earn the right to membership in the Club are seated. These, needless to say, become the object of considerable good-natured chiding from the more fortunate members seated at the other table.

It is possible to make an almost endless variety of adaptations of this plan, both in the field of automobile salesmanship and in other fields of selling.

The justification for its use is that it pays!

It pays not only the leader or manager of the or‑ ganization, but every member of the sales force as well.

This plan has been briefly described for the purpose of showing the student of this course how to make practical application of the principles outlined in this course.

The final acid test of any theory or rule or prin‑ ciple is that it will ACTUALLY WORK! The law of the "Master Mind" has been proved sound because it WORKS.

If you understand this law you are now ready to proceed with Lesson Two, in which you will be further and much more deeply initiated in the application of the principles described in this Introductory Lesson.

A WINNER NEVER
QUITS, AND A
QUITTER NEVER
WINS!

NOTICE

Study this chart carefully and compare the ratings of these ten men before grading yourself, in the two columns at the right.

THE FIFTEEN LAWS OF SUCCESS	HENRY FORD	BENJAMIN FRANKLIN	GEORGE WASHINGTON	THEODORE ROOSEVELT
I. Definite Chief Aim --	100	100	100	100
II. Self-Confidence - - - -	100	80	90	100
III. Habit of Saving - - - -	100	100	75	50
IV. Initiative & Leadership	100	60	100	100
V. Imagination - - - - - -	90	90	80	80
VI. Enthusiasm - - - - - - -	75	80	90	100
VII. Self-Control - - - - - -	100	90	50	75
VIII. Habit of Doing More Than Paid For -	100	100	100	100
IX. Pleasing Personality - -	50	90	80	80
X. Accurate Thinking - - -	90	80	75	60
XI. Concentration - - - -	100	100	100	100
XII. Cooperation - - - - -	75	100	100	50
XIII. Profiting by Failure - -	100	90	75	60
XIV. Tolerance - - - - - - -	90	100	80	75
XV. Practising Golden Rule -	100	100	100	100
GENERAL AVERAGE - - - -	91	90	86	82

The ten men who have been analyzed, in the above chart, are well known throughout the world. Eight of these are known to be successful, while two are generally considered to have been failures. The failures are Jesse James and Napoleon Bonaparte. They have been analyzed for comparison. Carefully observe where these two men have been graded zero and you will see why they failed. *A grading of zero on any one of the Fifteen Laws of Success is sufficient to cause failure,* even though all other grades are high.

Abraham Lincoln	Woodrow Wilson	William H. Taft	Napoleon Bonaparte	Calvin Coolidge	Jesse James	Grade yourself in these two columns, before and after completing the Law of Success course. BEFORE	AFTER
100	100	100	100	100	0		
75	80	50	100	60	75		
20	40	30	40	100	0		
60	90	20	100	25	90		
70	80	65	90	50	60		
60	90	50	80	50	80		
95	75	80	40	100	50		
100	100	100	100	100	0		
80	75	90	100	40	50		
90	80	80	90	70	20		
100	100	100	100	100	75		
90	40	100	50	60	50		
60	60	60	40	40	0		
100	70	100	10	75	0		
100	100	100	0	100	0		
81	79	75	70	71	37		

Notice that all the successful men grade 100% on a Definite Chief Aim. This is a prerequisite to success, in all cases, without exception. If you wish to conduct an interesting experiment replace the above ten names with the names of ten people whom you know, five of whom are successful and five of whom are failures, and grade each of them. When you are through, GRADE YOURSELF, taking care to see that you really know what are your weaknesses

YOUR SIX MOST DANGEROUS ENEMIES

An After-the-Lesson Visit With the Author

*The Six Specters are labeled: Fear of Pov-
erty, Fear of Death, Fear of Ill-Health, Fear
of the Loss of Love, Fear of Old Age, Fear
of Criticism.*

Every person on earth is afraid of something.
Most fears are inherited. In this essay you
may study the six basic fears which do the
most damage. Your fears must be mastered
before you can win in any worth-while undertaking in life. Find out how many of the six
fears are bothering you, but more important
than this, determine, also how to conquer these
fears.

IN this picture you have the opportunity to study
your six worst enemies.

These enemies are not beautiful. The artist who
drew this picture did not paint the six characters as
ugly as they really are. If he had, no one would have
believed him.

As you read about these ugly characters analyze yourself and find out which of them does YOU the most damage!

.   .   .   .

The purpose of this essay is to help the readers of this course throw off these deadly enemies. Observe that the six characters are at your back, where you cannot conveniently see them.

Every human being on this earth is bound down to some extent by one or more of these unseen FEARS. The first step to be taken in killing off these enemies is to find out where and how you acquired them.

They got their grip upon you through two forms of heredity. One is known as physical heredity, to which Darwin devoted so much study. The other is known as social heredity, through which the fears, superstitions and beliefs of men who lived during the dark ages have been passed on from one generation to another.

Let us study, first, the part that physical heredity has played in creating these six BASIC FEARS. Starting at the beginning, we find that Nature has been a cruel builder. From the lowest form of life to the highest, Nature has permitted the stronger to prey upon the weaker forms of animal life.

The fish prey upon the worms and insects, eating them bodily. Birds prey upon the fish. Higher forms of animal life prey upon the birds, and upon one another, all the way up the line to man. And, man preys upon all the other lower forms of animal life, and upon MAN!

The whole story of evolution is one unbroken chain of evidence of cruelty and destruction of the weaker by the stronger. No wonder the weaker forms of animal life have learned to FEAR the stronger. The Fear consciousness is born in every living animal.

. . . .

So much for the FEAR instinct that came to us through physical heredity. Now let us examine social heredity, and find out what part it has played in our make-up. The term "social heredity" has reference to everything that we are taught, everything we learn or gather from observation and experience with other living beings.

Lay aside any prejudices and fixed opinions you may have formed, at least temporarily, and you may know the truth about your Six Worst Enemies, starting with:

THE FEAR OF POVERTY! It requires courage to tell the truth about the history of this enemy of mankind, and still greater courage to hear the truth after it has been told. The Fear of Poverty grows out of man's habit of preying upon his fellow men, economically. The animals which have instinct, but no power to THINK, prey upon one another physically. Man, with his superior sense of intuition, and his more powerful weapon of THOUGHT, does not eat his fellow man bodily; he gets more pleasure from eating him FINANCIALLY.

So great an offender is man, in this respect, that nearly every state and nation has been obliged to pass laws, scores of laws, to protect the weak from the strong. Every blue-sky law is indisputable evidence of man's nature to prey upon his weaker brother economically.

The second of the Six Basic Fears with which man is bound down is:

THE FEAR OF OLD AGE!   This Fear grows out of two major causes.   First, the thought that Old Age may bring with it POVERTY.   Secondly, from false and cruel sectarian teachings which have been so well mixed with fire and brimstone that every human being learned to Fear Old Age because it meant the approach of another and, perhaps, a more horrible world than this.

The third of the Six Basic Fears is:

THE FEAR OF ILL HEALTH: This Fear is born of both physical and social heredity.   From birth until death there is eternal warfare within every physical body; warfare between groups of cells, one group being known as the friendly builders of the body, and the other as the destroyers, or "disease germs."   The seed of Fear is born in the physical body, to begin with, as the result of Nature's cruel plan of permitting the stronger forms of cell life to prey upon the weaker. Social heredity has played its part through lack of cleanliness and knowledge of sanitation.   Also, through the law of suggestion cleverly manipulated by those who profited by ILL HEALTH.

The fourth of the Six Basic Fears is:

THE FEAR OF LOSS OF LOVE OF SOMEONE: This Fear fills the asylums with the insanely jealous, for jealousy is nothing but a form of insanity.   It also fills the divorce courts and causes murders and other forms of cruel punishment.   It is a holdover, handed down through social heredity, from the stone age when man preyed upon his fellow man by stealing his mate by physical force. The method, but not the practice, has now changed to some extent. Instead of physical force man now steals his fellow man's mate with pretty colorful ribbons and fast motor cars and bootleg whisky, and sparkling rocks and stately mansions.

Man is improving. He now "entices" where once he "drove."

The fifth of the Six Basic Fears is:

THE FEAR OF CRITICISM: Just how and where man got this Fear is difficult to determine, but it is certain that he has it. But for this Fear men would not become bald-headed. Bald heads come from tightly fitting hat-bands, which cut off the circulation from the roots of the hair. Women seldom are bald because they wear loose fitting hats. But for Fear of Criticism man would lay aside his hat and keep his hair.

The makers of clothing have not been slow to capitalize this Basic Fear of mankind. Every season the styles change, because the clothes makers know that few people have the courage to wear a garment that is one season out of step with what "They are all wearing." If you doubt this (you gentlemen) start down the street with last year's narrow-brimmed straw hat on, when this year's style calls for the broad brim. Or (you ladies), take a walk down the street on Easter morning with last year's hat on. Observe how uncomfortable you are, thanks to your unseen enemy, the FEAR OF CRITICISM.

The sixth, and last of the Six Basic Fears is the most dreaded of them all. It is called:

THE FEAR OF DEATH! For tens of thousands

of years man has been asking the still unanswered questions—"WHENCE?" and "WHITHER?"   The more crafty of the race have not been slow to offer the answer to this eternal question, "Where did I come from and where am I going after Death?"   "Come into my tent," says one leader, "and you may go to Heaven after Death."   Heaven was then pictured as a wonderful city whose streets were lined with gold and studded with precious stones.   "Remain out of my tent and you may go straight to hell."   Hell was then pictured as a blazing furnace where the poor victim might have the misery of burning forever in brimstone.

No wonder mankind FEARS DEATH!

.   .   .   .

Take another look at the picture at the beginning of this essay and determine, if you can, which of the Six Basic Fears is doing you the greatest damage. An enemy discovered is an enemy half whipped.

Thanks to the schools and colleges man is slowly discovering these Six Enemies.   The most effective tool with which to fight them is ORGANIZED KNOWLEDGE.   Ignorance and Fear are twin sisters. They are generally found together.

But for IGNORANCE and SUPERSTITION the Six Basic Fears would disappear from man's nature in one generation.   In every public library may be found the remedy for these six enemies of mankind, providing you know what books to read.

Begin by reading The Science of Power, by Benjamin Kidd, and you will have broken the strangle hold of most of your Six Basic Fears.   Follow this by reading Emerson's essay on Compensation. Then select some good book on auto-suggestion (self-suggestion) and inform yourself on the principle through which your beliefs of today become the realities of tomorrow. Mind In the Making, by Robinson, will give you a good start toward understanding your own mind.

.   .   .   .

Through the principle of social heredity the IGNORANCE and SUPERSTITION of the dark ages have been passed on to you. But, you are living in a modern age. On every hand you may see evidence that every EFFECT has a natural CAUSE. Begin, now, to study effects by their causes and soon you will emancipate your mind from the burden of the Six Basic Fears.

Begin by studying men who have accumulated great wealth, and find out the CAUSE of their achievements. Henry Ford is a good subject to start with. Within the short period of twenty-five years he has whipped POVERTY and made himself the most powerful man on earth. There was no luck or chance or accident back of his achievement. It grew out of his careful observation of certain principles which are as available to you as they were to him.

Henry Ford is not bound down by the Six Basic Fears; make no mistake about this.

If you feel that you are too far away from Ford to study him accurately, then begin by selecting two people whom you know close at hand; one representing your idea of FAILURE and the other corresponding to your idea of SUCCESS. Find out what made

one a failure and the other a success. Get the real
FACTS. In the process of gathering these facts you
will have taught yourself a great lesson on CAUSE
and EFFECT.

Nothing ever just "happens." Everything, from
the lowest animal form that creeps on the earth or
swims in the seas, on up to man, is the EFFECT of
Nature's evolutionary process. Evolution is "orderly
change." No "miracles" are connected with this
orderly change.

Not only do the physical shapes and colors of animals undergo slow, orderly change from one generation
to another, but the mind of man is also undergoing
constant change. Herein lies your hope for improvement. You have the power to force your mind through
a process of rather quick change. In a single month
of properly directed self-suggestion you may place
your foot upon the neck of every one of your Six
Basic Fears. In twelve months of persistent effort you
may drive the entire herd into the corner where it will
never again do you any serious injury.

You will resemble, tomorrow, the DOMINATING
THOUGHTS that you keep alive in your mind today!
Plant in your mind the seed of DETERMINATION
to whip your Six Basic Fears and the battle will have
been half won then and there. Keep this intention in
your mind and it will slowly push your Six Worst
Enemies out of sight, as they exist nowhere except in
your own mind.

The man who is powerful FEARS nothing; not even
God. The POWERFUL man loves God, but FEARS
Him never! Enduring power never grows out of
FEAR. Any power that is built upon FEAR is bound

to crumble and disintegrate. Understand this great
truth and you will never be so unfortunate as to try
to raise yourself to power through the FEARS of
other people who may owe you temporary allegiance.

Man is of soul and body formed for deeds
Of high resolve; on fancy's boldest wing
To soar unwearied, fearlessly to turn
The keenest pangs to peacefulness, and taste
The joys which mingled sense and spirit yield;

Or he is formed for abjectness and woe,
To grovel on the dunghill of his fears,
To shrink at every sound, to quench the flame
Of natural love in sensualism, to know
That hour as blest when on his worthless days
The frozen hand of death shall set its seal,
Yet fear the cure, though hating the disease.

The one is man that shall hereafter be,
The other, man as vice has made him now.
                                        —SHELLEY

Lesson Two

A DEFINITE CHIEF AIM

The best rose bush, after all, is not that which has the fewest thorns, but that which bears the finest roses.

—*Henry van Dyke.*

THE LAW OF SUCCESS
Lesson Two
A DEFINITE CHIEF AIM

"You Can Do It if You Believe You Can!"

OU are at the beginning of a course of philosophy which, for the first time in the history of the world, has been organized from the known factors which have been used and must always be used by successful people.

Literary style has been completely subordinated for the sake of stating the principles and laws included in this course in such a manner that they may be quickly and easily assimilated by people in every walk of life.

Some of the principles described in the course are familiar to all who will read the course. Others are here stated for the first time. It should be kept in mind, from the first lesson to the last, that the value of the philosophy lies entirely in the thought stimuli it will produce in the mind of the student, and not merely in the lessons themselves.

Stated in another way, this course is intended as a mind stimulant that will cause the student to organize

and direct to a DEFINITE end the forces of his ot
her mind, thus harnessing the stupendous power which
most people waste in spasmodic, purposeless thought.

Singleness of purpose is essential for success, no
matter what may be one's idea of the definition of
success. Yet singleness of purpose is a quality which
may, and generally does, call for thought on many allied subjects.

This author traveled a long distance to watch Jack
Dempsey train for an oncoming battle. It was observed that he did not rely entirely upon one form of
exercise, but resorted to many forms. The punching
bag helped him develop one set of muscles, and also
trained his eye to be quick. The dumb-bells trained
still another set of muscles. Running developed the
muscles of his legs and hips. A well balanced food
ration supplied the materials needed for building muscle without fat. Proper sleep, relaxation and rest
habits provided still other qualities which he must have
in order to win.

The student of this course is, or should be, engaged
in the business of training for success in the battle of
life. To win there are many factors which must have
attention. A well organized, alert and energetic mind
is produced by various and sundry stimuli, all of
which are plainly described in these lessons.

It should be remembered, however, that the mind
requires, for its development, a variety of exercise,
just as the physical body, to be properly developed,
calls for many forms of systematic exercise.

Horses are trained to certain gaits by trainers who
hurdle-jump them over handicaps which cause them
to develop the desired steps, through habit and repe-

tition. The human mind must be trained in a similar manner, by a variety of thought-inspiring stimuli.

You will observe, before you have gone very far into this philosophy, that the reading of these lessons will superinduce a flow of thoughts covering a wide range of subjects. For this reason the student should read the course with a note-book and pencil at hand, and follow the practice of recording these thoughts or "ideas" as they come into the mind.

By following this suggestion the student will have a collection of ideas, by the time the course has been read two or three times, sufficient to transform his or her entire life-plan.

By following this practice it will be noticed, very soon, that the mind has become like a magnet in that it will attract useful ideas right out of the "thin air," to use the words of a noted scientist who has experimented with this principle for a great number of years.

You will do yourself a great injustice if you undertake this course with even a remote feeling that you do not stand in need of more knowledge than you now possess. In truth, no man knows enough about any worth-while subject to entitle him to feel that he has the last word on that subject.

In the long, hard task of trying to wipe out some of my own ignorance and make way for some of the useful truths of life, I have often seen, in my imagination, the Great Marker who stands at the gateway entrance of life and writes "Poor Fool" on the brow of those who believe they are wise, and "Poor Sinner" on the brow of those who believe they are saints.

Which, translated into workaday language, means that none of us know very much, and by the very na-

ture of our being can never know as much as we need
to know in order to live sanely and enjoy life while
we live.

Humility is a forerunner of success!

Until we become humble in our own hearts we are
not apt to profit greatly by the experiences and
thoughts of others.

Sounds like a preachment on morality? Well, what
if it does?

Even "preachments," as dry and lacking in interest
as they generally are, may be beneficial if they serve
to reflect the shadow of our real selves so we may get
an approximate idea of our smallness and superficial-
ity.

Success in life is largely predicated upon our knowing men!

The best place to study the man-animal is in your
own mind, by taking as accurate an inventory as possible of YOURSELF. When you know yourself thoroughly (if you ever do) you will also know much about
others.

To know others, not as they seem to be, but as they
really are, study them through:

1—The posture of the body, and the way they walk.

2—The tone of the voice, its quality, pitch, volume.

3—The eyes, whether shifty or direct.

4—The use of words, their trend, nature and quality.

Through these open windows you may literally
"walk right into a man's soul" and take a look at the
REAL MAN!

Going a step further, if you would know men study
them:

When angry

When in love

When money is involved

When eating (alone, and unobserved, as they believe)

When writing

When in trouble

When joyful and triumphant

When downcast and defeated

When facing catastrophe of a hazardous nature

When trying to make a "good impression" on others

When informed of another's misfortune

When informed of another's good fortune

When losing in any sort of a game of sport

When winning at sport

When alone, in a meditative mood.

Before you can know any man, as he really is, you must observe him in all the foregoing moods, and perhaps more, which is practically the equivalent of saying that you have no right to judge others at sight.

Appearances count, there can be no doubt of that, but appearances are often deceiving.

This course has been so designed that the student who masters it may take inventory of himself and of others by other than "snap-judgment" methods. The student who masters this philosophy will be able to look through the outer crust of personal adornment, clothes, so-called culture and the like, and down deep into the heart of all about him.

This is a very broad promise!

It would not have been made if the author of this philosophy had not known, from years of experimentation and analysis, that the promise can be met.

Some who have examined the manuscripts of this

No person is "Educated" who has not at least a "Speaking Acquaintance" with the Law of Compensation, as it is described by Emerson.

course have asked why it was not called a course in Master Salesmanship. The answer is that the word "salesmanship" is commonly associated with the marketing of goods or services, and it would, therefore, narrow down and circumscribe the real nature of the course. It is true that this is a course in Master Salesmanship, providing one takes a deeper-than-the-average view of the meaning of salesmanship.

This philosophy is intended to enable those who master it to "sell" their way through life successfully, with the minimum amount of resistance and friction. Such a course, therefore, must help the student organize and make use of much truth which is overlooked by the majority of people who go through life as mediocres.

Not all people are so constituted that they wish to know the truth about all matters vitally affecting life. One of the great surprises the author of this course has met with, in connection with his research activities, is that so few people are willing to hear the truth when it shows up their own weaknesses.

We prefer illusions to realities!

New truths, if accepted at all, are taken with the proverbial grain of salt. Some of us demand more than a mere pinch of salt; we demand enough to pickle new ideas so they become useless.

For these reasons the Introductory Lesson of this course, and this lesson as well, cover subjects intended to pave the way for new ideas so those ideas will not be too severe a shock to the mind of the student.

The thought the author wishes to "get across" has been quite plainly stated by the editor of the American

Magazine, in an editorial which appeared in a recent issue, in the following words:

"On a recent rainy night, Carl Lomen, the reindeer king of Alaska, told me a true story. It has stuck in my crop ever since. And now I am going to pass it along.

" 'A certain Greenland Eskimo,' said Lomen, 'was taken on one of the American North Polar expeditions a number of years ago. Later, as a reward for faithful service, he was brought to New York City for a short visit. At all the miracles of sight and sound he was filled with a most amazed wonder. When he returned to his native village he told stories of buildings that rose into the very face of the sky; of street cars, which he described as houses that moved along the trail, with people living in them as they moved; of mammoth bridges, artificial lights, and all the other dazzling concomitants of the metropolis.

" 'His people looked at him coldly and walked away. And forthwith throughout the whole village he was dubbed "Sagdluk," meaning "the Liar," and this name he carried in shame to his grave. Long before his death his original name was entirely forgotten.

" 'When Knud Rasmussen made his trip from Greenland to Alaska he was accompanied by a Greenland Eskimo named Mitek (Eider Duck). Mitek visited Copenhagen and New York, where he saw many things for the first time and was greatly impressed. Later, upon his return to Greenland, he recalled the tragedy of Sagdluk, and decided that it would not be wise to tell the truth. Instead, he would narrate stories that his people could grasp, and thus save his reputation.

" 'So he told them how he and Doctor Rasmussen maintained a kayak on the banks of a great river, the Hudson, and how, each morning, they paddled out for their hunting. Ducks, geese and seals were to be had a-plenty, and they enjoyed the visit immensely.

" 'Mitek, in the eyes of his countrymen, is a very honest man. His neighbors treat him with rare respect.'

"The road of the truth-teller has always been rocky. Socrates sipping the hemlock, Christ crucified, Stephen stoned, Bruno burned at the stake, Galileo terrified into retraction of his starry truths—forever could one follow that bloodly trail through the pages of history.

"Something in human nature makes us resent the impact of new ideas."

We hate to be disturbed in the beliefs and prejudices that have been handed down with the family furniture. At maturity too many of us go into hibernation, and live off the fat of ancient fetishes. If a new idea invades our den we rise up snarling from our winter sleep.

The Eskimos, at least, had some excuse. They were unable to visualize the startling pictures drawn by Sagdluk. Their simple lives had been too long circumscribed by the brooding arctic night.

But there is no adequate reason why the average man should ever close his mind to fresh "slants" on life. He does, just the same. Nothing is more tragic —or more common—than mental inertia. For every ten men who are physically lazy there are ten thousand with stagnant minds. And stagnant minds are the breeding places of fear.

An old farmer up in Vermont always used to wind up his prayers with this plea: "Oh, God, give me an open mind!" If more people followed his example they might escape being hamstrung by prejudices. And what a pleasant place to live in the world would be.

.   .   .   .

Every person should make it his business to gather new ideas from sources other than the environment in which he daily lives and works.

The mind becomes withered, stagnant, narrow and closed unless it searches for new ideas. The farmer should come to the city quite often, and walk among the strange faces and the tall buildings. He will go back to his farm, his mind refreshed, with more courage and greater enthusiasm.

The city man should take a trip to the country every so often and freshen his mind with sights new and different from those associated with his daily labors.

Everyone needs a change of mental environment at regular periods, the same as a change and variety of food are essential. The mind becomes more alert, more elastic and more ready to work with speed and accuracy after it has been bathed in new ideas, outside of one's own field of daily labor.

As a student of this course you will temporarily lay aside the set of ideas with which you perform your daily labors, and enter a field of entirely new (and in some instances, heretofore unheard-of) ideas.

Splendid! You will come out, at the other end of this course, with a new stock of ideas which will make you more efficient, more enthusiastic and more courageous, *no matter in what sort of work you may be engaged.*

Do not be afraid of new ideas! They may mean to you the difference between success and failure.

Some of the ideas introduced in this course will require no further explanation or proof of their soundness because they are familiar to practically everyone. Other ideas here introduced are new, and for that very reason many students of this philosophy may hesitate to accept them as sound.

Every principle described in this course has been thoroughly tested by the author, and the majority of the principles covered have been tested by scores of scientists and others who were quite capable of distinguishing between the merely theoretic and the practical.

For these reasons all principles here covered are known to be workable in the exact manner claimed for them. However, no student of this course is asked to accept any statement made in these lessons without having first satisfied himself or herself, by tests, experiments and analysis, that the statement is sound.

The major evil the student is requested to avoid is that of forming opinions without definite FACTS as the basis, which brings to mind Herbert Spencer's famous admonition, in these words:

"There is a principle which is a bar against all information; which is proof against all argument; and which cannot fail to keep a man in everlasting ignorance. This principle is contempt prior to examination."

It may be well to bear this principle in mind when you come to study the Law of the Master Mind de-

B^Y and Large, there

is no such thing as

"Something for Noth-

ing." In the long run you

get exactly that for which

you pay, whether you are

buying an automobile or

a loaf of bread.

scribed in these lessons. This law embodies an entirely new principle of mind operation, and, for this reason alone, it will be difficult for many students to accept it as sound until after they have experimented with it.

When the fact is considered, however, that the Law of the Master Mind is believed to be the real basis of most of the achievements of those who are considered geniuses, this Law takes on an aspect which calls for more than "snap-judgment" opinions.

It is believed by many scientific men whose opinions on the subject have been given the author of this philosophy, that the Law of the Master Mind is the basis of practically all of the more important achievements resulting from group or co-operative effort.

The late Dr. Alexander Graham Bell said he believed the Law of the Master Mind, as it has been described in this philosophy, was not only sound, but that all the higher institutions of learning would soon be teaching that Law as a part of their courses in psychology.

Charles P. Steinmetz said he had experimented with the Law and had arrived at the same conclusion as that stated in these lessons, long before he talked to the author of the Law of Success philosophy about the subject.

Luther Burbank and John Burroughs made similar statements!

Edison was never interrogated on the subject, but other statements of his indicate that he would endorse the Law as being a possibility, if not in fact a reality.

Dr. Elmer Gates endorsed the Law, in a conversation with this author more than fifteen years ago. Dr. Gates is a scientist of the highest order, ranking along with Steinmetz, Edison and Bell.

The author of this philosophy has talked to scores
of intelligent business men who, while they were not
scientists, admitted they believed in the soundness of
the Law of the Master Mind. It is hardly excusable,
therefore, for men of less ability to judge such matters,
to form opinions as to this Law, without serious, systematic investigation.

.   .   .   .

Let me lay before you a brief outline of what this
lesson is and what it is intended to do for *you!*

Having prepared myself for the practice of law I will
offer this introduction as a "statement of my case."
The evidence with which to back up my case will be
presented in the sixteen lessons of which the course is
composed.

The facts out of which this course has been prepared
have been gathered through more than twenty-five
years of business and professional experience, and my
only explanation of the rather free use of the personal
pronoun throughout the course is that I am writing
from *first-hand experience.*

Before this Reading Course on the Law of Success
was published the manuscripts were submitted to two
prominent universities with the request that they be
read by competent professors with the object of eliminating or correcting any statements that appeared to
be unsound, from an economic viewpoint.

This request was complied with and the manuscripts
were carefully examined, with the result that not a
single change was made with the exception of one or
two slight changes in wording.

One of the professors who examined the manuscripts expressed himself, in part, as follows: "It is a tragedy that every boy and girl who enters high school is not efficiently drilled on the fifteen major parts of your Reading Course on the Law of Success. It is regrettable that the great university with which I am connected, and every other university, does not include your course as a part of its curriculum."

Inasmuch as this Reading Course is intended as a map or blueprint that will guide you in the attainment of that coveted goal called "Success," may it not be well here to define success?

Success is the development of the power with which to get whatever one wants in life without interfering with the rights of others.

I would lay particular stress upon the word "power" because it is inseparably related to success. We are living in a world and during an age of intense competition, and the law of the survival of the fittest is everywhere in evidence. Because of these facts all who would enjoy enduring success must go about its attainment through the use of power.

And what is *power?*

Power is *organized* energy or effort. This course is properly called the Law of Success for the reason that it teaches how one may organize *facts* and *knowledge* and the faculties of one's mind into a unit of power.

This course brings you a definite promise, namely:

That through its mastery and application you can get whatever you want, with but two qualifying words —"within reason."

This qualification takes into consideration your education, your wisdom or your lack of it, your physical endurance, your temperament, and all of the other

qualities mentioned in the sixteen lessons of this course
as being the factors most essential in the attainment
of success.

Without a single exception those who have attained
unusual success have done so, either consciously or
unconsciously, through the aid of all or a portion of
the fifteen major factors of which this course is compiled. If you doubt this statement, then master these
sixteen lessons so you can go about the analysis with
reasonable accuracy and analyze such men as Carnegie,
Rockefeller, Hill, Harriman, Ford and others of this
type who have accumulated great fortunes of material
wealth, and you will see that they understood and applied the principle of *organized effort* which runs, like
a golden cord of indisputable evidence, throughout
this course.

Nearly twenty years ago I interviewed Mr. Carnegie for the purpose of writing a story about him.
During the interview I asked him to what he attributed
his *success*. With a merry little twinkle in his eyes
he said:

"Young man, before I answer your question will
you please define your term 'success'?"

After waiting until he saw that I was somewhat
embarrassed by his request he continued: "By success
you have reference to my money, have you not?" I
assured him that money was the term by which most
people measured success, and he then said: "Oh, well
—if you wish to know how I got my money—*if that is
what you call success*—I will answer your question by
saying that we have a master mind here in our business, and that mind is made up of more than a score
of men who constitute my personal staff of superin-

tendents and managers and accountants and chemists and other necessary types. No one person in this group is the master mind of which I speak, but the sum total of the minds in the group, co-ordinated, organized and directed to a *definite* end in a spirit of harmonious co-operation is the power that got my money for me. No two minds in the group are exactly alike, but each man in the group does the thing that he is supposed to do and he does it better than any other person in the world could do it."

Then and there the seed out of which this course has been developed was sown in my mind, but that seed did not take root or germinate until later. This interview marked the beginning of years of research which led, finally, to the discovery of the principle of psychology described in the Introductory Lesson as the "Master Mind."

I heard all that Mr. Carnegie said, but it took the knowledge gained from many years of subsequent contact with the business world to enable me to assimilate that which he said and clearly grasp and understand the principle back of it, which was nothing more nor less than the principle of *organized effort* upon which this course on the Law of Success is founded.

Carnegie's group of men constituted a "Master Mind" and that mind was so well organized, so well co-ordinated, so powerful, that it could have accumulated millions of dollars for Mr. Carnegie in practically any sort of endeavor of a commercial or industrial nature. The steel business in which that mind was engaged was but an incident in connection with the accumulation of the Carnegie wealth. The same wealth could have been accumulated had the "Master

IF you can run a losing race without blaming your loss on someone else, you have bright prospects of success further down the road in life.

Mind" been directed in the coal business or the banking business or the grocery business, for the reason that back of the mind was *power*—that sort of power which *you* may have when you shall have organized the faculties of your own mind and allied yourself with other well organized minds for the attainment of a *definite chief aim* in life.

A careful check-up with several of Mr. Carnegie's former business associates, which was made after this course was begun, proves conclusively not only that there is such a law as that which has been called the "Master Mind," but that this law was the chief source of Mr. Carnegie's success.

Perhaps no man was ever associated with Mr. Carnegie who knew him better than did Mr. C. M. Schwab. In the following words Mr. Schwab has very accurately described that "subtle something" in Mr. Carnegie's personality which enabled him to rise to such stupendous heights.

"I never knew a man with so much imagination lively intelligence and instinctive comprehension You sensed that he probed your thoughts and took stock of everything that you had ever done or might do. He seemed to catch at your next word before it was spoken. The play of his mind was dazzling and his habit of close observation gave him a store of knowledge about innumerable matters.

"But his outstanding quality, from so rich an en dowment, was the power of inspiring other men. Con· fidence radiated from him. You might be doubtful about something and discuss the matter with Mr. Carnegie. In a flash he would make you see that it was right and then absolutely believe it; or he might settle your doubts by pointing out its weakness. This quality of attracting others, then spurring them on, arose from his own strength.

"The results of his leadership were remarkable. Never before in history of industry, I imagine, was there a man who, without understanding his business in its working details, making no pretense of technical knowledge concerning steel or engineering, was yet able to build up such an enterprise.

"Mr. Carnegie's ability to inspire men rested on something deeper than any faculty of judgment."

In the last sentence Mr. Schwab has conveyed a thought which corroborates the theory of the "Master Mind" to which the author of this course has attributed the chief source of Mr. Carnegie's power.

Mr. Schwab has also confirmed the statement that Mr. Carnegie could have succeeded as well in any other business as he did in the steel business. It is obvious that his success was due to his understanding of his own mind and the minds of other men, and not to mere knowledge of the steel business itself.

This thought is most consoling to those who have not yet attained outstanding success, for it shows that success is solely a matter of correctly applying laws and principles which are available to all; and these laws, let us not forget, are fully described in the Sixteen Lessons of this course.

Mr. Carnegie learned how to apply the law of the "Master Mind." This enabled him to organize the faculties of his own mind and the faculties of other men's minds, and co-ordinate the whole behind a DEFINITE CHIEF AIM.

Every strategist, whether in business or war or industry or other callings, understands the value of *organized*, co-ordinated effort. Every military strate-gist understands the value of sowing seeds of dissension in the ranks of the opposing forces, because this breaks up the power of co-ordination back of the opposition. During the late world war much was heard about the effects of propaganda, and it seems not an exaggeration to say that the disorganizing forces of propaganda were much more destructive than were all the guns and explosives used in the war.

One of the most important turning-points of the world war came when the allied armies were placed under the direction of the French General, Foch. There are well informed military men who claim that this was the move which spelled doom for the opposing armies.

Any modern railroad bridge is an excellent example of the value of *organized effort,* because it demonstrates quite simply and clearly how thousands of tons of weight may be borne by a comparatively small group of steel bars and beams so arranged that the weight is spread over the entire group.

There was a man who had seven sons who were always quarreling among themselves. One day he called them together and informed them that he wished to demonstrate just what their lack of co-operative effort meant. He had prepared a bundle of seven sticks which he had carefully tied together. One by one he asked his sons to take the bundle and break it. Each son tried, but in vain. Then he cut the strings and handed one of the sticks to each of his sons and asked him to break it over his knee. After the sticks had all been broken, with ease, he said:

"When you boys work together in a spirit of harmony you resemble the bundle of sticks, and no one
can defeat you; but when you quarrel among yourselves anyone can defeat you one at a time."

There is a worth-while lesson in this story of the
man and his seven quarrelsome sons, and it may be
applied to the people of a community, the employees
and employers in a given place of employment, or to
the state and nation in which we live.

Organized effort may be made a power, but it may
also be a dangerous power unless guided with intelligence, which is the chief reason why the sixteenth lesson of this course is devoted largely to describing how
to direct the power of organized effort so that it will
lead to *success;* that sort of success which is founded
upon truth and justice and fairness that lead to ultimate *happiness.*

One of the outstanding tragedies of this age of struggle and money-madness is the fact that so few people
are engaged in the effort which they like best. One of
the objects of this course is to help each student find
his or her particular niche in the world's work, where
both material prosperity and *happiness* in abundance
may be found. To accomplish this purpose the various lessons of this course are skillfully designed to
help the student take inventory of himself and find out
what latent ability and hidden forces lie sleeping
within him.

This entire course is intended as a stimulus with
which to enable you to see yourself and your hidden
forces as they are, and to awaken in you the ambition
and the vision and the determination to cause you to go
forth and claim that which is rightfully yours.

Less than thirty years ago a man was working in the same shop with Henry Ford, doing practically the same sort of work that he was doing. It has been said that this man was really a more competent workman, in that particular sort of work, than Ford. Today this man is still engaged in the same sort of work, at wages of less than a hundred dollars a week, while Mr. Ford is the world's richest man.

What outstanding difference is there between these two men which has so widely separated them in terms of material wealth? Just this—Ford understood and applied the principle of *organized effort* while the other man did not.

In the little city of Shelby, Ohio, as these lines are being written, for the first time in the history of the world this principle of *organized effort* is being applied for the purpose of bringing about a closer alliance between the churches and the business houses of a community.

The clergymen and business men have formed an alliance, with the result that practically every church in the city is squarely back of every business man, and every business man is squarely back of every church. The effect has been the strengthening of the churches and the business houses to such an extent that it has been said that it would be practically impossible for any individual member of either class to fail in his calling. The others who belong to the alliance will permit no such failures.

Here is an example of what may happen when groups of men form an alliance for the purpose of placing the combined power of the group back of each individual unit. The alliance has brought both ma-

A GOOD Encyclopæ-
dia contains most of the
known facts of the world,
but they are as useless as
Sand Dunes until organ-
ized and expressed in
terms of action.

terial and moral advantages to the city of Shelby such
as are enjoyed by but few other cities of its size in
America. The plan has worked so effectively and so
satisfactorily that a movement is now under way to
extend it into other cities throughout America.

That you may gain a still more concrete vision of
just how this principle of *organized effort* can be made
powerful, stop for a moment and allow your imagination to draw a picture of what would likely be the
result if every church and every newspaper and every
Rotary Club and every Kiwanis Club and every Advertising Club and every Woman's Club and every
other civic organization of a similar nature, in your
city, or in any other city in the United States, should
form an alliance for the purpose of pooling their
power and using it for the benefit of all members of
these organizations.

The results which might easily be attained by such
an alliance stagger the imagination!

There are three outstanding powers in the world of
organized effort. They are: The churches, the schools
and the newspapers. Think what might easily happen if these three great powers and molders of public
opinion should ally themselves together for the purpose
of bringing about any needed change in human conduct. They could, in a single generation, so modify
the present standard of business ethics, for example,
that it would practically be business suicide for anyone to try to transact business under any standard
except that of the Golden Rule. Such an alliance
could be made to produce sufficient influence to
change, in a single generation, the business, social and
moral tendencies of the entire civilized world. Such

an alliance would have sufficient power to *force* upon the minds of the oncoming generations any ideals desired.

Power is *organized effort,* as has already been stated! Success is based upon power!

That you may have a clear conception of what is meant by the term "organized effort" I have made use of the foregoing illustrations, and for the sake of further emphasis I am going to repeat the statement that the accumulation of great wealth and the attainment of any high station in life such as constitute what we ordinarily call *success,* are based upon the vision to comprehend and the ability to assimilate and apply the major principles of the sixteen lessons of this course.

This course is in complete harmony with the principles of economics and the principles of Applied Psychology. You will observe that those lessons, which depend, for their practical application, upon knowledge of psychology, have been supplemented with sufficient explanation of the psychological principles involved to render the lessons easily understood.

Before the manuscripts for this course went to the publisher they were submitted to some of the foremost bankers and business men of America, that they might be examined, analyzed and criticized by the most practical type of mind. One of the best known bankers in New York City returned the manuscripts with the following comment:

"I hold a master's degree from Yale, but I would willingly exchange all that this degree has brought me in return for what your course on the Law of Success would have brought me had I been afforded the privi-

lege of making it a part of my training while I was
studying at Yale.

"My wife and daughter have also read the manuscripts, and my wife has named your course 'the master key-board of life' because she believes that all who
understand how to apply it may play a perfect symphony in their respective callings, just as a pianist
may play any tune when once the key-board of the
piano and the fundamentals of music have been mastered."

No two people on earth are exactly alike, and for
this reason no two people would be expected to attain
from this course the same viewpoint. Each student
should read the course, understand it and then appropriate from its contents whatever he or she needs to
develop a well rounded personality.

Take your measure; make a self-analysis. See
page 363 of my book "THINK AND GROW RICH."
If you will answer all these questions truthfully, you
will know more about yourself than the majority of
people. Study the questions carefully, come back to
them once each week for several months, and be astounded at the amount of additional knowledge of
great value to yourself, you will have gained by answering the questions truthfully. If you are not certain concerning the answers to some of the questions,
seek the counsel of those who know you well, especially those who have no motive in flattering you, and
see yourself through their eyes.

This course has been compiled for the purpose of
helping the student find out what are his or her natural
talents, and for the purpose of helping organize, co-
ordinate and put into use the knowledge gained from

experience. For more than twenty years I have been gathering, classifying and organizing the material that has gone into the course. During the past fourteen years I have analyzed more than 16,000 men and women, and all of the vital facts gathered from these analyses have been carefully organized and woven into this course. These analyses brought out many interesting facts which have helped to make this course practical and usable. For example, it was discovered that ninety-five per cent of all who were analyzed were failures, and but five per cent were successes. (By the term "failure" is meant that they had failed to find happiness and the ordinary necessities of life without struggle that was almost unbearable.) Perhaps this is about the proportion of successes and failures that might be found if all the people of the world were accurately analyzed. The struggle for a mere existence is terrific among people who have not learned how to organize and direct their natural talents, while the attainment of those necessities, as well as the acquiring of many of the luxuries, is comparatively simple among those who have mastered the principle of *organized effort*.

One of the most startling facts brought to light by those 16,000 analyses was the discovery that the ninety-five per cent who were classed as failures were in that class *because they had no definite chief aim in life,* while the five per cent constituting the successful ones not only had purposes that were *definite,* but they had, also, *definite plans* for the attainment of their purposes.

Another important fact disclosed by these analyses was that the ninety-five per cent constituting the failures were engaged in work which they did not like, while the five per cent constituting the successful ones were doing that which they liked best. It is doubtful whether a person could be a failure while engaged in work which he liked best. Another vital fact learned from the analyses was that all of the five per cent who were succeeding had formed the habit of systematic saving of money, while the ninety-five per cent who were failures saved nothing. This is worthy of serious thought.

One of the chief objects of this course is to aid the student in performing his or her chosen work in such a manner that it will yield the greatest returns in both money and happiness.

NO POSITION IN
LIFE CAN BE SE-
CURE, AND NO
ACHIEVEMENT
CAN BE PERMA-
NENT UNLESS
BUILT UPON TRUTH
AND JUSTICE.

A Definite Chief Aim

The key-note of this entire lesson may be found in the word "definite."

It is most appalling to know that ninety-five per cent of the people of the world are drifting aimlessly through life, without the slightest conception of the work for which they are best fitted, and with no conception whatsoever of even the need of such a thing as a *definite* objective toward which to strive.

There is a psychological as well as an economic reason for the selection of a *definite chief aim* in life. Let us devote our attention to the psychological side of the question first. It is a well established principle of psychology that a person's acts are always in harmony with the dominating thoughts of his or her mind.

Any *definite chief aim* that is deliberately fixed in the mind and held there, with the determination to realize it, finally saturates the entire subconscious mind until it automatically influences the physical action of the body toward the attainment of that purpose.

Your *definite chief aim* in life should be selected with deliberate care, and after it has been selected it should be written out and placed where you will see it at least once a day, the psychological effect of which is to impress this purpose upon your subconscious mind so strongly that it accepts that purpose as a pattern or blueprint that will eventually dominate your activities in life and lead you, step by step, toward the attainment of the object back of that purpose.

The principle of psychology through which you can impress your *definite chief aim* upon your subconscious mind is called Auto-suggestion, or suggestion which you repeatedly make to yourself. It is a degree of self-hypnotism, but do not be afraid of it on that account, for it was this same principle through the aid of which Napoleon lifted himself from the lowly station of poverty-stricken Corsican to the dictatorship of France. It was through the aid of this same prin-ciple that Thomas A. Edison has risen from the lowly beginning of a news butcher to where he is accepted as the leading inventor of the world. It was through the aid of this same principle that Lincoln bridged the mighty chasm between his lowly birth, in a log cabin in the mountains of Kentucky, and the presidency of the greatest nation on earth. It was through the aid of this same principle that Theodore Roosevelt became one of the most aggressive leaders that ever reached the presidency of the United States.

You need have no fear of the principle of Auto-suggestion as long as you are sure that the objective for which you are striving is one that will bring you happiness of an enduring nature. Be sure that your *definite purpose* is constructive; that its attainment will bring hardship and misery to no one; that it will bring you peace and prosperity, then apply, to the limit of your understanding, the principle of self-suggestion for the speedy attainment of this purpose.

On the street corner, just opposite the room in which I am writing, I see a man who stands there all day long and sells peanuts. He is busy every minute. When not actually engaged in making a sale he is roasting and packing the peanuts in little bags. He is one of that great army constituting the ninety-five per cent who have no *definite purpose* in life. He is selling peanuts, not because he likes that work better than anything else he might do, but because he never sat down and thought out a *definite purpose* that would bring him greater returns for his labor. He is selling peanuts because he is a drifter on the sea of life, and one of the tragedies of his work is the fact that the same amount of effort that he puts into it, if directed along other lines, would bring him much greater returns.

Another one of the tragedies of this man's work is the fact that he is unconsciously making use of the principle of self-suggestion, but he is doing it to his own disadvantage. No doubt, if a picture could be made of his thoughts, there would be nothing in that picture except a peanut roaster, some little paper bags and a crowd of people buying peanuts. This man could get out of the peanut business if he had the vision and the ambition first to imagine himself in a more profitable calling, and the perseverance to hold that picture before his mind until it influenced him to take the necessary steps to enter a more profitable calling. He puts sufficient labor into his work to bring him a substantial return if that labor were directed toward the attainment of a *definite purpose* that offered bigger returns.

One of my closest personal friends is one of the best known writers and public speakers of this country. About ten years ago he caught sight of the possibilities of this principle of self-suggestion and began, immediately, to harness it and put it to work. He worked out a plan for its application that proved to be very effective.   At that time he was neither a writer nor a speaker.

Each night, just before going to sleep, he would shut his eyes and see, *in his imagination,* a long council table at which he placed (in his imagination) certain well known men whose characteristics he wished to absorb into his own personality.   At the end of the table he placed Lincoln, and on either side of the table he placed Napoleon, Washington, Emerson and Elbert Hubbard.   He then proceeded to talk to these imaginary figures that he had seated at his imaginary council table, something after this manner:

Mr. Lincoln: I desire to build in my own character those qualities of patience and fairness toward all mankind and the keen sense of humor which were your outstanding characteristics.   I need these qualities and I shall not be contented until I have developed them.

Mr. Washington: I desire to build in my own character those qualities of patriotism and self-sacrifice and leadership which were your outstanding characteristics.

Mr. Emerson: I desire to build in my own character those qualities of vision and the ability to interpret the laws of Nature as written in the rocks of prison walls and growing trees and flowing brooks and growing flowers and the faces of little children, which were your outstanding characteristics.

Napoleon: I desire to build in my own character those qualities of self-reliance and the strategic ability to master obstacles and profit by mistakes and develop strength out of defeat, which were your outstanding characteristics.

Mr. Hubbard: I desire to develop the ability to equal and even to excel the ability that you possessed with which to express yourself in clear, concise and forceful language.

Night after night, for many months, this man saw these men seated around that imaginary council table until finally he had imprinted their outstanding characteristics upon his own subconscious mind so clearly that he began to develop a personality which was a composite of their personalities.

The subconscious mind may be likened to a magnet, and when it has been vitalized and thoroughly saturated with any *definite purpose* it has a decided tendency to attract all that is necessary for the fulfillment of that purpose. Like attracts like, and you may see evidence of this law in every blade of grass and every growing tree. The acorn attracts from the soil and the air the necessary materials out of which to grow an oak tree. It never grows a tree that is part oak and part poplar. Every grain of wheat that is planted in the soil attracts the materials out of which to grow a stalk of wheat.

It never makes a mistake and grows both oats and wheat on the same stalk.

And men are subject, also, to this same Law of Attraction. Go into any cheap boarding house district in any city and there you will find people of the same general trend of mind associated together. On the other hand, go into any prosperous community and there you will find people of the same general tendencies associated together. Men who are successful always seek the company of others who are successful. while men who are on the ragged side of life always

DO NOT "TELL"
THE WORLD
WHAT YOU CAN
DO—
"SHOW" IT!

seek the company of those who are in similar circumstances. "Misery loves company."

Water seeks its level with no finer certainty than
man seeks the company of those who occupy his own
general status financially and mentally. A professor
of Yale University and an illiterate hobo have nothing
in common. They would be miserable if thrown together for any great length of time. Oil and water
will mix as readily as will men who have nothing in
common.

All of which leads up to this statement:

That you will attract to you people who harmonize
with your own philosophy of life, whether you wish it
or not. This being true, can you not see the importance of vitalizing your mind with a *definite chief aim*
that will attract to you people who will be of help to
you and not a hindrance? Suppose your *definite chief
aim* is far above your present station in life. What of
it? It is your privilege—nay, your *DUTY,* to aim
high in life. You owe it to yourself and to the community in which you live to set a high standard for
yourself.

There is much evidence to justify the belief that
nothing *within reason* is beyond the possibility of attainment by the man whose *definite chief aim* has been
well developed. Some years ago Louis Victor Eytinge
was given a life sentence in the Arizona penitentiary.
At the time of his imprisonment he was an all-around
"bad man," according to his own admissions. In addition to this it was believed that he would die of tuberculosis within a year.

Eytinge had reason to feel discouraged, if anyone
ever had. Public feeling against him was intense and

he did not have a single friend in the world who came forth and offered him encouragement or help. Then something happened in his own mind that gave him back his health, put the dreaded "white plague" to rout and finally unlocked the prison gates and gave him his freedom.

What was that "something"?

Just this: He made up his mind to whip the white plague and regain his health. That was a very *definite chief aim*. In less than a year from the time the decision was made he had won. Then he extended that *definite chief aim* by making up his mind to gain his freedom. Soon the prison walls melted from around him.

No undesirable environment is strong enough to hold the man or woman who understands how to apply the principle of Auto-suggestion in the creation of a *definite chief aim*. Such a person can throw off the shackles of poverty; destroy the most deadly disease germs; rise from a lowly station in life to power and plenty.

All great leaders base their leadership upon a *definite chief aim*. Followers are willing followers when they know that their leader is a person with a *definite chief aim* who has the courage to back up that purpose with action. Even a balky horse knows when a driver with a *definite chief aim* takes hold of the reins; and yields to that driver. When a man with a *definite chief aim* starts through a crowd everybody stands aside and makes a way for him, but let a man hesitate and show by his actions that he is not sure which way he wants to go and the crowd will step all over his toes and refuse to budge an inch out of his way.

Nowhere is the lack of a *definite chief aim* more noticeable or more detrimental than it is in the relationship between parent and child. Children sense very quickly the wavering attitude of their parents and take advantage of that attitude quite freely. It is the same all through life—men with a *definite chief aim* command respect and attention at all times.

So much for the psychological viewpoint of a *definite purpose*. Let us now turn to the economic side of the question.

If a steamship lost its rudder, in mid-ocean, and began circling around, it would soon exhaust its fuel supply without reaching shore, despite the fact that it would use up enough energy to carry it to shore and back several times.

The man who labors without a *definite purpose* that is backed up by a definite plan for its attainment, resembles the ship that has lost its rudder. Hard labor and good intentions are not sufficient to carry a man through to success, for how may a man be sure that he has attained success unless he has established in his mind some definite object that he wishes?

Every well built house started in the form of a *definite purpose* plus a definite plan in the nature of a set of blueprints. Imagine what would happen if one tried to build a house by the haphazard method, without plans. Workmen would be in each other's way, building material would be piled all over the lot before the foundation was completed, and everybody on the job would have a different notion as to how the house ought to be built. Result, chaos and misunderstandings and cost that would be prohibitive.

Yet had you ever stopped to think that most people

finish school, take up employment or enter a trade or profession without the slightest conception of anything that even remotely resembles a *definite purpose* or a definite plan? In view of the fact that science has provided reasonably accurate ways and means of analyzing character and determining the life-work for which people are best fitted, does it not seem a modern tragedy that ninety-five per cent of the adult population of the world is made up of men and women who are failures because they have not found their proper niches in the world's work?

If *success* depends upon power, and if power is *organized effort,* and if the first step in the direction of organization is a *definite purpose,* then one may easily see why such a purpose is essential.

Until a man selects a *definite purpose* in life he dissipates his energies and spreads his thoughts over so many subjects and in so many different directions that they lead not to power, but to indecision and weakness.

With the aid of a small reading glass you can teach yourself a great lesson on the value of *organized effort.* Through the use of such a glass you can focus the sun-rays on a *definite* spot so strongly that they will burn a hole through a plank. Remove the glass (which represents the *definite purpose*) and the same rays of sun may shine on that same plank for a million years without burning it.

A thousand electric dry batteries, when properly organized and connected together with wires, will produce enough power to run a good sized piece of machinery for several hours, but take those same cells singly, disconnected, and not one of them would exert enough energy to turn the machinery over once. The faculties of your mind might properly be likened to those dry cells. When you organize your faculties, according to the plan laid down in the sixteen lessons of this Reading Course on the Law of Success, and direct them toward the attainment of a *definite purpose* in life, you then take advantage of the co-operative or accumulative principle out of which *power* is developed, which is called Organized Effort.

Andrew Carnegie's advice was this: "Place all your eggs in one basket and then watch the basket to see that no one kicks it over." By that advice he meant, of course, that we should not dissipate any of our energies by engaging in side lines. Carnegie was a sound economist and he knew that most men would do well if they so harnessed and directed their energies that some one thing would be done well.

When the plan back of this Reading Course was first born I remember taking the first manuscript to a professor of the University of Texas, and in a spirit of enthusiasm I suggested to him that I had discovered a principle that would be of aid to me in every public speech I delivered thereafter, because I would be better prepared to organize and marshal my thoughts.

He looked at the outline of the fifteen points for a few minutes, then turned to me and said:

"Yes, your discovery is going to help you make better speeches, but that is not all it will do. It will help you become a more effective writer, for I have noticed in your previous writings a tendency to scatter your thoughts. For instance, if you started to describe a beautiful mountain yonder in the distance you would be apt to sidetrack your description by calling atten-

THE BEST COM-
PENSATION
FOR DOING THINGS
IS THE ABILITY TO
DO MORE.

tion to a beautiful bed of wild flowers, or a running
brook, or a singing bird, detouring here and there, zig-
zag fashion, before finally arriving at the proper point
from which to view the mountain. In the future you
are going to find it much less difficult to describe an
object, whether you are speaking or writing, because
*your fifteen points represent the very foundation of
organization.*"

A man who had no legs once met a man who was
blind. To prove conclusively that the lame man was
a *man of vision* he proposed to the blind man that
they form an alliance that would be of great benefit
to both. "You let me climb upon your back," said he
to the blind man, "then I will use your legs and you
may use my eyes. Between the two of us we will
get along more rapidly."

Out of allied effort comes greater power. This is a
point that is worthy of much repetition, *because it
forms one of the most important parts of the foundation of this Reading Course.* The great fortunes of
the world have been accumulated through the use of
this principle of allied effort. That which one man can
accomplish single handed, during an entire life-time,
is but meagre at best, no matter how well organized
that man may be, but that which one man may accomplish through the principle of alliance with other
men is practically without limitation.

That "master mind" to which Carnegie referred during my interview with him was made up of more than
a score of minds. In that group were men of practically every temperament and inclination. Each man
was there to play a certain part and he did nothing
else. There was perfect understanding and team-

work between these men.   It was Carnegie's business
to keep harmony among them.

And he did it wonderfully well.

If you are familiar with the game of football you
know, of course, that the winning team is the one that
best co-ordinates the efforts of its players.   Team-work
is the thing that wins.   It is the same in the great
game of life.

In your struggle for *success* you should keep constantly in mind the necessity of knowing what it is that
you want—of knowing precisely what is your *definite
purpose*—and the value of the principle of *organized
effort* in the attainment of that which constitutes your
definite purpose.

In a vague sort of way nearly everyone has a definite
purpose—namely, the desire for *money!*   But this is
not a *definite purpose* within the meaning of the term
as it is used in this lesson.   Before your purpose could
be considered *definite,* even though that purpose were
the accumulation of money, you would have to reach a
decision as to the precise method through which you
intend to accumulate that money.   It would be insuf-
ficient for you to say that you would make money by
going into some sort of business.   You would have to
decide just what line of business.   You would also
have to decide just where you would locate.   You
would also have to decide the business policies under
which you would conduct your business.

In answering the question, "What Is Your Definite
Purpose In Life," that appears in the questionnaire
which I have used for the analysis of more than 16,000
people, many answered about as follows:

"My definite purpose in life is to be of as much

service to the world as possible and earn a good living."

That answer is about as *definite* as a frog's conception of the size of the universe is accurate!

The object of this lesson is not to inform you as to what your life-work should be, for indeed this could be done with accuracy only after you had been completely analyzed, but it is intended as a means of impressing upon your mind a clear conception of the value of a *definite purpose* of some nature, and of the value of understanding the principle of *organized effort* as a means of attaining the necessary power with which to materialize your *definite purpose*.

Careful observation of the business philosophy of more than one hundred men and women who have attained outstanding success in their respective callings, disclosed the fact that each was a person of prompt and definite decision.

The habit of working with a *definite chief aim* will breed in you the habit of prompt decision, and this habit will come to your aid in all that you do.

Moreover, the habit of working with a *definite chief aim* will help you to concentrate all your attention on any given task until you have mastered it.

Concentration of effort and the habit of working with a *definite chief aim* are two of the essential factors in success which are always found together. One leads to the other.

The best known successful business men were all men of prompt decision who worked always with one main, outstanding purpose as their chief aim.

Some notable examples are as follows:

Woolworth chose, as his *definite chief aim*, the belt-

ing of America with a chain of Five and Ten Cent
Stores, and concentrated his mind upon this one task
until he "made it and it made him."

Wrigley concentrated his mind on the production
and sale of a five-cent package of chewing gum and
turned this one idea into millions of dollars.

Edison concentrated upon the work of harmonizing
natural laws and made his efforts uncover more useful
inventions than any other man who ever lived.

Henry L. Doherty concentrated upon the building
and operation of public utility plants and made himself a multimillionaire.

Ingersoll concentrated on a dollar watch and girdled
the earth with "tickers" and made this one idea yield
him a fortune.

Statler concentrated on "homelike hotel-service" and
made himself wealthy as well as useful to millions of
people who use his service.

Edwin C. Barnes concentrated on the sale of Edison
Dictating Machines, and retired, while still a young
man, with more money than he needs.

Woodrow Wilson concentrated his mind on the
White House for twenty-five years, and became its
chief tenant, thanks to his knowledge of the value
of sticking to a *definite chief aim*.

Lincoln concentrated his mind on freeing the slaves
and became our greatest American President while
doing it.

Martin W. Littleton heard a speech which filled him
with the desire to become a great lawyer, concentrated
his mind on that one aim, and is now said to be the
most successful lawyer in America, whose fees for a
single case seldom fall below $50,000.00.

Rockefeller concentrated on oil and became the richest man of his generation.

Ford concentrated on "flivvers" and made himself the richest and most powerful man who ever lived.

Carnegie concentrated on steel and made his efforts build a great fortune and plastered his name on public libraries throughout America.

Gillette concentrated on a safety razor, gave the entire world a "close shave" and made himself a multimillionaire.

George Eastman concentrated on the kodak and made the idea yield him a fortune while bringing much pleasure to millions of people.

Russell Conwell concentrated on one simple lecture, "Acres of Diamonds," and made the idea yield more than $6,000,000.

Hearst concentrated on sensational newspapers and made the idea worth millions of dollars.

Helen Keller concentrated on learning to speak, and, despite the fact that she was deaf, dumb and blind, realized her *definite chief aim*.

John H. Patterson concentrated on cash registers and made himself rich and others "careful."

The late Kaiser of Germany concentrated on war and got a big dose of it, let us not forget the fact!

Fleischmann concentrated on the humble little cake of yeast and made things hump themselves all over the world.

Marshall Field concentrated on the world's greatest retail store and lo! it rose before him, a reality.

Philip Armour concentrated on the butchering business and established a great industry, as well as a big fortune.

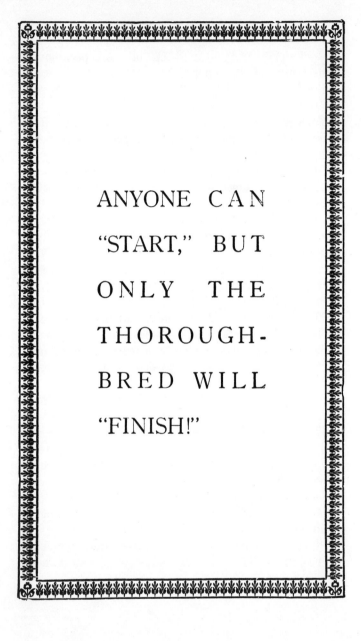

ANYONE CAN
"START," BUT
ONLY THE
THOROUGH-
BRED WILL
"FINISH!"

Millions of people are concentrating, daily, on POVERTY and FAILURE and getting both in over-abundance.

Wright Brothers concentrated on the airplane and mastered the air.

Pullman concentrated on the sleeping car and the idea made him rich and millions of people comfortable in travel.

The Anti-Saloon League concentrated on the Prohibition Amendment and (whether for better or worse) made it a reality.

Thus it will be seen that all who succeed work with some definite, outstanding aim as the object of their labors.

There is some one thing that you can do better than anyone else in the world could do it. Search until you find out what this particular line of endeavor is, make it the object of your *definite chief aim* and then organize all of your forces and attack it with the belief that you are going to win. In your search for the work for which you are best fitted, it will be well if you bear in mind the fact that you will most likely attain the greatest success by finding out what work you like best, for it is a well known fact that a man generally best succeeds in the particular line of endeavor. into which he can throw his whole heart and soul.

Let us go back, for the sake of clarity and emphasis, to the psychological principles upon which this lesson is founded, because it will mean a loss that you can ill afford if you fail to grasp the real reason for establishing a *definite chief aim* in your mind. These principles are as follows:

First: Every voluntary movement of the human body is caused, controlled and directed by *thought,* through the operation of the mind.

Second: The presence of any thought or idea in your consciousness tends to produce an associated feeling and to urge you to transform that feeling into appropriate muscular action that is in perfect harmony with the nature of the thought.

For example, if you think of winking your eyelid and there are no counter influences or thoughts in your mind at the time to arrest action, the motor nerve will carry your thought from the seat of government, in your brain, and appropriate or corresponding muscular action takes place immediately.

Stating this principle from another angle: You choose, for example, a *definite purpose* as your life-work and make up your mind that you will carry out that purpose. *From the very moment that you make this choice, this purpose becomes the dominating thought in your consciousness, and you are constantly on the alert for facts, information and knowledge with which to achieve that purpose.* From the time that you plant a *definite purpose* in your mind, your mind begins, both consciously and unconsciously, to gather and store away the material with which you are to accomplish that purpose.

Desire is the factor which determines what your *definite purpose* in life shall be. No one can select your dominating *desire* for you, but once you select it yourself it becomes your *definite chief aim* and occupies the spotlight of your mind until it is satisfied by transformation into reality, unless you permit it to be pushed aside by conflicting desires.

To emphasize the principle that I am here trying to make clear, I believe it not unreasonable to suggest that to be sure of successful achievement, one's *definite chief aim* in life should be backed up with a *burning desire* for its achievement. I have noticed that boys and girls who enter college and pay their way through by working seem to get more out of their schooling than do those whose expenses are paid for them. The secret of this may be found in the fact that those who are willing to work their way through are blessed with a *burning desire* for education, and such a desire, if the object of the desire is within reason, is practically sure of realization.

Science has established, beyond the slightest room for doubt, that through the principle of Auto-suggestion any deeply rooted *desire* saturates the entire body and mind with the nature of the desire and literally transforms the mind into a powerful magnet that will attract the object of the desire, if it be within reason. For the enlightenment of those who might not properly interpret the meaning of this statement I will endeavor to state this principle in another way. For example, merely desiring an automobile will not cause that automobile to come rolling in, but, if there is a *burning desire* for an automobile, that desire will lead to the appropriate action through which an automobile may be paid for.

Merely desiring freedom would never release a man who was confined in prison if it were not sufficiently strong to cause him to do something to entitle himself to freedom.

These are the steps leading from *desire* to fulfillment: First the *burning desire*, then the crystallization of that desire into a *definite purpose,* then sufficient appropriate *action* to achieve that purpose. *Remember that these three steps are always necessary to insure success.*

I once knew a very poor girl who had a *burning desire* for a wealthy husband, and she finally got him, but not without having transformed that desire into the development of a very attractive personality which, in turn, attracted the desired husband.

I once had a *burning desire* to be able to analyze character accurately and that desire was so persistent and so deeply seated that it practically drove me into ten years of research and study of men and women.

George S. Parker makes one of the best fountain pens in the world, and despite the fact that his business is conducted from the little city of Janesville, Wisconsin, he has spread his product all the way around the globe and he has his pen on sale in every civilized country in the world. More than twenty years ago, Mr. Parker's *definite purpose* was established in his mind, and that purpose was to produce the best fountain pen that money could buy. He backed that purpose with a *burning desire* for its realization and if you carry a fountain pen the chances are that you have evidence in your own possession that it has brought him abundant success.

You are a contractor and builder, and, like men who build houses out of mere wood and brick and steel, you must draw up a set of plans after which to shape your *success building.* You are living in a wonderful age, when the materials that go into *success* are plentiful and cheap. You have at your disposal, in the archives of the public libraries, the carefully compiled results of two thousand years of research covering practically every possible line of endeavor in which one would wish to engage. If you would become a preacher you have at hand the entire history of what has been learned by men who have preceded you in this field. If you would become a mechanic you have at hand the entire history of the inventions of machines and the discovery and usages of metals and things metallic in nature. If you would become a lawyer you have at your disposal the entire history of law procedure. Through the Department of Agriculture, at Washington, you have at your disposal all that has been learned about farming and agriculture, where you may use it should you wish to find your life-work in this field.

The world was never so resplendent with *opportunity* as it is today. On every hand there is an ever-increasing demand for the services of the man or the woman who makes a better mouse-trap or performs better stenographic service or preaches a better sermon or digs a better ditch or runs a more accommodating bank.

This lesson will not be completed until you shall have made your choice as to what your *definite chief aim* in life is to be and then recorded a description of that purpose in writing and placed it where you may see it every morning when you arise and every night when you retire.

Procrastination is—but why preach about it? You know that *you* are the hewer of your own wood and the drawer of your own water and the shaper of your own *definite chief aim* in life; therefore, why dwell upon that which you already know?

A definite purpose is something that you must create

Every line a man writes,
and every act in which he
indulges, and every word he
utters serves as unescapable
evidence of the nature of
that which is deeply imbedded in his own heart, a confession that he cannot dis-
avow.

for yourself. No one else will create it for you and it will not create itself. What are you going to do about it? and when? and how?

Start now to analyze your desires and find out what it is that you wish, then make up your mind to get it. Lesson Three will point out to you the next step and show you how to proceed. Nothing is left to chance, in this Reading Course. Every step is marked plainly. Your part is to follow the directions until you arrive at your destination, which is represented by your *definite chief aim*. Make that aim clear and back it up with persistence which does not recognize the word "impossible."

When you come to select your *definite chief aim* just keep in mind the fact that you cannot *aim* too high.

Also keep in mind the never-varying truth that you'll get nowhere if you start nowhere. If your aim in life is vague your achievements will also be vague, and it might well be added, very *meager*. *Know what you want, when you want it, why you want it and HOW you intend to get it.* This is known to teachers and students of psychology as the WWWH formula— "what, when, why and how."

Read this lesson four times, at intervals of one week apart.

You will see much in the lesson the fourth time you read it that you did not see the first time.

Your success in mastering this course and in making it bring you success will depend very largely, if not entirely, upon how well you follow ALL the instructions it contains.

Do not set up your own rules of study. Follow those laid down in the Course, as they are the result of years of thought and experimentation. If you wish to experiment wait until you master this course in the manner suggested by its author. You will then be in position to experiment more safely. For the present content yourself by being the student. You will, let us hope, become the teacher as well as the student after you have followed the Course until you have mastered it.

If you follow the instructions laid down in this Course for the guidance of its students, you can no more fail than water can run uphill above the level of its source.

INSTRUCTIONS FOR APPLYING THE
PRINCIPLES OF THIS
LESSON

Through the Introductory Lesson of this course you became familiar with the principle of psychology known as the "Master Mind."

You are now ready to begin use of this principle as a means of transforming your *definite chief aim* into reality. It must have occurred to you that one might as well have no *definite chief aim* unless one has, also, a very definite and practical plan for making that aim become a reality.

Your first step is to decide what your major aim in life shall be. Your next step is to write out a clear, concise statement of this aim. This should be followed by a statement, in writing, of the plan or plans through which you intend to attain the object of your aim.

Your next and final step will be the forming of an alliance with some person or persons who will co-operate with you in carrying out these plans and transforming your *definite chief aim* into reality.

The purpose of this friendly alliance is to employ the law of the "Master Mind" in support of your plans. The alliance should be made between yourself and those who have your highest and best interests at heart. If you are a married man your wife should be one of the members of this alliance, providing there exists between you a normal state of confidence and sympathy. Other members of this alliance may be your mother, father, brothers or sisters, or some close friend or friends.

If you are a single person your sweetheart, if you have one, should become a member of your alliance. This is no joke—you are now studying one of the most powerful laws of the human mind, and you will serve your own best interests by seriously and earnestly following the rules laid down in this lesson, even though you may not be sure where they will lead you.

Those who join with you in the formation of a friendly alliance for the purpose of aiding you in the creation of a "Master Mind" should sign, with you, your statement of the object of your *definite chief aim.* Every member of your alliance must be fully acquainted with the nature of your object in forming the alliance. Moreover, every member must be in hearty accord with this object, and in full sympathy with you. Each member of your alliance must be supplied with a written copy of your statement of your *definite chief aim.* With this exception, however, *you are explicitly instructed to keep the object of your chief aim to yourself.* The world is full of "Doubting Thomases" and it will do your cause no good to have these rattle-brained people scoffing at you and your ambitions. Remember, what you need is friendly encouragement and help, not derision and doubt.

If you believe in prayer you are instructed to make your *definite chief aim* the object of your prayer at least once every twenty-four hours, and more often if convenient. If you believe there is a God who can and will aid those who are earnestly striving to be of constructive service in the world, surely you feel that you have a right to petition Him for aid in the attainment of what should be the most important thing in life to you.

If those who have been invited to join your friendly alliance believe in prayer, ask them, also, to include the object of this alliance as a part of their daily prayer.

Comes, now, one of the most essential rules which you *must follow*. Arrange with one or all of the members of your friendly alliance to state to you, in the most positive and definite terms at their command, that THEY KNOW YOU CAN AND WILL REALIZE THE OBJECT OF YOUR DEFINITE CHIEF AIM. This affirmation or statement should be made to you at least once a day; more often if possible.

These steps must be followed persistently, with full faith that they will lead you where you wish to go! It will not suffice to carry out these plans for a few days or a few weeks and then discontinue them. YOU MUST FOLLOW THE DESCRIBED PROCEDURE UNTIL YOU ATTAIN THE OBJECT OF YOUR DEFINITE CHIEF AIM, REGARDLESS OF THE TIME REQUIRED.

From time to time it may become necessary to change the plans you have adopted for the achievement of the object of your *definite chief aim*. Make these changes without hesitation. No human being has sufficient foresight to build plans which need no alteration or change.

If any member of your friendly alliance loses faith in the law known as the "Master Mind," immediately remove that member and replace him or her with some other person.

Andrew Carnegie stated to the author of this course that he had found it necessary to replace some of the members of his "Master Mind." In fact he stated

"Yes, he succeeded—but—he almost failed!" So did Robert Fulton and Abraham Lincoln and nearly all the others whom we call successful. No man ever achieved worth-while success who did not, at one time or other, find himself with at least one foot hanging well over the brink of failure.

tnat practically every member of whom his alliance was originally composed had, in time, been removed and replaced with some other person who could adapt himself more loyally and enthusiastically to the spirit and object of the alliance.

You cannot succeed when surrounded by disloyal and unfriendly associates, no matter what may be the object of your *definite chief aim*. Success is built upon loyalty, faith, sincerity, co-operation and the other positive forces with which one must surcharge his environment.

Many of the students of this course will want to form friendly alliances with those with whom they are associated professionally or in business, with the object of achieving success in their business or profession. In such cases the same rules of procedure which have been here described should be followed. The object of your *definite chief aim* may be one that will benefit you individually, or it may be one that will benefit the business or profession with which you are connected. The law of the "Master Mind" will work the same in either case. If you fail, either temporarily or permanently, in the application of this law *it will be for the reason that some member of your alliance did not enter into the spirit of the alliance with faith, loyalty and sincerity of purpose.*

The last sentence is worthy of a second reading!

The object of your *definite chief aim* should become your "hobby." You should ride this "hobby" continuously; you should sleep with it, eat with it, play with it, work with it, live with it and THINK with it.

Whatever you want you may get if you want it with sufficient intensity, and keep on wanting it, providing

the object wanted is one within reason, and you
ACTUALLY BELIEVE YOU WILL GET IT! There
is a difference, however, between merely "wishing" for
something and ACTUALLY BELIEVING you will
get it. Lack of understanding of this difference has
meant failure to millions of people. The "doers" are
the "believers" in all walks of life. Those who BE-
LIEVE they can achieve the object of their *definite
chief aim* do not recognize the word impossible.
Neither do they acknowledge temporary defeat. They
KNOW they are going to succeed, and if one plan
fails they quickly replace it with another plan.

Every noteworthy achievement met with some sort
of temporary setback before success came. Edison
made more than ten thousand experiments before he
succeeded in making the first talking machine record
the words, "Mary had a little lamb."

If there is one word which should stand out in your
mind in connection with this lesson, it is the word
PERSISTENCE!

You now have within your possession the pass-key
to achievement. You have but to unlock the door
to the Temple of Knowledge and walk in. But you
must go to the Temple; it will not come to you. If
these laws are new to you the "going" will not be easy
at first. You will stumble many times, but keep
moving! Very soon you will come to the brow of the
mountain you have been climbing, and you will behold,
in the valleys below, the rich estate of KNOWLEDGE
which shall be your reward for your faith and efforts.

Everything has a price. There is no such possibility
as "something for nothing." In your experiments
with the Law of the Master Mind you are jockeying

with Nature, in her highest and noblest form. Nature cannot be tricked or cheated. She will give up to you the object of your struggles only after you have paid her price, which is CONTINUOUS, UNYIELDING, PERSISTENT EFFORT!

What more could be said on this subject?

You have been shown *what to do, when to do it, how to do it* and *why you should do it*. If you will master the next lesson, on Self-confidence, you will then have the faith in yourself to enable you to carry out the instructions laid down for your guidance in this lesson.

Master of human destinies am I!
Fame, love, and fortune on my footsteps wait.
Cities and fields I walk; I penetrate
Deserts and seas remote, and passing by
Hovel and mart and palace—soon or late
I knock, unbidden, once at every gate!
If sleeping, wake—if feasting, rise before
I turn away. It is the hour of fate,
And they who follow me reach every state
Mortals desire, and conquer every foe
Save death; but those who doubt or hesitate,
Condemned to failure, penury, and woe,
Seek me in vain and uselessly implore.
I answer not, and I return no more!

                                        —INGALLS.

NEGLECTING TO

BROADEN

THEIR VIEW HAS

KEPT SOME MEN

DOING ONE THING

ALL THEIR LIVES.

Lesson Three

SELF-CONFIDENCE

A MIDST all the mysteries by which we are surrounded, nothing is more certain than that we are in the presence of an Infinite and Eternal Energy from which all things proceed.

—*Herbert Spencer.*

THE LAW OF SUCCESS
Lesson Three
SELF-CONFIDENCE

"You Can Do It if You Believe You Can!"

EFORE approaching the fundamental prin-. ciples upon which this lesson is founded it will be of benefit to you to keep in mind the fact that it is practical—that it brings you the discoveries of more than twenty-five years of research—that it has the approval of the leading scientific men and women of the world who have tested every principle involved.

Skepticism is the deadly enemy of progress and self-development. You might as well lay this book aside and stop right here as to approach this lesson with the feeling that it was written by some long-haired theorist who had never tested the principles upon which the lesson is based.

Surely this is no age for the skeptic, because it is an age in which we have seen more of Nature's laws uncovered and harnessed than had been discovered in all past history of the human race. Within three decades we have witnessed the mastery of the air; we have explored the ocean; we have all but annihi-

71

lated distances on the earth; we have harnessed the lightning and made it turn the wheels of industry; we have made seven blades of grass grow where but one grew before; we have instantaneous communication between the nations of the world. Truly, this is an age of illumination and unfoldment, but we have as yet barely scratched the surface of knowledge. However, when we shall have unlocked the gate that leads to the secret power which is stored up within us it will bring us knowledge that will make all past discoveries pale into oblivion by comparison.

Thought is the most highly organized form of energy known to man, and this is an age of experimentation and research that is sure to bring us into greater understanding of that mysterious force called thought, which reposes within us. We have already found out enough about the human mind to know that a man may throw off the accumulated effects of a thousand generations of *fear,* through the aid of the principle of *Auto-suggestion.* We have already discovered the fact that *fear* is the chief reason for poverty and failure and misery that takes on a thousand different forms. We have already discovered the fact that the man who masters *fear* may march on to successful achievement in practically any undertaking, despite all efforts to defeat him.

The development of *self-confidence* starts with the elimination of this demon called *fear,* which sits upon a man's shoulder and whispers into his ear, *"You can't do it—you are afraid to try—you are afraid of public opinion—you are afraid that you will fail—you are afraid you have not the ability."*

This *fear* demon is getting into close quarters.

Science has found a deadly weapon with which to put it to flight, and this lesson on *self-confidence* has brought you this weapon for use in your battle with the world-old enemy of progress, *fear*.

THE SIX BASIC FEARS OF MANKIND: Every person falls heir to the influence of six basic fears. Under these six fears may be listed the lesser fears. The six basic or major fears are here enumerated and the sources from which they are believed to have grown are described.

The six basic fears are:

a The fear of Poverty
b The fear of Old Age
c The fear of Criticism
d The fear of Loss of Love of Someone.
e The fear of Ill Health
f The fear of Death.

Study the list, then take inventory of your own fears and ascertain under which of the six headings you can classify them.

Every human being who has reached the age of understanding is bound down, to some extent, by one or more of these six basic fears. As the first step in the elimination of these six evils let us examine the sources from whence we inherited them.

PHYSICAL AND SOCIAL HEREDITY

All that man is, both physically and mentally, he came by through two forms of heredity. One is known as physical heredity and the other is called social heredity.

Through the law of physical heredity man has slowly

evolved from the amœba (a single-cell animal form), through stages of development corresponding to all the known animal forms now on this earth, including those which are known to have existed but which are now extinct.

Every generation through which man has passed has added to his nature something of the traits, habits and physical appearance of that generation. Man's physical inheritance, therefore, is a heterogeneous collection of many habits and physical forms.

There seems little, if any, doubt that while the six basic fears of man could not have been inherited through physical heredity (these six basic fears being mental states of mind and therefore not capable of transmission through physical heredity), it is obvious that through physical heredity a most favorable lodging place for these six fears has been provided.

For example, it is a well known fact that the whole process of physical evolution is based upon death, destruction, pain and cruelty; that the elements of the soil of the earth find transportation, in their upward climb through evolution, based upon the death of one form of life in order that another and higher form may subsist. All vegetation lives by "eating" the elements of the soil and the elements of the air. All forms of animal life live by "eating" some other and weaker form, or some form of vegetation.

The cells of all vegetation have a very high order of intelligence. The cells of all animal life likewise have a very high order of intelligence.

Undoubtedly the animal cells of a fish have learned, out of bitter experience, that the group of animal cells known as a fish hawk are to be greatly feared.

By reason of the fact that many animal forms (including that of most men) live by eating the smaller and weaker animals, the "cell intelligence" of these animals which enter into and become a part of man brings with it the FEAR growing out of their experience in having been eaten alive.

This theory may seem to be far-fetched, and in fact it may not be true, but it is at least a logical theory if it is nothing more. The author makes no particular point of this theory, nor does he insist that it accounts for any of the six basic fears. There is another, and a much better explanation of the source of these fears, which we will proceed to examine, beginning with a description of social heredity.

By far the most important part of man's make-up comes to him through the law of social heredity, this term having reference to the methods by which one generation imposes upon the minds of the generation under its immediate control the superstitions, beliefs, legends and ideas which it, in turn, inherited from the generation preceding.

The term "social heredity" should be understood to mean any and all sources through which a person acquires knowledge, such as schooling of religious and all other natures; reading, word of mouth conversation, story telling and all manner of thought inspiration coming from what is generally accepted as one's "personal experiences."

Through the operation of the law of social heredity anyone having control of the mind of a child may, through intense teaching, plant in that child's mind any idea, whether false or true, in such a manner that the child accepts it as true and it becomes as much a

REMEMBER that when you make an appointment with another person you assume the responsibility of punctuality, and that you have not the right to be a single minute late.

part of the child's personality as any cell or organ of its physical body (and just as hard to change in its nature).

It is through the law of social heredity that the religionist plants in the child mind dogmas and creeds and religious ceremonies too numerous to describe, holding those ideas before that mind until the mind accepts them and forever seals them as a part of its irrevocable belief.

The mind of a child which has not come into the age of general understanding, during an average period covering, let us say, the first two years of its life, is plastic, open, clean and free. Any idea planted in such a mind by one in whom the child has confidence takes root and grows, so to speak, in such a manner that it never can be eradicated or wiped out, no matter how opposed to logic or reason that idea may be.

Many religionists claim that they can so deeply implant the tenets of their religion in the mind of a child that there never can be room in that mind for any other religion, either in whole or in part. The claims are not greatly overdrawn.

With this explanation of the manner in which the law of social heredity operates the student will be ready to examine the sources from which man inherits the six basic fears. Moreover, any student (except those who have not yet grown big enough to examine truth that steps upon the "pet corns" of their own superstitions) may check the soundness of the principle of social heredity as it is here applied to the six basic fears, without going outside of his or her own personal experiences.

Fortunately, practically the entire mass of evidence

submitted in this lesson is of such a nature that all who sincerely seek the truth may ascertain, for themselves, whether the evidence is sound or not.

For the moment at least, lay aside your prejudices and preconceived ideas (you may always go back and pick them up again, you know) while we study the origin and nature of man's Six Worst Enemies, the six basic fears, beginning with:

THE FEAR OF POVERTY: It requires courage to tell the truth about the origin of this fear, and still greater courage, perhaps, to accept the truth after it has been told. The fear of poverty grew out of man's inherited tendency to prey upon his fellow man economically. Nearly all forms of lower animals have instinct but appear not to have the power to reason and think; therefore, they prey upon one another physically. Man, with his superior sense of intuition, thought and reason, does not eat his fellow men bodily; he gets more satisfaction out of eating them FINANCIALLY!

Of all the ages of the world of which we know anything, the age in which we live seems to be the age of money worship. A man is considered less than the dust of the earth unless he can display a fat bank account. Nothing brings man so much suffering and humiliation as does POVERTY. No wonder man FEARS poverty. Through a long line of inherited experiences with the man-animal man has learned, for certain, that this animal cannot always be trusted where matters of money and other evidences of earthly possessions are concerned.

Many marriages have their beginning (and oftentimes their ending) solely on the basis of the wealth possessed by one or both of the contracting parties. It is no wonder that the divorce courts are busy!

"Society" could quite properly be spelled "$ociety," because it is inseparably associated with the dollar mark. So eager is man to possess wealth that he will acquire it in whatever manner he can; through legal methods, if possible, through other methods if necessary.

The fear of poverty is a terrible thing!

A man may commit murder, engage in robbery, rape and all other manner of violation of the rights of others and still regain a high station in the minds of his fellow men, PROVIDING always that he does not lose his wealth. Poverty, therefore, is a crime—an unforgivable sin, as it were.

No wonder man fears it!

Every statute book in the world bears evidence that the fear of poverty is one of the six basic fears of mankind, for in every such book of laws may be found various and sundry laws intended to protect the weak from the strong. To spend time trying to prove either that the fear of poverty is one of man's inherited fears, or that this fear has its origin in man's nature to cheat his fellow man, would be similar to trying to prove that three times two are six. Obviously no man would ever fear poverty if he had any grounds for trusting his fellow men, for there is food and shelter and raiment and luxury of every nature sufficient for the needs of every person on earth, and all these blessings would be enjoyed by every person except for the swinish habit that man has of trying to push all the other "swine" out of the trough, even after he has all and more than he needs.

The second of the six basic fears with which man is bound is:

THE FEAR OF OLD AGE: In the main this fear grows out of two sources. First, the thought that Old Age may bring with it POVERTY. Secondly, and by far the most common source of origin, from false and cruel sectarian teachings which have been so well mixed with "fire and brimstone" and with "purgatories" and other bogies that human beings have learned to fear Old Age because it meant the approach of another, and possibly a much more HORRIBLE, world than this one which is known to be bad enough.

In the basic fear of Old Age man has two very sound reasons for his apprehension: the one growing out of distrust of his fellow men who may seize whatever worldly goods he may possess, and the other arising from the terrible pictures of the world to come which were deeply planted in his mind, through the law of social heredity, long before he came into possession of that mind.

Is it any wonder that man fears the approach of Old Age?

The third of the six basic fears is:

THE FEAR OF CRITICISM: Just how man acquired this basic fear it would be hard, if not impossible, definitely to determine, but one thing is certain, he has it in well developed form.

Some believe that this fear made its appearance in the mind of man about the time that politics came into existence. Others believe its source can be traced no further than the first meeting of an organization of females known as a "Woman's Club." Still another school of humorists charges the origin to the contents of the Holy Bible, whose pages abound with some very vitriolic and violent forms of criticism. If the latter claim is correct, and those who believe literally all they find in the Bible are not mistaken, then God is responsible for man's inherent fear of Criticism, because God caused the Bible to be written.

This author, being neither a humorist nor a "prophet," but just an ordinary workaday type of person, is inclined to attribute the basic fear of Criticism to that part of man's inherited nature which prompts him not only to take away his fellow man's goods and wares, but to justify his action by CRITICISM of his fellow man's character.

The fear of Criticism takes on many different forms, the majority of which are petty and trivial in nature, even to the extent of being childish in the extreme.

Bald-headed men, for example, are bald for no other reason than their fear of Criticism. Heads become bald because of the protection of hats with tight fitting bands which cut off the circulation at the roots of the hair. Men wear hats, not because they actually need them for the sake of comfort, but mainly because "everybody's doing it," and the individual falls in line and does it also, lest some other individual CRITICIZE him.

Women seldom have bald heads, or even thin hair, because they wear hats that are loose, the only purpose of which is to make an appearance.

But it must not be imagined that women are free from the fear of Criticism associated with hats. If any woman claims to be superior to man with reference to this fear, ask her to walk down the street wearing a hat that is one or two seasons out of style!

IN every soul there has
been deposited t h e
seed of a great future, but
that seed will never ger-
minate, much less grow to
maturity, except through
the rendering of useful
service.

The makers of all manner of clothing have not been slow to capitalize this basic fear of Criticism with which all mankind is cursed. Every season, it will be observed, the "styles" in many articles of wearing apparel change. Who establishes the "styles"? Certainly not the purchaser of clothes, but the manufacturer of clothes. Why does he change the styles so often? Obviously this change is made so that the manufacturer can sell more clothes.

For the same reason the manufacturers of automobiles (with a few rare and very sensible exceptions) change styles every season.

The manufacturer of clothing knows how the man-animal fears to wear a garment which is one season out of step with "that which they are all wearing now."

Is this not true? Does not your own experience back it up?

We have been describing the manner in which people behave under the influence of the fear of Criticism as applied to the small and petty things of life. Let us now examine human behavior under this fear when it affects people in connection with the more important matters connected with human intercourse. Take, for example, practically any person who has reached the age of "mental maturity" (from thirty-five to forty-five years of age, as a general average), and if you could read his or her mind you would find in that mind a very decided disbelief of and rebellion against most of the fables taught by the majority of the religionists.

Powerful and mighty is the fear of CRITICISM!

The time was, and not so very long ago at that,

when the word "infidel" meant ruin to whomsoever it was applied. It is seen, therefore, that man's fear of CRITICISM is not without ample cause for its existence.

The fourth basic fear is that of:

THE FEAR OF LOSS OF LOVE OF SOMEONE: The source from which this fear originated needs but little description, for it is obvious that it grew out of man's nature to steal his fellow man's mate; or at least to take liberties with her, unknown to her rightful "lord" and master. By nature all men are polygamous, the statement of a truth which will, of course, bring denials from those who are either too old to function in a normal way sexually, or have, from some other cause, lost the contents of certain glands which are responsible for man's tendency toward the plurality of the opposite sex.

There can be but little doubt that jealousy and all other similar forms of more or less mild dementia præcox (insanity) grew out of man's inherited fear of the Loss of Love of Someone.

Of all the "sane fools" studied by this author, that represented by a man who has become jealous of some woman, or that of a woman who has become jealous of some man, is the oddest and strangest. The author, fortunately, never had but one case of personal experience with this form of insanity, but from that experience he learned enough to justify him in stating that the fear of the Loss of Love of Someone is one of the most painful, if not in fact the most painful, of all the six basic fears. And it seems reasonable to add that this fear plays more havoc with the human mind than do any of the other six basic fears, often leading to the more violent forms of permanent insanity.

The fifth basic fear is that of:

THE FEAR OF ILL HEALTH: This fear has its origin, to considerable extent also, in the same sources from which the fears of Poverty and Old Age are derived.

The fear of Ill Health must needs be closely associated with both Poverty and Old Age, because it also leads toward the border line of "terrible worlds" of which man knows not, but of which he has heard some discomforting stories.

The author strongly suspects that those engaged in the business of selling good health methods have had considerable to do with keeping the fear of Ill Health alive in the human mind.

For longer than the record of the human race can be relied upon, the world has known of various and sundry forms of therapy and health purveyors. If a man gains his living from keeping people in good health it seems but natural that he would use every means at his command for persuading people that they needed his services. Thus, in time, it might be that people would inherit a fear of Ill Health.

The sixth and last of the six basic fears is that of:

THE FEAR OF DEATH: To many this is the worst of all the six basic fears, and the reason why it is so regarded becomes obvious to even the casual student of psychology.

The terrible pangs of fear associated with DEATH may be charged directly to religious fanaticism, the source which is more responsible for it than are all other sources combined.

So-called "heathen" are not as much afraid of DEATH as are the "civilized," especially that portion of the civilized population which has come under the influence of theology.

For hundreds of millions of years man has been asking the still unanswered (and, it may be, the unanswerable) questions, "W H E N C E?" and "WHITHER?" "Where did I come from and where am I going after death?"

The more cunning and crafty, as well as the honest but credulous, of the race have not been slow to offer the answer to these questions. In fact the answering of these questions has become one of the so-called "learned" professions, despite the fact that but little learning is required to enter this profession.

Witness, now, the major source of origin of the fear of DEATH!

"Come into my tent, embrace my faith, accept my dogmas (and pay my salary) and I will give you a ticket that will admit you straightway into heaven when you die," says the leader of one form of sectarianism. "Remain out of my tent," says this same leader, "and you will go direct to hell, where you will burn throughout eternity."

While, in fact, the self-appointed leader may not be able to provide safe-conduct into heaven nor, by lack of such provision, allow the unfortunate seeker after truth to descend into hell, the possibility of the latter seems so terrible that it lays hold of the mind and creates that fear of fears, the fear of DEATH!

In truth no man knows, and no man has ever known, what heaven or hell is like, or if such places exist, and this very lack of definite knowledge opens the door of the human mind to the charlatan to enter and control that mind with his stock of legerdemain and various brands of trickery, deceit and fraud.

The truth is this—nothing less and nothing more—That NO MAN KNOWS NOR HAS ANY MAN EVER KNOWN WHERE WE COME FROM AT BIRTH OR WHERE WE GO AT DEATH. Any person claiming otherwise is either deceiving himself or he is a conscious impostor who makes it a business to live without rendering service of value, through play upon the credulity of humanity.

Be it said, in their behalf, however, the majority of those engaged in "selling tickets into heaven" actually believe not only that they know where heaven exists, but that their creeds and formulas will give safe passage to all who embrace them.

This belief may be summed up in one word—CREDULITY!

Religious leaders, generally, make the broad, sweep-ing claim that the present civilization owes its existence to the work done by the churches. This author, as far as he is personally concerned, is willing to grant their claims to be correct, if, at the same time he be permitted to add that even if this claim be true the theologians haven't a great deal of which to brag.

But, it is not—cannot be—true that civilization has grown out of the efforts of the organized churches and creeds, if by the term "civilization" is meant the un-covering of the natural laws and the many inventions to which the world is the present heir.

If the theologians wish to claim that part of civili-zation which has to do with man's conduct toward his fellow man they are perfectly welcome to it, as far

YOU are fortunate if you have learned the difference between temporary defeat and failure; more fortunate still, if you have learned the truth that the very seed of success is dormant in every defeat that you experience.

as this author is concerned; but, on the other hand,
if they presume to gobble up the credit for all the
scientific discovery of mankind the author begs leave
to offer vigorous protest.

.   .   .   .

It is hardly sufficient to state that social heredity
is the method through which man gathers all knowledge that reaches him through the five senses. It is
more to the point to state HOW social heredity works,
in as many different applications as will give the student a comprehensive understanding of that law.

Let us begin with some of the lower forms of animal life and examine the manner in which they are
affected by the law of social heredity.

Shortly after this author began to examine the major
sources from which men gather the knowledge which
makes them what they are, some thirty-odd years ago,
he discovered the nest of a ruffed grouse. The nest
was so located that the mother bird could be seen
from a considerable distance when she was on the
nest. With the aid of a pair of field glasses the bird
was closely watched until the young birds were
hatched out. It happened that the regular daily observation was made but a few hours after the young
birds came out of the shell. Desiring to know what
would happen, the author approached the nest. The
mother bird remained near by until the intruder was
within ten or twelve feet of her, then she disarranged
her feathers, stretched one wing over her leg and went
hobbling away, making a pretense of being crippled.
Being somewhat familiar with the tricks of mother
birds, the author did not follow, but, instead, went to

the nest to take a look at the little ones. Without the slightest signs of fear they turned their eyes toward him, moving their heads first one way and then another. He reached down and picked one of them up. With no signs of fear it stood in the palm of his hand. He laid the bird back in the nest and went away to a safe distance to give the mother bird a chance to return.

The wait was short. Very soon she began cautiously to edge her way back toward the nest until she was within a few feet of it, when she spread her wings and ran as fast as she could, uttering, meanwhile, a series of sounds similar to those of a hen when she has found some morsel of food and wishes to call her brood to partake of it.

She gathered the little birds around and continued to quiver in a highly excited manner, shaking her wings and ruffling her feathers. One could almost hear her words as she gave the little birds their first lesson in self-defense, through the law of SOCIAL HEREDITY:

"You silly little creatures! Do you not know that men are your enemies? Shame on you for allowing that man to pick you up in his hands. It's a wonder he didn't carry you off and eat you alive! The next time you see a man approaching make yourselves scarce. Lie down on the ground, run under leaves, go anywhere to get out of sight, and remain out of sight until the enemy is well on his way."

The little birds stood around and listened to the lecture with intense interest. After the mother bird had quieted down the author again started to approach the nest. When within twenty feet or so of the guarded household the mother bird again started to lead him in the other direction by crumpling up her wing and hobbling along as if she were crippled. He looked at the nest, but the glance was in vain. The little birds were nowhere to be found! They had learned rapidly to avoid their natural enemy, thanks to their natural instinct.

Again the author retreated, awaited until the mother bird had reassembled her household, then came out to visit them, but with similar results. When he approached the spot where he last saw the mother bird not the slightest signs of the little fellows were to be found.

.   .   .   .

When a small boy the author captured a young crow and made a pet of it. The bird became quite well satisfied with its domestic surroundings and learned to perform many tricks requiring considerable intelligence. After the bird was big enough to fly it was permitted to go wherever it pleased. Sometimes it would be gone for many hours, but it always returned home before dark.

One day some wild crows became involved in a fight with an owl in a field near the house where the pet crow lived. As soon as the pet heard the "caw, caw, caw" of its wild relatives it flew up on top of the house, and with signs of great agitation, walked from one end of the house to the other. Finally it took wing and flew in the direction of the "battle." The author followed to see what would happen. In a few minutes he came up with the pet. It was sitting on the lower branches of a tree and two wild crows were sitting on a limb just above, chattering and walking back and forth, acting very much in the same fashion that angry parents behave toward their offspring when chastising them.

As the author approached, the two wild crows flew away, one of them circling around the tree a few times, meanwhile letting out a terrible flow of most abusive language, which, no doubt, was directed at its foolish relative who hadn't enough sense to fly while the flying was good.

The pet was called, but it paid no attention. That evening it returned home, but would not come near the house. It sat on a high limb of an apple tree and talked in crow language for about ten minutes, saying, no doubt, that it had decided to go back to the wild life of its fellows, then flew away and did not return until two days later, when it came back and did some more talking in crow language, keeping at a safe distance meanwhile. It then went away and never returned.

Social heredity had robbed the author of a fine pet!

The only consolation he got from the loss of his crow was the thought that it had shown fine sportsmanship by coming back and giving notice of its intention to depart. Many farm hands had left the farm without going to the trouble of this formality.

.   .   .   .

It is a well known fact that a fox will prey upon all manner of fowl and small animals with the exception of the skunk. No reason need be stated as to why Mr. Skunk enjoys immunity. A fox may tackle a skunk once, but never twice! For this reason a skunk hide, when nailed to a chicken roost, will keep all but the very young and inexperienced foxes at a safe distance.

The odor of a skunk, once experienced, is never to be forgotten. No other smell even remotely resembles it. It is nowhere recorded that any mother fox ever taught her young how to detect and keep away from the familiar smell of a skunk, but all who are informed on "fox lore" know that foxes and skunks never seek lodgment in the same cave.

But one lesson is sufficient to teach the fox all it cares to know about skunks. Through the law of social heredity, operating via the sense of smell, one lesson serves for an entire life-time.

.   .   .   .

A bullfrog can be caught on a fish-hook by attaching a small piece of red cloth or any other small red object to the hook and dangling it in front of the frog's nose. That is, Mr. Frog may be caught in this manner, provided he is hooked the first time he snaps at the bait, but if he is poorly hooked and makes a get-away, or if he feels the point of the hook when he bites at the bait but is not caught, he will never make the same mistake again. The author spent many hours in stealthy attempt to hook a particularly desirable specimen which had snapped and missed, before learning that but one lesson in social heredity is enough to teach even a humble "croaker" that bits of red flannel are things to be let alone.

The author once owned a very fine male Airedale dog which caused no end of annoyance by his habit of coming home with a young chicken in his mouth.

IS it not strange that we fear most that which never happens? That we destroy our initiative by the fear of defeat, when, in reality, defeat is a most useful tonic and should be accepted as such.

Each time the chicken was taken away from the dog and he was soundly switched, but to no avail; he continued in his liking for fowl.

For the purpose of saving the dog, if possible, and as an experiment with social heredity, this dog was taken to the farm of a neighbor who had a hen and some newly hatched chickens. The hen was placed in the barn and the dog was turned in with her. As soon as everyone was out of sight the dog slowly edged up toward the hen, sniffed the air in her direction a time or two (to make sure she was the kind of meat for which he was looking), then made a dive toward her. Meanwhile Mrs. Hen had been doing some "surveying" on her own account, for she met Mr. Dog more than halfway; moreover, she met him with such a surprise of wings and claws as he had never before experienced. The first round was clearly the hen's. But a nice fat bird, reckoned the dog, was not to slip between his paws so easily; therefore he backed away a short distance, then charged again. This time Mrs. Hen lit upon his back, drove her claws into his skin and made effective use of her sharp bill! Mr. Dog retreated to his corner, looking for all the world as if he were listening for someone to ring the bell and call the fight off until he got his bearings. But Mrs. Hen craved no time for deliberation; she had her adversary on the run and showed that she knew the value of the offensive by keeping him on the run.

One could almost understand her words as she flogged the poor Airedale from one corner to another, keeping up a series of rapid-fire sounds which for all the world resembled the remonstrations of an angry mother who had been called upon to defend her off-spring from an attack by older boys.

The Airedale was a poor soldier! After running around the barn from corner to corner for about two minutes he spread himself on the ground as flat as he could and did his best to protect his eyes with his paws. Mrs. Hen seemed to be making a special attempt to peck out his eyes.

The owner of the hen then stepped in and retrieved her—or, more accurately stating it, he retrieved the dog—which in no way appeared to meet with the dog's disapproval.

The next day a chicken was placed in the cellar where the dog slept. As soon as he saw the bird he tucked his tail between his legs and ran for a corner! He never again attempted to catch a chicken. One lesson in social heredity, via the sense of "touch," was sufficient to teach him that while chicken-chasing may offer some enjoyment, it is also fraught with much hazard.

All these illustrations, with the exception of the first, describe the process of gathering knowledge through direct experience. Observe the marked difference between knowledge gathered by direct experience and that which is gathered through the training of the young by the old, as in the case of the ruffed grouse and her young.

The most impressive lessons are those learned by the young from the old, through highly colored or emotionalized methods of teaching. When the mother grouse spread her wings, stood her feathers on end, shook herself like a man suffering with the palsy and chattered to her young in a highly excited manner, she planted the fear of man in their hearts in a manner which they were never to forget.

The term "social heredity," as used in connection with this lesson, has particular reference to all methods through which a child is taught any idea, dogma, creed, religion or system of ethical conduct, by its parents or those who may have authority over it, before reaching the age at which it may reason and reflect upon such teaching in its own way; estimating the age of such reasoning power at, let us say, seven to twelve years.

.   .   .   .

There are myriads of forms of *fear*, but none are more deadly than the fear of poverty and old age. We drive our bodies as if they were slaves because we are so afraid of poverty that we wish to hoard money for—*what*—*old age!* This common form of *fear* drives us so hard that we overwork our bodies and bring on the very thing we are struggling to avoid.

What a tragedy to watch a man drive himself when he begins to arrive along about the forty-year mile post of life—the age at which he is just beginning to mature mentally. At forty a man is just entering the age in which he is able to see and understand and assimilate the handwriting of Nature, as it appears in the forests and flowing brooks and faces of men and little children, yet this devil *fear* drives him so hard that he becomes blinded and lost in the entanglement of a maze of conflicting *desires*. The principle of *organized effort* is lost sight of, and instead of laying hold of Nature's forces which are in evidence all around him, and permitting those forces to carry him to the heights of great achievement, he defies them and they become forces of destruction.

Perhaps none of these great forces of Nature are more available for man's unfoldment than is the principle of Auto-suggestion, but ignorance of this force is leading the majority of the human race to apply it so that it acts as a hindrance and not as a help.

Let us here enumerate the facts which show just how this misapplication of a great force of Nature takes place:

Here is a man who meets with some disappointment; a friend proves false, or a neighbor seems indifferent. Forthwith he decides (through self-suggestion) all men are untrustworthy and all neighbors unappreciative. These thoughts so deeply imbed themselves in his subconscious mind that they color his whole attitude toward others. Go back, now, to what was said in Lesson Two, about the dominating thoughts of a man's mind attracting people whose thoughts are similar.

Apply the Law of Attraction and you will soon see and understand why the unbeliever attracts other unbelievers.

Reverse the Principle:

Here is a man who sees nothing but the best there is in all whom he meets. If his neighbors seem indifferent he takes no notice of that fact, for he makes it *his business* to fill his mind with dominating thoughts of optimism and good cheer and faith in others. If people speak to him harshly he speaks back in tones of softness. Through the operation of this same eternal Law of Attraction he draws to himself the attention of people whose attitude toward life and whose dominating thoughts harmonize with his own.

Tracing the principle a step further:

Here is a man who has been well schooled and has the ability to render the world some needed service. Somewhere, sometime, he has heard it said that modesty is a great virtue and that to push himself to the front of the stage in the game of life savors of egotism. He quietly slips in at the back door and takes a seat at the rear while other players in the game of life boldly step to the front. He remains in the back row because he *fears* "what *they* will say." Public opinion, or that which he believes to be public opinion, has him pushed to the rear and the world hears but little of him. His schooling counts for naught because he is *afraid* to let the world know that he has had it. He is constantly *suggesting* to *himself* (thus using the great force of Auto-suggestion to his own detriment) that he should remain in the background lest he be criticized, as if criticism would do him any damage or defeat his purpose.

Here is another man who was born of poor parents. Since the first day that he can remember he has seen evidence of poverty. He has heard talk of poverty. He has felt the icy hand of poverty on his shoulders and it has so impressed him that he fixes it in his mind as a curse to which *he must submit*. Quite unconsciously he permits himself to fall victim of the belief "once poor always poor" until that belief becomes the dominating thought of his mind. He resembles a horse that has been harnessed and broken until it forgets that it has the potential power with which to throw off that harness. Auto-suggestion is rapidly relegating him to the back of the stage of life. Finally he be-

YOUR work and mine are peculiarly akin; I am helping the laws of Nature create more perfect specimens of vegetation, while you are using those same laws, through the Law of Success philosophy, to create more perfect specimens of thinkers.

—*Luther Burbank.*

comes a *quitter*. Ambition is gone. Opportunity comes his way no longer, or if it does he has not the vision to see it. *He has accepted his FATE!* It is a well established fact that the faculties of the mind, like the limbs of the body, atrophy and wither away if not used. Self-confidence is no exception. It develops when used but disappears if not used.

One of the chief disadvantages of inherited wealth is the fact that it too often leads to inaction and loss of Self-confidence. Some years ago a baby boy was born to Mrs. E. B. McLean, in the city of Washington. His inheritance was said to be around a hundred million dollars. When this baby was taken for an airing in its carriage it was surrounded by nurses and assistant nurses and detectives and other servants whose duty was to see that no harm befell it. As the years passed by this same vigilance was kept up. This child did not have to dress himself; he had servants who did that. Servants watched over him while he slept and while he was at play. He was not permitted to do anything that a servant could do for him. He had grown to the age of ten years. One day he was playing in the yard and noticed that the back gate had been left open. In all of his life he had never been outside of that gate alone, and naturally that was just the thing that he wished to do. During a moment when the servants were not looking he dashed out at the gate, and was run down and killed by an automobile before he reached the middle of the street.

He had used his servants' eyes until his own no longer served him as they might have done had he learned to rely upon them.

Twenty years ago the man whom I served as secre-tary sent his two sons away to school. One of them went to the University of Virginia and the other to a college in New York. Each month it was a part of my task to make out a check for $100.00 for each of these boys. This was their "pin money," to be spent as they wished. How profitably I remember the way I envied those boys as I made out those checks each month. I often wondered why the hand of fate bore me into the world in poverty. I could look ahead and see how these boys would rise to the high stations in life while I remained a humble clerk.

In due time the boys returned home with their "sheep-skins." Their father was a wealthy man who owned banks and railroads and coal mines and other property of great value. Good positions were waiting for the boys in their father's employ.

But, twenty years of time can play cruel tricks on those who have never had to struggle. Perhaps a better way to state this truth would be that *time gives those who have never had to struggle a chance to play cruel tricks on themselves!* At any rate, these two boys brought home from school other things besides their sheep-skins. They came back with well de-veloped capacities for strong drink—*capacities which they developed because the hundred dollars which each of them received each month made it unneces-sary for them to struggle.*

Theirs is a long and sad story, the details of which will not interest you, but you will be interested in their "finis." As this lesson is being written I have on my desk a copy of the newspaper published in the town where these boys lived. Their father has been bankrupted and his costly mansion, where the boys were born, has been placed on the block for sale. One of the boys died of delirium tremens and the other one is in an insane asylum.

Not all rich men's sons turn out so unfortunately, but the fact remains, nevertheless, that inaction leads to atrophy and this, in turn, leads to loss of ambition and self-confidence, and without these essential qualities a man will be carried through life on the wings of uncertainty, just as a dry leaf may be carried here and there on the bosom of the stray winds.

Far from being a disadvantage, struggle is a decided advantage, because it develops those qualities which would forever lie dormant without it. Many a man has found his place in the world because of having been forced to struggle for existence early in life. Lack of knowledge of the advantages accruing from struggle has prompted many a parent to say, "I had to work hard when I was young, *but I shall see to it that my children have an easy time!*" Poor foolish creatures. An "easy" time usually turns out to be a greater handicap than the average young man or woman can survive. There are worse things in this world than being forced to work in early life. Forced idleness is far worse than forced labor. Being forced to work, and forced to *do your best,* will breed in you temperance and self-control and strength of will and content and a hundred other virtues which the idle will never know.

Not only does lack of the necessity for struggle lead to weakness of ambition and will-power, but, what is more dangerous still, it sets up in a person's mind a state of lethargy that leads to the loss of Self-confidence. The person who has quit struggling because effort is no longer necessary is literally applying the principle of Auto-suggestion in undermining his own power of Self-confidence. Such a person will finally drift into a frame of mind in which he will actually look with more or less contempt upon the person who is forced to carry on.

The human mind, if you will pardon repetition, may be likened to an electric battery. It may be positive or it may be negative. Self-confidence is the quality with which the mind is re-charged and made positive.

Let us apply this line of reasoning to salesmanship and see what part Self-confidence plays in this great field of endeavor. One of the greatest salesmen this country has ever seen was once a clerk in a newspaper office.

It will be worth your while to analyze the method through which he gained his title as "the world's leading salesman."

He was a timid young man with a more or less retiring sort of nature. He was one of those who believe it best to slip in by the back door and take a seat at the rear of the stage of life. One evening he heard a lecture on the subject of this lesson, Self-confidence, and that lecture so impressed him that he left the lecture hall with a firm determination to pull himself out of the rut into which he had drifted.

He went to the Business Manager of the paper and asked for a position as solicitor of advertising and was put to work on a commission basis. Everyone in the office expected to see him fail, as this sort of salesmanship calls for the most positive type of sales ability. He went to his room and made out a list of

a certain type of merchants on whom he intended to
call. One would think that he would naturally have
made up his list of the names of those whom he believed he could sell with the least effort, *but he did
nothing of the sort.* He placed on his list only the
names of the merchants on whom other advertising
solicitors had called without making a sale. His list
consisted of only twelve names. Before he made a
single call he went out to the city park, took out his
list of twelve names, read it over a hundred times, saying to himself as he did so, *"You will purchase advertising space from me before the end of the month."*

Then he began to make his calls. The first day he
closed sales with three of the twelve "impossibilities."
During the remainder of the week he made sales to
two others. By the end of the month he had opened
advertising accounts with all but one of the merchants
that he had on the list. For the ensuing month he
made no sales, for the reason that he made no calls
except on this one obstinate merchant. Every morning when the store opened he was on hand to interview this merchant and every morning the merchant
said *"No."* The merchant knew he was not going to
buy advertising space, but this young man didn't know
it. When the merchant said *No* the young man did
not hear it, but kept right on coming. On the last
day of the month, after having told this persistent
young man *No* for thirty consecutive times, the merchant said:

"Look here, young man, you have wasted a whole
month trying to sell me; now, what I would like to
know is this—why have you wasted your time?"

"Wasted my time nothing," he retorted; "I have

NO man can become a great leader of men unless he has the milk of human kindness in his own heart, and leads by suggestion and kindness, rather than by force.

been going to school and you have been my teacher. Now I know all the arguments that a merchant can bring up for not buying, and besides that I have been drilling myself in Self-confidence."

Then the merchant said: "I will make a little confession of my own. I, too, have been going to school, and you have been my teacher. You have taught me a lesson in persistence that is worth money to me, and to show you my appreciation I am going to pay my tuition fee by giving you an order for advertising space."

And that was the way in which the Philadelphia North American's best advertising account was brought in. Likewise, it marked the beginning of a reputation that has made that same young man a millionaire.

He succeeded because he deliberately charged his own mind with sufficient Self-confidence to make that mind an irresistible force. When he sat down to make up that list of twelve names he did something that ninety-nine people out of a hundred would not have done—he selected the names of those whom he believed it would be hard to sell, because he understood that out of the resistance he would meet with in trying to sell them would come strength and Self-confidence. He was one of the very few people who understand that all rivers and *some men* are crooked because of following the line of least resistance.

   .   .   .   .

I am going to digress and here break the line of thought for a moment while recording a word of advice to the wives of men. Remember, these lines are intended only for wives, and husbands are not expected to read that which is here set down.

From having analyzed more than 16,000 people, the majority of whom were married men, I have learned something that may be of value to wives. Let me state my thought in these words:

You have it within your power to send your husband away to his work or his business or his profession each day with a feeling of Self-confidence that will carry him successfully over the rough spots of the day and bring him home again, at night, smiling and happy. One of my acquaintances of former years married a woman who had a set of false teeth. One day his wife dropped her teeth and broke the plate. The husband picked up the pieces and began examining them. He showed such interest in them that his wife said:

"You could make a set of teeth like those if you made up your mind to do it."

This man was a farmer whose ambitions had never carried him beyond the bounds of his little farm until his wife made that remark. She walked over and laid her hand on his shoulder and encouraged him to try his hand at dentistry. She finally coaxed him to make the start, and today he is one of the most prominent and successful dentists in the state of Virginia. I know him well, for he is my father!

No one can foretell the possibilities of achievement available to the man whose wife stands at his back and urges him on to bigger and better endeavor, for it is a well known fact that a woman can arouse a man so that he will perform almost superhuman feats. It is your right and your duty to encourage your husband and urge him on in worthy undertakings until he shall have found his place in the world. You can induce him to put forth greater effort than can any other person in the world. Make him believe that nothing within reason is beyond his power of achievement and you will have rendered him a service that will go a long way toward helping him win in the battle of life.

.   .   .   .

One of the most successful men in his line in America gives entire credit for his success to his wife. When they were first married she wrote a creed which he signed and placed over his desk. This is a copy of the creed:

I believe in myself. I believe in those who work with me. I believe in my employer. I believe in my friends. I believe in my family. I believe that God will lend me everything I need with which to succeed if I do my best to earn it through faithful and honest service. I believe in prayer and I will never close my eyes in sleep without praying for divine guidance to the end that I will be patient with other people and tolerant with those who do not believe as I do. I believe that success is the result of intelligent effort and does not depend upon luck or sharp practices or double-crossing friends, fellow men or my employer. I believe I will get out of life exactly what I put into it, therefore I will be careful to conduct myself toward others as I would want them to act toward me. I will not slander those whom I do not like. I will not slight

my work no matter what I may see others doing.
I will render the best service of which I am capable
because I have pledged myself to succeed in life
and I know that success is always the result of
conscientious and efficient effort. Finally, I will
forgive those who offend me because I realize that
I shall sometimes offend others and I will need their
forgiveness.

Signed ....

The woman who wrote this creed was a practical
psychologist of the first order. With the influence and
guidance of such a woman as a helpmate any man
could achieve noteworthy success.

Analyze this creed and you will notice how freely
the personal pronoun is used. It starts off with the
affirmation of Self-confidence, which is perfectly
proper. No man could make this creed his own without developing the positive attitude that would attract
to him people who would aid him in his struggle for
success.

This would be a splendid creed for every salesman
to adopt. It might not hurt your chances for success
if *you* adopted it. Mere adoption, however, is not
enough. You must *practice* it! Read it over and
over until you know it by heart. Then repeat it at
least once a day until you have literally transformed
it into your mental make-up. Keep a copy of it before you as a daily reminder of your pledge to practice
it. By doing so you will be making efficient use of the
principle of Auto-suggestion as a means of developing
Self-confidence. Never mind what anyone may say
about your procedure. Just remember that it is your

business to succeed, and this creed, if mastered and applied, will go a long way toward helping you.

You learned in Lesson Two that any idea you firmly fix in your subconscious mind, by repeated affirmation, automatically becomes a plan or blueprint which an unseen power uses in directing your efforts toward the attainment of the objective named in the plan.

You have also learned that the principle through which you may fix any idea you choose in your mind is called Auto-suggestion, which simply means a suggestion that you give to your own mind. It was this principle of Auto-suggestion that Emerson had in mind when he wrote:

"Nothing can bring you peace but yourself!"

You might well remember that *Nothing can bring you success but yourself.* Of course you will need the co-operation of others if you aim to attain success of a far-reaching nature, but you will never get that co-operation unless you vitalize your mind with the positive attitude of Self-confidence.

Perhaps you have wondered why a few men advance to highly paid positions while others all around them, who have as much training and who seemingly perform as much work, do not get ahead. Select any two people of these two types that you choose, and study them, and the reason why one advances and the other stands still will be quite obvious to you. You will find that the one who advances *believes in himself.* You will find that he backs this belief with such dynamic, aggressive action that he lets others know that he believes in himself. You will also notice that this Self-confidence is contagious; it is impelling; it is persuasive; it attracts others.

IF you want a thing done well, call on some busy person to do it. Busy people are generally the m o s t painstaking and thorough in all they do.

You will also find that the one who does not advance shows clearly, by the look on his face, by the posture of his body, by the lack of briskness in his step, by the uncertainty with which he speaks, that he lacks Self-confidence. No one is going to pay much attention to the person who has no confidence in himself.

He does not attract others because his mind is a negative force that repels rather than attracts.

In no other field of endeavor does Self-confidence or the lack of it play such an important part as in the field of salesmanship, and you do not need to be a character analyst to determine, the moment you meet him, whether a salesman possesses this quality of Self-confidence. If he has it the signs of its influence are written all over him. He inspires you with confidence in him and in the goods he is selling the moment he speaks.

We come, now, to the point at which you are ready to take hold of the principle of Auto-suggestion and make direct use of it in developing yourself into a positive and dynamic and self-reliant person. You are instructed to copy the following formula, sign it and commit it to memory:

SELF-CONFIDENCE FORMULA

First: I know that I have the ability to achieve the object of my *definite purpose,* therefore I *demand* of myself persistent, aggressive and continuous action toward its attainment.

Second: I realize that the dominating thoughts of my mind eventually reproduce themselves in outward, bodily action, and gradually transform themselves into physical reality, therefore I will concentrate

my mind for thirty minutes daily upon the task of
thinking of the person I intend to be, by creating
a mental picture of this person and then transforming that picture into reality through practical
service.

Third: I know that through the principle of Auto-
suggestion, any desire that I persistently hold in my
mind will eventually seek expression through some
practical means of realizing it, therefore I shall devote ten minutes daily to demanding of myself the
development of the factors named in the sixteen
lessons of this Reading Course on the Law of
Success.

Fourth: I have clearly mapped out and written down
a description of my *definite purpose* in life, for the
coming five years. I have set a price on my services for each of these five years; a price that I
intend to *earn* and *receive*, through strict application
of the principle of efficient, satisfactory service
which I will render in advance.

Fifth: I fully realize that no wealth or position can
long endure unless built upon truth and justice,
therefore *I will engage in no transaction which does
not benefit all whom it affects.* I will succeed by
attracting to me the forces I wish to use, and the
co-operation of other people. I will induce others
to serve me because I will first serve them. I will
eliminate hatred, envy, jealousy, selfishness and
cynicism by developing love for all humanity, because I know that a negative attitude toward others
can never bring me success. I will cause others to
believe in me because I will believe in them and in
myself.

I will sign my name to this formula, commit it to memory and repeat it aloud once a day with full *faith* that it will gradually influence my entire life so that I will become a successful and happy worker in my chosen field of endeavor.

Signed.............................

Before you sign your name to this formula make sure that you intend to carry out its instructions. Back of this formula lies a law that no man can explain. The psychologists refer to this law as Auto-suggestion and let it go at that, but you should bear in mind one point about which there is no uncertainty, and that is the fact that whatever this law is it *actually works!*

Another point to be kept in mind is the fact that, just as electricity will turn the wheels of industry and serve mankind in a million other ways, or snuff out life if wrongly applied, so will this principle of Auto-suggestion lead you up the mountain-side of peace and prosperity, or down into the valley of misery and poverty, according to the application you make of it. If you fill your mind with doubt and unbelief in your ability to achieve, then the principle of Auto-suggestion takes this spirit of unbelief and sets it up in your subconscious mind as your dominating thought and slowly but surely draws you into the whirlpool of *failure.* But, if you fill your mind with radiant Self-confidence, the principle of Auto-suggestion takes this belief and sets it up as your dominating thought and helps you master the obstacles that fall in your way until you reach the mountain-top of *success.*

THE POWER OF HABIT

Having, myself, experienced all the difficulties that stand in the road of those who lack the understanding to make practical application of this great principle of Auto-suggestion, let me take you a short way into the principle of habit, through the aid of which you may easily apply the principle of Auto-suggestion in any direction and for any purpose whatsoever.

Habit grows out of environment; out of doing the same thing or thinking the same thoughts or repeating the same words over and over again. Habit may be likened to the groove on a phonograph record, while the human mind may be likened to the needle that fits into that groove. When any habit has been well formed, through repetition of thought or action, the mind has a tendency to attach itself to and follow the course of that habit as closely as the phonograph needle follows the groove in the wax record.

Habit is created by *repeatedly* directing one or more of the five senses of seeing, hearing, smelling, tasting and feeling, in a given direction. It is through this repetition principle that the injurious drug habit is formed. It is through this same principle that the desire for intoxicating drink is formed into a habit.

After habit has been well established it will automatically control and direct our bodily activity, wherein may be found a thought that can be transformed into a powerful factor in the development of *Self-confidence*. The thought is this: *Voluntarily, and by force if necessary, direct your efforts and your thoughts along a desired line until you have formed the habit that will lay hold of you and continue.*

voluntarily, to direct your efforts along the same line.
The object in writing out and repeating the Self-confidence formula is to form the habit of making *belief in yourself* the dominating thought of your mind until that thought has been thoroughly imbedded in your subconscious mind, through the principle of *habit.*

You learned to write by repeatedly directing the muscles of your arm and hand over certain outlines known as letters, until finally you formed the habit of tracing these outlines. Now you write with ease and rapidity, without tracing each letter slowly. Writing has become a *habit* with you.

The principle of habit will lay hold of the faculties of your mind just the same as it will influence the physical muscles of your body, as you can easily prove by mastering and applying this lesson on Self-confidence. Any statement that you repeatedly make to yourself, or any *desire* that you deeply plant in your mind through repeated statement, will eventually seek expression through your physical, outward bodily efforts. The principle of habit is the very foundation upon which this lesson on Self-confidence is built, and if you will understand and follow the directions laid down in this lesson you will soon know more about the law of habit, from first-hand knowledge, than could be taught you by a thousand such lessons as this.

You have but little conception of the possibilities which lie sleeping within you, awaiting but the awakening hand of vision to arouse you, and you will never have a better conception of those possibilities unless you develop sufficient Self-confidence to lift you

A HOME is some-
thing that cannot be
bought. You can buy a
house but only a woman
can make of it a home.

above the commonplace influences of your present environment.

The human mind is a marvelous, mysterious piece of machinery, a fact of which I was reminded a few months ago when I picked up Emerson's Essays and re-read his essay on Spiritual Laws. A strange thing happened. I saw in that essay, which I had read scores of times previously, much that I had never noticed before. I saw more in this essay than I had seen during previous readings because the unfoldment of my mind since the last reading had prepared me to interpret more.

The human mind is constantly unfolding, like the petals of a flower, until it reaches the maximum of development. What this maximum is, where it ends, or whether it ends at all or not, are unanswerable questions, but the degree of unfoldment seems to vary according to the nature of the individual and the degree to which he keeps his mind at work. A mind that is forced or coaxed into analytical thought every day seems to keep on unfolding and developing greater powers of interpretation.

Down in Louisville, Kentucky, lives Mr. Lee Cook, a man who has practically no legs and has to wheel himself around on a cart. In spite of the fact that Mr. Cook has been without legs since birth, he is the owner of a great industry and a millionaire through his own efforts. He has proved that a man can get along very well without legs if he has a well developed Self-confidence.

In the city of New York one may see a strong able-bodied and able-headed young man, without legs, rolling himself down Fifth Avenue every afternoon, with cap in hand, begging for a living. His head is perhaps as sound and as able to think as the average.

This young man could duplicate anything that Mr. Cook, of Louisville, has done, if *he thought of himself as Mr. Cook thinks of himself.*

Henry Ford owns more millions of dollars than he will ever need or use. Not so many years ago, he was working as a laborer in a machine shop, with but little schooling and without capital. Scores of other men, some of them with better organized brains than his, worked near him. Ford threw off the poverty consciousness, developed confidence in himself, thought of success and attained it. Those who worked around him could have done as well had they *thought* as he did.

Milo C. Jones, of Wisconsin, was stricken down with paralysis a few years ago. So bad was the stroke that he could not turn himself in bed or move a muscle of his body. His physical body was useless, but there was nothing wrong with his brain, so it began to function in earnest, probably for the first time in its existence. Lying flat on his back in bed, Mr. Jones made that brain create a *definite purpose.* That purpose was prosaic and humble enough in nature, but it was *definite* and it was a *purpose,* something that he had never known before.

His *definite purpose* was to make pork sausage. Calling his family around him he told of his plans and began directing them in carrying the plans into action. With nothing to aid him except a sound mind and plenty of *Self-confidence,* Milo C. Jones spread the name and reputation of "Little Pig Sausage" all over the United States, and accumulated a fortune besides

All this was accomplished after paralysis had made it impossible for him to work with his hands.

Where *thought* prevails power may be found!

Henry Ford has made millions of dollars and is still making millions of dollars each year because *he believed in Henry Ford* and transformed that belief into a *definite purpose* and backed that purpose with a definite plan. The other machinists who worked along with Ford, during the early days of his career, visioned nothing but a weekly pay envelope and that was all they ever got. They demanded nothing out of the ordinary of themselves. If you want to *get more* be sure to *demand* more of yourself. Notice that this demand is to be made on *yourself!*

There comes to mind a well known poem whose author expressed a great psychological truth:

If you think you are beaten, you are;
    If you think you dare not, you don't;
If you like to win, but you think you can't,
    It is almost certain you won't.

If you think you'll lose you've lost,
    For out of the world we find
Success begins with a fellow's will—
    It's all in the state of mind.

If you think you are outclassed, you are—
    You've got to think high to rise.
You've got to be sure of yourself before
    You can ever win a prize.

> Life's battles don't always go
> To the stronger or faster man;
> But soon or late the man who wins
> Is the man who thinks he can.

It can do no harm if you commit this poem to memory and use it as a part of your working equipment in the development of Self-confidence.

Somewhere in your make-up there is a "subtle something" which, if it were aroused by the proper outside influence, would carry you to heights of achievement such as you have never before anticipated. Just as a master player can take hold of a violin and cause that instrument to pour forth the most beautiful and entrancing strains of music, so is there some outside influence that can lay hold of your mind and cause you to go forth into the field of your chosen endeavor and play a glorious symphony of *success*. No man knows what hidden forces lie dormant within *you*. You, yourself, do not know your capacity for achievement, and you never will know until you come in contact with that particular stimulus which arouses you to greater action and extends your vision, develops your Self-confidence and moves you with a deeper *desire* to achieve.

It is not unreasonable to expect that some statement, some idea or some stimulating word of this Reading Course on the Law of Success will serve as the needed stimulus that will re-shape your destiny and re-direct your thoughts and energies along a pathway that will lead you, finally, to your coveted goal of life. It is strange, but true, that the most important turning-points of life often come at the most unexpected times and in the most unexpected ways. I have in mind a typical example of how some of the seemingly unimportant experiences of life often turn out to be the most important of all, and I am relating this case because it shows, also, what a man can accomplish when he awakens to a full understanding of the value of Self-confidence. The incident to which I refer happened in the city of Chicago, while I was engaged in the work of character analysis. One day a tramp presented himself at my office and asked for an interview. As I looked up from my work and greeted him he said, "I have come to see the man who wrote this little book," as he removed from his pocket a copy of a book entitled Self-confidence, which I had written many years previously. "It must have been the hand of fate," he continued, "that slipped this book into my pocket yesterday afternoon, because I was about ready to go out there and punch a hole in Lake Michigan. I had about come to the conclusion that everything and everybody, including God, had it in for me until I read this book, and it gave me a new viewpoint and brought me the courage and the hope that sustained me through the night. I made up my mind that if I could see the man who wrote this book he could help me get on my feet again. Now, I am here and I would like to know what you can do for a man like me."

While he was speaking I had been studying him from head to foot, and I am frank to admit that down deep in my heart I did not believe there was anything I could do for him, but I did not wish to tell him so. The glassy stare in his eyes, the lines of discouragement in his face, the posture of his body, the ten days'

THE only man who makes no mistakes is the man who never does anything. Do not be afraid of mistakes providing you do not make the same one twice.

—*Roosevelt.*

growth of beard on his face, the nervous manner about this man all conveyed to me the impression that he was hopeless, but I did not have the heart to tell him so, therefore I asked him to sit down and tell me his whole story. I asked him to be perfectly frank and tell me, as nearly as possible, just what had brought him down to the ragged edge of life. I promised him that after I had heard his entire story I would then tell him whether or not I could be of service to him. He related his story, in lengthy detail, the sum and substance of which was this: He had invested his entire fortune in a small manufacturing business. When the world war began in 1914, it was impossible for him to get the raw materials necessary in the operation of his factory, and he therefore failed. The loss of his money broke his heart and so disturbed his mind that he left his wife and children and became a tramp. He had actually brooded over his loss until he had reached the point at which he was contemplating suicide.

After he had finished his story, I said to him: "I have listened to you with a great deal of interest, and I wish that there was something which *I* could do to help you, but *there is absolutely nothing.*"

He became as pale as he will be when he is laid away in a coffin, and settled back in his chair and dropped his chin on his chest as much as to say, "That settles it." I waited for a few seconds, then said:

"While there is nothing that I can do for you, there is a man in this building to whom I will introduce you, if you wish, who can help you regain your lost fortune and put you back on your feet again." These words had barely fallen from my lips when he jumped up, grabbed me by the hands and said, "For God's sake lead me to this man."

It was encouraging to note that he had asked this "for God's sake." This indicated that there was still a spark of hope within his breast, so I took him by the arm and led him out into the laboratory where my psychological tests in character analysis were conducted, and stood with him in front of what looked to be a curtain over a door. I pulled the curtain aside and uncovered a tall looking-glass in which he saw himself from head to foot. Pointing my finger at the glass I said:

"There stands the man to whom I promised to introduce you. There is the only man in this world who can put you back on your feet again, and unless you sit down and become acquainted with that man, as you never became acquainted with him before, you might just as well go on over and 'punch a hole' in Lake Michigan, because you will be of no value to yourself or to the world until you know this man better."

He stepped over to the glass, rubbed his hands over his bearded face, studied himself from head to foot for a few moments, then stepped back, dropped his head and began to weep. I knew that the lesson had been driven home, so I led him back to the elevator and sent him away. I never expected to see him again, and I doubted that the lesson would be sufficient to help him regain his place in the world, because he seemed to be too far gone for redemption. He seemed to be not only *down*, but almost *out*.

A few days later I met this man on the street. His

transformation had been so complete that I hardly recognized him. He was walking briskly, with his head tilted back. That old, shifting, nervous posture of his body was gone. He was dressed in new clothes from head to foot. He looked prosperous and he felt prosperous. He stopped me and related what had happened to bring about his rapid transformation from a state of abject failure to one of hope and promise.

"I was just on my way to your office," he explained, "to bring you the good news. I went out the very day that I was in your office, a down-and-out tramp, and despite my appearance I sold myself at a salary of $3,000.00 a year. *Think of it, man, three thousand dollars a year!* And my employer advanced me money enough with which to buy some new clothes, as you can see for yourself. He also advanced me some money to send home to my family, and I am once more on the road to success. It seems like a dream when I think that only a few days ago I had lost hope and faith and courage, and was actually contemplating suicide.

"I was coming to tell you that one of these days, when you are least expecting me, I will pay you another visit, and when I do I will be a successful man. I will bring with me a check, signed in blank and made payable to you, and you may fill in the amount because you have saved me from *myself* by introducing me to *myself*—that self which I never knew until you stood me in front of that looking-glass and pointed out the *real* me."

As that man turned and departed in the crowded streets of Chicago I saw, for the first time in my life, what strength and power and possibility lie hidden in the mind of the man who has never discovered the value of *Self-reliance*. Then and there I made up my mind that I, too, would stand in front of that same looking-glass and point an accusing finger at myself for not having discovered the lesson which I had helped another to learn. I did stand before that same looking-glass, and as I did so I then and there fixed in my mind, as my *definite purpose* in life, the determination to help men and women discover the forces that lie sleeping within them. The book you hold in your hands is evidence that my definite purpose is being carried out.

The man whose story I have related is now the president of one of the largest and most successful concerns of its kind in America, with a business that extends from coast to coast and from Canada to Mexico.

A short while after the incident just related, a woman came to my office for personal analysis. She was then a teacher in the Chicago public schools. I gave her an analysis chart and asked her to fill it out. She had been at work on the chart but a few minutes when she came back to my desk, handed back the chart and said, "I do not believe I will fill this out." I asked her why she had decided not to fill out the chart and she replied: "To be perfectly frank with you, one of the questions in this chart put me to thinking and I now know what is wrong with me, therefore I feel it unnecessary to pay you a fee to analyze me." With that the woman went away and I did not hear from her for two years. She went to New York City, became a writer of advertising copy for one of the largest agencies in the country and her income at the time she wrote me was $10,000.00 a year.

This woman sent me a check to cover the cost of my analysis fee, because she felt that the fee had been earned, even though I did not render her the service that I usually render my clients. It is impossible for anyone to foretell what seemingly insignificant incident may lead to an important turning-point in one's career, but there is no denying the fact that these "turning-points" may be more readily recognized by those who have well-rounded-out confidence in themselves.

One of the irreparable losses to the human race lies in the lack of knowledge that there is a definite method through which Self-confidence can be developed in any person of average intelligence. What an immeasurable loss to civilization that young men and women are not taught this known method of developing Self-confidence before they complete their schooling, for no one who lacks faith in himself is really educated in the proper sense of the term.

Oh, what glory and satisfaction would be the happy heritage of the man or woman who could pull aside the curtain of *fear* that hangs over the human race and shuts out the sunlight of understanding that Self-confidence brings, wherever it is in evidence.

Where *fear* controls, noteworthy achievement becomes an impossibility, a fact which brings to mind the definition of *fear*, as stated by a great philosopher:

"Fear is the dungeon of the mind into which it runs and hides and seeks seclusion. Fear brings on superstition and superstition is the dagger with which hypocrisy assassinates the soul."

In front of the typewriter on which I am writing

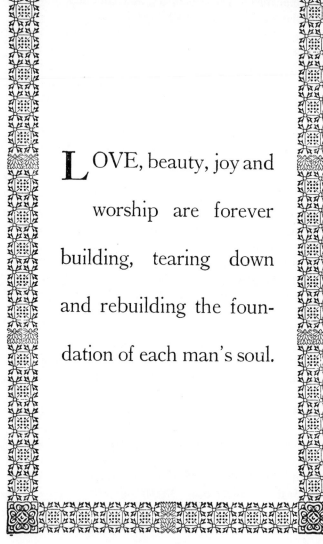

L OVE, beauty, joy and worship are forever building, tearing down and rebuilding the foundation of each man's soul.

the manuscripts for this Reading Course hangs a sign with the following wording, in big letters:

"Day by day in every way I am becoming more *successful.*"

A skeptic who read that sign asked if I really believed "that stuff" and I replied, "Of course not. All it ever did for me was to help me get out of the coal mines, where I started as a laborer, and find a place in the world in which I am serving upwards of 100,000 people, in whose minds I am planting the same positive thought that this sign brings out; therefore, why should I believe in it?"

As this man started to leave he said: "Well, perhaps there is something to this sort of philosophy, after all, for I have always been afraid that I would be a failure, and so far my fears have been thoroughly realized."

You are condemning yourself to poverty, misery and failure, or you are driving yourself on toward the heights of great achievement, solely by the thoughts you think. If you *demand* success of yourself and back up this demand with intelligent action you are sure to win. Bear in mind, though, that there is a difference between *demanding* success and just merely wishing for it. You should find out what this difference is, and take advantage of it.

Do you remember what the Bible says (look it up, somewhere in the book of Matthew) about those who have faith as a grain of mustard seed? Go at the task of developing Self-confidence with at least that much faith if not more. Never mind "what *they* will say" because you might as well know that "*they*" will be of little aid to you in your climb up the mountain-side of life toward the object of your *definite purpose.* You have within you all the power you need with which to get whatever you want or need in this world, and about the best way to avail yourself of this power is to *believe in yourself.*

"Know thyself, man; know thyself."

This has been the advice of the philosophers all down the ages. When you *really* know yourself you will know that there is nothing foolish about hanging a sign in front of you that reads like this: "Day by day in every way I am becoming more successful," with due apologies to the Frenchman who made this motto popular. I am not afraid to place this sort of suggestion in front of my desk, and, what is more to the point, I am not afraid to believe that it will influence me so that I will become a more positive and aggressive human being.

More than twenty-five years ago I learned my first lesson in Self-confidence building. One night I was sitting before an open fire-place, listening to a conversation between some older men, on the subject of Capital and Labor. Without invitation I joined in the conversation and said something about employers and employees settling their differences on the Golden Rule basis. My remarks attracted the attention of one of the men, who turned to me, with a look of surprise on his face and said:

"Why, you are a bright boy, and if you would go out and get a schooling you would make your mark in the world."

Those remarks fell on "fertile" ears, even though that was the first time anyone had ever told me that I was bright, or that I might accomplish anything worth while in life. The remark put me to thinking, and the more I allowed my mind to dwell upon that thought the more certain I became that the remark had back of it a possibility.

It might be truthfully stated that whatever service I am rendering the world and whatever good I accomplish, should be credited to that off-hand remark.

Suggestions such as this are often powerful, and none the less so when they are deliberate and self-expressed. Go back, now, to the Self-confidence formula and master it, for it will lead you into the "power-house" of your own mind, where you will tap a force that can be made to carry you to the very top of the Ladder of Success.

Others will believe in you only when you believe in yourself. They will "tune in" on your thoughts and feel toward you just as you feel toward yourself. The law of mental telepathy takes care of this. You are continuously broadcasting what you think of yourself, and if you have no faith in yourself others will pick up the vibrations of your thoughts and mistake them for their own. Once understand the law of mental telepathy and you will know why Self-confidence is the second of the Fifteen Laws of Success.

You should be cautioned, however, to learn the difference between Self-confidence, which is based upon sound knowledge of what you know and what you can do, and egotism, which is only based upon what you *wish* you knew or could do. Learn the difference between these two terms or you will make yourself boresome, ridiculous and annoying to people of culture and understanding. Self-confidence is something which should never be proclaimed or announced except through intelligent performance of constructive deeds.

If you have Self-confidence those around you will discover this fact. Let them make the discovery. They will feel proud of their alertness in having made the discovery, and you will be free from the suspicion of egotism. Opportunity never stalks the person with a highly developed state of egotism, but brick-bats and ugly remarks do. Opportunity forms affinities much more easily and quickly with Self-confidence than it does with egotism. Self-praise is never a proper measure of self-reliance. Bear this in mind and let your Self-confidence speak only through the tongue of constructive service rendered without fuss or flurry.

Self-confidence is the product of knowledge. Know yourself, know how much you know (and how little), why you know it, and how you are going to use it. "Four-flushers" come to grief, therefore, do not pretend to know more than you actually do know. There's no use of pretense, because any educated person will measure you quite accurately after hearing you speak for three minutes. What you really are will speak so loudly that what you "claim" you are will not be heard.

If you heed this warning the last four pages of this one lesson may mark one of the most important turning-points of your life.

Believe in yourself, but do not tell the world what you can do—SHOW IT!

You are now ready for Lesson Four, which will take you the next step up the Ladder of Success.

DISCONTENTMENT

An After-the-Lesson Visit With the Author

The marker stands at the Entrance Gate of Life and writes "Poor Fool" on the brow of the wise man and "Poor Sinner" on the brow of the saint.

The supreme mystery of the universe is life! We come here without our consent, from whence we know not! We go away without our consent, whither, we know not!

We are eternally trying to solve this great riddle of "LIFE," and, for what purpose and to what end?

That we are placed on this earth for a definite reason there can be no doubt by any thinker. May it not be possible that the power which placed us here will know what to do with us when we pass on beyond the Great Divide?

Would it not be a good plan to give the Creator who placed us here on earth, credit for having enough intelligence to know what to do with us after we pass on; or, should we assume the intelligence and the ability to control the future life in our own way? May it not be possible that we can co-operate with the Creator very intelligently by assuming to con-

155

trol our conduct on this earth to the end that
we may be decent to one another and do all
the good we can in all the ways we can during
this life, leaving the hereafter to one who
probably knows, better than we, what is best
for us?

THE artist has told a powerful story in the picture
at the top of this page.

From birth until death the mind is always reaching
out for that which it does not possess.

The little child, playing with its toys on the floor,
sees another child with a different sort of toy and
immediately tries to lay hands on that toy.

The female child (grown tall) believes the other
woman's clothes more becoming than her own and
sets out to duplicate them.

The male child (grown tall) sees another man with
a bigger collection of railroads or banks or merchandise and says to himself: "How fortunate! How fortunate! How can I separate him from his belongings?"

F. W. Woolworth, the Five and Ten Cent Store
king, stood on Fifth Avenue in New York City and
gazed upward at the tall Metropolitan Building and
said: "How wonderful! I will build one much
taller." The crowning achievement of his life was
measured by the Woolworth Building. That building
stands as a temporary symbol of man's nature to
excel the handiwork of other men. A MONUMENT
TO THE VANITY OF MAN, WITH BUT LITTLE
ELSE TO JUSTIFY ITS EXISTENCE!

.   .   .   .

The little ragged newsboy on the street stands, with
wide-open mouth, and envies the business man as he

alights from his automobile at the curb and starts into his office. "How happy I would be," the newsboy says to himself, "if I owned a Lizzie." And, the business man seated at his desk inside, thinks how happy he would be if he could add another million dollars to his already overswollen bank roll.

The grass is always sweeter on the other side of the fence, says the jackass, as he stretches his neck in the attempt to get to it.

Turn a crowd of boys into an apple orchard and they will pass by the nice mellow apples on the ground. The red, juicy ones hanging dangerously high in the top of the tree look much more tempting, and up the tree they will go.

The married man takes a sheepish glance at the daintily dressed ladies on the street and thinks how fortunate he would be if his wife were as pretty as they. Perhaps she is much prettier, but he misses that beauty because—well, because "the grass is always greener on the other side of the fence." Most divorce cases grow out of man's tendency to climb the fence into the other fellow's pastures.

.   .   .   .

Happiness is always just around the bend; always in sight but just out of reach. Life is never complete, no matter what we have or how much of it we possess. One thing calls for something else to go with it.

Milady buys a pretty hat. She must have a gown to match it. That calls for new shoes and hose and gloves, and other accessories that run into a big bill far beyond her husband's means.

Man longs for a home—just a plain little house setting off in the edge of the woods. He builds it, but it is not complete; he must have shrubbery and flowers and landscaping to go with it. Still it is not complete; he must have a beautiful fence around it, with a graveled driveway.

That calls for a motor car and a garage in which to house it.

All these little touches have been added, but to no avail! The place is now too small. He must have a house with more rooms. The Ford Coupe must be replaced by a Cadillac sedan, so there will be room for company in the cross country tours.

On and on the story goes, ad infinitum!

    .   .   .   .

The young man receives a salary sufficient to keep him and his family fairly comfortable. Then comes a promotion and an advance in salary of a thousand dollars a year. Does he lay the extra thousand dollars away in the savings account and continue living as before? He does nothing of the sort. Immediately he must trade the old car in for a new one. A porch must be added to the house. The wife needs a new wardrobe. The table must be set with better food and more of it. (Pity his poor, groaning stomach.) At the end of the year is he better off with the increase? He is nothing of the sort! The more he gets the more he wants, and the rule applies to the man with millions the same as to the man with but a few thousands.

The young man selects the girl of his choice, believing he cannot live without her. After he gets her he is not sure that he can live with her. If a man remains a bachelor he wonders why he is so stupid as to deprive himself of the joys of married life. If

he marries he wonders how she happened to catch
him off guard long enough to "harpoon" him.

And the god of Destiny cries out "O fool, O fool!
You are damned if you DO and you are damned if
you DON'T."

At every crossroad of Life the imps of Discontent-
ment stand in the shadows of the back-ground, with
a grin of mockery on their faces, crying out "Take
the road of your own choice!   We will get you in
the end!"

.   .   .   .

At last man becomes disillusioned and begins to
learn that Happiness and Contentment are not of this
world.   Then begins the search for the pass-word that
will open the door to him in some world of which he
knows not.   Surely there must be Happiness on the
other side of the Great Divide.   In desperation his
tired, care-worn heart turns to religion for hope and
encouragement.

But, his troubles are not over; they are just starting!

"Come into our tent and accept our creed," says
one sect, "and you may go straight to heaven after
death."   Poor man hesitates, looks and listens.   Then
he hears the call of another brand of religion whose
leader says:

"Stay out of the other camp or you'll go straight
to hell!   They only sprinkle water on your head, but
we push you all the way under, thereby insuring you
safe passage into the Land of Promise."

In the midst of sectarian claims and counter-claims
poor man becomes undecided.   Not knowing whether
to turn this way or that, he wonders which brand of

religion offers the safest passage-way, until Hope vanishes.

> "Myself when young
>   did eagerly frequent
> Doctor and Saint and heard
>   great argument
> About it and about; but
>   evermore
> Came out by the same door
>   where in I went."

Always seeking but never finding—thus might be
described man's struggle for Happiness and Contentment.   He tries one religion after another, finally
joining the "Big Church" which the world has named
the "Damned."   His mind becomes an eternal question mark, searching hither and yon for an answer to
the questions—"Whence and Whither?"

> "The worldly hope men set
>   their Hearts upon
> Turns Ashes—or it prospers;
>   and anon,
> Like Snow upon the Desert's
>   Dusty Face
> Lighting a little Hour or two—
>   is gone."

Life is an everlasting question-mark!

That which we want most is always in the embryonic distance of the future.   Our power to acquire
is always a decade or so behind our power to DE-
SIRE!

And, if we catch up with the thing we want we no longer want it!

Fortunate is the young woman who learns this great truth and keeps her lover always guessing, always on the defensive lest he may lose her.

Our favorite author is a hero and a genius until we meet him in person and learn the sad truth that, after all, he is only a man. "How often must we learn this lesson? Men cease to interest us when we find their limitations. The only sin is limitation. As soon as you once come up with a man's limitations, it is all over with him."—EMERSON.

How beautiful the mountain yonder in the distance; but, the moment we draw near it we find it to be nothing but a wretched collection of rocks and dirt and trees.

Out of this truth grew the oft-repeated adage "Familiarity breeds contempt."

Beauty and Happiness and Contentment are states of mind. They can never be enjoyed except through vision of the afar. The most beautiful painting of Rembrandt becomes a mere smudge of daubed paint if we come too near it.

Destroy the Hope of unfinished dreams in man's heart and he is finished.

The moment a man ceases to cherish the vision of future achievement he is through. Nature has built man so that his greatest and only lasting Happiness is that which he feels in the pursuit of some yet unattained object. Anticipation is sweeter than realization. That which is at hand does not satisfy. The only enduring satisfaction is that which comes to the person who keeps alive in his heart the HOPE of

future achievement.   When that hope dies write
FINIS across the human heart.

·   ·   ·   ·   ·   ·   ·

Life's greatest inconsistency is the fact that most
of that which we believe is not true.   Russel Conwell
wrote the most popular lecture ever delivered in the
English language.   He called it "Acres of Diamonds."
The central idea of the lecture was the statement that
one need not seek opportunity in the distance; that
opportunity may be found in the vicinity of one's
birth.   Perhaps! but, how many believe it?

Opportunity may be found wherever one really
looks for it, and nowhere else!   To most men the
picking looks better on the other side of the fence.
How futile to urge one to try out one's luck in the
little home-town when it is man's nature to look for
opportunity in some other locality.

Do not worry because the grass looks sweeter on
the other side of the fence.   Nature intended it so.
Thus does she allure us and groom us for the life-long
task of GROWTH THROUGH STRUGGLE.

SOME MODERN "MIRACLES"

Some people doubt the authenticity of the Bible because they believe that if miracles could be performed over two thousand years ago, before the dawn of science, while the world was still steeped in illiteracy and superstition, it should be just as easy to perform them today.

I have read the Bible very carefully; some parts of it many times; and I am convinced that it contains no account of any alleged miracle which has not been more than matched during the past seventy years, in the open light of science. Moreover, these modern day "miracles" are subject to analysis and proof. Any child of average intelligence, above the age of twelve years, may understand the "miracles" of to-day, and for this reason I here concern myself about these modern "revelations" by faith.

THE GREATEST OF ALL MIRACLES IS FAITH

This is a wonderful age! It is an age of provable miracles.

These are the modern "miracles" which have impressed me most:

The miracle which Edison performed when, after thousands of temporary failures, he wrested from Nature the secret by which the sound of the human voice may be recorded on a wax record and reproduced perfectly. That miracle was wrought through Edison's FAITH! He had no precedent to guide him. No other person had ever performed such a "miracle" as far as civilization knows.

One of the strange things about this "miracle" is the fact that Edison began at the very outset to experiment with the rudimentary principle and the mechanical apparatus through which the secret of the talking machine was later revealed. The principle was vibration and the apparatus was a tube made of wax which revolved on a cylinder which contacted the point of a needle. Nothing but faith could have enabled Edison to have begun so near the source of the secret which he sought, and nothing but faith could have given him the persistence to stick to his experiments through more than ten thousand "failures."

It was faith which enabled Edison to concentrate his mind upon the task which led him through many thousand "failures" before he created the incandescent lamp with which he harnessed the energy known as electricity and made it serve to light the world.

It was faith which prompted Edison to continue his experiments with the moving picture machine until he made it actually perform the "miracle" which he must have seen through his own imagination before he even began.

It was faith which sustained the Wright brothers through the years of hazardous experiments before they conquered the air and created a machine that excels, in both speed and endurance, the swiftest bird of the air.

It was faith which drove Lee DeForest through years of seemingly fruitless struggle before he perfected the apparatus with which man now "tunes in" and sends the sound of the voice around the earth in the fraction of a second, through the agency of a form of energy which was unknown to man when the Books of the Bible were being written and the "miracles" recorded therein were being described.

It was faith which prompted Christopher Columbus to set sail on an unchartered sea, in search of a land which, as far as he was concerned, existed nowhere excepting in his own imagination. Considering the frailties of the little sailing vessels in which he embarked on that momentous voyage, his faith must have been of that variety which enables a man to see the object of his labor already attained even before he begins it.

It was faith which inspired Copernicus to "see" that portion of a universe which human eyes had never beheld, and at a time in the history of the world when such revelations as those which he wrought through his faith and his crude mechanical equipment might mean his destruction at the hands of his contemporaries who BELIEVED there were no stars excepting those within range of the human eyes.

It was faith which revealed to Joseph Smith fragmentary evidences of a civilization which preceded the American Indians on this continent at least a hundred years before positive evidence of such a civilization was unearthed on the North and South American Continents. Incidentally, the revelations wrought by his faith led to his assassination at the hands of a mob whose leaders resented this modern day revelation of "miracles" through faith, thus indicating how doggedly mankind has fought all who dared to turn the spotlight of understanding on the principle of faith.

It was faith which enabled "Golden Rule" Nash to transform a modern business failure into a shining example of success, through the simple procedure of dealing with his associates in business and the public they served on the Golden Rule basis which Christ recommended nearly two thousand years ago. Arthur Nash turned to the principle of faith after every other principle which had been tried by modern business had

failed him.   Following that principle the remainder of
his life he accumulated a vast fortune in money to say
nothing of leaving the world about him richer in spirit,
because of his example.

It was his faith in a cause which enabled the Ma-
hatma Gandhi, of India, to blend into a single mass
the minds of more than two hundred millions of his
countrymen, every individual of whom would do
Gandhi's bidding even though it meant immediate
death.   No other influence excepting faith could have
performed this "miracle."   Because he has a mind
which is capable of sustained faith, Gandhi wields this
power passively.   Gandhi has proved that faith can
accomplish that which trained soldiers and money and
implements of warfare cannot achieve.

It was faith which cut the shackles of limitation
from the mind of Professor Einstein and revealed to
him mathematical principles which the world had not
even suspected to exist.   No fear-bound mind could
have uncovered such a "miracle."

It was faith which sustained our own beloved Washington and drove him on to victory in opposition to
vastly superior physical forces; a form of faith which
was born of his love for freedom for mankind.

The profound principle known as faith is as available to YOU as it ever was to any human being who
has passed this way.

*If your world is one of limitation, misery and want
it is because you have not been quickened to the realization that you have in your own mind a laboratory
which is equipped to engender the power of faith.*

If we may judge the possibilities of the future by
the achievements of the past, the "miracles" remaining to be uncovered are vastly greater in number and

in nature than those which have been revealed in the past. It is not yet revealed what our destiny may be. This is an age of revelation!

Those who believe that the power of revelation passed away with the superstition and ignorance which prevailed a few hundred years ago have but little comprehension of our modern history.

Men like Watt, Whitney, Bell, Howe, Steinmetz, Morse, Edison, the Wright Brothers, Lee DeForest, Henry Ford, Simon Lake, Arthur Nash, Einstein and Gandhi are all miracle men. They have removed the horizons of men's minds and discovered unto us new worlds. Ours is a day of miracles; and this is an age of faith.

The world is passing through an experience which will call for many forms of readjustment of human relationships. The real leadership, during this period will be found among those who have great capacity for faith. There will be no place in the programme of the immediate future for the weaklings and those who still believe that "miracles" belong only in the age of the dead past, or, that they are wrapped up in unfathomable mystery. *THE MIRACLES OF THE FUTURE WILL BE REVEALED BY SCIENCE.* The research carried on in the fields of science, has already uncovered the approach to revelations incomparably greater than any of the past. The "changed world" brought about by the 1929 economic collapse has given to all who are ready, an abundance of OPPORTUNITY to make practical use of these newly discovered "miracles."

Lesson Four

THE HABIT OF SAVING

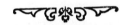

T HE only lasting favor which the parent may confer upon the child is that of helping the child to help itself.

"Man is a combination of flesh, bone, blood, hair and brain cells. These are the building materials out of which he shapes, through the Law of Habit, his own personality."

O advise one to save money without describing how to save would be somewhat like drawing the picture of a horse and writing under it, "This is a horse." It is obvious to all that the saving of money is one of the essentials for success, but the big question uppermost in the minds of the majority of those who do not save is:

"How can I do it?"

The saving of money is solely a matter of *habit*. For this reason this lesson begins with a brief analysis of the Law of Habit.

It is literally true that man, through the Law of Habit, shapes his own personality. Through repetition, any act indulged in a few times becomes a habit, and the mind appears to be nothing more than a mass of motivating forces growing out of our daily habits.

When once fixed in the mind a habit voluntarily impels one to action. For example, follow a given route to your daily work, or to some other place that you frequently visit, and very soon the habit has been formed and your mind will lead you over that route without thought on your part. Moreover, if you start out with the intention of traveling in another direction, without keeping the thought of the change in routes constantly in mind, you will find yourself following the old route.

Public speakers have found that the telling over and over again of a story, which may be based upon pure fiction, brings into play the Law of Habit, and very soon they forget whether the story is true or not.

WALLS OF LIMITATION BUILT THROUGH HABIT

Millions of people go through life in poverty and want because they have made destructive use of the Law of Habit. Not understanding either the Law of Habit or the Law of Attraction through which "like attracts like," those who remain in poverty seldom realize that they are where they are as the result of their own acts.

Fix in your mind the thought that your ability is limited to a given earning capacity and you will never earn more than that, because the law of habit will set up a definite limitation of the amount you can earn.

your subconscious mind will accept this limitation, and very soon you will feel yourself "slipping" until finally you will become so hedged in by FEAR OF POVERTY (one of the six basic fears) that opportunity will no longer knock at your door; your doom will be sealed; your fate fixed.

Formation of the Habit of Saving does not mean that you shall limit your earning capacity; it means just the opposite—that you shall apply this law so that it not only conserves that which you earn, in a systematic manner, but it also places you in the way of greater opportunity and gives you the vision, the self-confidence, the imagination, the enthusiasm, the initiative and leadership actually to increase your earning capacity.

Stating this great law in another way, when you thoroughly understand the Law of Habit you may insure yourself success in the great game of money-making by "playing both ends of that game against the middle."

You proceed in this manner:

First, through the law of Definite Chief Aim you set up, in your mind, an accurate, definite description of that which you want, including the amount of money you intend to earn. Your subconscious mind takes over this picture which you have created and uses it as a blueprint, chart or map by which to mold your thoughts and actions into practical plans for attaining the object of your Chief Aim, or purpose. Through the Law of Habit you keep the object of your Definite Chief Aim fixed in your mind (in the manner described in Lesson Two until it becomes firmly and permanently implanted there. This practice will destroy the poverty consciousness and set up, in its place, a prosperity consciousness. You will actually begin to DEMAND prosperity, you will begin to expect it, you will begin to prepare yourself to receive it and to use it wisely, thus paving the way or setting the stage for the development of the Habit of Saving.

Second, having in this manner increased your earning power you will make further use of the Law of Habit by provision, in your written statement of your Definite Chief Aim, for saving a definite proportion of all the money you earn.

Therefore, as your earnings increase, your savings will, likewise, increase in proportion.

By ever urging yourself on and demanding of yourself increased earning power, on the one hand, and by systematically laying aside a definite amount of all your earnings, on the other hand, you will soon reach the point at which you have removed all imaginary limitations from your own mind and you will then be well started on the road toward financial independence.

Nothing could be more practical or more easily accomplished than this!

Reverse the operation of the Law of Habit, by setting up in your mind the Fear of Poverty, and very soon this fear will reduce your earning capacity until you will be barely able to earn sufficient money to take care of your actual necessities.

The publishers of newspapers could create a panic in a week's time by filling their columns with news items concerning the actual business failures of the country, despite the fact that but few businesses, compared to the total number in existence, actually fail.

The so-called "crime waves" are very largely the products of sensational journalism. A single murder case, when exploited by the newspapers of the country, through scare headlines, is sufficient to start a regular "wave" of similar crimes in various localities. Following the repetition in the daily papers of the Hickman murder story, similar cases began to be reported from other parts of the country.

We are the victims of our habits, no matter who we are or what may be our life-calling. Any idea that is deliberately fixed in the mind, or any idea that is permitted to set itself up in the mind, as the result of suggestion, environment, the influence of associates, etc., is sure to cause us to indulge in acts which conform to the nature of the idea.

Form the habit of thinking and talking of prosperity and abundance, and very soon material evidence of these will begin to manifest itself in the nature of wider opportunity and new and unexpected opportunity.

Like attracts like! If you are in business and have formed the habit of talking and thinking about "business being bad" business will be bad. One pessimist, providing he is permitted to continue his destructive influence long enough, can destroy the work of half a dozen competent men, and he will do it by setting adrift in the minds of his associates the thought of poverty and failure.

Don't be this type of man or woman.

One of the most successful bankers in the state of Illinois has this sign hanging in his private office:

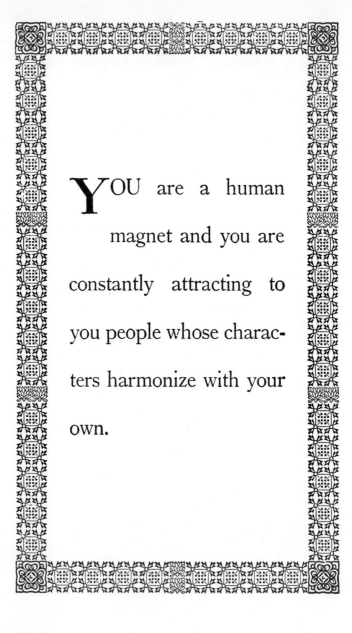

YOU are a human magnet and you are constantly attracting to you people whose characters harmonize with your own.

"WE TALK AND THINK ONLY OF ABUN-
DANCE HERE. IF YOU HAVE A TALE OF WOE
PLEASE KEEP IT, AS WE DO NOT WANT IT."

No business firm wants the services of a pessimist,
and those who understand the Law of Attraction and
the Law of Habit will no more tolerate the pessimist
than they would permit a burglar to roam around their
place of business, for the reason that one such person
will destroy the usefulness of those around him.

In tens of thousands of homes the general topic of
conversation is poverty and want, and that is just
what they are getting. They think of poverty, they
talk of poverty, they accept poverty as their lot in
life. They reason that because their ancestors were
poor before them they, also, must remain poor.

The poverty consciousness is formed as the result
of the habit of thinking of and fearing poverty.
"Lo! the thing I had feared has come upon me."

THE SLAVERY OF DEBT

Debt is a merciless master, a fatal enemy of the
savings habit.

Poverty, alone, is sufficient to kill off ambition,
destroy self-confidence and destroy hope, but add to it
the burden of debt and all who are victims of these
two cruel task-masters are practically doomed to
failure.

No man can do his best work, no man can express
himself in terms that command respect, no man can
either create or carry out a definite purpose in life,
with heavy debt hanging over his head. The man
who is bound in the slavery of debt is just as helpless

as the slave who is bound by ignorance, or by actual chains.

The author has a very close friend whose income is $1,000 a month. His wife loves "society" and tries to make a $20,000 showing on a $12,000 income, with the result that this poor fellow is usually about $8,000 in debt. Every member of his family has the "spending habit," having acquired this from the mother. The children, two girls and one boy, are now of the age when they are thinking of going to college, but this is impossible because of the father's debts. The result is dissension between the father and his children which makes the entire family unhappy and miserable.

It is a terrible thing even to think of going through life like a prisoner in chains, bound down and owned by somebody else on account of debts. The accumulation of debts is a habit. It starts in a small way and grows to enormous proportions slowly, step by step, until finally it takes charge of one's very soul.

Thousands of young men start their married lives with unnecessary debts hanging over their heads and never manage to get out from under the load. After the novelty of marriage begins to wear off (as it usually does) the married couple begin to feel the embarrassment of want, and this feeling grows until it leads, oftentimes, to open dissatisfaction with one another, and eventually to the divorce court.

A man who is bound by the slavery of debt has no time or inclination to set up or work out ideals, with the result that he drifts downward with time until he eventually begins to set up limitations in his own mind, and by these he hedges himself behind prison walls of FEAR and doubt from which he never escapes.

No sacrifice is too great to avoid the misery of debt!

"Think of what you owe yourself and those who are dependent upon you and resolve to be no man's debtor," is the advice of one very successful man whose early chances were destroyed by debt. This man came to himself soon enough to throw off the habit of buying that which he did not need and eventually worked his way out of slavery.

Most men who develop the habit of debt will not be so fortunate as to come to their senses in time to save themselves, because debt is something like quicksand in that it has a tendency to draw its victim deeper and deeper into the mire.

The Fear of Poverty is one of the most destructive of the six basic fears described in Lesson Three. The man who becomes hopelessly in debt is seized with this poverty fear, his ambition and self-confidence become paralyzed, and he sinks gradually into oblivion.

There are two classes of debts, and these are so different in nature that they deserve to be here described, as follows:

1. There are debts incurred for luxuries which become a dead loss.

2. There are debts incurred in the course of professional or business trading which represent service or merchandise that can be converted back into assets.

The first class of debts is the one to be avoided. The second class may be indulged in, providing the one incurring the debts uses judgment and does not go beyond the bounds of reasonable limitation. The moment one buys beyond his limitations he enters the realm of speculation, and speculation swallows more of its victims than it enriches.

Practically all people who live beyond their means are tempted to speculate with the hope that they may recoup, at a single turn of the wheel of fortune, so to speak, their entire indebtedness. The wheel generally stops at the wrong place and, far from finding themselves out of debt, such people as indulge in speculation are bound more closely as slaves of debt.

The Fear of Poverty breaks down the will-power of its victims, and they then find themselves unable to restore their lost fortunes, and, what is still more sad, they lose all ambition to extricate themselves from the slavery of debt.

Hardly a day passes that one may not see an account in the newspapers of at least one suicide as the result of worry over debts. The slavery of debt causes more suicides every year than all other causes combined, which is a slight indication of the cruelty of the poverty fear.

During the war millions of men faced the front-line trenches without flinching, knowing that death might overtake them any moment. Those same men, when facing the Fear of Poverty, often cringe and out of sheer desperation, which paralyzes their reason, sometimes commit suicide.

The person who is free from debt may whip poverty and achieve outstanding financial success, but, if he is bound by debt, such achievement is but a remote possibility, and never a probability.

Fear of Poverty is a negative, destructive state of

mind. Moreover, one negative state of mind has a tendency to attract other similar states of mind. For example, the Fear of Poverty may attract the fear of Ill Health, and these two may attract the Fear of Old Age, so that the victim finds himself poverty-stricken, in ill health and actually growing old long before the time when he should begin to show the signs of old age.

Millions of untimely, nameless graves have been filled by this cruel state of mind known as the Fear of Poverty!

Less than a dozen years ago a young man held a responsible position with the City National Bank, of New York City. Through living beyond his income he contracted a large amount of debts which caused him to worry until this destructive habit began to show up in his work and he was dismissed from the bank's service.

He secured another position, at less money, but his creditors embarrassed him so that he decided to resign and go away into another city, where he hoped to escape them until he had accumulated enough money to pay off his indebtedness. Creditors have a way of tracing debtors, so very soon they were close on the heels of this young man, whose employer found out about his indebtedness and dismissed him from his position.

He then searched in vain for employment for two months. One cold night he went to the top of one of the tall buildings on Broadway and jumped off Debt had claimed another victim.

WHO told you it couldn't be done? and, what great achievement has he to his credit that entitles him to use the w o r d "impossible" so freely?

HOW TO MASTER THE FEAR OF POVERTY

To whip the Fear of Poverty one must take two very definite steps, providing one is in debt. First, quit the habit of buying on credit, and follow this by gradually paying off the debts that you have already incurred.

Being free from the worry of indebtedness you are ready to revamp the habits of your mind and re-direct your course toward prosperity. Adopt, as a part of your Definite Chief Aim, the habit of saving a regular proportion of your income, even if this be no more than a penny a day. Very soon this habit will begin to lay hold of your mind and you will actually get joy out of saving.

Any habit may be discontinued by building in its place some other and more desirable habit. The "spending" habit must be replaced by the "saving" habit by all who attain financial independence.

Merely to discontinue an undesirable habit is not enough, as such habits have a tendency to reappear unless the place they formerly occupied in the mind is filled by some other habit of a different nature.

The discontinuance of a habit leaves a "hole" in the mind, and this hole must be filled up with some other form of habit or the old one will return and claim its place.

Throughout this course many psychological formulas, which the student has been requested to memorize and practice, have been described. You will find such a formula in Lesson Three, the object of which is to develop Self-confidence.

These formulas may be assimilated so they become a part of your mental machinery, through the Law of Habit, if you will follow the instructions for their use which accompany each of them.

It is assumed that you are striving to attain financial independence. The accumulation of money is not difficult after you have once mastered the Fear of Poverty and developed in its place the Habit of Saving.

The author of this course would be greatly disappointed to know that any student of the course got the impression from anything in this or any of the other lessons that Success is measured by dollars alone.

However, money does represent an important factor in success, and it must be given its proper value in any philosophy intended to help people in becoming useful, happy and prosperous.

The cold, cruel, relentless truth is that in this age of materialism a man is no more than so many grains of sand, which may be blown helter-skelter by every stray wind of circumstance, unless he is entrenched behind the power of money!

Genius may offer many rewards to those who possess it, but the fact still remains that genius without money with which to give it expression is but an empty, skeleton-like honor.

The man without money is at the mercy of the man who has it!

And this goes, regardless of the amount of ability he may possess, the training he has had or the native genius with which he was gifted by nature.

There is no escape from the fact that people will weigh you very largely in the light of bank balances, no matter who you are or what you can do. The first question that arises, in the minds of most people, when they meet a stranger, is, "How much money has he?" If he has money he is welcomed into homes and business opportunities are thrown his way. All sorts of attention are lavished upon him. He is a prince, and as such is entitled to the best of the land.

But if his shoes are run down at the heels, his clothes are not pressed, his collar is dirty, and he shows plainly the signs of impoverished finances, woe be his lot, for the passing crowd will step on his toes and blow the smoke of disrespect in his face.

These are not pretty statements, but they have one virtue—THEY ARE TRUE!

This tendency to judge people by the money they have, or their power to control money, is not confined to any one class of people. We all have a touch of it, whether we recognize the fact or not.

Thomas A. Edison is one of the best known and most respected inventors in the world, yet it is no misstatement of facts to say that he would have remained a practically unknown, obscure personage had he not followed the habit of conserving his resources and shown his ability to save money.

Henry Ford never would have got to first base with his "horseless carriage" had he not developed, quite early in life, the habit of saving. Moreover, had Mr. Ford not conserved his resources and hedged himself behind their power he would have been "swallowed up" by his competitors or those who covetously desired to take his business away from him, long, long years ago.

Many a man has gone a very long way toward success, only to stumble and fall, never again to rise, because of lack of money in times of emergency. The mortality rate in business each year, due to lack of reserve capital for emergencies, is stupendous. To this one cause are due more of the business failures than to all other causes combined!

Reserve Funds are essential in the successful operation of business!

Likewise, Savings Accounts are essential to success on the part of individuals. Without a savings fund the individual suffers in two ways: first, by inability to seize opportunities that come only to the person with some ready cash, and, second, by embarrassment due to some unexpected emergency calling for cash.

It might be said, also, that the individual suffers in still a third respect by not developing the Habit of Saving, through lack of certain other qualities essential for success which grow out of the practice of the Habit of Saving.

The nickels, dimes and pennies which the average person allows to slip through his fingers would, if systematically saved and properly put to work, eventually bring financial independence.

Through the courtesy of a prominent Building and Loan Association the following table has been compiled, showing what a monthly saving of $5.00, $10.00, $25.00 or $50.00 will amount to at the end of ten years. These figures are startling when one comes to consider the fact that the average person spends from $5.00 to $50.00 a month for useless merchandise or so-called "entertainment."

The making and saving of money is a science, yet

The Amazing Way Your Money Grows

SAVE $5 A MONTH (Only 17 cents a day)

	Amount Saved	Profit	Savings Plus Profits	Withdrawal Value
1st yr.	$ 60.00	$ 4.30	$ 64.30	$ $61.30
2nd yr.	$ 120.00	$ 16.55	$ 136.00	$ 125.00
3rd yr.	$ 180.00	$ 36.30	$ 216.30	$ 191.55
4th yr.	$ 240.00	$ 64.00	$ 304.00	$ 260.20
5th yr.	$ 300.00	$ 101.00	$ 401.00	$ 338.13
6th yr.	$ 360.00	$ 140.00*	$ 500.00*	$ 414.75*
7th yr.	$ 420.00	$ 197.10	$ 617.10	$ 495.43
8th yr.	$ 480.00	$ 257.05	$ 737.05	$ 578.32
9th yr.	$ 540.00	$ 324.95	$ 864.95	$ 687.15
10th yr.	$ 600.00	$ 400.00	$ 1000.00	$ 1000.00

SAVE $10 A MONTH (Only 33 cents a day)

	Amount Saved	Profit	Savings Plus Profits	Withdrawal Value
1st yr.	$ 120.00	$ 8.60	$ 128.60	$ 122.60
2nd yr.	$ 240.00	$ 33.11	$ 273.11	$ 250.00
3rd yr.	$ 360.00	$ 72.60	$ 432.60	$ 383.10
4th yr.	$ 480.00	$ 128.00	$ 608.00	$ 520.40
5th yr.	$ 600.00	$ 202.00	$ 802.00	$ 676.25
6th yr.	$ 720.00	$ 280.00	$ 1000.00*	$ 829.50*
7th yr.	$ 840.00	$ 394.20	$ 1234.20	$ 990.85
8th yr.	$ 960.00	$ 514.10	$ 1474.10	$ 1156.64
9th yr.	$1080.00	$ 649.90	$ 1729.90	$ 1374.30
10th yr.	$1200.00	$ 800.00	$ 2000.00	$ 2000.00

SAVE $25 A MONTH (Only 83 cents a day)

	Amount Saved	Profit	Savings Plus Profits	Withdrawal Value
1st yr.	$ 300.00	$ 21.50	$ 321.50	$ 306.50
2nd yr.	$ 600.00	$ 82.75	$ 682.75	$ 625.00
3rd yr.	$ 900.00	$ 181.50	$ 1081.50	$ 957.75
4th yr.	$1200.00	$ 320.00	$ 1520.00	$ 1301.00
5th yr.	$1500.00	$ 505.00	$ 2005.00	$ 1690.63
6th yr.	$1800.00	$ 700.00	$ 2500.00*	$ 2073.75*
7th yr.	$2100.00	$ 985.50	$ 3085.50	$ 2477.13
8th yr.	$2400.00	$1285.25	$ 3685.25	$ 2891.60
9th yr.	$2700.00	$1624.75	$ 4324.75	$ 3435.75
10th yr.	$3000.00	$2000.00	$ 5000.00	$ 5000.00

SAVE $50 A MONTH (Only $1.66 a day)

	Amount Saved	Profit	Savings Plus Profits	Withdrawal Value
1st yr.	$ 600.00	$ 43.00	$ 643.00	$ 613.00
2nd yr.	$1200.00	$ 165.50	$ 1365.50	$ 1250.00
3rd yr.	$1800.00	$ 363.00	$ 2163.00	$ 1915.50
4th yr.	$2400.00	$ 640.00	$ 3040.00	$ 2602.00
5th yr.	$3000.00	$1010.00	$ 4010.00	$ 3381.25
6th yr.	$3600.00	$1400.00	$ 5000.00*	$ 4147.50*
7th yr.	$4200.00	$1971.00	$ 6171.00	$ 4954.25
8th yr.	$4800.00	$2570.50	$ 7370.50	$ 5783.20
9th yr.	$5400.00	$3249.50	$ 8649.50	$ 6871.50
10th yr.	$6000.00	$4000.00	$10,000.00	$10,000.00

EVERY failure, every adversity, e v e r y heartache may be a blessing in disguise providing it softens the animal portion of our nature.

the rules by which money is accumulated are so simple that anyone may follow them.   The main prerequisite is a willingness to subordinate the present to the future, by eliminating unnecessary expenditures for luxuries.

A young man, who was earning only $20.00 a week as chauffeur for a prominent New York banker, was induced by his employer to keep an accurate account of every cent he spent for one week.   The following is an itemized list of his expenses:

Cigarettes ....$	.75
Chewing gum	.30
Soda fountain	1.80
Cigars for associates	.1.50
Moving picture show	1.00
Shaves, including tips, ...	1.60
Newspaper, daily and Sunday ..	.22
Shoe shines	.30
	$ 7.47
Board and room	$12.00
Money on hand	.53
	$20.00

These figures tell a tragic story which might as well apply to thousands of other people as to the young man who kept this account.   His actual savings out of $20.00 were only 53 cents.   He spent $7.47 for items, every one of which could have been greatly reduced, and most of which could have been eliminated entirely.   In fact, by shaving himself and shining his own shoes, he could have saved every cent of the $7.47.

Now turn to the table made up by the Building and Loan Association and observe what the saving of $7.47 a week would amount to. Suppose the amount this young man actually saved had been only $25.00 a month; the saving would have increased to the snug sum of $5,000.00 by the end of the first ten years.

The young man in question was twenty-one years old at the time he kept this expense account. By the time he reached the age of thirty-one years he could have had a substantial amount in the bank, had he saved $25.00 a month, and this saving would have brought him many opportunities that would have led directly to financial independence.

Some who are short-sighted, pseudo-philosophers, are fond of pointing to the fact that no one can become rich merely by saving a few dollars a week. This may be true enough, as far as the reasoning goes (which is not very far) but the other side of the story is that the saving of even a small sum of money places one in position where, oftentimes, this small sum may enable one to take advantage of business opportunities which lead directly and quite rapidly to financial independence.

The foregoing table, showing what a saving of $5.00 a month will amount to at the end of ten years, should be copied and pasted on your mirror, where it will stare you in the face every morning when you get up and every night as you retire, providing you have not already acquired the habit of systematic saving of money. This table should be reproduced, in letters and figures an inch tall, and placed on the walls of every public school throughout the land, where it might serve as a constant reminder to all school children of the value of the savings habit.

Some years ago, before giving serious thought to the value of the savings habit, this author made up an account of the money which had slipped through his fingers. The amount was so alarming that it resulted in the writing of this lesson, and adding the Habit of Saving as one of the Fifteen Laws of Success.

Following is an itemized statement of this account:

$ 4,000.00 inherited, invested in automobile supply business with a friend who lost the entire amount in one year.

3,600.00 extra money earned from sundry writing for magazines and newspapers, all spent uselessly.

30,000.00 earned from training 3,000 salesmen, with the aid of the Law of Success philosophy, invested in a magazine which was not a success because there was no reserve capital back of it.

3,400.00 extra money earned from public addresses, lectures, etc., all of which was spent as it came in.

6,000.00 estimated amount that could have been saved during a period of ten years, out of regular earnings, at the rate of only $50 a month.

$47,000.00

This amount, had it been saved and invested as received, in Building and Loan Associations, or in some other manner that would have earned compound interest, would have grown into the sum of $94,000.00 at the time this lesson is being written.

The author is not a victim of any of the usual habits of dissipation, such as gambling, drinking and excessive entertaining. It is almost unbelievable that a man whose habits of living are reasonably moderate could spend $47,000.00 within a little over ten years without having anything to show for the money, but it can be done!

A capital reserve of $94,000.00, working at compound interest, is sufficient to give any man all the financial freedom he needs.

I recall one occasion when the president of a large corporation sent me a check for $500.00 for an address I delivered at a banquet given to the employees, and I distinctly recall what went through my mind when I opened the letter and saw the check. I had wanted a new automobile and this check was exactly the amount required for the first payment. I had it spent before it had been in my hands thirty seconds.

Perhaps this is the experience of the majority of people. They think more of how they are going to SPEND what they have than they do about ways and means of SAVING. The idea of saving, and the self-control and self-sacrifice which must accompany it, is always accompanied by thoughts of an unpleasant nature, but oh, how it does thrill one to think of SPENDING.

There is a reason for this, and that reason is the fact that most of us have developed the habit of spending while neglecting the Habit of Saving, and any idea that frequents the human mind but seldom is not as welcome as that which frequents it often.

In truth, the Habit of Saving can be made as fascinating as the habit of spending, but not until it has become a regular, well grounded, systematic habit. We like to do that which is often repeated, which is but another way of stating what the scientists have discovered, that we are victims of our habits.

The habit of saving money requires more force of character than most people have developed, for the reason that saving means self-denial and sacrifice of amusements and pleasures in scores of different ways.

For this very reason one who develops the savings habit acquires, at the same time, many of the other needed habits which lead to success: especially Self-control, Self-confidence, Courage, Poise and Freedom from Fear.

HOW MUCH SHOULD ONE SAVE?

The first question that will arise is, "How Much Should One Save?" The answer cannot be given in a few words, for the amount one should save depends upon many conditions, some of which may be within one's control and some of which may not be.

Generally speaking, a man who works for a salary should apportion his income about as follows:

Savings Account 20%
Living—Clothes, Food and Shelter ... 50%
Education 10%
Recreation 10%
Life Insurance 10%
                                  ————
                                  100%

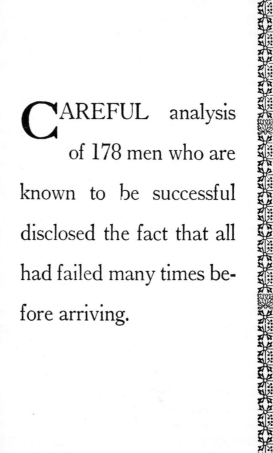

CAREFUL analysis of 178 men who are known to be successful disclosed the fact that all had failed many times before arriving.

The following, however, indicates the approximate distribution which the average man actually makes of his income:

Savings Account ....*NOTHING*
Living—Clothes, Food and Shelter ...60%
Education 0%
Recreation 35%
Life Insurance 5%
                                   ____
                                   100%

Under the item of "recreation" is included, of course, many expenditures that do not really "re-create," such as money spent for alcoholic drinks, dinner parties and other similar items which may actually serve to undermine one's health and destroy character.

An experienced analyst of men has stated that he could tell very accurately, by examining a man's monthly budget, what sort of a life the man is living; moreover, that he will get most of his information from the one item of "recreation." This, then, is an item to be watched as carefully as the greenhouse keeper watches the thermometer which controls the life and death of his plants.

Those who keep budget accounts often include an item called "entertainment," which, in a majority of cases, turns out to be an evil because it depletes the income heavily and when carried to excess depletes, also, the health.

We are living, right now, in an age when the item of "entertainment" is altogether too high in most budget allowances. Tens of thousands of people who earn not more than $50.00 a week are spending as much as one third of their incomes for what they call "entertainment," which comes in a bottle, with a questionable label on it, at anywhere from $6.00 to $12.00 a quart. Not only are these unwise people wasting the money that should go into a savings fund, but, of far greater danger, they are destroying both character and health.

Nothing in this lesson is intended as a preachment on morality, or on any other subject. We are here dealing with cold facts which, to a large extent, constitute the building materials out of which SUCCESS may be created.

However, this is an appropriate place to state some FACTS which have such a direct bearing on the subject of achieving success that they cannot be omitted without weakening this entire course in general and this lesson in particular.

The author of this course is NOT a reformer! Neither is he a preacher on morals, as this field of useful endeavor is quite well covered by others who are able workers. What is here stated, therefore, is intended as a necessary part of a course of philosophy whose purpose is to mark a safe road over which one may travel to honorable achievement.

During the year 1926 the author was in partnership with the late Don R. Mellett, who was, at that time, the publisher of the Canton (Ohio) Daily News. Mr. Mellett became interested in the Law of Success philosophy because it offered, as he believed, sound counsel to young men and young women who really wish to get ahead in life. Through the pages of the Daily News Mr. Mellett was conducting a fierce battle against the underworld forces of Canton. With the aid of detectives and investigators, some of whom were supplied by the Governor of Ohio, Mr. Mellett and the author gathered accurate data concerning the way most of the people in Canton were living.

In July, 1926, Mr. Mellett was assassinated from ambush, and four men, one of them a former member of the Canton police force, are now serving life sentences in the Ohio State Penitentiary for the crime.

During the investigation into crime conditions in Canton all reports came to the author's office, and the data here described are, therefore, known to be absolutely accurate.

One of the officials of a large industrial plant whose salary was $6,000.00 a year paid a Canton bootlegger an average of $300.00 a month for the liquor (if "stuff" can be called liquor) which he used for "entertaining." His wife participated in these "entertainments" which took place in his own home.

A paying teller in a bank, whose salary was $150.00 a month, was spending an average of $75.00 a month for liquor, and in addition to this unpardonable waste of money, out of a salary which was none too great at most, he was traveling at a pace and with a crowd which meant ruin for him later on.

The superintendent of a large manufacturing plant, whose salary was $5,000.00 a year, and who should have been saving at least $125.00 a month, was actually saving nothing. His bootlegger's bill averaged $150.00 a month.

A policeman whose income was $160.00 a month was spending over $400.00 a month on dinner parties at a near-by roadhouse. Where he got the difference between his legitimate income and his actual expenditures is a question that reflects no particular credit on the policeman.

A bank official whose income, as near as it could be estimated from his previous years' income tax reports, was about $8,000.00 a year, had a monthly bootlegger's bill of more than $500.00 during the three months that his activities were checked by the Mellett investigators.

A young man who worked in a department store, at a salary of $20.00 a week, was spending an average of $35.00 a week with one bootlegger. The assumption was that he was stealing the difference from his employer. Old Man Trouble awaited this young man, just around the corner, although it is not known by the author whether or not the two have come together as yet.

A salesman for a life insurance company, whose income was not known because he worked on a commission basis, was spending an average of $200.00 a month with one bootlegger. No record of any savings account was found, and the assumption is that he had none. This assumption was later confirmed when the company for which the young man worked had him arrested for embezzlement of its funds. No doubt he was spending the money which he should have turned in to the company. He is now serving a long sentence in the Ohio State Penitentiary.

A young lad who was attending high school was spending large sums for liquor. The actual amount was not obtainable for the reason that he paid cash as he got the liquor, and the bootlegger's records did not, therefore, disclose the actual amount. Later this boy's parents had him locked up "to save him from himself." It was found that he was stealing money from a savings fund kept by his mother, somewhere about the house. He had stolen and spent more than $300.00 of this money when discovered.

This author conducted a Lecture Bureau in forty-one high schools, where he lectured once a month during the entire school season. The principals of these high schools stated that less than two per cent of the students showed any tendency toward saving money, and an examination through the aid of a questionnaire prepared for that purpose disclosed the fact that only five per cent of the students, out of a total of 11,000, of the high-school age, believed that the savings habit was one of the essentials for success.

It is no wonder the rich are becoming richer and the poor are becoming poorer!

Call this a socialistic statement, if you please, but the facts bear out its accuracy. It is not difficult for any man to become rich, in a country of spendthrifts such as this, where millions of people spend every cent that comes into their possession.

Many years ago, before the present wave of mania for spending spread over the country, F. W. Woolworth devised a very simple method of catching the nickels and dimes that millions of people throw away for trash, and his system netted him over ONE HUNDRED MILLION DOLLLARS in a few years' time. Woolworth has died, but his system of saving nickels and dimes continues, and his estate is growing bigger and bigger.

Five and Ten Cent Stores are usually painted with a bright red front. That is an appropriate color, for red denotes danger. Every Five and Ten Cent Store

ALL salesmen will do well to remember that no one wants anything that someone else is trying to "get rid of."

is a striking monument that proves, to a nicety, that one of the cardinal faults of this generation is the SPENDING HABIT.

We are all victims of HABIT!

Unfortunately for most of us, we are reared by parents who have no conception whatsoever of the psychology of habit, and, without being aware of their fault, most parents aid and abet their offspring in the development of the spending habit by overindulgence with spending money, and by lack of training in the Habit of Saving.

The habits of early childhood cling to us all through life.

Fortunate, indeed, is the child whose parents have the foresight and the understanding of the value, as a character builder, of the Habit of Saving, to inculcate this habit in the minds of their children.

It is a training that yields rich rewards.

Give the average man $100.00 that he did not contemplate receiving, and what will he do with it? Why, he will begin to cogitate in his own mind on how he can SPEND the money. Dozens of things that he needs, or THINKS he needs, will flash into his mind, but it is a rather safe bet that it will never occur to him (unless he has acquired the savings habit) to make this $100.00 the beginning of a savings account. Before night comes he will have the $100.00 spent, or at least he will have decided in his mind how he is going to SPEND IT, thus adding more fuel to the already too bright flame of Habit of Spending.

We are ruled by our habits!

It requires force of character, determination and power of firm DECISION to open a savings account and then add to it a regular, if small, portion of all subsequent income.

There is one rule by which any man may determine, well in advance, whether or not he will ever enjoy the financial freedom and independence which is so universally desired by all men, and this rule has absolutely nothing to do with the amount of one's income.

The rule is that if a man follows the systematic habit of saving a definite proportion of all money he earns or receives in other ways, he is practically sure to place himself in a position of financial independence. If he saves nothing, he IS ABSOLUTELY SURE NEVER TO BE FINANCIALLY INDEPENDENT, no matter how much his income may be.

The one and only exception to this rule is that a man who does not save might possibly inherit such a large sum of money that he could not spend it, or he might inherit it under a trust which would protect it for him, but these eventualities are rather remote; so much so, in fact, that YOU cannot rely upon such a miracle happening to you.

This author enjoys a rather close acquaintance with many hundreds of people throughout the United States and in some foreign countries. For nearly twenty-five years he has been watching many of these acquaintances, and knows, therefore, from actual experience, how they live, why some of them have failed while others have succeeded, and the REASONS FOR BOTH FAILURE AND SUCCESS.

This list of acquaintances covers men who control hundreds of millions of dollars, and actually own many millions which they have acquired. Also men who have had millions of dollars, all of which passed through their fingers and they are now penniless.

For the purpose of showing the student of this philosophy just how the law of habit becomes a sort of pivotal point on which success or failure turns, and exactly why no man can become financially independent without developing the habit of SYSTEMATIC SAVING, the living habits of some of these many acquaintances will be described.

We will begin with a complete history, in his own words, of a man who has made a million dollars in the field of advertising, but who now has nothing to show for his efforts. This story first appeared in the American Magazine, and it is here reprinted through the courtesy of the publishers of that publication.

The story is true, in every respect, and it has been included as a part of this lesson because the author of the story, Mr. W. C. Freeman, is willing to have his mistakes made public with the hope that others may avoid them.

"I HAVE MADE A MILLION DOLLLARS BUT I HAVEN'T GOT A CENT"

While it is embarrassing, yes, humiliating, publicly to confess to an outstanding fault that has made a good deal of a mess of my life today, nevertheless I have decided to make this confession for the good it may do.

I am going to make a clean breast of how I let slip through my fingers all the money I have earned thus far in my life-time, which approximates one million dollars. This amount I made through my work in the field of advertising, except a few thousand dollars I earned up to twenty-five years of age by teaching in country schools and by writing news letters to some country weeklies and daily newspapers.

Maybe one lone million does not seem a lot of money in these days of many millions and even billions; but it is a big sum of money, just the same. If there are any who think to the contrary, let them count a million. I tried to figure out the other night how long it would take to do so. I found I could count an average of one hundred a minute. On this basis it would take me twenty days of eight hours each, plus six hours and forty minutes on the twenty-first day to do the stunt. I doubt very much if you or I were given an assignment to count one million one-dollar bills, upon the promise that all of them would be ours at the end of that time, that we could complete it. It would probably drive us mad—and a lot of use the money would be to us then, wouldn't it?

Let me say at the outset of my story that I do not regret, not for one minute, that I spent ninety per cent of the money I made. To wish any of this ninety per cent back at this time would make me feel that I would have denied much happiness to my family and to many others.

My only regret is that I spent *all* of my money, and more besides. If I had today the ten per cent I could have saved easily, I would have one hundred thousand dollars safely invested, and no debts. If I had this money I would feel really and truly that I was rich; and I mean just this, for I have never had a desire to accumulate money for money's sake.

Those school-teaching and newspaper-correspondence days of mine brought some cares and responsibilities, but they were met optimistically.

I married at the age of twenty-one, with the full approval of parents on both sides, who believed thoroughly in the doctrine preached by Henry Ward Beecher, that "early marriages are virtuous marriages."

Just one month and one day after I was married my father met a tragic death. He was suffocated by coal gas. Having been an educator all his life—and one of the best—he had not accumulated any money.

When he passed out of our family circle it was up to all of us to pull together and get along somehow, which we did.

Apart from the void left in our home by my father's death (my wife and I and my mother and only sister lived together), we had a joyful life, despite the fact that it was a tight squeeze to make ends meet.

My mother, who was exceptionally talented and resourceful (she had taught school with my father until I was born), decided to open our home to a married couple, old friends of the family. They came to live with us and their board helped to pay expenses. My mother was known far and wide for the wonderful meals she served. Later on, two well-to-do women friends of the family were taken into our home, thus increasing our revenue.

My sister helped very substantially by teaching a kindergarten class, which met in the big living-room of our home; my wife contributed her share to the household by taking charge of the sewing and mending.

Those were very happy days. Nobody in the house-

THINK well before you speak because your words may plant the seed of either success or failure in the mind of some other person.

hold was extravagant or had any extravagant tendencies except perhaps myself, for I was always
inclined to be free with money. I liked to make gifts
to the family and to entertain friends.

When the first baby came into our home—a boy—
we all thought heaven had opened its doors to us.
My wife's parents, who took the keenest and deepest
interest in our affairs, and who were always ready to
lend a helping hand, were equally happy over the
coming of their first grandchild. My brother-in-law,
much older than my wife, and a bachelor, could not
understand at first the joy we all felt; but even he
began to strut around like a proud peacock after a
while. What a difference a baby makes in a home!

I am injecting these details into my story merely
to emphasize how the early days of my life were lived.
I had no opportunity to spend much money, and yet
I had as much happiness in those days as I have ever
had since.

The strange thing about it all is that the experience
of those days did not teach me the value of money.
If anybody ever had a practical lesson to guide him
in his future, I certainly had it.

But let me tell you how this early experience affected me. The birth of my son inspired me to do
something that would make more money than I was
getting at teaching school and in writing for newspapers. I did not want my wife, mother and sister to
feel that they would have to continue indefinitely to
do their part in sustaining the household. Why should
a fellow, big and strong and healthy as I have always
been, and with a reasonable amount of ability, be
content to remain a spoke in the wheel? Why

shouldn't I be the whole wheel, as far as providing for the family was concerned?

Following my desire to make more money, I took on the selling of books in addition to teaching and writing for newspapers. This earned for me quite a little extra money. Finally, I gave up teaching and concentrated on selling books, and writing for newspapers.

My book-selling took me to Bridgeton, New Jersey. It was here that I got my first real start in making money. I had to be away from home a great deal to do this work, but the sacrifice was worth while. I earned enough money in a few weeks to send more money home than I had contributed to the household in any year from my school-teaching and newspaper correspondence. After combing the territory in the Bridgeton zone, I became interested in a newspaper in that city, the Morning Star. It seemed to me that the editor and publisher of this paper needed a helper. I called on him and told him so. He said, "Heavens, young man, how can I hire you? I am not earning enough money to pay for my own living!"

"That's just it," said I. "I believe together we can make the Star a success. I'll tell you what I'll do: I'll work for you for one week for one dollar a day. At the end of the week, if I have made good, I'll expect you to pay me three dollars a day for the second week; and then, if I continue to do well, I'll expect you to pay me six dollars a day for the third week, and will continue from then on until the paper makes enough money to pay me fifty dollars a week."

The owner agreed to my proposition. At the end of two months, I was being paid fifty dollars a week, which in those days was considered a big salary. I began to feel that I was well on my way toward making money—but all I wanted it for was to make my family more comfortable. Fifty dollars a week was just four times as much as I had made teaching school.

My job on the Star embraced editorial writing (not very brilliant), reporting (just ordinary), the writing and selling of advertisements (fairly successful), proof reading, bill collecting, and so forth. It kept me humping six days a week; but I could stand it, for I was strong and healthy, and, besides, the work was very interesting. I also contributed correspondence to the New York Sun, Philadelphia Record, and the Trenton (N. J.) Times, which brought me in an average of one hundred and fifty dollars a month, for this was a good news territory.

I learned a lesson on the Star which eventually shaped the course of my life. I found out that there is a great deal more money to be earned by selling advertising for newspapers than in writing for them. Advertising brings grist to the mill.

I put over one advertising stunt on the Star—a write-up of the south Jersey oyster industry, paid for by the oyster men—that brought in three thousand dollars cash, which the publisher divided with me fifty-fifty. I had never seen so much money at one time in all my life. Think of it! Fifteen hundred dollars—twenty-five per cent more than I had made in two years of school-teaching and odd tasks.

Did I save this money or any part of it? I did not. What was the use? I could do so much with it to make my wife, boy, mother and sister happy that I let it go far easier than I had made it.

But would it not have been a fine thing if I had put this money away for a rainy day?

My work in Bridegton attracted the attention of Sam Hudson, New Jersey correspondent of the Philadelphia Record, who was a shining example of that type of newspaper men whose greatest pleasure in life is doing things for others.

Sam told me that it was time for me to get located in a big city. He thought I had it in me to make good. He said he would get me a job in Philadelphia. He did, and I moved with my wife and baby to Germantown. I was given charge of the advertising department of the Germantown (Philadelphia) Gazette, a weekly newspaper.

At the start I did not make as much money as I had earned in Bridegton, because I had to give up my newspaper correspondence. The news for this section was covered by other correspondents. But very soon I was making twenty-five per cent more money. The Gazette increased its size three times to accommodate its advertising, and each time I received a very substantial increase in salary.

In addition to this, I was given a job to gather social news for the Sunday edition of the Philadelphia Press. Bradford Merrill, managing editor of that newspaper, now a very important New York newspaper executive, assigned me a big territory to cover. This kept me busy every night in the week except Saturdays. I was paid five dollars a column; but I averaged seven columns every Sunday; which made me thirty-five dollars a week extra.

It was more money for me to spend, and I spent it. I did not know anything about budgeting my expenses. I just let it go as it came. I did not have time, or thought I hadn't, to watch my step in spending.

A year later I was invited to join the advertising staff of the Philadelphia Press, a big opportunity for a young man, for I got wonderful training under the management of William L. McLean, now the owner of the Philadelphia Evening Bulletin. I still retained my job as gatherer of social news—so my income was just about the same as I had been making in Germantown.

But before long my work attracted the attention of James Elverson, Sr., publisher of the old Saturday Night and Golden Days, who had just purchased the Philadelphia Inquirer. I was offered and accepted the advertising management of this newspaper.

This meant a big increase in my income. And soon afterward there came a happy increase in my family, the birth of a daughter. Then I was able to do what I had longed to do since the birth of my son. I got the family together again under one roof—my wife and two babies, my mother and sister. At last I was able to relieve my mother of any cares or responsibilities, and never again did she have either as long as she lived. She died in her eighty-first year, twenty-five years after my father's death. I shall never forget her last words to me: "Will, you have never caused me a moment's worry since you were born, and I could not have had more than you have given me had I been the Queen of England."

I was making at this time four times more money than my father had made as superintendent of public schools in my home town of Phillipsburg, New Jersey.

I AM thankful for the adversities which have crossed my pathway, for they have taught me tolerance, sympathy, self-control, perseverance a n d some other virtues I might never have known.

All the money, however, passed out of my pockets as easily as water flows through a sieve. Expenses increased with every increase in my income, which is the habit, I suppose, with most people. There was no sane reason, though, for letting my expenses go beyond my income, which I did. I found myself piling up debts, and from this time on I was never out of debt. I did not worry about my debts, though, for I thought I could pay them off at any time. It never occurred to me—not until fully twenty-five years later—that debt eventually would bring upon me not only great anxiety and unhappiness, but that I would lose friends and credit as well.

But I must pat myself on the back for one thing: I was giving full rein to my big fault—spending money as fast as I made it, often faster; but I never shirked my work. I was always trying to find more things to do, and I always found them. I spent very little time with my family. I would go home to dinner every night and romp with the babies until their bedtime, then I would return to the office and often work.

So the years went by. Another daughter arrived. Presently I wanted my daughters to have a pony and cart, and I wanted my son to have a riding horse. Then I thought I needed a team to take me around with the family, driving them to a closed coupé or an open trap. I got them all. Instead of one horse and a carry-all, or perhaps a team, which would have been sufficient for our needs and something we could have afforded, I had to have a stable, with all that goes with it. This outfit cost me nearly one fourth of my annual income.

Then I took up golf. This was in my forty-first year. I went at my play the same as I went at my work—put my whole heart in it. I learned to play pretty well. My son and elder daughter played with me, and they learned to play well, too.

It was necessary that my younger daughter should spend the winter in the South and summers in the Adirondacks; but instead of her mother going with her alone, I felt it would be fine if the son and other daughter went along with them. This arrangement was carried out. They went to Pinehurst, North Carolina, every winter and to expensive resorts in the Adirondacks or in New Hampshire in the summer.

All this took a great deal of money. My son and elder daughter were keen about golf and spent a lot of money on it. I also disbursed quite a little on golf courses around New York. Between the three of us we won 80 prizes, most of which are now in storage. I sat down one day and calculated what these prizes had cost me. I discovered that each trophy had cost me $250.00 or a total of $45,000.00 over a period of fifteen years, an average of $3,000.00 a year. Ridiculous, wasn't it?

I entertained lavishly at my home. Montclair folks thought I was a millionaire. I frequently invited groups of business men to have a day of golf at the club, and then to have dinner with me in the evening. They would have been satisfied with a plain home dinner, but, no, I must serve them an elaborate affair staged by a famous caterer. These dinners never cost less than ten dollars a plate, which did not include the money spent for music while they were dining. I had a negro quartet come to the house. Our dining-room comfortably seated twenty people, and it was filled to capacity many times.

It was all very lovely, and I was glad to be their host. In fact, I was very happy over it. I never stopped to think how rapidly I was piling up debts. The day came when they began to bother me a lot. I had entertained so many guests at the golf club one month, paying for luncheons, cigars, and greens fees, that my bill was four hundred and fifty dollars. This attracted the attention of the directors of the club, who were all good friends of mine and very much interested in my welfare. They made it their business to tell me that I was spending entirely too much money, and they wished for my sake that I could check my expenses.

This gave me a bit of a jolt. It made me think seriously long enough to get rid of my horses and traps—at a big sacrifice, of course. I gave up our home and moved back to the city; but I did not leave any unpaid bills in Montclair. I borrowed the money to pay them. It was always easy for me to get all the money I wanted, despite my well known financial short-comings.

Here are two sidelights on my experience during my "flaring forties."

Besides spending money foolishly and perhaps recklessly, I loaned it with equal abandon. In cleaning out my desk at home before moving to the city I looked over a package of due bills, the total of which was over forty thousand dollars. That was money handed out to just anybody who came along. I tore them all up; but I realized that if I had that money in hand I wouldn't owe a dollar.

One of the prosperous business men I had entertained many times and who in turn had entertained me, said to me: "Billy, I've got to stop going on outings with you. You spend entirely too much money for me. I can't keep up with you."

Think of that coming from a man who was making more money than I was! It should have struck home, but it didn't. I went on spending just the same, and foolishly thinking that I was having a good time, and with no thought of the future. This man is now one of the vice presidents of one of New York's greatest financial institutions, and is reported to be worth many millions of dollars.

I should have taken his advice.

In the fall of 1908, after my disastrous experience of six months in another line of business following my resignation from the Hearst organization, I resumed newspaper work as advertising manager of the New York Evening Mail. I had known Henry L. Stoddard, editor and owner, back in the Philadelphia days, when he was political correspondent for the Press.

Despite the fact that I was bothered by debts, I did the best work of my life on the Evening Mail, and made more money during the five years I was associated with it than I had ever made before. Moreover, Mr. Stoddard gave me the privilege of syndicating advertising talks, which ran in his paper for one thousand consecutive publication days, and earned for me more than fifty-five thousand dollars.

Mr. Stoddard was very generous in many other ways, and frequently paid me special sums of money for doing what he considered unusual things in the way of developing business. During this period, I was so deeply in debt that, in order to keep things moving as smoothly as possible, but without retrenching in the slightest way in my expenses, I borrowed money from Peter to pay Paul and from Paul to pay Peter. That item of fifty-five thousand dollars earned from syndicating advertising talks would have more than paid all my debts and left a nice nest egg besides. But all of it was spent as easily as though I hadn't a care in the world.

In 1915 I went on my own in the advertising business. From that time until the spring of 1922 my fees ran into very big figures. I was still making more money than I ever did, and was spending it just as fast as I made it, until finally my friends got tired of making me loans.

If I had shown the slightest inclination to curb my expenses to the extent of only ten per cent, these wonderful men would have been willing to divide fifty-fifty with me, letting me pay them five per cent of it and saving five per cent. They did not care so much about the return of the money they had loaned me, as that they wanted to see me pull myself together.

The crash in my affairs came five years ago. Two friends who had stood by me loyally became impatient, and told me frankly that I needed a drastic lesson. They gave it to me all right. I was forced into bankruptcy, which nearly broke my heart. I felt that every person I knew was pointing the finger of scorn at me. This was very foolish. While there was comment, it was not at all unfriendly. It was expressive of keen regret that a man who had attained so much prestige in his profession, and had earned so

FORTUNATE is the person who has learned that the most certain way to "get" is to first "give" through some sort of useful service.

much money, should have allowed himself to get into financial difficulties.

Proud and sensitive to the core I felt the disgrace of bankruptcy so keenly that I decided to go to Florida, where I had once done a special piece of work for a client. It seemed to me to be the coming El Dorado. I figured that maybe I could make sufficient money in a few years so that I could return to New York, not only with a competency but with enough to pay all my debts in full. For a time it looked as though I would realize this ambition; but I was caught in the big real estate collapse. So here I am back in the old town where I once had big earning power and hundreds of friends and well-wishers.

It has been a strange experience.

One thing is certain: I have learned my lesson at last. I feel sure that opportunities will come my way to redeem myself, and that my earning power will be restored to me. And when that time comes I know that I shall be able to live as well as I ever did, on *forty* per cent of my income. Then I shall divide the remaining sixty per cent into two parts, setting aside thirty per cent to pay my creditors and thirty per cent for insurance and savings.

If I allowed myself to feel depressed over my past, or filled my mind with worries, I would not be capable of carrying on the fight to redeem myself.

Besides, I would be ungrateful to my Maker for having endowed me with wonderful health all my life. Is there any greater blessing?

I would be ungrateful to the memory of my parents, whose splendid training has kept me anchored pretty safely to moral standards. Slipping from moral moorings is infinitely more serious, in the end, than slipping from the thrift standard.

I would lack appreciation of the encouragement and support I have had in generous measure from hundreds of business men and to many good friends who helped me build a fine reputation in my profession.

These memories are the sunshine of my life. And I shall use them to pave the way to my future achievement.

With abundance of health, unfaltering faith, unflagging energy, unceasing optimism, and unbounded confidence that a man can win his fight, even though he commences late in life to realize the kind of fight he must make—is there anything but death to stop him?*

.   .   .   .

Mr. Freeman's story is the same as that which might be told by thousands of other men who save nothing, with the exception that the amounts of their incomes would vary. The manner of living, the way the money was spent, and why, as told in Mr. Freeman's narrative, show the way the spender's mind works.

.   .   .   .

Compilation of statistics covering family incomes and expenditures of over 16,000 families of men who have been analyzed by the author disclosed some facts that will be of help to the person who wishes to budget

* Reprinted by courtesy of The American Magazine. Copyright, The Crowell Publishing Company, 1927.

his income and disbursements on a practical working basis that is sound and economical.

The average income runs all the way from $100.00 to $300.00 per month. The budget allowance covering incomes within these two amounts should be about as follows:

A family consisting of two persons, whose income is $100.00 a month, should manage to set aside at least $10 or $12 a month for the savings account. The cost of shelter, or rent, should not exceed $25 or $30 a month. Food costs should average about $25 to $30. Clothing should be kept within an expenditure of $15 to $20 a month. Recreation and incidentals should be kept down to about $8 to $10 a month.

A family whose income is $100.00 a month, should that income be increased to $125.00, ought to save at least $20 of the amount.

A family of two persons, whose income is $150.00 a month, should budget their funds about as follows: Savings $25. Shelter or rent $35 to $40. Food $35 to $40. Clothes, $20 to $30. Recreation $10 to $15.

On a salary of $200 a month the budget should be: Savings $50. Shelter or rent $40 to $50. Food $35 to $45. Clothes $30 to $35. Recreation $15 to $20.

A family of two, on a salary or income of $300.00 a month, should apportion the income about thus: Savings $55 to $65. Shelter or rent $45 to $60. Food $45 to $60. Clothes $35 to $45. Recreation and education $50 to $75.

Some might argue that a family of two, making a salary of $300.00 a month, might live just as cheaply as one making but $100 or $125. However, this is not quite correct, because one who has the ability to earn $300.00 a month must as a rule associate with people who make better appearances and more entertainment necessary.

A single man, earning $100.00, $150.00 or $300.00 a month, should save considerably more than a man with a family could save on the same amounts. As a rule, a single man, who has no dependents, and who is not in debt, should live on a budget of $50 a month for room and food, and not to exceed $30 a month for clothes and perhaps $10 for recreation. These amounts might be slightly increased by one who earned from $150.00 to $300.00 a month.

A boy who lives away from home, and whose weekly income is only $20.00 should save $5 of the amount. The remainder should cover cost of food, room and clothes.

A girl, living away from home, on the same income, would require a slightly larger allowance for clothes, as women's wearing apparel is more costly than men's, and it is generally imperative that women watch, more closely than men, their personal appearance.

A family of three will be able to save considerably less than the amounts which can be saved by a family of two. With rare exceptions, however, such as cases where the family is involved in debt which must be absorbed out of the monthly income, any family can save at least five per cent of the gross income.

It is a common practice today for families to purchase automobiles on monthly payments which involve too great an expenditure compared to their income. A man with a Ford income has no business purchasing a Studebaker car. He should curb his desires and content himself with a Ford. Many single

men spend their entire incomes, and often go into
debt besides, because they maintain automobiles out
of keeping with their incomes. This common practice
is fatal to success as far as financial independence
may be considered a part of success, in thousands of
instances.

The instalment plan of buying has become so common, and it is so easy to purchase practically anything one desires, that the tendency to spend out of
proportion to one's income is rapidly increasing.
This tendency must be curbed by the person who has
made up his mind to gain financial independence.

It can be done by anyone who is willing to try.

Another evil, which is both an evil and a blessing,
is the fact that this country is so very prosperous that
money comes easily, and if not watched it goes still
more easily. Since the beginning of the World War
there has been a steady demand for practically everything manufactured in the United States, and this
condition of prosperity has caused people to lapse
into a state of careless, unjustified spending.

There is no virtue in "keeping up with the pace set
by neighbors" when this means sacrifice of the habit
of saving a regular part of one's income. It is far
better, in the long run, to be considered a bit behind
the times than it is to go along through youth, into
the days of maturity, and finally into old age, without
having formed the habit of systematic saving.

It is better to sacrifice during the age of youthful-
ness, than it is to be compelled to do so during the
age of maturity, as all who have not developed the
habit of saving generally have to do.

There is nothing quite so humiliating, that carries

I AM thankful that I was born poor—that I did not come into this world burdened by the whims of wealthy parents, with a bag of gold around my neck.

such great agony and suffering, as poverty in old age, when personal services are no longer marketable, and one must turn to relatives or to charitable institutions for existence.

A budget system should be maintained by every person, both the married and the single, but no budget system will work out if the person trying to keep it lacks the courage to cut expenses on such items as those of entertainment and recreation. If you feel so weak in will-power that you think it necessary to "keep up with the Smiths" with whom you associate socially, and whose income is greater than your own, or who spend all of their income foolishly, then no budget system can be of service to you.

Forming the savings habit means that, to some extent at least, you must seclude yourself from all except a well selected group of friends who enjoy you without elaborate entertaining on your part.

To admit that you lack the courage to trim down your expenditures so that you can save money, even if only a small amount, is the equivalent of admitting at the same time a lack of the sort of character which leads to success.

It has been proved times too numerous to be mentioned, that people who have formed the habit of saving money are always given preference in positions of responsibility; therefore, the saving of money not only adds advantages in the nature of preferred employment and a larger bank account, but it also increases the actual earning capacity. Any business man will prefer to employ a person who saves money regularly, not because of the mere fact that such person saves money, but because of the characteristics possessed by such a person which make him or her more efficient.

Many firms will not employ a man or a woman who does not save money.

It should be a common practice for all business houses to require all employees to save money. This would be a blessing to thousands of people who would not otherwise have the will-power to form the savings habit.

Henry Ford has gone a very long way, perhaps as far as is expedient, to induce his employees not only to save their money, but to spend what they do spend wisely, and to live sanely and economically. The man who induces his employees to form the habit of saving is a practical philanthropist.

OPPORTUNITIES THAT COME TO THOSE WHO HAVE SAVED MONEY

A few years ago a young man came to Philadelphia, from the farming district of Pennsylvania, and went to work in a printing plant. One of his fellow workmen owned some shares in a Building and Loan Company, and had formed the habit of saving $5.00 a week, through this Association. This young man was influenced by his associate to open an account with the Building and Loan Company. At the end of three years he had saved $900.00. The printing plant for which he worked got into financial difficulty and was about to fail. He came to the rescue with his $900.00 which he had saved in small amounts, and in return was given a half interest in the business.

By inaugurating a system of close economy he

helped the business to pay off its indebtedness, and today he is drawing out of it, as his half of the profits, a little better than $25,000.00 a year.

This opportunity never would have come, or, if it had, he would not have been prepared to embrace it, had he not formed the habit of saving money.

When the Ford automobile was perfected, during the early days of its existence, Henry Ford needed capital to promote the manufacture and sale of his product. He turned to a few friends who had saved up a few thousand dollars, one of whom was Senator Couzens. These friends came to his rescue, put in a few thousand dollars with him, and later drew out millions of dollars in profits.

When Woolworth first started his Five and Ten Cent Store Plan he had no capital, but he turned to a few friends who had saved, by the closest sort of economy and great sacrifice, a few thousand dollars. These friends staked him and later they were paid back hundreds of thousands of dollars in profits.

Van Heusen (of soft-collar fame) conceived the idea of producing a semi-soft collar for men. His idea was sound, but he had not a cent to promote it. He turned to a few friends who had only a few hundred dollars, who gave him a start, and the collar made each of them wealthy.

The men who started the El Producto Cigar business had but little capital, and what they did have was money they had saved from their small earnings as cigar makers. They had a good idea, and knew how to make a good cigar, but the idea would have died "a-bornin'" had they not saved a little money. With their meager savings they launched the cigar, and a few years later they sold out their business to the American Tobacco Company for $8,000,000.00.

Back of practically every great fortune one may find, as its beginning, a well developed habit of saving money.

John D. Rockefeller was an ordinary bookkeeper. He conceived the idea of developing the oil business, which was then not even considered a business. He needed capital, and because he had developed the habit of saving, and had thereby proved that he could conserve the funds of other people, he had no difficulty in borrowing what money he needed.

It may be truthfully stated that the real basis of the Rockefeller fortune is the habit of saving money which Mr. Rockefeller developed, while working as a bookkeeper at a salary of $40.00 a month.

James J. Hill was a poor young man, working as a telegrapher, at a salary of $30.00 a month. He conceived the idea of the Great Northern Railway System, but his idea was out of proportion to his ability to finance. However, he had formed the habit of saving money, and on the meager salary of $30.00 a month had saved enough to enable him to pay his expenses on a trip to Chicago, where he interested capitalists in financing his plan. The fact that he, himself, had saved money on a small salary was considered good evidence that he would be a safe man to trust with other people's money.

Most business men will not trust another man with their money unless he has demonstrated his ability to take care of his own and use it wisely. The test, while it is often embarrassing to those who have not formed the Habit of Saving, is a very practical one.

A young man who worked in a printing plant in the city of Chicago wanted to open a small print shop and go into business for himself. He went to a printing supply house manager and made known his wants, saying he desired credit for a printing press and some type and other small equipment.

The first question asked by the manager was: "Have you saved any money of your own?"

He had! Out of his salary of $30.00 a week he had saved $15.00 a week regularly for nearly four years. He got the credit he wanted. Later on he got more credit, until today he has built up one of the most successful printing plants in the city of Chicago. His name is George B. Williams, and he is well known, as are also the facts here stated, to the author of this course.

Many years after this incident, the author of this course became acquainted with Mr. Williams, and at the end of the war, in 1918, the author went to Mr. Williams and asked for credit amounting to many thousands of dollars, for the purpose of publishing the Golden Rule Magazine. The first question asked was: "Have you formed the habit of saving money." Despite the fact that all the money I had saved was lost in the war, the mere fact that I had actually formed the savings habit was the real basis on which I got credit for upward of $30,000.00.

There are opportunities on every corner, but they exist only for those who have ready money, or who can command money because they have formed the Habit of Saving, and developed the other characteristics which go with the formation of the savings habit known by the general term of "character."

L OVE and Justice are
the real arbiters of all
disputes. Give them a
chance and you will no
longer want to defeat a
brother sojourner by the
wayside of life.

The late J. P. Morgan once said he would rather loan a million dollars to a man of sound character, who had formed the habit of saving money, than he would a thousand dollars to a man without character, who was a spendthrift.

Generally speaking, this is the attitude which the world takes toward all men who save money.

It often happens that a small savings account of no more than two or three hundred dollars is sufficient to start one on the highway to financial independence. A few years ago a young inventor invented a household article which was unique and practical. He was handicapped, as inventors so often are, because he did not have the money to market his invention. Moreover, not having formed the savings habit he found it impossible to borrow money through banking sources.

His room-mate was a young machinist who had saved $200.00. He came to the inventor's aid with this small sum of money, and had enough of the articles manufactured to give them a start. They went out and sold, from house to house, the first supply, then came back and had another supply made up, and so on, until they had accumulated (thanks to the thrift and savings ability of the room-mate) a capital of $1,000.00. With this, plus some credit they secured, they bought the tools for manufacturing their own product.

The young machinist sold his half interest in the business, six years later, for $250,000.00. He never would have handled this much money, during his entire life, had he not formed the habit of saving, which enabled him to come to the rescue of his inventor friend.

This case might be multiplied a thousand times, with but slight variation as to details, as it is fairly descriptive of the beginning of many great fortunes that have been made and are now in the making, in the United States.

It may seem like a sad, cruel fact, but it is a FACT none the less, that if you have no money, and have not developed the habit of saving, you are "out of luck" as far as availing yourself of the opportunity to make money is concerned.

It can do no harm to repeat—in fact it should be repeated over and over again—that the real start of nearly all fortunes, whether great or small, is the formation of the habit of saving money!

Get this basic principle firmly founded in your mind and you will be well on the road toward financial independence!

It is a sad sight to see a man, well along in years, who has sentenced himself to the wearisome treadmill of hard labor all the days of his life because he has neglected forming the habit of saving money, yet there are millions of such men living, in the United States alone, today.

The greatest thing in life is FREEDOM!

There can be no real freedom without a reasonable degree of financial independence. It is a terrible thing to be compelled to be at a certain place, at a certain task (perhaps a task which one does not like) for a certain number of hours every working day of the week, for a whole life-time. In some ways this is the same as being in prison, since one's choice of action is always limited. It is really no better than being in prison with the privilege of a "trusty," and in some ways it is even worse because the man who is imprisoned has escaped the responsibility of providing a place to sleep, something to eat and clothes to wear.

The only hope of escape from this life-long toil which curtails freedom is to form the habit of saving money, and then live up to that habit, no matter how much sacrifice it may require. There is no other way out for millions of people, and unless you are one of the rare exceptions this lesson and all these statements of fact are meant for YOU, and apply to you!

> Neither a borrower, nor a
>   lender be:
> For loan oft loses both itself
>   and friend,
> And borrowing dulls the edge
>   of husbandry.
> This above all: to thine own
>   self be true,
> And it must follow, as the
>   night the day,
> Thou canst not then be false
>   to any man.
>   —SHAKESPEARE

EVERYTHING

PASSES AT PAR,

TEMPORARILY;

TRUTH ALONE

REMAINS

PERMANENTLY.

Lesson Five

INITIATIVE AND
LEADERSHIP

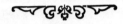

WHEN you do not know what to do or which way to turn, smile. This will relax your mind and let the sunshine of happiness into your soul.

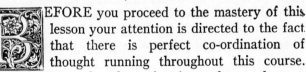

THE LAW OF SUCCESS
Lesson Five
INITIATIVE AND LEADERSHIP

"You Can Do It if You Believe You Can!"

BEFORE you proceed to the mastery of this lesson your attention is directed to the fact that there is perfect co-ordination of thought running throughout this course. You will observe that the entire sixteen lessons harmonize and blend with each other so that they constitute a perfect chain that has been built, link by link, out of the factors that enter into the development of power through *organized effort.*

You will observe, also, that the same fundamental principles of Applied Psychology form the foundation of each of these sixteen lessons, although different application is made of these principles in each of the lessons.

This lesson, on *Initiative* and *Leadership,* follows the lesson on Self-confidence for the reason that no one could become an efficient leader or take the initiative in any great undertaking without belief in him self.

Initiative and *Leadership* are associated terms in

71

this lesson for the reason that *Leadership* is essential
for the attainment of *Success,* and *Initiative* is the
very foundation upon which this necessary quality of
Leadership is built. *Initiative* is as essential to success as a hub is essential to a wagon wheel.

And what is *Initiative?*

It is that exceedingly rare quality that prompts—
nay, impels—a person to do that which ought to be
done *without being told to do it.* Elbert Hubbard expressed himself on the subject of *Initiative* in these
words:

"The world bestows its big prizes, both in money
and honors, for one thing, and that is *Initiative.*

"What is initiative? I'll tell you: It is doing the
right thing without being told.

"But next to doing the right thing without being
told is to do it when you are told once. That is to
say, 'Carry the message to Garcia.' Those who can
carry a message get high honors, but their pay is not
always in proportion.

"Next, there are those who do the right thing only
when necessity kicks them from behind, and these get
indifference instead of honors, and a pittance for pay.

"This kind spend most of the time polishing a bench
with a hard luck story.

"Then, still lower down in the scale than this we
have the fellow who will not do the right thing even
when someone goes along to show him how and stays
to see that he does it; he is always out of a job, and
receives the contempt he deserves, unless he has a rich
pa, in which case destiny patiently waits around the
corner with a stuffed club.

"To which class do *you* belong?"

Inasmuch as you will be expected to take inventory of yourself and determine which of the fifteen factors of this course you need most, after you have completed the sixteenth lesson, it may be well if you begin to get ready for this analysis by answering the question that Elbert Hubbard has asked:

To which class do you belong?

One of the peculiarities of *Leadership* is the fact that it is never found in those who have not acquired the *habit* of taking the initiative. *Leadership* is something that you must invite yourself into; it will never thrust itself upon you. If you will carefully analyze all leaders whom you know you will see that they not only exercised *Initiative,* but they went about their work with a *definite purpose* in mind. You will also see that they possessed that quality described in the third lesson of this course, *Self-confidence.*

These facts are mentioned in this lesson for the reason that it will profit you to observe that successful people make use of *all* the factors covered by the sixteen lessons of the course; and, for the more important reason that it will profit you to understand thoroughly the principle of *organized effort* which this Reading Course is intended to establish in your mind.

This seems an appropriate place to state that this course is not intended as a *short-cut* to success, nor is it intended as a mechanical formula that you may use in noteworthy achievement without effort on your part. The *real* value of the course lies in the *use* that you will make of it, and not in the course itself. The chief purpose of the course is to help you develop in yourself the fifteen qualities covered by the sixteen lessons of the course, and one of the most important of these qualities is *Initiative*, the subject of this lesson.

We will now proceed to apply the principle upon which this lesson is founded by describing, in detail, just how it served successfully to complete a business transaction which most people would call difficult.

In 1916 I needed $25,000.00 with which to create an educational institution, but I had neither this sum nor sufficient collateral with which to borrow it through the usual banking sources. Did I bemoan my fate or think of what I might accomplish if some rich relative or Good Samaritan would come to my rescue by loaning me the necessary capital?

I did nothing of the sort!

I did just what you will be advised, throughout this course, to do. First of all, I made the securing of this capital my *definite chief aim*. Second, I laid out a complete *plan* through which to transform this *aim* into reality. Backed by sufficient Self-confidence and spurred on by *Initiative*, I proceeded to put my plan into action. But, before the "action" stage of the plan had been reached, more than six weeks of constant, persistent study and effort and thought were embodied in it. If a plan is to be sound it must be built of carefully chosen material.

You will here observe the application of the principle of *organized effort*, through the operation of which it is possible for one to ally or associate several interests in such a way that *each of these interests* is greatly strengthened and each supports all the others, just as one link in a chain supports all the other links.

I wanted this $25,000.00 in capital for the purpose

of creating a school of Advertising and Salesmanship. Two things were necessary for the organization of such a school. One was the $25,000.00 capital, which I did not have, and the other was the proper course of instruction, which *I did have*. My problem was to *ally myself* with some group of men who needed that which I had, and who would supply the $25,000.00. This alliance had to be made through a plan that would benefit all concerned.

After my plan had been completed, and I was satisfied that it was equitable and sound, I laid it before the owner of a well known and reputable business college which just then was finding competition quite keen and was badly in need of a plan for meeting this competition.

My plan was presented in about these words:

Whereas, you have one of the most reputable business colleges in the city; and,

Whereas, you need some plan with which to meet the stiff competition in your field; and,

Whereas, your good reputation has provided you with all the credit you need; and,

Whereas, I have the plan that will help you meet this competition successfully.

Be it resolved, that we ally ourselves through a plan that will give you that which you need and at the same time supply me with something which I need.

Then I proceeded to unfold my plan, further, in these words:

I have written a very practical course on Advertising and Salesmanship. Having built this course out of my actual experience in training and directing salesmen and my experience in planning and directing

THE space you occupy and the authority you exercise may be measured with mathematical exactness by the service you render.

many successful advertising campaigns, I have back of it plenty of evidence of its soundness.

If you will use your credit in helping market this course I will place it in your business college, as one of the regular departments of your curriculum and take entire charge of this newly created department. No other business college in the city will be able to meet your competition, for the reason that no other college has such a course as this. The advertising that you do in marketing this course will serve, also, to stimulate the demand for your regular business course. You may charge the entire amount that you spend for this advertising, to my department, and the advertising bill will be paid out of that department, leaving you the accumulative advantage that will accrue to your other departments without cost to you.

Now, I suppose you will want to know where I profit by this transaction, and I will tell you. I want you to enter into a contract with me in which it will be agreed that when the cash receipts from my department equal the amount that you have paid out or contracted to pay out for advertising, my department and my course in Advertising and Salesmanship become my own and I may have the privilege of separating this department from your school and running it under my own name.

The plan was agreeable and the contract was closed.

(Please keep in mind that my *definite purpose* was to secure the use of $25,000.00 for which I had no security to offer.)

In a little less than a year the Business College had paid out slightly more than $25,000.00 for advertising and marketing my course and the other expenses incidental to the operation of this newly organized department, while the department had collected and turned back to the College, in tuition fees, a sum equaling the amount the College had spent, and I took the department over, as a going and self-sustaining business, according to the terms of my contract.

As a matter of fact this newly created department not only served to attract students for the other departments of the College, but at the same time the tuition fees collected through this new department were sufficient to place it on a self-sustaining basis before the end of the first year.

Now you can see that while the College did not loan me one penny of actual capital, it nevertheless supplied me with credit which served exactly the same purpose.

I said that my plan was founded upon equity; that it contemplated a benefit to all parties concerned. The benefit accruing to me was the use of the $25,000.00, which resulted in an established and self-sustaining business by the end of the first year. The benefit accruing to the college was the students secured for its regular commercial and business course as a result of the money spent in advertising my department, all advertising having been done under the name of the College.

Today that business college is one of the most successful schools of its kind, and it stands as a monument of sound evidence with which to demonstrate the value of *allied effort*.

This incident has been related, not alone because it shows the value of *initiative* and *leadership*, but for the reason that it leads up to the subject covered by the next lesson of this Reading Course on the Law of Success, which is *imagination*.

There are generally many plans through the operation of which a desired object may be achieved, and it often happens to be true that the obvious and usual methods employed are not the best. The usual method of procedure, in the case related, would have been that of borrowing from a bank. You can see that this method was impractical, in this case, for the reason that no collateral was available.

A great philosopher once said: *"Initiative is the pass-key that opens the door to opportunity."*

I do not recall who this philosopher was, but I know that he was *great* because of the soundness of his statement.

We will now proceed to outline the exact procedure that you must follow if you are to become a person of *initiative* and *leadership*.

First: You must master the habit of *procrastination* and eliminate it from your make-up. This habit of putting off until tomorrow that which you should have done last week or last year or a score of years ago is gnawing at the very vitals of your being, and you can accomplish nothing until you throw it off.

The method through which you eliminate *procrastination* is based upon a well known and scientifically tested principle of psychology which has been referred to in the two preceding lessons of this course as Autosuggestion.

Copy the following formula and place it conspicuously in your room where you will see it as you retire at night and as you arise in the morning:

INITIATIVE AND LEADERSHIP

Having chosen a *definite chief aim* as my life-work I now understand it to be my duty to transform this purpose into reality.

Therefore, I will form the habit of taking some *definite* action each day that will carry me one step nearer the attainment of my *definite chief aim*.

I know that *procrastination* is a deadly enemy of all who would become leaders in any undertaking, and I will eliminate this habit from my make-up by:

(*a*) Doing some one definite thing each day, that ought to be done, without anyone telling me to do it.

(*b*) Looking around until I find at least one thing that I can do each day, that I have not been in the habit of doing, and that will be of value to others, without expectation of pay.

(*c*) Telling at least one other person, each day, of the value of practicing this habit of doing something that ought to be done without being told to do it.

I can see that the muscles of the body become strong in proportion to the extent to which they are used, therefore I understand that the *habit of initiative* also becomes fixed in proportion to the extent that it is practiced.

I realize that the place to begin developing the *habit of initiative* is in the small, commonplace things connected with my daily work, therefore I will go at my work each day as if I were doing it solely for the purpose of developing this necessary *habit of initiative*.

I understand that by practicing this *habit* of taking

the *initiative* in connection with my daily work I will be not only developing that habit, but I will also be attracting the attention of those who will place greater value on my services as a result of this practice.

Signed..................................

Regardless of what you are now doing, every day brings you face to face with a chance to render some service, outside of the course of your regular duties, that will be of value to others. In rendering this additional service, of your own accord, you of course understand that you are not doing so with the object of receiving monetary pay. You are rendering this service because it provides you with ways and means of exercising, developing and making stronger the aggressive spirit of *initiative* which you must possess before you can ever become an outstanding figure in the affairs of your chosen field of life-work.

Those who work for *money* alone, and who receive for their pay nothing but money, are always under-paid, no matter how much they receive. Money is necessary, but the big prizes of life cannot be measured in dollars and cents.

No amount of money could possibly be made to take the place of the happiness and joy and pride that belong to the person who digs a better ditch, or builds a better chicken coop, or sweeps a cleaner floor, or cooks a better meal. Every normal person loves to create something that is better than the average. The joy of *creating* a work of art is a joy that cannot be replaced by money or any other form of material possession.

I have in my employ a young lady who opens, assorts

WHAT helped you over the great obstacles of life?" was asked of a highly successful man. "The other obstacles," he replied.

and answers much of my personal mail. She began in my employ more than three years ago. Then her duties were to take dictation when she was asked to do so. Her salary was about the same as that which others receive for similar service. One day I dictated the following motto which I asked her to typewrite for me:

Remember that your only limitation is the one that you set up in your own mind.

As she handed the typewritten page back to me she said, "Your motto has given me an idea that is going to be of value to both you and me."

I told her I was glad to have been of service to her. The incident made no particular impression on my mind, but from that day on I could see that it had made a *tremendous* impression on her mind. She began to come back to the office after supper and performed service that she was neither paid for nor expected to perform. Without anyone telling her to do it she began to bring to my desk letters that she had answered for me. She had studied my style and these letters were attended to as well as I could have done it; in some instances much better. She kept up this habit until my personal secretary resigned. When I began to look for someone to take his place, what was more natural than to turn to this young woman to fill the place. Before I had time to give her the position *she took it on her initiative*. My personal mail began to come to my desk with a new secretary's name attached, and she was that secretary. On her own time, after hours, without additional pay, she had prepared herself for the best position on my staff.

But that is not all. This young lady became so

noticeably efficient that she began to attract the attention of others who offered her attractive positions. I have increased her salary many times and she now receives a salary more than four times as large as the amount she received when she first went to work for me as an ordinary stenographer, and, to tell you the truth, I am helpless in the matter, because she has made herself so valuable to me that I cannot get along without her.

That is initiative transformed into practical, understandable terms. I would be remiss in my duties if I failed to direct your attention to an advantage, other than a greatly increased salary, that this young lady's *initiative* has brought her. It has developed in her a spirit of cheerfulness that brings her happiness which most stenographers never know. Her work is not work—it is a great interesting game at which she is playing. Even though she arrives at the office ahead of the regular stenographers and remains there long after they have watched the clock tick off *five o'clock* and *quitting time,* her hours are shorter by far than are those of the other workers. Hours of labor do not drag on the hands of those who are happy at their work.

This brings us to the next step in our description of the exact procedure that you must follow in developing *initiative* and *leadership.*

Second: You of course understand that the only way to get *happiness* is by giving it away, to others. The same applies to the development of *initiative.* You can best develop this essential quality in yourself by making it your business to interest those around you in doing the same. It is a well known fact that a man learns best that which he endeavors to teach others. If a man embraces a certain creed or religious faith, the first thing he does is to go out and try to "sell" it to others. And in exact proportion to the extent to which he impresses others does he impress *himself*.

In the field of salesmanship it is a well known fact that no salesman is successful in selling others until he has first made a good job of selling *himself*. Stated conversely, no salesman can do his best to sell others without sooner or later selling himself that which he is trying to sell to others.

Any statement that a person repeats over and over again for the purpose of inducing others to believe it, he, also, will come to believe, and this holds good whether the statement is false or true.

You can now see the advantage of making it your business to *talk initiative, think initiative, eat initiative, sleep initiative* and *practice initiative*. By so doing you are becoming a person of *initiative* and *leadership*, for it is a well known fact that people will readily, willingly and voluntarily follow the person who shows by his actions that he is a person of *initiative*.

In the place where you work or the community in which you live you come in contact with other people. Make it your business to interest every one of them who will listen to you, in the development of *initiative*. It will not be necessary for you to give your reasons for doing this, nor will it be necessary for you to an- nounce the fact that you are doing it. *Just go ahead and do it.* In your own mind you will understand, of course, that you are doing it because this practice will help you and will, at least, do those whom you influence in the same practice no harm.

If you wish to try an experiment that will prove both interesting and profitable to you, pick out some person of your acquaintance whom you know to be a person who never does anything that he is not expected to do, and begin selling him your idea of *initiative*. Do not stop by merely discussing the subject once; keep it up every time you have a convenient opportunity. Approach the subject from a different angle each time. If you go at this experiment in a tactful and forceful manner you will soon observe a change in the person on whom you are trying the experiment.

And, you will observe something else of more importance still: *You will observe a change in yourself!*

Do not fail to try this experiment.

You cannot talk *initiative* to others without developing a desire to practice it yourself. Through the operation of the principle of Auto-suggestion every statement that you make to others leaves its imprint on your own subconscious mind, and this holds good whether your statements are false or true.

You have often heard the saying: "He who lives by the sword will die by the sword."

Properly interpreted, this simply means that we are constantly attracting to ourselves and weaving into our own characters and personalities those qualities which our influence is helping to create in others. If we help others develop the habit of *initiative*, we, in turn, develop this same habit. If we sow the seeds of hatred and envy and discouragement in others, we, in turn, develop these qualities in ourselves. This principle through which a man comes to resemble in

his own nature those whom he most admires is fully
brought out in Hawthorne's story, The Great Stone
Face, a story that every parent should have his offspring read.

We come, now, to the next step in our description of
the exact procedure that you must follow in developing *initiative* and *leadership*.

Third: Before we go further let it be understood
what is meant by the term "Leadership," as it is used
in connection with this Reading Course on the Law
of Success. There are two brands of *leadership*, and
one of them is as deadly and destructive as the other
is helpful and constructive. The deadly brand, which
leads not to *success*, but to *absolute failure,* is the
brand adopted by pseudo-leaders who *force* their
leadership on unwilling followers. It will not be necessary here to describe this brand or to point out the
fields of endeavor in which it is practiced, with the
exception of the field of war, and in this field we will
mention but one notable example, that of Napoleon.

Napoleon was a *leader;* there can be no doubt about
this, but he led his followers and himself to destruction. The details are recorded in the history of France
and the French people, where you may study them
if you choose.

It is not Napoleon's brand of *leadership* that is
recommended in this course, although I will admit that
Napoleon possessed all the necessary fundamentals for
great leadership, excepting one—he lacked the spirit
of helpfulness to others as an objective. His desire
for the power that comes through leadership was based
solely upon self-aggrandizement. His desire for leadership was built upon personal ambition and not upon

CHERISH your visions and your dreams as they are the children of your soul; the blue-prints of your ultimate achievements.

the desire to lift the French people to a higher and nobler station in the affairs of nations.

The brand of *leadership* that is recommended through this course of instruction is the brand which leads to self-determination and freedom and self-development and enlightenment and justice. This is the brand that endures. For example, and as a contrast with the brand of *leadership* through which Napoleon raised himself into prominence, consider our own American commoner, Lincoln. The object of his *leadership* was to bring truth and justice and understanding to the people of the United States. Even though he died a martyr to his belief in this brand of *leadership,* his name has been engraved upon the heart of the world in terms of loving kindliness that will never bring aught but good to the world.

Both Lincoln and Napoleon led armies in warfare, but the objects of their *leadership* were as different as night is different from day. If it would give you a better understanding of the principles upon which this Reading Course is based, you could easily be cited to *leadership* of today which resembles both the brand that Napoleon employed and that which Lincoln made the foundation of his life-work, but this is not essential; your own ability to look around and analyze men who take the leading parts in all lines of endeavor is sufficient to enable you to pick out the Lincoln as well as the Napoleon types. Your own judgment will help you decide which type you prefer to emulate.

There can be no doubt in your mind as to the brand of *leadership* that is recommended in this Reading Course, and there should be no question in your mind as to which of the two brands described you will adopt as your brand. We make no recommendations on this subject, however, for the reason that this Reading Course has been prepared as a means of laying before its students the fundamental principles upon which power is developed, and not as a preachment on ethical conduct. We present both the constructive and the destructive possibilities of the principles outlined in this course, that you may become familiar with both, but we leave entirely to your own discretion the choice and application of these principles, believing that your own intelligence will guide you to make a wise selection.

THE PENALTY OF LEADERSHIP *

In every field of human endeavor, he that is first must perpetually live in the white light of publicity. Whether the leadership be vested in a man or in a manufactured product, emulation and envy are ever at work.

In art, in literature, in music, in industry, the reward and the punishment are always the same. The reward is widespread recognition; the punishment, fierce denial and detraction.

When a man's work becomes a standard for the whole world, it also becomes a target for the shafts of the envious few. If his work be merely mediocre, he will be left severely alone—if he achieve a masterpiece, it will set a million tongues a-wagging.

Jealousy does not protrude its forked tongue at the artist who produces a commonplace painting.

*(With the compliments of the Cadillac Motor Car Co.)

Whatsoever you write, or paint, or play, or sing or build, no one will strive to surpass or slander you, unless your work be stamped with the seal of a genius.

Long, long after a great work or a good work has been done, those who are disappointed or envious continue to cry out that it cannot be done.

Mean voices were raised against the author of the Law of Success before the ink was dry on the first textbooks. Poisoned pens were released against both the author and the philosophy the moment the first edition of the course was printed.

Spiteful little voices in the domain of art were raised against our own Whistler as a mountebank, long after the big world acclaimed him its greatest artistic genius.

Multitudes flocked to Beyreuth to worship at the musical shrine of Wagner, while the little group of those whom he had dethroned and displaced argued angrily that he was no musician at all.

The little world continued to protest that Fulton could never build a steamboat, while the big world flocked to the river banks to see his boat steam by.

Small, narrow voices cried out that Henry Ford would not last another year, but above and beyond the din of their childish prattle Ford went silently about his business and made himself the richest and most powerful man on earth.

The leader is assailed because he is a leader, and the effort to equal him is merely added proof of his leadership.

Failing to equal or to excel, the follower seeks to depreciate and to destroy—but only confirms the superiority of that which he strives to supplant.

There is nothing new in this.

It is as old as the world and as old as the human passions—envy, fear, greed, ambition and the desire to surpass.

And it all avails nothing.

If the leader truly leads, he remains the LEADER!

Master-poet, master-painter, master-workman, each in his turn is assailed, and each holds his laurels through the ages.

That which is good or great makes itself known, no matter how loud the clamor of denial.

A real leader cannot be slandered or damaged by lies of the envious, because all such attempts serve only to turn the spot-light on his ability, and real ability always finds a generous following.

Attempts to destroy real Leadership is love's labor lost, because that which deserves to live, lives!

.   .   .   .

We come back, now, to the discussion of the third step of the procedure that you must follow in developing *initiative* and *leadership*. This third step takes us back for a review of the principle of *organized effort,* as described in the preceding lessons of this course.

You have already learned that no man can accomplish enduring results of a far-reaching nature without the aid and co-operation of others. You have already learned that when two or more persons ally themselves in any undertaking, in a spirit of harmony and understanding, each person in the alliance thereby multiplies his own powers of achievement. Nowhere is this principle more evidenced than it is in an industry or business in which there is perfect team-work between the employer and the employees. Wherever you find this team-work you find prosperity and good-will on both sides.

Co-operation is said to be the most important word in the English language. It plays an important part in the affairs of the home, in the relationship of man and wife, parents and children. It plays an important part in the affairs of state. So important is this principle of co-operation that no leader can become powerful or last long who does not understand and apply it in his *leadership*.

Lack of Co-operation has destroyed more business enterprises than have all other causes combined. In my twenty-five years of active business experience and observation I have witnessed the destruction of all manner of business enterprises because of dissension and lack of application of this principle of Co-operation. In the practice of law I have observed the destruction of homes and divorce cases without end as a result of the lack of Co-operation between man and wife. In the study of the histories of nations it becomes alarmingly obvious that lack of Co-operative effort has been a curse to the human race all back down the ages. Turn back the pages of these histories and study them and you will learn a lesson in Co-operation that will impress itself indelibly upon your mind.

You are paying, and your children and your children's children will continue to pay, for the cost of the most expensive and destructive war the world has ever known, because nations have not yet learned that a part of the world cannot suffer without damage and suffering to the whole world.

SERVICE, Sacrifice and Self-Control are three words which must be well understood by the person who succeeds in doing something that is of help to the world.

This same rule applies, with telling effect, in the conduct of modern business and industry. When an industry becomes disorganized and torn asunder by strikes and other forms of disagreement, both the employers and employees suffer irreparable loss. But, the damage does not stop here; this loss becomes a burden to the public and takes on the form of higher prices and scarcity of the necessities of life.

The people of the United States who rent their homes are feeling the burden, at this very moment, of lack of co-operation between contractors and builders and the workers. So uncertain has the relationship between the contractors and their employees become that the contractors will not undertake a building without adding to the cost an arbitrary sum sufficient to protect them in the event of labor troubles. This additional cost increases rents and places unnecessary burdens upon the backs of millions of people. In this instance the lack of co-operation between a few men places heavy and almost unbearable burdens upon millions of people.

The same evil exists in the operation of our railroads. Lack of harmony and co-operation between the railroad management and the workers has made it necessary for the railroads to increase their freight and passenger rates, and this, in turn, has increased the cost of life's necessities to almost unbearable proportions. Here, again, lack of co-operation between a few leads to hardship for millions of people.

These facts are cited without effort or desire to place the responsibility for this lack of co-operation, since the object of this Reading Course is to help its students get at facts.

It may be truthfully stated that the high cost of living that everywhere manifests itself today has grown out of lack of application of the principle of co-operative *leadership*. Those who wish to decry present systems of government and industrial management may do so, but in the final analysis it becomes obvious to all except those who are not seeking the *truth* that the evils of government and of industry have grown out of lack of *co-operation*.

Nor can it be truthfully said that all the evils of the world are confined to the affairs of state and industry. Take a look at the churches and you will observe the damaging effects of lack of co-operation. No particular church is cited, but analyze any church or group of churches where lack of co-ordination of effort prevails and you will see evidence of disintegration that limits the service those churches could render. For example, take the average town or small city where rivalry has sprung up between the churches and notice what has happened; especially those towns in which the number of churches is far out of proportion to the population.

Through harmonized effort and through co-operation, the churches of the world could wield sufficient influence to render war an impossibility. Through this same principle of co-operative effort the churches and the leaders of business and industry could eliminate rascality and sharp practices, and all this could be brought about speedily.

These possibilities are not mentioned in a spirit of criticism, but only as a means of illustrating the power of co-operation, and to emphasize my belief in the potential power of the churches of the world. So there

will be no possibility of misinterpretation of my
meaning in the reference that I have here made to
the churches I will repeat that which I have so often
said in person; namely, that had it not been for the
influence of the churches no man would be safe in
walking down the street. Men would be at each
other's throat like wolves and civilization would still
be in the pre-historic age. My complaint is not against
the work that the churches have done, but the work
that *they could have done* through *leadership* that was
based upon the principle of co-ordinated, co-operative
effort which would have carried civilization at least a
thousand years ahead of where it is today. It is not
yet too late for such leadership.

That you may more fully grasp the fundamental
principle of co-operative effort you are urged to go to
the public library and read The Science of Power, by
Benjamin Kidd. Out of scores of volumes by some of
the soundest thinkers of the world that I have read
during the past fifteen years, no single volume has
given me such a full understanding of the possibilities
of co-operative effort as has this book. In recommending that you read this book it is not my purpose
to endorse the book in its entirety, for it offers some
theories with which I am not in accord. If you read
it, do so with an open mind and take from it only that
which you feel you can use to advantage in achieving
the object of your *definite chief aim.* The book will
stimulate *thought,* which is the greatest service that
any book can render. As a matter of fact the chief
object of this Reading Course on the Law of Success
is to stimulate deliberate *thought*: particularly that
brand of *thought* that is free from bias and prejudice

and is seeking *truth* no matter where or how or when it may be found.

During the World War I was fortunate enough to listen to a great soldier's analysis of how to be a *leader*. This analysis was given to the student-officers of the Second Training Camp at Fort Sheridan, by Major C. A. Bach, a quiet, unassuming army officer acting as an instructor. I have preserved a copy of this address because I believe it to be one of the finest lessons on *leadership* ever recorded.

The wisdom of Major Bach's address is so vital to the business man aspiring to *leadership,* or to the section boss, or to the stenographer, or to the foreman of the shop, or to the president of the works, that I have preserved it as a part of this Reading Course. It is my earnest hope that through the agency of this course this remarkable dissertation on *leadership* will find its way into the hands of every employer and every worker and every ambitious person who aspires to *leadership* in any walk of life. The principles upon which the address is based are as applicable to *leadership* in business and industry and finance as they are in the successful conduct of warfare.

Major Bach spoke as follows:

In a short time each of you men will control the lives of a certain number of other men. You will have in your charge loyal but untrained citizens, who look to you for instruction and guidance. Your word will be their law. Your most casual remark will be remembered. Your mannerisms will be aped. Your clothing, your carriage, your vocabulary, your manner of command will be imitated.

When you join your organization you will find there

a willing body of men who ask from you nothing more than the qualities that will command their respect, their loyalty and their obedience.

They are perfectly ready and eager to follow you so long as you can convince them that you have these qualities. When the time comes that they are satisfied you do not possess them you might as well kiss yourself good-bye. Your usefulness in that organization is at an end.

[How remarkably true this is in all manner of *leadership.*]

From the standpoint of society, the world may be divided into leaders and followers. The professions have their leaders, the financial world has its leaders. In all this leadership it is difficult, if not impossible, to separate from the element of pure leadership that selfish element of personal gain or advantage to the individual, without which any leadership would lose its value.

It is in military service only, where men freely sacrifice their lives for a faith, where men are willing to suffer and die for the right or the prevention of a wrong, that we can hope to realize leadership in its most exalted and disinterested sense. Therefore, when I say *leadership,* I mean *military leadership.*

In a few days the great mass of you men will receive commissions as officers. These commissions will not make you leaders; they will merely make you officers. They will place you in a position where you can become leaders if you possess the proper attributes. But you must make good, not so much with the men over you as with the men under you.

MAKE excuses for the shortcomings of others, if you wish, but hold yourself to a strict accountability if you would attain leadership in any undertaking.

Men must and will follow into battle officers who are not leaders, but the driving power behind these men is not enthusiasm but discipline. They go with doubt and trembling that prompts the unspoken question, "What will he do next?" Such men obey the letter of their orders but no more. Of devotion to their commander, of exalted enthusiasm which scorns personal risk, of *self-sacrifice* to insure his personal safety, they know nothing. Their legs carry them forward because their brain and their training tell them they *must* go. Their spirit does not go with them.

Great results are not achieved by cold, passive, unresponsive soldiers. They don't go very far and they stop as soon as they can. Leadership not only demands but receives the willing, unhesitating, unfaltering obedience and loyalty of other men; and a devotion that will cause them, when the time comes, to follow their uncrowned king to hell and back again, if necessary.

You will ask yourselves: "Of just what, then, does *leadership* consist? What must I do to become a leader? What are the attributes of leadership, and how can I cultivate them?"

Leadership is a composite of a number of qualities. [Just as *success* is a composite of the fifteen factors out of which this Reading Course was built.] Among the most important I would list Self-confidence, Moral Ascendency, Self-Sacrifice, Paternalism, Fairness, Initiative, Decision, Dignity, Courage.

Self-confidence results, first, from exact knowledge; second, the ability to impart that knowledge; and third,

the feeling of superiority over others that naturally
follows. All these give the officer poise. To lead,
you must *know!* You may bluff all of your men some
of the time, but you can't do it all the time. Men
will not have confidence in an officer unless he knows
his business, and he must know it from the ground up.

The officer should know more about paper work
than his first sergeant and company clerk put together;
he should know more about messing than his mess
sergeant; more about diseases of the horse than his
troop farrier. He should be at least as good a shot
as any man in his company.

If the officer does not know, and demonstrates the
fact that he does not know, it is entirely human for
the soldier to say to himself, "To hell with him. He
doesn't know as much about this as I do," and calmly
disregard the instructions received.

There is no substitute for accurate knowledge!

Become so well informed that men will hunt you
up to ask questions; that your brother officers will
say to one another, "Ask Smith—he knows."

And not only should each officer know thoroughly
the duties of his own grade, but he should study those
of the two grades next above him. A two-fold benefit
attaches to this. He prepares himself for duties which
may fall to his lot any time during battle; he further
gains a broader viewpoint which enables him to appreciate the necessity for the issuance of orders and
join more intelligently in their execution.

*Not only must the officer know but he must be able
to put what he knows into grammatical, interesting,
forceful English. He must learn to stand on his feet
and speak without embarrassment.*

I am told that in British training camps student-officers are required to deliver ten minute talks on any subject they choose. That is excellent practice. For to speak clearly one must think clearly, and clear, logical thinking expresses itself in definite, positive orders.

While self-confidence is the result of knowing more than your men, Moral Ascendency over them is based upon your belief that you are the better man. To gain and maintain this ascendency you must have self-control, physical vitality and endurance and moral force. You must have yourself so well in hand that, even though in battle you be scared stiff, you will never show fear. For if by so much as a hurried movement or a trembling of the hands, or a change of expression, or a hasty order hastily revoked, you indicate your mental condition it will be reflected in your men in a far greater degree.

In garrison or camp many instances will arise to try your temper and wreck the sweetness of your disposition. If at such times you "fly off the handle" you have no business to be in charge of men. For men in anger say and do things that they almost invariably regret afterward.

An officer should never apologize to his men; also an officer should never be guilty of an act for which his sense of justice tells him he should apologize.

Another element in gaining Moral Ascendency lies in the possession of enough physical vitality and endurance to withstand the hardships to which you and your men are subjected, and a dauntless spirit that enables you not only to accept them cheerfully but to minimize their magnitude.

Make light of your troubles, belittle your trials and you will help vitally to build up within your organization an esprit whose value in time of stress cannot be measured.

Moral force is the third element in gaining Moral Ascendency. To exert moral force you must live clean; you must have sufficient brain power to see the right and the will to do right.

Be an example to your men!

An officer can be a power for good or a power for evil. Don't preach to them—that will be worse than useless. Live the kind of life you would have them lead, and you will be surprised to see the number that will imitate you.

A loud-mouthed, profane captain who is careless of his personal appearance will have a loud-mouthed, profane, dirty company. *Remember what I tell you. Your company will be the reflection of yourself!* If you have a rotten company it will be because you are a rotten captain.

Self-sacrifice is essential to leadership. You will give, give, all the time. You will give of yourself physically, for the longest hours, the hardest work and the greatest responsibility are the lot of the captain. He is the first man up in the morning and the last man in at night. He works while others sleep.

You will give of yourself mentally, in sympathy and appreciation for the troubles of men in your charge. This one's mother has died, and that one has lost all his savings in a bank failure. They may desire help, but more than anything else they desire *sympathy*. Don't make the mistake of turning such men down with the statement that you have troubles of your own, for every time you do that you *knock a stone out of the foundation of your house.*

Your men are your foundation, and your house of *leadership* will tumble about your ears unless it rests securely upon them.   Finally, you will give of your own slender financial resources.   You will frequently spend your own money to conserve the health and well-being of your men or to assist them when in trouble.   Generally you get your money back.   Very frequently you must charge it off to profit and loss.

Even so, it is worth the cost.

When I say that paternalism is essential to leadership I use the term in its better sense.   I do not now refer to that form of paternalism which robs men of *initiative, self-reliance* and *self-respect.*   I refer to the paternalism that manifests itself in a watchful care for the comfort and welfare of those in your charge.

Soldiers are much like children.   You must see that they have shelter, food and clothing, the best that your utmost efforts can provide.   You must see that they have food to eat before you think of your own; that they have each as good a bed as can be provided before you consider where you will sleep.   You must be far more solicitous of their comfort than of your own.   You must look after their health.   You must conserve their strength by not demanding needless exertion or useless labor.

And by doing all these things you are breathing life into what would be otherwise a mere machine.   You are creating a soul in your organization that will make the mass respond to you as though it were one man. And that is esprit.

No accurate thinker will judge another person by that which the other person's enemies say about him.

And when your organization has this esprit you will wake up some morning and discover that the tables have been turned; that instead of your constantly looking out for them they have, without even a hint from you, taken up the task of looking out for you. You will find that a detail is always there to see that your tent, if you have one, is promptly pitched; that the most and the cleanest bedding is brought to your tent; that from some mysterious source two eggs have been added to your supper when no one else has any; that an extra man is helping your men give your horse a supergrooming; that your wishes are anticipated; that every man is "Johnny-on-the-spot." And then you have *arrived!*

You cannot treat all men alike! A punishment that would be dismissed by one man with a shrug of the shoulders is mental anguish for another. A company commander who, for a given offense, has a standard punishment that applies to all is either too indolent or too stupid to study the personality of his men. In his case justice is certainly blind.

Study your men as carefully as a surgeon studies a difficult case. And when you are sure of your diagnosis apply the remedy. And remember that you apply the remedy to effect a cure, not merely to see the victim squirm. It may be necessary to cut deep, but when you are satisfied as to your diagnosis don't be diverted from your purpose by any false sympathy for the patient.

Hand in hand with fairness in awarding punishment walks fairness in giving credit. Everybody hates a human hog. When one of your men has accomplished an especially creditable piece of work see that he gets the proper reward. *Turn heaven and earth upside down to get it for him.* Don't try to take it away from him and hog it for yourself. You may do this and get away with it, but you have lost the respect and loyalty of your men. Sooner or later your brother officers will hear of it and shun you like a leper. In war there is glory enough for all. Give the man under you his due. *The man who always takes and never gives is not a leader.* He is a parasite.

There is another kind of fairness—that which will prevent an officer from abusing the privileges of his rank. When you exact respect from soldiers be sure you treat them with equal respect. Build up their manhood and self-respect. Don't try to pull it down.

For an officer to be overbearing and insulting in the treatment of enlisted men is the act of a coward. He ties the man to a tree with the ropes of discipline and then strikes him in the face knowing full well that the man cannot strike back.

Consideration, courtesy and respect from officers toward enlisted men are not incompatible with discipline. They are parts of our discipline. Without initiative and decision no man can expect to lead.

In maneuvers you will frequently see, when an emergency arises, certain men calmly give instant orders which later, on analysis, prove to be, if not exactly the right thing, very nearly the right thing to have done. You will see other men in emergency become badly rattled; their brains refuse to work, or they give a hasty order, revoke it; give another, revoke that; in short, show every indication of being in a blue funk. Regarding the first man you may say: "That man is a genius. He hasn't had time to reason this thing out. He acts intuitively." Forget it! Genius is merely the capacity for taking infinite pains. The man who was ready is the man who has prepared himself. He has studied beforehand the possible situations that might arise; he has made tentative plans covering such situations. When he is confronted by the emergency he is ready to meet it. He must have sufficient mental alertness to appreciate the problem that confronts him and the power of quick reasoning to determine what changes are necessary in his already formulated plan. He must also have the decision to order the execution and stick to his orders.

Any reasonable order in an emergency is better than no order. The situation is there. Meet it. It is better to do something and do the wrong thing than to hesitate, hunt around for the right thing to do and wind up by doing nothing at all. And, having decided on a line of action, stick to it. Don't vacillate. Men have no confidence in an officer who doesn't know his own mind.

Occasionally you will be called upon to meet a situation which no reasonable human being could anticipate. If you have prepared yourself to meet other emergencies which you could anticipate, the mental training you have thereby gained will enable you to act promptly and with calmness.

You must frequently act without orders from higher authority. Time will not permit you to wait for them. Here again enters the importance of studying the work of officers above you. If you have a comprehensive grasp of the entire situation and can form an idea of the general plan of your superiors, that and your previous emergency training will enable you to determine that the responsibility is yours and to issue the necessary orders without delay.

The element of *personal dignity* is important in military leadership. Be the friend of your men, but do not become their intimate. Your men should stand in awe of you—not *fear!* If your men presume to become familiar it is your fault, and not theirs. Your actions have encouraged them to do so. And, above all things, don't cheapen yourself by courting their friendship or currying their favor. They will despise you for it. If you are worthy of their loyalty and respect and devotion they will surely give all these without asking. If you are not, nothing that you can do will win them.

It is exceedingly difficult for an officer to be dignified while wearing a dirty, spotted uniform and a three days' stubble of whiskers on his face. Such a man lacks self-respect, and self-respect is an essential of dignity.

There may be occasions when your work entails dirty clothes and an unshaved face. Your men all look that way. At such times there is ample reason for your appearance. In fact, it would be a mistake to look too clean—they would think that you were not doing your share. But as soon as this unusual occasion has passed set an example for personal neatness.

And then I would mention *courage*. Moral courage you need as well as mental courage—that kind of moral courage which enables you to adhere without faltering to a determined course of action, which your judgment has indicated is the one best suited to secure the desired results.

You will find many times, especially in action, that, after having issued your orders to do a certain thing, you will be beset by misgivings and doubts; you will see, or think you see, other and better means for accomplishing the object sought. You will be strongly tempted to change your orders. Don't do it until it is clearly manifested that your first orders were radically wrong. For, if you do, you will be again worried by doubts as to the efficacy of your second orders.

Every time you change your orders without obvious reason you weaken your authority and impair the confidence of your men. Have the moral courage to stand by your order and see it through.

Moral courage further demands that you assume the responsibility for your own acts. If your subordinates have loyally carried out your orders and the movement you directed is a failure the failure is *yours,* not theirs. Yours would have been the honor had it been successful. Take the blame if it results in disaster. Don't try to shift it to a subordinate and make him the goat. That is a cowardly act. Furthermore, you will need moral courage to determine the fate of those under you. You will frequently be called upon for recommendations for promotion or demotion of officers and non-commissioned officers in your immediate command.

Keep clearly in mind your *personal integrity* and the duty you owe your country. Do not let yourself be. deflected from a strict sense of justice by feelings of personal friendship. If your own brother is your sec-

THERE is something wrong about the man whose wife and children do not greet him affectionately on his homecoming.

ond lieutenant, and you find him unfit to hold his commission, eliminate him. If you don't your lack of moral courage may result in the loss of valuable lives.

If, on the other hand, you are called upon for a recommendation concerning a man whom, for personal reasons, you thoroughly dislike, do not fail to do him full justice. Remember that your aim is the general good, not the satisfaction of an individual grudge.

I am taking it for granted that you have physical courage. I need not tell you how necessary that is. Courage is more than bravery. Bravery is fearlessness —the absence of fear. The merest dolt may be brave, because he lacks the mentality to appreciate his danger; he doesn't know enough to be afraid.

Courage, however, is that firmness of spirit, that moral backbone which, while fully appreciating the danger involved, nevertheless goes on with the undertaking. Bravery is physical; courage is mental and moral. You may be cold all over; your hands may tremble; your legs may quake; your knees be ready to give way—that is fear. If, nevertheless, you go forward; if, in spite of this physical defection you continue to lead your men against the enemy, you have courage. The physical manifestations of fear will pass away. You may never experience them but once. They are the "buck fever" of the hunter who tries to shoot his first deer. You must not give way to them.

A number of years ago, while taking a course in demolitions, the class of which I was a member was handling dynamite. The instructor said, regarding its manipulation: "I must caution you gentlemen to be careful in the use of these explosives. One man has

but one accident." And so I would caution you. If
you give way to fear that will doubtless beset you in
your first action; if you show the white feather; if
you let your men go forward while you hunt a shell
crater, you will never again have the opportunity of
leading those men.

Use judgment in calling on your men for displays
of physical courage or bravery. *Don't ask any man to
go where you would not go yourself.* If your common
sense tells you that the place is too dangerous for you
to venture into, then it is too dangerous for him. You
know his life is as valuable to him as yours is to you.

*Occasionally some of your men must be exposed to
danger which you cannot share. A message must be
taken across a fire-swept zone. You call for volunteers. If your men know you and know that you are
"right" you will never lack volunteers, for they will
know your heart is in your work, that you are giving
your country the best you have, that you would willingly carry the message yourself if you could. Your
example and enthusiasm will have inspired them.*

And, lastly, if you aspire to leadership, I would
urge you to study men.

Get under their skins and find out what is inside.
Some men are quite different from what they appear
to be on the surface. Determine the workings of their
mind.

Much of General Robert E. Lee's success as a
leader may be ascribed to his ability as a *psychologist*.
He knew most of his opponents from West Point days;
knew the workings of their minds; and he believed
that they would do certain things under certain cir-

cumstances. In nearly every case he was able to anticipate their movements and block the execution.

You cannot know your opponent in this war in the same way. But you can know your own men. You can study each to determine wherein lies his strength and his weakness; which man can be relied upon to the last gasp and which cannot.

Know your men, know your business, know your-self!

.   .   .   .

In all literature you will not find a better description of *leadership* than this. Apply it to yourself, or to your business, or to your profession, or to the place where you are employed, and you will observe how well it serves as your guide.

Major Bach's address is one that might well be delivered to every boy and girl who graduates in high school. It might well be delivered to every college graduate. It might well become the book of rules for every man who is placed in a position of leadership over other men, no matter in what calling, business or profession.

In Lesson Two you learned the value of a *definite chief aim*. Let it be here emphasized that your aim must be active and not passive. A *definite aim* will never be anything else but a mere wish unless you become a person of initiative and *aggressively* and *persistently* pursue that aim until it has been fulfilled.

You can get nowhere without persistence, a fact which cannot be too often repeated.

The difference between persistence and lack of it is the same as the difference between wishing for a thing and positively determining to get it.

To become a person of initiative you must form the habit of *aggressively* and *persistently* following the object of your *definite chief aim* until you acquire it, whether this requires one year or twenty years. You might as well have no *definite chief aim* as to have such an aim without *continuous* effort to achieve it.

You are not making the most of this course if you do not take some step each day that brings you nearer realization of your *definite chief aim*. Do not fool yourself, or permit yourself to be misled to believe that the object of your *definite chief aim* will materialize if you only wait. The materialization will come through your own determination, backed by your own carefully laid plans and your own initiative in putting those plans into action, or it will not come at all.

One of the major requisites for Leadership is the power of quick and firm DECISION!

Analysis of more than 16,000 people disclosed the fact that Leaders are always men of ready decision, even in matters of small importance, while the follower is NEVER a person of quick decision.

This is worth remembering!

The follower, in whatever walk of life you find him, is a man who seldom knows what he wants. He vacillates, procrastinates, and actually refuses to reach a decision, even in matters of the smallest importance, unless a Leader induces him to do so.

To know that the majority of people cannot and will not reach decisions quickly, if at all, is of great help to the Leader who knows what he wants and has a plan for getting it.

Here it will be observed how closely allied are the two laws covered by Lesson Two and this lesson. The

Leader not only works with A DEFINITE CHIEF AIM, but he has a very definite plan for attaining the object of that aim. It will be seen, also, that the Law of Self-confidence becomes an important part of the working equipment of the Leader.

The chief reason why the follower does not reach decisions is that he lacks the Self-confidence to do so. Every Leader makes use of the Law of a Definite Purpose, the Law of Self-confidence and the Law of Initiative and Leadership. And if he is an outstanding, successful Leader he makes use, also, of the Laws of Imagination, Enthusiasm, Self-Control, Pleasing Personality, Accurate Thinking, Concentration and Tolerance. Without the combined use of all these Laws no one may become a really great Leader. Omission of a single one of these Laws lessens the power of the Leader proportionately.

A salesman for the LaSalle Extension University called on a real estate dealer, in a small western town, for the purpose of trying to sell the real estate man a course in Salesmanship and Business Management.

When the salesman arrived at the prospective student's office he found the gentleman pecking out a letter by the two-finger method, on an antiquated typewriter. The salesman introduced himself, then proceeded to state his business and describe the course he had come to sell.

The real estate man listened with apparent interest.

After the sales talk had been completed the salesman hesitated, waiting for some signs of "yes" or "no" from his prospective client. Thinking that perhaps he had not made the sales talk quite strong enough, he briefly went over the merits of the course he was

NO man may become
an accurate thinker
until he learns how to separate mere gossip and in-
formation from facts.

selling, a second time.   Still there was no response from the prospective student.

The salesman then asked the direct question, "You want this course, do you not?"

In a slow, drawling tone of voice, the real estate man replied:

"Well, I hardly know whether I do or not."

No doubt he was telling the truth, because he was one of the millions of men who find it hard to reach decisions.

Being an able judge of human nature the salesman then arose, put on his hat, placed his literature back in his brief case and made ready to leave.   Then he resorted to tactics which were somewhat drastic, and took the real estate man by surprise with this startling statement:

"I am going to take it upon myself to say something to you that you will not like, but it may be of help to you.

"Take a look at this office in which you work!   The floor is dirty; the walls are dusty; the typewriter you are using looks as if it might be the one Mr. Noah used in the Ark during the big flood; your pants are bagged at the knees; your collar is dirty; your face is unshaved, and you have a look in your eyes that tells me you are defeated.

"Please go ahead and get mad—that's just what I want you to do, because it may shock you into doing some thinking that will be helpful to you and to those who are dependent upon you.

"I can see, in my imagination, the home in which you live.   Several little children, none too well dressed, and perhaps none too well fed; a mother whose dress is three seasons out of style, whose eyes carry the same look of defeat that yours do. This little woman whom you married has stuck by you but you have not made good in life as she had hoped, when you were first married, that you would.

"Please remember that I am not now talking to a prospective student, because I would not sell you this course at THIS PARTICULAR MOMENT if you offered to pay cash in advance, because if I did you would not have the initiative to complete it, and we want no failures on our student list.

"The talk I am now giving you will make it impossible, perhaps, for me ever to sell you anything, but it is going to do something for you that has never been done before, providing it makes you think.

"Now, I will tell you in a very few words exactly why you are defeated; why you are pecking out letters on an old typewriter, in an old dirty office, in a little town: IT IS BECAUSE YOU DO NOT HAVE THE POWER TO REACH A DECISION!

"All your life you have been forming the habit of dodging the responsibility of reaching decisions, until you have come, now, to where it is well-nigh impossible for you to do so.

"If you had told me that you wanted the course, or that you did not want it, I could have sympathized with you, because I would have known that lack of funds was what caused you to hesitate, but what did you say? Why, you admitted you did not know whether you wanted it or not.

"If you will think over what I have said I am sure you will acknowledge that it has become a habit with you to dodge the responsibility of reaching clear-cut decisions on practically all matters that affect you."

The real estate man sat glued in his chair, with his under jaw dropped, his eyes bulged in astonishment, but he made no attempt to answer the biting indict-ment.

The salesman said good-bye and started for the door.

After he had closed the door behind him he again opened it, walked back in, with a smile on his face, took his seat in front of the astonished real estate man, and explained his conduct in this way:

"I do not blame you at all if you feel hurt at my remarks. In fact I sort of hope that you have been offended, but now let me say this, man to man, that I think you have intelligence and I am sure you have ability, but you have fallen into a habit that has whipped you. No man is ever down and out until he is under the sod. You may be temporarily down, but you can get up again, and I am just sportsman enough to give you my hand and offer you a lift, if you will accept my apologies for what I have said.

"You do not belong in this town. You would starve to death in the real estate business in this place, even if you were a Leader in your field. Get yourself a new suit of clothes, even if you have to borrow the money with which to do it, then go over to St. Louis with me and I will introduce you to a real estate man who will give you a chance to earn some money and at the same time teach you some of the important things about this line of work that you can capitalize later on.

"If you haven't enough credit to get the clothes you need I will stand good for you at a store in St. Louis where I have a charge account. I am in earnest and

my offer to help you is based upon the highest motive
that can actuate a human being. I am successful in
my own field, but I have not always been so. I went
through just what you are now going through, but, the
important thing is that I WENT THROUGH IT, and
got it over with, JUST AS YOU ARE GOING TO
DO IF YOU WILL FOLLOW MY ADVICE.

"Will you come with me?"

The real estate man started to arise, but his legs
wobbled and he sank back into his chair. Despite the
fact that he was a great big fellow, with rather pronounced manly qualities, known as the "he-man"
type, his emotions got the better of him and he actually wept.

He made a second attempt and got on his feet, shook
hands with the salesman, thanked him for his kindness, and said he was going to follow the advice, but
he would do so in his own way.

Calling for an application blank he signed for the
course on Salesmanship and Business Management,
made the first payment in nickels and dimes, and told
the salesman he would hear from him again.

Three years later this real estate man had an organization of sixty salesmen, and one of the most successful real estate businesses in the city of St. Louis.
The author of this course (who was advertising manager of the LaSalle Extension University at the time
this incident happened) has been in this real estate
man's office many times and has observed him over a
period of more than fifteen years. He is an entirely
different man from the person interviewed by the La-
Salle salesman over fifteen years ago, and the thing
that made him different is the same that will make

YOU different: it is the power of DECISION which is so essential to Leadership.

This real estate man is now a Leader in the real estate field. He is directing the efforts of other salesmen and helping them to become more efficient. This one change in his philosophy has turned temporary defeat into success. Every new salesman who goes to work for this man is called into his private office, before he is employed, and told the story of his own transformation, word for word just as it occurred when the LaSalle salesman first met him in his shabby little real estate office.

.   .   .   .

Some eighteen years ago the author of this course made his first trip to the little town of Lumberport, W. Va. At that time the only means of transportation leading from Clarksburg, the largest near-by center, to Lumberport, was the Baltimore & Ohio Railroad and an interurban electric line which ran within three miles of the town; one could walk the three miles if he chose.

Upon arrival at Clarksburg I found that the only train going to Lumberport in the forenoon had already gone, and not wishing to wait for the later afternoon train I made the trip by trolley, with the intention of walking the three miles. On the way down the rain began to pour, and those three miles had to be navigated on foot, through deep yellow mud. When I arrived at Lumberport my shoes and pants were muddy, and my disposition was none the better for the experience.

The first person I met was V. L. Hornor, who was

MASTERY of the Fifteen Laws of Success is the equivalent of an insurance policy against failure.

—*Samuel Gompers.*

then cashier of the Lumberport Bank. In a rather loud tone of voice I asked of him, "Why do you not get that trolley line extended from the junction over to Lumberport so your friends can get in and out of town without drowning in mud?"

"Did you see a river with high banks, at the edge of the town, as you came in?" he asked. I replied that I had seen it. "Well," he continued, "that's the reason we have no street cars running into town. The cost of a bridge would be about $100,000.00, and that is more than the company owning the trolley line is willing to invest. We have been trying for ten years to get them to build a line into town."

"Trying!" I exploded. "How hard have you tried?"

"We have offered them every inducement we could afford, such as free right of way from the junction into the town, and free use of the streets, but that bridge is the stumbling block. They simply will not stand the expense. Claim they cannot afford such an expense for the small amount of revenue they would receive from the three mile extension."

Then the Law of Success philosophy began to come to my rescue!

I asked Mr. Hornor if he would take a walk over to the river with me, that we might look at the spot that was causing so much inconvenience. He said he would be glad to do so.

When we got to the river I began to take inventory of everything in sight. I observed that the Baltimore & Ohio Railroad tracks ran up and down the river banks, on both sides of the river; that the county road crossed the river on a rickety wooden bridge, both approaches to which were over several strands of railroad track, as the railroad company had its switching yards at that point.

While we were standing there a freight train blocked the crossing and several teams stopped on both sides of the train, waiting for an opportunity to get through. The train kept the road blocked for about twenty-five minutes.

With this combination of circumstances in mind it required but little imagination to see that THREE DIFFERENT PARTIES were or could be interested in the building of the bridge such as would be needed to carry the weight of a street car.

It was obvious that the Baltimore & Ohio Railroad Company would be interested in such a bridge, because that would remove the county road from their switching tracks, and save them a possible accident on the crossing, to say nothing of much loss of time and expense in cutting trains to allow teams to pass.

It was also obvious that the County Commissioners would be interested in the bridge, because it would raise the county road to a better level and make it more serviceable to the public. And, of course the street railway company was interested in the bridge, but IT DID NOT WISH TO PAY THE ENTIRE COST.

All these facts passed through my mind as I stood there and watched the freight train being cut for the traffic to pass through.

A DEFINITE CHIEF AIM took place in my mind. Also, a definite plan for its attainment. The next day I got together a committee of townspeople, consisting of the mayor, councilmen and some leading citizens, and called on the Division Superintendent of the Bal-

timore & Ohio Railroad Company, at Grafton. We
convinced him that it was worth one third of the cost
of the bridge to get the county road off his company's
tracks. Next we went to the County Commissioners
and found them to be quite enthusiastic over the possibility of getting a new bridge by paying for only one
third of it. They promised to pay their one third
providing we could arrange for the other two thirds.

We then went to the president of the Traction
Company that owned the trolley line, at Fairmont, and
laid before him an offer to donate all the rights of
way and pay for two thirds of the cost of the bridge
providing he would begin building the line into town
promptly. We found him receptive, also.

Three weeks later a contract had been signed between the Baltimore & Ohio Railroad Company, the
Monongahela Valley Traction Company and the
County Commissioners of Harrison County, providing
for the construction of the bridge, one third of its cost
to be paid by each.

Two months later the right of way was being graded
and the bridge was under way, and three months after
that street cars were running into Lumberport on regular schedule.

This incident meant much to the town of Lumberport, because it provided transportation that enabled
people to get in and out of the town without undue
effort.

It also meant a great deal to me, because it served
to introduce me as one who "got things done." Two
very definite advantages resulted from this transaction. The Chief Counsel for the Traction Company
gave me a position as his assistant, and later on it was

the means of an introduction which led to my appointment as the advertising manager of the LaSalle Extension University.

Lumberport, W. Va., was then, and still is a small town, and Chicago was a large city and located a considerable distance away, but news of Initiative and Leadership has a way of taking on wings and traveling.

Four of the Fifteen Laws of Success were combined in the transaction described, namely: A DEFINITE CHIEF AIM, SELF-CONFIDENCE, IMAGINATION and INITIATIVE and LEADERSHIP. The Law of DOING MORE THAN PAID FOR also entered, somewhat, into the transaction, because I was not offered anything and in fact did not expect pay for what I did.

To be perfectly frank I appointed myself to the job of getting the bridge built more as a sort of challenge to those who said it could not be done than I did with the expectation of getting paid for it. By my attitude I rather intimated to Mr. Hornor that I could get the job done, and he was not slow to snap me up and put me to the test.

It may be helpful to call attention here to the part which IMAGINATION played in this transaction. For ten years the townspeople of Lumberport had been trying to get a street car line built into town. It must not be concluded that the town was without men of ability, because that would be inaccurate. In fact there were many men of ability in the town, but they had been making the mistake which is so commonly made by us all, of trying to solve their problem through one single source, whereas there were actually THREE SOURCES of solution available to them.

$100,000.00 was too much for one company to as-
sume, for the construction of a bridge, but when the
cost was distributed between three interested parties
the amount to be borne by each was more reasonable.

The question might be asked: "Why did not some of
the local townsmen think of this three-way solution?"

In the first place they were so close to their problem
that they failed to take a perspective, bird's-eye view
of it, which would have suggested the solution. This,
also, is a common mistake, and one that is always
avoided by great Leaders. In the second place these
townspeople had never before co-ordinated their efforts or worked as an organized group with the sole
purpose in mind of finding a way to get a street car
line built into town. This, also, is another common
error made by men in all walks of life—that of failure to work in unison, in a thorough spirit of co-
operation.

I, being an outsider, had less difficulty in getting
co-operative action than one of their own group might
have had. Too often there is a spirit of selfishness in
small communities which prompts each individual to
think that his ideas should prevail. It is an important part of the Leader's responsibility to induce people
to subordinate their own ideas and interests for the
good of the whole, and this applies to matters of a
civic, business, social, political, financial or industrial
nature.

Success, no matter what may be one's conception
of that term, is nearly always a question of one's ability to get others to subordinate their own individuali-
ties and follow a Leader. The Leader who has the
Personality and the Imagination to induce his follow-

TIME is the mighty hand that rocks the eternal cradle of progress and nurses struggling humanity through that period when man needs protection against his own ignorance.

ers to accept his plans and carry them out faithfully is always an able Leader.

The next lesson, on IMAGINATION, will take you still further into the art of tactful Leadership. In fact Leadership and Imagination are so closely allied and so essential for success that one cannot be successfully applied without the other. Initiative is the moving force that pushes the Leader ahead, but Imagination is the guiding spirit that tells him which way to go.

Imagination enabled the author of this course to analyze the Lumberport bridge problem, break it up into its three component parts, and assemble these parts in a practical working plan. Nearly every problem may be so broken up into parts which are more easily managed, as parts, than they are when assembled as a whole. Perhaps one of the most important advantages of Imagination is that it enables one to separate all problems into their component parts and to reassemble them in more favorable combinations.

It has been said that all battles in warfare are won or lost, not on the firing line, after the battle begins, but back of the lines, through the sound strategy, or the lack of it, used by the generals who plan the battles.

What is true of warfare is equally true in business, and in most other problems which confront us throughout life. We win or lose according to the nature of the plans we build and carry out, a fact which serves to emphasize the value of the Laws of Initiative and Leadership, Imagination, Self-confidence and a Definite Chief Aim. *With the intelligent use of these four laws one may build plans, for any purpose whatsoever, which cannot be defeated by any person or group of*

persons who do not employ or understand these laws.
There is no escape from the truth here stated!

ORGANIZED EFFORT is effort which is directed according to a plan that was conceived with the aid of Imagination, guided by a Definite Chief Aim, and given momentum with Initiative and Self-confidence. These four laws blend into one and become a power in the hands of a Leader. Without their aid effective leadership is impossible.

.   .   .   .

You are now ready for the lesson on Imagination. Read that lesson with the thought in mind of all that has been here stated and it will take on a deeper meaning.

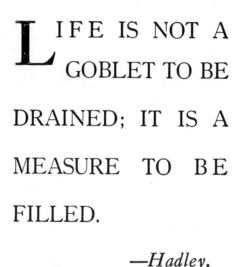

L IFE IS NOT A
GOBLET TO BE
DRAINED; IT IS A
MEASURE TO BE
FILLED.

—Hadley.

INTOLERANCE

An After-the-Lesson Visit With the Author

INTOLERANCE

If you must give expression to prejudice and hatred and intolerance, do not speak it, but write it; write it in the sands, near the water's edge.

When the dawn of Intelligence shall spread over the eastern horizon of human progress, and Ignorance and Superstition shall have left their last footprints on the sands of time, it will be recorded in the last chapter of the book of man's crimes that his most grievous sin was that of Intolerance.

The bitterest intolerance grows out of religious, racial and economic prejudices and differences of opinion. How long, O God, until we poor mortals will understand the folly of trying to destroy one another because we are of different religious beliefs and racial tendencies?

Our allotted time on this earth is but a fleeting moment. Like a candle, we are lighted, shine for a moment, and flicker out. Why can we not learn to so live during this brief earthly visit that when the great Caravan called Death

draws up and announces this visit completed
we will be ready to fold our tents and silently
follow out into the great unknown without fear
and trembling?

I am hoping that I will find no Jews or Gentiles, Catholics or Protestants, Germans, Englishmen or Frenchmen when I shall have
crossed the bar to the other side. I am hoping
that I will find there only human Souls,
Brothers and Sisters all, unmarked by race,
creed or color, for I shall want to be done with
intolerance so I may rest in peace throughout
eternity.

YOU will see at the top of the previous page a picture which describes the futility of combat.

The two male deer have engaged in a fight to the
finish, each believing that he will be the winner. Off
at the side the female awaits the victor, little dream-
ing that tomorrow the bones of both combatants will
be bleaching in the sun.

"Poor foolish animals," someone will say. Perhaps,
but not very different from the man family. Man
engages his brothers in mortal combat because of competition. The three major forms of competition are
sex, economic and religious in nature.

.   .   .   .

Twenty years ago a great educational institution
was doing a thriving business and rendering a worthy
service to thousands of students. The two owners of
the school married two beautiful and talented young
women, who were especially accomplished in the art
of piano playing. The two wives became involved in
an argument as to which one was the more accomplished in this art. The disagreement was taken up

by each of the husbands. They became bitter enemies. Now the bones of that once prosperous school
"lie bleaching in the sun."

The two bucks shown in the picture above locked
horns over the attention of the doe. The two "man
bucks" locked horns over the selfsame impulse.

. . . .

In one of the great industrial plants two young foremen "locked horns" because one received a promotion which the other believed he should have had. For
more than five years the silent undertow of hatred
and intolerance showed itself. The men under each
of the foremen became inoculated with the spirit of
dislike which they saw cropping out in their superiors. Slowly the spirit of retaliation began to spread
over the entire plant. The men became divided into
little cliques. Production began to fall off. Then
came financial difficulty and finally bankruptcy for the
company.

Now the bones of a once prosperous business "lie
bleaching in the sun," and the two foremen and several thousand others were compelled to start all over
again, in another field.

. . . .

Down in the mountains of West Virginia lived two
peaceful families of mountain-folk—the Hatfields and
the McCoys. They had been friendly neighbors for
three generations. A razor-back pig belonging to the
McCoy family crawled through the fence into the Hat-
field family's corn field. The Hatfields turned their
hound loose on the pig. The McCoys retaliated by
killing the dog. Then began a feud that has lasted

for three generations and cost many lives of the Hat-fields and McCoys.

In a fashionable suburb of Philadelphia certain gentlemen of wealth have built their homes. In front of each house the word "INTOLERANCE" is written. One man builds a high steel fence in front of his house. The neighbor next to him, not to be outdone, builds a fence twice as high. Another buys a new motor car and the man next door goes him one better by purchasing two new cars. One remodels his house adding a colonial style porch. The man next door adds a new porch and a Spanish style garage for good measure. The big mansion on top of the hill gives a reception which brings a long line of motor cars filled with people who have nothing in particular in common with the host. Then follows a series of "receptions" all down the "gold-coast" line, each trying to out-shine all the others.

The "Mister" (but they don't call him that in fash-ionable neighborhoods) goes to business in the back seat of a Rolls Royce that is managed by a chauffeur and a footman. Why does he go to business? To make money, of course! Why does he want more money when he already has millions of dollars? So he can keep on out-doing his wealthy neighbors.

Poverty has some advantages—it never drives those who are poverty-stricken to "lock horns" in the attempt to out-poverty their neighbors.

Wherever you see men with their "horns locked" in conflict you may trace the cause of the combat to one of the three causes of intolerance—religious dif-ference of opinion, economic competition or sex com-petition.

The next time you observe two men engaged in any sort of hostility toward each other, just close your eyes and THINK for a moment and you may see them, in their transformed nature, very much resembling the male deer shown in the picture above. Off at one side you may see the object of the combat—a pile of gold, a religious emblem or a female (or females).

Remember, the purpose of this essay is to tell some of the TRUTH about human nature, with the object of causing its readers to THINK. Its writer seeks no glory or praise, and likely he will receive neither in connection with this particular subject.

Andrew Carnegie and Henry C. Frick did more than any other two men to establish the steel industry. Both made millions of dollars for themselves. Came the day when economic intolerance sprang up between them. To show his contempt for Frick, Carnegie built a tall sky-scraper and named it the "Carnegie Building." Frick retaliated by erecting a much taller building, alongside of the Carnegie Building, naming it the "Frick Building."

These two gentlemen "locked horns" in a fight to the finish, Carnegie lost his mind, and perhaps more, for all we of this world know. What Frick lost is known only to himself and the keeper of the Great Records. In memory their "bones lie bleaching in the sun" of posterity.

The steel men of today are managing things differently. Instead of locking horns they now "interlock directorates," with the result that each is practically a solidified, strong unit of the whole industry. The steel men of today understand the dif-

ference between the meaning of the words COMPE-
TITION and CO-OPERATION; a difference which
the remainder of us would do well to understand, also.

.   .   .   .

In England the men who own the mines and those
who run the labor unions "locked horns." Had not
the cooler heads unlocked those horns the bones of
the British empire (including both the owners of industry and the labor unions) should soon have lain
"bleaching in the sun." One year of open combat between the unions and the owners of industry, in Great
Britain, would have meant annihilation of the British
empire. The other nations of the world would have
grabbed all the economic machinery now controlled by
Britain.

Let the leaders of American industry and unionism
not forget!

.   .   .   .

Fifteen factors enter into the attainment of SUC-
CESS. One of these is TOLERANCE. The other
fourteen are mentioned many times in this series of
lessons.

Intolerance binds man's legs with the shackles of
IGNORANCE and covers his eyes with the scales of
FEAR AND SUPERSTITION. Intolerance closes
the book of knowledge and writes on the cover "Open
not this book again. The last word has been herein
written."

It is not your DUTY to be tolerant; it is your
PRIVILEGE!

Remember, as you read this article, that sowing

the seed of INTOLERANCE is the sole and exclusive business of some men. All wars and all strikes and all other forms of human suffering bring profit to SOME. If this were not true there would be no wars or strikes or other similar forms of hostility.

In the United States today there is a well organized system of propaganda, the object of which is to stir up strife and hostility between the owners of industries and those who work in those industries. Take another look at the picture at the beginning of this article and you may see what will happen to all who lock horns in labor disagreements, and remember that it is always the bones of the workers (and not those of the leaders of either the unions or the industries) that "lie bleaching in the sun" after the fight is over.

.   .   .   .

When you feel yourself preparing to "lock horns" with someone remember that it will be more profitable if you LOCK HANDS instead! A warm, hearty hand-shake leaves no bones bleaching in the sun.

"LOVE is the only bow on life's dark cloud. It is the Morning and the Evening Star. It shines upon the cradle of the babe, and sheds its radiance upon the quiet tomb. It is the mother of Art, inspirer of poet, patriot and philosopher. It is the air and light of every heart, builder of every home, kindler of every fire on every hearth. It was the first to dream of immortality. It fills the world with melody, for Music is the voice of Love. Love is the magician, the enchanter, that changes worthless things to Joy, and makes right royal kings and queens of common clay. It is the perfume of the wondrous flower—the heart—and without that sacred passion, that divine swoon, we are less than beasts; but with it, earth is heaven and we are gods."

—INGERSOLL.

Cultivate LOVE for your fellow man and you will no longer want to lock horns with him in futile combat. Love makes every man his brother's keeper.

Love, indeed, is light from heaven;
A spark of that immortal fire
With angels shared, by Allah given,
To lift from earth our low desire.
Devotion wafts the mind above,
But heaven itself descends in love;
A feeling from the Godhead caught,
To wean from self each sordid thought;
A ray of Him who form'd the whole;
A glory circling round the soul:

—BYRON.

THE CALL FOR NEW LEADERS AND A NEW BRAND OF LEADERSHIP

The prolonged business depression which began in 1929 has served America as a moral physic which has cleansed it of a multitude of evils and paved the way for both a new group of leaders and a new brand of leadership.

The type of leadership of which America boasted before the depression, failed the people in the time of their greatest emergency. In practically no field of endeavor has this crisis brought into the limelight a real leader, a man of the qualities of genuine leadership. This astounding fact calls for a statement of the qualities which constitute leadership. These qualities are here outlined as a guide to those who aspire to leadership in the future.

20 QUALITIES WHICH FUTURE LEADERS MUST POSSESS

Rubber-spined men will have no part in the leadership of the future. They will have been supplanted because they lacked the qualities essential for leadership at a time when the whole country was literally bleeding to death because of poor leadership. Leaders of the future must possess these qualities:

(1) COMPLETE MASTERY OVER THE SIX BASIC FEARS.

(2) Willingness to subordinate personal interests for the good of their followers. Complete mastery over avarice and GREED.

(3) Singleness of purpose, represented by a definite program of leadership which harmonizes with the needs of the times.

143

(4) Understanding and application of the "Master Mind" principle, through which power may be achieved through coordination of effort in a spirit of HARMONY.

(5) Self-confidence in its highest form.

(6) Ability to reach DECISIONS quickly and to stand by them firmly.

(7) IMAGINATION sufficient to enable them to anticipate the needs of the times and to create plans for supplying those needs.

(8) INITIATIVE in its keenest form.

(9) Enthusiasm and the ability to transmit it to their followers.

(10) Self-control in its highest form.

(11) A willingness to render more service than that for which direct compensation is received.

(12) A pleasing, magnetic personality.

(13) The ability to THINK ACCURATELY.

(14) The ability to cooperate with others in a spirit of harmony.

(15) The persistence to concentrate thoughts and efforts upon a given task until it has been completed.

(16) The ability and "hind-sight" to profit by mistakes and failures.

(17) Tolerance in its highest form.

(18) Temperance in all of its forms.

(19) Intentional honesty of both purpose and deed.

(20) Last, but by no means least, strict adherence to the Golden Rule, as the basis of all relationships with others.

This may appear to be a formidable list of qualities with which the leader of the future must be equipped, but time will prove that those leaders who endure will possess and make use of every one of these qualities. Casual examination of the list will disclose the fact that the leaders of the future will be compelled to avoid the mistakes of the leaders of the past, the chief of which has been *exploitation of their followers.* Great fortunes accumulated at the expense of the masses will not be among the possessions of the leaders of the future.

Wise beyond room for comparison will be the aspirant to future leadership who realizes that no business or profession of the future may be successfully conducted without recognition of the fact that the followers and patrons of that business or profession are PARTNERS IN IT and, as such, are entitled to share in the benefits to be derived from it.

Successfully conducted businesses and professions of the future will be managed under a policy that is co-operative in nature and the leaders of such businesses and professions will regard themselves as quasi-public servants and not as individuals privileged to exploit the public for their own personal profit.

The politicians of the future will become servants of their constituency not in theory alone, but in FACT! The public official who fails to recognize this demand and to comply with it will be recalled from office IM-MEDIATELY. Special privilege in politics must pass. The future will not tolerate it. Government will be run on a business basis, and Government employees will give a full day's work for a day's pay, as in a well-managed business establishment. Moreover, employees will be chosen on merit rather than on the recommendation of politicians who have political debts to pay.

Before taking up the next lesson it may be helpful if you take inventory of yourself and determine your rating on the 20 qualities of leadership. Self-analysis always is beneficial, provided the analysis is accurate. Every essential for leadership can be cultivated by any person who makes a reasonable effort to apply the Law of Success philosophy.

If you wish to be certain that your self-analysis is accurate, give yourself a rating on the 20 qualities of leadership and then have it checked by two or three people who know you well enough to judge you accurately.

A simple method of rating yourself is this—

Copy the 20 qualities of leadership on a sheet of paper. After each of the qualities write the word "perfect, fair or poor" according to what you believe your rating to be. Perfect will entitle you to a rating of 5%, fair will entitle you to a rating of 2½% and poor should be rated as zero. Place these figures on your analysis sheet and add them. If the total gives you an average rating of less than 75% you will know that you are not yet passable as a leader in your chosen occupation. The chart will disclose where you are weak. Mastery of this philosophy will provide all you need with which to eliminate or bridge your weakness.

This self-analysis should be made before you pass on to the next lesson, because it will help you get more from that and all of the other lessons which follow. Remember, as you make this analysis, that its purpose is to let you see yourself as you are, through eyes that are dependable and friendly.

Lesson Six

IMAGINATION

I CALL THAT MAN

IDLE WHO

MIGHT BE BETTER

EMPLOYED.

—*Socrates.*

THE LAW OF SUCCESS
Lesson Six
IMAGINATION

"You Can Do It if You Believe You Can!"

MAGINATION is the workshop of the human mind wherein old ideas and established facts may be reassembled into new combinations and put to new uses. The modern dictionary defines *imagination* as follows:

"The act of constructive intellect in grouping the materials of knowledge or thought into new, original and rational systems; the constructive or creative faculty; embracing poetic, artistic, philosophic, scientific and ethical imagination.

"The picturing power of the mind; the formation of mental images, pictures, or mental representation of objects or ideas, particularly of objects of sense perception and of mathematical reasoning! also the reproduction and combination, usually with more or less irrational or abnormal modification, of the images or ideas of memory or recalled facts of experience."

Imagination has been called the creative power of the soul, but this is somewhat abstract and goes more deeply into the meaning than is necessary from the viewpoint of a student of this course who wishes to use the course only as a means of attaining material or monetary advantages in life.

If you have mastered and thoroughly understood the preceding lessons of this Reading Course you know that the materials out of which you built your *definite chief aim* were assembled and combined in your imagination. You also know that *self-confidence* and *initiative* and *leadership* must be created in your imagination before they can become a reality, for it is in the workshop of your imagination that you will put the principle of Auto-suggestion into operation in creating these necessary qualities.

This lesson on imagination might be called the "hub" of this Reading Course, because every lesson of the course leads to this lesson and makes use of the principle upon which it is based, just as all the telephone wires lead to the exchange office for their source of power. You will never have a *definite purpose* in life, you will never have *self-confidence,* you will never have *initiative* and *leadership* unless you first create these qualities in your *imagination* and see yourself in possession of them.

Just as the oak tree develops from the germ that lies in the acorn, and the bird develops from the germ that lies asleep in the egg, so will your material achievements grow out of the *organized* plans that you create in your *imagination.* First comes the thought; then organization of that thought into ideas and plans; then transformation of those plans into reality. The beginning, as you will observe, is in your *imagination.*

The imagination is both interpretative and creative in nature. It can examine facts, concepts and ideas, and it can create new combinations and plans out of these.

Through its interpretative capacity the imagination has one power not generally attributed to it; namely, the power to register vibrations and thought waves that are put into motion from outside sources, just as the radio-receiving apparatus picks up the vibrations of sound. The principle through which this interpretative capacity of the imagination functions is called telepathy; the communication of thought from one mind to another, at long or short distances, without the aid of physical or mechanical appliances, in the manner explained in the Introductory Lesson of this course.

Telepathy is an important factor to a student who is preparing to make effective use of imagination, for the reason that this telepathic capacity of the imagination is constantly picking up thought waves and vibrations of every description. So-called "snap-judgment" and "hunches," which prompt one to form an opinion or decide upon a course of action that is not in harmony with logic and reason, are usually the result of stray thought waves that have registered in the imagination.

The recently developed radio apparatus has enabled us to understand that the elements of the ether are so sensitive and alive that all manner of sound waves are constantly flying here and there with lightning-like speed. You have only to understand the modern radio outfit to understand, also, the principle of telepathy. So well has this principle been established, through psychological research, that we have abundance of proof that two minds which are properly attuned and in harmony with each other may send and receive thought at long distances without the aid of mechanical apparatus of any sort. Rarely have two minds become so well attuned that unbroken chains of thought could be registered in this manner, but there is evidence sufficient to establish the fact that parts of organized thought have been picked up.

That you may understand how closely interwoven are the fifteen factors upon which this Reading Course is based, consider, for example, what happens when a salesman who lacks confidence in himself, and in his goods, walks in to see a prospective buyer. Whether the prospective buyer is conscious of it or not, his imagination immediately "senses" that lack of confidence in the salesman's mind. The salesman's own *thoughts* are actually undermining his efforts. This will explain, from another angle, why *self-confidence* is one of the most important factors entering into the great struggle for success.

The principle of telepathy and the law of attraction, through which like attracts like, explain many a failure. If the mind has a tendency to attract from the ether those thought vibrations which harmonize with the dominating thoughts of a given mind, you can easily understand why a negative mind that dwells upon failure and lacks the vitalizing force of self-confidence would not attract a positive mind that is dominated by thoughts of *success*.

Perhaps these explanations are somewhat abstract to the student who has not made any particular study of the functioning processes of the mind, but it seems necessary to inject them into this lesson as a means of enabling the student to understand and make practical use of the subject of this lesson. The imagination is too often regarded merely as an indefinite, untraceable, indescribable something that does nothing but create fiction. It is this popular disregard of the powers of the imagination that has made necessary these more or less abstract references to one of the most important subjects of this course. Not only is the subject of imagination an important factor in this course; but, it is one of the most interesting subjects, as you will observe when you begin to see how it affects all that you do toward the achievement of your *definite chief aim.*

You will see how important is the subject of *imagination* when you stop to realize that it is the only thing in the world over which you have absolute control. Others may deprive you of your material wealth and cheat you in a thousand ways, but no man can deprive you of the control and use of your *imagination.* Men may deal with you unfairly, as men often do; they may deprive you of your liberty, but *they cannot* take from you the privilege of using your *imagination* as you wish.

The most inspiring poem in all literature was written by Leigh Hunt, while he was a poverty-stricken prisoner in an English prison, where he had been unjustly confined because of his advanced views on politics. This poem is entitled Abou Ben Adhem, and it is here re-printed as a reminder that one of the great things a man may do, in his own imagination, is to forgive those who have dealt unjustly with him:

Abou Ben Adhem (may his tribe increase)
Awoke one night from a deep dream of peace,

THE MAN WHO SLANDERS HIS FELLOWMAN UN- WITTINGLY UNCOV- ERS THE REAL NA- TURE OF HIS INNER SELF.

And saw within the moonlight of his room,
Making it rich and like a lily in bloom,
An angel writing in a book of gold,
Exceeding peace had made Ben Adhem bold,
And to the presence in the room he said:
"What writest thou?"—the vision raised its head,
And, with a look made of all sweet accord,
Answered, "The names of those who love the Lord."
"And is mine one?" said Abou. "Nay, not so,"
Replied the angel,—Abou spoke more low,
But cheerily still; and said, "I pray thee, then,
Write me as one that loves his fellow men."
The angel wrote, and vanished. The next night
It came again, with a great wakening light,
And showed the names whom love of God had blessed,
And, lo! Ben Adhem's name led all the rest!

Civilization, itself, owes its existence to such men as Leigh Hunt, in whose fertile *imaginations* have been pictured the higher and nobler standards of human relationship. Abou Ben Adhem is a poem that will never die, thanks to this man who pictured in his *imagination* the hope of an ideal that is constructive.

The major trouble with this world today lies in our lack of understanding of the power of *imagination*, for if we understood this great power we could use it as a weapon with which to wipe out poverty and misery and injustice and persecution, and this could be done in a single generation. This is a rather broad statement, and no one understands better than the author of this course how useless such a statement would be if the principle upon which it is founded were not explained in terms of the most practical, workaday

nature; therefore, let us proceed to describe what is
meant.

To make this description understandable we must
accept as a reality the principle of telepathy, through
the operation of which every thought we release is
registering itself in the minds of other people. We
need devote no time to proving that telepathy is a
reality, for the reason that this lesson on *imagination*
cannot be of the slightest value to the student who
has not sufficiently informed himself to understand
and accept telepathy as an established principle. We
will take it for granted that you are one who accepts
and understands this principle.

You have often heard of "mob psychology," which
is nothing more nor less than some strong, dominating
idea that has been created in the mind of one or more
persons and registers itself in the minds of other persons, through the principle of telepathy. So strong
is the power of mob psychology that two men fighting
in the street will often start a "free-for-all" fight in
which by-standers will engage each other in battle
without even knowing what they are fighting about,
or with whom they are fighting.

On armistice day, 1918, we had evidence in abundance to prove the reality of the principle of telepathy,
on a scale such as the world had never before witnessed. I remember, distinctly, the impression made
on my mind on that eventful day. So strong was this
impression that it awakened me at about 3:00 o'clock
in the morning, just as effectively as if someone had
aroused me by physical force. As I sat up in bed I
knew that something out of the ordinary had happened, and so strange and impelling was the effect of

this experience that I got up, dressed myself and went out in the streets of Chicago. where I was met by thousands of others who had felt the touch of the same influence. Everyone was asking: *"What has happened?"*

What had happened was this:

Millions of men had received instructions to cease fighting, and their combined joy set into motion a thought wave that swept the entire world and made itself felt in every normal mind that was capable of registering this thought wave. Perhaps never in the history of the world had so many millions of people *thought of the same thing, in the same manner, at the same time.* For once in the history of the world *every-body* felt something in common, and the effect of this harmonized thought was the world-wide "mob psy-chology" that we witnessed on armistice day. In connection with this statement it will be helpful if you recall what was said about the method of creating a "Master Mind," through the harmony of thought of two or more persons, in the Introductory Lesson of this course.

We will bring the application of this principle a little nearer home by showing how it may be made to make or break the harmonious working relationship of a business or industry. You may not have satisfied yourself that it was the harmony of thought of mil-lions of soldiers that registered in the minds of the people of the world and caused the "mob" psychologi-cal condition that was everywhere in evidence on armistice day, but you will need no proof that a dis-gruntled person always disturbs everyone with whom he comes in contact. It is a well established fact that

one such person in a place of employment will disrupt
the entire organization. The time is almost at hand
when neither the workers nor the employers will tolerate the typical "grouch" inside of a place of employment, for the reason that his state of mind registers
itself in the minds of those about him, resulting in
distrust, suspicion and lack of harmony. The time is
near at hand when the workers in a place of employment will no more tolerate one of their own rank and
file who is a typical "grouch" than they would a poisonous snake.

Apply the principle in another way: Place among
a group of workers one person whose personality is
of the positive, optimistic type, and who makes it his
business to sow the seeds of harmony around the place
where he works, and his influence will reflect itself in
every person who works with him.

If every business is "the extended shadow of one
man" as Emerson stated, then it behooves that one
man to reflect a shadow of confidence and good cheer
and optimism and harmony, that these qualities may,
in turn, reflect themselves in all who are connected
with the business.

In passing to the next step in our application of
the power of *imagination* in the attainment of success
we will cite some of the most recent and modern examples of its use in the accumulation of material
wealth and the perfection of some of the leading inventions of the world.

In approaching this next step it should be borne in
mind that "there is nothing new under the sun." Life
on this earth may be likened to a great kaleidoscope
before which the scenes and facts and material sub-

stances are ever shifting and changing, and all any man can do is to take these facts and substances and re-arrange them in new combinations.

The process through which this is done is called *imagination.*

We have stated that the *imagination* is both interpretative and creative in its nature. It can receive impressions or ideas and out of these it can form new combinations.

As our first illustration of the power of *imagination* in modern business achievement, we will take the case of Clarence Saunders, who organized the Piggly-Wiggly system of self-help grocery stores.

Saunders was a grocery clerk in a small southern retail store. One day he was standing in a line, with a tin tray in his hands, waiting his turn to secure food in a cafeteria. He had never earned more than $20.00 a week before that time, and no one had ever noticed anything about him that indicated unusual ability, but something took place in his mind, as he stood in that line of waiting people, that put his *imagination* to work. With the aid of his *imagination* he lifted that "self-help" idea out of the cafeteria in which he found it (not creating anything new, merely shifting an old idea into a new use) and set it down in a grocery store. In an instant the Piggly-Wiggly chain-store grocery plan had been created and Clarence Saunders the twenty-dollar-a-week grocery clerk rapidly became the million-dollar chain-store groceryman of America.

Where, in that transaction, do you see the slightest indication of a performance that you could not duplicate?

IT will make a big dif-
ference to you whether
you are a person with a
message or a person with
a grievance.

Analyze this transaction and measure it by the previous lessons of this course and you will see that Clarence Saunders created a very *definite purpose.* He supported this purpose with sufficient *self-confidence* to cause him to take the *initiative* to transform it into reality. His *imagination* was the workshop in which these three factors, *definite purpose, self-confidence* and *initiative* were brought together and made to supply the momentum for the first step in the organization of the Piggly-Wiggly plan.

Thus are great ideas changed into realities.

When Thomas A. Edison invented the incandescent electric light bulb he merely brought together two old, well known principles and associated them in a new combination. Mr. Edison and practically all others who were informed on the subject of electricity, knew that a light could be produced by heating a small wire with electricity, but the difficult problem was to do this without burning the wire in two. In his experimental research Mr. Edison tried out every conceivable sort of wire, hoping to find some substance that would withstand the tremendous heat to which it had to be subjected before a light could be produced.

His invention was half completed, but it was of no practical value until he could find the missing link that would supply the other half. After thousands of tests and much combining of old ideas in his *imagination,* Edison finally found this missing link. In his study of physics he had learned, as all other students of this subject learn, that there can be no combustion without the presence of oxygen. He of course knew that the difficulty with his electric light apparatus was the lack of a method through which to control the heat.

When it occurred to him that there could be *no* combustion where there was *no* oxygen he placed the little wire of his electric light apparatus inside of a glass globe, shut out *all* the oxygen, and lo! the mighty incandescent light was a reality.

When the sun goes down tonight you step to the wall, press a button and bring it back again, a performance that would have mystified the people of a few generations ago, and yet there is no mystery back of your act. Thanks to the use of Edison's *imagination*, you have simply brought together two principles both of which were in existence since the beginning of time.

No one who knew him intimately ever accredited Andrew Carnegie with unusual ability, or the power of genius, except in one respect, and that was his ability to select men who *could* and *would* co-operate in a spirit of harmony, in carrying out his wishes. But what additional ability did he need in the accumulation of his millions of dollars?

Any man who understands the principle of *organized effort*, as Carnegie understood it, and knows enough about men to be able to select just those types that are needed in the performance of a given task, could duplicate all that Carnegie accomplished.

Carnegie was a man of *imagination*. He first created a *definite purpose* and then surrounded himself with men who had the training and the vision and the capacity necessary for the transformation of that purpose into reality. Carnegie did not always create his own plans for the attainment of his *definite purpose*. He made it *his* business to know what he wanted, then found the men who could create plans through which to procure it. And that was not only *imagination*, it was genius of the highest order.

But it should be made clear that men of Mr. Carnegie's type are not the only ones who can make profitable use of *imagination*. This great power is as available to the beginner in business as it is to the man who has "arrived."

One morning Charles M. Schwab's private car was backed on the side-track at his Bethlehem Steel plant. As he alighted from his car he was met by a young man stenographer who announced that he had come to make sure that any letters or telegrams Mr. Schwab might wish to write would be taken care of promptly. No one told this young man to be on hand, but he had enough *imagination* to see that his being there would not hurt his chances of advancement. From that day on, this young man was "marked" for promotion. Mr. Schwab singled him out for promotion because he had done that which any of the dozen or so other stenographers in the employ of the Bethlehem Steel Company might have done, but didn't. Today this same man is the president of one of the largest drug concerns in the world and has all of this world's goods and wares that he wants and much more than he needs.

A few years ago I received a letter from a young man who had just finished Business College, and who wanted to secure employment in my office. With his letter he sent a crisp ten-dollar bill that had never been folded. The letter read as follows:

"I have just finished a commercial course in a first-class business college and I want a position in your office because I realize how much it would be worth to a young man, just starting out on his business career, to have the privilege of working under the direction of a man like you.

"If the enclosed ten-dollar bill is sufficient to pay for the time you would spend in giving me my first week's instructions I want you to accept it. I will work the first month without pay and you may set my wages after that at whatever I prove to be worth.

"I want this job more than I ever wanted anything in my life and I am willing to make any reasonable sacrifice to get it.   Very cordially,"

This young man got his chance in my office. His *imagination* gained for him the opportunity that he wanted, and before his first month had expired the president of a life insurance company who heard of this incident offered the young man a private secretaryship at a substantial salary. He is today an official of one of the largest life insurance companies in the world.

Some years ago a young man wrote to Thomas A. Edison for a position. For some reason Mr. Edison did not reply. By no means discouraged on this account the young man made up his mind that he would not only get a reply from Mr. Edison, but what was more important still, he would actually secure the position he sought. He lived a long distance from West Orange, New Jersey, where the Edison industries are located, and he did not have the money with which to pay his railroad fare. But *he did have imagination.* He went to West Orange in a freight car, got his interview, told his story in person and got the job he sought.

Today this same man lives in Bradentown, Florida.

He has retired from active business, having made all the money he needs. His name, in case you wish to confirm my statements, is Edwin C. Barnes.

By using his *imagination,* Mr. Barnes saw the advantage of close association with a man like Thomas A. Edison. He saw that such an association would give him the opportunity to study Mr. Edison, and at the same time it would bring him in contact with Mr. Edison's friends, who are among the most influential people of the world.

These are but a few cases in connection with which I have personally observed how men have climbed to high places in the world and accumulated wealth in abundance by making practical use of their *imagination.*

Theodore Roosevelt engraved his name on the tablets of time by one single act during his tenure of office as President of the United States, and after all else that he did while in that office will have been forgotten this one transaction will record him in history as a man of *imagination.*

He started the steam shovels to work on the Panama Canal.

Every President, from Washington on up to Roosevelt, could have started the canal and it would have been completed, but it seemed such a colossal undertaking that it required not only *imagination* but daring courage as well. Roosevelt had both, and the people of the United States have the canal.

At the age of forty—the age at which the average man begins to think he is too old to start anything new —James J. Hill was still sitting at the telegraph key, at a salary of $30.00 per month. He had no capital.

THE reason most people do not like to hear the story of your troubles is that they have a big flock of their own.

He had no influential friends with capital, but he did have that which is more powerful than either—*imagination*.

In his mind's eye he saw a great railway system that would penetrate the undeveloped northwest and unite the Atlantic and Pacific oceans. So vivid was his *imagination* that he made others see the advantages of such a railway system, and from there on the story is familiar enough to every school-boy. I would emphasize the part of the story that most people never mention—that Hill's Great Northern Railway system became a reality in his own *imagination* first. The railroad was built with steel rails and wooden cross ties, just as other railroads are built, and these things were paid for with capital that was secured in very much the same manner that capital for all railroads is secured, but if you want the real story of James J. Hill's success you must go back to that little country railway station where he worked at $30.00 a month and there pick up the little threads that he wove into a mighty railroad, with materials no more visible than the thoughts which he organized in his *imagination*.

What a mighty power is *imagination,* the workshop of the soul, in which *thoughts* are woven into railroads and skyscrapers and mills and factories and all manner of material wealth.

"I hold it true that thoughts are things;
    They're endowed with bodies and breath and wings;
    And that we send them forth to fill
    The world with good results or ill.
    That which we call our secret thought

Speeds forth to earth's remotest spot,
Leaving its blessings or its woes,
Like tracks behind it as it goes.
We build our future, thought by thought,
For good or ill, yet know it not,
Yet so the universe was wrought.
Thought is another name for fate;
Choose, then, thy destiny and wait,
For love brings love and hate brings hate."

If your *imagination* is the mirror of your soul, then you have a perfect right to stand before that mirror and see yourself as you wish to be. You have the right to see reflected in that magic mirror the mansion you intend to own, the factory you intend to manage, the bank of which you intend to be president, the station in life you intend to occupy. *Your imagination* belongs to you! Use it! The more you use it the more efficiently it will serve you.

At the east end of the great Brooklyn Bridge, in New York City, an old man conducts a cobbler shop. When the engineers began driving stakes and marking the foundation place for that great steel structure this man shook his head and said *"It can't be done!"*

Now he looks out from his dingy little shoe-repair shop, shakes his head and asks himself: *"How did they do it?"*

He saw the bridge grow before his very eyes and still he lacks the *imagination* to analyze that which he saw. The engineer who planned the bridge saw it a reality long before a single shovel of dirt had been removed for the foundation stones. The bridge became a reality in his *imagination* because he had trained that *imagination* to weave new combinations out of old ideas.

Through recent experiments in the department of electricity one of our great educational institutions of America has discovered how to put flowers to sleep and wake them up again, with electric "sunlight." This discovery makes possible the growth of vegetables and flowers without the aid of sunshine. In a few more years the city dweller will be raising a crop of vegetables on his back porch, with the aid of a few boxes of dirt and a few electric lights, with some new vegetable maturing every month of the year.

This new discovery, plus a little *imagination*, plus Luther Burbank's discoveries in the field of horticulture, and lo! the city dweller will not only grow vegetables all the year around, within the confines of his back porch, but he will grow bigger vegetables than any which the modern gardener grows in the open sunlight.

In one of the cities on the coast of California all of the land that was suitable for building lots had been developed and put into use. On one side of the city there were some steep hills that could not be used for building purposes, and on the other side the land was unsuitable for buildings because it was so low that the back-water covered it once a day.

A man of *imagination* came to this city. Men of *imagination* usually have keen minds, and this man was no exception. The first day of his arrival he saw the possibilities for making money out of real estate. He secured an option on those hills that were unsuitable for use because of their steepness. He also secured an option on the ground that was unsuitable for use

because of the back-water that covered it daily. He
secured these options at a very low price because the
ground was supposed to be without substantial value.

With the use of a few tons of explosives he turned
those steep hills into loose dirt. With the aid of a
few tractors and some road scrapers he leveled the
ground down and turned it into beautiful building lots,
and with the aid of a few mules and carts he dumped
the surplus dirt on the low ground and raised it above
the water level, thereby turning it into beautiful building lots.

He made a substantial fortune, *for what?*

For removing some dirt from where it was not needed
to where it was needed! *For mixing some useless dirt
with imagination!*

The people of that little city gave this man credit
for being a genius; and he was—the same sort of
genius that any one of them could have been had he
used his *imagination* as this man used his.

In the field of chemistry it is possible to mix two
or more chemical ingredients in such proportions that
the mere act of mixing gives each of the ingredients
a tremendous amount of energy that it did not possess.
It is also possible to mix certain chemical ingredients
in such proportions that *all the ingredients of the combination take on an entirely different nature,* as in the
case of H_2O, which is a mixture of two parts hydrogen
and one part oxygen, creating water.

Chemistry is not the only field in which a combination of various physical materials can be so assembled
that each takes on a greater value, or the result is a
product entirely foreign in nature to that of its component parts. The man who blew up those useless

hills of dirt and stone and removed the surplus from where it was not needed over to the low-land, where it was needed, gave that dirt and stone a value that it did not have before.

A ton of pig-iron is worth but little. Add to that pig-iron carbon, silicon, manganese, sulphur and phosphorus, in the right proportions, and you have transformed it into steel, which is of much greater value. Add still other substances, in the right proportion, including some skilled labor, and that same ton of steel is transformed into watch-springs worth a small fortune. But, in all these transformation processes the one ingredient that is worth most is the one that has no material form—*imagination!*

Here lie great piles of loose brick, lumber, nails and glass. In its present form it is worse than useless for it is a nuisance and an eye-sore. But mix it with the architect's *imagination* and add some skilled labor and lo! it becomes a beautiful mansion worth a king's ransom.

On one of the great highways between New York and Philadelphia stood an old ramshackle, time-worn barn, worth less than fifty dollars. With the aid of a little lumber and some cement, plus *imagination,* this old barn has been turned into a beautiful automobile supply station that earns a small fortune for the man who supplied the *imagination.*

Across the street from my office is a little print-shop that earns coffee and rolls for its owner and his helper, but no more. Less than a dozen blocks away stands one of the most modern printing plants in the world, whose owner spends most of his time traveling and has far more wealth than he will ever use. Twenty-two

I KNOW I am here. I know I had nothing to do with my coming, and I shall have but little, if anything, to do with my going, therefore I will not worry because worries are of no avail.

years ago those two printers were in business together.

The one who owns the big print-shop had the good judgment to ally himself with a man who mixed *imagination* with printing. This man of *imagination* is a writer of advertisements and he keeps the printing plant with which he is associated supplied with more business than it can handle by analyzing its clients' business, creating attractive advertising features and supplying the necessary printed material with which to make these features of service. This plant receives top-notch prices for its printing because the *imagination* mixed with that printing produces a product that most printers cannot supply.

In the city of Chicago the level of a certain boulevard was raised, which spoiled a row of beautiful residences because the side-walk was raised to the level of the second story windows. While the property owners were bemoaning their ill-fortune a man of *imagination* came along, purchased the property for a "song," converted the second stories into business property, and now enjoys a handsome income from his rentals.

As you read these lines please keep in mind all that was stated in the beginning of this lesson; especially the fact that the greatest and most profitable thing you can do with your *imagination* is the act of rearranging old ideas in new combinations.

If you properly use your imagination it will help you convert your failures and mistakes into assets of priceless value; it will lead you to discovery of a truth known only to those who use their *imagination;* namely, that the greatest reverses and misfortunes of life often open the door to golden opportunities.

One of the finest and most highly paid engravers in the United States was formerly a mail-carrier. One day he was fortunate enough to be on a street car that met with an accident and had one of his legs cut off. The street railway company paid him $5,000.00 for his leg. With this money he paid his way through school and became an engraver. The product of his hands, plus his *imagination*, is worth much more than he could earn with his legs, as a mail-carrier. He discovered that he had *imagination* when it became necessary to re-direct his efforts, as a result of the street car accident.

You will never know what is your capacity for achievement until you learn how to mix your efforts with *imagination*. The products of your hands, minus *imagination*, will yield you but a small return, but those selfsame hands, when properly guided by *imagination*, can be made to earn you all the material wealth you can use.

There are two ways in which you can profit by *imagination*. You can develop this faculty in your own mind, or you can ally yourself with those who have already developed it. Andrew Carnegie did both. He not only made use of his own fertile *imagination*, but he gathered around him a group of other men who also possessed this essential quality, for his *definite* purpose in life called for specialists whose *imagination* ran in numerous directions. In that group of men that constituted Mr. Carnegie's "master mind" were men whose *imaginations* were confined to the field of chemistry. He had other men in the group whose *imaginations* were confined to finances. He had still others whose *imaginations* were confined to salesmanship, one of whom was Charles M. Schwab, who is said to have been the most able salesman on Mr. Carnegie's staff.

If you feel that your own *imagination* is inadequate you should form an alliance with someone whose *imagination* is sufficiently developed to supply your deficiency. There are various forms of alliance. For example, there is the alliance of marriage and the alliance of a business partnership and the alliance of friendship and the alliance of employer and employee. Not all men have the capacity to serve their own best interests as employers, and those who haven't this capacity may profit by allying themselves with men of *imagination* who have such capacity.

It is said that Mr. Carnegie made more millionaires of his employees than any other employer in the steel business. Among these was Charles M. Schwab, who displayed evidence of the soundest sort of *imagination* by his good judgment in allying himself with Mr. Carnegie. It is no disgrace to serve in the capacity of employee. To the contrary, it often proves to be the most profitable side of an alliance since not all men are fitted to assume the responsibility of directing other men.

Perhaps there is no field of endeavor in which *imagination* plays such an important part as it does in salesmanship. The master salesman sees the merits of the goods he sells or the service he is rendering, in his own *imagination,* and if he fails to do so he will not make the sale.

A few years ago a sale was made which is said to have been the most far-reaching and important sale of its kind ever made. The object of the sale was not merchandise, but the freedom of a man who was confined in the Ohio penitentiary and the development of a prison reform system that promises a sweeping change in the method of dealing with unfortunate men and women who have become entangled in the meshes of the law.

That you may observe just how *imagination* plays the leading part in salesmanship I will analyze this sale for you, with due apologies for personal references, which cannot be avoided without destroying much of the value of the illustration.

A few years ago I was invited to speak before the inmates of the Ohio penitentiary. When I stepped upon the platform I saw in the audience before me a man whom I had known as a successful business man, more than ten years previously. That man was B——, whose pardon I later secured, and the story of whose release has been spread upon the front page of practically every newspaper in the United States. Perhaps you will recall it.

After I had completed my address I interviewed Mr. B—— and found out that he had been sentenced for forgery, for a period of twenty years. After he had told me his story I said:

"I will have you out of here in less than sixty days!"

With a forced smile he replied: "I admire your spirit but question your judgment. Why, do you know that at least twenty influential men have tried every means at their command to get me released, without success? *It can't be done!*"

I suppose it was that last remark—*It can't be done* —that challenged me to show him that it could be done. I returned to New York City and requested my wife to pack her trunks and get ready for an indefinite stay in the city of Columbus, where the Ohio penitentiary is located.

I had a *definite purpose* in mind! That purpose was to get B—— out of the Ohio penitentiary. Not only did I have in mind securing his release, but I intended to do it in such a way that his release would erase from his breast the scarlet letter of "convict" and at the same time reflect credit upon all who helped to bring about his release.

Not once did I doubt that I would bring about his release, for no salesman can make a sale if he doubts that he can do it. My wife and I returned to Columbus and took up permanent headquarters.

The next day I called on the governor of Ohio and stated the object of my visit in about these words:

"Governor: I have come to ask you to release B—— from the Ohio penitentiary. I have sound reason for asking his release and I hope you will give him his freedom at once, but I have come prepared to stay until he is released, no matter how long that may be.

"During his imprisonment B—— has inaugurated a system of correspondence instruction in the Ohio penitentiary, as you of course know. He has influenced 1729 of the 2518 prisoners of the Ohio penitentiary to take up courses of instruction. He has managed to beg sufficient textbooks and lesson materials with which to keep these men at work on their lessons, and has done this without a penny of expense to the state of Ohio. The warden and the chaplain of the penitentiary tell me that he has carefully observed the prison rules. Surely a man who can influence 1729 men to turn

IF you have been wise and successful I congratulate you; unless you are unable to forget how successful you have been, then I pity you.

their efforts toward self-betterment cannot be a very
bad sort of fellow.

"I have come to ask you to release B—— because
I wish to place him at the head of a prison school that
will give the 160,000 inmates of the other penitentiaries
of the United States a chance to profit by his influence.
I am prepared to assume full responsibility for his
conduct after his release.

"That is my case, but, before you give me your
answer, I want you to know that I am not unmindful
of the fact that your enemies will probably criticize
you if you release him; in fact if you release him it
may cost you many votes if you run for office again."

With his fist clinched and his broad jaw set firmly
Governor Vic Donahey of Ohio said:

"If that is what you want with B—— I will release
him if it costs me five thousand votes. However, before I sign the pardon I want you to see the Clemency
Board and secure its favorable recommendation. I
want you also to secure the favorable recommendation of the warden and the chaplain of the Ohio
penitentiary. You know a governor is amenable to
the Court of Public Opinion, and these gentlemen are
the representatives of that Court."

The sale had been made! and the whole transaction
had required less than five minutes.

The next day I returned to the governor's office,
accompanied by the chaplain of the Ohio penitentiary,
and notified the governor that the Clemency Board,
the Warden and the Chaplain all joined in recommending the release. Three days later the pardon was
signed and B—— walked through the big iron gates,
a free man.

I have cited the details to show you that there was nothing difficult about the transaction. The groundwork for the release had all been prepared before I came upon the scene. B—— had done that, by his good conduct and the service he had rendered those 1729 prisoners. When he created the world's first prison correspondence school system he created the key that unlocked the prison doors for himself.

Why, then, had the others who asked for his release failed to secure it?

They failed because they used no *imagination!*

Perhaps they asked the governor for B——'s release on the ground that his parents were prominent people, or on the ground that he was a college graduate and not a bad sort of fellow. *They failed to supply the governor of Ohio with a sufficient motive to justify him in granting a pardon,* for had this not been so he would undoubtedly have released B—— long before I came upon the scene and asked for his release.

Before I went to see the governor I went over all the facts and in my own *imagination* I saw myself in the governor's place and made up my mind what sort of a presentation would appeal most strongly to me if I were in reality in his place.

When I asked for B——'s release I did so in the name of the 160,000 unfortunate men and women inmates of the prisons of the United States who would enjoy the benefits of the correspondence school system that he had created. I said nothing about his prominent parents. I said nothing about my friendship with him during former years. I said nothing about his being a deserving fellow. All these matters might have been used as sound reasons for his release, but they seemed insignificant when compared with the bigger and sounder reason that his release would be of help to 160,000 other people who would feel the influence of his correspondence school system after his release.

When the governor of Ohio came to a decision I doubt not that B—— was of secondary importance as far as his decision was concerned. The governor no doubt saw a possible benefit, not to B—— alone, but to 160,000 other men and women who needed the influence that B—— could supply, if released.

And that was imagination!

It was also salesmanship! In speaking of the incident after it was over, one of the men who had worked diligently for more than a year in trying to secure B——'s freedom, asked:

"How did you do it?"

And I replied: "It was the easiest task I ever performed, because most of the work had been done before I took hold of it. In fact I didn't do it— B—— did it himself."

This man looked at me in bewilderment. He did not see that which I am here trying to make clear; namely, that practically all difficult tasks are easily performed if one approaches them from the right angle. There were two important factors entering B——'s release. The first was the fact that he had supplied the material for a good case before I took it in charge; and the second was the fact that before I called on the governor of Ohio I so completely convinced myself that I had a right to ask for B——'s release that I had no difficulty in presenting my case effectively.

Go back to what was stated in the beginning of this lesson, on the subject of telepathy, and apply it to this case. The governor could tell, long before I had stated my mission, that *I knew I had a good case.* If my brain did not telegraph this thought to his brain, then the look of self-confidence in my eyes and the positive tone of my voice made obvious my belief in the merits of my case.

Again I apologize for these personal references with the explanation that I have used them only because the whole of America was familiar with the B——— case that I have described. I disclaim all credit for the small part I played in the case, for I did nothing except use my *imagination* as an assembly room in which to piece together the factors out of which the sale was made. I did nothing except that which any salesman of *imagination* could have done.

It requires considerable courage to prompt one to use the personal pronoun as freely as it has been used in relating the facts connected with this case, but justification lies in the value of application of the principle of *imagination* to a case with which nearly everybody is familiar.

I cannot recall an incident in my entire life in connection with which the soundness of the fifteen factors that enter into this Reading Course was more clearly manifested than it was in securing the release of B———.

It is but another link in a long chain of evidence that proves to my entire satisfaction the power of *imagination* as a factor in salesmanship. There are endless millions of approaches to every problem, but there is *only one* best approach. Find this one best

approach and your problem is easily solved. No
matter how much merit your goods may have, there
are millions of *wrong* ways in which to offer them.
Your *imagination* will assist you in finding the *right*
way.

In your search for the *right* way in which to offer
your merchandise or your services, remember this peculiar trait of mankind:

*Men will grant favors that you request for the bene-
fit of a third person when they would not grant them
if requested for your benefit.*

Compare this statement with the fact that I asked
the governor of Ohio to release B——, not as a favor
to me, and not as a favor to B——, but, for the benefit of 160,000 unfortunate inmates of the prisons of
America.

Salesmen of *imagination* always offer their wares in
such terminology that the advantages of those wares to
the prospective purchaser are obvious. It is seldom
that any man makes a purchase of merchandise or
renders another a favor just to accommodate the salesman. It is a prominent trait of human nature that
prompts us all to do that which advances our own interests. This is a cold, indisputable fact, claims of
the idealist to the contrary notwithstanding.

To be perfectly plain, *men are selfish!*

To understand the truth is to understand how to
present your case, whether you are asking for the release of a man from prison or offering for sale some
commodity. In your own *imagination* so plan your
presentation of your case that the strongest and most
impelling advantages to the buyer are made plain.

This is *imagination!*

I NEVER see a person trying to disclose the scarlet letter on another's breast that I do not wonder if he doesn't carry some mark of disgrace which would have ruined him had he been overtaken by justice.

A farmer moved to the city, taking with him his well trained shepherd dog. He soon found that the dog was out of place in the city, so he decided to "get rid of him." (Note the words in quotation.) Taking the dog with him he went out into the country and rapped on the door of a farm-house. A man came hobbling to the door, on crutches. The man with the dog greeted the man in the house in these words:

"You wouldn't care to buy a fine shepherd dog, that I wish to get rid of, would you?"

The man on crutches replied, *"No!"* and closed the door.

The man with the dog called at half a dozen other farm-houses, asking the same question, and received the same answer. He made up his mind that no one wanted the dog and returned to the city. That evening he was telling of his misfortune, to a man of *imagination.* The man heard how the owner of the dog had tried in vain to "get rid of him."

"Let me dispose of the dog for you," said the man of *imagination.* The owner was willing. The next morning the man of *imagination* took the dog out into the country and stopped at the first farm-house at which the owner of the dog had called the day before. The same old man hobbled out on crutches and answered the knock at the door.

The man of *imagination* greeted him in this fashion:

"I see you are all crippled with rheumatism. What you need is a fine dog to run errands for you. I have a dog here that has been trained to bring home the cows, drive away wild animals, herd the sheep and perform other useful services. You may have this dog for a hundred dollars."

"All right," said the crippled man, "I'll take him!"
That, too, was *imagination!*

No one wants a dog that someone else wants to "get rid of," but most anyone would like to own a dog that would herd sheep and bring home the cows and perform other useful services.

The dog was the same one that the crippled buyer had refused the day before, but the man who sold the dog was not the man who had tried to "get rid of him." If you use your *imagination* you will know that no one wants anything that someone else is trying to "get rid of."

Remember that which was said about the Law of Attraction through the operation of which "like attracts like." If you look and act the part of a failure you will attract nothing but failures.

Whatever your life-work may be, it calls for the use of *imagination.*

Niagara Falls was nothing but a great mass of roaring water until a man of *imagination* harnessed it and converted the wasted energy into electric current that now turns the wheels of industry. Before this man of *imagination* came along millions of people had seen and heard those roaring falls, but lacked the *imagination* to harness them.

The first Rotary Club of the world was born in the fertile *imagination* of Paul Harris, of Chicago, who saw in this child of his brain an effective means of cultivating prospective clients and the extension of his law practice. The ethics of the legal profession forbid advertising in the usual way, but Paul Harris' *imagination* found a way to extend his law practice without advertising in the usual way.

If the winds of Fortune are temporarily blowing against you, remember that you can harness them and make them carry you toward your *definite purpose*, through the use of your *imagination*. A kite rises against the wind—not with it!

Dr. Frank Crane was a struggling "third-rate" preacher until the starvation wages of the clergy forced him to use his *imagination*. Now he earns upward of a hundred thousand dollars a year for an hour's work a day, writing essays.

Bud Fisher once worked for a mere pittance, but he now earns seventy-five thousand dollars a year by making folks grin, with his Mutt and Jeff comic strip. No art goes into his drawings, therefore he must be selling his *imagination*.

Woolworth was a poorly paid clerk in a retail store —poorly paid, perhaps, because he had not yet found out that he had *imagination*. Before he died he built the tallest office building in the world and girdled the United States with Five and Ten Cent Stores, through the use of his *imagination*.

You will observe, by analyzing these illustrations, that a close study of human nature played an important part in the achievements mentioned. To make profitable use of your *imagination* you must make it give you a keen insight into the motives that cause men to do or refrain from doing a given act. If your *imagination* leads you to understand how quickly people grant your requests when those requests appeal to their self-interest, you can have practically anything you go after.

I saw my wife make a very clever sale to our baby not long ago. The baby was pounding the top of our mahogany library table with a spoon. When my wife reached for the spoon the baby refused to give it up, but being a woman of *imagination* she offered the baby a nice stick of red candy; he dropped the spoon immediately and centered his attention on the more desirable object.

That was *imagination!* It was also salesmanship. She won her point without using force.

I was riding in an automobile with a friend who was driving beyond the speed limit. An officer rode up on a motorcycle and told my friend he was under arrest for speeding. The friend smiled pleasantly at the officer and said: "I'm sorry to have brought you out in all this rain, but I wanted to make the ten o'clock train with my friend here, and I was hitting it up around thirty-five miles an hour."

"No, you were only going twenty-eight miles an hour," replied the officer, "and as long as you are so nice about it I will let you off this time if you will watch yourself hereafter."

And that, too, was *imagination!* Even a traffic cop will listen to reason when approached in the right manner, but woe unto the motorist who tries to bully the cop into believing his speedometer was not reg istering properly.

There is one form of *imagination* against which I would caution you. It is the brand which prompts some people to *imagine* that they can get something for nothing, or that they can force themselves ahead in the world without observing the rights of others. There are more than 160,000 prisoners in the penal institutions of the United States, practically every one of whom is in prison because he *imagined* he could play the game of life without observing the rights of his fellow men.

There is a man in the Ohio penitentiary who has served more than thirty-five years of time for forgery, and the largest amount he ever got from his misapplication of *imagination* was twelve dollars.

There are a few people who direct their *imaginations* in the vain attempt to work out a way to show what happens when "an immovable body comes in contact with an irresistible force," but these types belong in the psychopathic hospitals.

There is also another form of misapplied *imagination;* namely, that of the young boy or girl who knows more about life than his or her "Dad." But this form is subject to modification with *time*. My own boys have taught me many things that my "Dad" tried, in vain, to teach me when I was their age.

Time and *imagination* (which is often but the product of time) teach us many things, but nothing of more importance than this:

That all men are much alike in many ways.

If you would know what your customer is thinking, Mr. Salesman, study yourself and find out what *you* would be thinking if you were in your customer's place.

Study yourself, find out what are the motives which actuate you in the performance of certain deeds and cause you to refrain from performing other deeds, and you will have gone far toward perfecting yourself in the accurate use of *imagination*.

The detective's biggest asset is *imagination*. The first question he asks, when called in to solve a crime is: *"What was the motive?"* If he can find out the

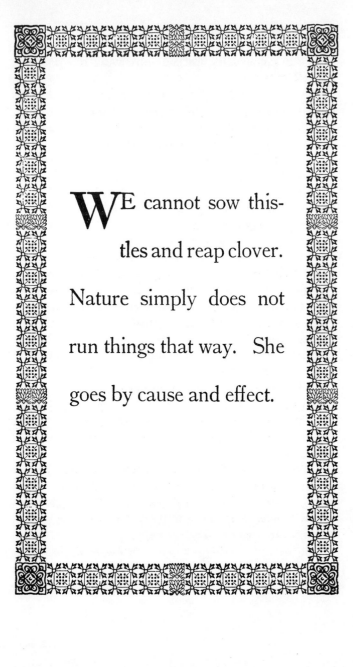

WE cannot sow this-
tles and reap clover.
Nature simply does not
run things that way. She
goes by cause and effect.

motive he can usually find the perpetrator of the crime.

A man who had lost a horse posted a reward of five dollars for its return. Several days later a boy who was supposed to have been "weak-minded" came leading the horse home and claimed the reward. The owner was curious to know how the boy found the horse. "How did you ever think where to look for the horse?" he asked, and the boy replied, "Well, I just thought where I would have gone if I had been a horse and went there, and he had." Not so bad for a "weak-minded" fellow. Some who are not accused of being weak-minded go all the way through life without displaying as much evidence of *imagination* as did this boy.

If you want to know what the other fellow will do, use your *imagination,* put yourself in his place and find out what you would have done. That's *imagination.*

Every person should be somewhat of a dreamer. Every business needs the dreamer. Every industry and every profession needs him. But, the dreamer must be, also, a doer; or else he must form an alliance with someone who can and does translate dreams into reality.

The greatest nation upon the face of this earth was conceived, born and nurtured through the early days of its childhood, as the result of *imagination* in the minds of men who combined dreams with *action!*

Your mind is capable of creating many new and useful combinations of old ideas, but the most important thing it can create is a *definite chief aim* that will give you that which you most desire.

Your *definite chief aim* can be speedily translated

into reality after you have fashioned it in the cradle
of your *imagination*. If you have faithfully followed
the instructions set down for your guidance in Lesson
Two you are now well on the road toward success, because you know what it is that you want, and you
have a plan for getting that which you want.

The battle for the achievement of success is half
won when one knows definitely what is wanted. The
battle is all over except the "shouting" when one knows
what is wanted and has made up his mind to get it,
whatever the price may be.

The selection of a *definite chief aim* calls for the use
of both *imagination* and decision! The power of decision grows with use. Prompt decision in forcing the
imagination to create a *definite chief aim* renders more
powerful the capacity to reach decisions in other
matters.

Adversities and temporary defeat are generally
blessings in disguise, for the reason that they force
one to use both *imagination* and decision. This is
why a man usually makes a better fight when his back
is to the wall and he knows there is no retreat. He
then reaches the decision to fight instead of running.

The *imagination* is never quite so active as it is
when one faces some emergency calling for quick and
definite decision and action.

In these moments of emergency men have reached
decisions, built plans, used their *imagination* in such
a manner that they became known as geniuses. Many
a genius has been born out of the necessity for unusual
stimulation of the *imagination,* as the result of some
trying experience which forced quick thought and
prompt decision.

It is a well known fact that the only manner in which an overpampered boy or girl may be made to become useful is by forcing him or her to become self-sustaining. This calls for the exercise of both *imagination* and decision, neither of which would be used except out of necessity.

The Reverend P. W. Welshimer is the pastor of a church in Canton, Ohio, where he has been located for nearly a quarter of a century. Ordinarily pastors do not remain at the head of one church for so great a length of time, and Reverend Welshimer would have been no exception to this rule if he had not mixed *imagination* with his pastoral duties.

Three years constitute the usual time that one pastor may remain in a given pastorate without wearing out his welcome.

The church of which Reverend Welshimer is the leader has a Sunday School of over 5,000 members— the largest membership enjoyed by any church in the United States.

No pastor could have remained at the head of one church for a quarter of a century, with the full consent of his followers, and have built up a Sunday School of this size, without employing the Laws of Initiative and Leadership, a Definite Chief Aim, Self-confidence and Imagination.

The author of this course made it his business to study the methods employed by Reverend Welshimer, and they are here described for the benefit of the students of this philosophy.

It is a well known fact that church factions, jealousy, etc., often lead to disagreements which make a change in leaders essential. Reverend Welshimer has steered around this common obstacle by a unique application of the Law of Imagination. When a new member comes into his church he immediately assigns a DEFINITE task to that member—one that suits the temperament, training and business qualifications of the individual, as nearly as possible—and, to use the minister's own words, he "keeps each member so busy pulling for the church that there is no time left for kicking or disagreeing with other members."

Not a bad policy for application in the field of business, or in any other field. The old saying that "idle hands are the devil's best tools" is more than a mere play upon words, for it is true.

Give any man something to do that he likes to do, and keep him busy doing it, and he will not be apt to degenerate into a disorganizing force. If any member of the Sunday School misses attendance twice in succession a committee from the church calls to find out the reason for the failure to attend. There is a "committee" job for practically every member of the church. In this way Reverend Welshimer delegates to the members, themselves, the responsibility of rounding up the delinquents and keeping them interested in church affairs. He is an organizer of the highest type. His efforts have attracted the attention of business men throughout the country, and times too numerous to be mentioned he has been offered positions, at fancy salaries, by banks, steel plants, business houses, etc., that recognized in him a real Leader.

In the basement of the church Reverend Welshimer operates a first-class printing plant where he publishes, weekly, a very creditable church paper that goes to all the members. The production and distribution of this paper is another source of employment which keeps the church members out of mischief, as practically all of them take some sort of an active interest in it. The paper is devoted exclusively to the affairs of the church as a whole, and those of the individual members. It is read by each member, line by line, because there is always a chance that each member's name may be mentioned in the news locals.

The church has a well trained choir and an orchestra that would be a credit to some of the largest theaters. Here Reverend Welshimer serves the double purpose of supplying entertainment and at the same time keeping the more "temperamental" members who are artists employed so they, also, remain out of mischief, incidentally giving them a chance to do that which they like best.

The late Dr. Harper, who was formerly president of the University of Chicago, was one of the most efficient college presidents of his time. He had a penchant for raising funds in large amounts. It was he who induced John D. Rockefeller to contribute millions of dollars to the support of the University of Chicago.

It may be helpful to the student of this philosophy to study Dr. Harper's technique, because he was a Leader of the highest order. Moreover, I have his own word for it that his leadership was never a matter of chance or accident, but always the result of carefully planned procedure.

The following incident will serve to show just how Dr. Harper made use of *imagination* in raising money in large sums:

He needed an extra million dollars for the construc-

WE all like commendation and many of us like flattery, but it is a debatable question as to whether the indulgence of these tendencies builds character and strength and individuality.

tion of a new building. Taking inventory of the wealthy men of Chicago to whom he might turn for this large sum, he decided upon two men, each of whom was a millionaire, and both were bitter enemies.

One of these men was, at that time, the head of the Chicago Street Railway system. Choosing the noon hour, when the office force and this man's secretary, in particular, would be apt to be out at lunch, Dr. Harper nonchalantly strolled into the office, and, finding no one on guard at the outer door, walked into the office of his intended "victim," whom he surprised by his appearance unannounced.

"My name is Harper," said the doctor, "and I am president of the University of Chicago. Pardon my intrusion, but I found no one in the outer office (which was no mere accident) so I took the liberty of walking on in.

"I have thought of you and your street railway system many many times. You have built up a wonderful system, and I understand that you have made lots of money for your efforts. I never think of you, however, without its occurring to me that one of these days you will be passing out into the Great Unknown, and after you are gone there will be nothing left as a monument to your name, because others will take over your money, and money has a way of losing its identity very quickly, as soon as it changes hands.

"I have often thought of offering you the opportunity to perpetuate your name by permitting you to build a new Hall out on the University grounds, and naming it after you. I would have offered you this opportunity long ago had it not been for the fact that one of the members of our Board wishes the honor to go to Mr. X—— (the street car head's enemy). Personally, however, I have always favored you and I still favor you, and if I have your permission to do so I am going to try to swing the opposition over to you.

"I have not come to ask for any decision today, however, as I was just passing and thought it a good time to drop in and meet you. Think the matter over and if you wish to talk to me about it again, telephone me at your leisure.

"Good day, sir! I am happy to have had this opportunity of meeting you."

With this he bowed himself out without giving the head of the street car company a chance to say either yes or no. In fact the street car man had very little chance to do any talking. Dr. Harper did the talking. That was as he planned it to be. He went into the office merely to plant the seed, believing that it would germinate and spring into life in due time.

His belief was not without foundation. He had hardly returned to his office at the University when the telephone rang. The street car man was on the other end of the wire. He asked for an appointment with Dr. Harper, which was granted, and the two met in Dr. Harper's office the next morning, and the check for a million dollars was in Dr. Harper's hands an hour later.

Despite the fact that Dr. Harper was a small, rather insignificant-looking man it was said of him that "he had a way about him that enabled him to get everything he went after."

And as to this "way" that he was reputed to have had—what was it?

It was nothing more nor less than his understanding of the power of Imagination. Suppose he had gone to the office of the street car head and asked for an appointment. Sufficient time would have elapsed between the time he called and the time when he would have actually seen his man, to have enabled the latter to anticipate the reason for his call, and also to formulate a good, logical excuse for saying, "No!"

Suppose, again, he had opened his interview with the street car man something like this:

"The University is badly in need of funds and I have come to you to ask your help. You have made lots of money and you owe something to the community in which you have made it. (Which, perhaps, was true.) If you will give us a million dollars we will place your name on a new Hall that we wish to build."

What might have been the result?

In the first place, there would have been no motive suggested that was sufficiently appealing to sway the mind of the street car man. While it may have been true that he "owed something to the community from which he had made a fortune," he probably would not have admitted that fact. In the second place, he would have enjoyed the position of being on the offensive instead of the defensive side of the proposal.

But Dr. Harper, shrewd in the use of Imagination as he was, provided for just such contingencies by the way he stated his case. First, he placed the street car man on the defensive by informing him that it was not certain that he (Dr. Harper) could get the permission of his Board to accept the money and name the Hall after the street car man. In the second place, he intensified the desire of the street car man to have his name on that building because of the thought that his enemy and competitor might get the honor if it got away from him. Moreover (and this was no accident, either), Dr. Harper had made a powerful appeal to one of the most common of all human weaknesses by showing this street car man how to perpetuate his own name.

All of which required a practical application of the Law of Imagination.

Dr. Harper was a Master Salesman. When he asked men for money he always paved the way for success by planting in the mind of the man of whom he asked it a good sound reason why the money should be given; a reason which emphasized some advantage accruing to the man as the result of the gift. Often this would take on the form of a business advantage. Again it would take on the nature of an appeal to that part of man's nature which prompts him to wish to perpetuate his name so it will live after him. But, always, the request for money was carried out according to a plan that had been carefully thought out, embellished and smoothed down with the use of Imagination.

.   .   .   .

While the Law of Success philosophy was in the embryonic stage, long before it had been organized into a systematic course of instruction and reduced to textbooks, the author was lecturing on this philosophy in a small town in Illinois.

One of the members of the audience was a young life insurance salesman who had but recently taken up that line of work. After hearing what was said on the subject of Imagination he began to apply what he had heard to his own problem of selling life insurance. Something was said, during the lecture, about the value of allied effort, through which men may enjoy greater success by co-operative effort, through a working arrangement under which each "boosts" the interests of the other.

Taking this suggestion as his cue, the young man in question immediately formulated a plan whereby he gained the co-operation of a group of business men who were in no way connected with the insurance business.

Going to the leading grocer in his town he made arrangements with that grocer to give a thousand dollar insurance policy to every customer purchasing no less than fifty dollars' worth of groceries each month. He then made it a part of his business to inform people of this arrangement and brought in many new customers. The groceryman had a large neatly lettered card placed in his store, informing his customers of this offer of free insurance, thus helping himself by offering all his customers an inducement to do ALL their trading in the grocery line with him.

This young life insurance man then went to the leading gasoline filling station owner in the town and made arrangements with him to insure all customers who purchased all their gasoline, oil and other motor supplies from him.

Next he went to the leading restaurant in the town and made a similar arrangement with the owner. Incidentally, this alliance proved to be quite profitable to the restaurant man, who promptly began an advertis-

CHARLES CHAPLIN makes a million dollars a year out of a funny, shuffling walk and a pair of baggy trousers, because he does "something different." Take the hint and "individualize" yourself with some distinctive idea.

ing campaign in which he stated that his food was so
pure, wholesome and good that all who ate at his place
regularly would be apt to live much longer, therefore
he would insure the life of each regular customer for
$1,000.00.

The life insurance salesman then made arrangements
with a local builder and real estate man to insure the
life of each person buying property from him, for an
amount sufficient to pay off the balance due on the
property in case the purchaser died before payments
were completed.

The young man in question is now the General
Agent for one of the largest life insurance companies
in the United States, with headquarters in one of the
largest cities in Ohio, and his income now averages
well above $25,000.00 a year.

The turning-point in his life came when he discovered how he might make practical use of the Law
of Imagination.

There is no patent on his plan. It may be duplicated over and over again by other life insurance men
who know the value of *imagination*. Just now, if I
were engaged in selling life insurance, I think I should
make use of this plan by allying myself with a group
of automobile distributors in each of several cities,
thus enabling them to sell more automobiles and at the
same time providing for the sale of a large amount of
life insurance, through their efforts.

.   .   .   .

Financial success is not difficult to achieve after one
learns how to make practical use of creative imagination. Someone with sufficient *initiative* and *leadership*,

and the necessary *imagination,* will duplicate the fortunes being made each year by the owners of Five and Ten Cent Stores, by developing a system of marketing the same sort of goods now sold in these stores, with the aid of vending machines. This will save a fortune in clerk hire, insure against theft, and cut down the overhead of store operation in many other ways. Such a system can be conducted just as successfully as food can be dispensed with the aid of automatic vending machines.

The seed of the idea has been here sown. It is yours for the taking!

Someone with an inventive turn of the mind is going to make a fortune and at the same time save thousands of lives each year, by perfecting an automatic railroad crossing "control" that will reduce the number of automobile accidents on crossings.

The system, when perfected, will work somewhat after this fashion: A hundred yards or so before reaching the railroad crossing the automobile will cross a platform somewhat on the order of a large scale platform used for weighing heavy objects, and the weight of the automobile will lower a gate and ring a gong. This will force the automobile to slow down. After the lapse of one minute the gate will again rise and the car may continue on its way. Meanwhile, there will have been plenty of time for observation of the track in both directions, to make sure that no trains are approaching.

Imagination, plus some mechanical skill, will give the motorist this much needed safe-guard, and make the man who perfects the system all the money he needs and much more besides.

Some inventor who understands the value of *imagination* and has a working knowledge of the radio principle, may make a fortune by perfecting a burglar alarm system that will signal police headquarters and at the same time switch on lights and ring a gong in the place about to be burglarized, with the aid of apparatus similar to that now used for broadcasting.

Any farmer with enough *imagination* to create a plan, plus the use of a list of all automobile licenses issued in his state, may easily work up a clientele of motorists who will come to his farm and purchase all the vegetables he can produce and all the chickens he can raise, thus saving him the expense of hauling his products to the city. By contracting with each motorist for the season the farmer may accurately estimate the amount of produce he should provide. The advantage to the motorist, accruing under the arrangement, is that he will be sure of direct-from-the-farm produce, at less cost than he could purchase it from local dealers.

The roadside gasoline filling station owner can make effective use of *imagination* by placing a lunch stand near his filling station, and then doing some attractive advertising along the road in each direction, calling attention to his "barbecue," "home-made sandwiches" or whatever else he may wish to specialize on. The lunch stand will cause the motorists to stop, and many of them will purchase gasoline before starting on their way again.

These are simple suggestions, involving no particular amount of complication in connection with their use, yet it is just such uses of *imagination* that bring financial success.

The Piggly-Wiggly self-help store plan, which made millions of dollars for its originator, was a very simple idea which anyone could have adopted, yet considerable *imagination* was required to put the idea to work in a practical sort of way.

The more simple and easily adapted to a need an idea is, the greater is its value, as no one is looking for ideas which are involved with great detail or in any manner complicated.

.   .   .   .

Imagination is the most important factor entering into the art of selling. The Master Salesman is always one who makes systematic use of *imagination*. The outstanding merchant relies upon *imagination* for the ideas which make his business excel.

Imagination may be used effectively in the sale of even the smallest articles of merchandise, such as ties, shirts, hosiery, etc. Let us proceed to examine just how this may be done.

I walked into one of the best known haberdasheries in the city of Philadelphia, for the purpose of purchasing some shirts and ties.

As I approached the tie counter a young man stepped forward and inquired:

"Is there something you want?"

Now if I had been the man behind the counter I would not have asked that question. He ought to have known, by the fact that I had approached the tie counter, that I wanted to look at ties.

I picked up two or three ties from the counter, examined them briefly, then laid down all but one light blue which somewhat appealed to me. Finally I laid this one down, also, and began to look through the remainder of the assortment.

The young man behind the counter then had a happy idea. Picking up a gaudy-looking yellow tie he wound it around his fingers to show how it would look when tied, and asked:

"Isn't this a beauty?"

Now I hate yellow ties, and the salesman made no particular hit with me by suggesting that a gaudy yellow tie is pretty. If I had been in that salesman's place I would have picked up the blue tie for which I had shown a decided preference, and I would have wound it around my fingers so as to bring out its appearance after being tied. I would have known what my customer wanted by watching the kinds of ties that he picked up and examined. Moreover, I would have known the particular tie that he liked best by the time he held it in his hands. A man will not stand by a counter and fondle a piece of merchandise which he does not like. If given the opportunity, any customer will give the alert salesman a clue as to the particular merchandise which should be stressed in an effort to make a sale.

I then moved over to the shirt counter. Here I was met by an elderly gentleman who asked:

"Is there something I can do for you today?"

Well, I thought to myself that if he ever did anything for me it would have to be today, as I might never come back to that particular store again. I told him I wanted to look at shirts, and described the style and color of shirt that I wanted.

The old gentleman made quite a hit with me when he replied by saying:

THE man who is afraid to give credit to those who help him do a piece of creditable work is so small that Opportunity will pass by without seeing him some day.

"I am sorry, sir, but they are not wearing that style this season, so we are not showing it."

I said I knew "they" were not wearing the style for which I had asked, and for that very reason, among others, I was going to wear it providing I could find it in stock.

If there is anything which nettles a man—especially that type of man who knows exactly what he wants and describes it the moment he walks into the store—it is to be told that "they are not wearing it this season."

Such a statement is an insult to a man's intelligence, or to what he thinks is his intelligence, and in most cases it is fatal to a sale. If I were selling goods I might think what I pleased about a customer's taste, but I surely would not be so lacking in tact and diplomacy as to tell the customer that I thought he didn't know his business. Rather I would prefer to manage tactfully to show him what I believed to be more appropriate merchandise than that for which he had called, if what he wanted was not in stock.

One of the most famous and highly paid writers in the world has built his fame and fortune on the sole discovery that it is profitable to write about that which people already know and with which they are already in accord. The same rule might as well apply to the sale of merchandise.

The old gentleman finally pulled down some shirt boxes and began laying out shirts which were not even similar to the shirt for which I had asked. I told him that none of these suited, and as I started to walk out he asked if I would like to look at some nice suspenders.

Imagine it! To begin with I do not wear suspenders, and, furthermore, there was nothing about my manner or bearing to indicate that I might like to look at suspenders.

It is proper for a salesman to try to interest a customer in wares for which he makes no inquiry, but judgment should be used and care taken to offer something which the salesman has reason to believe the customer may want.

I walked out of the store without having bought either shirts or ties, and feeling somewhat resentful because I had been so grossly misjudged as to my tastes for colors and styles.

A little further down the street I went into a small, one-man shop which had shirts and ties on display in the window.

Here I was handled differently!

The man behind the counter asked no unnecessary or stereotyped questions. He took one glance at me as I entered the door, sized me up quite accurately and greeted me with a very pleasant "Good morning, sir!"

He then inquired, "Which shall I show you first, shirts or ties?" I said I would look at the shirts first. He then glanced at the style of shirt I was wearing, asked my size, and began laying out shirts of the very type and color for which I was searching, without my saying another word. He laid out six different styles and watched to see which I would pick up first. I looked at each shirt, in turn, and laid them all back on the counter, but the salesman observed that I examined one of the shirts a little more closely than the others, and that I held it a little longer. No sooner had I laid this shirt down than the salesman picked it up and began to explain how it was made. He then went to the tie counter and came back with three very beautiful blue ties, of the very type for which I had been looking, tied each and held it in front of the shirt, calling attention to the perfect harmony between the colors of the ties and the shirt.

Before I had been in the store five minutes I had purchased three shirts and three ties, and was on my way with the package under my arm, feeling that here was a store to which I would return when I needed more shirts and ties.

I learned, afterwards, that the merchant who owns the little shop where I made these purchases pays a monthly rental of $500.00 for the small store, and makes a handsome income from the sale of nothing but shirts, ties and collars. He would have to go out of business, with a fixed charge of $500.00 a month for rent, if it were not for his knowledge of human nature which enables him to make a very high percentage of sales to all who come into his store.

.   .   .   .

I have often observed women when they were trying on hats, and have wondered why salespeople did not read the prospective buyer's mind by watching her manner of handling the hats.

A woman goes into a store and asks to be shown some hats. The salesperson starts bringing out hats and the prospective buyer starts trying them on. If a hat suits her, even in the slightest sort of way, she will keep it on a few seconds, or a few minutes, but if she does not like it she will pull it right off her head the moment the salesperson takes her hands off the hat.

Finally, when the customer is shown a hat that she likes she will begin to announce that fact, in terms which no well informed salesperson will fail to understand, by arranging her hair under the hat, or pulling it down on her head to just the angle which she likes best, and by looking at the hat from the rear, with the aid of a hand-mirror. The signs of admiration are unmistakable. Finally, the customer will remove the hat from her head, and begin to look at it closely; then she may lay it aside and permit another hat to be tried on her, in which event the clever salesperson will lay aside the hat just removed, and at the opportune time she will bring it back and ask the customer to try it on again.

By careful observation of the customer's likes and dislikes a clever saleswoman may often sell as many as three or four hats to the same customer, at one sitting, by merely watching what appeals to the customer and then concentrating upon the sale of that.

The same rule applies in the sale of other merchandise. The customer will, if closely observed, clearly indicate what is wanted, and, if the clue is followed, very rarely will a customer walk out without buying.

I believe it a conservative estimate when I say that fully seventy-five per cent of the "walk-outs," as the non-purchasing customers are called, are due to lack of tactful showing of merchandise.

.   .   .   .

Last Fall I went into a hat store to purchase a felt hat. It was a busy Saturday afternoon and I was approached by a young "extra" rush-hour salesman who had not yet learned how to size people up at a glance. For no good reason whatsoever the young man pulled down a brown derby and handed it to me, or rather tried to hand it to me. I thought he was trying to be funny, and refused to take the hat into my hands, saying to him, in an attempt to return his compliment and be funny in turn, "Do you tell bed-time stories also?" He looked at me in surprise, but didn't take the cue which I had offered him.

If I had not observed the young man more closely than he had observed me, and sized him up as an earnest but inexperienced "extra," I would have been highly insulted, for if there is anything I hate it is a derby of any sort, much less a brown derby.

One of the regular salesmen happened to see what was going on, walked over and snatched the brown derby out of the young man's hands, and, with a smile on his face intended as a sort of sop to me, said, "What the hell are you trying to show this gentleman, any-way?"

That spoiled my fun, and the salesman who had im-mediately recognized me as a gentleman sold me the first hat he brought out.

The customer generally feels complimented when a salesman takes the time to study the customer's per-sonality and lay out merchandise suited to that per-sonality.

.   .   .   .

I went into one of the largest men's clothing stores in New York City, a few years ago, and asked for a suit, describing exactly what was wanted, but not

HOT HEADS" go
with "cold feet."
He who loses his temper
is usually a bluffer and
when "called" is a quitter.

mentioning price. The young man, who purported
to be a salesman, said he did not believe they carried
such a suit, but I happened to see exactly what I
wanted hanging on a model, and called his attention
to the suit. He then made a hit with me by saying,
"Oh, that one over there? That's a high-priced suit!"

His reply amused me; it also angered me, so I inquired of the young man what he saw about me which
indicated that I did not come in to purchase a high-
priced suit? With embarrassment he tried to explain, but his explanations were as bad as the original
offense, and I started toward the door, muttering
something to myself about "dumb-bells." Before I
reached the door I was met by another salesman who
had sensed by the way I walked and the expression
on my face that I was none too well pleased.

With tact well worth remembering, this salesman
engaged me in conversation while I unburdened my
woes and then managed to get me to go back with him
and look at the suit. Before I left the store I purchased the suit I came in to look at, and two others
which I had not intended purchasing.

That was the difference between a salesman and
one who drove customers away. Moreover, I later
introduced two of my friends to this same salesman
and he made sizable sales to each of them.

.   .   .   .

I was once walking down Michigan Boulevard, in
Chicago, when my eye was attracted to a beautiful
gray suit in the window of a men's store. I had no
notion of buying the suit, but I was curious to know
the price, so I opened the door, and, without entering,

merely pushed my head inside and asked the first man I saw how much the suit in the window was.

Then followed one of the cleverest bits of sales maneuvering I have ever observed. The salesman knew he could not sell me the suit unless I came into the store, so he said, "Will you not step inside, sir, while I find out the price of the suit?"

Of course he knew the price, all the time, but that was his way of disarming me of the thought that he intended trying to sell me the suit. Of course I had to be as polite as the salesman, so I said, "Certainly," and walked inside.

The salesman said, "Step right this way, sir, and I will get the information for you."

In less than two minutes I found myself standing in front of a case, with my coat off, getting ready to try on a coat like the one I had observed in the window.

After I was in the coat, which happened to fit almost perfectly (which was no accident, thanks to the accurate eyes of an observing salesman) my attention was called to the nice, smooth touch of the material. I rubbed my hand up and down the arm of the coat, as I had seen the salesman do while describing the material, and, sure enough, it was a very fine piece of material. By this time I had again asked the price, and when I was told that the suit was only fifty dollars I was agreeably surprised, because I had been led to believe that it might have been priced much higher. However, when I first saw the suit in the window my guess was that it was priced at about thirty-five dollars, and I doubt that I would have paid that much for it had I not fallen into the hands of a man who knew

how to show the suit to best advantage. If the first
coat tried on me had been about two sizes too large,
or a size too small, I doubt that any sale would have
been made, despite the fact that all ready-to-wear
suits sold in the better stores are altered to fit the
customer.

I bought that suit "on the impulse of the moment,"
as the psychologist would say, and I am not the only
man who buys goods on that same sort of impulse. A
single slip on the part of the salesman would have lost
him the sale of that suit. If he had replied, "Fifty
dollars," when I asked the price I would have said,
"Thank you," and have gone my way without looking
at the suit.

Later in the season I purchased two more suits
from this same salesman, and if I now lived in Chicago the chances are that I would buy still other suits
from him, because he always showed me suits that
were in keeping with my personality.

· · · · · · ·

The Marshall Field store, in Chicago, gets more for
merchandise than does any other store of its kind in
the country. Moreover, people knowingly pay more
at this store, and feel better satisfied than if they
bought the merchandise at another store for less
money.

Why is this?

Well, there are many reasons, among them the fact
that anything purchased at the Field store which is not
entirely satisfactory may be returned and exchanged
for other merchandise, or the purchase price may be
refunded, just as the customer wishes. An implied

guarantee goes with every article sold in the Field store.

Another reason why people will pay more at the Field store is the fact that the merchandise is displayed and shown to better advantage than it is at most other stores. The Field window-displays are truly works of art, no less than if they were created for the sake of art alone, and not merely to sell merchandise. The same is true of the goods displayed in the store. There is harmony and proper grouping of merchandise throughout the Field establishment, and this creates an "atmosphere" that is more—much more—than merely an imaginary one.

Still another reason why the Field store can get more for merchandise than most other merchants is due to the careful selection and supervision of salespeople. One would seldom find a person employed in the Field store whom one would not be willing to accept as a social equal, or as a neighbor. Not a few men have made the acquaintance of girls in the Field store who later became their wives.

Merchandise purchased in the Field store is packed or wrapped more artistically than is common in other stores, which is still another reason why people go out of their way and pay higher prices to trade there.

. . . .

While we are on the subject of artistic wrapping of merchandise I wish to relate the experience of a friend of mine which will not fail to convey a very definite meaning to those engaged in the business of selling, as it shows how *imagination* may be used even in wrapping merchandise.

This friend had a very fine silver cigarette case which he had carried for years, and of which he was very proud because it was a gift from his wife.

Constant usage had banged the case up rather badly. It had been bent, dented, the hinges warped, etc., until he decided to take it to Caldwell the jeweler, in Philadelphia, to be repaired. He left the case and asked them to send it to his office when it was ready.

About two weeks later a splendid-looking new delivery wagon with the Caldwell name on it drew up in front of his office, and a nice-looking young man in a neat uniform stepped out with a package that was artistically wrapped and tied with a ribbon tape string.

The package happened to be delivered to my friend on his birthday, and, having forgotten about leaving the cigarette case to be repaired, and observing the beauty and size of the package that was handed to him, he naturally imagined that someone had sent him a birthday present.

His secretary and other workers in his office gathered around his desk to watch him open up his "present." He cut the ribbon and removed the outer covering. Under this was a covering of tissue paper, fastened with beautiful gold seals bearing the Caldwell initials and trade-mark. This paper was removed and behold! a most beautiful plush-lined box met his eyes. The box was opened, and, after removing the tissue paper packing, there was a cigarette case which he recognized, after careful examination, as the one he had left to be repaired, but it did not look like the same case, thanks to the *imagination* of the Caldwell manager.

E. M. STATLER BE-
CAME THE MOST
SUCCESSFUL HOTEL
MAN IN THE WORLD
BY RENDERING
MORE SERVICE and
BETTER SERVICE
THAN HIS GUESTS
WERE ASKED TO
PAY FOR.

Every dent had been carefully straightened out. The hinges had been trued and the case had been polished and cleaned so it shone as it did when it was first purchased.

Simultaneously a prolonged "Oo-o-o-o-o-o-Oh!" of admiration came from the onlookers, including the owner of the cigarette case.

And the bill! Oh, it was a plenty, and yet the price charged for the repair did not seem too high. As a matter of fact everything that entered into the transaction from the packing of the case, with the fine tissue paper cover, the gold seals, the ribbon tape string, the delivery of the package by a neatly uniformed boy, from a well appointed new delivery wagon, was based upon carefully calculated psychology which laid the foundation for a high price for the repair.

People, generally, do not complain of high prices, providing the "service" or embellishment of the merchandise is such as to pave the way for high prices. What people do complain of, and rightly so, is high prices and "sloppy" service.

To me there was a great lesson in this cigarette case incident, and I think there is a lesson in it for any person who makes a business of selling any sort of merchandise.

The goods you are selling may actually be worth all you are asking for them, but if you do not carefully study the subjects of advantageous display and artistic packing you may be accused of overcharging your customers.

.   .   .   .

On Broad Street, in the city of Philadelphia, there is a fruit shop where those who patronize the store are met at the door by a man in uniform who opens the door for them. He does nothing else but merely open the door, but he does it with a smile (even though it be a carefully studied and rehearsed smile) which makes the customer feel welcome even before he gets inside of the store. This fruit merchant specializes on specially prepared baskets of fruit. Just outside the store is a big blackboard on which are listed the sailing dates of the various ocean liners leaving New York City. This merchant caters to people who wish baskets of fruit delivered on board departing boats on which friends are sailing. If a man's sweetheart, or perhaps his wife or a very dear friend, happens to be sailing on a certain date he naturally wants the basket of fruit he purchases for her to be embellished with frills and "trimmings." Moreover, he is not necessarily looking for something "cheap" or even inexpensive.

All of which the fruit merchant capitalizes! He gets from $10.00 to $25.00 for a basket of fruit which one could purchase just around the corner, not more than a block away, for from $3.00 to $7.50, with the exception that the latter would not be embellished with the seventy-five cents' worth of frills which the former contains.

This merchant's store is a small affair, no larger than the average small fruit-stand store, but he pays a rent of at least $15,000.00 a year for the place and makes more money than half a hundred ordinary fruit stands combined, merely because he knows how to display and deliver his wares so they appeal to the vanity of the buyers. This is but another proof of the value of *imagination*.

The American people—and this means all of them, not merely the so-called rich—are the most extravagant spenders on earth, but they insist on "class" when it comes to appearances such as wrapping and delivery and other embellishments which add no real value to the merchandise they buy. The merchant who understands this, and has learned how to mix IMAGINATION with his merchandise, may reap a rich harvest in return for his knowledge.

And a great many are doing it, too.

The salesman who understands the psychology of proper display, wrapping and delivery of merchandise, and who knows how to show his wares to fit the whims and characteristics of his customers, can make ordinary merchandise bring fancy prices, and what is more important still, he can do so and still retain the patronage of his customers more readily than if he sold the same merchandise without the "studied" appeal and the artistic wrapping and delivery service.

In a "cheap" restaurant, where coffee is served in heavy, thick cups and the silverware is tarnished or dirty, a ham sandwich is only a ham sandwich, and if the restaurant keeper gets fifteen cents for it he is doing well; but just across the street, where the coffee is served in dainty thin cups, on neatly covered tables, by neatly dressed young women, a much smaller ham sandwich will bring a quarter, to say nothing of the cost of the tip to the waitress. The only difference in the sandwiches is merely in appearances; the ham comes from the same butcher and the bread from the same baker, whether purchased from the former or the latter restaurant. The difference in price is very considerable, but the difference in the merchandise is not a difference of either quality or quantity so much as it is of "atmosphere," or appearances.

People love to buy "appearance" or atmosphere! which is merely a more refined way of saying that which P. T. Barnum said about "one being born every minute."

It is no overstatement of fact to say that a master of sales psychology could go into the average merchant's store, where the stock of goods was worth, let us say, $50,000.00, and at very slight additional expense make the stock bring $60,000.00 to $75,000.00. He would do nothing except coach the salespeople on the proper showing of the merchandise, after having purchased a small amount of more suitable fixtures, perhaps, and re-packed the merchandise in more suitable coverings and boxes.

A man's shirt, packed one to the box, in the right sort of a box, with a piece of ribbon and a sheet of tissue paper added for embellishment, can be made to bring a dollar or a dollar and a half more than the same shirt would bring without the more artistic packing. I know this is true, and I have proved it more times than I can recall, to convince some skeptical merchant who had not studied the effect of "proper displays."

Conversely stated, I have proved, many times, that the finest shirt made cannot be sold for half its value if it is removed from its box and placed on a bargain counter, with inferior looking shirts, both of which examples prove that people do not know what they are buying—that they go more by appearances than they do by actual analysis of the merchandise they purchase.

This is noticeably true in the purchase of automobiles. The American people want, and DEMAND, style in the appearance of automobiles. What is under the hood or in the rear axle they do not know and really do not care, as long as the car looks the part.

Henry Ford required nearly twenty years of experience to learn the truth of the statement just made, and even then, despite all of his analytical ability, he only acknowledged the truth when forced to do so by his competitors. If it were not true that people buy "appearances" more than they buy "reality" Ford never would have created his new automobile. That car is the finest sort of example of a psychologist who appeals to the tendency which people have to purchase "appearance," although, of course, it must be admitted that in this particular example the real value of the car actually exists.

GREAT ACHIEVE-
MENT IS USU-
ALLY BORN OF
GREAT SACRIFICE,
AND IS NEVER THE
RESULT OF SELF-
ISHNESS.

Lesson Seven

ENTHUSIASM

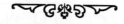

I GAVE a beggar a dime with the suggestion that he invest it in a copy of Elbert Hubbard's Message to Garcia.

THE LAW OF SUCCESS
Lesson Seven
ENTHUSIASM

"You Can Do It if You Believe You Can!"

NTHUSIASM is a state of mind that inspires and arouses one to put *action* into the task at hand. It does more than this —it is contagious, and vitally affects not only the enthusiast, but all with whom he comes in contact.

Enthusiasm bears the same relationship to a human being that steam does to the locomotive—it is the vital moving force that impels *action*. The greatest leaders of men are those who know how to inspire enthusiasm in their followers. Enthusiasm is the most important factor entering into salesmanship. It is, by far, the most vital factor that enters into public speaking.

If you wish to understand the difference between a man who is enthusiastic and one who is not, compare Billy Sunday with the average man of his profession. The finest sermon ever delivered would fall upon deaf ears if it were not backed with enthusiasm by the speaker.

HOW ENTHUSIASM WILL AFFECT YOU

Mix enthusiasm with your work and it will not seem hard or monotonous. Enthusiasm will so energize your entire body that you can get along with less than half the usual amount of sleep and at the same time it will enable you to perform from two to three times as much work as you usually perform in a given period, without fatigue.

For many years I have done most of my writing at night. One night, while I was enthusiastically at work over my typewriter, I looked out of the window of my study, just across the square from the Metropolitan tower, in New York City, and saw what seemed to be the most peculiar reflection of the moon on the tower. It was of a silvery gray shade, such as I had never seen before. Upon closer inspection I found that the reflection was that of the early morning sun and not that of the moon. It was daylight! I had been at work all night, but I was so engrossed in my work that the night had passed as though it were but an hour. I worked at my task all that day and all the following night without stopping, except for a small amount of light food.

Two nights and one day without sleep, and with but little food, without the slightest evidence of fatigue, would not have been possible had I not kept my body energized with *enthusiasm* over the work at hand.

Enthusiasm is not merely a figure of speech; it is a vital force that you can harness and use with profit. Without it you would resemble an electric battery without electricity.

Enthusiasm is the vital force with which you recharge your body and develop a dynamic personality. Some people are blessed with natural *enthusiasm*, while others must acquire it. The procedure through which it may be developed is simple. It begins by the doing of the work or rendering of the service which one likes best. If you should be so situated that you cannot conveniently engage in the work which you like best, for the time being, then you can proceed along another line very effectively by adopting a *definite chief aim* that contemplates your engaging in that particular work at some future time.

Lack of capital and many other circumstances over which you have no immediate control may force you to engage in work which you do not like, but no one can stop you from determining in your own mind what your *definite chief aim* in life shall be, nor can anyone stop you from planning ways and means for translating this aim into reality, nor can anyone stop you from mixing *enthusiasm* with your plans.

Happiness, the final object of all human effort, is a state of mind that can be maintained only through the hope of future achievement. Happiness lies always in the future and never in the past. The happy person is the one who dreams of heights of achievement that are yet unattained. The home you intend to own, the money you intend to earn and place in the bank, the trip you intend to take when you can afford it, the position in life you intend to fill when you have prepared yourself, and the preparation, itself—these are the things that produce happiness. Likewise, these are the materials out of which your *definite chief aim* is formed; these are the things over which you may become *enthusiastic,* no matter what your present station in life may be.

More than twenty years ago I became enthusiastic over an idea. When the idea first took form in my mind I was unprepared to take even the first step toward its transformation into reality. But I nursed it in my mind—I became *enthusiastic* over it as I looked ahead, in my imagination, and saw the time when I would be prepared to make it a reality.

The idea was this: I wanted to become the editor of a magazine, based upon the Golden Rule, through which I could inspire people to keep up courage and deal with one another squarely.

Finally my chance came! and, on armistice day, 1918, I wrote the first editorial for what was to become the material realization of a hope that had lain dormant in my mind for nearly a score of years.

With *enthusiasm* I poured into that editorial the emotions which I had been developing in my heart over a period of more than twenty years. My dream had come true. My editorship of a national magazine had become a reality.

As I have stated, this editorial was written with *enthusiasm.* I took it to a man of my acquaintance and with *enthusiasm* I read it to him. The editorial ended in these words: "At last my twenty-year-old dream is about to come true. It takes money, and a lot of it, to publish a national magazine, and I haven't the slightest idea where I am going to get this essential factor, but this is worrying me not at all because *I know I am going to get it somewhere!*" As I wrote those lines, I mixed *enthusiasm* and faith with them.

I had hardly finished reading this editorial when

the man to whom I read it—the first and only person
to whom I had shown it—said:

"I can tell you where you are going to get the
money, for I am going to supply it."

And he did!

Yes, *enthusiasm* is a vital force; so vital, in fact,
that no man who has it highly developed can begin
even to approximate his power of achievement.

Before passing to the next step in this lesson, I wish
to repeat and to emphasize the fact that you may develop *enthusiasm* over your *definite chief aim* in life,
no matter whether you are in position to achieve that
purpose at this time or not. You may be a long way
from realization of your *definite chief aim,* but if you
will kindle the fire of *enthusiasm* in your heart, and
keep it burning, before very long the obstacles that
now stand in the way of your attainment of that purpose will melt away as if by the force of magic, and
you will find yourself in possession of power that you
did not know you possessed.

HOW YOUR ENTHUSIASM WILL AFFECT
OTHERS

We come, now, to the discussion of one of the most
important subjects of this Reading Course, namely,
suggestion.

In the preceding lessons we have discussed the subject of *Auto-suggestion,* which is self-suggestion. You
saw, in Lesson Three, what an important part *Auto-
suggestion* played.

Suggestion is the principle through which your words
and your acts and even *your state of mind* influence

ONE of the most valuable things any man can learn is the art of using the knowledge and experience of others.

others. That you may comprehend the far-reaching power of *suggestion*, let me refer to the Introductory Lesson, in which the principle of telepathy is described. If you now understand and accept the principle of telepathy (the communication of thought from one mind to another without the aid of signs, symbols or sounds) as a reality, you of course understand why *enthusiasm* is contagious, and why it influences all within its radius.

When your own mind is vibrating at a high rate, because it has been stimulated with *enthusiasm*, that vibration registers in the minds of all within its radius, and especially in the minds of those with whom you come in close contact. When a public speaker "senses" the feeling that his audience is "en rapport" with him he merely recognizes the fact that his own *enthusiasm* has influenced the minds of his listeners until their minds are vibrating in harmony with his own.

When the salesman "senses" the fact that the "psychological" moment for closing a sale has arrived, he merely feels the effect of his own *enthusiasm* as it influences the mind of his prospective buyer and places that mind "en rapport" (in harmony) with his own.

The subject of *suggestion* constitutes so vitally an important part of this lesson, and of this entire course, that I will now proceed to describe the three mediums through which it usually operates; namely, what you say, what you do and what you *think!*

When you are *enthusiastic* over the goods you are selling or the services you are offering, or the speech you are delivering, your state of mind becomes obvious to all who hear you, *by the tone of your voice*. Whether you have ever thought of it in this way or not, it is the tone in which you make a statement, more than it is the statement itself, that carries conviction or fails to convince. No mere combination of words can ever take the place of a deep belief in a statement that is expressed with burning *enthusiasm*. Words are but devitalized sounds unless colored with feeling that is born of *enthusiasm*.

Here the printed word fails me, for I can never express with mere type and paper the difference between words that fall from unemotional lips, without the fire of *enthusiasm* back of them, and those which seem to pour forth from a heart that is bursting with eagerness for expression. The difference is there, however.

Thus, *what you say,* and the way in which you say it, conveys a meaning that may be just the opposite to what is intended. This accounts for many a failure by the salesman who presents his arguments in words which seem logical enough, but lack the coloring that can come only from *enthusiasm* that is born of sincerity and belief in the goods he is trying to sell. His words said one thing, but the tone of his voice *suggested* something entirely different; therefore, no sale was made.

That which you *say* is an important factor in the operation of the principle of *suggestion,* but not nearly so important as that which you *do.* *Your acts will count for more than your words,* and woe unto you if the two fail to harmonize.

If a man preach the Golden Rule as a sound rule of conduct his words will fall upon deaf ears if he does not practice that which he preaches. The most effective sermon that any man can preach on the soundness of the Golden Rule is that which he preaches, by *suggestion,* when he applies this rule in his relationships with his fellow men.

If a salesman of Ford automobiles drives up to his prospective purchaser in a Buick, or some other make of car, all the arguments he can present in behalf of the Ford will be without effect. Once I went into one of the offices of the Dictaphone Company to look at a dictaphone (dictating machine). The salesman in charge presented a logical argument as to the machine's merits, while the stenographer at his side was transcribing letters from a shorthand note-book. His arguments in favor of a dictating machine, as compared with the old method of dictating to a stenographer, did not impress me, because his actions were not in harmony with his words.

Your *thoughts* constitute the most important of the three ways in which you apply the principle of *suggestion,* for the reason that they control the tone of your words and, to some extent at least, your actions. If your *thoughts* and your *actions* and your *words* harmonize, you are bound to influence those with whom you come in contact, more or less toward your way of thinking.

We will now proceed to analyze the subject of *suggestion* and to show you exactly how to apply the principle upon which it operates. As we have already seen, *suggestion* differs from *Auto-suggestion* only in one way—we use it, consciously or unconsciously, when we influence others, while we use *Auto-suggestion* as a means of influencing ourselves.

Before you can influence another person through *suggestion,* that person's mind must be in a state of neutrality; that is, it must be open and receptive to your method of *suggestion*. Right here is where most salesmen fail—they try to make a sale before the mind of the prospective buyer has been rendered receptive or neutralized. This is such a vital point in this lesson that I feel impelled to dwell upon it until there can be no doubt that you understand the principle that I am describing.

When I say that the salesman must neutralize the mind of his prospective purchaser before a sale can be made I mean that the prospective purchaser's mind must be credulous. A state of confidence must have been established and it is obvious that there can be no set rule for either establishing confidence or neutralizing the mind to a state of openness. Here the ingenuity of the salesman must supply that which cannot be set down as a hard and fast rule.

I know a life insurance salesman who sells nothing but large policies, amounting to $100,000.00 and upward. Before this man even approaches the subject of insurance with a prospective client he familiarizes himself with the prospective client's complete history, including his education, his financial status, his eccentricities if he has any, his religious preferences and other data too numerous to be listed. Armed with this information, he manages to secure an introduction under conditions which permit him to know the prospective client in a social as well as a business way. Nothing is said about the sale of life insurance during his first visit, nor his second, and sometimes he does not approach the subject of insurance until he has become very well acquainted with the prospective client.

All this time, however, he is not dissipating his efforts. He is taking advantage of these friendly visits for the purpose of neutralizing his prospective client's mind; that is, he is building up a relationship of confidence so that when the time comes for him to talk life insurance that which he says will fall upon ears that *willingly listen.*

Some years ago I wrote a book entitled How to Sell Your Services. Just before the manuscript went to the publisher, it occurred to me to request some of the well known men of the United States to write letters of endorsement to be published in the book. The printer was then waiting for the manuscript; therefore, I hurriedly wrote a letter to some eight or ten men, in which I briefly outlined exactly what I wanted, but the letter brought back no replies. I had failed to observe two important prerequisites for success—I had written the letter so hurriedly that I had failed to inject the spirit of *enthusiasm* into it, and, I had neglected so to word the letter that it had the effect of neutralizing the minds of those to whom it was sent; therefore, I had not paved the way for the application of the principle of *suggestion.*

After I discovered my mistake, I then wrote a letter that was based upon strict application of the principle of *suggestion,* and this letter not only brought back replies from all to whom it was sent, but many of the replies were masterpieces and served, far beyond my fondest hopes, as valuable supplements to the book. For the purpose of comparison, to show you how the principle of *suggestion* may be used in writing a letter, and what an important part *enthusiasm* plays in giving the written word "flesh," the two letters are here reproduced. It will not be necessary to indicate which letter failed, as that will be quite obvious:

A CAREFUL inventory of all your past experiences may disclose t h e startling fact that everything has happened for the best.

My dear Mr. Ford:

I am just completing a manuscript for a new book entitled How to Sell Your Services. I anticipate the sale of several hundred thousand of these books and I believe those who purchase the book would welcome the opportunity of receiving a message from you as to the best method of marketing personal services.

Would you, therefore, be good enough to give me a few minutes of your time by writing a brief message to be published in my book? This will be a big favor to me personally and I know it would be appreciated by the readers of the book.

Thanking you in advance for any consideration you may care to show me, I am,

Yours very truly,

. . . .

Hon. Thomas R. Marshall,
Vice-President of the United States,
Washington, D. C.
My dear Mr. Marshall:

Would you care for the opportunity to send a message of encouragement, and possibly a word of advice, to a few hundred thousand of your fellow men who have failed to make their mark in the world as successfully as you have done?

I have about completed a manuscript for a book to be entitled How to Sell Your Services. The main point made in the book is that service rendered is *cause* and the pay envelope is *effect;* and that the latter varies in proportion to the efficiency of the former.

The book would be incomplete without a few words

of advice from a few men who, like yourself, have come up from the bottom to enviable positions in the world. Therefore, if you will write me of your views as to the most essential points to be borne in mind by those who are offering personal services for sale I will pass your message on through my book, which will insure its getting into hands where it will do a world of good for a class of earnest people who are struggling to find their places in the world's work.

I know you are a busy man, Mr. Marshall, but please bear in mind that by simply calling in your secretary and dictating a brief letter you will be sending forth an important message to possibly half a million people. In money this will not be worth to you the two cent stamp that you will place on the letter, but, if estimated from the viewpoint of the good it may do others who are less fortunate than yourself, it may be worth the difference between success and failure to many a worthy person who will read your message, believe in it, and be guided by it.

                    Very cordially yours,

Now, let us analyze the two letters and find out why one failed in its mission while the other succeeded. This analysis should start with one of the most important fundamentals of salesmanship, namely motive. In the first letter it is obvious that the motive is entirely one of self-interest. The letter states exactly what is wanted, but the wording of it leaves a doubt as to *why* the request is made or whom it is intended to benefit. Study the sentence in the second paragraph, "This will be a big favor to me personally, etc." Now it may seem to be a peculiar trait, but the truth is that most people will not grant favors just to please others. If I ask you to render a service that will benefit me, without bringing you some corresponding advantage, you will not show much enthusiasm in granting that favor; you may refuse altogether if you have a plausible excuse for refusing. But if I ask you to render a service that will benefit a third person, even though the service must be rendered through me; and if that service is of such a nature that it is likely to reflect credit on you, the chances are that you will render the service willingly.

We see this psychology demonstrated by the man who pitches a dime to the beggar on the street, or perhaps refuses even the dime, but willingly hands over a hundred or a thousand dollars to the charity worker who is begging in the name of others.

But the most damaging suggestion of all is contained in the last and most important paragraph of the letter, "Thanking you in advance for *any consideration you may care to show me.*" This sentence strongly suggests that the writer of the letter anticipates a refusal of his request. It clearly indicates lack of *enthusiasm*. It paves the way for a refusal of the request. There is not one single word in the entire letter that places in the mind of a man to whom it is sent a satisfactory reason why he should comply with the request. On the other hand, he can clearly see that the object of the letter is to secure from him a letter of endorsement that will help sell the book. The most important selling argument—in fact, the only selling argument available in connection with this request, has been lost because it was not brought out and established as the real motive for making the request. This argument was but faintly mentioned in the sentence, "I believe those who purchase the book would welcome the opportunity of receiving a message from you as to the best method of marketing personal services."

The opening paragraph of the letter violates an important fundamental of salesmanship because it clearly suggests that the object of the letter is to gain some advantage for its writer, and does not even hint at any corresponding advantage that may accrue to the person to whom it is sent. Instead of neutralizing the mind of the recipient of the letter, as it should do, it has just the opposite effect; it causes him to close his mind against all argument that follows; it puts him in a frame of mind that makes it easy for him to say no. It reminds me of a salesman—or, perhaps I should say, a man who wanted to be a salesman—who once approached me for the purpose of selling me a subscription to the Saturday Evening Post. As he held a copy of the magazine in front of me he suggested the answer I should make by this question:

"You wouldn't subscribe for the Post to help me out, would you?"

Of course I said no! He had made it easy for me to say no. There was no *enthusiasm* back of his words, and gloom and discouragement were written all over his face. He needed the commission he would have made on my subscription had I purchased; no doubt about that—but he suggested nothing that appealed to my self-interest motive, therefore he lost a sale. But the loss of this *one sale* was not the sad part of his misfortune; the sad part was that this same attitude was causing him to lose all other sales which he might have made had he changed his approach.

A few weeks later another subscription agent approached me. She was selling a combination of six magazines, one of which was the Saturday Evening Post, but how different was her approach. She glanced at my library table, on which she saw several magazines, then at my book shelves, and exclaimed with *enthusiasm:*

"Oh! I see you are a lover of books and magazines."

I *proudly* pleaded guilty to the charge. Observe the word *"proudly,"* for it has an important bearing on this incident. I laid down the manuscript that I was reading when this saleswoman came in, for I could see that she was a woman of intelligence. Just how I came to see this I will leave to your imagination. The important point is that I laid down the manuscript and actually felt myself wanting to hear what she had to say.

With the aid of eleven words, plus a pleasant smile, plus a tone of genuine *enthusiasm,* she had neutralized my mind sufficiently to make me want to hear her. She had performed her most difficult task, with those few words, because I had made up my mind when she was announced that I would keep my manuscript in my hands and thereby convey to her mind, as politely as I could, the fact that I was busy and did not wish to be detained.

Being a student of salesmanship and of *suggestion,* I carefully watched to see what her next move would be. She had a bundle of magazines under her arm and I expected she would unroll it and begin to urge me to purchase, but she didn't. You will recall that I said she was *selling* a combination of six magazines; not merely trying to sell them.

FIRST IMPRESSIONS
REALLY DO COUNT.
DRESS TO LOOK
THE PART YOU IN-
TEND TO PLAY IN
LIFE, BUT TAKE
CARE NOT TO
OVERDO IT.

She walked over to my book shelves, pulled out a copy of Emerson's Essays, and for the next ten minutes she talked about Emerson's essay on Compensation so interestingly that I lost sight of the roll of magazines that she carried. (She was neutralizing my mind some more.)

Incidentally, she gave me a sufficient number of new ideas about Emerson's works to provide material for an excellent editorial.

Then she asked me which magazines I received regularly, and after I told her she smiled as she began to unroll her bundle of magazines and laid them on the table in front of me. She analyzed her magazines one by one, and explained just why I should have each of them. The Saturday Evening Post would bring me the cleanest fiction; Literary Digest would bring me the news of the world in condensed form, such as a *busy man like myself* would demand; the American Magazine would bring me the latest biographies of the men who were leading in business and industry, and so on, until she had covered the entire list.

But I was not responding to her argument as freely as she thought I should have, so she slipped me this gentle *suggestion:*

"A man of your position is bound to be well informed and, if he isn't, it will show up in his own work!"

She spoke the truth! Her remark was both a compliment and a gentle reprimand. She made me feel somewhat sheepish because she had taken inventory of my reading matter—and six of the leading magazines were not on my list. (The six that she was selling)

Then I began to "slip" by asking her how much the six magazines would cost. She put on the finishing touches of a well presented sales talk by this tactful reply: "The cost? Why, the cost of the entire number is less than you receive for a single page of the typewritten manuscript that you had in your hands when I came in."

Again she spoke the truth. And how did she happen to guess so well what I was getting for my manuscript? The answer is, she didn't guess—*she knew!* She made it a part of her business to draw me out tactfully as to the nature of my work (which in no way made me angry). She became so deeply interested in the manuscript which I had laid down when she came in, that she actually induced me to talk about it. (I am not saying, of course, that this required any great amount of skill or coaxing, for have I not said that *it was my manuscript?*) In my remarks about that manuscript I suspect I *admitted* that I was receiving $250.00 for the fifteen pages; yes, *I am sure I was careless enough to admit that I was being well paid for my work.*

Perhaps she induced me to make the admission. At any rate, the information was valuable to her and she made effective use of it at the psychological moment. For all I know it was a part of her plan to observe carefully all that she saw and heard, with the object of finding out just what my weaknesses were and what I was most interested in discussing. Some salesmen take the time to do this; some do not. She was one of those who did.

Yes, she went away with my order for the six magazines; also my twelve dollars. But that was not all the benefit she derived from tactful *suggestion* plus *enthusiasm;* she got my consent to canvass my office, and before she left she had five other orders from my employees.

At no time during her stay did she leave the impression that I was favoring her by purchasing her magazines. Just to the contrary, she distinctly impressed me with the feeling that she was rendering me a favor. This was tactful suggestion.

Before we get away from this incident, I wish to make an admission—when she drew me into conversation she did it in such a way that I talked with *enthusiasm.* There were two reasons for this. She was one of them; and the other one was the fact that she managed to get me to talk *about my own work!* Of course I am not suggesting that *you* should be meddlesome enough to smile at my carelessness as you read this; or that you should gather from this incident the impression that this tactful saleswoman actually led me to talk of my own work for the purpose of neutralizing my mind so that I would listen to her, when she was ready to talk of her magazines, as patiently as she had listened to me. However, if you should be clever enough to draw a lesson from her method, there is no way for me to stop you from doing so.

As I have stated, when I talked I mixed *enthusiasm* with my conversation. Perhaps I caught the spirit of *enthusiasm* from this clever saleswoman, when she made that opening remark as she came into my study. Yes, I am sure this is where I caught it, and, I am just as sure that her enthusiasm was not a matter of accident. She had trained herself to look for something in her prospective purchaser's office, or his work, or his conversation, over which she could express *enthusiasm*.

Remember, *suggestion* and *enthusiasm* go hand in hand!

I can remember, as though it were yesterday, the feeling that came over me when that would-be salesman pushed that Saturday Evening Post in front of me, as he remarked:

"You wouldn't subscribe for the Post to help me out, would you?"

His words were chilled, they were lifeless; they lacked *enthusiasm;* they registered an impression in my mind, but that impression was one of coldness. I wanted to see the man go out at the door at which he had come in. Mind you, I am not naturally unsympathetic, but the tone of his voice, the look on his face, his general bearing *suggested* that he was there to ask a favor and not to offer one.

Suggestion is one of the most subtle and powerful principles of psychology. You are making use of it in all that you do and say and think, but, unless you understand the difference between negative suggestion and positive suggestion, you may be using it in such a way that it is bringing you defeat instead of success.

Science has established the fact that through the negative use of suggestion life may be extinguished. Some years ago, in France, a criminal was condemned to death, but before the time for his execution an experiment was performed on him which conclusively proved that through the principle of *suggestion* death could be produced. The criminal was brought to the guillotine and his head was placed under the knife, after he had been blindfolded. A heavy, sharp edged plank was then dropped on his neck, producing a shock similar to that of a sharp edged knife. Warm water was then gently poured on his neck and allowed to trickle slowly down his spine, to imitate the flow of warm blood. In seven minutes the doctors pronounced the man dead. His imagination, through the principle of suggestion, had actually turned the sharp edged plank into a guillotine blade and stopped his heart from beating.

In the little town where I was raised, there lived an old lady who constantly complained that she feared death from cancer. During her childhood she had seen a woman who had cancer and the sight had so impressed itself upon her mind that she began to look for the symptoms of cancer in her own body. She was sure that every little ache and pain was the beginning of her long-looked-for symptom of cancer. I have seen her place her hand on her breast and have heard her exclaim, "Oh, I am sure I have a cancer growing here. I can feel it." When complaining of this imaginary disease, she always placed her hand on her left breast, where she believed the cancer was attacking her.

For more than twenty years she kept this up.

A few weeks ago she died—*with cancer on her left breast!* If suggestion will actually turn the edge of a plank into a guillotine blade and transform healthy body cells into parasites out of which cancer will develop, can you not imagine what it will do in destroying disease germs, if properly directed? *Suggestion* is the law through which mental healers work what appear to be miracles. I have personally witnessed the removal of parasitical growths known as warts,

Half the wrecks that strew

life's ocean

If some star had been their

guide,

Might in safety now be

riding,

But they drifted with the

Tide.

through the aid of suggestion, within forty-eight hours.

You—the reader of this lesson—can be sent to bed with *imaginary* sickness of the worst sort, in two hours' time or less, through the use of *suggestion*. If you should start down the street and three or four people in whom you had confidence should meet you and each exclaim that you look ill you would be ready for a doctor. This brings to mind an experience that I once had with a life insurance salesman. I had made application for a policy, but was undecided as to whether I would take ten or twenty thousand dollars. Meanwhile, the agent had sent me to the life insurance company's doctor to be examined. The following day I was called back for another examination. The second time the examination was more searching, and the doctor carried a worried look on his face. The third day I was called back again, and this time two consulting physicians were there to look me over. They gave me the most searching examination I had ever received or even heard of.

The next day the agent called on me and addressed me as follows:

"I do not wish to alarm you! but the doctors who examined you do not agree on your analysis. You have not yet decided whether you will take ten or twenty thousand dollars' worth of insurance, and I do not think it fair for me to give you a report on your medical examination until you make this decision, because if I did you might feel that I was urging you to take the larger amount."

Then I spoke up and said: "Well, I have already decided to take the full amount." True enough; I had decided to take the full twenty thousand dollar policy.

*I decided the moment the agent planted the suggestion
in my mind that perhaps I had some constitutional
weakness that would make it hard for me to get as
much insurance as I wanted.*

"Very well," said the agent, "now that you have
decided I feel it my duty to tell you that two of the
doctors believe you have the tubercular germ in your
system, while the other two disagree with them." The
trick had been turned. Clever suggestion had pushed
me over the fence of indecision and we were all
satisfied.

Where does *enthusiasm* come in, do you ask? Never
mind, it "came in" all right, but if you wish to know
who brought it you will have to ask the life insurance
agent and his four medical *accomplices,* for I am sure
they must have had a hearty laugh at my expense.
But the trick was all right. I needed the insurance
anyway.

Of course, if you happen to be a life insurance agent
you will not grab this idea and work it out on the next
prospective client who is slow in making up his mind
about taking a policy. Of course you will not!

A few months ago I received one of the most effective pieces of advertising I ever saw. It was a neat
little book in which a clever automobile insurance
salesman had reprinted press dispatches that he had
gathered from all over the country, in which it was
shown that sixty-five automobiles had been stolen in a
single day. On the back page of the book was this
highly *suggestive* statement:

"Your car may be the next one to go. Is it insured?"

At the bottom of the page was the salesman's name
and address; also his telephone number. Before I had

finished reading the first two pages of the book I called the salesman on the telephone and made inquiry about rates. He came right over to see me, and you know the remainder of the story.

.   .   .   .

Go back, now, to the two letters and let us analyze the second one, which brought the desired replies from all to whom it was sent. Study, carefully, the first paragraph and you will observe that it asks a question which can be answered in but one way. Compare this opening paragraph with that of the first letter, by asking yourself which of the two would have impressed you most favorably. This paragraph is worded as it is for a two-fold purpose; first, it is intended to serve the purpose of neutralizing the mind of the reader so he will read the remainder of the letter in an open-minded attitude; and, second, it asks a question which can be answered in but one way, for the purpose of committing the reader to a viewpoint which harmonizes with the nature of the service that he is to be requested to render in subsequent paragraphs of the letter.

In the second lesson of this course you observed that Andrew Carnegie refused to answer my question, when I asked him to what he attributed his *success,* until he had asked me to define the word *success.* He did this to avoid misunderstanding. The first paragraph of the letter we are analyzing is so worded that it states the object of the letter and at the same time practically forces the reader to accept that object as being sound and reasonable.

Any person who would answer the question asked

in this paragraph of the letter under discussion, in the negative, would, by the same answer, convict himself on the charge of selfishness, and no man wants to face himself with a guilty conscience on such a charge. Just as the farmer first plows his ground, then fertilizes it, and perhaps harrows it and prepares it to receive the seed, in order that he may be sure of a crop, so does this paragraph fertilize the mind of the reader and prepare it for the seed which is to be placed there through the subtle *suggestion* that the paragraph contains.

Study, carefully, the second paragraph of the letter and you will observe that it carries a statement of fact which the reader can *neither question nor deny!* It provides him with no reason for argument because it is obviously based upon a sound fundamental. It takes him the second step of the psychological journey that leads straight toward compliance with the request that is carefully clothed and covered up in the third paragraph of the letter, but you will notice that the third paragraph begins by paying the reader a nice little compliment that was not designed to make him angry. "Therefore, if you will write me of your views as to the most essential points to be borne in mind by those who are offering personal services for sale," etc. Study the wording of this sentence, together with the setting in which it has been placed, and you will observe that it hardly appears to be a request at all, and certainly there is nothing about it to suggest that the *writer of the letter is requesting a favor for his personal benefit.* At most, it can be construed merely as a request for a favor for others.

Now study the closing paragraph and notice how

tactfully concealed is the suggestion that if the reader should refuse the request he is placing himself in the awkward position of one who does not care enough about those who are less fortunate than himself to spend a two cent stamp and a few minutes of time for their benefit.

From start to finish the letter conveys its strongest impressions by mere *suggestion,* yet this suggestion is so carefully covered that it is not obvious except upon careful analysis of the entire letter.

The whole construction of the letter is such that if the reader lays it aside without complying with the request it makes *he will have to reckon with his own conscience!* This effect is intensified by the last sentence of the last paragraph and especially by the last thirteen words of that sentence, "who will *read your message, believe in it, and be guided by it."*

This letter brings the reader up with a bang and turns his own conscience into an ally of the writer; it corners him, just as a hunter might corner a rabbit by driving it into a carefully prepared net.

The best evidence that this analysis is correct is the fact that the letter brought replies from every person to whom it was sent, despite the fact that every one of these men was of the type that we speak of as being a man of affairs—the type that is generally supposed to be too busy to answer a letter of this nature. Not only did the letter bring the desired replies, but the men to whom it was sent replied in person, with the exception of the late Theodore Roosevelt, who replied under the signature of a secretary.

John Wanamaker and Frank A. Vanderlip wrote two of the finest letters I have ever read, each a mas-

CONCEIT is a fog which envelops a man's real character beyond his own recognition. It weakens his native ability and strengthens all his inconsistencies.

terpiece that might well have adorned the pages of a more dignified volume than the one for which the letters were requested. Andrew Carnegie also wrote a letter that was well worth consideration by all who have personal services for sale. William Jennings Bryan wrote a fine letter, as did, also, the late Lord Northcliffe. None of these men wrote merely to please me, for I was unknown to all of them, with the exception of four. *They did not write to please me— they wrote to please themselves and to render a worthy service.* Perhaps the wording of the letter had something to do with this, but, as to that, I make no point other than to state that all of these men whom I have mentioned, and most others of their type, are generally the most willing men to render service for others when they are properly approached.

I wish to take advantage of this appropriate opportunity to state that all of the really big men whom I have had the pleasure of knowing have been the most willing and courteous men of my acquaintance when it came to rendering service that was of benefit to others. Perhaps that was one reason why they were *really* big men.

The human mind is a marvelous piece of machinery!

One of its outstanding characteristics is noticed in the fact that all impressions which reach it, either through outside *suggestion* or Auto-suggestion, are recorded together in groups which harmonize in nature. The negative impressions are stored away, all in one portion of the brain, while the positive impressions are stored in another portion. When one of these impressions (or past experiences) is called into the conscious mind, through the principle of memory, there is a tendency to recall with it all others of a similar nature, just as the raising of one link of a chain brings up other links with it. For example, anything that causes a feeling of doubt to arise in a person's mind is sufficient to call forth all of his experiences which caused him to become doubtful. If a man is asked by a stranger to cash a check, immediately he remembers having cashed checks that were not good, or of having heard of others who did so. Through the law of association all similar emotions, experiences and sense impressions that reach the mind are filed away together, so that the recalling of one has a tendency to bring back to memory all the others.

To arouse a feeling of distrust in a person's mind has a tendency to bring to the surface every doubt-building experience that person ever had. For this reason successful salesmen endeavor to keep away from the discussion of subjects that may arouse the buyer's "chain of doubt impressions" which he has stored away by reason of previous experiences. The successful salesman quickly learns that "knocking" a competitor or a competing article may result in bringing to the buyer's mind certain negative emotions growing out of previous experiences which may make it impossible for the salesman to "neutralize" the buyer's mind.

This principle applies to and controls every sense impression that is lodged in the human mind. Take the feeling of fear, for example; the moment we permit a single emotion that is related to fear to reach the conscious mind, it calls with it all of its unsavory relations. A feeling of courage cannot claim the attention of the conscious mind while a feeling of fear is there. One or the other must dominate. They make poor room-mates because they do not harmonize in nature. Like attracts like. Every thought held in the conscious mind has a tendency to draw to it other thoughts of a similar nature. You see, therefore, that these feelings, thoughts and emotions growing out of past experiences, which claim the attention of the conscious mind, are backed by a regular army of supporting soldiers of a similar nature, that stand ready to aid them in their work.

Deliberately place in your own mind, through the principle of Auto-suggestion, the ambition to succeed through the aid of a *definite chief aim,* and notice how quickly all of your latent or undeveloped ability in the nature of past experiences will become stimulated and aroused to action in your behalf. Plant in a boy's mind, through the principle of *suggestion,* the ambition to become a successful lawyer or doctor or engineer or business man or financier, and if you plant that suggestion deeply enough, and keep it there, by repetition, it will begin to move that boy toward the achievement of the object of that ambition.

If you would plant a *suggestion* "deeply," mix it generously with *enthusiasm;* for enthusiasm is the fertilizer that will insure its rapid growth as well as its permanency.

When that kind-hearted old gentleman planted in my mind the suggestion that I was a "bright boy" and that I could make my mark in the world if I would educate myself, it was not so much *what* he said, as it was the *way in which he said it* that made such a deep and lasting impression on my mind. It was the way in which he gripped my shoulders and the look of confidence in his eyes that drove his suggestion so deeply into my subconscious mind that it never gave me any peace until I commenced taking the steps that led to the fulfillment of the suggestion.

This is a point that I would stress with all the power at my command. *It is not so much what you say as it is the TONE and MANNER in which you say it that makes a lasting impression.*

It naturally follows, therefore, that sincerity of purpose, honesty and earnestness must be placed back of all that one says if one would make a lasting and favorable impression.

Whatever you successfully sell to others you must first sell to *yourself!*

Not long ago I was approached by an agent of the government of Mexico who sought my services as a writer of propaganda for the administration in charge at that time. His approach was about as follows:

"Whereas, Señor has a reputation as an exponent of the Golden Rule philosophy; and whereas, Señor is known throughout the United States as an independent who is not allied with any political faction, now, therefore, would Señor be gracious enough to come to Mexico, study the economic and political affairs of that country, then return to the United States and write a series of articles to appear in the newspapers, recommending to the people of America the immediate recognition of Mexico by the government of the United States, etc."

For this service, I was offered more money than I shall, perhaps, ever possess during my entire life; but I refused the commission, and for a reason that will fail to impress anyone except those who understand the principle which makes it necessary for all who would influence others to remain on good terms with their own conscience.

I could not write convincingly of Mexico's cause for the reason that I did not believe in that cause; therefore, I could not have mixed sufficient *enthusiasm* with my writing to have made it effective, even though I had been willing to prostitute my talent and dip my pen into ink that I knew to be muddy.

I will not endeavor further to explain my philosophy on this incident for the reason that those who are far enough advanced in the study of Auto-suggestion will not need further explanation, while those who are not far enough advanced would not and could not understand.

No man can afford to express, through words or acts, that which is not in harmony with his own belief, and if he does so he must pay by the loss of his ability to influence others.

Please read, aloud, the foregoing paragraph! It is worth emphasizing by repetition, for lack of observation of the principle upon which it is based constitutes the rocks and reefs upon which many a man's *definite chief aim* dashes itself to pieces.

I do not believe that I can afford to try to deceive anyone, about anything, but *I know that I cannot afford to try to deceive myself.* To do so would destroy the power of my pen and render my words ineffective. It is only when I write with the *fire of enthusiasm* burning in my heart that my writing impresses others favorably; and it is only when I speak from a heart that is bursting with belief in my message, that I can move my audience to accept that message.

IS there not food for thought in the fact that no newspaper has ever published any account of "Wild drinking parties" or other similar scandals in connection with the names of Edison, Ford, Rockefeller a n d most of the other really big fellows?

I would also have you read, aloud, the foregoing paragraph. Yes, I would have you commit it to memory. Even more than this, I would have you write it out and place it where it may serve as a daily reminder of a principle, nay, a *law* as immutable as the law of gravitation, *without which you can never become a power in your chosen life-work.*

There have been times, and many of them, when it *appeared* that if I stood by this principle it would mean starvation!

There have been times when my closest friends and business advisers have strongly urged me to shade my philosophy for the sake of gaining a needed advantage here and there, but somehow I have managed to cling to it, mainly, I suppose, for the reason that I have preferred peace and harmony in my own heart to the material gain that I might have had by a forced compromise with my conscience.

Strange as it may seem, my deliberations and conclusions on this subject of refusing to strangle my own conscience have seldom been based upon what is commonly called "honesty." That which I have done in the matter of refraining from writing or speaking anything that I did not believe has been solely a question of honor between my conscience and myself. I have tried to express that which my heart dictated because I have aimed to give my words "flesh." It might be said that my motive was based more upon self-interest than it was on a desire to be fair with others, although I have never desired to be unfair with others, so far as I am able to analyze myself.

No man can become a master salesman if he compromises with falsehood. Murder will out, and even though no one ever catches him red-handed in express-ing that which he does not believe, his words will fail in the accomplishment of their purpose because he cannot give them "flesh," if they do not come from his heart, and if they are not mixed with genuine, unadul-terated *enthusiasm.*

I would also have you read, aloud, the foregoing paragraph, for it embraces a great law that you must *understand and apply* before you can become a person of influence in any undertaking.

In making these requests, for the sake of emphasis, I am not trying to take undue liberties with you. I am giving you full credit for being an adult, a thinker, an intelligent person, yet I know how likely you are to skip over these vital laws without being sufficiently impressed by them to make them a part of your own workaday philosophy. *I know your weakness because I know my own.* It has required the better part of twenty-five years of ups and downs—mostly downs—to impress these basic truths upon my own mind so that they influenced me. I have tried both them and their opposites; therefore, I can speak, not as one who merely *believes* in their soundness, but as one who *knows.*

And what do I mean by "these truths"?

So that you cannot possibly misunderstand my meaning, and so that these words of warning cannot possibly convey an abstract meaning, I will state that by "these truths" I mean this:

You cannot afford to suggest to another person, by word of mouth or by an act of yours, that which you do not believe.

Surely that is plain enough.

And, the reason you cannot afford to do so, is this:

If you compromise with your own conscience, it will not be long before you will have no conscience; for your conscience will fail to guide you, just as an alarm clock will fail to awaken you if you do not heed it.

Surely, that is plain enough, also.

And how do I happen to be an authority on this vital subject, do you ask?

I am an authority because I have experimented with the principle until I know how it works!

"But," you may ask, "how do I know that you are telling the truth?"

The answer is that *you will know only by experimenting for yourself, and by observing others who faithfully apply this principle and those who do not apply it.*

If my evidence needs backing, then consult any man whom you know to be a person who has "tried to get by" without observing this principle, and if he will not or cannot give you the truth you can get it, nevertheless, by analyzing the man.

There is but one thing in the world that gives a man real and enduring power, and that is *character! Reputation,* bear in mind, is not *character.* Reputation is that which people are believed to be; character is that which people *are!* If you would be a person of great influence, then be a person of real *character.*

Character is the philosopher's lode-stone through which all who have it may turn the base metals of their life into pure gold. Without *character* you have nothing; you are nothing; and you can be nothing, except a pile of flesh and bone and hair, worth perhaps twenty-five dollars. Character is something that you cannot beg or steal or buy. You can get it only by *building it;* and you can build it by your own *thoughts* and *deeds,* and in no other way.

Through the aid of Auto-suggestion, any person can build a sound character, no matter what his past has been. As a fitting close for this lesson, I wish to emphasize the fact that all who have *character* have *enthusiasm* and personality sufficient to draw to them others who have character.

You will now be instructed as to how you shall proceed in developing *enthusiasm,* in the event that you do not already possess this rare quality.

The instructions will be simple, but you will be unfortunate if you discount their value on that account.

First: Complete the remaining lessons of this course, because other important instructions which are to be co-ordinated with this one will be found in subsequent lessons.

Second: If you have not already done so, write out your *definite chief aim* in clear, simple language, and follow this by writing out the plan through which you intend to transform your *aim* into reality.

Third: Read over the description of your *definite chief aim* each night, just before retiring, and as you read, see yourself (in your imagination) in full possession of the object of your *aim.* Do this with full faith in your ability to transform your *definite chief aim* into reality. *Read aloud, with all the enthusiasm at your command, emphasizing every word. Repeat this reading until the small still voice within you tells you that your purpose will be realized.* Sometimes you will feel the effects of this voice *from within* the

first time you read your *definite chief aim;* while at
other times, you may have to read it a dozen or fifty
times before the assurance comes, but do not stop until
you feel it.

If you prefer to do so you may read your *definite
chief aim* as a prayer.

The remainder of this lesson is for the person who
has not yet learned the power of *faith* and who knows
little or nothing of the principle of Auto-suggestion.

To all who are in this class, I would recommend the
reading of the seventh and eighth verses of the seventh
chapter, and the twentieth verse of the seventeenth
chapter of St. Matthew.

One of the greatest powers for good, upon the face
of this earth, is faith. To this marvelous power may
be traced miracles of the most astounding nature. It
offers peace on earth to all who embrace it.

Faith involves a principle that is so far-reaching in
its effect that no man can say what are its limitations,
or if it has limitations. *Write into the description of
your definite chief aim a statement of the qualities
that you intend to develop in yourself, and the station
in life that you intend to attain, and have faith, as you
read this description each night, that you can transform this purpose into reality.* Surely, you cannot
miss the suggestion contained in this lesson.

To become successful you must be a person of action. Merely to "know" is not sufficient. It is necessary both to *know* and *do.*

Enthusiasm is the mainspring of the mind which
urges one to put knowledge into action.

Billy Sunday is the most successful evangelist this
country has ever known. For the purpose of study-

IF you think your lot in
life has been hard
read "Up From Slavery"
by Booker T. Washing-
ton, and you may see how
fortunate you have been.

ing his technique and checking up on his psychological methods the author of this course went through three campaigns with Reverend Sunday.

His success is based very largely upon one word—
ENTHUSIASM!

By making effective use of the law of suggestion Billy Sunday conveys his own spirit of enthusiasm to the minds of his followers and they become influenced by it. He sells his sermons by the use of exactly the same sort of strategy employed by many Master Salesmen.

Enthusiasm is as essential to a salesman as water is to a duck!

All successful sales managers understand the psychology of enthusiasm and make use of it, in various ways, as a practical means of helping their men produce more sales.

Practically all sales organizations have get-together meetings at stated times, for the purpose of revitalizing the minds of all members of the sales force, and injecting the spirit of enthusiasm, which can be best done en masse, through group psychology.

Sales meetings might properly be called "revival" meetings, because their purpose is to revive interest and arouse enthusiasm which will enable the salesman to take up the fight with renewed ambition and energy.

During his administration as Sales Manager of the National Cash Register Company Hugh Chalmers (who later became famous in the motor car industry) faced a most embarrassing situation which threatened to wipe out his position as well as that of thousands of salesmen under his direction.

The company was in financial difficulty. This fact

had become known to the salesmen in the field and the effect of it was to cause them to lose their Enthusiasm. Sales began to dwindle until finally the conditions became so alarming that a general meeting of the sales organization was called, to be held at the company's plant in Dayton, Ohio. Salesmen were called in from all over the country.

Mr. Chalmers presided over the meeting. He began by calling on several of his best salesmen to get on their feet and tell what was wrong out in the field that orders had fallen off. One by one they got up, as called, and each man had a most terrible tale of grief to unfold. Business conditions were bad, money was scarce, people were holding off buying until after Presidential election, etc. As the fifth man began to enumerate the difficulties which had kept him from making his usual quota of sales Mr. Chalmers jumped up on top of a table, held up his hands for silence, and said "STOP! I order this convention to come to a close for ten minutes while I get my shoes shined."

Then turning to a small colored boy who sat near by he ordered the boy to bring his shoe-shine outfit and shine his shoes, right where he stood, on top of the table.

The salesmen in the audience were astounded! Some of them thought that Mr. Chalmers had suddenly lost his mind. They began to whisper among themselves. Meanwhile, the little colored boy shined first one and then the other shoe, taking plenty of time and doing a first-class job.

After the job was finished Mr. Chalmers handed the boy a dime, then went ahead with his speech:

"I want each of you," said he, "to take a good look

at this little colored boy. He has the concession for shoe-shining throughout our plant and offices. His predecessor was a white boy, considerably older than himself, and despite the fact that the company subsidized him with a salary of $5.00 a week he could not make a living in this plant, where thousands of people are employed.

"This little colored boy not only makes a good living, without any subsidy from the company, but he is actually saving money out of his earnings each week, working under the same conditions, in the same plant, for the same people.

"Now I wish to ask you a question: Whose fault was it that the white boy did not get more business? Was it his fault, or the fault of his buyers?"

In a mighty roar from the crowd the answer came back:

"IT WAS THE BOY'S FAULT, OF COURSE!"

"Just so," replied Chalmers, "and now I want to tell you this, that you are selling Cash Registers in the same territory, to the same people, with exactly the same business conditions that existed a year ago, yet you are not producing the business that you were then. Now whose fault is that? Is it yours, or the buyer's?"

And again the answer came back with a roar:

"IT IS OUR FAULT, OF COURSE!"

"I am glad that you are frank to acknowledge your faults," Chalmers continued, "and I now wish to tell you what your trouble is: You have heard rumors about this company being in financial trouble and that has killed off your enthusiasm so that you are not making the effort that you formerly made. If you will

go back into your territories with a definite promise
to send in five orders each during the next thirty days
this company will no longer be in financial difficulty,
for that additional business will see us clear. Will
you do it?"

They said they would, and they did!

That incident has gone down in the history of the
National Cash Register Company under the name of
Hugh Chalmers' Million Dollar Shoe Shine, for it is
said that this turned the tide in the company's affairs
and was worth millions of dollars.

Enthusiasm knows no defeat!   The Sales Manager
who knows how to send out an army of enthusiastic
salespeople may set his own price on his services, and
what is more important even than this, he can increase
the earning capacity of every person under his direction; thus, his enthusiasm benefits not only himself
but perhaps hundreds of others.

Enthusiasm is never a matter of chance.   There are
certain stimuli which produce enthusism, the most important of these being as follows:

1. Occupation in work which one loves best.

2. Environment where one comes in contact with
others who are enthusiastic and optimistic.

3. Financial success.

4. Complete mastery and application, in one's daily
work, of the Fifteen Laws of Success.

5. Good health.

6. Knowledge that one has served others in some
helpful manner.

7. Good clothes, appropriate to the needs of one's
occupation.

All of these seven sources of stimuli are self-explanatory with the exception of the last. The psychology of clothes is understood by very few people, and for this reason it will be here explained in detail. Clothes constitute the most important part of the embellishment which every person must have in order to feel self-reliant, hopeful and enthusiastic.

THE PSYCHOLOGY OF GOOD CLOTHES

When the good news came from the theater of war, on November the eleventh, 1918, my worldly possessions amounted to but little more than they did the day I came into the world.

The war had destroyed my business and made it necessary for me to make a new start!

My wardrobe consisted of three well worn business suits and two uniforms which I no longer needed.

Knowing all too well that the world forms its first and most lasting impressions of a man by the clothes he wears, I lost no time in visiting my tailor.

Happily, my tailor had known me for many years, therefore he did not judge me entirely by the clothes I wore. If he had I would have been "sunk."

With less than a dollar in change in my pocket, I picked out the cloth for three of the most expensive suits I ever owned, and ordered that they be made up for me at once.

The three suits came to $375.00!

I shall never forget the remark made by the tailor as he took my measure. Glancing first at the three bolts of expensive cloth which I had selected, and then at me, he inquired:

"Dollar-a-year man, eh?"

ALL anyone really requires, as a capital on which to start a successful career, is a sound mind, a healthy body and a genuine desire to be of as much service as possible to as many people as possible.

"No," said I, "if I had been fortunate enough to get on the dollar-a-year payroll I might now have enough money to pay for these suits."

The tailor looked at me with surprise. I don't think he got the joke.

One of the suits was a beautiful dark gray; one was a dark blue; the other was a light blue with a pin stripe.

Fortunately I was in good standing with my tailor, therefore he did not ask when I was going to pay for those expensive suits.

I knew that I could and would pay for them in due time, but could I have convinced him of that? This was the thought which was running through my mind, with hope against hope that the question would not be brought up.

I then visited my haberdasher, from whom I purchased three less expensive suits and a complete supply of the best shirts, collars, ties, hosiery and underwear that he carried.

My bill at the haberdasher's amounted to a little over $300.00.

With an air of prosperity I nonchalantly signed the charge ticket and tossed it back to the salesman, with instructions to deliver my purchase the following morning. The feeling of renewed self-reliance and success had begun to come over me, even before I had attired myself in my newly purchased outfit.

I was out of the war and $675.00 in debt, all in less than twenty-four hours.

The following day the first of the three suits ordered from the haberdasher was delivered. I put it on at once, stuffed a new silk handkerchief in the outside pocket of my coat, shoved the $50.00 I had borrowed on my ring down into my pants pocket, and walked down Michigan Boulevard, in Chicago, feeling as rich as Rockefeller.

Every article of clothing I wore, from my underwear out, was of the very best. That it was not paid for was nobody's business except mine and my tailor's and my haberdasher's.

Every morning I dressed myself in an entirely new outfit, and walked down the same street, at precisely the same hour. That hour "happened" to be the time when a certain wealthy publisher usually walked down the same street, on his way to lunch.

I made it my business to speak to him each day, and occasionally I would stop for a minute's chat with him.

After this daily meeting had been going on for about a week I met this publisher one day, but decided I would see if he would let me get by without speaking.

Watching him from under my eyelashes I looked straight ahead, and started to pass him when he stopped and motioned me over to the edge of the sidewalk, placed his hand on my shoulder, looked me over from head to foot, and said: "You look damned prosperous for a man who has just laid aside a uniform. Who makes your clothes?"

"Well," said I, "Wilkie & Sellery made this particular suit."

He then wanted to know what sort of business I was engaged in. That "airy" atmosphere of prosperity which I had been wearing, along with a new and different suit every day, had got the better of his curiosity. (I had hoped that it would.)

Flipping the ashes from my Havana perfecto, I said "Oh, I am preparing the copy for a new magazine that I am going to publish."

"A new magazine, eh?" he queried, "and what are you going to call it?"

"It is to be named Hill's Golden Rule."

"Don't forget," said my publisher friend, "that I am in the business of printing and distributing magazines. Perhaps I can serve you, also."

That was the moment for which I had been waiting. I had that very moment, and almost the very spot of ground on which we stood, in mind when I was purchasing those new suits.

But, is it necessary to remind you, that conversation never would have taken place had this publisher observed me walking down that street from day to day, with a "whipped-dog" look on my face, an unpressed suit on my back and a look of poverty in my eyes.

An appearance of prosperity attracts attention always, with no exceptions whatsover. Moreover, a look of prosperity attracts "favorable attention," because the one dominating desire in every human heart is to be prosperous.

.   .   .   .

My publisher friend invited me to his club for lunch. Before the coffee and cigars had been served he had "talked me out of" the contract for printing and distributing my magazine. I had even "consented" to permit him to supply the capital, without any interest charge.

For the benefit of those who are not familiar with

the publishing business may I not offer the information that considerable capital is required for launching a new nationally distributed magazine.

Capital, in such large amounts, is often hard to get, even with the best of security. The capital necessary for launching Hill's Golden Rule Magazine, which you may have read, was well above $30,000.00, and every cent of it was raised on a "front" created mostly by good clothes. True, there may have been some ability back of those clothes, but many millions of men have ability who never have anything else, and who are never heard of outside of the limited community in which they live. This is a rather sad truth!

To some it may seem an unpardonable extravagance for one who was "broke" to have gone in debt for $675.00 worth of clothes, but the psychology back of that investment more than justified it.

The appearance of prosperity not only made a favorable impression on those to whom I had to look for favors, but of more importance still was the effect that proper attire HAD ON ME.

I not only knew that correct clothes would impress others favorably, but I knew also that good clothes would give me an atmosphere of self-reliance, without which I could not hope to regain my lost fortunes.

I got my first training in the psychology of good clothes from my friend Edwin C. Barnes, who is a close business associate of Thomas A. Edison. Barnes afforded considerable amusement for the Edison staff when, some twenty-odd years ago, he rode into West Orange on a freight train (not being able to raise sufficient money for passenger fare) and announced at the Edison offices that he had come to enter into a partnership with Mr. Edison.

Nearly everybody around the Edison plant laughed at Barnes, except Edison himself. He saw something in the square jaw and determined face of young Barnes which most of the others did not see, despite the fact that the young man looked more like a tramp than he did a future partner of the greatest inventor on earth.

Barnes got his start, sweeping floors in the Edison offices!

That was all he sought—just a chance to get a toe-hold in the Edison organization. From there on he made history that is well worth emulation by other young men who wish to make places for themselves.

Barnes has now retired from active business, even though he is still a comparatively young man, and spends most of his time at his two beautiful homes in Bradentown, Florida, and Damariscotta, Maine. He is a multimillionaire, prosperous and happy.

I first became acquainted with Barnes during the early days of his association with Edison, before he had "arrived."

In those days he had the largest and most expensive collection of clothes I had ever seen or heard of one man owning. His wardrobe consisted of thirty-one suits; one for each day of the month. He never wore the same suit two days in succession.

Moreover, all his suits were of the most expensive type. (Incidentally, his clothes were made by the same tailors who made those three suits for me.)

He wore socks which cost six dollars per pair.

THERE is a suitable reward for every virtue and appropriate punishment for every sin a man commits. Both the reward and the punishment are effects over which no man has control, as they come upon him voluntarily.

His shirts and other wearing apparel cost in similar proportion. His cravats were specially made, at a cost of from five to seven dollars and a half each.

One day, in a spirit of fun, I asked him to save some of his old suits which he did not need, for me.

He informed me that he hadn't a single suit which he did not need!

He then gave me a lesson on the psychology of clothes which is well worth remembering. "I do not wear thirty-one suits of clothes," said he, "entirely for the impression they make on other people; I do it mostly for the impression they have on me."

Barnes then told me of the day when he presented himself at the Edison plant, for a position. He said he had to walk around the plant a dozen times before he worked up enough courage to announce himself, because he knew that he looked more like a tramp than he did a desirable employee.

Barnes is said to be the most able salesman ever connected with the great inventor of West Orange. His entire fortune was made through his ability as a salesman, but he has often said that he never could have accomplished the results which have made him both wealthy and famous had it not been for his understanding of the psychology of clothes.

.   .   .   .

I have met many salesman in my time. During the past ten years I have personally trained and directed the efforts of more than 3,000 salespeople, both men and women, and I have observed that, without a single exception, the star producers were all people who understood and made good use of the psychology of clothes.

I have seen a few well dressed people who made no outstanding records as salesmen, but I have yet to see the first poorly dressed man who became a star producer in the field of selling.

I have studied the psychology of clothes for so long, and I have watched its effect on people in so many different walks of life, that I am fully convinced there is a close connection between clothes and success.

.   .   .   .

Personally I feel no need of thirty-one suits of clothes, but if my personality demanded a wardrobe of this size I would manage to get it, no matter how much it might cost.

To be well dressed a man should have at least ten suits of clothes. He should have a different suit for each of the seven days of the week, a full dress suit and a Tuxedo, for formal evening occasions, and a cutaway for formal afternoon occasions.

For summer wear he should have an assortment of at least four appropriate light suits, with blue coat and white flannel trousers for informal afternoon and evening occasions. If he plays golf he should have at least one golf suit.

This, of course, is for the man who is a notch or two above the "mediocre" class. The man who is satisfied with mediocrity needs but few clothes.

It may be true, as a well known poet has said, that "clothes do not make the man," but no one can deny the fact that good clothes go a very long way toward giving him a *favorable start*.

A man's bank will generally loan him all the money he wants when he does not need it—when he is prosperous, but never go to your bank for a loan with a shabby-looking suit on your back and a look of poverty in your eyes, for if you do you'll get the gate.

Success attracts success! There is no escape from this great universal law; therefore, if you wish to attract success make sure that you look the part of success, whether your calling is that of day laborer or merchant prince.

For the benefit of the more "dignified" students of this philosophy who may object to resorting to "stunt" stimuli or "trick clothing" as a means of achieving success, it may be profitably explained that practically every successful man on earth has discovered some form of stimulus through which he can and does drive himself on to greater effort.

It may be shocking to members of the Anti-Saloon League, but it is said to be true, nevertheless, that James Whitcomb Riley wrote his best poems when he was under the influence of alcohol. His stimulus was liquor. (The author wishes it distinctly understood that he does not recommend the use of alcoholic or narcotic stimuli, for any purpose whatsoever, as either will eventually destroy both body and mind of all who use them.) Under the influence of alcohol Riley became imaginative, enthusiastic and an entirely different person, according to close personal friends of his.

Edwin Barnes spurred himself into the necessary action to produce outstanding results, with the aid of good clothes.

Some men rise to great heights of achievement as

the result of love for some woman. Connect this with the brief suggestion to the subject which was made in the Introductory Lesson and you will, if you are a person who knows the ways of men, be able to finish the discussion of this particular phase of enthusiasm stimulus without further comment by the author which might not be appropriate for the younger minds that will assimilate this philosophy.

Underworld characters who are engaged in the dangerous business of highway robbery, burglary, etc., generally "dope" themselves for the occasion of their operations, with cocaine, morphine and other narcotics. Even in this there is a lesson which shows that practically all men need temporary or artificial stimuli to drive them to greater effort than that normally employed in the ordinary pursuits of life.

SUCCESSFUL PEOPLE HAVE DISCOVERED WAYS AND MEANS WHICH THEY BELIEVE BEST SUITED TO THEIR OWN NEEDS, TO PRODUCE STIMULI WHICH CAUSE THEM TO RISE TO HEIGHTS OF ENDEAVOR ABOVE THE ORDINARY.

One of the most successful writers in the world employs an orchestra of beautifully dressed young women who play for him while he writes. Seated in a room that has been artistically decorated to suit his own taste, under lights that have been colored, tinted and softened, these beautiful young ladies, dressed in handsome evening gowns, play his favorite music. To use his own words, "I become drunk with enthusiasm, under the influence of this environment, and rise to heights I never know or feel on other occasions. It is then that I do my work. The thoughts pour in on me as if they were dictated by an unseen and unknown power."

This author gets much of his inspiration from music and art. Once a week he spends at least an hour in an art museum, looking at the works of the masters. On these occasions, again using his own words, "I get enough enthusiasm from one hour's visit in the museum of art to carry me for two days."

Edgar Allan Poe wrote "The Raven" when, it is reported, he was more than half intoxicated. Oscar Wilde wrote his poems under the influence of a form of stimulus which cannot be appropriately mentioned in a course of this nature.

Henry Ford (so it is believed by this author, who admits that this is merely the author's opinion) got his real start as the result of his love for his charming life-companion. It was she who inspired him, gave him faith in himself, and kept him keyed up so that he carried on in the face of adversities which would have killed off a dozen ordinary men.

These incidents are cited as evidence that men of outstanding achievement have, by accident or design, discovered ways and means of stimulating themselves to a high state of enthusiasm.

Associate that which has been here stated with what was said concerning the law of the "Master Mind," in the Introductory Lesson, and you will have an entirely new conception of the modus operandi through which that law may be applied. You will also have a somewhat different understanding of the real purpose of "allied effort, in a spirit of perfect harmony," which constitutes the best known method of bringing into use the Law of the Master Mind.

YOUR employer does not control the sort of service you render. You control that, and it is the thing that makes or breaks you.

At this point it seems appropriate to call your attention to the manner in which the lessons of this course blend. You will observe that each lesson covers the subject intended to be covered, and in addition to this it overlaps and gives the student a better understanding of some other lesson or lessons of the course.

In the light of what has been said in this lesson, for example, the student will better understand the real purpose of the Law of the Master Mind; that purpose being, in the main, a practical method of stimulating the minds of all who participate in the group constituting the Master Mind.

Times too numerous to be here described this author has gone into conference with men whose faces showed the signs of care, who had the appearance of worry written all over them, only to see those same men straighten up their shoulders, tilt their chins at a higher angle, soften their faces with smiles of confidence, and get down to business with that sort of ENTHUSIASM which knows no defeat.

The change took place the moment harmony of purpose was established.

If a man goes about the affairs of life in the same day-in and day-out, prosaic, lackadaisical spirit, devoid of enthusiasm, he is doomed to failure. Nothing can save him until he changes his attitude and learns how to stimulate his mind and body to unusual heights of enthusiasm AT WILL!

The author is unwilling to leave this subject without having stated the principle here described in so many different ways that it is bound to be understood and also respected by the students of this course, who, all will remember, are men and women of all sorts of natures, experiences and degrees of intelligence. For this reason much repetition is essential.

Your business in life, you are reminded once again, is to achieve success!

With the stimulus you will experience from studying this philosophy, and with the aid of the ideas you will gather from it, plus the personal co-operation of the author who will give you an accurate inventory of your outstanding qualities, you should be able to create a DEFINITE PLAN that will lift you to great heights of achievement. However, there is no plan that can produce this desirable result without the aid of some influence that will cause you to arouse yourself, in a spirit of enthusiasm, to where you will exert greater than the ordinary effort which you put into your daily occupation.

You are now ready for the lesson on Self-control!

As you read that lesson you will observe that it has a vital bearing on this lesson, just as this lesson has a direct connection with the preceding lessons on A Definite Chief Aim, Self-confidence, Initiative and Leadership and Imagination.

The next lesson describes the Law which serves as the Balance Wheel of this entire philosophy.

THE SEVEN DEADLY
HORSEMEN

An After-the-Lesson Visit With the Author

The "seven horsemen" are labeled, in order shown,—Intolerance, Greed, Revenge, Egotism, Suspicion, Jealously and "?"

The worst enemy that any man has is the one that walks around under his own hat.

If you could see yourself as others see you the enemies that you harbor in your own personality might be discovered and thrown out. The Seven Enemies named in this essay are the commonest which ride millions of men and women to failure without being discovered. Weigh yourself carefully and find out how many of the Seven you are harboring.

YOU see, in this picture, seven deadly warriors! From birth until death every human being must give battle to these enemies. Your success will be measured very largely by the way you manage your battle against these swift riders.

As you look at this picture you will say, of course,

that it is only imagination. True, the picture is imaginary, but the swift riders of destruction are REAL.

If these enemies rode openly, on real horses, they would not be dangerous, because they could be rounded up and put out of commission. But, they ride unseen, in the minds of men. So silently and subtly do they work that most people never recognize their presence.

Take inventory of yourself and find out how many of these seven horsemen you are harboring.

.   .   .   .

In the foreground you will find the most dangerous and the commonest of the riders. You will be fortunate if you discover this enemy and protect yourself against it. This cruel warrior, INTOLERANCE, has killed more people, destroyed more friendships, brought more misery and suffering into the world and caused more wars than all of the other six horsemen that you see in this picture.

Until you master INTOLERANCE you will never become an accurate thinker. This enemy of mankind closes up the mind and pushes reason and logic and FACTS into the back-ground. If you find yourself hating those whose religious viewpoint is different from your own you may be sure that the most dangerous of the seven deadly horsemen still rides in your brain.

.   .   .   .

Next, in the picture, you will observe REVENGE and GREED!

These riders travel side by side. Where one is found the other is always close at hand. GREED warps and twists man's brain so that he wants to build a fence around the earth and keep everyone else on the outside of it. This is the enemy that drives man to accumulate millions upon top of millions of dollars which he does not need and can never use. This is the enemy that causes man to twist the screw until he has wrung the last drop of blood from his fellow man.

And, thanks to REVENGE which rides alongside of GREED, the unfortunate person who gives brain-room to these cruel twins is not satisfied to merely take away his fellow man's earthly belongings; he wants to destroy his reputation in the bargain.

> "Revenge is a naked sword—
>   It has neither hilt nor guard.
> Would'st thou wield this brand of the Lord:
>   Is thy grasp then firm and hard?
> But the closer thy clutch of the blade,
>   The deadlier blow thou would'st deal,
> Deeper wound in thy hand is made—
>   It is thy blood reddens the steel.
> And when thou hast dealt the blow—
>   When the blade from thy hand has flown—
> Instead of the heart of the foe
>   Thou may'st find it sheathed in thine own."

If you would know how deadly are ENVY and GREED, study the history of every man who has set out to become RULER OF THIS WORLD!

If you do not wish to undertake so ambitious a program of research, then study the people around you; those who have tried and those who are now trying to "feather their own nests" at the cost of others. GREED and REVENGE stand at the crossroads of life, where they turn aside to failure and misery every person who would take the road that leads to success. It is a part of your business not to permit them to interfere with you when you approach one of these crossroads.

Both individuals and nations rapidly decline where GREED and ENVY ride in the minds of those who dominate.   Take a look at Mexico and Spain if you wish to know what happens to the envious and the greedy.

Most important of all, take a look at YOURSELF and make sure that these two deadly enemies are not riding in your brain!

. . . .

Turn your attention, now, to two more twins of destruction—EGOTISM and SUSPICION.   Observe that they, also, ride side by side.   There is no hope of success for the person who suffers either from too much self-love or lack of confidence in others.

Someone who likes to manipulate figures has estimated that the largest club in the world is the "IT CAN'T BE DONE CLUB."   It is claimed that there are approximately ninety-nine million members of this club in the United States of America alone.

If you have no FAITH in other people you have not the seed of success in you.   SUSPICION is a prolific germ.   If permitted to get a start it rapidly multiplies itself until it leaves no room for FAITH.

Without faith no man may enjoy enduring success.

Running, like a golden cord of illumination throughout the Bible, is the admonition to have FAITH. Before civilization lost itself in its mad rush for dollars men understood the power of FAITH.

"For verily I say unto you, if ye have faith as a grain of mustard seed, ye shall say unto this mountain, Remove hence to yonder place; and it shall remove; and nothing shall be impossible unto you."

The writer of this passage, which appears in the Bible, understood a great law which but few of today understand. Believe in people if you would have them believe in you. Kill off SUSPICION. If you do not it will kill you off.

If you would have power, cultivate FAITH in mankind!

EGOTISM thrives where SUSPICION exists. Interest yourself in others and you will be too busy to indulge in self-love. Observe those around you who begin every sentence with the personal pronoun, "I," and you will notice that they are suspicious of other people.

The man who can forget himself while engaging in useful service to other people is never cursed with SUSPICION. Study those about you who are both SUSPICIOUS and EGOTISTICAL and see how many of this type you can name who are successful in whatever work they may be engaged in.

And, while making this study of OTHERS, study, also, yourself!

Be sure that you are not bound down by EGOTISM and SUSPICION.

Bringing up the rear of this deadly group of riders you see two horsemen. One is JEALOUSY and the name of the other has been purposely omitted.

Each reader of this article may take inventory of himself and give the seventh rider a name that fits whatever he finds in his own mind.

Some will name this rider DISHONESTY. Others will name it PROCRASTINATION. A few will have the courage to name it UNCONTROLLED SEX DESIRE. As for you, name it whatever you please, but be sure to give it a name.

Perhaps your own imagination will supply an appropriate name as a fellow-traveler for JEALOUSY.

You will be better prepared to give the unnamed rider a name if you know that JEALOUSY is a form of insanity! Facts are sometimes cruel things to face. It is a fact that JEALOUSY is a form of insanity, known to the medical fraternity as "dementia praecox."

> "O jealousy,
> Thou ugliest fiend of hell! thy deadly venom
> Preys on my vitals, turns the healthful hue
> Of my fresh cheek to haggard sallowness,
> And drinks my spirit up!"

You will notice that JEALOUSY rides just back of SUSPICION. Some who read this will say that JEALOUSY and SUSPICION should have ridden side by side, as one often leads to the other in man's mind.

JEALOUSY is the most common form of insanity. It rides in the minds of both men and women; sometimes with a real cause, but more often without any cause whatsoever.

This deadly rider is a great friend of the divorce lawyers!

It also keeps detective agencies busy night and day. It takes its regular toll of murder. It breaks up homes and makes widows of mothers and orphans of innocent little children. Peace and happiness can never be YOURS as long as this rider remains unharnessed in your brain.

Man and wife may go through life together in poverty and still be very happy, if both are free from this child of insanity known as JEALOUSY. Examine yourself carefully and if you find any evidence of JEALOUSY in your mind begin, at once, to master it.

JEALOUSY rides in many forms.

When it first begins to creep into the brain it manifests itself in something after this fashion:

"I wonder where she is and what she is doing while I am away?"

Or, "I wonder if he does not see another woman when he is away from me?"

When these questions begin to arise in your mind do not call in a detective. Instead, go to the psychopathic hospital and have yourself examined, because more than likely you are suffering from a mild form of insanity.

Get your foot on JEALOUSY'S neck before it gets its clutches on your throat.

.   .   .   .

After you have read this essay lay it aside and THINK about it.

At first you may say "This does not apply to me. I have no imaginary horsemen in my brain." And, you may be right—ONE OUT OF EVERY TEN MILLION COULD SAY THIS AND BE RIGHT! The other nine million nine hundred and ninety-nine thousand nine hundred and ninety-nine would be wrong.

Do not fool yourself!   You may be in that larger class.   The purpose of this article is to get you to see yourself as YOU ARE!   If you are suffering failure and poverty and misery in any of their forms you are sure to discover one or more of these deadly riders in your brain.

Make no mistake about it—those who have all they want, including happiness and good health, have driven the seven horsemen out of their brains.

Come back to this essay a month from now, after you have had time to analyze yourself carefully. Read it again and it may bring you face to face with FACTS that will emancipate you from a horde of cruel enemies that now ride within your brain without your knowing it.

Lesson Eight

SELF-CONTROL

THE man who actually knows just what he wants in life has already gone a long way toward attaining it.

THE LAW OF SUCCESS
Lesson Eight
SELF-CONTROL

"You Can Do It if You Believe You Can!"

N the preceding lesson you learned of the value of enthusiasm. You also learned how to generate enthusiasm and how to transmit its influence to others, through the principle of *suggestion*.

You come, now, to the study of *self-control,* through which you may direct your *enthusiasm* to constructive ends. Without *self-control* enthusiasm resembles the unharnessed lightning of an electrical storm—it may strike *anywhere;* it may destroy life and property.

Enthusiasm is the vital quality that arouses you to *action,* while *self-control* is the balance wheel that directs your *action* so that it will build up and not tear down.

To be a person who is well "balanced," you must be a person in whom *enthusiasm* and *self-control* are equalized. A survey which I have just completed of the 160,000 adult inmates of the penitentiaries of the United States discloses the startling fact that ninety-two per cent of these unfortunate men and women are

in prison because they lacked the necessary *self-control*
to direct their energies constructively.

Read the foregoing paragraph again; it is authentic,
it is *startling!*

It is a fact that the majority of a man's griefs come
about through lack of *self-control.* The holy scriptures are full of admonition in support of *self-control.*
They even urge us to love our enemies and to forgive
those who injure us. The law of non-resistance runs,
like a golden cord, throughout the Bible.

Study the records of those whom the world calls
great, and observe that *every one of them possesses this
quality of self-control!*

For example, study the characteristics of our own
immortal Lincoln. In the midst of his most trying
hours he exercised patience, poise and *self-control.*
These were some of the qualities which made him the
great man that he was. He found disloyalty in some
of the members of his cabinet; but, for the reason that
this disloyalty was toward him, personally, and because those in whom he found it had qualities .which
made them valuable to his country, Lincoln exercised
self-control and disregarded the objectionable qualities.

How many men do you know who have *self-control*
to equal this?

In language more forceful than it was polished,
Billy Sunday exclaimed from the pulpit: *"There is
something as rotten as hell about the man who is always trying to show some other fellow up!"* I wonder if the "devil" didn't yell, "Amen, brother!" when
Billy made that statement?

However, *self-control* becomes an important factor

in this Reading Course on the Law of Success, not so much because lack of it works hardships on those who become its victims, as for the reason that those who do not exercise it suffer the loss of a great power which they need in their struggle for achievement of their *definite chief aim.*

If you neglect to exercise *self-control,* you are not only likely to injure others, but you are *sure to injure yourself!*

During the early part of my public career I discovered what havoc lack of *self-control* was playing in my life, and this discovery came about through a very commonplace incident. (I believe it not out of place here to digress by making the statement that most of the great truths of life are wrapped up in the ordinary, commonplace events of every-day life.)

This discovery taught me one of the most important lessons I have ever learned. It came about in this way:

One day, in the building in which I had my office, the janitor and I had a misunderstanding. This led to a most violent form of mutual dislike between us. As a means of showing his contempt for me, this janitor would switch off the electric lights of the building when he knew that I was there alone at work in my study. This happened on several occasions until I finally decided to "strike back." My opportunity came one Sunday when I came to my study to prepare an address that I had to deliver the following night. I had hardly seated myself at my desk when off went the lights.

I jumped to my feet and ran toward the basement of the building where I knew I would find the janitor.

When I arrived, I found him busily engaged, shoveling coal into the furnace, and whistling as though nothing unusual had happened.

Without ceremony I pitched into him, and for five minutes I hurled adjectives at him which were hotter than the fire that he was feeding. Finally, I ran out of words and had to slow down. Then he straightened himself up, looked back over his shoulder, and in a calm, smooth tone of voice that was full of poise and *self-control,* and with a smile on his face that reached from ear to ear, he said:

"Why, you-all's just a little bit excited this morning, ain't you?"

That remark cut as though it had been a stiletto!

Imagine my feelings as I stood there before an illiterate man who could neither read nor write, but who, despite this handicap, had defeated me in a duel that had been fought on grounds—and with a weapon —of my own choice.

My conscience pointed an accusing finger at me. I knew that not only had I been defeated but, what was worse, I knew that I was the aggressor and that I *was in the wrong,* which only served to intensify my humiliation.

Not only did my conscience point an accusing finger at me, but it placed some very embarrassing thoughts in my mind; it mocked me and it tantalized me. There I stood, a boasted student of advanced psychology, an exponent of the Golden Rule philosophy, having at least a fair acquaintance with the works of Shakespeare, Socrates, Plato, Emerson and the Bible; while facing me stood a man who knew nothing of literature or of philosophy, but who had, despite this lack of knowledge, whipped me in a battle of words.

I turned and went back to my office as rapidly as I could go. There was nothing else for me to do. As I began to think the matter over I saw my mistake, but, true to nature, I was reluctant to do that which I knew must be done to right the wrong. I knew that I would have to apologize to that man before I could place myself at peace in my own heart, much less with him. Finally, I made up my mind to go back down to the basement and suffer this humility which I knew I had to undergo. The decision was not easily reached, nor did I reach it quickly.

I started down, but I walked more slowly than I had when I went down the first trip. I was trying to think how I would make the second approach so as to suffer the least humiliation possible.

When I got to the basement I called to the janitor to come over to the door. In a calm, kindly tone of voice he asked:

"What do you wish this time?"

I informed him that I had come back to apologize for the wrong I had done, if he would permit me to do so. Again that smile spread all over his face as he said:

"For the love of the Lord, you don't have to apologize. Nobody heard you except these four walls and you and me. I ain't going to tell it and I know you ain't going to tell it, so just forget it."

And that remark hurt more than his first one, for he had not only expressed a willingness to forgive me, but he had actually indicated his willingness to help me cover the incident up, so it would not become known and do me an injury.

IF ye have faith as a grain of m u s t a r d seed, ye shall say unto this mountain, Remove hence to yonder place; and it shall remove; and nothing shall be impossible unto you."

But I walked over to him and took him by the hand. I shook with more than my hand—I shook with my heart—and as I walked back to my office I felt good for having summoned the courage with which to right the wrong I had done.

This is not the end of the story. *It is only the beginning!* Following this incident, I made a resolution that I would never again place myself in a position in which another man, whether he be an illiterate janitor or a man of letters, could humiliate me because I had lost my *self-control.*

Following that resolution, a remarkable change began to take place in me. My pen began to take on greater power. My spoken words began to carry greater weight. I began to make more friends and fewer enemies among men of my acquaintance. The incident marked one of the most important turning-points of my life. It taught me that no man can control others unless he first controls himself. It gave me a clear conception of the philosophy back of these words, "Whom the gods would destroy, they first make mad." It also gave me a clear conception of the law of non-resistance and helped me interpret many passages of the holy scriptures, bearing on the subject of this law, as I had never before interpreted them.

This incident placed in my hands the pass-key to a storehouse of knowledge that is illuminating and helpful in all that I do, and, later in life, when enemies sought to destroy me, it gave me a powerful weapon of defense that has never failed me.

Lack of *self-control* is the average salesman's most damaging weakness. The prospective buyer says something that the salesman does not wish to hear,

and, if he has not this quality of *self-control*, he will
"strike back" with a counter remark that is fatal to
his sale.

In one of the large department stores of Chicago I
witnessed an incident that illustrated the importance
of *self-control*. A long line of women were in front
of the "complaint" desk, telling their troubles and *the
store's faults* to the young woman in charge. Some of
the women were angry and unreasonable and some of
them made very ugly remarks. The young woman at
the desk received the disgruntled women without the
slightest sign of resentment at their remarks. With a
smile on her face she directed these women to the
proper departments with such charming grace and poise
that I marveled at her *self-control*.

Standing just back of her was another young woman
who was making notations on slips of paper and passing them in front of her, as the women in the line
unburdened their troubles. These slips of paper contained the gist of what the women in the line were
saying, minus the "vitriolic coloring" and the anger.

The smiling young woman at the desk who was
"hearing" the complaints was *stone deaf!* Her assistant supplied her with all the necessary facts, though
those slips of paper.

I was so impressed with the plan that I sought the
manager of the store and interviewed him. He informed me that he had selected a deaf woman for one
of the most trying and important positions in the store
for the reason that he had not been able to find any
other person with sufficient *self-control* to fill the
place.

As I stood and watched that line of angry women,

I observed what pleasant effect the smile of the young woman at the desk had upon them. They came before her growling like wolves and went away as meek and quiet as sheep. In fact some of them had "sheepish" looks on their faces as they left, because the young woman's *self-control* had made them ashamed of themselves.

Ever since I witnessed that scene, I have thought of the poise and self-control of that young woman at the desk every time I felt myself becoming irritated at remarks which I did not like, and often I have thought that everybody should have a set of "mental ear muffs" which they could slip over their ears at times. Personally, I have developed the habit of "closing" my ears against much of the idle chatter such as I used to make it my business to resent. Life is too short and there is too much constructive work to be done to justify us in "striking back" at everyone who says that which we do not wish to hear.

In the practice of law I have observed a very clever trick that trial lawyers use when they wish to get a statement of facts from a belligerent witness who answers questions with the proverbial "I do not remember" or "I do not know." When everything else fails, they manage to make such a witness angry; and in this state of mind they cause him to lose his *self-control* and make statements that he would not have made had he kept a "cool" head.

Most of us go through life with our "weather eye" cast skyward in quest of trouble. We usually find that for which we are looking. In my travels I have been a student of men whom I have heard in "Pullman car conversation," and I have observed that practically nine out of every ten have so little *self-control* that they will "invite" themselves into the discussion of almost any subject that may be brought up. But few men are contented to sit in a smoking compartment and listen to a conversation without joining in and "airing" their views.

Once I was traveling from Albany to New York City. On the way down, the "Smoking Car Club" started a conversation about the late Richard Croker, who was then chief of Tammany Hall. The discussion became loud and bitter. Everyone became angry except one old gentleman who was agitating the argument and taking a lively interest in it. He remained calm and seemed to enjoy all the mean things the others said about the "Tiger" of Tammany Hall. Of course, I supposed that he was an enemy of the Tammany Chief, but he *wasn't!*

He was Richard Croker, himself!

This was one of his clever tricks through which he found out what people thought of him and what his enemies' plans were.

Whatever else Richard Croker might have been, he was a man of *self-control*. Perhaps that is one reason why he remained undisputed boss of Tammany Hall as long as he did. *Men who control themselves usually boss the job, no matter what it may be.*

Please read, again, the last sentence of the preceding paragraph, for it carries a subtle suggestion that might be of profit to *you*. This is a commonplace incident, but it is in just such incidents that the great truths of life are hidden—hidden because the settings are ordinary and commonplace.

Not long ago I accompanied my wife on a "bargain-hunting" bee. Our attention was attracted by a crowd of women who were elbowing each other out of the way in front of a petticoat counter at which "bargains" were being offered. One lady who looked to be about forty-five years of age crawled on her hands and knees through the crowd and "bobbed" up in front of a customer who had engaged the attention of the saleswoman ahead of her. In a loud, high-pitched tone of voice she demanded attention. The saleswoman was a diplomat who understood human nature; she also possessed *self-control,* for she smiled sweetly at the intruder and said: "Yes, *Miss;* I will be with you in a moment!"

The intruder calmed herself!

I do not know whether it was the "Yes, *Miss,*" or the sweet tone in which it was said that modified her attitude; but it was one or the other; perhaps it was both. I do know, however, that the saleswoman was rewarded for her *self-control* by the sale of three petticoats, and the happy *"Miss"* went away feeling much younger for the remark.

Roast turkey is a very popular dish, but overeating of it cost a friend of mine, who is in the printing business, a fifty thousand dollar order. It happened the day after Thanksgiving, when I called at his office for the purpose of introducing him to a prominent Russian who had come to the United States to publish a book. The Russian spoke broken English and it was therefore hard for him to make himself easily understood. During the interview he asked my printer friend a question which was mistaken as a reflection upon his ability as a printer. In an unguarded moment he countered with this remark:

I WOULD RATHER
BEGIN AT THE BOT-
TOM AND CLIMB TO
THE TOP THAN TO
START AT THE TOP
AND HAVE TO RE-
MAIN THERE.

"The trouble with you Bolsheviks is that you look with suspicion on the remainder of the world just because of your own short-sightedness."

My "Bolshevik" friend nudged me on the elbow and whispered:

"The gentleman seems to be sick. We shall call again, when he is feeling better."

But, he never called again. He placed his order with another printer, and I learned afterward that the profit on that order was more than $10,000.00!

Ten thousand dollars seems a high price to pay for a plate of turkey, but that is the price that it cost my printer friend; for he offered me an apology for his conduct on the ground that his turkey dinner had given him indigestion and therefore he had lost his *self-control*.

One of the largest chain store concerns in the world has adopted a unique, though effective, method of employing salespeople who have developed the essential quality of *self-control* which all successful salespeople must possess. This concern has in its employ a very clever woman who visits department stores and other places where salespeople are employed and selects certain ones whom she believes to possess tact and *self-control;* but, to be sure of her judgment, she approaches these salespeople and has them show her their wares. She asks all sorts of questions that are designed to try their patience. If they stand the test, they are offered better positions; if they fail in the test, they have merely allowed a good opportunity to pass by without knowing it.

No doubt all people who refuse or neglect to exercise *self-control* are literally turning opportunity after

opportunity away without knowing it.   One day I was
standing at the glove counter of a large retail store
talking to a young man who was employed there.   He
was telling me that he had been with the store four
years, but on account of the "short-sightedness" of
the store, his services had not been appreciated and
he was looking for another position.   In the midst of
this conversation a customer walked up to him and
asked to see some hats.   He paid no attention to the
customer's inquiry until he had finished telling me his
troubles, despite the fact that the customer was obviously becoming impatient.   Finally, he returned to
the customer and said: "This isn't the hat department."   When the customer inquired as to where he
might find that department the young man replied:
"Ask the floor-walker over there; he will direct you."

For four years this young man had been standing on
top of a fine opportunity but he did not know it.   He
could have made a friend of every person whom he
served in that store and these friends could have made
him one of the most valuable men in the store, because they would have come back to trade with him.
"Snappy" answers to inquiring customers do not bring
them back.

One rainy afternoon an old lady walked into a Pittsburgh department store and wandered around in an
aimless sort of way, very much in the manner that
people who have no intention of buying often do.
Most of the salespeople gave her the "once over" and
busied themselves by straightening the stock on their
shelves so as to avoid being troubled by her.   One of
the young men saw her and made it his business to
inquire politely if he might serve her.   She informed

him that she was only waiting for it to stop raining; that she did not wish to make any purchases. The young man assured her that she was welcome, and by engaging her in conversation made her feel that he had meant what he said. When she was ready to go he accompanied her to the street and raised her umbrella for her. She asked for his card and went on her way.

The incident had been forgotten by the young man when, one day, he was called into the office by the head of the firm and shown a letter from a lady who wanted a salesman to go to Scotland and take an order for the furnishings for a mansion.

That lady was Andrew Carnegie's mother; she was also the same woman whom the young man had so courteously escorted to the street many months previously.

In the letter, Mrs. Carnegie specified that this young man was the one whom she desired to be sent to take her order. That order amounted to an enormous sum, and the incident brought the young man an opportunity for advancement that he might never have had except for his courtesy to an old lady who did not look like a "ready sale."

Just as the great fundamental laws of life are wrapped up in the commonest sort of every-day experiences that most of us never notice, so are the *real* opportunities often hidden in the seemingly unimportant transactions of life.

Ask the next ten people whom you meet why they have not accomplished more in their respective lines of endeavor, and at least nine of them will tell you that *opportunity does not seem to come around their way.* Go a step further and analyze each of these nine accurately by observing their actions for one single day, and the chances are that you will find that every one of them is turning away the finest sort of opportunities every hour of the day.

One day I went to visit a friend who was associated with a Commercial School, in the capacity of solicitor. When I asked him how he was getting along he replied: "Rotten! I see a large number of people but I am not making enough sales to give me a good living. In fact my account with the school is overdrawn and I am thinking about changing positions as there is no *opportunity* here."

It happened that I was on my vacation and had ten days' time that I could use as I wished, so I challenged his remark that he had no opportunity by telling him that I could turn his position into $250.00 in a week's time and show him how to make it worth that every week thereafter. He looked at me in amazement and asked me not to joke with him over so serious a matter. When he was finally convinced that I was in earnest he ventured to inquire how I would perform the "miracle."

Then I asked him if he had ever heard of *organized effort,* to which he replied: *"What do you mean by organized effort?"* I informed him that I had reference to the direction of his efforts in such a manner that he would enroll from five to ten students with the same amount of effort that he had been putting into the enrollment of one or of none. He said he was willing to be shown, so I gave him instructions to arrange for me to speak before the employees of one of the local department stores. He made the ap-

pointment and I delivered the address. In my talk
I outlined a plan through which the employees could
not only increase their ability so that they could earn
more money in their present positions, but it also offered them an opportunity to prepare themselves for
greater responsibilities and better positions. Following my talk, which of course was designed for that
purpose, my friend enrolled eight of those employees
for night courses in the Commercial School which he
represented.

The following night he booked me for a similar address before the employees of a laundry, and following
the address he enrolled three more students, two of
them *young women who worked over the washing machines at the hardest sort of labor.*

Two days later he booked me for an address before
the employees of one of the local banks, and following
the address he enrolled four more students, making a
total of fifteen students, and the entire time consumed
was not more than six hours, including the time required for the delivery of the addresses and the enrollment of the students.

My friend's commission on the transactions was a
little over four hundred dollars!

These places of employment were within fifteen minutes' walk of this man's place of business, but he had
never thought of looking there for business. Neither
had he ever thought of allying himself with a speaker
who could assist him in "group" selling. That man
now owns a splendid Commercial School of his own,
and I am informed that his net income last year was
over $10,000.00.

"No opportunities" come your way? Perhaps they

IT IS BETTER TO BE
TOO BIG FOR YOUR
JOB THAN TO HAVE
A JOB THAT IS TOO
BIG FOR YOU.

come but you do not see them. Perhaps you will see
them in the future as you are preparing yourself,
through the aid of this Reading Course on the Law of
Success, so that you can recognize an opportunity when
you see it. The sixth lesson of this course is on the
subject of *imagination,* which was the chief factor that
entered into the transaction that I have just related.
Imagination, plus a Definite Plan, plus Self-confidence,
plus Action, were the main factors that entered into
this transaction. You now know how to use all of
these, and before you shall have finished this lesson
you will understand how to direct these factors through
self-control.

Now let us examine the scope of meaning of the
term *self-control,* as it is used in connection with this
course, by describing the general conduct of a person
who possesses it. A person with well-developed *self-
control* does not indulge in hatred, envy, jealousy, fear,
revenge, or any similar destructive emotions. A person with well-developed *self-control* does not go into
ecstasies or become ungovernably enthusiastic over
anything or anybody.

Greed and selfishness and self-approval beyond the
point of accurate self-analysis and appreciation of one's
actual merits, indicate lack of *self-control* in one of
its most dangerous forms. Self-confidence is one of
the important essentials of success, but when this faculty is developed beyond the point of reason it becomes
very dangerous.

Self-sacrifice is a commendable quality, but when
it is carried to extremes, it, also, becomes one of the
dangerous forms of lack of *self-control.*

You owe it to yourself not to permit your emotions

to place your happiness in the keeping of another person. Love is essential for happiness, but the person who loves so deeply that his or her happiness is placed entirely in the hands of another, resembles the little lamb who crept into the den of the "nice, gentle little wolf" and begged to be permitted to lie down and go to sleep, or the canary bird that persisted in playing with the cat's whiskers.

A person with well-developed *self-control* will not permit himself to be influenced by the cynic or the pessimist; nor will he permit another person to do his thinking for him.

A person with well-developed *self-control* will stimulate his imagination and his enthusiasm until they have produced *action*, but he will then control that action and not permit it to control him.

A person with well-developed *self-control* will never, under any circumstances, slander another person or seek revenge for any cause whatsoever.

A person with *self-control* will not hate those who do not agree with him; instead, he will endeavor to understand the reason for their disagreement, and profit by it.

We come, now, to a form of lack of *self-control* which causes more grief than all other forms combined; it is the habit of forming opinions before studying the *facts*. We will not analyze this particular form in detail, in this lesson, for the reason that it is fully covered in Lesson Eleven, on *accurate thought*, but the subject of *self-control* could not be covered without at least a passing reference to this common evil to which we are all more or less addicted.

No one has any right to form an opinion that is not

based either upon that which he believes to be *facts*, or upon a reasonable hypothesis; yet, if you will observe yourself carefully, you will catch yourself forming opinions on nothing more substantial than your desire for a thing to be or not to be.

Another grievous form of lack of *self-control* is the "spending" habit. I have reference, of course, to the habit of spending beyond one's needs. This habit has become so prevalent since the close of the world war that it is alarming. A well known economist has prophesied that three more generations will transform the United States from the richest country in the world to the poorest if the children are not taught the *savings habit,* as a part of their training in both the schools and the homes. On every hand, we see people buying automobiles on the installment plan instead of buying homes. Within the last fifteen years the automobile "fad" has become so popular that literally tens of thousands of people are mortgaging their futures to own cars.

A prominent scientist, who has a keen sense of humor, has prophesied that not only will this habit grow lean bank accounts, but, if persisted in, it will eventually grow babies whose legs will have become transformed into wheels.

This is a speed-mad, money-spending age in which we are living, and the uppermost thought in the minds of most of us is to live faster than our neighbors. Not long ago the general manager of a concern that employs 600 men and women became alarmed over the large number of his employees who were becoming involved with "loan sharks," and decided to put an end to this evil. When he completed his investiga-

IT is better to be a big man in a small town than to be a small man in a big town, and ever so much easier.

tion, he found that only nine per cent of his employees had savings accounts, and of the other ninety-one per cent who had no money ahead, seventy-five per cent were in debt in one form or another, some of them being hopelessly involved financially. *Of those who were in debt 210 owned automobiles.*

We are creatures of imitation. We find it hard to resist the temptation to do that which we see others doing. If our neighbor buys a Buick, we must imitate him and if we cannot scrape together enough to make the first payment on a Buick we must, at least, have a Ford. Meanwhile, we take no heed of the morrow. The old-fashioned "rainy-day nest egg" has become obsolete. We live from day to day. We buy our coal by the pound and our flour in five pound sacks, thereby paying a third more for it than it ought to cost, because it is distributed in small quantities.

Of course this warning does not apply to you!

It is intended only for those who are binding themselves in the chains of poverty by spending beyond their earning capacity, and who have not yet heard that there are definite laws which must be observed by all who would attain *success*.

The automobile is one of the modern wonders of the world, but it is more often a luxury than it is a necessity, and tens of thousands of people who are now "stepping on the gas" at a lively pace are going to see some dangerous skidding when their "rainy days" arrive.

It requires considerable *self-control* to use the street cars as a means of transportation when people all around us are driving automobiles, but all who exercise this *self-control* are practically sure to see the day when many who are now driving cars will be either riding the street cars or walking.

It was this modern tendency to spend the entire income which prompted Henry Ford to safe-guard his employees with certain restrictions when he established his famous $5.00 a day minimum wage scale.

Twenty years ago, if a boy wanted a wagon, he fashioned the wheels out of boards and had the pleasure of building it himself. Now, if a boy wants a wagon, he cries for it—*and gets it!*

Lack of *self-control* is being developed in the oncoming generations by their parents who have become victims of the spending habit. Three generations ago, practically any boy could mend his own shoes with the family cobbling outfit. Today the boy takes his shoes to the corner shoe-shop and pays $1.75 for heels and half soles, and this habit is by no means confined to the rich and well-to-do classes.

I repeat—*the spending habit is turning America into a nation of paupers!*

I am safe in assuming that *you* are struggling to attain success, for if you were not you would not be reading this course. Let me remind you, then, that a little savings account will attract many an opportunity to you that would not come your way without it. The size of the account is not so important as is the fact that you have *established the savings habit,* for this habit marks you as a person who exercises an important form of *self-control.*

The modern tendency of those who work for a salary is to spend it all. If a man who receives $3,000.00 a year and manages to get along on it fairly well, receives an increase of $1,000.00 a year, does he continue to live on $3,000.00 and place the increased portion of his income in the savings bank? No, not unless he is one of the few who have developed the savings *habit*. Then, what does he do with this additional $1,000.00? He trades in the old automobile and buys a more expensive one, and at the end of the year he is poorer on a $4,000.00 income than he was the previous year on a $3,000.00 income.

This is a "modern, twentieth century model" American that I am describing, and you will be lucky if, upon close analysis, you do not find yourself to be one of this class.

Somewhere between the miser who hoards every penny he gets his hands on, in an old sock, and the man who spends every cent he can earn or borrow, there is a "happy medium," and if you enjoy life with reasonable assurance of average freedom and contentment, you must find this half-way point and adopt it as a part of your *self-control* program.

Self-discipline is the most essential factor in the development of personal power, because it enables you to control your appetite and your tendency to spend more than you earn and your habit of "striking back" at those who offend you and the other destructive habits which cause you to dissipate your energies through non-productive effort that takes on forms too numerous to be catalogued in this lesson.

Very early in my public career I was shocked when I learned how many people there are who devote most of their energies to tearing down that which the builders construct. By some queer turn of the wheel of fate one of these destroyers crossed my path by making it his business to try to destroy my reputation

ASK any wise man what he most desires and he will, more than likely, say "more wisdom."

At first, I was inclined to "strike back" at him, but as I sat at my typewriter late one night, a thought came to me which changed my entire attitude toward this man. Removing the sheet of paper that was in my typewriter, I inserted another one on which I stated this thought, in these words:

You have a tremendous advantage over the man who does you an injury: you have it within your power to forgive him, while he has no such advantage over you.

As I finished writing those lines, I made up my mind that 1 had come to the point at which I had to decide upon a policy that would serve as a guide concerning my attitude toward those who criticize my work or try to destroy my reputation. I reached this decision by reasoning something after this fashion: Two courses of action were open to me. I could waste much of my time and energy in striking back at those who would try to destroy me, or I could devote this energy to furthering my life-work and let the result of that work serve as my sole answer to all who would criticize my efforts or question my motives. I decided upon the latter as being the better policy and adopted it.

"By their deeds you shall know them!"

If your deeds are constructive and you are at peace with yourself, in your own heart, you will not find it necessary to stop and explain your motives, for they will explain themselves.

The world soon forgets its destroyers. It builds its monuments to and bestows its honors upon none but its builders. Keep this fact in mind and you will more easily reconcile yourself to the policy of refusing to waste your energies by "striking back" at those who offend you.

Every person who amounts to anything in this world comes to the point, sooner or later, at which he is forced to settle this question of policy toward his enemies, and if you want proof that it pays to exercise sufficient *self-control* to refrain from dissipating your vital energies by "striking back" then study the records of all who have risen to high stations in life and observe how carefully they curbed this destructive habit.

It is a well known fact that no man ever reached a high station in life without opposition of a violent nature from jealous and envious enemies. The late President Warren G. Harding and ex-President Wilson and John H. Patterson of the National Cash Register Company and scores of others whom I could mention, were victims of this cruel tendency, of a certain type of depraved man, to destroy reputation. But these men wasted no time explaining or "striking back" at their enemies. They exercised *self-control*.

I do not know but that these attacks on men who are in public life, cruel and unjust and untruthful as they often are, serve a good purpose. In my own case, I know that I made a discovery that was of great value to me, as a result of a series of bitter attacks which a contemporary journalist launched against me. I paid no attention to these attacks for four or five years, until finally they became so bold that I decided to override my policy and "strike back" at my antagonist. I sat down at my typewriter and began to write. In all of my experience as a writer I do not believe I ever assembled such a collection of biting adjectives as those which I used on this occasion. The more I wrote, the more angry I became, until I had written all that I could think of on the subject. As the last line was finished, a strange feeling came over me—it was not a feeling of bitterness toward the man who had tried to injure me—it was a feeling of compassion, of sympathy, of forgiveness.

I had unconsciously psycho-analyzed myself by releasing, over the keys of my typewriter, the repressed emotions of hate and resentment which I had been unintentionally gathering in my sub-conscious mind over a long period of years.

Now, if I find myself becoming very angry, I sit down at my typewriter and "write it out of my system," then throw away the manuscript, or file it away as an exhibit for my scrapbook to which I can refer back in the years to come—after the evolutionary processes have carried me still higher in the realm of understanding.

Repressed emotions, especially the emotion of hatred, resemble a bomb that has been constructed of high explosives, and unless they are handled with as much understanding of their nature as an expert would handle a bomb, they are as dangerous. A bomb may be rendered harmless by explosion in an open field, or by disintegration in a bath of the proper sort. Also, a feeling of anger or hatred may be rendered harmless by giving expression to it in a manner that harmonizes with the principle of psycho-analysis.

Before *you* can achieve success in the higher and broader sense you must gain such thorough control over yourself that you will be a person of *poise*.

WHILE others may side-track your ambitions not a few times, remember that discouragement most frequently comes from within.

You are the product of at least a million years of evolutionary change. For countless generations preceding you Nature has been tempering and refining the materials that have gone into your make-up. Step by step, she has removed from the generations that have preceded you the animal instincts and baser passions until she has produced, in you, the *finest specimen of animal that lives*. She has endowed you, through this slow evolutionary process, with reason and poise and "balance" sufficient to enable you to control and do with yourself whatever you will.

No other animal has ever been endowed with such *self-control* as you possess. You have been endowed with the power to use the most highly organized form of energy known to man, that of *thought*. It is not improbable that *thought* is the closest connecting link there is between the material, physical things of this world and the world of Divinity.

You have not only the power to *think* but, what is a thousand times more important still, you have the power to *control your thoughts and direct them to do your bidding!*

We are coming, now, to the really important part of this lesson. Read slowly and meditatively! I approach this part of this lesson almost with fear and trembling, for it brings us face to face with a subject which but few men are qualified to discuss with reasonable intelligence.

I repeat, *you have the power to control your thoughts and make them do your bidding!*

Your brain may be likened to a dynamo, in this respect, that it generates or sets into motion the mysterious energy called *thought*. The stimuli that start your brain into action are of two sorts; one is Auto-suggestion and the other is Suggestion. You can select the material out of which your thinking is produced, and that is Auto-suggestion (or self-suggestion). You can permit others to select the material out of which your thinking is produced and that is Suggestion. It is a humiliating fact that most thought is produced by the outside suggestions of others, and it is more humiliating, still, to have to admit that the majority of us accept this suggestion without either examining it or questioning its soundness. We read the daily papers as though every word were based upon fact. We are swayed by the gossip and idle chatter of others as though every word were true.

Thought is the only thing over which you have absolute control, yet, unless you are the proverbial exception, which is about one out of every ten thousand, you permit other people to enter the sacred mansion of your mind and there deposit, through suggestion, their troubles and woes, adversities and falsehoods, just as though you did not have the power to close the door and keep them out.

You have within your control the power to select the material that constitutes the dominating thoughts of your mind, and just as surely as you are reading these lines, those thoughts which dominate your mind will bring you success or failure, according to their nature.

The fact that *thought* is the only thing over which you have absolute control is, within itself, of most profound significance, as it strongly suggests that *thought* is your nearest approach to Divinity, on this earthly plane. This fact also carries another highly impressive suggestion; namely, that *thought* is your most important tool; the one with which you may shape your worldly destiny according to your own liking.   Surely, Divine Providence did not make *thought* the sole power over which you have absolute control without associating with that power potentialities which, if understood and developed, would stagger the imagination.

Self-control is solely a matter of *thought-control!*

Please read the foregoing sentence aloud; read it thoughtfully and meditate over it before reading further, because it is, without doubt, the most important single sentence of this entire course.

You are studying this course, presumably because you are earnestly seeking truth and understanding sufficient to enable you to attain some high station in life.

You are searching for the magic key that will unlock the door to the source of power; and yet you have the key in your own hands, and you may make use of it the moment you learn to *control your thoughts*.

Place in your own mind, through the principle of Auto-suggestion, the positive, constructive thoughts which harmonize with your *definite chief aim* in life, and that mind will transform those thoughts into physical reality and hand them back to you, as a finished product.

This is thought-control!

When you deliberately choose the thoughts which dominate your mind and firmly refuse admittance to outside suggestion, you are exercising *self-control* in its highest and most efficient form.   Man is the only living animal that can do this.

How many millions of years Nature has required in which to produce this animal no one knows, but every intelligent student of psychology knows that the dominating thoughts determine the actions and the nature of the animal.

The process through which one may think accurately is a subject that has been reserved for Lesson Eleven, of this course. The point we wish clearly to establish, in this lesson, is that *thought,* whether accurate or inaccurate, is the most highly organized functioning power of your mind; and that *you are but the sum total of your dominating or most prominent thoughts.*

If you would be a master salesman, whether of goods and wares or of personal services, you must exercise sufficient *self-control* to shut out all adverse arguments and suggestions. Most salesmen have so little *self-control* that they hear the prospective purchaser say "no" even before he says it. Not a few salesmen hear this fatal word "no" even before they come into the presence of their prospective purchaser. They have so little *self-control* that they actually *suggest to themselves that their prospective purchaser will say "no" when asked to purchase their wares.*

How different is the man of *self-control!* He not only suggests to himself that his prospective purchaser will say "yes," but if the desired "yes" is not forthcoming, he stays on the job until he breaks down the opposition and forces a "yes." If his prospective purchaser says "no," he does not hear it. If his prospective purchaser says "no"—a second, and a third, and a fourth time—he does not hear it, for he is a man of *self-control* and he permits no suggestions to reach his mind except those which he desires to influence him.

The master salesman, whether he be engaged in selling merchandise, or personal services, or sermons, or public addresses, understands how to control his own *thoughts.*   Instead of being a person who *accepts, with meek submission, the suggestions of others,* he is a person who persuades others to accept *his suggestions.* By controlling himself and by placing only positive thoughts in his own mind, he thereby becomes a dominating personality, a master salesman.

This, too, is self-control!

A master salesman is one who takes the offensive, and never the defensive side of an argument, if argument arises.

Please read the foregoing sentence again!

If you are a master salesman you know that it is necessary for you to keep your prospective purchaser on the defensive, and you also know that it will be fatal to your sale if you permit him to place you on the defensive and keep you there.   You may, and of course you will at times, be placed in a position in which you will have to assume the defensive side of the conversation for a time, but it is your business to exercise such perfect poise and *self-control* that you will change places with your prospective purchaser without his noticing that you have done so, by placing him back on the defensive.

This requires the most consummate skill and *self-control!*

Most salesmen sweep this vital point aside by becoming angry and trying to scare the prospective purchaser into submission, but the master salesman remains calm and serene, and usually comes out the winner

PEOPLE like to use their excess energy by "chewing the rag." Wm. Wrigley, Jr., capitalized this human trait by giving them a stick of Spearmint.

The word "salesman" has reference to all people who try to persuade or convince others by logical argument or appeal to self-interest. We are all salesmen; or, at least, we should be, no matter what form of service we are rendering or what sort of goods we are offering.

The ability to negotiate with other people without friction and argument is the outstanding quality of all successful people. Observe those nearest you and notice how few there are who understand this art of tactful negotiation. Observe, also, how successful are the few who understand this art, despite the fact that they may have less education than those with whom they negotiate.

It is a knack that can be cultivated.

The art of successful negotiation grows out of patient and painstaking *self-control*. Notice how easily the successful salesman exercises *self-control* when he is handling a customer who is impatient. In his heart such a salesman may be boiling over, but you will see no evidence of it in his face or manner or words.

He has acquired the art of tactful negotiation!

A single frown of disapproval or a single word denoting impatience will often spoil a sale, and no one knows this better than the successful salesman. He makes it his business to control his feelings, and as a reward he sets his own salary mark and chooses his own position.

To watch a person who has acquired the art of successful negotiation is a liberal education, within itself. Watch the public speaker who has acquired this art; notice the firmness of his step as he mounts the platform; observe the firmness of his voice as he begins to speak; study the expression on his face as he sweeps his audience with the mastery of his argument. *He has learned how to negotiate without friction.*

Watch the physician who has acquired this art, as he walks into the sick room and greets his patient with a smile. His bearing, the tone of his voice, the look of assurance on his face, all mark him as one who has acquired the art of successful negotiation, and the patient begins to feel better the moment he enters the sick room.

Watch the foreman of the works who has acquired this art, and observe how his very presence spurs his men to greater effort and inspires them with confidence and enthusiasm.

Watch the lawyer who has acquired this art, and observe how he commands the respect and attention of the court, the jury and his fellow-practitioners. There is something about the tone of his voice, the posture of his body, and the expression on his face which causes his opponent to suffer by comparison. He not only knows his case, but he convinces the court and the jury that he knows, and as his reward he wins his cases and claims big retaining fees.

And all of this is predicated upon *self-control!*

And *self-control* is the result of *thought-control!*

Deliberately place in your own mind the sort of *thoughts* that you desire there, and keep out of your mind those *thoughts* which others place there through *suggestion,* and you will become a person of *self-control.*

This privilege of stimulating your mind with suggestions and thoughts of your own choosing is your prerogative power that Divine Providence gave you, and if you will exercise this holy right there is nothing within the bounds of reason that you cannot attain.

"Losing your temper," and with it your case, or your argument, or your sale, marks you as one who has not yet familiarized himself with the fundamentals upon which *self-control* is based, and the chief one of these fundamentals is the privilege of choosing the *thoughts* that dominate the mind.

A student in one of my classes once asked how one went about controlling one's thoughts when in a state of intense anger, and I replied: *"In exactly the same way that you would change your manner and the tone of your voice if you were in a heated argument with a member of your family and heard the door bell ring, warning you that company was about to visit you. You would control yourself because you would desire to do so."*

If you have ever been in a similar predicament, where you found it necessary to cover up your real feelings and change the expression on your face quickly, you know how easily it can be done, and you also know that it can be done *because one wants to do it!*

Back of all achievement, back of all *self-control*, back of all *thought control*, is that magic something called DESIRE!

It is no misstatement of fact to say that you are limited only by the depth of your *desires!*

When your *desires* are strong enough you will appear to possess superhuman powers to achieve. No one has ever explained this strange phenomenon of the mind, and perhaps no one ever will explain it, but

if you doubt that it exists you have but to experiment
and be convinced.

If you were in a building that was on fire, and all
the doors and windows were locked, the chances are
that you would develop sufficient strength with which
to break down the average door, because of your intense *desire* to free yourself.

If you *desire* to acquire the art of successful negotiation, as you undoubtedly will when you understand
its significance in relation to your achievement of your
definite chief aim, you will do so, providing your *desire*
is intense enough.

Napoleon *desired* to become emperor of France and
did rule.   Lincoln *desired* to free the slaves, and he
accomplished it.   The French *desired* that "they shall
not pass," at the beginning of the world war, and *they
didn't pass!*   Edison *desired* to produce light with
electricity, and he produced it—although he was many
years in doing so.   Roosevelt *desired* to unite the Atlantic and Pacific oceans, through the Panama Canal,
and he did it.   Demosthenes *desired* to become a great
public speaker, and despite the handicap of serious impediment of speech, he transformed his desire into
reality.   Helen Keller *desired* to speak, and despite
the fact that she was deaf, dumb and blind, she now
speaks.   John H. Patterson *desired* to dominate in the
production of cash registers, and he did it.   Marshall
Field *desired* to be the leading merchant of his time,
and he did.   Shakespeare *desired* to become a great
playwright, and, despite the fact that he was only a
poor itinerant actor, he made his desire come true.
Billy Sunday *desired* to quit playing base-ball and become a master preacher, and he did.   James J. Hill

desired to become an empire builder; and, despite the fact that he was only a poor telegraph operator, he transformed that desire into reality.

Don't say, "It can't be done," or that you are different from these and thousands of others who have achieved noteworthy success in every worthy calling. If you are "different," it is only in this respect: *they desired the object of their achievement with more depth and intensity than you desire yours.*

Plant in your mind the seed of a *desire* that is constructive by making the following your creed and the foundation of your code of ethics:

"I wish to be of service to my fellow men as I jour ney through life. To do this I have adopted this creed as a guide to be followed in dealing with my fellow-beings:

"To train myself so that never, under any circumstances, will I find fault with any person, no matter how much I may disagree with him or how inferior his work may be, as long as I know he is sincerely trying to do his best.

"To respect my country, my profession and myself. To be honest and fair with my fellow men, as I expect them to be honest and fair with me. To be a loyal citizen of my country. To speak of it with praise, and act always as a worthy custodian of its good name. To be a person whose name carries weight wherever it goes.

"To base my expectations of reward on a solid foundation of service rendered. To be willing to pay the price of success in honest effort. To look upon my work as an opportunity to be seized with joy and made

IT is a peculiar trait of human nature, but it is true, that the most successful men will work harder for the sake of rendering useful service than they will for money alone.

the most of, and not as a painful drudgery to be reluctantly endured.

"To remember that success lies within myself—in my own brain. To expect difficulties and to force my way through them.

"To avoid procrastination in all its forms, and never, under any circumstances, put off until tomorrow any duty that should be performed today.

"Finally, to take a good grip on the joys of life, so I may be courteous to men, faithful to friends, true to God—a fragrance in the path I tread."

The energy which most people dissipate through lack of *self-control* would, if organized and used constructively, bring all the necessities and all the luxuries desired.

The time which many people devote to "gossiping" about others would, if controlled and directed constructively, be sufficient to attain the object of their *definite chief aim* (if they had such an aim).

All successful people grade high on *self-control!* All "failures" grade low, generally zero, on this important law of human conduct.

Study the comparative analysis chart in the Introductory Lesson, and observe the *self-control* gradings of Jesse James and Napoleon.

Study those around you and observe, with profit, that all the successful ones exercise *self-control,* while the "failures" permit their THOUGHTS, WORDS and DEEDS to run wild!

One very common and very destructive form of lack of *self-control* is the habit of talking too much. People of wisdom, who know what they want and are

bent on getting it, guard their conversation carefully
There can be no gain from a volume of uninvited, un,
controlled, loosely spoken words.

It is nearly always more profitable to listen than it
is to speak. A good listener may, once in a great
while, hear something that will add to his stock of
knowledge. It requires *self-control* to become a good
listener, but the benefits to be gained are worth the
effort.

"Taking the conversation away from another person" is a common form of lack of *self-control* which is
not only discourteous, but it deprives those who do
it of many valuable opportunities to learn from others.

After completing this lesson you should go back to
the self-analysis chart, in the Introductory Lesson, and
re-grade yourself on the Law of Self-control. Perhaps you may wish to reduce your former grading
somewhat.

Self-control was one of the marked characteristics of
all successful leaders whom I have analyzed, in gathering material for this course. Luther Burbank said
that, in his opinion, *self-control* was the most important of the Fifteen Laws of Success. During all his
years of patient study and observation of the evolutionary processes of vegetable life he found it necessary to exercise the faculty of *self-control,* despite the
fact that he was dealing with inanimate life.

John Burroughs, the naturalist, said practically the
same thing; that *self-control* stood near the head of
the list, in importance, of the Fifteen Laws of Success.

The man who exercises complete *self-control* cannot
be permanently defeated, as Emerson has so well

stated in his essay on Compensation, for the reason that obstacles and opposition have a way of melting away when confronted by the determined mind that is guided to a definite end with complete *self-control*.

Every wealthy man whom I have analyzed (referring to those who have become wealthy through their own efforts) showed such positive evidence that *self-control* had been one of his strong points that I reached the conclusion that no man can hope to accumulate great wealth and keep it without exercising this necessary quality.

The saving of money requires the exercise of *self-control* of the highest order, as, I hope, has been made quite clear in the fourth lesson of this course.

I am indebted to Edward W. Bok for the following rather colorful description of the extent to which he found it necessary to exercise *self-control* before he achieved success and was crowned with fame as one of the great journalists of America:

WHY I BELIEVE IN POVERTY AS THE RICHEST EXPERIENCE THAT CAN COME TO A BOY

I make my living trying to edit the Ladies' Home Journal. And because the public has been most generous in its acceptance of that periodical, a share of that success has logically come to me. Hence a number of my very good readers cherish an opinion that often I have been tempted to correct, a temptation to which I now yield. My correspondents express the conviction variously, but this extract from a letter is a fair sample:

"It is ll very easy for you to preach economy to

us when you do not know the necessity for it: To tell us how, as for example in my own case, we must live within my husband's income of eight hundred dollars a year, when you have never known what it is to live on less than thousands. Has it occurred to you, born with the proverbial silver spoon in your mouth, that theoretical writing is pretty cold and futile compared to the actual hand-to-mouth struggle that so many of us live, day by day and year in and year out—an experience that you know not of?"

"An experience that you know not of!"

Now, how far do the facts square with this statement?

Whether or not I was born with the proverbial silver spoon in my mouth, I cannot say. It is true that I was born of well-to-do parents. But when I was six years old my father lost all his means, and faced life at forty-five, in a strange country, without even necessaries. There are men and their wives who know what that means; for a man to try to "come back" at forty-five, and in a strange country!

I had the handicap of not knowing one word of the English language. I went to a public school and learned what I could. And sparse morsels they were! The boys were cruel, as boys are. The teachers were impatient, as tired teachers are.

My father could not find his place in the world. My mother who had always had servants at her beck and call, faced the problems of housekeeping that she had never learned nor been taught. And there was no money.

So, after school hours, my brother and I went home, but not to play. After-school hours meant for us to help a mother who daily grew more frail under the burdens that she could not carry. Not for days, but for years, we two boys got up in the gray cold winter dawn when the beds feel so warm to growing boys, and we sifted the coal ashes of the day-before's fire for a stray lump or two of unburned coal, and with what we had or could find we made the fire and warmed up the room. Then we set the table for the scant breakfast, went to school, and directly after school we washed the dishes, swept and scrubbed the floors. Living in a three-family tenement, each third week meant that we scrubbed the entire three flights of stairs from the third story to the first, as well as the doorsteps and the sidewalk outside. The latter work was the hardest; for we did it on Saturdays, with the boys of the neighborhood looking on none too kindly, so we did it to the echo of the crack of the ball and bat on the adjoining lot!

In the evening when the other boys could sit by the lamp or study their lessons, we two boys went out with a basket and picked up wood and coal in the adjoining lots, or went after the dozen or so pieces of coal left from the ton of coal put in that afternoon by one of the neighbors, with the spot hungrily fixed in mind by one of us during the day, hoping that the man who carried in the coal might not be too careful in picking up the stray lumps!

"An experience that you know not of!" Don't I?

At ten years of age I got my first job, washing the windows of a baker's shop at fifty cents a week. In a week or two I was allowed to sell bread and cakes behind the counter after school hours for a dollar a week—handing out freshly baked cakes and warm, de-

OUR DOUBTS ARE
TRAITORS, AND
MAKE US LOSE
THE GOOD WE OFT
MIGHT WIN BY
FEARING TO
ATTEMPT.

—*Shakespeare.*

licious-smelling bread, when scarcely a crumb had passed my mouth that day!

Then on Saturday mornings I served a route for a weekly paper, and sold my remaining stock on the street. It meant from sixty to seventy cents for that day's work.

I lived in Brooklyn, New York, and the chief means of transportation to Coney Island at that time was the horse car. Near where we lived the cars would stop to water the horses, the men would jump out and get a drink of water, but the women had no means of quenching their thirst. Seeing this lack I got a pail, filled it with water and a bit of ice, and, with a glass, jumped on each car on Saturday afternoon and all day Sunday, and sold my wares at a cent a glass. And when competition came, as it did very quickly when other boys saw that a Sunday's work meant two or three dollars, I squeezed a lemon or two in my pail, my liquid became "lemonade" and my price two cents a glass, and Sunday meant five dollars to me.

Then, in turn, I became a reporter during the evenings, an office boy day-times, and learned stenography at midnight.

My correspondent says she supports her family of husband and child on eight hundred dollars a year, and says I have never known what that means. I supported a family of three on six dollars and twenty-five cents a week—less than one-half of her yearly income. When my brother and I, combined, brought in eight hundred dollars a year we felt rich!

I have for the first time gone into these details in print so that you may know, at first hand, that the editor of the Ladies' Home Journal is not a theorist when he writes or prints articles that seek to preach economy or that reflect a hand-to-hand struggle on a small or an invisible income. There is not a single step, not an inch, on the road of direct poverty that I do not know of or have not experienced. And, having experienced every thought, every feeling and every hardship that come to those who travel that road, I say today that I rejoice with every boy who is going through the same experience.

Nor am I discounting or forgetting one single pang of the keen hardships that such a struggle means. I would not today exchange my years of the keenest hardship that a boy can know or pass through for any single experience that could have come to me. I know what it means to earn—not a dollar, but to earn two cents. I know the value of money as I could have learned it or known it in no other way. I could have been trained for my life-work in no surer way. I could not have arrived at a truer understanding of what it means to face a day without a penny in hand, not a loaf of bread in the cupboard, not a piece of kindling wood for the fire—with nothing to eat, and then be a boy with the hunger of nine and ten, with a mother frail and discouraged!

"An experience that you know not of!" Don't I?

And yet I rejoice in the experience, and I repeat: I envy every boy who is in that condition and going through it. But—and here is the pivot of my strong belief in poverty as an undisguised blessing to a boy —I believe in poverty as a condition to experience, to go through, and then to get out of: not as a condition to stay in. "That's all very well," some will say; "easy enough to say, but how can you get out of it?"

No one can definitely tell another that. No one told me. No two persons can find the same way out. Each must find his way for himself. That depends on the boy. I was determined to get out of poverty, because my mother was not born in it, could not stand it and did not belong in it. This gave me the first essential: a purpose. Then I backed up the purpose with effort and willingness to work and to work at anything that came my way, no matter what it was, so long as it meant "the way out." I did not pick and choose; I took what came and did it in the best way I knew how; and when I didn't like what I was doing I still did it well while I was doing it, but I saw to it that I didn't do it any longer than I had to do it. I used every rung in the ladder as a rung to the one above. It meant effort, but out of the effort and the work came the experience; the upbuilding, the development; the capacity to understand and sympathize; the greatest heritage that can come to a boy. And nothing in the world can give that to a boy, so that it will burn into him, as will poverty.

That is why I believe so strongly in poverty, the greatest blessing in the way of the deepest and fullest experience that can come to a boy. But, as I repeat: always as a condition to work out of, not to stay in.

Before you can develop the habit of perfect *self-control* you must understand the real need for this quality. Also, you must understand the advantages which *self-control* provides those who have learned how to exercise it.

By developing *self-control* you develop, also, other qualities that will add to your personal power. Among

other laws which are available to the person who exercises *self-control* is the Law of Retaliation.

You know what "retaliate" means!

In the sense that we are using here it means to
"return like for like," and not merely to avenge or to
seek revenge, as is commonly meant by the use of
this word.

If I do you an injury you retaliate at first opportunity. If I say unjust things about you, you will
retaliate in kind, even in greater measure!

On the other hand, if I do you a favor you will reciprocate even in greater measure if possible.

Through the proper use of this law *I can get you to
do whatever I wish you to do.* If I wish you to dislike me and to lend your influence toward damaging
me, I can accomplish this result by inflicting upon
you the sort of treatment that I want you to inflict
upon me through retaliation.

If I wish your respect, your friendship and your
co-operation I can get these by extending to you my
friendship and co-operation.

On these statements I know that we are together.
You can compare these statements with your own experience and you will see how beautifully they harmonize.

How often have you heard the remark, "What a
wonderful personality that person has." How often
have you met people whose personalities you coveted?

The man who attracts you to him through his pleasing personality is merely making use of the Law of
Harmonious Attraction, or the Law of Retaliation,
both of which, when analyzed, mean that "like attracts
like "

If you will study, understand and make intelligent **use** of the Law of Retaliation you will be an efficient and successful salesman.   When you have mastered **this** simple law and learned how to use it you will have learned all that can be learned about salesmanship.

The first and probably the most important step **to** be taken in mastering this law is to cultivate complete *self-control.* You must learn to take all sorts of punishment and abuse without retaliating in kind.   This *self-control* is a part of the price you must pay for mastery of the Law of Retaliation.

When an angry person starts in to vilify and abuse you, justly or unjustly, just remember that if you retaliate in a like manner you are being drawn down to that person's mental level, therefore *that person is dominating you!*

On the other hand, if you refuse to become angry, if you retain your self-composure and remain calm and serene you retain all your ordinary faculties through which to reason.   You take the other fellow by surprise.   You retaliate with a weapon with the use of which he is unfamiliar, consequently you easily dominate him.

Like attracts like!   There's no denying this!

Literally speaking, every person with whom you come in contact is a mental looking-glass in which you may see a perfect reflection of your own mental attitude.

As an example of direct application of the Law of Retaliation, let us cite an experience that I recently had with my two small boys, Napoleon Junior and James.

IT is well worth remembering that the customer is the most important factor in any business. If you don't think so, try to get along without him for a while.

We were on our way to the park to feed the birds and squirrels. Napoleon Junior had bought a bag of peanuts and James had bought a box of "Crackerjack." James took a notion to sample the peanuts. Without asking permission he reached over and made a grab for the bag. He missed and Napoleon Junior "retaliated" with his left fist which landed rather briskly on James' jaw.

I said to James: "Now, see here, son, you didn't go about getting those peanuts in the right manner. Let me show you how to get them." It all happened so quickly that I hadn't the slightest idea when I spoke what I was going to suggest to James, but I sparred for time to analyze the occurrence and work out a better way, if possible, than that adopted by him.

Then I thought of the experiments we had been making in connection with the Law of Retaliation, so I said to James: "Open your box of 'Crackerjack' and offer your little brother some and see what happens." After considerable coaxing I persuaded him to do this. Then a remarkable thing happened—a happening out of which I learned my greatest lesson in salesmanship! *Before Napoleon would touch the "Crackerjack" he insisted on pouring some of his peanuts into James' overcoat pocket.* He "retaliated in kind!" Out of this simple experiment with two small boys I learned more about the art of managing them than I could have learned in any other manner. Incidentally, my boys are beginning to learn how to manipulate this Law of Retaliation which saves them many a physical combat.

None of us have advanced far beyond Napoleon Junior and James as far as the operation and influence of the Law of Retaliation is concerned. We are all just grown-up children and easily influenced through this principle. The habit of "retaliating in kind" is so universally practiced among us that we can properly call this habit the Law of Retaliation. If a person presents us with a gift we never feel satisfied until we have "retaliated" with something as good or better than that which we received. If a person speaks well of us we increase our admiration for that person, and we "retaliate" in return!

Through the principle of retaliation we can actually convert our enemies into loyal friends. If you have an enemy whom you wish to convert into a friend you can prove the truth of this statement if you will forget that dangerous millstone hanging around your neck, which we call "pride" (stubbornness). Make a habit of speaking to this enemy with unusual cordiality. Go out of your way to favor him in every manner possible. He may seem immovable at first, but gradually he will give way to your influence and "retaliate in kind!" The hottest coals of fire ever heaped upon the head of one who has wronged you are the coals of human kindness.

One morning in August, 1863, a young clergyman was called out of bed in a hotel at Lawrence, Kansas. The man who called him was one of Quantrell's guerrillas, and he wanted him to hurry downstairs and be shot. All over the border that morning people were being murdered. A band of raiders had ridden in early to perpetrate the Lawrence massacre.

The guerrilla who called the clergyman was impatient. The latter, when fully awake, was horrified by what he saw going on through his window. As he

came downstairs the guerrilla demanded his watch and
money, and then wanted to know if he was an abolitionist. The clergyman was trembling. But he decided that if he was to die then and there it would not
be with a lie on his lips. So he said that he was, and
followed up the admission with a remark that immediately turned the whole affair into another channel.

He and the guerrilla sat down on the porch, while
people were being killed through the town, and had
a long talk. It lasted until the raiders were ready to
leave. When the clergyman's guerrilla mounted to
join his confederates he was strictly on the defensive.
He handed back the New Englander's valuables, apologized for disturbing him and asked to be thought
well of.

That clergyman lived many years after the Lawrence massacre. What did he say to the guerrilla?
What was there in his personality that led the latter
to sit down and talk? What did they talk about?

"Are you a Yankee abolitionist?" the guerrilla had
asked. "Yes, I am," was the reply, "and you know
very well that you ought to be ashamed of what you're
doing."

This drew the matter directly to a moral issue. It
brought the guerrilla up roundly. The clergyman was
only a stripling beside this seasoned border ruffian.
But he threw a burden of moral proof on to the raider,
and in a moment the latter was trying to demonstrate
that he might be a better fellow than circumstances
would seem to indicate.

After waking this New Englander to kill him on account of his politics, he spent twenty minutes on the
witness stand trying to prove an alibi. He went into

his personal history at length. He explained matters from the time when he had been a tough little kid who wouldn't say his prayers, and became quite sentimental in recalling how one thing had led to another, and that to something worse, until—well, here he was, and "a mighty bad business to be in, pardner." His last request in riding away was: "Now, pardner, don't think too hard of me, will you?"

The New England clergyman made use of the Law of Retaliation, whether he knew it at that time or not. Imagine what would have happened had he come downstairs with a revolver in his hand and started to meet physical force with physical force!

But he didn't do this! He mastered the guerrilla because he fought him with a force that was unknown to the brigand.

Why is it that when once a man begins to make money the whole world seems to beat a pathway to his door?

Take any person that you know who enjoys financial success and he will tell you that he is being constantly sought, and that opportunities to make money are constantly being urged upon him!

"To him that hath shall be given, but to him that hath not shall be taken away even that which he hath."

This quotation from the Bible used to seem ridiculous to me, yet how true it is when reduced to its concrete meaning.

Yes, *to him that hath shall be given!* If he "hath" failure, lack of self-confidence, hatred or lack of *self-control*, to him shall these qualities be given in still greater abundance! But, if he "hath" success, self-confidence, *self-control*, patience, persistence and determination, to him shall these qualities be increased!

Sometimes it may be necessary to meet force with force until we overpower our opponent or adversary, but while he is down is a splendid time to complete the "retaliation" by taking him by the hand and showing him a better way to settle disputes.

Like attracts like! Germany sought to bathe her sword in human blood, in a ruthless escapade of conquest. As a result she has drawn the "retaliation in kind" of most of the civilized world.

It is for you to decide what you want your fellow men to do and *it is for you to get them to do it through the Law of Retaliation!*

"The Divine Economy is automatic and very simple: we receive only that which we give."

How true it is that "we receive only that which we give"! It is not that which we *wish for* that comes back to us, but that *which we give.*

I implore you to make use of this law, not alone for material gain, but, better still, for the attainment of happiness and good-will toward men.

This, after all, is the only real success for which to strive.

SUMMARY

In this lesson we have learned a great principle— probably the most important major principle of psychology! We have learned that our *thoughts* and *actions toward others* resemble an electric magnet which attracts to us the same sort of thought and the same sort of action that we, ourselves, create.

We have learned that "like attracts like," whether in thought or in expression of thought through bodily

A GOOD HEARTY LAUGH IS WORTH TEN THOUSAND "GROANS" AND A MILLION "SIGHS" IN ANY MARKET ON EARTH.

action. We have learned that the human mind responds, in kind, to whatever thought impressions it receives. We have learned that the human mind resembles mother earth in that it will reproduce a crop of muscular action which corresponds, in kind, to the sensory impressions planted in it. We have learned that kindness begets kindness and unkindness and injustice beget unkindness and injustice.

We have learned that our actions toward others, whether of kindness or unkindness, justice or injustice, come back to us, *even in a larger measure!* We have learned that the human mind responds in kind, to all sensory impressions it receives, therefore we know what we must do to influence any desired action upon the part of another. We have learned that "pride" and "stubbornness" must be brushed away before we can make use of the Law of Retaliation in a constructive way. *We have not learned what the Law of Retaliation is, but we have learned how it works and what it will do;* therefore, it only remains for us to make intelligent use of this great principle.

.   .   .   .

You are now ready to proceed with Lesson Nine, where you will find other laws which harmonize perfectly with those described in this lesson on Self-control.

It will require the strongest sort of *self-control* to enable the beginner to apply the major law of the next lesson, on the Habit of Doing More Than Paid For, but experience will show that the development of such control is more than justified by the results growing out of such discipline.

IF you are successful remember that somewhere, sometime, someone gave you a lift or an idea that started you in the right direction. Remember, also, that you are indebted to life until you help some less fortunate person, just as you were helped.

THE EVOLUTION OF TRANSPORTATION

An After-the-Lesson Visit With the Author

Nothing is permanent except change. Life resembles a great kaleidoscope before which Time is ever shifting, changing and rearranging both the stage setting and the players. New friends are constantly replacing the old. Everything is in a state of flux. In every heart is the seed of both rascality and justice. Every human being is both a criminal and a saint, depending upon the expediency of the moment as to which will assert itself. Honesty and dishonesty are largely matters of individual viewpoint. The weak and the strong, the rich and the poor, the ignorant and the well-informed are exchanging places continuously.

Know YOURSELF and you know the entire human race. There is but one real achievement, and that is the ability to THINK ACCURATELY. We move with the procession, or behind it, but we cannot stand still.

NOTHING is permanent except change!

In the picture above you see proof that the law of evolution is working out improvements in the methods of travel. Remember, as you study this picture, that all these changes took place first in the minds of men.

At the extreme left you see the first crude method of transportation. Man was *not satisfied* with this slow process. Those two little words "not satisfied," have been the starting point of all advancement. Think of them as you read this article.

Next, in the picture, you see the history of transportation step by step, as man's brain began to expand. It was a long step forward when man discovered how to hitch a bullock to a wagon and thereby escape the toil of pulling the load. That was practical utility. But, when the stage-coach was ushered into use that was both utility and style. Still man was "not satisfied" and this dissatisfaction created the crude locomotive that you see in the picture.

Now all these methods of travel have been discarded except in certain uncivilized (or uncommercialized) parts of the world. The man drawing the cart, the bullock drawing the cart, the stage-coach and the crude locomotive all belong to ages that have passed.

At the right you see the transportation methods of the present. Compare them with those of the past and you may have a fair idea of the enormous expansion that has taken place in the brain and mind of man. Man now moves about more rapidly than in the past. From the first type of locomotive there has been evolved a powerful machine capable of hauling a hundred cars of freight, compared with the one small, light car that could be drawn with the original. Automobiles that travel at the speed of seventy-five miles an hour are now as common as were the two-wheel carts in ages past. Moreover, they are within the means of all who want them.

And still man's mind was "not satisfied." Travel on the earth was too slow. Turning his eyes upward he watched the birds soaring high in the elements and became "DETERMINED" to excel them. Study, also, the word "determined," for whatever man becomes determined to do man does! Within the brief period of fifteen years man has mastered the air and now travels in the airplane at the rate of a hundred and fifty miles an hour.

Not only has man made the air carry him at amazingly rapid speed, but he has harnessed the ether and made it carry his words all the way around the earth in the fractional part of a second.

.   .   .   .

We have been describing the PAST and the PRESENT!

At the bottom of the picture we may see the next step forward that man will take in methods of travel; a machine that will fly in the air, run on the ground and swim in the water, at the discretion of man.

The purpose of this essay and the picture at the top of the page is to provide food for THOUGHT!

Any influence that causes one to think causes one, also, to grow stronger mentally. Mind stimulants are essential for growth. From the days of the man-drawn cart to the present days of air mastery the only progress that any man has made has been the result of some influence that stimulated his mind to greater than normal action.

The two great major influences that cause the mind of man to grow are the urge of necessity and the urge of desire to create. Some minds develop only after they have undergone failure and defeat and other forms of punishment which arouse them to greater action. Other minds wither away and die under punishment, but grow to unbelievable heights when provided with the opportunity to use their imaginative forces in a creative way.

Study the picture of the evolution of transportation and you will observe one outstanding fact worth remembering, namely, that the whole story has been one of development and advancement that grew out of *necessity*. The entire period described in the picture as "THE PAST" was one wherein the urge was that of necessity.

In the period described in the picture above as "THE PRESENT" the urge has been a combination of both necessity and the desire to create. The period described as "THE FUTURE" will be one in which the strong desire to create will be the sole urge that will drive man's mind on and on to heights as yet undreamed of.

It is a long distance from the days of the man-drawn cart to the present, when man has harnessed the lightning of the clouds and made it turn machinery that will perform as much service in a minute as ten thousand men could perform in a day. But, if the distance has been long the development of man's mind has been correspondingly great, and that development has been sufficient to eventually do the work of the world with machines operated by Nature's forces and not by man's muscles.

The evolutionary changes in the methods of transportation have created other problems for man's mind to solve. The automobile drove man to build better roads and more of them. The automobile and the speedy locomotive, combined, have created dangerous crossings which claim thousands of lives annually. Man's mind must now respond to the urge of "necessity" and meet this emergency.

Keep this essay and remember this prophecy:

Within five years every railroad crossing in the country will be amply protected against automobile accidents, and, the automobile, itself, will manipulate the system that will do the protecting; a system that will be fool-proof and effective; a system that will work whether the driver of the automobile is asleep or awake, drunk or sober.

Come, now, for a brief glimpse at the machinery of the imagination of man, as it works under the stimulant of desire to create.

Some imaginative man; perhaps some fellow who never did anything else of note and who will never do anything worth while again; will create a system of railroad crossing protection that will be operated by the weight of the passing automobile. Within the required distance from the crossing a platform similar to the platform of a large freight scale will cover an entire section of the roadway. As soon as an automobile mounts this platform the weight of the machine will lower a gate, ring a gong and flash a red light in front of the motorist. The gate will rise in one minute, allowing the motorist to pass over the track, thus forcing him to "stop, look and listen."

If you have a highly imaginative mind YOU may

be the one who will create this system and collect the royalties from its sale.

To be practical the imaginative mind should be always on the alert for ways and means of diverting waste motion and power into useful channels. Most automobiles are far too heavy in comparison with the load they carry. This weight can be utilized by making it provide the motorist with railroad crossing protection.

Remember, the purpose of this essay is to give you merely the seed of suggestion; not the finished product of an invention ready to set up and render service. The value to you, of this suggestion, lies in the possibility of THOUGHT that you may devote to it, thereby developing and expanding your own mind.

Study yourself and find out to which of the two great major urges to action your mind responds most naturally—the urge of necessity or the desire to create. If you have children, study them and determine to which of these two motives they respond most naturally. Millions of children have had their imagination dwarfed and retarded by parents who removed as much as possible of the urge of necessity. By "making it easy" for your child you may be depriving the world of a genius. Bear in mind the fact that most of the progress that man has made came as the result of bitter, biting NECESSITY!

.   .   .   .

You need no proof that methods of transportation have undergone a continuous process of evolution. So marked has the change been that the old one-lung type of automobile now provokes a laugh wherever it is found on the street.

The law of evolution is always and everywhere at work, changing, tearing down and rebuilding every material element on this earth and throughout the universe. Towns, cities and communities are undergoing constant change. Go back to the place where you lived twenty years ago and you will recognize neither the place nor the people. New faces will have made their appearance. The old faces will have changed. New buildings will have taken the place of the old. Everything will appear differently because everything will be different.

The human mind is also undergoing constant change. If this were not true we would never grow beyond the child-mind age. Every seven years the mind of a normal person becomes noticeably developed and expanded. It is during these periodical changes of the mind that bad habits may be left off and better habits cultivated. Fortunate for the human being that his mind is undergoing a continuous process of orderly change.

The mind that is driven by the urge of necessity, or out of love to create, develops more rapidly than does the mind that is never stimulated to greater action than that which is necessary for existence.

The imaginative faculty of the human mind is the greatest piece of machinery ever created. Out of it has come every man-made machine and every man-made object.

Back of the great industries and railroads and banking houses and commercial enterprises is the all-powerful force of IMAGINATION!

Force your mind to THINK! Proceed by combining old ideas into new plans. Every great invention and every outstanding business or industrial achievement that you can name is, in final analysis, but the application of a combination of plans and ideas that have been used before, in some other manner.

"Back of the beating hammer
    By which the steel is wrought,
Back of the workshop's clamor
    The seeker may find the Thought;
The thought that is ever Master
    Of iron and steam and steel,
That rises above disaster
    And tramples it under heel.

"The drudge may fret and tinker
    Or labor with lusty blows,
But back of him stands the Thinker,
    The clear-eyed man who knows;
For into each plow or saber,
    Each piece and part and whole,
Must go the brains of labor,
    Which gives the work a soul.

"Back of the motor's humming,
    Back of the bells that ring,
Back of the hammer's drumming,
    Back of the cranes that swing,
There is the Eye which scans them,
    Watching through stress and strain,
There is the Mind which plans them—
    Back of the brawn, the Brain.

"Might of the roaring boiler,
　　Force of the engine's thrust,
Strength of the sweating toiler,
　　Greatly in these we trust;
But back of them stands the schemer,
　　The Thinker who drives things through,
Back of the job—the Dreamer
　　Who's making the dream come true."

Six months or a year from now come back and read this essay again and you will observe how much more you will get from it than you did at first reading. TIME gives the law of evolution a chance to expand your mind so it can see and understand more.

I HAVE YET TO FIND THE FIRST MAN WHO AMOUNTED TO VERY MUCH WHO HAD NOT THE COURAGE TO ASSUME RESPONSIBILITY FOR HIS OWN MISTAKES WITHOUT BEING ACCUSED.

Lesson Nine

HABIT OF DOING MORE
THAN PAID FOR

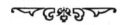

9

THERE are ten weaknesses against which most of us must guard ourselves. One of these is the habit of trying to reap before we have sown, and the other nine are all wrapped up in the one practice of creating alibis to cover every mistake made.

THE LAW OF SUCCESS
Lesson Nine
HABIT OF DOING MORE THAN PAID FOR

"You Can Do It if You Believe You Can!"

IT may seem to be a departure from the subject of this lesson to start the lesson with a discussion of love, but, if you will reserve your opinion until you have completed the lesson, you may be ready to agree that the subject of love could not have been omitted without impairing the value of the lesson.

The word "love" is here used in an all-embracing sense!

There are many objects, motives and people which arouse one's love-nature. There is some work which we do not like, some that we do like moderately, and, under certain conditions, there may be work that we actually LOVE!

Great artists, for example, generally love their work. The day laborer, on the other hand, usually not only dislikes his work, but may actually hate it.

Work which one does merely for the sake of earning a living is seldom liked. More often it is disliked, or even hated.

79

When engaged in work which he loves, a man may labor for an unbelievably long period of hours without becoming fatigued. Work that a man dislikes or hates brings on fatigue very quickly.

A man's endurance, therefore, depends very largely on the extent to which he likes, dislikes or loves that which he is doing.

We are here laying the foundation, as you will of course observe, for the statement of one of the most important laws of this philosophy, viz.:

A man is most efficient and will more quickly and easily succeed when engaged in work that he loves, or work that he performs in behalf of some person whom he loves.

Whenever the element of love enters into any task that one performs, the quality of the work becomes immediately improved and the quantity increased, without a corresponding increase in the fatigue caused by the work.

Some years ago a group of socialists, or perhaps they called themselves "co-operators," organized a colony in Louisiana, purchased several hundred acres of farm land, and started to work out an ideal which they believed would give them greater happiness in life and fewer of the worries through a system that provided each person with work at the sort of labor he liked best.

Their idea was to pay no wages to anyone. Each person did the work he liked best, or that for which he might be best equipped, and the products of their combined labors became the property of all. They had their own dairy, their own brick-making plant, their own cattle, poultry, etc. They had their own schools and a printing plant through which they published a paper.

A Swedish gentleman from Minnesota joined the colony, and at his own request he was placed at work in the printing plant. Very soon he complained that he did not like the work, so he was changed and put to work on the farm, operating a tractor. Two days of this was all he could stand, so he again applied for a transfer, and was assigned to the dairy. He could not get along with the cows, so he was once more changed, to the laundry, where he lasted but one day. One by one he tried every job on the works, but liked none of them. It had begun to look as if he did not fit in with the co-operative idea of living, and he was about to withdraw when someone happened to think of one job he had not yet tried—in the brick plant, so he was given a wheelbarrow and put to work wheeling bricks from the kilns and stacking them in piles, in the brick yard. A week's time went by and no complaint was registered by him. When asked if he liked his job he replied, "This ban chust the job I like."

Imagine anyone preferring a job wheeling bricks! However, that job suited the Swede's nature, he worked alone, at a task which called for no thought, and placed upon him no responsibility, which was just what he wanted.

He remained at the job until all the bricks had been wheeled out and stacked, then withdrew from the colony because there was no more brick work to be done. "The nice quiet job ban finished, so I t'ank I ban go back to Minney-so-tie," and back to "Minney-so-tie" he went!

When a man is engaged in work that he loves it is no hardship for him to do more work and better work than that for which he is paid, and for this very reason every man owes it to himself to do his best to find the sort of work he likes best.

I have a perfect right to offer this advice to the students of this philosophy for the reason that I have followed it, myself, without reason to regret having done so.

This seems to be an appropriate place to inject a little personal history concerning both the author and the Law of Success philosophy, the purpose of which is to show that labor performed in a spirit of love for the sake of the labor, itself, never has been and never will be lost.

This entire lesson is devoted to the offering of evidence that it really pays to render more service and better service than one is paid to render. What an empty and useless effort this would be if the author had not, himself, practiced this rule long enough to be able to say just how it works out.

For over a quarter of a century I have been engaged in the labor of love out of which this philosophy has been developed, and I am perfectly sincere when I repeat that which I have stated elsewhere in this course, that I have been amply paid for my labors, by the pleasure I have had as I went along, even if I received nothing more.

My labors on this philosophy made it necessary, many years ago, for me to choose between immediate monetary returns, which I might have enjoyed by directing my efforts along purely commercial lines, and remuneration that comes in later years, and which is represented by both the usual financial standards and other forms of pay which can be measured only in terms of accumulated knowledge that enables one to enjoy the world about him more keenly.

The man who engages in work that he loves best does not always have the support, in his choice, of his closest friends and relatives.

Combating negative suggestions from friends and relatives has required an alarming proportion of my energies, during the years that I have been engaged in research work for the purpose of gathering, organizing, classifying and testing the material which has gone into this course.

These personal references are made solely for the purpose of showing the students of this philosophy that seldom, if ever, can one hope to engage in the work one loves best without meeting with obstacles of some nature. Generally, the chief obstacles in the way of one engaging in the sort of work one loves best is that it may not be the work which brings the greatest remuneration at the start.

To offset this disadvantage, however, the one who engages in the sort of work he loves is generally rewarded with two very decided benefits, namely; first, he usually finds in such work the greatest of all rewards, HAPPINESS, which is priceless, and secondly, his actual reward in money, when averaged over a life-time of effort, is generally much greater, for the reason that labor which is performed in a spirit of love is usually greater in quantity and finer in quality than that which is performed solely for money.

The most embarrassing and, I might without any intention of disrespect say, the most disastrous oppo-

THERE is no more dangerous person—dangerous to himself and to others—than the person who passes judgment without pretending to know the facts.

sition to my choice of a life-work came from my wife. This, perhaps, will explain why I have made frequent references, in many of the lessons of this course, to the fact that a man's wife may either "make" or "break" him, according to the extent to which she gives or withholds co-operation and encouragement in connection with his chosen work.

My wife's idea was that I should accept a salaried position that would insure a regular monthly income, because I had shown, by the few salaried positions I had held, that I had marketable ability which should command an income of from $6,000.00 to $10,000.00 a year without any very great effort on my part.

In a way I saw my wife's viewpoint and was in sympathy with it, because we had young growing children coming on who needed clothes and education, and a regular salary, even though it were not large, seemed to be a necessity.

Despite this logical argument, however, I chose to override my wife's counsel. Came, then, to her rescue, the combined forces of her family and mine, and collectively they charged me, head-on, with what amounted to a command to right-about-face and settle down on a salary basis.

Studying other people might be all right for a man who had the time to spend in this "unprofitable" manner, they reasoned, but for a young married man with a growing family this seemed hardly the thing to do.

But I remained adamant! I had made my choice and I was determined to stand by it.

The opposition did not yield to my viewpoint, but gradually, of course, it melted away. Meanwhile, the knowledge that my choice had worked at least a temporary hardship on my family, combined with the thought that my dearest friends and relatives were not in harmony with me, greatly increased my labors.

Fortunately, not all of my friends believed my choice unwise!

There were a few friends who not only believed I was following a course that would ultimately bring me out somewhere near the top of the mountain of useful achievement, but, in addition to believing in my plans, they actually went out of their way to encourage me not to be whipped by either adversity or the opposition of relatives.

Of this small group of faithful ones who gave me encouragement at a time when it was badly needed, perhaps one man should have the fullest credit, and this man is Edwin C. Barnes, a business associate of Thomas A. Edison.

Mr. Barnes became interested in my chosen work nearly twenty years ago, and I owe it to him to state here that had it not been for his unwavering faith in the soundness of the Law of Success philosophy I would have yielded to the persuasion of my friends and sought the way of least resistance via the salary route.

This would have saved me much grief and an almost endless amount of criticism, but it would have wrecked the hopes of a life-time, and in the end I would in all probability have lost, also, the finest and most desirable of all things, HAPPINESS! for I have been extremely happy in my work, even during the periods when the remuneration it brought me could be measured by nothing but a mountain of debts which I could not for the moment pay.

Perhaps this may explain, to some extent, why the subject of slavery through debt was so extensively emphasized in Lesson Four, on the Habit of Saving.

We want that lesson to "sink in."

Edwin Barnes not only believed in the soundness of the Law of Success philosophy, but his own financial success had demonstrated, as had also his close business relationship with the greatest inventor on earth, that he had the right to speak with authority on the subject of the laws through which success may be achieved.

I began my work of research with the belief that success could be attained, by anyone with reasonable intelligence and a real desire to succeed, by following certain (then by me unknown) rules of procedure. I wanted to know what these rules were and how they could be applied.

Mr. Barnes believed as I did. Moreover, he was in a position to know that the astounding achievements of his business associate, Mr. Edison, came about entirely through the application of some of the principles which later were tested and included as a part of this philosophy. From his way of thinking it seemed that the accumulation of money, enjoying peace of mind and finding happiness could be brought about by the application of never-varying laws which anyone might master and apply.

That was my belief, also. That belief has now been transformed into not merely a provable, but a PROVED reality, as I hope every student of this course will have reason to understand when the course shall have been mastered.

Please keep in mind that during all these years of

research I was not only applying the law covered by this lesson, by DOING MORE THAN PAID FOR, but, I was going much further than this by doing work for which I did not, at the time I was doing it, hope ever to receive pay.

Thus, out of years of chaos, adversity and opposition this philosophy was finally completed and reduced to manuscripts, ready for publication.

For a time nothing happened!

I was resting on my oars, so to speak, before taking the next step toward placing the philosophy in the hands of people who I had reason to believe would welcome it.

"God moves in a mysterious way, His wonders to perform!"

During the earlier years of my experience I thought these words to be empty and meaningless, but I have since modified my belief considerably.

I was invited to deliver an address in Canton, Ohio. My coming had been well advertised and there was reason to expect that I would have a large audience. To the contrary, conflicting meetings being held by two large groups of business men reduced my audience to the lucky number of "thirteen."

It has always been my belief that a man should do his best, regardless of how much he receives for his services, or the number of people he may be serving or the class of people served. I went at my subject as though the hall were filled. Somehow there arose in me a sort of feeling of resentment on account of the way the "wheel of fate" had turned against me, and if I ever made a convincing speech I made it that night.

Down deep in my heart, however, I thought I had failed!

I did not know until the next day that I was making history the night before that was destined to give the Law of Success philosophy its first real impetus.

One of the men who sat in my audience, as one of the "thirteen," was the late Don R. Mellett, who was then the publisher of the Canton Daily News, brief reference to whom I made in the Introductory Lesson of this course.

After I had finished speaking I slipped out at the back door and returned to my hotel, not wanting to face any of my "thirteen" victims on the way out.

The next day I was invited to Mr. Mellett's office.

Inasmuch as it was he who had taken the initiative by inviting me in to see him I left it to him to do most of the talking. He began in something like this fashion:

"Would you mind telling me your entire life-story, from the days of your early childhood on up to the present?"

I told him I would do so if he could stand the burden of listening to so long a narrative. He said he could, but before I began he cautioned me not to omit the unfavorable side.

"What I wish you to do," said he, "is to mix the fat with the lean and let me take a look at your very soul, not from its most favorable side, but from all sides."

For three hours I talked while Mellett listened!

I omitted nothing. I told him of my struggles, of my mistakes, of my impulses to be dishonest when the tides of fortune swept against me too swiftly, and of

AMONG the other
things you intend to
"cut out" in your New
Year's resolution, include
the word "Impossible!"

my better judgment which prevailed in the end, but only after my conscience and I had engaged in prolonged combat. I told him how I conceived the idea of organizing the Law of Success philosophy, how I had gone about gathering the data that had gone into the philosophy, of the tests I had made which resulted in the elimination of some of the data and the retention of other parts of it.

After I had finished Mellett said: "I wish to ask you a very personal question, and I hope you will answer it as frankly as you have told the remainder of your story. Have you accumulated any money from your efforts, and, if not, do you know why you have not?"

"No!" I replied. "I have accumulated nothing but experience and knowledge and a few debts, and the reason, while it may not be sound, is easily explained. The truth is that I have been so busy all these years in trying to eliminate some of my own ignorance so I could intelligently gather and organize the data that have gone into the Law of Success philosophy, that I have had neither the opportunity nor the inclination to turn my efforts to making money."

The serious look on Don Mellett's face, much to my surprise, softened into a smile as he laid his hand on my shoulder and said:

"I knew the answer before you stated it, but I wondered if you knew it. You probably know that you are not the only man who has had to sacrifice immediate monetary remuneration for the sake of gathering knowledge, for in truth your experience has been that of every philosopher from the time of Socrates down to the present."

Those words fell as the sound of music upon my ears!

I had made one of the most embarrassing admissions of my life; I had laid my soul bare, admitting temporary defeat at almost every cross-road which I had passed in my struggles, and I had capped all this off by admitting that an exponent of the Law of Success was, himself, a temporary failure!

How incongruous it seemed! I felt stupid, humiliated and embarrassed as I sat in front of the most searching pair of eyes and the most inquisitive man I had ever met.

The absurdity of it all came over me like a flash— THE PHILOSOPHY OF SUCCESS, CREATED AND BROADCASTED BY A MAN WHO WAS OBVIOUSLY A FAILURE!

This thought struck me so forcibly that I expressed it in words.

"What?" Mellett exclaimed, "a failure?

"Surely you know the difference between failure and temporary defeat," he continued. "No man is a failure who creates a single idea, much less an entire philosophy, that serves to soften the disappointments and minimize the hardships of generations yet unborn."

I wondered what was the object of this interview. My first conjecture was that Mellett wanted some facts on which to base an attack, in his newspaper, on the Law of Success philosophy. Perhaps this thought grew out of some of my previous experiences with newspaper men, a few of whom had been antagonistic toward me. At any rate, I decided at the outset of the interview to give him the facts, without embellishment, come from it what would.

Before I left Mellett's office we had become business partners, with the understanding that he would resign as publisher of the Canton Daily News and take over the management of all my affairs, as soon as this could be arranged.

Meanwhile, I began writing a series of Sunday feature-page editorials which were published in the Canton Daily News, based upon the Law of Success philosophy.

One of these editorials (the one entitled "Failure," which appears in the back of one of the lessons of this course) came to the attention of Judge Elbert H. Gary, who was at that time the Chairman of the Board of the United States Steel Corporation. This resulted in the opening of communication between Mellett and Judge Gary, which, in turn, led to Judge Gary's offer to purchase the Law of Success course for the use of the employees of the Steel Corporation, in the manner described in the Introductory Lesson.

The tides of fortune had begun to turn in my favor!

The seeds of service which I had been sowing over a long period of toilsome years, by DOING MORE THAN PAID FOR, were beginning to germinate at last!

Despite the fact that my partner was assassinated before our plans had much more than started, and Judge Gary died before the Law of Success philosophy could be re-written so it conformed to his requirements, the "love's labor lost" on that fateful night, when I spoke to an audience of thirteen in Canton, Ohio, started a chain of events which now move rapidly without thought or effort on my part.

It is no abuse of confidences to enumerate here a few of the events which show that no labor of love is ever performed at a total loss, and that those who render more service and better service than that for which they are paid sooner or later receive pay for much more than they actually do.

As this lesson is ready to go to the publisher some of the following well known concerns are considering favorably the purchase of the Law of Success course for all their employees, while others have actually arranged for the purchase of the course:

Mr. Daniel Willard, President of the Baltimore & Ohio Railroad Co.

Indian Refining Company

Standard Oil Company

New York Life Insurance Company

The Postal Telegraph Commercial-Cable Company

The Pierce-Arrow Motor Car Company

The Cadillac Motor Car Company

And some fifty other concerns of a similar size.

In addition to this, a newly organized club for boys, similar in nature to the Y. M. C. A., has contracted for the use of the Law of Success course as the basis of its educational program, and estimates that it will distribute more than 100,000 courses of the philosophy within the next two years.

Quite aside from these sources of distribution, the Ralston University Press, of Meriden, Conn., has contracted to publish and distribute the course to individuals throughout the United States, and perhaps in some foreign countries. How many courses they will distribute cannot be accurately estimated, but when one stops to consider the fact that they have a mailing

list of approximately 800,000 people who have faith
in anything they offer for sale, it seems very reasonable to suppose that their distribution will place tens
of thousands of courses in the hands of men and women
who are earnestly searching for the knowledge conveyed by the Law of Success philosophy.

Perhaps it is unnecessary, but I wish to explain that
my only object in here relating the story of how the
Law of Success philosophy has gained the recognition
described is to show how the law upon which this lesson is based actually works out in the practical affairs
of life.

If I could have made this analysis without the use
of the personal pronoun I would have done so.

.   .   .   .

With this background of history concerning the Law
of Success philosophy as a whole, and this lesson in
particular, you are better prepared to accept as sound
the law on which this lesson is based.

There are more than a score of sound reasons why
you should develop the habit of performing more
service and *better service* than that for which you are
paid, despite the fact that a large majority of the
people are not rendering such service.

There are two reasons, however, for rendering such
service, which transcend, in importance, all the others;
namely,

First: By establishing a reputation as being a person who always renders more service and better service
than that for which you are paid, you will benefit by
comparison with those around you who do not render
such service, and the contrast will be so noticeable that

IF you have tried and met with defeat; if you have planned and watched your plans as they were crushed before your eyes; just remember that the greatest men in all history were the products of courage, and courage, you know, is born in the cradle of adversity.

there will be keen competition for your services, no matter what your life-work may be.

It would be an insult to your intelligence to offer proof of the soundness of this statement, because it is obviously sound. Whether you are preaching sermons, practicing law, writing books, teaching school, or digging ditches, you will become more valuable and you will be able to command greater pay the minute you gain recognition as a person who does more than that for which he is paid.

Second: By far the most important reason why you should render more service than that for which you are paid; a reason that is basic and fundamental in nature; may be described in this way: Suppose that you wished to develop a strong right arm, and suppose that you tried to do so by tying the arm to your side with a rope, thus taking it out of use and giving it a long rest. Would disuse bring strength, or would it bring atrophy and weakness, resulting, finally, in your being compelled to have the arm removed?

You know that if you wished a strong right arm you could develop such an arm *only by giving it the hardest sort of use.* Take a look at the arm of a blacksmith if you wish to know how an arm may be made strong. Out of resistance comes strength. The strongest oak tree of the forest is not the one that is protected from the storm and hidden from the sun, but it is the one that stands in the open, where it is compelled to struggle for its existence against the winds and rains and the scorching sun.

It is through the operation of one of Nature's unvarying laws that struggle and resistance develop strength, and the purpose of this lesson is to show you

how to harness this law and so use it that it will aid
you in your struggle for success. By performing more
service and better service than that for which you are
paid, you not only exercise your service-rendering
qualities, and thereby develop skill and ability of an
extraordinary sort, but you build reputation that is
valuable. If you form the habit of rendering such
service you will become so adept in your work that
you can *command* greater remuneration than those
who do not perform such service. You will eventually develop sufficient strength to enable you to remove yourself from any undesirable station in life,
and no one can or will desire to stop you.

If you are an employee you can make yourself so
valuable, through this habit of performing more service than that for which you are paid, that you can
practically set your own wages and no sensible employer will try to stop you. If your employer should
be so unfortunate as to try to withhold from you the
compensation to which you are entitled, this will not
long remain as a handicap because other employers
will discover this unusual quality and offer you employment.

The very fact that most people are rendering as
little service as they can possibly get by with serves
as an advantage to all who are rendering more service
than that for which they are paid, because it enables
all who do this to profit by comparison. You can "get
by" if you render as little service as possible, but that
is all you will get; and when work is slack and re-
trenchment sets in, you will be one of the first to be
dismissed.

For more than twenty-five years I have carefully

studied men with the object of ascertaining why some achieve noteworthy success while others with just as much ability do not get ahead; and it seems significant that every person whom I have observed applying this principle of rendering more service than that for which he was paid, was holding a better position and receiving more pay than those who merely performed sufficient service to "get by" with.

Personally I never received a promotion in my life that I could not trace directly to recognition that I had gained by rendering more service and better service than that for which I was paid.

I am stressing the importance of making this principle a habit as a means of enabling an employee to promote himself to a higher position, with greater pay, for the reason that this course will be studied by thousands of young men and young women who work for others. However, the principle applies to the employer or to the professional man or woman just the same as to the employee.

Observance of this principle brings a two-fold reward. First, it brings the reward of greater material gain than that enjoyed by those who do not observe it; and, second, it brings that reward of happiness and satisfaction which come only to those who render such service. If you receive no pay except that which comes in your pay envelope, you are underpaid, no matter how much money that envelope contains.

.   .   .   .

My wife has just returned from the Public Library with a book for me to read. The book is entitled

"*Observation;* Every Man His Own University," by Russell H. Conwell.

By chance I opened this book at the beginning of the chapter entitled Every Man's University, and, as I read it through, my first impulse was to recommend that *you* go to the Public Library and read the entire book; but, upon second thought, I will not do this; instead, I will recommend that you purchase the book and read it, not once but a hundred times, because it covers the subject of this lesson as though it had been written for that purpose; covers it in a far more impressive manner than I could do it.

The following quotation from the chapter entitled Every Man's University will give you an idea of the golden nugget of truth to be found throughout the book:

"The intellect can be made to look far beyond the range of what men and women ordinarily see, but not all the colleges in the world can alone confer this power —this is the reward of *self-culture;* each must acquire it for himself; and perhaps this is why the power of observing deeply and widely is so much oftener found in those men and those women who have never crossed the threshold of any college but the *University of Hard Knocks.*"

Read that book as a part of this lesson, because it will prepare you to profit by the philosophy and psychology upon which the lesson is built.

.   .   .   .

We will now analyze the law upon which this entire lesson is founded, namely—

THE LAW OF INCREASING RETURNS!

Let us begin our analysis by showing how Nature employs this law in behalf of the tillers of the soil. The farmer carefully prepares the ground, then sows his wheat and waits while the Law of Increasing Returns brings back the seed he has sown, *plus a manyfold increase.*

But for this Law of Increasing Returns, man would perish, because he could not make the soil produce sufficient food for his existence. There would be no advantage to be gained by sowing a field of wheat if the harvest yield did not return more than was sown.

With this vital "tip" from Nature, which we may gather from the wheat fields, let us proceed to appropriate this Law of Increasing Returns and learn how to apply it to the service we render, to the end that *it may yield returns in excess of and out of proportion to the effort put forth.*

First of all, let us emphasize the fact that there is no trickery or chicanery connected with this Law, although quite a few seem not to have learned this great truth, judging by the number who spend all of their efforts either trying to get something for nothing, or something for less than its true value.

It is to no such end that we recommend the use of the Law of Increasing Returns, for no such end is possible, within the broad meaning of the word *success.*

Another remarkable and noteworthy feature of the Law of Increasing Returns is the fact that it may be used by those who purchase service with as great returns as it can be by those who render service, for proof of which we have but to study the effects of

ULTIMATELY, nothing matters very much. The defeat that seems to break your heart today will be but a ripple among the waves of other experiences in the ocean of your life further ahead.

Henry Ford's famous Five-Dollar-a-day minimum wage scale which he inaugurated some years ago.

Those who are familiar with the facts say that Mr. Ford was not playing the part of a philanthropist when he inaugurated this minimum wage scale; but, to the contrary, he was merely taking advantage of a sound business principle which has probably yielded him greater returns, in both dollars and good-will, than any other single policy ever inaugurated at the Ford plant.

By paying more wages than the average, he received more service and better service than the average!

At a single stroke, through the inauguration of that minimum wage policy, Ford attracted the best labor on the market and placed a premium upon the privilege of working in his plant.

I have no authentic figures at hand bearing on the subject, but I have sound reason to conjecture that for every five dollars Ford spent, under this policy, he received at least seven dollars and fifty cents' worth of service. I have, also, sound reason to believe that this policy enabled Ford to reduce the cost of supervision, because employment in his plant became so desirable that no worker would care to run the risk of losing his position by "soldiering" on the job or rendering poor service.

Where other employers were forced to depend upon costly supervision in order to get the service to which they were entitled, and for which they were paying, Ford got the same or better service by the less expensive method of placing a premium upon employment in his plant.

Marshall Field was probably the leading merchant

of his time, and the great Field store, in Chicago, stands today as a monument to his ability to apply the Law of Increasing Returns.

A customer purchased an expensive lace waist at the Field store, but did not wear it. Two years later she gave it to her niece as a wedding present. The niece quietly returned the waist to the Field store and exchanged it for other merchandise, despite the fact that it had been out for more than two years and was then out of style.

Not only did the Field store take back the waist, but, what is of more importance it did so *without argument!*

Of course there was no obligation, moral or legal, on the part of the store to accept the return of the waist at that late date, which makes the transaction all the more significant.

The waist was originally priced at fifty dollars, and of course it had to be thrown on the bargain counter and sold for whatever it would bring, but the keen student of human nature will understand that the Field store not only did not lose anything on the waist, but it actually profited by the transaction to an extent that cannot be measured in mere dollars.

The woman who returned the waist knew that she was not entitled to a rebate; therefore, when the store gave her that to which she was not entitled the transaction won her as a permanent customer. But the effect of the transaction did not end here; it only began; for this woman spread the news of the "fair treatment" she had received at the Field store, far and near. It was the talk of the women of her set for many days, and the Field store received more advertising from the transaction than it could have purchased in any other way with ten times the value of the waist.

The success of the Field store was built largely upon Marshall Field's understanding of the Law of Increasing Returns, which prompted him to adopt, as a part of his business policy, the slogan, "The customer is always right."

When you do only that for which you are paid, there is nothing out of the ordinary to *attract favorable comment* about the transaction; but, when you willingly do more than that for which you are paid, your action attracts the favorable attention of all who are affected by the transaction, and goes another step toward establishing a reputation that will eventually set the Law of Increasing Returns to work in your behalf, for this reputation will create a demand for your services, far and wide.

Carol Downes went to work for W. C. Durant, the automobile manufacturer, in a minor position. He is now Mr. Durant's right-hand man, and the president of one of his automobile distributing companies. He promoted himself into this profitable position solely through the aid of the Law of Increasing Returns, which he put into operation by rendering more service and better service than that for which he was paid.

In a recent visit with Mr. Downes I asked him to tell me how he managed to gain promotion so rapidly. In a few brief sentences he told the whole story.

"When I first went to work with Mr. Durant," said he, "I noticed that he always remained at the office long after all the others had gone home for the day, and I made it my business to stay there, also. No one

TO love praise, but not worship it, and fear condemnation, but not go down under it, is evidence of a well balanced personality.

asked me to stay, but I thought someone should be there to give Mr. Durant any assistance he might need. Often he would look around for someone to bring him a letter file, or render some other trivial service, and *always he found me there ready to serve him.* He got into the habit of calling on me; that is about all there is to the story."

"He got into the habit of calling on me!"

Read that sentence again, for it is full of meaning of the richest sort.

Why did Mr. Durant get into the habit of calling on Mr. Downes? Because *Mr. Downes made it his business to be on hand where he would be seen.* He deliberately placed himself in Mr. Durant's way in order that he might render service that would place the Law of Increasing Returns back of him.

Was he told to do this? *No!*

Was he paid to do it? *Yes!* He was paid by the opportunity it offered for him to bring himself to the attention of the man who had it within his power to promote him.

We are now approaching the most important part of this lesson, because this is an appropriate place at which to suggest that *you* have the same opportunity to make use of the Law of Increasing Returns that Mr. Downes had, and you can go about the application of the Law in exactly the same way that he did, *by being on hand and ready to volunteer your services in the performance of work which others may shirk because they are not paid to do it.*

Stop! Don't say it—don't even think it—if you have the slightest intention of springing that old time-worn phrase entitled, "But *my employer is different."*

Of course he is different. All men are different in most respects, but they are very much alike in this— they are somewhat *selfish;* in fact they are selfish enough not to want a man such as Carol Downes to cast his lot with their competitor, and this very self-ishness may be made to serve you as an asset and not as a liability *if—*

You have the good judgment to make yourself so useful that the person to whom you sell your services cannot get along without you.

One of the most advantageous promotions I ever received came about through an incident which seemed so insignificant that it appeared to be unimportant. One Saturday afternoon, a lawyer, whose office was on the same floor as that of my employer, came in and asked if I knew where he could get a stenographer to do some work which he was compelled to finish that day.

I told him that all of our stenographers had gone to the ball game, and that I would have been gone had he called five minutes later, but that I would be very glad to stay and do his work as I could go to a ball game any day and his work had to be done then.

I did the work for him, and when he asked how much he owed me I replied, "Oh, about a thousand dollars, as long as it is you; if it were for anyone else, I wouldn't charge anything." He smiled, and thanked me.

Little did I think, when I made that remark, that he would ever pay me a thousand dollars for that afternoon's work, but *he did!* Six months later, after I had entirely forgotten the incident, he called on me again, and asked how much salary I was receiving.

When I told him he informed me that he was ready to pay me that thousand dollars which I had laughingly said I would charge him for the work I had performed for him and he *did pay it* by giving me a position at a thousand dollars a year increase in salary.

Unconsciously, I had put the Law of Increasing Returns to work in my behalf that afternoon, by giving up the ball game and rendering a service which was obviously rendered out of a desire to be helpful and not for the sake of a monetary consideration.

It was not my duty to give up my Saturday afternoon, but—

It was my privilege!

Furthermore, it was a profitable privilege, because it yielded me a thousand dollars in cash and a much more responsible position than the one I had formerly occupied.

It was Carol Downes' *duty* to be on hand until the usual quitting time, but it was his *privilege* to remain at his post after the other workers had gone, and that privilege properly exercised brought him greater responsibilities and a salary that yields him more in a year than he would have made in a life-time in the position he occupied before he exercised the privilege.

I have been thinking for more than twenty-five years of this *privilege* of performing more service and better service than that for which we are paid, and my thoughts have led me to the conclusion that a single hour devoted each day to rendering service for which we are not paid, can be made to yield bigger returns than we received from the entire remainder of

THE educated man is the man who has learned how to get everything he needs without violating the rights of his fellow men. Education comes from within; you get it by struggle and effort and thought.

the day during which we are merely performing our *duty.*

(We are still in the neighborhood of the *most important part* of this lesson, therefore, *think* and assimilate as you pass over these pages.)

The Law of Increasing Returns is no invention of mine, nor do I lay claim to the discovery of the principle of rendering more service and better service than paid for, as a means of utilizing this Law. I merely appropriated them, after many years of careful observation of those forces which enter into the attainment of success, just as *you will appropriate them* after you understand their significance.

You might begin this appropriation process now by trying an experiment which may easily open your eyes and place back of your efforts powers that you did not know you possessed.

Let me caution you, however, not to attempt this experiment in the same spirit in which a certain woman experimented with that Biblical passage which says something to the effect that *if you have faith the size of a grain of mustard, and say to yonder mountain be removed to some other place, it will be removed.* This woman lived near a high mountain that she could see from her front door; therefore, as she retired that night she commanded the mountain to remove itself to some other place.

Next morning she jumped out of bed, rushed to the door and looked out, but lo! the mountain was still there. Then she said:

"Just as I had expected!   I knew it would be there."

I am going to ask you to approach this experiment

with full *faith* that it will mark one of the most important turning-points of your entire life. I am going to ask you to make the object of this experiment the removal of a mountain that is standing where *your temple of success should stand,* but where it never can stand until you have removed the mountain.

You may never have noticed the mountain to which I refer, but it is standing there in your way just the same, unless you have already discovered and removed it.

"And what is this mountain?" you ask!

It is the feeling that you have been cheated unless you receive material pay for all the service you render.

That feeling may be unconsciously expressing itself and destroying the very foundation of your *temple of success* in scores of ways that you have not observed.

In the very lowly bred type of humanity, this feeling usually seeks outward expression in terms something like this:

"I am not paid to do this and I'll be blankety-blankety-blank if I'll do it!"

You know the type to which reference is made; you have met with it many times, but you have never found a single person of this type who was successful, and you *never will.*

Success must be *attracted* through understanding and application of laws which are as immutable as is the law of gravitation. It cannot be driven into the corner and captured as one would capture a wild steer. For this reason you are requested to enter into the following experiment with the object of familiarizing yourself with one of the most important of these laws; namely, the Law of Increasing Returns.

The experiment:

During the next six months make it your business to render useful service to at least one person every day, for which you *neither expect nor accept monetary pay.*

Go at this experiment with *faith* that it will uncover for your use one of the most powerful laws that enter into the achievement of enduring success, and *you will not be disappointed.*

The rendering of this service may take on any one of more than a score of forms. For example, it may be rendered personally to one or more specific persons; or it may be rendered to your employer, in the nature of work that you perform after hours.

Again, it may be rendered to entire strangers whom you never expect to see again. It matters not to whom you render this service so long as you render it with willingness, and solely for the purpose of bene-fiting others.

If you carry out this experiment in the proper attitude of mind, you will discover that which all others who have become familiar with the law upon which it is based have discovered; namely, that—

You can no more render service without receiving compensation than you can withhold the rendering of it without suffering the loss of reward.

"Cause and effect, means and ends, seed and fruit, cannot be severed," says Emerson; "for the effect already blooms in the cause, the end pre-exists in the means, the fruit in the seed."

.   .   .   .

"If you serve an ungrateful master, serve him the more. Put God in your debt. Every stroke shall be

THE person who sows a single beautiful thought in the mind of another, renders the world a greater service than that rendered by all the faultfinders combined.

repaid. The longer the payment is withholden, the better for you; for compound interest on compound interest is the rate and usage of this exchequer."

.   .   .   .

"The law of Nature is, Do the thing and you shall have the power; but they who do not the thing have not the power."

.   .   .   .

"Men suffer all their life long, under the foolish superstition that they can be cheated. But it is as impossible for a man to be cheated by anyone but himself, as for a thing to be, and not to be, at the same time. There is a third silent party to all our bargains. The nature and soul of things takes on itself the guaranty of fulfillment of every contract, so that *honest service cannot come to loss*."

Before you begin the experiment that you have been requested to undertake, read Emerson's essay on Compensation, for it will go a very long way toward helping you to understand *why* you are making the experiment.

Perhaps you have read Compensation before. Read it again! One of the strange phenomena that you will observe about this essay may be found in the fact that every time you read it you will discover new truths that you did not notice during previous readings.

A few years ago I was invited to deliver the graduation address before the students of an eastern college. During my address I dwelt at length, and with all the emphasis at my command, on the importance of rendering more service and better service than that for which one is paid.

After the address was delivered, the president and the secretary of the college invited me to luncheon. While we were eating, the secretary turned to the president and said:

"I have just found out what this man is doing. He is putting himself ahead in the world by first helping others to get ahead."

In that brief statement he had epitomized the most important part of my philosophy on the subject of success.

It is literally true that you can succeed best and quickest by helping others to succeed.

Some ten years ago, when I was engaged in the advertising business, I built my entire clientele by the application of the fundamentals upon which this lesson is founded. By having my name placed on the follow-up lists of various mail order houses I received their sales literature. When I received a sales letter or a booklet or a folder which I believed I could improve I went right to work on it and made the improvement, then sent it back to the firm that had sent it to me, with a letter stating that this was but a trifling sample of what I could do—that there were plenty of other good ideas where that one came from —and, that I would be glad to render regular service for a monthly fee.

Invariably this brought an order for my services.

On one occasion I remember that the firm was dishonest enough to appropriate my idea and use it without paying me for it, but this turned out to be an advantage to me, in this way: A member of the firm who was familiar with the transaction started another business and as a result of the work I had done for his former associates, for which I was not paid, he engaged me to serve him, on a basis that paid me more than double the amount I would have realized from his original firm.

Thus the Law of Compensation gave back to me, and with compound interest added, that which I had lost by rendering service to those who were dishonest.

If I were looking for a profitable field of employment today, I could find it by again putting into action this plan of re-writing sales literature as a means of creating a market for my services. Perhaps I would find others who would appropriate my ideas without paying for them, but by and large people would not do this for the simple reason that it would be more profitable to them to deal fairly with me and thereby avail themselves of my continued services.

Several years ago I was invited to deliver a lecture before the students of the Palmer School, at Davenport, Iowa. My manager completed arrangements for me to accept the invitation under the regular terms in effect at that time, which were $100.00 for the lecture and my traveling expenses.

When I arrived at Davenport, I found a reception committee awaiting me at the depot and that evening I was given one of the warmest welcomes I had ever received during my public career, up to that time. I met many delightful people from whom I gathered many valuable facts that were of benefit to me; therefore, when I was asked to make out my expense account so the school could give me a check, I told them that I had received my pay, many times over, by that which I had learned while I was there. I refused my fee and returned to my office, in Chicago, feeling well repaid for the trip.

The following morning Dr. Palmer went before the two thousand students of his school and announced what I had said about feeling repaid by what I had learned, and added:

"In the twenty years that I have been conducting this school I have had scores of speakers address the student body, but this is the first time I ever knew a man to refuse his fee because he felt that he had been repaid for his services in other ways. This man is the editor of a national magazine and I advise every one of you to subscribe for that magazine, because such a man as this must have much that each of you will need when you go into the field and offer your services."

By the middle of that week I had received more than $6,000.00 for subscriptions to the magazine of which I was editor, and during the following two years these same two thousand students and their friends sent in more than $50,000.00 for subscriptions.

Tell me, if you can, how or where I could have invested $100.00 as profitably as this, by refusing to accept my $100.00 fee and thereby setting the Law of Increasing Returns to work in my behalf?

We go through two important periods in this life; one is that period during which we are gathering, classifying and organizing knowledge, and the other is that period during which we are struggling for recognition. We must first learn something, which requires more effort than most of us are willing to put into the job; but, after we have learned much that can be of useful service to others. we are still confronted with the problem of convincing them that we can serve them.

One of the most important reasons why we should always be not only ready but *willing* to render service, is the fact that every time we do so, we gain thereby another opportunity to prove to someone that we have ability; we go just one more step toward gaining the necessary recognition that we must all have.

Instead of saying to the world, "Show me the color of your money and I will show you what I can do," reverse the rule and say, "Let me show you the color of my service so that I may take a look at the color of your money if you like my service."

In 1917 a certain woman who was then nearing the fifty-year milepost of life, was working as a stenographer, at fifteen dollars a week. Judging by the salary she must have been none too competent in that work.

Now note this change:

Last year, this same woman cleared a little over $100,000.00 on the lecture platform.

What bridged that mighty chasm between these two earning capacities? you ask, and I answer:

The habit of performing more service and better service than that for which she was paid, thereby taking advantage of the Law of Increasing Returns.

This woman is well known throughout the country, as she is now a prominent lecturer on the subject of Applied Psychology.

Let me show you how she harnessed the Law of Increasing Returns. First, she goes into a city and delivers a series of fifteen free lectures. All may attend who will, without money and without price. Dur-

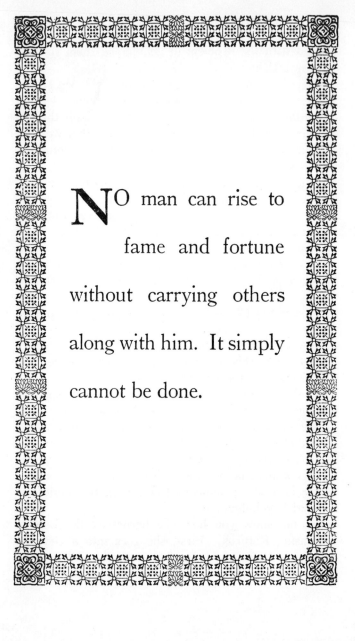

NO man can rise to fame and fortune without carrying others along with him. It simply cannot be done.

ing the delivery of these fifteen lectures she has the opportunity of "selling herself" to her audience, and at the end of the series she announces the formation of a class for which she charges twenty-five dollars per student.

That's all there is to her plan!

Where she is commanding a small fortune for a year's work there are scores of much more proficient lecturers who are barely getting enough from their work to pay their expenses, simply because they have not yet familiarized themselves with the fundamentals upon which this lesson is based, as she has done.

Now, I would like to have you stop right here and answer this question:

If a fifty-year-old woman, who has no extraordinary qualifications, can harness the Law of Increasing Returns and make it raise her from the position as stenographer at fifteen dollars a week to that of lecturer at over $100,000.00 a year—*why cannot you apply this same law so that it will give you advantages that you do not now possess?*

Never mind what is to come in the remainder of this lesson until you have answered this question and —*answered it AS IT SHOULD BE ANSWERED!*

You are struggling, either meekly or earnestly, to make a place for yourself in the world. Perhaps you are exerting enough effort to bring you success of the highest order, if that effort were coupled with and supported by the Law of Increasing Returns.

For this reason, you owe it to yourself to find out just how you can apply this law to best advantage.

Now go back to that question, again; for I am determined that you shall not pass it by lightly, without giving yourself the benefit of at least trying to answer it.

In other words, there is no mistaking the fact that you are being brought face' to face with a question that vitally affects your future, and, if you evade it, the fault will be with you.

You may lay this lesson aside after you have read it, and it is your privilege to do so, without making any attempt to profit by it; but, if you do so, you will never again be able to look at yourself in a mirror without being haunted by the feeling that—

YOU HAVE DELIBERATELY CHEATED YOURSELF!

Perhaps this is telling the truth in an undiplomatic way; but, when you purchased this course on the Law of Success, you did so because you wanted facts, and you are getting them, without the embellishment of apology.

After you have finished this lesson, if you will go back and review the lessons on *Initiative and Leadership* and *Enthusiasm*, you will better understand those lessons.

Those lessons and this one clearly establish the necessity of *taking the initiative, following it with aggressive action* and *doing more than you are paid to do*. If you will *burn* the fundamentals of these three lessons into your consciousness you will be a changed person, and I make this statement regardless of *who you are* or *what your calling may be*.

If this plain language has made you angry, I am glad; for it indicates that you can be moved! Now, if you would profit by the counsel of one who has made many more mistakes than you ever made, and for that reason learned a few of the fundamental truths of life, harness this anger and focus it on *yourself* until it drives you forth to render the service of which you are capable.

If you will do this you can collect a king's ransom as your reward.

.   .   .   .

Now let us turn our attention to still another important feature of this habit of performing more service and better service than that for which we are paid; namely, the fact that we can develop this habit without asking for permission to do so.

Such service may be rendered through your own initiative, without the consent of any person. You do not have to consult those to whom you render the service, for it is a privilege over which you have entire control.

There are many things you could do that would tend to promote your interests, but most of them require the co-operation or the consent of others. If you render *less* service than that for which you are paid you must do so by leave of the purchaser of the service, or the market for your service will soon cease.

I want you to get the full significance of this right of prerogative, which you have, to render more service and better service than that for which you are paid, for this places squarely *upon your shoulders* the responsibility of rendering such service, and if you fail to do so, you haven't a plausible excuse to offer or an "alibi" upon which to fall back, if you fail in the achievement of your *definite chief aim* in life.

One of the most essential yet the hardest truths

that I have had to learn, is that every person should
be his own hardest task-master.

We are all fine builders of "alibis" and creators of
"excuses" in support of our short-comings.

We are not seeking *facts* and *truths* as they *are*, but,
as we wish them to be. We prefer honeyed words of
flattery to those of cold, unbiased truth, wherein lies
the weakest spot of the man-animal.

Furthermore, we are up in arms against those who
dare to uncover the truth for our benefit.

One of the most severe shocks I received in the
early part of my public career was the knowledge that
men are still being crucified for the high crime of
telling the *truth*. I recall an experience I had some
ten years ago, with a man who had written a book
advertising his business school. He submitted this
book to me and paid me to review it and give him my
candid opinion of it. I reviewed the book with painstaking care, then did my duty by showing him wherein
I believed the book was weak.

Here I learned a great lesson, for that man became
so angry that he has never forgiven me for allowing
him to look at his book through my eyes. When he
asked me to tell him frankly what "criticism" I had
to offer of the book, what he really meant was that I
should tell him what I saw in the book that I could
"compliment."

That's human nature for you!

We court flattery more than we do the *truth*. I
know, because I am human.

All of which is in preparation for the "unkindest
cut of all" that I am duty-bound to inflict upon you;
namely, to suggest that you have not done as well as

you might have done for the reason that you have not applied a sufficient amount of truth set out in Lesson Eight, on *Self-control*, to charge yourself with your own mistakes and short-comings.

To do this takes *self-control* and plenty of it.

If you paid some person who had the ability and the *courage* to do it, a hundred dollars to strip you of your vanity and conceit and love for flattery, so that you might see the weakest part of your make-up, the price would be reasonable enough.

We go through life stumbling and falling and struggling to our knees, and struggling and falling some more, making asses of ourselves, and going down, finally, in defeat, largely because we either neglect or *flatly refuse* to learn the *truth* about ourselves.

Since I have come to discover some of my own weaknesses through my work of helping others discover theirs, I blush with shame when I take a retrospective view of life and think how ridiculous I must have seemed in the eyes of those who could see me as I *wouldn't* see myself.

We parade before the enlarged shadows of our own vanity and imagine that those shadows are our real selves, while the few knowing souls with whom **we** meet stand in the background and look at us with **pity** or with scorn.

Hold on a minute!   I am not through with you yet.

You have paid me to delve into the depths of your real self and give you an introspective inventory of what is there, and I am going to do the job right, as nearly as I can.

Not only have you been fooling yourself as to the real cause of your failures of the past, but you have

ALL salesmen will profit by remembering that none of us want anything that someone else wishes to "get rid of."

tried to hang these causes on the door of someone else.

When things did not go to suit you, instead of accepting full responsibility for the cause, you have said, "Oh, hang this job!—I don't like the way *'they'* are treating me, so I'm going to *quit!"*

Don't deny it!

Now let me whisper a little secret in your ear—a secret which I have had to gather from grief and heartaches and unnecessary punishment of the hardest sort—

Instead of "quitting" the job because there were obstacles to master and difficulties to be overcome, you should have faced the facts and then you would have known that life, itself, is just one long series of mastery of difficulties and obstacles.

The measure of a man may be taken very accurately by the extent to which he adapts himself to his environment and makes it his business to accept responsibility for every adversity with which he meets, whether the adversity grows out of a cause within his control or not.

Now, if you feel that I have "panned" you rather severely, have pity on me, O Fellow-Wayfarer, for you surely must know that I have had to punish myself more sorely than I have punished you *before I learned the truth that I am here passing on to you for your use and guidance.*

I have a few enemies—*thank God for them!*—for they have been vulgar and merciless enough to say some things about me that *forced* me to rid myself of some of my most serious short-comings; mainly those which I did not know I possessed. I have profited by the criticism of these enemies without having to pay them for their services in dollars, although I have paid in other ways.

However, it was not until some years ago that I caught sight of some of my most glaring faults which were brought to my attention as I studied Emerson's essay on Compensation, particularly the following part of it:

"Our strength grows out of our weakness.

"Not until we are pricked, and stung, and sorely shot at, awakens the indignation which arms itself with secret forces. *A great man is always willing to be little.* While he sits on the cushion of advantage he goes to sleep. When he is pushed, tormented, defeated, he has a chance to learn something; he has been put on his wits, on his manhood; he has *gained facts;* learned his ignorance; is cured of the insanity of conceit; has got moderation and real skill. The wise man always throws himself on the side of his assailants. It is more his interest than it is theirs to find his weak point. Blame is safer than praise. I hate to be defended in a newspaper. As long as all that is said is said against me, I feel a certain assurance of success. But as soon as honeyed words of praise are spoken of me, I feel as one that lies unprotected before his enemies."

Study this, the philosophy of the immortal Emerson, for it may serve as a modifying force that will temper your metal and prepare you for the battles of life, as carbon tempers the steel.

If you are a very young person, you need to study it all the more, for it often requires the stern realities of many years of experience to prepare one to assimilate and apply this philosophy.

Better that you should understand these great truths as a result of my undiplomatic presentation of them than to be forced to gather them from the less sympathetic sources of cold experience. Experience is a teacher that knows no favorites. When I permit you to profit by the truths I have gathered from the teachings of this cold and unsympathetic teacher called "experience," I am doing my best to show you favoritism. which reminds me, somewhat, of the times when my father used to "do his duty" by me, in the woodshed, always starting with this bit of encouraging philosophy: ·

"Son, this hurts me worse than it does you."

·   ·   ·   ·   ·   ·   ·

Thus we approach the close of this lesson without having exhausted the possibilities of the subject; nay, without having more than scratched the surface of it.

There comes to my mind the story of a romance of long ago through which I can leave in your mind the main import of this lesson. This story had its setting in the city of Antioch, in ancient Rome, two thousand years ago, when the great city of Jerusalem and all the land of Judea were under the oppressive heel of Rome.

The star figure of the story was a young Jew by the name of Ben Hur, who was falsely accused of crime and sentenced to hard labor, at the galley's oar. Chained to a bench in the galley, and being forced to tug wearily at the oars, Ben Hur developed a powerful body. Little did his tormentors know that out of his punishment would grow the strength with which he would one day gain his freedom. Perhaps Ben Hur, himself, had no such hopes.

Then came the day of the chariot races: the day that was destined to break the chains that bound Ben Hur to the oars of the galley and give him his freedom.

One span of horses was without a driver. In desperation the owner sought the aid of the young slave because of his mighty arms, and begged him to take the place of the missing driver.

As Ben Hur picked up the reins, a mighty cry went up from the onlookers.

"Look! Look! Those arms!—where did you get them?" they howled, and Ben Hur answered:

"At the galley's oar!"

The race was on. With those mighty arms Ben Hur calmly drove that charging span of horses on to victory; victory that won for him his freedom.

Life, itself, is a great chariot race, and the victory goes only to those who have developed the strength of character and determination and will-power to win.

What matters it that we develop this strength through cruel confinement at the galley's oar, as long as we use it so that it brings us, finally, to victory and freedom.

It is an unvarying law that strength grows out of resistance. If we pity the poor blacksmith who swings a five pound hammer all day long, we must also admire the wonderful arm that he develops in doing it.

". . . Because of the dual constitution of all things, in labor as in life, there can be no cheating," says Emerson. "The thief steals from himself. The swindler swindles himself. *For the real price of labor is knowledge and virtue, whereof wealth and credit are signs.* The signs, like paper money, may be counterfeited or stolen, but that which they represent; namely, knowledge and virtue, cannot be counterfeited or stolen."

Henry Ford receives fifteen thousand letters a week from people who are begging for a part of his wealth; yet how few of these poor ignorant souls understand that Ford's real wealth is not measured by the dollars he has in the bank, nor the factories he owns, but by the *reputation* he has gained through the rendering of useful service at a reasonable price.

And how did he gain that *reputation?*

Certainly not by rendering as little service as possible and collecting for it *all he could filch from the purchasers.*

The very warp and woof of Ford's business philosophy is this:

"Give the people the best product at the lowest price possible."

When other automobile manufacturers raise their prices, Ford lowers his. When other employers lower wages, Ford increases them. What has happened? This policy has placed the Law of Increasing Returns back of Ford so effectively that he has become the richest and most powerful man in the world.

Oh, you foolish and short-sighted seekers after wealth, who are returning from the daily chase empty-handed,—why do you not take a lesson from men like Ford? Why do you not reverse your philosophy and *give* in order that you may *get?*

I am finishing this lesson on Christmas Eve!

In the room next to my study our children are deco-rating their Christmas tree, and the rhythm of thei`

THERE are no lazy men. What may appear to be a lazy man is only an unfortunate person who has not found the work for which he is best suited.

voices falls as music upon my ears. They are happy, not alone because they expect to *receive*, but for the deeper reason that they have presents hidden away which they expect to *give*.

From the window of my study, I can see the neighbor's children as they, too, are gleefully engaged in preparing for this wonderful event.

Throughout the civilized world, millions of people are preparing to celebrate the birth of this Prince of Peace who, more than any other man, set forth the reasons why it is more blessed to give than to receive, and why enduring happiness comes not from *possessing* material wealth, but from rendering service to humanity.

It seems a queer co-incidence that the completion of this particular lesson should have happened on Christmas Eve, yet I am glad that it has, for this has provided me with sufficient justification for reminding you that nowhere in the entire history of civilization could I have found stronger support of the fundamentals of this lesson than may be found in the Sermon on the Mount, in the book of Matthew.

Christianity is one of the greatest and most far-reaching influences in the world today, and I hardly need apologize for reminding you that the tenets of Christ's philosophy are in absolute harmony with the fundamentals upon which this lesson, in the main, is founded.

As I see the happy faces of the children and watch the hurrying crowds of belated Christmas shoppers, all radiant with the splendor of the spirit of *giving*, I cannot help wishing that every eve was Christmas Eve, for then this would be a better world in which the struggle for existence would be reduced to a minimum, and hatred and strife outlawed.

Life is but a short span of years at best. Like a candle we are lighted, flicker for a moment, and then *go out!* If we were placed here for the purpose of laying up treasures for use in a life that lies beyond the dark shadow of Death, may it not be possible that we can best collect these treasures by rendering all the service we can, to all the people we can, in a loving spirit of kindness and sympathy?

I hope you agree with this philosophy.

Here this lesson must end, but it is by no means *completed.* Where I lay down the chain of thought it is now *your duty* to take it up and develop it, in your own way, and to your own benefit.

By the very nature of the subject of this lesson it can never be finished, for it leads into the heart of all human activities. Its purpose is to cause you to take the fundamentals upon which it is based and use them as a stimulus that will cause your mind to unfold, thereby releasing the latent forces that are yours.

This lesson was not written for the purpose of teaching you, but it was intended as a means of causing you to teach yourself one of the great truths of life. It was intended as a source of education, in the true sense of educing, drawing out, developing from within, those forces of mind which are available for your use.

When you deliver the best service of which you are capable, striving each time to excel all your previous efforts, you are making use of the highest form of education. Therefore, when you render more service and better service than that for which you are paid, you, more than anyone else, are profiting by the effort.

It is only through the delivery of such service that mastery in your chosen field of endeavor can be attained. For this reason you should make it a part of your *definite chief aim* to endeavor to surpass all previous records in all that you do. Let this become a part of your daily habits, and follow it with the same regularity with which you eat your meals.

Make it your business to render more service and better service than that for which you are paid, and lo! before you realize what has happened, you will find that THE WORLD IS WILLINGLY PAYING YOU FOR MORE THAN YOU DO!

Compound interest upon compound interest is the rate that you will be paid for such service. Just how this pyramiding of gains takes place is left entirely to you to determine.

Now, what are you going to do with that which you have learned from this lesson? and when? and how? and why? This lesson can be of no value to you unless it moves you to adopt and use the knowledge it has brought you.

Knowledge becomes POWER only through organization and USE! Do not forget this.

You can never become a Leader without doing more than you are paid for, and you cannot become successful without developing leadership in your chosen occupation.

THERE is always room for the man who can be relied upon to deliver the goods when he said he would.

THE MASTER MIND

An After-the-Lesson Visit With the Author

A Power That Can Bring You Whatever You Want On This Earth

SUCCESS is achieved through the application of power.

In the picture at the top of this page you see two forms of POWER!

At the left you see physical power, produced by Nature, with the aid of organized raindrops pouring over Niagara Falls. Man has harnessed this form of power.

At the right you see another, and a much more intensive form of power, produced through the *harmonious* co-ordination of THOUGHT in the minds of men. Observe that the word "harmonious" has been emphasized. In this picture you see a group of men seated at the Directors' Table in a modern business office. The powerful figure rising above the group represents the "Master Mind" which may be created wherever men blend their minds in a spirit of perfect harmony, with some DEFINITE objective in view.

137

Study this picture! It interprets the greatest POWER known to man.

.   .   .   .

With the aid of the MIND man has discovered many interesting facts about the earth on which he lives, the air and the ether that fill the endless space about him, and the millions of other planets and heavenly bodies that float through space.

With the aid of a little mechanical contrivance (which his MIND conceived) called a "spectroscope," man has discovered, at a distance of 93,000,000 miles, the nature of the substances of which the sun is made.

We have lived through the stone age, the iron age, the copper age, the religious fanatic age, the scientific research age, the industrial age and we enter, now, the age of THOUGHT.

Out of the spoils of the dark ages through which man has passed he has saved much material that is sound food for THOUGHT. While for more than ten thousand years the battle between IGNORANCE, SUPERSTITION and FEAR on the one side, and INTELLIGENCE on the other, has raged, man has picked up some useful knowledge.

Among other fragments of useful knowledge gathered by man, he has discovered and classified the 83 elements of which all physical matter consist.. By study and analysis and comparison man has discovered the "bigness" of the material things in the universe as they are represented by the suns and stars, some of them over ten million times as large as the earth on which he lives. On the other hand, man has discovered the "littleness" of things by reducing matter to molecules, atoms, and finally, to the smallest known particle, the electron. An atom is so inconceivably small that a grain of sand contains millions of them.

The molecule is made up of atoms, which are said to be little particles of matter that revolve around each other in one continuous circuit, at lightning speed, very much as the earth and other planets whirl around the sun in an endless circuit.

The atom, in turn, is made up of electrons which are constantly in rapid motion; thus it is said that in every drop of water and every grain of sand the entire principle upon which the whole universe operates, is duplicated.

How marvelous! How stupendous! How do we know these things to be true? Through the aid of the MIND.

You may gather some slight idea of the magnitude of it all the next time you eat a beef-steak, by remembering that the steak on your plate, the plate itself, and the table on which you are eating and the silverware with which you are eating are all, in final analysis, made of exactly the same material, electrons.

In the physical or material world, whether one is looking at the largest star that floats through the heavens or the smallest grain of sand to be found on earth, the object under observation is but an organized collection of molecules, atoms and electrons. (An electron is an inseparable form of power, made up of a positive and a negative pole.)

Man knows much about the physical facts of the universe!

The next great scientific discovery will be the fact, which already exists, that every human brain is both a broadcasting and a receiving station; that every thought vibration released by the brain may be picked up and interpreted by all other brains that are in harmony, or in "tune" with the rate of vibration of the broadcasting brain.

.   .   .   .

How did man acquire the knowledge that he possesses concerning the physical laws of this earth? How did he learn what has taken place before his time, and during his uncivilized period? He gathered this knowledge by turning back the pages of Nature's Bible and there viewing the unimpeachable evidence of millions of years of struggle among animals of a lower intelligence. By turning back the great stone pages man has uncovered the bones, skeletons, footprints and other unmistakable evidence which Mother Nature has held for his inspection throughout unbelievable periods of time.

Now man is about to turn his attention to another section of Nature's Bible—the one wherein has been written a history of the great mental struggle that has taken place in the realm of THOUGHT. This page is represented by the boundless ether which has picked up and still carries every thought vibration that was ever released from the mind of man.

This great page in Nature's Bible is one that no human being has been able to tamper with. Its records are positive, and soon they may be clearly interpreted. No interpolations by man have been permitted. Of the authenticity of the story written on this page there can be no doubt.

Thanks to EDUCATION (meaning the unfolding,

educing, drawing out, developing from within of the human mind) Nature's Bible is now being interpreted. The story of man's long, perilous struggle upward has been written on the pages of this, the greatest of all Bibles.

All who have partly conquered the Six Basic Fears described in another "author's visit" in this series, and who have succesfully conquered SUPERSTITION and IGNORANCE, may read the records that have been written in Nature's Bible. To all others this privilege is denied. For this reason there are probably fewer than one thousand people in the entire world at this time who are in even the primary grade as far as the reading of this Bible is concerned.

In the entire world there are probably fewer than one hundred people, today, who know anything about or have ever heard of the chemistry of the mind, through which two or more minds—

—MAY BE BLENDED, IN A SPIRIT OF PERFECT HARMONY, IN SUCH A MANNER THAT THERE IS BORN A THIRD MIND POSSESSING THE SUPERHUMAN POWER TO READ THE STORY OF THE VIBRATION OF THOUGHT AS IT HAS BEEN WRITTEN AND NOW EXISTS IN THE IMPERISHABLE RECORDS OF THE ETHER.

The newly-discovered radio principle has shut the mouths of the Doubting Thomases and sent the scientist scurrying into new fields of experimentation. When they emerge from this field of research they will show us that the mind as we understand it today, as compared to the mind of tomorrow, is about the same as comparing the intelligence of a polliwog to that of a professor of biology who has read the entire life-line of animal life, from the amoeba on up to man.

.   .   .   .

Come for a short visit with a few of the POWER-FUL men of recent years who made use of power created through the blending, in a spirit of harmony, of two or more minds.

We will begin with three well known men, who are known to be men of great achievement in their respective fields of endeavor.   Their names are Henry Ford, Thomas A. Edison and Harvey Firestone.

Of the three Henry Ford is the most POWERFUL, having reference to economic power.   Mr. Ford is the most powerful man now living on earth, and is believed to be the most powerful who ever lived.   So great is his power that he may have anything of a physical nature that he desires, or its equivalent. Millions of dollars, to him, are but playthings, no harder to acquire than the grains of sand with which the child builds sand-tunnels.

Mr. Edison has such a keen insight into Mother Nature's Bible that he has harnessed and combined for the good of man, more of Nature's laws than any other man who ever lived.   It was he who brought together the point of a needle and a piece of wax in such a way that they record and preserve the human voice.   It was he who first made the lightning serve to light our houses and streets, through the aid of the incandescent light.   It was he who made the camera record and produce all sorts of motion, through the modern moving picture apparatus.

Mr. Firestone's industrial achievement is so well

known that it needs no comment. He has made dollars multiply themselves so rapidly that his name has become a by-word wherever automobiles are operated.

All three men began their business and professional careers with no capital and but little schooling of the nature usually referred to as "education."

Perhaps Mr. Ford's beginning was, by far, the most humble of the three. Cursed with poverty, retarded by lack of even the most elementary form of schooling, and handicapped by ignorance in many forms, he has mastered all of these in the inconceivably short period of twenty-five years.

Thus might we briefly describe the achievements of three well known, successful men of POWER!

But, we have been dealing with EFFECT only!

The true philosopher wishes to know something of the cause which produced these desirable EFFECTS.

It is a matter of public knowledge that Mr. Ford, Mr. Edison and Mr. Firestone were close personal friends; that they went away to the woods once a year for a period of recuperation and rest.

But, it is not generally known—it is doubtful if these three men, themselves, even knew it—

—THAT THERE EXISTED BETWEEN THE THREE MEN A BOND OF HARMONY OUT OF WHICH HAS GROWN A MASTER MIND THAT IS BEING USED BY EACH OF THE THREE. A MIND OF SUPERHUMAN ABILITY, THAT HAS THE CAPACITY TO "TUNE IN" ON FORCES WITH WHICH MOST MEN ARE TO NO EXTENT FAMILIAR.

Let us repeat the statement that out of the blending and harmonizing of two or more minds (twelve or thirteen minds appear to be the most favorable number) may be produced a mind which has the capacity to "tune in" on the vibrations of the ether and pick up, from that source, kindred thoughts, on any subject.

.   .   .   .

Through the principle of harmony of minds, Ford, Edison and Firestone have created a Master Mind that now supplements the efforts of each of the three, and WHETHER CONSCIOUSLY OR UNCONSCIOUSLY, THIS "MASTER MIND" IS THE CAUSE OF THE SUCCESS OF EACH OF THE THREE.

There is no other answer to their attainment of great power, and their far-reaching success in their respective fields of endeavor, and this is true despite the fact that neither of them may be conscious of the power they have created, or the manner in which they have done so.

In the city of Chicago live six powerful men known as the Big Six. These six men are said to be the most powerful group of men in the middle west. It is said that their combined income totals more than twenty-five million dollars a year.

Every man in the group began in the most humble of circumstances.

Their names are:

Wm. Wrigley, Jr., who owns the Wrigley Chewing Gum business, and whose income is said to be over fifteen million dollars a year. John R. Thompson, who owns the chain of Thompson self-help lunch rooms throughout the country. Mr. Lasker, who owns the Lord & Thomas Advertising Agency. Mr. McCullough, who owns the largest express business in the world. And, Mr. Ritchie and Mr. Hertz, who own the Yellow Taxicab business of the country.

There is nothing startling about a man who does nothing more than become a millionaire, as a rule. However, there is something connected with the financial success of these particular millionaires that is more than startling, for it is well known that there exists between them a bond of friendship out of which has grown the condition of harmony that produces a Master Mind.

These six men, whether by accident or design, have blended their minds in such a way that the mind of each has been supplemented by a superhuman power known as a "Master Mind," and that mind has brought each of them more worldly gain than any person could possibly use to advantage.

The law upon which the principle of a Master Mind operates was discovered by Christ, when he surrounded himself with twelve disciples and created the first Thirteen Club of the world.

Despite the fact that one of the thirteen (Judas) broke the chain of harmony, sufficient seed was sown during the period of harmony that originally existed between these thirteen people, to insure the continuation of THE GREATEST AND MOST FAR-REACHING PHILOSOPHY KNOWN TO THE INHABITANTS OF THIS EARTH.

Many millions of people believe themselves to possess WISDOM. Many of these do possess wisdom, in certain elementary stages, but no man may possess real wisdom without the aid of the power known as a Master Mind, and such a mind cannot be created except through the principle of blending, in harmony, of two or more minds.

Through many years of practical experimentation it has been found that thirteen minds, when blended in a spirit of perfect harmony, produce the most practical results.

Upon this principle, whether consciously or unconsciously, is founded all of the great industrial and commercial successes that are so abundant in this age.

The word "merger" is becoming one of the most popular words in newspaper parlance, because hardly a day goes by that one may not read of some big industrial, commercial, financial or railroad merger. Slowly the world is beginning to learn (in a very few minds only) that through friendly alliance and co-operation great POWER may be developed.

     .   .   .   .

The successful business and industrial and financial enterprises are those managed by leaders who either consciously or unconsciously apply the principle of co-ordinated effort described in this article. If you would be a great leader in any undertaking, surround yourself with other minds that can be blended in a spirit of co-operation so that they act and function as one.

If you can grasp this principle and apply it you may have, for your efforts, whatever you want on this earth!

Lesson Ten

PLEASING PERSONALITY

10

EMPLOYERS are always on the lookout for a man who does a better job of any sort than is customary, whether it be wrapping a package, writing a letter or closing a sale.

THE LAW OF SUCCESS

Lesson Ten

PLEASING PERSONALITY

WHAT is an *ATTRACTIVE personality?*

Of course the answer is: *A personality that attracts.*

But what *causes* a personality to attract? Let us proceed to find out. *Your* personality is the sum total of your characteristics and appearances which distinguish you from all others. The clothes you wear, the lines in your face, the tone of your voice, the thoughts you think, the character you have developed by those thoughts, all constitute parts of your *personality.*

Whether your *personality* is attractive or not is another matter.

By far the most important part of your *personality* is that which is represented by your character, and is therefore the part that is not visible. The style of your clothes and their appropriateness undoubtedly constitute a very important part of your personality, for it is true that people form first impressions of you from your outward appearance.

Even the manner in which you shake hands forms an important part of your *personality*, and goes a very long way toward attracting or repelling those with whom you shake hands.

This art can be cultivated.

The expression of your eyes also forms an important part of your *personality*, for there are people, and they are more numerous than one might imagine, who can look through your eyes into your heart and see that which is written there by the nature of your most secret thoughts.

The vitality of your body—sometimes called personal magnetism—also constitutes an important part of your *personality*.

Now let us proceed to arrange these outward mediums through which the nature of our *personality* is expressed, so that it will *attract* and not repel.

There is one way in which you can so express the composite of your *personality* that it will *always attract*, even though you may be as homely as the circus "fat woman," and this is by—

Taking a keen heart-interest in the other fellow's "game" in life.

Let me illustrate exactly what is meant, by relating an incident that happened some years ago, from which I was taught a lesson in *master salesmanship*.

One day an old lady called at my office and sent in her card with a message saying that she must see *me personally*. No amount of coaxing by secretaries could induce her to disclose the nature of her visit, therefore I made up my mind that she was some poor old soul who wanted to sell me a book, and remembering that my own mother was a woman, I decided to go out to the reception room and buy her book, whatever it might be.

Please follow every detail thoughtfully; for you, too, may learn a lesson in master salesmanship from this incident.

As I walked down the hall-way from my private office this old lady, who was standing just outside of the railing that led to the main reception room, began to smile.

I had seen many people smile, but never before had I seen one who smiled so sweetly as did this lady. It was one of those contagious smiles, because I caught the spirit of it and began to smile also.

As I reached the railing the old lady extended her hand to shake hands with me. Now, as a rule, I do not become too friendly on first acquaintance when a person calls at my office, for the reason that it is very hard to say "no" if the caller should ask me to do that which I do not wish to do.

However, this dear old lady looked so sweetly innocent and harmless that I extended my hand and *she began to shake it!* whereupon, I discovered that she not only had an attractive smile, but she also had a magnetic hand-shake. She took hold of my hand firmly, but not too firmly, and the very manner in which she went about it telegraphed the thought to my brain that it *was she* who was doing the honors. She made me feel that she was really and truly *glad* to shake my hand, and I believe that she was. I believe that her hand-shake came from the heart as well as from the hand.

I have shaken hands with many thousands of people during my public career, but I do not recall having ever done so with anyone who understood the art of doing it as well as this old lady did. The moment she touched my hand I could feel myself "slipping," and I knew that whatever it was that she had come after she would go away with it, and that I would aid and abet her all I could toward this end.

In other words, that penetrating smile and that warm hand-shake had disarmed me and made me a "willing victim." At a single stroke this old lady had shorn me of that false shell into which I crawl when salesmen come around selling, or *trying to sell,* that which I do not want. To go back to an expression which you found quite frequently in previous lessons of this course, this gentle visitor had "neutralized" my mind and made me want to listen.

Ah, but here is the stumbling point at which most salespeople fall and break their necks, figuratively speaking, for it is as useless to try to sell a man something until you have first made him *want* to listen, as it would be to command the earth to stop rotating.

Note well how this old lady used a smile and a hand-shake as the tools with which to pry open the window that led to my heart; but the most important part of the transaction is yet to be related.

Slowly and deliberately, as if she had all the time there was in the universe (which she did have, as far as I was concerned at that moment) the old lady began to crystallize the first step of her victory into reality by saying:

"I just came here to tell you (what seemed to me to be a long pause) *that I think you are doing the most wonderful work of any man in the world today."*

Every word was emphasized by a gentle, though

firm, squeeze of my hand, and *she was looking through my eyes and into my heart as she spoke.*

After I regained consciousness. (for it became a standing joke among my assistants at the office that I fainted dead away) I reached down and unlocked the little secret latch that fastened the gate and said:

"Come right in, dear lady,—come right into my private office," and with a gallant bow that would have done credit to the cavaliers of olden times, I bade her come in and "sit awhile."

As she entered my private office, I motioned her to the big easy-chair back of my desk while I took the little hard-seated chair which, under ordinary circumstances, I would have used as a means of discouraging her from taking up too much of my time.

For three-quarters of an hour I listened to one of the most brilliant and charming conversations I have ever heard, and my visitor was doing *all* of the conversing. From the very start she had assumed the initiative and taken the lead, and, up to the end of that first three-quarters of an hour, she found no inclination, on my part, to challenge her right to it.

I repeat, lest you did not get the full import of it, that I was *a willing listener!*

Now comes the part of the story which would make me blush with embarrassment, if it were not for the fact that you and I are separated by the pages of this book; but I must summon the courage with which to tell you the facts because the entire incident would lose its significance if I failed to do this.

As I have stated, my visitor entranced me with brilliant and captivating conversation for three-

TO do much clear thinking a man must arrange for regular periods of solitude when he can concentrate and indulge his imagination without distraction.

—*Thomas A. Edison.*

quarters of an hour. Now, what do you suppose she was talking about all that time?

No! You are wrong.

She was not trying to sell me a book, nor did she once use the personal pronoun "I."

However, she was not only *trying,* but actually *selling* me something, and *that something was myself.*

She had no sooner been seated in that big cushioned chair than she unrolled a package which I had mistaken for a book that she had come to sell me, and sure enough, there was a book in the package—in fact, several of them; for she had a complete year's file of the magazine of which I was then editor (Hill's Golden Rule). She turned the pages of those magazines and read places that she had marked here and there, assuring me, in the meanwhile, that *she had always believed the philosophy back of that which she was reading.*

Then, after I was in a state of complete mesmerism, and thoroughly receptive, my visitor tactfully switched the conversation to a subject which, I suspect, she had in mind to discuss with me long before she presented herself at my office; but—*and this is another point at which most salespeople blunder*—had she reversed the order of her conversation and begun where she finished, the chances are that she never would have had the opportunity to sit in that big easy-chair.

During the last three minutes of her visit, she skillfully laid before me the merits of some securities that she was selling. She did not ask me to purchase; but, the way in which she told me of the merits of the securities (plus the way in which she had so impressively told me of the merits of my own "game") had the psychological effect of causing me to want to purchase; and, even though I made no purchase of securities from her, she *made a sale*—because I picked up the telephone and introduced her to a man to whom she later sold more than five times the amount that she had intended selling me.

If that same woman, or another woman, or a man, who had the tact and *personality* that she possessed, should call on me, I would again sit down and listen for three-quarters of an hour.

We are all human; and we are all more or less vain!

We are all alike in this respect—we will listen with intense interest to those who have the tact to talk to us about that which lies closest to our hearts; and then, out of a sense of reciprocity, we will also listen with interest when the speaker finally switches the conversation to the subject which lies closest to his or her heart; and, at the end, we will not only "sign on the dotted line" but we will say, *"What a wonderful personality!"*

In the city of Chicago, some years ago, I was conducting a school of salesmanship for a securities house which employed more than 1,500 salespeople. To keep the ranks of that big organization filled, we had to train and employ six hundred new salespeople every week. Of all the thousands of men and women who went through that school, there was but one man who grasped the significance of the principle I am here describing, the first time he heard it analyzed.

This man had never tried to sell securities and frankly admitted, when he entered the salesmanship class, that he was not a salesman. Let's see whether he was or not.

After he had finished his training, one of the "star" salesmen took a notion to play a practical joke on him, believing him to be a credulous person who would believe all that he heard, so this "star" gave him an inside "tip" as to where he would be able to sell some securities without any great effort. This star would make the sale himself, so he said; but the man to whom he referred as being a likely purchaser was an ordinary artist who would purchase with so little urging that he, being a "star," did not wish to waste his time on him.

The newly made salesman was delighted to receive the "tip," and, forthwith, he was on his way to make the sale. As soon as he was out of the office, the "star" gathered the other "stars" around him and told of the joke he was playing; for in reality the artist was a very wealthy man and the "star," himself, had spent nearly a month trying to sell him, but without success. It then developed that all of the "stars" of that particular group had called on this same artist but had failed to interest him.

The newly made salesman was gone about an hour and a half. When he returned he found the "stars" waiting for him with smiles on their faces.

To their surprise, the newly made salesman also wore a broad smile on his face. The "stars" looked at each other inquiringly, for they had expected that this "green" man would not return in a joyful mood.

"Well, did you sell to your man?" inquired the originator of this "joke."

"Certainly," replied the uninitiated one, "and I found that artist to be all you said he was—a perfect gentleman and a very interesting man."

Reaching into his pocket he pulled out an order and a check for $2,000.00.

The "stars" wanted to know how he did it.

"Oh, it wasn't difficult," replied the newly made salesman; "I just walked in and talked to him a few minutes and he brought up the subject of the securities himself, and said he wanted to purchase; therefore, I really did not sell to him—he purchased of his own accord."

When I heard of the transaction, I called the newly made salesman in and asked him to describe, in detail, just how he made the sale, and I will relate it just as he told it.

When he reached the artist's studio, he found him at work on a picture. So engaged in his work was the artist that he did not see the salesman enter; so the salesman walked over to where he could see the picture and stood there looking at it without saying a word.

Finally the artist saw him; then the salesman apologized for the intrusion and began to talk—

about the picture that the artist was painting!

He knew just enough about art to be able to discuss the merits of the picture with some intelligence; and he was really interested in the subject.

He liked the picture and frankly told the artist so, which, of course, *made the artist very angry!*

For nearly an hour those two men talked of nothing but art; particularly that picture that stood on the artist's easel.

Finally, the artist asked the salesman his name and his business, and the *salesman* (yes, the *master* salesman) replied, "Oh, never mind my business or my name; I am more interested in *you and your art!*"

The artist's face beamed with a smile of joy.

Those words fell as sweet music upon his ears. But, not to be outdone by his polite visitor, he insisted on knowing what mission had brought him to his studio.

Then, with an air of genuine reluctance, this *master salesman*—this real "star"—introduced himself and told his business.

Briefly he described the securities he was selling, and the artist *listened as if he enjoyed every word that was spoken.* After the salesman had finished the artist said:

"Well, well! I have been very foolish. Other salesmen from your firm have been here trying to sell me some of those securities, but they talked nothing but business; in fact, they annoyed me so that I had to ask one of them to leave. Now let me see—what was that fellow's name—oh, yes, it was Mr. Perkins." (Perkins was the "star" who had thought of this clever trick to play on the newly made salesman.) "But you present the matter so differently, and now I see how foolish I have been, and I want you to let me have $2,000.00 worth of those securities."

Think of that—*"You present the matter so differently!"*

And how did this newly made salesman present the matter so differently? Putting the question another way, what did this *master salesman* really sell that artist? Did he sell him securities?

No! he sold him his own picture which he was painting on his own canvas.

The securities were but an incident.

Don't overlook this point. *That master salesman*

NO MAN ACHIEVES
GREAT SUCCESS
WHO IS UNWILLING
TO MAKE PER-
SONAL SACRIFICES.

had remembered the story of the old lady who enter-
tained me for three-quarters of an hour by talking
about that which was nearest my heart, and it had so
impressed him that he made up his mind to study his
prospective purchasers and find out what would inter-
est them most, so he could talk about that.

This "green," newly made salesman earned
$7,900.00 in commissions the first month he was in the
field, leading the next highest man by more than double, and the tragedy of it was that not one person out
of the entire organization of 1,500 salespeople took
the time to find out *how and why* he became the real
"star" of the organization, a fact which I believe fully
justifies the rather biting reprimand suggested in
Lesson Nine to which you may have taken offense.

A Carnegie, or a Rockefeller, or a James J. Hill, or
a Marshall Field accumulates a fortune, through the
application of the selfsame principles that are available to all the remainder of us; but we envy them their
wealth without ever thinking of studying their philosophy and appropriating it to our own use.

We look at a successful man in the hour of his
triumph, and wonder how he did it, but we overlook
the importance of analyzing his methods and we forget the price he had to pay in careful, well organized
preparation which had to be made before he could reap
the fruits of his efforts.

Throughout this course on the Law of Success, you
will not find a single new principle; every one of them
is as old as civilization itself; yet you will find but
few people who seem to understand how to apply
them.

The salesman who sold those securities to that artist

was not only a *master salesman*, but he was a **man** with an *attractive personality*. He was not much to look at; perhaps that is why the "star" conceived the idea of playing that cruel (?) joke on him; but even a homely person may have a very *attractive personality* in the eyes of those whose handiwork he has praised.

Of course, there are some who will get the wrong conception of the principle I am here trying to make clear, by drawing the conclusion that any sort of cheap flattery will take the place of *genuine heart interest*. I hope that *you* are not one of these. I hope that you are one of those who understand the real psychology upon which this lesson is based, and that you will make it your business to study other people closely enough to find something about them or their work that you *really* admire. Only in this way can you develop a personality that will be irresistibly *attractive*.

Cheap flattery has just the opposite effect to that of constituting an attractive personality. It repels instead of attracting. It is so shallow that even the ignorant easily detect it.

.   .   .   .

Perhaps you have observed—and if you have not I wish you to do so—that this lesson emphasizes at length the importance of making it your business to take a keen interest in other people and in their work. business or profession. *This emphasis was by no means an accident.*

.   .   .   .

You will quickly observe that the principles upon which this lesson is based are very closely related to those which constitute the foundation of Lesson Six, on Imagination.

Also, you will observe that this lesson is based upon much the same general principles as those which form the most important part of Lesson Thirteen, on Co-operation.

Let us here introduce some very practical suggestions as to how the laws of Imagination, Co-operation and Pleasing Personality may be blended, or co-ordinated to profitable ends, through the creation of usable ideas.

Every thinker knows that "ideas" are the beginning of all successful achievement. The question most often asked, however, is, "How can I learn to create ideas that will earn money?"

In part we will answer this question in this lesson by suggesting some new and novel ideas, any of which might be developed and made very profitable, by almost anyone, in practically any locality.

IDEA NUMBER ONE

The world war has deprived Germany of her enormous trade in toys. Before the war we bought most of our toys from Germany. We are not likely to buy any more toys from German manufacturers in our time, or for a long while afterward.

Toys are in demand, not alone in the United States, but in foreign countries, many of which will not buy toys from Germany. Our only competitor is Japan and her toys are of so poor a quality that her competition means nothing.

But what sort of toys shall I manufacture and where

will I get the capital with which to carry on the business, you will ask?

First, go to a local toy dealer and find out just which class of toys sells most rapidly. If you do not feel competent to make improvements on some of the toys now on the market, advertise for an inventor "with an idea for a marketable toy" and you will soon find the mechanical genius who will supply this missing link in your undertaking. Have him make you a working model of just what you want, then go to some small manufacturer, woodworker, machine shop or the like, and arrange to have your toys manufactured.

You now know just what your toy will cost, so you are ready to go to some big jobber, wholesaler or distributor and arrange for the sale of your entire product.

If you are an able salesman you can finance this whole project on the few dollars required with which to advertise for the inventor. When you find this man you can probably arrange with him to work out a model for you during his spare evening hours, with a promise that you will give him a better job when you are manufacturing your own toys. He will probably give you all the time you want in which to pay him for his labor; or he may do the work in return for an interest in the business.

You can get the manufacturer of your toys to wait for his money until you are paid by the firm to which you sell them; and, if necessary, you can assign to him the invoices for the toys sold and let the money come direct to him.

Of course if you have an unusually pleasing and

convincing personality and considerable ability to organize, you will be able to take the working model of your toy to some man of means and, in return for an interest in the business, secure the capital with which to do your own manufacturing.

If you want to know what will sell, watch a crowd of children at play, study their likes and dislikes, find out what will amuse them and you will probably get an idea on which to build your toy. It requires no genius to invent! Common sense is all that is necessary. Simply find out what the people want and then produce it. Produce it well—better than anyone else is doing. Give it a touch of individuality. Make it distinctive.

We spend millions of dollars annually for toys with which to entertain our children. Make your new toy useful as well as interesting. Make it educational if possible. If it entertains and teaches at the same time it will sell readily and live forever. If your toy is in the nature of a game make it teach the child something about the world in which it lives, geography, arithmetic, English, physiology, etc. Or, better still, produce a toy that will cause the child to run, jump or in some other way exercise. Children love to move about and moving about is of benefit to them, especially when stimulated by the play motive.

An indoor baseball game would be a ready seller, especially in the cities. Work out an arrangement for attaching the ball to a string that will be suspended from the ceiling so one child may throw the ball against the wall and then stand back and strike it with a bat as it rebounds. A one-child baseball game, in other words.

FEAR no man, hate
no man, wish no one
misfortune, and more
than likely you will have
plenty of friends.

PLAN NUMBER TWO

This will be of interest only to the man or woman who has the self-confidence and the ambition to "run the risk" of making a big income, which, we may add, most people have not.

It is a suggestion that could be put into practical operation by at least forty or fifty people in every large city throughout the United States, and by a smaller number in the smaller cities.

It is intended for the man or woman who can write or will learn to write advertising copy, sales literature, follow-up letters, collection letters and the like, using the ability to write which we will suppose that you possess.

To make practical and profitable use of this suggestion you will need the co-operation of a good advertising agency and from one to five firms or individuals who do enough advertising to warrant their appropriations going through an agency.

You should go to the agency first and make arrangements with it to employ you and pay you seven per cent on the gross expenditures of all acounts which you bring to it; this seven per cent to compensate you for getting the account and for writing the copy and otherwise serving the client in the management of his advertising appropriation. Any reliable agency will gladly give you this amount for all the business you will bring.

Then you go to a firm or individual whose advertising account you wish to handle and say in effect that you wish to go to work *without compensation*. Tell what you can do and what you intend to do for that particular firm that will help it sell more goods.   If the firm employs an advertising manager you are to become virtually his assistant *without pay,* on one condition, namely, that the advertising appropriation is to be placed through the agency with which you have the connection.   Through this arrangement the firm or individual whose account you thus secure will get the benefit of your personal services, *without cost,* and pay no more for placing its advertising through your agency than it would through any other.   If your canvass is convincing and you really take the time to prepare your case, you will get your account without much argument.

You can repeat this transaction until you have as many accounts as you can handle advantageously, which, under ordinary conditions, will be not more than ten or twelve; probably less if one or more of your clients spends upwards of $25,000.00 a year in advertising.

If you are a competent writer of advertising copy and have the ability to create new and profitable ideas for your clients you will be able to hold their business from year to year.   You of course understand that you are not to accept more accounts than you can handle individually.   You should spend a portion of your time in the place of business of each of your clients; in fact you should have a desk and working equipment right on the grounds, so you can get first-hand information as to your clients' sales problems as well as accurate information as to their goods and wares.

Through this sort of effort you will give the advertising agency a reputation for effective service such as it would get in no other way, and you will please your clients because they will see satisfactory returns from your efforts. As long as you keep the agency and the clients whom you serve satisfied your job is safe and you will make money. A reasonable expectation of returns under this plan would be a gross business of $250,000.00 a year, on which your seven per cent would amount to $17,500.00.

A man or woman of unusual ability could run the figure much higher than this, up to, say, an income of $25,000.00 a year, while the tendency would be, however, to drop down to around $5,000.00 to $7,500.00, which are the figures that the "average" man or woman might reasonably expect to earn.

You can see that the plan has possibilities. It supplies independent work and gives you one hundred per cent of your earning power. It is better than a position as advertising manager, even if the position paid the same money, because it practically places you in a business of your own—one in which your name is constantly developing a survival value.

PLAN NUMBER THREE

This plan can be put into operation by almost any man or woman of average intelligence, and with but little preparation. Go to any first-class printer and make arrangements with him to handle all the business you bring to him, allowing you a commission of say ten per cent on the gross amount. Then go to the largest users of printed matter and get samples of everything in the way of printing that they use.

Form a partnership or working arrangement with a

commercial artist who will go over all this printed matter and wherever suitable or appropriate he will improve the illustrations or make illustrations where none were used before, making a rough pencil sketch which can be pasted to the original printed matter.

Then, if you are not a writer of copy, form a working arrangement with someone who is and get him or her to go over the copy of the printed matter and improve it in every respect possible.

When the work is complete go back to the firm from whom you get the printed matter, taking with you quotations on the work and show what can be done in the way of improvement. Say nothing about your quotations, however, until you have shown how much you could improve the printed matter. You will probably get the entire business of that firm by giving that sort of service in connection with every job of printing it has done.

If you perform your service properly you will soon have all the business that your commercial artist, your copy writer and you can handle. It ought to be good for $5,000.00 a year apiece for you.

Any profits that you earn from the work of others in connection with any of these plans will be a legitimate profit—a profit to which you will be entitled in return for your ability to organize and bring together the necessary talent and ability with which to perform satisfactory service.

If you go into the toy business you will be entitled to a profit on the work of those who make the toys because it will be through your ability that employment for them is available.

It is more than likely that your brains and your

ability, when added to that of those who work with you or for you, will greatly increase their earning capacity—even to the extent that they can well afford to see you make a small amount from their efforts *because they will be still earning much more than they could earn without your guidance!*

You are willing to take any of these plans and make a profit out of them, are you not? You see nothing wrong on your part, do you? If you are an employee, working for some other person or firm, may it not be possible that the head of that firm or that individual, with his ability to organize, finance, etc., is increasing your own earning capacity right now?

You want to get out of the employee class and become an employer. We do not blame you for that. Nearly every normal person wants to do the same. The one best first step to take is to serve the firm or individual for whom you are working just as you would wish to be served if you were that individual or the head of that firm.

Who are the big employers of help, today? Are they the rich men's sons who fell heir to employership? Not on your life! They are the men and women who came up from the ranks of the most lowly sort of labor; men and women who have had no greater opportunity than you have. They are in the positions that they hold because their superior ability has enabled them intelligently to direct others. You can acquire that ability if you will try.

Right in the town or city where you live there are people who probably could benefit by knowing you, and who could undoubtedly benefit you in return. In one section of the city lives John Smith who wishes

ASPIRATION is greater than realization, because it keeps us eternally climbing upward toward some unattained goal.

to sell his grocery store and open a moving picture theater. In another section of the city is a man who has a moving picture theater that he would like to trade for a grocery store.

Can you bring them together?

If you can, you will serve both and earn a nice remuneration.

In your town or city are people who want the products raised on the farms in the surrounding community. On those farms are farmers who raise farm products and who want to get them into the hands of those who live in town. If you can find a way of carrying the farm products direct from the farm to the city or town consumer you will enable the farmer to get more for his products and the consumer to get those products for less, and still there will be a margin to pay you for your ingenuity in shortening the route between producer and consumer.

In business there are, broadly speaking, two classes of people—the Producers and the Consumers. The tendency of the times is to find some way of bringing these two together without so many intermediaries. Find a way to shorten the route between producer and consumer and you will have created a plan that will help these two classes and handsomely profit you.

The laborer is worthy of his hire. If you can create such a plan you are entitled to a fair proportion of that which you *save* for the consumer and also a fair proportion of that which you *make* for the producer.

Let us warn you that whatever plan you create as a means of making money you had better see that it slices off a little of the cost to the consumer instead of adding a little to that cost.

The business of bringing producer and consumer together is a profitable business when it is conducted fairly to both, and without a greedy desire to *get all there is in sight!* The American public is wonderfully patient with profiteers who impose upon it, but there is a pivotal point beyond which even the shrewdest of them dare not go.

It may be all right to corner the diamond market and run up enormously high the price of those white rocks which are dug out of the ground in Africa without trouble, but when the prices of food and clothing and other necessities begin to soar skyward there is a chance of someone getting into the bad graces of the American public.

If you crave wealth and are really brave enough to shoulder the burdens which go with it, reverse the usual method of acquiring it by giving your goods and wares to the world at the lowest possible profit you can afford instead of exacting all that you can with safety. Ford has found it profitable to pay his workers, *not as little as he can get them for, but as much as his profits will permit.* He has also found it profitable to reduce the price of his automobile to the consumer while other manufacturers (many of whom have long since failed) continued to increase their price.

There may be some perfectly good plans through the operation of which you could squeeze the consumer and still manage to keep out of jail, but you will enjoy much more peace of mind and in all probability more profits in the long run if your plan, when you complete it, is built along the Ford lines.

You have heard John D. Rockefeller abused considerably, but most of this abuse has been prompted by sheer envy upon the part of those who would like to have his money but who haven't the inclination to earn it. Regardless of your opinion of Rockefeller, do not forget that he began as a humble bookkeeper and that he gradually climbed to the top in the accumulation of money because of his ability to organize and direct other and less able men intelligently. This author can remember when he had to pay twenty-five cents for a gallon of lamp oil and walk two miles through the hot sun and carry it home in a tin can in the bargain. Now, Rockefeller's wagon will deliver it at the back door, in the city or on the farm, at a little over half that sum.

Who has a right to begrudge Rockefeller his millions as long as he has reduced the price of a needed commodity. He could just as easily have increased the price of lamp oil to half a dollar, but we seriously doubt that he would be a multi-millionaire today if he had done so.

There are a lot of us who want money, but ninety-nine out of every hundred who start to create a plan through which to get money give all their thought to the scheme through which to get hold of it and *no thought to the service to be given in return for it.*

A Pleasing Personality is one that makes use of Imagination and Co-operation. We have cited the foregoing illustrations of how ideas may be created to show you how to co-ordinate the laws of Imagination, Co-operation and a Pleasing Personality.

Analyze any man who does not have a Pleasing Personality and you will find lacking in that man the faculties of Imagination and Co-operation also.

This brings us to a suitable place at which to introduce one of the greatest lessons on *personality* ever placed on paper. It is also one of the most effective lessons on salesmanship ever written, for the subjects of *attractive personality* and salesmanship must always go hand in hand; they are inseparable.

I have reference to Shakespeare's masterpiece, Mark Antony's speech at the funeral of Caesar. Perhaps you have read this oration, but it is here presented with interpretations in parentheses which may help you to gather a new meaning from it.

The setting for that oration was something like the following:

Caesar is dead, and Brutus, his slayer, is called on to tell the Roman mob, that has gathered at the undertaker's, why he put Caesar out of the way. Picture, in your imagination, a howling mob that was none too friendly to Caesar, and that already believed that Brutus had done a noble deed by murdering him.

Brutus takes the platform and makes a short statement of his reasons for killing Caesar. Confident that he has won the day he takes his seat. His whole demeanor is that of one who believes his word will be accepted without question; it is one of haughtiness.

Mark Antony now takes the platform, knowing that the mob is antagonistic to him because he is a friend of Caesar. In a low, humble tone of voice Antony begins to speak:

Antony: "For Brutus' sake, I am beholding to you."
Fourth Citizen: "What does he say of Brutus?"
Third Citizen: "He says, for Brutus' sake, he finds himself beholding to us all."

Fourth Citizen: " 'Twere best he speak no harm of
    Brutus here."
First Citizen: "This Caesar was a tyrant."
Third Citizen: "Nay, that's certain; we are blest that
    Rome is rid of him."
Second Citizen: "Peace! Let us hear what Antony
    can say." (Here you will observe, in Antony's
    opening sentence, his clever method of "neutral-
    izing" the minds of his listeners.)
Antony: "You gentle Romans,—"
    (About as "gentle" as a gang of Bolsheviks in
    a revolutionary labor meeting.)
All: "Peace, ho! Let us hear him."
    (Had Antony begun his speech by "knocking"
    Brutus, the history of Rome would have been
    different.)
Antony: "Friends, Romans, Countrymen, lend me
    your ears;
    I come to bury Caesar, not to praise him."
    (Allying himself with what he knew to be the
    state of mind of his listeners.)
    "The evil that men do lives after them;
    The good is oft interred with their bones;
    So let it be with Caesar. The noble Brutus
    Hath told you Caesar was ambitious;
    If it were so, it was a grievous fault;
    And grievously hath Caesar answered it.
    Here, under leave of Brutus and the rest,—
    For Brutus is an honorable man;
    So are they all, all honorable men—
    Come I to speak at Caesar's funeral.
    He was my friend—faithful, and just to me;
    But Brutus says he was ambitious;

C ONGRATULATE yourself when you reach that degree of wisdom which prompts you to see less of the weaknesses of others and more of your own, for you will then be walking in the company of the really great.

And Brutus is an honorable man;
He hath brought many captives home to Rome,
Whose ransoms did the general coffers fill;
Did this in Caesar seem ambitious?
When the poor have cried, Caesar hath wept;
Ambition should be made of sterner stuff;
Yet Brutus says he was ambitious;
And Brutus is an honorable man.
You all did see that on the Lupercal
I thrice presented him a kingly crown,
Which he did thrice refuse. Was this ambition?
Yet Brutus says he was ambitious;
And, surely, he is an honorable man.
I speak not to disprove what Brutus spoke,
But here I am to speak what I do know.
You all did love him once, not without cause;
What cause withholds you then to mourn for him?
O judgment! thou art fled to brutish beasts,
And men have lost their reason. Bear with me,
My heart is in the coffin there with Caesar,
And I must pause till it come back to me."

(At this point Antony paused to give his audience a chance to discuss hurriedly, among themselves, his opening statements. His object in doing this was to observe what effect his words were having, just as a master salesman always encourages his prospective purchaser to talk so he may know what is in his mind.)

First Citizen: "Methinks there is much in his sayings."
Second Citizen: "If thou consider rightly of the matter, Caesar has had great wrong."

Third Citizen: "Has he, masters? I fear there will be
worse come in his place."

Fourth Citizen: "Mark'd ye his words? He would
not take the crown? Therefore 'tis certain he
was not ambitious."

First Citizen: "If it be found so, someone will dear
abide it."

Second Citizen: "Poor soul! his eyes are red as fire
with weeping."

Third Citizen: "There's not a nobler man in Rome
than Antony."

Fourth Citizen: "Now mark him, he begins again to
speak."

Antony: "But yesterday the word of Caesar might
Have stood against the world; now lies he there,
And none so poor to do him reverence.
O masters (appealing to their vanity) if I were
disposed to stir
Your hearts and minds to mutiny and rage,
I should do Brutus wrong and Cassius wrong,
Who, you all know, are honorable men;"

(Observe how often Antony has repeated the term
"honorable." Observe, also, how cleverly he brings in
the first suggestion that, perhaps, Brutus and Cassius
may not be as honorable as the Roman mob believes
them to be. This suggestion is carried in the words
"mutiny" and "rage" which he here uses for the first
time, after his pause gave him time to observe that
the mob was swinging over toward his side of the
argument. Observe how carefully he is "feeling" his
way and making his words *fit that which he knows to
be the frame of mind of his listeners.*)

Antony: "I will not do them wrong; I rather choose
   To wrong the dead, to wrong myself and you,
   Than I will wrong such honorable men."

(Crystallizing his suggestion into hatred of Brutus
and Cassius, he then appeals to their curiosity and
begins to lay the foundation for his climax—a climax
which he knows will win the mob because he is reaching it so cleverly that the mob believes it to be its
own conclusion.)

Antony: "But here's a parchment, with the seal of
      Caesar;
   I found it in his closet; 'tis his will;
   Let but the commons hear this testament,
   Which, pardon me, I do not mean to read—"

(Tightening up on his appeal to their curiosity by
making them believe he does not intend to read the
will.)

   "And they would go and kiss dead Caesar's
      wounds
   And dip their napkins in his sacred blood,
   Yea, beg a hair of him for memory,
   And, dying, mention it within their wills,
   Bequeathing it as a rich legacy
   Unto their issue."

(Human nature *always* wants that which is difficult
to get, or that of which it is about to be deprived.
Observe how craftily Antony has awakened the interest of the mob and made them want to hear the reading of the will, thereby preparing them to hear it with
open minds. This marks his second step in the process of "neutralizing" their minds.)

All: "The will, the will!   We will hear Caesar's will."

Antony: "Have patience, gentle friends, I must not read it;

It is not meet you know how Caesar loved you.

You are not wood, you are not stones, but men;

And, being men, hearing the will of Caesar,

It will inflame you; (Exactly what he wishes to do)

It will make you mad;

'Tis good you know not that you are his heirs,

For if you should, O what will come of it!"

Fourth Citizen: "Read the will; we'll hear it, Antony;

You shall read us the will; Caesar's will."

Antony: "Will you be patient?   Will you stay awhile?

I have o'ershot myself to tell you of it;

I fear I wrong the honorable men

Whose daggers have stabb'd Caesar, I do fear it."

("Daggers" and "stabb'd" suggest cruel murder. Observe how cleverly Antony injects this suggestion into his speech, and observe, also, how quickly the mob catches its significance, because, unknown to the mob, Antony has carefully prepared their minds to receive this suggestion.)

Fourth Citizen: "They were traitors, honorable men!"

All: "The will!   The testament!"

Second Citizen: "They were villains, murderers; the will!" (Just what Antony would have said in the beginning, but he knew it would have a more desirable effect if he planted the thought in the minds of the mob and permitted them to say it themselves.)

Antony: "You will compel me then to read the will?
Then make a ring about the corpse of Caesar,
And let me show you him that made the will.
Shall I descend, and will you give me leave?"

(This was the point at which Brutus should have begun to look for a back door through which to make his escape.)

All: "Come down."

Second Citizen: "Descend."

Third Citizen: "Room for Antony, most noble Antony."

Antony: "Nay, press not so upon me, stand far off."

(He knew this command would make them want to draw nearer, which is what he wanted them to do.)

All: "Stand back. Room."

Antony: "If you have tears, prepare to shed them now.
You all do know this mantle; I remember
The first time ever Caesar put it on;
'Twas on a summer's evening, in his tent,
That day he overcame the Nervii;
Look, in this place ran Cassius' dagger through;
See what a rent the envious Casca made;
Through this the well-beloved Brutus stabb'd;
And as he pluck'd his cursed steel away,
Mark how the blood of Caesar followed it,
As rushing out of doors, to be resolved
If Brutus so unkindly knock'd or no;
For Brutus, as you know, was Caesar's angel;
Judge, O you gods, how dearly Caesar loved him!
This was the most unkindest cut of all;

THE word educate has its roots in the Latin word "educo," which means to educe, to draw out, to develop from within. The best educated man is the one whose mind has been the most highly developed.

For, when the noble Caesar saw him stab,
Ingratitude, more strong than traitor's arms,
Quite vanquish'd him; then burst his mighty
   heart;
And, in his mantle muffling up his face,
Even at the base of Pompey's statua,
Which all the while ran blood, great Caesar fell.
O, what a fall was there, my countrymen!
Then I, and you, and all of us fell down
While bloody treason flourish'd over us.
O, now you weep, and I perceive you feel
The dint of pity; these are gracious drops.
Kind soul, why weep you when you but behold
Our Caesar's vesture wounded?   Look you here;
Here is himself, marr'd, as you see, with traitors."

(Observe how Antony now uses the words "traitors" quite freely, because he knows that it is in harmony with that which is in the minds of the Roman mob.)

First Citizen: "O piteous spectacle!"
Second Citizen: "O woeful day!"
Third Citizen: "O woeful day!"
First Citizen: "O most bloody sight!"
Second Citizen: "We will be revenged."

(Had Brutus been a wise man instead of a braggart he would have been many miles from the scene by this time.)

All: "Revenge! About! Seek! Burn! Fire! Kill!
   Slay! Let not a traitor live!"

(Here Antony takes the next step toward crystallizing the frenzy of the mob into *action;* but, clever salesman that he is, does not try to *force* this action.)

Antony: "Stay, countrymen."

First Citizen: "Peace there! Hear the noble Antony."

Second Citizen: "We'll hear him, we'll follow him, we'll die with him.".

(From these words Antony knows that he has the mob with him. Observe how he takes advantage of this psychological moment—the moment for which all *master salesmen* wait.)

Antony: "Good friends, sweet friends, let me not stir you up to such a sudden flood of mutiny.
They that have done this deed are honorable.
What private griefs they have, alas, I know not,
That made them do it; they were wise and honorable,
And will, no doubt, with reasons answer you.
I come not, friends, to steal away your hearts:
I am no orator as Brutus is;
But, as you know me all, a plain, blunt man,
That love my friend; and that they know full well
That gave me public leave to speak of him;
For I have neither wit, nor words, nor worth,
Action, nor utterance, nor the power of speech,
To stir men's blood; I only speak right on;
I tell you that which you yourselves do know;
Show you sweet Caesar's wounds, poor, poor, dumb mouths.
And bid them speak for me; but were I Brutus,
And Brutus Antony, there an Antony
Would ruffle up your spirits, and put a tongue
In every wound of Caesar that should move
The stones of Rome to rise and mutiny."

All: "We'll mutiny."

First Citizen: "We'll burn the house of Brutus."

Third Citizen: "Away, then! Come, seek the conspirators."

Antony: "Yet hear me, countrymen; yet hear me speak!"

All: "Peace, ho! Hear Antony. Most noble Antony!"

Antony: "Why, friends, you go to do you know not what;

Wherein hath Caesar thus deserved your love?

Alas, you know not; I must tell you, then;

You have forgot the will I told you of."

(Antony is now ready to play his trump card; he is ready to reach his climax. Observe how well he has marshaled his suggestions, step by step, saving until the last his most important statement; the one on which he relied for *action*. In the great field of salesmanship and in public speaking many a man tries to reach this point too soon; tries to "rush" his audience or his prospective purchaser, and thereby loses his appeal.)

All: "Most true; the will! Let's stay and hear the will."

Antony: "Here is the will, and under Caesar's seal.

To every Roman citizen he gives,

To every several man, seventy-five drachmas."

Second Citizen: "Most noble Caesar! we'll revenge his death."

Third Citizen: "O royal Caesar!"

Antony: "Hear me with patience."

All: "Peace, ho!"

Antony: "Moreover, he hath left you all his walks,

His private arbors and new planted orchards,
On this side Tiber; he hath left them you,
And to your heirs forever; common pleasures,
To walk abroad and recreate yourself.
Here was a Caesar! When comes such another?"
First Citizen: "Never, never. Come, away, away:
We'll burn his body in the holy place,
And with the brands fire the traitors' houses.
Take up the body."
Second Citizen: "Go fetch fire."
Third Citizen: "Pluck down benches."
Fourth Citizen: "Pluck down forms, windows, anything."

And that was Brutus' finish!

He lost his case because he lacked the *personality* and the good judgment with which to present his argument *from the viewpoint of the Roman mob,* as Mark Antony did. His whole attitude clearly indicated that he thought pretty well of himself; that he was proud of his deed. We have all seen people, in this day and time, who somewhat resemble Brutus in this respect, but, if we observe closely, we notice that they do not accomplish very much.

Suppose that Mark Antony had mounted the platform in a "strutting" attitude, and had begun his speech in this wise:

"Now *let me* tell you Romans something about this man Brutus—*he is a murderer at heart and—*" he would have gone no further, for the mob would have howled him down.

Clever salesman and practical psychologist that he was, Mark Antony so presented his case that it appeared not to be *his* own idea at all, but that of the Roman mob, itself.

Go back to the lesson on *initiative and leadership* and read it again, and as you read, compare the psychology of it with that of Mark Antony's speech. Observe how the *"you"* and not *"I"* attitude toward others was emphasized. Observe, if you please, how this same point is emphasized throughout this course, and especially in Lesson Seven, on *enthusiasm.*

Shakespeare was, by far, the most able psychologist and writer known to civilization; for that reason, all of his writings are based upon unerring knowledge of the human mind. Throughout this speech, which he placed in the mouth of Mark Antony, you will observe how carefully he assumed the *"you"* attitude; so carefully that the Roman mob was sure that its decision was of its own making.

I must call your attention, however, to the fact that Mark Antony's appeal to the self-interest of the Roman mob was of the crafty type, and was based upon the stealth with which dishonest men often make use of this principle in appealing to the cupidity and avarice of their victims. While Mark Antony displayed evidence of great self-control in being able to assume, at the beginning of his speech, an attitude toward Brutus that was not real, at the same time it is obvious that his entire appeal was based upon his knowledge of how to influence the minds of the Roman mob, through flattery.

The two letters reproduced in Lesson Seven, of this course, illustrate, in a very concrete way, the value of the *"you"* and the fatality of the *"I"* appeal. Go back and read these letters again and observe how the more

I HAVE great wealth that can never be taken away from me; that I can never squander; that cannot be lost by declining stocks or bad investments; I have the wealth of contentment with my lot in life.

successful of the two follows closely the Mark Antony
appeal, while the other one is based upon an appeal of
just the opposite nature. Whether you are writing a
sales letter, or preaching a sermon or writing an advertisement, or a book, you will do well to follow the
same principles employed by Mark Antony in his
famous speech.

Now let us turn our attention to the study of ways
and means through which one may develop a *pleasing
personality*.

Let us start with the first essential, which is *character*, for no one may have a *pleasing personality*
without the foundation of a sound, positive character.
Through the principle of telepathy you "telegraph"
the nature of your character to those with whom you
come in contact, which is responsible for what you
have often called an "intuitive" feeling that the person
whom you had just met, but about whom you did not
know very much, was not trustworthy.

You may embellish yourself with clothes of the
neatest and latest design, and conduct yourself in a
most pleasing manner as far as outside appearances
go; but if there is greed, and envy, and hatred, and
jealousy, and avarice, and selfishness in your heart,
you will never *attract* any, except those characters
which harmonize with your own. Like attracts like,
and you may be sure, therefore, that those who are
attracted to you are those whose inward natures
parallel your own.

You may embellish yourself with an artificial smile
that belies your feelings, and you may practice the art
of hand-shaking so that you can imitate, perfectly, the
hand-shake of the person who is an adept at this art,

but, if these outward manifestations of an *attractive personality* lack that vital factor called *earnestness of purpose* they will repel instead of attract.

How, then, may one build *character?*

The first step in *character* building is rigid *self-discipline:*

In both the second and eighth lessons of this course, you will find the formula through which you may shape your *character* after any pattern that you choose; but I repeat it here, as it is based upon a principle that will bear much repetition, as follows:

First: Select those whose characters were made up of the qualities which you wish to build into your own character, and then proceed, in the manner described in Lesson Two, to appropriate these qualities, through the aid of *Auto-suggestion.* Create, in your imagination, a council table and gather your characters around it each night, first having written out a clear, concise statement of the particular qualities that you wish to appropriate from each. Then proceed to affirm or suggest to yourself, in outspoken, audible words, that you are developing the desired qualities in yourself. As you do this close your eyes and see, in your imagination, the figures seated around your imaginary table, in the manner described in Lesson Two.

Second: Through the principles described in Lesson Eight, on *self-control,* control your thoughts and keep your mind vitalized with thoughts of a positive nature. Let the dominating thought of your mind be a picture of the person that you intend to be: the person *that you are deliberately building,* through this procedure. At least a dozen times a day, when you have a few minutes to yourself, shut your eyes and direct your thoughts to the figures which you have selected to sit at your imaginary council table; and feel, with a *faith* that knows *NO LIMITATION,* that you are actually growing to resemble in character those figures of your choice.

Third: Find at least one person each day, and more if possible, in whom you see some good quality that is worthy of praise, and *praise it.* Remember, however, that this praise must not be in the nature of cheap, insincere flattery; it must be genuine. Speak your words of praise with such earnestness that they will impress those to whom you speak; then watch what happens. You will have rendered those whom you praise a decided benefit of great value to them; and, you will have gone just one more step in the direction of developing the habit of looking for and finding the good qualities in others. I cannot over-emphasize the far-reaching effects of this habit of praising, openly and enthusiastically, the good qualities in others; for this habit will soon reward you with a feeling of self-respect and manifestation of gratitude from others, that will modify your entire personality. Here, again, the law of attraction enters, and those whom you praise will see, in you, the qualities that you see in them. Your success in the application of this formula will be in exact proportion to your *faith* in its soundness.

I do not merely believe that it is sound—*I know that it is*—and the reason *I know* is that I have used it successfully and I have also taught others how to use it successfully; therefore, I have a right to promise you that you can use it with equal success.

Furthermore, you can, with the aid of this formula

develop an *attractive personality* so speedily that you will surprise all who know you. The development of such a personality is entirely within your own control, a fact which gives you a tremendous advantage and at the same time places upon you the responsibility if you fail or neglect to exercise your privilege.

I now wish to direct your attention to the reason for speaking, aloud, the affirmation that you are developing the desired qualities which you have selected as the materials out of which to develop an *attractive personality.*

This procedure has two desirable effects; namely—

First: It sets into motion the vibration through which the thought back of your words reaches and imbeds itself in your sub-conscious mind, where it takes root and grows until it becomes a great moving force in your outward, physical activities, leading in the direction of transformation of the thought into reality.

Second: It develops in you the ability to speak with force and conviction which will lead, finally, to great ability as a public speaker. No matter what your calling in life may be, you should be able to stand upon your feet and speak convincingly, as this is one of the most effective ways of developing an *attractive personality.*

Put feeling and emotion into your words as you speak, and develop a deep, rich tone of voice. If your voice is inclined to be high pitched, tone it down until it is soft and pleasing. You can never express an *attractive personality,* to best advantage, through a harsh or shrill voice. You must cultivate your voice until it becomes rhythmical and pleasing to the ear.

Remember that speech is the chief method of expressing your personality, and for this reason it is to your advantage to cultivate a style that is both forceful and pleasing.

I do not recall a single outstanding *attractive personality* that was not made up, in part, of ability to speak with force and conviction. Study the prominent men and women of today, wherever you find them, and observe the significant fact that the more prominent they are the more efficient are they in speaking forcefully.

Study the outstanding figures of the past in politics and statesmanship and observe that the most successful ones were those who were noted for their ability to speak with force and conviction.

In the field of business, industry and finance it seems significant, also, that the most prominent leaders are men and women who are able public speakers.

In fact no one may hope to become a prominent leader in any noteworthy undertaking without developing the ability to speak with forcefulness that carries conviction. While the salesman may never deliver a public address, he will profit, nevertheless, if he develops the ability to do so, because this ability increases his power to talk convincingly in ordinary conversation.

Let us now summarize the chief factors which enter into the development of an *attractive personality*, as follows:

First: Form the habit of interesting yourself in other people; and make it your business to find their good qualities and speak of them in terms of praise.

Second: Develop the ability to speak with force

ENTHUSIASM is the mainspring of the soul. Keep it wound up and you will never be without power to get what you actually need.

and conviction, both in your ordinary conversational tones and before public gatherings, where you must use more volume.

Third: Clothe yourself in a style that is becoming to your physical build and the work in which you are engaged.

Fourth: Develop a positive character, through the aid of the formula outlined in this lesson.

Fifth: Learn how to shake hands so that you express warmth of feeling and enthusiasm through this form of greeting.

Sixth: Attract other people to you by first "attracting yourself" to them.

Seventh: Remember that your only limitation, within reason, is the one which YOU set up in YOUR OWN mind.

These seven points cover the most important factors that enter into the development of an *attractive personality,* but it seems hardly necessary to suggest that such a personality will not develop of its own accord. It *will develop, if you submit yourself to the discipline herein described, with a firm determination to transform yourself into the person that you would like to be.*

As I study this list of seven important factors that enter into the development of an *attractive personality* I feel moved to direct your attention to the second and the fourth as being the *most important.*

If you will cultivate those finer thoughts, and feelings, and actions, out of which a positive character is built, and then learn to express yourself with force and conviction, you will have developed an *attractive personality,* for it will be seen that out of this attainment will come the other qualities here outlined.

There is a great power of *attraction* back of the person who has a positive character, and this power expresses itself through unseen as well as visible sources. The moment you come within speaking distance of such a person, even though not a word is spoken, the influence of the "unseen power within" makes itself felt.

Every "shady" transaction in which you engage, every negative thought that you think, and every destructive act in which you indulge, destroys just so much of that "subtle something" within you that is known as *character*.

"There is full confession in the glances of our eyes; in our smiles; in salutations; in the grasp of the hands. His sin bedaubs him, mars all his good impression. Men know not why they do not trust him, but they do not trust him. His vice glasses his eye, demeans his cheek, pinches the nose, sets the mark of beast on the back of the head, and writes, 'O fool! fool!' on the forehead of a king." (Emerson.)

I would direct your attention, now, to the first of the seven factors that enter into the development of an *attractive personality*. You have observed that all through this lesson I have gone into lengthy detail to show the material advantages of *being agreeable* to other people.

However, the biggest advantage of all lies, not in the possibility of monetary or material gain which this habit offers, but in the beautifying effect that it has upon the character of all who practice it.

Acquire the habit of making yourself agreeable and you profit both materially and mentally; for you will never be as happy in any other way as you will be when you know that you are making others happy.

Remove the chips from your shoulders and quit challenging men to engage you in useless arguments! Remove the smoked glasses through which you see what you believe to be the "blueness" of life and behold the shining sunlight of friendliness in its stead. Throw away your hammer and quit knocking, for surely you must know that the big prizes of life go to the *builders* and not the *destroyers*.

The man who builds a house is an artist; the man who tears it down is a junkman. If you are a person with a *grievance* the world will listen to your vitriolic "ravings," providing it does not "see you coming"; but, if you are a person with a *message* of friendliness and optimism, it will listen because it wishes to do so.

No person with a grievance can be also a person with an attractive personality!

The art of being agreeable—

—Just that one simple trait—

—is the very foundation of all successful salesmanship.

I drive my automobile five miles into the outskirts of the city to purchase gasoline which I could procure within two blocks of my own garage—

Because the man who runs the filling station is an artist; he makes it his business to be agreeable. I go there, not because he has cheaper gasoline, but because I enjoy the vitalizing effect of his *attractive personality!*

I purchase my shoes at the Regal Shoe Store, at Fiftieth Street and Broadway, in New York, not because I cannot find other good shoes at the same price, but for the reason that Mr. Cobb, the manager of that particular Regal Store, has an *attractive personality.* While he is fitting me with shoes, he makes it his business to talk to me on subjects which he *knows to be close to my heart.*

I do my banking at the Harriman National Bank, at Forty-fourth Street and Fifth Avenue, not because there are not scores of other good banks much nearer my place of business; but for the reason that the tellers, and the cashiers, and the lobby detective, and Mr. Harriman, and all of the others, with whom I come in contact, make it their business to *be agreeable.* My account is small but they receive me as though it were large.

I greatly admire John D. Rockefeller, Jr., not because he is the son of one of the world's richest men; but for the better reason that he, too, has acquired the art of *being agreeable.*

In the little city of Lancaster, Pennsylvania, lives M. T. Garvin, a very successful merchant whom I would travel hundreds of miles to visit, not because he is a wealthy merchant, but for the reason that he makes it his business to *be agreeable.* However, I have no doubt that his material success is closely related to this noble art of affability which he has acquired.

I have in my vest pocket a Parker fountain pen, and my wife and children have pens of the same brand, not because there are not other good fountain pens, but for the reason that *I have been attracted to George S. Parker on account of his habit of being agreeable.*

My wife takes the Ladies' Home Journal, not because there are not other good magazines of a similar
nature, but for the reason that we became attracted
to the Journal several years ago, while Edward Bok
was its editor, because he had acquired the art of
being agreeable.

O ye struggling pilgrims, who are searching for the
rainbow's end; ye drawers of water and hewers of
wood, tarry for a moment by the wayside and learn
a lesson from the successful men and women who
have succeeded because they acquired the art of—
being agreeable!

You can win, for a time, through ruthlessness and
stealth; you can garner in more of this world's goods
than you will need, by sheer force and shrewd strategy,
without taking the time or going to the trouble of
being agreeable; but, sooner or later, you will come
to that point in life at which you will feel the pangs
of remorse and the emptiness of your well filled
purse.

I never think of power and position and wealth that
was attained by force, without feeling, very deeply,
the sentiment expressed by a man whose name I dare
not mention, as he stood at the tomb of Napoleon:

"A little while ago I stood by the grave of the old
Napoleon—a magnificent tomb of gilt and gold, fit
almost for a deity dead—and gazed upon the sar-
cophagus of rare and nameless marble, where rest at
last the ashes of that restless man. I leaned over the
balustrade and thought about the career of the greatest soldier of the modern world. I saw him at Toulon.
I saw him walking upon the banks of the Seine contemplating suicide. I saw him putting down the mob

NO man has the right to strain the relationship of friendly acquaintance to the breaking point by asking or expecting of a friend that which might prove to be a burden to the friend.

in the streets of Paris. I saw him at the head of the army in Italy. I saw him crossing the bridge at Lodi with the tri-color in his hand. I saw him in Egypt, in the shadows of the pyramids; I saw him conquer the Alps and mingle the eagles of France with the eagles of the crags. I saw him at Marengo, at Ulm and at Austerlitz. I saw him in Russia, when the infantry of the snow and the cavalry of the wild blast scattered his legions like winter's withered leaves. I saw him at Leipsic in defeat and disaster—driven by a million bayonets back upon Paris—clutched like a wild beast—banished to Elba. I saw him escape and re-take an empire by the force of his genius. I saw him upon the frightful field of Waterloo, where chance and fate combined to wreck the fortunes of their former king. And I saw him at St. Helena, with his hands crossed behind him, gazing out upon the sad and solemn sea.

"I thought of the widows and orphans he had made, of the tears that had been shed for his glory, and of the only woman who ever loved him, pushed from his heart by the cold hand of ambition. And I said I would rather have been a French peasant and worn wooden shoes; I would rather have lived in a hut with a vine growing over the door, and the grapes growing purple in the amorous kisses of the autumn sun; I would rather have been that poor peasant, with my wife by my side knitting as the day died out of the sky, with my children upon my knees and their arms about me; I would rather have been this man and gone down to the tongueless silence of the dreamless dust, than to have been that imperial personation of force and murder, known as Napoleon the Great."

I leave with you, as a fitting climax for this lesson, the thought of this deathless dissertation on a man who lived by the sword of force and died an ignominious death, an outcast in the eyes of his fellow men; a sore to the memory of civilization; a failure because—

He did not acquire the art of being agreeable! Because he could not or would not subordinate "self" for the good of his followers.

Lesson Eleven

ACCURATE THOUGHT

~⦿⦿⦿~

11

IT is pardonable to tell your friends, by tactful suggestion, of your needs, but take care not to ask them outright for assistance if you would retain their friendship.

THE LAW OF SUCCESS
Lesson Eleven
ACCURATE THOUGHT

"You Can Do It if You Believe You Can!"

HIS is at one and the same time the most *important*, the most *interesting* and the most difficult to present lesson of this entire course on the Law of Success.

It is important because it deals with a principle which runs through the entire course. It is interesting for the same reason. It is difficult to present for the reason that it will carry the average student far beyond the boundary line of his common experiences and into a realm of *thought* in which he is not accustomed to dwell.

Unless you study this lesson with an open mind, you will miss the very key-stone to the arch of this course, and without this stone you can never complete your Temple of Success.

This lesson will bring you a conception of *thought* which may carry you far above the level to which you have risen by the evolutionary processes to which you have been subjected in the past; and, for this reason, you should not be disappointed if, at first reading, you

63

do not fully understand it. Most of us *disbelieve* that which we cannot understand, and it is with knowledge of this human tendency in mind that I caution you against closing your mind if you do not grasp all that is in this lesson at the first reading.

For thousands of years men made ships of wood, and of nothing else. They used wood because they believed that it was the only substance that would float; but that was because they had not yet advanced far enough in their *thinking* process to understand the truth that steel will float, and that it is far superior to wood for the building of ships. They did not know that anything could float which was lighter than the amount of water is displaced, and until they learned of this great truth they went on making ships of wood.

Until some twenty-five years ago, most men thought that only the birds could fly, but now we know that man can not only equal the flying of the birds, but he can excel it.

Men did not know, until quite recently, that the great open void known as the air is more alive and more sensitive than anything that is on the earth. They did not know that the spoken word would travel through the ether with the speed of a flash of lightning, without the aid of wires. How could they know this when their minds had not been unfolded sufficiently to enable them to grasp it? The purpose of this lesson is to aid *you* in so unfolding and expanding your mind that you will be able to *think* with accuracy, for this unfoldment will open to you a door that leads to all the power you will need in completing your Temple of Success.

All through the preceding lessons of this course you observed that we have dealt with principles which anyone could easily grasp and apply. You will also observe that these principles have been so presented that they lead to *success* as measured by material wealth. This seemed necessary for the reason that to most people the word *success* and the word *money* are synonymous terms. Obviously, the previous lessons of this course were intended for those who look upon worldly things and material wealth as being all that there is to *success*.

Presenting the matter in another way, I was conscious of the fact that the majority of the students of this course would feel disappointed if I pointed out to them a roadway to *success* that leads through other than the doorways of business, and finance, and industry; for it is a matter of common knowledge that most men want success that is spelled $UCCE$$!

Very well—let those who are satisfied with this standard of *success* have it; but some there are who will want to go higher up the ladder, in search of *success* which is measured in other than material standards, and it is for their benefit in particular that this and the subsequent lessons of this course are intended.

. . . .

Accurate thought involves two fundamentals which all who indulge in it must observe. First, to think accurately you must separate *facts* from mere *information*. There is much "information" available to you that is not based upon facts. Second, you must separate *facts* into two classes; namely, the *important* and the *unimportant,* or, the *relevant* and the *irrelevant.*

Only by so doing can you think clearly.

All *facts* which you can use in the attainment of your *definite chief aim* are important and relevant; all that you cannot use are unimportant and irrelevant. It is mainly the neglect of some to make this distinction which accounts for the chasm which separates so widely people who appear to have equal ability, and who have had equal opportunity. Without going outside of your own circle of acquaintances you can point to one or more persons who have had no greater opportunity than you have had, and who appear to have no more, and perhaps less, ability than you, who are achieving far greater success.

And you wonder why!

Search diligently and you will discover that all such people have acquired the habit of combining and using the *important facts* which affect their line of work. Far from working harder than you, they are perhaps working less and with greater ease. By virtue of their having learned the secret of separating the *important facts* from the *unimportant,* they have provided themselves with a sort of fulcrum and lever with which they can move with their little fingers loads that you cannot budge with the entire weight of your body.

The person who forms the habit of directing his attention to the *important facts* out of which he is constructing his Temple of Success, thereby provides himself with a power which may be likened to a triphammer which strikes a ten-ton blow as compared to a tack-hammer which strikes a one-pound blow!

If these similes appear to be elementary you must

keep in mind the fact that some of the students of this course have not yet developed the capacity to think in more complicated terms, and to try to force them to do so would be the equivalent of leaving them hopelessly behind.

That you may understand the importance of distinguishing between *facts* and mere *information,* study that type of man who is guided entirely by that which he hears; the type who is influenced by all the "whisperings of the winds of gossip"; that accepts, without analysis, all that he reads in the newspapers and judges others by what their enemies and competitors and contemporaries say about them.

Search your circle of acquaintances and pick out one of this type as an example to keep before your mind while we are on this subject. Observe that this man usually begins his conversation with some such term as this—*"I see by the papers,"* or *"they say."* The *accurate thinker* knows that the newspapers are not always accurate in their reports, and he also knows that what "they say" usually carries more falsehood than truth. If you have not risen above the *"I see by the papers,"* and the *"they say"* class, you have still far to go before you become an *accurate thinker.* Of course, much truth and many *facts* travel in the guise of idle gossip and newspaper reports; but the *accurate thinker* will not accept as such all that he sees and hears.

This is a point which I feel impelled to emphasize, for the reason that it constitutes the rocks and reefs on which so many people flounder and go down to defeat in a bottomless ocean of false conclusions.

In the realm of legal procedure, there is a principle

THE great Edison failed ten thousand times before he made the incandescent electric light work. Do not become discouraged and "quit" if you fail once or twice before making your plans work.

which is called the law of *evidence;* and the object of this law is to get at the *facts.* Any judge can proceed with justice to all concerned, if he has the *facts* upon which to base his judgment, but he may play havoc with innocent people if he circumvents the law of *evidence* and reaches a conclusion or judgment that is based upon *hearsay information.*

The law of Evidence varies according to the subject and circumstances with which it is used, but you will not go far wrong if, in the absence of that which you know to be *facts,* you form your judgments on the hypothesis that only that part of the evidence before you which furthers your own interests *without working any hardship on others* is based upon *facts.*

This is a crucial and *important* point in this lesson; therefore, I wish to be sure that you do not pass it by lightly. Many a man mistakes, knowingly or otherwise, expediency for *fact;* doing a thing, or refraining from doing it, for the sole reason that his action furthers his own interest without consideration as to whether it interferes with the rights of others.

No matter how regrettable, it is true that most thinking of today, far from being *accurate,* is based upon the sole foundation of expediency. It is amazing to the more advanced student of *accurate thought,* how many people there are who are "honest" when it is profitable to them, but find myriads of facts (?) to justify themselves in following a dishonest course when that course seems to be more profitable or advantageous.

No doubt you know people who are like that.

The *accurate thinker* adopts a standard by which he guides himself, and he follows that standard at all times, whether it works always to his immediate ad‹ vantage, or carries him, now and then, through the fields of disadvantage (as it undoubtedly will).

The *accurate thinker* deals with *facts,* regardless of how they affect his own interests, for he knows that ultimately this policy will bring him out on top, in full possession of the object of his *definite chief aim* in life. He understands the soundness of the philosophy that the old philosopher, Croesus, had in mind when he said:

"There is a wheel on which the affairs of men revolve, and its mechanism is such that it prevents *any* man from being *always* fortunate."

The *accurate thinker* has but one standard by which he conducts himself, in his intercourse with his fellow men, and that standard is observed by him as faithfully when it brings him temporary disadvantage as it is when it brings him outstanding advantage; for, being an *accurate thinker,* he knows that, by the law of averages, he will more than regain at some future time that which he loses by applying his standard to his own temporary detriment.

You might as well begin to prepare yourself to understand that it requires the staunchest and most unshakable *character* to become an *accurate thinker,* for you can see that this is where the reasoning of this lesson is leading.

There is a certain amount of temporary penalty attached to *accurate thinking;* there is no denying this fact; but, while this is true, it is also true that the compensating *reward,* in the aggregate, is so overwhelmingly greater that you will gladly pay this penalty.

In searching for *facts* it is often necessary to gather them through the sole source of knowledge and experience of others. It then becomes necessary to examine carefully both the evidence submitted and the person from whom the evidence comes; and when the evidence is of such a nature that it affects the interest of the witness who is giving it, there will be reason to scrutinize it all the more carefully, as witnesses who have an interest in the evidence that they are submitting often yield to the temptation to color and pervert it to protect that interest.

If one man slanders another, his remarks should be accepted, if of any weight at all, with at least a grain of the proverbial salt of caution; for it is a common human tendency for men to find nothing but evil in those whom they do not like. The man who has attained to the degree of *accurate thinking* that enables him to speak of his enemy without exaggerating his faults, and minimizing his virtues, is the exception and not the rule.

Some very able men have not yet risen above this vulgar and self-destructive habit of belittling their enemies, competitors and contemporaries. I wish to bring this common tendency to your attention with all possible emphasis, because it is a tendency that is fatal to *accurate thinking*.

Before you can become an *accurate thinker,* you must understand and make allowance for the fact that the moment a man or a woman begins to assume leadership in any walk of life, the slanderers begin to circulate "rumors" and subtle whisperings reflecting upon his or her character.

No matter how fine one's character is or what service he may be engaged in rendering to the world, he cannot escape the notice of those misguided people who delight in *destroying* instead of *building*. Lincoln's political enemies circulated the report that he lived with a colored woman. Washington's political enemies circulated a similar report concerning him. Since both Lincoln and Washington were southern men, this report was undoubtedly regarded by those who circulated it as being at one and the same time the most fitting and degrading one they could imagine.

But we do not have to go back to our first President to find evidence of this slanderous nature with which men are gifted, for they went a step further, in paying their tributes to the late President Harding, and circulated the report that he had negro blood in his veins.

When Woodrow Wilson came back from Paris with what he believed to be a sound plan for abolishing war and settling international disputes, all except the *accurate thinker* might have been led to believe, by the reports of the *"they say"* chorus, that he was a combination of Nero and Judas Iscariot. The little politicians, and the cheap politicians, and the "interest-paid" politicians, and the plain ignorants who did no thinking of their own, all joined in one mighty chorus for the purpose of destroying the *one and only man in the history of the world who offered a plan for abolishing war*.

The slanderers killed both Harding and Wilson—murdered them with vicious lies. They did the same to Lincoln, only in a somewhat more spectacular manner, by inciting a fanatic to hasten his death with a bullet.

Statesmanship and politics are not the only fields in

which the *accurate thinker* must be on guard against the *"they say"* chorus.   The moment a man begins to make himself felt in the field of industry or business, this chorus becomes active.   If a man makes a better mouse-trap than his neighbor, the world will make a beaten path to his door; no doubt about that; and in the gang that will trail along will be those who come, not to commend, but to condemn and to destroy his reputation.   The late John H. Patterson, president of the National Cash Register Company, is a notable example of what may happen to a man who builds a better cash register than that of his neighbor; yet, in the mind of the *accurate thinker*, there is not one scintilla of evidence to support the vicious reports that Mr. Patterson's competitors circulated about him.

As for Wilson and Harding, we may only judge how posterity will view them by observing how it has immortalized the names of Lincoln and Washington. Truth, alone, endures.   All else must pass on with Time.

The object of these references is not to eulogize those who stand in no particular need of eulogy; but, it is to direct your attention to the *fact* that *"they say"* evidence is always subject to the closest scrutiny; and all the more so when it is of a negative or destructive nature.   No harm can come from accepting, as *fact*, hearsay evidence that is constructive; but its opposite, if accepted at all, should be subjected to the closest inspection possible under the available means of applying the law of evidence.

As an *accurate thinker*, it is both your privilege and your duty to avail yourself of facts, even though you

YOU are well on the road toward success if you have such a keen conception of life that you never build a plan which contemplates your requesting another person to do that which does not bring that person some corresponding advantage in return for compliance with your request.

must go out of your way to get them. If you permit yourself to be swayed to and fro by all manner of information that comes to your attention, you will never become an *accurate thinker;* and if you do not *think accurately,* you cannot be sure of attaining the object of your *definite chief aim* in life.

Many a man has gone down to defeat because, due to his prejudice and hatred, he underestimated the virtues of his enemies or competitors. The eyes of the *accurate thinker* see *facts*—not the delusions of prejudice, hate and envy.

An *accurate thinker* must be something of a good sportsman—in that he is fair enough (with himself at least) to look for virtues as well as faults in other people, for it is not without reason to suppose that all men have some of each of these qualities.

"I do not believe that I can afford to deceive others —*I know I cannot afford to deceive myself!*"

This must be the motto of the *accurate thinker.*

.   .   .   .   .   .

With the supposition that these "hints" are sufficient to impress upon your mind the importance of searching for *facts* until you are reasonably sure that you have found them, we will take up the question of organizing, classifying and using these *facts.*

Look, once more, in the circle of your own acquaintances and find a person who appears to accomplish more with less effort than do any of his associates. Study this man and you observe that he is a strategist in that he has learned how to arrange *facts* so that he brings to his aid the Law of Increasing Returns which we described in a previous lesson.

The man who *knows* that he is working with *facts* goes at his task with a feeling of *self-confidence* which enables him to refrain from temporizing, hesitating or waiting to make sure of his ground. He knows in advance what the outcome of his efforts will be; therefore, he moves more rapidly and accomplishes more than does the man who must "feel his way" because he is not sure that he is working with *facts*.

The man who has learned of the advantages of searching for *facts* as the foundation of his thinking has gone a very long way toward the development of *accurate thinking,* but the man who has learned how to separate *facts* into the *important* and the *unimportant* has gone still further. The latter may be compared to the man who uses a trip-hammer, and thereby accomplishes at one blow more than the former, who uses a tack-hammer, can accomplish with ten thousand blows.

Let us analyze, briefly, a few men who have made it their business to deal with the *important* or *relevant* *facts* pertaining to their life-work.

If it were not for the fact that this course is being adapted to the practical needs of men and women of the present workaday world, we would go back to the great men of the past—Plato, Aristotle, Epictetus, Socrates, Solomon, Moses and Christ—and direct attention to their habit of dealing with *facts.* However, we can find examples nearer our own generation that will serve our purpose to better advantage at this particular point.

Inasmuch as this is an age in which money is looked upon as being the most concrete proof of *success,* let us study a man who has accumulated almost as much

of it as has any other man in the history of the world
—John D. Rockefeller.

Mr. Rockefeller has one quality that stands out,
like a shining star, above all of his other qualities; it
is his habit of dealing only with the *relevant facts*
pertaining to his life-work.   As a very young man
(and a very poor young man, at that) Mr. Rockefeller
adopted, as his *definite chief aim,* the accumulation of
great wealth.   It is not my purpose, nor is it of any
particular advantage, to enter into Mr. Rockefeller's
method of accumulating his fortune other than to observe that his *most pronounced quality* was that of
insisting on *facts* as the basis of his business philosophy.   Some there are who say that Mr. Rockefeller
was not always fair with his competitors.   That may
or may not be true (as accurate thinkers we will leave
the point undisturbed), but no one (not even his competitors) ever accused Mr. Rockefeller of forming
"snap-judgments" or of underestimating the strength
of his competitors.   He not only recognized *facts* that
affected his business, wherever and whenever he found
them, but *he made it his business to search for them
until he was sure he had found them.*

Thomas A. Edison is another example of a man
who has attained to greatness through the organization, classification and use of *relevant facts.*   Mr.
Edison works with natural laws as his chief aids;
therefore, he *must* be sure of his *facts* before he can
harness those laws.   Every time you press a button
and switch on an electric light, remember that it was
Mr. Edison's capacity for organizing *relevant facts*
which made this possible.

Every time you hear a phonograph, remember that

Mr. Edison is the man who made it a reality, through his persistent habit of dealing with *relevant facts*.

Every time you see a moving picture, remember that it was born of Mr. Edison's habit of dealing with *important* and *relevant facts*.

In the field of science *relevant facts* are the tools with which men and women work. Mere information, or hearsay evidence, is of no value to Mr. Edison; yet he might have wasted his life working with it, as millions of other people are doing.

Hearsay evidence could never have produced the incandescent electric light, the phonograph or the moving picture, and if it had, the phenomenon would have been an "accident." In this lesson we are trying to prepare the student to avoid "accidents."

The question now arises as to what constitutes an *important* and *relevant fact*.

The answer depends entirely upon what constitutes your *definite chief aim* in life, for an *important* and *relevant fact* is any fact which you can use, without interfering with the rights of others, in the attainment of that purpose.

All other *facts,* as far as you are concerned, are superfluous and of minor importance at most.

However, you can work just as hard in organizing, classifying and using *unimportant* and *irrelevant facts* as you can in dealing with their opposites, but *you will not accomplish as much.*

.   .   .   .

Up to this point we have been discussing only **one** factor of *accurate thought,* that which is based upon deductive reasoning. Perhaps this is the point at which some of the students of this course will have to *think* along lines with which they are not familiar, for we come, now, to the discussion of *thought* which does much more than gather, organize and combine *facts*.

Let us call this *creative thought!*

That you may understand why it is called *creative thought* it is necessary briefly to study the process of evolution through which the *thinking man* has been created.

Thinking man has been a long time on the road of evolution, and he has traveled a very long way. In the words of Judge T. Troward (in Bible Mystery and Bible Meaning), "Perfected man is the apex of the Evolutionary Pyramid, and this by a necessary sequence."

Let us trace *thinking man* through the five evolutionary steps through which we believe he has traveled, beginning with the very lowest; namely—

1. The Mineral Period. Here we find life in its lowest form, lying motionless and inert; a mass of mineral substances, with no power to move.

2. Then comes the Vegetable Period. Here we find life in a more active form, with intelligence sufficient to gather food, grow and reproduce, but still unable to move from its fixed moorings.

3. Then comes the Animal Period. Here we find life in a still higher and more intelligent form, with ability to move from place to place.

4. Then comes the Human or Thinking Man Period, where we find life in its highest known form; the highest, because man can *think,* and because *thought* is the highest known form of organized energy. In

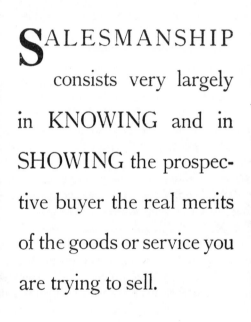

SALESMANSHIP consists very largely in KNOWING and in SHOWING the prospective buyer the real merits of the goods or service you are trying to sell.

the realm of *thought* man knows no limitations. He can send his *thoughts* to the stars with the quickness of a flash of lightning. He can gather facts and assemble them in new and varying combinations. He can create hypotheses and translate them into physical reality, through *thought*. He can reason both inductively and deductively.

5. Then comes the Spiritual Period. On this plane the lower forms of life, described in the previously mentioned four periods, converge and become infinitude in nature. At this point *thinking man* has unfolded, expanded and grown until he has projected his thinking ability into *infinite intelligence*. As yet, *thinking man* is but an infant in this fifth period, for he has not learned how to appropriate to his own use this *infinite intelligence* called Spirit. Moreover, with a few rare exceptions, man has not yet recognized *thought* as the connecting link which gives him access to the power of *infinite intelligence*. These exceptions have been such men as Moses, Solomon, Christ, Plato, Aristotle, Socrates, Confucius and a comparatively small number of others of their type. Since their time we have had many who partly uncovered this great *truth;* yet the *truth,* itself, is as available now as it was then.

To make use of *creative thought,* one must work very largely on *faith,* which is the chief reason why more of us do not indulge in this sort of *thought.* The most ignorant of the race can *think* in terms of deductive reasoning, in connection with matters of a purely physical and material nature, but to go a step higher and *think* in terms of *infinite intelligence* is another question. The average man is totally at sea the moment he gets beyond that which he can comprehend with the aid of his five physical senses of seeing, hearing, feeling, smelling and tasting. *Infinite intelligence* works through none of these agencies and we cannot invoke its aid through any of them.

How, then, may one appropriate the power of *infinite intelligence?* is but a natural question.

And the answer is:

Through creative thought!

To make clear the exact manner in which this is done I will now call your attention to some of the preceding lessons of this course through which you have been prepared to understand the meaning of *creative thought.*

In the second lesson, and to some extent in practically every other lesson that followed it, up to this one, you have observed the frequent introduction of the term "Auto-suggestion." (Suggestion that you make to yourself.) We now come back to that term again, because Auto-suggestion is the telegraph line, so to speak, over which you may register in your subconscious mind a description or plan of that which you wish to *create* or acquire in physical form.

It is a process you can easily learn to use.

The sub-conscious mind is the intermediary between the conscious *thinking* mind and *infinite intelligence,* and you can invoke the aid of *infinite intelligence* only through the medium of the sub-conscious mind, by giving it clear instructions as to what you want. Here you become familiar with the psychological reason for a *definite chief aim.*

If you have not already seen the importance of creating a *definite chief aim* as the object of your life-work, you will undoubtedly do so before this lesson shall have been mastered.

Knowing, from my own experience as a beginner in the study of this and related subjects, how little I understood such terms as "Sub-conscious Mind" and "Auto-suggestion" and *"Creative Thought,"* I have taken the liberty, throughout this course, of describing these terms through every conceivable simile and illustration, with the object of making their meaning and the method of their application so clear that no student of this course can possibly fail to understand. This accounts for the repetition of terms which you will observe throughout the course, and at the same time serves as an apology to those students who have already advanced far enough to grasp the meaning of much that the beginner will not understand at first reading.

The sub-conscious mind has one outstanding char- acteristic to which I will now direct your attention; namely, *it records the suggestions which you send it through Auto-suggestion, and invokes the aid of infi- nite intelligence in translating these suggestions into their natural physical form, through natural means which are in no way out of the ordinary.* It is im- portant that you understand the foregoing sentence, for, if you fail to understand it, you are likely to fail, also, to understand the importance of the very founda- tion upon which this entire course is built—*that foundation being the principle of infinite intelligence,* which may be reached and appropriated at will through aid of the law of the "Master Mind" described in the Introductory Lesson.

Study carefully, thoughtfully and with meditation, the entire preceding paragraph.

The sub-conscious mind has another outstanding characteristic—it accepts and acts upon all suggestions that reach it, whether they are constructive or destructive, and whether they come from the outside or from your own conscious mind.

You can see, therefore, how essential it is for you to observe the law of evidence and carefully follow the principles laid down in the beginning of this lesson, in the selection of that which you will pass on to your sub-conscious mind through Auto-suggestion. You can see why one must search diligently for *facts,* and why one cannot afford to lend a receptive ear to the slanderer and the scandalmonger—for to do so is the equivalent of feeding the sub-conscious mind with food that is poison and ruinous to *creative thought.*

The sub-conscious mind may be likened to the sensitive plate of a camera on which the picture of any object placed before the camera will be recorded. The plate of the camera does not choose the sort of picture to be recorded on it, it records anything which reaches it through the lens. The conscious mind may be likened to the shutter which shuts off the light from the sensitized plate, permitting nothing to reach the plate for record except that which the operator wishes to reach it. The lens of the camera may be likened to Auto-suggestion, for it is the medium which carries the image of the object to be registered, to the sensitized plate of the camera. And *infinite intelligence* may be likened to the one who develops the sensitized plate, after a picture has been recorded on it, thus bringing the picture into physical reality.

The ordinary camera is a splendid instrument with which to compare the whole process of *creative thought*. First comes the selection of the object to be exposed before the camera. This represents one's *definite chief aim* in life. Then comes the actual operation of recording a clear outline of that *purpose*, through the lens of Auto-suggestion, on the sensitized plate of the sub-conscious mind. Here *infinite intelligence* steps in and develops the outline of that *purpose* in a physical form appropriate to the nature of the *purpose*. The part which *you* must play is clear!

You select the picture to be recorded (*definite chief aim*). Then you fix your conscious mind upon this purpose with such intensity that it communicates with the sub-conscious mind, through Auto-suggestion, and registers that picture. You then begin to watch for and to expect manifestations of physical realization of the subject of that picture.

Bear in mind the fact that you do not sit down and wait, nor do you go to bed and sleep, with the expectation of awaking to find that *infinite intelligence* has showered you with the object of your *definite chief aim*. You go right ahead, in the usual way, doing your daily work in accordance with the instructions laid down in Lesson Nine of this course, *with full faith and confidence that natural ways and means for the attainment of the object of your definite purpose will open to you at the proper time and in a suitable manner.*

The way may not open suddenly, from the first step to the last, but it may open one step at a time. Therefore, when you are conscious of an opportunity

ANY man may become great by doing the common-place things of life in a great spirit, with a genuine desire to be of helpful service to others, regardless of his calling.

to take the first step, take it without hesitation, and do the same when the second, and the third, and all subsequent steps, essential for the attainment of the object of your *definite chief aim,* are manifested to you.

Infinite intelligence will not build you a home and deliver that home to you, ready to enter; but *infinite intelligence* will open the way and provide the necessary means with which *you* may build your own house.

Infinite intelligence will not command the cashier of your bank to place a definite sum of money to your credit, just because you suggested this to your subconscious mind; but *infinite intelligence* will open to you the way in which you may earn or borrow that money and place it to your own credit.

Infinite intelligence will not throw out the present incumbent of the White House and make you President in his place; but *infinite intelligence* would most likely proceed, under the proper circumstances, to influence you to prepare yourself to fill that position with credit and then help you to attain it through the regular method of procedure.

Do not rely upon the performance of miracles for the attainment of the object of your *definite chief aim;* rely upon the power of *infinite intelligence* to guide you, through natural channels, and with the aid of natural laws, for its attainment. Do not expect *infinite intelligence* to bring to you the object of your *definite chief aim;* instead, expect *infinite intelligence* to *direct you toward that object.*

As a beginner, do not expect *infinite intelligence* to move quickly in your behalf; but, as you become more adept in the use of the principle of Auto-suggestion, and as you develop the *faith* and *understanding* required for its quick realization, you can create a *definite chief aim* and witness its immediate translation into physical reality. You did not walk the first time you tried, but now, as an adult (an adept at walking), you walk without effort. You also look down at the little child as it wobbles around, trying to walk, and laugh at its efforts. As a beginner in the use of *creative thought*, you may be compared to the little child who is learning to take its first step.

I have the best of reasons for knowing that this comparison is accurate, but I will not state them. I will let you find out your own reason, in your own way.

Keep in mind, always, the principle of *evolution* through the operation of which everything physical is eternally reaching upward and trying to complete the cycle between *finite* and *infinite* intelligences.

Man, himself, is the highest and most noteworthy example of the working of the principle of evolution. First, we find him down in the minerals of the earth, where there is life but no intelligence. Next, we find him raised, through the growth of vegetation (evolution), to a much higher form of life, where he enjoys sufficient intelligence to feed himself. Next, we find him functioning in the animal period, where he has a comparatively high degree of intelligence, with ability to move around from place to place. Lastly, we find him risen above the lower species of the animal kingdom, to where he functions as a *thinking* entity, with ability to appropriate and use *infinite intelligence.*

Observe that he did not reach this high state all at one bound.   He climbed—step by step, perhaps through many reincarnations.

Keep this in mind and you will understand why you cannot reasonably expect *infinite intelligence* to circumvent the natural laws and turn man into the storehouse of *all knowledge* and *all power* until he has prepared himself to use this knowledge and power with higher than finite intelligence.

If you want a fair example of what may happen to a man who suddenly comes into control of power, study some newly-rich or someone who has inherited a fortune.   Money-power in the hands of John D. Rockefeller is not only in safe hands, but it is in hands where it is serving mankind throughout the world, blotting out ignorance, destroying contagious disease and serving in a thousand other ways of which the average individual knows nothing.

But place John D. Rockefeller's fortune in the hands of some young lad who has not yet finished high school and you might have another story to tell, the details of which your own imagination and your knowledge of human nature will supply.

I will have more to say on this subject in Lesson Fourteen.

If you have ever done any farming, you understand that certain preparations are necessary before a crop can be produced from the ground.   You know, of course, that grain will not grow in the woods, that it requires sunshine and rain for its growth.   Likewise, you understand that the farmer must plow the soil and *properly plant the grain*.

After all this has been done, he then waits on *Nature*

to do her share of the work; and she does it in due time, without outside help.

This is a perfect simile which illustrates the method through which one may attain the object of one's *definite chief aim*. First comes the preparing of the soil to receive the seed, which is represented by *faith* and *infinite intelligence* and understanding of the principle of Auto-suggestion and the sub-conscious mind through which the seed of a *definite purpose* may be planted. Then comes a period of waiting and working for the realization of the object of that *purpose*. During this period, there must be continuous, intensified *faith*, which serves as the sunshine and the rain, without which the seed will wither and die in the ground. Then comes realization, harvest-time.

And a wonderful harvest *can* be brought forth.

I am fully conscious of the fact that much of that which I am stating will not be understood by the beginner, at the first reading, for I have in mind my own experiences at the start. However, as the evolutionary process carries on its work (and it will do so; make no mistake about this) all the principles described in this and in all other lessons of this course, will become as familiar to you as did the multiplication table after you had mastered it; and, what is of greater importance still, these principles will work with the same unvarying certainty as does the principle of multiplication.

Each lesson of this course has provided you with *definite* instructions to follow. The instructions have been simplified as far as possible, so anyone can understand them. Nothing has been left to the student except to follow the instructions and supply the *faith* in their soundness without which they would be use-less.

In this lesson you are dealing with four major factors to which I would again direct your attention with the request that you familiarize yourself with them. They are:

Auto-suggestion, the Sub-conscious Mind, Creative Thought and Infinite Intelligence.

These are the four roadways over which you must travel in your upward climb in quest of knowledge. Observe that *you* control three of these. Observe, also —and this is especially emphasized—that upon the manner in which you traverse these three roadways will depend the *time* and *place* at which they will converge into the fourth, or *infinite intelligence*.

You understand what is meant by the terms Auto-suggestion and Sub-conscious Mind. Let us make sure that you understand, also, what is meant by the term Creative Thought. This means *thought* of a positive, non-destructive, creative nature. The object of Lesson Eight, on Self-control, was to prepare you to understand and successfully apply the principle of Creative Thought. If you have not mastered that lesson you are not ready to make use of Creative Thought in the attainment of your *definite chief aim*.

Let me repeat a simile already used by saying that your sub-conscious mind is the field or the soil in which you sow the seed of your *definite chief aim*. Creative Thought is the instrument with which you keep that soil fertilized and conditioned to awaken that seed into growth and maturity. Your sub-conscious mind will not germinate the seed of your *definite chief aim* nor will *infinite intelligence* translate that

REMEMBER that
your real wealth can
be measured, not by what
you have, but, by what
you are.

purpose into physical reality if you fill your mind with hatred, and envy, and jealousy, and selfishness and greed. These negative or *destructive thoughts* are the weeds which will choke out the seed of your *definite purpose*.

Creative thought pre-supposes that you will keep your mind in a state of expectancy of attainment of the object of your *definite chief aim;* that you will have full *faith* and confidence in its attainment in due course and in due order.

If this lesson does that which it was intended to do, it will bring you a fuller and deeper realization of the third lesson of this course, on Self-confidence. As you begin to learn how to plant the seed of your *desires* in the fertile soil of your sub-conscious mind, and how to fertilize that seed until it springs into life and action, you will then have reason, indeed, to believe in yourself.

And, after you have reached this point in the process of your evolution, you will have sufficient knowledge of the real source from which you are drawing your power, to give full credit to *infinite intelligence* for all that you had previously credited to your Self-confidence.

. . . .

Auto-suggestion is a powerful weapon with which one may rise to heights of great achievement, when it is used constructively. Used in a negative manner, however, it may destroy all possibility of success, and if so used continuously it will actually destroy health.

Careful comparison of the experiences of leading physicians and psychiatrists disclosed the startling in-

formation that approximately seventy-five per cent of
those who are ill are suffering from hypochondria,
which is a morbid state of mind causing useless anxiety
about one's health.

Stated in plain language, the hypochondriac is a
person who believes he or she is suffering with some
sort of imaginary disease, and often these unfortunates
believe they have every disease of which they ever
heard the name.

Hypochondriacal conditions are generally superinduced by auto-intoxication, or poisoning through failure of the intestinal system to throw off the waste
matter. The person who suffers with such a toxic condition is not only unable to think with accuracy, but
suffers from all sorts of perverted, destructive, illusory
thoughts. Many sick people have tonsils removed, or
teeth pulled, or the appendix taken out, when their
trouble could have been removed with an internal bath
and a bottle of Citrate of Magnesia (with due apologies to my friends, the physicians, one of the leading
of whom gave me this information).

Hypochondria is the beginning of most cases of
insanity!

Dr. Henry R. Rose is authority for the following
typical example of the power of Auto-suggestion:

" 'If my wife dies I will not believe there is a God.'
His wife was ill with pneumonia, and this is the way
he greeted me when I reached his home. She had
sent for me because the doctor had told her she could
not recover. (Most doctors know better than to make
a statement such as this in the presence of a patient.)
She had called her husband and two sons to her bed-
side and bidden them good-by. Then she asked that

I, her minister, be sent for. I found the husband in the front room sobbing and the sons doing their best to brace her up. When I went into her room she was breathing with difficulty, and the trained nurse told me she was very low.

"I soon found that Mrs. N—— had sent for me to look after her two sons after she was gone. Then I said to her: 'You mustn't give up. YOU ARE NOT GOING TO DIE! You have always been a strong and healthy woman and I do not believe God wants you to die and leave your boys to me or anyone else.'

"I talked to her along this line and then read the 103d Psalm and made a prayer in which I prepared her to get well rather than to enter eternity. I told her to put her faith in God and throw her mind and will against every thought of dying. Then I left her, saying, 'I will come again after the church service, and I will then find you much better.'

"This was on Sunday morning. I called that afternoon. Her husband met me with a smile. He said that the moment I had gone his wife called him and the boys into the room and said: 'Dr. Rose says that I am not going to die; that I am going to get well, and I am.'

"She did get well. But what did it? Two things: Auto-suggestion, superinduced by the suggestion I had given her, and faith on her part. I came just in the nick of time, and so great was her faith in me that I was able to inspire faith in herself. It was that faith that tipped the scales and brought her through the pneumonia. No medicine can cure pneumonia. The physicians admit that. There are cases of pneumonia, perhaps, that nothing can cure. We all sadly agree to that, but there are times, as in this case, when the mind, if worked upon and worked with in just the right way, will turn the tide. While there is life there is hope; but hope must rule supreme and do the good that hope was intended to do.

"Here is another remarkable case showing the power of the human mind when used constructively. A physician asked me to see Mrs. H——. He said there was nothing organically wrong with her, but she just wouldn't eat. Having made up her mind that she could not retain anything on her stomach, she had quit eating, and was slowly starving herself to death. I went to see her and found, first, that she had no religious belief. She had lost her faith in God. I also found that she had no confidence in her power to retain food. My first effort was to restore her faith in the Almighty and to get her to believe that He was with her and would give her power. Then I told her that she could eat anything she wanted. True, her confidence in me was great and my statement impressed her. She began to eat from that day! She was out of her bed in three days, for the first time in weeks. She is a normal, healthy and happy woman today.

"What did it? The same forces as those described in the preceding case; outside suggestion (which she accepted in faith and applied, through self-suggestion) and inward confidence.

"There are times when the mind is sick and it makes the body sick. At such times it needs a stronger mind to heal it by giving it direction and especially by giving it confidence and faith in itself. This is called suggestion. It is transmitting your confidence and power to another, and with such force as to make the other believe as you wish and do as you will. It need not be hypnotism. You can get wonderful results with the patient wide awake and perfectly rational. The patient must believe in you and you must understand the workings of the human mind in order to meet the arguments and questions of the patient. Each one of us can be a healer of this sort and thus help our fellow men.

"It is the duty of every person to read some of the best books on the forces of the human mind and learn what amazing things the mind can do to keep people well and happy. We see the terrible things that wrong thinking does to people, even going to such lengths as to make them positively insane. It is high time we found out the good things the mind can do, not only to cure mental disorders, but physical diseases as well."

You should delve deeper into this subject.

I do not say the mind can cure everything. There is no reliable evidence that certain forms of cancer have been cured by thinking or faith or any mental or religious process. If you would be cured of cancer you must take it at the very beginning and treat it surgically. There is no other way, and it would be criminal to suggest that there is. But the mind can do much with so many types of human indisposition and disease that we ought to rely upon it more often than we do.

Napoleon, during his campaign in Egypt, went among his soldiers who were dying by the hundreds of the black plague. He touched one of them and lifted a second, to inspire the others not to be afraid,

WE climb to heaven mostly on the ruins of our cherished plans, finding our failures were but friendly guide-posts that led us onward and upward to success.

for the awful disease seemed to spread as much by the aid of the imagination as in any other way. Goethe tells us that he himself went where there was malignant fever and never contracted it because he put forth his will. These giants among men knew something WE ARE SLOWLY BEGINNING TO FIND OUT—*the power of Auto-suggestion!* This means the influence we have upon ourselves by believing we cannot catch a disease or be sick. There is something about the operation of the automatic or sub-conscious mind by which it rises above disease germs and bids defiance to them when we resolve not to let the thought of them frighten us, or when we go in and out among the sick, even the contagiously sick, without thinking anything about it.

"Imagination will kill a cat," so runs the old adage. It certainly will kill a man, or, on the other hand, it will help him rise to heights of achievement of the most astounding nature, providing he uses it as the basis of self-confidence. There are authentic cases on record of men having actually died because they imagined they were cut by a knife across the jugular vein, when in reality a piece of ice was used and water was allowed to drip so they could hear it and imagine their blood was running out. They had been blindfolded before the experiment was begun. No matter how well you may be when you start for work in the morning, if everyone you meet should say to you, "How ill you look; you should see a doctor," it will not be long before you begin to feel ill, and if this keeps up a few hours you will arrive at home in the evening as limp as a rag and ready for a doctor. Such is the power of the imagination or Auto-suggestion.

The imaginative faculty of the human mind is a marvelous piece of mental machinery, but it may, and usually does, play queer tricks on us unless we keep constantly on guard and control it.

If you allow your imagination to "expect the worst" it will play havoc with you. Young medical students not infrequently become frightened and believe they have every disease on the medical calendar, as the result of medical lectures and class-room discussions of the various diseases.

As has been stated, hypochondria may often be superinduced by toxic poisoning, through improper elimination of the waste matter of the body; also, it may be brought on by false alarm, through improper use of the imagination. In other words, the hypochondriacal condition may have as its cause a real physical basis, or it may arise entirely as the result of allowing the imagination to run wild.

Physicians are pretty well agreed upon this point!

Dr. Schofield describes the case of a woman who had a tumor. They placed her on the operating table and gave her anesthetics, when lo! the tumor immediately disappeared, and no operation was necessary. But when she came back to consciousness the tumor returned. The physician then learned that she had been living with a relative who had a real tumor, and that her imagination was so vivid that she had imagined this one upon herself. She was placed on the operating table again, given anesthetics and then she was strapped around the middle so that the tumor could not artificially return. When she revived she was told that a successful operation had been performed but that it would be necessary to wear the bandage for several days. She believed the doctor, and when the bandage was finally removed the tumor did not return. No operation whatever had been performed. She had simply relieved her sub-conscious mind of the thought that she had a tumor and her imagination had nothing to work upon save the idea of health, and, as she had never really been sick, of course she remained normal.

The mind may be cured of imaginary ills in exactly the same manner that it became diseased with those ills, by Auto-suggestion. The best time to work on a faulty imagination is at night, just as you are ready to go to sleep, for then the automatic or sub-conscious mind has everything its own way, and the thoughts or suggestions you give it just as your conscious or "day" mind is about to go off duty will be taken up and worked on during the night.

This may seem impossible, but you can easily test the principle by the following procedure: You wish to get up at seven o'clock tomorrow morning, or at some hour other than your regular time to awaken. Say to yourself, as you are about ready to go to sleep, "I must arise at seven o'clock tomorrow without fail." Repeat this several times, at the same time impressing the fact upon your mind that you must actually arise at the precise moment mentioned. Turn this thought over to your sub-conscious mind with absolute confidence that you will awaken at seven o'clock, and when that hour arrives your sub-conscious mind will awaken you. This test has been successfully made hundreds of times. The sub-conscious mind will awaken you, at any hour you demand, just as if someone came to your bed and tapped you on the shoulder.

But you must give the command in no uncertain or indefinite terms.

Likewise, the sub-conscious mind may be given any other sort of orders and it will carry them out as readily as it will awaken you at a given hour. For example, give the command, as you are about to go to sleep each night, for your sub-conscious mind to develop self-confidence, courage, initiative or any other quality, and it will do your bidding.

If the imagination of man can create imaginary ills and send one to bed with those ills, it can also, and just as easily, remove the cause of those ills.

.   .   .   .

Man is a combination of chemical equivalents the value of which is said to be about twenty-six dollars, with the exception, of course, of that stupendous power called the human mind.

In the aggregate the mind seems to be a complicated machine, but in reality, as far as the manner in which it may be used is concerned, it is the nearest thing to perpetual motion that is known. It works automatically when we are asleep; it works both automatically and in conjunction with the will, or voluntary section, when we are awake.

The mind is deserving of the minutest possible analysis in this lesson because the mind is the energy with which all thinking is done. To learn how to THINK ACCURATELY, the teaching of which is the sole object of this lesson, one must thoroughly understand:

First: That the mind can be controlled, guided and directed to creative, constructive ends.

Second: That the mind can be directed to destructive ends, and, that it may, voluntarily, tear down and destroy unless it is with plan and deliberation controlled and directed constructively.

Third: That the mind has power over every cell of the body, and can be made to cause every cell to do its intended work perfectly, or it may, through neglect or wrong direction, destroy the normal functionary purposes of any or all cells.

Fourth: That all achievement of man is the result of thought, the part which his physical body plays being of secondary importance, and in many instances of no importance whatsoever except as a housing place for the mind.

Fifth: That the greatest of all achievements, whether in literature, art, finance, industry, commerce, transportation, religion, politics or scientific discoveries, are usually the results of ideas conceived in one man's brain but ACTUALLY TRANSFORMED INTO REALITY BY OTHER MEN, through the combined use of their minds and bodies. (Meaning that the conception of an idea is of greater importance than the transformation of that idea into more material form, because relatively few men can conceive useful ideas, while there are hundreds of millions who can develop an idea and give it material form after it has been conceived.)

Sixth: The majority of all thoughts conceived in the minds of men are not ACCURATE, being more in the nature of "opinions" or "snap-judgments."

When Alexander the Great sighed because he had no more worlds (as he believed) that could be conquered he was in a frame of mind similar to that of the pres-

WHEN a man really finds himself, at the top of the Ladder of Success, he is never alone, because no man can climb to genuine success without taking others along with him.

ent-day "Alexanders" of science, industry, invention, etc., whose "accurate thoughts" have conquered the air and the sea, explored practically every square mile of the little earth on which we live, and wrested from Nature thousands of "secrets" which, a few generations ago, would have been set down as "miracles" of the most astounding and imponderable sort.

In all this discovery and mastery of mere physical substances is it not strange, indeed, that we have practically neglected and overlooked the most marvelous of all powers, the human mind!

All scientific men who have made a study of the human mind readily agree on this—that the surface has not yet been scratched in the study of the wonderful power which lies dormant in the mind of man, waiting, as the oak tree sleeps in the acorn, to be aroused and put to work. Those who have expressed themselves on the subject are of the opinion that the next great cycle of discovery lies in the realm of the human mind.

The possible nature of these discoveries has been suggested, in many different ways, in practically every lesson of this course, particularly in this and the following lessons of the course.

If these suggestions appear to lead the student of this philosophy into deeper water than he or she is accustomed to, bear in mind the fact that the student has the privilege of stopping at any depth desired, until ready, through thought and study, to go further.

The author of this course has found it necessary to take the lead, and to keep far enough ahead, as it were, to induce the student to go at least a few paces ahead of the normal average range of human thought.

It is not expected that any beginner will, at first, try to assimilate and put into use all that has been included in this philosophy. But; if the net result of the course is nothing more than to sow the seed of constructive thought in the mind of the student the author's work will have been completed. Time, plus the student's own desire for knowledge, will do the rest.

This is an appropriate place to state frankly that many of the suggestions passed on through this course would, if literally followed, lead the student far beyond the necessary bounds and present needs of what is ordinarily called business philosophy. Stated differently, this course goes more deeply into the functioning processes of the human mind than is necessary as far as the use of this philosophy as a means of achieving business or financial success is concerned.

However, it is presumed that many students of this course will wish to go more deeply into the study of mind power than may be required for purely material achievement, and the author has had in mind these students throughout the labor of organizing and writing this course.

SUMMARY OF PRINCIPLES INVOLVED IN ACCURATE THINKING

We have discovered that the body of man is not singular, but plural—that it consists of billions on top of billions of living, intelligent, individual cells which carry on a very definite, well organized work of building, developing and maintaining the human body.

We have discovered that these cells are directed, in their respective duties, by the sub-conscious or automatic action of the mind, that the subconscious section of the mind can be, to a very large extent, controlled and directed by the conscious or voluntary section of the mind.

We have found that any idea or thought which is held in the mind, through repetition, has a tendency to direct the physical body to transform such thought or idea into its material equivalent. We have found that any order that is PROPERLY given to the subconscious section of the mind (through the law of Auto-suggestion) will be carried out unless it is sidetracked or countermanded by another and stronger order. We have found that the sub-conscious mind does not question the source from which it receives orders, nor the soundness of those orders, but it will proceed to direct the muscular system of the body to carry out any order it receives.

This explains the necessity for guarding closely the environment from which we receive suggestions, and by which we are subtly and quietly influenced at times and in ways of which we do not take cognizance through the conscious mind.

We have found that every movement of the human body is controlled by either the conscious or the subconscious section of the mind; that not a muscle can be moved until an order has been sent out by one or the other of these two sections of the mind, for the movement.

When this principle is thoroughly understood we understand, also, the powerful effect of any idea or thought which we create through the faculty of IMAGINATION and hold in the conscious mind until the sub-conscious section of the mind has time to take over that thought and begin the work of transforming it into its material counterpart. When we understand the principle through which any idea is first placed in the conscious mind, and held there until the sub-conscious section of the mind picks it up and appropriates it, we have a practical working knowledge of the Law of Concentration, covered by next lesson (and, it might be added, we have also a thorough understanding of the reason why the Law of Concentration is necessarily a part of this philosophy).

When we understand this working relationship between the imagination, the conscious mind and the sub-conscious section of the mind, we can see that the very first step in the achievement of any *definite chief aim* is to create a definite picture of that which is desired. This picture is then placed in the conscious mind, through the Law of Concentration, and held there (through the formulas described in next lesson) until the sub-conscious section of the mind picks it up and translates it into its ultimate and desired form.

Surely this principle has been made clear. It has been stated and restated, over and over, not only for the purpose of thoroughly describing it, but, of greater importance, to IMPRESS UPON THE MIND OF THE STUDENT THE PART IT PLAYS IN ALL HUMAN ACHIEVEMENT.

THE VALUE OF ADOPTING A CHIEF AIM

This lesson on Accurate Thought not only describes the real purpose of a *definite chief aim,* but it explains in simple terms the principles through which such an aim or purpose may be realized. We first create the objective toward which we are striving, through the imaginative faculty of the mind, then transfer an outline of this objective to paper by writing out a definite statement of it in the nature of a *definite chief aim*. By daily reference to this written statement the idea or thing aimed for is taken up by the conscious mind and handed over to the sub-conscious mind, which, in turn, directs the energies of the body to transform the desire into material form.

DESIRE

Strong, deeply rooted desire is the starting point of all achievement. Just as the electron is the last unit of matter discernible to the scientist, DESIRE is the seed of all achievement; the starting place, back of which there is nothing, or at least there is nothing of which we have any knowledge.

A *definite chief aim*, which is only another name for DESIRE, would be meaningless unless based upon a deeply seated, strong desire for the object of the *chief aim*. Many people "wish" for many things, but a wish is not the equivalent of a strong DESIRE, and therefore wishes are of little or no value unless they are crystallized into the more definite form of DESIRE.

It is believed by men who have devoted years of research to the subject, that all energy and matter throughout the universe respond to and are controlled by the Law of Attraction which causes elements and forces of a similar nature to gather around certain centers of attraction. It is through the operation of this same universal Law of Attraction that constant.

WM.WRIGLEY, Jr., has amassed a tremendous fortune by concentrating all his efforts on the manufacture and distribution of the "best" package of chewing gum, proving, once more, that the seed of success lies wrapped up in the little things of life.

deeply seated, strong DESIRE attracts the physical equivalent or counterpart of the thing desired, or the means of securing it.

We have learned, then, if this hypothesis is correct, that all cycles of human achievement work somewhat after this fashion: First, we picture in our conscious minds, through a *definite chief aim* (based upon a strong desire), some objective; we then focus our conscious mind upon this objective, by constant thought of it and belief in its attainment, until the subconscious section of the mind takes up the picture or outline of this objective and impels us to take the necessary physical action to transform that picture into reality.

SUGGESTION AND AUTO-SUGGESTION

Through this and other lessons of the Law of Success course the student has learned that sense impressions arising out of one's environment, or from statements or actions of other people, are called suggestions, while sense impressions that we place in our own minds are placed there by self-suggestion, or Auto-suggestion.

All suggestions coming from others, or from environment, influence us only after we have accepted them and passed them on to the sub-conscious mind, through the principle of Auto-suggestion, thus it is seen that suggestion becomes, and must become, Auto-suggestion before it influences the mind of the one receiving it.

Stated in another way, no one may influence another without the consent of the one influenced, as the influencing is done through one's own power of Auto-suggestion.

The conscious mind stands, during the hours when one is awake, as a sentinel, guarding the sub-conscious mind and warding off all suggestions which try to reach it from the outside, until those suggestions have been examined by the conscious mind, passed upon and accepted. This is Nature's way of safeguarding the human being against intruders who would otherwise take control of any mind desired at will.

It is a wise arrangement.

THE VALUE OF AUTO-SUGGESTION IN ACCOMPLISHING THE OBJECT OF YOUR DEFINITE CHIEF AIM

One of the greatest uses to which one may direct the power of Auto-suggestion is that of making it help accomplish the object of one's *definite chief aim* in life.

The procedure through which this may be accomplished is very simple. While the exact formula has been stated in Lesson Two, and referred to in many other lessons of the course, the principle upon which it is based will be here, again, described, viz.:

Write out a clear, concise statement of that which you intend to accomplish, as your *definite chief aim,* covering a period of, let us say, the next five years. Make at least two copies of your statement, one to be placed where you can read it several times a day, while you are at work, and the other to be placed in the room where you sleep, where it can be read several times each evening before you go to sleep and just after you arise in the morning.

The suggestive influence of this procedure (impractical though it may seem) will soon impress the object of your *definite chief aim* on your sub-conscious mind and, as if by a stroke of magic, you will begin to observe events taking place which will lead you nearer and nearer the attainment of that object.

From the very day that you reach a definite decision in your own mind as to the precise thing, condition or position in life that you deeply desire, you will observe, if you read books, newspapers and magazines, that important news items and other data bearing on the object of your *definite chief aim* will begin to come to your attention; you will observe, also, that opportunities will begin to come to you that will, if embraced, lead you nearer and nearer the coveted goal of your desire. No one knows better than the author of this course how impossible and impractical this may seem to the person who is not informed on the subject of mind operation; however, this is not an age favorable to the doubter or the skeptic, and the best thing for any person to do is to experiment with this principle until its practicality has been established.

To the present generation it may seem that there are no more worlds to conquer in the field of mechanical invention, but every thinker (even those who are not accurate thinkers) will concede that we are just entering a new era of evolution, experiment and analysis as far as the powers of the human mind are concerned.

The word "impossible" means less now than ever before in the history of the human race. There are some who have actually removed this word from their vocabularies, believing that man can do anything he can imagine and BELIEVE HE CAN DO!

We have learned, for sure, that the universe is made up of two substances: matter and energy. Through patient scientific research we have discovered what we believe to be good evidence that everything that is or ever has been in the way of matter, when analyzed to the finest point, can be traced back to the electron, which is nothing but a form of energy. On the other hand, every material thing that man has created began in the form of energy, through the seed of an idea that was released through the imaginative faculty of the human mind. In other words, the beginning of every material thing is energy and the ending of it is energy.

All matter obeys the command of one form or another of energy. The highest known form of energy is that which functions as the human mind. The human mind, therefore, is the sole directing force of everything man creates, and what he may create with this force in the future, as compared with that which he has created with it in the past, will make his past achievements seem petty and small.

We do not have to wait for future discoveries in connection with the powers of the human mind for evidence that the mind is the greatest force known to mankind. We know, now, that any idea, aim or purpose that is fixed in the mind and held there with a will to achieve or attain its physical or material equivalent, puts into motion powers that cannot be conquered.

Buxton said: "The longer I live the more certain I am that the great difference between men, between the feeble and the powerful, the great and the insignificant. is energy—invincible determination—a purpose once fixed, and then death or victory. That quality will do anything that can be done in this world—and no talents, no circumstances, no opportunities will make a two-legged creature a man without it."

Donald G. Mitchell has well said: "Resolve is what makes a man manifest. Not puny resolve; not crude determinations; not errant purposes—but that strong and indefatigable will which treads down difficulties and danger, as a boy treads down the heaving frostlands of winter, which kindles his eye and brain with proud pulse-beat toward the unattainable. WILL MAKES MEN GIANTS!"

The great Disraeli said: "I have brought myself, by long meditation, to the conviction that a human being with a settled purpose must accomplish it, and that nothing can resist a will which will stake even existence upon its fulfillment."

Sir John Simpson said: "A passionate DESIRE and an unwearied will can perform impossibilities, or what may seem to be such to the cold, timid and feeble."

And John Foster adds his testimony when he says: "It is wonderful how even the casualties of life seem to bow to a spirit that will not bow to them, and yield to subserve a design which they may, in their first apparent tendency, threaten to frustrate. When a firm, decisive spirit is recognized, it is curious to see how the space clears around a man and leaves him room and freedom."

Abraham Lincoln said of General Grant: "The great thing about Grant is his cool persistency of purpose. He is not easily excited, and he has got the grip of a

THE most successful
physicians are those
who mix hope and faith
with the medicines they
prescribe.

bull-dog. When he once gets his teeth in, nothing can shake him off."

It seems appropriate to state here that a strong desire, to be transformed into reality, must be backed with persistency until it is taken over by the sub-conscious mind. It is not enough to feel very deeply the desire for achievement of a *definite chief aim*, for a few hours or a few days, and then forget all about that desire. The desire must be placed in the mind and held there, with PERSISTENCE THAT KNOWS NO DEFEAT, until the automatic or sub-conscious mind takes it over. Up to this point you must stand back of the desire and push it; beyond this point the desire will stand back of you and push you on to achievement.

Persistence may be compared to the dropping of water which finally wears away the hardest stone. When the final chapter of your life shall have been completed it will be found that your persistence, or lack of this sterling quality, played an important part in either your success or your failure.

This author watched the Tunney-Dempsey fight, in Chicago. He also studied the psychology leading up to and surrounding their previous bout. Two things helped Tunney defeat Dempsey, on both occasions, despite the fact that Dempsey is the stronger of the two men, and, as many believe, the better fighter.

And these two things, which spelled Dempsey's doom, were, first, his own lack of self-confidence—the fear that Tunney might defeat him; and, second, Tunney's complete self-reliance and his belief that he would whip Dempsey.

Tunney stepped into the ring, with his chin in the

air, an atmosphere of self-assurance and certainty written in his every movement. Dempsey walked in, with a sort of uncertain stride, eying Tunney in a manner that plainly queried, "I wonder what you'll do to me?"

Dempsey was whipped, in his own mind, before he entered the ring. Press agents and propagandists had done the trick, thanks to the superior thinking ability of his opponent, Tunney.

And so the story goes, from the lowest and most brutal of occupations, prize-fighting, on up to the highest and most commendable professions. Success is won by the man who understands how to use his power of thought.

Throughout this course much stress has been laid upon the importance of environment and habit out of which grow the stimuli that put the "wheels" of the human mind into operation. Fortunate is the person who has found how to arouse or stimulate his or her mind so that the powers of that mind will function constructively, as they may be made to do when placed back of any strong, deeply seated desire.

Accurate thinking is thinking that makes intelligent use of all the powers of the human mind, and does not stop with the mere examination, classification and arranging of ideas. Accurate thought creates ideas and it may be made to transform these ideas into their most profitable, constructive form.

.   .   .   .

The student will perhaps be better prepared to analyze, without a feeling of skepticism and doubt, the principles laid down in this lesson if the fact is kept

Although all forms of the Methodist revival would use societies as one of their basic methods of organization, they would envision them as associations of the converted. The Holy Club at Oxford, however, had its heyday before any of its members had undergone a conversion experience. Its members, therefore, would look back on its activities as fruitless works before grace. Whitefield was the only member of the group who underwent that experience while he was still at the university, which he did under the influence of a book to which Charles Wesley introduced him.

Ordained a deacon on June 20, 1736, about a month before he received his B.A., Whitefield began preaching around London, not having been appointed to a cure. In what Stout calls the "filiopietistic" accounts of the beginning of the Methodist revival, a good bit of shock is expressed over the way that the founders were denied pulpits in the Church of England. Such a reaction is hardly justified. The account of the latitudinarian church in the previous chapter does not reveal it to be seething with zeal, but the synagogue at Nazareth when our Lord preached there may have been the last pulpit open to anyone who wanted to occupy it. The clergy appointed to the parishes were the only persons with an automatic right to preach in them. Those who complain today about the exclusion of Whitefield and the Wesleys probably keep close watch over who preaches in their own churches, and it is only the conviction that the Methodist leaders were voices crying in the wilderness that makes the closed pulpits seem at all exceptional.

The truly extraordinary fact is that they received so many invitations to preach so early in their ministries. That does not happen today to many twenty-two-year-old, newly ordained deacons. Yet young Whitefield seems to have been the sensation of the season. The Wesleys had already gone to Georgia as missionaries of the Society for the Propagation of the Gospel, and Whitefield soon came to see it as his vocation to follow them there. Meanwhile, he took advantage of every opportunity to preach the necessity of the rebirth he had just experienced.

The effects were astonishing: someone complained to the bishop of London that in his first sermon, Whitefield had driven fifteen people mad. The bishop's response was to wish that "the madness might not be forgotten before the next Sunday." Other clergy must have felt the same way because invitations poured in and, wherever he went, the churches were overflowing. In the year and a half before he could sail to America, Whitefield created such a taste for his sermons that it had to be met by printed transcripts for those unable to hear them. Indeed, most of the

---

content to the later preaching of revivals, some of the external forms of such preaching also can be traced back to British Calvinists in the early-seventeenth century—although in this case they were not English Puritans, but Scottish and Irish Presbyterians. Among them a tradition had developed of preparing for their infrequent celebrations of the Eucharist by having sacramental meetings at which people were encouraged to ready themselves to receive Holy Communion by repenting of their sins in the assurance that justification should produce a sanctified life. The preaching was often quite emotional, and people came under conviction of their sins and experienced conversion.

Such meetings began as activities of the local congregation, but they came to be such moving experiences that visitors from some distance were attracted. At times the crowds were so large that the meeting had to be moved out-of-doors. These meetings were suppressed by Charles I, but, by the time of the Restoration when they were outlawed again, they had become the principal institutional form of the religious life of the Scottish and Irish Calvinists, who continued to hold such meetings under clandestine conditions. Access to the churches being forbidden them, open-air meetings became the norm. Since their clergy had been ejected from their "livings," they wandered around preaching revivals at these sacramental meetings. These conditions continued until the Glorious Revolution of 1688, when William and Mary came to the throne.

> By 1688 there was a long-established tradition of periodic sacramental meetings, involving enthusiastic preaching and the expectation of experiences of conviction and conversion, hosted by a semi-independent fellowship of traveling (or itinerant) preachers. The precedents for the Evangelical Revival (and American Awakenings) were well in place.[6]

THE EVANGELICAL REVIVAL

Wales

Although the Evangelical revival is explained by some historians against the background of the industrial revolution, deism, Lockean psychology and epistemology, and the emergence of moralism and voluntary societies in the sphere of religion, its first manifestation was in one area of the British Isles least affected by all of these forces, Wales. Unlike the movement a century before among Scottish and Irish Calvinists, this one began (although it did not remain) within the established church. Nor was the Welsh revival unhoped for. **The Reverend Griffith Jones** of the parish of Llandowrer, who served as a sort of godfather for the movement, had been praying for it as far back as 1714. His own way of preparing the way of the Lord was to establish schools in which children could become literate enough to read the Bible in Welsh. He was able to found 3,225 such schools, in which 150,000 had learned to read before he died in 1761; he also distributed 30,000 Welsh Bibles.

Two young men in particular are credited with the first preaching of the revival. One of them, **Howell Harris,** was not ordained. After a dramatic conversion experience in 1735 when he was twenty-one, he went to Oxford with the ministry in mind, but he was so distressed by the low moral level of the university that he stayed only a few weeks. Returning home, he began a ministry of teaching and preaching. He became an overseer of some of Griffith Jones's schools and began evangelizing from house to house, establishing societies of his converts.

Soon his witnessing attracted crowds, and he began preaching out-of-doors and itinerating between his congregations. Harris's preaching drew power from his strongly emotional nature, a nature that also made him hard to get along with. In fact, at one time he dropped out of the Methodist conference for twelve years, establishing instead a community not unlike Zinzendorf's Herrnhut at his home at Trevecka. Later, though, he became reconciled. Through him the Welsh revival was to influence the British revival, especially through his contacts with George Whitefield, John Wesley, and Lady Huntingdon.

The other young man, **Daniel Rowland,** was ordained in the established church and presented to the parish of Llangeitho, which served both as a base for his itinerate preaching and as a center for the revival. Although no direct influence has been traced, Rowland's work bore many resemblances to the Scottish and Irish revivals of the previous century. Harris has left an account of the preaching in preparation for a celebration of the Eucharist in Rowland's parish:

> I was last Sunday at the Ordinance with Brother Rowlands where I saw, felt, and heard such things as I cant send on Paper any Idea of. . . . Such Crying out and Heart Breaking Groans, Silent Weeping and Holy Joy, and shouts of Rejoicing I never saw. Their Amens and Cryings Glory in the Highest &c would inflame your soul was you there. Tis very common when he preaches for Scores to fall down by the Power of the Word, pierced and wounded or overcom'd by the love of God and Sights of the Beauty and Excellency of Jesus, and lie on the ground.[7]

It was upon the foundation of these two men that the Me ment, which became the most notable aspect of Welsh cult ations to come, was built.

A study of the preaching of the Welsh pioneers was ma their successors, Gwyn Walters, who taught preaching for n Gordon-Conwell Theological Seminary.[8] He described th style of the Welsh folk preachers covering a period of 250 ye strating what remarkable eloquence in the gospel some of th Several characteristics of their style remind one of class American preaching, especially a form of dialogue with the "amen corner" that resembles the black tradition of "call and and the way preachers would break out in an extemporaneou their words, what the Welsh call the *hwyl*, which resembles portions of American folk preaching.

The Homeless Pilgrim with Dubious Name[9]

The link between the Welsh and British expressions of the Awakening was in the person of Howell Harris, who came to association with both Whitefield, for whom he furnished the field preaching and later served as a marriage broker, and We association to be discussed below.[10]

Born to innkeeping parents[11] in Gloucester in 1714, **George** showed great interest in both religion and drama as a child. financial circumstances of the family meant that the only way go to the university to prepare for ordination was as a "servit had to perform chores for his college and for "gentleman" There he met the Wesley brothers (who occupied the midd of "commoners") and became involved in their pious circle, k the university by such opprobrious terms as the "Holy C "Methodists."

Although the name Methodists was later to be picked up and worn as a badge, what it came to stand for was very different fr to which it was originally applied. The circle at Oxford was typi sort of voluntary association being formed at the time, one tha something to the influence of both the Puritan "conventicles" of th vious century and the *collegia* of Spener and the German Pietists. "societies," founded on models established by Anthony Hornec Josiah Woodword, were "a means by which Christians could hol other accountable for their personal moral behavior and for their p of benevolent enterprises."[12]

sermons that he ever edited for publication himself (forty-six out of sixty-three) were written by the time he was twenty-five.[13]

This early adulation was accorded before Whitefield's preaching had acquired two of the characteristics that were to make it most appealing and accessible to mass audiences: it was done without notes and in the open air. Extempore preaching had been an ideal of the Holy Club at Oxford, but Whitefield began it only on the eve of his departure for America. Field preaching was inaugurated after he returned from his short sojourn abroad[14] for ordination to the priesthood and appointment to the orphanage he had founded in Georgia as his cure. Since canon law of the Church of England did not provide for itinerate preaching, Whitefield found his excuse in the need to raise money for the orphans, as John Wesley was to find his in the claim that a fellow of an Oxford college was licensed to preach anywhere.

By this time, however, the publication of Whitefield's *Journal* of his travels had already turned many of the clergy against him so that the popularity he had enjoyed the year before was now withheld. Pulpits were closed to him, especially after an incident in which he appears to have intruded into that of St. Margaret's, Westminster, by force. But he had heard of Howell Harris's field preaching as early as 1737, and now he experimented with it himself.

Less than two weeks after the St. Margaret's affair, Whitefield and his friend William Seward were visiting Bristol and went out to the collieries of nearby Kingswood. There he decided to preach to the miners, about two hundred of whom assembled. A week later he was preaching to five thousand, and that number doubled two days later. In March, the number had doubled again to twenty thousand. After that he was ready to try out this technique developed in the countryside on urban London. He had found his medium. Before moving into London, however, he made two visits to Harris in Wales and preached with him there, establishing in person the friendship already begun by mail.

Thus all the pieces were in place for what must be one of the most extraordinary preaching careers of all time. Soon Whitefield was to preach to a crowd in Hyde Park that he estimated to number eighty thousand. "Even discounting that number substantially leaves a staggering total, a crowd the size of which had not been seen in all England since the great battles of the Civil War."[15] The following October he preached to twenty thousand in Boston, and "there had never been a larger crowd in America to that date."[16]

He was to keep up the pace for thirty years, preaching an average of nine times per week to congregations that regularly ran to the tens of thousands. He toured America seven times, meeting his death on the last round there, and became what Stout has called "an American icon—the first intercolonial hero."[17] He made twice as many trips to Scotland and also visited Wales and Ireland; he even went to Holland and Spain. Inside England he traversed distances that were geographically short but socially cosmic, having been heard on many occasions by the leading members of the nobility and intelligentsia.

Even though there were popular preachers in the Middle Ages who attracted vast crowds, it is doubtful that any human being was heard by as many fellow mortals as Whitefield before the advent of modern mass communication. And it is even more doubtful that as many of any other preacher's listeners experienced what they understood to be conversion as a result of their preaching, until at least the nineteenth century and possibly the twentieth.

As interesting as it would be to follow Whitefield the rest of his journey—to observe his breach with John Wesley, his association with Lady Huntingdon, his friendship with Benjamin Franklin—it is more to the purpose of this book to try to ascertain what made his preaching unique, to determine as far as possible both what made him attract such vast audiences and also why there was at the time and has remained ever since such disagreement about him—what makes his name "dubious," as Whittier called it. (For an example of Whitefield's preaching, **see Vol. 2, pp. 349-62.**)

The first observation to be made is that while Whitefield created the basic pattern that evangelistic preaching has retained ever since, it does not differ greatly in terms of outline from the neoclassical pattern followed by Tillotson and his successors. This is to say that the pattern was essentially topical. The sermon was based on a short text, and, after an introduction and some background, there was an announcement of the points that would be made. Each of the heads would have several subheadings, and all led to a conclusion.

Here, though, the resemblance ended, for the greatest dread of the neoclassicists was what they called "enthusiasm." They did recognize the need for emotional appeals, but these were never to exceed the bounds of good taste. What Whitefield was aiming at, however, was conversion, and he believed that could occur only when people were brought under conviction of their sins, when they were brought to believe in the depths of their being that they were sinners whose only chance of escaping hell was a divine intervention. Hammer away at this as he did, however, his emphasis was not on God's wrath so much as on the divine love and pity that sought the lost sheep and the rejoicing in heaven whenever one was reclaimed. However much the grounds for fear are gone over in the sermon, the conclusion is always joyful doxology. It is no wonder that Whitefield himself was frequently in tears and that most of his hearers were; often the emotional manifestations were more extreme.

In addition to creating a formula, Whitefield also had extraordinary personal gifts. One was a voice that not only carried to audiences larger than any addressed before amplification, but also was the envy of actors because of the feeling it could put into a word. The actor David Garrick is reported to have said that Whitefield could "make his audiences weep or tremble merely by varying his pronunciation of the word Mesopotamia."[18] He also said, "I would give a hundred guineas if I could only say 'O!' like Mr. Whitefield."[19] Another talent he possessed was the ability to register in his face and gestures all of the feelings he invoked; in this he was at one with the elocutionary movement in rhetoric of that time, which sought to bring liveliness to delivery.[20] Beyond that, he had a genius as a raconteur to make a scene from biblical history and other illustrative material palpably present to his hearers.

To these qualities he added the other techniques of popular speakers. One student has enumerated them in this way:

> the element of surprise; travellers' tales; anecdotes to lighten the strain or to point a moral; the selection of the dramatic parts of scripture for his most successful expositions; such rhetorical devices as the formal introduction to an imaginative flight, antithesis, the intermingling of long and short sentences, and the enforcing of a point by a pithy saying; counter-attacks upon his critics by way of declamations; the comic interlude in which wit, satire, and whimsy, humour, and even puns are used; the direct form of address to individuals or to groups in the auditory and particular applications in the exhortations of his sermons; the great range of his appeal to sentiment, arousing pity (he was a master of pathos), indignation, or terror; the use of homely and telling illustrations; and the employment of topical references and impromptu illustrations.[21]

To this must be added the mastery that came through the privilege of an itinerant, that of repeating a sermon many times. Benjamin Franklin said:

> By hearing him often I came to distinguish easily between sermons newly composed and those which he had often preached in the course of his travels. His delivery of the latter was so improved by frequent repetition, that every accent, every emphasis, every modulation of

voice, was so perfectly well turned, and well placed, that without being interested in the subject, one could not help being pleased with the discourse: a pleasure of much the same kind with that received from an excellent piece of music.[22]

All of this effort to list traits is not intended to explain Whitefield's power, but rather to show that the only possible explanation for it is that in him came together that rare combination of ability called genius. There must be few speakers in human history who have matched his ability to move audiences by eloquence.

Since these and similar gifts in preachers are often described as dramatic, it may be worthwhile to make important distinctions between effective public speaking and acting. The actor says words written by someone else and says them in the role of another person, a character in a play, while preachers speak their own words as their own. The speech of actors is ostensibly spoken to other actors on the stage and is meant to be heard by the audience as interaction between the characters portrayed, while preachers address congregations, usually parishioners, communicating directly with them.

Effective acting, then, is the ability to be convincing in the portrayal of emotions that are not the actor's own, while effective preaching is the ability to convey one's own deepest convictions with power. The two skills are different, and not everyone good at the one activity is good at the other. This, of course, is not to say that preachers cannot improve their delivery by study and application, and even less is it to claim that all preachers, or even all widely heard preachers, have been sincere. But even if they are frauds, it is their own thoughts and feelings that they are feigning, and they intend for their words to be received as direct address. Their performances, then, are not theater, but a confidence game.

The question raised in the Whittier quotation, therefore, is essentially one of Whitefield's sincerity. Yet the issue is more complex. Since the preserved documentation does not furnish explicit evidence of duplicity, the issue is simply one of trust. But trust in such a matter depends largely upon whether one favors or opposes the kind of activity in which the figure in question was engaged. In this case, that means whether one considers dramatic conversion experiences in response to emotional preaching to be the ordinary channel of the grace of God or regards them instead as hysterical responses to manipulative behavior. A mediating position would be that such preaching and conversion experiences are one of the many channels through which God reaches out to reclaim estranged children, the channels differing according to the needs of the individuals.

As for Whitefield, any evaluation must do justice to these data: on the one hand, even many of those who admire him most, the "filiopietists," admit that he was not always judicious. On the other hand, he was convincing to a skeptic like Benjamin Franklin, who knew him well, and many of his converts were permanently changed for the better.[23]

Institutionalizing the Revival

In American folklore there is the story of how the legendary hero of the Southwest, Pecos Bill, lassoed a tornado. **John Wesley** accomplished something on the same order by the way he harnessed the religion of the heart movement in Britain (as his followers were to do in America) and organized it into a denomination. His having done so is not without irony, since he insisted to the end of his life that he was utterly opposed to his movement's separating from the Church of England. There are other ironies as well, including the fact that most of the techniques he used to domesticate the revival had been used by others before him, but without his fixity of purpose, so that they were never as productive for those from whom Wesley copied them as they were for Wesley himself. For instance, Wesley learned field preaching from Whitefield, who, in turn, had learned it from Howell Harris.

In many ways, it appears that Whitefield began most things before Wesley did but that Wesley was the one who hung around and garnered the results. While it can be argued that in his devotion to preaching the revival himself rather than organizing its results, Whitefield was maximizing the gifts he had as Wesley maximized his own, it is nevertheless true that Whitefield was the first of the two to be converted, the first to itinerate, the first to preach in the open, and the first to organize a network of societies. Of course, all these things had been done by Harris and the Welsh revivalists before Whitefield, by the seventeenth-century Scotch and Irish Calvinists before Harris, and many by continental Pietists as well.

Yet Wesley was the one able to launch an international religious movement by these actions. The Welsh Calvinistic Methodists, as they came to be called, were to dominate Welsh culture well into the twentieth century. Whitefield's clergy seem to have become Independents or Congregationalists, and Lady Huntingdon's Connexion became dissenting chapels. As closely connected and intertwined as these movements were at various times—especially before the breach between the "Arminian" Wesleyans and the "Calvinist" others—it is for their association with Wesley's Methodists that the others are chiefly remembered.

For over a third of his long life, however, no one looked less likely to lead a mass religious movement than John Wesley. It would have seemed much more likely that he would develop into the fussy sort of scholarly priest his father was. Educated at Charterhouse and at Christ Church College, Oxford, he was ordained and elected as a fellow of Lincoln College. After taking a couple of years off to serve as his father's curate, he resumed the life of a fellow of an Oxford college. As long as he remained a bachelor he would receive an adequate fellow's stipend while engaging in the educational tasks of the college and pursuing his own studies. While doing so, he also showed himself to be an earnest and pious, not to say scrupulous, Christian. With the kindred souls of the Holy Club or "Bible Moths," he took on a strict regimen of prayer, fasting, self-examination, and corporal works of mercy. It was because he and his friends went about these duties so systematically that they came to be derisively called "Methodists."

Several of the Methodists, including John and his brother Charles, decided to become SPG[24] missionaries to Georgia and set out for that purpose late in 1735 when John was thirty-two. After a voyage of almost four months, they arrived at their destination to begin a ministry that lasted less than two years and was characterized by misguided zeal and pastoral ineptitude. Arriving back in England at the end of January 1737, Wesley's evaluation of his time abroad was expressed in his *Journal*:

> It is now two years and almost four months since I left my native country in order to teach the Georgian Indians the nature of Christianity. But what have I learned myself in the meantime? Why, what I the least of all suspected, that I, who went to America to convert others, was never myself converted to God.[25]

That lesson did not come directly from his time in Georgia but from the voyages over and back. Storms at sea revealed to Wesley his fear of death, a fear obviously not shared by Moravian fellow travelers. Their peace and calm convinced him that he stood in need of conversion, an experience that came to him on the evening of May 24, 1738, when he was attending a meeting of a Moravian society in Aldersgate Street. The following month he began a trip to the Continent for the principal purpose of visiting Zinzendorf's Moravian community at Herrnhut. There he was refused Communion on the grounds that he was *homo perturbatus*, but he was greatly impressed with what he saw. Even though he was eventually to break with the Moravians over their quietism, they provided the occasion on which his previously divided self could be united through a great emotional upheaval. It is probably more accurate to speak of a process rather than a single experience of conversion for Wesley, but the Aldersgate experience was the turning point. Soon after his thirty-fifth birthday, he was ready to begin his life's work.

The direction his work was to take was shown him by Whitefield, who returned from Georgia at the end of 1738. Whitefield had already begun his own experiments in field preaching, and now he called on Wesley to join him. Always a stickler for propriety in many ways, Wesley was at first reluctant to go. Yet he had already begun preaching out of his experience of conversion with two results: (1) people responded in profoundly emotional ways, and (2) the pulpits of staid Anglican parishes came to be closed to him. Thus he joined Whitefield at Bristol, and his *Journal* entry for April 2, 1739, tells the tale:

> At four in the afternoon I submitted to be more vile, and proclaimed in the highways the glad tidings of salvation, speaking from a little eminence in a ground adjoining to the city, to about three thousand people.

The text of his sermon was, "The Spirit of Lord is upon me, because he hath anointed me to preach the gospel to the poor."[26]

And preach it he did. In the remaining fifty-two years of his life, he preached more than forty thousand sermons. Although he did not draw the crowds that Whitefield did, his were large enough, sometimes over twenty thousand. While he left it to his representatives to cross the Atlantic, his travels—on horseback until he was almost seventy—have been estimated at 225,000 miles. And what of the results? When he died three-quarters of the way through his eighty-eighth year, he left behind seventy thousand Methodists in Great Britain. This number represents rolls that he was continually trying to strip of deadwood. There were also sixty thousand of his followers in America—even though he had opposed their Revolution. Nor do these figures represent isolated adherents. The secret of the movement's strength was the complex infrastructure he devised to keep the fires of faith burning ardently among his followers. Ronald Knox has provided an economical list of the components of this infrastructure:

> When he died he left behind him a powerful religious body, Anglican in its inspiration, and for the most part in its membership, but ripe for schism. . . . It had its cadre, not only of itinerate preachers and local preachers, but of class leaders, band leaders, helpers, stewards, and schoolmasters; it had band-meetings, class-meetings, quarterly meetings, love-feasts over and above its ordinary services. Nominally it was

only an aggregation of "religious societies" organized in various cen-
tres. . . . But in fact a church had formed in embryo within the womb
of the Establishment, with John Wesley as its visible head.[27]

This unparalleled ministry is not only impressive in its own right but
also significant for the history of preaching in at least three ways. First,
those forty thousand sermons call for attention, not so much for their
number as for the light they cast on the modes of evangelistic preaching.
While the outward form of Wesley's sermons was similar to that of
Whitefield's, the strategy of persuasion was very different. Looking at
Wesley's sermons after examining Whitefield's can offer a sense of the
range of expression possible in this genre. Then Wesley also has importance in the history of preaching as a writer of homiletical instruction for
his itinerate and local preachers. Manuals on how to preach for those
who have not undergone formal theological education are relatively rare,
and it is indicative of Wesley's thoroughness that he thought to produce
them. Finally, Wesley chose published sermons (many of which had never
been delivered orally) as his own most distinctive catechetical form in the
library he created to provide all his followers needed to know in addition
to the Bible. This use of the sermon form divorced from oral delivery as
the most effective pattern for forming his movement intellectually casts
some light on the effectiveness of the form itself as a vehicle for the communication of Christian faith and knowledge.

Wesley's Live Preaching[28]

The term "live," taken from modern telecommunications media where
it distinguishes performances being broadcast as they occur from a
recorded form to be aired later, is chosen to call attention to an issue even
more problematic for John Wesley than for others in the history of
preaching: the relation of published sermons to what was delivered
orally to a congregation. The reason it was more problematic is that his
spoken and written sermons are not necessarily different forms of the
same composition: "Many of Wesley's favorite texts for oral preaching
do not appear at all in the corpus of his written sermons and vice
versa."[29] And the reason for that is: "He saw an important difference
between the principal aims of an oral and a written sermon: the former
is chiefly for *proclamation* and invitation; the latter is chiefly for *nurture*
and reflection."[30]

Even though this difference in purpose would suggest a difference in
method, which in turn would ordinarily mean a published document

440

would offer an unreliable guide to the oral event, there is at least one printed sermon that probably comes close to what was spoken to congregations. Sermon 43, "The Scripture Way of Salvation," is on Ephesians 2:8, "ye are saved through faith," a text from which Wesley's record tells us he preached over ninety times.[31] Since its form is the neoclassical structure followed by both the latitudinarians and Whitefield, a detailed look at this sermon may give a sense of how variation in content and in the faculties to which appeal is made can produce enormous difference in the dynamics of sermons constructed to satisfy ostensibly the same criteria.

Sermon 43 begins with a short proem that distinguishes between the complexity of religion as it is often described and the simplicity of the "genuine religion of Jesus Christ," which has salvation as its end and faith as the means to that end. In order to see what those important terms mean, he proposes the partition:

> I.   What is salvation?
> II. What is that faith whereby we are saved? and
> III. How we are saved by it.

I. What is salvation?

1. First of all, negatively, it "is not what is frequently understood by that word, the going to heaven, eternal happiness." Rather, it is something his hearers already possess.

2. This includes "all that is wrought in the soul by what is frequently termed 'natural conscience,' but more properly, 'preventing grace.'"

3. But the salvation spoken of by the apostle in the text "consists of two general parts, justification and sanctification," with the understanding that "justification is another word for pardon."

4. Sanctification begins at the moment of justification.

5. The experience of pardon at justification leaves those who undergo it with a sense that "all sin is gone."

6. "But it is seldom long before they are undeceived, finding sin was only suspended, not destroyed."

7. Macarius expressed that point well fourteen hundred years previously.

8. The work of sanctification takes place gradually "while we take up our cross and deny ourselves every pleasure that does not lead us to God."

9. The process of sanctification is "go[ing] on to perfection," the perfection of perfect love. "It is love excluding sin; love filling the heart, taking up the whole capacity of the soul."

II. "But what is that 'faith through which we are saved'?"

1. It is what the apostle calls "the evidence of things not seen," which is both a supernatural evidence and a supernatural perception of God, a "twofold operation of the Holy Spirit" by which we see "the spiritual world" and "the eternal world."

2. Most particularly, "faith is a divine evidence and conviction, not only that 'God was in Christ,' . . . but also that Christ 'loved *me*, and gave himself for *me*.'"

3. Such a faith is both the "faith of assurance" and that of "adherence," "for a man cannot have a childlike confidence in God till he knows he is a child of God."

4. "It is by this faith we . . . [are both] justified and sanctified."

III. How are we justified and sanctified by faith?

1. We are justified by faith in the sense that "faith is the condition, and the only condition, of our justification."

2. While both repentance and the fruits of repentance are necessary for justification, they are not necessary in the same sense nor to the same degree as faith.

3. And just as we are justified, so also are we sanctified by faith because "no man is sanctified till he believes; every man when he believes is sanctified."

4. But since Wesley teaches the need for repentance after as well as before justification, is that repentance not then a condition for salvation in addition to faith?

5. This second repentance (as well as good works), rightly understood, is necessary to salvation.

6. This repentance after justification differs from that before in that it is "a conviction wrought by the Holy Ghost of the 'sin' which still 'remains' in our heart," "a conviction of our proneness to evil, of an heart 'bent to backsliding,' of the still continuing tendency of the 'flesh' to 'lust against the Spirit.'"

7. "With this conviction of the sin *remaining* in our hearts there is joined a clear conviction of the sin remaining in our lives."

8. "One thing more is implied in this repentance, namely, a conviction of our helplessness, of our utter inability to think one good thought."

9. Of the good works that must be practiced for sanctification, the first kind is "works of piety."

10. The second kind is "works of mercy."

11. "Hence may appear the extreme mischievousness of that seemingly innocent opinion that 'there is no sin in a believer' . . . By totally preventing that repentance it quite blocks up the way to sanctification."

12. Yet "there is no possible danger in *thus* expecting full salvation."

13. "Though it be allowed that both this repentance and its fruits are necessary to full salvation, yet they are not necessary either in the *same sense* with faith or in the *same degree*."

14. The "faith whereby we are sanctified, saved from sin and perfected in love" is "a divine evidence and conviction, first, that God hath promised it in the Holy Scripture."

15. "It is a divine evidence and conviction, secondly, that what God hath promised he is *able* to perform."

16. It is, thirdly, a divine evidence and conviction that he is able and willing to do it *now*."

17. To this there needs to be added a fourth thing, "a divine evidence and conviction that *he doth it*."

18. This "great work in the soul"... "may be gradually wrought in some," but "it is infinitely desirable, were it the will of God, that it should be done instantaneously."[32]

(At this point, without any change in the division, there is a shift to application/ exhortation.)

Thou therefore look for it every moment. . . . But you shall not be disappointed of your hope: it will come, and will not tarry. Look for it then every day, every hour, every moment.[33]

(This exhortation ends in a call, complete with the verse of a hymn.)

Do *you* believe we are sanctified by faith? Be true then to your principle, and look for this blessing just as you are, neither better, nor worse; as a poor sinner that has still nothing to pay, nothing to plead but "Christ died." And if you look for it as you are, then expect it *now*. Stay for nothing. Why should you? Christ is ready. And he is all you want. He is waiting for you. He is at the door! Let your inmost soul cry out,

> Come in, come in, thou heavenly Guest!
> Nor hence again remove:
> But sup with me, and let the feast
> Be everlasting love.[34]

The contrast with Whitefield is diametrical. Indeed, were it not for the subject matter and the final exhortation, this sermon of Wesley's would have more in common with the rational addresses of the latitudinarians. There is nothing in the way of ornament, nothing that will impede the clear flow of thought. At the end of a detailed analysis of the preaching styles of the two evangelists, Horton Davies says in summary:

> The conclusion of our consideration of the techniques of the discourses of Whitefield and Wesley can only be that Whitefield was the spell-binding orator and preacher par excellence, while Wesley was the best of pulpit teachers.[35]

While this is true as far as it goes, it probably makes the mistake of assuming that the matter and style of the oral and written sermons were the same. Since, however, it is known that Wesley expected them to accomplish different purposes, that assumption cannot be safely made. The oral sermons were for proclamation and invitation. How else can one account for the tens of thousands of persons converted through them? Could this religion of the head appeal successfully to a generation yearning for a religion of the heart? The answer would appear to be no, especially in light of the emotional appeal of the exhortation in the sermon just summarized. Nor does "head work"—to contrast this intellectual appeal to the term "heart work," which Wesley loved to speak of—appear to be all there was to his preaching.

This much is suggested by one of the sophisticates of the time who heard him out of curiosity. The earl of Orford, Horace Walpole, a litterateur and a pioneer in the Gothic revival, wrote an unsympathetic account:

> I have been at one opera, Mr. Wesley's. . . . Wesley is a lean elderly man, fresh-coloured, his hair smoothly combed, but with a *soupçon* of curl at the ends. Wondrous clean, but as evidently an actor as Garrick. He spoke his sermon, but so fast and with so little accent, that I am sure he has often uttered it, for it was like a lesson. There were parts and eloquence in it; but towards the end he exalted his voice, and acted very vulgar enthusiasm; decried learning, and told stories, like Latimer, of the fool of his college, who said, "I *thanks* God for everything."[36]

One does not have to depend, however, on such unsympathetic accounts. In his *Journal*, Wesley often notes that he was powerfully moved while preaching and that his congregation shared that experience. Further, he also notes that some of his hearers shouted, fainted, or were seized with convulsions.[37] The only conclusion is that in his oral preaching Wesley made strong emotional appeals, the nature of which his published sermons do little to suggest. It is hard to believe that he employed any of the rhetorical means that came so naturally to Whitefield; nothing in his writings suggests that he had such weapons in his arsenal. Perhaps it was something about his presence, the sort of overwhelming compassionate concern conveyed in the Hone portrait, or his urgent conviction. It is utterly unlikely that so many would have been converted through his preaching unless it had a large element of enthusiasm. Though whether one would agree with Walpole that the enthusiasm was ugly is another matter.

His Instructions to His Preachers

What has been said about the difference between the preaching style of Wesley and that of Whitefield refers to a difference in personality. It certainly should not suggest that Wesley was unconscious of his manner of speaking or that he had not given considerable thought and study to the principles of effective speech. It would have been entirely out of character for him to overlook anything so important to his mission.[38] He not only applied such insight to his own practice, but also distilled it for the instruction of his lay preachers. While some of his thoughts on the subject are inserted in letters to various persons, most of them are collected in two documents: the "Large Minutes," which served as the nearest approach of his Connexion to being a codex of canon law,[39] and *Directions Concerning Pronunciation and Gesture,* an abridgement he made of an anonymous rhetorical manual of his time.[40]

Before going into his instructions about preaching, it would perhaps be helpful to say something about his cadre of preachers. He does not regard them as clergy. Rather, they are intended to be Helpers of the Ministers of the Church of England. They are "extraordinary messengers," who "provoke regular Ministers to jealousy"[41] and "supply their lack of service toward those who are perishing from lack of knowledge" (Q. 24). Their duties include preaching morning and evening, meeting regularly with societies and bands and their leaders, catechizing families in the method recommended by Richard Baxter in *The Reformed Pastor,* and studying at least five hours a day. They also have records to keep. What they did not do was administer any sacraments, since doing so would imply that they were a dissenting Christian body and not what today would be called a renewal movement within Anglicanism.[42]

There were both local and itinerating preachers, although Wesley thought it bad for anyone to settle down in one place. There were also assistants, who were supervisors somewhat in the manner of modern American district superintendents. All of them owed complete allegiance to Wesley, and any that did not wish to follow the minute rules he laid down were free to leave (Q. 27.5).

The same condition applied to laypeople, so there were frequent departures and the rolls were continually purged—although the founder was never satisfied with the state of purity achieved. Wesley is often spoken of as a good organizer, but that does not mean he delegated authority well. It means rather that he wanted to have oversight of the souls of all his seventy thousand followers and those who preached to them. It was this discipline that lassoed the tornado.[43]

The advice he gives to his preachers on the best general method of preaching is: (1) to invite, (2) to convince, (3) to offer Christ, and (4) to build up, "and to do this in some measure in every sermon" (Q. 36). He follows this with "smaller advices relative to preaching," which include beginning and ending at precisely the time appointed; letting one's whole deportment before the congregation be serious, weighty, and solemn; suiting one's subject to the congregation; choosing the plainest texts possible; not rambling; limiting one's use of allegorical or spiritual interpretation; and avoiding anything either awkward or affected in gesture, phrase, or pronunciation. The list continues after that, but with admonitions that have less and less to do directly with preaching, touching such matters as singing no hymns of one's own composition, not spelling words like "honour" and "vigour" without the *u,* not wearing a slouched hat, and taking care of one's horse (Q. 37).

While such preaching was obviously intended to be evangelistic, Wesley was contemptuous of what were often spoken of as "gospel sermons."[44] The implication is that preaching such can relieve the necessity of requiring behavioral standards consistent with what God had required of converted sinners. He says:

> The most effectual way of preaching Christ, is to preach him in all his offices,[45] and to declare his law as well as his gospel, both to the believers and unbelievers. Let us strongly and closely insist upon inward and outward holiness, in all its branches. (Q. 38)

One of the objections to Calvinism, "the direct antidote to Methodism," and its doctrine of "heart-holiness," is that "it seems to magnify Christ; although in reality it supposes him to have died in vain" (Q. 74). But Methodists had leaned too much in the direction of Calvinism by soft-pedaling the need for redemption to express itself in good works. There was thus a need for them to attend to the strong practical and ethical thrust of Wesley's own preaching and that which he expected of his preachers. For example, to Question 21, "Do not Sabbath-breaking, dram-drinking, evil-speaking, unprofitable conversation, lightness, expensiveness or gaiety of apparel, and contracting debts without due care to discharge them, still prevail in some places?" he responds by saying, "Let us preach expressly on each of these heads."

The content of Methodist preaching, then, was a combination of evangelizing those not yet converted and exhortation on holiness of life to the justified, who were supposed to be "going on to perfection."

To see that these messages get across, the founder also had some sage advice on delivery.[46] Preachers should imitate only good examples. They should develop their voices so that they could be heard, and they should practice their enunciation. Faults to be avoided were speaking either too loudly or too low; speaking in a "thick, cluttering manner," mumbling and swallowing words or syllables; speaking too fast or slow or with an irregular, desultory, and uneven voice; or, the worst fault of all, speaking with a "tone" (and Wesley has an interesting list of the varieties of such affected pronunciation that are available). Instead, one should speak in public as one does in conversation. This involves working to achieve a voice that is soft and sweet. Preachers should not cough or spit while they are speaking.

They should, however, learn to vary their voice so that it is appropriate to their subject matter. There are three qualities of voice in which such variation is possible: volume, vehemence, and speed; and Wesley gives the ways for achieving the proper combination of these qualities for the different moods in sermons (e.g., "In congratulating the happy events of life, we speak with a lively and cheerful accent").[47]

Preachers who wish to improve the way they communicate their thoughts and feelings through the expressions on their faces and their gestures should work with a mirror or a friend who will give them reliable reactions. The preacher should neither be constantly in motion nor stand stock-still. The head is to be "kept modestly and decently upright, in its natural state and position," looking occasionally to the right or left but otherwise straight forward. Facial expressions should be practiced. Preachers should move from looking one hearer in the eye to so looking at another, with "an air of affection and regard."[48]

> The mouth must never be turned awry; neither must you bite or lick your lips, or shrug your shoulders, or lean upon your elbow; all which give just offense to the spectators.[49]

The hands can be used in "a thousand different ways." The preacher should not clap or thump the pulpit. The right hand is used most in gestures; the left is never used alone. When speaking of one's own "faculties, heart, or conscience," one may gently apply the right hand to the breast[50]—and other such advice. But when speaking, one should use the gestures that arise naturally. Wesley trained his preachers with these and other such instructions, apparently giving them little leeway about either what they should say or how they should say it.

Wesley's Printed Sermons

The familiarity of published sermons could blind one to the significance of Wesley's in his total plan for the religious community he founded. Publication for him was not simply an effort to make available to people a transcript of what they had heard and wished to go back over, or what they had not heard and were sorry they missed. Indeed, as has been noted, not all of his oral sermons were published, nor were all his published sermons delivered.

The purpose of this published corpus has to be understood in terms of Wesley's role in relation to his movement. Outler has described this by saying: "His chief intellectual interest, and achievement, was in what one could call a folk theology: the Christian message in its fullness and integrity, in 'plain words for plain people.'"[51] Expanding this, he goes on to say:

> Wesley was a prolific author, editor and publisher. But in his literary work, as in all else, it was the requirements of the Revival that dictated what he wrote and what he published. He regarded himself—and was so regarded—as the chief theological tutor of the Methodist people. In this role he undertook to supply them with an abundance of edifying literature which was cheap enough to buy, concise enough to read.[52]

This means that he personally set out to provide the Methodists, preachers and laity alike, with everything they needed to know—which amounted to a great deal: witness the five hours a day he expected his preachers to read. He did this by writing prolifically himself, but even more by editing others' works for his people's use, sometimes producing a tract of only thirty pages from a volume that ran into the hundreds.

Most of the reading and editing he did on horseback, which prompted Ronald Knox to quip that "he is not a good advertisement for reading on horseback,"[53] suggesting that he had misunderstood what he read. The truth is more likely that his interest was not in passing along the thought of others so much as it was in providing edifying reading for his people. If what he wrote was not what his sources had said, it was what they should have said. In his fifty-volume "Christian Library" of devotional and theological literature drawn from every age, as well as in his *Arminian Magazine,* he set out to supply all his people would need to read—every bit of it predigested for them by the leader himself.[54]

It is in the total context of Wesley's efforts to supply his movement with all the reading material it needed that the purpose of his published sermons is to be understood: they were the keystone of the arch. I noted above that he saw a difference in purpose between oral and published sermons: the first were for proclamation and invitation, and the latter were for nurture and reflection. This didactic purpose lay behind his publication of his sermons. They were to be the distinctive theological literature of his people as creeds, confessions, or theological treatises had been that of other Christian bodies. They were to be his main medium for communicating what he thought Methodists were about.

Wesley began publishing his sermons in collected form less than ten years after his Aldersgate experience. He originally intended a three-volume set of his *Sermons on Several Occasions*. Volume 1, containing those that dealt with his soteriology, appeared in 1746; volume 2, devoted to the *ordo salutis*, appeared in 1748; and volume 3, "a sort of ellipse with its twin foci (:) Wesley's understanding of the graciousness of grace . . . and the fullness of grace,"[55] in 1750. A fourth volume, bringing the total of published sermons to forty-three, appeared in 1760. When he brought out his *Works* in 1770, the four volumes of sermons, now containing an additional nine, appeared first in the set.

Eight years later he felt that his controversy with Calvinists demanded a medium through which he could communicate his views to his people. The medium he chose was the eventually ten-volume *Arminian Magazine*, for which he began to write sermons that had never been delivered orally. Finally, in 1787 he collected these new sermons, along with the older ones, into an eight-volume edition of *Sermons on Several Occasions*, the last four volumes being devoted to what can be lumped together as pastoral theology.

All the various editions of the sermons that appeared over a forty-year period were introduced with the same preface (**see Vol. 2, pp. 362-66**), a document that thus has great importance in indicating the author's intentions in publishing them. Outler has summarized these:

> (1) to describe the enterprise and to explain Wesley's choice of the sermon form as the medium of his theology; (2) to defend his style and role as a folk theologian, renouncing his academic identification; (3) to stress soteriology as the focus of his entire theology; (4) to leave the way open for dialogue and reconciliation. . . .[56]

The sentence in which Wesley explains his choice of sermons as his theological medium is: "Every serious man who peruses these will therefore see in the clearest manner what those doctrines are which I embrace and teach as the essentials of true religion."[57] This seems to be saying that, since preaching has been the normal mode of his teaching, it should also be the normal mode for publishing that teaching.

Whether there are deeper reasons for the choice of the medium is open to question. Outler has suggested at least two reasons. The first is that the standard collection of the Church of England's theological teachings was the two *Books of Homilies*,[58] published under Edward VI and Elizabeth, formularies to which Wesley was ever eager to confess his allegiance. Always anxious to be understood as an Anglican, perhaps he thought sermons were the genre for the expression of Anglican theology. The second reason is that "sermons, as a genre, do not lend themselves to legalistic interpretation."[59] This is related to the fourth purpose stated in the preface, leaving the way open for dialogue and reconciliation. To this could be added the popularity of sermons as a form of literature at the time.[60]

While much more could be said about all of this, enough has already been said to show that the Wesleyan revival was at heart a preaching movement, as may be seen from the indefatigable oral preaching of the founder, the oral preaching also of the cadre of preachers he appointed and trained through his manuals, and the choice of published sermons as the definitive medium for the communication of his thought.

Reviving the Establishment

The early-twentieth-century revivalist Billy Sunday is supposed to have called the Episcopal Church in the USA a "sleeping giant." If that term appropriately described the American expression of Anglicanism of his time, how much more does it apply to the mother church in the wake of latitudinarianism! All that Whitefield and the Wesleys were trying to do could be understood as an effort to arouse Gulliver.

That should not leave the impression, however, that no one else in the Church of England shared their concerns. The same impulse to a religion of the heart was stirring in other clergy who would remain within the established church and try to revive it. They had some contact with the Methodists, but, since most of them had Calvinist leanings, they felt more in common with Whitefield than Wesley. By and large, they did not itinerate or do field preaching; instead, they remained within their parishes, preached the cross of Christ as the only hope of salvation, and hoped to instill in their parishioners an acceptance and assurance of that salvation, and to encourage them to lead lives totally given to living out the implications of their redemption.

Later, through the influence of members of the so-called "Clapham Sect,"[61] especially William Wilberforce, Evangelicals were to be involved in a variety of good works ranging from the abolition of slavery and the slave trade, and reform of child labor, to foreign missions and the organization of the British and Foreign Bible Society.

Some of the pioneers of the movement include John Fletcher, Henry Venn, William Romaine, and John Newton. The most famous name associated with the movement, though, and that which is most important for the history of preaching, belongs to a member of the second generation, **Charles Simeon** (1759–1836), who spent fifty-four years as vicar of Holy Trinity, Cambridge. When Simeon went up to Cambridge from Eton, he discovered that one of the ways in which the universities were still fiefdoms of the established church was that all students were required to receive Holy Communion, and that he would have to do so in three weeks. Although he had not been devout before, he was afraid that unworthy reception would cause him to eat and drink damnation to his soul. He therefore involved himself in a frenzy of preparation.

When he went through that experience without achieving the peace he sought, he continued his search until Easter, not knowing how to relate his sense of guilt to the sacrifice of Christ. The key came to him from Bishop Thomas Wilson's *Instruction for the Lord's Supper,* in which he read that there was wisdom in the Jewish practice of transferring the people's guilt to the scapegoat on the Day of Atonement. He immediately knew that he did not have to bear the weight of his own sins, that he could transfer them to Christ. As he told it,

> Accordingly I sought to lay my sins upon the sacred head of Jesus; and on the Wednesday began to have a hope of mercy; on the Thursday that hope increased; on the Friday and Saturday it became more strong; and on the Sunday morning, Easter Day, April 4th, I awoke early with those words upon my heart and lips, "Jesus Christ is risen today! Hallelujah! Hallelujah!"[62]

After his conversion, Simeon appears to have gone from strength to strength. When he graduated from Cambridge he was ordained deacon and during the summer filled in at St. Andrew's church, where he occupied Latimer's old pulpit and, much to everyone's surprise, drew large congregations. He was also made a fellow of King's, his old college. When he became a priest, the bishop of Ely appointed him vicar of Holy Trinity in the center of both the town and the university. He was to occupy these positions for the rest of his life, living in rooms at King's and ministering to his parish flock. He had not been his parishioners' choice, and for a number of years he was quite unpopular with them; they went so far as to lock their pews so no one could sit in them and tried to lock him out of the church. Evangelicals were so unpopular in the university that students tried to break up his services and threw unpleasant things at him in the street.

In the end, the effects of his conversion and (what may amount to the same thing) his rare sweetness of character won out. He filled his church with his preaching, attracting not only parishioners but undergraduates as well in a way that few clergy in Cambridge have ever been able to. And he sent many "sons in the gospel" out into the ministry. In time, his influence was so great that the historian Thomas Macaulay said:

> If you knew what his authority and influence were, and how they extended from Cambridge to the most remote corners of England, you would allow that his real sway in the church was far greater than that of any primate.[63]

One of the more prominent ways in which he influenced the church of his day was by sharing his conviction of the importance of preaching. He did this through four media: his own preaching, sermon classes and "conversation parties" he held for serious students preparing for ordination, a neoclassical French homiletics text he annotated, and a series of sermon outlines he produced on what he considered to be virtually all the preachable texts in the Bible. While records remain of the impression made by the first two,[64] the others exist today in their full form.

The preaching textbook in question was the *Traité de la composition d'un sermon*, written by Jean Claude in 1688 and translated into English by Robert Robinson, a Baptist minister in Cambridge shortly before the incumbency of Simeon at Holy Trinity.[65] Simeon, however, did not come across the book until he had already been preaching for some years, during the first seven of which he was apparently without any sense of how sermons work. By the time he read Claude, though, he had learned enough to recognize in the work of the Frenchman a systematic presentation of an understanding very similar to his own. He made it the basis of his sermon classes and finally included it as an appendix to his twenty-one volumes of sermon outlines.[66] He called his version of Claude "an improved edition of a translation," which is to say that he found Robinson's violently antiestablishment introduction and notes offensive. Nor was he entirely satisfied with the work of Claude himself, believing that not all the examples of his principles taken from sermons of the

Frenchman were entirely accurate and offering some of his own in their place.

Scholars who are more interested in Simeon than they are in the history of preaching are inclined to give both Claude and Simeon more credit for originality than they are strictly entitled to. First, they fail to recognize that Claude came toward the end of the neoclassical movement in France and that he tended to epitomize the particular development of Protestant homiletics in that movement, a development that had more in common with Roman Catholic preaching at the time than might be expected. Second, as the term "neoclassical" implies, the movement was an effort to apply the insights of Greco-Roman rhetoricians to homiletics. For instance, in the introduction to a selection of sermon outlines from *Horae Homileticae,* James M. Houston says, "Simeon had . . . not two but three aims in his preaching: to instruct, to please, and to affect his audience,"[67] failing to recognize in this list Cicero's enumeration of the *officia* of the orator *(reddere auditores benevolos, attentos, dociles)* as that had been adapted to preaching by Augustine in *De doctrina christiana.* Even more amazing is Hugh Evan Hopkins's conclusion that Claude's conviction that a sermon should be composed of three parts, an introduction, discussion, and conclusion, "was in fact largely original" with Simeon.[68]

The basic sermon pattern advocated by Claude and Simeon has been spelled out by Peter Bayley:

> After the reading of the text, he begins with a general exordium which sometimes discusses the sacred author, sometimes the circumstances in which the sermon is being preached, and sometimes more abstract topics. This is followed by a close examination of the text, its historical background, its context in the book from which it is taken, and the difficulties raised by its language. This is often the place for a display of etymological scholarship. Then comes the *propositio* or division, almost always into three points. The body of the sermon is followed by a sort of extended peroration often entitled "Applications" or "Enseignements et consolations." . . . It is to this model that the majority of the Protestant preachers in the second half of our period approximate. . . . It was, as the sermons of Jean Claude show, to remain the model for many decades.[69]

The basic differences between this type of preaching and the sermon form of the latitudinarians are differences between French and English preaching, summarized in such statements as: "The 'inflamed orations' of the French preachers were no doubt less suited to the English genius than 'the sober reasonings' of British divines."[70] But Evangelistic preaching necessarily calls for more feeling than that of rationalists like Tillotson. What distinguishes the Claude-Simeon method from that of Wesley, however, is that the former is more exegetical and less topical, allowing the sermon's structure to be determined by the text. Yet the form is not simply exegesis.

> Some say, preaching is designed only to make Scripture understood . . . but this is a mistake; for preaching is not only intended to give the sense of Scripture, but also of theology in general; and, in short, to explain the whole of religion.[71]

These transchannel collaborators do insist, however, that the sermon should clearly and purely explain a text and that the sermon should give the entire sense of the whole text.[72] What is most distinctive about their method is the four methods they have of developing the sermon so that it succeeds in giving the entire sense of the text. The first method, *discussion*, as the body of the sermon is called, is by way of explication, in which everything in the text that needs to be explained is explained. The second is by way of *observation*, involving many of the *topoi* of classical rhetoric: from species to genus or vice versa; the diverse characters of something; the relation of one subject to another; the person speaking or acting; time, place, person addressed; and so on, through twenty-seven areas of observation. Explication and observation are called textuary ways of preaching because they keep to the text. That is not true of discussion by *continual or perpetual application* or by *propositions*. The first moves directly from the teaching of the text to the lives of the congregation, while the second reduces the text to between two and four propositions that have mutual dependence and connection.[73]

Simeon recognized that beginning preachers would have difficulty in applying all these principles to the composition of their own sermons. He wished to preserve them from the habit of the time of repreaching the sermons of others, so he tried to provide them with an intermediate alternative, that of preparing sermons following outlines (or "skeletons," as he called them) written by him until they developed sufficient skill to write their own. His collection of these, which began with the publication of 100 in 1796, continually grew until the full edition of *Horae Homileticae* contained 2,536 outlines on what were regarded as all the preachable texts of the Bible. "If one were to read a single sermon a day, it would take seven years to get through them all."[74]

Since the total work went through eight editions within sixteen years, it must have been a success. Indeed, Hopkins notes that Simeon's profits from the sale of the work (all of which he gave to evangelical causes) would amount in time to twice what James Boswell ever received for his famous account of the life of Samuel Johnson.[75] As everyone knows, however, buying a book is not the same as reading it and following its instructions.

> In consequence, Victorian dust collected upon the one and twenty volumes of the *Horae Homileticae*: and Anglican preachers of a later generation forsook the formal intricacies of the Claudian system in favour of a simpler method which had developed naturally under the influence of Tillotson, and which had never been abandoned. This method consisted in the division, not of the text, but of the sermon, into two or three, or at most into four or five, main heads.[76]

Thus, if one is to look for the influence of Charles Simeon on Anglican Evangelical preaching, it will not be so much in the particular method he taught. Nor will it be subsumed into the general preaching of the Evangelical Awakening in England, since the Evangelicals of the established church did not preach in fields, itinerate, or conduct revivals. Most of their preaching was to people who were already baptized and who had come to church on Sunday for an ordinary Prayer Book service. More than anywhere else, Simeon's influence on Anglican Evangelical preaching will be found in the sincerity of the converted man who knew the joy of being a saved sinner and who devoted his life to seeing that as many others as possible would have the same experience. Simeon himself preached in a church crowded with townspeople and undergraduates, whom he inspired to seek the same awareness he had of divine grace poured out efficaciously in one's own behalf. From there the influence went out over all England and the world.

BRINGING THE AWAKENING INDOORS: THE PREACHING OF CHARLES HADDON SPURGEON

The next stage of the religion of the heart movement in British preaching can be seen as a combination of the sort of mass evangelism characteristic of the Methodist revival (Wesleyan and Calvinist) with a parochial base as favored by the Anglican Evangelicals. A church became the site of a revival, and the masses flocked to it instead of having the preacher come to them. Since the preacher himself was one of the extraordinary geniuses who appear from time to time in the history of preaching, it could be thought that discussion of his work does not belong to a narrative more concerned with movements than individuals. Yet it is true that movements are often begun by and summed up in particular preachers and that these preachers are thus determinative for much that is to follow. Such is the case of Charles Haddon Spurgeon.

The basic facts of Spurgeon's life can be told quickly. Born in Essex in 1834 into a working-class family that produced a number of Dissenting clergy, he grew up as a physically awkward child who did well at his books and acquired a precocious taste for John Bunyan and other Puritan writers. As a youth, he was oppressed with such a sense of sin that he began a systematic search for a church and preacher to relieve him of his burden and give him assurance of pardon. His goal was achieved on a Sunday morning in January of his fifteenth year in a Primitive Methodist chapel in Colchester, where he heard a lay preacher expound on Isaiah 45:22: "Look unto me, and be ye saved, all the ends of the earth" (KJV).

Being convinced, however, that only believers should be baptized, he joined a Baptist church. He then secured employment as an usher (assistant teacher) in a Cambridge academy and began to engage in a vigorous program of Sunday school teaching, visitation, and tract distribution.[77] Next he involved himself in the work of the Lay Preachers Association, and served as the pastor of the little chapel at Waterbeach for two years. He remained a lay preacher all his life, refusing ordination and eschewing the title of "Reverend." The little congregation grew under his leadership to four hundred members, and there were other improvements in the community.

The reputation of the "boy preacher" grew so much that he was called to be pastor of New Park Street Baptist Church, which had been a major congregation in London but had diminished because of a changing neighborhood. Even at that, it was an extraordinary invitation for someone who was only nineteen. He remained with the same congregation the rest of his life, forcing it constantly to expand its seating capacity, moving temporarily to music halls or other locations while remodeling was going on, until finally it was necessary to build the Metropolitan Tabernacle which could hold, standees included, almost six thousand people—and Spurgeon filled it twice on Sundays for thirty years. It has been estimated that no other English preacher has been heard in a church building by so many people.

Spurgeon in Action

While he had many other remarkable accomplishments, Spurgeon's importance for the history of preaching lies in three areas: his live preaching to congregations, his published sermons, and his lectures on homiletics. To imagine Spurgeon preaching in his prime is to think of him at the Metropolitan Tabernacle.[78] Although the exterior of the building was Greek Revival, the interior had the form of a long oval given to it by a lower and an upper balcony, both supported by columns rising from the floor and extending just behind their front railings to an architrave above that supported the vaulted ceiling. The pews faced the baptistery, which was set off by rails in front that curved at the sides and ascended to the first balcony level as guards for a flight of stairs on each side. The staircases led up to a platform that projected with a semicircular floor surmounted by a smaller semicircle at its center. The inside stair rails continued and joined in front of the platform. To the left of the smaller semi-circle was a table on which a Bible rested.

Imagine all five thousand–plus seats filled and all faces looking toward the semicircular platform at the level of the first balcony, because it was from there that Spurgeon preached in a voice that could be clearly heard by all. The tabernacle had no pulpit because Spurgeon hated pulpits, considering them too confining to permit graceful gesture. The second series of *Lectures to My Students* includes woodcuts contrasting "Paul Preaching at Athens" in the open air with free movement to "The Very Reverend Dr. Paul Preaching in London," which depicts the apostle hedged in by a pulpit that came up over his elbows, with a cushion in front and gas lamps level with the lower part of his face on either side.[79]

This is not to say that Spurgeon strutted and strode like some televangelists today; he had no desire to be compared to "the polar bear, at the Zoological Gardens, which for ever goes backwards and forwards in its den."[80] He just wanted to be unfettered when he proclaimed the Word. He sought a golden mean between excess and woodenness in gesture, following the principles of the elocutionary movement. Photographs and caricatures often showed him with an upper arm extended straight out to the side and parallel to the floor, while the forearm reached up at a right angle, the forefinger pointing to heaven.

Spurgeon had almost certainly prayed the pastoral prayer, involving the congregation in the petitions that he had already been earnestly offering in private. On the table he would have at most an outline of his points and subpoints. He had written that only the night before, although he had been thinking all week about his topic, studying it, setting secretaries to look up information for him. On Saturday afternoon he'd had friends in to tea and then excused himself early to go to his final preparation. That began with choosing the best text to preach from in order to convey the message he had in mind. That done, he would work up an outline. Or, rather, he would usually work up a number of outlines, until he finally found the way of most tellingly and effectively saying what was on his heart. He then would have his wife read to him from various commentaries on the passage from which his text was taken.

Apparently that was all it took to enable him to be fluent in speech the next morning. His words, as they have been transcribed, seem to have come cascading from his mouth; semicolons dot the page, suggesting a cumulative force of urgency in the words that tumble forth, yet each of the words (sturdy Anglo-Saxon words; no Latinisms here) seems as carefully chosen as though a manuscript had been labored over for months. And never does the rush obscure the meaning. The skeleton of the sermon is always visible. Each point or subpoint is illustrated by an anecdote, a quotation, an analogy or metaphor that renders the principle in utter clarity. Even though the message has an eschatological seriousness, there is also time for joy and humor. One could even speak of a breeziness about the enterprise. Finally, at the end comes the invitation, communicated with all the pathos and power of one who believes completely in the reality of the salvation he is offering and in the effectiveness of the means he is extending to his hearers to enable them to experience that reality. There is almost always at least one conversion, and usually there are more.

Then, as now, people had diametrically opposed opinions about the quality of his preaching. Many of the objections were simply to popular preaching as such, to someone more interested in getting the message across than in the decorum with which that is done. Clergy of all denominations, including his own, had vitriolic things to say about him, some undoubtedly in envy of his widespread appeal. For a while, most newspapers pilloried him.[81] Echoing their spirit over a century later are the words of a British poet and literary critic who recently lectured at Cambridge on nonconformist literature:

> Spurgeon's vulgarities led him to misinterpret both the Scriptural text and Scriptural doctrine, and to let his exhortatory didacticism swamp out the sacramental aspects of worship. . . . In any case, it is plain that from a standpoint concerned with the cultural implications of English Dissent, Spurgeon's ministry, and the influence he exerted, were disastrous.[82]

In marked contrast is the advice given by the famous post–World War II pastor and theologian of Heidelberg, Helmut Thielicke:

> I am almost tempted to shout out to those who are serving the eternal
> Word as preachers, and to those who are preparing to do so, in what I
> hope will be a productive hyperbole: Sell all that you have (not least of
> all some of your stock of current sermonic literature) and buy Spurgeon
> (even if you have to grub through the second-hand bookstores).[83]

These words have been quoted often enough to become a cliché. What is
not said nearly so often is where they appear: at the end of the introduction to a volume published by Thielicke and composed of selections from
Lectures to My Students plus a couple of Spurgeon's sermons. Which is
to say that Thielicke thought enough of his advice to make it possible for
people to follow it.[84]

About the only response to these differences of opinion that can
advance beyond remarks of the *de gustibus* ilk is to notice Lewis
Drummond's efforts to account for the popularity of Spurgeon's preaching in terms of its being in service of a revival sent by the Holy Spirit.[85]
People will respond to Spurgeon's preaching in the way that they respond
to the idea of such revivals. Everything from his Calvinism and absolute
conviction that souls will be eternally damned or saved on the basis of
whether they have undergone a conversion experience or not, to his use
of language that working-class and poor people can understand and
respond to, is to be assessed upon the basis of whether one believes that
a basic dynamic of God's relation with human beings is the sending of
periodic revivals. This is to say that the judgment is theological rather
than aesthetic or merely homiletic. In any case, there is no doubt that he
was popular and effective. The membership of his congregation in
London grew from 313 when he arrived in 1854, to a peak of 5,427 in
1882.

Publish Glad Tidings

Beyond the growth of his own congregation and even the effects upon
countless visitors of hearing him preach is the impact of Spurgeon's
printed sermons. There must be few preachers in history who have published so many different sermons in so many copies. During his second
year in London, a publisher began to print one of Spurgeon's sermons
each week and continued that practice until long after Spurgeon's death,
up until World War I. These weekly "Penny Pulpit" sermons were annually collected into a book, resulting in six volumes of *The New Park
Street Pulpit* and fifty-seven of *The Metropolitan Tabernacle Pulpit*, each
of which contains between fifty-two and sixty sermons. That brings the
total number of sermons published to around thirty-five hundred. For

many years, the average press run of the weekly sermon was twenty-five thousand. Over the years, the number of copies of individual Penny Pulpit sermons published totaled more than one hundred million.[86] This, of course, does not count the bound volumes, the other collections, the American newspaper publication of weekly sermons, or the translations into as many as twenty-three languages.

There are enough stories of people being converted through reading one of Spurgeon's sermons to constitute a *Gattung* for form critics to analyze. Yet the influence of the sermons is wider yet, for one must consider the number of clergy who have imitated the sermons' style in their own preaching or quoted from them—or preached them as their own. Drummond even has a story of Spurgeon himself being helped by one when he was suffering from one of his bouts of depression and wandered into a small church, where he heard the preacher delivering a Spurgeon sermon.[87] It seems safe to say that no other preacher's sermons in history have been read by so many people. And they are still in print. Even as these words are being written, catalogs offer a ten-volume set of 250.

A Teacher of Preachers

Finally, Spurgeon's influence on preaching was exercised through his lectures on homiletics. These had an impact not only on the hundreds of students who heard Spurgeon deliver them in his Friday afternoon visits to the Pastors' College of the Metropolitan Tabernacle, but on the half million people who have purchased copies of *Lectures to My Students* as well. The lectures were published in three series. The first begins with several talks on the spiritual condition of the preacher: He should practice what he preaches. He should have the call to preach, which includes physical as well as spiritual qualifications (e.g., having a chest wide enough to have lung power).[88] Next follows a treatment of the necessity of the preacher's life of private prayer and advice on leading public prayer.

Then Spurgeon shifts to preaching itself, beginning with the content of the sermon. Since he outlined so meticulously himself, it is surprising that the only advice he gives on the subject is that "our matter should be well arranged according to the true rules of mental architecture" (1:80). After that comes a section on how to choose a text to preach upon, which is virtually the same as choosing the subject of a sermon. While it is not surprising that he does not favor following the lectionary (on which he says Church of England sermons were based at the time [1:87]), it is more so that he does not favor course preaching either (1:99-101).

The treatment of the chosen text is dealt with to the extent of saying that occasionally it is permissible to spiritualize it—an admission that horrified many of his contemporaries. Then comes an excellent little section of what may be called the stewardship of the preacher's voice, which is followed by words from a master of the subject on how to get and hold attention and by techniques for acquiring the ability to speak impromptu on the rare occasions when it is necessary and therefore to be allowed.

"The Minister's Fainting Fits" is a touching presentation of the incidence of depression among clergy by one who himself suffered grievously from it. The first series then concludes with notice of how one's preaching ministry carries over into conversations with parishioners and seekers, and a lecture on how preachers who cannot afford one can get by without a large library—a sensitive empathy from a man who had a personal collection of twelve thousand volumes.

The second series of lectures also begins with spirituality, including the necessity of commitment to the truth of the gospel, before going on to deal with the history and value of open-air preaching and then with body language in preaching. In the two lectures on the latter subject, Spurgeon is at the top of his form, caricaturing formalists on the one hand and ranters on the other. To be certain that the point gets across, he even commissioned woodcut illustrations, showing such monstrosities as the preacher who looks like he is boxing or hammering, or whose arms perform the motions of a whirligig. Then, to offer a positive example, he includes several pages of illustrations from that classic of the elocutionary movement, Austin's *Chironomia* (2:137-43). There follows another lecture on spirituality and one on pastoral discretion, followed by a reminder that the conversion of sinners is the aim of preaching, which purpose is to be achieved by preaching the basic doctrines of Calvinism in the manner that the president of Pastors' College details. (For the text of the lecture on conversion, **see Vol. 2, pp. 366-79.**)

The third series of lectures, devoted to illustration, will probably disappoint most modern readers, being occupied as most of it is with Spurgeon's assessment of Puritan and contemporary encyclopedias of support material as quarries for preachers. Of more use to most will be the study of the other lectures to see how Spurgeon himself went about making certain that his meaning would be inescapable. A brilliant case in point is the lecture "Illustrations in Preaching," which is organized by a sustained metaphor: illustrations as the windows of sermons (3:1-14).

When one asks what religion of the heart preaching looked like in the last half of the nineteenth century, no better answer can be given than to point to the "boy preacher" who captivated London and the world by the power of his own preaching, both orally and in printed transcripts, and who tried to show other pulpit fledglings how he went about doing what he did. None of those who followed commanded so large a hearing, but it is doubtful that any in his tradition ever went into the pulpit without carrying with him echoes of Spurgeon. He had shown his generation and several to follow what it meant to preach a revival in one's own congregation.

This account of preaching movements emphasizing affective involvement, which grew up along with and in response to many of the same conditions as rationalist preaching, has traced its development for two hundred years. Any stopping point is arbitrary. The Moody-Sankey revival, which Spurgeon favored, is worth noting but will be considered in the treatment of American evangelical preaching. The Salvation Army developed their own methods for bringing the gospel to the attention of the poorest of the urban poor, but their homiletical tradition was too oral to leave much in the way of written records.

Yet there is a sense that the movement has tamed. While Spurgeon drew many thousands, he drew them to a building. As much as he advocated open-air preaching and even practiced it on occasion, his chief concern seems to have been with his congregation. Nor do we hear of the converts at the Metropolitan Tabernacle being torn by paroxysms of emotion. We are told of no one who yelled, leaped, rolled on the ground, or fainted. Everything appears to have been in good taste; a bourgeois decorum was observed. One almost gets the impression that religion of the heart had evolved from emotion to sentimentality.

Much has changed in the two centuries from the Restoration to the time of Victoria. The next chapter deals with religion of the heart preaching in America, and the two following chapters look at side effects of that preaching. Then it will be time to see that religion of the heart had other manifestations, manifestations not so much of sentimentality as of sentiment. That will call for a survey of the effect of the Romantic movement on preaching.

FOR FURTHER READING

Campbell, Ted A. *The Religion of the Heart: A Study of European Religious Life in the Seventeenth and Eighteenth Centuries.* Columbia: University of South Carolina Press, 1991.

Hopkins, Hugh Evan. *Charles Simeon of Cambridge.* Grand Rapids, Mich.: Eerdmans, 1977.

Select Sermons of George Whitefield, With an Account of His Life by J. C. Ryle. Edinburgh: Banner of Truth Trust, 1958.

Spurgeon, C. H. *Lectures to My Students: Addresses Delivered to the Students of the Pastors' College, Metropolitan Tabernacle.* One-volume edition of the first, second, and third series published in London, 1875–94. Grand Rapids, Mich.: Baker, 1977.

Stout, Harry S. *The Divine Dramatist: George Whitefield and the Rise of Modern Evangelicalism.* Grand Rapids, Mich.: Eerdmans, 1991.

The Works of John Wesley: Volume 1: Sermons I. Edited with introduction by Albert C. Outler. The Bicentennial Edition of the Works of John Wesley. Nashville: Abingdon, 1984.

Thielicke, Helmut J. *Encounter with Spurgeon.* Translated by John W. Doberstein. Philadelphia: Fortress, 1963.

Notes

1. Speaking of these movements as responses to historical situations is in no way intended to preclude other levels of description, including the theological. There is some sense in which Christians have to regard at least some of them as providential, the work of the Holy Spirit. Divine causation, however, is not susceptible to empirical observation and thus not a factor in historical explanation as such.

2. What follows is based upon Ted A. Campbell, *The Religion of the Heart: A Study of European Religious Life in the Seventeenth and Eighteenth Centuries* (Columbia: University of South Carolina Press, 1991).

3. In his tracing of the synchronicity of these movements, Ted Campbell has noted that in addition to their emphasis on the feeling element in religion, they had four concomitant traits, traits that do not define the movements but do show their similarity. These include: "the phenomena of religious excitation, the threats posed to them by sectarianism and mysticism, the leadership roles exercised by women, and their offering of a cultural parallel to the Enlightenment" (ibid., 173-76, with this summary passage on the last of these pages). His explanation of why so many groups should turn to the cultivation of affective piety at the same time is that in each church there were those who were "disgusted with what corporate Christian states had done to one another since the Reformation (and) disillusioned with 'objective' appeals to scripture and tradition." In reaction, these "turned inwardly to a more individualistic and (in a certain sense) 'subjective' appropriation of the Christian faith" (ibid., 177).

4. He has already been encountered as the author of the most influential Puritan homiletics textbook, *The Arte of Prophesying.* See above, p. 365.

5. Campbell, *The Religion of the Heart*, 44-53. The *ordo salutis* was to become one of the most important topics in evangelical theology, and strategies of evangelistic preaching were framed on the basis of theories about that order.

6. Ibid., 53-57.

7. Quoted by Derec Llwyd Morgan, *The Great Awakening in Wales*, trans.

Dyfnallt Morgan (London: Epworth, 1988), 23, from Harris's *Selected Trevecka Letters,* ed. G. M. Roberts (Caernarfon, 1956–62), 1:81. Morgan's book is the fullest treatment of the Welsh revival in English.

8. In the year that he was president of the Academy of Homiletics, he shared his findings in his address (Toronto, 1983). Seven years later, at the twenty-fifth anniversary meeting of the academy at Princeton Theological Seminary on December 8, 1990, he repeated the lecture. The report above is based on the tape recorded by the Audio-Visuals Department of Princeton Theological Seminary. For the conventions of African American preaching, see below, pp. 529-31.

9. Lo, by the Merrimack WHITEFIELD stands
   In the temple that never was made by hands,
   Curtains of azure, and crystal wall,
   And dome of sunshine over all!
   A homeless pilgrim, with dubious name
   Blown about on the winds of fame;
   Now as an angel of blessing classed,
   And now as a mad enthusiast.

John Greenleaf Whittier, "The Preacher" (*The Complete Works of John Greenleaf Whittier,* Cambridge ed. [Boston: Houghton Mifflin, 1894], 69-74. See specifically p. 71.

10. Whitefield was eventually to break with Harris after the latter fell so under the influence of Sidney Griffith as to occasion scandal. Harry S. Stout, *The Divine Dramatist: George Whitefield and the Rise of Modern Evangelicalism* (Grand Rapids, Mich.: Eerdmans, 1991), 221.

11. There is disagreement about the social status of the Whitefields. Stout sees his going to Oxford to study for the ministry to have been an effort on his part and that of his mother to reverse the declining social status of the family (ibid., 2-3, and passim). Arnold A. Dallimore, on the other hand, sees the family as one of Gloucester's more prominent families, in *George Whitefield: God's Anointed Servant in the Great Revival of the Eighteenth Century* (Westchester, Ill.: Crossway, 1990), 11. Opinion seems to vary on the basis of whether one approves or disapproves of Whitefield. The work of Dallimore cited is a condensation of a work of 1,200 pages from the same publisher, *George Whitefield: The Life and Times of the Great Evangelist of the Eighteenth-Century Revival* (1970–79), a work described by Stout as "filiopietistic" (i.e., hagiographic).

12. Campbell, *The Religion of the Heart,* 101.

13. The relatively few of his other sermons to be published were taken down and published by others. While some of these are poorly transcribed, probably the best indication of what Whitefield was like in his prime comes from *Eighteen Sermons . . . Taken Verbatim in Shorthand and Faithfully Transcribed by Joseph Gurney,* rev. Andrew Gifford (Newburyport: Edmund Blunt, 1797). This superiority is due in part to being a transcript of what was actually said rather than what was edited for publication, and in part to coming from near the end rather than the beginning of the preacher's career.

14. February 2 to December 8, 1738.

15. Stout, *The Divine Dramatist,* 84.

16. Ibid., 125.

17. Ibid., 252.

18. Joseph Beaumont Wakeley, *The Prince of Pulpit Orators* (New York: Carlton & Lanahan, 1871), 225-26. While Wakeley claims in his preface to use many sources that had not been available before, he does not cite them for particular anecdotes in this very anecdotal account.

19. Ibid.

20. As stated in note 27 of chapter 16.

21. Horton Davies, *From Watts and Wesley to Maurice, 1690–1850,* vol. 3 of *Worship and Theology in England* (Princeton: Princeton University Press, 1961), 162-63.

22. Quoted by Stout, *The Divine Dramatist,* 104, without citation.

23. For other efforts to account for the effectiveness of Whitefield's preaching, see not only those of Stout and Davies already referred to, but also that of Edwin Dargan, *A History of Preaching* (New York: Burt Franklin, 1968), 2:313-15; Edward S. Ninde, *George Whitefield: Prophet-Preacher* (New York: Abingdon, 1924), 161-79; and Clyde E. Fant Jr. and William M. Pinson Jr., eds., *20 Centuries of Great Preaching: An Encyclopedia of Preaching* (Waco, Tex.: Word, 1971), 3:111-16. The most complete edition of the sermons of Whitefield was published in 1771 in the last two of a six-volume set of his works. Oddly enough, they have not been much reprinted. The most available collection is *Select Sermons of George Whitefield, With an Account of His Life by J. C. Ryle* (Edinburgh: Banner of Truth Trust, 1958). For samples of the *Eighteen Sermons* transcribed in shorthand by Joseph Gurney and edited by Andrew Gifford, see Volume 2, chapter 17, and the Fant and Pinson volume.

24. The Society for the Propagation of the Gospel in Foreign Parts, an Anglican voluntary association for missions that sent out a high percentage of the priests who went to America.

25. *John Wesley,* ed. Albert C. Outler, Library of Protestant Thought (New York: Oxford University Press, 1964), 48.

26. Ibid., 17.

27. Ronald A. Knox, *Enthusiasm: A Chapter in the History of Religion* (Oxford: University Press, 1950), 427.

28. W. L. Doughty has published a volume called *John Wesley: Preacher* (London: Epworth, 1955), but since it is more anecdotal and hagiographic than analytical, it is not referred to in the discussion that follows.

29. Albert C. Outler, "Introduction" to *The Works of John Wesley: Vol. 1: Sermons I,* The Bicentennial Edition of the Works of John Wesley (Nashville: Abingdon, 1984), 14. While the sermons of Wesley have been published in many editions both during his lifetime and ever since, the Bicentennial Edition is the first critical edition ever published. Outler's edition, which draws on the textual work of Frank Baker, the first general editor of the series, runs to four volumes. A handy edition of the most important of these sermons is *John Wesley's Sermons: An Anthology,* ed. Albert C. Outler and Richard P. Heitzenrater (Nashville: Abingdon, 1991). Heitzenrater began as assistant editor in chief to Frank Baker for the Bicentennial Edition and now serves as general editor. Outler, a beloved teacher of the present

writer, entered the church expectant before the publication of this latter volume. *Requiescat in pace.*

30. Outler, "Introduction" to *The Works of John Wesley, Vol. 1: Sermons I,* 14.

31. Outler and Heitzenrater, *John Wesley's Sermons,* 371-80.

32. Ibid., 379-80.

33. Ibid., 380.

34. Ibid.

35. Davies, *From Watts and Wesley to Maurice,* 172. This is the closing sentence of a section that begins on p. 160 and that will repay in insight the energy spent reading.

36. In a letter written to John Chute on October 10, 1766. *Horace Walpole's Correspondence with John Chute et al.,* ed. W. S. Lewis et al., The Yale Edition of Horace Walpole's Correspondence, vol. 35 (New Haven: Yale University Press, 1973), 118-19.

37. These entries have been collected and reflected on by Knox in a chapter entitled "Wesley and the Religion of Experience," in *Enthusiasm,* 513-48.

38. It is important to recognize how much Wesley was a man of his time in his interest in all things scientific. His *Journals* have frequent reference to his curiosity about new inventions and, in general, how things work. He shares some of the optimism of his time that almost any skill can be reduced to written law on the basis of observation. "Experimental" has for him the double significance of efforts to gain such knowledge and reference to experience, especially religious experience. Without thinking that evangelism could be done with mechanistic determinism, he nevertheless thought that one could learn how things ought to be done.

39. *Minutes of Several Conversations between the Rev. Mr. Wesley and Others from the Year 1744, to the Year 1789.* The edition consulted was the Zondervan reprint of the Wesleyan Conference Office edition published in London in 1872, 8:299-338. Reference, however, will be made within the text by question rather than page number (e.g., Q. 2). The "Conversations" in question were Wesley's "Conferences" with his preachers, the beginning of that conspicuous feature of Methodist polity. The Methodist term for canon law is "discipline."

40. *The Art of Speaking in Publick: Or an Essay on the Action of an Orator as to His Pronunciation and Gesture* (1727); see Outler, "Introduction," 24. The edition of *Directions* consulted is the Zondervan, 13:518-27.

41. Here "jealousy" probably means "zealousness."

42. Keeping Methodism within the Church of England was one of the areas in which Wesley had the greatest difficulty imposing his will on the Methodists—although it must be admitted that he initiated many of the aspects of Methodist life that made the breach inevitable.

43. Deborah M. Valenze, *Prophetic Sons and Daughters: Female Preaching and Popular Religion in Industrial England* (Princeton: Princeton University Press, 1985). Valenze gives a fascinating account of a few women whom Wesley allowed to preach while he was alive and many more who became preachers in Methodist sects that withdrew from the Wesleyans after his death. Since, however, her interest is in the way their preaching was a form of resistance to social and economic change, she

understandably neglects providing the information about their preaching per se that would be such an enrichment to this history.

44. See Sermon 123, "On Knowing Christ After the Flesh," or Wesley's letter to Mary Bishop of October 18, 1778: "Let but a pert, self-sufficient animal, that has neither sense nor grace, bawl out something about Christ, or his blood, or justification by faith, and his hearers cry out, 'What a fine gospel sermon!' Surely the Methodists have not so learnt Christ. We know no gospel without salvation from sin." See Outler, "Introduction," 25.

45. That is, as prophet, priest, and king.

46. What follows is drawn from *Directions Concerning Pronunciation and Gesture* (Grand Rapids, Mich.: Zondervan), 13:518-27.

47. Ibid., 523.

48. Ibid., 526.

49. Ibid.

50. The influence of the elocutionary movement is to be seen in all of this.

51. *John Wesley*, ed. Albert C. Outler, vii.

52. Ibid., xi.

53. Knox, *Enthusiasm*, 447.

54. For the sources and formative influences of his thought see Outler, "Introduction," 66-96.

55. Ibid., 45.

56. Introductory comment on the Preface, *Sermons*, 1:103.

57. Ibid.

58. See above, p. 358.

59. Outler, "Introduction," 40. Cf. p. 55.

60. See above, pp. 392-414.

61. A group of wealthy evangelical families who lived in the London suburb of Clapham and attended the parish church where John Venn was rector. The best account is the memoir of James Stephen, who grew up in the group, in his *Essays in Ecclesiastical Biography*, Silver Library ed. (London: Longmans, Green & Co., 1907), 2:187-248. For the beginnings of the movement, see L. E. Elliott-Binns, *The Early Evangelicals: A Religious and Social Study* (London: Lutterworth, 1953). For the generation after the Clapham Sect, see Michael Hennell, *Sons of the Prophets: Evangelical Leaders of the Victorian Church* (London: SPCK, 1979). For the theological position of the Evangelicals in contrast to that of the Oxford movement, see Peter Toon, *Evangelical Theology 1833–1856: A Response to Tractarianism*, New Foundations Theological Library (Atlanta: John Knox, 1979).

62. Quoted in Hugh Evan Hopkins, *Charles Simeon of Cambridge* (Grand Rapids, Mich.: Eerdmans, 1977), 28, from a personal memoir quoted in William Carus, *Memoirs of the Life of the Rev. Charles Simeon* (London: Hatchard, 1847), 9.

63. Quoted in Hopkins, *Charles Simeon of Cambridge*, 118, from G. O. Trevelyan, *The Life and Letters of Lord Macaulay* (1876), 1:68 n. "Primate" in this context refers to the archbishop of either Canterbury or York.

64. Abner William Brown has left *Recollections of the Conversation Parties of the Rev. Charles Simeon, Senior Fellow of King's College, and Perpetual Curate of Trinity Church, Cambridge* (1863), which I have not seen. An impression of Simeon's

delivery can be formed from silhouettes cut out at the time that depict him expounding, imparting, acquiring, entreating, imploring, and concluding. These silhouettes, which are the property of King's College, are reproduced in the inside front cover of Hopkins, *Charles Simeon of Cambridge.*

65. John Claude, *An Essay on the Composition of a Sermon,* trans. with notes Robert Robinson, 2 vols. (London and Cambridge, 1778, 1779).

66. Charles Simeon, "Claude's Essay on the Composition of a Sermon," *Horae Homileticae, or Discourses Digested into One Continuous Series, and Forming a Commentary, Upon Every Book of The Old and New Testament,* 8th ed. (London: Henry G. Bohn, 1847), 21:287-435.

67. *Evangelical Preaching: An Anthology of Sermons by Charles Simeon,* ed. John M. Houston with intro. John R. W. Stott (Portland, Ore.: Multnomah, 1986), xvii.

68. Hopkins, *Charles Simeon of Cambridge,* 58.

69. Peter Bayley, *French Pulpit Oratory 1598–1650: A Study in Themes and Styles with a Descriptive Catalogue of Printed Texts* (Cambridge: Cambridge University Press, 1980), 110. More is said of Bayley's contribution in the section above on the preaching of the Catholic Reform, pp. 343-45.

70. Attributed to George Colman and Bonnell Thornton in Rolf P. Lessenich, *Elements of Pulpit Oratory in Eighteenth-Century England (1660–1800)* (Cologne and Vienna: Böhlau Verlag, 1972), 61. His treatment of the differences between the styles of French and English exordia, 60-64, has humor that may be unconscious. This same section indicates more knowledge of French rhetorical thought in England during this period than the observations of Charles Smyth, *The Art of Preaching: A Practical Survey of Preaching in the Church of England 747–1939* (London: SPCK; New York: Macmillan 1940), 181, seem to suggest. Yet Smyth speaks guardedly of "direct and significant influence upon the English pulpit." Hugh Blair showed detailed knowledge of the French literature in his textbook of rhetoric, *Lectures on Rhetoric and Belles Lettres,* that was published a little before Simeon's edition of Claude, but Blair was a Scot. For Blair, see the treatment of belletristic preaching in the discussion of the Romantic movement in preaching in chapter 22.

71. Simeon, "Claude's Essay on the Composition of a Sermon," 292.

72. Ibid., 294.

73. Ibid., 325-97. Simeon gives outlines of four sermons on the same text using each of these methods, pp. 411-27. An excellent summary of the Essay is given by Smyth, *The Art of Preaching,* 179-201.

74. John Stott, in "Introduction" to Houston, *Evangelical Preaching,* xxvii.

75. Hopkins, *Charles Simeon of Cambridge,* 60. Simeon's work, however, was much more than twice as long as Boswell's.

76. Smyth, *The Art of Preaching,* 201.

77. There he became a member of St. Andrew's Baptist Church, where Robert Robinson, the translator of Claude, had been pastor.

78. The following description of the Metropolitan Tabernacle is based on the remarkable collection of photographs in Craig Skinner's biography of Spurgeon's son Thomas, *Lamplighter and Son* (Nashville: Broadman, 1984), 120-57. Some of these are reproduced with better quality in Lewis A. Drummond, *Spurgeon: Prince of Preachers* (Grand Rapids, Mich.: Kregel, 1992). Skinner's Spurgeon scholarship is

also reflected in his article "The Preaching of Charles Haddon Spurgeon," *Baptist History and Heritage* 19 (1984): 16-26.

79. C. H. Spurgeon, *Lectures to My Students: Addresses Delivered to the Students of the Pastors' College, Metropolitan Tabernacle,* one-volume edition of the first, second, and third series published in London, 1875–94 (Grand Rapids, Mich.: Baker, 1977), 2:102-3.

80. Ibid., 2:109.

81. For many quotations from both clergy and the press, see Drummond, *Spurgeon,* 175-274. While this 895-page volume is the most complete source of information on Spurgeon, it has little critical distance on its subject, falling into the genre of hagiography. For the person who would like to search further, there is also the disadvantage that many interesting pieces of information and even quotations are undocumented.

82. Donald Davie, *A Gathered Church: The Literature of the English Dissenting Interest, 1700–1930* (New York: Oxford University Press, 1978), 89.

83. Helmut Thielicke, *Encounter with Spurgeon,* trans. John W. Doberstein (Philadelphia: Fortress, 1963), 45.

84. For praise of Spurgeon from an unexpected source, see the quotation from the leader of the Oxford movement, E. B. Pusey, in Drummond, *Spurgeon,* 320-21. Unfortunately, the admiration was not mutual. For Spurgeon's remarks about the followers of Pusey, see ibid., 492.

85. Drummond, *Spurgeon,* 258-74.

86. These figures are drawn from idid., 320-25.

87. Ibid., 328.

88. Spurgeon, *Lectures to My Students,* 1:34-35. Further references will be inserted parenthetically into the text with the volume number, a colon, and the page number(s).

CHAPTER 18

AMERICAN REVEILLE

THE PURITANS

The first distinctive American homiletical tradition was that of the Puritans—although, to be sure, this tradition had its origins in England.[1] Within it were both of the characteristic English responses to the challenge of early modernism, religion of the head and religion of the heart. Before it can be seen how these two impulses, which seemed so contrary to one another in England, were entwined in the colonies, however, something must be said about the distinctiveness of American Puritanism.

Puritanism as such lasted much longer in America than it did in England. In some sense, Puritanism as a movement ended in England with the Restoration in 1660. Before that time, it had largely been an effort within the established church to change its polity from episcopacy to a presbyterian structure and to pursue other goals of the Calvinist agenda, such as doing nothing in the church not explicitly called for in the Bible. When Puritanism was excluded from the established church in the Restoration settlement, it gained recognition as a tolerated form of dissent. Puritans and Independents became Nonconformists, forming Presbyterian, Congregationalist, and Baptist denominations. For the

Presbyterians and Congregationalists, at any rate, this soon led to a loss of much that had been distinctive about Puritan ethos. In New England, however, the basic pattern of thought and preaching lasted through the Revolution and into the beginning of the nineteenth century.

The Pilgrims landed at Plymouth Rock in 1620 and were soon followed by the Puritans at Massachusetts Bay, whose colony eventually absorbed that of their Pilgrim neighbors. Twenty thousand Puritans eventually migrated to what are now the states of Massachusetts and Connecticut. From the beginning they had their own theological emphases, which distinguished them from Puritans who remained in England.[2] First, while most of the English Puritans believed in a presbyterial polity, those who went to New England appear to have been Congregationalists all along.

That distinction means more than a difference in church government. The English Presbyterian Puritans were like other Anglicans in believing that all citizens should belong to the national church. Those who went to New England, however, thought of the church as a congregation of the elect. They wished to erase the distinction between the visible and invisible church by not extending the possibility of church membership to any but visible saints. To be eligible, a person had to be able to recite his or her story of conversion as a demonstration of election. Churches were formed by the saints in a local area covenanting with one another. The primary ecclesial reality was, therefore, not the holy church universal but a local congregation of those elected to salvation. The even more basic Christian reality was the individual soul predestined to salvation.

This does not mean, however, that those who could not demonstrate their election never darkened the meetinghouse door. Rather, it was assumed that all who immigrated to New England shared in the Puritan construction of reality and wished to be in the covenant. They were required to attend church and thus be exposed to the preaching through which election usually occurred. While they were not guaranteed election, they would nevertheless wish to be in position for it to occur if it were decreed.

So taken for granted was this desire of the not-yet-visibly-chosen that civil law required church attendance. Indeed, since right religious behavior and right behavior as citizens were considered to be obeying two aspects of the law of God, it was further agreed that only the saints, those capable of recognizing God's law, should be allowed to vote in civil elections. As unjust as this may appear to later generations that have different theories of the bases of civil law, it made sense to the New Englanders of the time, both the enfranchised and the disenfranchised.

Perry Miller says:

> The effort of the Massachusetts Bay Company to set up a due form of government both civil and ecclesiastical came ultimately to the one purpose of gathering men and women together in orderly congregations that they might sit under a "powerful" and a literate ministry, that they might hear the Word of God ... as it was expounded by that ministry.[3]

This shows how important preaching was in their whole scheme of things: the Puritans left England and endured the dangers of sea travel and the hardships of the frontier so that they could guarantee, as far as humanly possible, that the people in their community would be exposed to sermons preached as they ought to be. The reason they felt so strongly about this is an extension of the general Calvinist assumption that preaching was the most common medium through which election was effected.

Their expression of this belief, however, had a few refinements of the Puritans' own. These were functions of Puritan presuppositions about psychology on the one hand, and logic and rhetoric on the other. The psychology was of a faculty variety that could be traced ultimately back to Aristotle. The way the faculties operated has been succinctly and amusingly illustrated by Miller in this example of a man who sees a bear:

> So the bear, encountered in the wilderness, causes in the *eye* a phantasm of the bear, which is identified as belonging to the species bear in *common sense*, recognized as dangerous in *imagination*, associated with remembered dangers in *memory*, declared an object to be fled in *reason*, made the signal of command to the *will*, which then excites the *affection* of fear, which finally prompts the muscles of the legs to run.[4]

The importance of this psychology for the understanding of preaching grows out of the Puritan desire at one and the same time to preserve God's absolute sovereignty in election while making human beings, who are predestined to reprobation, responsible for their own damnation. While more is involved in that effort, the relevant aspects were in the assumption that all of the faculties had been distorted in the fall and that an effect of conversion was the restoration of the faculties to their Edenic accuracy. It is this restored capacity of the faculties that enables a person to accept the salvation extended in preaching. While God has to renew the faculties for them to be able to work aright, nevertheless, the one who rejects or accepts the gospel does so by the employment of all that person's faculties. The one who refuses to accept, therefore, does so naturally, and the results are that person's own fault and not something for which God is to be blamed.

The underlying assumptions are what caused the Puritans to decide preaching that can be an effective medium for election must appeal mainly to the faculties of reason and will. This insistence upon the conversions of both understanding and the will shows how intertwined religion of reason and religion of the heart were in Puritan thought.

Puritan understanding of what is meant by reason and will comes from the theories of Pierre Ramus. While the impact of Ramus's thought on the structure of English Puritan sermons was discussed above, more needs to be said of his system here. Briefly, his dialectic was an effort to simplify the logic of Aristotle. Ramus reduced logic to two, or, more accurately, three operations. The first, which he called *invention*, consisted of identifying the objects of thought and their relations. Confusingly to modern readers, he calls both the "things" and their relations "arguments." The second part of dialectic is *judgment*, which involves taking the arguments (things and their relations) discovered by invention and stating them propositionally as "axioms." Ideally and most often, these axioms will be self-evident propositions. When they are not so evident, however, difficulties are to be resolved by means of syllogisms. Finally, *method* (sometimes treated as a subdivision of judgment) disposes axioms in their best possible order.

Ramist logic was thought to be not the contrivance of a clever man, but the way the universe was constructed by God, which Ramus merely discerned. By this logic, all of the arts arrive at the true depiction of their subject matter and at the laws by which their operations are performed. While *truth* is one, a result of the fall is that humans can only discern it piecemeal as separate arts, but all the arts are consistent with one another, and not the smallest element of that consistency is the way their science is arrived at through the use of Ramist dialectic.

This is as true of rhetoric as it is of other arts. In fact, rhetoric was one of the disciplines most radically redefined by the Ramist system. Ramus saw no need for a special art for oral persuasion, assuming that all persuasion should be by the use of reason (i.e., Ramist logic). Thus the invention of Aristotelian rhetoric (discovering the available means of persuasion) and its disposition (finding the most effective sequence for a speech) should be coextensive with Ramist dialectical invention, judgment, and method. Ramus also saw no need for treating *memory* as a separate part of rhetoric. All that was left as a subject matter proper to rhetoric was *style* (*elocutio*: figures of thought and speech) and *delivery*. Ramus's friend Omer Talon wrote the handbook of rhetoric, which perfectly incorporated Ramus's theories and came to have almost the status of revelation among the Puritans. The specifically homiletical implications of Ramism were worked out by William Perkins in *The Arte of Prophesying.*[5]

Preaching theory built on the foundations of Ramus, Talon, and Perkins was quite consistent with Puritan understanding of the way preaching was the ordinary means through which election occurred. Both reason and the will needed to be converted. Reason that has been restored by election recognizes the truth of axioms derived by Ramist judgment from the arguments it invented. The will is moved by the tropes and schemata recognized by Ramist rhetoric. These are not ornament for the sake of ornament; there is here no "carnall eloquence" from a "blubber-lipt Ministry."[6] Rather, the purpose of figures (mostly metaphors) is to humble sinners by helping them feel the extent to which they deserve damnation.[7]

The exclusion of useless ornamentation is extended to exordia and perorations, introductions and conclusions. All that is necessary or even appropriate is a succession of axioms disposed in their natural order. This is not to say, of course, that the sermon does not have parts. It begins with the "opening" of the text, which generally consists of taking the figurative statements of Holy Scripture and translating them into the literal language of Ramist self-evident axioms. These are *doctrines,* for which there must be *proofs,* which are either (1) parallel biblical passages or principles of systematic theology, (2) principles in nature, universal rules, or (3) common experience and sense. With this establishment of doctrines as sound, it remains only to show their relevance to the life of the congregation, their *uses.*

It is in uses that the will is moved through the appropriate figures. While the basic use was to be the means through which those predestined to salvation were elected, a variety of application types were made. William Ames, who played Elisha to Perkins's Elijah, listed as the main types:

> information in proving a truth; refutation in confuting error; instruction in demonstrating a life to be followed; correction in condemning a life to be shunned; consolation to remove or mitigate grief or fear; exhortation to start or strengthen an inward virtue; and admonition to correct a vice.[8]

Such was the homiletical diet of the Puritans. And it is doubtful that many other groups in history have been so systematically stuffed.

Twice on Sunday and often once during the week, every minister in New England delivered sermons lasting between one and two hours in length. . . . The average weekly churchgoer in New England (and there were far more churchgoers than church members) listened to something like seven thousand sermons in a lifetime, totaling somewhere around fifteen thousand hours of concentrated listening.[9]

Because of the quantity of preaching to which the average New Englander listened in a lifetime, and because no other opinion-shaping medium came even close to rivaling this saturation, Harry S. Stout has argued that sermons were the most important influence on the way reality was constructed socially among the Puritans:

Unlike modern mass media, the sermon stood alone in local New England contexts as the only regular (at least weekly) medium of public communication. As a channel of communication, it combined religious, educational, and journalistic functions, and supplied all the key terms necessary to understand existence in this world and the next. As the only event in public assembly that regularly brought the entire community together, it also represented the central ritual of social order and control.[10]

Because he sees preaching to have been so influential in the lives of the settlers in Massachusetts and Connecticut, Stout is eager to correct what he considers to be a misunderstanding on the part of many scholars about the persistence of Puritan theology's great themes in that preaching. A similar misunderstanding exists of the results of the Reforming Synod convoked in 1679.

Historians from Perry Miller onward have emphasized the reformers' concern with external civil reform and "outward" ritual to the virtual exclusion of their pietistic concern with covenant renewal and revival. From this one-sided examination, they have concluded that the synod's "preoccupation" with external morality signaled a dilution of Puritan thought and piety; having lost their parents' piety, the children settled for outward shows of morality that preserved the husk of religiosity without the nourishing kernel of inner spirituality.[11]

Most such studies are concerned with trying to find the roots of the radical resistance and violence that prompted New Englanders, along with other American colonists, to revolt against the English Crown. The offered explanations include secular "republicanism," "civil millennialism," and class-conscious "popular ideology."[12]

475

The studies all suffer, however, from the way they have used evidence from sermons to support their arguments. In doing so, they have assumed that the published sermons were the more influential. Stout points out, however, that 85 percent of the sermons published were weekday "occasional" sermons. Yet the regular Sunday sermons were the steady homiletical diet of the people and much more influential than the considerably less frequent weekday sermons that appeared in print.[13] In order to see whether there was any such falling away as has been suggested, it would be necessary to study the manuscripts of ordinary Sunday sermons rather than the published occasional sermons.

Stout himself spent nine years reading more than two thousand Sunday sermons in manuscript form. In doing so, he discovered that the sermons offered little support for previous interpretations of New England culture made on the basis of sermons. For example, he discovered no shift from piety to moralism, no "decline" or subsequent "secularization" of Puritanism. From the landing of the *Mayflower* through the Revolution, the regular Sunday sermons continued to be about the great classical themes of Calvinist Christianity: sin, salvation, and service.

Stout's thesis is that other historians have misunderstood the occasional sermons. They assumed that the published sermons were the most "successful," the most representative of the way public attitudes were developing. He argues that these sermons should instead be understood as variations on the themes of the much more frequent and normative regular Sunday sermons. The basic categories for understanding human existence in general, and covenant experience in New England in particular, were set forth on Sunday. The details were worked out in the occasional sermons when principles were applied to particular circumstances.

A natural disaster, for instance, would indicate that God was angry because the people had been unfaithful. A fast would then be called so the unfaithfulness that accounted for the disaster could be specified and the people could repent, following which the hand of God would be turned.[14] Thus such sermons were preoccupied with external events and issues of morality. When these are the only sermons read by historians, it is not surprising that they assume faith was being replaced by morality and religious explanation was giving way to secular interpretation. If, however, occasional sermons are seen in the perspective of the more massive regular preaching that never departed from the basic themes of Calvinism, they are revealed to document the continuing appeal of Puritanism rather than to bring it into question.

Stout divides preachers into five "generations" based on when they graduated from college, and names the generations after the five divisions of classical rhetoric:

> *Inventio*—"Invention," discovering what to say, 1620–65
> *Dispositio*—Arrangement, 1666–1700
> *Elocutio*—Style, 1701–30
> *Pronuntiatio*—Delivery, 1731–63
> *Memoria*—Memory, 1764–76[15]

As artificial as this sounds, it works astonishingly well as a device for characterizing the issues of the various periods.

It was in the first generation, for instance, that the "founders" developed the basic covenantal theology of this "special people." The second generation worked out the details of what this would look like in practice by instituting such things as the "Halfway Covenant" and the various forms of occasional preaching, as well as founding Harvard College to prepare new preachers. They showed their adaptability in relating the founders' covenantal theology to new situations ranging from King Philip's War to the decline of clerical social status. The third generation was a time of Anglicization when influence of the neoclassical preaching style was felt—and even a dab of latitudinarian thought, which, however, never compromised Calvinist orthodoxy. The period of the Great Awakening was a time of controversies over delivery, whether one preached in the polished neoclassical manner or followed the impromptu method of George Whitefield. Finally, it was precisely the memory of the founders' theology that enabled preachers on the eve of the Revolution to justify opposition to the English Crown through appeals to the parallels between threats to the covenant people of the Old Testament and to those in New England.[16]

A study of New England preaching that overlaps the periods surveyed by Stout and goes beyond, *The Art of Prophesying: New England Sermons and the Shaping of Belief* by Teresa Toulouse,[17] is valuable for showing how much variety there can be in sermons constructed according to the same theory and structure. The theory and structure she studies is the classic for English and American Puritans, that enunciated by William Perkins in *The Arte of Prophesying*. She shows that Perkins himself used it as a way of preparing those who had not yet become aware of their election to receive assurance of it. John Cotton, however, who was of the generation of the founders in New England, used it to reassure those who had already become aware of their election. And Benjamin Colman, of the generation of style that brought the influence of Tillotson back to New England from London, was able to preserve the Perkins form and Calvin's theology in a way that nevertheless undercut the whole Puritan system.

Toulouse's analysis of the preaching of Channing and Emerson will be drawn on below. For now, it is enough to note the perspective her analysis gives on Stout's thesis. One could almost reverse the old French proverb and say that the more Puritan preaching remained the same, the more it changed. Before the Revolution, this can be seen in the Old Light/New Light controversy, and afterward, the extent of the change can be discerned in the Unitarian reaction.

JONATHAN EDWARDS AND THE GREAT AWAKENING

The preacher under whom the Great Awakening was inaugurated, Jonathan Edwards, was a loyal follower of the Perkins sermon form. While, as seen above, the preacher with whom the Awakening is most associated is George Whitefield,[18] the one under whose preaching it began was very different in both preaching style and approach. Enough was said about Whitefield in the discussion of the Evangelical Awakening in Britain. Even though Edwards shared Whitefield's Calvinism, the two of them were even more different in their preaching styles than were Whitefield and Wesley. Whitefield preached in an evangelical adaptation of the neoclassical style, while Edwards was loyal to Perkins's form. Whitefield was one of the most dramatic preachers of all time and Edwards one of the most staid.[19]

This makes it even more ironic that at least in the Anglo-American revival tradition, it was Edwards who seems to have popularized "hell-fire and damnation" preaching and justified it theologically.[20] The primary association with Edwards in the minds of most products of American schools is his sermon "Sinners in the Hands of an Angry God." A reaction to that sermon that is atypical only in the charm of its expression is Phyllis McGinley's poem "The Theology of Jonathan Edwards":

> Whenever Mr. Edwards spake
>   In church about Damnation,
> The very benches used to quake,
>   For awful agitation.
>
> Good men would pale and roll their eyes
>   While sinners rent their garments

478

To hear him so anatomize
  Hell's orgiastic torments,

The blood, the flames, the agonies
  In store for frail or flighty
New Englanders who did not please
  A whimsical Almighty.

Times were considered out of tune
  When half a dozen nervous
Female parishioners did not swoon
  At every Sunday service;

And, if they had been taught aright,
  Small children, carried bedwards,
Would shudder lest they meet that night
  The God of Mr. Edwards.

Abraham's God, the Wrathful One,
  Intolerant of error—
Not God the Father or the Son
  But God the Holy Terror.[21]

Such an attitude represents a cultural lag in what Henry F. May calls "the nineteenth century revulsion against Edwards as a cruel monster, dangerous because of his great talents." Or maybe it is what May calls the twentieth-century tendency to patronize Edwards.[22]

All things considered, though, Jonathan Edwards seems an odd person to have introduced this innovation in homiletical theory and practice. He was, after all, "the most astute American philosopher up to the time of Charles Pierce," in the opinion of the Dominican scholar Brian Davies,[23] which may differ from a more common view only in stating a *terminus ad quem*. But there is more to it than that: in trying to voice the consensus of contemporary scholarship, May says: "We can agree that Edwards was somehow a great man, whether we admire him most as artist, psychologist, preacher, theologian, or philosopher."[24] How could such a universal genius be responsible for establishing a trend that many find shameful?

This, after all, was the man who expressed his mystical appreciation of the blessings of election and his awareness of the specialness of the woman he would eventually marry when she was only thirteen:

They say there is a young lady in [New Haven] who is beloved of that Great Being, who made and rules the world, and that there are certain seasons in which this Great Being, in some way or other invisible, comes to her and fills her mind with exceeding sweet delight, and that she hardly cares for any thing, except to meditate on him—that she expects after a while to be received up where he is, to be raised up out of the world and caught up into heaven.[25]

To understand how this could happen, it is necessary to have some knowledge of Jonathan Edwards's life. Born in East Windsor, Connecticut, in 1703, he was the son of one and grandson of another New England cleric of good reputation whose congregation had experienced revival. The only son in a family of eleven children, he grew up as a precociously religious and scholarly boy who was socially awkward. He entered Yale at the age of thirteen and, when he graduated four years later, stayed on for another two years of study. Sometime along the way, he experienced conversion (without, however, experiencing the classical stage of "legal fear") and decided to enter the ministry.

His first call was to the new Presbyterian congregation in New York City, where he stayed less than a year because of the church's financial stress. Returning to Yale as a tutor, he received an M.A., wrote his famous essay on spiders, and, more important, began work on "his central philosophical concept"[26] of excellence. Then he was called to assist his famous grandfather, Solomon Stoddard, in the role of heir apparent at the church in Northampton, Massachusetts. The following year he married Sarah Pierrepont.

Although Northampton at the time was little more than a frontier town, it was known throughout New England for its minister, one of the most articulate theologians and influential clergy of the period, the one known as "the Congregational Pope of the Connecticut Valley." Solomon Stoddard's main claim to fame was that he had taken even further the logic of the "Halfway Covenant," by which the children of visible saints could be baptized before they were capable of narrating the tales of their own conversions, by admitting them to Communion as well if they exhibited godliness. When Edwards arrived, his grandfather had been at the Northampton church for fifty-three years and was a recognized authority on preaching. It must have been intimidating for the twenty-three-year-old to alternate Sundays in the pulpit with his famous grandfather. In two years, though, Stoddard was dead, and young Edwards was the spiritual leader of the congregation.

He had almost twenty good years before the events occurred that would eventually lead to his dismissal. Indeed, he was very popular at first, especially with the young adults in the congregation. He was even given the honor of being invited to preach before the clergy of Boston only two years after he had succeeded Stoddard, a sign that he was already recognized as a brilliant young theologian. A revival that occurred in his parish, and the account of it that he then published, was what brought Edwards to the attention of a wider world. This revival was the immediate occasion of the Great Awakening.

It began in late 1733 when he was disturbed by the way the young people of the congregation spent their Sunday evenings socializing—after, of course, they had attended his afternoon lecture, not to mention the morning worship service and sermon. While to later tastes this activity may seem harmless and even desirable, to their minister it was an unbecoming worldliness, so he suggested their parents see that they stay home instead.

Later he suggested they come together in small groups for religious conversation. Parental intervention proved unnecessary because the young people complied at once on their own. A couple of deaths in the community and a threat of Arminianism that arose helped heighten the atmosphere of religious seriousness. Soon there came to be numerous conversions, at first among the youth but in time among the middle-aged parishioners and children as well, and as much among males as females.[27] Before long, the influence of the revival spread to thirty-two churches in the Connecticut River valley of Massachusetts and Connecticut.[28]

Although the number of communicants at the Northampton church was around 620, which included most of the town's adults, Edwards, using the tests applied by clergy of the time, was convinced that around 300 valid conversions had occurred by the end of 1735, when the revival seemed to have run its course. Several attempts at suicide suggested to some that the atmosphere had become too intense, and much of the movement's momentum was dissipated.

Edwards's part in the inspiration of the Great Awakening was largely in the reception accorded his account of this revival in Northampton, which he called *A Faithful Narrative of the Surprising Work of God in the Conversion of Many Hundred Souls in Northampton, and the Neighboring Towns and Villages of New-Hampshire in New-England.*[29] He was such a meticulous observer that his descriptive morphology of conversion in that work was taken by many at the time and by large numbers of evangelicals ever since as being a normative morphology, an effect that he lived to regret, since it seemed to place more emphasis on the "bodily manifestations" of conversion than on the effect of election on the will. A good bit of the rest of his literary output had to be devoted to redressing the balance, to insisting upon the reality of revivals and their importance while treating the emotional manifestations that often accompanied them as epiphenomena of conversion rather than its essence.

Understanding Edwards's convictions on this subject can take us a long way toward understanding his approach to preaching, including his countenancing and practicing the stirring up of the terror of damnation and hell. The place to begin is with the realization that Edwards was an utter Calvinist in his assumption that there is absolutely nothing any human being can do to contribute toward that person's own conversion and salvation or that of anyone else. While such Calvinism was still the official theology of New England, its erosion was evident in the Halfway Covenant and the admission of persons baptized under that covenant to Holy Communion, which were advocated and practiced by Edwards's grandfather and predecessor, Solomon Stoddard. Such relaxations of the Puritan determination to have churches of the visible elect would lead to further theological derelictions as time went on, first Arminianism and, after the Revolution, even Unitarianism. But the initial vision had not faded one whit for Jonathan Edwards.

This raises the question that has recurred constantly in the history of reactions to predestination: Why preach to those who have already been elected to salvation or reprobation? To the classical Calvinist response that preaching is the normal medium through which election is effected, Edwards added additional understanding of what preaching could contribute. Since people were not converted through persuasion, the preacher's purpose was not to persuade.

> Rather than attempt to persuade the unconverted, Edwards tried by means of his preaching, in addition to offering the Word, (1) to provide the optimal conditions and circumstances within which conversion might take place, (2) to offer the logical connections between guilt and repentance so that those who have been or are being converted might better understand what is happening to them, and (3) to prevent the misinterpretation of pseudo-religious experience, especially by those who believe they have experienced grace but have not.[30]

This theory about what preaching can accomplish grows out of Edwards's understanding of the will. He had abandoned the Puritan faculty psychology that assumed reason inevitably preceded volition. Rather, a person has two wills, the rational and another that is an "inclination arising from the liveliness of the idea of, or sensibleness of the good of, the object presented to the mind."[31] At other times, he refers to what he calls "inclination" here as "appetite," "heart," or "will." The emphasis is on the affective rather than the logical dimension of will.

What is attractive to the will is the perfection of God, the superiority of infinite being to finite being. While this could sound like Aristotle's understanding of the Unmoved Mover as moving the universe by the *eros* of all things for its perfection and beauty, that is precisely what Edwards's understanding is not. For the attractiveness of the Unmoved Mover could be expected to move all things equally, but conversion for Edwards is the divine alteration of the human will of one elected to salvation, which enables it to consent to the infinite will and purpose of God and to find it overwhelmingly attractive.

What is so transcendently beautiful for Edwards is the idea of God's sovereignty, which elects some to salvation and others to reprobation. Election is manifested in the ability to recognize the excellency of that sovereignty and consent to it joyfully.

The excellency of that sovereignty is the central concept in Edwards's thought to which I have already alluded.[32] Edwards's understanding of that concept is stated in a sermon he preached on the eve of the revival in Northampton, "A Divine and Supernatural Light." (For the text, see **Vol. 2, pp. 380-97**.) A look at that sermon will show not only his thought on the subject but also his use of the Perkins sermon form of "doctrines and uses." The text for the sermon is Matthew 16:17 (KJV): "And Jesus answered and said unto him, Blessed art thou, Simon Bar-jona: for flesh and blood have not revealed it unto thee, but my Father which is in heaven."

The sermon begins with the explication of the text. It may be observed in the text that:

> Peter is blessed because of what has been revealed to him.
> What makes him blessed or happy is that God and God alone made the revelation to Peter, since this shows that:
> God favored him more than others.
> The knowledge was greater than any of which flesh and blood are capable, any merely natural knowledge.

From this text he draws the doctrine that "there is such a thing as a spiritual and divine light, immediately imparted to the soul by God, of a different nature from any that is obtained by natural means." He expounds this doctrine by showing three things (the "reasons" for the doctrine):

What that spiritual and divine light is. This is first shown negatively by stating what the light is not. It is not

Convictions of their sin and misery that persons have in a state of nature, as from conscience. Such convictions come rather from the Spirit of God who operates very differently in the souls of the redeemed from the way that Spirit operates in the unregenerate (111).

"Any impression made upon the imagination" (although such impressions may accompany such spiritual discoveries) (112).

"New truths or propositions not contained in the word of God" (which would be inspiration of the sort the sacred writers and no one else had) (113).

An *"affecting view"* of religious things, since those can be received from other human beings and not exclusively from God.[33]

Next, he shows positively what the divine and spiritual light is. It is "a true sense of the divine excellency of the things revealed in the word of God, and a conviction of the truth and reality of them thence arising. . . . There is therefore in this spiritual light . . . ":

1. *"A true sense of the divine and superlative excellency of the things of religion; a real sense of the excellency of God and Jesus Christ, and of the work of redemption, and the ways and works of God revealed in the gospel"* (113). This is not merely notional knowledge, but a sense of the heart. The difference between the two is that between "having a rational judgment that honey is sweet, and having a sense of its sweetness" (114).

2. "A conviction of the truth and reality" of the excellency of the things revealed in scripture that is both indirect and direct. It is indirect in two ways:

When prejudices against the divine truth are removed, the mind is opened to rational arguments for the truth.

Reason is helped positively because the light makes speculative notions more lively.

It is also direct because "the excellency of these things is so superlative" (115).

The truth "is immediately given by God, and not obtained by natural means." This does not mean, however, that

". . . the natural faculties are not used in it."

"Outward means have no concern in this affair."

It does mean, though, that

"It is given by God without making use of any means that operate by their own power or natural force" (116).

The doctrine is true, "there is such a thing as that spiritual light that has been described, thus immediately let into the mind by God" (116). This may be demonstrated

By scripture (with a number of texts cited and inferences drawn from them).

Rationally.

The superlative excellency of divine things is built into the definition of God.

Yet, again by definition, it cannot be expected that wicked persons should be able to see that excellency.

Thus the knowledge of this excellency must be communicated by God directly and not obtained through natural means.

With his doctrine thus clearly delineated, Edwards moves on to apply it with a "brief improvement."

The members of his congregation are led "to reflect on the goodness of God" in so ordering revelation that a knowledge of truth is not limited to the brilliant and well educated, but can be given as well to persons of little ability or training.

The doctrine should lead them to reflect on whether they have received such a revelation or not.

They all should seek that light earnestly, since:

"This is the most excellent and divine wisdom that any creature is capable of."

"This knowledge is that which is above all others sweet and joyful."

"This light is such as effectually influences the inclination, and changes the nature of the soul" (122).

"This light, and this only, has its fruit in an universal holiness of life" (123).

The second point in the application calls for members of the congregation to reflect on whether or not they have received the divine and spiritual light. This means that Edwards, in this and all sermons, assumes he has two audiences, those who have and those who have not received the light, those who have experienced election and conversion and those who have not, the redeemed and the reprobate.

The unredeemed are shown to fall short. Their fears, their confusions, their inadequacies, are explained by their departures from biblical expectations. In contrast, the redeemed are reminded of their present difference from their past life and from their fellows who remain unsaved.[34]

This twofold audience is as much a presupposition for sermons in which he held up the horrors of damnation as it is for those that speak of the joys of salvation. As time goes on, however, a shift is discernible in his preaching, from emphasizing the latter to making more of the former. Part of that is undoubtedly a matter of young preachers having to preach largely from their own experience because they do not have much knowledge of the experience of others—and the spiritual life of the young Edwards was full of affective satisfaction. As he came to better know parishioners, however, he discovered that they were not so much a company of visible saints as he had expected. And the longer he knew them, the worse they appeared to get. After the revival there were various signs of worldliness: a diminished respect for ministerial authority, the introduction of pews into the meetinghouse with the structuralization of social distinctions that involved, and the erection of a secular building for town meetings that seemed to deny the peculiar vocation of New England.

Yet even these negative sermons presupposed two audiences. And it is the failure to recognize this that causes contemporary readers to assume that all of his hearers must have responded to such preaching with terror.

> Saints may hear his sermons as psalmlike celebrations of God's glory— the rolling thunder and leaping fire may, in Edwards' words, "rejoice" one. . . . Grounded in assurance, saints are able to discern the awesome beauty of God's justice.[35]

As calloused as such a reaction may appear to modern readers, it reached to the heart of Edwards's conviction that election was manifested in a love for the excellency of God, especially in the excellency of God's justice in calling some to election and others to reprobation. Sinners' reactions to such sermons, however, would not likely be of terror. The worst proof of their condition could be a smug assumption that they were of the elect and that the terrible words applied to others and not to themselves; or they might be merely apathetic about the whole business. Stark terror on the part of a listener, then, could be a sign of hope, since it takes the grace of God to realize the extent of the loss that threatens and to realize God's justice in condemning sinners such as oneself.

Not only that, the sermon may aid those who have been awakened to the point of fear, since preaching is the ordinary medium through which election occurs. Stephen Yarborough and John Adams interpret this homiletical strategy of Edwards as a use of what Aristotle considered to be the main characteristic of oral persuasion, the *enthymeme*. An enthymeme is an incomplete syllogism, one with a suppressed minor premise that must be supplied by the audience. The major premise in Edwards's sermons is his description of the way that God works with souls. The minor premise to be supplied is the confirmation or ratification of what has been said from one's own experience. The converting potential of sermons like "Sinners in the Hands of an Angry God" is enthymematic, "the 'missing premise' is in the unwilled inclination of a saint to experience the Word in a saving way—with an uncommon affection."[36]

Such sermons, therefore, do not have a character of their own that causes conversion; that cause lies only in the excellent and inscrutable will of God. Yet such sermons can achieve the first of Edwards's three purposes in preaching: "to provide the optimal conditions and circumstances within which the conversion might take place." Hence in defending such preaching, Edwards says:

> Another thing that some ministers have been greatly blamed for, and I think unjustly, is speaking terror to them that are already under great terrors, instead of comforting them. Indeed, if ministers in such a case go about to terrify persons with that which is not true, or to affright 'em by representing their case worse than it is, or in any respect otherwise than it is, they are to be condemned; but if they terrify 'em only by still holding forth more light to them, and giving them to understand more of the truth of their case, they are altogether to be justified. When sinners' consciences are greatly awakened by the Spirit of God, it is by light imparted to the conscience, enabling them to see their case to be, in some measure, as it is; and if more light be let in, it will terrify 'em still more. . . . Why should we be afraid to let persons that are in an infinitely miserable condition, know the truth, or bring 'em into the light, for fear it should terrify them? 'Tis light that must convert them, if ever they are converted.[37]

In all this may be seen the way it came about that Jonathan Edwards was the great advocate and theorist of hellfire and damnation preaching. Yet not all that was to follow in this genre would have met with his approval. In his high Calvinist way of denying that conversion could be effected by anything human beings do, he would have been aghast at suggestions soon to be made that fear could be used to induce conversion. He may have paved the way for such preaching, but he would never have been willing to walk down the paths by which others extended his route.[38]

FOR FURTHER READING

American Sermons: The Pilgrims to Martin Luther King, Jr. Edited by Michael Warner. The Library of America. New York: Library Classics of the United States, 1999.

The Great Awakening. Vol. 4 of *The Works of Jonathan Edwards.* Edited by C. C. Goen. New Haven and London: Yale University Press, 1972.

Miller, Perry. *The New England Mind: The Seventeenth Century.* Cambridge: Belknap Press of Harvard University Press, 1939.

Sermons and Discourses 1720–23. Vol. 10 of *The Works of Jonathan Edwards.* Edited by Wilson H. Kimnach. New Haven and London: Yale University Press, 1992.

Stout, Harry S. *The New England Soul: Preaching and Religious Culture in Colonial New England.* New York and Oxford: Oxford University Press, 1986.

Yarborough, Stephen R., and John C. Adams. *Delightful Conviction: Jonathan Edwards and the Rhetoric of Conversion.* Great American Orators, no. 20. Westport, Conn., and London: Greenwood, 1993.

Notes

1. See above, chapter 15.

2. What follows is based on Perry Miller, *The New England Mind: The Seventeenth Century* (Cambridge: Belknap Press of Harvard University Press, 1939).

3. Ibid., 298.

4. Ibid., 241. Emphasis added to identify faculties.

5. William Perkins, *The Arte of Prophesying*, trans. Thomas Tuke, in *The Works of William Perkins*, ed. and intro. Ian Breward, Courtenay Library of Reformation Classics (Appleford and Abingdon, Berkshire County): Sutton Courtenay, 1970), 3:331-49.

6. Quoted in ibid., 301.

7. For something of the range of "similitudes" in Puritan sermons, see Babette M. Levy, *Preaching in the First Half Century of New England History* (New York: Russell & Russell, 1967; reprinted from American Society of Church History edition of 1945), 98-130.

8. Quoted by Horton Davies from Ames's *The Marrow of Sacred Divinity,* a 1638

translation of *Medulla Theologica,* in *The Worship of the American Puritans, 1629–1730* (New York, Bern, Frankfort am Main, and Paris: Peter Lang, 1990), 84. Chapter 5 of Davies's work, pp. 77-113, is a useful analysis of Puritan preaching. Others have written about Puritan preaching from a number of different perspectives. Ralph G. Turnbull's effort to write a third volume for E. C. Dargan's *A History of Preaching* that would deal with American preaching as well as European preaching in the first half of the twentieth century (Grand Rapids, Mich.: Baker, 1974) is not really a scholarly work and should be used with caution. Dargan himself produced a manuscript for a third volume that is in the library of Southern Baptist Theological Seminary, Louisville, Kentucky, where he taught. Microfilm copies of the manuscript are in a few other libraries, such as that of the Princeton Theological Seminary. The article of Eugene E. White titled "Puritan Preaching and the Authority of God" in *Preaching in American History: Selected Issues in the American Pulpit, 1630–1967,* ed. DeWitte Holland, assoc. eds. Jess Yoder and Hubert Vance Taylor (Nashville and New York: Abingdon, 1969), deals more with the theology preached by the Puritans, especially their understanding of the various covenants, than with any specifically homiletical issues, but it does have a useful bibliography. In the companion volume, *Sermons in American History,* edited by the same people and published by the same press two years later, White introduces two sermons dealing with those issues: John Cotton's "A Sermon" and Peter Bulkeley's "Three Differences More Betwixt the Two Covenants." Emory Elliott, *Power and the Pulpit in Puritan New England* (Princeton: Princeton University Press, 1975), a learned, interesting, and informative work, is concerned about the way sermons and other Puritan religious literature furnished the symbols and myths that enabled the people to deal with the psychological stress inherent to their situation. Again, the concern of the book is not really germane to the history of preaching as such. For examples of Puritan preaching see *American Sermons: The Pilgrims to Martin Luther King, Jr.,* ed. Michael Warner, Library of America (New York: Library Classics of the United States, 1999), which devotes about half of its 900-plus pages to examples.

9. Harry S. Stout, *The New England Soul: Preaching and Religious Culture in Colonial New England* (New York and Oxford: Oxford University Press, 1986), 3-4. In an endnote to this passage, Stout notes that this lifetime load of sermon listening is about ten times the time spent listening to lectures in a college undergraduate degree program. What is said here about Stout's book and that of Toulouse follows very closely my review article, "Preaching in New England," *ATR* 71 (1989): 191-200.

10. Stout, *The New England Soul,* 3.

11. Ibid., 97.

12. Ibid., 7.

13. The times at which occasional sermons were preached include fast days, days of thanksgiving, and election days. Ibid., 27-31. On occasional services, see Davies, *The Worship of the American Puritans,* 51-73.

14. For a full discussion of such fast-day sermons and their subsequent influence on American literature, see Sacvan Bercovitch's classic study, *The American Jeremiad* (Madison: University of Wisconsin Press, 1978).

15. Stout, *The New England Soul,* 5.

16. An ambitious effort to interpret the last of Stout's periods is made by Donald Weber in *Rhetoric and History in Revolutionary New England* (New York: Oxford University Press, 1988), where he attempts to use an interdisciplinary method to enter the thought world of "New Divinity" preachers like Jonathan Edwards Jr. He does not succeed, however, in making either his thesis or the case for it clear enough for evaluation. See my review "Preaching in New England," 194-96.

17. Teresa Toulouse, *The Art of Prophesying: New England Sermons and the Shaping of Belief* (Athens and London: University of Georgia Press, 1987).

18. The respective influences of Whitefield and Edwards on American revivalism have been distinguished by C. C. Goen: "While Whitefield, by virtue of his flamboyant itinerancy and its consequent influence on evangelistic method, may be called the 'founder' of American revivalism, it was Jonathan Edwards who began the historical documentation and theological defense which have sustained as an ongoing tradition." "Editor's Introduction" in *The Great Awakening,* vol. 4 of *The Works of Jonathan Edwards* (New Haven and London: Yale University Press, 1972), 1.

19. For a comparison of the two homiletical styles, see Stephen R. Yarborough and John C. Adams, *Delightful Conviction: Jonathan Edwards and the Rhetoric of Conversion,* Great American Orators, no. 20 (Westport, Conn., and London: Greenwood, 1993), 43. We owe to Ola Elizabeth Winslow the oft-quoted observation that Whitefield gave New England "its first taste of theater under the flag of salvation" in her foreword to the volume she edited, *Jonathan Edwards: Basic Writings* (New York: Meridian, 1966), xviii.

20. For a demonstration of the rarity of such preaching by the earlier Puritans, see Levy, *Preaching in the First Half Century of New England History,* 25-39. It was not, however, unheard of. For example, Edwards's grandfather, Solomon Stoddard, said: "When men don't Preach much about the danger of Damnation, there is want of good Preaching. Men need to be terrified and have the arrows of the Almighty in them that they may be converted," in *The Defects of the Preacher Reproved* (Boston, 1724), 13, 14, quoted by Wilson H. Kimnach, ed., *Sermons and Discourses 1720–23,* vol. 10 of *The Works of Jonathan Edwards* (New Haven and London: Yale University Press, 1992), 14. Yet it was Edwards's fame as the theologian and harbinger of the Great Awakening that gave widespread currency to the practice.

21. Phyllis McGinley, *Times Three: Selected Verse from Three Decades* (Garden City, N.Y.: Image Books, 1975), 35-36.

22. Henry F. May, "Jonathan Edwards and America," in *Jonathan Edwards and the American Experience,* ed. Nathan O. Hatch and Harry S. Stout (New York and Oxford: Oxford University Press, 1988), 23, 25. This collection of papers read at a conference at Wheaton College in 1984 represents an effort "to pull together some of [the disparate strands of the contemporary proliferation of Edwards studies] and to make accessible the best of the current thinking about this remarkable individual," p. 5.

23. Editorial foreword to John E. Smith, *Jonathan Edwards: Puritan, Preacher, Philosopher* (Notre Dame: University of Notre Dame Press, 1992), vii.

24. May, "Jonathan Edwards and America," 30.

25. Winslow, *Jonathan Edwards: Basic Writings,* 66. For a delightful picture of the home life of the Edwards family and its positive influence on the Edwards children,

see Elisabeth D. Dodds, *Marriage to a Difficult Man: The "Uncommon Union" of Jonathan and Sarah Edwards* (Philadelphia: Westminster, 1971).

26. Yarborough and Adams, *Delightful Conviction*, 4.

27. For a socioeconomic theory of why the young people in Northampton were so responsive to Edwards, see ibid., 24-27.

28. For a list of the churches and their ministers and a map of their dispersion, see Goen, *The Great Awakening*, 22-25.

29. A critical edition of this work is given by Goen in *The Great Awakening*, 97-211.

30. Yarborough and Adams, *Delightful Conviction*, 10.

31. Quoted ibid., 11, from the Edwards notebooks.

32. Ibid., 11-21. This paragraph represents an effort to give a simple and concise summary of a position to which Yarborough and Adams give a nuanced presentation.

33. Yarborough and Adams, *Delightful Conviction*, 113. Page numbers used parenthetically throughout this sermon are also from this work.

34. Ibid., 30.

35. Ibid., 54.

36. Ibid., 56.

37. "Some Thoughts Concerning the Revival" in *The Great Awakening,* ed. C. C. Goen, 389-90.

38. In his introduction to *Sermons and Discourses 1720–23,* which extends over 250 pages, Wilson H. Kimnach contributes greatly to our knowledge of many aspects of Jonathan Edwards's preaching: the influences on his preaching, the way he constructed his manuscripts, his recycling of material in later sermons and books, his thoughts about writing, and his homiletical and literary techniques (the subject of Kimnach's 1971 University of Pennsylvania dissertation). Since, however, the present purpose is not to concentrate on the genius of individual preachers but rather to study movements, this section has been confined to the area in which Edwards was most influential on preaching to come, hellfire and damnation preaching. The stir caused by itinerants such as Gilbert Tennent and James Davenport, while interesting in their own right, had little direct influence on later preaching. For a good short treatment of Edwards's preaching, see chapter 3, "Word and Spirit," in Conrad Cherry, *The Theology of Jonathan Edwards: A Reappraisal* (Garden City, N.Y.: Anchor Books, 1966), 44-55.

THE SECOND CALL

THE SECOND GREAT AWAKENING

The discontinuities between the First and Second Great Awakenings are at least as great as the continuities. Some have to do with the cultural setting. Jonathan Edwards's Northampton and the other sites of the First Awakening were places where there had been almost a century of Puritan culture, while much of the Second Awakening took place beyond the borders of the original thirteen colonies in areas newly opened to white settlement. The first occurred in a British colony not yet grown dissatisfied, while the second was set in a self-consciously independent America that was moving beyond its original boundaries. The first came at a time when Calvinism was still the taken-for-granted construction of reality, and the second was at a time when the whole belief system was up for grabs.

A religious movement can be described in many ways, none of which call into question its religious reality. The fact that sociological, psychological, anthropological, or economic interpretations can be given for the sequence of events is not to say that it is any less a revival sent by God. And many scholars have sought to offer such interpretations of the Second Great Awakening. William G. McLoughlin, for instance, has undertaken to use the tools of social anthropology to gain insight into the dynamics of all "revitalizations," as he calls them.[1] Using analytical tools developed by Anthony F. C. Wallace, he argues that there is a standard pattern in which these occur:

> A great awakening occurs, Wallace says, when a society finds that its day-to-day behavior has deviated so far from the accepted (traditional) norms that neither individuals nor large groups can honestly (consistently) sustain the common set of religious understandings by which they believe (have been taught) they should act.[2]

This statement can be paraphrased in the vocabulary of the sociology of knowledge by saying that when a society can no longer assimilate its experience to its social construction of reality, that construction must be revised to accommodate experience. That revision is normally accomplished by individuals who undergo the accommodation in their own religious experience and then proclaim the transformation to others.

> If they are lucky, [the members of the society] will find leaders able to articulate a new accommodation with "reality," a new sense of reality, of identity, and of self-confidence, and, above all, a revision of their institutional structure that will return daily life to regularity and order.[3]

The Second Great Awakening enabled the new American nation to negotiate the changes listed above by giving the country a new way to articulate the basic myths of its culture so they were consistent with the way life was being experienced at that time, thus making it possible for the culture to continue until the next crisis of discontinuity occurred.[4]

While McLoughlin has a chapter on the Second Great Awakening, the basic thing to be learned from him is the pattern of awakenings in general. Insight into this particular awakening can be gained from Nathan O. Hatch's study, *The Democratization of American Christianity*.[5] Hatch argues against those scholars who have seen the Second Great Awakening as having an essentially conservative social force by looking at the populism unleashed by the Revolution, which he calls "the most crucial event in American history."[6]

> The generation overshadowed by it and its counterpart in France stands at the fault line that separates an older world, premised on standards of deference, patronage, and ordered succession, from a newer one that continues to shape our values. . . . Above all, the Revolution dramatically expanded the circle of people who considered themselves

493

capable of thinking for themselves about issues of freedom, equality, sovereignty, and representation. Respect for authority, tradition, station, and education eroded.[7]

This populism was as obvious in religion as in any other aspect of culture. That meant the Puritanism that had predominated in religious life up to that point and had even furnished the rationale for the Revolution was suddenly out of fashion. It represented an elite establishment that was anti-egalitarian. Its clergy expected deference to their authority because of their station and the education they had acquired to prepare for it. Theirs was the way of tradition, but the time had come when that no longer drew any water. One person was thought to be as good an interpreter of the Bible as another, whether ordained or lay, educated or not. And along with this populism went an optimism that was aghast at the assumption that a revival occurred only following the inscrutable decision of Providence to send it. God wanted revivals, and it took only faithful souls devoted to the cause and actively promoting it to bring one about. By the same token, salvation was not open just to those elected to it; it was available to any who would trust and accept God's promises. Thus while the Second Great Awakening shared many presuppositions with the First, there were other presuppositions in which it could not have differed more. These differences gave both a very different dynamic to the later movement and a very different style of preaching to mediate it.

But, as noted above, the explanation of the events given by those who participated in them was theological. To those who were in favor of them, they appeared God-sent. To those who opposed them, they were of infernal inspiration. The issue at stake was whether souls would be saved or damned for all eternity.

SOUTHERN BEGINNINGS

The Cane Ridge Sacrament

There were two major streams of the Second Great Awakening, one coming out of New England and going to the upper Midwest, and one that was southern and moved into the whole area, reaching from the lower Midwest to the Gulf of Mexico. Since the latter was the earlier and also reflected a greater break with tradition, it seems the place to begin.

The southern revival began among Presbyterians, although they were quickly to lose this leadership and were actually to suffer schism because of the revival. While the Presbyterian Church in this country began

494

among Puritan colonists from England, it had its largest growth and fastest spread among Scotch-Irish who settled in Pennsylvania and farther south. These made up more than half of the first white Americans who crossed the Appalachians as pioneer settlers.[8] Since their pattern of settlement met the standard of Daniel Boone, who considered himself crowded if he could see the smoke from a neighbor's chimney, it was hard to find enough people who lived close together to form a church. The learned ministers expected by their tradition were also in short supply. Since a majority of these settlers had come from the ardent tradition of Ulster, being deprived of their church was very hard on them and probably caused them to feel guilty as well.

In some ways it is misleading to separate the two Great Awakenings, because there was no intervening period in which a revival[9] was not going on somewhere. This was especially true of Scotch-Irish Presbyterians, who had brought with them the tradition of sacramental meetings, which had been the occasion of great revivals among them in the seventeenth and eighteenth centuries and which also had been the inspiration of the Welsh revival and had developed most of what were to become the conventions of the Methodist Awakening in Great Britain.[10]

> Nothing was as conducive to cyclical revivals as the traditional communion service, with its day of fasting and prayer, its intensive all-day preparatory services, the careful screening of candidates and allocation of tokens (which very conspicuously identified those outside the church), the intense experience of the sacrament itself, and the follow-up thanksgiving service, all in an intercongregational context with huge throngs of people, outdoor preaching tents, and frequent all-night prayer services.[11]

As Presbyterianism moved down through Virginia into the Carolinas and then over into Kentucky and Tennessee, there was a succession of communion meetings led by clergy who had been converted in such meetings themselves and then acquired the education that allowed them to be ordained. By the summer of 1800, there was a small group of such clergy in Logan County, Kentucky, under the leadership of James McGready, who preached with extraordinary power in spite of using a manuscript. The area clergy planned to have their summer sacramental meetings so synchronized that none would conflict, permitting members of one congregation to attend the meeting of another and create the critical mass of people necessary for such an event.

Much to everyone's surprise, what some consider to be the first camp meeting occurred at the communion of one of McGready's churches, that of Gasper River.[12] People came from more than one hundred miles, which means that they could have come from Tennessee, Illinois, or Indiana, as well as Kentucky. By the time of the opening session on Friday, twenty to thirty wagons were encamped. Four clergy shared the preaching and ministration of the sacrament. The anticipation shown by the flocking of people from such a wide area was not disappointed. Many were caught up in the excitement of the occasion, experiencing a variety of physical manifestations of the grace they felt, and a large number were converted. This spark ignited a flame of revival that spread to Carolina and east Tennessee.

Religious stirrings had been felt not only by the Presbyterian congregations in central Kentucky, but by Methodists and Baptists as well, although the Presbyterian sacraments were always the most explosive. By the time the next summer came, anticipation was intense. The excitement was canalized by the Presbyterians through what they called societies or socials, groups very similar to Methodist classes. Clergy became involved by hearing of the things that were happening in other churches and going to witness them for themselves.

An example of this was Barton Stone, the pastor of Cane Ridge and Concord churches in Bourbon County east of Lexington. He had been in his cure and indeed had been ordained only three years when he visited his old classmates at Gasper River to see what their communion was like in May of 1801. He returned to his flocks and saw signs of a great stirring at the Concord sacrament. The Cane River communion in August, however, was to prove, to the amazement of all concerned, to be the unleashing of the Second Great Awakening in the South.

Since he did not take a leading part in the preaching, it is unclear what Barton Stone's exact role was in what happened at his Cane Ridge sacrament that year. Indeed, it is hard to know the contribution of any or all of the clergy there, since what happened appears to have been, humanly speaking, a function of the expectations of the people who arrived. They came like lemmings eager to drown in a sea of grace.

Although there are a number of eyewitness accounts, some written down at the time and others not until years later,[13] reliable numbers are hard to come by. While estimates range as high as twenty thousand, half that number of attendants seems more likely. Methodists and Baptists came as well as Presbyterians, although the Baptists' practice of close Communion would have excluded them from the sacrament. Blacks participated as well as whites, but in a segregated manner on the grounds. Not all who came were devout; there were many who were curious, cynical, or thrill seekers. Seventeen ministers preached during the course of the event, while hundreds of laity exhorted—including one seven-year-old girl. At this communion meeting it is likely that no more than 200 received, but Stone estimated that somewhere between 500 and 1,000 persons were converted. Many more than that number were said to be "slain" (i.e., to have fainted from religious agitation).

What most impressed contemporary observers as well as historians and their readers ever since was the bodily manifestations[14] of religious emotions displayed at Cane Ridge and in the camp meetings to follow. The descriptions are impressive, as this example from one of the clergy present:

> Sinners dropping down on every hand, shrieking, groaning, crying for mercy, convoluted; professors [of religion] praying, agonizing, fainting, falling down in distress, for sinners, or in raptures of joy! Some singing, some shouting, clapping their hands, hugging and even kissing, laughing; others talking to the distressed, to one another, or to opposers of the work, and all this at once.[15]

The writer's reaction to the events he reported was to say, "No spectacle can excite a stronger sensation," a verdict few would question.

In addition to weeping, shouting, and fainting, the physical manifestations of religious emotion were so varied that a taxonomy had to be created to classify them. One written by Stone is worth quoting at length:

> The jerks cannot be so easily described . . . When the whole system was affected, I have seen a person stand in one place and jerk backward and forward in quick succession, their head nearly touching the floor behind and before. All classes . . . were thus affected. They could not account for it; but some have told me that they were among the happiest seasons of their lives.
>
> The dancing exercise . . . The subject, after jerking awhile, began to dance, and the jerks would cease . . . While thus exercised, I have heard their solemn praises and prayers ascending to God.
>
> The barking exercise (as opposers contemptuously called it) was nothing but the jerks. A person affected with the jerks, especially in his head, would often make a grunt or a bark, if you please, from the suddenness of the jerk.
>
> The singing exercise . . . The subject in a very happy state of mind would sing most melodiously not from the mouth or nose, but entirely in the breast, the sounds issuing thence. Such music silenced everything, and attracted the attention of all.[16]

Then as now, such descriptions have repulsed many people. Some have tried to distance themselves from this type of behavior by attributing it to the effect of the frontier on ignorant people, but, as Paul Conkin has pointed out, "no revivals took place, or could take place, among the first scattered white settlers in any area of the West,"[17] and one of the diary records of the event shows that "the people most stricken were often sturdy landowners or prominent women, leaders in the local congregations, people in the upper ranks of early Kentucky society."[18]

Conkin also has a good perspective on these exercises that sound as alien to many contemporary Christians as they do to religion's "cultured despisers":

> What the exercises revealed were religiously serious people who, in a powerfully suggestive environment, chose, or were forced, to reenact the drama of Jesus' passion and the ever-recurring drama of their own tortured quest for salvation. . . . Tears, either of remorse or of joy, are at the heart of any affectional religion. Beyond tears are the more extreme but equally involuntary effects—verbal or muscular or neurological. These, too, are within the range of almost everyone's experience, as in rare and often unwanted moments of overwhelming feeling, such as at the death of a loved one. Who can then resist tears? Or cries of despair? Or even the writhing and convulsive movements that may provide an outlet for complete personal desolation? Surely no one expects a quiet demeanor or reasonable rationalization at such moments. Nor for those often unsought, often inexplicable moments of sheer exaltation which, for some people, may be approached in a sexual orgasm. In other words, some form of physical expression fitted these occasions, whether in an avowedly religious or a secular setting. Physical effects are not in themselves different whatever the stimulant. After all, some people largely identify swooning with rock concerts or find in Woodstock the clearest parallel to Cane Ridge.[19]

The kind of preaching done at Cane Ridge encouraged responses of ecstatic frenzy. Since the preaching was impromptu, we have no manuscript texts of sermons preached there, but do know of some devices employed:

> Certain repeated and familiar verbal images, those with great resonance for an audience, worked better than others. In many of the greatest revivals the spark was a type of confession—the telling of what had happened to oneself there or at an earlier revival. Some ministers learned the most evocative ways of telling their stories. Several sermonic

devices—timing, phrasing, pauses, and above all the display of intense feeling—worked.[20]

Undoubtedly the mood of the crowd contributed to an emotional state open to intense religious experience. There is bound to be something contagious about being in the middle of a group caught up in despair or ecstasy. The fact that there were always several clergy preaching at the same time from different platforms on the grounds must have heightened the excitement. Add to that hundreds of people, clergy and lay, "exhorting" groups and individuals, and you have conditions highly conducive to emotional release. This, too, affected the preaching:

> In the tumult the distinction between prepared sermons (with a theme or text taken from the Bible and carefully developed points or arguments) and more spontaneous exhortations (extemporaneous or even impromptu practical advice, or tearful appeals or warnings) dissolved, particularly when outlying members of the audience could not even hear the sermons.[21]

In the Kentucky revivals around the turn of the nineteenth century, a style of preaching was perfected that was very effective for creating revivals in which large numbers of people received the spiritual release for which they were hoping and praying. It was to become characteristic of the camp meetings and most revivals that have taken place since.

Before moving on to the camp meetings, however, a word needs to be said about the immediate effects of Cane Ridge. One is that the camp meeting as such, rather than the Presbyterian sacrament meeting, came to be the characteristic occasion of revivals. This meant, first of all, that the centrality of the Eucharist was lost for Presbyterians.[22] It also meant that the initiative for the Awakening in the South passed from the Presbyterians to the Methodists and, to a lesser extent, the Baptists.

The Presbyterians, indeed, were to suffer two schisms as a result of disagreements over the Kentucky revivals.[23] Most of the clergy involved in the Cane Ridge revival, including Barton Stone, would separate over a nexus of issues that included how worship should be conducted, whether clergy should be given privileged status, the doctrine of Christ, and freedom of the will. In time, the majority of these ministers became involved in the Restoration movement that created the Christian Church,[24] the Disciples of Christ, and the Church of Christ—although some became Shakers.

The heirs of the McGready revivals in Logan County found themselves at loggerheads with less evangelical clergy in the Cumberland Presbytery.

All the issues of decorum versus emotion in worship were involved, but the original issue around which controversy centered was educational qualifications for ordination: Was English education enough or did one need classical and biblical languages as well? In time, however, the issue shifted to Arminianism. The result was that the orthodox pronounced anathemas, and the evangelicals formed the Cumberland Presbyterian Church.

Circuit Riders and Camp Meetings

The growth of Methodists in the years following Cane Ridge was phenomenal. Shortly before the Revolution, they had small groups in New York and Philadelphia and a few in the South, but by 1820 they had a quarter of a million members, and ten years later they doubled that number.[25] The Baptists did almost as well, increasing their membership tenfold by 1813. These two groups would come to claim the allegiance of two-thirds of America's Protestants. By contrast, the Congregationalists, who had two times as many clergy as any other American church at the beginning of the Revolution, had less than one-tenth the number of the Methodists by 1845.

The reason for this rapid increase of the Methodists is that they had the infrastructures that enabled them to grow with the westward expansion of the country. Primary among these were an itinerant ministry recruited from the settlers and the camp meeting. This is to say that the system of Wesley flourished in America at the very time that it was disappearing in England. In its native land, Methodism had gone respectable: "The circuit horse was almost extinct in England by 1815,"[26] and camp meetings were considered egregious breaches of decorum. What makes this especially ironic is that American Methodists actually revoked their former commitment to obey Wesley at their General Conference of 1787 and removed his name from their minutes.[27] Yet they were much truer to his spirit than the parent church.

Bishop Asbury

The main reason the American Methodists were so loyal to the evangelistic method of their founder was a man who resembled him closely in almost every respect other than being a fellow of an Oxford college. Francis Asbury was as tireless in his labors, as thorough an organizer, and as authoritarian in his leadership as John Wesley, the man who had chosen him for his work.[28] He was born in 1745 into the family of a skilled gardener and farmer, and his formal education took place between the ages of seven and twelve. He was apprenticed to a trade, but after his conversion at the age of fourteen and his discovery of the Methodists, preaching came to be his only interest. He was appointed to his first circuit as an itinerant when he was twenty-one.

His lack of formal education does not mean that he was ignorant. Wesley's reading program for his preachers was never more assiduously followed. A commitment of Asbury's rule of life was to read a hundred pages a day, an extraordinary achievement under the most adverse circumstances.[29] He regretted that travel by horseback was not as conducive to reading in America as it was in England, but he used the time to review Hebrew grammar.[30]

In 1771, five years after his first itinerant appointment, Wesley sent him to America in response to a request from Methodists here for help. Since soul winning was the ruling passion of Francis Asbury's life, he became constantly on the alert for ways in which the infant Methodist movement in this country could become more effective. He came to be the best-informed person in the church about its state in every place. His efforts to improve things had its ups and downs until after the Revolution, when Wesley saw the need for clergy in America who could administer the sacraments. In 1784 he said that Asbury and Thomas Coke should be appointed superintendents—by which he meant bishops, although he never admitted it. Since Coke spent more time in England than America, Asbury was virtually dictator of the American branch of the church.

This did not mean that he ceased to be an itinerant preacher. Quite the contrary; it meant only that his circuit was enlarged. In his entire ministry in America, Asbury would travel 270,000 miles, mostly on horseback, but in a carriage after he became infirm. He would preach 16,500 sermons and ordain 4,000 preachers.[31] He never married, he accepted no salary larger than that of his circuit riders, beginning at the rate of sixty-four dollars a year, and most of the time he was sick and in pain. Yet until his death in 1816, American Methodism bore his imprint as clearly as the original movement bore that of John Wesley.

Asbury's journals (for a sample, see **Vol. 2, pp. 398-403**) permit us to know a good bit about his preaching—which was not atypical of Methodist preaching in general at the time. He was always on the go and preached wherever he went. Like Wesley, he often preached at 5:00 A.M. and also preached almost every evening. Frequent notes in his journal not only mention the occasions of his sermons, but also often give the texts and even say how successful the sermon was. Occasionally the outline is given as well. He did not write out his sermons; to preach from a manuscript on the frontier would have been counterproductive. He did believe in preparation, however, which probably consisted of prayer and thinking through the outline he would follow. Yet his constant study also lay behind each sermon.

While he almost always preached from a text, neither the outline nor the content necessarily grew out of the text. Rather,

> Asbury's most common practice was to take the wording of a biblical text and reconstruct from that wording a topical outline of his own for preaching. Where he knew the historical background of the text he might use it. If the text was obviously and directly applicable he might apply it literally. . . . But there was no guarantee that the topical out-line drawn from a text would have any direct connection with the pri-mary meaning of the text itself. . . . If the text mentioned salvation, the topic headings would almost certainly cover the full range of crucial Methodist doctrines. . . . The topics of the sermon tended to come out the same no matter what the text. There was (1) conviction—under awful weight of our sin; (2) repentance and justification—to be taken on now; (3) perseverance in good works—no backsliding; and (4) sanc-tification—going on to perfect love.[32]

When described this way, his sermons do not sound very biblical, but there is a more profound sense in which they were very much so: he was saturated with the Bible and from it drew his most basic thought forms. His illustrations also were taken from Holy Scripture, unless they were taken from current events.

He generally preached for about an hour, although if the response jus-tified it, he could go on for several hours. He was not emotional in his delivery, but if he sensed that his congregation was being stirred, he sometimes allowed himself free rein and continued as long as the response did. He was not a great preacher, but those who heard him most often best appreciated him.

Peter Cartwright and Circuit Riding

No system could have been better devised than Methodist itinerancy for bringing religion to the settlers moving westward. Even the Baptist system of having unpaid preachers who were fellow settlers and farmers did not work as well; their settled condition limited their ability to fol-low every movement of population. But wherever pioneer families moved, circuit riders found their way to them and established classes with their leaders and local preachers. They would appoint a regular time to preach in a home in an area and make that a point on their circuit, although they may not visit more often than once a month. They would appear at the appointed time, pray, preach, and learn from class leaders the spiritual state of every class member.

The circuit riders, in turn, were visited by their presiding elders, who would meet with them and the lay preachers of the area in quarterly conferences. Then all the clergy of an annual conference would meet annually with Asbury. Every four years there was a General Conference, attended by preachers elected by their annual conference and presided over by Asbury. Further, the Methodist Book Concern, organized by Asbury, turned all the circuit riders into colporteurs of Methodist literature, by which they reinforced their doctrinal preaching and, incidentally, added to their scanty income. It is hard to imagine a system better devised for evangelizing the westward movement of American settlers.

What the life of a circuit rider was like can be learned from a remarkable document written by a remarkable man, *The Autobiography of Peter Cartwright, the Backwoods Preacher.* Cartwright was born in Logan County and converted at one of McGready's sacramental meetings at the age of fifteen. Two years later, when his family moved three counties west and he asked for his letter of transfer of church membership, he discovered that it commissioned him to establish a preaching circuit there. At first he demurred on the basis of his lack of education, but went on to become an autodidact in the great tradition of Wesleyan preachers.

> From then on Peter Cartwright rode circuits in Kentucky, Tennessee, Indiana, Ohio, and Illinois when the distances between preaching appointments were often measured by hundreds of miles and when at times the indefatigable riders were guided only by the evening star or dead reckoning.[33]

Within ten years he was made what modern Methodists call a district superintendent, which eventually enabled him to publish a second autobiographical volume called *Fifty Years as a Presiding Elder.* He became a sort of folk hero and acquired national fame, at least in part because he was willing to use his fists when other means of persuasion failed. He also was a vigorous polemicist, advocating a sectarian exclusiveness shocking to the ecumenical ears of later generations.[34] Although he considered slavery one of the greatest evils in the history of the world, he seemed to think abolitionists ran a close second. He even served in the Illinois legislature, the only opponent ever to win an election over Abraham Lincoln for a seat in that body—although Lincoln was to have his revenge in a congressional election.

Yet Cartwright's passion, his monomania, was soul winning. His *Autobiography* has fascinating accounts of the exposure to weather and other hardships to which circuit riders subjected themselves in their loyalty to their vocation, the sort of experience that gave rise to the proverbial remark about stormy days: "There is nothing out today but crows and Methodist preachers."[35] As absorbing as these are, more to the present purpose are his remarks about the kind of preaching it took (and did not take!) to exercise the vocation of a frontier evangelist. One of the most hilarious of his negative examples is the account of the New School preacher whose response upon being sent to minister to those in anguish on the anxious bench was, "Be composed; be composed, brother."[36] Writing in his early seventies, Cartwright had lived to see Methodism overtaken by the sort of refinement that made Presbyterians so ill-adapted to following the settlers west. More store was set by the education and good taste of clergy than their passion for souls. This was not the spirit that had won a million souls in sixty years.[37]

Although he had devoted much effort to the promotion of education, Cartwright's reaction to this development was an indignant snort. The following passage is typical:

> About this time there were a great many young missionaries sent out to this country to civilize and Christianize the poor heathen of the West. They would come with a tolerable education, and a smattering knowledge of the old Calvinistic system of theology. They were generally tolerably well furnished with old manuscript sermons, that had been preached, or written, perhaps a hundred years before. Some of these sermons they had memorized, but in general they read them to the people. This way of reading sermons was out of fashion altogether in this Western world, and of course they produced no good effect among the people. The great mass of our Western people wanted a preacher that could mount a stump, a block, or old log, or stand in the bed of a wagon, and without note or manuscript, quote, expound, and apply the word of God to the hearts and consciences of the people.[38]

Camp Meetings

So much for the preaching of circuit riders in general. Now for the particular sort of proclamation that was done in that other infrastructure of Methodist expansion during the Second Great Awakening, the camp meeting. While other denominations made some use of camp meetings, it was the Methodists who really capitalized on the opportunities they afforded. With the regular life of the class with its leaders and local preachers, and the regular but less frequent presence of the circuit rider, the Methodist system had need for the occasional sessions of rally and reinforcement that came from having camp meetings around the last quarterly conference of the year and around the annual conference each year.

Such regularity involved a certain "routinization of charisma," as did other aspects of the way the meetings evolved. The two main differentiae between Cane Ridge and true camp meetings were that Cane Ridge was unplanned and had no set rules governing the conduct of those who attended. Rules and planning as characteristics of the events already involve a degree of routinization. A paradox of the camp meeting movement was that, while the emotional extravagance of Cane Ridge and Logan County were the evidences that the Holy Spirit was sending a revival, the emotion itself was regarded as dangerous, and those who wanted to imitate the earlier successes wished at the same time to tame them.[39] Small wonder that camp meetings were progressively refined until they evolved into such programs as Chataqua and summer camping; or that later historians would look on the achievements of the movement more in terms of "civilizing" the West than evangelizing it.[40]

The fire did not leave the backwoods revivals all at once, though. As Charles Johnson says:

> While a public display of one's inner feelings is unthinkable by today's standards [1955], it was regarded as merely the expression of convictions "very pungent and deep" in the harvest time of the camp meeting. This mode of behavior was common even in the populous East. The point at which tension, confusion, and strife between the old sinful ways and the new were overcome by the awesome sermons, prolonged prayers, and crowd pressures was often accompanied by strange bodily manifestations. Automatisms (bodily excitement, crying out, and hallucinations), while not considered positive evidence of conversion, were viewed as probable tokens of God's presence and attested to the power of preaching.[41]

What were the events like that elicited such strong responses? They were held at the end of the summer, when there was a natural lull in farmwork and the weather was still warm enough to permit meeting out-of-doors. An area of two to four acres would be prepared for the camp (**See Vol. 2, pp. 403-4, for a firsthand report**). It had to be near a good source of water. The ground would be laid out in one of several patterns: round, horseshoe, or rectangular. The outer border would contain the horses and mules, and inside their ring were drawn up the wagons and carriages in which participants traveled to the meeting. In front of those, tents were raised, and in front of the tents, campfires were built. At each end of the open area in the middle was erected an elevated speaker's stand, in front of which was usually an area for "mourners" (those under conviction of sin who had not yet been converted). The area in between was filled with benches made of split logs or boards between tree stumps.

The meetings would occupy a four-day weekend or sometimes a longer period. The days would begin early with family prayers and breakfast, followed by a marathon of preaching that lasted into the night. Preaching rotated among the clergy present, with the better known and more accomplished taking the prime times. The intervals between sermons were filled with exhorters and the singing of emotional revival music. Exhorters were also active during the sermons. Those who were "affected" were constantly being ushered into the mourners' area. There they would be surrounded by clergy and others who would try to help pray them through. There were probably as many curiosity seekers as devout in attendance and not a few tradespeople were hawking their wares—including whiskey. Sometimes agitators would try to interrupt the proceedings and would have to be coped with by those in charge. Anything else that brought as much excitement into the backwoods as a camp meeting had the disadvantage of being life-threatening.

The preaching that occurred on these occasions had much in common with other preaching of the circuit riders, but a few generalizations about it are worth making. Naturally, the delivery was extempore. Not only was an inability to preach without manuscript regarded as an indication of practical incompetence, it was also taken as prima facie evidence that the preacher was unconverted: the Spirit would tell the truly called what they should say. The vocabulary and diction of the preachers were in the idiom of those who heard them. Picturesque expression and vigorous delivery were highly prized. A loud voice was necessary to be heard over the hubbub. The vocal endurance of the preachers was remarkable; they could sustain the volume for as many as two or three hours. At the same time, the preachers were capable of great pathos. Poetic imagery and sentimental stories were part of their stock in trade. Much of the spirit of these events was captured by Abraham Lincoln's statement that "when I see a man preach I like to see him act as if he were fighting bees."[42] These backwoods preachers felt they were engaged in an eschatological struggle with evil for the eternal souls of men and women, and they were prepared for strenuous combat. As the evangelist in the film *The Return of Frank James* said: "It's gonna be me and the devil and no holds barred."

Most, but not all, of the sermons were evangelistic in the sense of calling upon those who heard them to escape hell and accept salvation. Altar calls were their climax. Yet many other sermons were preached to the converted, telling them how to live the new lives they had received. In the Methodist tradition, this involved the assumption that they were going on to perfection, and the demands made were stern and uncompromising. A radical difference between the new and old lives was expected.

Whiskey drinking, vanity in dress, and slavery were a triad of evils frequently attacked.

> In pungent language the evils of the day were fearlessly denounced: immorality, intemperance, tobacco, blasphemy, dueling, card playing, horse racing, and gambling.[43]

Hatch's claim that this period in church history was characterized by "the democratization of American religion" is documented by the frequency with which liberty was a sermon topic at camp meetings. There were also doctrinal sermons, especially polemical ones against the perceived shortcomings of other denominations. Thus there was considerable variety in the homiletical diet of a camp meeting. All in all, the camp meeting was one of the most effective means the Methodists used to accomplish their phenomenal growth in the first half of the nineteenth century.

THE URBANIZATION AND UPWARD SOCIAL MOVEMENT OF THE AWAKENING

Stirrings

One of the curious aspects of the northern manifestation of the Second Great Awakening is its ambivalent attitude toward the man whose activity was the occasion of the First, Jonathan Edwards. Indications of this attitude were shown in disagreements about the theological system to which Edwards was in some ways so loyal, Calvinism. As time went on, the great center of Calvinist orthodoxy migrated from Congregationalist New England to Presbyterian Princeton. Those who were closest to Edwards in terms of common history, denomination, and even family ties were no longer so captured as he had been by an overwhelming view of God's absolute sovereignty. They did, however, cling to his devotion to the cause of revival. Indeed, it was their concern for conversions—along with influences from the spirit of the times—that caused them to modify their views on election.

The herald of the Second Awakening in the North was Edwards's grandson, **Timothy Dwight.** A Congregationalist minister who had been a chaplain in the Revolution, Dwight felt that the Puritan world of his ancestors was threatened by many conditions that prevailed in the post-war world. Deism and Unitarianism showed how far gone New England was from original righteousness. Part and parcel with these was the Jeffersonian Republicanism that was disestablishing the church, depriving learned clergy of their elevated position in the community, and banishing respect for all constituted authority. With such an apocalyptic view of the situation, it is no wonder that Dwight thought a revival of religion was needed to get the country back on course. Thus when he became president of Yale in 1795, Dwight immediately began preaching revival in the chapel. Notable outpourings were felt in 1802, 1807, 1812, 1815, and 1820.

The significance of this for the Second Great Awakening was in the graduates who went forth from Yale to spread the revival. There were three who were especially important. The revivalist was **Asahel Nettleton,** who appears to have been launched in that role almost by accident and to have succeeded in it as much by accident as any intention or skill. About the time he became accepted as the very model of a modern gospel preacher, however, illness interrupted his ministry, and his activity was greatly abated from the early 1820s on. He lived to become an embittered man who would find the reason for his existence in resisting the new methods of evangelism that were to sweep the country.

The churchman who would organize the party and rally the troops to the flag was **Lyman Beecher.** He became the most influential leader in the Congregational Church and could succeed in getting accepted almost any program he sponsored. The theologian was **Nathaniel Taylor,** who was the first to occupy Yale's chair in theology, established in 1822. He would furnish a theoretical basis for revivals more congenial than Edwards's assumption that they were sent by an inscrutable Providence for reasons unaffected by human thought or efforts. "For many years in his ministerial study he was absorbed in working on a new system of divinity which left man free to repent and virtually promised that he would be saved if he did."[44]

While these heirs of Edwards were important in the history of the northern expression of the Second Great Awakening, they were not influential on the future of preaching. Of his own preaching, Beecher said:

> I always preached right to the conscience. Every sermon with my eye on the gun to hit somebody. Went through the doctrines; showed what they didn't mean; what they did; then the argument; knocked away objections, and drove home on the conscience.[45]

This is obviously the old Perkins form of "doctrines and uses" and represents no change in preaching style. Nor did the delivery of such sermons violate earlier norms of decorum. While Beecher had a great reputation as a preacher during his lifetime, Nettleton did not attempt to stir the congregation in one of his revivals; "if the meeting began to show signs of violent feeling, Nettleton was apt to break it up."[46]

Charles Grandison Finney, Prosecuting Attorney

Timothy Dwight's disciples were greatly upset when someone came along who changed the rules of the game considerably. As will be seen, they were to put forth energetic effort to set roadblocks in the way of Charles Grandison Finney, who was to adapt the techniques of the southern awakening to the North. The irony is that Finney was to do so in a way that would recommend itself to areas much more stably settled than the southern backwoods and to an audience higher on the social scale than farmer-settlers. Before he finished, Finney numbered among his supporters some of the wealthiest people in the country, and he was invited by them to conduct revivals in the largest cities of the East.

Although Charles G. Finney was actually born in New England, his parents joined the westward migration when he was only two and moved to Oneida County, New York. There the young Finney eventually gained enough education to become a schoolteacher, but he afterward turned to an apprenticeship in law as the path to his chosen career.

Finney's parents had not been religious, and he lived in the region for which he supplied the name that has stuck, "the burned-over district."

> There had been, a few years previously, a wild excitement [passing through that region], which they called a revival, but which turned out to be spurious. It was reported as having been a very extravagant excitement; and resulted in a reaction so extensive and profound as to leave the impression on many minds that religion was a mere delusion.[47]

Finney spent only three years in the study and practice of law. He already attended church, but his motives for doing so were not basically religious. Discovering, however, that the Bible was cited in his legal texts as the authority for many of the principles of common law, he bought his first Bible and began to study it. Yet when he started reading the Bible, he was led to consider the condition of his own soul. He came under deep conviction of sin and remained that way for about a week. At the end of that ordeal, he had an overwhelming conversion experience that filled

him with great joy and a sense of being called to preach. On the morning of his conversion, he had been scheduled to appear in court, but he
told his client, "Deacon B_____, I have a retainer from the Lord Jesus
Christ to plead his cause, and I cannot plead yours."[48]

He began studying for the Presbyterian ministry under the guidance of
his pastor, having refused to go to seminary because he found seminary
graduates so poorly prepared for their work—although his
Autobiography probably exaggerates the extent to which he differed
from his instructor on Calvinism at the time.[49] After two years of study,
he was taken under care by the presbytery. Six months later he was
licensed, and seven months after that he was ordained as a teaching elder
for a ministry of evangelism rather than that of a settled pastor. He began
to work in the small villages of the surrounding area, and his preaching
met with an enthusiastic response.[50]

He immediately began to acquire a local reputation, and success in one
area would lead to an invitation to a larger one. In the rural villages
where he began, his method was the sort of sensational hellfire and
damnation preaching that was common at first in southern camp meetings, but as he moved to larger towns, he recognized that more restraint
was needed if he was going to reach a more refined set of sinners.[51]

Even toned down, however, his methods met the objections of
Nettleton, who to that time had been the reigning revivalist in New York
and New England. Finney was accused of using "new measures" in
evangelism.

> Although opponents such as Asahel Nettleton would later list as many
> as twenty-nine practices they considered objectionable, only five or six
> caused widespread controversy: public praying by women in mixed
> audiences; protracted series of meetings (i.e., daily services); colloquial
> language used by the preacher; the anxious seat or bench; the practice
> of praying for people by name; and immediate church membership for
> converts.[52]

While Methodists and others had used such means for some time, they
were, nevertheless, offensive to the sense of decorum of some
Presbyterians and Congregationalists. Unitarians and Universalists were
also very opposed to Finney, but he could take their disapproval almost
as a commendation.

By 1827 Nettleton and Lyman Beecher were involved with others in a
conspiracy to halt Finney's influence and had begun publishing attacks
on his methods in the church press. A conference was proposed in New

Lebanon, New York, where Finney had been preaching, to see if the two sides could iron out their differences. Each side had nine representatives. When they convened on July 18, it was the hope of the New Englanders that Finney would be so discredited that his effectiveness would vanish. They treated the occasion almost as a trial of him and his methods.

In the end, however, they overextended themselves; they had very inadequate information about what he was actually doing and were abashed to discover that the measures they could get condemned by the group had apparently never been practiced by Finney. The upshot was that he left the conference without a mark against him and thus with the appearance of the blessing of the New England establishment. Beecher was eventually to be somewhat reconciled to Finney and even to join Boston clergy in inviting him to conduct a revival.[53] Nettleton, however, would not accept the inevitable and found himself progressively isolated and embittered. When Finney's measures were next subjected to a major attack, it was not from New School Calvinists but from the Old School tradition of Princeton, after the publication of his *Lectures on Revivals*.

From New Lebanon on he began to have citywide, ecumenically supported revivals in the major metropolitan centers of the East Coast. His successes there, however, were never so overwhelming and unqualified as they were in western New York. His greatest triumph was in Rochester, where he preached from September 10, 1830, to March 6, 1831. Although conditions had been very unpromising when he arrived, the response was total. The establishment backed the revival completely. Church membership increased by almost ten thousand. And, in one of the first major associations of evangelism with social action, a city that was a center of distilleries was converted to the cause of temperance.

The most important results of the revival, however, were not confined to Rochester:

> It was almost singularly responsible for bringing about the national revival of 1831, in which what had been building up for years throughout the country seemed almost to explode in that one year. . . . Between 1800 and 1835 the portion of Protestant church members to the national population almost doubled, from 7 to 12 1/2 percent, but most of that growth came after 1830. . . . Everywhere, ordinary citizens desired to have duplicated in their town what had happened so sanely and so respectably in Rochester.[54]

The Second Great Awakening, which had begun among the widely scattered farmer-settlers of the Trans-Appalachian South, was now completely at home among the business leaders as well as the rank-and-file population of the urban North.

Even though Finney was to continue preaching revivals for many years and was even to make two evangelistic tours of England, the exacting demand of the revival schedule had begun to wear down his health so that in 1832, at the age of forty, he accepted his first appointment as pastor of a congregation, the Second Free Church (also called Chatham Street Chapel) in New York City. Two years later he transferred to Broadway Tabernacle, where a church was built to his specifications.

The following year, he accepted the professorship of theology at the infant Oberlin College and for a while divided his year between his parish and the campus. Although not the founder of Oberlin, Finney was the person around whom it was built. His main understanding of his work there was that he was to raise up a generation of young evangelists who would carry on his work. Finney was deeply involved in the development of "Oberlin perfectionism," a belief similar to Wesley's understanding of sanctification. He became president of Oberlin in 1852, and the college remained his home until his death twenty-three years later.

The key to Finney's success as an evangelist was the power of his preaching. He was a tall, slim, commanding figure, his appearance not unlike that of the film actor Charlton Heston. His most impressive feature was his eyes, which even in printed reproductions of photographs have an amazingly piercing, hypnotic quality.[55] One gets the impression that he must have been a riveting speaker. We can gain an idea of what—beyond the sheer physical impact of his appearance—made his preaching so effective by reading, even more than his sermons, two of his other writings, his *Lectures on Revivals of Religion*[56] and his *Autobiography*.

The *Lectures on Revivals* were not only an end in themselves but also a means to raise money. They were given at his Chatham Street Chapel in New York in 1834, after Finney returned from an unsuccessful voyage to restore his health only to discover that the *New York Evangelist* was almost bankrupt because, contrary to his instructions, the editor had used the newspaper to crusade for abolition.[57] Publication of the lectures in the *Evangelist* did succeed in regaining its lost subscribers. Modern readers who turn to the work expecting to find "how-to" gimmicks will be disappointed. While the work is prescriptive, the perspective is much more spiritual than practical. More than the first third of the book is devoted to the work of prayer that must be done in advance and during the meeting for a revival to occur.

Only the twelfth lecture is devoted to preaching. Its outline shows not only his thoughts on the subject but also the form Finney's sermons usually took:

How to Preach the Gospel

I. Several passages of scripture ascribe conversion to human agency.

II. These are not inconsistent with those that ascribe it to God.

III. Several particulars about preaching the gospel will be listed which show that practical wisdom is needed to win souls for Christ.

First, with regard to the matter of preaching.

1. "All preaching should be *practical*." Doctrine that does not have practical implications is irrelevant.

2. "Preaching should be *direct*," preached to people instead of about them.

3. The minister should hunt for sinners and for Christians entrenched in inaction.

4. The preacher should dwell on the points most needed.

5. The minister should not introduce distracting controversy.

6. The whole gospel should be brought to the mind of the people.

7. Sinners should be made to feel their guilt and not left with the impression that they are merely unfortunate.

8. "A prime objective with the preacher must be to make the *present obligation* felt."

9. Sinners should be made to feel that they should repent and repentance is something no one else can do for them.

10. "Ministers should never rest satisfied, until they have ANNI-HILATED every excuse of sinners."[58]

11. "Sinners should be made to feel that if they *now* grieve away the Spirit of God, it is very probable that they will be *lost forever*."

Secondly, a few remarks about the manner of preaching.

1. It should be *conversational*.

2. It must be in the *language of common life*.

3. Preaching should be *parabolical*.

4. The illustrations should be drawn *from common* life.

5. Preaching should be *repetitious*.

6. "A minister should always feel deeply his subject, and then he will suit the action to the word and the word to the action, so as to make the full impression which the truth is calculated to make."

7. "A minister should aim to *convert his congregation*."

8. The preacher should anticipate and answer the objections of sinners.

9. The preacher must not be monotonous.

10. "A minister should address the feelings enough to secure attention, and then deal with the conscience, and probe to the quick."

Remarks[59]

1. To convert the leading minds of the community, ministers must reason with them so that they see the truth of the gospel.

2. The success of the gospel requires extempore preachers.

    a. there is not time to write all the sermons that will be needed.

    b. written sermons do not produce the necessary effect.

    c. "it is impossible for a man who writes his sermons to arrange his matter, and turn and choose his thoughts, so as to produce the same effect as when he addresses the people directly, and makes them feel that he means them."

3. Education for ministers should all be theological in the sense that secular disciplines should only be studied from a theological perspective.

4. "All ministers should be revival ministers, and all preaching should be revival preaching" in the sense that it promotes holiness, it inculcates doctrines to be practiced.

5. Two mistaken objections have been made to such preaching:

    a. it lets down the dignity of the pulpit.

    b. it is theatrical.

6. Ministers should be chosen not on the basis of whether they are popular or learned but on that of whether they are wise to win souls.

"Finally It is the duty of the church to pray for us, ministers."[60]

Nearly everything that needs to be said about Finney's understanding of how preaching should be done is included in that outline, but the significance of some of his remarks needs to be underlined by reference to parallel statements in his *Autobiography*. At the outset, the difference between him and his predecessors in the Congregationalist-Presbyterian tradition needs to be noted.[61] He summarized their objections to him in a paragraph:

> They used to complain that I let down the dignity of the pulpit, that I was a disgrace to the ministerial profession, that I talked like a lawyer at the bar, that I talked to the people in a colloquial manner, that I said "you," instead of preaching about sin and sinners, and saying "they," that I said "hell," and with such an emphasis as often to shock people;

furthermore, that I urged people with such vehemence as if they might not have a moment to live; and sometimes they complained that I blamed people too much.[62]

His opponents considered talking like a lawyer at the bar a shortcoming, but he regarded it as a virtue. He said that he had interpreted the Bible from the beginning "as I would have understood the same or like passages in a law book" (42, cf. 89). The qualities of legal speech that appealed to him were its simplicity, its logic, and the way that it was directed to getting a verdict on the spot. Thus preachers should define their terms and not assume what needs to be proved (8, 7). His hyper-Calvinist opponents did not preach that way; the biblical passages with which they supported their doctrines would not have been considered at all conclusive in a court of law (60).

He quoted against them the remarks of a supreme court judge: "Our object in addressing a jury, is to get their minds settled before they leave the jury box. . . . We are set on getting a verdict. Hence we are set upon being understood." Most ministers, the judge said, do not share that purpose; "They rather seem to aim at making fine literary productions, and displaying great eloquence and an ornate use of language" (85-86). Finney says in another place, "If advocates at the bar should pursue the same course in pleading the cause of their clients, that ministers do in pleading the cause of Christ with sinners, they would not gain a single case" (155).

On the whole, Finney seems to have approved of the members of his former profession more than he did those of his latter. He said, "As a general thing, they take a more intelligent view of the whole plan of salvation, than any other class of men to whom I have preached" (368). In one of his Rochester revivals, he had a special course of sermons for them. He certainly thought more highly of legal than ministerial training (85-97). And he always taught doctrine more like someone with legal than with theological training. There is also in his teaching a certain legalism, as in such remarks as "For me the Law and Gospel have but one rule of life; and every violation of the spirit of the Law, is also a violation of the spirit of the Gospel" (339). (For a sermon that shows how much he was shaped by a legal approach, see **Vol. 2, pp. 405-19**.)

Ways in which his preaching resembled an attorney's efforts to win a verdict are his use of colloquial speech and his illustrations.

I used to meet from ministers a great many rebuffs and reproofs, particularly in respect to my manner of preaching. . . . They would reprove me for illustrating my ideas by reference to the common affairs of men, as I was in the habit of doing. Among farmers and mechanics, and other classes, I borrowed illustrations from their various occupations. I tried also to use such language as they would understand. I addressed them in the language of the common people. (I sought to express all my ideas in few words, and in words that were in common use.) (81)

The result was that "people have often said to me: 'Why, you do not preach. You talk to the people....He don't preach; he only explains what other people preach.' Or, again, 'You talk as if you were as much at home as if you sat in the parlor'" (91). To be effective, sermons must also repeat the main points over and over until they have entered the consciousness of the congregation (83 passim).

His own practice and the response to it gave him distinct opinions about how seminarians should be trained:

Men cannot learn to preach by study without practice. The students should be encouraged to exercise, and prove, and improve their gifts and calling of God, by going out into any places open to them, and holding Christ up to the people in earnest talks. They must thus learn to preach. Instead of this, the students are required to write what they call sermons, and present them for criticism; to preach—that is, read—them to a class and a professor. Thus they play at preaching. . . . This reading of elegant literary essays, is not to [the people] preaching. . . . The students are taught to cultivate a fine, elevated style of writing. As for real eloquence, that gushing, impressive and persuasive oratory, that naturally flows from an educated man whose soul is on fire with his subject, and who is free to pour out his heart to a waiting and earnest people, they have none of it. (90)

In addition to being in conversational language and clearly illustrated from the experience of the congregation, preaching must be extemporaneous. Finney not only often castigates written sermons, but also describes his own method of sermon preparation.

My habit has always been to study the Gospel, and the best application of it, all the time. . . . Then, in the light of the Holy Spirit, I take a subject that I think will meet their present necessities. I think intensely on it, and pray much over the subject on Sabbath morning, for example, and get my mind full of it, and then go and pour it out to the people. . . . I think I have studied all the more for not having written my sermons. . . . I simply note the heads upon which I wish to dwell in the briefest possible manner, and in language not a word of which I use, perhaps, in preaching. (94)[63]

The frequency of his sermons and the demand of other duties meant that he often did not have opportunity to think of what he was going to say until the last minute.[64]

Some of the most telling sermons I have ever preached in Oberlin, I have thus received after the bell had rung for church; and I was obliged to go and pour them off from my full heart, without jotting down more than the briefest possible skeleton, and that sometimes not covering half the ground that I covered in my sermon. (96)

For him, this dearth of immediate preparation was not irresponsible, but was instead a dependence upon divine inspiration.

I held that the Holy Spirit operates in the preacher, clearly revealing these truths in their proper order, and enabling him to set them before the people in such proportion and in such order as is calculated to convert them. (155, cf. 55)

The reason such plain and persuasive language and, even more, such inspiration is necessary is that the eternal destiny of precious souls is at stake:

A reflecting mind will feel as if it were infinitely out of place to present in the pulpit to immortal souls, hanging upon the verge of everlasting death, such specimens of learning and rhetoric. They know that men do not do so on any subject where they are really in earnest. The captain of a fire company, when a city is on fire, does not read to his company an essay, or exhibit a fine specimen of rhetoric, when he shouts to them and directs their movements. . . . This is the reason why, formerly, the ignorant Methodist preachers and the earnest Baptist preachers produced so much more effect than our most learned theologians and divines. . . . Great sermons lead the people to praise the preacher. Good preaching leads the people to praise the Savior. (90-91)

That, however, was not the way of his opponents:

You would scarcely get the idea from the sermons that are heard, either in this country or in England, that ministers expect or intend, to be instrumental in converting, at any time, anybody in the house. (410, cf. 43, 155)

They often preach about the Gospel instead of preaching the Gospel. They often preach about sinners instead of preaching to them. . . . I have often said, "Do not think I am talking about anybody else; but I mean you, and you, and you." (92)

Evangelistic preaching aimed at conversions then and there was the only sort of preaching for which Finney had any use. That preoccupation determined both the way he went about preaching and all of the other "means" that he used in his revivals. His method of preaching was to hammer away at his congregation for two hours at a time or more, to break down the unconverted until they had to admit they were sinners who deserved eternal damnation if they did not repent and accept salvation at that very moment.

It often appeared brutal to others, but he felt that anything else would make him a party to the loss of their souls. "It seemed to myself as if I could rain hail and love upon them at the same time; or in other words, that I could rain upon them hail, in love" (101). "It was a fire and a hammer breaking the rock and as a sword that was piercing to the dividing asunder of soul and spirit" is the way he described his preaching on another occasion (65).

He tried to show his listeners that all delay was only an evasion of present duty (80).

> We insisted then, as I have ever done since, on immediate submission, as the only thing that God could accept at their hands; and that all delay, under any pretext whatever, was rebellion against God. (190)

His message was consistent with his medium:

> Sinners were not encouraged to expect the Holy Ghost to convert them, while they were passive; and never told to wait God's time, but were taught, unequivocally, that their first and immediate duty was, to submit themselves to God, to renounce their own will, their own way, and themselves, and instantly to deliver up all that they were, and all that they had, to their rightful owner, the Lord Jesus Christ. They were taught here, as everywhere in those revivals, that the only obstacle in the way was their own stubborn will; that God was trying to gain their unqualified consent to give up their sins, and accept the Lord Jesus Christ as their righteousness and salvation. . . . [In meetings of inquiry he made a course of remarks] calculated to strip them of every excuse, and bring them face to face with the great question of present, unqualified, universal acceptance of the will of God in Christ Jesus. . . . The doctrine of the justice of endless punishment was fully insisted upon; and not only its justice, but

the certainty that sinners will be endlessly punished, if they die in their sins, was strongly held forth. (363-64, cf. 77, 134-35, 189)

Finney not only pressed for an immediate decision, but also provided means by which those under conviction could respond then and there. He did not introduce the Methodist mourners' bench or "anxious seat" until his first great revival at Rochester, but he began very early in his ministry to see that people had an opportunity to respond to the pressure for conversion by some simple act such as standing or kneeling (116, 164 passim). The other means he used also reinforced the emotional pressure to submit to his call for conversion:

> The means that I had all along used, thus far, in promoting revivals, were much prayer, secret and social, public preaching, personal conversation, and visitation from house to house; and when inquirers became multiplied, I appointed meetings for them, and invited those that were inquiring to meet for instruction, suited to their necessities. These were the means and the only means, that I had thus far used, in attempting to secure the conversion of souls.[65] (160, cf. 77, 80)

For all that his revivals were designed to be emotional pressure cookers, however, Finney remained enough of a Presbyterian (or was concerned enough about his reputation and influence in the areas to which he wished to take the revival) to see that things were done decently and in order. In his autobiography he often takes pains to show that "converts were sound, and the work permanent and genuine" (105). He also stresses that revivals were not emotionally excessive, as, for example, the meeting at Rome, New York: "It is difficult to conceive so deep and universal a state of religious feeling, with no instance of disorder, or tumult, or fanaticism, or anything that was objectionable" (170). In much the same spirit are countless remarks about the upper-class status of those who were converted or who supported and called for the revivals.

In many ways, the culmination of Finney's work as an evangelist was the Awakening of 1858, which began in Hamilton, Ontario, and quickly spread through the northern United States. Triggered by the financial panic of the previous year, it began in many cities with businessmen gathering spontaneously for noonday prayers; as many as ten thousand met in various places in New York City. James Gordon Bennett and Horace Greeley made coverage of the Awakening a regular feature in their newspapers. College campuses were as affected as business districts.

> Estimates of the total number of converts in the Awakening of 1858 have varied somewhat. Finney declared, "It was estimated that during

this revival not less than five hundred thousand souls were converted in this country," and this may be one of the lower approximations. At times the reports from various places seemed to indicate that, for the climactic five months from February to June 1858, some fifty thousand persons were making commitments each week, which would raise the estimate considerably above Finney's. The total will never be known, but the fact that the Awakening of 1858 was utterly lacking in fanaticism, solemn, devoted to prayer, and led by laymen, makes it unique in American history.[66]

Largely through the efforts of Charles Grandison Finney, the shape of revivals in America had changed. The Calvinism of the First Great Awakening was dead and buried. The excesses of the southern Second Awakening had been tamed. The decorous demurrals of conservative northern revivalists were silenced. The soul of the North, and especially its urban aristocracies, was reflexively evangelical. And Finney's "new measures" were everywhere accepted as the way to have a revival. Indeed, his *Lectures on Revivals* is still the accepted textbook for almost anyone who wishes to have a protractive meeting.[67]

FOR FURTHER READING

The Autobiography of Peter Cartwright, the Backwoods Preacher. Edited with introduction by Charles L. Wallis. Pierce & Washabaugh, 1956: reprint, Nashville: Abingdon, 1984.

Conkin, Paul K. *Cane Ridge: America's Pentecost.* The Curti Lectures. Madison and London: University of Wisconsin Press, 1990.

Finney, Charles G. *An Autobiography.* Old Tappan, N.J.: Fleming H. Revell, 1876, renewed 1908.

_____. *Lectures on Revivals of Religion.* New revised edition. Oberlin, Ohio: E. J. Goodrich, 1868.

Hardman, Keith J. *Charles Grandison Finney, 1792–1875: Revivalist and Reformer.* Syracuse: Syracuse University Press, 1987; republished by Baker Book House in 1990.

Johnson, Charles A. *The Frontier Camp Meeting: Religion's Harvest Time.* Dallas: Southern Methodist University Press, 1955; reprinted in 1985 with new introduction by Ferenc M. Szasz.

Rudolph, L. C. *Francis Asbury.* Nashville: Abingdon, 1966.

Weisberger, Bernard A. *They Gathered at the River: The Story of the Great Revivalists and Their Impact upon Religion in America.* Boston and Toronto: Little, Brown, 1958.

Notes

1. William G. McLoughlin, *Revivals, Awakenings, and Reform: An Essay on Religion and Social Change in America, 1607–1977,* Chicago History of American Religion (Chicago and London: University of Chicago Press, 1978).

2. Ibid., 12.

3. Ibid.

4. The basic American myths that have perdured and been accommodated in each revitalization of our history are: "the chosen nation, the covenant with God, the millennial manifest destiny; the higher (biblical or natural) law, against which private and social behavior is to be judged; the moral law (the Ten Commandments, the Sermon on the Mount); the laws of science, presumed to be from the Creator, and evolutionary or progressive in their purpose; the free and moral responsible individual, whose political liberty and liberty of conscience are inalienable; the work ethic (or 'Protestant ethic'), which holds that equal opportunity and hard work will bring economic success and public respect to all who assert and discipline themselves; and the benevolence of nature under the exploitative or controlling hand of man (i.e., nature was made for man)" (ibid., 103).

5. Nathan O. Hatch, *The Democratization of American Christianity* (New Haven and London: Yale University Press, 1989).

6. Ibid., 5.

7. Ibid.

8. Paul K. Conkin, *Cane Ridge: America's Pentecost,* The Curti Lectures (Madison and London: University of Wisconsin Press, 1990), 27. This admirable monograph is drawn on heavily for this treatment of the Cane Ridge Revival.

9. In the sense that a congregation or an area was experiencing intensified religious emotions. Revival in the sense of a protracted meeting held to bring in such a period is anachronistic for the time.

10. See above, chapter 17. Marilyn J. Westerkamp has seen the Scotch-Irish sacraments as the inspiration of the First as well as the Second Great Awakening in America. She also has identified a lay rather than a clerical impetus for the Awakening. *The Triumph of the Laity: Scots-Irish Piety and the Great Awakening, 1625–1760* (New York and Oxford: Oxford University Press, 1988).

11. Conkin, *Cane Ridge,* 31. Although tents in the modern sense of fabric-covered shelters came to be a standard feature of camp meetings, and even though Charles Finney and others were to hold tent revivals, in the passage quoted "tent" is used in the technical sense of Presbyterians of the time that referred to the permanent outdoor canopied platform from which preaching was done at a communion meeting. Ibid., 19.

12. There is much disagreement over what was the original camp meeting, depending on how one defines that event and other factors, including the denominational allegiance of the particular scholar. Conkin, however, says judiciously that "by most later images of camps, [the Gasper River meeting] scarcely qualified; there had been no planning, no tents or cabins, no regulations." Ibid., 61.

13. Ibid., 97-98 n. 22.

14. "Exercises" was the term used at the time.

15. Quoted, ibid., 93-94, in a letter from a Kentucky minister included in a letter from Moses Hoge to Dr. Ashbel Green, September 10, 1801, in William Wallis Woodward, *Increase of Piety, or Revival of Religion in the United States of America* (Newburyport, Conn.: Angier March, 1802), 53.

16. *The Biography of Eld. Barton Warren Stone, Written by Himself: With Additions and Reflections by Elder John Rogers* (Cincinnati: J. A. and U. P. James, 1847), 39-42. Quoted in Max Ward Randall, *The Great Awakenings and the Restoration Movement* (Joplin, Mo.: College Press, 1983), 51-52. See also Bernard A. Weisberger, *They Gathered at the River: The Story of the Great Revivalists and Their Impact upon Religion in America* (Boston and Toronto: Little, Brown, 1958), 34-35.

17. Conkin, *Cane Ridge*, 65.

18. Ibid., 103.

19. Ibid., 104-5. Nor are such religious exercises confined to the remote past. Near the time this section was being written, a story appeared in a national newsmagazine concerning the spread of the phenomenon known as the "Toronto Blessing," which causes people caught up in ecstatic worship to fall to the floor in uncontrollable laughter, some jerking spasmodically. Apparently more than one hundred thousand persons have already undergone this experience. Furthermore, "Anglicans—known for their reserve at worship—seem especially prone to catching the new spirit" (*Newsweek*, February 20, 1995, 54). Another point Conkin made later about the emotionalism of the Cane Ridge revival was that "such a warm religion enabled humble people, whose lives were so much more insecure and cruel than our own, to have fun. That was not a mean achievement" (*Cane Ridge*, 178).

20. Ibid., 106.

21. Ibid., 91.

22. For a much more extensive discussion of the loss of that centrality, see Doug Adams, *Meeting House to Camp Meeting: Toward a History of American Free Church Worship from 1620 to 1835* (Saratoga, Fla.: Modern Liturgy-Resource Publications; Austin, Tex.: Sharing Company, 1981, 1984).

23. Those who left the Presbyterian Church at that time, of course, were to view their actions not as schisms, but as founding churches in which a more scriptural form of Christianity was taught and practiced.

24. Now part of the United Church of Christ, having merged with Congregationalists in 1931.

25. Hatch, *The Democratization of American Christianity*, 3.

26. Ibid., 91. On this general subject, see also pp. 7, 8, 50-52, and 92.

27. L. C. Rudolph, *Francis Asbury* (Nashville: Abingdon, 1966), 70. Wesley's name was restored in 1789 as a courtesy, but he died without accepting the independence of the American branch of the movement he founded.

28. It is amazing that a critical biography of Asbury has yet to appear. The most often cited work is that of a descendant who was a journalist and not a follower in the faith; Herbert Asbury, *A Methodist Saint: The Life of Bishop Asbury* (New York: Knopf, 1927). Asbury's journal was republished in three volumes by Abingdon Press in 1958 (*The Journal and Letters of Francis Asbury*, ed. Elmer T. Clark, J. Manning Potts, and Jacob S. Payton), but, as informative as that is, it can hardly be considered objective. Perhaps the best treatment available is the short work of Rudolph cited above.

29. Ibid., *The Journal and Letters of Francis Asbury*, for July 29, 1776 (1:195).

30. Ibid. for March 6, 1793 (1:750).

31. Merrill R. Abbey, *The Epic of United Methodist Preaching: A Profile in American Social History* (Lanham, N.Y.: University Press of America, 1984), 20.

32. Rudolph, *Francis Asbury*, 84-85. This description of Asbury's preaching is based on ibid., 80-94.

33. Charles L. Wallis, "Introduction," in *The Autobiography of Peter Cartwright* (Pierce & Washabaugh, 1956; Nashville: Abingdon, 1984), 6.

34. In this he was not unlike Asbury, who thought the Reformation small potatoes beside the Wesleyan awakening and believed that true episcopacy had not existed between the apostle's times and its itinerant restoration by American Methodists. Rudolph, *Francis Asbury*, 171-73, 186-206.

35. Quoted in Charles A. Johnson, *The Frontier Camp Meeting: Religion's Harvest Time* (Dallas: Southern Methodist University Press, 1955, as reprinted in 1985 with new intro. by Ferenc M. Szasz), 151.

36. Wallis, *The Autobiography of Peter Cartwright*, 245.

37. Ibid., 266.

38. Ibid., 236. For similar passages, see pp. 63-66, 114, 204, 212, 236-37, 244-46, 265, 316, and especially 267-68.

39. This is not unlike the fate of the legacy of Jonathan Edwards. It came to be overtaken by the Genteel Tradition, as in Edwards Amasa Park, who wrote: "We bow before this father of our New England theology with the profoundest veneration. . . . Yet we can not help wishing that he had been something more of a brother and somewhat less of a champion." He goes on to say that they needed a theology to take with them into the flower garden. Quoted by Herbert May, "Jonathan Edwards and America," in *Jonathan Edwards and the American Experience*, ed. Nathan O. Hatch and Harry S. Stout (New York: Oxford University Press, 1988), 22.

40. The author of the standard monograph on camp meetings, Charles A. Johnson, begins his preface by saying: "Among all of the weapons forged by the West in its struggle against lawlessness and immorality, few were more successful than the frontier camp meeting" (*The Frontier Camp Meeting*, xix). In this he followed the interpretation of his mentor, William Warren Sweet.

41. Ibid., 173.

42. Quoted ibid., 188. This paragraph and the next are based on pp. 170-91.

43. Ibid., 177.

44. Weisberger, *They Gathered at the River*, 84.

45. Quoted from his *Autobiography*, 1:100-101, in ibid., 72-73.

46. Ibid., 66.

47. Charles G. Finney, *An Autobiography* (Old Tappan, N.J.: Fleming H. Revell, 1876, renewed 1908), 63. Finney's actual term was "burnt district," but the other form has been standard at least since Whitney R. Cross published his book with that title in 1950.

48. Ibid., 24.

49. Keith J. Hardman, *Charles Grandison Finney, 1792–1875: Revivalist and*

Reformer (Syracuse: Syracuse University Press, 1987; republished by Baker in 1990), 52. This is the only modern scholarly biography.

50. For a map of Finney's evangelistic activity, see ibid., 1.

51. Ibid., 82.

52. Ibid., 84.

53. The differences between Beecher and Finney were more political than theological, Beecher being a Federalist defender of the established order of New England and Finney showing a Jacksonian democratic spirit.

54. Ibid., 220.

55. A hint of their effect can be given by saying that they remind one of the eyes of master villains in superhero comic books. They seem to emit X-rays that can see right through you and laser beams that can saw you in half.

56. Charles G. Finney, *Lectures on Revivals of Religion,* new rev. ed. (Oberlin, Ohio: E. J. Goodrich, 1868). Finney regarded these lectures as sermons and they follow his typical sermon outline. Yet the lectures do not represent his *ipsissima verba:* they were taken down while he delivered them by the editor of the *Evangelist,* who did not know shorthand. Finney said that the lectures averaged an hour and three-quarters in length while one in published form can be read aloud in half an hour (Finney, *An Autobiography,* 330).

57. Finney was an ardent opponent of slavery, but he considered promoting abolition to be a distraction from the even more important cause of winning souls. His strategy for eliminating slavery was to have churches universally condemn it as sin, with the expected result that "in three years, a public sentiment would be formed that would carry all before it, and there would not be a shackled slave, nor a bristling, cruel slaveowner, in this land" (ibid., 302).

58. Emphasis in all quotations from this chapter is Finney's.

59. "Remarks" is Finney's usual designation for the application section of his sermons.

60. Finney, *Lectures on Revivals of Religion,* 185-212.

61. By this time, the two traditions were so alike that it was even possible to have united "Presbygational" congregations, although there were groups in both churches that stoutly insisted on differences.

62. Finney, *An Autobiography,* 83. Hereafter in this section, page numbers of quoted material from this work will be cited parenthetically in the text.

63. Finney says that he wrote down nothing for his first twelve years of preaching. His first sermon "skeletons" were written after he preached the sermon rather than before. Yet he found he could never reuse one of those sermon outlines. A specimen skeleton in his handwriting is reproduced in his *Autobiography,* on facing pp. 96-97.

64. At the beginning of his ministry, his presbytery, having heard of his impromptu preaching, arranged an occasion on which he would have to do it before them (ibid., 82).

65. To this list should be added the apparatus and infrastructure created for citywide revivals, at least from Rochester on.

66. Hardman, *Charles Grandison Finney,* 433.

67. Finney even shaped the architecture of evangelism. In his directions for the construction of Broadway Tabernacle, he anticipated most of the provisions

Spurgeon would make at his Metropolitan Tabernacle to have every eye in the church focused on the preacher, and did so in the year Spurgeon was born (Finney, *An Autobiography*, 326). He even commissioned an enormous tent that was largely used to make up for the lack of an auditorium of adequate size at Oberlin, but it "was used, to some extent also, for holding protracted meetings in the region round about" (ibid., 336), possibly making Finney the first tent evangelist.

"THE FRUITS OF FERVOR" (A)

AMONG AFRICAN AMERICANS

THE SOCIAL IMPLICATIONS OF GOSPEL PREACHING[1]

Revivalism was the dominant influence on all major denominations in the United States between 1840 and 1865, especially in the larger cities. During this period, American Protestantism took on four qualities that have characterized it ever since: (1) lay leadership, (2) interdenominational cooperation, (3) an emphasis on ethics over theology, and (4) the replacement of the Calvinist doctrine of election with belief in the human acceptance of salvation as determinative. Furthermore, this regnant revivalism both reflected and helped shape an interconnected series of elements in the American *zeitgeist* during that era, which included optimism, perfectionism,[2] and millennialism.

These elements of mid-nineteenth-century urban revivalism had inevitable social implications. It used to be assumed that revivalism as a force had pretty well run its course before the Civil War and that it would not reemerge until the end of the century and then only among socially marginal groups. It was further assumed that the emphasis on social ethics in American Christianity owed its origins entirely to the liberal tradition. It is now recognized, however, that "Evangelical Protestantism reached the summit of its influence in America during the last half of the nineteenth century."[3] Furthermore, during the quarter century ending with the end of war,

> a widespread aspiration for Christian perfection complemented in many ways the social idealism which endeavored to reform the drunkard, free the slaves, elevate womankind, and banish poverty and vice from the country.[4]

This is not to say that exclusive credit for these social movements should go to revivalism. Rather, as Timothy Smith has said:

> Whatever may have been the role of other factors, the quest for perfection joined with compassion for poor and needy sinners and a rebirth of millennial expectation to make popular Protestantism a mighty social force long before the slavery conflict erupted into war.[5]

Many of these points can be documented in the persons and movements surveyed in the previous chapter. John Wesley told William Wilberforce in a letter dated February 24, 1791, that he considered American slavery to be "the vilest that ever saw the sun."[6] Almost twenty years earlier he had published his negative *Thoughts upon Slavery*. Thomas Coke and Francis Asbury shared the founder's opinion and did all in their power to make it impossible for anyone who owned slaves to be a Methodist in good standing. Southerners in the General Conference, however, refused to permit rules against slavery to stay on the books. Asbury ultimately had to settle for evangelizing the slaves instead of working to free them.[7]

Peter Cartwright shared the opinion of Brother Axley that "a preacher that was good and true, had a trinity of devils to fight, namely: superfluous dress, whiskey, and slavery."[8] Cartwright moved from Kentucky to Illinois so that his children would not have to grow up in a state where slavery was practiced, and then ran for the legislature in order to oppose efforts to open his new state to slavery.[9]

Charles G. Finney was equally opposed. He wrote:

> Deprive a human being of liberty who has been guilty of no crime; rob him of himself—his body—his soul—his time, and his earnings, to promote the interests of his master, and attempt to justify this on the principles of moral law! It is the greatest absurdity, and the most revolting wickedness.[10]

Finney would not permit slaveowners to receive Communion at Chatham Street Chapel, and he made the admission of African American students one of the conditions of his joining the faculty at Oberlin.

None of these men, however, could be considered an abolitionist in the strict sense. Each saw eternal salvation as a higher good than earthly freedom. Besides, William Garrison and other abolitionists often expressed anti-Christian sentiments, making it hard for clergy to align themselves with the cause. Further, Cartwright was even more committed to preventing the schism of southern Methodists than he was to opposing slavery. And Finney was not an integrationist; he insisted on segregated seating in the Chatham Street Chapel, even over the opposition of his largest donors, Arthur and Lewis Tappan.

Another moral crusade in which all these evangelists were engaged is that of total abstinence, which was just coming into vogue as an easier goal to reach than true temperance. Peter Cartwright admired the wisdom of John Wesley in interdicting dram drinking in the Rules of his United Societies, and, although in the United States the rule was (to misinterpret Hamlet) more honored in the breach than the observance, this prototypical circuit rider was not at all inclined to go along with the laxity of the prevailing fashion—especially when, as was often the case, the offender was ordained.[11]

As noted in the previous chapter, Finney included the cause of temperance in his first great campaign in Rochester. He invited his young convert Theodore Weld to come and lead that aspect of the work. Finney even consented to suspending evangelistic work for a while so that the cause of temperance could be given exclusive attention. Weld later would become one of the leading abolitionists of the Oberlin group. This eventually was to come between Weld and Finney, since the young disciple began to consider ending slavery to be the most urgent demand upon Christian conscience and activity. For Finney, the most pressing insight (and also the most elusive) was to comprehend that all evils afflicting human society—wrongs done to women, slavery, drunkenness, war, and all the rest—were but natural consequences of *sin*, and that if faithful pastors attacked this central evil by the cure of conversion, in time all subordinate evils would begin to diminish.[12]

Nevertheless, Finney did speak out against the other evils, considering it the evangelist's duty not only to convert the unsaved but also to help reborn souls know how to live out the life into which they had been initiated. Thus revival preaching always included a strong dose of attacks upon the ills of the day. What Charles Johnson said of the preachers at camp meetings could apply to all revivalists of the Second Great Awakening and their heirs:

The itinerants were not socially myopic, as their sermon themes indicate. They considered it their spiritual obligation to strike out against all forms of sin. In pungent language the evils of the day were fearlessly denounced: immorality, intemperance, tobacco, blasphemy, dueling, card playing, horse racing, and gambling.[13]

To contemporary consciousness, that list of evils must appear a curious blend of the personal and the corporate. Yet the lines were not so clearly drawn then as they are today; for example, much of the passion behind the abstinence movement was a conviction that drunkenness was a major cause of poverty. In any case, having these social evils and bad habits blended together so indiscriminately does not weaken Smith's assertion that a major by-product of the Second Great Awakening was the preaching of social reform.

ETHIOPIA STRETCHES OUT HER HANDS UNTO GOD:[14] THE BEGINNING OF AFRICAN AMERICAN PREACHING

The extension of preaching topics to include social reform was not the only fruit of the Second Awakening fervor. One of the most obvious and beneficial was a broadening of understanding about the social groups whose members were eligible to preach. Until this time in America, it had been generally assumed that preaching was beyond the capacity of any but a white male. A result of the Awakening was that there came to be significant numbers of women and African American preachers. Of the two groups, the latter was the larger, and we will consider it first.

The majority of African American slaves did not become Christians until after the second decade of the nineteenth century.[15] There is a variety of reasons for that, including a desire of their owners that they not do so, a shortage of clergy to evangelize them, and an effort to get them to accept Christianity through the uncongenial method of catechesis rather than conversion. The more emotional means of evangelization introduced in the Second Great Awakening—means that had something in common with African traditional religion—however, made Christianity, especially in its Methodist and Baptist manifestations, more attractive to some slaves and free persons of color. And some of their number began to preach; "Black Harry" Hosier, for instance, who accompanied Asbury and other Methodist leaders, was often regarded as a better preacher than the white clergy with whom he traveled.

Black Christians were either included in white congregations or founded their own, and preachers of their race were heard in both configurations.

The founding of African American denominations occurred largely in the North and was the work of free blacks, yet there were congregations in the South composed largely of slaves. The ability of persons in bondage to participate in any public religious activities varied considerably from time to time and place to place. For instance, owners for a long time refused to allow their slaves to be baptized, under the impression that doing so would imply manumission. Most owners also would not allow the people belonging to them to be educated, for fear they would become less subservient. And, after some slave rebellions grew out of Methodist groups, especially those connected with Nat Turner and Denmark Vessey, many southern states passed laws against preaching by slaves. Instead, white missionary activity directed to this human chattel was promoted on the theory that it would make them more obedient servants. At other times, black preaching was permitted, but only when whites were present to make certain nothing subversive was said.

The condition of slavery was so oppressive, however, that such participation in public institutions was not to be the rule of slave religion. The norm was to be the "invisible institution" mentioned by Albert J. Raboteau in the subtitle of *Slave Religion*: secret and illegal gatherings of African Americans for worship on plantations. These often occurred in the middle of the night in fields, gullies, or thickets—places away from the observation of the whites. Even more than their other gatherings, these clandestine praise meetings, or "shouts," were times of fervent emotional outbursts in which tormented people sought the strength to endure their difficult lives. Shouting, hand-clapping, ring dancing, and transports of ecstasy, often choreographed by one of their own who had been called to preach, marked these precious moments of release.

Their own Christian congregations, whether churches or the clandestine gatherings on plantations, were the only institution over which African Americans had complete control.[16] It is not surprising, therefore, that these congregations became a natural sphere for the development of leadership within their number. One of the first to point out the significance of that leadership was W. E. B. DuBois, who wrote in 1903:

> The Preacher is the most unique personality developed by the Negro on American soil. A leader, a politician, an orator, a "boss," an intriguer, an idealist,—all these he is, and ever, too, the centre of a group of men, now twenty, now a thousand in number.[17]

Some of these clergy proved to be among the most eloquent preachers of their day. They seem to have developed two distinct homiletical styles, styles that can be seen in the African American church to this day. One labored (successfully) to show that members of their race were as intellectually capable as whites, and that they could produce sermons that were as eloquent and closely argued as the best white preaching of the time. The other style discovered kinship between the ecstatic preaching of the Second Great Awakening and African religious traditions that enabled them to meet their congregations at the deepest emotional level. Thus the different types of preaching served different social functions within the African American community.

William E. Montgomery has criticized the tendency to speak of "the black church" as though it were monolithic, and has pointed to the social stratification within its different expressions of Christian faith.[18] He designates the two types of congregation—and preaching—as "elite" and "folk." These are not mutually exclusive or polar opposite categories, but instead represent the extreme positions on a spectrum. They are, however, a convenient distinction for looking at African American preaching.

Both preaching methods are worthy of study. Unfortunately, they cannot both be studied in the same way. Inevitably, the literary tradition has left much more extensive documentation. The ecstatic tradition, however, has been so impressive that it has been the object of a great deal of analytical attention. Consequently, the two preaching styles will have to be studied separately. The literary tradition can be examined in the ministries and pulpit work of two of its greatest exemplars: C. T. Walker and Charles Albert Tindley.[19] The ecstatic tradition is accessible mainly through secondhand reports and the efforts of scholars to interpret what they have heard or heard about, although it can be seen in part in the preaching of John Jasper.

Learned Preaching

The elite tradition can be seen as early as the late-eighteenth century in the life of **Lemuel Haynes.** The son of a black father, Haynes was abandoned by his white mother in infancy, but he was taken into the home of a white church deacon and raised as a member of the family. Well educated, he prepared for the ministry after serving in the American army during the Revolution. Apparently his racial mixture did not limit him in any way; he served in several pastorates with great success, had sermons published, and was consulted by the presidents of Yale and Amherst on matters of doctrine. In a famous sermon against the doctrine of universal salvation, he attributed the doctrine to Satan in the Garden of Eden, when he said: "Ye shall not surely die!" This proclamation of doctrine, Haynes said, made Satan a preacher, of whom it could be said that he was old, cunning, laborious, heterogeneous, presumptuous, and successful.[20]

While the preaching of Haynes can be called elite, and it is the work of a man of some African ancestry, it hardly represents the preaching of the black church as such. To see that in its fullest development, it helps to look at the proclamation of a minister who was born into slavery and, to show that talent was not the result of an admixture of white blood, one who was "a Negro in every drop of his blood."[21] Such a person was the preacher who came to be called "the Black Spurgeon," **Charles T. Walker.** The son of a black deacon who was his master's coachman and who died the day before he was born, Walker lived his first seven years as a slave.[22] Two of his uncles were preachers, however, one of whose freedom was purchased by his congregation, Franklin Covenant Baptist Church, founded in 1848 near Hepzibah, Georgia. His mother died during her first year of freedom, and her eight-year-old son was passed from relative to relative until he could care for himself. He worked as a field hand on his pastor uncle's large farm, and was converted at the age of fifteen after a struggle of three days.

His call to preach came not long afterward, and he felt the need to become educated. His mother had taught him his ABC's and how to read John 14. He had also spent two five-month terms in a school operated by the Freedman's Bureau. In the fall of his sixteenth year, he began to study at the Augusta Institute, a school formed to train black preachers by a former slaveowner, which later became Atlanta Baptist Seminary and then Atlanta Baptist College. After two years there he graduated and was ordained. Already popular as a "boy preacher," he soon had four churches to serve. Two years later he married. Moving to LaGrange, Georgia, he preached two revivals in the church he served for three years, during which four hundred were converted, three hundred of whom became church members.

Walker was then called to and eventually became pastor of what later became known as Tabernacle Baptist Church in Augusta. Under his leadership it soon had a new brick building that seated eight hundred and had a pipe organ. It was paid for within two years. During the fourteen years he was pastor at Tabernacle Baptist, there were two thousand conversions and fourteen hundred baptisms. He was also active in civic affairs, helping to found a weekly newspaper as well as a high school and a normal school for his people, and leading an exposition to demonstrate the progress of the Negro. He also saved many from jail; paid fines and rent; furnished food, clothing, and fuel; reconciled marriages; sent children to school; got jobs for adults; and brought many to Christ.[23] During the same period, he conducted revivals throughout the state, served in many church offices, was a trustee of colleges, acted as a member of the State Executive Committee for the Republican Party, and became "the best known Negro minister in the state."[24] He became the first cleric of his race to be sent to Europe and the Holy Land by his congregation, and his lectures about the trip were eventually published as a book.

During all this time, Walker was becoming known nationally. He was a leader of the National Baptist Convention and had been awarded a D.D. by the State University of Kentucky. He served as a chaplain in Cuba during the Spanish-American War, and became a vice president of the International Sunday School Convention in 1899. He also began preaching revivals in many of the major cities of the country. When he preached in the Exposition Park in Atlanta to audiences of eight thousand whites and blacks, the *Constitution* said that he had drawn as many if not more people than the legendary white evangelists Sam Jones and Dwight L. Moody.[25]

These successes resulted in his being called in 1899 to Mt. Olivet Baptist Church in New York City, a church to whose building fund John D. Rockefeller and other prominent Baptists had contributed. Its membership increased from 430 to 1,800 in two years, with the result that Walker preached to "the largest regular congregation of any man in New York City, white or black."[26] Thus, in accordance with the custom of the times, his sermons were regularly and favorably reviewed by the New York press.

His sermon preparation consisted of prayer, Bible reading, and meditation. He said: "I know what I'm going to say before I come into the pulpit. I know the hymns I am going to sing, the chapter I'm going to read, and I know where the text is to be found."[27] The daily newspaper was his favorite source of information outside the Bible. According to his biographer:

> When he enters the pulpit, free from the narrowness that muts [sic] come to the man who uses only his Bible commentary, he seems to feel himself under divine compulsion to deliver a message of transcendent importance to dying men; there is an air about him of a soldier who has a divine commission to fight a great battle for humanity. He speaks directly to the heart, in language all hearts can understand. Humor and pathos, pleading and scorn, impassioned exhortation and cutting sarcasm, are all used in his discourses with tremendous effect.[28]

An example of his preaching that is also informative about the history of the black church can be seen in an excerpt from the sermon he was invited to deliver at the Missionary Baptist State Convention in Georgia to commemorate the one-hundredth anniversary of the Negro Baptist Church in Georgia. His text was Numbers 23:23 (KJV): "According to this time it shall be said of Jacob and of Israel, What hath God wrought!"

> We stand today upon an eminence from which we may take a retrospective view of a one hundred years' journey. This is a glorious day. We have come to celebrate the progress and triumphs of a century. We are here to speak of the vicissitudes through which we have passed, the conflicts we have encountered . . . and the victories yet to be achieved. We are here to pass up and down the line of march from 1788 to 1888. Old fathers, worn and weary with burdens and cares of long and useful lives, their heads whitened by the frosts of many winters, infirm and superannuated, have come up to shake hands with the century, to bid Godspeed to their brethren, and, like Simeon of old, to exclaim, "Lord, now lettest thou thy servant depart in peace, for mine eyes have seen thy salvation." Young men have come to get inspiration from a review of the works of the fathers and to return to their various fields stimulated, electrified and encouraged.
>
> We shall discuss, first, what God has wrought in the permanent establishment of His church. The founder of the true church is Jesus Christ. He is the Son of Abraham, according to the flesh, and He is also the Son of God. Two natures and three offices mysteriously meet his person. He is the foundation of the true church, the chief corner stone, the lawgiver in Zion. He has given us a kingdom which cannot be moved. He began in Asia to ride in the gospel chariot. He sent out twelve small boats at first. On the day of Pentecost, 3,000 were added to the number. In 1630, He sent Roger Williams to America. In the spirit of his Master, he planted churches in New England, and the stone continued to roll until it reached the sunny South. In 1788, the oppressed, rejected and enslaved brother in black, for the first time in Georgia, lifted the Baptist flag under the leadership of Andrew Bryan. The handful of corn was sown not on the high, wild and rocky mountains, but on the seaboard; but the wind carried the seed to every part of Georgia and the barren rocks and sandy deserts became gardens of the Lord. From that handful of corn have sprung more than 1,500 churches, 500 ordained preachers, and 166,429 communicants. The little one has become a thousand. In the entire United States there are today more than 1,250,000 colored Baptists. I make bold to say here and now that the progress of the Baptists in this country has been due to the earnest, faithful and simple preaching of Christ crucified. The

fathers in their preaching did not preach philosophy, nor did they strive to reach the people with rhetorical strains of eloquence, but they strove to reach the people by preaching the plain, old-fashioned, simple truths of the gospel. The gospel declared in its truth and simplicity will make Baptists.

Third, we shall discuss what God has wrought for our race during this century. For our race, this century was one of hardship, oppression, persecution and sore trial. We were slaves; we had no moral training; no intellectual advantages during the greater part of this century and the two preceding; we were run by bloodhounds; sometimes whipped to death; we were sold from the auction block, husbands and fathers being separated from wives and children at the behest of some white man; we had to get a ticket to go to church; we had to get permission from some white man before we could join the church; we were out-casts. But all that has changed. God was against slavery, and in his own time and way He removed the foul blot from the national escutcheon. Emancipated without a dollar, without education, without friends and without competent leaders, like Hagar and Ishmael, we were turned out to die. But despite all obstacles, the Negro in Georgia has today $10,000,000 worth of property and has proven himself worthy of citizenship. We have thousands of children in our public schools. Our men will be found in the law, in the practice of medicine, in legislative halls, among teachers and professors, on the list of authors, skilled musicians, journalists, theologians, and business men. God has wrought wonderfully among us. God is still opening the way for greater progress. The cry is loud and long all the line for consecrated workers. The harvest truly is white, but the laborers are few.[29]

In recording the progress of his people, he incarnates and epitomizes it. Remarkable accomplishments, all of them.

The second example of a preacher in the literary tradition who was born in slavery is **Charles Albert Tindley.** The exact date of Tindley's birth is unknown, and details of his early life are hard to come by. Some records say he was born in 1856, but others say 1851.[30] His parents were among the few slaves owned by a farmer near Berlin on the Eastern Shore of Maryland. His mother died when he was two and his father was unable to keep him, so he was placed in the homes of others to work for his keep.[31] Some of the people who kept him were cruel, and none allowed him to own a book or go to church. He nevertheless developed a great desire for education. He says:

> I used to find bits of newspaper on the roadside and put them in my bosom (for I had no pockets), in order to study the A,B,C's from them.

During the day I would gather pine knots, and when the people were asleep at night I would light these pine knots, and, lying flat on my stomach to prevent being seen by any one who might still be about, would, with fire-coals, mark all the words I could make out on these bits of newspaper. I continued in this way, and without any teacher, until I could read the Bible almost without stopping to spell the words.[32]

Emancipation occurred at some time during his youth, and he grew up to support himself as a hod carrier[33] and to marry. Hearing of better opportunities in Philadelphia (directly north through the state of Delaware), he took his wife there and found lodgings and a job. His landlord invited the young couple to worship with him at John Wesley Methodist Episcopal Church, affiliated with the Delaware Annual Conference, an administrative provision for black congregations in the Middle Atlantic region within a basically white denomination. Tindley threw himself into the life of the congregation, participating in every activity, and even becoming its volunteer sexton when the congregation moved to a location on Bainbridge Street (from which it would take its name in 1890).

His passion for learning continued. Not being able to attend the Institute for Colored Youths because he had to work days when it was in session, he studied at night and was examined by local schoolteachers subject by subject. Somewhere along the way, he discovered his vocation to the ministry and began reading for preordination examinations under the guidance of his pastor and with the approval of his presiding elder and the encouragement of his bishop. To the surprise of the contemptuous seminary graduates with whom he was examined, he scored highly on the tests and was admitted to the conference on probation. He never lost his desire for learning. He completed the theological course at Brandywine Institute and learned both Greek and Hebrew in order to be as well prepared as possible for his ministerial work. In time, he received the doctor of divinity degree from Bennett College and Morgan College. Nevertheless, he was plagued the rest of his life by the detractions of clergy with more formal credentials; indeed, these were to subvert his election to the episcopate.

When he was admitted to the conference on probation in 1885, Tindley was sent to his first charge in Cape May, New Jersey, where he served for two years. At the end of that time, he was ordained deacon and reassigned to South Wilmington, Delaware. After ordination as an elder in 1889, he served in a variety of charges until he became pastor of the prestigious Ezion Church in Wilmington, Delaware, in 1897; he was promoted to presiding elder of that district in 1900.

From the district, Tindley went to the church he would serve the rest of his life, Bainbridge Street Methodist Episcopal—which, during his tenure, would change its name two more times: once to East Calvary and then, in his honor, to Tindley Temple. When he first arrived, however, some parishioners were embarrassed to discover that their former sexton was now their pastor. When he became pastor of the congregation it had only 130 members, but under his leadership it grew to seven thousand.[34] A church building seating thirty-two hundred that he called a cathedral was constructed while he was there, and he filled it twice on Sundays. His congregation came to have a wide variety of programs, from literary societies to the provision of meals for large numbers of the poor. Tindley had an extraordinary street ministry in which he greeted, counseled, and prayed with everyone from derelicts to the sporting crowd.

As pastor of an influential church, he became a power within the city of Philadelphia and had friendships with such figures as Russell Conwell,[35] the founder of Temple University, and John Wanamaker, the department store magnate. He also became very influential in the General Conference of the Methodist Episcopal Church, to which he was a regular delegate and at which he was a frequent preacher. And, on top of everything else, he was a talented musician and composer with more than forty-five gospel songs to his credit, five of which are in *The United Methodist Hymnal.* Two have become popular favorites: "I'll Overcome Someday"[36] and "Stand By Me."

It was for his preaching, however, that Tindley was most famous. He must have been an impressive figure in the pulpit. He was six feet three inches tall, had a booming baritone speaking voice, and a walk that "exuded self-confidence without injecting the least semblance of swagger."[37] He seems to have preached topical sermons[38] that were developed with a list of qualities. His sermon "The World's Conqueror," based upon John 16:33 (KJV) ("I have overcome the world"), has as its points "the forces which heaven employed to conquer the powers of the devil and to bring man, with all his possession, back to God."[39] These are: truth, peace, and love.

We can gain a taste of his eloquence from his definition of *love* in this sermon:

> It is the soul of one person going out, with all of its possession and pow-
> ers, to make another happy. It is this going out to make others happy
> that is healing the scars and wiping up the blood caused by Cain's

murderous club, and Samaritan-like, healing the wounded, providing for their comfort and paying the bill. This is the mightiest possession that any soul can have. It is the sunlight of heaven caught and stored up in the human life to shine among men. Like chunks of coal a heartful of the Love of God has banked the fires that are destined to burn up and melt the coldness of this world into the springtime of heaven. It is a flower garden in every life through which perennial streams flow. It is the songbird whose notes of melody drown the croaking of the frogs, the hiss of serpents and the growl of beast.[40]

This is little more than half of what he says on the subject, but it is enough to show the eloquence of which he was capable. (For another of Tindley's sermons, see **Vol. 2, pp. 420-30.**)

The Folk Tradition of the Chanted Sermon

The elite literary tradition represented above was always eager to distance itself from the tradition to be considered now, which was regarded as undignified, emotional, illiterate, and embarrassing. There is no standard term for referring to a sermon of this second sort. It has been called anything from "the black folk sermon" to "old-time country preaching," but Albert J. Raboteau prefers to call it "the chanted sermon" because, as he says, its defining characteristic is "the metrical, tonal, rhythmic chant with which the preacher climaxes the sermon."[41]

More on the chant later. The place to begin a description of this genre is with the recognition that, as Raboteau points out, verbal skill has always been highly valued in the black community.[42] This is as true of the elite as of the folk portion of the community,[43] but the impressive phenomenon to be noted here is the ability of persons with no access to written language to construct oral music of extraordinary beauty. Because the folk preachers could expect audiences composed of connoisseurs of linguistic sound, those who were most appreciated were virtuosos.

Thus the power of their preaching was felt by many who, in consciousness of their sophistication, were embarrassed by their own reaction of being deeply moved. But others recognized the richness of the resources displayed and went on in time to combine the technique of the folk preachers with a more rigorous theological content.[44]

The classical folk or chanted sermon always began with a text from the Bible, shaped as it was by the example of the preaching of the Great Awakening—and, indeed, most of the Christian tradition. Dependence upon a printed book posed a considerable challenge to slaves whose masters were afraid to allow them to learn to read, but many showed incredible ability to remember not only narratives but also long passages of text they had only heard. The tradition of preaching as an explication of text was so strong that

> some illiterate slave preachers of the antebellum South had their texts read for them or, lacking a Bible, pretended to read scriptural words from their hand or from a handkerchief.[45]

Henry Mitchell has a good bit to say about the use of the Bible in African American preaching. He begins by noting that while the Bible is the ultimate authority for what is preached, the black church has not tended to be Fundamentalist.

> The Black preacher is more likely to think of the Bible as an inexhaustible source of good preaching material than as an inert doctrinal and ethical authority....His intuitively flexible approach to the Bible leads him to ask, "What is the Lord trying to tell me today in this passage of scripture?"[46]

The basic use of the Scripture is narrative, and details to enliven the story are drawn from the text itself, from biblical scholarship, and from analogy to the lives of the people. Apposite parallels from contemporary life are also used, both to bring the story to life and to show its relevance. Black illustrations tend to stick very close to the gut-level issues of life and death, of struggle and frustration. And black preachers tend to illustrate passages already chosen from the Bible on the basis of the same criteria.[47]

This means that an effective preacher in the tradition must be a first-rate storyteller, which involves dramatizing the story, playing every part in it, and making the congregation feel present at the described events. As entertaining as such storytelling is, it is never done purely for entertainment. Rather, it is through this engagement that the preacher enlists the congregation's commitment to the truth being communicated. For that involvement to occur, the suspense of the story must be maintained, no matter how familiar it is. The preacher must be a master of timing.[48]

Classical folk sermons on particular texts were repreached by others and in this manner were "passed with only slight modifications from preacher to preacher and from locality to locality."[49] These, however, were not "vain repetitions," since in the slave church there was an unspoken recognition that preaching is, among other things, a performance art, and thus the expectation of the community was not so much for originality as it was for "skill, fluency, spontaneity, and intensity."[50] The slave preachers recognized instinctively something understood by the seventeenth-century English metaphysical school of preaching: the content of a sermon cannot be separated from the way in which it is communicated.[51]

To say that the folk sermon began with a text is not to say that it was necessarily confined to its exposition. An old joke has it that clergy preach from a text—often very far from it, and this applies to most traditions. But the Bible was the main source of the language, images, and stories of the slave preachers' sermons. In this appropriation, nothing was more important than the story of Moses and the exodus: "Slaves prayed for the future day of deliverance to come, and they kept hope alive by incorporating as part of *their* mythic past the Old Testament exodus of Israel out of slavery."[52]

The basic outline of these sermons covered the announcement of the text, an elaboration of the context of the passage, and then an application of it to the lives of those who heard it. Mitchell observes that many sermons consist of retelling a Bible story with continuous application as the story unfolds. Certainly the structure is seldom deductive and tightly argued; the preacher "guides his seekers rather than arguing with his opponents."[53]

In addition to this pattern of content, there was also a pattern of sound, the structure of performance style. This justifies the designation of "chanted" sermons.[54]

> The preacher begins calmly, speaking in conversational, if oratorical and occasionally grandiloquent, prose; he then gradually begins to speak more rapidly, excitedly, and to chant his words in time to a regular beat; finally, he reaches an emotional peak in which his chanted speech becomes tonal and merges with the singing, clapping, and shouting of the congregation. Frequently, the preacher ends the sermon by returning briefly to conversational prose.[55]

The only thing that needs to be added to this description is to say that many of the sermons do not have just one peak of intensity, but will reach several minor climaxes before the major one is achieved.

The art of preaching such sermons is improvisational, because it is expected that they will be delivered extempore. This does not mean they are unprepared; indeed, the fact that many of them are repeated shows that all could not be created in the process of delivery. But the preacher must have a capacity to adjust rapidly to the immediate situation. The adjustments call for a high artistry because of the rhythmic pattern that has been established. Words must be composed on the spot to fit that pattern, and any adjustment to an earlier form of the same sermon that adapts it to the new situation has to be made in the full flow of delivery.

Bruce Rosenberg conducted research to see if connections could be made between the improvisational skill involved in the chanted sermons and that of the bards who performed the Homeric poems or *Beowulf*, and with Yugoslav *guslars* of more recent times, all of whom were able to create verse on the spur of the moment that satisfied many formal requirements.[56] While doing so, he became aware of significant differences between the material he was working with and that of the oral poets, and he became more and more interested in American folk preaching in its own right. Rosenberg did, however, see a connecting link between the preachers' art and that of the poem performers in his experience of hearing an African American preacher repeat the same phrases again and again in the course of delivering a chanted sermon.

Albert Lord had argued that what enabled the poets to compose epics spontaneously while performing them was the use of "formulas," which he defined as: "a group of words regularly employed under the same metrical conditions to express a given essential idea."[57] The repeated phrases in the sermons seemed to serve a similar purpose. Rosenberg calls the repeated phrases of the preachers "stall" formulas, meaning that they are interjected in order to give the preacher time to think of what to say next. Closely related to these are what he calls "themes,"[58] "a formulary portion of a sermon," that is, a set piece that can be inserted anywhere—a tape to be played, in current slang. These also put a preacher on automatic pilot as a way of gaining time to think.

Related to this need to establish a rhythmic pattern is the preacher's tendency to gasp for air at the end of each line. This practice and its purpose were noticed as early as James Weldon Johnson. He referred to the gasps as the oral punctuation of sermons by "a certain sort of pause that is marked by a quick intaking and an audible expulsion of breath." He saw it as a part of a "syncopation of speech—the crowding in of many syllables or the lengthening out of a few to fill one metrical foot."[59]

The folklorist Gerald L. Davis has pointed out that the rhythm established by the preachers is not nearly so exact as the meter of the poets. While the sermon is being preached it may seem that all the lines are of the same length, but actually their length may vary widely. He describes the process more precisely by saying that "the principle morphologic unit of the African-American sermon is a *group of hemistich phrases shaped into an irrhythmic metrical unit when performed.*"[60]

In any case, the rhythm is important. The preacher may even rap it out on the pulpit with his hand to emphasize the beat. The preacher may also clap his hands and even dance around the podium. It is in response to the established rhythm and other aspects of the sermon that the congregation becomes involved. They join in the clapping or tap their feet.[61] Their bodies may sway. And they find their own voices. They may moan or shout, but they also become involved in a dialogue with the preacher. This is to say that a black folk sermon is not a solo performance by a preacher, but a verbal activity involving the whole congregation. This flow between the preacher and the congregation is the pattern of "call-and-response" that is distinctive of preaching in this tradition.

Although he does not use the vocabulary of form criticism, Davis treats the performed sermon as a *Gattung* with certain necessary elements. Several of these have to do with the introduction:

- The preacher must indicate that the sermon text was provided by divine inspiration.
- The theme or subject of the sermon must be stated.
- The biblical passage on which the sermon is based must be interpreted, first literally and then more broadly.

The requirements for the body are more complex, but Davis states them as a single element:

The body of the African-American sermon is constructed of independent theme-related formulas. Each unit of the formula develops or retards a secular and sacred tension and moves between abstract and concrete example. Each generated formula is an aspect of the "argument" of the announced theme and advances the discovery and examination of the sermon theme.

The final element is not so much a conclusion as an end.

Closure is rarely found at the end of an African-American sermon. The sermon is open-ended.[62]

The successful sermon satisfies these criteria and others as well. It is in the recognition of these formal criteria that the significance of call-and-response is to be seen: the different responses (including relative lack of response) indicate the congregation's judgment of whether the criteria of the genre are being satisfied. They thus constitute either the congregation's permission for the preacher to go ahead or indicate a need to go back and complete the foundation.[63]

There is considerable debate among those who have studied these folk sermons about what they are supposed to accomplish. Most of the early interpreters sided with the elite tradition in seeing the purpose to be emotional release. Johnson, for instance, noted that he had seen congregations "moved to ecstasy by the rhythmic intoning of sheer incoherences."[64] According to William Pipes, the sermons "reflected the need for an escape mechanism by a people held in bondage." In addition to instructing people in biblical teaching and persuading them to live accordingly, the purpose of the preaching is "to impress the audience, so that there will be an outburst (escape) of emotion in shouting and frenzy."[65] And, beginning as he did with his concern for rhythm as the counterpart in folk preaching to the meter of the oral poets, Rosenberg understandably considered the tempo established in the sermon to be more important than semantic content. He thus saw the essential dynamic of such preaching to be an emotional catharsis achieved through crescendo and climax of the rhythm.[66]

For Gerald Davis, on the other hand, the semantic content is primary: "In sermon performance, the African American preacher is primarily concerned with the organization and language of his sermon."[67] The feel of rhythm is a vehicle of content and is generated simultaneously with the sermon's linguistic structure.

The element of overall argument is often lost on the outside observer of African American preaching because of the coded quality of language, a quality necessary in slave times and at least prudent ever since.[68] Over time, the habit of communicating in code became ingrained and reflexive. Therefore,

> both preacher and congregation share in the encoding and deciphering of sermon element. When this complex, concurrent activity is most intense, the only suitable responses are sound or word-absent phrases— those "moans," "cries," and "shouts" so underestimated by [Lawrence] Davis, [Daniel] Crowley, and [William] Pipes and appreciated by [Henry] Mitchell.[69]

What is encoded here is the preacher's exercise of a pastor's role as guide to the congregation in both religious and secular life. In Davis's interpretation, every sermon has to deal with both. But more attention is given to the secular than the sacred. The secular factor in the sermon is "weighted." According to Davis, the preacher "may use the perfection of the Christian life as example, as framework, but his focus is riveted on his congregation's need to live a fully experiencing daily, secular existence."[70] Even this is still somewhat encoded, because it does not say that the daily existence must be lived in a world dominated by whites. Living in such a world is like "living with a hatchet over your head every day," to use a description given a therapist of my acquaintance.

This understanding has been further refined by Cleophus J. LaRue.[71] His thesis is that the power of black preaching comes from a combination of three elements: (1) a particular method of interpreting the Bible, (2) a deep awareness of the black experience, and (3) particular aspects of the life of the black church. The key employed in the interpretation of Scripture is to discern in all its pages the work of "a sovereign God who acts in concrete and practical ways on behalf of the marginalized and powerless."[72] This belief that God is powerful to act and uses that power for those who suffer gives meaning to what black people have experienced, first in slavery and later in prejudice and discrimination. The hope and expectation of power that enable God's people to overcome all obstacles are applied to one of four "domains of experience": (1) personal piety, (2) care of the soul ("encouragement, exhortation, consolation, renewal, instruction, or admonishment"[73] to the wounded and broken), (3) social action, corporate concerns that "particularly and peculiarly affect black life,"[74] and (4) maintenance of the institutional church.

Sermons in the tradition of the black church create a powerful conviction that the people of God will be given the strength to endure and to overcome in all areas of their lives in Christ. Decoded, that means black Christians will be able to survive all the oppression heaped upon them by a white world. As LaRue shows, this purpose is discernible in the whole tradition, whether in slave times or contemporarily, and in the sermons of the learned as well as those of folk preachers. To what LaRue said may be added the point that whites have felt the power of such preaching but because racism is so systemic, they have not identified themselves with the oppressors in the biblical stories and the sermons based upon them, but with the oppressed because of their own life struggles.

It would be a false dichotomy, however, to contrast this emphasis on content with another on the catharsis or ecstasy experienced by worshipers when the traditional folk method of preaching is employed. In defending celebrative climaxes against the charges that they are emotional and manipulative, Henry Mitchell says:

> People live by emotion. Emotions move people, while ideas which do not generate some emotion are powerless to change anybody's life. In the black climax at its best, the idea—the point which has been made—

is embraced and celebrated. It is, as it were, burned into the consciousness of the hearer. Embrace and celebration are emotional. And a good Black climax will appeal to the highest and noblest emotions of a man, whether Black or white.[75]

The conviction with which those who have participated leave the church is not simply a rational belief in an intellectual proposition about God's power and activity. It is an existential certainty that has been reinforced while doubts have been resolved in the whole process of the experience of the sermon. People are enabled to go back into a hostile world and live another week because of their persuasion of a truth that has been accomplished at every level of their being. "In the chanted sermon, African-American Christians did not merely talk about God, they experienced his power, and found that in the experience their own spirits were renewed."[76]

The remaining question to be discussed about black chanted sermons is whether the predominant influence on their development was white or African. Rosenberg takes the position that it began in the efforts of Africa American preachers to imitate the preaching style of the white preachers of the Second Great Awakening under whom they were converted. As documentation for this thesis, he points out that some white preachers in eastern Kentucky, where the awakening began, continue to preach that way to this very day.[77] In stating his own position, he does not discuss the extensive and prolonged argument over whether traditional African American Christian worship, including preaching, owes more of its inspiration to African traditional religion than to white American Christianity.

The classical debate over the question was between Melville J. Herskovits, who used his anthropological fieldwork in Africa to argue for that origin, and the African American anthropologist E. Franklin Frazier, who insisted that slavery had successfully expunged any memories of African culture.[78] Rosenberg referred to the work of Frazier but not to that of Herskovits.[79] There is, nevertheless, a good bit to be said for the Herskovits position in its basic claim, if not in its detailed argument.

Raboteau has summarized the current status of the debate very judiciously. He notes that there were many survivals of African traditional religion in Caribbean and Latin American countries, but that there were considerable cultural differences between the slave populations there and those in the United States, differences that prevented many detailed influences in this country. The African past, then, is not so determinative of the exact shape of the worship and preaching of African Americans as it is of those in the Caribbean and Latin America.

> Nevertheless, even as the gods of Africa gave way to the God of Christianity, the African heritage of singing, dancing, spirit possession, and magic continued to influence Afro-American spirituals, ring shouts, and folk beliefs.[80]

The ring shout, the dance in which Christian slaves shuffled, clapped, and sang spirituals, closely resembles call-and-response, including the sort of congregational involvement that Rosenberg considers to be the cathartic release toward which the rhythm of folk preaching is aimed.[81] African religious traditions thus predisposed the slaves to respond more readily to the emotional presentation of Christianity made in the Second Great Awakening than to catechetical presentations that were largely rational in their appeal.[82] Anyone who has heard classical African American chanted sermons has reason to be grateful for this fruit of the fervor of the Awakening.[83]

John Jasper: A Case Study in Folk Preaching

Just as Walker and Tindley enable one to have a vision of the elite tradition of African American preaching in action, a similar perspective on the folk tradition can be gained by looking at the life and ministry of John Jasper. Like Walker and Tindley, Jasper was born into slavery. What accounts for the difference in the path he took is probably that he was born so much earlier than they. Instead of being a child or at most an early teenager when he was given his freedom, he was a half century old and had already preached for half that time.

Anyone who writes about Jasper labors under the difficulty that the only source of information about him is a collection of articles[84] written by a Baptist minister who occupied the pulpit of one of the most prominent white churches in Richmond, the city where Jasper's ministry occurred. That cleric, William Eldridge Hatcher, was a Virginian of colonial ancestry and a person of great sophistication.[85] Thus he maintained an ambivalent attitude toward his subject throughout the book. There can be no doubt that he admired and even loved him. Indeed, he almost appears obsessed with him. For twenty-five years he sat under his preaching, even when influential members of his congregation criticized him for doing so. When Jasper died, he preached a eulogy for him to a packed house in his large white church. It is said that Hatcher's dying words were, "John Jasper, we're brothers now, and we'll live forever round the throne of God."[86] Yet he was able to refer to social equality between the races as a "hideous dogma."[87] He shared many of the prejudices of the elite against folk preaching, and much that he says sounds patronizing to modern ears. An example is the way he recorded Jasper's words in conversation and preaching in dialectical spelling, even though at times one cannot distinguish between the sounds of his transcription and standard spelling (e.g., "great palace" sounds exactly like "grate pallis") (178).[88] In depending upon the Hatcher account, therefore, it is a challenge not to sound condescending at times.

John Jasper was born into slavery on the plantation of the Peachy family in Fluvanna County, Virginia, in 1812, the last of the twenty-four children of Philip and Nina Jasper. His father, who was also a preacher, died two months before John was born, but his mother lived until she was almost one hundred and held many responsible positions, from being head of the working women on the Peachy plantation, to serving as chief of the servant force in a wealthy home, to being nurse to the sick in the negro quarters.

John originally served as a field hand, but he was moved around from place to place because of his owners' fluctuating fortunes. After he became an adult, he was sent to live in Williamsburg, and while there he became engaged, but was forced to move on the day he married. Since he could not live with her, his wife eventually asked to be released from the union.

After the Peachy family broke up, he was sold to various masters and used for different kinds of work. When he came to live in Richmond, he worked for a time in foundries and also as a house servant, but his last owner, Samuel Hargrove, put him to work removing stems from tobacco leaves in his plant. Jasper had gone to school for only six weeks, but around the beginning of 1839, he found a man who taught him to read from a *New York Speller.*

On July 4 of that year, he came under conviction of sin and was converted at work one day after six weeks of searching for God. His elation was so great that he wanted to share it, and tried to do so quietly, but his emotion overcame his restraint. The overseer quieted him and sent him back to work, but his owner asked what the commotion was about. On hearing, he sent for Jasper, took his hand, and told him they shared the same faith and were brothers in the Lord (27). Then he told him to witness throughout the factory and to take the rest of the day off to tell his folks and his neighbors about what had happened to him. Afterward, Jasper always regarded this as his call to preach, which came from God but was mediated through his master.

Since slaves were permitted to go only where their owners allowed, it was difficult for one called to preach to get around very much or to make any regular commitments. One concession allowed slaves to take off for a loved one's funeral, and the master would arrange for someone to preach it. Often a white minister was summoned, but a few slave preachers like Jasper achieved a considerable reputation as funeral preachers and received invitations their owners allowed them to accept. Stories remain of how, when he competed with a white preacher on such an occasion, Jasper outshone him by far. In time, his master allowed him to go to Petersburg two Sundays a month, and he acquired a large following there. The war brought that to an end, however. During the war, though, he visited the Confederate hospitals in Richmond to preach to the wounded. Although he preached for twenty-five years before liberation, the oppressive conditions of slavery meant that "his ministry had been migratory, restricted, and chiefly of ungathered fruit" (58).

When freedom came at last, Jasper was like most other released slaves in having no financial resources, and he had to make his way in the world as best he could. His first job was cleaning bricks from ruined buildings so they could be reused. But his great ambition was to build a church. He began preaching on an island in the James River where many of the newly freed lived. Sometimes they met in a house and sometimes in a deserted stable. When the congregation outgrew those meeting places, they found a larger building that was unoccupied. All along, his flock multiplied as sinners were converted and Jasper baptized them in the river. They bought a deserted Presbyterian mission church for $2,025 but soon had to enlarge it at a cost of $6,000. By then the congregation numbered two thousand, and Jasper was more than sixty years old. Yet they went on to build another church that "would be respectable in almost any part of Richmond" (60-61). The name of the church was Sixth Mount Zion Baptist.

While Jasper was a devoted and tireless pastor, the church was built on his preaching. That was in the folk tradition, but he practiced it with rare genius. Hargrove describes the first sermon he ever heard Jasper preach:

> Did ever mortal lips gush with such torrents of horrible English! Hardly a word came out clothed and in its right mind. And gestures! He circled around the pulpit with his ankle in his hand; and laughed and sang and shouted and acted about a dozen characters within the space of three minutes. Meanwhile, in spite of these things, he was pouring out a gospel sermon, red hot, full of love, full of invective,

full of tenderness, full of bitterness, full of tears, full of every passion that ever flamed in the human breast. He was a theatre within himself, with the stage crowded with actors. He was a battle-field;—himself the general, the staff, the officers, the common soldiery, the thundering artillery and the rattling musketry. He was the preacher; likewise the church and the choir and the deacons and the congregation. (9)

That experience drew the white minister back as long as Jasper lived and led him to write essays during that time as "a tribute to the brother in black—the one unmatched, unapproachable, and wonderful brother" (10).

Of his preaching style, it can be said that he documented every point he made with a quotation from the Bible, citing chapter and verse, and often saying, "If you don't find it just exactly as I tells you, you can meet me on the street the next day and say to me, 'John Jasper, you are a liar,' and I won't say a word" (63). Many of his sermons were retellings of Bible stories that turned each successive scene into a vivid verbal picture. Yet at other times he would give an exposition on a point of Christian doctrine, and his logic was "his tower of strength" (96). "His ministrations fairly covered the theological field, were strongly doctrinal, and he grappled with honest vigour the deepest principles of the Gospel" (66). There were even times when his sermons were "sober and deliberate, sometimes even dull" (67). He studied his Bible with the asceticism of a hermit and came to have an encyclopedic knowledge of its text that he drew upon freely as he preached.

> There was a kinship between the Bible and himself, and, untaught of the schools, he studied himself in the light of the Bible and studied the Bible in the darkness of himself. This kept him in contact with people and whenever he preached he invaded their experience and made conscious their wants to themselves. (48)

His delivery was in the classical style of the chanted sermon, and "he intoned his sermons,—at least, in their more tender passages" (95). And the congregation participated in call-and-response (128). After the preacher died, Hatcher interviewed one of his former parishioners, who said, "It look like Brother Jasper couldn't stop preaching. It was his food and drink" (81). She went on to say what it was like to hear him:

> Brother Jasper was mighty fond of walking in the pulpit. It was a great, large place, and he frisked around most like he was a boy.

When he was filled up with the arousement of the gospel on him, it was just glorious to see him as he whirled around the stand; the faces of his folks shone with the brightness of the sun, and they often made the house ring with laughter and with their shouts.

One thing that always made his congregations rock with joy, and that was [for him] to sing while he was preaching. He was almost ninety years old, but he never lost his power to sing, and when he struck a tune the note of it shot in the people like arrows from angels' quivers. You couldn't hold still when Jasper sung. Soon as he started, the people would begin to swing and join in till the music filled the house. (82)

He soon attracted a following among Richmond's white population. Members of the legislature, judges, governors, and other distinguished people, including some of the most prominent ministers in the country, thronged to hear him. "He was justly ranked as one of the attractions of Richmond" (107). For many who came for the first time, the expectation was that they would be amused by the ridiculous posturings of an ignorant semi-savage, but those who came to scoff, stayed to pray.

He achieved a national reputation that was based largely on one sermon he preached arguing that when Joshua fought the battle of Gibeon, the sun actually stood still (Josh. 10:13). He did not preach it to seek notoriety, but simply to settle a theological debate between his sexton and another church member. He later repreached it 250 times to raise money to pay off the church debt, and even made an abortive venture on the lecture circuit. While he was ridiculed by many for the position he took, he simply took his stand on the plenary verbal inspiration of the Bible, a doctrine still held by many Christians. Like John Wesley, he was a man of one book. But he knew that book thoroughly, and he arrayed his argument with great logic and rhetorical power. "He had ferreted out of the Bible every passage that bore upon the motions of the sun, and he had them all printed in a sort of tract" (159), which he distributed beforehand so that everyone could follow his argument and its proof. His biographer responded by saying: "I believed in his sincerity, and to me he was a philosopher, sound in his logic, mighty in his convictions, though he might be wrong in his premises" (171).[89]

A final point needs to be made before turning to an example of Jasper's preaching. In the account given above of the first sermon by Jasper that he heard, Hatcher speaks of the preacher's atrocious grammar and pronunciation. In the essays that he collected into a book, Hatcher makes many such slighting remarks. One passage, however, suggests that with Jasper's lifetime of study, his diction grew progressively closer to the norms of standard English:

> During his long ministerial life his reading and contact with edu-
> cated people rooted out many of his linguistic excrescences. There
> were times when he spoke with approximate accuracy, and even
> with elegance; and yet he delighted, if indeed he was conscious of it,
> in returning to his dialect and in pouring it forth unblushingly in its
> worst shape, and yet always with telling effect. (96)

In the interview mentioned above, his former church member said much the same thing, noting that many of the white people who came to hear him commented on his elegant language. "I know," she said, "he could handle great words when he wanted to, but he could talk in the old way, and he often loved to do that" (88).

A sample of his preaching can be seen in his sermon on "The Stone Cut Out of the Mountain" (108-20; **see Vol. 2, pp. 430-37**). This is a narrative sermon based upon Daniel 2:45. It begins with an introduction in which Jasper affirms his call to preach and says he knows that it angers the devil to see him ascend the pulpit. Then he moves without transition into the story, saying that God sets up the rulers of the people, even though he does not always pick out good people for the job. Temple-robbing Nebuchadnezzar was a case in point, and he was a very powerful ruler.

But Nebuchadnezzar had a frightening dream that none of the experts in his court could tell or explain to him. When he threatened to have all of them killed, Daniel heard of it and prayed. Receiving the insight for which he prayed (for "one thing the Lord can't do: he can't refuse to answer the cries of his people"), he went to the king and explained the dream. The stone from the rock that struck the idol's feet of clay was the kingdom of God, and it would destroy and replace the Babylonian Empire.

Then Jasper said that Nebuchadnezzar did not learn from this experi-ence but built an image ninety feet high and nine feet wide, which he commanded people to worship on the signal of a musical group. He did so despite the fact that Daniel had already explained that Nebuchadnez-zar's kingdom would be destroyed by the kingdom of Jesus Christ. God will destroy all the foundations of sin, and Jasper could hear the Savior saying to his Father that it was time for Gabriel to blow his horn. "I am going out to call my people from the field; they have been abused and laughed at, and made a scoffing long enough for my name's sake." God is going to bring his people home, and Jasper and his people will be among them. Then the proud from whom they have suffered will be told by King Jesus, "I don't know you, and I don't want to know you, and I don't want to see you." The stone out of the mountain will roll through the kingdom of darkness and crush the enemies of God.

Shadrach, Meshach, and Abednego refused to worship Nebuchadnezzar's golden image, and the Chaldeans reported them. When the king offered them another chance, they refused it, so he ordered that the furnace be heated seven times hotter than usual and commanded giants to throw in the Hebrew children. The giants were burned up, but the king looked into the furnace and saw that the three men were totally undamaged and that a fourth man was with them who looked like the Son of God. "The righteous always comes out conquerors and more than conquerors. Kings may hate you, friends despise you, and cowards backbite you, but God is your deliverer."

But Jasper had forgotten that some people believed what he was saying was "old fogy religion." He, however, wanted his church filled with old fogies, who would participate in the unceasing worship in heaven that John of Patmos had foreseen. The "saints of God that was all bruised and mangled by the fiery darts of the wicked" would be there to enjoy it. While Jasper did not have as much religion as he wanted, he had enough to give free salvation to all who wanted it. "If in this big crowd there is one lost sinner that have not felt the cleansing touch of my Savior's blood, I ask him to come today and he shall never die."

In form, this is a fairly standard narrative sermon, but one that could be decoded and seen to have all the power of the tradition, because it used the hermeneutical key to the Bible mentioned by LaRue, combined it with the black experience, and focused it on a particular aspect of life in the church. Anyone reading the entire text can understand why people, black and white, hastened to hear this man who had lived the first half of his life as the possession of another human being.

Thus in the generation before the Civil War, the fruits of the fervor of the Second Awakening came to be visible in a number of efforts at social reform. White evangelicals preached against slavery (without identifying themselves with the strict abolitionists), initiated the campaign against alcoholic beverages that would eventually result in prohibition by constitutional amendment, and pushed other ethical and social implications of their theology. One of the most bountiful fruits of the Awakening, however, was the attraction of significant numbers of African Americans, first to Christianity and then to a preaching ministry. Two manifestations of black Christianity ultimately developed: the elite, which wanted to demonstrate that African Americans are capable of the same achievements as whites, and the folk, which built upon links between the emotionalism of the Awakening and elements of traditional African religion. Both manifestations were to produce preachers of great power. An additional fruit of fervor was the acceptance of women as preachers, which will be the subject of the next chapter.

FOR FURTHER READING

Hatcher, William E. *John Jasper: The Unmatched Negro Philosopher and Preacher.* New York: Fleming H. Revell, 1908.

Johnson, James Weldon. *God's Trombones: Seven Negro Sermons in Verse.* New York: Viking, 1927.

Jones, Ralph H. *Charles Albert Tindley, Prince of Preachers.* Nashville: Abingdon Press, 1982.

McArthur, Robert Stuart. Introduction to *Life of Charles T. Walker, D.D. ("The Black Spurgeon") Pastor of Mt. Olivet Baptist Church, New York City,* by Silas Xavier Floyd. 1902. Reprint, New York: Negro Universities Press, 1960.

Mitchell, Henry H. *Black Preaching: The Recovery of a Powerful Art.* 1970, 1979. Rev. ed. Nashville: Abingdon Press, 1990.

Raboteau, Albert J. *Slave Religion: The "Invisible Institution" in the Antebellum South.* New York: Oxford University Press, 1978.

Smith, Timothy L. *Revivalism and Social Reform: American Protestantism on the Eve of the Civil War.* 1957. Reprint, New York: Harper & Row, 1965.

Notes

1. The title of this chapter is borrowed from a chapter in Timothy L. Smith, *Revivalism and Social Reform: American Protestantism on the Eve of the Civil War* (Nashville: Abingdon, 1957; reprint, New York: Harper & Row, 1965).

2. The theological roots in this belief lie in the theology of John Wesley, who regarded perfection as a second work of grace, an experience parallel to and following conversion. Finney developed a different form of the doctrine as part of his revision of Calvinism. More of this will be considered in the next chapter in the discussion of the Holiness movement.

3. Smith, *Revivalism and Social Reform,* 15.

4. Ibid.

5. Ibid., 149.

6. *John Wesley,* ed. Albert C. Outler (New York: Oxford University Press, 1964), 86.

7. L. C. Rudolph, *Francis Asbury* (Nashville: Abingdon, 1966), 193.

8. Charles L. Wallis, ed., *The Autobiography of Peter Cartwright* (Pierce & Washabaugh, 1956; Nashville: Abingdon, 1984), 72.

9. Ibid., 176.

10. Charles G. Finney, *Lectures on Systematic Theology*, 2:446, quoted in Keith J. Hardman, *Charles Grandison Finney, 1792–1875: Revivalist and Reformer* (Syracuse: Syracuse University Press, 1987), 370.

11. Wallis, *The Autobiography of Peter Cartwright*, 145-46 passim.

12. Hardman, *Charles Grandison Finney, 1792–1875*, 316.

13. Charles A. Johnson, *The Frontier Camp Meeting: Religion's Harvest Time* (Dallas: Southern Methodist University Press, 1955, as reprinted in 1985 with new intro. by Ferenc M. Szasz), 177.

14. "Princes shall come out of Egypt; Ethiopia shall soon stretch out her hands unto God" (Ps. 68:31 KJV). For the interpretation of this verse in the black church, see Albert J. Raboteau, *A Fire in the Bones: Reflections on African American Religious History* (Boston: Beacon, 1995), 37-56.

15. Albert J. Raboteau, *Slave Religion: The "Invisible Institution" in the Antebellum South* (Oxford: Oxford University Press, 1978), 149.

16. On the importance of this institution, see C. Eric Lincoln and Lawrence H. Mamiya, *The Black Church in the African American Experience* (Durham: Duke University Press, 1990).

17. W. E. B. DuBois, *The Souls of Black Folk* (Chicago: A. C. McClurg, 1903; reprint, New York: Blue Heron, 1953; reprint, with intro. Herbert Apteker, Millwood, N.Y.: Kraus-Thomson, 1973), 190-91.

18. William E. Montgomery, *Under Their Own Vine and Fig Tree: The African American Church in the South, 1865–1900* (Baton Rouge: Louisiana State University Press, 1994), 256-66.

19. I am grateful to Prof. Henry Mitchell for the suggestion of these two names.

20. Lemuel Haynes, "Universal Salvation—A Very Ancient Doctrine," in *Black Writers of America: A Comprehensive Anthology*, ed. Richard Barksdale and Keneth Kinnamon (New York: Macmillan, 1972), 226-29. Haynes follows the Perkins sermon form of doctrines and uses, and the characteristics of Satan he lists are aspects of his first point of doctrine, the character of the preacher.

21. Born February 5, 1858. Silas Xavier Floyd, *Life of Charles T. Walker, D.D. ("The Black Spurgeon") Pastor of Mt. Olivet Baptist Church, New York City*, intro. Robert Stuart McArthur (National Baptist Publishing Board, 1902; reprint, New York: Negro Universities Press, 1960).

22. Robert Stuart MacArthur, introduction to ibid.

23. Ibid., 52.

24. Ibid., 57.

25. Ibid., 93.

26. Ibid., 103.

27. Ibid., 182.

28. Ibid.

29. Ibid., 125-28.

30. Ralph H. Jones, *Charles Albert Tindley, Prince of Preachers* (Nashville: Abingdon, 1982). 13. Tindley was less fortunate in his biographer than Walker. Jones wrote largely on the basis of archival information and the memory of former parishioners, and what he wrote is more like a chronicle than a coherent effort to interpret

Tindley's life and ministry. There is, however, an advantage to this approach because information about such things as Tindley's disappointment in not being elected a bishop, the politics behind that, the misbehavior of his children, and factions within his congregation is not filtered out.

31. His memory of this, recorded in a sermon (ibid., 19-20), implies that his father had disposition of him, which sounds inconsistent with his being a slave.

32. Ibid., 20.

33. A workman who carried bricks and mortar to masons.

34. There may have been as many as ten thousand, but his biographer is not consistent in the statistics he provides.

35. A Baptist minister famous for an inspirational speech he gave six thousand times called "Acres of Diamonds."

36. "We Shall Overcome" of civil rights fame.

37. Jones, *Charles Albert Tindley,* 15.

38. I have been able to see only two.

39. Jones, *Charles Albert Tindley,* 157.

40. Ibid., 162.

41. In an essay entitled "The Chanted Sermon" in Raboteau, *Fire in the Bones,* 141-51; the quoted words are from p. 151. There is a wide literature on this subject that begins with James Weldon Johnson's introductory essay to his *God's Trombones* (New York: Viking , 1927) and includes: William H. Pipes, *Say Amen, Brother! Old-Time Negro Preaching: A Study in American Frustration* (New York: William-Frederick, 1951); Bruce Rosenberg, *The Art of the American Folk Preacher* (New York: Oxford University Press, 1970), revised as *Can These Bones Live?* (Urbana and Chicago: University of Illinois Press, 1988); Gerald L. Davis, *I Got the Word in Me and I Can Sing It, You Know: A Study of the Performed African American Sermon* (Philadelphia: University of Pennsylvania Press, 1985); Evans E. Crawford with Thomas H. Troeger, *The Hum: Call and Response in African American Preaching* (Nashville: Abingdon, 1995); and Henry H. Mitchell, *Black Preaching* (San Francisco: Harper & Row, 1970, 1979; rev. ed. Nashville: Abingdon, 1990).

42. Raboteau, *Fire in the Bones,* 142.

43. T. G. Steward, "The Influence of Euphony upon the Employment of Language," *A.M.E. Zion Church Review (Quarterly)* 2 (1885): 41-43.

44. Among those can be numbered such contemporary preachers as James Forbes, senior pastor of Riverside Church and former homiletics professor at Union Seminary, and Michael Curry, bishop of the Episcopal Diocese of North Carolina.

45. Raboteau, "The Chanted Sermon," 143.

46. Mitchell, *Black Preaching,* 113.

47. Ibid., 129.

48. Ibid., 112-47.

49. Johnson, *God's Trombones,* 1.

50. Raboteau, "The Chanted Sermon," 142.

51. See above, chapter 15.

52. Raboteau, *Slave Religion,* 311. On the influence of the Bible in slave religious thought, see ibid., 239-66.

53. Mitchell, *Black Preaching,* 179.

54. Johnson refers to this use of voice as "intoning." "This intoning is always a matter of crescendo and dimuendo in the intensity—a rising and falling between plain speaking and wild chanting" (*God's Trombones,* 10).

55. Raboteau, "The Chanted Sermon," 143-44.

56. Bruce Rosenberg, *The Art of the American Folk Preacher* and *Can These Bones Live?*

57. Albert Lord, *The Singer of Tales* (New York: Athenaeum, 1965), 30, quoted in *Can These Bones Live?*, 84.

58. The term used by folklorists, apparently, although what it means closely approximates what classical rhetoricians called *topi.*

59. Johnson, *God's Trombones*, 11.

60. Davis, *I Got the Word in Me and I Can Sing It, You Know*, 49.

61. A number of studies have been made about the musical aspect of this preaching, including Jon Michael Spenser, *Sacred Symphony: The Chanted Sermon of the Black Preacher* (Westbury, Conn.: Greenwood, 1987); and Marion Joseph Franklin, *The Relationship of Black Preaching to Black Gospel Music* (Unpublished Drew D.Min. thesis, 1982). See also the treatment of spirituals in Raboteau, *Slave Religion*, passim. There have also been linguistic studies such as the unpublished 1976 University of Texas Ph.D. dissertation of Richard Louis Wright, *Linguistic Standards and Communicative Style in the Black Church.*

62. Davis, *I Got the Word in Me and I Can Sing It, You Know*, 64-80. The criteria are stated in Davis's language.

63. Ibid., 26-38. This point is documented in an amusing way by Evans Crawford's use of typical sermon responses to furnish criteria by which a homiletics class can evaluate a student's sermon:
Help 'em, Lord (the search is on for the connections and we start out in need of prayer),
Well? (You're hinting to the witness with a chantable refrain or "riff"),
That's all right! (There are Good News and gospel possibilities; the sermon is becoming persuasive),
Amen! (The truth is affirmed and the pitch is right for the people and Scripture passage),
Glory Hallelujah! (the point of the loudest praise, highest joy, and praise to God). (Crawford, *The Hum*, 13).

64. Johnson, *God's Trombones*, 5.

65. Pipes, *Say Amen, Brother!*, 71-72.

66. Rosenberg, *Can These Bones Live?*, 131; cf. 71-72, 139-40.

67. Davis, *I Got the Word in Me and I Can Sing It, You Know*, 51.

68. On the ambiguity of language in spirituals, see Raboteau, *Slave Religion*, 248-50.

69. Davis, *I Got the Word in Me and I Can Sing It, You Know*, 66.

70. Ibid., 64.

71. Cleophus J. LaRue, *The Heart of Black Preaching* (Louisville, Ky.: Westminster John Knox, 2000).

72. Ibid., 18.

73. Ibid., 22.

74. Ibid., 23.

75. Mitchell, *Black Preaching*, 195.

76. Raboteau, "The Chanted Sermon," 151.

77. Ibid., 21. Cf. Howard Dorgan, *Giving Glory to God in Appalachia: Worship Practices of Six Baptist Subdenominations* (Knoxville: University of Tennessee Press, 1987), 56-85, for an excellent description of such preaching. See also what was said above about Welsh preaching, above, chapter 17.

78. Raboteau, *Slave Religion*, 48-55. See E. Franklin Frazier, *The Negro Church in America* (New York: Schocken, 1964), 1-19, and other books as well.

79. In contrast, see the treatment of Pipes, *Say Amen, Brother!*, 55 n. 13, pp. 169-70.

80. Raboteau, *Slave Religion*, 92.

81. Ibid., 66-73.

82. There is something problematic about the time references of the studies of African American preaching that have been reviewed here. This chapter is concerned with fruits of the Second Great Awakening, and thus is mainly interested in African American preaching during slave times and Reconstruction, the period studied by Raboteau and referred to by DuBois. Johnson was writing just before the Great Depression. Pike wrote during the Korean War, but in an effort to see if preaching in rural Georgia was still like slave preaching. Rosenberg and Davis, however, did their fieldwork mostly in California, the first in the late 1960s and the latter in the early 1980s. To what extent can it be assumed that essentially the same phenomenon is being described? The only answer that can be given is that the qualities to which Rosenberg and Davis call attention are present in the descriptions of the earliest black preaching. Undoubtedly there are differences between times and places, but they do not seem to affect the overall picture that has been presented.

83. I will say more of African American preaching in the section that deals with preaching after World War II, including the civil rights movement, the way that Negro preaching came to the attention of white culture, how black preachers came to occupy positions of national leadership, African Americans giving the Beecher Lectures on Preaching at Yale, and the development of homiletical textbooks and other pedagogical tools in this tradition. See below, chapter 28.

84. William E. Hatcher, *John Jasper: The Unmatched Negro Philosopher and Preacher* (New York: Fleming H. Revell, 1908).

85. *Dictionary of American Biography*, ed. Dumas Malone (New York: Scribner's, 1932), 8:395.

86. Richard Ellsworth Day, *Rhapsody in Black: The Life Story of John Jasper*, A Broad Brim Book (Philadelphia: Judson, 1953), 12.

87. Hatcher, *John Jasper*, 131. Hereafter, references to this work will be given parenthetically in the text by page number alone.

88. On the advice of Prof. Larry Murphy of Garrett-Evangelical Theological Seminary, quotations from Jasper will be given here in standard spelling, but grammatical irregularities will be allowed to stand.

89. It is ironic that Hatcher, a Southern Baptist minister, accepted the scientific explanation one hundred years ago, while today many members of his denomination would agree with Jasper in a creationist understanding.

CHAPTER 21

"THE FRUITS OF FERVOR" (B)

"YOUR DAUGHTERS SHALL PROPHESY"

Women preachers have appeared occasionally throughout the history of the church, but the first significant trend toward making their activity the norm, rather than an exception, in what became the mainline churches in America was another fruit of the Second Great Awakening. Yet, to vary the metaphor, the ground was prepared and a seed was planted that did not achieve its full fruitfulness until the last half of the twentieth century. In the intervening time, sprigs grew into trees that dropped their own seed until, finally, there was an orchard.

There is, however, one major exception to this otherwise accurate generalization.

THE SOCIETY OF FRIENDS

The first tradition in America to have women ministers on a regular basis was the Religious Society of Friends, commonly known as the

Quakers.[1] During the first three-quarters of the eighteenth century, this body became the third largest religious group among Americans of European descent,[2] and their women who "traveled in ministry" were a common sight. Among Quakers, women preachers had been recognized equally with men from the beginning. The principle on which that recognition was based had been stated succinctly by William Penn: "Sexes make no Difference; since in Souls there is none."[3]

This revolutionary attitude originated in the cauldron of social and religious change that was seventeenth-century England. Quakers have been classified as one of the more radical spiritual reform groups that arose during the age of the Puritans and Independents.[4] George Fox, the founder of the Friends, proclaimed that men and women had been restored to their pre-fall purity. Upon the basis of the quotation in Acts 2 of Joel 2:28-32, the existence of women who prophesied was taken as evidence that the last days had arrived.[5] Accordingly, it was necessary and even inevitable that women should preach, but their doing so meant the end of the world was very near. The spirit of Christ had come as Light to dwell in human beings and to fill them with concerns that they should relay to others. By the end of the century, however, these imminent apocalyptic expectations had faded from the movement and the motivating dynamic had become the experience of Light itself, which "had come to be viewed more as a divine spiritual principle working in all people and ages."[6]

The apocalyptic interpretation of Acts 2:17 did not relieve the early Friends from the necessity of justifying the preaching of women in the face of the widely perceived Pauline ban on women speaking in church. Fox himself wrote two tracts on the subject. The first, published in 1656, had the misleading title of *The Woman Learning in Silence: or, the Mysterie of the Woman's Subjection to Her Husband, as Also, the Daughter Prophesying, Wherein the Lord Hath, and Is Fulfilling That He Spake by the Prophet Joel, I Will Pour Out My Spirit unto All Flesh.* The second was titled *Concerning Sons and Daughters, and Prophetesses Speaking and Prophesying in the Law and the Gospel.* Both showed that women in the Bible had prophesied and been the vehicles of messages from God. Another tract, *Womens Speaking Justified, Proved, and Allowed of by the Scriptures,* was published in 1666 by the "Nursing Mother of Quakerism," Margaret Fell.

To say that Quakers had women preachers can be confusing, since the Religious Society of Friends did not have pastors.[7] Furthermore, their meetings for worship were silent gatherings unless someone present— anyone present—felt moved by the Spirit to share some light received. To clarify the matter, it is necessary to distinguish among ministry as order (i.e., conferred by ordination), ministry as office (i.e., a professional appointment), and ministry as function. Only in the functional sense can we speak of early Quakers, male or female, as ministers. From the beginning, they had decried a professional ministerial class as a "hireling" clergy. Those among them who performed ministerial functions had other employment and ministered only occasionally and as they were led by the Spirit.

But, as Carol Stoneburner said, "Over time Quakers created a leadership class."[8] While it was still believed that the Spirit dwelled in all human beings and could lay a concern to speak on any member attending a meeting, experience showed that the Spirit spoke through some persons more often, more effectively, and at greater length than through others. Those whose gifts had been noticed were recorded as ministers. Meetinghouses came to be constructed with a slightly raised bench at the front that faced the other benches. Elders and recorded ministers sat on these. There could be several ministers in one congregation, and there was no expectation that each would speak at every meeting. Only a person who felt that she or he had been given an insight by the Spirit, as well as a command to share it with the meeting, would speak. And when speaking, only the message received was to be communicated and then as concisely as possible, without any rhetorical embellishment or addition of thoughts by the speaker.

In a study of twenty-five women from the first five generations of English Quakers, Elise Boulding writes of stages of call to ministry:

> All the women struggle mightily against being called to the ministry. There are usually three crises. The first is in accepting an inward call to serious holiness. The second is accepting a call to speak in Meeting. Some women struggled so hard against the inner call to speak that they became seriously ill, and the struggle could go on for several years.[9]

The effective preachers among those who responded to this call were "recorded" as ministers. The third crisis mentioned by Boulding was the call to travel in ministry outside one's local meeting.

Again, this call could come to either a woman or a man, and at times came to a wife and husband together. They would report to their local meeting for business that a concern had been laid upon their hearts for a particular task in a particular place. In the seventeenth century, this could be to carry the Quaker message in evangelism or proselytism, but in the eighteenth, it was more often a matter of building up or reforming other

Quaker meetings.[10] The meeting, after a process of discernment as to whether the concern was really a prompting of the Spirit, would decide whether to record in a minute the sense of the meeting that the person should travel in this ministry. Such decisions were often accompanied by a commitment of the meeting to underwrite the travel expenses and to look after the traveling minister's local responsibilities while away. The journey might be short or long. It could be the only one on which a particular person ever went or it could be one of a number, but the commission in the enabling minute was for only the particular trip.

The records of some of these journeys are heroic in the extreme. Seventeenth-century preaching could involve disrupting services of the established church to claim the superiority of Quaker worship, street preaching in the marketplace, or even addressing the king at court. Those who went on such journeys often had to pay severely for their witness, being either beaten or imprisoned. When Mary Fisher and Elizabeth Williams rebuked the undergraduates of Oliver Cromwell's old college at Cambridge, calling them "Antichrists" and "a Cage of Unclean Birds and the Synagogue of Satan," the magistrate ordered them to be whipped until the blood ran down their bodies. This same Mary Fisher was eventually to preach before the sultan of Turkey, by whom she was received with far greater courtesy than was accorded her in either old or New England.

The following year, two others who tried to preach in Cambridge received the same punishment. One, Elizabeth Fletcher, never recovered from the beating, but she did go back the following year and walked naked through the streets "as a sign for the hypocritical profession they made there."[11] Mary Dyer, one of a number of English women Friends who attempted to preach in New England, was eventually hanged in Boston under a law of the Massachusetts General Court banishing Quakers on pain of death.[12]

Not only did British women Quakers receive minutes authorizing them to travel to America, American women also became Public Friends, as those who received such minutes were called, to travel in ministry to England. Women accounted for 42 of the 103 American Public Friends who visited Britain in the eighteenth century.[13] While travel remained hazardous, the danger of outright persecution had lessened, and perhaps the ministries had become more sedate. As noted above, imminent apocalyptic expectations had faded from the movement by the end of the seventeenth century, and its motivating dynamic had become the experience of Light itself. This shift within the movement coincided with a shift in the culture at large toward toleration and other Enlightenment virtues.

As a result, Quaker women who traveled in ministry to America were no longer regarded as witches; instead, some were even welcomed as "celebrated preachers."[14]

As the eighteenth century turned into the nineteenth, the Society of Friends became an established part of American life, but continued to lead in every activity for the amelioration of society, from prison reform to abolition. Two sisters from a slaveowning family in South Carolina, Angelina and Sarah Grimké, moved north to Philadelphia to join the Quakers and speak out against slavery and the oppression of women, although they did not find their own meeting there as supportive as they had hoped.

This speaking on social issues from a religious perspective by the Grimké sisters does not appear to have been mandated by a minute to travel, but some of their coworkers in these causes were definitely women ministers. The most prominent was certainly Lucretia Mott. Many know her primarily for her advocacy of a wide range of reforms, including feminism, abolition, peace, Native American rights, and immigrant welfare, among others. A close study of her correspondence, sermons, and speeches, however, convinced one scholar that "her secret source of strength was her implicit faith in the promptings of the Divine Spirit."[15]

Born Lucretia Coffin in Nantucket in 1793, she was educated at a Quaker school in New York State, where she met and eventually married a young instructor named James Mott. By the time of their marriage they had moved to Philadelphia, which remained their home the rest of their lives. The mother of six children, Lucretia also devoted herself to many activities outside the house. The death of one of her children in 1817 caused her to turn to her faith more deeply than before. It was out of this experience that she became a recorded minister in the Society of Friends. From then on, she traveled in ministry, preached widely, and lectured and otherwise labored for the many causes listed above. Her husband, also a recorded minister, was not nearly as articulate as she, but was content to enable her ministry in any way possible.[16]

Influences on Mott's thought, in addition to the Quaker tradition and the abolitionism of William Lloyd Garrison, were Unitarianism and New England transcendentalism.[17] Her belief system was thus an amalgam that fitted in with the optimistic progressivist liberalism of her time. It is not surprising, then, that Mott's sermons were neither expository nor textual, but topical. She did, however, quote extensively from the Bible and from other sources, especially poetry. She was invited to preach in churches of other denominations and, of course, she gave platform addresses in support of her many causes.

But, in accord with the Quaker tradition, her sermons at regular meetings for worship were delivered extempore, and their preservation is due to stenographic recording. (For an example, see **Vol. 2, pp. 438-44.**) In her sermons, she holds up the superiority of the Quaker tradition to that of other denominations (decrying rites, dogmas, and "hireling" clergy). She exhorts her hearers to act upon the testimony of the Spirit within them, root out their own sin, and extirpate social evil in a manner consistent with their nonviolent tradition. And she looks forward to a time when all of that will be accomplished.

Quaker women proclaimed the message that characterized each century of the existence of their movement: in the seventeenth they were apocalyptic, in the eighteenth they focused on Inner Light and reform in a deeply Christian way, and in the nineteenth they advocated progressive social causes, many also identifying themselves with liberal religion.

THE WESLEYAN/HOLINESS TRADITION

By the nineteenth century, the number of women preaching afforded their being classified according to tradition and typical experience. While an extensive literature upon the subject exists, until recently it has concentrated more upon the effort to have women's eligibility to preach recognized than what made their pulpit activity distinctive from that of their male counterparts.[18] A great service has been done the history of preaching by Catherine A. Brekus, who has rescued from oblivion more than a hundred women preachers in this country before the Civil War. In *Strangers & Pilgrims: Female Preaching in America, 1740–1845*,[19] she has been able to reconstruct a detailed picture of preaching by women in a period when it was believed that little occurred. Very few of these women were ordained clergy, but most had recognized positions within their denominations that allowed them to engage in proclamation, even to "promiscuous" audiences (as those containing both men and women were called at the time).

One of the most useful of Brekus's services is her recognition of periods in which different groups of women preachers were enlisted. Most of the women active in the time of the First Great Awakening were exhorters, who encouraged those under conviction to accept conversion. During the period of the Revolution, two charismatic women started their own sects: Mother Ann Lee, founder of the Shakers; and the woman known as Jemima Wilkinson before the experience in which she was reborn as the Public Universal Friend and began to gather other Universal Friends around her.

563

The majority of the women preachers chronicled by Brekus, however, were itinerant lay evangelists of the Second Great Awakening who were recognized by denominations that came into existence in America during that time: the Methodists, the African Methodists, the Free Will Baptists, and the Christian Connection.[20] Brekus's essential thesis is that these bodies used women evangelists to help them grow from small sects into flourishing denominations, and then were embarrassed by them as their churches became respectable in the age of the cult of domesticity. In that culture, where women were expected to refine and purify the private sphere and be invisible in the public sphere, the raucous evangelists of the frontier no longer had a place. Indeed, there was an effort to purge denominational histories of any hint they had ever existed.

The preaching of women evangelists did get a new lease on life in the Millerite movement, out of which the Adventists were eventually to be formed, but most of Brekus's study is devoted to the earlier and larger group. In addition to a chapter on their message (typical of evangelistic preaching at the time), other chapters are devoted to their autobiographical writings and their use of marketing techniques being developed at the time while deploring the marketing revolution.

One shortcoming of Brekus's work, however, is a failure to recognize the impetus given to such preaching by the Holiness movement. It could be argued that Mott's understanding of guidance by the Inner Light was an example of the yearning for perfection, which, according to Timothy Smith, characterized so many American religious movements in the quarter century before the Civil War. In the Wesleyan movement, however, the understanding of Christian perfection, sanctification as a second work of grace was on its native soil. And it is not accidental that the number of women who felt called to preach in this tradition and its branches were usually persons who claimed to have undergone that experience.

African American Pioneers

Among the earliest women to preach in the Wesleyan tradition were a number of African American evangelists, several of whom have left accounts of their lives. The best known of these, the woman who received the name Sojourner Truth (1797–1883), was the least typical. In spite of early membership in a Methodist congregation, she was not affiliated with any denomination for most of her life—although she worked with a number—nor was she ever authorized by any to preach. Although Truth was a person of commanding presence and penetrating insight, the relatively short time during which preaching was her main activity suggests that the most appropriate category in which to understand her is that put forward by Marta Tomhave Blauvelt, "wandering seer."[21]

After Sojourner Truth, the best known is probably Amanda Smith, a member of the African Methodist Episcopal Church who was an independent evangelist and served as a missionary in the United States, Great Britain, India, and Africa between 1878 and 1890.[22] As impressive as she was, there are autobiographical accounts of the ministries of several women who labored much earlier than she. Jarena Lee first felt the call to preach in 1811 and was licensed as an A.M.E. exhorter by Bishop Richard Allen in 1819. In the year that Lee was licensed, Zilpha Elaw felt the call to preach at a camp meeting. She did not enter full-time ministry until 1825, however, and, while she was never officially licensed, Elaw did receive endorsement from various Methodist clergy and others. Born later than the other two, Julia Foote did not begin preaching until the early 1840s. She was "read out" of her A.M.E. congregation for preaching, but was nevertheless welcomed into the pulpits of other A.M.E. churches, as well as those of other denominations, including the Methodists. After many years, she became an official missionary for her church and was even ordained elder before her death in 1900.[23]

A number of common threads run through the stories of Lee, Elaw, and Foote. All members of the A.M.E. Church, their common sense of vocation to preach grew out of their experiences of sanctification. All had visionary experiences. Each had difficulty in accepting her call because the assumption of the time was that women should not preach.[24] The husbands of all three opposed their ministries, and it was not until after the spouses' deaths that they were able to give themselves unremittingly to their work. Relations with official church structures were tenuous at best, yet each found willing audiences and was welcomed into the pulpits of many clergy. Their preaching was heard with appreciation by members of different denominations,[25] by white as well as black, the educated and socially prominent as well as the poor and illiterate.

Each suffered from racial bigotry, from prejudice against women in preaching, and from resentment of evangelism.[26] Each traveled many difficult miles, enduring great hardships and dangers. Elaw, for instance, carried her ministry into slave states where she was in danger of being sold into slavery herself and also spent several years preaching in England. Their sense of being led by God to do things opposed in the society of their time means that their autobiographies are accounts of extraordinary heroism in the service of the gospel.

What can be said of the way they preached? For one thing, their styles must have had much in common with the evangelistic preaching of men

during the Second Great Awakening. Lee and, even more, Elaw sometimes record the texts from which they preached, and most are the sort
that suggest the challenge given by the coming judgment to repent and
accept the gospel. The responses to their preaching also sound very much
like the responses recorded by men from the *Journals* of John Wesley
on.[27] They also proclaimed the blessings of sanctification in such a manner that, at times, mere conversion sounded like only a half-safe step.

The most informative of the three autobiographies from a homiletical
point of view is that of Foote. Its title is taken from Zechariah 3:2 (KJV),
"a brand plucked out of the fire," and these words recur as a refrain
throughout the book to proclaim that the author had been providential-
ly rescued many times.[28] A common homiletical device is thus used in
giving structure to a book. Further, many chapters end in an exhortation
to the reader that sounds for the world like the end of a sermon, such as:

> Dear reader, have you innocent children, given you from the hand of
> God? Children, whose purity rouses all that is holy and good in your
> nature? Do not, I pray, give to these little ones of God the accursed cup
> which will send them down to misery and death. Listen to the voice of
> conscience, the woes of the drunkard, the wailing of poverty-stricken
> women and children, and touch not the accursed cup. From Sinai come
> the awful words of Jehovah, "No drunkard shall inherit the kingdom
> of heaven" [1 Cor. 6:10].[29]

Foote also gives evidence in several places of having consulted commentaries or other tools of biblical study in the preparation of her sermons. When, for example, she tries to answer the supposed Pauline ban
on women preaching, she refers to the meaning of the Greek term by
which Paul refers to Priscilla, notes how the same word is translated in
other places, and concludes by saying: "When Paul said, 'Help those
women who labor with me in the Gospel,' he certainly meant that they
did more than to pour out tea."[30]

Biblical scholarship is used again in a sermon she was asked to preach
on Micah 4:13 (KJV), "Arise and thresh, O daughter of Zion," when she
contrasts the method of threshing used in biblical times with that utilized
in her own day.[31] She seems to give an outline of the sermon (it surely
must have been longer), the first of several that occur near the end of her
book. She interprets the passage as referring to preachers and says that
the metaphor works as well with modern as with ancient means of
threshing. Either way, the devil is threshed out of sinners, an unpleasant
but necessary experience for all to undergo.

To repeat, the sermons of these African American women evangelists seem to be calls for conversion and sanctification, common themes of Awakening preaching.

Mainstreaming Holiness

Lee, Foote, and Elaw had experienced sanctification some years before it came to be sought by white Methodists, especially those with any social prominence. There were, however, calls for greater holiness from the highest circles of the Methodist Episcopal Church, including a pastoral address on the subject from the bishops at General Conference in 1835. The critical turn occurred that same year when Sarah Lankford combined the prayer meetings of two Methodist churches in New York City to form the "Tuesday Meeting for the Promotion of Holiness." Her sister, **Phoebe Palmer,** soon experienced sanctification and became the leader of the movement. Within five years a number of prominent clergy had been enlisted in the cause, women in other places started similar groups, and expectation of the experience became common rather than rare.

This was about the time that Charles G. Finney and the Oberlin faculty were beginning to teach their doctrine of perfection, which had Wesleyan roots although it also grew out of Finney's teaching on free will. Holiness was an idea whose time had come.

Palmer's understanding of holiness grew out of Wesley's teaching about sanctification as a second work of grace after conversion, but she adapted the doctrine somewhat:

> Wesley's emphasis on the disciplined life that led to an eventual attainment of this "perfect love" was, in her mind, an unnecessary prolongation of a "blessing" that was available the moment a Christian consecrated everything to God and claimed this promise of "perfect love." All an individual needed to do was to become a "living sacrifice on the altar of Jesus Christ."[32]

Part of the explanation for her change was that her approach was more analytical than emotional. She had never felt the affective satisfaction that converted Methodists were expected to enjoy. When she experienced sanctification herself, it came as a matter of faith, of deciding to believe that God could be relied upon to keep the divine promises. "Signs and wonders" were not to be relied upon:

> She would instead rely on nothing except the Bible, which she held to be the word of God to man, and "faith," which she defined as . . . taking "God at his word, whatever [one's] emotions might be."[33]

Phoebe Palmer was quick to express the grace she had received in her life, handing out tracts in the slums, visiting prisons, and doing pioneer settlementhouse work, especially in the Five Points Mission she founded. She also wrote several books to communicate her understanding. And she and her physician husband, Walter, began in the late 1850s to travel around, conducting revivals. They were so successful that by the time she died in 1874, Phoebe Palmer was credited with having brought twenty-five thousand people to Christ.[34]

There is an evolution in the form Palmer's leadership took at religious gatherings. The Tuesday Meetings were largely occasions at which those gathered testified to their experience of grace or the need for it, and at these she presided unobtrusively. As she began to receive invitations to speak, she developed an ability to address a group in a more complex way, so that by the time she began preaching revivals, she was an accomplished speaker:

> In the church or hall meeting . . . Palmer was the preacher of the hour, doing all the things a Finney would do; occupying the pulpit, taking a text, presenting an exhortation calculated to persuade hearers to repent and turn to God or seek to more fully enter the "way of holiness" (always replete with stories and illustrations), issuing an "invitation" to the anxious to pray and be prayed for, and praying with an[d] instructing those who responded to the invitation. According to the evidence, this was perhaps Palmer's *most* effective medium of all, as well as being the one in which the participation of a woman was the most exceptional.[35]

Palmer, then, was one of the great women preachers of the nineteenth century. Yet at first she would have rejected the description, since she did not believe it right for women to preach. In time, however, she came to distinguish between what she did and "technical preaching," the sort of thing done by ordained clergy. (For her discussion of "the gift of prophecy," **see Vol. 2, pp. 446-57.**) Her definition of "nontechnical preaching" was elastic enough to cover anything from the personal witness of one individual to another to addresses from the pulpit to large crowds. She did not so much oppose the ordination of women and technical preaching by them as prescind the questions of their appropriateness. She seemed to think the sort of thing she was doing was much more crucial. As she said,

> The word *preach* taken in connection with its attendant paraphernalia, oratorical display, onerous titles, and pulpits of pedestal eminence,

means so much more than we infer was signified by the word *preach*, when used in connection with the ministrations of Christ and his apostles, that we were disposed to withhold our unreserved assent to women's preaching in the technical sense.[36]

So modest was she and so traditional in her view of the role of women that at first she did not even allow her name to appear on the title pages of her books. *Promise of the Father,* for instance, says only that it is by the author of her other works. She changed her mind, however, when she was walking past the Bowery Theater one day and saw a lurid placard that listed female as well as male members of the cast. Her reaction was: "Here are the servants of Satan who are not afraid or ashamed to let their names appear. And shall the servants of the Heavenly King be less bold?" From then on, she published under her name.[37]

Palmer was born only sixteen years after the death of John Wesley, the daughter of a man who was proud that he had received his ticket of membership in the Methodist society from the founder himself.[38] She came along at a time when American Methodism

> was seeking its way from an association of "societies" founded for spiritual discovery and fellowship within the Church of England to an autonomous denomination operating according to the American pattern of free-for-all competition among pluralistic religious bodies.[39]

Under Wesley's regime, all Methodist preachers were assumed to be laypersons, but in America they came to be ordained. It was inevitable that the time would come when ordination would be extended to women.

The first Methodist Episcopal woman to be licensed to preach was **Maggie Newton Van Cott.**[40] Born in 1830 into a prosperous middle-class Episcopal family, Margaret Newton married Peter Van Cott a couple of months before her seventeenth birthday. Her husband later contracted tuberculosis and was an invalid on and off for the rest of his life. His illness forced Mrs. Van Cott to help in the support of the family, and she became something of an entrepreneur, manufacturing medicines and selling them to stores.

Converted while riding the Fulton Street ferry, she became a class member at Duane Street Methodist Episcopal Church and began to speak a little at class meetings. After her husband died, she joined The Methodist Church. Before long she began conducting a meeting in an ecumenical mission in Five Points that lasted twenty-one months and included the organization of a Sunday school.[41] Then, early in 1868, she was asked to preach in the Catskills. She accepted the invitation but refused to call what she was doing "preaching," saying that she was only "talking about Jesus." Yet host clergy insisted that she speak from the pulpit.

It seems that wherever Van Cott went to speak, a revival broke out and she had to remain several weeks. Then further invitations would come from the surrounding area. By the middle of 1868, the urgent invitations for her to preach had become so numerous that she had to give up her business. In September of that year, she was licensed as an exhorter by the Methodist Episcopal Church and six months later was licensed to preach by that church—although she herself had little interest in such credentials.

In her first year as an itinerant evangelist, she preached 335 hour-long sermons, traveled 3,000 miles, and saw 500 probationers added to The Methodist Church (222). She expanded the circle of her travels first into New England and then to the Midwest. When she preached in Evanston, Illinois, Frances Willard said that all but two of her "girls" at the Evanston College for Ladies became members of the church. In 1870 she preached 339 times and had a total of 2,949 converts, 1,735 of whom became Methodist probationers (276). She "was on the sawdust trail for thirty years" and was compared to Dwight L. Moody in effectiveness.[42]

It is possible to get an impression of Van Cott's preaching because her biographer included in an appendix a number of press clippings that contain reports of her sermons, and he also reprinted newspaper transcriptions of two of her sermons. A sense of what it was like to hear her can be gained from one of the reviews, that in *Harper's Bazaar*. At the time it was still a Methodist publication in spirit if not officially, and it contained many favorable remarks about her preaching. This report, which describes the qualities indicative of the time's successful revival preaching, justifies extended quotation:

> Like most revivalists, she is more declamatory than argumentative, appealing more to the passions than the reason. Her articulation is distinct and easily heard in any part of the church (we had almost said of the village), and her style being varied does not fatigue the hearer. At times she amuses the fancy with familiar talk, filled with flowery imagery, fixing the attention and winning the confidence of her hearers, till rising with her theme, she rushes on with the excitement of inspiration, breaking down the fortifications of the ungodly and carrying their works by storm. She is not an educated woman, in the strict sense, and her influence, as a consequence, is chiefly felt among her own class. She is gifted with a remarkable flow of language, her gestures are graceful,

and her general style would give rise to the remark that she must have derived her ideas of public speaking from dramatic performers. Her powers of endurance are very remarkable, speaking nearly three hours every evening through the week, and twice on Sundays. (327)

A Return to the Soil

Much humbler were the circumstances of **Lydia Sexton,** a woman who ministered in the church that has been called the "German phase of Methodism in America," the United Brethren in Christ.[43] Born the daughter of a Baptist minister in Rockport, New Jersey, she came to experience extreme deprivation. When her father died, her mother remarried and had to farm out her own children in order to take care of her husband's children by a former marriage and other dependents. Consequently, while growing up, Sexton was exploited as free labor while living in the homes of various relatives. She married out of such dependency twice, only to have her husbands die. When her *Autobiography* was published, however, she had been living with her third husband for more than fifty years. Her story is a fascinating account of life on the frontier as she moved from New Jersey to Ohio to Indiana and finally to Kansas.

Converted in a United Brethren revival, Sexton was eventually urged to begin preaching. She was licensed by her quarterly conference in 1851, a license that had to be renewed every quarter. Eventually, though, she was given not a license but a "recommendation" by her annual conference. She was not appointed to a circuit but gave out appointments to preach (i.e., she accepted invitations). Her preaching was revivalistic, and she held many protracted meetings—the sort of ministry Maggie Van Cott had. Finally, in 1870 she was appointed chaplain to the Kansas State Prison for men, a post in which she was very effective.

One sample of Sexton's preaching is included in her book. There is a gusto and humor about her writing that are seen in her description of the situation in which the sermon was preached:

I greatly doubted the propriety and actual benefit of my preaching at St. Marys [Indiana]; but the appointment had gone out and I must submit. They had procured the largest room in the place, which was in part used for the storage of groceries and liquors. When I entered the room the fumes of whiskey were very rank—indeed almost intolerable. I had my misgivings as to duty; but I thought of what Brother Griffith said when asked whether he would preach in a Universalist Church. His answer was, "I will preach anywhere on this side of hell, if it is a decent place." As the audience was very large I thought it best not to disappoint them. (309)

Her sermon was suited to the setting. She preached mainly on Leviticus 14:33, but actually on all that Leviticus has to say about leprosy. She spent some time talking about how it was diagnosed, how it could attack a house as well as a person, the precautions a priest had to take in visiting the contagion, and what must be done about it—with the destruction of the house as the remedy of last resort. Then she said that various moral failings were like leprosy: swearing, dancing, gambling, and, worst of all, selling liquor.

The sermon is illustrated with anecdotes of people she had known whose lives one or another of these vices had ruined. The language is vigorous, and there is the occasional bit of comic relief, as when she tells a long tale proving that men who are stingy will seldom become drunkards (316-17). She is convinced that woman suffrage would close the saloons (318). Rum sellers should be held accountable for the damage they do in the same way as the owner of an ox that gores someone. The only remedy for sin is the death of Jesus, a point that is made by a catena of verses from all over the Bible.

She heard the next day that the owner of the building "liked [her] sermon first-rate, only he wished [she] had not spoken so strongly against dancing and drinking and grocery-keepers" (321).

Early Pentecostalism

As the century moved on, the Holiness movement became separated from mainline churches and formed into independent denominations and even congregations. While many of these have continued their existence to the present day, they also furnished the environment in which the Pentecostal movement began at the turn of the century.[44] A woman in whose ministry this trajectory of the Wesleyan Holiness tradition can be observed is the proto-Pentecostal preacher, **Maria Beulah Woodworth-Etter**.[45] Almost forgotten for a time, Woodworth-Etter had great success as an evangelist in Indiana and Illinois in the closing decades of the nineteenth century, attracting crowds of as many as twenty-five thousand people. Originally from Ohio, she had been born in Lisbon in 1844. Her family did not become religious until her father almost died when she was twelve. Thereafter they became Disciples of Christ, and although Maria had a conversion of sorts when she was thirteen, it was not until 1879 that she experienced what led her to begin preaching.

By then she had married a Civil War veteran and farmer, Philo Harrison Etter, and had six children by him, five of whom succumbed to illness. Her sense of call came in her bereavement. Or, rather, in that condition she felt a renewal of a call that had stirred her when she was a teenager. She began reviving churches in the area. The Disciples did not ordain women, but several denominations offered her jobs. She began with the United Brethren but soon switched to the Church of God (Winebrenner), which asked her to return her ministerial credentials after she had preached in their connection for twenty years.

She held successful meetings in places like Muncie and Kokomo. She was best known for a sort of trance into which she and some of her converts fell. She also engaged in healing and other displays of charismatic power, but the gift of tongues is not mentioned in connection with her until after the Azusa Street revival in Los Angeles in 1906, the most commonly given date for the beginning of the Pentecostal movement.[46]

She lost credibility in 1909 when she prophesied a tidal wave and earthquake in Oakland, California, that did not happen,[47] but somehow she kept at it until 1914 when she began to identify with Pentecostalism, the movement for which she seems to have been born. Many communities where she held revivals were embarrassed by what they considered to be excesses, and as a result she was often harassed by the law and arrested on trumped-up charges. She finally settled down and built a tabernacle in Indianapolis, where she remained as pastor until she was eighty. And her congregation survived her death.

A skeptical but impressed reporter for the Muncie *Daily News* provided a vivid account of one of Woodworth's revivals for their edition of September 21, 1885.[48] The service described was attended by an estimated twenty thousand people. The preacher's platform, surrounded by mourner's benches, was in a large tent. In order to be seen and heard by the throng, she had to stand on two chairs held together by some men.

The writer gives an account of the sort of trance into which Woodworth[49] went:

> Mrs. Woodworth had risen to a dread and awful majestic grandeur. Her lips moved, but she said nothing. Throwing her head back she gazed upward with a reverential and earnest, though frightful and terrible, yet fascinating,[50] and with an alluring charm her hands supplicantly and helplessly extended in the direction of her gaze and her whole frame was quivering as though laboring under intense excitement.[51]

Woodworth-Etter's biographer includes excerpts from three of her sermons as appendixes to his book. The first, a defense of women in ministry, is based upon most of the same texts that had been used since George Fox and Margaret Fell saw prophesying women as a sign of the end. In this sermon, she says that "Paul worked with women in the gospel more than any of the apostles."[52] Instead of seeing Phoebe as likely to be the owner of a house where the church met, she says that Paul and Phoebe had been holding revivals together and that she had been successful in winning souls to Christ. The Pauline ban on women speaking in church is dealt with by saying that the statement is law, but we are under grace. This direction of Paul is no more binding than that which says it is better not to marry. The response of the Samarian people after the woman at the well told them about Jesus is described as "a great revival there at the well." The sermon ends with an exhortation:

> My dear sister in Christ, as you hear these words may the Spirit of God come upon you, and make you willing to do the work the Lord has assigned to you. . . . The world is dying, the grave is filling, hell is boasting; it will all be over soon.[53]

The next female star to rise in the Pentecostal firmament could easily be the most famous woman preacher of all times, one who did not suffer in comparison with male revivalists such as Dwight L. Moody and Billy Sunday. **Aimee Semple McPherson** attracted an extraordinary amount of attention during her lifetime, having, for instance, her returns to Los Angeles greeted by tickertape parades that rivaled those of the most popular moviestars.[54] Such success inevitably inspired envy on the part of many, making it hard to get a straightforward view of her life. By the same token, Sister's homiletical use of her own life story does not make it any easier to strive after the Rankean will-o'-the-wisp, history "as it actually happened."

Aimee Kennedy grew up on a prosperous farm in southern Ontario, the daughter of an older man and his young second wife, a Salvation Army lassie. A child of ability and attractive appearance, Aimee early on acquired a local reputation for her dramatic and writing abilities as well as her interest in religious questions. It was not, however, until a Pentecostal mission opened in town during 1907, her final year of school, that she found her destiny. It seemed personified in the young Irish evangelist under whose preaching she was converted, Robert Semple. They were married the following summer and, after a short ministry in Canada, went to Chicago, where they both received ordination.

Their deepest sense of call, however, was to missionary work in China, and by the beginning of 1910 they were on their way. They arrived on June 1, and by August 19, Robert had died from dysentery. On September 17, Aimee gave birth to their daughter, Roberta. At the age of nineteen, she found herself in a foreign country, a widow, and a single parent.

Her mother wired her money to come home, but she returned to New York City rather than to the farm in Ontario. Mother Minnie was there, having reached an agreement with her seventy-four-year-old husband that allowed her to go to New York to do administrative work for the Salvation Army. Minnie tried to involve her daughter in this work, but, depressed and lonely, she responded to the attentions of a cashier in a fashionable restaurant, Harold McPherson. They were married in February of 1913.

Harold wanted nothing but domesticity, but his wife had strong guilt feelings about having forsaken the ministry to which she had been called—not to mention energy and creativity her husband could never understand. Her sense of vocation drove her to leave him in June of 1915, going home to her mother, who was temporarily back in Canada. There she became involved in a Pentecostal revival and found that people easily received the gift of tongues through her. She received invitations to conduct revivals and began her first in a town called Mount Forest. This was so successful that she bought a tent, and the future seemed set.

Her husband became reconciled with her and even tried to be her partner in evangelism. In the winter of 1916–17 they made an evangelistic tour of Florida, going north to Long Island and Boston for the summer. Then it was back to Florida again. By this time, Harold had discovered that he was not suited to the life of a revivalist, and the McPhersons separated. Aimee carried on with her ministry, embarking on a transcontinental tour in the fall of 1918. Her mother became, in effect, her business manager or executive officer and took care of all the arrangements necessary for the sorts of campaigns Sister Aimee was now conducting in major cities all over the country.

Such an itinerant life, however, can go on only so long. By February of 1921, McPherson had already purchased land in Los Angeles and broken ground for her permanent mission center, the Angelus Temple. In less than two years, the enormous church complex had been built, paid for, and dedicated. Having a flexible seating capacity of between five thousand and seventy-five hundred, it was filled for three services on Sundays and heavily used every other day of the week as well. Programs proliferated. Sister became one of the first religious broadcasters, opening station KFSG early in 1924. At the end of 1925, she opened a school for ministry, L.I.F.E. Bible College. During the depression, the Temple carried on a huge feeding program for the hungry.

As time went on, the toll of such total dedication began to show. In the spring of 1926, Aimee Semple McPherson disappeared after a swim at Ocean Park and did not appear again until more than a month later. Although scandalmongers then and since have argued that she was with a lover, Edith Blumhofer is right in saying that "the historical evidence is simply too ambiguous to be resolved conclusively in a responsible way."[55] Her final years show the enormous psychic energy demanded by a ministry as vast as hers and the difficulty of sustaining the pace indefinitely. In trying to sum up Sister's impact, Blumhofer gets as close to the reality as one could hope:

> Her singularity resulted more from her extraordinary application of her ordinariness than from unusual traits as such. She found the stamina to persist when others lagged; she had the practical creativity to make or acquire what she wanted while others simply craved it; she had the knack of enlisting cooperation and putting everyone to work. She loved people, and she lived out—at considerable personal cost—dreams many shared but for which few were willing to pay the price.
>
> Perhaps this apparent determination not to consider the personal toll at first set her apart from the crowd.[56]

It was undoubtedly McPherson's power as a preacher that most moved the immense crowds she attracted. The content of her preaching is hardly surprising. Her Foursquare Gospel included the four points of Pentecostalism: (1) justification, (2) Holy Ghost baptism, (3) healing, and (4) the imminent return of Christ, although as time went on she soft-pedaled distinctive Pentecostal emphases for a more general "Bible Christianity" that had a wider appeal.

Her method of presentation was what made her different from hundreds of other preachers. She had a flair for the dramatic and could pick up on the latest slogan and use that as a medium for conveying her traditional message. For instance, during World War I, she took the patriotic expression "Buy a Liberty Bond" and worked it into a catena of biblical expressions that were a call for conversion.[57] The use of a maid's or nurse's uniform as a vestment was originally an expedient of indigence, but she immediately recognized its effectiveness. There was also an erotic element to her appeal that somehow shone through utter decorum. And she used props and devices of all kinds, from musical presentations to flowers to live animals, to make her sermons more vivid.

This use of audiovisual aids in preaching came about in two stages. First was the use of charts to enable congregations to keep track of her outline, a device hit upon when she was developing a core of about sixty sermons that were her basic repertoire.[58] Other revivalists before and since have used similar charts, but she did it with a special flair.

A case in point is the chart used for the sermon "A Certain Man Went Down," based upon the parable of the good Samaritan.[59] At the top of the chart is the legend "A Certain Man Went Down from Jerusalem to Jericho" (**see Vol. 2, pp. 457-71**). Under this appears a picture of a shining walled city with two gates and the name Jerusalem written on the wall. Roads from the two gates merge quickly into a winding road, which leads down to a similar but unshining city labeled Jericho.

Along the road are small numbered signs in two sets, one a group of seven and the other a group of nine. The numbers stand for the letters in the names of the two cities, and on each side there is a list of qualities, the initials of which spell the name of one of the cities. The list used to spell *Jerusalem* is: Jesus, Enjoyment, Rest, Usefulness, Salvation, Adoration, Love, Enrichment, Mercy; and to spell *Jericho*: Jollification, Evil, Restlessness, Indifference, Calousness [*sic*], Hatred, and Obstinacy.

The chart makes the allegorical treatment of the text obvious. Sister begins by saying that the sermon is especially directed to backsliders and admits that she had an experience of their sin herself, not going into detail, but suggesting that it could have been in her marriage to Harold McPherson. What she derives from her text is not the example of the Samaritan as a person of compassion; indeed, the Samaritan signifies Christ. Rather, the two cities represent the two possible eternal destinations of life.

> Let *Jerusalem* on the chart stand for all that is holy and pure and Christlike, for all that is embodied in the New Jerusalem that is soon coming down from God out of Heaven, and *Jericho* for all that is sinful and profane and ungodly.[60]

Within that typology, each word in the story is interpreted anagogically. For instance, after the words "and fell" (among thieves), she says: "Oh you cannot walk a single step without Jesus, no matter how strong you are, or how many years you have been a Christian; the moment you let go of his dear hand, that moment you will cease to stand, and you will fall." The qualities for which the names of the cities are acronyms represent the clothing worn by the citizens of each, with the apparel of

Jerusalem representing what the backslider is stripped of. The beast on which the victim is set is salvation. The inn is the church, and the host is the preacher.

In many ways, the treatment is very patristic, although it is hard to imagine one of the fathers having such an unctuous style as to say in response, "I will repay thee."

> Why! Just one glimpse of his beautiful face—fairer than the lilies, brighter than the sun—just one smile from his tender eyes—just one "well done," and we would be a million times repaid for any little labor of love that is naught but our reasonable service when all is said and done.[61]

Other examples could be given, but the point is clear. A barrel of sixty such sermons would be adequate for a protracted meeting a month long.

After Sister Aimee settled in Los Angeles, built the Angelus Temple, and had a regular congregation, however, it was necessary to employ a wider repertoire and to introduce more variety. While her preaching of weekday sermons remained in her old basic style, the Sunday sermons in time came to be more dramatic—perhaps in keeping with the expectations of Tinseltown. She began to produce what are called "illustrated sermons," complete with costumes, props, and scenery.[62] The message or even the approach does not appear to have changed much; the difference seems to be that she could enlist much more elaborate audiovisual aids than the simple charts of the revival tent. But what she wanted to get across remained the same. As time went on, the productions became extravaganzas, and the streetcar company had to run extra trolleys on the route that led to the Temple when a new illustrated sermon began its run.[63] It was said that with George Whitefield, America got its first taste of theater under the banner of religion. That was not to be its last. But, contrary to the implication of Harry S. Stout's characterization of Whitefield as "the divine dramatist," dramatic presentation is not incompatible with utter sincerity. Few things are so impressive, in fact, as the ring of complete conviction.

This trajectory of women preaching in the Wesleyan Holiness/ Pentecostal tradition can be completed by reference to a study made of the sermons of **contemporary Pentecostal women preachers** in central Missouri by Elaine J. Lawless, a folklorist who teaches English at the University of Missouri.[64] While the current division of this history of preaching is supposed to survey a period that ends with World War II, homiletical conventions within this faith community can be expected to have remained nearly enough the same for an analysis of current practice to be informative about the way earlier preaching was done. Studies by folklorists in the field of contemporary African American preaching certainly contributed to the interpretation of classical preaching in that tradition advanced in the previous chapter.

The women studied by Lawless ministered in small Pentecostal churches in impoverished agricultural communities either as evangelists or, less commonly, as pastors. The most significant result of her study for the concerns of this book is the difference she discovered between the preaching of those who were invited into congregations in which someone else was pastor, and the preaching of those who were the regular minister of a congregation. Lawless says of one woman revivalist's pulpit behavior:

> Sister Linda's style of preaching is close to what we have come to expect from inspired, spontaneous evangelistic preachers in general. . . . She speaks quickly and, for the most part, in a loud dramatic performance style. Her rhythmic, punctuated style yields "line" formations that are balanced symmetrically, metered, and phonetically pleasing. In the most clearly "chanted" portions of her sermons, she terminates each line with the standard sermon performative "ah." She utilizes simple assonance and alliteration and persistently employs "formulas" for emphasis and for transition during certain portions of her sermons. She characteristically repeats formulaic sequences for effect.[65]

As Lawless says, the style is familiar; it sounds like the African American preaching described by Bruce Rosenberg and Gerald Davis and that of white male clergy of Baptist subdenominations in the Appalachians reported upon by Howard Dorgan. What Lawless calls the "cheerleading" approach of Sister Linda is the familiar pattern of "call-and-response."

The main differences Lawless finds between the preaching of the evangelist and that of the pastor result from the intimate acquaintance the latter has with members of the congregation and the different purpose of helping them lead the life of faith rather than converting them to it.[66] Hence there is less need to work up the congregation or to establish a relation with them; instead, everything can be more "businesslike":

> She mentions child abuse, drugs, divorce, adultery, Alcoholics Anonymous, and compromise in an evil and sinful world. These are real-life, everyday issues for the people she knows so well. Poverty and unemployment are common in the lives of her congregation. Unwed

mothers attend her church; young men whose wives have left them with three babies come to Sister Anna for help. She cannot be a stranger talking to an anonymous audience. She knows them too well.[67]

THE PREACHING OF LIBERAL WOMEN

The history of women in preaching is very different from that of women serving as ordained ministers and pastors of congregations, acceptance being far easier to come by in the former role than in the latter. Most of the women studied so far preached as itinerant evangelists rather than as parish clergy.

Even as late as 1888, when Willard published her classic *Woman in the Pulpit,* there were only an estimated twenty women in the United States serving as pastors. That figure did not include the some five hundred women evangelists or the Quaker women "preachers," whose numbers were estimated to be around 350. Nor did it include Salvation Army officers.[68]

Even when women were ordained, they did not necessarily stay in the pastorate very long. Much is made of the fact that Antoinette Brown was "the first fully ordained woman in a recognized American denomination," but less is said about the way her initial parish ministry lasted less than a year.[69] As Edwina Hunter has said:

> Congregationalists (United Church of Christ), Disciples (Christian Church), and American Baptists have ordained women for almost one hundred years; however, real progress in full acceptance of women in parish ministry has come only recently.[70]

There is, however, one group of women clergy in a liberal denomination who functioned over a number of decades, preached regularly in their own congregations, and whose ministry is well enough documented to permit a reconstruction of what they did and how they did it. In *Prophetic Sisterhood: Liberal Women Ministers of the Frontier, 1880–1930,*[71] Cynthia Grant Tucker has traced the growth of a network of Unitarian women clergy that arose in Iowa at the end of the nineteenth century and continued to influence their church for several decades. The pivotal figure was **Mary A. Safford,** who had been born just across the Mississippi near Hamilton, Illinois, the daughter of a religious liberal. Near her home was that of another family with Unitarian connections. Their daughter **Eleanor Gordon** was Safford's best friend. In their early twenties, the two "made a pledge that they would spend their lives together serving the world as a team."[72] Gordon was already a school-teacher, but Safford soon decided to become a Unitarian minister. Unable to earn degrees, the two began to educate themselves as best they could. The Unitarians' Western secretary, Jenkin Lloyd Jones, helped them to begin a congregation in Hamilton. By the end of the year, the little congregation was flourishing. The Sunday school organized by Gordon had a weekly attendance of more than 150, and Safford had organized another small church eight miles away.

Jones asked Safford to become the minister of a parish in Humboldt, Iowa, where Gordon became school principal. Even with their different professions, the two lived together and worked as a team. As the work grew rapidly, Gordon became more and more involved in the life of the congregation, so that the sensible thing seemed for her to become ordained herself and work full-time for the church. They took into their home four young women who assisted in the parish while attending Humboldt's Normal College, and some of whom entered the ministry. They also began forming a network of women in ministry throughout an area encompassing several states. In time, the women who entered the ministry under the tutelage of Safford and Gordon began to influence others to seek that goal. After five years in Humboldt, the two ministers moved to a parish in Sioux City, leaving a vacancy that was filled by other women.

The "sisterhood" that grew up around Safford and Gordon expanded in time to include twenty-one women engaged in promoting the cause of liberal religion.[73] Not all accepted ordination, and some of those who did were eventually to leave parochial ministry. But for a while, Iowa seemed a Camelot for liberal women ministers. There they engaged in an imaginative and energetic form of ministry that evoked an enthusiastic response. Operating out of an egalitarian perspective, they conceived of the church as a family. This domestic model shaped the way they built churches, conducted worship, and involved parishioners in study projects.

The women had received much of their own vision from eastern male Unitarians, Universalists, and transcendalists including William Ellery Channing, Theodore Parker, and Ralph Waldo Emerson. Yet the heirs of these men in the East, the Unitarian national leadership, disapproved of and eventually discouraged the frontier ministries simply because they were performed by women, even though they were proving more effective than those of male clergy. Many of the women ultimately left for work with other causes where they expected their efforts to meet with a better response. Others remained, but became too hedged in by bureaucracy to be able to exercise much influence. For a while, though, it must have been a heady experience.

These women took their preaching responsibilities very seriously. In this regard, they resembled their male counterparts in the Unitarian ministry. Since their church had accepted the new biblical criticism coming out of Germany, they felt no necessity to engage in traditional exegesis in order to demonstrate a system of orthodox doctrine. Instead, they felt free to range the whole expanse of human experience. And, while they generally took a biblical text to preach from,

> their themes and "proof passages," topical illustrations, and language were just as likely to come from current events and history as from the Bible or to draw on ancient and modern philosophy, world religions, science, and art.[74]

They were excited about ideas, especially those of the new science and contemporary philosophy, yet they resisted some of the fashions of the age such as phrenology, mind cure, and social Darwinism. Their sermons were thoughtful presentations of ideas rather than efforts to stir up emotions. And, although the majority of listeners in their day were no more eager than the majority today to hear sermons advocating social change, these women used their pulpits as platforms from which they could prophetically call for reform.[75]

This overview of their preaching can be made more concrete by a look at a few of their sermons.[76] One preached by Safford on Matthew 19:17 was published in the July 1856 issue of *Old and New,* the journal of the Iowa conference. It begins with a contrast between a former age, in which teachings of the church were considered authoritative in their own right, and the present age, in which demonstration by scientific experiment was required. That did not mean, however, that the day of religion had passed:

> Because religion rests on a sure foundation, because it is as real as the law of gravitation or as the solar system, it will bear the test of reason and experiment, it can be tried in the crucible of life and not be found wanting.

To show the empirical basis of religion, however, one had to go much deeper than what the revivalists meant by experiencing religion. Instant conversion was not deep enough to accommodate all that is involved in religion, "for the religious life is above all things else, the honest, loving, reverent life." Just as flowers need to incarnate sunshine in the very tissues of their being, so human beings must use everything that comes their way to build noble characters. This point is documented first by a quotation from Emerson and then by the text "If thou wouldest enter into life, keep the Commandments."

> Religion has been too divorced from life. Too long have men tried to embody it in creeds and forms and rituals instead of striving to express its divine strength and beauty, its sweetness and light in loyal, loving lives.

Conversion, then, is not the end of religious development, but only its beginning. In the past, conversion has often been the occasion for someone to claim superiority over others, rather than to acquire the sort of humility exemplified by Dickens's "poor little Joe." In contrast to such arrogance, true religious experience is "our delight in finding truth, our satisfaction in honest, faithful work, our joy in noble love." A life devoted to the activities that produce those satisfactions will permit someone eventually to attain to an experimental knowledge of religion.

A sermon by Eleanor Gordon making a similar point but taking a very different form appeared in the February 1906 issue of *Old and New.* (The text of this sermon is in **Vol. 2, pp. 471-75.**) The form has become common since then, but it must have been rare in sermons at the time. Gordon says that her text was an entire novel by Edith Wharton, *The House of Mirth,* which had appeared the previous year. This text could be reduced to several biblical verses, however.

The novel is a "picture of a society where the one aim is pleasure," and thus one in which the one essential is money. Members of the group who did not have money had to devote all their efforts to marrying someone who did. The two characters in the story who did not share this preoccupation remained, nevertheless, unattractive. One of the two was a woman philanthropist, but she did not truly represent the modern settlement worker, because such a person would not fit the environment of the story. The main character in the novel is Lily Bart, who had grace, charm, and beauty, but in order to have money she had to marry it. Hers is a divided self, too good to accept the proposal when it came, but too weak to leave the group to support herself; too good to expose the false friend who smeared her reputation, but too weak to go on living on her own.

Gordon suggests that her congregation must wonder how a depiction of such a social world can offer any insight into their own lives. In reply, she points out that if a line could be drawn separating good from evil, "this line would not pass between any two of us. It would divide each and every one into two parts...." Thus the evils of the more elegant social group found their counterparts in the humbler one. The need for excitement that had turned weekends in the House of Mirth into gambling parties caused the local school to have football and other rough sports so that boys would not be too bored to attend. Unless the young women of Des Moines were trained to support themselves with honest and useful labor, they would not be any better off than Lily Bart. Even those who would inherit means had a debt to the universe that they owed for their subsistence, a debt that should be repaid by usefulness. The suggestion of the novel that "licentiousness and flagrant violation of the moral law" can grow out of seemingly so small a thing as "love of luxury and a desire to take things easy" is absolutely true to life. People must learn that "the one really essential thing in this world is personal honor." The novel is nothing but an extended paraphrase of Jesus' question: "What shall it profit a man if he gain the whole world and lose his own soul?"

Thus the emergence of women preachers can be seen as one of the fruits of the Second Great Awakening. While Quaker women had been accustomed to engaging in ministry on a par with men from their origins in the seventeenth century, it was only with the Awakening that such openness was met in other traditions. The emphasis placed by the Awakening upon religious experience in contrast to theological sophistication meant that the qualifications for preaching became less of a barrier—although there remained much resistance. Since the tradition of which the Awakening was characteristic was a Wesleyan trajectory that went through the African American churches, white Methodist Episcopalians, the United Brethren, and Holiness and Pentecostal denominations, it is not surprising to find a succession of women preachers there. Although some of the liberal denominations pioneered in opening ordination and parish ministry to women, there was so much opposition that these permissions generally fell into desuetude. Yet there are notable exceptions, such as the group of Unitarian women in Iowa who were so active for a time. While the total number of women who preached remained small, the quality of their work was an earnest of good things to come.

CONCLUSION

The three main homiletical fruits of the fervor of the Second Great Awakening were (1) preaching on the social implications of the gospel, (2) the beginnings of African American preaching, and (3) the first admission of a significant number of women to the ranks of those who preached. It would be possible to go on to consider another fruit of the Second Awakening to be the Third.[77] That temptation will be resisted, though, because while D. L. Moody, Sam Jones, and Billy Sunday did have their own distinctive styles of preaching, in many ways what they did can be understood as a decline rather than a development of the "Religion of the Heart" movement.

Certainly the emotionalism that was characteristic of the First and Second Awakenings had so declined that these evangelists would have removed from the congregation anyone who became too excited. Then, too, what was understood as conversion had tamed considerably. Instead of turmoil that included being slain in the Spirit and struggles that could go on for days or even weeks, it came to be nothing more than a willingness to hold up one's hand, sign a card, or walk down the sawdust trail to shake the evangelist's hand. Most of the people who attended these revivals were already active in churches, and their conversion meant little more than committing themselves to living in a way more consistent with the profession of faith they had already made. Revivals had come a long way from Northampton and Cane Ridge. Revival no longer meant any great upheaval in either the culture at large or the lives of individual Christians.

FOR FURTHER READING

Blumhofer, Edith L. *Aimee Semple McPherson: Everybody's Sister.* Library of Religious Biography. Grand Rapids, Mich.: Eerdmans, 1993.

Brekus, Catherine A. *Strangers & Pilgrims: Female Preaching in America, 1740–1845: Gender and American Culture.* Chapel Hill: University of North Carolina Press, 1998.

Larson, Rebecca. *Daughters of Light: Quaker Women Preaching and Prophesying in the Colonies and Abroad, 1700–1775.* Chapel Hill: University of North Carolina Press, 1999.

Lucretia Mott: Her Complete Speeches and Sermons. Edited by Dana Greene. Studies in Women and Religion, vol. 4. Lewiston, N.Y.: Edwin Mellen, 1980.

McPherson, Aimee Semple. *This Is That: Personal Experiences, Sermons, and Writings.* Los Angeles: Echo Park Evangelistic Association, 1923.

Palmer, Phoebe. *Promise of the Father; or, A Neglected Speciality [sic] of the Last Days, Addressed to the Clergy and Laity of All Christian Communities.* Boston: Henry V. Degen, 1859.

Raser, Harold E. *Phoebe Palmer: Her Life and Thought.* Studies in Women and Religion, vol. 22. Lewiston, N.Y.: Edwin Mellen, 1987).

Sisters of the Spirit: Three Black Women's Autobiographies of the Nineteenth Century. Edited with introduction by William L. Andrews. Religion in North America. Bloomington: Indiana University Press, 1986.

Tucker, Cynthia Grant. *Prophetic Sisterhood: Liberal Women Ministers of the Frontier, 1880–1930.* Boston: Beacon, 1990.

Notes

1. There were, of course, individuals such as Anne Hutchinson who engaged in activity that could be called preaching, but no religious bodies other than the Quakers accepted preaching by women.

2. Rebecca Larson, *Daughters of Light: Quaker Women Preaching and Prophesying in the Colonies and Abroad, 1700–1775* (Chapel Hill: University of North Carolina Press, 1999), 339.

3. William Penn, *Fruits of Solitude* (London: Northcott, 1693), 33, quoted by Margaret Bacon in *Mothers of Feminism: The Story of Quaker Women in America* (San Francisco: Harper & Row, 1986), 2.

4. Horton Davies has graphically set out the various degrees of radicalism in movements of the period by describing the progression of interiorization from Roman Catholics to Quakers in *Worship and Theology in England: 1603–1690* (Princeton: University Press, 1975), 495-96. It should be noted that the Quakers were not the only body at the time to have women preachers: more radical Independents such as the Brownists had them as well. See Antonia Fraser, *The Weaker Vessel* (George Weidenfeld & Nicholson, and Knopf, 1984; New York: Vintage, 1985), 244-64.

5. The passage begins: "In the last days it will be, God declares, that I will pour out my Spirit upon all flesh, and your sons and your daughters shall prophesy."

6. Catherine M. Wilcox, *Theology and Women's Ministry in Seventeenth-Century English Quakerism: Handmaids of the Lord,* Studies in Women and Religion, vol. 35 (Lewiston, N.Y.: Edwin Mellen , 1995), 235. The understanding given above of how the Quakers originally understood the preaching of women is an attempt to summarize the thesis of Wilcox's book.

7. An exception is the heirs of the Gurneyite faction of Quakers, who had pastors after the Second Great Awakening; their meetings for worship were very much like general Protestant services.

8. Carol Stoneburner, "Drawing a Profile of American Female Public Friends as

Shapers of Human Space" in *The Influence of Quaker Women on American History: Biographical Studies,* ed. Carol and John Stoneburner, Studies in Women and Religion, vol. 21 (Lewiston, N.Y.: Edwin Mellen, 1986), 6.

9. Elise Boulding, "Mapping the Inner Journey of Quaker Women," in ibid., 89.

10. A sense of the way this worked can be gained from *The Journal of John Woolman.* The edition consulted was the John Greenleaf Whittier text with intro. Frederick B. Tolles (New York: Citadel, 1961). I am grateful to Dr. Ann Riggs for this insight.

11. Fraser, *The Weaker Vessel,* 365-66; Bacon, *Mothers of Feminism,* 18-19.

12. Ibid., 26. It has been estimated that twenty-nine of the first eighty-seven Friends who traveled in ministry to New England between 1656 and 1700 were women. This does not include those who accompanied their husbands. Ibid., 29.

13. Bacon, *Mothers of Feminism,* 34.

14. Larson, *Daughters of Light,* 232-95, traces this evolution in status.

15. Margaret H. Bacon, "Lucretia Mott: Holy Obedience and Human Liberation," in Stoneburner and Stoneburner, eds., *The Influence of Quaker Women on American History,* 203-4.

16. Mott was in the wool business, having abandoned cotton because it was a product of slave labor.

17. The introductory essay in *Lucretia Mott: Her Complete Speeches and Sermons,* ed. Dana Greene, Studies in Women and Religion, vol. 4 (Lewiston, N.Y.: Edwin Mellen, 1980), 12.

18. This may be seen, for instance, in the section devoted to the topic in the standard history edited by Rosemary Radford Ruether and Rosemary Skinner Keller, *Women and Religion in America* (San Francisco: Harper & Row, 1981). Written by Barbara Brown Zikmund, the chapter is entitled, "The Struggle for the Right to Preach," 1:193-205. A guide to literature in the field is Robert R. Howard, "Women and Preaching: A Bibliography," *Homiletic* 17 (1992): 7-10; 18 (1993): 34-36; 19 (1994): 28-30; 20 (1995): 7-10. Susie C. Stanley has compiled *Wesleyan/Holiness Women Clergy: A Preliminary Bibliography* (Portland, Ore.: Western Evangelical Seminary, 1994). I am grateful to President Zikmund, Dr. Howard, and Professor Stanley for assistance in several ways.

19. Catherine A. Brekus, *Strangers & Pilgrims: Female Preaching in America, 1740–1845: Gender and American Culture* (Chapel Hill: University of North Carolina Press, 1998).

20. Followers of Barton Stone who did not go with him into the merger with Alexander Campbell's denomination that created the Disciples of Christ.

21. Marta Tomhave Blauvelt, "Women and Revivalism," in *Women and Religion in America,* ed. Ruether and Keller, 1:5. Carleton Mabee corrects the tendency to turn Sojourner Truth into a legend by using critical scholarship to establish her real contribution, in *Sojourner Truth: Slave, Prophet, Legend* (New York and London: New York University Press, 1993).

22. Amanda Smith, *An Autobiography: The Story of the Lord's Dealing with Mrs. Amanda Smith the Colored Evangelist,* intro. Jualynne E. Dodson (Chicago: Meyer, 1893; reprint, Schaumburg Library of Nineteenth-Century Women Writers, New York: Oxford University Press, 1988).

23. *Sisters of the Spirit: Three Black Women's Autobiographies of the Nineteenth Century,* ed. with intro. William L. Andrews, Religion in North America (Bloomington: Indiana University Press, 1986). Andrews gives short synopses of the women's lives on pp. 4-10.

24. This and other patterns recur with such consistency in the life stories of these and other women of the period that one wonders how much such statements are the conventions of a literary genre. This, of course, is not to question the historicity of the experience. Such conventions, among other things, tell people what to expect in their own experiences.

25. Lee and Elaw had significant contacts with Quakers and observed some of their conventions.

26. In the introduction to Foote's book, the editor of *Christian Harvester,* Thomas K. Doty, says ironically that Foote was "guilty of three great crimes": color, womanhood, and evangelism. Andrews, *Sisters of the Spirit,* 164.

27. Though seldom in such elegant language as Elaw uses to justify emotional response to preaching. Andrews, *Sisters of the Spirit,* 107.

28. Julia Foote, *A Brand Plucked from the Fire: An Autobiographical Sketch* (Cleveland: privately printed, 1879).

29. Andrews, *Sisters of the Spirit,* 168.

30. Ibid., 209.

31. Ibid., 222.

32. Ruth A. Tucker and Walter L. Liefeld, *Daughters of the Church: Women and Ministry from New Testament Times to the Present* (Grand Rapids, Mich.: Zondervan, 1987), 262.

33. Harold E. Raser, *Phoebe Palmer: Her Life and Thought,* Studies in Women and Religion, vol. 22 (Lewiston, N.Y.: Edwin Mellen, 1987), 47. The internal quotation is from Palmer's *The Way of Holiness, With Notes by the Way* (New York: W. C. Palmer, 1843, ed. of 1867), 37-38.

34. For an enthusiastic estimation of Palmer's place in American church history, see the editorial introduction of Thomas C. Oden to *Phoebe Palmer: Selected Writings,* Sources of American Spirituality (New York: Paulist, 1988), 1-22. Perhaps more measured is the assessment of Raser, *Phoebe Palmer,* 289-98.

35. Raser, *Phoebe Palmer,* 115-16.

36. Phoebe Palmer, *Promise of the Father; or, A Neglected Speciality [sic] of the Last Days, Addressed to the Clergy and Laity of All Christian Communities* (Boston: Henry V. Degen, 1859), 36.

37. George Hughes, *Fragrant Memories of the Tuesday Meeting and the Guide to Holiness and Their Fifty Years' Work for Jesus* (New York: Palmer & Hughes, 1886), 182.

38. Raser, *Phoebe Palmer,* 23.

39. Ibid., 290.

40. John O. Foster, *Life and Labors of Mrs. Maggie Newton Van Cott, The First Lady Licensed to Preach in the Methodist Episcopal Church in the U.S.A.,* intro. Gilbert Haven and David Sherman, Women in American Protestant Religion 1800–1930 (Cincinnati: Hitchcock & Walden, 1872; reprint. New York: Garland, 1987). Hereafter, references to this work will be given parenthetically in the text by page number alone.

41. I do not know if this was the settlementhouse started by Phoebe Palmer.

42. Van Cott's biography ends in 1872, near the beginning of her ministry. The words in quotation marks appeared as an undocumented quotation in Tucker and Liefeld, *Daughters of the Church*, 269.

43. *Autobiography of Lydia Sexton: The Story of Her Life Through a Period of Over Seventy-two Years, From 1799 to 1872. Her Early Privates, Adventures, and Reminiscences, Clouds and Sunshine, As Child, Wife, Mother, and Widow; As a Minister of the Gospel; As Prison Chaplain,* Women in American Protestant Religion 1800–1930 (Dayton, Ohio: United Brethren Publishing House, 1882; reprint, New York: Garland, 1987). References to page numbers in this source will be indicated parenthetically in the text.

44. Donald W. Dayton, *Theological Roots of Pentecostalism* (Grand Rapids, Mich.: Francis Asbury Press of Zondervan, 1987). See also Robert M. Anderson, *Vision of the Disinherited: The Making of American Pentecostalism* (New York: Oxford University Press, 1979; reprint, Peabody, Mass.: Hendrickson, 1992).

45. Wayne E. Warner, *The Woman Evangelist: The Life and Times of Charismatic Evangelist Maria B. Woodworth-Etter,* Studies in Evangelicalism, no. 8 (Meteuchen, N.J.: Scarecrow, 1986).

46. The other birthday commonly assigned is when Agnes N. Ozman spoke in tongues at Charles F. Parham's Bethel College in Topeka, in late 1900 or early 1901. See Anderson, *Vision of the Disinherited*, 51-58.

47. Warner, *The Woman Evangelist*, 309-11.

48. Ibid., 52-57.

49. Her name at the time.

50. This is one of several places where the reporter omitted words or Warner failed to transcribe them. I incline to the former explanation.

51. Members of the congregation who went into a trance, however, would become stiff and could remain that way for hours. Warner, *The Woman Evangelist*, 54.

52. Ibid., 297-98.

53. Ibid., 300.

54. Two recent biographies are past the muckraking that characterized some earlier ones: Daniel Mark Epstein, *Sister Aimee: The Life of Aimee Semple McPherson* (San Diego: A Harvest Book of Harcourt, Brace & Co., 1993), and Edith L. Blumhofer, *Aimee Semple McPherson: Everybody's Sister,* Library of Religious Biography (Grand Rapids, Mich.: Eerdmans, 1993).

55. Blumhofer, *Aimee Semple McPherson: Everybody's Sister*, 300.

56. Ibid., 21.

57. Described by Epstein, *Sister Aimee*, 130.

58. Blumhofer, *Aimee Semple McPherson: Everybody's Sister*, 155.

59. Aimee Semple McPherson, *This Is That: Personal Experiences, Sermons, and Writings* (Los Angeles: Echo Park Evangelistic Assoc., 1923), 599-614.

60. Ibid., 601.

61. Ibid., 338.

62. The illustrated sermons are discussed in Blumhofer, *Aimee Semple McPherson: Everybody's Sister*, 258-62, and in Epstein, *Sister Aimee*, 253-59.

63. The reality was vivid enough, but journalists could not help improving on something that lent itself so naturally to caricature. Thus they said that one night, dressed

in a traffic cop's uniform, she came down the aisle of the Temple on a motorcycle and roared up a ramp to stop in mid-stage. She merely stood by a motorcycle parked onstage and, while sirens sounded in the background, raised a white-gloved hand and said: "Stop! You've been arrested for speeding." She quickly sketched in a number of vignettes in which persons seemed destined for every success, and then began to list the sort of incident that could arrest any such progress, thus reminding her congregation of the contingency of human life and the necessity of depending upon God at every moment.

64. Elaine J. Lawless, *Handmaidens of the Lord: Pentecostal Women Preachers and Traditional Religion* (Philadelphia: University of Pennsylvania Press, 1988).

65. Ibid., 90.

66. Even the sermons of the pastors end in an altar call, however, as they do when the pastors are male clergy in any strongly evangelistic tradition.

67. Ibid., 105.

68. Zikmund, "The Struggle for the Right to Preach," 208.

69. Tucker and Liefeld, *Daughters of the Church*, 281. It was almost fifty years before she returned to the pastorate, then as a Unitarian, in a church she founded and remained in for twenty years, All Souls' in Elizabeth, New Jersey. She died in 1921.

70. Edwina Hunter, in intro. to "Contemporary Women Preachers," in *And Blessed Is She: Sermons by Women*, ed. David Albert Farmer and Edwina Hunter (San Francisco: Harper & Row, 1990), 88.

71. Cynthia Grant Tucker, *Prophetic Sisterhood: Liberal Women Ministers of the Frontier, 1880–1930* (Boston: Beacon, 1990).

72. Ibid., 18.

73. Biographical sketches of these twenty-one women are given in Tucker, *Prophetic Sisterhood*, 235-40.

74. Ibid., 161.

75. This paragraph is an effort to summarize Tucker's chapter on "Preaching Reform," in ibid., 159-70.

76. I am grateful to Professor Tucker for making the texts of these sermons available to me.

77. The identification of four Great Awakenings is the work of William G. McLoughlin. His designation of the exact period of the Third Awakening changed between his initial presentation of the concept in *Modern Revivalism: Charles Grandison Finney to Billy Graham* (New York: Ronald Press, 1959) and his presentation of it in *Revivals, Awakenings, and Reform: An Essay on Religion and Social Change in America, 1607–1977*, Chicago History of American Religion (Chicago and London: University of Chicago Press, 1978).

CHAPTER 22

THE PREACHING OF ROMANTICISM IN BRITAIN

DEFINITION

The rationalistic preaching inaugurated by the latitudinarians and the emotional preaching of the "Religion of the Heart" were both born in the aftermath of the religious wars at the end of the seventeenth century. Rationalistic preaching lasted into the nineteenth century, while heart preaching is still practiced today in some circles. By the end of the eighteenth century, a third mode of preaching began to appear that had elements in common with both of the others while having a spirit different from that of either. For instance, it stressed emotion, but did not try to furnish the occasion for religious experiences such as conversion. Rather, it saw feeling as a path that ultimately gave greater access to knowledge than reason. This epistemological understanding of feeling, however, did not mean that those who held it were anti-intellectual or opposed to critical thought. To the contrary, it was in their circles that, for instance, historical-critical biblical interpretation developed.

The intellectual movement of which this sort of preaching was a manifestation is called Romanticism. While in many ways it was essentially a literary movement, from its earliest days in Germany and Great Britain it caught the imagination of the day's greatest philosophical minds, and theologians were numbered among its most seminal thinkers. Unfortunately, it seems virtually impossible to get scholars, especially literary critics, to agree on what constitutes the essence of Romanticism. There is, however, no need to supply the correct definition here. It is enough to list qualities that have been associated with Romanticism by reputable scholars and see how these qualities became standard in the preaching that will occupy this chapter and the next two.

The task may be performed by looking at what historians of doctrine have pointed to as characteristics of the thought of theologians admitted to have been Romantic in their outlook. The list compiled by Bernard M. G. Reardon is a good example. He has said that Romanticism can be defined negatively by opposing it to classicism.[1] Its essence, however, is not to be found in this antithesis nor in the horror of reality attributed to it by Emile Faguet, but rather in a deep sense that behind and within the finite there is always "an infinite beyond" that shines through. Thus there is always a coincidence of the finite and infinite. Taken to extremes, this Romantic conviction easily boils over into pantheism; it certainly finds idealistic philosophy congenial. But the basic conviction is that behind the finite and transfiguring it there is always the infinite.

The sense of the ultimate unity of things involved in this stance caused Romanticists to yearn for final reconciliation and peace, although they did not expect to achieve it without endless struggle. And their recognition of the need to strive fitted into the Romantic understanding of perfection as being dynamic rather than static. Thus meaning was found in process, and reality was seen as always being brought into being and never finally achieved.

The struggle to achieve reconciliation and peace was—as all else—considered to be highly individual, and the reality perceived through it was therefore subjective. The ego became the measure of reality. This premium on uniqueness can be illustrated in the way the standard Romantic hero was an exile. An outcome of this egotism was an intense emotionalism. And in this emphasis on emotion, there was an understanding that feeling had an epistemological function: It was through the strength and depth of feeling that knowledge was attained. Religious truth, for instance, was considered to be subjective, but that subjectivity made it more rather than less reliable.

In a similar way, an aestheticism was also related to this emotionalism; indeed, as Reardon says, "aesthetics itself becomes a religion, with art as its dogma and liturgy."[2] Aesthetics itself was highly subjective, and that subjectivity gave it much of its importance. The uniquely individual had never before been so prized.

Since Romanticists believed every moment of the past was, on the one hand, unique and, on the other, a finite moment in which the infinite was present, they also shared a new appreciation for history. Beginning with a taste for the culturally most alien period, the Gothic, this love of the past led in time to the development of critical historiography. Yet it also gave birth to a new respect for tradition and continuity—an ironic turn of events, since nothing was more Romantic than a contempt for convention and a "bohemian" delight in shocking respectability. Still, modern historical consciousness began with Romanticism.[3]

EARLY INFLUENCES

To this list of traits have to be added only a couple of the period's characteristics commonly noted by literary critics—love of nature and interest in common people—in order to have criteria for recognizing that a tradition of preaching deserves to be considered Romanticist. Not surprisingly, most of these traits are apparent in the thought and work of "the father of modern theology," Friedrich Daniel Ernst Schleiermacher (1768–1834), whom Reardon calls the Protestant theologian *par excellence* of the Romantic movement.[4]

As in Germany, the beginnings of the Romantic movement in England had an important connection with preaching. The first major literary monument of the movement in Britain was *Lyrical Ballads,* published in 1798 by William Wordsworth and Samuel Taylor Coleridge. While Coleridge was a poet of genius in his younger days, that muse seems to have deserted him as he aged. In his maturity, however, he became an unusually perceptive critic as well as a theological writer of distinction.

He was one of the few British thinkers of his time to read German, and he kept abreast of what was being written in that language. As a result he became, with Connop Thirlwall, one of the first to introduce German historical-critical biblical scholarship to the British Isles. Yet the efforts of these two were not much heeded, for it was only with the publication of Benjamin Jowett's contribution to *Essays and Reviews* (1860) that the English church became aware enough of that scholarship to be disturbed by it.[5] Nevertheless, since the introduction of historical-critical exegetical perspective was one of the most revolutionary elements of Romanticist preaching, it is worth noting that one of the fathers of Romanticism in Britain was a pioneer in this perspective.

While Coleridge had alluded to the topic in earlier works, the fullest statement of his position (itself quite short) was published posthumously in 1840. *Confessions of an Inquiring Spirit*[6] appears in the form of seven letters written to a friend about biblical inspiration. In this work Coleridge says he cannot accept the doctrine that biblical books were dictated word for word by the Holy Spirit and provides some critical analysis of biblical books to show the reasons why.

The principles that Coleridge had learned from Herder, Eichhorn, Lessing, and Schleiermacher seem self-evident to mainstream Christianity today, Catholic as well as Protestant, but they were shocking then. It was hard for his contemporaries to recognize that he occupied a mediating position between those who idolized the Bible and those who rejected it. He accepted the Bible as the medium through which Christian faith and morals were mediated and valued it above all other books put together. He was grateful for the way it spoke to his deepest needs. Yet he also had to admit that its excellence was not uniform, that there were traces of chaff still in the well-winnowed wheat. And he was convinced that what was valuable in it had a far greater chance of being recognized and lived by if those who found it were not required to treat the rest as having the same level of merit.[7] As his sources indicate, his position was thoroughly Romantic and was to be the view that informed Romanticist preaching.

PRE-ROMANTIC RHETORIC

While it is fairly easy to date the beginning of the Romantic movement, that does not mean it emerged instantly and full-grown. All through the eighteenth century in Great Britain, there were anticipations of attitudes that would be considered to be characteristically Romantic in the following century, and in France these began to appear even earlier.

Longinus

For rhetoric, the most noteworthy harbinger was the publication in 1674 of Boileau's translation of an obscure[8] Greek rhetorical treatise called *On the Sublime* by an otherwise unknown writer whose name was thought to be "Longinus." The impact of this work on the thought of the time, however, has been compared with that of Freud's ideas on contemporary thought.[9] "*On the Sublime* added to Neoclassical rhetorical criticism an element it badly needed, a theory of genius and inspiration to rise above pedantic rules of composition without contradicting them."[10] Nothing could have been better calculated to appeal to the Romantic consciousness that was to emerge than ideas of inspiration, genius, and rising above pedantic rules.

What makes the seventeenth-century publication of this work so important in the history of rhetoric in general and homiletics in particular is that it contained the first statement of the view that persuasion was not the only purpose of oratory. It also had the aim of enabling an audience to experience sublimity. The sublime *(hypsos)* is defined as "a kind of height and conspicuous excellence in speeches and writings."

> What is beyond nature drives the audience not to persuasion, but to ecstasy. What is wonderful, with its stunning power, prevails every-where over that which aims merely at persuasion and at gracefulness.[11]

Longinus's view that the aim of public speaking was not so much to persuade an audience of the truth of a proposition as it was to enable them to experience ecstasy was to have enormous influence on Romantic thought. In the critical thought of Coleridge, for instance, "we can see the Romantic attempt to adopt Longinus' principle of intense emotion as the central and organic element of art."[12]

British Rhetorical Thought

The influence of Longinus on British preaching, however, was to be mediated by three rhetorical writers, all clergy deeply concerned about preaching whose books were to be the subject's most influential treatments in both England and America through the nineteenth century.[13] The late-eighteenth century was a time when rhetoric occupied some of the best minds of the age—such thinkers as Edmund Burke, Adam Smith, David Hume, Lord Kames, and others—so that writers speak of this as the period of New Rhetoric.

It was also a time when the intellectual life of the Scottish universities was more exciting than that of the ancient English ones. This was the world of the first two authors of textbooks in rhetoric to be noted, Hugh Blair and George Campbell. The third, Richard Whately, was to write half a century later in Oxford. These three, by writing textbooks that would shape the understanding of public speaking of English and American university students and schoolboys through the nineteenth century, furnished the basic understanding of preaching held by those who practiced the skill during the Romantic period.[14] Each influenced this understanding in a way different from that of the other two.

The fullest heir of Longinus was **Hugh Blair** (1718–1800), who for the last half of his life was minister of Edinburgh's prestigious High Church of St. Giles and regius professor of rhetoric and belles lettres at the

university. The conjunction in the title of his chair suggests the distinctiveness of his influence. "Belles lettres" was the term used in Blair's day
to refer to literature and thus shows that, like Longinus, he combined the
discussion of oratory with that of creative writing, and that he thought
to engage in either activity one must become a critic in the field. The term
also indicates that Blair's Longinian perspective was mediated and filtered through French neoclassical rhetorical thought. In France the belles
lettres movement was associated with that of the beaux arts, and thus
displayed a self-conscious aestheticism that was to be characteristic of
the Romantic period. To all of this Blair was an heir.[15]

It is possible to make too much of the pre-Romanticism of Blair's work
on rhetoric. Most of what he has to say about oratory as such is a translation of Quintilian's principles into the vocabulary of eighteenth-century Edinburgh. He was, after all, giving practical instruction to college
students, mostly in their mid-teens, on how to write, speak in public, and
assess others' attempts to do the same things. The whole effort was considered to be as elementary as college textbooks on rhetoric are today.

Yet the pre-Romanticism of the twenty or so lectures he devoted to
oratory is seen in his decision to concentrate on only one of the five tasks
the classical rhetoricians saw as necessary in preparing a speech: *elocutio*. His main emphasis, more than half his effort, goes to the details of
style. He is almost contemptuous of invention and disposition as set forth
in Aristotle's *Rhetoric*. Memory is barely touched on. Delivery is compressed into one lecture.[16]

This focus meant he was preoccupied with an aesthetic interest that
was to become characteristically Romantic. The preacher was now to be
considered a creative writer, sermons were to be thought of as works of
art, their style was to be evaluated critically in terms of taste, and the
results of that critique reflected the genius of the preacher or lack of it.[17]

Blair, however, was no mere aesthete. Indeed, he said that the preacher
should shun above all things the "air of foppishness" (116).[18] He had a
high view of the ministerial calling, and his definition of *preaching* was
very serious, even if it was short on theological and christological content for an heir of Calvin.[19] He says, "The end of all preaching is to make
men good" (105).[20] Or, again, the proper idea of a sermon is that of "a
serious persuasive Oration, delivered to a multitude, in order to make
them better men" (114). Or, finally, the "great end for which a Preacher
mounts the pulpit" is "to infuse good dispositions into his hearers, to
persuade them to serve God, and to become better men" (125).

This understanding of the purpose of preaching dictates that a sermon
should be a popular speech in the best sense of the word, one "calculated

to make impression on the people; to strike and to seize their hearts" (106). Thus the qualities that distinguish preaching from other forms of public speaking are gravity and warmth. These qualities are hard to combine, but when they are properly joined they create the quality the French call *onction*: "the affecting, penetrating, interesting manner, flowing from a strong sensibility of heart in the Preacher to the importance of those truths which he delivers, and an earnest desire that they may make full impression on the hearts of his Hearers" (107).

Further, to be most effective a sermon should be about a single subject and as concrete as possible. Some of the best sermons are those that follow a biblical character in a way that "can trace and lay open, some of the most secret windings of man's heart" (113), sermons such as Bishop Butler's on the character of Balaam, and, though he would have been too modest to say so, his own on Joseph and on Hazael.[21] The Romantics would share his conviction that truth is experienced more deeply in narratives of individual human lives than in abstract reasoning. Frederick Robertson, for instance, would also preach biographical sermons about biblical characters.

Blair's advice about preaching is very practical. He is aware that a preacher has advantages over other public speakers, such as being free from interruption, but the preacher also has to contend with the fact that "his[22] subjects of discourse are, in themselves, noble and important, but they are subjects trite and familiar" (102). The first rule of homiletical style is that sermons should be perspicuous. No quality of a sermon is so important as its being clear and understandable. Rightly employed, scriptural quotations and allusions are a great ornament to sermons, but "in a Sermon, no points or conceits should appear, no affected smartness or quaintness of expression" (116). Preachers must decide for themselves whether to memorize their sermons, preach them extemporaneously, or speak from notes, but "the practice of reading Sermons, is one of the greatest obstacles to the Eloquence of the Pulpit in Great Britain, where alone this practice prevails" (118).

Blair's knowledge of neoclassical rhetoric allows him to distinguish between French and English preaching:

> The French Preachers address themselves chiefly to the imagination and the passions; the English, almost solely to the understanding. It is the union of these two kinds of composition, of the French earnestness and warmth, with the English accuracy and reason, that would form, according to my idea, the model of the perfect Sermon. (119)

In a brief review of British preaching, Blair notes the traditionally alleged faults of the metaphysical preachers, but insists that they did have "warm pathetic addresses to the consciences of their hearers" (122). And he considers that a much more appealing quality than the "argumentative manner, bordering on the dry and unpersuasive" that was characteristic of the latitudinarians. In Blair's opinion, no finer compliment could be paid to a sermon than that of Louis XIV to Massillon after a sermon at Versailles: "Whenever I hear you, I go away displeased with myself, for I see more of my own character" (126). Such a criterion would probably have seemed "enthusiastic" to the latitudinarians, but it would prove very congenial to the Romantic emphasis on feeling.

The approach of the next New Rhetorician to be considered was very different from the aesthetic emphasis of Blair. Blair had produced what George Kennedy called a technical rhetoric, a "how-to-do-it" manual, but **George Campbell** (1719–96) was, among other things, a philosopher. His *Philosophy of Rhetoric* (1776),[23] as its title indicates, was intended to be what Kennedy calls philosophical rhetoric. To say that Blair wrote a technical and Campbell a philosophical rhetoric is not to say their understandings of rhetoric were fundamentally different. They share many of the same presuppositions and, indeed, often state them in almost the same words. The difference is rather in the aspect of rhetoric to which they devote their attention.

Most of Campbell's life and ministry were spent in Aberdeen. There he attended Marischal College in his youth and became its principal and professor of divinity in his maturity. His writings grew out of his teaching duties; they include volumes on miracles, church history, systematic theology, and pulpit eloquence,[24] as well as his translation of the New Testament.

His *Philosophy of Rhetoric*, however, was not written as a general textbook, nor was its content originally addressed to students. Most of its chapters began as papers he read to a small group he helped found, the Philosophical Society of Aberdeen, which met twice a month to discuss a presentation of one of the members. He had little interest in practical rhetoric; what occupied his thought was the relationship between rhetoric and what was called "human nature" at the time, most of which today would be considered aspects of psychology.[25] Campbell's understanding of human nature was based on the work of the British empiricist philosophers, especially David Hume, whom Bitzer describes as "the absent member of the Philosophical Society of Aberdeen."[26]

The way Campbell understands rhetoric in the light of human nature may be seen in his conviction that what causes attention to be paid to an idea and credence given to it is the idea's vivacity, its liveliness, energy, force, or brilliancy. Rhetoric, which includes all forms of communication for Campbell, may have as its purpose to inform, convince, please, arouse passion, or persuade. In order to fulfill any of these purposes, though, the rhetor must "communicate ideas which feel lively and vivid to his hearers or readers."[27]

For Campbell, there are three kinds of perceptions immediately present to the mind. The first is *sensations,* feelings, which include both sense data and emotions.[28] The next kind of perception is *ideas of memory,* recollections of earlier sensations. The third sort, *ideas of the imagination,* are constructs the mind makes from its ideas of memory. Thus ideas of imagination include everything from hypotheticals[29] to judgments about the real existence of things not being sensed or remembered at the present moment.

It works out that sensations are the perceptions with the greatest vivacity, ideas of memory come next, and ideas of imagination have the least. The challenge to the rhetor is that most of what he wishes to communicate are ideas of imagination. Therefore, the rhetor must find ways of lending vivacity to those perceptions that have the least of it.

Those ways are furnished by the patterns of the association of ideas in the mind, the most important of which, to Campbell's way of thinking, are resemblance, contiguity, and causation. Such associations can transfer vividness from a more to a less lively idea. Most of the work of the rhetor is in finding such associations by which vivacity can be given to the rhetor's ideas of imagination.

The other means by which the rhetor is persuasive involve the use of grammar and language. The phrasing of one's ideas must be "pure" in the sense of expressing them exactly and in not misleading the hearers in any way. It must also be perspicuous. Stylistic devices are another quality of language that gives it vivacity. Rhetorical strategy, then, involves using the association of ideas, purity and perspicuity of language, and stylistic devices to give to one's ideas of imagination the vivacity of sensations, thus providing the passion by which persuasion occurs.

This is the way Campbell draws on contemporary studies of human nature, especially that of Hume, to construct a theory of how rhetoric works. This empiricism makes his understanding of persuasion very different from the rationalism of the latitudinarians. Although his approach to emotion differs from that of Blair, his emphasis on it made it easy for the Romantics who came afterward to use his book.

The third of the New Rhetoricians was even more unlike the other two than they were unlike one another. **Richard Whately** (1787–1863) was born

599

almost seventy years after Blair and Campbell, he was English rather than Scottish, an Anglican rather than a Presbyterian, and affiliated with Oxford rather than a Scottish university. He resembled Campbell in that he was more interested in persuasion than in style, but like Blair in that he wrote a beginner's textbook rather than a philosophical treatise on rhetoric.

He became a fellow of Oriel College on taking his degree and was identified with the "Noetics," the group involved in restoring the intellectual life of Oxford. After marrying he took a parish for several years, but returned to Oxford as principal of St. Alban's Hall. There he remained until he became the Anglican archbishop of Dublin in 1831.

Not a Romantic himself, Whately did have connections with those who were in the previous and following generations. Both his *Elements of Logic* and his *Elements of Rhetoric* were originally created in manuscript form for use with students preparing for ordination.[30] The first published form of both works, however, was as articles in the *Encyclopedia Metropolitana*, a publication for which Coleridge had the idea and was originally to have been the editor.[31] The Romantic link in the following generation was John Henry Newman, a new fellow at Oriel whom Whately had taken in hand. Newman credited Whately with being the one who "opened (his) mind, taught (him) to think and to use (his) reason."[32] Part of that opening was to enlist Newman's help in rewriting Whately's manuscripts on logic and rhetoric for the encyclopedia articles.[33]

The editor of the modern edition of the *Elements* claims that it is essentially an ecclesiastical rhetoric to prepare future clergy for their work.[34] He sees traces of that purpose in such features as the inclusion of a section on oral reading and the selection of a number of illustrations from theological literature. Ehninger identifies the "chief business" of the book to be:

> to arm the pulpit orator for his task of conveying to an unlettered congregation the indisputable doctrines of the Christian faith, and (2) to arm the Christian controversialist who is called upon to defend the evidences of religion against the onslaughts of the skeptic.[35]

Whately considered the preacher's task to be basic catechesis of a particular apologetic sort in which the articles of faith are to be defended against challenges. Outside the pulpit and in other fora, the preacher was to take on the gainsayers themselves.

Whately makes this polemical understanding of rhetoric clear in his introduction. He states that he is going to follow a middle course in his book, neither treating rhetoric exclusively as persuasive speaking nor broadly as any sort of prose composition, but presenting it instead as argumentative composition generally and exclusively (4).[36] The argumentative character of the rhetoric taught by Whately is further brought out by his statement that he considers rhetoric to be "an off-shoot of logic." This prepares the reader for the way roughly the first half of the book is devoted to argumentation, leaving the impression of a textbook on debate more than one on homiletics.

Whately, then, expected polemics and controversy to be the order of the day in preaching. Ehninger describes him as a person who was "by dedication a life-long defender of religion against the attacks of the rationalists and the skepticism of science."[37] He devoted himself to preparing other clergy to continue in the fight that had gone on since the rise of deism, a fight in which the latitudinarians had been engaged with less sense of a sharp line dividing the two sides. Since, however, Whately was an early friend of the leaders of the Oxford movement and he would become their opponent, perhaps he had an awareness that a period was beginning in which a good deal of preaching would be more concerned with controversy than the simple proclamation of the gospel. And, living at a time when geology and evolution as well as biblical criticism would present severe challenges to the faithful, perhaps a rhetoric of argumentative composition was what would be most needed.

THE ROMANTICISM OF VICTORIAN PREACHERS

While it is customary for critics of English literature to distinguish between the Romantic and Victorian periods, from a religious perspective, "the whole of the nineteenth century exudes an aura of Romanticism to a greater or lesser degree."[38] The truth of that claim becomes apparent when one looks at the characteristics of Victorian British preachers. These, as noted by Horton Davies, are: They preached topical sermons in response to the challenges to traditional faith that arose in that era. They made frequent appeals to the emotions, especially pity and fear. They delighted in scenic grandeur. And, perhaps their least Romantic trait, they included wit and humor among the weapons in their rhetorical armory.[39]

John Henry Newman

From the number of eminent Victorian preachers, two can be selected as representative, Frederick Robertson and John Henry Newman. The latter was certainly the better known of the two during their lifetimes, but both continue to be read as homiletical models to this day. Born into a middle-class family of comfortable means, Newman had a conversion experience as a schoolboy, and he arrived at Oxford an earnest Evangelical when he was seventeen.[40] He did well enough academically to be made a fellow of Oriel College after taking his B.A. The senior common room of Oriel at the time was the center of the noetic movement; there the shy and serious Newman was taken in hand by Whately and whipped into shape both intellectually and socially. After ordination in the established church,[41] Newman became Whately's vice-principal at St. Alban's Hall in 1825. Three years later he was made vicar of St. Mary's, the university church.

He toured southern Europe in 1832–33 and returned to Oxford to learn that John Keble had preached an assize sermon at the university, declaring that the effort of the government to suppress ten Irish bishoprics was tantamount to "National Apostasy." For Keble, the issue was not whether so many Anglican bishops were needed in Ireland but whether the state had the right to decide how many bishops the church should have. This and other examples of what was regarded as Erastianism were the precipitating causes of the Oxford movement, the Catholic revival of the Church of England.

Newman quickly became involved in the cause, and he and others began writing a series of "Tracts for the Times,"[42] in which were set forth a renewal of the Anglo-Catholic theology of Caroline divines such as William Laud and Lancelot Andrewes. They claimed that the apostolic succession of the established church's bishops, and the continuity and validity of its sacramental practice, made it the ancient and legitimate branch of the church Catholic in England. The original inspiration for this theology was patristic, and the Tractarians contributed greatly to the study and publication of the Fathers, using their scholarship to assert that the Church of England was the *via media* between Rome and Protestantism. As time went on, a widespread stir arose over the tracts, associating them with Roman Catholicism. A certain number of the younger and more enthusiastic members of the group did begin to find Roman claims persuasive, and even Newman himself was received into the Roman church in 1845.

As a Roman Catholic, Newman joined the Oratorians, an order founded during the Catholic Reformation by Philip Neri, and opened a house in Birmingham. Except for five years when he was in Dublin organizing a short-lived Roman Catholic university, he spent the rest of his life quietly in the Oratory as a priest, preaching to the working-class people who came to church there. For most of this second half of his life he was viewed with suspicion by his co-religionists, although he was made a cardinal by Leo XIII eleven years before his death. His most important theological treatises were written during this period, however, including his *Essay on the Development of Doctrine, A Grammar of Assent,* and *The Idea of a University.* These works have caused some to see anticipations in his thought of some of the most important insights of contemporary Roman Catholic theology. Perhaps his best-known book was the autobiography he wrote to defend himself against Charles Kingsley's charge of dishonesty, *Apologia pro vita sua.* He also wrote novels and poetry.

While he was vicar of St. Mary's, Newman's preaching made him the pied piper of undergraduates. (For a sample of his preaching there, see **Vol. 2, pp. 476-85.**) Accounts of the effect of his preaching have been left by J. A. Froude, Matthew Arnold, and W. E. Gladstone. Perhaps the best description, however, is that of Principal Shairp:

> The service was very simple,—no pomp, no ritualism[43] . . . the most remarkable thing was the beauty, the silver intonation, of Mr. Newman's voice, as he read the Lessons. It seemed to bring new meaning out of the familiar words. . . . When he began to preach, a stranger was not likely to be much struck, especially if he had been accustomed to pulpit oratory of the Boanerges sort. Here was no vehemence, no declamation, no show of elaborated argument, so that one who came prepared to hear "a great intellectual effort" was almost sure to go away disappointed. . . . The delivery had a peculiarity which it took a new hearer some time to get over. Each separate sentence, or at least each short paragraph, was spoken rapidly, but with great clearness of intonation; and then at its close there was a pause lasting for nearly half a minute; and then another rapidly but clearly spoken sentence, followed by another pause. It took some time to get over this, but, that once done, the wonderful charm began to dawn on you. . . . He laid his finger—how gently, yet how powerfully!—on some inner place in the hearer's heart, and told him things about himself he had never known till then. Subtlest truths, which it would have taken philosophers pages of circumlocution and big words to state, were dropt out by the way in a sentence or two of the most transparent Saxon. . . . And the tone of the voice in which they were spoken, once you grew accustomed to it, sounded like a fine strain of unearthly music. Through the silence of that high Gothic building the words fell on the ear like the measured drippings of water in some vast dim cave.[44]

The appeal to idealistic undergraduates was so magnetic that the dons of other colleges, suspicious of this influence on their students and perhaps jealous of it as well, changed the hour of Sunday dinner in hall to coincide with that of Newman's sermon at St. Mary's. Even then many of the young men chose to satisfy the hunger of their souls rather than that of their bodies.

What did he preach that had such an effect? What was his homiletical theory? It will be easier to first answer the latter question. Newman published two treatises on preaching, one negative on what to avoid and the other positive on what to strive for. The last of his *Lectures on the Doctrine of Justification* (1838) was "On Preaching the Gospel."[45] It grew out of a sense Newman shared with the other Oxford leaders that Anglican Evangelicals had unduly exalted preaching in their understanding of the Christian life. Thus the chapter is a rousing critique of the evangelical theory and practice of preaching.

> It summarizes the Tractarian attitudes toward the Evangelicals: it attacks their emphasis upon feeling, their insistence upon "internal" versus "external" religion, their unnatural and strained idiom, their elevation of preaching to primacy over baptism and other sacraments, their innate tendency to dissent, their substituting faith in faith for faith in Christ—in short, their allegiance to what Newman would see as a human system replacing the system ordained by God for the proclamation of the gospel.[46]

What worries Newman about all this is its subjectivism, its emphasis on the evangelicals' interior state of feeling rather than on Christ, the object of their faith. It is also a reliance on the rhetorical skill of preachers who are able to engender these emotional states in others, a tendency "to rely upon words, vehemence, eloquence, and the like."[47] All of this is a substitute for the means of grace provided by God in the historic church with its catholic faith, apostolic ministry, sacramental system, and disciplinary practices. Thus it substitutes a human program for the divinely ordained program of salvation.

The positive treatise on what a preacher should strive for is called "University Preaching" and appeared first in *Lectures and Essays on University Subjects* (1859), but, like much of that volume's content, it is much more accessible in *The Idea of a University* (definitive edition, 1873).[48] Written when he was rector of the Catholic University of Ireland in Dublin, the article was a response to those invited to preach university sermons who had asked for guidelines.

His advice is given in two stages, the first having to do with preaching in general and the second with specifically university preaching. He begins by noting that "the preacher's object is the spiritual good of his hearers." That immediately leads him to the strategic consideration that "as a marksman aims at the target and its bull's-eye, and at nothing else, so the preacher must have a definite point before him, which he has to hit" (304-5).

This means that any consideration of eloquence, intellect, or learning has to be subordinated to the single purpose of getting across to the congregation the one point identified as the best way at that moment to effect their spiritual good.

Nothing contributes so much to getting that point across as the earnestness of the preacher in trying to. This does not mean that the preacher should strive to be earnest or, even worse, to appear earnest: "He must aim at his *object,* which is to do some spiritual good to his hearers . . . which will at once *make* him earnest" (306). The object of doing some spiritual good involves having before the preacher's mental eye the Four Last Things.[49] "It is this earnestness, in the supernatural order, which is the eloquence of saints; and not of saints only, but of all Christian preachers, according to the measure of their faith and love" (307).

To be effective, the good the preacher tries to do for the congregation must be specific rather than general. "No one will carry off much from a discourse which is on the general subject of virtue, or vaguely and feebly entertains the question of the desirableness of attaining Heaven, or the rashness of incurring eternal ruin." Or, again, "so necessary is it to have something to say, if we desire any one to listen" (308). This involves deciding, before composing a sermon, exactly what one wishes it to communicate.

Every temptation to include anything—however valuable it might be in itself—that does not contribute to the one unified impact must be sternly resisted. Included in this ban on extraneous material is "the habit of preaching on three or four subjects at once," which amounts to "the delivery of three sermons in succession without break between them." The best way of achieving such definiteness is to "select some distinct fact or scene, some passage in history, some truth, simple or profound, some doctrine, some principle, or some sentiment, and ... study it well and thoroughly, and first make it (one's) own" (ibid.). Making it one's own begins with bringing that point home to oneself.

So much for preaching in general. Why and how should university preaching be different? The why is that a sermon should always be prepared to meet the needs of a specific audience: "We cannot determine how in detail we ought to preach, till we know whom we are to address"

(311). In most important respects, all hearers are the same: redeemed sinners and members of the church. The first thing to be noticed about a university congregation, however, is that it is composed largely of undergraduates: "an assemblage of the young, the inexperienced, the lay and the secular" (312), which means that no Christian doctrine is too basic or simple. Beyond that, however, in Newman's time the university congregation would consist of "men, not women; of the young rather than the old; and of persons either highly educated or under education" (312).

A series of university sermons should not be considered the draft of a book on the subject. Rather, Newman thought, such lectures belonged to the Divinity School instead of the pulpit. "Nevertheless, it is not asking too much to demand for academical discourses a more careful study beforehand, a more accurate conception of the idea which they are to enforce, a more cautious use of words, a more anxious consultation of writers of authority, and somewhat more of philosophical and theological knowledge" (314-15).

Even more important, however, is the principle that university sermons should be addressed to the temptations faced by the congregation.

> The temptations which ordinarily assail the young and the intellectual are two kinds: those which are directed against their virtue, and those which are directed against their faith. . . . As youth becomes the occasion of excess and sensuality, so does the intellect give accidental opportunity to religious error, rash speculation, doubt, and infidelity. (313)

In trying to help students resist such temptations, however, preachers should first be very certain they understand their congregation, or they could do more harm than good. The other caution Newman gives to a university preacher is that "even when he addresses himself to some special danger or probable deficiency or need of his hearers, he should do so covertly, not showing on the surface of his discourse what he is aiming at" (314). This is to say that "infidelity, orthodoxy, or virtue, or the pride of reason, or riot, or sensual indulgence" should not be approached head-on—explicitly, and as a block. Instead, one should preach about such subjects as, for instance, the improvement of time, avoiding the occasions of sin, frequenting the sacraments, divine warnings, the inspirations of grace, the mysteries of the rosary, natural virtue, beauty of the rites of the church, consistency of the Catholic faith, relation of Scripture to the church, the philosophy of tradition, and any others, which may touch the heart and conscience, or may suggest trains of thought to the intellect, without proclaiming the main reason why they had been chosen (314).

The last advice Newman gives to university preachers is that they not use a manuscript in the pulpit if they can possibly avoid doing so. While his approach to the question is strategic, nuanced, and perhaps extended unnecessarily, his conclusion is that it is "no extravagance to say that a very inferior sermon, delivered without book, answers the purposes for which all sermons are delivered more perfectly than one of great merit, if it be written and read" (320-21).

Newman's own observance of this last principle was an accomplishment of his Roman Catholic days. His sermons to the undergraduates of Oxford were delivered from manuscripts, and he began to preach extempore only as a Roman Catholic, apparently because doing so was expected at that time. This is only one of the differences between the eight[50] volumes of *Parochial and Plain Sermons* preached at St. Mary's and the *Discourses Addressed to Mixed Congregations* and *Sermons Preached on Various Occasions* from his Roman Catholic period. Each series is faithful to the principle of being aimed at a particular audience: the *Parochial and Plain* for Oxford, those to *Mixed Congregations* for the working-class neighborhood of Birmingham where the Oratory was, and those *on Various Occasions* for university audiences, his brothers of the Oratory, and distinguished public occasions.[51]

A very different sort of sermon from those in these three series appears in his *Oxford University Sermons*,[52] which deal with the theological issue of the relation of faith to reason, rather than the issues of personal spirituality that are the standard topics of the others. Indeed, the *University Sermons* are considered to be the preliminary working out of the argument developed and completed in *The Grammar of Assent*.

This serves as a reminder that Newman was a complex thinker who wrote in a number of literary genres. Perhaps he was most famous as a controversialist, one of whom Whately could have been proud if their paths had not diverged so greatly. But he also had an acute philosophical mind. And he found different means of persuasion appropriate for different tasks. It has been shown by Jouett L. Powell that Newman's "discourse concerned with 'coming to faith' features implicit persuasive reasoning, that with 'exercising faith' reliance on mental imagery, and that with 'explicating faith' dependence on abstract argument."[53] Thus Newman advocates different strategies of persuasion for different stages of faith.

The majority of the sermons have to do with what Powell calls "exercising faith" and so rely heavily on mental imagery and imagination.[54]

That is responsible for their effect described so vividly by Principal Shairp: "He laid his finger—how gently, yet how powerfully!—on some inner place in the hearer's heart, and told him things about himself he had never known till then."[55]

And in all this we have "the typical Romantic appeal to the past, to tradition, to the continuing organic life of the community, as against the atomistic individualism brought about by the irresponsible use of critical reason."[56] Newman was without doubt one of the great English Romantic preachers.

Frederick Robertson

Even more obviously a Romanticist, however, was Frederick W. Robertson. Robertson, who has been posthumously awarded such superlative homiletical accolades as being called the greatest English-speaking preacher of the nineteenth century, would appear at first blush an unlikely candidate for such laurels. None of the conditions that have usually accompanied such status can be discovered in his life. To begin with, it was too short; he died when he was only thirty-seven after an ordained ministry that lasted a mere thirteen years. He served a curacy among the poor in Winchester, then he filled an assistantship in fashionable Cheltenham for five years, and his last six years were spent in the fashionable watering place of Brighton, not as vicar of the parish church, but as rector of Trinity, a proprietary chapel.[57]

He did none of the things that would have called attention to himself or his ministry. He was stationed neither in London nor at a cathedral or a university. He did not preach at court. He was granted no titles and he did not seek preferment. Only one of his sermons was published while he lived, and he appeared in a London pulpit but once. During his ministry at Brighton he became something of a local celebrity, yet his fame scarcely extended beyond the city limits.

His anonymity, however, faded quickly after his death. His family published four volumes of his sermons, and these did not go out of print for at least a century after his death.[58] Further fame came with the issuance of *The Life and Letters of Frederick W. Robertson, M.A.* by Stopford A. Brooke in 1865.[59] Which is to say that the enormous reputation of Robertson as a preacher is based entirely on the impression made by his printed sermons on people who never heard him. This is the more remarkable because the published form of the sermons is not a transcript of what was spoken from the pulpit. Rather, they are simply "Recollections":

sometimes dictated by the Preacher himself to the younger members of the family in which he was interested, at their entreaty; sometimes written out by himself for them when they were at a distance and unable to attend his ministry.[60]

To account for the homiletical phenomenon that was Frederick Robertson, it is necessary to understand two things: the effect he had on his Brighton congregation, and his appeal to later generations of preachers. One of a number of possible ways of approaching the first of these issues is to note that Robertson was a perfect Romantic figure. That is apparent in his Byronic good looks. He was a little above average in height, and he had a well-made but not heavy body—the sort of figure one associates with an officer of the guards. His posture was of a military erectness and his gait was sprightly. His thick, wavy brown hair crowned a high forehead, and bushy sideburns set off the features of his face. He had a long, straight nose that began with so little indentation under the brow that it was almost Greek, leaving his dark blue eyes deep set. His lips were gracefully curved and capable of registering a wide range of emotion. The overall impression was of "a man of great moral elevation of character, and of large intellectual power."[61]

The ideal and language of chivalry came naturally to his lips. As a boy, "he loved to fancy himself a knight—seeking adventures, redressing wrongs, laying down his life for maidens in distress" (1:4).[62] He came from a military family and he wanted passionately to be a soldier. When his father suggested the ministry, he replied that he was not good enough for it, but did hope that as an officer he could have a Christian influence on his men like that of Cornelius the centurion. His commission as an officer of the dragoons came through just days after his acceptance at Oxford to study for holy orders, so he could have had a military career. By then, however, he had almost reluctantly admitted that duty lay elsewhere. Much of the military man clung to him the rest of his life.[63]

At the same time that he appeared so vigorous and dashing, his ministry, as noted above, was beset by health problems. Each of his three appointments[64] was terminated by illness: Winchester by problems with his lungs, thought to be, and treated as, the tuberculosis to which other members of his family had succumbed, Cheltenham by what sounds like a bout of deep depression, and Brighton by a fatal illness described as "abscess in the cerebellum" (2:221) or as something that affected "the *ganglia* or bunches of nerves which are at the roots of the brain" (2:223).[65] As early as his year in Winchester he had premonitions of an early death (1:64), and was much impressed with the lives of David

Brainerd and Henry Martyn (1:60), both of whom died young in the service of the gospel.

All this poor health must have had an enormous Romantic appeal at the time. Susan Sontag notes that in the nineteenth century, melancholy and tuberculosis came to be socially regarded as a sign of a special nature: "The melancholy character—or the tubercular one—was a superior one: sensitive, creative, a being set apart."[66] These were the ailments of artists; they made people interesting. Keats, Shelley, and, it seems, half the poets of the time were "consumptive." Robertson's first illness was thought to be tuberculosis; his second seems to have been melancholy. The third was most Romantic of all, a mysterious illness that sapped away life and led to an early death.

None of this is to suggest that Robertson was a poseur or in any way insincere. As James R. Blackwood says, "Intensity was the secret of his power." And he backs up the statement by quoting Lady Byron's statement that "his very calm is a hurricane."[67] There is nothing more obvious than his earnestness. And he agonized over everything. Nor is it to suggest that he was weak. Few clergy have shown greater courage in the pulpit. He did not allow suffering to keep him from his work; he labored on silently in great pain, trying not to let it show to those to whom he was ministering. It is only to say that he would have been recognizable to his contemporaries as a much admired type of the time, the candle that burned so brightly, it had quickly to burn itself out.

Consistent with this intensity was a high degree of sensitivity. He loved friends, had a great need for their support, felt loneliness intensely, and yet had a code or pride that made it nearly impossible for him to confide what was troubling him or the degree of his pain. Thus, not surprisingly, he spent a good bit of his time depressed—and yet tried not to let it show and to work as hard as ever. Preaching was an agony to him, and he seemed useless for a day or so after a Sunday. There was no group for which he had such contempt as popular preachers, those who used their power over crowds to advance their own cause rather than that of the Kingdom.

He was also impatient with party strife in the Church of England at the time, which seemed to be polarized between evangelicals and Tractarians like Newman, and, because he would not repeat the slogans of either side, he was pilloried by both. He felt some sympathy with the liberalism of Thomas Arnold and the Christian socialism of F. D. Maurice and Charles Kingsley, but disagreed with both positions in some matters and resented having their opinions attributed to him. He was an isolated individual who suffered to preserve integrity through much struggle.

He loved poetry and read all the Romantics deeply, offering his critical insight into their work frequently in his letters and occasionally giving public lectures about them. He was also immersed in earlier poetry and especially loved and studied Shakespeare and Dante. Nor was that the end of his reading.[68] In his correspondence he frequently discussed the latest novels, reading not only English books but a surprising number of American works of all kinds as well. In addition to the biblical languages and Latin, he read in French, Italian, and German. The Germans were important to him for their philosophers, notably Kant, Fichte, and Lessing, and for their biblical scholars. He was also conversant with the science of his age, especially enjoying chemistry and ornithology.

Thoroughly Romantic also was his appreciation for the beauty of nature, whether awesome Alpine landscapes[69] or the less dramatic scenery of the hills around Cheltenham or the Brighton seashore. Equally Romantic was his appreciation of common people, but discussion of that will be postponed for inclusion in the treatment of what has made his preaching so influential in recent generations. Enough has been said, however, to indicate that Frederick Robertson summed up most of the cultural themes of his age, he was aware of and evaluated calmly and soundly all that was going on in his society, and he did so utilizing the categories that reflected the spirit of the age. He epitomized a Christian appropriation of Romantic consciousness, and thus what he said spoke directly to most of his hearers.

As to what made him a natural role model to preachers of later generations, that, too, can be approached from a number of directions, but none sums it up so well as saying that he was one of the first to face the issues that have been characteristic for mainline Christianity ever since, and that he dealt with them in ways that were effective. He did so without rejecting the issues, but by presupposing them and going on matter-of-factly to consider their ramifications. In this way he remained relevant to preachers who lived in later times, when it was no longer thought that if the difficulties were ignored, they would go away. While in many ways his age seems as alien to the present as many that are more remote, the situation of the church in the world was so much the same that his example can still be followed with profit.

This is to say that he assumed the people who filled Trinity Chapel Sunday after Sunday found Christian faith hard rather than easy. Their Christian construction of reality had been eroded by their experiences of the week, and they needed to have it reinforced. Thus most of Robertson's preaching can be considered problem solving, but he addressed a range of kinds of problems.

Some of his sermons were essays in apologetics, defending the faith in an age in which new knowledge—scientific, historical, or biblical—seemed to call it into question. Others had to do with the difficulties individuals had in living out their faith, so that he became one of the first great psychological preachers who practiced pastoral care from the pulpit. And others had to do with a society in which the wealth of empire and industrial revolution was distributed very inequitably and in which the gulf between social classes seemed an abyss over which even Victorian engineers could not erect a bridge. Social problems, personal problems, impediments to belief—they all sound very familiar, and Robertson of Brighton showed how all of them could be dealt with helpfully through sermons. It is not surprising that preachers who have come after him have wanted to look back and see how he did it.

While the way he dealt homiletically with each of these three kinds of problems will need to be examined, those examinations must be informed by an awareness of what Robertson considered to be the basic principles of his approach to Christian theology.

> First. The establishment of positive truth, instead of the destruction of error.
> Secondly. That truth is made up of two opposite propositions, and not found in a *via media* between the two.
> Thirdly. That spiritual truth is discerned by the spirit, instead of intellectually in propositions, and, therefore, Truth should be taught suggestively, not dogmatically.
> Fourthly. That belief in the Human character of Christ's Humanity must be antecedent to belief in His Divine Origin.
> Fifthly. That Christianity, as its teachers should, works from the inward to the outward, and not *vice versa*.
> Sixthly. The soul of goodness in things evil. (2:153)

Such an approach is hard to imagine in any period prior to the Romantic era.

With these principles understood, the approach he made to dealing with the problems of belief, practice, and society that he faced in common with his colleagues in the twentieth century becomes clear. This approach may be seen first in his work as an apologist.

His was the first generation of Christians to deal with the challenges to faith that have become so familiar, the challenges to the historicity of Genesis posed by the study of geology and biological evolution. In the 1830s Sir Charles Lyell and William Buckland[70] had used the evidence of rocks and fossils to show that the world was much older than the six thousand years the standard reconstruction of biblical chronology claimed.[71] And, although Darwin's *Origin of the Species* would not be published until six years after Robertson's death, an anonymous book called *The Vestiges of the Natural History of Creation* had appeared in 1844 with a theory of the development of animal life, with which Darwin's would agree in principle. For the first time, evidence existed that would bring into question the literal historical truth of the Bible.

At the same time, German scholars had begun to study the Bible like any other book and to raise questions about its historical accuracy on literary grounds. Although Coleridge and Thirwall had already introduced the German scholarship to English readers, it remained unnoticed by most clergy and theologians until the publication of *Essays and Reviews* in 1860—seven years after Robertson's death. Ten years earlier, Robertson lectured on Genesis in his parish and, "while declaring that the Mosaic cosmogony could not be reconciled with geological facts, still succeeded in showing its inner harmony, in principle, with the principles of scientific geology" (1:233; cf. 2:139). He also distinguished between the J and E documents and questioned the universality of the flood, but approached all these questions in a positive rather than a negative way, in accordance with his principles. That is what made it possible for people to leave the chapel "deeply opposed, it is true, to the popular theory of Inspiration, but deeply convinced of *an* Inspiration" (ibid.).

Robertson also preached a sermon on inspiration in that same year of 1850.[72] (For the text of this sermon, see **Vol. 2, pp. 486-92.**) In the introduction he listed the kinds of questions to be raised. A sampling includes: "What the Bible is, and what the Bible is not? What is meant by inspiration? Whether inspiration is the same thing as infallibility? When God inspired the minds, did he dictate the words? Did the inspiration of men mean the infallibility of their words? Is inspiration the same as dictation?" In regard to these questions he says:

> Upon these things there are many views, some of them false, some superstitious; but it is not our business now to deal with these; our way is rather to teach positively than negatively; we will try to set up the truth, and error may fall before it.[73]

Instead of exposing erroneous principles of interpretation, he invokes the principles by which the apostles read the Bible, two of them constituting the divisions of the body of the sermon. The first is that Scripture is of universal application. By that he means, while passages in the Bible tell of individual persons, they apply to not just those individuals but to all who are in that "particular state of character." The second point is that all the lines of Scripture converge toward Christ.

> Every unfulfilled aspiration of humanity in the past; all partial repre-
> sentation of perfect character; all sacrifices, nay even those of idolatry,
> point to the fulfillment of what we want, the answer to every longing—
> the type of perfect humanity, the Lord Jesus Christ.[74]

In a time when few English Christians knew that science and biblical scholarship had brought the historicity of parts of the Bible into question, when even Maurice still spoke of the universe as only six thousand years old,[75] it is astonishing to see the rector of a proprietary chapel in a fashionable watering place finding no threat to full Christian faith in the issues. He assured his congregation that if the popular theory of inspiration is wrong, the Scriptures are nevertheless the inspired Word of God, from which all true insight into the human condition is derived. He was dealing calmly with the problem before most clergy knew there was a problem.

The first point in his sermon on "Inspiration" is the principle on which Robertson dealt with personal problems from the pulpit. Assuming that "scripture is of universal application," he would identify a personal or spiritual problem on which he thought he ought to preach and then compose the sermon as a study of a biblical character who suffered from it. He brought the issue so to life that his hearers would recognize themselves and their own situations and be given insight accordingly. In this way, he became one of the first "psychological" preachers.[76] Horton Davies lists examples of such sermons when he says that Robertson discoursed on the skepticism of Pilate, on Thomas as the type of the doubter, on Elijah as the victim of despondency, on Christ as the supreme image of heroic loneliness, on religious depression, on the faith of the centurion, on the victory of faith, and on how to attain rest.[77]

What gave Robertson such acute psychological insight was his own experience of many of the problems discussed, experience that caused him acute suffering. Such an understanding of what made the sermons work could not be stated better than it was by their anonymous editor:

> Suppose a preacher goes down into the depths of his own being, and
> has the courage and fidelity to carry all he finds there, first to God in
> confession and prayer, and then to his flock as some part of the gener-
> al experience of Humanity, do you not feel that he must be touching
> close upon some brother-man's sorrows and wants? . . . Does not the
> man feel that here is a revelation of God's truth as real and fresh as if

he had stood in the streets of Jerusalem and heard the Savior's very voice?[78]

The third area in which Robertson's sermons have been an inspiration and model for later preachers is the way they addressed social problems. The radicality of what he did cannot be understood without knowledge of the condition of English Christianity in general, from Roman Catholics to Unitarians, at the time. England had been frightened into reaction by the French and American revolutions, and thus its class system had become yet more rigid. Even Coleridge can be cited as an example of this tendency. He argued in 1829 for a National Church (a temporal body separate from the spiritual Church of Christ), which would have a clerisy whose responsibility would be "to form and train up the people of the country to be obedient, free, useful, organizable subjects, citizens, and patriots, living to the benefit of the state and prepared to die for its defense."[79]

The main difference between Coleridge and many of his clerical contemporaries is that they would see no need for the National Church to be separate from the Church of Christ, or for its clerisy to be a body other than the clergy. To them the most important teachings of the Catechism in the Book of Common Prayer were:

> To honour and obey the King, and all that are put in authority under him: To submit myself to all my governors, teachers, spiritual pastors, and masters, . . . to learn and labor truly to get mine own living, and to do my duty in that state of life, unto which it shall please God to call me.

This was a time of much social unrest, when Chartists and Socialists were threatening the status quo. At the same time, it was a period in which to be a "gentleman" and a member of polite society meant having private income and not having to work or engage in trade, the age of *Vanity Fair.*

Robertson was not a revolutionary. He felt the ambiguity of his position, saying, "My tastes are with the aristocrat, my principles with the mob" (2:118). Nor was he even a Christian Socialist like Maurice or Kingsley, much less a Socialist in the ordinary sense of the word. He felt that Socialism would only create a new ruling class with all the faults of the present one.

> Dragged aside by two extremes, he fell back on Christianity, not as a *via media,* but as declaring truths that embraced in their ample round

the wisdom of conservatism and the progressive spirit of liberalism, which solved the questions of the day—neither by laying down laws, nor by coercive measures for oppression or for liberty, but by spreading in all classes a spirit of love, of duty, and of mutual respect (1:161).

However unsatisfactory this may seem to contemporary analysts who consider social evil systemic, he was at least as demanding that the upper classes do their Christian duty as he was that the poor do so. In a sermon on Sabbath observance, for instance, he pointed out that clergy have been inconsistent in demanding that the poor not break the day in ways the wealthy were permitted to.[80] In reply to Evangelical threats that God would punish England by a foreign war for its breach of the holy day, he said that God's judgment would not fall because the working class had a few hours recreation, but because "we are selfish men; and we prefer pleasure to duty, and traffic to honor; and because we love party more than our Church, and our Church more than our Christianity; and our Christianity more than truth, and ourselves more than all."[81]

Certainly the poor were a main concern all through his ministry. His work at Winchester was among them, he chafed among the prosperous in Cheltenham, he accepted a poor parish in Oxford before the bishop urged him to go to Brighton instead. There his congregation was largely of the merchant class, but he preached sermons that were appreciated by the working class and servants as well. He was interested in the young men who came to Brighton to work in stores and offices. He helped in the organization of a Working-Man's Institute, which would make a library and reading room available to its members. He visited the poor assiduously and helped as he could in all their troubles. And he preached on social and economic issues.

The one sermon he preached in London was in a series for working people at St. John's, Fitzroy Street, in which Maurice and Kingsley were also to preach. For a text he took the story of David's response following Nabal's refusal to make a contribution to the band that had protected his property. Robertson said that "whenever two classes are held apart by rivalry and selfishness, instead of drawn together by the law of love, . . . there exist the forces of inevitable collision."[82] The sermon division he proposed, then, was: "I. The causes of this false social state. II. The message of the Church to the man of wealth." The cause of the false social state was a social falsehood to the effect that "wealth constitutes superiority, and has a right to the subordination of inferiors." Thus he branded as false what was generally assumed to be the basis of English society at the time. The church's message to the wealthy was that "a

Scientific Political Economy" would coincide with the Christian revelation, which is that "the law, which alone can interpret the mystery of life, is the self-sacrifice of Christ."[83] To be Christian, the wealthy must live by that example. That they have not been aware of that duty was the fault of the clergy: "For three long centuries we have taught submission to the powers that be. . . . Rarely have we dared to demand of those powers that be, justice; of the wealthy man and the titled, duties."

Robertson did not preach that way only when he was out of his parish. The two that follow this example in the *Sermons* were equally forthright and were preached at Trinity Chapel. His biography lists other sermons on social questions at the time (2:2). It also includes letters that demonstrate his willingness to justify such preaching to members of the nobility and the wealthy (e.g., 2:6-8, 54-55).

He did not set himself up as an expert on social conditions, although he was deeply aware of them from his ministry among the poor; nor did he believe that one social group was less tainted by original sin than another. His profound conviction was that the church should participate in the improvement of society by being the channel through which God changed the hearts of its members. As an ordained minister, he thought his field of competence was sin and grace, and that the repentance of one and the acceptance of the other were what was needed to improve society. As a cobbler, he stuck to his last. While later generations may recognize that social structures as well as individuals need to be made more just, no one can deny the prophetic courage with which Robertson took stands rare among the clergy of his age. Thus his sermons on social issues, personal problems, and impediments to faith have made him one of the few preachers of the past with whom today's clergy can feel immediate empathy and from whom they can derive new inspiration and dedication.

FOR FURTHER READING

Brooke, Stopford A. *The Life and Letters of Frederick W. Robertson, M.A.* New ed. of 1868. London: Kegan, Paul, Trench, Trübner, & Co., 1891.

Golden, James L., Goodwin F. Berquist, and William E. Coleman. *The Rhetoric of Western Thought.* 3rd. ed. Dubuque, Iowa: Kendall/ Hunt, 1976–83.

Ker, Ian. *John Henry Newman: A Biography.* Oxford: Oxford University Press, 1988.

Longinus. *On the Sublime.* Translated with commentary by James A. Arieti and John M. Crossett. Texts and Studies in Religion, vol. 21. Lewiston, N.Y.: Edward Mellen, 1985.

The Preaching of John Henry Newman. Edited with introduction by W. D. White. The Preacher's Paperback Library. Philadelphia: Fortress, 1969.

Reardon, Bernard M. G. *Religion in the Age of Romanticism: Studies in Early Nineteenth Century Thought.* Cambridge: Cambridge University Press, 1985.

Robertson, Frederick W. *Sermons Preached at Brighton.* New York: Harper & Brothers, 1905.

Notes

1. Bernard M. G. Reardon, *Religion in the Age of Romanticism: Studies in Early Nineteenth Century Thought* (Cambridge: Cambridge University Press, 1985), 1. If it may be said that Romanticism is, in part, a reaction against classicism, then classicism becomes its *terminus a quo.* In that sense, its *terminus ad quem* would be realism.

2. Ibid., 10.

3. The foregoing represents an effort to summarize ibid., 1-15. For a comparable but much terser effort to characterize Romanticism, see the summary of Claude Welch, *Protestant Thought in the Nineteenth Century, Vol. I, 1799–1870* (New Haven: Yale University Press, 1972), 52-55:

> 1. A protest, in the name of freedom and dynamism, against the formalism and structure of neoclassicism, rationalism, and moral asceticism and discipline.
>
> 2. A stress on individuality that at times amounted almost to worship of originality and genius.
>
> 3. An exaltation of the immediacy of feeling "in the self, for humanity, and for the world," which involved vitalism and an aesthetic approach to nature.
>
> 4. A concern and feeling for history.
>
> 5. The dominance of the twin principles of plenitude (as opposed to the restriction of content by formal rules) and diversity (as opposed to uniformity and simplicity).

4. Reardon, *Religion in the Age of Romanticism*, 29. For a look at his preaching, see *Servant of the Word: Selected Sermons of Friedrich Schleiermacher,* trans. with intro. Dawn De Vries, Fortress Texts in Modern Theology (Philadelphia: Fortress, 1987).

5. Stephen Neill and Tom Wright, *The Interpretation of the New Testament 1861–1986,* 2nd. ed. (Oxford: Oxford University Press, 1988), 3 (Coleridge), 8-10 (Thirlwall), 31-34 *(Essays and Reviews).*

6. *Confessions of an Inquiring Spirit,* intro. David Jasper, 3rd ed. of 1853, Fortress Texts in Modern Theology (Philadelphia: Fortress, 1988).

7. For the influence of Coleridge on later English theology, see Charles Richard Sanders, *Coleridge and the Broad Church Movement: Studies in S. T. Coleridge, Dr. Arnold of Rugby, J. C. Hare, Thomas Carlyle, and F. D. Maurice* (Durham, N.C.: Duke University Press, 1942). Sanders gives a concise statement of Coleridge's understanding of inspiration, pp. 82-83.

8. The work is not mentioned in any classical writing.

9. Longinus, *On the Sublime,* trans. with comm. by James A. Arieti and John M. Crossett, Texts and Studies in Religion, vol. 21 (Lewiston, N.Y.: Edward Mellen, 1985), x.

10. George A. Kennedy, *Classical Rhetoric and Its Christian and Secular Tradition from Ancient to Modern Times* (Chapel Hill: University of North Carolina Press, 1980), 226.

11. Arieti and Crossett, *Longinus,* 9.

12. Ibid., 39.

13. James L. Golden, Goodwin F. Berquist, and William E. Coleman, *The Rhetoric of Western Thought,* 3rd. ed. (Dubuque, Iowa: Kendall/Hunt, 1976–83), 103-87.

14. Nan Johnson, *Nineteenth-Century Rhetoric in North America* (Carbondale: Southern Illinois University Press, 1991).

15. One of the tasks to which Schleiermacher devoted himself in his first parish was translating Blair's sermons into German (*Servant of the Word,* ed. De Vries, 2).

16. Hugh Blair, *Lectures on Rhetoric and Belles Lettres,* ed. with intro. Harold F. Harding with a foreword by David Potter (Carbondale: Southern Illinois University Press, 1965), xviii.

17. *The Rhetoric of Blair, Campbell, and Whately, with Updated Bibliography,* ed. James L. Golden and Edward P. J. Corbett, Landmarks in Rhetoric and Public Address (Carbondale: Southern Illinois University Press, 1990), 37-73.

18. Parenthetical numbers refer to pages in the second volume of the Harding edition of Blair's *Lectures.*

19. He represents the "Common Sense" school of Scottish philosophy and theology regnant at the time. The edition of Blair's *Sermons* consulted is the single volume published in London by T. and J. Allman in 1825 with "A Short Account of the Life and Character of the Author" by James Finlayson.

20. Obviously, Blair lived at a time when "men" was thought to be gender inclusive.

21. Blair, *Sermons,* 269-88.

22. Blair assumes that all preachers will be male.

23. *The Philosophy of Rhetoric,* ed. Lloyd F. Bitzer with foreword by David Potter, Landmarks in Rhetoric and Public Address (Carbondale: Southern Illinois University Press, 1963). Although Campbell's book on rhetoric was published six years before that of Blair, Blair's thought on the subject is earlier, since he had lectured on the subject since 1759 and he made very little change in the text of his lectures prior to their publication.

24. Since, however, it was not these lectures but his book on rhetoric that was to be so influential on future preaching, attention here will be focused on the latter work.

25. This interpretation follows very closely that of Lloyd Bitzer in his introduction to the Southern Illinois edition of Campbell. For alternative approaches, see Golden, Berquist, and Coleman, *The Rhetoric of Western Thought,* 148-63, and Johnson, *Nineteenth-Century Rhetoric,* 20-31.

26. Bitzer, "Introduction," xiii.

27. Ibid., xxv.

28. Campbell recognizes, however, that there is no necessary connection between what the mind perceives as sensation and any external reality.

29. Ranging from a purple cow to the heavenly city.

30. Undergraduates in their teens rather than postgraduates in a professional degree program. It was not even required that they "read" ("major in") divinity; general education was the goal with the assumption that professional readiness could be acquired on one's own.

31. The first publication of the *Logic* as a separate book was in 1826 and that of the *Rhetoric* was in 1828. Whately continued to revise the latter work all his life, seeing it through seven editions, four of which involved at least some revision. Richard Whately, *Elements of Rhetoric, Comprising an Analysis of the Laws of Moral Evidence and of Persuasion, with the Rules for Argumentative Composition and Elocution*, intro. Douglas Ehninger, Landmarks in Rhetoric and Public Address (Carbondale: Southern Illinois University Press, 1963), xvi-xix.

32. The words are from *Apologia pro Vita Sua*, quoted without page citation in Ian Ker, *John Henry Newman: A Biography* (Oxford: Oxford University Press, 1988), 19. For the relation of Whately and Newman, see Geoffrey Faber, *Oxford Apostles: A Character Study of the Oxford Movement* (London: Faber & Faber, 1935; reprint, Harmondsworth: Penguin, 1954) 108-11.

33. Whately also arranged for the twenty-three-year-old Newman to contribute the article on Cicero to the *Encyclopedia,* an article that is held in high regard. Walter Jost, *Rhetorical Thought in John Henry Newman* (Columbia: University of South Carolina Press, 1989), 9. And, when Whately became principal of St. Alban's Hall, he invited Newman to become his vice-principal.

34. Ehninger, "Editor's Introduction," ix.

35. Ibid., xi.

36. Ibid., 4.

37. Ibid., ix.

38. Reardon, *Religion in the Age of Romanticism*, 2.

39. Horton Davies, *Worship and Theology in England, From Newman to Martineau, 1850–1900*, vol. 4, Worship and Theology in England (Princeton: Princeton University Press, 1962), 4:287-301.

40. The standard treatment of his life has become, Ker, *John Henry Newman.* On it and several other recent books about Newman, see my review article, "A Centennial Perspective on Newman as Rhetor," *ATR* 73 (1991), 477-83.

41. The only church possible for a member of either university, since religious tests excluding Dissenters were not abolished until 1871.

42. From which came the designation of the Oxford movement as the Tractarians.

43. The first generation of Tractarians was not liturgically demonstrative. It was the second generation, the "millinerians," who began to imitate the vestments and ceremonial of contemporary Roman Catholics.

44. I have taken the quotation from Faber, *Oxford Apostles,* 187. It is from the *Studies in Poetry and Philosophy* (1868) of John Campbell Shairp, a Scottish scholar who became professor of poetry at Oxford long after Newman left.

45. John Henry Newman, "On Preaching the Gospel" in *Lectures on the Doctrine of Justification* (London: Longmans, Green & Co, 1892). The best analysis of

Newman's preaching I have seen is W. D. White's introduction to *The Preaching of John Henry Newman*, The Preacher's Paperback Library (Philadelphia: Fortress, 1969).

46. Ibid., 14-15.

47. John Henry Newman, "On Preaching the Gospel," 371.

48. *The Idea of a University Defined and Illustrated in Nine Discourses Delivered to the Catholics of Dublin in Occasional Lectures and Essays Addressed to the Members of the Catholic University,* ed. with intro. and notes by Martin J. Svaglic (Notre Dame: University of Notre Dame Press, 1982), 303-21. Further page references to this work will be made parenthetically in the text.

49. Death, judgment, heaven, and hell.

50. Originally seven.

51. For a succinct description of the differences between the three series, see Davies, *Worship and Theology in England,* 4:302-5.

52. John Henry Newman, *Fifteen Sermons Preached Before the University of Oxford Between A.D. 1826 and 1843.* The edition consulted was that of 1898 published by Longmans, Green, & Co.

53. Jouett L. Powell, *Three Uses of Christian Discourse in John Henry Newman: An Example of Nonreductive Reflection on the Christian Faith,* AARDS, no. 10 (Missoula, Mont.: Scholars Press, 1975). The quotation is from Jost, *Rhetorical Thought in John Henry Newman.*

54. Powell, *Three Uses of Christian Discourse,* 90-91.

55. John Campbell Shairp, *Studies in Poetry and Philosophy,* quoted in Faber, *Oxford Apostles,* 187.

56. Reardon, *Religion in the Age of Romanticism,* 14. The extent to which Newman was a man of his time and a Romantic is discussed by David Nicholls and Fergus Kerr in the introduction to the collection of essays they edited titled *John Henry Newman: Reason, Rhetoric, and Romanticism* (Carbondale: Southern Illinois University Press, 1991), 3-4, and by Valerie Pitt in her contribution to that volume, "Demythologizing Newman," 13-27. Most of the essayists of that volume doubt the ongoing significance of Newman's thought (p. 4). A much more thorough effort to understand the life and work of Newman in terms of the great motifs of Romanticism is David Goslee, *Romanticism and the Anglican Newman* (Athens: Ohio University Press, 1996).

57. That is, a church that was not a part of the diocesan structure, but one that was privately organized and supported.

58. *Sermons Preached at Trinity Chapel, Brighton, by the Late Rev. Frederick W. Robertson, M.A., the Incumbent.* The copy consulted was the frequently reprinted Harper & Brothers one-volume edition, which appeared originally in 1870, but I am very grateful to Prof. Sam Hill for the gift of a set of the edition published by Bernhard Tauchnitz of Leipzig, 1861–66.

59. Stopford A Brooke, *The Life and Letters of Frederick W. Robertson, M.A.* The copy consulted is the New Edition of 1868, published in London by Kegan, Paul, Trench, Trübner, & Co., Ltd. in 1891.

60. Frederick W. Robertson, *Sermons Preached at Brighton* (New York: Harper & Brothers, 1905), 5.

61. Brooke, *Life and Letters,* 2:265. The description above is based on the letter from which the quotation was made, a passage from his biography (2:229), an engraving of his bust that is the frontispiece for that volume, and the portrait sketch that is the frontispiece for the Harper & Brothers edition of the *Sermons.*

62. Parenthetical numbers refer to pages of Brooke, *The Life and Letters of Frederick W. Robertson.*

63. It is hard for post–Vietnam Christians to consider anything warlike to be consistent with their religion, but that is simply one of the cultural differences between them and nineteenth-century Europeans, who believed that war kept nations morally healthy. Cf. Owen Chadwick, *The Secularization of the European Mind in the Nineteenth Century,* Canto (Cambridge: Cambridge University Press, 1990), 132-34, although in this passage Chadwick is discussing a period slightly later than that of Robertson.

64. There was a fourth, St. Ebbe's at Oxford, but he was there only two months.

65. Davies says that he died of a brain tumor, but does not cite his authority for that diagnosis. *Worship and Theology,* 4:312. In response to my summary of symptoms, Dr. Samuel A. Trufant, who taught neurology at the medical schools of Cincinnati and Tulane Universities for many years, said that an aneurysm or a cerebellar or other form of cyst seems more likely.

66. Susan Sontag, *Illness as a Metaphor* (New York: Farrar, Straus & Giroux, 1978), 32.

67. James R. Blackwood, *The Soul of Frederick W. Robertson, the Brighton Preacher* (New York: Harper & Brothers, 1947), 117.

68. At the same time, he was an advocate of studying a few books thoroughly rather than reading many superficially.

69. Some of his best descriptions of natural beauty occur in letters he wrote to his wife while walking through the Alps after the collapse of his work in Cheltenham. Brooke, *The Life and Letters of Frederick W. Robertson,* 1:115-33.

70. The Dean of Westminster Abbey!

71. Archbishop Ussher set the date of creation as 4004 B.C.

72. Frederick W. Robertson, *Sermons Preached at Brighton.*

73. Ibid., 826.

74. Ibid., 831.

75. Alec R. Vidler, *The Church in an Age of Revolution: 1789 to the Present Day,* The Pelican History of the Church, vol. 5 (Harmondsworth: Penguin, 1961), 114.

76. Charles Smyth, *The Art of Preaching: A Practical Survey of Preaching in the Church of England 747-1939* (London: SPCK; New York: Macmillan, 1940), 229-30.

77. Davies, *Worship and Theology,* 4:290. For an analytical summary of one such sermon see Smyth, *The Art of Preaching,* 226-29. The sermon treated is "The Skepticism of Pilate," *Sermons,* 226-34.

78. Brooke, *The Life and Letters of Frederick W. Robertson,* ix.

79. "On the Constitution of the Church and State," *Works,* 10:54, quoted in Robert Hole, *Pulpit, Politics, and Public Order in England 1762–1832* (Cambridge: Cambridge University Press, 1989), 253.

80. "The Sydenham Palace, and the Religious Non-Observance of the Sabbath," *Sermons*, 343-52.

81. Ibid., 352.

82. Robertson, *Sermons Preached at Brighton*, 186.

83. Ibid., 195.

CHAPTER 23

TRANSATLANTIC ROMANTICISM

UNITARIAN ROMANTICISM

Although most previous trends in preaching moved from east to west, Romantic preaching was heard in America before it began in Britain. Theological liberalism in the U.S. was receptive to Romantic influence at an earlier date. British radical thought began in the late-seventeenth century with Enlightenment rationalism rather than with Romanticism, which developed later. The eroding tendencies of the Enlightenment, however, were pretty well kept in check in New England through the American Revolution, at least in regard to the doctrine of the Trinity.[1] By the time this traditional orthodoxy came to be questioned, therefore, the mood of the culture had shifted from the Augustan exaltation of reason to one more congenial to the Romantic spirit.

For some time before that, double predestination had ceased to be presupposed by many New England Congregationalists; the sort of Arminianism that developed in the Second Great Awakening could be found even among the more staid clergy of Boston. This left them open to other liberalizing tendencies. Then, near the beginning of the nineteenth century, liberal clergy moving away from Trinitarian orthodoxy

624

took key positions at Harvard. In this way an atmosphere developed, but there was not yet any movement toward institutionalizing it.

Pre-Romantic Liberalism

The catalyst that turned the theological trend into a denomination was a sermon preached by William Ellery Channing (1780–1842) at the 1819 ordination of Jared Sparks in Baltimore. The young minister of the Federal Street Church in Boston had already appeared as the champion of modernist theology in 1815, when he led the defense against a call from the orthodox for the exposure of heretics. In an open letter to Samuel Thatcher, his colleague at the Brattle Street Church, he had warded off that attack and turned a beleaguered position into a positive plat-form. But the ordination sermon, "Unitarian Christianity,"[2] initiated a movement that culminated in the formation of the American Unitarian Association in 1825.

Channing, however, represented a position that was still pre-Romantic, one that was in transition from neoclassic rationalism. He still showed some of the attitudes of the Enlightenment, but he worked out their implications differently from the way of his British predecessors. His Christology, for instance, was Arian rather than Socinian; that is, he regarded Jesus as a preexistent divine being rather than as a human being with a special divine mission.

He also showed other tendencies that would have a fuller place among the Romantics, nor were these exclusively theological. When he needed to travel for his health, he went to England and looked up William Wordsworth, who introduced him to Samuel Coleridge, who, in turn, induced him to read Friedrich Schelling and Johann Fichte. His interest in Wordsworth and his poetry was a result of his love of nature and a "mystical sense of the universe as the outer garment of God."[3] All this was thoroughly Romantic.

The heart of Channing's theology was not the doctrine of God, nor was it Christology. Rather, his characteristic interest was anthropology, and he entertained a very high understanding of the spiritual capacity of human beings. His reaction against Calvinism is most apparent in his estimate of human capacity. He came "to define the religious life as a continual pursuit of self-culture."[4] The possibilities of self-improvement were infinite; its goal was perfection. This is not to say that he was unaware of the human capacity for evil, but only that he felt it did not have to be indulged.

While the later transcendentalists shared Channing's "intractable faith in the potential divinity of the individual," they carried it farther than he, fitting it in with the pantheism to which Romanticism was always inclined, while he "clung much more firmly to a Christ-centered religion."[5] In other ways as well he remained pre-Romantic in his theology, his rationalism being seen, for instance, in an epistemology derived from John Locke and the Scottish Common Sense philosophers. In early American Unitarianism, the closer one got to Romanticism, the farther one became removed from traditional Christianity. Coming at the very beginning of the process, Channing was thus nearer to historic Christianity and less Romantic than many to follow.

Channing's preaching was shaped by Hugh Blair, in both form and content.[6] With his commitment to self-cultivation, it was only natural that he should find congenial Blair's belief that the purpose of preaching was to make people better. Indeed, one of his major objections to Trinitarianism was that the preaching of its doctrines did not have this effect.[7] Channing used the same criterion to evaluate both doctrines and the rhetorical method by which they were communicated: the value of either was seen in its capacity to improve people morally. Beliefs also needed the unity, consistency, and harmony that Blair required of speeches if they were to contribute to the improvement of human morals.[8]

Emerson's Pastorate

True Romantic preaching in America was first practiced by one whose very Romantic impulses would eventually lead him from the pulpit and even from such a place in the Christian tradition as his Unitarian mentors retained. Ralph Waldo Emerson (1803–82) was the son of a Unitarian minister who died when Waldo was eight, leaving his widow and their children in straitened circumstances. The one of these five who would grow up to be called "the Sage of Concord" showed no particular literary, philosophical, or religious precocity in his youth. One of his earliest vague senses of vocational direction, however, was a desire to "put on eloquence as a robe," and it was from his preacher father that he claimed to derive "a passionate love for the strains of eloquence."[9] Yet when he graduated from Harvard he was not able to pursue that goal, since he had to start working immediately as a schoolteacher to supplement the family income.

The influences on his life pointed him toward the Unitarian pulpit. Among these were the Channing brothers, with William Ellery supplying the theological framework and Edward Tyrrel having taught him how to write and speak. After he decided to enter the ministry and prepare for it at Harvard Divinity School, he contracted tuberculosis, which not only threatened his vision but also left him weak for his studies. When eventually he was licensed to preach, he delayed finding a church of his own and becoming ordained both to protect his health and because it was still expected that a New England minister would be wedded to his parish for life. He wanted to make sure that the place he accepted was one in which he could devote more energy to scholarly preaching than to wider pastoral duties.

His eventual settlement came after he began in July 1828 to fill in at Second Church, Boston,[10] because of the illness of its pastor, Henry Ware Jr., one of the most distinguished Unitarian ministers of the period. The following January he was called to be junior pastor of Second Church.[11] It was recognized that because of Ware's illness, most of the work would fall upon Emerson; he would, however, succeed Ware as senior minister. The succession occurred on July 1, 1829, when Ware joined the Harvard faculty.

Far from being lifelong, his tenure as pastor lasted less than two and a half years. The secular literary scholars who have been the main students of Emerson have assumed that he was miscast as a minister all along, and that his resignation of his pastorate was an escape from the shackles of an institution and its dogmas that he found confining.[12] While it is true that his transcendentalist manifesto, "Nature," was published in 1836, he nevertheless continued to fill pulpits on occasion until 1839.

The transition was far more gradual than has been understood, and the discontinuity less than has been assumed. Wesley Mott, for instance, argues that the roots of Emerson's most transcendental teachings lie not in Platonism or Eastern religions, as has been thought, but in biblical and Puritan theology, and David Robinson takes a very similar position.

The occasion of his resignation was his unwillingness to administer Holy Communion, but this was not because he had lost his religion. The issue, rather, was his concern with the relation of what he called "forms" to religious experience. He was probably not so much a philosophical idealist as someone who was convinced that spirit is much more important than matter. Sacraments or ordinances, the Bible, morality, and church were all in conflict to a certain degree with the experience of the true religion in the soul. The sacramental assumption that forms can be means of grace was foreign to him; such things seemed to Emerson more likely to block than to convey the Spirit. Hence his quarrel with Unitarianism was not that it was too religious but rather that it was not religious enough; in his Romantic antiformalism he saw popular religion, including Unitarianism, as a constable religion.[13]

The important human trait for Emerson was what he called "Mind," which is the same as what Coleridge called "Reason"; this is to be distinguished from the analytical faculty that most people call reason (and Coleridge designated as mere "Understanding").[14] This Mind in the individual participates in the spiritual reality of the universe that Emerson can describe interchangeably as Reason, Universal Mind, or the Oversoul. Therefore, religion can be self-evident to all minds open to perceiving it, and Emerson can say that spiritual religion "has no other evidence than its own intrinsic probability."[15] Such a religion, of course, would have slight need of forms.

Slight, but some—just as Reason would always have need of Understanding. The sort of preaching Emerson believed in and wanted to do while he was still a minister was one of the right sort of forms, because he conceived preaching to be the middle term between Spirit and letter. The preacher enunciates the inner testimony of Spirit that he perceives and thus calls it to the attention of the congregation, who can recognize it because the same Spirit is testifying to the same truth within them.

The Spirit "speaks," makes itself heard, through the medium of the external word, but the hearing is of two kinds. The external word simply helps to activate (not to cause) the inner hearing of the inner Word. Listeners respond initially to external words only by an external hearing, but all who truly desire to do so are capable of hearing the Spirit's voice "through" external words.[16]

Such an understanding of the purpose of preaching would obviously have implications for the form of preaching. To begin with, it meant that a sermon was not complete when the preacher spoke; it had to be completed within and by the hearers. Its meaning had to be recognized and carried further by them. And the medium for enabling that process was not discursive reasoning, but a "suggestiveness" that did not override the audience's freedom. Thus Emerson came to reject Hugh Blair's rhetorical theory, which he had learned from Edward Tyrrel Channing, having a different sense of the hearers' needs and believing that "the individual self must express itself outward in forms that are not imposed from without."[17]

He began to deride what he called the "gingerbread distinctions" of sermons and to recognize that truths to be communicated have their own organic form; in this way, sermons are "composed" as a system of interrelations. "For Emerson, it is the idea, the unity infusing the parts of a lecture, just as it is the law immanent in the parts of nature (such as a shell) that a speaker should suggest."[18]

Emerson went on to experiment with the sermon form in an effort to see how self-evident truth could be relayed to an audience.[19] Before he could perfect that form, however, another, Holy Communion, came to appear too inconsistent with his understanding of ministry for him to continue in that calling. He became a lecturer and a writer as his thought evolved in a more transcendental direction. Even then, however, the degree of his alienation from Christianity can be overestimated. (For an example of a sermon by Emerson, see **Vol. 2, pp. 493-502.**)

Theodore Parker, a Transcendental Preacher

The Unitarian transcendentalist who would remain in the ministry and anticipate many trends of later Romantic preaching in liberal Christianity was Theodore Parker (1810–60), a grandson of the John Parker who led the American minutemen in the first battle of the Revolutionary War. Theodore exhibited throughout his life the spirit of the words his forebear is supposed to have said just before the fighting began: "Don't fire unless fired upon; but if they mean to have a war, let it begin here!"[20]

From his father he inherited an omnivorous appetite for reading but little in a material way, since his father was a not very successful farmer. Theodore had to take his Harvard degree by examination because he could not afford tuition, but both his diligence and his capacity for learning meant that by graduation he was already on his way to becoming a polymath.[21] At first he taught school but had some of the same difficulty with teaching that he was later to have with preaching: he expected from those who heard him commitment, application, and ability equal to his own. Gifted in languages, he read deeply in German Romantic philosophers and biblical criticism, not to mention the sacred writings of other religions in their original tongues.

By the time he took his first pastorate in West Roxbury, he had identified himself with the transcendentalists. Like Channing, he signaled the next stage of Unitarian thought in an ordination sermon; his was later to be published as "The Transient and Permanent in Christianity." His distinction between the permanent and transient was essentially the one others were to make later between "the religion of Jesus" and "the religion about Jesus." The transient elements were forms and doctrines, which had changed in every age and place. Examples of such evanescent dogmas were doctrines of scriptural revelation and Christologies. What was abiding could be reduced to Jesus' summary of the law: love God completely and your neighbor as yourself.

Implicit to all this is a transcendental epistemology. The religion of

Jesus is not reliable because it was taught with either his authority or that of the Bible. "It is hard to see why the great truths of Christianity rest on the personal authority of Jesus, more than the axioms of geometry rest on the personal authority of Euclid or Archimedes."[22] Great religious truth is recognized intuitively because God has constructed the human soul to have that capacity.

> Such ideas, capable of this legitimation, transcend experience, require and admit no further proof; as true before experience as after; true before time, after time, eternally; absolutely true.[23]

People do not differ on these truths; because they were implanted in the human consciousness by God, they are the same for all. That self-evidence, however, was less than self-evident. What Parker said at the ordination of Charles Shackleford was as threatening to the cozy establishment of his fellow Unitarian clergy as what Channing had said was to the orthodox Congregationalists of his day. They wished to exclude him from their fellowship, but they could never muster enough votes, and he refused to resign.

He continued to work on a number of fronts. One of his most important contributions was a heavily revised translation of Wilhelm De Wette's *Critical and Historical Introduction to the Canonical Scriptures of the Old Testament*. Although German thought was influential in Boston at the time,[24] this was one of the first if not the very first translation into English of contemporary German biblical scholarship. In this Parker contributed to the beginning of what was to become a norm in Christian preaching, its relying upon historical-critical biblical scholarship.

As little welcome to the Unitarian clergy as Parker and his message were, they were very welcome to a large number of laity. In 1845 he was called from his West Roxbury pulpit to a new congregation in Boston that would become the Twenty-Eighth Congregational Society there. They had no building in the beginning, nor did they wish to erect one large enough for the crowds they could expect. Instead, they held their services first at the Melodeon theater and then, when it was completed, at the new Music Hall, which held three thousand persons. Parker had one thing in common with successful evangelists of the period like Charles Grandison Finney and Charles Haddon Spurgeon: needing a theater to hold the huge audiences that turned out to hear them.

What Parker considered to be the permanent elements of Christianity, love of God and love of neighbor, determined the content of his preaching. He was, in his opinion, a reformer of faith and a reformer of morals.

His way of reforming faith has already been indicated. Soon after he moved to Boston, however, his way of reforming morals became clear. He saw eight "prominent evils" that needed to be opposed: intemperance, covetousness, ignorance, the condition of women, improper politics, war, slavery, and false theology.[25]

He was deeply concerned about all these issues. For instance, his concern for women is reflected in a practice modern feminists may have thought they invented, praying to "Our Father and Our Mother God."[26] He also anticipated the preaching of the "Social Gospel" to be discussed below. Soon, however, his passionate commitment to the abolitionist cause forced him to neglect other areas of social evil to concentrate on that massive one. His tireless work in the cause of abolition may have contributed to the tuberculosis that forced his early retirement, which was to be shortly followed by his death.

Although he published a great deal, the main medium for the dissemination of Parker's thought was his sermons.[27] These usually lasted about an hour and tended to be deductive, beginning with the widest possible generalization and working down progressively to the point under consideration. Words were chosen to be effective when heard rather than read. A standard technique was classification, which allowed him to break the material discussed into several categories that could be analyzed. Into this rhetorical framework he would fit vast amounts of statistics, history, and arcane lore.

In no case, however, was the appeal to authority, since the only source of religious truth he recognized was innate intuitions and perceptions of the divine. Thus "The Transient and Permanent in Christianity" was an exception among his sermons because it took a biblical text as a point of departure. In this way, Parker's transcendental epistemology led him away from what had always been a main characteristic of Christian preaching, the explication of a biblical text. The next wave of Unitarian theological change would regard theism as optional. And so it happened that the tradition to first produce Romantic preaching in English came in time to abandon anything that with precision could be labeled Christian proclamation.

THE THREE Bs OF AMERICAN PREACHING[28]

Horace Bushnell

By a quirk of fate, the three preachers most highly regarded in America during the middle to the end of the nineteenth century had family names

631

that begin with the letter *B*: Bushnell, Beecher, and Brooks. All three were Romantics who were loyal to the traditional Christian faith, but wished to state it in a vocabulary that would have meaning to the men and women of their day.

Chronologically the first of these, and theologically the most innovative and influential, was Horace Bushnell (1802–76). The son of a farmer in Litchfield County, Connecticut, Bushnell grew up to attend Yale. Upon graduation he worked for a while as a newspaperman before returning to Yale to tutor undergraduates and study law. During the time he was in that capacity in 1831, a religious revival occurred of the sort that had been a regular event at Yale earlier in the century during the presidency of Timothy Dwight.[29] Bushnell, who had been something of a skeptic before, was converted, although as much out of a desire to set a good example, apparently, as from any other internal crisis.[30] Nevertheless, the experience was enough to cause him to transfer to the Divinity School to prepare for ordination. Upon graduation he became the minister of North Congregational Church in Hartford, Connecticut, where he remained until ill health forced him to retire in 1859. Afterward, he was able to write and even to travel; he remained a force until his death in 1876, and his influence lasted on after that.

Even though he never held an academic post and was always contemptuous of academic theology, he came to be regarded as "the American Schleiermacher" and "the father of American religious liberalism,"[31] and has been described as "the greatest theologian of his generation and one of the most important thinkers in the history of American Protestantism."[32] As H. Shelton Smith has pointed out, the main issues on which Bushnell was to reflect theologically had become the agenda for New England theology after being raised by William Ellery Channing in his Baltimore ordination sermon.[33] The issues were the Trinity, Christology, human depravity, and the nature of the redemption brought by Christ. Bushnell's position on these issues was very different from that of Channing, however. He was also careful to distinguish his position from the other two influential systems of the time, Scholastic Calvinist Orthodoxy (as then taught) and revivalism.

Bushnell wished to affirm the Trinity, the divinity of Christ, human sinfulness, and the need for redemption.[34] What made him different from his orthodox contemporaries was a conviction learned from one of the books that influenced his thought most deeply, Coleridge's *Aids to Reflection*, the conviction that "Christianity is not a theory, or a speculation; but a life;—not a philosophy of life, but a life and a living process."[35] This organic perspective on life is typically Romantic. It was shocking to Bushnell's orthodox contemporaries, however, who thought that Christian preaching consisted of accurately arguing the doctrines of Calvin as they had received them. And it was equally unsatisfactory to the Unitarians, whether of Channing's Christian variety or Parker's transcendentalist persuasion.

Bushnell's position was also offensive to the revivalists because his understanding of Christian growth had led him to publish his views on Christian nurture—in many ways merely an extension of the old Puritan concept of the "Halfway Covenant."[36] He assumed that children born into Christian families and baptized could "grow up in love with all goodness, and remember no definite time when they became subjects of Christian principle."[37] This meant that it was not necessary to undergo a dramatic conversion experience in order to be saved. He thought the revivalist understanding "denied the manner in which one could grow into the faith and thereby ignored the need for the structures of family, church, and society, which nurture the person into the religious life."[38] Yet Bushnell—particularly after a near mystical experience in 1848—was convinced that growth had to involve significant change. Otherwise, the "religious nature," a longing for God shared by all human beings, never developed into the "religious life," which for him was the state of salvation.[39] Thus he believed in conversion, but thought that it could be a process spread over a lifetime as well an event of which one could remember the day and the hour.

Bushnell's characteristic medium for developing and communicating his theological positions was his sermons. Even though he published treatises in addition to his volumes of sermons, the longer works generally grew out of his preaching. His theological perspective caused him to object to the major preaching styles of his day, whether the arid rationalism of Orthodoxy, the Romanticism of transcendentalism, or the emotional manipulation of the revivalists.

One of the reasons he opposed Scholastic Orthodoxy was his understanding of the way language works. From his professor of biblical languages at Yale, Josiah Willard Gibbs, he learned that all language began as physical descriptions, which came to be used in abstract thought only as analogies; no abstract language is literal.[40] Yet it took Bushnell to see the implication that theological language therefore cannot be univocal, cannot be literal, objective, or scientific. The Scholastics' insistence that it could be would "only serve to produce a theology even more ambiguous than its metaphorical language already makes it."[41]

Bushnell recognized that the language of theology is artistic and even poetic. While such language does not encapsulate truth in exact formulas, it can do something better: it can get closer to the religious life as it is actually lived. And what is true of the language of theology is true a fortiori of the language of preaching. "Preaching should be an art form which stirs the symbolic consciousness and invites one to undertake the pilgrimage of faith."[42] Thus preaching involves all the instruments of eloquence, but its aim is vastly more serious than that of mere eloquence: it is a call to faith.

These principles can be seen at work in Bushnell's sermons, in which he takes a subject that has become stale in the arid formulas of the orthodox and brings it alive by graphic language, lively analogies, and the sheer power of imagination. For instance, in "The Power of an Endless Life," he admits at the outset that the subject of immortality as usually presented is "one of the dullest subjects," largely because of a concentration on its merely mathematical duration.[43] He wishes it to be understood as growth and sees an analogy in the way gigantic California redwoods develop from tiny seed. The emphasis is on achieving one's full potential. He goes on to show how many areas there are in which human beings develop in addition to the spiritual: "intelligence, reason, conscience, observation, choice, memory, enthusiasm." A catalog of the areas of human achievement made possible by those developments is given. Then he goes on to say, "And yet we have, in the power thus developed, nothing more than a mere hint or initial sign of what is to be the real stature of his personality in the process of his everlasting development."[44]

Having said that, though, he goes on to show how sin has inhibited the realization of this potential. He must speak, therefore, of the redemption wrought in Christ. The greatest impediment to appreciating this is the assumption by human beings that they are too far beneath such attention from God: "The expense of the sacrifice wears a look of extravagance."[45] In the conclusion he says people also fear a diminished humanity in salvation, but, to the contrary, it is far expanded beyond anything they can imagine. He quickly sketches in a virtual presence of humanity in the achievement of its full potential among the principalities and powers of the heavenly kingdom. The overall effect is to take what has been regarded as dullness itself and show it in such vividness that hearers begin to aspire to it with an exalted yearning that is itself a proleptic presence of the glory to be revealed. The hallmark of Bushnell's preaching is his ability to reconceive traditional Christian teaching in a way that brings it startlingly to life and makes it a real option to be sought.

Henry Ward Beecher

The revivalism against which Bushnell reacted was not just that of Finney's heirs, but also that urged by Finney's early opponents: Asahel Nettleton, Nathaniel Taylor, and Lyman Beecher.[46] While they had come to revise Jonathan Edwards's Calvinist belief in predestination, they were as insistent upon divine judgment as the hard-shell Presbyterians of Princeton, the orthodox Scholastics opposed by Bushnell. But when Lyman Beecher's son Henry Ward Beecher (1813–87)[47] entered the ministry, he discovered, after an initial commitment to the revivalist camp, that Bushnell's God of love appealed to him more than his father's God of wrath. Thus, although the younger Beecher was more of a communicator than a thinker, his theology, insofar as it was systematic, developed very much in the spirit of Bushnell's.[48]

The eleven children of Lyman Beecher are a strong argument for the importance of either heredity or environment in the development of talent. Two of Henry Ward's sisters were among the most influential women of the nineteenth century, Catherine being one of the major theoreticians of the cult of true womanhood and Harriet the author of *Uncle Tom's Cabin*, the novel that did more than anything else to galvanize Northern opinion against slavery.[49] Henry was the eighth child born to the Beechers and was not regarded by his parents as one of their more promising. He was not, for instance, considered up to following in the family tradition of Yale. Instead, he was sent to Mount Pleasant School in Amherst, Massachusetts, for his secondary education, and he stayed on in the same town for college. He was a rather weak student in such basic courses as Greek and Latin, but he became thoroughly grounded in rhetoric and developed a power of delivery that was to stay with him and grow for the rest of his life.[50]

When his father accepted the presidency of Lane Seminary in Cincinnati out of a deep sense of mission to evangelize the West with the religion and culture of New England, much of the family followed, including Henry, who enrolled in the seminary. After graduation he stayed in the area to assist in that winning of the West, serving first as minister of the Presbyterian church of Lawrenceville, Indiana (1837–39), and then going on to become pastor of Second Presbyterian in Indianapolis (1839–47). In this work on what was still essentially the frontier, his ministry began to develop emphases for which he would later become famous. In Indianapolis, for instance, he preached his first sermons against slavery, and gave his *Lectures to Young Men*, warning them against the moral dangers of life in the city. He also became involved in editorial work and even wrote for a periodical on agriculture.[51]

In 1847 he was called to be the first pastor of Plymouth Congregational Church in Brooklyn. There his pulpit became what William McLoughlin has called "the spiritual center of the republic for almost half a century."[52] His principal work at Plymouth Church was preaching; he did little pastoral work in the usual sense. The rest of his energy was spent in what could be considered extensions of his preaching: lecturing, writing, and editorial work. So effective was his communication that his preaching came to be regarded as one of the tourist attractions of the metropolitan area that every visitor from this country or abroad had to experience.[53]

The impact of his proclamation was phenomenal, especially as he began to address social issues in general and slavery in particular.[54] He had been concerned about slavery during college, had tried to protect an abolitionist printer against mob action while in seminary, and had begun preaching against slavery in Indianapolis. But now Henry went so far as to raise money to provide rifles (the notorious "Beecher's Bibles") for antislavery settlers in Kansas. Abraham Lincoln is supposed to have greeted Henry's sister Harriet with the words: "So you're the little woman who wrote the book that started this great war!"[55] She and her brother were certainly among the most effective antislavery publicists.

Many at the time thought that Beecher's speaking tour in Britain was the main factor in dissuading the British from recognizing the Confederacy. President Lincoln invited him to be the speaker when the Union flag was raised again at Fort Sumter at the end of the war. After the war, his became an important voice on many issues disrupting the society, issues ranging from woman's rights to the acceptance of evolution. Although he remained a conservative on such questions as the accumulation of wealth and labor unions, he was nevertheless a forerunner of the Social Gospel preaching of Washington Gladden and Walter Rauschenbusch.

The most significant aspect of the preaching of Henry Ward Beecher is that pointed out by Clifford E. Clark Jr. Beecher was the public thinker who provided Americans with the words and ideas to negotiate their transition from a rural agricultural society to an urban industrial one. He was the one who articulated the ideals of American Victorian culture, and he did so by calling upon a core of Romantic Christian themes.

> As espoused by Beecher, romantic Christianity was a religion of the heart, an appeal to the feelings and emotions that replaced the cold, formalistic evangelical theology of the previous generation and accepted

the new theories of evolution and biblical criticism. Using the natural world as a source of inspiration, Beecher preached a new experiential Christianity that emphasized God's love for man and the availability of salvation for all. It was a cheerful and optimistic faith that gave people the confidence to attack vice and crime and encouraged them to work for a general reformation of society.[56]

This is to say that the significance of Beecher's preaching was that it furnished the thoughts and words from which a generation was able to construct their reality socially and thus to articulate for themselves the meaning of the new world in which they were living.[57] In many ways Beecher was like Lincoln: the attitudes of both men enabled them to win more support for their side than others who were closer to what was later to be called political correctness. Beecher had such a sensitive finger on the public's pulse that he seemed to know the exact moment when they were ready to arrive at a new understanding, and he stood ready to provide for them the words and concepts in which to phrase that understanding. If effective preaching is more a matter of getting people to see something in a new way than it is of stating what they ought to believe before they are willing to accept it, Henry Ward Beecher has to be regarded as one of the most effective preachers in American history.

Phillips Brooks

The influence of the third of the three *B*'s, Phillips Brooks (1835–93), was due entirely to his preaching and the impact of his personality through it. As one scholar noted, he "was not an ecclesiastical statesman, an energetic executive, or an adventurous missionary. He led no movement; he wrought no reforms; and except for his sermons and lectures he wrote no books."[58] Yet it would be hard to think of anyone else who has had as much influence on American preaching. Edgar De Witt Jones has said that Beecher and Brooks are "the two most written about preachers in America" and that their Beecher Lectures on Preaching at Yale are the series most often referred to by other lecturers.[59] One has the impression, however, that the long-term influence of Brooks has been greater than that of Beecher and that his lectures have been reprinted more regularly.[60] Certainly no homiletical mot is more quoted than Brooks's definition of *preaching* as "truth through personality."[61]

His life is quickly summarized because it appears as almost without incident. Born on December 13, 1835, he was the second of the six sons of his parents, both of whom came from old New England families. When he was four, the family changed its membership from a Congregational church that was too Unitarian for their orthodox taste to an evangelical Episcopal parish. Young Brooks went to Boston Latin School and received a thorough grounding in classical languages and then to Harvard, where he was known for writing effective prose.

Almost the only ripple ever to disturb his life's placid surface was connected with his first employment, teaching at the Latin School. He was an utter failure. Unable to maintain discipline, he resigned after only four months and spent the rest of the academic year in depression. By the end of the summer, however, he began to emerge from his gloom and started reading again, especially the English and German Romanticists. "In the midst of his discouragement, the English poet Percy Bysshe Shelley provided him with the kind of heroic defiance of adverse circumstances that he desperately needed."[62] Reading the Romantics was both therapy and a conversion of sorts. Even though he had not yet been confirmed, he enrolled that fall in the Virginia Theological Seminary.

Although Brooks's background was in the Evangelical wing of the Episcopal Church, which had founded the seminary in Alexandria, he was put off by much he found there. He thought his classmates used piety as an excuse to avoid intellectual effort, most of the faculty fell far below the standards of Harvard, and he found slavery abhorrent. Yet he settled in, studied hard on his own, began a lifelong habit of notebook keeping, completed the course, and was ordained to the diaconate in June 1859.

From the beginning, his preaching attracted large crowds. His first call was to the Church of the Advent in Philadelphia, but his success there led to his being called three years later to Holy Trinity in the same city, one of the largest Episcopal churches in the country—an extraordinary appointment for a young man of twenty-six. Even then his preaching was so impressive that it was reported in New York papers. Unlike Beecher, however, he was a devoted pastor. He loved his people—and indeed all people—and gave himself unstintingly to them. During the Civil War years, he ministered to the soldiers in their camps and hospitals as much as he could.

Then, after ten years in Philadelphia, he accepted a call back to Boston to Trinity, the old downtown church. There he remained as rector, preaching three times a week to a full church, for twenty-two years. Having resisted many prestigious calls to other parishes, to the episcopate, and to academic appointments, he agreed to become the bishop of his own diocese. His health held out in that office for only fifteen months. He died on January 23, 1893, deeply mourned by the whole city of Boston and by thousands all over the world who had been blessed by his ministry.

When Brooks was in seminary, his devout Evangelical mother wrote to him, warning against the theology of Horace Bushnell, saying that she would prefer that he never preach the gospel to his perverting it as Bushnell did.[63] She was to be disappointed, for both his theology and his homiletical method were to be closer to Bushnell's than to those of the clergy she admired.

While Brooks has been described as a liberal or a Broad Churchman, the Incarnation was nevertheless the center of his faith, and he had a passionate devotion to the Trinity. But he did accept evolution, finding that it strengthened rather than weakened his faith, and, while he did not put much emphasis on exegesis, he welcomed biblical criticism.

When he was elected to the episcopate, there were accusations of heresy leveled against him by Anglo-Catholics, and efforts were made to prevent his consecration, but today most of what he was charged with would be regarded merely as ecumenism. Although he valued it, he did not consider the threefold ministry of bishops, priests, and deacons to be of the *esse* of the church as the Anglo-Catholics claimed. Even in those days of more conservative theology, however, the necessary number of dioceses and bishops approved his candidacy and he was consecrated. These questions about his orthodoxy were the closest he ever came to being criticized publicly; otherwise, his reputation was without blemish.

Brooks's Beecher lectures on preaching are in some ways more of a spirituality of preaching than a how-to manual. The key is the principle enunciated in the first lecture that "preaching is the bringing of truth through personality."[64] "Personality" here does not so much have its modern sense of charm (as in the expression "He has a good personality") as it does of personhood. In other words, Brooks was as incarnational in his understanding of preaching as he was in his theology. Preaching is interpersonal communication, but it is even more the communication of the deepest truth embodied in the communicator. The preacher, therefore, must be a person who is totally alert in two directions—listening attentively to God and observing people as closely as possible—so that what God has to say to the people can be relayed to them in the most effective manner. For such preaching to occur, the "primary necessity" is "that the Christian preacher should be a Christian first" (16).

Since it is the personality of the preacher that mediates truth, the preacher's own person has to be considered. The work of the preacher is then attended under the heads of its nature, method, and spirit. The nature of the work is that one is at once a preacher and a pastor; one is also a leader. As disastrous as having no method in the work is having the wrong method, too small or narrow, a hobbyhorse that is ridden. "The first necessity for the preacher and the hod-carrier[65] is the same. Be faithful, and do your best always" (101). The preacher's work should be done in the spirit of a servant to one's parishioners, of one who never feels equal to the task, who is profoundly honest, and who is vitally alive.

This concern with the spirituality of the preacher carries over into the lecture on the idea of the sermon. The idea grows out of the purpose. "A sermon exists in and for its purpose. That purpose is the persuading and moving of men's souls" (110).[66] The lecture that sounds as though it will come nearest to nuts and bolts is that on the making of the sermon, but its concern, too, is loftier than that. When speaking of deciding upon a subject, Brooks says:

> Care not for your sermon, but for your truth, and for your people; and subjects will spring up on every side of you, and the chances to preach upon them will be all too few. (152)

Within that framework, factors in the choice of a subject should be the peculiar needs of the people, the symmetry and "scale" of all the preacher's preaching, and the bent of the preacher's inclination. Even in the discussion of style, the issues seem more moral than rhetorical.

In considering the congregation to which one preaches, Brooks calls attention to the categories of people who make it up, but says that sermons should be directed to those who are "earnest seekers after truth" (200). Next he notes special qualities of his age that affected the way one preached: what he calls a fatalism brought on by a scientific worldview, tolerance and relativism, not to mention commercialism, preoccupation with fashion, and sentimentalism. Another condition of preaching in that age was the changed status of the Bible. Evaluating the situation, he says: "While there have been many centuries in which it was easier, there has been none in which it was more interesting or inspiring for a man to preach" (254).

He was able to maintain this enthusiasm and even joy in his vocation because of his deep belief in the value of the human soul, which is the topic of the final lecture (**see Vol. 2, pp. 502-16**). Few passages ever written have this lecture's capacity to rekindle the ardor of a preacher's vocation. Rereading it annually on the anniversary of one's ordination would be a good addition to any cleric's rule of life.

How did the practice of Brooks's preaching match his theory? His power in the pulpit has been well described by one of his friends, an English scholar named James Bryce:

> There was no sign of art about his preaching, no touch of self-consciousness. He spoke to his audience as a man might speak to his friend,

pouring forth with swift, yet quiet and seldom impassioned earnestness the thoughts and feelings of his singularly pure and lofty spirit. The listeners never thought of style or manner, but only of the substance of the thoughts. They were entranced and carried out of themselves by the strength and sweetness and beauty of the aspects of religious truth and its helpfulness to weak human nature which he presented. There was a wealth of keen observation, fine reflection, and insight both subtle and imaginative, all touched with warmth and tenderness which seemed to transfuse and irradiate the thought itself.[67]

Small wonder that the day of Brooks's death, January 23, has been chosen by the Episcopal Church for inclusion as a day of optional commemoration in its calendar of saints' days and holy days.[68] Truth was brought through his personality.

CONCLUSION

A short summary of the characteristics of Romanticism noted at the beginning of the previous chapter follows:

1. A protest, in the name of freedom and dynamism, against the formalism and structure of neoclassicism, rationalism, and moral asceticism and discipline.
2. A stress on individuality that at times amounted almost to worship of originality and genius.
3. An exaltation of the immediacy of feeling "in the self, for humanity, and for the world," which involved vitalism and an aesthetic approach to nature.
4. A concern and feeling for history.
5. The dominance of the twin principles of plenitude (as opposed to the restriction of content by formal rules) and diversity (as opposed to uniformity and simplicity).

It would be tedious to parcel out this list of traits among the preachers of Britain and America who have exemplified some or all of them. Yet a simple review of the persons encountered should be enough to establish that a major tradition of proclamation of the Word was begun in Britain and America that can be understood only in the context of the Romantic movement. This is especially clear when we remember that the alternatives available at the time were either the rationalistic preaching of the latitudinarians or the "religion of the heart" preaching characteristic of the Evangelical Awakenings. Romantic preaching represents a new consciousness and a new style.

Its great German pioneer, Friedrich Schleiermacher, was both a foundational theoretician of the Romantic movement and a parish pastor and preacher. Samuel Coleridge, who, with William Wordsworth, began the English manifestation of Romanticism, was deeply interested in theology and, among other things, introduced historical-critical study of the Bible to the British Isles.

A necessary precondition for the development of a Romantic rhetoric was Nicolas Boileau's translation of Longinus's treatise *On the Sublime,* which claimed aesthetic experience to be as much a purpose of oratory as persuasion. The pre-Romantic rhetoricians, Hugh Blair, George Campbell, and Richard Whately, enunciated a homiletic that would be an appropriate medium for the new preaching when it appeared. In very different ways, John Henry Newman and Frederick Robertson, among the British, took full advantage of the opportunities this afforded for the expression of Christian faith in the vocabulary of the spirit of the new age.

In America, true Romantic preaching began earlier because of the Unitarians' openness to its spirit. William Channing anticipated this efflorescence, but it was seen in full blossom in the short pulpit ministry of Ralph Waldo Emerson and the longer ministry of Theodore Parker. The great orthodox theologian of Romanticism was Horace Bushnell, and his insights were given voice in the proclamation of his disciples, Henry Ward Beecher and Phillips Brooks.

Partly because of such products of Romanticism as biblical criticism, Protestant Christianity was about to separate into three main branches: (1) the liberal, which would become progressively more radical until it ceased to feel the need to be theistic (by far the smallest of the streams), (2) the critical orthodox, which would become "mainline," and (3) the conservative evangelical, which would be as large, if not as socially prominent, as the mainline. In the mainline, Romantic preaching would become the norm rather than the exception.

FOR FURTHER READING

Abbott, Lyman. *Henry Ward Beecher.* Boston: Houghton Mifflin, 1903. Reprint, with introduction by William G. McLoughlin, New York: Chelsea House, 1980.
Brooks, Phillips. *Lectures on Preaching: The Yale Lectures on Preaching,*

1877. Edited by Ralph G. Turnbull. New York: E. P. Dutton, 1907. Reprint, Grand Rapids, Mich.: Baker, 1969, 1981.

Commager, Henry Steele. *Theodore Parker.* Boston: Little, Brown, 1936.

Horace Bushnell: Sermons. Edited with introduction by Conrad Cherry. Sources of American Spirituality. NewYork: Paulist, 1985.

Mott, Wesley T. *"The Strains of Eloquence": Emerson and His Sermons.* University Park: Pennsylvania State University Press, 1989.

William Ellery Channing: Selected Writings. Edited by David Robinson. Sources of American Spirituality. New York: Paulist, 1985.

Notes

1. William R. Hutchinson, *The Modernist Impulse in American Protestantism* (Cambridge: Harvard University Press, 1976), 14.

2. The sermon has been reprinted often; the edition consulted was in *William Ellery Channing: Selected Writings,* ed. David Robinson, Sources of American Spirituality (New York: Paulist, 1985), 70-102.

3. Van Wyck Brooks, *The Flowering of New England 1815–1865* (New York: E. P. Dutton, 1937), 104.

4. Robinson, ed., *William Ellery Channing,* 6.

5. Ibid., 31.

6. William Ellery's brother, Edward T. Channing, was professor of rhetoric at Harvard and is one of the American teachers whose textbooks were based on the New Rhetoric of Blair, Campbell, and Whately (Nan Johnson, *Nineteenth-Century Rhetoric in North America* [Carbondale: Southern Illinois University Press, 1991], 70 passim). His pupils included the great writers of the period, many of whom gave him credit for teaching them their craft. Brooks, *The Flowering of New England,* 43.

7. This moral criticism of the results of preaching Calvinism may be seen all through "Unitarian Christianity." The following example, however, is sufficient to make the position clear: "(This religious system) tends to discourage the timid, to give excuses to the bad, to feed the vanity of the fanatical, and to offer shelter to the bad feelings of the malignant. By shocking, as it does, the fundamental principles of morality, and by exhibiting a severe and partial Deity, it tends strongly to pervert the moral faculty, to form a gloomy, forbidding, and servile religion, and to lead men to substitute censoriousness, bitterness, and persecution, for a tender and impartial charity" (Robinson, *William Ellery Channing,* 89-90).

8. Channing's homiletical strategy changed over the years as he strove to make his own preaching more effective in enabling the moral development of members of his congregation. Teresa Toulouse, *The Art of Prophesying: New England Sermons and the Shaping of Belief* (Athens: University of Georgia Press, 1987), 75-117.

9. Ralph Waldo Emerson, *Journals and Miscellaneous Notebooks,* 2:242, 238, as quoted by Wesley T. Mott, *"The Strains of Eloquence": Emerson and His Sermons* (University Park: Pennsylvania State University Press, 1989), 4-5. Mott's interpretation of Emerson's preaching is generally consistent with that of Toulouse, *The Art of*

Prophesying, 118-84. The following account also draws on David M. Robinson, "The Sermons of Ralph Waldo Emerson: An Introductory Historical Essay," in *The Complete Sermons of Ralph Waldo Emerson* (Columbia: University of Missouri Press, 1989), 1:1-32. Albert J. von Frank edited vol. 1; Toulouse and Mott edited other volumes.

10. Both Increase and Cotton Mather were numbered among its earlier ministers.

11. He was then ordained the following March 11.

12. "Emerson's resignation of his only full-time pastorate in October 1832 has been seen as a sloughing off of religious orthodoxy and stifling convention." Mott, *"The Strains of Eloquence,"* 2.

13. Emerson, *Journals and Miscellaneous Notebooks,* 4:363-64, quoted in Toulouse, *The Art of Prophesying,* 119. Most of what follows is an attempt to summarize her understanding of Emerson's preaching.

14. "That part of the mind which takes in, classifies, divides, and arranges sensuous information" (ibid., 123).

15. Ibid.

16. Ibid., 125.

17. Ibid., 144.

18. Ibid., 145.

19. Ibid., 148-75. Toulouse analyzes four of Emerson's sermons—his first, two from the middle of his ministry, and his last at Second Church—to show his developing understanding of the preacher's task.

20. R. C. Albrect, *Theodore Parker,* Twayne's United States Authors Series, no. 179 (New York: Twayne, 1971), 17.

21. His personal library would number twenty-five thousand volumes.

22. "The Transient and the Permanent," in *Theodore Parker: American Transcendentalist: A Critical Essay and a Collection of his Writings,* ed. Robert E. Collins (Meteuchen, N.J.: Scarecrow, 1973), 88.

23. "Transcendentalism" (ibid., 70).

24. Brooks, *The Flowering of New England,* 73-88 passim.

25. The list comes from a report he wrote to his congregation after ill health forced his retirement, *Theodore Parker's Experience as a Minister,* which has been preserved in several collections of his works. For citations, see Albrecht, *Theodore Parker,* 132, 148 n. 7.

26. See, for instance, Henry Steele Commager, *Theodore Parker* (Boston: Little, Brown, 1936), 120.

27. For an extended description of his preaching, see Commager, *Theodore Parker,* 115-20.

28. A form of this section appeared as "The Preaching of Romanticism in America," *ATQ: 19th C. American Literature and Culture* n.s. 14 (2000): 297-312.

29. See above, 526-29.

30. His sermon on "The Gentleness of God" tells how souls are led to conversion in a lifelong process of which they are hardly conscious at the time (*Horace Bushnell: Sermons,* ed. with intro. Conrad Cherry, Sources of American Spirituality [New York: Paulist, 1985], 148-62; reprinted from *Christ and His Salvation, In Sermons Variously Related Thereto* [New York: Scribner's, 1864], 28-50). The sermon could be autobiographical in detailing how Bushnell himself came to faith.

31. The two titles are set in quotation marks but not identified as to source by Sidney Ahlstrom, *A Religious History of the American People* (New Haven: Yale University Press, 1972), 610, 613.

32. Gardiner H. Shattuck Jr., "Bushnell, Horace," in *The Encyclopedia of American Religious History,* ed. Edward L. Queen II, Stephen R. Prothero, and Gardiner H. Shattuck Jr. (New York: Facts on File, 1996), 1:93.

33. H. Shelton Smith, *Horace Bushnell,* A Library of Protestant Thought (New York: Oxford University Press, 1965), 4-22. For the Channing sermon, see above, 625-26.

34. Apparently he was not completely successful in the beginning of his efforts to proclaim the traditional form of these doctrines. Ahlstrom, *A Religious History of the American People,* 611-12.

35. Quoted by Cherry in his introduction to *Horace Bushnell: Sermons,* 1. The reference is to *Aids to Reflection* (4th ed. of 1840; reprint, New York: Kennikat, 1971), 201.

36. On the publication history of Bushnell's writings on the subject, see Smith, *Horace Bushnell,* 376-78.

37. Quoted in ibid., 375, from "The Kingdom of God as a Grain of Mustard Seed," *New Englander* 2 (1844): 610. In nothing is Bushnell more Romantic than in his view of education. Jean-Jacques Rousseau, who has been called "the first major Romantic," revolutionized educational theory in his work of 1762, *Émile, ou de l'Éducation.* His protest, however, was against the corrupting effect of society and was a plea for bringing up children naturally. Bushnell was reacting against revivalism more than Enlightenment rationalism, but in his organic view of life and his emphasis on feeling he had much in common with Rousseau.

38. Cherry, *Horace Bushnell,* 4.

39. See the sermon "Religious Nature, and Religious Character," published in his *Sermons on Living Subjects* (New York: Scribner, Armstrong & Co., 1872), 129-47, and reprint, Cherry, *Horace Bushnell,* 26-37.

40. Gibbs, in turn, learned this from Schleiermacher's friend, Karl Ferdinand Becker.

41. Cherry, *Horace Bushnell,* 10.

42. Ibid., 12.

43. In ibid., 119-33 (the quotation is from p. 119); reprint from *Sermons for the New Life* (New York: Scribner, Armstrong & Co., 1873), 304-25.

44. Ibid., 123.

45. Ibid., 129.

46. See above, 507-9.

47. Eleven years after the birth and the death of Bushnell.

48. See Clifford E. Clark Jr., *Henry Ward Beecher: Spokesman for Middle-Class America* (Urbana: University of Illinois Press, 1978), 81-86, for a comparison of the theologies of the two.

49. For information about this remarkable family, see Joan D. Hedrick, *Harriet Beecher Stowe: A Life* (New York: Oxford University Press, 1994). Harriet was Henry's next oldest and his closest sibling.

50. The training he received in preparatory school was in the tradition of the

elocutionary movement, which stressed vocal exercises and gesture. The vocal exercises meant both that he had great nuance of expression and that he knew how to use his voice without straining it. He drilled himself so in gesture that as an adult he never had to think about it, doing automatically what would best communicate his point. See the hagiographic but informative biography by his successor at Plymouth Church, Lyman Abbott, *Henry Ward Beecher* (Boston: Houghton Mifflin, 1903; reprint, with intro. William G. McLoughlin, New York: Chelsea House, 1980), 104-5.

51. His editorial activity had begun in Cincinnati, but in Indianapolis he edited the agricultural section of the *Indiana Journal*, "The Western Farmer and Gardener," displaying a Romantic interest in nature that stayed with him all his life (ibid., 328).

52. Ibid., xvi.

53. An indication of how well known he became and remained is a limerick that puns on his name:

> A great Congregational preacher
> Said, "The hen is an elegant creature."
> > The hen, liking that,
> > Laid an egg in his hat
> And thus did the hen reward Beecher.

54. So great was his popularity that his reputation survived both civil and ecclesiastical trials over the charge that he committed adultery with the wife of Theodore Tilton, one of his supporters. Beecher was acquitted in the church trial, but the civil jury was unable to agree, although a majority of them considered him innocent. Nevertheless, many since have believed that he was guilty. Some writers have enjoyed capitalizing on the sensational aspects of the trial of so famous a preacher for actions inconsistent with his profession; a case in point is Robert Shaplen, *Free Love and Heavenly Sinners: The Story of the Great Henry Ward Beecher Scandal* (London: Andre Deutsch, 1956).

55. Hedrick, *Harriet Beecher Stowe*, vii.

56. Clark, *Henry Ward Beecher*, 4. The book that follows is essentially Clark's development of this thesis.

57. That being the case, there is little need to detail the specifics of his homiletical technique. That task has been performed often enough, however, first by Beecher himself. One of Henry's church members endowed what has become the most prestigious series of lectures on homiletics in the country, the Beecher Lectures at Yale, in honor of Beecher's father. Henry himself gave the first three sets, although only the first dealt with preaching. He published these as *Yale Lectures on Preaching* (Boston: Pilgrim, 1874). A good summary of them is given by Abbott, *Henry Ward Beecher*, 353-73. Lionel G. Crocker has published two books on Beecher's homiletics: *Henry Ward Beecher's Art of Preaching* (Chicago: University of Chicago Press, 1934), and *Henry Ward Beecher's Speaking Art* (New York: Fleming H. Revell, 1937). Finally, Halford R. Ryan has written *Henry Ward Beecher: Peripatetic Preacher*, Great American Orators, no. 5 (New York: Greenwood, 1990). Ryan's knowledge of the history of oratory is greater than his familiarity with church history and theology, and thus he often misses the point.

58. James Thayer Addison, *The Episcopal Church in the United States, 1789–1931* (New York: Scribner's, 1951), 262.

59. Edgar De Witt Jones, *The Royalty of the Pulpit: A Survey and Appreciation of the Lyman Beecher Lectures on Preaching Founded at Yale Divinity School 1871 and Given Annually (with Four Exceptions) Since 1872* (New York: Harper & Brothers, 1951), 19.

60. The edition consulted was Phillips Brooks, *Lectures on Preaching: The Yale Lectures on Preaching, 1877,* ed. Ralph G. Turnbull (New York: E. P. Dutton, 1907; reprint, Grand Rapids, Mich.: Baker, 1969, 1981).

61. Ibid., 5.

62. John F. Woolverton, *The Education of Phillips Brooks* (Urbana: University of Illinois Press, 1995), 53. The classical biography is Alexander V. G. Allen, *Life and Letters of Phillips Brooks,* 2 vols. (New York: E. P. Dutton, 1900). The standard modern biography is Raymond W. Albright, *Focus on Infinity: A Life of Phillips Brooks* (New York: Macmillan, 1961).

63. Her letter of November 27, 1864, quoted in Albright, *Focus on Infinity,* 106.

64. Brooks, *Lectures on Preaching,* 5. Hereafter, references to this work will be given parenthetically in the text by page number alone.

65. A menial laborer on construction sites at the time whose duty was to carry bricks and mortar to those who would use them.

66. Brooks obviously lived in an age when it was thought that masculine terms could be generic and therefore inclusive.

67. James Bryce, quoted in Addison, *The Episcopal Church in the United States, 1789–1931,* 267.

68. *The Book of Common Prayer and the Administration of the Sacraments and Other Rites and Ceremonies of the Church Together with the Psalter or Psalms of David According to the Use of the Episcopal Church* (New York: Church Hymnal Corp. and Seabury Press, 1979), 19. Cf. *The Proper for the Lesser Feasts and Fasts, Together with the Fixed Holy Days,* 4th ed. (New York: Church Hymnal Corporation, 1988), 130-31.

CHAPTER 24

THE TRIUMPH OF ROMANTICISM

THE SOCIAL GOSPEL

The Romantic preaching of liberal orthodoxy helped American Protestants to adjust to the great social change of the years after the Civil War, that of moving from an agricultural to an industrial society. Horace Bushnell, Henry Ward Beecher, and Phillips Brooks all were concerned with the social problems they saw, such as slavery and the status of women, but they were too involved in the rise of middle-class Victorian culture and an urban, industrial economy to identify the characteristic evils they entailed.[1] It remained for the next two generations of preachers to help their congregations understand that these new social and economic arrangements had spawned human suffering that Christian conscience could not tolerate. This preaching was to manifest a number of continuing Romantic emphases and outgrowths, including concern for the common people, the influence of German philosophy and theology, historical-critical biblical interpretation, and evolutionary thought.

A group of clergy and social scientists, who came to be known collectively as the "Social Gospel" movement, called attention to the moral crises brought on by the industrial revolution. Charles Howard Hopkins has chronicled the movement from 1865 to 1915, dividing the time into four periods that are characterized as stages in a person's life: birth, youth, coming of age, and maturity.[2] Birth (1865–80) was a time of vague awakenings; youth (1880–90) a period of discussion rather than action, for lack of a well-developed sociology; the coming of age (1890–1900) saw action being taken in the formation of organizations and founding of periodicals; and maturation (1900–15) involved both a theoretical grounding of the movement and its incorporation into the mainstream of American Protestant life, accomplished through denominational agencies committed to its cause and the organization, largely around social concerns, of the Federal Council of Churches.

Washington Gladden

For the purposes of the history of preaching, the first three stages can be seen in the life of one man, Washington Gladden, and the last stage in the life of another, Walter Rauschenbusch.[3]

Gladden[4] (1836–1918) is deservedly known as the "father of the Social Gospel." Orphaned at an early age, he grew up on an uncle's farm near Oswego, New York, where he helped with the chores and acquired a good but irregular basic education. He was apprenticed to a local newspaper publisher when he was sixteen, but became attracted to the ministry and prepared for it through study at Oswego Academy and Williams College. Immediately after college he taught school and privately studied theology. He was called to a small Congregational church in Brooklyn and was ordained on November 15, 1860.

Like most of the Romantic preachers studied above, he had a nervous breakdown. He resigned his church but was soon called to another in suburban Morrisania, New York, where he was able to recuperate, attend lectures at Union, and read Frederick Robertson and Horace Bushnell, thus acquiring the theological perspective from which his life's work would be done.

That work began, in a sense, when he was called to a church in North Adams, Massachusetts, where he witnessed the tension between capital and labor. After serving in North Adams for five years, he became religious editor of the *Independent,* a leading newspaper of the time, and participated in the paper's crusade against the Tweed Ring in New York.[5]

Returning to the pastorate in 1875, he went to North Church in Springfield, Massachusetts. When an economic depression led to wide-scale unemployment, Gladden tried to speak to the problem in addresses, first to workers in Springfield and then to the employers. The series of lectures so begun was published as *Working People and Their Employers,* the first of his thirty-eight books.[6]

In 1882 he accepted a call to First Congregational Church in Columbus, Ohio, a position in which he remained until his retirement in 1914. There he became one of the best-known clerics in the country and was widely invited to speak at important events. He was, for instance, twice the Beecher lecturer at Yale.

Most of his fame came through his many books, but these, in turn, were by-products of his preaching. He said in his *Recollections,*[7] "Of the thirty-one volumes [as of then] of which the encyclopedias accuse me, all but six have gone through my pulpit, and are printed as they were preached, with almost no revision."[8]

Gladden's pulpit practice is responsible for an unusual twist to his pioneering Social Gospel preaching.[9] His Sunday morning sermons were fairly ordinary, preached on biblical texts and devoted to issues of personal religion. On Sunday and Wednesday evenings, however, he would lecture on a wider range of topics, usually not starting from Holy Scripture, but "keeping the discussion close to the issues of life and character."[10]

Although the Sunday morning sermons were by no means devoid of reference to the social issues of the day, it was in the evening lectures that he dealt most explicitly and fully with the problems of an industrial society. It could be argued that these discourses were not sermons in a strict sense, lacking a scriptural base, but they were proclaimed from the pulpit, and it is obvious that Gladden considered them all part of the same work.

"Thy Kingdom Come," in a series on the Lord's Prayer, is an example of a Sunday morning sermon that includes Christian social teaching (**see Vol. 2, pp. 517-25**).[11] In this sermon, he is able to take the standard Social Gospel position that the kingdom of God is to come on earth as a perfect social order. "When we intelligently offer this petition, then, we are asking for nothing less than this—that the light and love and power of God may increase and abound everywhere in the world."[12]

The petition is seen as not being confined to Christian countries, and it is answered wherever attention is paid to the needs of women, prisoners, the insane, and slaves. He ends this exposition of the meaning of the Lord's Prayer, as he understands it, with a personal challenge to his hearers:

> You pray that the Kingdom of God may come? Do you want it to come
> to Massachusetts? Do you desire that it should come to Springfield? Do
> you wish to have it come to your store, your office, your shop, your

study, your table, your toilet, your closet, your heart? How near to you do you desire that the Kingdom of God should come?[13]

The lectures are very different, in that they do not explain a biblical passage nor apply it to the lives of the congregation, and they are what the name implies: expository speeches that inform their audience about an issue. A case in point is the lecture on "Labor and Capital," given to the working men of Springfield and included in *Working People and Their Employers*, which talks of the three different systems by which capital and labor have been brought together—slavery, wages, or cooperation—with a recommendation of cooperation as the Christian ideal.[14] But even this lecture is from the perspective of Christian theology and ends with an appeal to its audience:

> The power that has stricken the shackles from the laborer, that has lightened his burdens, that has lifted him up to a happier and nobler life, and that has put into his hands the key of a great future, is the power that came into the world when Christ was born.[15]

This shows that even the lectures have a right to be considered as sermons proclaiming the Social Gospel. Thus Gladden appears to have devised a new genre of Christian preaching.

Walter Rauschenbusch

While most of Gladden's ministry was as a parish pastor and much of his self-identity was tied up in preaching,[16] the other great spirit of the movement spent only eleven years in parochial ministry as a regular preacher to a congregation. For most of his professional life, Walter Rauschenbusch (1861–1918) was a member of a seminary faculty, doing the work that entitles him to be known as "the theologian of the Social Gospel." His father was a German pastor who came to this country as a Lutheran missionary, but later changed to Baptist views and ministry and went on to teach at Rochester Theological Seminary. His father also had a drinking problem, which in 1864 caused his mother to take young Walter and two sisters back to Germany for four years.[17]

Indeed, the German connection was to be very important for him. After high school he completed the classics course in the Gymnasium in Gütersloh. Then in 1891 he took a leave from his church to study social movements in England and the New Testament in Germany. His seminary training after the Gymnasium and before ordination was in the German department of Rochester.

His parochial ministry was served in a German Baptist church in the "Hell's Kitchen" area of New York City, a neighborhood where he became an eyewitness of "the terrible human effects of insecurity, unemployment, poverty, wretched housing, malnutrition, disease, ignorance, and crime."[18] In 1897 he returned to Rochester as a member of the faculty, first in the German department and then in the English, a position he held until his death.

In response to the conditions around him when he was a pastor, Rauschenbusch became involved in studying the social situation to see how it could be ameliorated. He became active in the campaign to elect Henry George, the single-tax theorist, as mayor of New York. In 1889 he tried to start a newspaper for working people.

Most of all, though, he tried to find a basis for Christian ministry that was not just interested in saving people's souls, but was concerned for their bodies as well. This he eventually found, with the help of Horace Bushnell, Friedrich Ritschl, Julius Wellhausen, and Adolf Harnack, in the ethical teaching of Jesus:

> When the kingdom of God dominated our landscape, the perspective of life shifted into a new alignment. I felt a new security in my social impulses. . . . I found that this new conception of the purpose of Christianity was strangely satisfying. It responded to all the old and all the new elements of my religious life. The saving of the lost, the teaching of the young, the pastoral care of the poor and frail, the quickening of starved intellects, the study of the Bible, church union, political reform, the reorganization of the industrial system, international peace—it was all covered by the one aim of the reign of God on earth.[19]

While it would be interesting to trace the development of Rauschenbusch's theology,[20] the present purpose is to look at his preaching, most of which occurred before his thought became so theoretical. Until recently it has been hard to study that preaching, because Rauschenbusch published no volumes of sermons and did not even leave complete or easily legible manuscripts. Instead, he left sermon notes that were partly in German and partly in shorthand. Fortunately, eight sets of these notes for sermons on social topics were deciphered and translated by Robert Payne and Clyde Fant Jr. for the section on Rauschenbusch in *20 Centuries of Great Preaching*.[21]

Even these notes, however, are not entirely for sermons preached to his congregation, and some sound more like Gladden's "lectures" than sermons based upon Scripture. For instance, the set on "The Kingdom of God in the Parables of Jesus" (146-54), while an excellent exegetical study from the perspective of the time, was written as a study for the Brotherhood of the Kingdom, a fellowship of socially involved Baptist clergy that was an important support group for Rauschenbusch. Although "The Social Problem, Our Problem" (154-57) gives the first chapter of Isaiah as a text, the passage is referred to only obliquely in the course of this address concerning poverty. Instead, Rauschenbusch calls upon his audience to overthrow poverty by the abolition of privilege and by association (Christian and Socialist). The methods recommended are thought and agitation. "Peace" (158-62) also lists a text, but it is an address given to the International Peace Conference.[22]

There are, however, several sermons for his congregation that show both traditional sermonic structure and concern for social issues. An example is "The Kingship of Christ" (162-64), which is organized by a series of questions about the title of "King" offered to Jesus. Words from the text (Matt. 28:18-20) are given as answers to the questions:

1. Did Jesus claim the title? Yes, *"to me is given all power in heaven and earth."*
2. "Has he an army and ministers to present and enforce his claims? Yes, '*Go ye.*'"
3. "What are the weapons of warfare? *Teach.*"
4. "The extent of the Kingdom. *All nations.*"
5. "Is there a badge of citizenship? *Baptizing them.*"
6. "Is there a law in this kingdom? *All things whatsoever I commanded you.*"
7. "Has it glory and splendor like other kingdoms? Yes, *Lo, I am with you.*"
8. "How long shall it endure?" ... "*Always, unto the end of the world.*"

Rauschenbusch's empathy with his congregation comes out clearly in the introduction to his sermon on "The New Jerusalem":

We have met together as a band of brothers after a week of toil, weariness, and failing, as an army rallies after one assault to prepare for the next. We have felt weak and starved; we have come to take the bread of life, to have peace and love, and faith, and a brighter hope. It is hope that beckons us on. (164)

Such preaching in a hellish environment must have sounded like good news indeed.

The preachers of the Social Gospel have been criticized by later generations for a number of shortcomings,[23] one of which is that they concentrated only on labor issues and did not deal with the whole range of problems besetting the society, especially issues of race. The only reply that can be made is that the preachers were aware of most of these problems and spoke out about them, but they concentrated upon what seemed the most pressing issue of their time.

More subtly, Janet Forsythe Fishburn has pointed to a number of paradoxes involved in the movement. The major one, she says, is that the Social Gospel

> differs so little from the evangelical piety that Rauschenbusch so disdained in the "conservative" evangelical. Although the social gospel was theoretically the application of humanitarian concern to the social order, in practice the salvation of the social order depended on the influence of individual Christians as the primary mode of evangelism. This was not significantly different from the practice and methods of the conservative evangelical tradition.[24]

This is probably only what was to be expected, since so much of Christian concern with social issues was an outgrowth of the Second Great Awakening, as Timothy Smith pointed out.[25] It also reflects the difficulties Hopkins pointed to in his periodization of the Social Gospel movement.[26] Seeing a need and devising a strategy for meeting it are two very different activities. But both preaching and writing are aimed at the individual member of the audience; they can persuade only one at a time. The hope is that enough will be enlisted in a cause to constitute a group that can effect change. While the civil rights movement of the 1960s and 1970s became much more sophisticated about how change is effected in society, it, too, found social evil to be far less tractable than it had anticipated. "This kind goeth not out but by prayer and fasting" (Matt. 17:21 KJV)—if even then. But the cause of the kingdom—understood either eschatologically or socially—has always depended upon "the foolishness of preaching" (1 Cor. 1:21 KJV). As Rauschenbusch said, teaching is the only weapon in our warfare.

THE ROMANTIC BECOMES ORDINARY: JOHN A. BROADUS

The Social Gospel movement lasted until World War I, but long before that Romantic preaching had become the rule rather than the exception.

654

This may be seen in a textbook published in 1870 that was to be revised and remain the standard work in the field for more than a century: *A Treatise on the Preparation and Delivery of Sermons* by John A. Broadus.[27]

Almost as informative on the triumph of Romanticism in preaching as a look at this book would be a glance at the life of its remarkable author. Broadus was born in 1827 on a farm in Virginia, where he grew up and helped his father. A major in the county militia and for many years a member of the state legislature,[28] his father had made some bad investments that reduced the family's resources. Yet so great was his commitment to his talented son that he took a position as the steward for boarding state students at the University of Virginia to enable his son to continue his education there.

The university was one of the best in the country at the time, and John stayed on to receive an M.A. in 1850, becoming an excellent classicist and all-around scholar. He also married the daughter of the chair of the faculty. Although he had already begun to receive the invitations to teach at institutions of higher education that would continue throughout his life, he had answered the call to preach. Since seminary training was unavailable, he spent a year as tutor in a private household so that he could study theology on his own.

He was called back to Charlottesville to become pastor of the Baptist church there. The university asked him to teach, as well, and he stayed for eight years, proving effective in various combinations of parochial and university positions. In him, the scholar and the minister were always to be deeply connected. He was finally prevailed upon in 1859 to become one of four learned young clergy to found the Southern Baptist Theological Seminary at Greenville, South Carolina. His teaching responsibilities were in the areas of New Testament and homiletics. The recognition he had already received as a rising scholar was indicated in the two honorary doctorates bestowed upon him at the time, one from William and Mary.

The seminary was just getting started when the Civil War broke out. Although Broadus opposed secession, he did support the Southern cause when hostilities came and even served as a missionary to Confederate troops, winning the admiration of Stonewall Jackson and Robert E. Lee. Meanwhile, it was a struggle to keep the seminary going and his family fed. After the seminary closed in 1862, Broadus supported his family by preaching every Sunday at several small Baptist churches.

Reconstruction was hard on the seminary, but it did get going again. During the first term, which began November 1, 1865, Broadus had only one student in homiletics and that one blind, but the professor gave him his conscientious best, which seemed his only standard for performing any duty. The result of this course was the lectures that became his textbook.

The heroic efforts he had been required to make for so long weakened his health, and in 1870 he was forced, like many other preachers in this period, to travel for the benefit to his health. He spent a year in Britain, Europe, and the Middle East, seeing the sights and making firsthand acquaintance with scholars he had previously known only through correspondence and exchange of writings. In 1877 the seminary moved to Louisville, where it has remained and flourished. When his dear friend James P. Boyce died in 1889, Broadus succeeded him in the seminary's presidency, remaining in that office until his own death in 1895.

Broadus and his friends gave their lives for the seminary, turning down flattering offers elsewhere in order to see that Southern Baptist theological education got off to a good start. Broadus himself was offered the presidencies of Chicago University,[29] Brown University, and Crozer Seminary, as well as teaching positions on many faculties, some of them very prestigious.

During his lifetime, Broadus was more famous as a New Testament scholar than as a homiletician. His best-known work in that field is a commentary on Matthew, but he wrote many articles and was also involved in biblical translation revision and the International Sunday School lessons. Philip Schaff invited him to contribute to the first series of *Nicene and Post-Nicene Fathers* by revising and supplying additional notes for the Oxford translation of Chrysostom's homilies on Philippians, Colossians, and Thessalonians.[30]

Yet he was much in demand as a preacher, supplying in prominent eastern and northern pulpits in the summer, and being invited to preach on significant occasions at churches, universities, and seminaries. His Beecher lectures at Yale were given in 1889, almost twenty years after *A Treatise on the Preparation and Delivery of Sermons* was published. They were given from notes—Broadus's characteristic method of preaching and lecturing—and never published, although E. C. Dargan did integrate much from them into the second edition of the textbook. The five lectures on the history of preaching that Broadus gave at Newton Theological Seminary in 1876 were published, however—after his children copied them with his corrections.[31]

For one who came from a rural area, received all his formal education near to home, served but one church full time, and taught only in a new and struggling seminary of a denomination that was not yet known for its scholarship,[32] his international fame and respect are remarkable.

The claim that *A Treatise on the Preparation and Delivery of Sermons* inculcates a Romantic homiletic can be first established negatively by saying that it does not commend either the rationalistic preaching of the latitudinarians or the emotional preaching of the revivalists. The positive case, however, is to be made on the basis of the book's treatment of imagination.

When Broadus comes to discuss "Application," he says that it is not enough to convince people or to let them see that the message applies to them; they must also be persuaded. And persuasion is largely a matter of supplying them with motives for acting as the preacher recommends (232).[33] Yet

> so mighty is the opposition which the gospel encounters in human nature, so averse is the natural heart to the obedience of faith, so powerful are the temptations of life, that we must arouse men to intense earnestness and often to impassioned emotion, if we would bring them to surmount all obstacles, and to conquer the world, the flesh, and the devil. (235)

How are people so aroused? "In order to excite any passions by speech, we have to operate chiefly through the *imagination*" (238). Thus Broadus includes a section on imagination in its relation to eloquence, which deals not only with the many high uses of imagination but also with how it is to be acquired (395-405) (see **Vol. 2, pp. 526-32**). This section ends his treatment of the preparation of sermons as such. The rest of the book is devoted to delivery and conducting public worship. But to end with imagination is to end in Romantic territory. Romantic preaching has become the norm rather than the eccentricity of a few.

FOR FURTHER READING

Broadus, John A. *A Treatise on the Preparation and Delivery of Sermons*. Philadelphia: Smith, English & Co.; New York: Sheldon & Co., 1870.

Gladden, Washington. *Recollections: An Autobiography*. Boston: Houghton, Mifflin & Co., 1909.

_____. *The Lord's Prayer: Seven Homilies*. Boston: Houghton, Mifflin & Co., 1881.

Robertson, A. T. *Life and Letters of John Albert Broadus*. Philadelphia: American Baptist Publication Society, 1910.

*The Social Gospel in America 1870–1920: Gladden, Ely,
Rauschenbusch.* Edited by Robert T. Handy. A Library of
Protestant Thought. New York: Oxford University Press, 1966.
"Walter Rauschenbusch, 1861–1918." In *20 Centuries of Great
Preaching.* Edited by Clyde E. Fant Jr. and Walter M. Pinson Jr.,
7:125-72. Waco, Tex.: Word, 1971.

Notes

1. For a picture of the challenges to faith arising in the last third of the nineteenth century, see Paul A. Carter, *The Spiritual Crisis of the Gilded Age* (DeKalb: Northern Illinois University Press, 1971).

2. Charles Howard Hopkins, *The Rise of the Social Gospel in American Protestantism 1865–1915*, Yale Studies in Religious Education, no. 14 (New Haven: Yale University Press, 1940). For an interesting attempt to set the movement in a wider cultural context, see Janet Forsythe Fishburn, *The Fatherhood of God and the Victorian Family: The Social Gospel in America* (Philadelphia: Fortress, 1981).

3. Gaius Glenn Atkins said these two "did more between them to direct the mind of the churches toward the social problem than any of their contemporaries" (*Religion in Our Times* [New York, 1931], quoted in *The Social Gospel in America 1870–1920: Gladden, Ely, Rauschenbusch,* ed. Robert T. Handy, A Library of Protestant Thought [New York: Oxford University Press, 1966], 15).

4. His first name, Solomon, is seldom used in references to him.

5. A notoriously corrupt group of political leaders in New York City in the third quarter of the nineteenth century headed by William M. "Boss" Tweed.

6. Washington Gladden, *Working People and Their Employers* (Boston: Houghton, Mifflin & Co., 1876); in Handy, *The Social Gospel in America 1870–1920,* 38-48.

7. Washington Gladden, *Recollections: An Autobiography* (Boston: Houghton, Mifflin & Co., 1909).

8. Quoted in Handy, *The Social Gospel in America 1870–1920,* 24.

9. While Gladden epitomizes the movement during this period, he was by no means its sole representative. For a much fuller list, see the names cited by Hopkins in the various stages of *The Rise of the Social Gospel in American Protestantism 1865–1915.*

10. Gladden, *Recollections,* 411.

11. Washington Gladden, *The Lord's Prayer: Seven Homilies* (Boston: Houghton, Mifflin & Co., 1881), 59-81.

12. Ibid., 64. This was before Johannes Weiss and Albert Schweitzer demonstrated the eschatological nature of the term in the teaching of Jesus.

13. Ibid., 80-81.

14. Washington Gladden, *Working People and Their Employers* (Boston: Houghton, Mifflin & Co., 1876), 30-51; in Handy, *The Social Gospel in America 1870–1920,* 38-48.

15. Ibid., 48.

16. Fant and Pinson, *20 Centuries of Great Preaching,* 6:181, quotes him as saying: "I have never tried to do anything else but preach. I have no other ambition."

17. Fishburn, *The Fatherhood of God and the Victorian Family,* 8.

18. Handy, *The Social Gospel in America 1870–1920,* 254.

19. Walter Rauschenbusch, *Christianizing the Social Order* (New York: Macmillan, 1912), 93, quoted in Handy, *The Social Gospel in America 1870–1920,* 255-56.

20. For the development of his theology, see Hopkins, *The Rise of the Social Gospel in American Protestantism 1865–1915,* 215-44.

21. Robert Payne and Clyde Fant Jr., "Walter Rauschenbusch, 1861–1918," in *20 Centuries of Great Preaching,* ed. Clyde E. Fant Jr. and William J. Pinson Jr. (Waco, Tex.: Word, 1971), 7:125-72.

22. This, the only sermon preached at the conference, is printed in full from a newspaper account instead of being mere notes.

23. For an evaluation of the accomplishments of the moment that is extremely nuanced for the time in which it was written (1940), see Hopkins, *The Rise of the Social Gospel in Protestantism 1865–1915,* 318-27.

24. Fishburn, *The Fatherhood of God and the Victorian Family,* 166.

25. See above, 526-29.

26. See above, 648-49.

27. John A. Broadus, *A Treatise on the Preparation and Delivery of Sermons* (Philadelphia: Smith, English & Co.; New York: Sheldon & Co., 1870). The first revision was made in 1897 according to the intentions of the author by his colleague, the noted historian of preaching, E. C. Dargan. The next revision was not made until 1943, this one by J. B. Witherspoon, who still was able to consult a daughter of Dr. Broadus. Vernon L. Stanfield revised the fourth edition in 1979. Dargan could say of the first edition that it had gone through twenty-two printings in this country and two in England, was used in English as a textbook in Japan, and was translated to be used in China and again to be used in Brazil (Dargan's preface to the 2nd ed. as reprinted in Stanfield's 4th ed., xvii).

28. A critical biography of Broadus is badly needed. The standard work is still the original: A. T. Robertson, *Life and Letters of John Albert Broadus* (Philadelphia: American Baptist Publication Society, 1910). While the genre of "life and letters" was popular at the time and could produce good results, as in the case of Stopford A. Brooke's treatment of Frederick Robertson (above, 608-17), this Robertson did not provide enough context for letters to enable the reader to understand what they were about. A good condensation of the *Life and Letters* is given in Fant and Pinson, *20 Centuries of Great Preaching,* 5:43-59.

29. An earlier institution than the University of Chicago, which did not incorporate until 1892. Broadus, however, was known and admired by both William Rainey Harper, the first president of the University of Chicago, and John D. Rockefeller, who endowed it.

30. *NPNF*[1] 13:v-vii. Broadus also provided a short essay on "St. Chrysostom as a Homilist" as a preface to the volume.

31. Robertson, *Life and Letters of John Albert Broadus,* 300.

32. It could be argued now, however, that no other seminary has made quite the contribution to homiletics that Southern Baptist at Louisville has.

33. Broadus, *A Treatise on the Preparation and Delivery of Sermons.* Page numbers cited parenthetically are to the first edition of 1870.

PART V

THE CENTURY OF CHANGE

CHAPTER 25

PASTORAL COUNSELING THROUGH PREACHING

THE LULL BEFORE THE STORM

The twentieth century seems to have seen more changes than most previous centuries put together. In the same way, there has been greater variety in the kinds of preaching developed during these recent decades than appeared in all previous periods. The homily, after all, was nearly the only form available for well over half the Christian era, and the thematic sermon was the only other major development before the Reformation. During the era of Renaissance and Reformation there was a great deal of homiletical creativity, but since then most efforts could be subsumed under the categories of rationalistic, revivalistic, and Romantic preaching. The trends treated in this section, therefore, should lead readers to conclude that preachers during the late-twentieth century tried to accomplish a greater variety of things through their sermons than any of their predecessors attempted.

Yet this creativity was not evenly distributed throughout the century and was by no means evident in the beginning. One way of showing this is to look at the textbooks used to teach clergy to preach, on the assumption that different understandings of the undertaking require different methods of execution. "During the first half of this century, John A. Broadus's *On the Preparation and Delivery of Sermons* dominated the teaching of homiletics. . . . Not until 1958 was its dominance seriously challenged."[1] H. Grady Davis's 1958 *Design for Preaching*[2] was still being used by more than half the homiletics professors polled in 1974. Ten years later, however, the situation had changed completely again. Davis's share of the market was less than one-fourth of what it had been, with eight other books doing as well or better, yet none of them were used by as many as one-seventh of the respondents to a questionnaire on the subject.[3]

All of this suggests that the majority of the new movements in homiletics reported on began after World War II and, indeed, from the Vietnam era on. A corollary to this is that the new kinds of preaching surveyed are closely tied to the changes going on within the larger society. To reflect these changes, the chapters ahead will deal with eight areas of homiletical development: (1) pastoral counseling through preaching, (2) the impact of biblical theology, (3) the influence of the liturgical movement, (4) the emergence of African American preaching in the majority culture, (5) new forms of social protest preaching, (6) the homiletical results of the widespread opening of ordination to women, (7) changes in evangelistic preaching, and (8) the trends referred to collectively as "the New Homiletic."

Since most of these trends are still developing, since they are so numerous, and since they are much more likely than what has preceded to be familiar to anyone with interest in homiletics, no effort will be made to provide as detailed a history for these movements as that given for those that came before them. Instead, what will follow will be more in the nature of progress reports or bulletins and often will pay more attention to the theory enunciated in books than to sermons actually delivered. To attempt more would be to create something intolerably long and something that is bound to be outdated before it could be printed.

THE FIRST CATALYST

Not only were changes in homiletical thought slow to emerge, they were not even always recognized at the time as interruptions of the status quo. The general situation of Protestant churches in general and their preaching in particular seemed better than ever through the first half of the century. Indeed, William B. Lawrence has referred to the years

1930–55 as "the crest of the Protestant mainstream."[4] Exploring the metaphor of "mainstream" as it is commonly applied to these denominations, he says:

> At the beginning of the twentieth century, their level of cultural influence and ecclesiastical domination was rising. At the end of the twentieth century, they are receding. Somewhere during these hundred years, the mainstream denominations crested.[5]

And, as he says, "one only knows that the crest has occurred after it has passed."[6]

Lawrence dates the beginning of the mainstream's crest as October 5, 1930, with the dedication of Riverside Church, constructed at the cost of $4 million by John D. Rockefeller to afford a suitable platform for his pastor, Harry Emerson Fosdick. By then Fosdick was already one of the most influential clerics in the country, and he had developed the theory of preaching that is the subject of this chapter: pastoral counseling through preaching.

The historical significance of this development, however, is not basically that it was the accomplishment of Fosdick. Rather, its relevance is as an early indicator of what Philip Rieff has called "the triumph of the therapeutic."[7]

The present concern, however, is with only the homiletical aspects of that historical movement. There is no need to trace here, for instance, the evolution of pastoral counseling in its own right.[8] The effort to sketch the progress of the pulpit's use for pastoral counseling must begin with Fosdick, however, because "it was Fosdick who persuaded a large section of the liberal Protestant clergy to refashion the sermon in the image of the counseling session."[9]

Harry Emerson Fosdick

Harry Emerson Fosdick[10] (1878–1969) was born into the home of one of the most beloved secondary educators in Buffalo, New York. His parents were devout but not narrow Baptists, and religion was an important element in his upbringing. After going though the local school system, Fosdick attended Colgate University, where he experienced a crisis of faith that ended in a sense of call to the ministry. He started his theological education at Hamilton Theological Seminary, but transferred to Union Theological Seminary, near Columbia University in New York City. Despite a nervous breakdown after his first year at Union, he graduated with an impressive record. He immediately got married, and began his ministry.

His beginning pastorate was First Baptist Church in Montclair, New Jersey, where he remained for eleven years. Most of the things that were to distinguish his ministry were evident in its beginning. Before his Montclair tenure was over, he had seen his church grow, had made an impact on the local community, and was in demand as a speaker all over the country. He also had published six devotional books, two of which were to be printed in millions of copies and translated into many languages.[11] It was also in Montclair that he developed his personal approach to homiletics, which will be considered below.

While still at Montclair he began teaching at Union Seminary, first in Baptist principles and polity and then in homiletics. In 1915 he was invited to become a full-time faculty member. Nine years later he gave the prestigious Lyman Beecher Lectures on Preaching at Yale, although the topic he chose was not preaching as such but biblical interpretation.[12] Yet his academic involvement did not mean that he had quit preaching. In 1918 he went on a six-month mission to minister to American soldiers in France. He later reflected on what he saw of war and became a staunch pacifist, a commitment he maintained throughout World War II.

After his return from France, he was engaged as an interim preacher at First Presbyterian Church in Manhattan, which had just been formed by the consolidation of three historic congregations. When asked to become the pastor, he refused to become a Presbyterian. The search committee then recommended that someone else be designated as pastor, but that Fosdick do most of the preaching. This arrangement was agreed to.

While at First Presbyterian, Fosdick preached a sermon titled "Will the Fundamentalists Win?" This sermon not only established him as one of the most visible leaders in the fundamentalist-modernist controversy,[13] but also occasioned a fierce battle within the Presbyterian Church, U.S.A. The upshot was that Fosdick was given the choice of becoming a Presbyterian or leaving that pulpit. Thus two preaching engagements Fosdick undertook in 1918 eventually resulted in two of the stands for which he was best known, modernism and pacifism.

Fosdick's reluctance to allow First Presbyterian to suffer because of his theological principles left him open to the invitation of Park Avenue Baptist Church to become its pastor. The invitation was all the more welcome because, through the generosity of Rockefeller, one of its lay leaders, the congregation promised to build a new church to be established according to Fosdick's principles. That, of course, became Riverside Church. By then his fame was enormous, but it soon grew even greater when he became a pioneer radio preacher on the National Vespers Radio Hour and had a weekly audience of millions. By this means, he came to be heard by more people than any preacher who had ever lived up until that time.

While Fosdick made many contributions to homiletics, the one to be considered here is his understanding of the way sermons should work and the way he organized his sermons to accomplish that purpose. In his autobiography he tells how he arrived at that insight during his pastorate in Montclair:

> Little by little . . . the vision grew clearer. People come to church on Sunday with every kind of personal difficulty and problem flesh is heir to. A sermon was meant to meet such needs; it should be pastoral counseling on a group scale. . . . Every sermon should have for its main business the head-on constructive meeting of some problem which was puzzling minds, burdening consciences, distracting lives, and no sermon which so met a real human difficulty, with light to throw on it and help to win a victory over it, could possibly be futile.[14]

It is easy for contemporary readers to misunderstand what Fosdick meant by "personal counseling on a group scale," because of the radical change in meaning the expression "pastoral counseling" underwent in the 1950s and 1960s. Then, largely under the influence of Carl Rogers, pastoral counseling was understood as psychotherapy done in the context of the church.[15] Fosdick's list of problems that puzzle minds, burden consciences, and distract lives shows that by pastoral counseling he meant all the kinds of issues parishioners might like to discuss privately with their pastor, whether personal, family, ethical, theological, or what-have-you.

He was interested in the new psychology, aware of William James, the mental health movement, and Freud,[16] but he would not have considered himself competent to do what psychoanalysts, psychiatrists, or psychotherapists did, nor would he have felt theirs was a higher calling.[17]

Fosdick's own experience of having a nervous breakdown gave him an empathy he called "clairvoyant," and there are many records to show that his counseling was penetrating and helpful. Since, however, most of his sessions lasted only fifteen minutes, it is likely that there was as much preaching in his counseling as there was counseling in his preaching.

The most obvious breakthrough in his use of the pulpit to do pastoral counseling on a group scale was in the way he constructed his sermons. While he saw much good in the classical expository sermon that grew out of Puritan homiletics, he worried about the way sermons began with issues of exegesis, saying, "Only the preacher proceeds still upon the idea that folk come to church desperately anxious to discover what happened to the Jebusites."[18] (For the magazine article from which this quotation is taken, see **Vol. 2, pp. 535-47.**) He had less respect for topical preaching, which he associated with a loss of faith that eventually caused clergy to leave the ministry.

He was led to what he called "the project method," which he used as a technical term in educational psychology. He said, "Modern pedagogy starts not with the subject, but with the child."[19] Information is taught by showing the relevance of the information. Hence he began his sermon with a problem he thought some of his hearers might be facing.

It has been thought that Fosdick's sermon arrangement, in which he began with the problem,[20] reflected the thought of John Dewey,[21] but that is only partially true. Dewey believed that the best teaching was done in five steps:

1. A felt difficulty
2. Location and definition of the difficulty
3. Suggestion of possible solutions
4. Development by reasoning of bearings of suggestions
5. Further observation and exploration leading to acceptance or rejection of the solution.[22]

The difficulty with this interpretation is that, while Fosdick's sermons begin with a felt difficulty, they do not follow the rest of the outline.[23]

This can be seen in a fairly typical sermon, "When Life Reaches Its Depths," which was preached after America's entry into World War II.[24] This sermon is based on a clause from Psalm 42:7 (ASV), "Deep calleth unto deep at the noise of thy waterfalls," which is understood analogically to mean: "Every serious life has had that experience, where the profundities within ask for an answering profundity."[25] That experience accounts for "the deathless hold that religious faith has upon the human experience," because irreligion offers no answering profundity to the deep situations in which people find themselves. This is what Fosdick called "the major idea"[26] of the sermon.

The rest of the sermon is a testing of that thesis in five areas of human experience. Was it true when one had to deal with trouble, love, moral need, ethical devotion, and spiritual insight? Fosdick may have learned from Dewey's pedagogical theory to begin with difficulties members of the congregation were feeling, but he did not follow the other four of Dewey's five steps in learning as the rest of his outline.

The opening section of a Fosdick sermon first served to show that the problem being discussed was a problem for his hearers, was important, and was consistent with life as it is depicted in the Bible. Then he went on to state the main idea around which the rest of the sermon was organized.

The way in which the other points related to the main idea were seen by Fosdick as analogous to either a *box,* a *tree,* or a *river.* The points in the first sort of sermon are enumerated one after another, as boards are nailed together in the construction of a box. Those of the second sort fork off from the main idea, as do limbs from the trunk of a tree. "The message with 'riverlike' structure flows along without giving the hearers points sharply marked off from one another. It surges forward, opening up one new vista after another."[27] To repeat, none of these patterns follows Dewey's five steps.

The opening section in which Fosdick stated his main idea is the *introduction* to his sermon, and the points he makes in relation to that idea are thus its *body.* These two sections were there to lead to the *conclusion.* As Fosdick said:

> Starting a sermon with a problem, however vital and urgent, suggests a discussion, a dissertation, a treatise. A sermon, however, is more than that. The preacher's business is not merely to discuss repentance but to persuade people to repent; not merely to debate the meaning and possibility of Christian faith, but to produce Christian faith in the lives of his listeners; not merely to talk about the available power of God to bring victory over trouble and temptation, but to send people out from their worship on Sunday with victory in their possession. A preacher's task is to create in his congregation the thing he is talking about.[28]

Of course, the entire sermon was designed to lead to this result, but it was in the conclusion that Fosdick challenged his listeners to live by what he had said.

PREACHING IN THE HEYDAY OF PASTORAL COUNSELING

This pattern of stating in the introduction a main idea about a problem facing members of the congregation, making points about it in the body of the sermon, and appealing to them to live by that message in the conclusion is Fosdick's main contribution to the effort to do pastoral counseling from the pulpit. It was some time before thought about how such preaching should be done advanced beyond what he had said.[29] Tracing that advance when it came is a matter of surveying the literature in which it appeared.

A pioneering work was Edgar N. Jackson's *A Psychology for Preaching,* which appeared in 1961 with a preface by Fosdick.[30] It is a disappointment, however, to anyone who expects to find in it either a personality theory or much insight into how one can achieve Fosdick's goal of preaching as counseling on a group scale. Instead, it is the sort of book that flooded the market in the years after World War II, one that promised professional practitioners psychological insight to help them understand their customers or clients and thus be more successful.

The next book on the subject, *Preaching and Pastoral Care* by Arthur L. Teikmanis, appeared in a distinguished series of books edited by pastoral counseling pioneer Russell L. Dicks.[31] It did not advance the theory of how counseling was done through preaching, however, consisting as it did of introductory chapters on the importance of preaching, the value of pastoral calling, and aspects of preparing to preach, followed by chapters consisting of nothing but outlines of sermons the author had preached on five categories of problems faced by parishioners. Perhaps the greatest contribution of this book was its defense of the value of preaching, something rare in the counseling field at the time, when the two activities were often viewed as antithetical alternatives.

The first book I have known to relate preaching to the pastoral care movement, which emerged after World War II under the influence of Carl Rogers, did not appear until 1979. David K. Switzer's *Pastor, Preacher, Person: Developing a Pastoral Ministry*[32] is not devoted exclusively to the relation of pastoral counseling and preaching. Rather, it seeks to bring insights from the field of psychotherapy to bear on "ministers' ways of thinking about themselves, their operational context within the church, and two central ministerial functions—preaching and pastoral care."[33] Only two of the five chapters are about preaching, the first having to do with the pastor's sense of his or her role, and the other examining the metaphor of the church as the family of God by applying to it the traits of a healthy family.

Switzer, who taught at Southern Methodist University, thinks that such descriptions of preaching as calling it "counseling on a group scale" are essentially reductionistic (especially after the Rogerian understanding of counseling took over). He does recognize, however, that the two activities share a desire to meet human needs and that both are "interpersonal, primarily verbal processes engaged in by the minister with others, and as such there are *some* common goals and necessary relational ingredients."[34] In reference to meeting human needs, he argues that preaching can change lives, although some authorities in pastoral counseling doubt that. His reasons for thinking so, however, are theoretical and theological rather than empirical.

The necessary relational ingredients held in common by counseling and preaching are also shared with all the helping professions: empathy, respect, concreteness, genuineness, self-disclosure, confrontation, and immediacy. The desirability of such ingredients is self-evident, but may be like other self-evident things: they are only so after being pointed out.

In this way Switzer undertook to illuminate the preaching task with psychotherapeutic insight. In doing so he did not reduce the church's ministry to therapy but recognized the transcendent claims of Christians. It would have been interesting to see what he would have said, however, had he gone on to analyze what is unique to the work of the pastor and thus discontinuous with other helping relationships.

The next major effort to relate pastoral counseling and preaching was *Pastoral Counseling and Preaching: A Quest for an Integrated Ministry,* by Donald Capps of Princeton Theological Seminary.[35] Capps claims that efforts to relate counseling and preaching from Fosdick on had failed to show that they are "two foci of an integrated ministry."[36] His thesis is that counseling and preaching share a formal structure: (1) identification of the problem, (2) reconstruction of the problem, (3) diagnostic interpretation, and (4) pastoral intervention.

His understanding of diagnosis is Rogerian, trying to understand a problem from the counselee's internal frame of reference. Yet he recognizes that there are different types of diagnosis done in preaching, each of which is akin to a type of counseling. The correlations he makes are:

1. "Identify[ing] underlying personal motivations" (psychoanalysis and others, including transactional analysis).
2. "Identify[ing] the range of potential causes" (various social therapies, such as social psychology and family counseling).
3. "Expos[ing] inadequate formulations of the problem" (depth psychology).
4. "Drawing attention to untapped personal and spiritual resources" (humanistic psychology).
5. "Bring[ing] clarity to the problem" (various therapies clarify various things).
6. "Assess[ing] problems in terms of the deepest intentions of shared human experience" (the client-centered approach).[37]

Capps sees value in each of these approaches, but thinks a pastor should be consistent in using only one of them in both preaching and counseling. Though his formal structure is not necessarily significant, his recognition of the theological nature of diagnosis, and of the need for proclamation in counseling, points toward an overarching theological vision of the church and its ministry, one in which pastoral counseling and preaching belong together as parts of the same work.

All the writers since Fosdick surveyed here represent the era of pastoral counseling's hegemony in practical theology. The swing of the pendulum back to the center can be seen in the last book to be studied on the relation of counseling to preaching. In *Pastoral Preaching: Timeless Truth for Changing Needs*,[38] Gary D. Stratman, a Presbyterian pastor in Nashville, Tennessee, looks for a wider definition of "pastoral" that can arise from a study of the biblical image of the shepherd (for which, of course, the Latin word is *pastor*). He draws on a study by David Steere, which sees the essential elements of the biblical concept of shepherding to be:

1. A positive pattern of action meeting need
2. A negative pattern of action constituting a withdrawal of the first
3. A sacrificial expenditure of life
4. Love as spontaneous, creative, and initiating.[39]

Stratman thinks the pastoral counseling approach to preaching has been strong on the first and last of these elements, but weak on the second and third. Weakness on the second element has been seen in an unwillingness to judge. Moral judgments, however, are a necessary part of pastoral leadership. Though counseling sermons have dealt with true and important matters, they have not treated everything of concern to Christians. Thus, Stratman says, "pastoral preaching will be marked by a shepherd's compassion and concern which desires nothing less for Christ's flock than the whole counsel of God."[40]

Stratman is concerned that preaching deal not just with some truth but with the *whole* truth. This, for him, is a theological concern. The source of truth is the Bible, and preaching that presents the whole truth cannot be limited by drawing upon only restricted portions of the Scriptures; for the whole truth, one needs the whole Bible.

Most of the rest of Stratman's book is dedicated to the way he prepares to preach, which does not need to be considered here. It is to be regretted that he did not pursue the biblical metaphor of shepherding further to specify in more detail what he means by "pastoral," and that he did not say more about what is the "whole" truth of the Bible. The development of Stratman's thought is more homiletical than analytical. Since his insights, in an area in which analysis is badly needed, seem so sound, it is to be regretted that he did not go on to make a wider contribution.

THE CURRENT SITUATION

As Stratman's work indicates, the period in which pastoral counseling enjoyed a hegemony in practical theology has passed, and the esteem in which the two pastoral activities of counseling and preaching are held is now more even. Having begun with reference to homiletics textbooks to see what was important in the preaching of a period, this chapter can end the same way by heeding what a popular manual has to say on this subject:

> The distance between preaching and pastoring has been manufactured out of exaggerated descriptions and caricatured portraits of both. On the one hand, the preacher was sketched as a drone, full of authoritarian harangues, moralistic scoldings, sectarian loyalties, and promotional trivia. On the other hand, the pastor was cartooned as a passive pseudo-psychologist, relishing the intimate details of parishioners' private lives.
>
> The past tense was used in the sentences above because preaching and pastoring now enjoy a healthier relationship of mutual enrichment.[41]

In summary, it can be said that it is axiomatic for most preachers today that one of the purposes of their preaching is to do pastoral counseling on a group scale. Furthermore, it seems obvious to many that sermons should begin with issues that are relevant to members of the congregation—whether those of personal psychology or of theology or ethics or whatever else is appropriate to preach about—in order to engage their interest and prepare them to see the relevance of what will be said. And so the influence of Fosdick continues, although it is not as dominant as it was during his ministry.

FOR FURTHER READING

Fosdick, Harry Emerson. *The Living of These Days: An Autobiography.* New York: Harper & Brothers, 1956.

_____. *A Great Time to Be Alive: Sermons on Christianity in Wartime*. New York: Harper & Brothers, 1944.

Harry Emerson Fosdick's Art of Preaching: An Anthology. Edited by Lionel Crocker. Springfield, Ill.: Charles C. Thomas, 1971.

Holifield, E. Brooks. *A History of Pastoral Care in America: From Salvation to Self-Realization*. Nashville: Abingdon, 1983.

Stratman, Gary D. *Pastoral Preaching: Timeless Truth for Changing Needs*. Nashville: Abingdon, 1983.

Notes

1. Lucy Atkinson Rose, *Sharing the Word: Preaching in the Roundtable Church* (Louisville, Ky.: Westminster John Knox, 1997), 7.

2. H. Grady Davis, *Design for Preaching* (Philadelphia: Fortress, 1958).

3. Donald F. Chatfield, "Textbooks Used by Teachers of Preaching," *Homiletic* 9 (1984): 2:1-5.

4. William B. Lawrence, *Sundays in New York: Pulpit Theology at the Crest of the Protestant Mainstream 1930–1955*, ATLA Monograph Series, no. 41 (Lanham, Md.: American Theological Library Association and Scarecrow Press, 1996). While this book is a treasure trove of fascinating information, it seems to argue that a good bit of the loss of mainstream Protestantism's influence on American society was due to the "tangentially" Protestant theology of Harry Emerson Fosdick and Ralph W. Sockman; this sounds like a "great man" theory of historical change with a vengeance. See especially pp. 224-26.

5. Ibid., vii.

6. Ibid.

7. Philip Rieff, *The Triumph of the Therapeutic: Uses of Faith after Freud* (New York: Harper & Row, 1966).

8. An excellent account of that has been provided by E. Brooks Holifield in *A History of Pastoral Care in America: From Salvation to Self-Realization* (Nashville: Abingdon, 1983), 210-356.

9. Ibid., 220. What is meant by "pastoral counseling" in this context will be defined below. For the present, it is enough to note that the practice is in part a function of the growing popularity of psychology in America immediately after World War I.

10. The bibliography on Fosdick is enormous. His own account of his life and ministry is *The Living of These Days: An Autobiography* (New York: Harper & Brothers, 1956). The standard biography is Robert Moats Miller, *Harry Emerson Fosdick: Preacher, Pastor, and Prophet* (New York and Oxford: Oxford University Press, 1985). Miller also wrote the article on Fosdick in the *Concise Encyclopedia of Preaching*, ed. William H. Willimon and Richard Lischer (Louisville: Westminster John Knox, 1995), 154-57. The major collection of Fosdick's writings and those of others about his preaching is *Harry Emerson Fosdick's Art of Preaching: An Anthology*, comp. and ed. Lionel Crocker (Springfield, Ill.: Charles C. Thomas, 1971). Two of the most useful essays in that collection are Robert D. Clark, "Harry

Emerson Fosdick: The Growth of a Great Preacher" (pp. 128-85, reprinted from *A History and Criticism of American Public Address*, ed. Marie Kathryn Hochmuth [New York: Russell & Russell, 1955]), and Edmund H. Linn, "Harry Emerson Fosdick and the Techniques of Organization" (pp. 186-209, reprinted from *ANQ* 1 [1961]: 19-40). Linn later went on to construct the sort of homiletics textbook Fosdick might have written had he been inclined to do so, *Preaching as Counseling: The Unique Method of Harry Emerson Fosdick* (Valley Forge, Pa.: Judson, 1966), which incorporates much of the earlier essay. Another study of Fosdick's rhetoric is Halford R. Ryan, *Harry Emerson Fosdick: Persuasive Preacher*, Great American Orators, no. 2 (New York: Greenwood, 1989). Clyde Fant's introduction to the sermons of Fosdick included in Clyde E. Fant Jr. and William M. Pinson Jr., eds., *20 Centuries of Great Preaching: An Encyclopedia of Preaching* (Waco, Tex.: Word, 1971), 9:3-27, is another good summary.

11. Harry Emerson Fosdick, *The Meaning of Faith*; and *The Meaning of Prayer*.

12. Harry Emerson Fosdick, *The Modern Use of the Bible* (New York: Macmillan, 1924).

13. About whether the Bible was to be understood as literally true or to be interpreted by the historical-critical method. While Beecher and Brooks had been strong advocates of critical method a half century before, the clash over biblical interpretation did not really begin to tear Protestant churches apart until the 1920s.

14. Fosdick, *The Living of These Days*, 94.

15. Holifield, *A History of Pastoral Care in America*, 259-306.

16. His knowledge of Freud was superficial and his attitude toward him antagonistic. Miller, *Harry Emerson Fosdick*, 260-64.

17. See ibid., 251-84, and Holifield, *A History of Pastoral Care*, 219-21.

18. Fosdick, "What Is the Matter With Preaching?" in *Harper's Magazine* (July 1928), reprinted in Crocker, *Harry Emerson Fosdick's Art of Preaching*, 30.

19. Ibid., 32.

20. Charles Kemp called this kind of sermon "Life Situation" preaching in "Harry Emerson Fosdick: The Methods of a Master," *Life Situation Preaching* (St. Louis: Bethany Press, 1956), 88, in Crocker, *Harry Emerson Fosdick's Art of Preaching*, 225. I was introduced to this term in the early 1950s in a course on public speaking at Duke Divinity School taught by John J. Rudin III. The concept was summarized as: "You have to start with people where they are in order to get them where you want them to go," but I do not know with whom this statement originated.

21. See, for example, Halford E. Luccock, *In the Minister's Workshop*, Notable Books on Preaching (Whitmore & Stone, 1944; reprint, Grand Rapids, Mich.: Baker, 1977), 52-58. I accepted this theory in my book *The Living and Active Word: One Way to Preach from the Bible Today* (New York: Seabury, 1975), 47-48.

22. Luccock, *In the Minister's Workshop*, 56.

23. A speech outline based on Dewey is Alan Monroe's "Motivated Sequence," for which the five steps are: (1) *Attention*. The creation of interest and desire, (2) *Need*. The development of the problem, through an analysis of things wrong in the world and through a relating of those wrongs to individuals' interests, wants, or desires, (3) *Satisfaction*. The proposal of a plan of action which will alleviate the problem and satisfy the individuals' interests, wants, or desires, (4) *Visualization*. The verbal depiction of the world as it will look if the plan is put into operation, (5) *Action*. The final call for personal commitments and deeds" (David Ehninger, Bruce E. Gronbeck, and

Alan H. Monroe, *Principles of Speech Communication,* 9th Brief Ed. (Glenview, Ill.: Scott, Foresman & Co., 1984), 249. Monroe first published this pattern in 1935.

24. In Harry Emerson Fosdick, *A Great Time to Be Alive: Sermons on Christianity in Wartime* (New York: Harper & Brothers, 1944), 192-200.

25. Ibid., 192.

26. This term was used in a letter to Edmund H. Linn, dated April 15, 1951, and quoted in "Techniques of Organization," in Crocker, *Harry Emerson Fosdick's Art of Preaching,* 189.

27. Ibid., 200. While Fosdick was more concerned with psychological than logical order in his sermons, Gilbert Stillman MacVaugh's idea that his longest point was always his main idea in the introduction and that his subordinate points grew progressively shorter appears not to be true. ("Structural Analysis of the Sermons of Dr. Harry Emerson Fosdick," in Crocker, *Harry Emerson Fosdick's Art of Preaching,* 210-224; reprinted from *The Quarterly Journal of Speech,* 19:531-46). See Linn letter, ibid., 204-5. Linn's analysis of the organization of Fosdick's sermons is the most astute study of *dispositio* as practiced by a particular preacher that I have seen.

28. Fosdick, *The Living of These Days,* 99.

29. The rest of this chapter builds on my essay "Preaching and Pastoral Care," in *Anglican Theology and Pastoral Care,* ed. James E. Griffiss, Anglican Study Series (Wilton, Conn.: Morehouse-Barlow, 1985), 133-58.

30. Edgar N. Jackson, *A Psychology for Preaching* (1961; reprint, San Francisco: Harper & Row, 1981).

31. Arthur L. Teikmanis, *Preaching and Pastoral Care,* Successful Pastoral Counseling, ed. Russell L. Dicks (Englewood Cliffs, N.J.: Prentice-Hall, 1964).

32. David K. Switzer, *Pastor, Preacher, Person: Developing a Pastoral Ministry* (Nashville: Abingdon, 1979).

33. Ibid., 9.

34. Ibid., 53.

35. Donald Capps, *Pastoral Counseling and Preaching: A Quest for an Integrated Ministry* (Philadelphia: Westminster, 1980). He taught at Phillips University at the time of this writing.

36. Ibid., 91-103.

37. This list brings to mind Walker Percy's question: "Can you explain why it is that there are, at last count, sixteen schools of psychotherapy with sixteen theories of the personality and its disorders and that patients treated in one school seem to do as well or as badly as patients treated in any other—while there is only one generally accepted theory of the cause and cure of pneumococcal pneumonia and only one generally accepted theory of the orbits of the planets and the gravitational attraction of our galaxy and the galaxy M31 in Andromeda?" (*Lost in the Cosmos: The Last Self-Help Book* (New York: Washington Square Press Division of Pocket Books, 1983), 11.

38. Gary D. Stratman, *Pastoral Preaching: Timeless Truth for Changing Needs* (Nashville: Abingdon, 1983).

39. Ibid., p. 20.

40. Ibid., p. 37.

41. Fred B. Craddock, *Preaching* (Nashville: Abingdon, 1985), 38.

CHAPTER 26

THE RESURGENCE OF ORTHODOXY

THE RISE OF BIBLICAL THEOLOGY

From the late-nineteenth century through the middle of the twentieth, a prevailing climate had developed in mainstream American— and, to a lesser extent, British—preaching, in which the primary concerns of the pulpit seemed to be pastoral counseling or problem solving à la Fosdick,[1] social reform, and moral exhortation. The last of these reflected, among other things, the concentration during that period of New Testament scholarship upon efforts to reconstruct the life of Jesus historically.[2] Such a preoccupation with the ministry of Jesus led by default to a lessened emphasis on the incarnation, crucifixion, resurrection, and ascension. Thus it came about that clergy, many of whom still held a traditional Christology, found themselves treating Jesus homiletically as the great teacher and example of ethical life.

In the years following World War II,[3] this picture was to undergo considerable change brought about by a number of factors. One was a revolution in the way New Testament scholars looked at Jesus. It was the historian of Life of Jesus research,[4] **Albert Schweitzer** (1875–1965),[5] among others, who showed that Jesus' life and teaching must be understood in light of the belief Jesus shared with most of his contemporaries,

677

that the present age of history was coming to a sudden and cataclysmic end, after which would be ushered in the reign of God. Therefore, sound biblical interpretation did not support the view that Jesus taught a time-less ethic or that the kingdom of God was something human beings were to bring in through their personal and corporate efforts at social reform. While Schweitzer's own evaluation of Jesus' eschatological teaching was to assume that it was brilliantly and gloriously mistaken, scholars were beginning to assume by the mid-1930s that there had to be some way in which Jesus' views were both true and normative for Christianity.

A change in the dominant method of studying the Gospels occurred simultaneously with some of these developments. Life of Jesus research had been predicated upon the assumption that differences in the Gospels were to be explained by differences in the sources available to the Evangelists, and much of synoptic study was directed toward separating and identifying these sources, the assumption being that the earliest was the most reliable historically. During World War I, however, a new method of synoptic study was devised by a trio of German scholars: **K. L. Schmidt** (1891–1956), **Rudolf Bultmann** (1884–1976), and **Martin Dibelius** (1883–1947). This method, called "Form Criticism" in English,[6] investigated the time between Jesus' ministry and when the first account of it was written down in Mark's Gospel, an interval of slightly less than forty years. During that interval, the stories and sayings of Jesus were handed down by word of mouth. When such transmission occurs, as studies in the oral tradition of folkloric material indicate, various kinds of material tend to settle into characteristic patterns. Thus by ana-lyzing the way that such patterns were preserved or altered, it should be possible to establish the relative age of different versions of the same unit of tradition.

When the form-critical method was first applied to the Gospels, the question was raised of why the church preserved some stories and say-ings and not others. It was immediately recognized that the only materi-al handed down was that useful to the early church in its effort to evangelize the Greco-Roman world. This means that nothing was passed down just because it satisfied curiosity about Jesus; the purpose was not reminiscence but conversion. Each story or saying was kept because it led to the conclusion that "Jesus is the Messiah, the Son of God, and that through believing you may have life in his name" (John 20:31).

It became an axiom of form criticism that each individual unit of tra-dition, each story or saying, had such christological implications that it was the entire gospel in a nutshell. And this meant that the whole nine-teenth-century quest of the historical Jesus had been based upon a misunderstanding. It had hoped to get behind the supernatural picture of Jesus to show him as a historical person, when the very reason all the sources drawn upon had been preserved was to serve as evidence for the supernatural interpretation. One could not get behind them to a purely historical account; every pericope of the Gospels proclaims the ultimacy of Christ.

New Testament scholars learned the method of form criticism from Old Testament scholars, who had also used it to move behind source criticism. Late in the nineteenth century, **Julius Wellhausen** (1844–1918), professor at Marburg and Göttingen, published a theory of how the Pentateuch was put together, identifying the J (Yahwistic), E (Elohistic), P (Priestly), and D (Deuteronomic) accounts as the sources from which the finished document was assembled. Combined with this literary analysis was a Hegelian and evolutionary interpretation of the history of the religion of Israel that traced its progress from primitive superstition to the enlightened ethical monotheism of the prophets. Form criticism shifted the emphasis to the individual units of tradition that lay behind the sources of not only the Pentateuch but other parts of the Hebrew Bible as well. Sagas from Genesis were analyzed, psalms were sorted into their various types, and the structure of prophetic oracles was studied.

Creedal statements that took the form of recitals of the history of God's dealings with Israel were identified, and these dealings were seen in relation to the succession of covenants God formed with Israel. In this manner, the emphasis shifted from an evolutionary view of Israel's search for God to the proclamation of the God who acted in the history of Israel. In the process, philosophical interpretation of biblical religion was branded as illegitimate, and there was much insistence upon the difference between Hebrew and Greek thought, with an implied claim of the superiority of the former over the latter. Connected with this was an interest in the theological vocabulary of the Bible, such as was manifested in the *Theologisches Wörterbuch zum Neuen Testament,* edited by **Gerhard Kittel** (1888–1948) and Gerhard Friedrich. Although the vocabulary of the New Testament was Greek, it was thought to represent the Semitic thought world from which Jesus and his first followers came.

Another development in biblical scholarship that was to have a profound impact on homiletics was **C. H. Dodd's** (1884–1973) study of *The Apostolic Preaching and Its Developments.*[7] In the book Dodd argued that the New Testament word for preaching, *kerygma,* and its cognates, did not refer to moral instruction, which instead was designated as *didache* (teaching), *paraklesis* (exhortation), or *homilia* (informal discussion of the Christian life). To preach was to proclaim the good news of

God's saving activity in Jesus Christ. "While the church was concerned to hand on the teaching of the Lord, it was not by this that it made converts. It was by *kerygma,* says Paul, not by *didache,* that it pleased God to save men."[8]

These changes in biblical studies paralleled shifting emphases in theology. A voice crying in the wilderness for such changes had been **Søren Kierkegaard** (1813–55), a Danish philosopher and theologian who challenged the regnant theology of German idealism that derived from Hegel. His concern with the position of a human being existing before God made him the father of existentialism (a term he coined). Furthermore, his criticism of the Danish church of his time for seeking to accommodate the Christian revelation to human desires makes him the ancestor of the "crisis" or "dialectical" theology of the twentieth century, a movement largely identified with the Swiss theologian Karl Barth.

Also influential in English-speaking countries was **P(eter) T(aylor) Forsyth** (1848–1921), a Scottish Congregationalist theologian who in his early life and ministry had espoused the liberal theology of Hegel and Albrecht Ritschl. When he came to be convinced of the inadequacy of that approach, however, he also knew that he could not espouse instead the rigorous biblicism that was the other option in Scottish theology at the time. Although he continued to appreciate much about modernism, he nevertheless insisted upon the radical pervasiveness of human sin and, therefore, the utter dependence of human beings upon the atoning death of Christ, through which God reconciled a lost humanity to God's self.[9] Forsyth has been called "a Barth before Barth," and he did indeed anticipate many of what were to be the characteristic emphases the Swiss theologian would later display.

Generally recognized as the most influential theologian of the twentieth century, **Karl Barth** (1886–1968) demonstrated to the Christian world that the optimistic liberal assumption of inevitable progress was inconsistent with the realities of human nature. Two world wars, separated by a worldwide depression, were to reveal to many the shallowness of liberal Christian theology's optimistic understanding of human nature. For Barth, however, that insight came before even World War I. Trained by the leading liberal theologians of Germany, he found the worldview he had been taught inadequate in his efforts to be a pastor in the Swiss town of Safenwil. To gain a deeper understanding of his parishioners' lives, he turned to a study of Paul's Letter to the Romans.

This study was incorporated into a commentary, and through its revised second edition he both established what was to be his characteristic position and was established as one of the leading theologians in

Europe. Biblical truth could not be understood as progressive human discovery but only as the self-revelation of a holy God who is totally different from sinful human beings. The upshot was that all human activity—whether philosophical, ethical, or religious—was thoroughly compromised by human pride and self-centeredness and thus not to be relied upon for any insight. The only serious truth available to humanity is what God discloses of God's self in biblical revelation.

The response of the theological world to Barth's commentary on Romans was overwhelming; university appointments in Germany came his way, and he began his *Kirchliche Dogmatik*, which was to run to thirteen thick volumes in its English translation.[10]

While the theological world responded to Barth's call to recognize the infinite qualitative distance between God and human beings, most thinkers were not prepared to state the disjunction between divine and human thought so starkly as he. They were more likely to side with **Emil Brunner** (1889–1966) in recognizing the possibility of some natural knowledge of God. The theological school of Barth, Brunner, and others was called "dialectical" and "crisis" theology, but the wider movement that reaffirmed the transcendence of God and the human need for salvation was called "neoorthodoxy." In the United States, the most influential spokespersons for this wider theological movement were the brothers **Reinhold** (1892–1971) and **H. Richard Niebuhr** (1894–1962). By the end of World War II, there was a pervasive rejection of old-school liberalism in American and British theology and a call for a more biblical understanding of God's relations with human beings.

As a result of these and other trends, a characteristic approach to biblical study developed that referred to itself as the **"biblical theology" movement**. While the movement was always very fluid and comprised a great variety of positions, it nevertheless had a number of emphases that were shared by most of those who made it up. These emphases included a reaction against abstract and philosophical thought in general, and a rejection of efforts to systematize the theology of the Bible on the grounds that it was too organic to be susceptible to that sort of presentation without distortion. Instead, it showed a preference for what was considered the more dynamic quality of biblical ("Hebrew") thought over what was believed to be the static quality of Greek thought. It was believed that the New Testament had to be interpreted in light of the Old, since it belonged to the Hebrew thought world. There was, therefore, a deep sense of the unity of the Bible. A favored method for getting at the Hebrew structure of thought was the study of individual words, as in the Kittel *Wörterbuch*.

And, just as New Testament thought was distinguished from that of the Greeks, so Old Testament thought was sharply separated from that of Israel's Near Eastern neighbors. One of the qualities of Hebrew thought admired by the movement was its understanding that revelation occurs in history rather than in the delivery of abstract propositions. Thus the reason for scholars to study the Bible was to discover the theology that had been revealed in history. By the same token, other theological disciplines should have biblical theology as their point of departure. But this theology was not to be remote and academic. It should be concerned with the life of the church in the world and have its most important expression in preaching.[11]

THE INFLUENCE OF EXEGESIS UPON PROCLAMATION

The impact of biblical theology upon preaching was mainly through seminary courses in Bible and theology. There was not, at any rate, a single textbook devoted to the method that dominated the teaching of homiletics from the midforties to the midsixties, the heyday of the movement. There were, however, a number of significant books on preaching that reflected the movement's assumptions. Oddly enough, Barth's own lectures on homiletics were not among the most influential. That was undoubtedly because he did not publish them himself; rather, they survived in the form of student notes. The earlier form of these was not published in English until 1963, and the more complete form did not appear until the movement was over.[12]

A book that was a review of the changed situation in theology and designed to persuade preachers to change their way of preaching was among the more significant. Theodore O. Wedel, who was warden of the College of Preachers at the National Cathedral in Washington, began *The Pulpit Rediscovers Theology*[13] by describing the liberal theology that had been the homiletical staple up until that time, and the doubts that must have arisen in regard to it, especially noting that ethical exhortation that does not grow out of the gospel of grace, is an invitation to despair in the way that it sets perfectionist standards to be met by human effort alone. Jesus must be our Savior before he can be our Master.

Saying that recognizes the need for dogma, however repugnant the word was to liberals. The pulpit needed the biblical theology that was making such an impact at the time, with its recognition of the reality of sin and the need for grace. After summarizing the main tenets of biblical theology and its critique of liberalism, Wedel ended his book by noting the implications of the liturgical movement[14] for preaching and giving a review of the doctrine of the church.

682

While Wedel tried to persuade preachers of their need for biblical theology, he did not tell them how to preach from its insights. There were, however, a number of textbooks that did attempt to do so—some of which were written by biblical scholars rather than homileticians—although, as noted above, none of these were accepted as the standard work.[15]

One of the clearest examples of such an effort may be seen in two books by Donald G. Miller, *Fire in the Mouth*[16] and *The Way to Biblical Preaching*.[17] Miller was a Presbyterian pastor who also taught in several seminaries and served as president of one, as well as the editor of *Interpretation,* one of the leading journals to grow out of the biblical theology movement. The first of the two books deals with presuppositions behind biblical preaching, and the second tells how to construct sermons that reflect the understanding of the first. *The Way to Biblical Preaching* begins with a summary of the perspective of *Fire in the Mouth*. After criticizing several definitions of biblical preaching and rejecting the older understanding of expository preaching, the author states his ideal:

> Expository preaching is an act wherein the living truth of some portion of Holy Scripture, understood in the light of solid exegetical and historical study and made a living reality to the preacher by the Holy Spirit, comes alive to the hearer as he is confronted by God in Christ through the Holy Spirit in judgment and redemption.[18]

Two aspects of that definition call for attention. The first is that the approach to exegesis is historical-critical, but depends upon the perspective of biblical theology. The second is the implicit understanding of the nature of the preaching event. "The *end* of preaching is that the sermon situation should be transformed from a human encounter between the preacher and his congregation into a divine encounter between God and both preacher and people."[19]

Having set forth such a high doctrine of preaching, Miller goes on to outline a process of sermon preparation. He begins with the exegesis of the biblical text, recognizing the necessity of understanding the passage in its context within the Bible, but focusing more on lexicographical study than any other sort. He has little to say about the historical situation reflected in the passage, for instance. The next task is to discover the theme of the sermon: "Every sermon should have a theme, and that theme should be the theme of the portion of scripture on which it is based."[20]

Miller writes in a homiletical style, finding examples of good and bad usage in published sermons of unidentified preachers, and offering abundant analogies to the principles he states. In successive chapters he argues that preaching should be balanced, reflecting all sides of the truth, and that every sermon's message should be reducible to one sentence and should have a clear structure that is an outgrowth of the biblical passage upon which it is based. And it should have a particular purpose. Finally, the sermon must be delivered in the proper emotional tone. "Fire is kindled by fire. Let us capture the Bible's fire and lay it on the dry faggots of our own lives and those of our people. The world needs to know again that 'our God is a consuming fire.' "[21] While it might be difficult to construct a sermon with no more guidance than this, any that were constructed in this way would certainly represent the perspectives of the biblical theology movement.

The overall success of the movement in influencing preaching can be seen in the way that many of its teachings were presupposed by the next textbook to dominate the field, *Design for Preaching* by H. Grady Davis, which was used by over half the homiletics professors polled in 1974.[22] Yet for Davis, the emphases were presuppositions rather than his main concern. And, in looking at sermons produced in the heyday of the movement, it is hard to find many that seem to have been constructed according to a hard and fast formula. As Brevard Childs says of the impact of the movement upon preaching, "At least for a time, one gains the impression that many pastors tried to put the suggestions into practice while holding on to a typical American homiletical style."[23]

This is to say that the change had more to do with content than pattern. There were fewer sermons of the sort Wedel designated as the "we must" type, sermons that urged ethical imitation of Jesus. And there were more that proclaimed the reality of sin and the need for the grace of God, who acts and who has acted most visibly in Jesus Christ for the redemption of a lost world. There also was a visible shift in pulpit demeanor from that of exhorters, who were earnestly urging more effort in moral practice, to that of proclaimers, who believed that through human words the omnipotent God was communicating urgent messages to the people of God. (**See Vol. 2, pp. 548-52** for an example of British tradition of this sort of preaching.)

Even though many influences of the biblical theology movement continue to be felt in preaching today, there is no question that it has long since ceased to be the dominant consciousness in homiletics. It has not had that prominence since the mid-1960s, when the civil rights movement and other forms of social action came to the forefront of churches' attention. In that period there was a sense, as Childs has said, that "God has abandoned the sanctuary and gone out into the streets."[24] He went on to say:

Many pastors who continued to hold the major tenets of the movement struggled unsuccessfully to apply the theology to concrete issues. Neither the concept of the biblical mentality nor the redemptive history of the people of God provided the needed insights or carried the required authority for the issues of the day. Suddenly the familiar approach to the Bible began to seem as outdated as had Harry Emerson Fosdick's theology to the biblical theologians of the forties. The growing uncertainty regarding the place of the Bible reflected itself again in the form of the sermon. Whatever criticisms one could aim at the older liberals in respect to its content, one had to admit that the preaching of Fosdick, Luccock, and Sockman had at least been interesting, lucid, and relevant. These qualities appeared to many modern preachers to claim top priority.[25]

FOR FURTHER READING

Barth, Karl. *Homiletics.* Translated by Geoffrey W. Bromiley and Donald E. Daniels, with foreword by David Buttrick. Louisville: Westminster John Knox, 1991.

Bonhoeffer, Dietrich. *Worldly Preaching: Lectures on Homiletics.* Edited and translated with critical commentary by Clyde E. Fant. New York: Crossroad, 1991.

Childs, Brevard S. *Biblical Theology in Crisis.* Philadelphia: Westminster, 1970.

Davis, H. Grady. *Design for Preaching.* Philadelphia: Fortress, 1958.

Miller, Donald G. *The Way to Biblical Preaching.* New York and Nashville: Abingdon, 1957.

Wedel, Theodore O. *The Pulpit Rediscovers Theology.* Greenwich, Conn.: Seabury, 1956.

Notes

1. See the previous chapter for the way that Fosdick and those who followed him understood preaching as pastoral counseling on a group scale.

2. The history of nineteenth-century German efforts in this enterprise is recounted in Albert Schweitzer, *The Quest of the Historical Jesus,* trans. W. Montgomery, pref. F. C. Burkitt, 2nd ed. (1911; New York: Macmillan, 1948); the title in German was *Von Reimarus zu Wrede* (1906). For American and English activity in this field, see Stephen Neill and Tom Wright, *The Interpretation of the New Testament 1861–1986,* passim.

3. There was a time lag between what was going on in German biblical scholarship, where most of the new movements were launched, and their acceptance by

American and English scholars. While the main changes discussed here happened in the first quarter of the twentieth century in German scholarship, they were not widely accepted by English and American scholars until the third quarter.

4. *Lebenjesuforschung.*

5. A man of many talents, Schweitzer was considered one of the greatest interpreters of the organ works of J. S. Bach. By midcentury he was widely regarded as a saint for devoting his life to service as a medical missionary in French Equatorial Africa, receiving a Nobel Peace Prize in 1953. Since then his reputation has been diminished by a belief that he had racist attitudes toward his African patients. Yet few people have ever made such distinguished contributions in such diverse fields as biblical scholarship and theology, philosophy and ethics, music (both as a scholar and a performer), and medicine—in which he could have had a brilliant career in research.

6. German: *Formgeschichte.*

7. C. H. Dodd, *The Apostolic Preaching and Its Developments* (Chicago and New York: Willett, Clark & Co., 1937).

8. Ibid., 8.

9. A highly respected preacher himself, Forsyth was invited to give the prestigious Beecher Lectures in Preaching. These were published as *Positive Preaching and the Modern Mind* (London: Independent Press Ltd., 1907).

10. The size of the set together, with the color of the cloth in which the original German edition was bound, led him to refer to it deprecatingly as his Moby Dick, his "great white whale."

11. The most extensive discussion of this movement's rise is in Brevard S. Childs, *Biblical Theology in Crisis* (Philadelphia: Westminster, 1970), 9-87. An excellent short treatment is James Barr, "Biblical Theology," *IDB*, Supplementary Vol., 104-11. Krister Stendahl gave a concise statement of the movement's European background in his article "Biblical Theology," *IDB*, 1:418-32. Childs considered the movement to be more American than British or continental, and attributed its attractiveness to the depth of memories of the still recent fundamentalist-modernist controversy. Barr, on the other hand, saw it as an international and essentially uniform movement. In the discussion of the impact of biblical theology upon preaching that is to follow, I am grateful for bibliographical suggestions from David Buttrick, Don Wardlaw, Bruce Shields, and Richard Lischer.

12. The earlier form was *The Preaching of the Gospel* (Philadelphia: Westminster, 1963), trans. B. E. Hooke from *Le proclamation de l'Évangile*, ed. A. Roulin (Neuchâtel: Delachaux et Niestlé, 1961), while the later was *Homiletics*, trans. Geoffrey W. Bromiley and Donald E. Daniels, with foreword by David Buttrick (Louisville.: Westminster John Knox, 1991). Barth's approach to preaching was to eschew introductions, conclusions, and efforts at relevance or to relate the biblical message to the contemporary thought world. Instead, he called for a reiteration of the text's message. Like many other writers of homiletical textbooks, however, he was not completely consistent in carrying out his own principles. See Clyde Fant in Clyde E. Fant Jr. and William M. Pinson Jr., eds., *20 Centuries of Great Preaching: An Encyclopedia of Preaching* (Waco, Tex.: Word, 1971), 10:104-7. Some of Barth's sermons may be read in the Fant work. Much of his preaching was done at the prison

in Basel. A sampler of these sermons is Karl Barth, *Deliverance to the Captives,* trans. Marguerite Wieser (New York: Harper & Bros., 1961). For thoughts about preaching that are close to those of Barth in many ways while having significant differences, cf. Dietrich Bonhoeffer, *Worldly Preaching: Lectures on Homiletics,* ed. and trans. with critical commentary by Clyde E. Fant (New York: Crossroad, 1991).

13. Theodore O. Wedel, *The Pulpit Rediscovers Theology* (Greenwich, Conn.: Seabury, 1956).

14. The influence of the liturgical movement upon preaching is the subject of the next chapter of this history.

15. Examples include Jean-Jacques von Allmen, *Preaching and Congregation,* trans. B. L. Nicholas, Ecumenical Studies in Worship, no. 10 (Richmond, Va.: John Knox, 1962); Ernest Best, *From Text to Sermon: Responsible Use of the New Testament in Preaching* (Atlanta: John Knox, 1978); Leander E. Keck, *The Bible in the Pulpit: The Renewal of Biblical Preaching* (Nashville: Abingdon, 1978); and Paul Scherer, *The Word God Sent* (New York: Harper & Row, 1965). For a conservative evangelical approach to the subject, see Edmund P. Clowney, *Preaching and Biblical Theology* (Grand Rapids, Mich.: Eerdmans, 1961).

16. Donald G. Miller, *Fire in the Mouth,* Notable Books on Preaching (Pierce & Washabaugh, 1954; reprint, Grand Rapids, Mich.: Baker, 1976).

17. Donald G. Miller, *The Way to Biblical Preaching* (New York and Nashville: Abingdon, 1957).

18. Ibid., 26.

19. Ibid.

20. Ibid., 55.

21. Ibid., 153.

22. See chapter 25, p. 664.

23. Childs, *Biblical Theology in Crisis,* 28.

24. Ibid., 85.

25. Ibid.

PREACHING AS AN ELEMENT OF WORSHIP

THE IMPACT OF THE LITURGICAL MOVEMENT ON ROMAN CATHOLIC PREACHING

Biblical theology was by no means the only influence on the mainline American churches during the 1950s and 1960s. Equally exciting were the ecumenical movement, which had little influence on their homiletics,[1] and the liturgical movement, which had a good bit. This latter movement, however, did not begin among these churches; instead, it began in continental Roman Catholicism.[2]

To understand how drastically Roman Catholic worship has changed in response to the liturgical movement, contemporary readers have to be reminded of what it was like before. The Mass was in Latin. Much of the emphasis was on its daily celebration as part of the priests' rule of life; those who did not preside for a congregation said private Masses. Because of this concentration on the priest, the norm became the "Low" or said celebration. Thus when the service was sung ("Solemn"[3] or "High" Mass), the celebrant would, in effect, say a Low Mass while the choir sang.

For instance, when the priest finished saying the creed, he moved to the sedilia and sat until the choir finished singing it, and often he would be well into the eucharistic prayer before the choir had finished the sanctus. While the choir sang the people's parts in the liturgy, the altar boy said those parts to the priest, whose back was to the congregation. At Low Mass, only the altar boy made the responses while the faithful, who did not understand the Latin, occupied themselves with some other devotion, such as private recitation of the rosary or adoration of the sacrament exposed in a monstrance.

For the laity, the value of assisting at Mass was understood to be receiving remission of days in purgatory. Missing Sunday Mass was considered a mortal sin. Communion by the faithful was infrequent, mainly because one had to be in a state of grace with no mortal sins committed since the last confession in order to receive. Even then, it was often the case at Solemn Masses that only the sanctuary party were communicated. When there was a sermon, which was not always the case, it would likely be a topical treatment of a doctrinal or moral issue, rather than an effort to apply the biblical passages read (in Latin) to the lives of the people.

Thus there was a highly individualistic understanding of the whole affair. The liturgical movement in Roman Catholicism can be understood as the effort to change most of these aspects of eucharistic celebration to those that are the norm today.

The beginning of the movement[4] is generally dated to the restoration of Benedictine monasticism (which had been greatly disrupted during the French Revolution) at the abbey of Solesmes by **Dom Prosper Guéranger** (1805–75). After the fabric of the monastery had been put in order, the full Benedictine life was instituted, with its corporate recitation of the offices and celebrations of the feasts of the church year. For that to be done properly, Guéranger thought it was necessary to revive plainsong, or Gregorian chant as it is called. Prior to this, French liturgical life had been chaotic, with a number of "neo-Gallican" rites being used in addition to that of Rome. After Solesmes became a showcase of the transcendent beauty with which the liturgy could be offered, parishes and cathedrals, as well as monasteries, adopted its model.[5]

Solesmes was also influential at a theoretical level, producing a widely read study of the liturgical year that ran to five thousand pages, the purpose of which was to deepen the congregation's participation through greater understanding of the liturgical texts and the scriptural lectionary. While this emphasis on participation did not entail any desire to revise the Roman liturgy or to translate it into the vernacular, it set in motion a progression of thought that would end there. Another result was that the use of plainsong rather than "concert" Mass settings shortened musical responses drastically, and so provided a far greater synchronicity of the celebrant's actions with those of the choir, making it more obvious that all were involved in a joint undertaking.

The next stage of the movement was to see the Eucharist understood as an action of the entire church. As early as 1883, Dom Gerhard Van Caloen began to advocate lay participation in the rite and published a small bilingual missal that would make it possible for the laity to follow the action of the Mass. Another Belgian Benedictine, **Dom Lambert Beauduin,** believed that the way to restore Christian spirituality was to work for the sung Mass's restoration as the norm for Sundays, with the faithful participating by singing and by an informed following of the rites and texts.

Beauduin's openness to Eastern Christians and Anglicans led in 1926 to his being expelled from the monastery of Mont César and indeed all of Belgium, but his exile's effect was to spread the influence of his thought. Among those who felt the force of his convictions were Virgil Michel, an American Benedictine who returned home to spread the movement here, and the papal nuncio in Paris when Beauduin taught there, the future pope John XXIII.

By the end of World War I, there was considerable lay interest in the liturgy. One of those who did most to satisfy that curiosity was **Pius Parsch** (1884–1954), an Augustinian canon of Klosterneuberg in Austria. While a chaplain in the war, "he discovered the two ideas that were to dominate his later years, the Bible as the people's book and the liturgy as the people's work."[6] He came to advocate many reforms, such as having the Sunday Mass at the center of the life of the people. To be such, it would have to be what was called a dialogue Mass, one in which the faithful made the responses. Congregational hymn singing was another important ingredient of Sunday worship as it ought to be. Parsch even came to encourage use of the vernacular. And, not surprisingly in the light of his devotion to Scripture, he published sermons for both the Sunday cycle and the great feasts, as well as a five-volume commentary on the Sunday Masses and their biblical texts.[7] Michael Mathis said that this latter work may have "won more adherents to the liturgical movement than any other book ever written."[8]

Romano Guardini (1885–1968) was another great popularizer of the movement. He was also one of the earliest priests to set a good example of liturgical preaching.

> He realized that for each homily he needed a "fuse," a burning question that interested him personally. He followed the church year, but chose his subjects based only on his own questions embedded in themes of the feasts and seasons.[9]

He also discovered that the homilist "had to use the same language from the pulpit that he used in the words and deeds of his personal life,"[10] rather than an artificial rhetorical language.

The primary theological insight upon which all the reforms advocated by the liturgical movement were based was that of the church as the mystical body of Christ. This insight, recognizing Christian worship's corporate nature, called for greater participation of all the faithful to make practice consistent with this understanding. The most influential theologian of the liturgical movement was **Odo Casel** (1886–1948), a Benedictine of Maria Laach. Casel's "mystery theology," as it was called, was seen as offering an adequate conceptualization of what the mystical body does in liturgy. His understanding of liturgical theology grew out of his study of pagan mystery religions.[11] He wrote at a time when scholars of the *Religionsgeschichtliche Schule* ("History of Religions School"), such as Richard Reitzenstein and Wilhelm Bousset, were suggesting that sacraments and much else in early Christianity were derived from these mystery religions. As Louis Bouyer said, Casel's "great and courageous feat was . . . to accept all the materials brought forward by the 'comparative' school and to propound new interpretations of these materials, much deeper and richer than that of his opponents."[12]

Casel's theology has been well summarized by Ernest B. Koenker:

> In the liturgical rites of sacrifice and sacrament we meet the mystical making-present-again of the *totum opus redemptionis*;[13] not only the Passion of Christ but his whole life, from the Incarnation to his Second Coming, is rendered sacramentally present in the cultic mysteries. It is not an empty commemoration or pious meditation; neither is this action something psychological or ethical. It is rather ontological action, a *signum efficax*,[14] a reality which efficaciously heightens man's natural existence through an activity in a higher sphere; as such, of course, it works *ex opere operato*.[15]

Through the combined force of its pioneers' insights, the way was paved for total triumph of the liturgical movement's point of view at the Second Vatican Council, as may be seen in its *Constitution on the Sacred Liturgy,* which was ratified on December 4, 1963. Now when the faithful gather for the liturgy, they have a text in their own language and all participate in dialogue with the priest, who presides facing them over the holy table. It is, after all, the action of the whole people of God, the mystical body of Christ, and thus a corporate activity.

On Sundays and during great feasts, at any rate, there is likely to be a great deal of singing—which may be anything from traditional chants of the church, to hymns from the rich tradition of the Protestant Reformation, to songs from the contemporary renewal movement accompanied by a guitar. Laypeople often read biblical lections other than the gospel and may also help in administration of Holy Communion.

A sermon is called for at all major celebrations, and the guidelines for such sermons say that they will help the congregation understand their lives in the light of these scriptures and the liturgy. The importance of such preaching in the liturgy is stated in the council's *Decree on the Ministry and Life of Priests*: "The primary duty of priests is the proclamation of the gospel of God to all."[16]

The revival of biblical scholarship in the Roman Catholic Church was contemporaneous with the liturgical movement's latter phase, and there was much cross-fertilization between the two activities. As far back as the time of Guéranger, the importance of the scripture readings at Mass was recognized. This gave new impetus to biblical interpretation. Some suspicion became attached to use of the historical-critical method developed by Protestant scholars because it had been taken too far by the modernist movement within Roman Catholicism, a movement condemned by Pope Pius X in his 1893 encyclical *Providentissimus Deus*.

By 1943, however, the appreciation of the Bible's importance to the church had sufficiently increased, and the recognition of the value of critical interpretation had sufficiently advanced, that Pius XII could issue *Divino afflante spiritu*, which was a reinterpretation as well as a reiteration of the earlier encyclical. In retrospect, it is recognized that a new era of Catholic biblical scholarship had been opened.[17] That opening was widened by the publication of the Vatican II document on revelation, *Verbum Dei*. A natural culmination of these trends was the publication of a new three-year lectionary cycle to begin with Advent 1971.

This changing climate had made it possible for the liturgical movement to be informed by the biblical theology movement, using many of the latter's insights in its own liturgy interpretations. New Catholic translations of the Bible into English became available at about the time the liturgy itself appeared in the vernacular. These included *The Jerusalem Bible* in 1973, greatly influenced by a French translation prepared by the École Biblique in Jerusalem, and *The New American Bible* in 1970–86. Both have excellent critical notes.

All of these trends come together in comments about preaching in Vatican II's *Constitution on the Sacred Liturgy*, which speaks of "the two parts which, in a certain sense, go to make up the mass, namely, the liturgy of the word and the eucharistic liturgy" and says these two parts are "so closely connected with each other that they form but a single act of worship" (56).

Indeed, the homily "is to be highly esteemed as a part of the liturgy itself; in fact, at those masses which are celebrated with the assistance of the people on Sundays and feasts of obligation, it should not be omitted except for a serious reason" (52). The content of the sermon is also specified:

> The sermon, moreover, should draw its content mainly from the scriptural and liturgical sources, and its character should be that of a proclamation of God's wonderful works in the history of salvation, the mystery of Christ, ever made present and active within us, especially in the celebration of the liturgy. (35)

Similarly, #24 states that "it is from scripture that lessons are read and explained in the homily."

It was, of course, much easier to arrange for a wholesale change in the way the liturgy was celebrated than to see that there was a similarly drastic alteration in the way preaching was done. For the liturgy, a priest had only to receive the revised rites and celebrate them according to the rubrics, but for preaching he almost needed to be "sent back to the factory and reprogrammed."

Some excellent resources were developed to assist in the change, however. Within five years of the *Constitution on the Sacred Liturgy,* a volume on preaching, edited by no less an authority than Karl Rahner, appeared in the Concilium series. Titled *The Renewal of Preaching: Theory and Practice,*[18] it includes articles on such subjects as the New Testament theology of the Word, "translation from the language of scripture and tradition into a language that can be understood today,"[19] an application of communications theory to preaching, an analysis of preaching's relation to sacramental worship, a study of preaching's contribution to reconciliation, a consideration of whether the laity may preach, and an essay on radio preaching. This is followed by reports on preaching in various European and American countries, with another look at preaching in relation to mass media. This volume, therefore, is not so much a statement of how the council's decrees concerning preaching were to be carried out as a look at the issues that have to be considered in making such a statement.

A number of individuals have written "how-to" manuals consistent with the criteria of the *Constitution on the Sacred Liturgy,*[20] but perhaps the best place to gain a post–Vatican II American Roman Catholic perspective on the nature of the homiletical task is a document published by the Bishop's Committee on Priestly Life and Ministry of the United States Conference of Catholic Bishops, *Fulfilled in Your Hearing: The Homily in the Sunday Assembly*.[21] After an introduction in which it is noted that the Sunday homily is "the normal and frequently the formal way in which [the majority of Catholics] hear the Word of God proclaimed" (2), the document looks at the three major elements of liturgical preaching: the assembly, the preacher, and the homily, in that order. This analysis of elements is followed by a consideration of homiletic method; after that the work concludes with an epilogue on "The Power of the Word."

The analysis begins with the assembly not only because communications theory points to the importance of the audience, but even more basically because "the primary reality is Christ in the assembly, the People of God" (4).

> The community that gathers Sunday after Sunday comes together to offer God praise and thanksgiving, or at least to await a word that will give meaning to their lives and enable them to celebrate Eucharist. (8)

The priest helps the people to make connections between their lives and the Word of God by listening prayerfully both to the biblical readings appointed for the Sunday and to his people. For interpretation of the Scriptures, the priest must do the best exegesis he is capable of, and he must study his people with the same attentiveness. Study of either the Word or the people will not be infallible, but "what the Word of God offers us is a way to interpret our human lives, a way to face the ambiguities and challenges of the human condition, not a pat answer to every problem and question that comes along" (15).

The purpose of the liturgical homily is that "a community of believers who have gathered to celebrate the liturgy may do so more deeply and more fully—more faithfully—and thus be formed for Christian witness in the world."[22] Thus one of the major differences between liturgical preaching and other varieties is that this form derives a lot of its meaning from the way it relates to the other liturgical elements. As William Skudlarek said, "To celebrate and offer thanks for the good news we have heard: that ultimately is the reason preaching and liturgy go together. We need to know why we should lift up our hearts."[23] Therefore, it is "preaching that proclaims the good news of the great and wonderful things God has done and is doing for his people, rather than preaching that lists the dos and don'ts that people must follow if they are to gain the favor of God."[24] Such preaching would meet with the approval of the biblical theology movement, rehearsing as it does the mighty acts of God, but it is also preaching that gives meaning and purpose to the eucharistic celebration of which it is an integral part. Implicit in this liturgical grounding is celebration of the *magnalia*[25] that reflect a particular day's theme in the church year and their rehearsal in the lectionary-appointed scriptural lessons.

The method of homily preparation taught in *Fulfilled in Your Hearing* could have been a godsend to the priest who had no idea of how to go about the kind of preaching the council expected him to do, but it is not otherwise innovative enough to require summary here. An appropriate closing to this account of the difference the liturgical movement has made in Roman Catholic preaching, however, is the sense of the joy and privilege of preaching with which the booklet ends:

> We too stand in sacred space, aware of our personal inadequacy, yet willing to share how the scriptural story has become integrated into our thoughts and actions while we walked among those who turn their faces toward us. The words we speak are human words describing how God's action has become apparent to us this week. Is it any wonder then that excitement and tension fill us in the moments before we preach? With a final deep breath may we also breathe in the Spirit of God who will animate our human words with divine power (42).[26]

THE ANGLICAN/EPISCOPAL EXPERIENCE

Among Western churches not in obedience to the pope, the Anglican Communion is unique in that it has "never ceased to be a *liturgical* church." This is to say that "it finds its nexus of unity, its spiritual regimen, its tradition and way of life in the Book of Common Prayer."[27] Moreover, Anglicanism's sense of continuity with the undivided early church had been strengthened for many by the nineteenth-century Catholic revival known as the Oxford or Tractarian movement.[28] That movement, however, had the effect of polarizing the communion into those who identified primarily with either its Catholic or its Protestant heritage. While all Anglican worship was liturgical, and the majority of parishes had an early celebration of the Eucharist without music or sermon, the main service on most Sundays tended in "Low Church" parishes to be choral Morning Prayer with sermon,[29] and in "High Churches" to be the Eucharist, celebrated as nearly as possible to the Roman Catholic manner described at the beginning of this chapter, with the exception that it was usually in English rather than Latin.

There had always been liturgical scholars in Anglicanism, and some of their efforts culminated in a 1928 attempt to revise the Church of England's Prayer Book and bring an end to the chaos into which Anglicanism's liturgical life had degenerated. While the necessary legislation passed the church's governing body, it failed to get through Parliament, which had to approve such major changes in the established church.[30] In the aftermath of that failure, two changes began slowly to occur. One was a reduction of tension between the High and Low Church, and the other was a growing appreciation for the Eucharist as the central act of Christian worship.

The attitude developing toward the Eucharist was given a rallying point in the concept of the "parish communion" publicized in a 1937 book edited by A. G. Hebert.[31] Gabriel Hebert, a monk of the Society of the Sacred Mission at Kelham, had already translated the great study by the Swedish Lutheran archbishop Yngve Brilioth, *Eucharistic Faith and Practice: Evangelical and Catholic.*[32] He had also established himself as a liturgical theologian in *The Liturgy and Society: The Function of the Church in the Modern World,*[33] an effort to consider the continental liturgical movement's implications for the Church of England and, indeed, for modern Europe.

The parish communion, which had originated in the parish of Temple Balsall in rural Warwickshire in 1913, was a manner of celebrating the Eucharist so that its status as the central act of Christian worship would be obvious and honored. It was held around nine o'clock on Sunday morning and was designed to be as participatory as possible. Often it was followed by a parish breakfast, a sort of modern agape meal in which members of the parish could become better acquainted and could interact as fellow members of the body of Christ. Often there was an offertory procession in which the elements were brought to the altar from the back of the church, where each person intending to receive had placed a communion bread in the ciborium when entering.

In other words, the parish communion in the Church of England exemplified most of the liturgical movement's ideals. And, as Horton Davies says, "The parish communion has, in subsequent years, become almost the normative celebration of the eucharist in the Church of England."[34] The practice quickly spread from England to other parts of the Anglican Communion, including the Episcopal Church in the United States.

Father Hebert came to devote more of his energy to biblical theology and less to liturgics, another of many instances when the two movements cross-fertilized each other. Meanwhile, Anglican preaching got a new lease on life from the parish communion, at which priests felt it necessary to teach about the liturgy, especially the seasons of the church year, and about the biblical lections that were read to proclaim the mighty acts of God on which the calendar was based. Thus it is not surprising that one of the most important representatives of the biblical theology movement in England, Reginald H. Fuller, should write a book called *What Is Liturgical Preaching?*[35] (For a later version of Fuller's thought, see **Vol. 2, pp. 553-67.**)

Although scriptural passages read at their services had always been those appointed in the lectionary, Anglican clergy had never been as likely to preach on one of these "propers" as Lutheran pastors were to preach from the "pericopes." Further, as Brilioth has pointed out, after Tillotson, "the Anglican sermon to a disheartening extent became an oral essay on a religious or ethical subject."[36] The result was that, in spite of the occasional great preachers who were exceptions to the rule, Anglican preaching stood in real need of being rescued by the liturgical movement.

Fuller explained that the purpose of the sermon was not merely to explain obscure passages in the Bible, nor to relate them to the lives of modern congregations, nor to be analogous to "the type of public speaking which takes place at the annual festal gathering of a society or club."[37] Neither is it the sort of preaching to non-Christians that the New Testament *kerygma* was, nor the kind of instruction in doctrine and ethics that *didache* was. Rather, it should be *paraklesis*: "a renewal and deepening of the apprehension of the *kerygma* in the already converted."[38] Close to Skudlarek's saying that it should tell us why we should lift up our hearts is Fuller's understanding of the purpose of the sermon:

> to extract from the scripture readings the essential core and content of the gospel, to penetrate behind the day's pericope to the proclamation of the central act of God in Christ which it contains, in order that the central act of God can be made the material for recital in the prayer of thanksgiving.[39]

As the parish communion became the norm in Anglicanism, this sort of preaching accompanied it and has been the basic form of preaching in the communion ever since.

THE LITURGICAL MOVEMENT AND NONLITURGICAL CHURCHES

In the subtitle for the fifth volume of his history of *Worship and Theology in England,* Horton Davies refers to the twentieth as the "ecumenical century." Nowhere is that more obvious than in attitudes toward Christian worship. As Davies said:

> What is fascinating about (the liturgical) movement is that it has enabled Protestant churches to recover in part the Catholic liturgical heritage, while the Catholics seem to have appropriated the Protestant valuation of preaching, of shared worship in the vernacular tongue, and the importance of the laity as the people of God.[40]

These trends in England are traced only to 1965, the year the Davies volume was published.[41] James F. White, however, sees Catholic and Protestant worship traditions growing even closer in the years after Vatican II (1962–65). He says:

> If the postwar period was a time of Protestant ideas coming to the fore-front in Roman Catholic thinking, the post–Vatican II era has been a time of Roman Catholic ideas shaping Protestant worship. Protestants have now returned the compliment by borrowing much that is new in Roman Catholic worship. Indeed, new service books from Roman Catholic, Methodist, Lutheran, Reformed, and Anglican traditions seem to be similar recensions of a single text.[42]

The degree of accord that has been achieved may be seen in the *Baptism, Eucharist, and Ministry* document of the Faith and Order Commission of the World Council of Churches, which was completed in January 1982 at Lima, Peru. While the response to this document has not been without dissension, it has, nevertheless, been adequately positive to indicate the high degree of agreement achieved in the three areas of theology indicated by its title, areas in which sharp polemics had raged since the Reformation.[43]

The changes that have occurred in the worship of the Free Churches of Great Britain parallel those in American Protestant churches. As listed by Davies, changes for England have included the following:

1. A loss of prejudice against set forms of worship and, in some places a welcoming of liturgical forms.
2. The increasing use of the seasons and feasts of the Christian year.
3. A diminishing antipathy to the recitation of creeds in worship.[44]
4. A greatly enhanced appreciation of the gospel sacraments of Baptism and the Eucharist.
5. The improvement of the solemnity of ordination services.
6. A better balance between Word and sacrament.[45]

Of these, those that affect preaching the most deeply are concerned with greater acceptance of the Christian year and better balance between Word and sacrament. Wider use of the lectionary is implicit to the acceptance of the liturgical calendar. How widespread that has become may be seen in a popular series of homiletical preparation aids that list in parallel columns the passages to be read on a given Sunday or holy day according to the usage of a number of churches. These include the Lutheran, Roman Catholic, Episcopal, Presbyterian/United Church of Christ/Christian, and United Methodist/COCU lectionaries. To these can be added *The Common Lectionary,* which was drawn up by the North American Committee on a Common Lectionary. All of these are three-year reading cycles that have a high incidence of agreement on the second lessons and Gospels appointed for particular days, but show greater variation in the readings from the Hebrew Scriptures.

A result of the mainline Protestant churches' greater openness to preaching from the lectionary, observing the Christian year, and achieving a better balance between Word and sacrament, has been that the homilies preached by clergy from the different faith communities show the same sort of convergence displayed by the liturgies in their new service books. Therefore, the liturgical movement, combined as it has been with the biblical theology and ecumenical movements, has been a major change agent in twentieth-century preaching.

FOR FURTHER READING

Fulfilled in Your Hearing: The Homily in the Sunday Assembly. Bishop's Committee on Priestly Life and Ministry of the United States Conference of Catholic Bishops. Washington: United States Conference of Catholic Bishops, 1982.

Fuller, Reginald H. *What Is Liturgical Preaching?* Studies in Worship and Ministry. London: SCM, 1957.

How Firm a Foundation: Leaders of the Liturgical Movement. Compiled and introduction by Robert L. Tuzik. Chicago: Liturgy Training Publications, Archdiocese of Chicago, 1990.

The Parish Communion. Edited by A. G. Hebert. London: SPCK, 1937.

Skudlarek, William. *The Word in Worship: Preaching in a Liturgical Context.* Abingdon Preacher's Library. Nashville: Abingdon, 1981.

White, James F. *Protestant Worship: Traditions in Transition.* Louisville: Westminster John Knox, 1989.

Notes

1. Preaching theory had been agreed upon among these churches for some time.

2. The involvement of the Roman Catholic Church in the ecumenical movement did open it to both the biblical theology movement and, as will be seen below, the influence of Protestant homiletics.

3. At a Solemn Mass, a deacon and a subdeacon assisted the officiating priest.

4. A concise history of the continental Roman Catholic phase of the liturgical movement appears in Horton Davies, *The Ecumenical Century, 1900–1965*, vol. 5 of *Worship and Theology in England* (Princeton: Princeton University Press, 1970), 5:13-49. The contribution of individuals is detailed in *How Firm a Foundation: Leaders of the Liturgical Movement*, comp. and intro. Robert L. Tuzik (Chicago: Liturgy Training Publications, Archdiocese of Chicago, 1990). This latter volume is ecumenical, includes Americans as well as Europeans, and traces the movement down to recent times, treating "the dead and the elderly, though a few in their 60s" at the time of writing. See also Louis Bouyer, *Liturgical Piety*, Liturgical Studies (Notre Dame: University of Notre Dame Press, 1955), and the article on "The History of the Liturgical Renewal," by Massey H. Shepherd Jr., in the volume he edited for the Associated Parishes, *The Liturgical Renewal of the Church* (New York: Oxford University Press, 1960), 21-52.

5. The revival of Gregorian chant was greatly aided by a *motu proprio*, published by Pope Pius X in 1903 on music and liturgy.

6. Michael Kwatera, "Pius Parsch, Evangelist of the Liturgy," in Tuzik, *How Firm a Foundation*, 30.

7. *Sermons on the Liturgy for Sundays and Feasts*, trans. Philip T. Weller (Milwaukee: Bruce, 1953), and *The Church's Year of Grace*, trans. William G. Heidt (Collegeville, Minn.: Liturgical Press, 1953–59).

8. Quoted in Kwatera, "Pius Parsch, Evangelist of the Liturgy," 34.

9. Regina Kuehn, "Romano Guardini," in Tuzik, *How Firm a Foundation*, 40.

10. Ibid.

11. Casel wrote two doctoral dissertations, one on the eucharistic theology of Justin Martyr, and the other on mysticism and Greek philosophy.

12. Bouyer, *Liturgical Piety*, 87. Bouyer, however, goes on to say that Casel could have questioned the findings of the History of Religions School far more radically than he did.

13. "The whole work of redemption."

14. "Effective sign."

15. "On the basis of the action performed." Ernest B. Koenker, *The Liturgical Renaissance in the Roman Catholic Church* (Chicago: University of Chicago Press, 1954), 107, quoted in Shepherd, *The Liturgical Renewal of the Church*, 31-34.

16. *Decree on the Ministry and Life of Priests*, Presbyterorum Ordinis, *Promulgated by His Holiness, Pope Paul VI on December 7, 1965*, chapter 2, section 1, paragraph 4, http://www.microbookstudio.com/secondv.htm.

17. Robert Grant and David Tracy, *A Short History of the Interpretation of the Bible*, 2nd ed., rev. and enl. (Philadelphia: Fortress, 1984), 119-25.

18. *The Renewal of Preaching: Theory and Practice*, ed. Karl Rahner, Concilium:

Theology in the Age of Renewal, vol. 33 (New York and Glen Rock, N.J., 1968).

19. Ibid., 23. This article is by Rahner himself and is titled "Demythologization and the Sermon," but the words quoted above are what he means by the title.

20. An excellent example is *The Word in Worship: Preaching in a Liturgical Context,* Abingdon Preacher's Library (Nashville: Abingdon, 1981) written by a Benedictine, William Skudlarek, for an ecumenical series of volumes on preaching. My own *Elements of Homiletic: A Method for Preparing to Preach* (New York: Pueblo, 1982), was commissioned by a Roman Catholic publisher to serve that purpose.

21. *Fulfilled in Your Hearing: The Homily in the Sunday Assembly,* Bishop's Committee on Priestly Life and Ministry of the United States Conference of Catholic Bishops (Washington: United States Conference of Catholic Bishops, 1982). The principal writer was the author of the book listed in the previous note, William Skudlarek, O.S.B. The team included such capable homileticians as David Buttrick and Fred Baumer, C.P.P.S., in addition to members of the hierarchy. The priestly sociologist and novelist Andrew Greeley was a consultant to the project. (Hereafter, parenthetical references in text are to page numbers in this document.)

22. Ibid., 18. In the text there is an extensive footnote commenting on this passage.

23. Skudlarek, *The Word in Worship,* 70.

24. Ibid., 71.

25. The "mighty acts" of God.

26. That the kingdom has no more fully come in the Roman church than any other, however, is suggested by Keith F. Pecklers in *The Unread Vision: The Liturgical Movement in the United States of America: 1926–55* (Collegeville, Minn.: Liturgical Press, 1998). He says: "We are in the midst of a liturgical malaise. Liturgical presiding, preaching, and music are in need of help" (p. 285).

27. Davies, *Worship and Theology in England,* 5:38. Davies gives a convenient summary of the history of the liturgical movement within Anglicanism on pp. 38-44, although he wrote before the Prayer Book revisions made by virtually every province of the communion had appeared. See also Shepherd, "The History of the Liturgical Renewal," 45-50. For the American branch of the Anglican Communion, the Episcopal Church, see Urban T. Holmes, "Education for Liturgy: An Unfinished Symphony in Four Movements," in *Worship Points the Way: Celebration of the Life and Work of Massey H. Shepherd, Jr.,* ed. Malcolm C. Burson (New York: Seabury, 1981), 116-41. For the importance of the Book of Common Prayer for all Anglican understandings of ministry, see my essay "Anglican Pastoral Tradition," in *The Study of Anglicanism,* ed. Stephen Sykes, John Booty, and Jonathan Knight, rev. ed. (London: SPCK; Minneapolis: Fortress, 1998), 378-91.

28. See above, chapter 22, 601-8.

29. Prayer Book rubrics call for a sermon with the Eucharist but do not do so for Morning Prayer.

30. For an account of this process, see Davies, *Worship and Theology in England,* 5:284-306.

31. *The Parish Communion,* ed. A. G. Hebert (London: SPCK, 1937).

32. Yngve Brilioth, *Eucharistic Faith and Practice: Evangelical and Catholic*, trans. A. G. Hebert (London: SPCK, 1930).

33. A. G. Hebert, *The Liturgy and Society: The Function of the Church in the Modern World* (London: Faber & Faber, 1936).

34. Davies, *Worship and Theology in England*, 5:321.

35. Reginald H. Fuller, *What Is Liturgical Preaching?*, Studies in Worship and Ministry (London: SCM, 1957). By the time the book was published, Fuller had already joined the faculty of Seabury-Western Theological Seminary in Evanston, Illinois. As another incidence of the overlap of the biblical theology and liturgical movements, see Theodore O. Wedel, *The Pulpit Rediscovers Theology* (Greenwich, Conn.: Seabury, 1956), 128-58.

36. Yngve Brilioth, *A Brief History of Preaching*, trans. Karl E. Mattson (Philadelphia: Fortress, 1965), 179.

37. Fuller, *What Is Liturgical Preaching?*, 17.

38. Ibid., 22.

39. Ibid.

40. Davies, *Worship and Theology in England*, 5:7.

41. Davies has since written a sixth volume to *Worship and Theology*, entitled *Crisis and Creativity, 1965-Present* (Grand Rapids, Mich.: Eerdmans, 1996), but that is primarily concerned with developments in baptism and the Eucharist and says very little about changes in preaching in the generation covered.

42. James F. White, *Protestant Worship: Traditions in Transition* (Louisville: Westminster John Knox, 1989), 34. White himself is not in favor of too much assimilation of Protestant worship to Catholic forms, however, saying: "If the convergence becomes too prominent, we must ask whether some of the richness of the variety of Protestant worship will suffer. *The richness of Protestant worship consists in its diversity and in its consequent ability to serve a wide variety of people*" (ibid., 212).

43. See *Baptism, Eucharist, and Ministry, 1982–1990: Report on the Process and Responses*, Faith and Order Paper, no. 149 (Geneva: WCC Publications, 1990).

44. Davies did not number this as a separate trend, but he did devote a page to discussing the matter. *Worship and Theology in England*, 5:391-92.

45. These are discussed in ibid., 5:387-97. On the last point of the relation of Word and sacrament, it is interesting to note that the intimate connection between them was maintained by Karl Barth (*Homiletics*, transl. Geoffrey W. Bromiley and Donald E. Daniels, foreword David Buttrick [Louisville: Westminster John Knox, 1991], 56-63).

CHAPTER 28

A HOMILETICAL EPIPHANY

THE EMERGENCE OF AFRICAN AMERICAN PREACHING IN MAJORITY CONSCIOUSNESS

"THE PREACHER KING"

Among the many streams of tradition that converged to form late-twentieth-century understanding of the nature of preaching, none showed the proclaimed word's potentialities to move people and change society as did the classical homiletic of the African American church. As much as its pulpit had done to sustain its people through slavery, reconstruction, and segregation, it was hardly known to the rest of American society until the civil rights movement got under way in the late-1950s. Then, however, it burst on the national scene with dazzling brightness.

The brilliance of that impression is the product of two factors: the homiletical ability of the Reverend Dr. Martin Luther King Jr., and the coverage the news media, especially television, gave to the campaigns in which he was involved. The events were startling enough to be given full coverage, to be served up to white Americans in their living rooms on a daily basis. And always at the center was a man who could articulate the issues in such a way that they had to be taken seriously. Whether the viewers were inspired, reluctantly persuaded, or stirred to rage by him, he and his message could not be ignored.

This is not to say that Martin Luther King was the only civil rights leader, that he was the only Christian minister among the leaders, or even that he was the best preacher of the lot. Working with him were such gifted proclaimers of the word as Ralph Abernathy, Andrew Young, Wyatt Tee Walker, C. T. Vivian, Jesse Jackson, Bernard Lee, Walter Fauntroy, James Lawson, Charles Sherrod, Bernard Lafayette, John Lewis, and James Bevel. Local clergy were involved in every campaign, and other civil rights organizations, some with their own clergy, were engaged in additional campaigns. But the TV cameras focused on King, and, therefore, it was he who showed the rest of the country a homiletical tradition of startling power.

Ironically, King's own preaching at the beginning of his ministry was not in the tradition of the black church, but more akin to that of liberal white clergy at the time. He grew up in the classic tradition and saw it modeled by his father at Ebenezer Baptist Church in Atlanta's "Sweet Auburn" district, and by William Holmes Borders at the nearby Wheat Street Church. Although he and his friends studied the techniques of preachers in the neighborhood, when he went to Morehouse College he undertook the formal study of rhetoric and began to be influenced by the liberal preaching of the college president, Benjamin Mays.[1]

That liberal influence was intensified when King enrolled in the predominantly white Crozer Seminary in Chester, Pennsylvania. And it achieved its ultimate impact when he focused his Ph.D. on the personalist theology of Edgar S. Brightman at Boston University.[2] Thus he absorbed the pulpit tradition of such nineteenth-century figures as Henry Ward Beecher and Phillips Brooks, and that of contemporary luminaries like Harry Emerson Fosdick, George A. Buttrick, and Halford E. Luccock. At the same time, however, he studied the examples of great African American preachers like Gardner Taylor, who could "generate passion while retaining his composure," and J. Pius Barbour, who could combine "theological erudition with old-time religion."[3]

When King arrived in Montgomery, Alabama, to begin his first pastorate in September of 1954, his new congregation included the most distinguished people of his race in the city, and they expected a dignity in their worship that was commensurate with their achievement.[4] Thus the

704

previous January when he preached his trial sermon auditioning for a call to the church, he used a sermon called "The Three Dimensions of a Complete Life," which he had preached in the Boston area several times.[5] It was an allegorical interpretation of Revelation 21:16, which gives the dimensions of the New Jerusalem. He treats a healthy self-respect as the length, love of neighbor as the breadth, and love of God as the height.[6] According to the historians of the church at its centennial, King at some time during his tenure there said: "I revolt against the emotionalism of Negro[7] religion, the shouting and the stamping. I don't understand it and it embarrasses me."[8] At the beginning of his ministry, he and his parishioners apparently saw eye to eye.

This is not to say, however, that he had forgotten his roots. A sermon he preached in Detroit the month after his Dexter trial sermon was much more the combination of traditional homiletic with learned content that was to be the hallmark of his later preaching. More important, his reflexes were ready for the supreme challenge when it came. The occasion of its coming was Rosa Parks's now legendary refusal to give up her bus seat to a white man. Clergy and other leaders in the African American community quickly called a boycott of buses and organized the Montgomery Improvement Association, naming King as their president. He was to speak, virtually without preparation, on the evening after her trial at a mass meeting called at Holt Street Baptist Church.

At that meeting on December 5, 1955, Martin Luther King Jr. discovered his calling, his principle, and his method. The calling was to lead the civil rights movement, his principle was to combine militancy with nonviolence, and his method was to use oratory that combined intellectual content with the power of classical African American preaching. As Stephen Oates said:

> It was as though he had been preparing for that speech all his life . . . He sat down, trembling from his effort. Across the church, people were yelling and waving their arms, clapping and singing as he had never seen them do before. Imagine Martin Luther King, a twenty-six-year-old scholar, making people rock with such emotion.[9]

The bus boycott ended triumphantly a year later when the Supreme Court struck down the laws that segregated public transportation in Alabama. Although Dr. King continued as pastor at Dexter, his presence was continually being sought elsewhere to help in the struggle. Thus King organized the Southern Christian Leadership Conference in August of 1957. Eventually, however, the conflict between being pastor of a local church and heading a movement that covered the Deep South and had international involvement became too great. At the end of January 1960, he resigned from Dexter and moved to Atlanta, where he would receive most of his income from being his father's assistant pastor at Ebenezer and devote most of his time and energy to being president of SCLC.

The story of what was accomplished has been told too often to need recounting here. Besides, at first glance, much of it would appear to have little to do with the history of preaching. Yet overprecise distinctions would be hard to maintain. Lischer has shown that from 1960 on, King practiced three basic forms of public address:[10] he preached often at Ebenezer and other African American churches, he addressed mass meetings held nightly during campaigns, and he occupied distinguished public rostra in the white world.[11]

Yet there was not as much difference among these genres of speech as might be expected. The mass meetings were held in churches, hymns were sung and prayers offered, and ordained men who often based what they said on a biblical text gave most of the speeches.[12] And, while the public addresses argued from civic rather than biblical texts and were intended to appeal to a wider audience, even in them appear many of the preacher's mannerisms and techniques. A small example of this is his "adroitly juxtaposing quotations from the scriptures with the lyrics of patriotic anthems" in the most famous of such occasions, his "I Have a Dream" speech at the March on Washington of August 28, 1963.[13] Hence the key to all of King's rhetorical activity is an understanding of his preaching.

To understand the preaching of the mature King, it is necessary to look at the sermons he preached during the eight and a quarter years he served as his father's assistant at Ebenezer Baptist Church in Atlanta. While he did not preach there every Sunday during that period, he did so often enough to reveal a clear pattern to his sermons:[14]

> The bent of King's gospel follows the contours of the Christian story of redemption. It begins with the human condition, which is nothing other than the experience of one of life's many perplexities. The perplexity suggests a larger problem, the problem yields a sin, the sin opens onto a social concern (always related to race or war), the concern invites a generalization about "man" or "life," and the stage is set for the next phase of the message.[15]

By "sin," King means a human effort to accomplish what only God can do. What starts out as the presentation of a problem always ends up as a cry for redemption. Along the way, however, the universal problem is particularized in ways that it is experienced by the African American community, both in terms of what has been done to them (the "triple ghetto" of poverty, race, and misery) and also in the sinful responses these crimes evoke in their victims.

The only answer to any of these problems is the God of the Bible: the Creator of the world, the liberator of Israel, and the Father of Jesus Christ. "It goes without arguing that God wills to liberate Negroes from captivity in America because that is the kind of God we have."[16] This God of love grants deliverance through Jesus Christ, the caring one who can heal all personal wounds and overcome all social problems, the one who can not only forgive sins but also change sinners. King's hearers could be transformed into people who love their enemies, and their love would be the means God used to transform those who persecuted them.

Thus the vision of a glorious future kingdom of God that he held up to his congregation was not of a heavenly home but of a transformed society. And the agent of that deliverance was not the Christian church in general—he had seen too many failures of white Christians—but the African American church, with its willingness to suffer in order to bring about reconciliation.

King's Ebenezer sermons always ended with a celebration of the glory and goodness of God, the ecstatic climax of African American preaching, but this element was consistently eliminated when he preached to a white congregation and from printed editions of his sermons. Also at Ebenezer, he always ended with that staple of Southern evangelical churches, an altar call. The "doors of the church" were opened, but, more important, the possibility of a personal relation with Jesus was extended. The way to achieve that was through repentance and conversion. And then, "the services at Ebenezer often ended on a chaotic note when the invitation would degenerate into general announcements."[17] This, too, was standard in thousands of churches, black and white.

Dr. King seldom had time to prepare his Ebenezer sermons in detail, and his ability to virtually extemporize homiletical masterpieces depended on his having available in his memory a variety of sermon titles and outlines, and a collection of set pieces that he could interject wherever they were needed. This is not to say that his sermons were simply rehashes of his own and other preachers' previous efforts, but rather that having available such a useful collection of frameworks left him free to devote his creativity to the immediate situation and its needs.

The titles and outlines generally went together, and he had been using most of them since at least his first year at Dexter; many had been borrowed or adapted from other preachers. In this use of borrowed materials, King was like all preachers of his time:

> A survey of the sermon volumes of the 1950s reveals a pronounced lack of originality among the twentieth-century princes of the pulpit not only in the canned illustrations that circulated among them but also with regard to their themes.[18]

What is impressive, however, is not his sources but his use of them. They were merely hooks on which he was able to hang his analysis of the racial situation in the country. The real content of his sermons was uniquely his. This can be seen especially by comparing the recordings made over a period of years of sermons involving the same title and outline, such as the "Three Dimensions" sermon he used for his audition at Dexter. These are versions of the same thing only in the most limited sense. In terms of real content and effect, each version is unique, and thus entitled to respect from even the perspective of the Romantic preoccupation with originality. (For a version of this sermon, see **Vol. 2, pp. 568-79.**)

More important for his oratory's effectiveness than King's reused titles and outlines was what Lischer calls his "set pieces"—the "enormous disassembled inventory of rhetorical parts ready for immediate installation."[19] The more usual rhetorical term is "commonplaces," a literal translation of both the Latin *loci communes* and the Greek *koinoi topoi.* This term is defined as "a general argument, observation, or description a speaker could memorize for use on a number of possible occasions."[20] King's quiver of commonplaces embraced a range of complexity, the simplest form of which was the epithet, a brief metaphoric expression such as "the iron feet of oppression."

> In addition to the Homeric epithet, King developed a repertoire of borrowed formulas that included assemblages of poems, paragraphs drawn from popular white preachers, gospel climax formulas absorbed in the black church, and much longer poetic-like pieces of his own composition.[21]

"Commonplace" is a basket term, embracing the two meanings "of the things that people generally consider persuasive, and of methods that have persuasive effects."[22] King's collection of set pieces were sermonic elements that he knew from experience would elicit a response, would stir up the sort of emotion that would cause people to identify with the cause and enlist in its program. And his whole purpose in preaching was to achieve that result.

It would be possible to think of the stylistic elements in King's sermons as a collection of techniques he had amassed in general that could be applied to the specific goal of participation in the movement. In doing so, however, one would miss the strategic dimension of all King did in his preaching. It was all motivated behavior, intended to accomplish the particular task and to do so in the most efficient way possible. He recognized with Cicero that the purposes of the orator are to teach, to please, and to move—and that teaching and pleasing are done in order to move, to enlist one's hearers in the cause.

A basic goal was to enable all to realize that their particular campaigns were not small struggles on local issues, but were instead key episodes in the eternal struggle between right and wrong. These were not things "done in a corner," but events of cosmic significance. A key element of King's rhetorical strategy was to indicate by the elevated tone of his discourse the importance of what was at stake in the struggle.

A case in point is the use of epithets noted above. Many of these involve metaphors: gradualism is a drug, despair a "dark and desolate valley," pessimism a chamber, etc. In these epithets, "King often combines an archetypal image, for example, a *valley* or a *sunlit path*, with an equally universal value, such as *despair* or *peace*."[23] In so doing he indicates the universal scope of the issues at stake in the local struggle. "King framed what was an exceedingly mean-spirited conflict between protesters and state troopers in the abstract language of light and darkness, justice and injustice."[24] At the same time, by his elevated diction, King showed that he—and, by implication, all members of his race—were not servile, but persons of intelligence and ability, deserving of a place in society as good as their oppressors'. His diction was so elevated that many passages of his sermons could be set down in stanza form and read as poetry.

The elevation of his style involves use of all the standard figures of sound. One encounters alliteration and assonance. Anaphora, which begins successive clauses with the same group of words, is balanced by its opposite, epistrophe, where the repetition occurs at the end. Key to these figures is repetition, which is also seen in such forms of amplification as copiousness (saying the same thing in a number of different ways) and intensification (statements in an ascending order of gravity). His strategy of elevation also involves sacred or heroic association, at times in explicit and logical ways, but at others through unexpected parataxis.

These are devices of sound, but they represent only a fraction of King's ability to pattern sound to achieve his effect. In addition to these, for instance, he was able to establish rhythm in his sermons by the way he spoke them. This effect was heightened by his use of anaphora and other repetitive figures. He would often rap out the cadence on the side of the pulpit or its Bible. He would reinforce the effect by variations in the stress and pitch he gave to syllables. Then he would emphasize the pattern by altering it in places with a syncopated stammer or a run-on effect, as when the third time around he said "I have a dream" at the close of one sentence rather than the beginning of the next.

Much of the way he was able to pattern sound was a function of the total control he had of his magnificent voice:

> The gradual ascendancy of his pitch from a low growl at the beginning of the sermon to a piercing shout at the upper range of his high baritone, the predictable rhythm of the rise and fall of his voice, and the relentless increase in the *rate* of his speech—all contribute to the melodiousness, the songlike quality, of his voice.[25]

Among the musical techniques that he, in common with other African American preachers, employed vocally were blue notes, glissando, grace notes, falloffs, and tremolo. The range of his power of expression was extraordinary.

Blend all of this with the antiphony of the call-and-response interaction between a black preacher and his congregation, and the effect was hypnotic and ecstatic, especially when the sermon rose to the final climax in which the goodness and glory of God were celebrated. There is no doubt that King was a rhetorical and vocal artist who could carry out a strategy for enlistment. In the end, however, all the technique was just a vehicle for his message. More than his rhetorical ability but reinforced by it, what really allowed him to demonstrate to the wider public the power of classical African American preaching was a combination of two factors: the axiomatic nature of his appeal's moral principles and his unhesitating, undeviating, fearless commitment to carrying them out.

TEACHERS TO THE NATION: AFRICAN AMERICAN BEECHER LECTURERS

While the television coverage of Martin Luther King Jr.'s leadership of the civil rights movement revealed to the nation at large the richness of the African American church's classical homiletical tradition, it was through different channels that those who practiced other preaching methods were instructed in how to acquire for themselves something of the black pulpit's power. One of these channels—and, even more, an indication of the extent to which such instruction was sought—were the invitations extended to African American clergy to deliver the Lyman Beecher Lectures at Yale, the most distinguished forum in the country for the imparting of homiletical wisdom. Eight sets of lectures have been delivered by African Americans, all given in the second half of the twentieth century.[26]

James H. Robinson

The first series stands apart from the others in a number of ways. Given in 1955, it preceded the next set by almost twenty years. And it was delivered a few months before the bus boycott in Montgomery, and so was prior to when the civil rights movement seized the general public's attention. Further, the lecturer, the Reverend Dr. James H. Robinson, was a minister of the Presbyterian Church, rather than one of the historic African American denominations, and had trained at Union seminary. Although possibly the youngest person ever to give the lectures, he was already a world-famous speaker who often had been invited to address prestigious white groups.

His parish, the Church of the Master on the western edge of Harlem, was large enough to justify having assistant pastors and a number of other professional staff who administered a number of social and pastoral programs. The church was located in a changing neighborhood in which the black population had increased from 25 to 65 percent in a decade. But the congregation still drew faculty and students from not only Union but Columbia and City College of New York as well. Reinhold Niebuhr wrote the preface to his published lectures.

Shortly after giving the lectures, Dr. Robinson went on to found and become executive director of Operation Crossroads Africa, a program that arranged for a number of students to spend the summer in Africa after their graduation from prep school.[27]

Thus for all his concern about race relations, Robinson was not really a representative of the classical African American homiletical tradition. Further, his lectures deal more with what to preach about than how to do it.[28] The first is devoted to the loss of status in the culture that clergy had experienced for some time, even though at the time of writing, during the Eisenhower administration, there was at least a superficial "revival of religion." The next has to do with the preacher's need for a deep spiritual life; for a relation with God, laypeople, and fellow clergy, with whom could occur a "fellowship of confession." The third is a passionate call for urban churches to remain in changing neighborhoods and minister to the people around them. Then follows an analysis of the deteriorating condition of Western civilization and the church in the post–World War II world, with challenges to Christianity from Communism and from other religions, especially in Asia and Africa, where the integrity of the gospel had been compromised by its association with Western exploitation. After that there is a prophetic insistence on the inseparability of religion and politics. The book ends with lectures on the gospel's inclusiveness and the grounds for hope given by faith in situations that encourage despair. An excellent set of lectures by a very impressive man, but not one that extends to others the resources of the classical African-American homiletic.

Henry H. Mitchell

The next African American Beecher lecturer attended both the same university and the same seminary as Robinson, but remained closer to the black church. Indeed, he was one of the first to pay serious homiletical attention to classical African American preaching, and it was the publication of his *Black Preaching* in 1970 that led to his invitation to give the lectures in 1974.[29] Published as *The Recovery of Preaching*,[30] his lectures had the purpose of assisting the white pulpit to preach with the power of the black. Sermons in the classical African American tradition "have had great impact and given great support and guidance in both communal and individual life."

> By way of contrast it may at least be argued that this has not been true of White middle-class Protestant preaching, which has been carried on in an academically oriented counterculture to the folk idiom of America's majority.[31]

The reason Mitchell sees for white preaching's failure, as implied in the quotation, is that it has been directed too exclusively to the intellect instead of to the whole person. In this vein, he begins his lectures with a sermon from Ezekiel 3:15 on the way the prophet sat where the people sat before he began preaching to them. Drawing on depth psychology and the history of religions, he says that the whole person includes what Jung inaccurately calls the "unconscious," and Eliade more accurately describes as "transconsciousness."

In order to reach the depth dimension of human persons, an artistic homiletic is necessary, one that makes use of stories and images: "vivid and realistic pictures or dramas of truth and symbol and of experience" (32). The goal is not achieved by art alone, however, since no one can communicate an experience that he or she has not had. The stories to be

told are mainly from the Bible, and the preacher must combine information and imagination, first internalizing a story in order to make it meaningful to others. The meaning of these biblical stories is not separable
from the stories themselves; rather, "Moses and David and Jeremiah and
Jesus are their own content" (40).

At the same time, however, the sermons must relate to the congregation's deepest needs, corporately and individually. "The desperate need is
for patterns of life-sustaining meaning, targeted to reach 'what's happening' and hurting *now*" (40). For this storytelling to be effective at the
meaning level, the congregation has to be given time to experience each
important point, and no point should be made that cannot be expressed
in a story or word picture filled with graphic details.[32] The ability to supply those details is the fruit of a life devoted to searching them out.

Such preaching is not only proclamation, but celebration as well—
both literal celebration and a symbolic and ritual expression of praise
and joy. This type of celebration enhances the retention of the gospel and
contributes to the way the congregation understands it and acts on it.
This ecstasy also contributes to the hearer's personhood and identity by
giving it free expression. The celebration also transforms a congregation
into a community. Further, it can be recalled and drawn on as a spiritual resource. And, finally, it is an appropriate climax to a well-balanced
sermon. Such celebration, then, is not just one of the conventions of
African American preaching, it is an effective ingredient for all good
preaching.

Celebration like this occurs only when a sermon is on a great theme.
It must also minister effectively to deep-seated human needs, offering fulfillment to persons. In addition to having such seriousness of purpose
and content, a sermon must be rhetorically effective to engender celebration. Specifically, it must have good timing and provide a medium for
summing up and celebrating the theme. An ingredient of good timing, an
appropriate emotional pace, is introducing new insights early rather than
dragging them in at the last minute. And the celebration at the end
should be of what the sermon is about: "the climactic utterance should
be especially characterized by celebrative feelings matching the ideas"
(64).[33]

Recognizing that something so emotionally powerful can be used
manipulatively, Mitchell gives a list of safeguards to prevent that misuse,
ending with the caution that "the preacher who would ask God to confer on his or her feeble utterance the charismatic gift of climactic celebration must diminish or hide self, and be possessed by the message and
its Giver" (67). He then goes on to give the criteria for material to be

used in the climax, noting the necessity for imagination and the preacher's deep involvement.

This ends the summary of the first four chapters of *The Recovery of Preaching*, the only ones given as Beecher lectures. The other chapters, however, presented as lectures elsewhere, also serve the intention to help white preachers achieve the homiletical power of their black colleagues. As Dr. Mitchell says, "The rest of this work is devoted to a kind of unpacking of the three preceding chapters."[34] The remaining chapters give practical instruction on effective biblical storytelling, preaching in the folk vocabulary of the congregation, and achieving dialogue through a cultural equivalent to call-and-response.

Like many good sermons, the book ends with a summary of all that has been said. Ministers from other racial or ethnic groups who wish to learn from African American colleagues how to make their sermons come alive could hardly find a better place to begin than with this book, written for the specific purpose of offering them such help.[35]

Gardner Taylor

The next African American Beecher lecturer was Dr. Gardner C. Taylor. Originally asked to be a colecturer with Mitchell,[36] Taylor was reinvited to deliver the series in 1976. In doing so he became the first lecturer who was pastor of a large congregation in a traditional black denomination. Concord Baptist Church in Brooklyn has a congregation of twelve thousand members. During the forty years of his pastorate, ten thousand have been added to the church rolls. Destroyed by fire in 1952, the church was rebuilt at a cost of $2 million before runaway inflation. Deeply involved in the life of its community, Concord has a fully accredited elementary school, a 121-bed hospital, a clothing exchange, and a credit union.

Although he has taught homiletics at Colgate Rochester, Harvard, and Union, Taylor's reputation is based mainly on his preaching to his own congregation. The effectiveness of that proclamation has been recognized in countless other ways as well, including his election as president of his denomination, the Progressive National Baptist Convention; presidency of the New York City Council of Churches; appearance on the National Radio Pulpit; and being selected by *Time* magazine as one of the top seven preachers in the country.[37]

Educated at Leland College and Oberlin Graduate School of Theology, Taylor is a master of the grand style of preaching in the African American tradition. Thus he was a homiletical model for many other preachers,

714

including Martin Luther King Jr. Comparing them, Lischer deems Taylor to have been better than King both in the use of his voice and in his rhetoric. In comparing their capacity for vocal expression, Lischer cites many qualities they have in common, but goes on to say: "Taylor's high is purer, his low more richly resonant, and the mastery of his vocal instrument more complete than King's."[38]

In comparing the two rhetorically, he says:

> Taylor's allusions . . . are more organic to his sermons, his metaphors more original and intellectually satisfying, and his powers of biblical reportrayal far more vivid than young King's.[39]

High praise indeed!

In his lectures, Dr. Taylor is like Phillips Brooks in that he does not so much seek to instruct in the mechanics of homiletics as he does to provide a spiritual perspective on the preaching task. Accordingly, his first lecture deals with the presumptuousness of preaching and his second treats its foolishness. The third seems more likely to give practical advice, bearing as it does the title of "Building a Sermon."

It begins by recognizing that "the heart of the preacher's dilemma is how to trust God wholly and at the same time to prepare diligently."[40] Ideas for sermons come in many ways, with Bible study being the first. But ideas can come from anywhere, with the observation of nature being a good source. And,

> any preacher greatly deprives himself or herself who does not study the recognized masters of pulpit discourse, not to copy them but rather to see what has been the way in which they approached the scriptures, their craftsmanship, their feel for men's hearts.[41]

To preach well, human hearts must be studied, beginning with one's own. Such study will note not only "the sense of melancholy which possesses most of the ablest preachers"[42] but the sense of being visited by God as well. In this lecture there is much that every preacher needs to hear, but little that relates to what the rhetoricians call invention, disposition, and style.

The final lecture is called "Preaching the Whole Counsel of God" and deals with the duty of preaching to cover the full range of biblical teaching and all the needs of "people who are solitary-social animals."[43] Even here, however, one suspects that what must have been most valuable in this series, certainly to those present but to readers as well, is the sense of being in contact with a great soul who personifies a great tradition. Even in the lecture format, the conventions of the African American preaching genre shine through.[44] There is wonderfully imaginative retelling of the biblical narratives, there is involvement of the audience—at least in the range of human experience addressed, and there are even celebratory climaxes.

The only one of Mitchell's criteria for the classic tradition of African American preaching that Taylor's writing does not meet is that of "folk language." Or, if it does, it is a very special category, because, as Lischer said, Taylor belongs to the "grand" tradition. He uses an elevated diction that he attributes to home influence:

> I am thankful that I was born to parents who, though not highly educated by today's standards, had a natural feel for the essential music of the English language wedded to an intimate and emotional affection for the great transactions of the scriptures. Somehow, in the way they thought and spoke, what is African found a cordial meeting with what is Anglo-Saxon.[45]

His way of putting things can be imagined from this and other quotations from his writings, although the sustained beauty of his expression can only be seen in extended passages, especially from the sermons.[46] It is no wonder that so many sought to imitate him.

Kelly Miller Smith

The next African American Beecher lecturer not only set out to help the white pulpit achieve something of the black pulpit's power, but did so specifically in the area of social justice preaching. Kelly Miller Smith, the lecturer for 1982–83, had studied at Morehouse College and Howard University Divinity School. After an early pastorate in Vicksburg, he went to First Baptist Church, Capitol Hill, in Nashville. While in Nashville, he also served as assistant dean of the Divinity School of Vanderbilt University, where he lectured in church, ministry, and community. Having been a close associate of Martin Luther King Jr., Smith's lectures, published under the title of *Social Crisis Preaching*,[47] draw liberally upon King's preaching for illustration.

His four lectures, titled with homiletical alliteration, deal with the Purview, Perception, Perspective, and Proclamation and beyond of social crisis preaching.

> Under the caption of "Purview," the terrain was observed in order to see its composition. Questions were asked as to what and where the danger points are and what can be learned of the topography. (79)

716

Noting that a number of previous Beecher lecturers had been characterized as "prophets of social change," Smith states that there has been such preaching all through church history and that, indeed, all religion is concerned with the social problems people face. "The social relevance of Christianity is axiomatic" (8), growing as it does from the tradition of the Hebrew prophets and Jesus of Nazareth. The black church owes its existence to social crisis.

That is not to say, however, that preaching on social issues is always expected or welcome. Nor, on the other hand, does everyone think preaching is capable of effecting social change. To do so, its quality must be high, it must be courageous, and it must be "proclamation of *what God continues to say* to the present condition" (18). Through the impact of the ancient Word of God in preaching, "the oppressed become aware that they are not hapless orphans deserted on the doorsteps of destiny, but are sons and daughters of a caring God" (23).

In his lecture on Perception, which deals with how social crisis preaching is perceived both by the preacher and by the congregation, Smith defines such preaching as "the proclamation of that which is crucially relevant within the context of the Christian gospel in times of social upheaval and stress." As part of the definition, he goes on to say that such preaching "aims at setting corrective measures into motion" (33). To get his own perception straight, the preacher needs to ask: What social crisis? Recognizing that there is one, the preacher must recognize his or her own limitations of experience and theological orientation and deal honestly with the pressure of practical considerations. To overcome those limitations, the preacher should call on those who better understand the situation, study what is written on the issue, and become directly involved in working toward a solution.

Acquiring a more accurate perception of the congregation involves recognizing that "they are people who are not excited about the social issue that the preacher is going to present in sermon context. They are people with their own priorities" (41). The preacher must know what those priorities are, and what the people's needs are as well—which may not be the same thing. To avoid answering questions that no one is asking, the preacher has the task of showing the congregation how the crisis reflects their own needs as well as those of the people more directly involved. With that correct perception of the preacher and the congregation, the preacher can then see that one of the most effective things that can be done is to preach about the crisis. "The power inherent in that word conjoined with the perceptiveness, commitment, and faithfulness of the preacher who proclaims that word and the people who hear it, will bring results" (45).

For social crisis preaching to be done effectively, it must be seen in Perspective, it must take cognizance of the dimensions of history, the Bible, and the black experience. History shows that such preaching characterized the prophets of the Old Testament, the writers of the New Testament, the great Fathers of the early church, the Social Gospel movement, and, especially those who are victims of the crisis. The biblical perspective on social crisis preaching demands that it demonstrate the relationship between experience and exegesis, that between extrabiblical tradition and the Word of God in Scripture, and that between exegesis and proclamation. The perspective of the black experience recognizes that

> the Black church in America not only provides the care necessary for those wounded in the fray; it also provides the experience of liberation itself for an oppressed people. (73)

Coming as it does out of that experience, "the preaching of Dr. Martin Luther King, Jr. represents social crisis preaching at its best" (74).[48]

Smith's final lecture, on Proclamation, gives practical advice on social crisis sermons. He begins by saying that for the individual sermon on a social issue to be effective, it must not be an isolated event, but instead must be part of an ongoing effort to involve the congregation in social ministry. The sermon itself should be based on an idea "rooted in an expression of God's concern for some human condition" (82). In crafting the sermon, the preacher needs to pay careful attention to language to make sure that what is said is clear, that the emotional freight of words is not overlooked, that what is offered as the Word of God is no mere venting of the preacher's spleen, and that the power of language to move people is drawn upon positively. Even then, however, the words will "still fail to convey the total message which is in the heart of one committed minister" (85).

Like all good preaching, social crisis sermons will have focus and structure. Homiletical strategy will determine the kind of structure chosen. A "miniature inductive"[49] form will move a reluctant congregation "gently but positively onto the basic thesis of the sermon," but at times "the abruptly direct order may be chosen for its shock value." And an inductive structure may work best with a conservative congregation. There are outlines that are also especially appropriate for social crisis sermons, including the interrogative, the problem solving, and the Hegelian pattern of thesis, antithesis, and synthesis.[50]

Delivery may be from or without a manuscript, if proper safeguards are taken against the dangers of each method. The preacher's emotion should be controlled but obvious. Different preachers have different gifts, but variety in pitch and force is always appropriate, and diaphragmatic breathing, clarity of enunciation, and projection of the voice always help. Finally, the sermon must be consistent with the life of the preacher: "effective social crisis preaching requires life commitment to the cause of justice and liberation" (99). One hears in Smith the voice of experience in effective preaching on social issues.

James Forbes

If it is true that Gardner Taylor's Beecher lectures were a spiritual perspective on the preaching task, then the same description may be applied a fortiori to those of James Forbes in 1986.[51] Indeed, they constitute a homiletical pneumatology, since Forbes's thesis is that in order to preach effectively, one must have been anointed by the Holy Spirit. The son of a bishop in the United Holy Church of America, a Pentecostal denomination, Forbes was educated at Howard and Union Seminary. He found at Union, in the teaching of H. Pitney Van Dusen, Paul Tillich, and others, an openness to the work of the Spirit that allowed him to state his Pentecostal convictions in the language of academic theology at that time. After graduation, he served as assistant pastor at a large Southern Baptist church in Chapel Hill, North Carolina, and then went on to pastor churches of his own denomination in Wilmington and Roxboro, North Carolina, and in Richmond, Virginia. From Richmond he was called back to Union to teach preaching, which he continued to do until he succeeded William Sloane Coffin Jr. as senior minister at Riverside Church. He has been an extremely popular visiting preacher, lecturer, and workshop conductor all over the country.

Forbes sees much of the weakness of contemporary preaching to be attributable to a Holy Spirit shyness among many Christians. Since it is the Spirit who inspired the Bible at every stage of its origin and transmission, and it is the Spirit who guides both preachers and congregations today in their understanding of how its message applies to them, not to be aware of the Spirit's action is to miss a great deal of what is going on. And, as a result, "many of the biblical provisions for Holy Spirit empowerment often are left unrealized like unclaimed packages and unopened letters" (22).

For that power to be reclaimed, there must be preachers who have been anointed by the Holy Spirit in much the way that Jesus was. While the relation of Jesus to God was unique, there is also a sense in which the relation of anyone to God is unique. In calling for this anointing, Forbes is not suggesting that there is only one pattern for its bestowal; he is open ecumenically to all the ways the gift of the Spirit has been understood in church history. Nor does he wish to say that it has to come in an unvarying series of steps. He finds that Tillich's reference to dimensions of spiritual growth gives a more accurate sense of the way things happen.

The marks of the Spirit's anointing include, first, its wholeness in the sense that it covers every aspect of the anointed. Thus "the anointed person is *willing to witness* in word and deed to the lordship of Jesus and the kingdom of God" (48). Then, faithfulness makes one attentive to the Spirit's guidance. With the guidance comes power from on high. Therefore, "those who testify to the anointing of the Spirit will go forth in ministry fully convinced that their efforts will make a difference" (51).

With these marks of the anointed, a preacher should be able to raise the dead in the way that Ezekiel saw the Spirit giving life to dry bones.[52] Taking a physician's definition of *death* as the point at which "there is no longer any prospect of meaningful, powerful, human existence" (59), Forbes points to conditions in the lives of individuals and society that can only be called death. It is in such situations that the anointed preacher must prophesy, not knowing what to say but depending upon guidance. In such moments, the preacher is gripped by a fear of losing control, but love casts out fear. The preacher says what God says, but before giving that word, "God gives the prophet the sense of the despair of the people"—the death from which they are yearning to be raised (64).

Speaking from such an orientation, it is not surprising that when Forbes comes to writing a chapter titled "Sermon Preparation and Preaching," he does not give "how-to" instructions, but rather talks about waiting on the Spirit for the message one is to proclaim. That does not mean, however, that he thinks the anointed preacher can avoid the hard work of exegesis and the other preparation tasks. Rather, he tells what may be expected in that process: the guiding presence of the Spirit. And the same Spirit will be preparing the congregation to receive the message the Spirit gave the preacher.

Forbes's final chapter, "The Spiritual Formation of Anointed Preachers," is a homiletical tour de force. It is an interpretation of the sixteenth chapter of Mark, a traditional problem for exegetes. Most believe that Mark ended his Gospel with verse 8 of chapter 16, which has the women fleeing the empty tomb, saying nothing to anyone because of their fear. It is usually thought that a later redactor added verses 9-20 as a summary of the resurrection appearance stories in the other Gospels. These verses also state that believers will be able to speak in tongues, handle snakes, not be overcome by poison, and cure the sick. Forbes treats the blank space between verses 8 and 9 in modern translations as the hiatus in which the anointing of the disciples occurred and their fear of speaking was taken away. Then he interprets these abilities of believers as the effects of anointed preaching, the sort of results that one should be able to expect. It is a glorious vision of the difference preaching can make.

Samuel D. Proctor

The 1990 Beecher lectures, given by Samuel D. Proctor,[53] are like those of James H. Robinson in that they have more to do with the content than the method of preaching[54] and that little distinguishes them as representative of African American preaching. Born in Norfolk in 1921, Proctor graduated from Virginia Union University and preceded Martin Luther King Jr. at both Crozer and Boston, studying at Penn and Yale as well along the way.

After an early pastorate in Providence, Proctor spent most of his career in education, government, and institutional service. Returning to his alma mater, he taught religion and ethics at Virginia Union, and became first dean of the School of Religion and then president of the university. After that he was president of North Carolina A & T State University. Then came work with the Peace Corps and O.E.O., and offices in the National Council of Churches and the Institute for Services to Education. A deanship at the University of Wisconsin and a professorship at Rutgers followed. While remaining on the Rutgers faculty, he succeeded Congressman Adam Clayton Powell Jr. as pastor of Abyssinian Baptist Church in Harlem. In retirement he taught preaching at Vanderbilt, Duke, and United Seminary in Dayton.[55]

The content Proctor recommends for sermons comprises four propositions that he developed as his lecture topics:

> First, basic to the Christian belief system is the understanding of God as absolute, wholly "other," yet present, participating, and aware of the details of all creation, history, and human endeavor, and who can and does intervene on our behalf in the affairs of the world.
>
> Second, it is also basic to our faith that human nature can be renewed; we can be born again and become new creatures.
>
> Third, is the conviction that, dismal and remote as it may seem at the moment, the human family can become a genuine community.
>
> Fourth, also basic is the belief that our earthbound condition, our mundaneness, is given meaning and purpose by the dimension of eternity that is the ever-present potential in our midst. Immortality begins now; eternity flows in the midst of time.[56]

Proctor's lectures include reminiscences of classical African American preaching through his frequent completion of a point in a quotation from Scripture, poetry, or a hymn, and in his use of language reminiscent of Taylor's. And there is certainly notice taken of racial justice issues and the contributions of African Americans. Yet, on the whole, while Proctor's recommendations about sermon content are worthy contributions to homiletics,[57] there is little reminder that this help is coming from the black church.

Thomas Hoyt

The Beecher lecturer in 1993 was Thomas Hoyt, a New Testament scholar and ecumenist. Born in Fayette, Alabama, Hoyt received his Ph.D. from Duke University. He was a pastor in Chapel Hill, North Carolina, and then taught at the Interdenominational Theological Center, an African American seminary consortium in Atlanta, before becoming professor of Biblical Studies at Hartford Seminary, the position he held at the time of the lectures. Since then he has become bishop of the Christian Methodist Episcopal Church[58] in Shreveport, Louisiana, and president of the National Council of Churches of Christ in the U.S.A. An ardent ecumenist, he has served on the Faith and Order Commissions of both the National and the World Councils of Churches.

Titled "The Church's Preaching in a Pluralistic and Ecumenical Context,"[59] Hoyt's three lectures[60] have three foci that represent his commitments. The first, on tradition, reflects his work as a New Testament scholar. His thesis is that Christian proclamation has focused too exclusively on Paul's understanding of the crucifixion and resurrection and has not done justice to Jesus' teaching about the kingdom of God, a theme important for the hope it gives to all oppressed peoples.[61]

His second lecture, titled "Particularity: Let the Church Say Amen," begins with the recognition that biblical interpreters look for a hermeneutical key that will unlock the meaning of Scripture. Such a key, however, is often "a canon within the canon" for the interpreter. All such approaches are partial and need to be supplemented with others to do justice to the full gospel. Each particular expression must be heard as a part of the whole and he will present the African American tradition. The African American approach to biblical interpretation has emphasized such biblical motifs as the exodus, creation in the image of God, Jesus' suffering and overcoming, and hope for those struggling ("after awhile" and "by-and-by"). The emphasis on these motifs in preaching has been the way in which the biblical tradition has been made contemporary to the black church.

While the preaching of the African American pulpit has been too rich, diverse, and creative to be characterized in a simple formula, it can be said that it is an oral tradition that cannot be fully understood from sermon manuscripts or transcripts.[62] That orality is only one aspect of the way black preaching grew out of a history of slavery and oppression. Black people have gone to church to hear the good news that they are some-bodies in a land where they are called nobodies. As diverse as the congregations and their preachers are, however, certain generalizations can be made. Hoyt agrees with Eugene Stratton that black sermons are marked by congregational participation, prophetic boldness, creativity on the part of the preacher, storytelling, spontaneity and movement of the Spirit, and accompaniment by a liturgy of singing, praying, and general celebration.[63] The congregation becomes involved in the end of the sermon as well.

Hoyt's third lecture is on "Universality: What, in View of the World's Disorder, Shall We Preach?" The black church does not agree with white politicians who have seen "a new world order." Their experience has been of disorder instead. There has been a need, as Walter Wink has said, to confront the powers, those who spread the delusions that those who hold power in society deserve to and are entitled to its rewards by their virtue. But for this disorder to be overcome, differing Christian and religious traditions will have to cooperate rather than compete. White people of Europe and America have dominated and exploited the rest of the world for their comfort and convenience, and this cannot continue. Even an assumption of the religious superiority of white Christians can no longer be made.

In the face of this world disorder, however, is the amazing truth pointed out by Kelly Miller Smith[64] that these issues can be addressed by the preaching of the gospel. Such preaching, though, cannot be from the perspective of an ideology. It must have as its content what God has done and will do in Jesus Christ, it must challenge the powers that be, and it must expect a cross. And, as Smith said, it must get over Cartesian compartmentalization and preach to the whole person and to a pluralistic society.

The church is called upon to go into all the world where there is a need for repentance, and to proclaim the inauguration of the reign of God. In doing so, it must resist the temptation of power and assume the role of a servant in a world where violence and force have been determinative of all outcomes.

Along with this proclamation must also go teaching, calling people to obedience as well as belief, and recognizing that an evangelism that does not address the social order is not evangelism. Such preaching will share with the fifth chapter of Revelation a vision of community that is multiethnic, multinational, multiracial, and multilinguistic. God is creating such a community in the secularity of life, and if we do not get it now, we will by-and-by.

Peter Gomes

The most recent Beecher lectures delivered by an African American resemble the first in that they are "an excellent set of lectures by a very impressive man, but not one that extends to others the resources of the classical African American homiletic." Although he has worked for causes important to the black community,[65] the homiletical tradition that lay behind the lectures of Peter Gomes was that of Harvard's Memorial Chapel, where he had preached for twenty-eight years, rather than the African American pulpit. Building on his popular volume *The Good Book: Reading the Bible with Mind and Heart*,[66] Gomes's 1999 lectures[67] deal with preaching from the Psalms, Epistles, and parables.[68]

This brings up to date the efforts of African American preachers through Beecher lectures to tutor their colleagues of other traditions in how to appropriate some of the power that has traditionally been attached to black preaching. The lecturers are a variegated group. Several of them (Robinson, Gomes, and, to an extent, Proctor) have shown in their lectures little that was distinctively African American. Only Mitchell has concentrated exclusively on preaching method. Robinson, Smith, Proctor, and Gomes have dealt instead with the content of preaching, while Taylor and Forbes were concerned with homiletical spirituality.

The lecturers represent a variety of denominations: three come from black Baptist churches, two are American Baptists,[69] one is from a historical black Methodist body, one began in a black Pentecostal church but is now a Baptist, and one is a Presbyterian. Most of them represent the hybrid sort of black congregation in that they have combined the emotion of the folk tradition with the rationality of bourgeois parishes.

All of them, however, further document what was first revealed to the majority culture through television coverage of Dr. Martin Luther King Jr.: the existence of a homiletical tradition with sufficient power to effect change.

FOR FURTHER READING

A Knock at Midnight: Inspiration From the Great Sermons of Reverend Martin Luther King, Jr. Edited by Clayborne Carson and Peter Holloran. New York: Warner, 1998.

Lischer, Richard. *The Preacher King: Martin Luther King, Jr. and the Word That Moved America.* New York: Oxford University Press, 1995.

Mitchell, Henry H. *The Recovery of Preaching.* Harper's Ministerial Paperback Library. San Francisco: Harper & Row, 1977.

Smith, Kelly Miller. *Social Crisis Preaching.* Macon, Ga.: Mercer University Press, 1984.

Taylor, Gardner C. *How Shall They Preach?* (Elgin, Ill.: Progressive Baptist Publishing House, 1977).

Notes

1. Richard Lischer, *The Preacher King: Martin Luther King, Jr. and the Word That Moved America* (New York: Oxford University Press, 1995), 42-44. I am grateful to Professor Lischer for a prepublication copy of the book manuscript. Most of the interpretation of King's preaching that follows is based on Lischer's insights. He also wrote the article on King in the *Concise Encyclopedia of Preaching,* which he edited with William Willimon (Louisville: Westminster John Knox, 1995), 288-90. For other biographical information, I have relied on Stephen B. Oates, *Let the Trumpet Sound: The Life of Martin Luther King, Jr.,* A Plume Book (New York: New American Library, 1982).

2. Like any public figure, especially one who has effectively challenged entrenched social patterns, King has his detractors. One of the more frequent charges made against him is that of plagiarism. The most thorough statement of the case for that charge is in Keith D. Miller, *The Voice of Deliverance: The Language of Martin Luther King, Jr. and Its Sources* (New York: Free Press, 1992). While it would be hard to question the facts Miller presents, his interpretation of them is another matter. He says, for example, that "his professors' ivory-tower formalism failed to engage his mind" (ibid., 62).

What Lischer says in response to a charge made by David Garrow that King was out of his element in an academic environment applies to Miller's view as well: "The problem with this portrait is that it does not square with King's academic record at Crozer, including his top examination scores." Nor does it accord with the memory of his fellow students at Boston that he "had the intellectual capacity to carry on prolonged theological debates with his professor while the rest of the class respectfully watched" (Lischer, *The Preacher King,* 63). As Lischer says, "The dilemma [of his plagiarism] cannot be resolved, but for the purposes of understanding King's preaching two points must be made. The first is that despite carelessness and lapses in academic honesty, King's immersion in academic theology was real and significant for his development as a preacher.... The second point is closely related to this observation. He approached all intellectual learning as raw material for the rhetoric of his sermons" (ibid., 63-64).

It is also true, as Miller shows, that King appropriated other preachers' sermon outlines and much of their language. Partly, that is a tradition of both black and white homiletics. As William Sloane Coffin said: "While most preachers are incurable magpies, I am a shameless one" (*Living the Truth in a World of Illusion* [San Francisco: Harper & Row, 1985], Preface). The other point to be made relates to the use King made of his sources. Shakespeare, after all, used as a source for *Hamlet* a play that is now lost and forgotten. None of the sermons on which King drew had the impact that his own did.

3. Lischer, *The Preacher King*, 51, 68.

4. Something it had not always had from King's erudite, brilliant, and unpredictable predecessor, Vernon Johns—the first African American to have his work published in one of the annual volumes of *Best Sermons*.

5. Many clergy have had popular sermons they preached frequently, and King was no exception. Caught up as he became in his duties as a leader of the civil rights movement, King found less and less time to prepare for sermons or any other kind of public speaking. Though he went through most of his life repreaching the sermons he composed during his first year at Dexter, a given sermon was never simply repeated; it was always altered to fit the circumstances of its delivery and in the light of King's evolving understanding of the world. When word-for-word documentation is not available, and all we have is the sermon title, it is hard to know what he said on a particular occasion. Besides, his sermons were edited for publication. Many of the Dexter sermons were published in *Strength to Love* (New York: Harper & Row, 1963), but, as Lischer says, "King and his editors removed all local and personal references from these sermons and polished them up as timeless masterpieces of the pulpit. In their printed form, they are scarcely distinguishable from the liberal commonplaces of the white, mainline pulpit during the Eisenhower era. Anything resembling the African-Baptist gospel in which King was nurtured or the prophetic rage that often seized him was removed in order to lend his utterances universality and to recommend his Movement to as wide a reading audience as possible" (Lischer, *Preacher King*, 4-5).

The transcriptions in *A Knock at Midnight: Inspiration from the Great Sermons of Reverend Martin Luther King, Jr.*, ed. Clayborne Carson and Peter Holloran (New York: Warner, 1998) follow, with a few exceptions, the editorial principles developed by the Martin Luther King Jr. Papers Project, and thus are much more accurate representations of what was actually said. But, precisely because of that, the form of each sermon is only the one preached on the occasion of the recording; there is no way the countless variations could be included. The best anthology of King's other writings is *A Testament of Hope: The Essential Writings of Martin Luther King, Jr.*, ed. James M. Washington (San Francisco: Harper & Row, 1986).

6. According to Miller, he took the outline from Phillips Brooks's sermon "The Harmony of Life" (Miller, *The Voice of Deliverance*, 75).

7. This was still the preferred way of referring to his race during most of King's ministry.

8. Quoted in Lischer, *The Preacher King*, 82, from *The Dexter Avenue Baptist Church, 1877–1977*, ed. Zelia S. Evans with J. T. Alexander (1978), 69.

9. Oates, *Let the Trumpet Sound*, 72.

10. Of course, he had practiced all of them before, but during his time at Dexter the roles were not so clearly separated. In addition to recognizing the different gen-

res in which King spoke, it is necessary to be aware of the periodization of his public utterances. During the first period, he spoke from a strategy of identification with the values of mainstream Western virtues to develop a consensus between all whites and blacks except what he originally believed was only a minority of racists. Next was a period in which he recognized that the movement had to provoke racists to engage in acts of violence that would elicit white sympathy when they were shown on television, and thus become a force for change. The last period was when the Vietnam War revealed to King that American society was and always had been racist to the core. Then he began to attack the system rather the shortcomings of individuals (Lischer, *The Preacher King*, 142-62).

11. Ibid., 221-66.

12. King's associates said that his speeches in these meetings were all the same (ibid., 253). Lischer gives a nine-point outline of the typical mass-meeting speech (ibid., 257).

13. The quoted words are from ibid., 178. The text of the speech can be found in Washington, *A Testament of Hope*, 217-20.

14. What follows is based on Lischer, *The Preacher King*, 221-42.

15. Ibid., 221-22.

16. Ibid., 225.

17. Ibid., 241.

18. Ibid., 106. Such mutual dependence is characteristic not only of all preachers in all times, but of others whose profession requires frequent public expression, including politicians and stand-up comics. In his analysis of King's usage of "What He Received: Units of Tradition," Lischer gives a masterful analysis of what is involved in sermon composition for all preachers (ibid., 93-118).

19. Ibid., 102.

20. Richard A. Lanham, *A Handlist of Rhetorical Terms*, 2nd ed. (Berkeley and Los Angeles: University of California Press, 1991), 169. Lanham's entire article on commonplaces is informative.

21. Lischer, *The Preacher King*, 104.

22. Kenneth Burke, quoted in Lanham, *A Handlist of Rhetorical Terms*, 169.

23. Lischer, *The Preacher King*, 123. In this passage, Lischer speaks of metonymy as a "predictable metaphor" (ibid.), apparently in dependence on Bernard Brandon Scott (ibid., 292). More commonly, *metonymy* denotes the substitution of one "name" for another, for example, *cause* for *effect* or vice versa. This confusing use of terms, however, does not make his analysis of King's strategy of elevation any less perceptive.

24. Ibid., 124.

25. Ibid., 133.

26. I am grateful for the assistance of Prof. Harry Adams of Yale Divinity School, Prof. Richard Lischer of Duke, and Prof. Henry Mitchell of the Interdenominational Theological Center in Atlanta for assistance in the identification of these lecturers. The last two of these advisers are themselves Beecher lecturers.

27. See James H. Robinson's *Africa at the Crossroads*, Christian Perspectives on Social Problems (Philadelphia: Westminster, 1962), and *Education for Decision*, eds. Frank E. Gaebelein, Earl G. Harrison Jr., and William L. Swing, for which he and

D. Elton Trueblood, Ernest Gordon, and John Crocker are listed as authors (New York: Seabury, 1963).

28. James H. Robinson, *Adventurous Preaching*, The Lyman Beecher Lectures at Yale (Great Neck, N.Y.: Channel, 1956).

29. Henry H. Mitchell, *Black Preaching* (San Francisco: Harper & Row, 1970, 1979; rev. ed. Nashville: Abingdon, 1990). This book is discussed above, chapter 20. For Mitchell's biography, see his *Festschrift, Preaching on the Brink: The Future of Homiletics*, ed. Martha J. Simmons (Nashville: Abingdon, 1996), 16-25.

30. Henry H. Mitchell, *The Recovery of Preaching*, Harper's Ministerial Paperback Library (San Francisco: Harper & Row, 1977).

31. Ibid., 11. This point is stated even more strongly on p. 98 where Mitchell says, "Everyone in the ghetto fancies that white preachers 'can't preach a lick,'" reminding one of a 1992 humorous film about pickup basketball games, *White Men Can't Jump*. (Parenthetical references that follow in this text section are to page numbers in *The Recovery of Preaching*.)

32. In an arresting simile of his own, Mitchell compares stories as they appear in the Bible with dried milk: they do not become palatable until they are mixed with an ordinary substance like water (ibid., 47).

33. A similar point will be made by Thomas Hoyt (see below), who said that he prefers his gravy to be made with the juice of the meat.

34. Ibid., 73. It will be recalled that the first chapter was a sermon.

35. In many ways, Mitchell's Beecher lectures were brought up to date in his *Celebration and Experience in Preaching* (Nashville: Abingdon, 1990). In 1993, Martha J. Simmons collaborated with him in writing a privately published *Studyguide to Accompany Celebration and Experience in Preaching*. Dr. Mitchell's colleague in all his homiletical enterprises is his wife, Dr. Ella Pearson Mitchell. In her own right, she has called attention to the homiletical achievements of African American women, as in the two volumes she edited titled *Those Preaching Women: (More) Sermons by Black Women Preachers* (Valley Forge, Pa.: Judson, 1985). In 2000, the Mitchells were copresidents of the Academy of Homiletics.

36. Dr. Mitchell told this to me in a telephone conversation.

37. This information was garnered from the dust jackets of Dr. Taylor's Beecher lectures, *How Shall They Preach* (Elgin, Ill.: Progressive Baptist Publishing House, 1977); his collection of sermons, *Chariots Aflame* (Nashville: Broadman, 1988); and the homiletical aid volume on which he and I collaborated, *Proclamation 2: Aids for Interpreting the Lessons of the Church Year: Pentecost 3* (Philadelphia: Fortress, 1980).

38. Lischer, *The Preacher King*, 50-51.

39. Ibid.

40. Taylor, *How Shall They Preach*, 57.

41. Ibid., 63-64.

42. Ibid., 72.

43. Ibid., 81.

44. This is true as well of Taylor's suggestions for homiletical development in the *Proclamation* volume, of which he was coauthor. And it is true a fortiori of his actual sermons, including the four he uses to make his lectures a book-length volume as well as those in *Chariots Aflame*.

45. Taylor, *How Shall They Preach*, 13.

46. A good sample of this eloquence can be seen in ibid., 68-72, in the passage discussing the depression that has afflicted so many great preachers.

47. Kelly Miller Smith, *Social Crisis Preaching* (Macon, Ga.: Mercer University Press, 1984). An example of Smith's own preaching can be seen in *Outstanding Black Sermons*, vol. 2, ed. Walter B. Hoard (Valley Forge, Pa.: Judson, 1979), 107-13. Parenthetical references that follow in the text section are to page numbers in *Social Crisis Preaching*.

48. Smith provides a good list of the accomplishments of Dr. King in *Social Crisis Preaching*, 75-76.

49. For what is meant by inductive preaching, see the discussion of Fred Craddock below, pp. 800-6.

50. Sermon outline patterns were a favorite topic of mid-twentieth-century homiletics manuals; see, for example, Halford E. Luccock, *In the Minister's Workshop*, Notable Books on Preaching (Whitmore & Stone, 1944; reprint, Grand Rapids, Mich.: Baker, 1977), 134-47.

51. James Forbes, *The Holy Spirit in Preaching* (Nashville: Abingdon, 1989). Parenthetical references that follow in this text section are to page numbers from *The Holy Spirit in Preaching*.

52. In Forbes's lectures are a number of extended expositions of scripture that effectively turn them into sermons.

53. Samuel D. Proctor, *"How Shall They Hear?": Effective Preaching for Vital Christian Faith* (Valley Forge, Pa.: Judson, 1992).

54. Proctor has also written a "how-to" book on preaching, *The Certain Sound of the Trumpet: Crafting a Sermon of Authority* (Valley Forge, Pa.: Judson, 1994).

55. See Samuel Proctor's autobiography, *The Substance of Things Hoped For: A Memoir of African-American Faith* (New York: G. P. Putnam's Sons, 1996).

56. Proctor, *How Shall They Hear?*, 16-17.

57. Lischer calls Proctor "one of the most formidable black preachers of our century" and says that he may have been the only one tutored by Pius Barbour in Chester, Pennsylvania, who was more promising than King (Lischer, *The Preacher King*, 110, 70).

58. One of the three major historic African American churches in the Wesleyan tradition.

59. Hoyt's lectures have not yet been published in book form, although a cassette recording of them is available from Berkeley Divinity School at Yale, the Episcopal presence at Yale Divinity School. I am grateful to the former dean of Berkeley, Dr. William Franklin, for a set of these cassettes.

60. In contrast to the usual four.

61. A more nuanced view of Hoyt's hermeneutic than he was able to give in his lecture appears in "Interpreting Biblical Scholarship for the Black Church Tradition," the chapter he contributed to *Stony the Road We Trod: African American Biblical Interpretation*, ed. Cain Hope Felder (Minneapolis: Fortress, 1991), 17-39. This entire volume is useful for understanding contemporary African American preaching.

62. Even here there are differences in congregations. As Hoyt points out, some are largely composed of traditional folk hearers, others of bourgeois hearers (who expect a preacher with educational credentials whose sermons are rationally persuasive), and still others of a hybrid type that expects sermons to be both rationally persuasive and emotionally stirring.

63. This last element is especially characteristic of the folk-type church.

64. See above, pp. 716-19.

65. For example, his first work assignment was as director of the Freshman Experimental Program at Tuskegee Institute.

66. Peter Gomes, *The Good Book: Reading the Bible with Mind and Heart* (New York: William Morrow, 1996).

67. Unpublished in book format so far, they may be heard on cassettes recorded by Biomedical Communications, Audio Visual Services, Yale University School of Medicine and distributed through Yale's Student Book Supply under the title of *The Texture of Biblical Preaching: Songs, Letters, and Stories.*

68. Examples of Gomes's preaching can be seen in his *Sermons: Biblical Wisdom for Daily Living* (New York: William Morrow, 1998).

69. This could be misleading, since many African American congregations have a dual membership in the American Baptist Churches.

CHAPTER 29

MAINSTREAM PROPHECY

The civil rights movement did not affect preaching in African American churches alone. The mainstream denominations of the white majority in the United States were deeply challenged by the charges of complicity in the subjugation and exploitation that still victimized the descendants of slaves. Their guilt acknowledged and their consciences aroused, the white churches took up the cause of working with their black brothers and sisters to purge their institutions and the country as a whole of the racism that was as pervasive as it was contrary to the gospel.

One of the main agents employed in the purging was the prophetic voice of the pulpit. Yet churches had been so separated along racial lines that conventions of preaching in the white denominations were very different from those of the communions that had been mobilized into militant involvement by the sermons of Dr. King and his clerical comrades in the struggle. While white America was awestruck by the eloquence of the black pulpit, it would take more familiar rhetorical strategies to move its churches to accept the cause as their own. Thus there came to be developed a type of sermon on racial justice that fit into the homiletical tradition of white American churches that could still be called mainline at that time.

A CRISIS IN VALUES

The raising of this one major issue of social morality, however, was only the beginning. Soon it became apparent that there were many other injustices to be acknowledged and dealt with. The crisis in the social values of America was just beginning. The country was on the verge of another of what Mark Noll[1] has called its "turbulent decades."

The 1960s were so tumultuous that it is hard for even those who lived through them and participated in the events of the time to believe all that actually happened. When the decade began, Eisenhower was still president, and memories of McCarthyism were fresh. There was doubt whether a Roman Catholic like John F. Kennedy could be elected to the country's highest office. The Russians had already launched their first spaceship and would soon put the first human being into orbit around the earth. In addition to competition in space, the cold war produced the Cuban missile crisis and the Berlin Wall.

All that seems like a continuation of the 1950s, but change was in the air. Lunch-counter sit-ins had begun, and a voting rights bill had passed Congress. By 1961, African American and white Freedom Riders were challenging Jim Crow segregation of interstate travel facilities. The following year, the University of Mississippi admitted its first black student, James Meredith, even though three thousand federal troops were needed to quell riots. In some ways, the climax of the civil rights movement was the March on Washington of August 28, 1963, when Dr. King gave his "I Have a Dream" speech. The next summer saw campaigns to register African American voters in southern states—and the martyrdom of some of the workers in that effort. But it also saw the passage of the Civil Rights Act, which banned racial discrimination in voting, jobs, public accommodations, and federally funded programs.

That legislative accomplishment, however, did not mean racial problems were over for the country, as the riots that broke out in major cities during the rest of the decade demonstrated. The assassination of Dr. King on April 4, 1968, was tragic evidence of how far the struggle was from being over. Indeed, racism remains the most serious social problem in the United States at the time of this writing.

President Lyndon Johnson tried to involve the country in efforts to eliminate other social problems such as poverty, which, although one of the worst aspects of racism, was not confined to racial minorities. While he did get his War on Poverty Bill passed in the summer of 1964, he had already become embroiled in a cause that would put him at loggerheads with most of those who supported his efforts to create "the Great Society."

American cold war strategy had become captive to a metaphor. The manner in which one European country after another had become communist after World War II was compared to what happens to dominoes stood on end and in line with one another: If the first is tilted, they all will fall. When North Vietnam became Marxist after the expulsion of the French, this was understood not as a move for national self-determination, but as part of an international communist conspiracy that would initiate a domino effect throughout Southeast Asia.

As a result, a small cadre of American military advisers was sent to South Vietnam quite early on, and President Kennedy decided that they should protect themselves if fired upon. Johnson used an alleged attack on American naval vessels in the Gulf of Tonkin to obtain congressional approval for military action in Vietnam. As early as 1967, there were four hundred thousand American troops there, and a saturation bombing campaign was being carried out against the North.

By then the war had become increasingly unpopular at home, and a vast peace movement organized protests and demonstrations all over the country. After North Vietnam launched an all-out offensive in early 1968 and it became obvious how far the war was from being won, Johnson grew so discouraged that he stopped the bombing raids and decided not to run for another term as president. Six weeks later, peace talks began in Paris. After Richard Nixon took office and the peace negotiations dragged on, the protest movement increased in vehemence, culminating in a march of a quarter million people on Washington. The cease-fire and withdrawal of American troops did not occur until early 1973.

While the civil rights and the peace movements were the most obvious social actions in the sixties, other changes were occurring in society that would be just as far-reaching. The most obvious date assigned to the beginning of the sexual mores revolution that has changed so much in American social life is 1960, when approval was given for marketing the birth control "pill." The modern environmental movement may be said to have gotten its initial impulse from the publication of Rachel Carson's book *The Silent Spring* in late 1962. And the women's movement can be dated from the release of Betty Friedan's *The Feminine Mystique* a few months later. The growing ethnic and religious pluralism of the country was documented when the Supreme Court declared in 1963 that requiring prayers and Bible reading in public schools was unconstitutional. It was also seen in Cesar Chavez's organization of migrant farmworkers, not to mention the fact that somewhere along the way an interest in Eastern religions developed in the country.

The triumphal tour of the Beatles in 1964 demonstrated a basic shift in taste in popular music, a shift that had become complete by the summer of 1969 when a half million young people assembled for a music festival near Woodstock, New York. Woodstock also showed how far the sexual revolution had gone and how much drug use had become a part of youth culture. And, while Medicare for the nation's elderly was instituted in 1965, the decade belonged to the young. Thus a students' rights movement disrupted the nation's college campuses. Along with that occurred a free speech movement, which resulted in the entry into the public vocabulary of many words and expressions that had formerly been considered obscene or profane. Another cause supported in the sexual revolution was the gay rights movement, which began with the Stonewall Inn riot on June 27, 1969. A turbulent decade, indeed, and a decade during which more accepted values were in dispute than during any comparable period in American history.

A PRIVILEGED PROPHET

As in any dispute about values, clergy felt an obligation to speak out on the controversies of the sixties and early seventies, to try to cast some Christian light on the situation. While there was a great deal of advocacy for some of the changes being called for at the time, there was also a sense that others had to be resisted. And all clergy did not take the same side on a particular issue, nor did their parishioners always agree with them or favor their expressing opinions from the pulpit. While it was by no means a unanimous voice and may not even have been a majority voice, there did develop in the United States at the time a highly visible and even more audible strain of preaching. It intended to be prophetic, to rally Christians to work for social justice involving many conflicts of value and the confrontations of groups that disagreed vigorously and sometimes violently.

While in many ways this movement was the heir of the Social Gospel movement before World War I, it also differed from it markedly in a number of other ways. The earlier movement grew out of Romanticism and shared many of its liberal presuppositions. These included the understanding of the kingdom of God as the establishment of a perfect society on earth and the belief that, on the one hand, this society was to be the result of inevitable evolutionary progress in history, and that, on the other, it was to be brought in by the concerted efforts of Christians who could be exhorted by preaching to make the effort. Involved in this point of view is an optimistic understanding of human nature that considered people capable of such achievements if they would use their free will to accomplish them. Thus a distinction was made between evil institutions and essentially good human beings.

The prophetic preaching of the sixties, on the other hand, was influenced by the realism regarding human nature that came after two world wars and a depression in one generation, and by biblical scholarship that understood the kingdom of God in the teaching of Jesus as an eschatological and apocalyptic concept. Another difference between the social preaching in the two eras is that the first concentrated on labor questions, while the latter extended to all the questions of value raised in the 1960s. As a result, the main common factors between the two movements were a sense of Christian duty to improve society and an assumption that preaching could help effect such change.

As with many other movements in the history of preaching, this one can be studied mainly in the ministry of one cleric. It cannot be said that William Sloane Coffin Jr. (1924–) was the first to engage in such preaching or that he was typical of those who did, but he became by far the best-known exemplar of this homiletical trend. Not only that, he also did social protest preaching with a power and persuasiveness that few could achieve and with an integrity and wisdom that were hard to match.

It would be difficult to claim that Bill Coffin is typical of anything, since he came to his work with gifts and privileges few can equal. He was born into a position of affluence and social prominence. Much of the family wealth was lost in the Great Depression and more after his father died when Coffin was nine, but even in such relative financial straits, he was better off than most. He and his siblings were provided a secondary education in prep schools at home or abroad, and undergraduate and graduate schooling in the Ivy League.

Then, too, their social position remained secure. Very few clergy, for instance, have been lucky enough to have as an uncle someone like Henry Sloane Coffin, who had been, among other things, pastor of Madison Avenue Presbyterian Church in Manhattan, president of Union Theological Seminary, and moderator of the Presbyterian Church. But the family connections were not exclusively nor even mainly ecclesiastical.

Yet family and affluence are not the most extraordinary things about Coffin. His great talents in a number of areas are more impressive than anything else. He is so musically gifted, for instance, that when still high-school age, he was in Paris studying piano under Jacques Février and composition under the legendary Nadia Boulanger. The French virtuoso of the piano, Alfred Corot, told him that he had an enormous talent,[2] and, if World War II had not intervened, he probably would have achieved his ambition to become a conductor.

He also has a rare facility for languages. After living in Paris for a short while, he was able to pass himself off as French.[3] Later, as an army intelligence officer in the war, he learned enough Russian in three months to serve as a liaison officer between U.S. and Soviet military units stationed in Czechoslovakia.[4] Finally, he was a far better athlete than the majority of clergy. To cite but one instance: When he was in the sixth grade he was able to put up a respectable resistance to a muscular seventeen-year-old who was already boxing professionally.[5] In all of this Coffin finds "the source of the paradoxes and tensions" that complicated his later life: "I was an elitist who came to question such principles; a combative young squirt who espoused nonviolence; a boy with a gift for music and languages who became a preacher."[6]

When he returned home from World War II, Coffin went to Yale, where he received advanced placement for his various accomplishments. At the time he was anticipating a career in diplomacy and majored in political science, but already his interest was being captured by issues of good and evil as those were discussed by atheistic existentialists like Sartre and Camus and Christian theologians such as the Niebuhr brothers and Tillich.

After graduation he began to prepare for the ministry at Union Seminary, but the Korean War broke out in the summer after his first year, and his patriotism caused him to accept the CIA appointment he had considered before. He spent almost three years in Germany training anticommunist Russians for clandestine operations within the Soviet Union. Then he returned to his preparation for ordination—at Yale, however, rather than Union, so he could be near his aging mother in New Haven.

Coffin had originally hoped to serve in an inner-city slum parish, but his engagement to the daughter of the famous pianist Arthur Rubinstein led him to accept a call to be chaplain at Phillips Andover. After a year there and another at Williams College, he began the ministry through which he would become known to the Christian world: eighteen years as chaplain of his alma mater Yale. That attention came because of his public involvement in some of the most visible of the social protest movements. For the civil rights movement, that meant his participation in a "Freedom Ride" through Georgia and Alabama in the spring of 1961 to try to integrate travel facilities in accordance with the regulations of the Interstate Commerce Commission. He was also with Dr. King in Birmingham two years later.

His interest in the war in Vietnam was stimulated in the spring of 1964 by Paul Jordan, a graduate student in music. In the summer of 1965, he founded Americans for the Reappraisal of Far Eastern Policy, and the following winter he helped organize the National Emergency Committee of Clergy Concerned About Vietnam. He was convicted of conspiracy along with other prominent people like Dr. Benjamin Spock for counseling young men to turn in their draft cards. Nothing he did, however, shocked the country so much as his going with a delegation to Hanoi in 1972 to accept the release of three American prisoners of war. In a similar way, he went to Tehran during the Iran hostage crisis.

In 1977 he became senior minister of Manhattan's famous Riverside Church, which had been founded by another preacher against war, Harry Emerson Fosdick. Coffin held that position for ten years before he left to organize SANE/FREEZE, the country's largest peace and justice organization. As William J. Carl III has pointed out, each major phase of his ministry had its characteristic social issue:

> His practice has been to immerse himself in one major problem for a period of time. In the early sixties it was civil rights. In the late sixties to early seventies it was Vietnam. In the late seventies it was hunger and American intervention in places like El Salvador. In the eighties it has been the arms race.[7]

In retirement, he continues to witness for the justice demanded by the gospel.

Coffin's Homiletic

The difference between Coffin's social action preaching and any of his other sermons—or those of his contemporaries in the pulpit—was not so much in structure as in content. He usually preached from the lectionary, and he has said that his best sermons had an introduction, three points, and a conclusion.[8] Nor was his preaching exclusively about social issues. He said that he much preferred pastoral counseling to prophetic preaching,[9] and printed collections of his sermons include more dealing with pastoral than social issues—although the pastoral sermons are at least as aware of the social aspects of problems as they are of their personal dimensions.

Yet the issue here is how he preached social action sermons. The first point, then, is that he did so only occasionally. And the second is that he was well prepared when he did so. One of the most obvious features of his sermons is the large number of illustrations and quotations, drawn from a wide range of reading. He decries the fact that the average Christian cleric reads only a third as much as the average rabbi.[10] His own reading of the Bible, books, and magazines is voluminous, covering not only theology and ethics but also literature and technical studies of the topics with which he deals.[11] It is these latter that give authority to what he has to say on such subjects. To be taken seriously on social issues, clergy must make it obvious that they know whereof they speak. Not stated in so many words but clearly implied is the assumption that many clergy are not respected for what they say on controversial issues because they go off half-cocked without bothering to inform themselves on what they are talking about.

One of the reasons Coffin concentrated on one major problem at a time was so that his study of it could be cumulative and deep. "At Yale and at Riverside his practice has been to do his homework and make his statement clearly and early to the congregation only once, and not badger them with it week after week."[12]

Nor was his reading on just one side of the issue. He believes that one should be able to "state the opposition's position to the opposition's satisfaction."[13] It is easier for people to accept refutation of a position that they know has been understood and taken seriously. Of equal importance is the fact that fairness to the other side will show his hearers that they, too, are being taken seriously. Coffin thus often quoted with approval words spoken to him by a Yale freshman: "If it's both true and painful, say it softly."[14]

And on his own he said:

> Whenever possible, I believe we should challenge people kindly. Nothing, for example, prevents any of us, in the middle of a sermon, from saying, "What I now want to say is hard for me to say, so I can imagine how painful it's going to be for some of you to hear. But here we are in church, where unity is based not on agreement, but on mutual concern. So let me tell you what's on my mind and heart and, after the service, those of you who disagree can bring your coffee into the library and tell me where you think I went wrong."[15]

At the same time, however, he was insistent that the preacher's own need to be loved should not encourage soft-pedaling what ought to be proclaimed from the housetops.

In addition to being informed and pastoral, Coffin thought that social action preaching had also to be theological. It was only the theological dimension of the issue that made it an appropriate subject for preaching.

In this way he distinguished between what he himself did in press conferences and what he did from the pulpit. Yet "Coffin believes that we preachers should speak theologically about not only ecclesiastical but [*sic*] political matters. For this reason, he always speaks as a 'reverend,' whether he is in church or the local Rotary Club."[16]

He says that his own orthodoxy has increased over the years, but for theological rather than psychological reasons. He finds that the world is always bearing out the Bible, and the Bible is always illuminating the world.[17] He can, therefore, make it clear to people that his insistence on social justice derives from his concern for their souls.

A Case in Point

An example of the way Coffin practiced his own homiletical principles is a sermon on homosexuality. (For the text of this sermon, see **Vol. 2, pp. 580-85.**) It was published in *The Courage to Love*[18] in 1982 and had already appeared in the journal *Christianity and Crisis*[19] previously, so it must have been preached only about a decade after the Stonewall Inn riot, the beginning of the gay rights movement.[20] He introduces the question by asking his congregation if they know what a long list of famous and talented people of both sexes and many fields of endeavor have in common. By announcing that the common factor is homosexuality he has gained their attention and made them aware that the issue is serious.

He admits that the subject is the most divisive in the church since slavery, and, by identifying it with slavery, suggests on which side people should be. The previously unmentionable subject has become unavoidable because some Christian clergy are claiming that homosexuals are sinfully different from other people. "Gay men and women are being physically and psychologically abused; they are being excluded from their families, frozen out of churches, and discriminated against in a variety of painful legal ways" (40).

The basis for the claim of these clergy is their understanding of biblical teaching. To counter that, Coffin begins by interpreting his sermon's text, the story in Acts 10:1-20 of Peter's vision on a roof in Joppa in which he was commanded to eat nonkosher food. The revelation to Peter was that "God shows no partiality, but in every nation any one who fears him and does what is right is acceptable to him" (Acts 10:34 RSV). The passage seems likely to have been appointed in the lectionary, and, after studying it, the preacher must have asked what would be an apt application and extension of it in the present. He concludes that "in every sexual orientation any one who fears him and does what is right is acceptable to him" (41).

Coffin then quotes ethicist James B. Nelson to the effect that there are four primary theological stances toward homosexuality: the rejecting-punitive, the rejecting nonpunitive, the conditional acceptance, and the unconditional acceptance positions. These four attitudes become the four points discussed in the body of the sermon. Consideration of the rejecting-punitive stance involves a close look at what the Bible has to say on the subject of homosexuality. It is true that Leviticus calls a male homosexual act an abomination, but it uses the same Hebrew word *(toevah)* in reference to "eating pork, to misuse of incense, and to intercourse during menstruation" (41). Other passages are related to participating in pagan rites that included both male and female prostitutes, where the issue was idolatry. And others to anal rape as a way of humiliating captured enemy soldiers.

Further, the understanding of conception in that culture was that only the male seed carried life, "women providing only the incubating space." In a society in which it was desirable to have as many children as possible, any waste of sperm in homoerotic acts or masturbation was viewed as a form of abortion. As for Sodom and Gomorrah, their sin as viewed by Ezekiel, Isaiah, and Jesus seems to have been more a violation of hospitality than a sin against nature. In thus rejecting the interpretation of his opponents, Coffin shows that he takes the Bible more seriously than they do. He is not content with hurling proof texts; he exerts considerable effort to learn what the sacred writers meant.

In addressing the rejecting-nonpunitive position, Coffin responds to the charge that a homosexual orientation is a psychic disorder that needs to be cured. He points out that the psychotherapeutic community does not agree. Then he considers the conditional acceptance attitude, which would permit the ordination of homosexuals while not being able to "picture a gay spouse in the parsonage" (45). He sees an analogy between their position and that of those who think Jews should enjoy the same rights as Christians, but nevertheless consider Judaism inferior to Christianity. Recognizing the dilemma involved, he says, "The worst thing we can do with a dilemma is to resolve it prematurely because we lack the courage to live with uncertainty" (45).

Finally, with the unconditional acceptance stance that is his own, he points out analogies to "the black problem" and "the woman problem": "The 'homosexual problem' is really the homophobia of many heterosexuals" (45). While he was appalled at the promiscuity of some gays in those days before the AIDS epidemic, so were other gays, and it was no worse than straight promiscuity.

In his conclusion, Coffin returns to his text, saying that Peter widened his horizons and we should do the same, perceiving that God shows no partiality in regard to sexual orientation. And he ends by saying: "What St. Augustine called the duty of the preacher is the obligation of all: 'to teach what is right and to refute what is wrong, and in the performance of this task to conciliate the hostile [and] to rouse the careless'" (46). It would be hard to find a better statement of Coffin's homiletic or a better description of what he did than this sermon.

THE PERSPECTIVE OF THE UNDERPRIVILEGED

The prophetic preaching of mainstream clergy who spoke out on social issues was mostly delivered to middle-class whites by males of their own social group and reflected the group's attitudes toward its social role. This is not to question the sincerity of the clergy in call for change, but rather to say that they assumed that they and their audience, working with others like themselves, could effect the changes they called for. It is to say that they thought they could work within the social and economic system to improve it.

Another strain of social protest preaching that was never as large as the first in the United States was more in touch with the attitude of those oppressed by society and was more likely to assume that social and economic systems needed to be replaced rather than improved. This tradition was shaped by the liberation theology of Latin America and took as its model the preaching done in that area. (For an example of such preaching, see **Vol. 2, pp. 592-95.**) That point of view can be seen in a popular manual on preaching from a liberation perspective, *The Liberating Pulpit* by Justo L. González and Catherine G. González.[21] The five chapters of the book deal with the stance of liberation theology; impediments to understanding the Bible as the underprivileged do; resources for doing that; techniques to help in that endeavor; and the integration of biblical interpretation, preaching, and liturgy to communicate the insights gained.

The starting point of liberation theology is that traditional theology has carried an often unidentified agenda of oppression as the result of "an unconscious process through which the values, goals, and interests of those in power are read into scripture and expressed in supposedly universal theology" (16). That process began with the conversion of Constantine, although the greatest of the church fathers resisted this inclination. Centuries of such conditioning have led those speaking in the name of the church to offer theological justification for the continuation of oppressed people's suffering. Most of those who did this were not cruel so much as unaware of the way their theology had been shaped by the agenda of the powerful.

The corrective proposed by liberation theology is to notice that "the major portion of the Bible records the perspective of those who, in their own social situation, are the powerless and oppressed" (18). That being so, it becomes obvious that the Bible is best understood by those whose situation is most analogous to that of the people of God in Scripture. Often the only way the elite can hear what the Bible really says is to hear it from a powerless person. Such a hearing can be difficult to achieve because those who speak from this perspective are frequently regarded as communists and as advocates of violence and revolution. This reaction fails to note the violence by which subjugation has been maintained and the burning desire of those who have suffered from it to escape.

While liberation theology arises out of the concrete situation of oppressed people, it is not solely concerned with their own practical situation. Rather, their experience has given them important perspectives on every Christian doctrine. For them a basic insight is the recognition that the biblical principle of *Heilsgeschichte* ("redemption history") does not apply merely to Israel and the early church, but is relevant to all times and all places. Thus, "history is not simply the narration of past events. History is a project, both divine and human, for the redemption of God's creation" (24).

And part of this understanding of history as the arena of redemption is to notice that oppressive systems enslave not only the underprivileged but the elite as well, those for whom their comfort is the bribe for their compliance. That may be observed in our consumerist society, "where human beings are seen as either means of production or agents of consumption, and where the poor are valued according to how much they can produce, while the rich are valued according to how much they consume" (26).

Preaching that is shaped by a liberation perspective concentrates on interpreting the Bible from the point of view of the oppressed peoples about whom it was written rather than from the point of view of the powerful that has shaped post-Constantinian theology. So engrained is the elitist interpretation, however, that there are impediments to hearing the outlook of the original text. These impediments include the way that the Reformation principle of *sola scriptura* has led to the confusion of what the Bible actually says with the traditional elitist interpretation of its text. In fact, that traditional interpretation has been presupposed so reflexively that it has shaped translations of the Bible into other languages.

Furthermore, lectionaries, for all their merits, are drawn up by representatives of the mainline churches that use them and thus reflect their values; many texts that would raise issues of social justice are never read. Finally, biblical commentaries are often written from an Enlightenment perspective of rationality that assumes it knows what ancient documents originally meant and is unconcerned with what they might mean to people of faith today. For this reason, anyone who would expound the Bible from a liberation perspective has an uphill struggle to arrive at that interpretation.

The way to achieve the liberation interpretation always involves what Juan Luis Segundo has called "the hermeneutical circle."[22] This process begins when one brought up on the traditional interpretation becomes aware of oppression in the world and wants to do something about it as a Christian. At that point, representatives of the mainstream declare such an attitude unbiblical and unchristian. The circle is completed if, instead of giving in to the majority position, a person becomes suspicious of the methods of biblical interpretation that led to conclusions so apparently inconsistent with the attitude of Christ. The suspicion results in a new approach to the Bible, resulting in the discovery that it was written from the perspective of oppressed people and has to be interpreted in that light.

The rest of the book is concerned with exegesis in preparation for constructing a sermon and with the interrelation between biblical interpretation, the sermon, and the liturgy rather than with homiletics as such. Therefore, it need not be considered here.

More relevant to the actual history of preaching is the consideration of particular sermons constructed from the perspective of liberation theology. The most influential collection is from Latin America rather than the United States: *The Gospel in Solentiname*, edited by Ernesto Cardenal.[23]

Solentiname is an archipelago on Lake Nicaragua where Cardenal, a Roman Catholic priest, went with some companions to form a community or lay monastery.[24] The community worked with the local residents *(campesinos)*, and a number of artistic and agricultural projects were begun, projects that attracted worldwide attention.[25] As a religious community, however, its activity was centered in Word and sacrament.

The sermons were not delivered by the priest alone, but were instead group reflections—or, as Cardenal calls them, dialogues—on the texts of the lectionary Gospels. At first Cardenal reconstructed these from memory, but then he began to record and transcribe them. Anyone reading through the collection will notice that most of the comments were made by a small group of regulars who become recognizable over time for their points of view.

743

Marcelino is a mystic. Olivia is more theological. Rebeca, Marcelino's wife, always stresses love. Laureano refers everything to the Revolution. Elvis always thinks of the perfect society of the future. Felipe, another young man, is very conscious of the proletarian struggle. Old Tomás Peña, his father, doesn't know how to read, but he talks with great wisdom. Alejandro, Olivia's son, is a young leader, and his commentaries are usually directed toward everyone, and especially toward other young people. Pancho is a conservative. Julio Mairena is a great defender of equality. His brother Oscar always talks about unity. (Introduction, ix)

The discussion is led by the priest, and the two other founding adults of the community, the Colombian poet William Agudelo and his wife, Teresita, also make contributions.

The dialogues took place either at Mass or in a thatched hut afterward. Copies of the Gospel were distributed to those who could read and then read aloud for those who could not. The translation used was *Dios llega al hombre,* made by Protestants in the language of the campesinos. The passage was discussed verse by verse. The simplest way to convey the flavor of what took place is by quotation of randomly chosen facing pages. The text under consideration is the parable of the mustard seed from Matthew 13. (The full text of this sermon may be read in **Vol. 2, pp. 586-92.**) The pages begin with the conclusion of a remark by a visiting poet that started on the previous page. Then

LAUREANO: "And the guerilla groups are small, insignificant, poor. And they're often wiped out. But they're going to change society. Can't we apply also to them the parable of the mustard seed?"

MARCELINO, with his calm voice, said: "I don't know about the mustard seed, but I do know about the *guasima* seed, which is tiny. I'm looking at that *guasima* tree over there. It's very large, and the birds come to it too. I say to myself: that's what we are, this little community, a *guasima* seed. It doesn't seem there's any connection between a thing that's round and tiny, like a pebble, and that great big tree. It doesn't seem either that there's any connection between some poor *campesinos* and a just and well-developed society, where there is abundance and everything is shared. And we are the seed of that society. When the tree will develop we don't know. But we know that we are a seed and not a pebble."

I [Cardenal] said: "The great tree with all its branches and its leaves is already present in the seed, even though in a hidden form. In the same way the kingdom of heaven, which is a cosmic kingdom, is already present in us, but in a hidden way. A tree is the product of the evolution of a seed, and in nature everything is produced by a process of evolution. And it seems to me that with this parable of the seed Christ is also telling us here that the kingdom of heaven is the product of the same process of evolution that formed stars, plants, animals, people. And it grows in us impelled by the same forces of nature that impelled the evolution of the whole cosmos, which is to say that the kingdom of heaven is evolution itself."[26]

ELVIS: "The birds that make their nests in the branches, it seems to me, are humanity now free: people who can go freely everywhere without borders of any kind and who will feel safe in the universe, without any of them ever being in need."

TERESITA: "This parable also teaches us that we must be patient, because a tree isn't created in a single day, and all the processes of nature take their time."

OLIVIA: "The kingdom of heaven or the kingdom of love begins with a tiny bit. When we work on it, that seed grows and grows."

"I've seen that seed growing here, blessed be God," said DOÑA ADELITA in her faint voice.

OLIVIA continued: "The kingdom of heaven is also taking shape in our homes with our growing children that we are shaping. They are growing up, and the kingdom of love is taking shape, which is the kingdom of heaven. It has to take shape in a child. And then it goes on developing, and if the children develop well they are going to extend that kingdom of love also. Yes, you can notice also how the kingdom of heaven is growing inside the child."[27]

In time a group of young people decided, precisely out of their Christian commitment, to participate in the Sandinista revolution against the Samoza dictatorship. In reprisal, Solentiname was devastated. The revolution succeeded, however, on July 19, 1979, and Ernesto Cardenal became the minister of culture for Nicaragua. The Sandinista government was voted out of office in 1990.

The preaching method devised by Cardenal for Solentiname has been taken up in other communities that see the cause of liberation to be related to the cause of the kingdom of God. It is used, for instance, in several ministries to homeless urban people. In commenting on the volumes collected by Cardenal, González and González say:

There is . . . in the comments of many of these uneducated people an insight into the meaning of various texts, an ability to see what scholarly commentators hardly ever note, which seems to prove the contention that the poor and the oppressed have an edge when it comes to understanding the meaning of the Bible.[28]

That insight is ratified by those who have had the privilege of being present when this sermonic method was being used.[29]

Thus the practice of preaching for social justice that started in the black church spread quickly to others. Clergy in mainly white mainline churches began speaking out on all the social issues that came to be debated in the 1960s. No one exemplified the prophetic stance of such preaching better than William Sloane Coffin Jr. in his ministry as chaplain of Yale University and as senior pastor of Riverside Church in New York City. Coffin, a multitalented person who grew up in an atmosphere of privilege, offered a very responsible model of prophetic preaching by the way he informed himself thoroughly on any subject he discussed from the pulpit, alternated such preaching with a more pastoral kind, always showed fairness to those who disagreed, and had genuine concern for those to whom he preached.

There was always the danger in such mainline preaching, however, that it would be done from the perspective of the powerful rather than that of the oppressed. Those who really wanted to speak in the name of the least of Christ's brothers and sisters had to learn a new hermeneutic that recognized the Bible's "preferential option for the poor" and to preach from that perspective. The way to do that has been spelled out by Justo and Catherine González, and examples of it exist in abundance in the four volumes of *The Gospel in Solentiname*.

FOR FURTHER READING

Coffin, William Sloane, Jr. *Living the Truth in a World of Illusion.* San Francisco: Harper & Row, 1985.

———. *Once to Every Man: A Memoir.* New York: Athenaeum, 1977.

González, Justo L., and Catherine G. González. *The Liberating Pulpit.* Nashville: Abingdon, 1994.

The Gospel in Solentiname. Edited by Ernesto Cardenal. Translated by Donald D. Walsh. 4 vols. Maryknoll, N.Y.: Orbis Books, 1976–82.

Proclaiming the Acceptable Year: Sermons from a Perspective of Liberation. Edited by Justo González. Valley Forge, Pa.: Judson, 1982.

Notes

1. Mark Noll, *A History of Christianity in the United States and Canada* (Grand Rapids, Mich.: Eerdmans, 1992), 441-46.

2. William Sloane Coffin Jr., *Once to Every Man: A Memoir* (New York: Athenaeum, 1977), 20.

3. Ibid., 19.

4. Ibid., 52, 62. His ability to speak Russian was also an important factor in his being recruited by the CIA.

5. Ibid., 10-11.

6. Ibid., 14.

7. William J. Carl III, *Preaching Christian Doctrine* (Philadelphia: Fortress, 1984), 122.

8. Audiotape, "Discussion of Homiletics," at Union Theological Seminary, Richmond, Va., April 21, 1975, from the seminary's Reigner Recording Library. Other main sources for what Coffin says about preaching are his 1980 Beecher Lectures, "Preaching in the 80s," which were not published as such in book form, but are available in audiocassette from the Visual Educational Service of Yale Divinity School, and "Epilogue: A Word to the Preachers," in his *A Passion for the Possible: A Message to U.S. Churches* (Louisville: Westminster John Knox, 1993). The latter volume appears to be fragments of sermons and speeches integrated into a book. He describes his *The Courage to Love* as an edited form of sermons (San Francisco: Harper & Row, 1982), 8. The content of his *Living the Truth in a World of Illusion* (San Francisco: Harper & Row, 1985), however, is described simply as "sermons" (ix) and is probably closest to what was actually delivered from the pulpit. The first three of Coffin's four Beecher lectures were sermons, and they appear in edited form in *The Courage to Love*. (Indeed, like any preacher asked to speak often on the same subjects, Coffin reuses the language in which he phrases his thought as well as quotations and illustrations a number of times.) His fourth Beecher lecture, however, was addressed to clergy about the work he shares with them.

9. Coffin, *A Passion for the Possible*, 85. I can believe this from watching him conduct a workshop at the College of Preachers in 1994. He noted whenever a visitor appeared in the refectory for a meal and made a point of introducing himself and learning as much about that person as he could, without focusing any attention on himself as the celebrity that he was.

10. Ibid., 86. He also deals with this issue in the fourth Beecher lecture and in the "Discussion on Homiletics."

11. The indices and endnotes (if any) of his books show the range of his reading.

12. Carl, *Preaching Christian Doctrine*, 122.

13. Coffin, *A Passion for the Possible*, 86.

14. Ibid., 84.

15. Ibid., 85.

16. Carl, *Preaching Christian Doctrine*, 124. Carl identifies the position of Coffin with that of Reinhold Niebuhr: "They both reject political passivity and thoughtless activism and encourage a politically active posture informed by scripture, tradition,

and obedience to Christ" (120). He also sees similarities between Coffin's position and that of social-minded Evangelicals such as Richard Mouw and Richard Quebedeaux.

17. Coffin, "Discussion on Homiletics."

18. Coffin, *The Courage to Love*, 39-47. Hereafter, parenthetical references that follow in this text section are to page numbers in this work.

19. In the *Christianity and Crisis* issue for November 2, 1981, where it had a somewhat different form and appeared under the title "Homosexuality Revisited: Whose Problem?"

20. This means that it was preached before the AIDS epidemic had begun. The way that affected his thinking on the subject can be seen in the chapter called "Homophobia" in *A Passion for the Possible*, 62-68.

21. Justo L. González and Catherine G. González, *The Liberating Pulpit* (Nashville: Abingdon, 1994). This work is a thorough revision and expansion of their *Liberation Preaching: The Pulpit and the Oppressed* (Nashville: Abingdon, 1980). See also their article on "Liberation Preaching" in *Concise Encyclopedia of Preaching*, ed. William H. Willimon and Richard Lischer (Louisville: Westminster John Knox, 1995), 307-8. Hereafter, parenthetical references that follow in this text section are to page numbers in *The Liberating Pulpit*.

22. Juan Luis Segundo, *The Liberation of Theology* (Maryknoll, N.Y.: Orbis Books, 1976), 9; cited in González and González, *Liberation Preaching*, 32.

23. *The Gospel in Solentiname*, ed. Ernesto Cardenal, trans. Donald D. Walsh, 4 vols. (Maryknoll, N.Y.: Orbis Books, 1976–82). Justo González has also edited *Proclaiming the Acceptable Year: Sermons from a Perspective of Liberation* (Valley Forge, Pa.: Judson, 1982).

24. This information comes from an introduction that is the same in all four volumes and occupies pp. vii-x in each.

25. From the epilogue that also appears in each volume. Located at the end, its page numbers vary with the length of the individual volumes.

26. The evolutionary interpretation of Cardenal does not reflect older liberal Protestant theology, which interpreted parables as teaching progressive growth. More likely, it shows the influence of the thought of the French Jesuit Pierre Teilhard de Chardin, which was very popular in Roman Catholic circles at the time.

27. Ibid., 2:54-55.

28. González and González, *The Liberating Pulpit*, 59.

29. I have been very impressed by insights that emerged in such discussions at the Church of the Advocate, a church for the homeless formed in Asheville, North Carolina, by the Reverend Judith Whelchel and the Reverend William Jamieson.

CHAPTER 30

A GREAT COMPANY OF WOMEN[1]

Among the issues of social justice clamoring for attention in the 1960s was that of equal rights for women. At the same time as the feminist movement was getting started, an unprecedented number of women were entering the seminaries and ordained ministries of the mainline Christian churches in America. The exact correlation of the women's rights movement with the sudden increase in the number of ordained women is unclear.

On the one hand, most of the denominational decisions to permit such ordinations antedated the movement. Congregationalists and some Baptists were already ordaining women in the nineteenth century. The Methodists agreed to extend full ministerial privileges to women in 1956. Northern Presbyterians[2] decided that women could become teaching elders the same year, and their southern counterpart[3] followed suit eight years later. In 1970, the American Lutheran Church and the Lutheran Church in America both decided that women could become pastors.[4] And the General Convention of the Episcopal Church voted in 1976 to permit women to become priests. Since Sarah M. Evans calls the 1960s the "decade of discovery" for the feminist movement,[5] obviously it was possible for women to be ordained in some of the country's largest denominations before the movement really got under way.

Yet, on the other hand, the possibility that women could be ordained did not make it probable that many would be. Expectations of what women clergy might do were generally circumscribed until the influence of feminism was felt in the churches. There was, for instance, an article in *Monday Morning,* a Presbyterian weekly magazine for clergy, that welcomed the 1956 decision precisely because it saw the role of ordained women as subservient to that of male pastors:

> An ordained woman, among many other specializing tasks, can con-
> duct junior congregations, relieve or supplement the pastor in calling,
> assist in the pulpit, take the sacraments to the sick and aged, perform
> certain types of personal work, counsel with young women on person-
> al problems, even marry them, and lay away those of their sex.[6]

Small wonder there was not an immediate rush to the seminaries to prepare for such a challenging vocation.

When the influence of the women's rights movement came to be felt, however, and the possibility of full equality in ministry was opened, min-
isterial vocation came to be taken much more seriously by women in the churches in which they could be ordained. "In 1972 the Association of Theological Schools in the United States and Canada reported that bare-
ly 10 percent of the students in its member institutions were women, whereas by 1987 that figure had climbed to over 27 percent."[7] By 1998, the percentage had increased to 33.6, although only 29.9 percent were in the preordination degree program.[8] In the same year, women made up almost 10 percent of the total number of clergy in the country, an impressive number in view of the fact that three-quarters of American Christians belong to churches that do not ordain women.[9]

While the basic work of ministry in most of the churches that ordain women would appear very much the same to a casual observer, the rela-
tive timing of denominational decisions to ordain is related to the polity or form of governance in each body. The Congregationalists and Baptists needed only the agreement of the local congregation. For Methodists, the crucial issue was not so much the ministry of Word and sacrament as it was the full membership in an annual conference that entitled a cleric to a local church appointment. Presbyterians distinguished between ruling elders, who were the local governing board, and teaching elders, who preached and administered sacraments. Lutherans had only one order of ministry of Word and sacrament, that of pastors. Episcopalians claimed

to have the threefold ministry of the early church and recognized as priests only those who were ordained by a bishop in apostolic succession.

As Barbara Brown Zikmund has pointed out, however, "in most mainstream denominations, no progress is made towards the recognition of women clergy until women gain significant power and influence as laity."[10] They have to be able to speak and vote in congregational meetings, serve on the local governing board, and be eligible for election as delegates to national bodies before service as ordained ministers becomes a likely possibility. Thus the issue is essentially one of power and the right of women to an equal share of it. Since that is the sort of issue feminists were calling attention to in all other structures of society, it is not surprising that it was raised in the churches.

Most of the women who had preached earlier had done so as evangelists, an activity that was not thought to require ordination. Even then they had functioned mainly in denominations that were in an early stage of transition from sect to church and at a time when there was a shortage of male clergy.[11] Therefore, the large numbers of women who began to be ordained in the 1970s represented a new stage in the histories of both the church and preaching, a stage in which a good deal of Christian preaching was to be done by women for the first time. What difference did that make in the way preaching was done?

PERCEIVED DIFFERENCES BETWEEN THE SPEAKING OF MEN AND WOMEN

An element of the ideology that previously had barred women from the pulpit was an assumption of differences in the psychological makeup of the two sexes. From classical antiquity at least, there had been an assumption that any public speaking done by women would be very different from that done by men:

> Because it was presumably driven by emotion, womanly speech was thought to be personal, excessive, disorganized, and unduly ornamental. Because it was presumably driven by reason, the manly style was thought to be factual, analytic, organized, and impersonal. Where womanly speech sowed disorder, manly speech planted order. Womanly speech corrupted an audience by inviting it to judge the case on spurious grounds; manly speech invited judicious judgment.[12]

Congregations in which some of the first ordained women served noted similar differences between the preaching of men and women. The

751

College of Preachers in Washington, D.C., held a conference on "Women and Preaching" in 1979 that was attended by about thirty female clergy from all over the country. Part of their preparation for the conference was to gather data from their congregations on the differences members perceived between the preaching of women and that of men. The approximately 150 responses revealed the pattern displayed in the table below.[13]

Perceived Gender Differences in Preaching

1980

Male	Female
Content	
Intellectual	Down-to-earth
Theological	Emotional
Jargon	Personal
Hard questions	Experiential
Abstract	Life issues
Traditional and	No point
male illustrations	Too personal
Delivery	
Confident	Solicitous
Controlled	Inviting
Voice-rich	Apologetic
Strong	Hesitant
Bigger	Animated
	Hard to hear
	Expressive
	Warm
Style	
Formal	Informal
Forceful	Warm
Rational	Personal
Organized	Apologetic
Authoritarian	Ingratiating
Remote	

On the whole, men's preaching was considered more effective. Yet, when a similar poll was taken in 1994, the confidence that had come to women from experience and the greater exposure of congregations to women's preaching resulted in a much better scorecard for them.

> Women's preaching is described in more positive, receptive tones and words than in the earlier study.... Hearers appear to register a stronger feeling response to women preaching than to men.[14]

LEVELING THE PLAYING FIELD

One of the first efforts by a woman homiletician to delineate the strengths and weaknesses of preaching by members of her sex and to assist her sisters in building on the one and overcoming the other is **Carol Norén**'s book *The Woman in the Pulpit*.[15] The author, who moved from Duke into an endowed chair at North Park seminary in Chicago, begins by offering advice on overcoming hurdles in the process of becoming accepted as a candidate for ordination. Then she notes the lack of role models up until that time for women who would fill the pulpit. Next she says that women find it easier to claim authority in preaching and leading worship than in other parochial duties. This claim is made on the basis of polls taken among ordained women, and the author offers explanations of why both elements of the statement are true. She then goes on to suggest strategies for dealing with the imbalance.

Norén's fourth chapter is concerned with the way women preachers disclose themselves in the pulpit through their illustrations and autobiographical references and through their nonverbal communication. She says that when they preach from narrative texts in the Bible, they often identify with the character in the story who is weakest or who is "the object of the action rather than the initiator" (65). Sometimes, too, women preachers forget that personal illustrations are to be used when the speaker can be "the representative I" for all members of the congregation rather than for revealing their own need for intimacy. In these ways, the preachers are in danger of perpetuating stereotypes.

Noting that some authorities believe that 90 percent of a speaker's influence depends on nonverbal communication, Norén goes on to indicate the importance of pulpit attire that suggests professional competence. She points out that a woman who tilts or bobs her head while preaching, or breathes in a shallow way, crosses her legs like scissors, or has a rising inflection at the end of sentences is likely to suggest a daughterly diffidence to her congregation rather than spiritual leadership.

"More often," however, "the preacher's gestures and changes in posture communicate, 'Listen to your mother!'" (84).

In looking at ways in which the biblical interpretation of women preachers differs from that of men, Norén points out that "women's sermons regularly manifest several features in exegetical method that concur with liberation and/or feminist hermeneutics as set forth by Justo and Catherine González and Elisabeth Schüssler Fiorenza" (91). That often involves preaching from a familiar biblical text, but calling attention to aspects of it that had escaped notice or not been thought important before, especially the oppressiveness of patriarchy that can be discovered in many passages. Women also tend to show a more concrete relation than men do between the situation in the biblical text and the situation today. "Perhaps the strongest affinity between feminist/liberation hermeneutics and preaching by women in general is the way that both favor narrative/historical texts" (96). Another technique is to identify with the people addressed by a prophet rather than with the prophet, or otherwise "reassign the cast of characters." Finally, women's sermons assume implicitly that the congregation's task is to do everything possible to bring God's new social order to pass.

Female clergy have other characteristic ways of interpreting biblical texts that are not derived from a feminist hermeneutic. These include retelling the story of the text in an amplified way and then drawing an analogy to it in the present context. Often, too, the preachers studied by Norén identify with the least powerful character in the story and thus implicitly expect members of their congregation to do so. "A third characteristic of women's interpretive method is choosing to focus on the dynamics of relationship evidenced in the text, and preach a sermon that works for reconciliation in the divine-human and interpersonal relationships" (107). The last tendency shown by the preaching of the women studied was to interpret the text "from the perspective of the preacher's internal authority, based on her own experiences" (109).

Norén goes on to offer advice pertaining to the use of inclusive language about people and God and women's participation in liturgy, but these get away from characterizing the preaching of women as such. In summarizing what she has to say about the pulpit performance of ordained women, she does note some particular virtues, but on the whole directs her efforts toward helping her sisters avoid some of the practices that played into the hands of those who earlier had wished to denigrate their efforts.

Very different from Norén's book is one written a couple of years earlier, *Weaving the Sermon* by **Christine M. Smith**.[16] While Norén certainly does not want to make women preach like men, her primary goal is to help them avoid practices that could diminish the effectiveness of their proclamation. Smith, on the other hand, writes in a prescriptive way to encourage a new homiletical method that she thinks would result in a great improvement in preaching. That method is indicated in the book's subtitle, *Preaching in a Feminist Perspective*.[17]

The structure of Smith's book comes from the metaphor of weaving that appears in her title. This metaphor, she says, emerged in feminist writing "as an organizing image in women's lives" (7). Her entire project assumes that "there is some qualitative distinctiveness surrounding the preaching of feminist women" (9).[18] The metaphor of weaving points to that distinctiveness: "This image has at its heart the interlacing of conflict and struggle with vision and hope" (15). Or, again: "The essence of the craft [of weaving] is that it always involves the process of uniting and integrating separate strands into an interwoven whole" (21).

Each of Smith's chapters deals with an element of preaching to which an element of weaving is seen to be analogous. Inevitably, in the first the preacher is treated as the weaver. This is the only chapter in which Smith does not draw from feminists as such. Her sources here are women who have written on the psychology of their sex. It is necessary to point out that there is not one psychology for men and women; there are important differences between them:

> While men, particularly white men, appear to have autonomy, individuality, and detachment as integral focus points in their development and growth, women appear to have at the heart of their development qualities of affiliation and interconnectedness. (24)

The basic themes that recur in the psychological studies are of intimacy and relatedness. For the preaching task, this means "women preachers feel that the relationship established in the moment of preaching is as crucial to life and faith as the truths of the biblical witness" (40). It also means the experience of women will be a basic source and norm for that preaching. Anything untrue to that criterion has no place in feminist preaching.

The loom on which the feminist preacher weaves her sermons is her authority. It is, after all, a loom that holds the warp threads under tension and in order, so that the weft may be woven in to create a tapestry with its own pattern. But the authority of the feminist preacher is not "special rights, power, knowledge, and capacity to influence or transform" (46), which male preachers have traditionally claimed. Rather, many women would not speak of authority as that which gives them the "right" to speak. Authority has to do with a quality of content, a mode of communication, and an authenticity of message which makes the preaching craft and the moment of proclamation credible, honest, and life-transforming for speaker and listener alike. (47)

That quality, mode, and authenticity are the mutuality and solidarity that make up the loom of feminists' preaching: "The loom of our transforming, creative power, the loom of our life and faith weaving, is our woman's wisdom—a large source of our authority" (54).

The warp threads spread on the loom to undergird feminist preaching are a critique of traditional God language, Christology, and biblical hermeneutics. This is the prophetic dimension of such preaching. One approach to dealing with the traditional masculine and even macho language used about God has been to replace it with feminine images. Women need to hear such images, but that is not all that needs to be done:

> To incorporate the strands of our tradition that point to a prophetic God, a liberating sovereign, and a God who breaks through all idolatries is a much more radical stance in Christian preaching than to articulate equivalent female images in addition to male God images. (75)

Even more radical is the feminist critique of traditional Christology. It postulates that the male Jesus of Nazareth cannot be the normative model for all human beings. What is claimed instead is that "Jesus is not God, but Jesus' activity as justice bearer, healer of pain-filled humanity, and profound relational presence embodies and incarnates God in our world" (81). The most that can be said is that Jesus is a parable of God.[19] And, if feminist theology finds traditional God language and Christology wanting, how much more is it dissatisfied with biblical interpretation that ignores the way the Bible reflects the patriarchal societies in which it was written, and the consequent suppression in its text of women's lives, witness, and worth.[20]

The weft of feminist preaching is a vision for the transformation of the world. Such preaching could be called "weft-faced" because the threads that dominate it will not be those of tradition but those of transformation. This vision should come from feminist thought, music, art, and spirituality. It recognizes the interconnectedness of all forms of oppression; it is committed to peace, disarmament, and living in ecological and relational harmony with all creation; and draws on new feminist understandings of spirituality. While Smith lists as interconnected forms of oppression sexism, racism, classism, militarism, heterosexism, and lack of access, she highlights two: the oppression of the aged and the differently abled.[21] Then, referring to those who have suffered from the interconnected forms of oppressions, she says:

> Until all preachers are willing to open themselves to the voices in their communities and to be changed by those voices and insights, the preaching act will remain individualistic in nature, and the content of sermons will be less than inclusive, isolated from the needs and wisdom of the whole people of God. (123)

The commitment to peace and disarmament and to harmony with creation, the second weft thread of the transforming vision, is obvious enough. The third weft thread of feminist spirituality, however, needs to have its content specified in greater detail. Smith calls attention to three aspects of it: its recognition that spirituality that does not result in political action and social transformation is not worth the name; its affirmation and celebration of the human body; and an appreciation for a wide diversity of spiritual disciplines, perspectives, and practices. Preaching with these three weft threads will be prophetic preaching, shaped as it is by a vision for the transformation of society and individuals.

Design is the final element of weaving either fabrics or sermons. Noting the great freedom and creativity possible in sermon design, Smith quotes a weaving textbook: "One speaks of a design as being *effective* or *successful,* and any design is so when it satisfies the artist's aesthetic impulse and communicates with the audience."[22] The first element of design, proportion, is related to the phenomenon of beginning with women's lives, the process of naming. "One woman's weaving ought never to be more important in *proportion* to the whole, nor should one woman's weaving ever be less important in *proportion* to the whole" (144). The enterprise is collective!

Balance is the second element of design, and it is treated as the weft of transformation's relation to the warp of tradition. Even if the design is weft-faced, "to preach without a strong commitment to the tradition, even in the midst of transforming it, is to stand rootless as a preacher" (145). Emphasis is the element of design that catches and holds the viewer's attention. Two emphases noted in the preaching of women are their tendency to reveal themselves in their sermons and the greater imagination with which they preach. And on the rhythm of a feminist sermon Smith says: "At its very finest [it] should feel like an art piece and have the spirit of transformation" (150).

Preaching, then, that is woven by a woman on the loom of the authority given by mutuality and solidarity, in which the warp is Christian tradition that has undergone a feminist critique and the weft is the transforming vision of global feminism, that follows a design with the proportion of the one woman's voice to that of others, with a balance between tradition (as critiqued) and vision, the emphasis of self-revelation and imagination, and the balance of a work of art, will, in the opinion of Christine Smith, be transforming indeed.[23]

THE METAPHOR OF VOICE

Smith observed the importance of the weaving metaphor for feminist thought, but in more recent years another metaphor has occupied the attention of women homileticians, that of voice. For instance, **Lee McGee** of Yale Divinity School addressed that issue in *Wrestling with the Patriarchs*. Her title probably has a double reference. On the one hand, it refers to the difficulty many ordained women have experienced in preaching, a difficulty a seminarian described by saying:

> For me, the preaching experience is best conveyed in the image of God and Jacob wrestling. There is a combination of feelings, like a wound and a blessing. I'm never sure if I'm meeting an angel or a demon in the sermon preparation and delivery. (13, 29)

In this instance, the woman sees herself in analogy to the patriarch Jacob. On the other hand, a good bit of the struggle is caused by the way women have grown up in a patriarchal society in which their voices were not listened to or valued.

McGee was prompted to this study by her discovery of the way many women agonized over sermon preparation. This led her to research that Carol Gilligan and others engaged in as a collaborative endeavor of Harvard University and the Stone Center at Wellesley College.[24] Their work concerns the psychological development of girls and women. They have found that during adolescence, girls experience an increased desire for relationship, one result of which is their fear of saying anything that may alienate a male or female peer or adult.

A dramatic example of this desire's effect is revealed in the way girls at age fourteen say "I know" only a third as many times as they did at age twelve. Instead, they say "you know" to interviewers, teachers, or friends. This decline is referred to as "loss of voice." "[The girl] seems to be refusing to say what she knows, probably due to a loss of confidence about self, reality, and relationship security" (46).

The need to be true to God, her congregation, and herself while staying in relationship with her congregation is what McGee thinks is responsible for the anxiety women feel in preparing to preach. To help women deal with that anxiety, she developed a five-session workshop process, which she has used in her teaching and in conferences she has conducted. She gives the format for such a program in the last chapter of her book (97-113). In this process for "voice retrieval," women seminarians and clergy are invited to study the lives of great women in church history to see the barriers to being heard they faced and how they overcame them. Then they are exposed to the findings of the Harvard-Wellesley scholars on the psychological development of women and how that affects their willingness to speak.

Next they are taught an adaptation of a counseling method developed by Mary Ballou and Nancy Gabalac to help women overcome "harmful adaptation."[25] The method has five phases. The first is *separation*: "For the woman preacher this step involves separating herself from situations and persons who, either consciously or unconsciously, try to stifle, inhibit, or intimidate her voice" (74). The next step, *validation*, involves the preacher's stating her understanding of everything from personal relations to biblical interpretation to other women who reinforce those perceptions.

Then, by an *association* with other women during at least six sessions, she comes to see that her voice is valued because it is hers, rather than because everyone else shares or even welcomes her insight. After this association has gone on for a while, each member begins to feel an *authorization* of her voice by the group, because what she says is listened to with attention and respect for her situation. The final phase is one of *negotiation*, which involves testing the use of her voice and learning to weigh the relative costs and benefits of using it. "In this phase, women preachers attempt to make conscious decisions about and take risks with voice in preaching. Women preachers discuss how to alter sermon preparation so as to nurture voice" (80).

This, then, is the process McGee has developed to assist seminarians and ordained women to overcome the loss of voice they experienced in their adolescent development—the loss that made sermon preparation an agony for them—and to retrieve their voices so that they can freely and effectively share their insights with the church. Although they go over much the same ground, **Mary Donovan Turner** and **Mary Lin Hudson** have produced a very different book in their *Saved from Silence: Finding Women's Voices in Preaching*.[26] McGee has designed a process while Turner and Hudson have written an essay; their book is more discursive and analytical.

Turner and Hudson begin with a survey of feminist literature in which the metaphor of voice has been important. From that they abstract the following summary:

> "Voice" offers a new possibility for understanding the nature of self and world in relation to God and others. It is distinctive. It can call forth authentic selfhood. It is the self's authoritative expression. Sometimes it is resistant, but always it speaks of relationship. It opens the world to new perceptions, new action, and new ways of living. Voice subverts. Voice transforms. (17)

They go on to say that the metaphor also provides a new way of understanding "revelation, liberation, memory, longing, and justice" (17). They begin their justification for that claim with a two-chapter look at biblical revelation, with one chapter on the Old Testament and the other on the New. In the Bible, the God of Israel is one who speaks and one who listens. Persons and all things were brought into being when God spoke, and what God said came into being. And God is open to hearing the people God has made and responding to their distress; yet, the people of God are not always faithful and need to hear God's judgment spoken by the prophets. "God, through speech, discloses new meaning and becomes a living presence on our journey—even when we fail to be a hearing people" (33).

The authors limit their study of the New Testament to Luke–Acts, which carries forward the Israelite understanding of prophetic speech as an effect of the Holy Spirit:

> The Spirit breathes through Jesus in a limitless way, combining into one single voice the harmony of the voices of prophets throughout the ages. In turn, Jesus promises power to the disciples, and the Spirit sweeps through their silence and draws forth multiple voices alive with the presence of God. . . . They find that their voices offer a unique, unmistakable, essential tone to the sound of God's liberation of the world. (47)

Theological reflection on the biblical understanding of voice leads to the insight that "to be made in the image of God is to be made in the sound of God" (49). This is to say that after the death of Jesus, the prophetic authority of his voice was passed on to all his followers who seek God's realm. The authors say that this theology of voice challenges the traditional Protestant notion of an "unchanging and static Word that somehow comes to expression through women and men unaltered and unscathed" (54). Such a notion perpetuates the status quo and thus promotes disempowerment. On the other hand,

> a metaphor of "voice" suggests that the Holy Spirit still speaks, gives voice to ongoing revelation in the lives of many who have been silenced, often in the name of the very God who is thus represented. (55)

This means that the preacher must not only listen to the biblical text; she must also listen to her own experience in the world. In doing so, she would be trusting in the one who has called her all along and given her voice, rather than obeying the ecclesiastical authorities that have tried to stifle voices like hers through the centuries.

Like McGee, Turner and Hudson believe that women gain strength from the examples of women in church history who have resisted all efforts to silence them in order to use the voices God gave them. They cite New Testament examples and pay particular attention to Hildegard of Bingen among medieval models. They also look at Louisa Maria Layman Woolsey, ordained by the Cumberland Presbyterians in 1889. They look as well at Beverly Wildung Harrison, who rose to power in the United Presbyterian Church by conforming to masculine role models before she began to read feminists, who enabled her to accept herself as a woman and to begin to assist other women in holding on to their vocations.

The large numbers of women in seminaries today and in at least entry-level positions in ordained ministry could leave the impression that finding their voice is no longer a problem for women in the church. Turner and Hudson insist, however, that such is not the case. Referring to the research of Carol Gilligan and others that McGee also mentioned, and to numerous studies of adolescent girls in contemporary America, they show that outer and inner voices still conspire to silence women. Worse, they show that the church has colluded in this conspiracy to prevent women from speaking and to make them mistrust their own voices.

As a result, women are still hindered in their psychological, intellectual, and emotional development. And, since the descriptions of reality they hear come from those who oppress them, the descriptions often do not describe reality as they experience it. Thus there is a necessity for the woman in the church to begin a search, "looking for new theological language, new liturgical language to describe her experience of life, love, God, salvation, redemption, joy as true and good" (91). For a woman to be able to stand in the pulpit and speak that new theological language is a redemptive experience for her. It is also a prophetic act.

This means that for a woman, learning to preach is not just acquiring a set of skills to be added to others. It is the process by which she comes to value her own voice and to believe that she has something to say worth hearing. Key elements in reaching that assurance are imagination and listening: imaginative consideration of the possibilities that lead to a recognition that she has something valuable to say, and listening to voices from other silenced groups so that she will speak not just for herself but for all the oppressed.

Such imagining and listening will assist the preacher in "naming the old worlds out of which we would like to move" (111). Involved in this coming to voice through imagining, listening, and naming is the acquisition of new hermeneutical, exegetical, homiletic, narrative, and feminist and womanist theories. These theories "demand that the preacher bring forth the gospel in her own distinctive, authentic, authoritative, resistant, and relational voice, born of spirit and expressive of [her] own god-likeness" (99). When that happens, women in the church will have found their voice in preaching; they will have been saved from silence.[27]

PREACHING AS A MULTISTRANDED HELIX

While the metaphors of weaving and voice have been important to women homileticians, a different analogy has seemed more appropriate to an ethnographer who has made a specialty of studying women who preach. The work of Elaine J. Lawless, who teaches at the University of Missouri, was drawn on above in our study of women preachers in the Wesleyan/Holiness/ Pentecostal trajectory.[28] From there she has gone on to make the acquaintance of a sizable group of women clergy in mainline churches in the vicinity of Columbus, Missouri. In 1983, she began visiting their churches and recording their sermons. The first fruit of this work was a study of the women themselves, published as *Holy Women: Wholly Women: Sharing Ministries of Wholeness Through Life Stories and Reciprocal Ethnography.*[29] From there she went on, however, to make a study of the way they preach.[30] (**See Vol. 2, pp. 596-601,** for one of their sermons.)

Her method for doing this was to continue visiting the churches of the women and recording their sermons, but she added meeting with them in their groups. These included bimonthly luncheon meetings of as many as twenty-five women in ministry. More to the point was a smaller group that met weekly to study the readings from the Common Lectionary appointed for the following Sunday. She also met with a small number drawn from both groups who were interested in helping her with this book. In addition, there were some who met regularly as friends. In this way, she was in on the sermon preparation process and could also get reactions from the women to her efforts to interpret what they were doing; she calls her method "reciprocal ethnography" (4-6).

On the basis of this research, Lawless was able to find a list of qualities that characterize the preaching of her clergy friends. The qualities she found overlap with a number that have been mentioned above, but she finds all of these to be virtues, while some of the other analyses treat them as ambivalent.[31]

She found storytelling to be a key element in women's pulpit work: "I felt a concerted effort on their part to make the scriptures relevant to modern audiences, not in an ahistorical way, but by bringing the scriptures and people's lives into praxis through storytelling" (87).[32] "In their sermons, the speakers seem to be re-thinking the messages in biblical stories and in the process of preaching often disrupt the listeners' typical response to time-worn sermon analyses and expectations" (89). Thus "the sermons [are] unorthodox in the way they question things," and "some of them suggest that following the rules and regulations, the prescribed ways of doing things, is not necessarily the appropriate plan of action" (91).

The fact that the sermons are "about the outsider, the outcast, the marginal, the youngest, the meek, the quiet one, the unlikely one getting chosen by God" suggests to Lawless that the women are more concerned about "*Where* is God" than with "*Who* is God?" (91). And their sermons locate God in connection, relationship, the interconnectedness of all things, gratitude, the intuitive and the experienced (as opposed to the factual and the cerebral), dialogue, the fluid characteristics of an image, God's actions, their own stories, and being vulnerable (91-93).

Hence the sermons are rarely didactic (93). "Rhetorically, in these sermons, the women relate their beliefs 'about where God is' to their style of preaching by relinquishing typical pulpit hierarchical authority and claiming, instead, an authority based on equality and connection" (94). Appropriately, therefore, "the language used in these sermons is often poetic, powerful, sensuous, intimate, and evocative" (95).

Then, "above and beyond the significance of the characteristics outlined thus far in this chapter lies the power of personal experience stories used by women in their sermons to frame their messages" (95). Women do not use stories to illustrate sermons as men do, especially not canned material from encyclopedias of illustration. Lawless finds that amazing because the women were socialized to share with children the quality of being seen but not heard. "For the first time I am hearing women's stories and experiences from the pulpit. From whence comes the courage, the audacity, the willingness to take such a risk?...In these settings, women's stories become stories enhanced, sanctified, endorsed, validated, confirmed, experienced, enjoyed, shared, and celebrated" (96).

Through the stories, Lawless realized "just how much being female affected their sermons" (97). "Through their first-person stories, women's stories, the women were providing a new validation for the connection between women's lives and their personal, intimate relationship with the sacred. . . . The stories of the women authenticate the immediacy of an immanent God prepared and willing to enter into relationship with them and with all other humans, in mutual and collective connection in spite of differences" (97). "Their personal stories are poignant, deeply private, and sometimes angry" (98). But at any rate, they do not reflect a picture of God as "distant, judging, inaccessible, and 'watching'" (98) to catch them out.

Lawless says in summary, "Relationships, vulnerability, love, empathy, shared concerns, dialogue, and connection are the crucial themes that run throughout the sermons in every aspect—structure, language, storytelling, personal experience stories, and points of view" (99). On the basis of her study, Lawless concludes that there has been a paradigm shift in the church. She builds on Loren Mead's thesis that a shift from "the Christendom paradigm" to a "new paradigm," is occurring. She differs from Mead's belief that the shape of the new paradigm is not yet clear, insisting instead that it has emerged in the preaching of women (161).[33]

> Women's voices offer diverse approaches, reflective attitudes, different perspectives, and stimulating avenues for exploration. The women seem fearless to me, afraid of nothing. Speaking no longer only from the margins, they have broken through the fissures of the "old" Christendom paradigm and offer Christians new cooperative, reciprocal, and dialogic ways of being. (175)

Whether this is a new paradigm for Christianity remains to be seen, but it is clearly an improvement in the church.

BEECHER LECTURERS

In addition to these women who have written about the preaching of women, there have been others who delivered the prestigious Beecher Lectures on Preaching at Yale. Yet none of the four thus honored have chosen to focus on the preaching of women as such. The first, **Helen Kenyon,** was a member of a panel of laypersons[34] asked in 1950 to speak of the way preaching looked from the pew. At the time, Kenyon was moderator of the General Council of the Congregational Christian Churches, having served previously for six years as the chair of the Missions Council of the Congregationalists.

Her topic was "Walking Together."[35] She did not speak primarily as a woman, but rather as a nonprofessional layperson to the assembled clergy and future clergy. Speaking from the perspective of the old covenants between Puritan congregations and their pastors, she was concerned about how they should walk together into the presence of God. She addressed her audience as teachers, preachers, and pastors. She said laypeople need to be taught the Bible and to read good works of theology; they need to be taught to think—and to worship. She stated that preachers should train their congregations in worship, both private and corporate. And she called upon pastors to trust their people more, to allow a member of the congregation to preach occasionally, and to encourage lay evangelism.

Thirty-two years passed before another woman gave the lectures. By then the feminist movement was in full stride, and the distinguished scholar of the Hebrew Bible, **Phyllis Trible,** spoke on *Texts of Terror: Literary-Feminist Readings of Biblical Narratives.*[36] These lectures were written to be a companion volume to her earlier work, *God and the Rhetoric of Sexuality,*[37] although, as she says, the two books differ in emphasis and spirit: "The first is a time to laugh and dance; the second, a time to weep and mourn."[38] Neither book deals with preaching as such, but with the sort of exegetical work that should be done in preparation for preaching. In the first, Trible uses literary analysis to call attention to the way the power of women and life-giving images of their experience shine through essentially patriarchal texts in the stories in Genesis, Ruth, and the Song of Solomon. In her Beecher lectures, she shows how the brutalization, rape, and violation of women have been obscured in biblical accounts such as the stories of Hagar, Tamar, Jephthah's daughter, and the unnamed woman in Judges 19: Texts of Terror, indeed! Since, however, what Trible contributes is a resource for preaching rather than a consideration of the preaching of women as such, it cannot be considered at length here.

A similar verdict must be passed on the next Beecher lectures by a woman, those of **Peggy Brainard Way,** delivered in 1995.[39] Way has taught pastoral theology and directed field education at the University of Chicago Divinity School, the Urban Training Center, the Vanderbilt

765

Divinity School, and Eden Theological Seminary. She gave a marvelous series of lectures on the way that the voices of pastoral persons have been undervalued as resources for the privileged knowledge of the academic theological disciplines; they should be required listening for everyone involved in theological education or in church judicatories. Yet even though she is an ordained woman and a feminist, her lectures do not address the concerns of this chapter.

The only woman Beecher lecturer to speak about preaching as such is **Barbara Brown Taylor.** Her 1998 lectures were titled *Famine in the Land: Homiletical Restraint and the Silence of God,* but they were published as *When God Is Silent.*[40] An Episcopal priest, Taylor spent six years in administrative posts at the seminaries of Emory and Yale before she was ordained. For the next nine years she was on the staff of a large parish in Atlanta. Next she served as rector of the parish in Clarkesville, a small town in north Georgia.

Her preaching attracted attention from the beginning of her ordained life. She was, for example, asked to assist the legendary Fred Craddock in the instruction of preaching at Emory while she was in Atlanta. She won an award for the series of sermons she preached on *The Protestant Hour* in 1990, she was named by Baylor University as one of the twelve most effective preachers in the English-speaking world, and she has been widely invited to preach and to lecture on preaching. Now she holds an endowed chair at Piedmont College in Demorest, Georgia.[41]

Much of the literature about the preaching of women has dealt with difficulties they have experienced in that task. Therefore, it is helpful to be able to look at the work of Taylor, who has concentrated on preaching, to see how the Word's proclamation has been enriched by the ordination of women.[42] The qualities that make her such an effective preacher are also evident in her Beecher lectures.

The first of the lectures deals with a famine of the Word of God. Part of the problem, she recognizes, is with the way language has been abused. Some of that abuse has been by clergy: "most preachers wield words such as *God* or *faith* as if they were made of steel instead of air" (7). But our society is in crisis over a lack of trust in the power of words to convey meaning. Much of that is a result of consumerism, "which forces words to make promises they cannot keep" (9). Some of the fault also lies with journalism, which Taylor sees as a variety of consumerism. And more lies with the proliferation of words; their sheer quantity makes it hard for us to listen to any of them. She agrees with George Steiner that "we are living in the aftermath of the broken covenant between the word and the world."[43] As for preachers, "at best, we contribute more persuasive words to a world already glutted with them. At worst, we engage in more false advertising" (20). In the presence of so much sound, people are hungry for the Word of God. In all this noise, God seems silent.

In her second lecture, Taylor addresses the perceived silence of God. She says that of those who come to her for counseling,

> the large majority come because they cannot get God to say anything at all. They have asked as sincerely as they know how for answers, for guidance, for peace, but they are still missing those things. (51)

A search of the Scriptures, however, shows that this is not a new experience. "After the delivery of the commandments, God never spoke directly to the people again" (54). Only in Jesus did he speak again, but not all could recognize his voice there. Much of God's silence can be interpreted as for our protection. "Many people pray for an encounter with the living God. Those whose prayers are answered rarely ask for the same thing twice" (57). After hearing the voice of God directly at Sinai, the people of Israel decided they needed a mediator. After Mount Moriah, Abraham never again talked to God. And the resistance of the prophets to the word of God is "legendary."

How we have changed! "When we speak of God, we do not sound so much like people with fire shut up in our bones as we do like people who are blowing on gray coals" (65). We have turned away from God, but apparently God has also turned away from us. "This game of divine hide and seek is part of God's pedagogy in Isaiah, which makes silence a vital component of God's speech" (67). And silence is as much a characteristic of the Christian as of the Hebrew Scriptures. "Even when he spoke, Jesus created silence. Many of his sayings were so cryptic that no response was possible, while others were so offensive that replies were withheld" (75). Furthermore, Jesus himself experienced the silence of God when he prayed from the cross. And such things should surely produce silence in us.

> With the cross and the empty tomb, God has provided us with two events that defy all our efforts to domesticate them. Before them, and before the God who is present in them, our most eloquent words turn to dust. (80)

In her last lecture, Taylor talks about "how we may approach this God with all due respect, proclaiming the Word without violating the silence, by speaking with restraint" (80). Thus she disagrees with those who say that one should preach without restraint. "One big gulp of Gatorade is not the answer"[44] for people dying of thirst; what they need instead is a series of sips. Preaching exists in tension with the silence of God: "We must finally make peace with the incompleteness of our saying, which draws near to but cannot penetrate the silence of God's pure being" (90). Yet when we dare speak, what we say must give evidence of the time spent in waiting before the silence.

That, of course, raises the question: "How does one preach silence? More to the point, how does one preach without profaning God's silence?" (99). Taylor believes that three qualities are needed for such preaching: economy, courtesy, and reverence in the language we use. Preachers address both God and their people, acting as matchmakers between them. "Our job is to find the fewest, best words that will allow them to find one another and then to get out of the way" (101). The economy of preaching, then, will be expressed in short, well-crafted sermons. This means, among other things, that the words of the sermon will be the preacher's own, rather than those garnered from someone else; they must be the truest thing one can say about the subject. They must be like the food a hungry person finds crawling on her belly on the forest floor.

By courtesy in preaching, Taylor means the opposite of coercion. She means respecting the autonomy of those who hear. That involves "leaving partly described what can only be partly described" (111). The preaching of Jesus displayed this courtesy, this respect for the listener, with its stories and images that always have "great pockets of silence in them" (114). Too often preachers are made nervous by God's silence and compensate for it by talking more themselves. But,

> our job is not to pierce that mystery with our language, but to reverence it. Our understanding, such as it is, is never a result of trespassing the bounds of the holy but of knowing where they are, and of having the good sense not to say what cannot be said. (118-19)

This is true because "our duty in this time of famine is not to end the human hunger and thirst for God's word but to intensify it, until the whole world bangs its forks for God's food" (120).

Such a description of the preaching task is bound to raise the question of what sermons that meet these criteria would be like. One that comes very close is Taylor's Lenten sermon, "Life-Giving Fear."[45] For the text of this sermon, see **Vol. 2, pp. 601-4.**) She tells of making a hospital visit with the mother of a five-year-old girl who had a large tumor on her optic nerve. The mother was convinced that the child's illness was pun-

768

ishment for the mother's smoking. Taylor told her she did not believe in such a God, but saw that in doing so, what she said was more threatening than helpful. "If there was something wrong with her daughter, then there had to be a reason. She was even willing to be the reason. At least that way she could get a grip on the catastrophe" (70). In this the mother was much like the rest of us, who seek for a perspective that will give us some sense of control over the chaos of our lives.

Taylor is a lectionary preacher, and this sermon was for the Third Sunday in Lent, Year C. The Gospel is Luke 13:1-9, in which Jesus tells of the Galileans "whose blood Pilate mingled with their sacrifices." Jesus asks if those Galileans were worse sinners than all others. His answer to his own question seemed to give with one hand what was taken away with the other. "*No*, Jesus says, *there is no connection between the suffering and the sin. Whew. But unless you repent, you are going to lose some blood too. Oh*" (71).

Jesus responds to the panic the Galileans feel that the terrible things happening around them are the results of their failings. While he denies that to be the case, he recognizes the vulnerability the panic has caused, and urges them to take advantage of it and turn toward the light.

> That torn place your fear has opened up inside you is a holy place. Look around while you are there. Pay attention to what you feel. It may hurt you to stay there and it may hurt you to see, but it is not the kind of hurt that leads to death. It is the kind that leads to life. (72)

That sounds like preaching appropriate for a time when God is silent. It is also a good example of how Christian preaching has been enriched by the widespread ordination of women. It has most of the qualities that women homileticians have claimed are characteristic of the preaching of women. While Lawless may be premature in claiming that a shift of paradigms has occurred in church history, it is at least true that turning over the responsibility for a good bit of it to women has improved the quality of preaching.

FOR FURTHER READING

Lawless, Elaine J. *Women Preaching Revolution: Calling for Connection in a Disconnected Time.* Philadelphia: University of Pennsylvania Press, 1996.

McGee, Lee, with Thomas H. Troeger. *Wrestling with the Patriarchs: Retrieving Women's Voices in Preaching.* Nashville: Abingdon, 1996.

Norén, Carol. *The Woman in the Pulpit.* Nashville: Abingdon, 1991.

Smith, Christine M. *Weaving the Sermon.* Louisville: Westminster John Knox, 1989.

Taylor, Barbara Brown. *When God Is Silent.* Cambridge, Mass.: Cowley, 1998.

Turner, Mary Donovan, and Mary Lin Hudson. *Saved from Silence: Finding Women's Voices in Preaching.* St. Louis: Chalice, 1999.

Notes

1. "The Lord gave the word; great was the company of women who bore the tidings" (Ps. 68:11 BCP 1979 trans).

2. The Presbyterian Church in the USA.

3. The Presbyterian Church, U.S.

4. These were among the Lutheran bodies that merged in 1987 to become the Evangelical Lutheran Church in America.

5. Sarah M. Evans, *Born for Liberty: A History of Women in America* (New York: Free Press, 1989), 263-85.

6. Quoted by Barbara Brown Zikmund, "Winning Ordination for Women in Mainstream Protestant Churches," in Rosemary Radford Ruether and Rosemary Skinner Keller, *Women and Religion in America,* vol. 3 (San Francisco: Harper & Row, 1981), 367.

7. Mark A. Noll, *A History of Christianity in the United States and Canada* (Grand Rapids, Mich.: Eerdmans, 1992), 512. This figure is misleading in that it includes seminaries of denominations that do not yet ordain women, including the Roman Catholic Church and Southern Baptist Convention. There are, however, women students in some of these two churches' seminaries.

8. *Fact Book of Theological Education for the Academic Year 1998–99,* ed. Matthew Zyniewicz and Daniel Aleshire (Pittsburgh: ATS, 1999), 23.

9. *Employment and Earnings* 46 (1999): 214, gives the total number of clergy as 275,000, of whom 25,000 are women. The fraction of three-quarters is an estimate based on an awareness of the total number of Roman Catholics, Eastern Orthodox, Southern Baptists, and conservative evangelicals in the country.

10. Zikmund, "Winning Ordination for Women in Mainstream Protestant Churches," 339.

11. Catherine A. Brekus, *Strangers & Pilgrims: Female Preaching in America, 1740–1845: Gender and American Culture* (Chapel Hill: University of North Carolina Press, 1998).

12. Kathleen Hall Jamieson, *Eloquence in an Electronic Age: The Transformation of Political Speechmaking* (New York: Oxford University Press, 1988), 76. Some speeches delivered by men were considered feminine, but that was regarded as a disgraceful occurrence. Jamieson's thesis, however, is that television, with its scale of living room intimacy, has made what was previously regarded as feminine speech the currently most effective means of oral communication. "The intimate medium of tel-

evision requires that those who speak comfortably through it project a sense of private self, unself-consciously self-disclose, and engage the audience in completing messages that are mere dots and dashes on television's screen. The traditional male style is, in McLuhan's terms, too hot for the cool medium of television" (81). See my review article "Exempla 10," *ATR* 73 (1991): 188-93.

13. Lee McGee with Thomas H. Troeger, *Wrestling with the Patriarchs: Retrieving Women's Voices in Preaching* (Nashville: Abingdon, 1996), 26.

14. Ibid., 28.

15. Carol Norén, *The Woman in the Pulpit* (Nashville: Abingdon, 1991). Parenthetical references in the following text refer to page numbers in this book.

16. Christine M. Smith, *Weaving the Sermon: Preaching in a Feminist Perspective* (Louisville: Westminster John Knox, 1989). Parenthetical references in the following text refer to page numbers in this book.

17. Ibid. She considers what she says to be relevant to the preaching of men as well as that of women, as she frequently makes clear throughout the book.

18. She is aware that what she says applies most directly to the preaching of white Protestant women (ibid., 10), although she is very supportive of the "womanist" movement among African Americans, the "mujerista" movement among Hispanics, and movements in other ethnic groups.

19. Smith notes that African American womanists do not share this feminist critique of Christology (ibid., 89).

20. More will be said about feminist biblical interpretation below when the Beecher lectures of Phyllis Trible are discussed.

21. Smith discusses the need for preaching against most of these forms of oppression in *Preaching as Weeping, Confession, and Resistance: Radical Responses to Radical Evil* (Louisville: Westminster John Knox, 1992). A resource for those committed to doing such preaching is *Sermons Seldom Heard: Women Proclaim Their Lives,* ed. Annie Lally Milhaven, foreword Elisabeth Schüssler Fiorenza (New York: Crossroad, 1991). This collection includes sermons by women on all these topics and more, each followed by an autobiographical statement by the writer, and background information on the subject. A homiletics textbook not explicitly labeled as feminist but sharing much of Smith's perspective is the posthumously published work of Lucy Atkinson Rose, *Sharing the Word: Preaching in a Roundtable Church* (Louisville: Westminster John Knox, 1997).

22. Smith, *Weaving the Sermon,* 141. The quotation is from Shirley E. Held, *Weaving: A Handbook for Fiber Craftsmen* (New York: Holt, Rinehart & Winston, 1973), 310. This is but one of a number of books on weaving that are cited.

23. Similar, although much shorter, descriptions of feminine preaching occur in two introductions to collections of sermons by women, that by Edwina Hunter in the book she edited with David A. Farmer, *And Blessed Is She: Sermons by Women,* ed. David Albert Farmer and Edwina Hunter (San Francisco: Harper & Row, 1990), 91-97, and that by E. Lee Handcock in *The Book of Women's Sermons: Hearing God in Each Other's Voices* (New York: Riverhead, 1999), 1-11. An earlier anthology of sermons by women that has no introduction is *Spinning a Sacred Yarn: Women Speak from the Pulpit,* no editor named (New York: Pilgrim, 1982). Ella Pearson Mitchell has also edited two volumes of *Those Preaching Women: [More] Sermons by Black Women Preachers* (Valley Forge, Pa.: Judson, 1985–88).

24. The best-known publication of this group is *Making Connections: The*

Relational World of Adolescent Girls at Emma Willard School, eds. Carol Gilligan, Nona P. Lyons, and Trudy J. Hammer (Cambridge: Harvard University Press, 1988). Others are listed in McGee and Troeger, *Wrestling with the Patriarchs,* 125 (bibliography).

25. Mary Ballou and Nancy Gabalac, *A Feminist Position on Mental Health* (Springfield, Ill.: Thomas, 1985).

26. Mary Donovan Turner and Mary Lin Hudson, *Saved from Silence: Finding Women's Voices in Preaching* (St. Louis: Chalice, 1999). Turner teaches at Pacific School of Religion and Hudson at Memphis Theological Seminary.

27. The last chapter is followed by three sermons, one by each of the authors and one by Cheryl Cornish, with analyses that show how they exemplify the sort of preaching the book was written to encourage.

28. For Lawless's study of Pentecostal women preachers, see above, pp. 578-80.

29. Elaine J. Lawless, *Holy Women: Wholly Women: Sharing Ministries of Wholeness through Life Stories and Reciprocal Ethnography,* Publications of the American Folklore Society, n.s. (Philadelphia: University of Pennsylvania Press, 1993).

30. Elaine J. Lawless, *Women Preaching Revolution: Calling for Connection in a Disconnected Time* (Philadelphia: University of Pennsylvania Press, 1996). Just as in the former volume Lawless intercalated life stories of the women clergy with the chapters of her analysis, so in this one she interleaves sermons. Parenthetical references following in this section of text are to page numbers from this book.

31. Perhaps, as with other things, the shortcomings of an individual or group are the defects of their virtues.

32. Lawless used italics to set off her first mention of each quality from the discussion of it, but they have been omitted here since only these first mentions are quoted.

33. Her reference is to Loren B. Mead, *The Once and Future Church* (Washington, D.C.: Alban Institute, 1991).

34. The name of the series is "The Church and Its Ministry." The other members of the panel and their topics are, Henry M. Wriston, "The Preacher as Teacher"; Arthur S. Flemming, "The Objectives of the Local Church"; W. H. Auden, "The Witness of the Layman"; Edmund Sinnott, "The Church in an Age of Science"; and Charles P. Taft, "The Social and Economic Program of the Churches." The only one of these lectures that has been published is that of Sinnott, which was issued as a pamphlet by the Edward W. Hazen Foundation in 1950 as "Science and Religion—A Necessary Partnership."

35. Helen Kenyon, "Walking Together" (Cornwall, Conn.: privately printed at Hayloft Press, 1964). I am grateful to Martha Smalley of the Library of Yale Divinity School for providing me with a photocopy of this lecture.

36. Phyllis Trible, *Texts of Terror: Literary-Feminist Readings of Biblical Narratives,* OBT, no. 13 (Philadelphia: Fortress, 1984). The lectures were given two years earlier.

37. Phyllis Trible, *God and the Rhetoric of Sexuality* (Philadelphia: Fortress, 1978).

38. Ibid., xiii.

39. Peggy Brainard Way, *Pastoral Epistemology: Method, Metaphor, Metatheology* has not yet been published in print form. Cassette recordings of these lectures can be obtained from the Yale Divinity School bookstore.

40. Barbara Brown Taylor, *When God Is Silent* (Cambridge, Mass.: Cowley, 1998). Hereafter, parenthetical references that follow in this text section are to page numbers in this work.

41. There are autobiographical elements in the first five chapters of Taylor's *The Preaching Life* (1993); the second half of the book is sermons. Other volumes of her sermons are *Gospel Medicine* (1995), *Bread of Angels* (1997), and *Home by Another Way* (1999). All are published by Cowley Press of Cambridge, Massachusetts. I am grateful to Cynthia Shattuck, editor-in-chief at the time, for sending me copies of these volumes as they have appeared.

42. Although her writings make it obvious that Taylor has a strong social conscience in regard to women's issues as well as other problems, she does not often identify herself as a feminist or even as a woman.

43. Taylor, *Home by Another Way*, 71. Her reference is to George Steiner's *Language & Silence: Essays on Language, Literature, and the Inhuman* (New York: Atheneum, 1986).

44. Taylor quotes these words from the letter of an unnamed friend in ibid., 86.

45. Taylor, *Home by Another Way*, 69-72. This sermon was originally published in *Christian Century*, March 4, 1998.

CHAPTER 31

EVANGELISM IN AN ELECTRONIC AGE

E vangelistic preaching was the form of the earliest Christian proclamation, beginning with the apostles at Pentecost. Through the ages
it has been a major activity of the church, especially as new populations have become open to the extension of the Christian community.
There is a more restricted use of the term "evangelistic preaching," however, that applies particularly to a sort of preaching that began in the
Scotch-Irish Presbyterian sacramental meetings in the seventeenth century. These, in turn, paved the way for the Evangelical Awakening in
Britain and the Great Awakenings in America beginning in the eighteenth
century. Since then, such evangelistic preaching has become almost
indigenous to the United States, where charismatic leaders of revivals
have been the instruments of periods of heightened spiritual interest and
religious activity.[1]

Most of the chapters so far in this section have been concerned with
the effects of social change of one sort or another on how preaching was
done. This chapter explores the effects of technological change on the
way evangelistic preaching occurs. While revivals have taken place all
through the twentieth century and into the twenty-first,[2] technological

change has critically influenced three forces in evangelistic preaching: the ministry of Billy Graham, televangelism, and megachurches.

THE CRUSADER FOR CHRIST[3]

Speaking of Billy Graham demands superlatives. In 1956, only seven years after Graham had become a national celebrity through his Los Angeles campaign, Stanley High, an editor of the *Reader's Digest*, said that "Billy Graham has probably preached to more people than any spokesman for the faith in all Christian history."[4] High reckoned the number then to have been twenty million, of whom one million were estimated to have made "decisions for Christ."[5] In the approximately fifty years that have passed since then, the yearly average has probably increased. Indeed, at his 1973 crusade in South Korea, crowds averaged around half a million, and attendance at the final service was more than one million. No other human being has ever had a larger live audience.

Technological change enabling Graham and his team to travel rapidly to all parts of the world made such numbers possible, but even these numbers are dwarfed by statistics for the audience reached by the extensions of his voice through advances in the technology of communication. As he has said, "It has literally become possible to proclaim the Gospel to the entire world."[6] That possibility can be documented by the fact that telecasts of his crusade in Hong Kong were translated into forty-eight languages and were heard by an estimated one hundred million viewers a night.[7] It is not improbable that more people have made decisions in response to his preaching than have even heard any other evangelist. His influence has been felt in yet further ways, such as his acquaintance with many world political leaders, especially his access to every American president since Truman.

Little wonder, then, that biographers have often asked of him the question the apostles asked of Jesus after he calmed the storm at sea: "What manner of man is this?"[8] The facts are fairly straightforward, however little they account for the phenomenon. He was born in Charlotte, North Carolina, on November 7, 1918, the son of a dairy farmer. He grew up in a devout Associate Reformed Presbyterian family, and was converted near his sixteenth birthday at a citywide revival conducted by Mordecai Ham. Although he was unaware of his vocation at a conscious level, he soon began doing things that were usual preparations for ministry. He enrolled at Bob Jones University but, finding it too strict, he transferred to Florida Bible Institute. After doing a good bit of preaching there, he acknowledged his vocation and was ordained as a Southern Baptist preacher.

With that vocational commitment, he felt the need for further education and went to Wheaton College in Illinois. Upon graduation he married classmate Ruth Bell, the daughter of a medical missionary to China and the one whom he identifies as his inspiration and closest adviser. He became pastor of Western Springs Baptist Church in a Chicago suburb and soon attracted enough attention to take over a weekly radio program with the help of singer George Beverly Shea, who has worked with him ever since. During the World War II years he considered the military chaplaincy, but gave that up to become the international organizer for Youth for Christ, a program being developed then to provide one-night rallies in cities that would be an alternative to nights on the town for service personnel on leave. It was through these rallies that he became an itinerant evangelist.

Even though he continued his work with Youth for Christ, Graham was persuaded in 1948 to become president of a Bible college in Minneapolis, Northwestern Schools, despite the facts that he was only thirty and had just a bachelor's degree. While the school grew under his leadership, his heart was truly in evangelism, and he had already begun holding citywide campaigns before he went to Northwestern.

He had previously led revivals in cities as large as Miami and Baltimore, but what he calls the watershed of his ministry was the 1949 campaign in Los Angeles. Held in a giant circus tent, the meeting was originally scheduled for three weeks; it lasted eight. The involvement of movie stars, a gangster, and other celebrities—and overall attendance in the hundreds of thousands and decisions in the thousands, brought media attention from all over the country. During the Los Angeles campaign, William Randolph Hearst instructed his chain of newspapers to "puff Graham." Since that time, few names have been so familiar or been able to open as many doors as that of Billy Graham.

Los Angeles was followed by other campaigns as spectacular, from New England to the South to the Northwest. He easily raised $25,000 in order to begin his weekly network radio program, and that was the occasion of the incorporation of the Billy Graham Evangelistic Association. By 1952, Graham had resigned his other jobs and was ready to devote himself full-time to evangelism.

Even before Los Angeles, however, he and the team he had formed had already drawn up the principles that would govern the conduct of all their campaigns and their strategy for waging them. First, to avoid the pitfalls into which other evangelists had stumbled, they would be strictly accountable for all funds while downplaying their efforts to raise them. They committed themselves to avoiding any situation that could possibly be thought conducive to sexual impropriety. They would cooperate fully with local churches instead of criticizing them. And they would never inflate reports of their results.[9] As a further hedge against any suggestion of avarice, they decided that team members would be compensated by salary alone, with Graham's salary to "compare favorably with that of a typical minister in any average large-city church."[10]

Their campaign strategy was always to have as broad-based an involvement of local churches as possible, to have widespread prayer in preparation for the meeting, and to have as much honest publicity in advance as they could arrange.[11] They also discovered the advantage of placing a member of their staff in the city to supervise preparation well in advance of the campaign. And they arranged for the recruitment and training of thousands of persons to serve as door-to-door callers, members of the choir, ushers, and counselors to those who made decisions. All the expenses for the campaign were to be raised and administered by the local committee and thoroughly audited.

By 1955, their crusades had extended to England and Scotland, with exploratory rallies on the Continent. The next year saw them in Asia, from India to Korea and Japan. It was not until the following year that they felt confident enough to carry their work into New York City. From May through August, the old Madison Square Garden was filled nightly, with even larger services in Yankee Stadium and Times Square. After that it was Australia, Africa, the Middle East, South and Central America, and eventually behind the Iron Curtain. In time, Graham was even allowed to preach in China and North Korea. And for fifty years the world over, the response was greater than anyone had anticipated. "He has preached in person to eighty million people in more than eighty countries and has seen more than two million respond to the invitation at the end of his sermons."[12]

Such statistics prompt the question of what sort of preaching could elicit such a response. The answer hardly seems adequate to the question, because everyone, including his team members and Graham himself, admits that homiletically they are not outstanding. To begin with, one has to note that he is an evangelist. His definition of that term is

a person who has been called and especially equipped by God to declare the Good News to those who have not yet accepted it, with the goal of challenging them to turn to Christ in repentance and faith and to follow Him in obedience to His will.[13]

This means that the message of all his sermons is the same. God created human beings in his image, but we all have sinned. Yet God loves us still and wishes to forgive us so that we can live with him forever. To make that possible he sent his Son, Jesus Christ, to die on the cross for our salvation. In order to receive this salvation, we have to respond by confessing our sins and committing our lives to Christ as our Lord and Savior. Thus those in the congregation who have not already done so are invited to accept Jesus Christ. When they do that, they will be changed forever.[14]

This means, among other things, that his sermons are not expository.

> What he calls his "text" is actually an introductory Scripture to gain attention for John 3:16, which is invariably his real text. That is true whether he is dealing with "Teenage Vandalism," "Nonconformity to the World," or "The Ten Commandments." In each of these sermons he uses other "texts" to illustrate man's need, to describe a given human problem, to present an illustration of God's provision, or to state a condemnation of specific sins. In each case, however, he is presenting a lengthy introduction to his real business of inviting men to accept God's provision in Christ.[15]

While Graham has had essentially one message through his entire preaching career, his delivery has changed considerably over the years. In the beginning he had a frenetic style that Martin has called "assault."[16] He would move from one end of the platform to the other, with his arms in constant motion and his words coming in a constant flow, almost browbeating his congregation into submission. Through the years, however, he has evolved a calmer and quieter delivery. This moderation is not simply an effect of the aging process, but reflects as well a change of attitude. While earlier a great deal of anger was detected in his manner, he now realizes that the preacher's attitude toward rebellious sinners should be the compassion of the God who became incarnate in order to deliver them from sin. This is part and parcel of a mellowing process, an indication that he takes his own medicine and has continued to mature spiritually.

Attempts to explain the power of his attraction differ from writer to writer, depending on the disposition of each toward him. Some regard him as a special agent of the Holy Spirit sent to be a channel of redemption in a sinful age. Others would offer a demonic explanation if they believed in demons. Most, however, are convinced that besides being an extraordinarily charismatic person, he has a transparent conviction of his message's utter truth. His most persuasive argument is *ethos,* the trustworthiness of the speaker, rather than *logos*, reason, or *pathos*, the capacity to stir emotion.[17] To the extent that it can be accounted for, much of that impression seems to derive from his trust in the authority of the Bible.

His absolute conviction of that issue dates back to slightly before the Los Angeles campaign. His Youth for Christ colleague Chuck Templeton had intellectual doubts that activated Graham's own. On a moonlight stroll in the San Bernardino Mountains, he wrestled with his uncertainty until he was able to pray: "Father, I am going to accept this as thy Word—*by faith!* I'm going to allow faith to go beyond my intellectual questions and doubts, and I will believe this to be your inspired Word."[18] After that he never looked back. One of the traits of his preaching that has been noted most often is the absolute conviction with which he exclaims, "The Bible says . . . !"

Almost as remarkable as Graham's impact on those who have come into his presence, is the way he has taken advantage of technology to extend that impact. It goes back at least to his days as pastor of the Western Springs church when he took over a popular religious broadcast in the Chicago area. This was continued in 1950 when he began a week-ly radio broadcast, *The Hour of Decision,* over ABC. That program grew until it was carried on a thousand stations and had an audience of more than twenty-five million. A few months after he began network broad-casting, he started writing a syndicated daily newspaper column, "My Answer," which soon had a daily circulation of twenty million.[19]

In 1951, the Billy Graham Evangelistic Association made the first of its many religious motion pictures. As early as his 1954 crusade in London, his sermons were relayed by telephone line to theaters and halls all over England so that four hundred thousand more people could hear his message. His use of television has already been mentioned. He was quick to see the advantage of satellites for extending the range of virtual presence at one of his meetings. Now BGEA is assessing the effectiveness of a Web site on the Internet, www.billygraham.org.

Along with the newspaper column, books he has written, and maga-zines he has founded, from *Christianity Today* to *Decision,* these uses of media technology have been extensions of his preaching as such.[20] They have multiplied his audiences beyond even the thousands and hundreds of thousands who could hear him preach in person, to millions at a time, a homiletical development of some significance.

All this is a demonstration of the tendency to fall into superlatives when discussing the ministry of Billy Graham. Yet he is not without fault, nor is he superior to others who proclaim God's Word, as he would be the first to say. Regret can be felt for what appears to be his tendency to dwell on the number of celebrities with whom he has come in contact—although it must be admitted that they seem just as eager to claim association with him. Those who have what they consider to be a more nuanced theological position may wish that his did not seem oversimplified to them, although, again, there has been development over the years, and he has suffered much from fellow evangelicals who think he has sold their faith down the river. These conservatives also deplore his willingness to work not only with liberal Protestants, but with Roman Catholics, Eastern Orthodox, and even Jews as well. Like him or not, one must admit that Christianity had no more visible advocate in the twentieth century.

TELEVANGELISTS

As effective at using television as Billy Graham has been, he has not attempted a weekly program—much less, a more frequent one—because of the high cost of doing so.[21] Where he has hesitated, however, others have not. Something about the very nature of Evangelicalism makes that inevitable. If the belief exists that anyone who has not been converted to Christ will spend eternity in hell, then there also exists the obligation to rescue as many as possible. And if conversion is understood as "the life-changing experience of turning one's life over to Jesus,"[22] then the obligation is to provide opportunities for that to occur.

Since evangelists concentrate on conversion rather than the pastoral care and spiritual development of parishioners with whom they are in a long-term relation, the impetus is to reach as many people as possible.[23] This motive is reinforced for many who are premillennialists[24] because of their interpretation of Matthew 24:14 (KJV): "And this gospel of the kingdom shall be preached in all the world for a witness unto all nations; and then shall the end come." Providing opportunity for everyone on earth to hear the gospel would hasten the second coming of Christ.[25]

Television's potential for reaching the widest possible audience is seen in the way that Billy Graham's 1990 Hong Kong telecasts were translated into forty-eight languages and heard nightly by one hundred million people. This technology magnifies enormously the number of people who can be reached by a given evangelist. Small wonder, then, that so many of this calling rushed to avail themselves of such an opportunity to maximize their efforts.

Of course, something of this potential for reaching larger audiences was already present in radio and many, including Graham, took advantage of it. The first radio station to broadcast on a regular basis was KDKA, Pittsburgh, which went on the air November 2, 1920. Two months later, it broadcast its first religious program by airing the evening service of Calvary Episcopal.[26] The promise of religious broadcasting was soon recognized, and many churches even experimented in owning radio stations. Stable patterns did not begin to appear, however, until the late 1920s, when networks of stations were first formed. The earliest of these, NBC, developed a policy toward the end of 1928 to protect itself from religious groups' requests for public service time. It decided that responsibility for Protestant airtime would be lodged with the Federal Council of Churches, while the National Council of Catholic Men and the Jewish Theological Seminary of America would administer the time allotted to their constituencies. At the same time, they said airtime would not be sold for religious broadcasts. CBS and ABC followed NBC's approach. Only Mutual dissented, deciding to make no free time available to religious groups, but to market it to those who were willing to pay.[27]

The effect of this was to virtually exclude from the airways representatives of the Evangelical and Pentecostal traditions. This arbitrary decision was not based on the percentage of the population represented by these different traditions. When the radio networks were being founded, conservative Christians were admittedly in decline as a result of the fundamentalist/modernist controversy, but their numbers were never small. The relevant distinction between them and the members of the Federal Council of Churches as far as this policy is concerned was social: they did not belong to the elite. There was a gulf of social class between the churches that were given public service time on radio and those that had to purchase their airtime. The Evangelicals and Pentecostals, who have since formed the National Association of Evangelicals, as well as those who agreed with them, were trying to convert a world in which they counted for little.

The first preacher to demonstrate television's potential for religious propagation was a Roman Catholic, Bishop Fulton J. Sheen, whose *Life Is Worth Living* series became a commercially sponsored part of ABC programming in 1952. He attracted an audience competitive with that for the entertainment provided by other channels for five years. When he stopped broadcasting, he did so because of ecclesiastical opposition rather than any decline in popularity.

By the 1950s, Billy Graham had begun televising his crusades, but he made no other use of the medium. Within a few years, Oral Roberts also began using TV to air his tent revival and healing services, but as his fame spread, he began to broadcast his program from a television studio instead. In the 1960s, Rex Humbard became the first evangelist to build a church especially for telecasting. In the early days of televangelism, the format of its programs came from evangelistic services in tents and stadia, but gradually some of the preachers began to develop approaches more compatible with the medium, as when Pat Robertson copied the structure of television talk shows for his *700 Club*. Robertson was also a pioneer in the next stage of religious telecasting, when he led the way in forming a network of stations and satellites to carry conservative Christian programs.

It is difficult to characterize the preaching of the televangelists because several have developed such individual styles. Perhaps the best that can be done is to follow the admittedly breezy taxonomy created by Jeffrey Hadden and Charles Swann to enumerate the main types of television preachers.[28] Their first category is "Supersavers," by which they mean the pioneers of religious telecasting. There are, however, distinctions to be made among them. Graham's sermons were simply those he preached at his crusades. Jerry Falwell's sermons on his *Old-Time Gospel Hour* are like Graham's in that they are what he prepared for a live audience. But they differ in that Falwell's were for the regular congregation of his seventeen-thousand-member Thomas Road Baptist Church in Lynchburg, Virginia, instead of for those attending an evangelistic meeting. When Oral Roberts moved to the studios of the university he founded in Tulsa, he set his sermons in the context of what was essentially a religious entertainment show, with music and guest stars. Rex Humbard was like Falwell in telecasting the services of his church (the Cathedral of Tomorrow in Akron, Ohio), but these had a format similar to Roberts's entertainment pattern.

The next category of Hadden and Swann, "Mainliner," has only one member, Robert Schuller, who is a minister of a nonfundamentalist denomination, the Reformed Church of America. His message, however, is not as typical of the mainline churches as it is of the "power of positive thinking" approach of his fellow RCA cleric, Norman Vincent Peale. The third category is "The Talkies," named for televangelists who use the format of a TV talk show, and includes Jim Bakker, Pat Robertson, and Paul Crouch. These shows do not have extended sermons as such, but fit short meditations into the flow of their magazine format.

"The Entertainers," which includes evangelists like Jimmy Swaggart, have essentially a musical show into which preaching is inserted. "The Teachers" includes evangelists with a more didactic style who conduct

Bible study from a set created to look like a living room. Richard De Haan, Paul Van Gorder, and Frank Pollard belong to this group. What "The Rising Stars"—James Robinson, Kenneth Copeland, and Jack Van Impe—have in common is not so much a style as a popularity that was increasing when *Prime Time Preachers* was published in 1981. The last category, "The Unconventional," is another that has only one member, Ernest Angley, who, the authors say, has been called "the lunatic fringe" of religious broadcasting because of his claim to have seen demons leaving those he healed, angels standing by his side, and even God.

Obviously, the medium of each of these televangelist groups colors the way they preach. Therefore, to find a common denominator for the preaching of the entire group, it is necessary to look at content rather than style. With the exception of Schuller, they share a theology and a worldview—though Pentecostals add an expectation of the gifts of the Holy Spirit to the evangelical creed. They all have a strong doctrine of biblical inspiration, and most are fundamentalists. They believe in a God who is intimately involved in the world and the lives of individuals and nations, so that nothing happens without divine causation or at least permission. And they tend to have great confidence in their ability to discern why God intervenes in a particular way.

God's overall purpose is the salvation of all, and the evangelists are God's agents in the conversion of souls. The Pentecostals also hope to be the media through whom people are baptized in the Holy Spirit and receive such charismata as the gift of tongues. Many of the televangelists also believe that God has given them the gift of healing the physical as well as spiritual ailments of those who hear them, and some also claim to be able to cast out demons.

All of them see the world as a battleground where the forces of God contend with those of Satan, and many of them think that the warfare is approaching a climax. They expect Jesus to return soon and begin his thousand-year reign, but before that happens they expect the "rapture," the instant and simultaneous taking-up into heaven of all saved souls. In the first seven years after the rapture, Jews will be converted to Christianity, and the antichrist will rise and contend against Israel. When the antichrist is defeated, Jesus will return.

What are regarded as biblical prophecies of these events are closely correlated with world events today in an effort to show that these are the last days. Even among those who put less emphasis on the approaching end, however, the United States is generally given a special role. Communism is often identified with the antichrist, and America has the vocation to oppose it. In order to do so, however, the nation will have to return to what are understood as the religious roots of the country. It will have to oppose evil in every form. Most of the evil tendencies in the culture are lumped together under the rubric of secular humanism, "man's attempt to solve his problems independently of God."[29] Crucial to this restoration of righteousness is the protection of the nuclear family from the threats of feminism, abortion, and homosexuality. The restoration of public prayer to the schools is also vital.[30]

Another item that has high priority on this agenda is the evangelists' ability to continue their ministries. First and foremost, that means they must continue to receive the donations necessary to purchase very expensive airtime, which has led to an emphasis on fund-raising that many have found distressing. While a few of the televangelists have been shown to have feathered their own nests by this means, such charlatanism does not seem to be the major dynamic in this emphasis on raising money. Most of the religious broadcasters seem to be sincere people who are caught up in the catch-22 of their situation. They feel the need to go on TV in order to save as many souls as possible. To do that, they have to meet an enormous regular budget. To meet this budget, they have to spend so much time encouraging donations that they have less time to preach the gospel. And some have been led by this necessity into a theology that promises material as well as spiritual benefits to those who both respond to God's grace and give financial support to the TV ministry.[31]

In the late 1980s, a series of scandals connected with television ministries left the impression with many people in the general culture that all such preachers' credibility had been so thoroughly damaged that they lost all influence and following. Jim Bakker was accused of adultery and later of wider sexual irregularity. It then transpired that he and his wife, Tammy Faye, had lived a life of luxury on the offerings to their ministry, and he consequently spent time in federal prison for a number of financial irregularities. Jimmy Swaggart was then discovered to have visited a prostitute, and Oral Roberts claimed that God would take his life unless he raised $8 million in a month.[32]

What has happened, however, is not that such broadcasting has disappeared or even lost its audience. Bobby C. Alexander said:

> By January 1989, almost two years after news of the Bakker scandal broke, television religion showed signs of recovering audiences and contributions. Many stations had returned controversial personalities to the air. The number of organizations producing religious television had increased. And contributions were holding steady.[33]

What really happened was that televangelism dropped from the consciousness of the mainstream of American culture. That, however, did little to diminish its audience, because that audience had always been composed largely of Evangelical and Pentecostal Christians who remained loyal to this expression of their faith.[34] In fact, these groups have become a progressively larger percentage of the American public without the rest of the country's having really noticed.[35] At the time of this writing, about half of the Christians in the United States are Roman Catholic. Approximately half of those remaining belong to liberal churches of the sort that make up the National Council of Churches, while the other half belong to conservative churches of the sort that belong to the National Association of Evangelicals.[36] Thus part of the significance of the public ado over televangelism in the 1970s and 1980s is that it brought a large segment of American Christianity into its overall consciousness.[37]

MEGACHURCHES

One of televangelism's curiosities is that while its audience is isolated individuals, it has the capacity to communicate to the viewer a sense of being part of a wider body, called the "virtual church." This phenomenon is to be accounted for in terms of the two main technologies these ministries use: television and the computer. It has been pointed out that the scale of television is living room intimacy. Listening to a person whose face seems almost life-sized in the comfort of home creates a sense of personally knowing the speaker.[38] Regulars on a program, especially the preacher, come to seem like old friends, far more familiar, for instance, than one's pastor. Then the capacity of the computer to personalize letters, to retrieve information about the addressee that can be fitted into the boilerplate of a solicitation, to take note of prayer requests, and to offer counseling increases further the sense of being a member of an intimate group. A person is known and valued as he or she knows and values the evangelist. Yet, obviously, this sense of intimacy is an illusion. A single listener among hundreds of thousands or millions can hardly rise to the consciousness of the broadcasters. The community is only virtual. Or, as a poster of the Episcopal Ad Project trenchantly expressed it: "You can't receive holy communion from a Sony!"

By contrast, the third phenomenon of late-twentieth-century evangelism to be considered, the megachurch, is far more ecclesial in its orientation than the evangelical community has traditionally been. As noted above, most of the effort in the past has gone to convert people, with the assumption that those who have been saved will somehow continue in the life of grace and become integrated into a local church. The megachurch movement, however, is congregationally based, uses its own worship to evangelize, and has as its goal the integration of converts into its life.

For instance, the vision of founder Bill Hybels for Willow Creek Community Church in the Chicago suburb of Barrington, the prototypical megachurch, is the second chapter of Acts as expounded by Trinity College professor Gilbert Bilezikian. As Hybels said:

> What motivated me twenty years ago, and what motivates me today, is the priceless goal of seeing redeemed people become the church. To one another. I am reenergized every time I see people who were formerly lost in darkness now giving and receiving love, walking through valleys with one another, rescuing each other, and helping each other with their physical and spiritual needs.[39]

The presentation of megachurches that follows is based primarily on Willow Creek.[40] Megachurches can be defined as "large churches with more than 2,000 persons in attendance at Sunday services."[41] A brief sketch of how this church, which averages sixteen thousand in weekend attendance, came into being provides a perspective from which megachurch preaching can be understood.

From a human point of view, it would seem that Willow Creek was begun almost by accident. Hybels did not start out to enter the ministry; in fact, to the best of my knowledge, he has never been ordained. While he was converted at summer camp when he was sixteen, and attended a "Christian" (i.e., evangelical) liberal arts college, he dropped out after two years to work in his father's successful wholesale produce business. There is an affluence and even a sophistication in his background that are rare in some evangelical circles. He learned to sail in his father's oceangoing yacht and fly in his plane, and was given a sporty car and a motorcycle of his own. He grew up in a Dutch evangelical culture that had begun in Michigan and spread through the Midwest, a culture that combined Calvinist orthodoxy with intense interest in education. While Evangelicalism makes up a larger proportion of the total population in the South than in other parts of the country,[42] there are European ethnic communities in the Midwest that have been an important part of the movement since at least the end of the nineteenth century.[43]

Even as Hybels threw himself into work in the family business, he began to have deeper vocational stirrings, wondering if God was calling him to some form of ministry. The following summer, that of 1972, he went, as had become his custom, to serve on the staff of the church camp where he had been converted. While there he was visited by Dave Holmbo, an old friend who had recently taken a job as assistant music director of a church in the Chicago suburb of Park Ridge. To provide the music at a contemporary service the church had recently begun offering, he had founded a Christian rock-and-roll group called Son City that was already giving concerts all around the area. By the end of the summer, Hybels had decided to move to Chicago and work for the association that sponsored his camp. Once he was there, Holmbo asked him to become one of the group's guitarists and to begin a Bible class for them on Wednesday evenings. Everything that happened later seems to have grown out of that.

The Bible study grew so rapidly that Hybels and Holmbo decided to organize a weekly outreach program to which the Christian young people could invite their unchurched friends. In planning for this, the Bible study class, most members of which attended a high school that placed great emphasis on the arts, insisted that the program be one that eliminated the "cringe factor" so frequently experienced by young evangelicals who invited their friends to church. Hybels, remembering this from his own efforts to evangelize as a teenager, said:

> The typical traditional church is no place for the unchurched. To anybody but the already convinced, the average church service seems grossly abnormal. It makes no sense to those who haven't grown up in it, to those who don't know the drill. The music we sing, the titles we choose, the way we dress, the language we use, the subjects we discuss, the poor quality of what we do—all of these lead the average unchurched person to say, "This is definitely not for me."[44]

The suggestions the young people made at that meeting were to determine the basic approach that Willow Creek Church would take when it was organized a couple of years later. They had to have a more attractive setting than the basement room in which they sat on carpet squares. The music had to be the sort of Christian rock and roll played by Son City. It would help to have a short dramatic presentation that raised the question dealt with by the sermon. A media presentation would add to the effect. And Hybels was not to do the sort of expository treatment of the next section of a biblical book that had characterized the Bible studies he had led. "Make a point that is biblical but relevant to the kids' lives, tell

787

some good stories to illustrate it, and keep it down to about twenty-five minutes," he was told.[45] Within six months, the group had grown to three hundred. And, since the outreach program was designed for the unchurched, it was necessary to add a Sunday evening event in which the converted members could be fed spiritually. This was called Son Village, while the outreach program was designated by the band's name, Son City.

The high point of Son City was an evening in May 1974 when there was a major outreach program. Six hundred young people turned out and, when Hybels issued an altar call, half of the group made decisions for Christ. By that time, however, relations between the host church and Son City had become strained; the impact of so many excited teenagers on an ordinary congregation was too jarring, even though many approved of the good work.

At the same time, Hybels had been finishing his undergraduate degree at Trinity College in Deerfield, Illinois, where he was exposed to the vision of Dr. Bilezikian. In that context, Hybels began to wonder if this vision of Acts 2 could be applied to adults as well as high school students. By then Son City had an average attendance of twelve hundred young people, but Hybels resigned in May of 1975 to start a church, and Holmbo decided to help him. The core idea for the adult congregation was the sort of "seeker service," as they had come to call it, that they had used at Son City: "a regularly scheduled, high-quality, Spirit-empowered outreach service where irreligious people can come and discover that they matter to [God] and that Christ died for them."[46]

Many of the young people who had worked on the Son City team joined Hybels in founding Willow Creek. They decided that the nearby suburb of Palatine was the place to start, and they wanted to focus on the unchurched. To make sure they avoided the things that kept people away, they made a door-to-door survey, asking those who did not attend why they did not.[47] They were looking for things to avoid in their church, because it was not to be formed from Christians who transferred in from other congregations; it was to be recruited entirely from the unchurched. For a meeting place, they rented a local movie house for Sunday morning hours when it was unused, because it was easy to get to, had a large parking lot, and could seat nearly a thousand people. The theater was used for their evangelistic "seeker service," while, initially, the service for believers was held in a conference room they added on to a warehouse in which their equipment was stored. Placing the seeker event at the usual time for church services while asking church members to come on a weekday evening reversed what had been standard practice, but reflected the priority of putting evangelism first. And the seeker service followed the format of Son City's outreach programs, which was not dissimilar to that of televangelism's entertainment style.[48]

The opening service, which attracted 125 people, was held at Willow Creek Theater on October 12, 1975. The midweek New Community services for believers began the following January. Within two years, the Sunday service was filling the theater twice; within three, they had bought the ninety-acre property in South Barrington that has become their home, although they did not move into their own building until 1981. The story of how they came to their present system of four week-end services, almost filling their forty-five-hundred-seat auditorium for each, and two midweek New Community services is interesting. So is the way the team developed their program to meet needs and offer services.[49] Such information is not necessary, however, to understand the homiletical strategy of Willow Creek and other megachurches, both in their seeker and in their believer services.

People wishing to attend a weekend service at Willow Creek will turn from a major road onto a well-marked drive leading to an enormous parking lot, into which a corps of attendants welcomes and directs them. As seen from the road, the building could be any of a number of large corporate headquarters that dot the area. An elegant modern building sprawls above a pond on a spacious and well-landscaped tract. Entering the building through a vast open space with information booths and other services, the visitor is welcomed again and pointed toward the auditorium. It resembles an immense theater with unusually comfortable seats more than it does a church building as commonly conceived. There are several tiers of seating, and the area is wider than it is long. No traditional religious symbol is to be seen anywhere. The stage is wide, with a bandstand that accommodates a fifteen- to twenty-piece orchestra occupying the rear center. Up high on each side is an enormous television screen. The nearest thing to ordinary church furniture is a pulpit of sorts, but the resemblance is slight. It is made of Plexiglas and is hardly noticeable, even when it is being used. The center pedestal is narrow, but the ledge on which a manuscript, a Bible, and other things can be placed has room for all. There is an air of expectancy in the audience, and those who see friends visit with animation.

The service opens with an energetic prelude played by the orchestra. The TV screens magnify what is taking place on the stage as seen from a number of camera angles. A group of perhaps eight vocalists, male and female, clad in upscale, informal mod clothing, line up in front of the band with individual microphones and belt out the opening song. All the songs, like everything else in the service, are on the theme of the sermon that day—and could indeed be considered a part of it. There is no unscripted moment. For all that anyone unacquainted with the repertoire of Christian rock might know, the songs could have been written for the service, so well do they serve its theme.

The musicians then vacate the stage so that a short dramatic presentation can be given. On the last weekend in September 1999, this was a monologue by someone dressed as the Lone Ranger who talked about the way that American individualism and self-reliance often cut people off from the needed support of others. Next came a testimony to the difference that faith and a church family make. This September Sunday, it was given by a staff member who had experienced major illness in his family and had been given the support that made it endurable. After another song and announcements, an offering was taken, with the admonition that visitors were not expected to contribute. A seeker service ends with the "message" from Hybels or one of the other teachers. This particular Sunday, he began a series of sermons entitled "Nobody Stands Alone."[50] (For the sermon, see **Vol. 2, pp. 605-17.**)

He began by noting that persons who suddenly erupt into violence and kill a number of others are generally found to be loners. By the same token, the failure of a schoolchild to make friendships, or a potential mate's lack of relationships, is a serious warning sign. That is because friendships are so important in the scheme of things. There are few issues about which God is more concerned than friendships, especially the sort that move people from loneliness into rich, Christ-honoring community. The Bible is full of warnings about the danger of isolation. So the question is: How do we move from standing alone to standing together? And the answer grows out of the nature of true friendship. It is not about trying to get someone else to take care of you in one way or another, but about seeking that person's well-being.

Starting and building such friendships is a risky, inexact, lengthy, and frustrating challenge, but success is worth the effort. A tip to those accepting the challenge is to look for friends in an environment conducive to such mutual commitments. Willow Creek has been such an environment for many, since such relationships are one of the two main purposes for which the Christian church exists. Ways of going about trying to form these relationships include joining one of their many small groups,[51] volunteering for a ministry team at the church, or becoming a member of a sports or fitness group, but the person seeking such relationships has to take the initiative. The idea for Willow Creek originated because Hybels took the initiative in forming a friendship with Dr. Bilezikian.

When such preliminary initiative has been taken, ways to deepen the relationship involve asking questions that encourage confidences about what is going on in the life of the other. It is by forming such friendships that one discovers how much they are a part of what life is all about. Although there are thousands who attend Willow Creek who have never become more involved, Hybels's dream for the church is that no one will have to stand alone for the rest of their life. The closing prayer was for those who were still lonely and for the other members to reach out to them.

It is clear that this service as a whole followed Hybels's norms for a seeker service: it was "a regularly scheduled, high-quality, Spirit-empowered outreach service where irreligious people [could] come and discover that they matter to [God] and that Christ died for them." It is also obvious that this sermon met the criteria the teenagers had set for Hybels in the original Son City outreach program: "Make a point that is biblical but relevant to the kids' lives, tell some good stories to illustrate it, and keep it down to about twenty-five minutes."

This sermon was topical life-situation preaching, in which an alternative was offered to the meaninglessness of much of contemporary life. While intended to be entirely biblical, it did not depend on a single text, much less present an exposition of an extended passage. Instead, it sought to condense the meaning of the Bible as a whole, with a number of citations of particular verses (although these were often given a modern paraphrase) and general summaries of biblical teaching. The remedy for the diagnosed condition was not merely that the Willow Creek community was a good place to make friends, because there was always the implication that such relationships are a by-product of relationship with God through Christ. It was, as it was intended to be, an invitation to seekers to satisfy their longings in the Body of Christ.[52]

The other kind of services held at Willow Creek, the "New Community" midweek services for believers, begins with somewhere from one-half to three-quarters of an hour of praise to God in word and song. The Lord's Supper is celebrated once a month. And they "learn together, going through the Bible book by book and focusing on themes—such as 'downward mobility' from Philippians 2—that become rallying cries throughout the church."[53] So the preaching is the continuous exposition of a biblical book. Many evangelicals assume that such *lectio continuo* expository preaching is normative among the converted. Rick Warren shares that conviction:

> When preaching to believers I like to teach through books of the Bible, verse-by-verse. . . . Verse-by-verse, or book, exposition builds up the

body of Christ. It works great when you're speaking to believers who accept the authority of God's Word and are motivated to learn the Scriptures.[54]

This acceptance of expository preaching as the norm for the faithful reflects the Reform tradition of Calvin and the Puritans, in which the public exegesis of Scripture is expected to convey grace *ex opere opera-to*. Not surprisingly, then, preaching is often spoken of as teaching, and Hybels designates those who deliver sermons as teachers more often than as preachers. He also does not refer to traditional orders of ministry, but instead has a charismatic understanding of office in the church, based on 1 Corinthians 12:28 and Galatians 5:22-23. He considers his own gifts to be leader,[55] evangelist, and teacher, in that order.[56]

His understanding of the relative relations of teaching and leadership is that both are vital to the church. "The church *needs* great teachers. Preaching is the core ministry of the church, and lives will not change without powerful and Spirit-inspired teaching from the Word of God." But,

> when teachers stand in front of people, their chief desire is to accurately and compellingly communicate biblical truth in the hopes of impacting lives. But when leaders have the microphone, there's another agenda. Usually they have a purpose, mission, or cause that they want to get people fired up about."[57]

Willow Creek is perhaps the only local church that has ever been studied by Harvard Business School to see how well it serves its constituents. In the discussion, a student was asked what she thought of the congregation's mission statement. Her reply was: "It sounds to me like they're . . . well . . . *they're trying to turn atheists into missionaries.* And frankly, I see that as one hell of a challenge!"[58] Hybels agrees. The church exists to transform the lives of all its members in the way lives were transformed in Acts 2, and the role of preaching in the transformation of lives is crucial.

> In a biblically functioning community, the leaders make sure the preaching is done only by those who have the appropriate spiritual gifts, who have yielded themselves to the spiritual disciplines, and who have been anointed by the Holy Spirit to teach. When that happens, life starts pulsating through a place.[59]

Megachurches that share the goal of Willow Creek do not see their purpose so much to be big as to be church.

The unifying theme of this chapter on late-twentieth-century evangelistic preaching has been the ways in which technology has been employed to make the preaching more effective. The uses of technology in megachurches have been implicit rather than explicit in the foregoing discussion, but it is easy enough to raise them to consciousness. The technologies have been mainly the television projection screens, which have made it possible for all the people in a large auditorium to have an intimate view of those leading in the worship; and the sound systems, which have enabled all to hear the music and the preaching without straining.[60] The combination has also made seekers feel at home in an environment as familiar as their TVs, computer screens, stereos, and the rock concerts they attend. This combination of the familiar and the ecstatic opens them to the proclaimed word of invitation. Therefore, the defining characteristic of evangelistic preaching in this era has been its use of technology.

FOR FURTHER READING

Alexander, Bobby C. *Televangelism Reconsidered: Ritual in the Search for Human Community.* American Academy of Religion Studies in Religion, no. 68. Atlanta: Scholars Press, 1994.

Graham, Billy. *Just As I Am: The Autobiography of Billy Graham.* San Francisco: HarperCollins, 1997.

_____. *The Challenge: Sermons Delivered from Madison Square Garden.* New York: Doubleday, 1969.

Hadden, Jeffrey K., and Charles E. Swann. *Prime Time Preachers: The Rising Power of Televangelism.* Reading, Mass.: Addison-Wesley, 1981.

Hybels, Lynne and Bill. *Rediscovering Church: The Story and Vision of Willow Creek Community Church.* Grand Rapids, Mich.: Zondervan, 1995.

Warren, Rick. *The Purpose-Driven Church: Growth Without Compromising Your Message & Mission.* Grand Rapids, Mich.: Zondervan, 1995.

Notes

1. The process by which that was accomplished is the subject of chapters 18 and 19, in this book.

2. A sense of these can be gained from Richard M. Riss, *A Survey of 20th-Century Revival Movements in North America* (Peabody, Mass.: Hendrickson, 1988). Riss, however, is primarily interested in Pentecostal movements, and many important campaigns in other traditions are entered only by title.

3. This term was used by the *Boston Sunday Globe* in its January 1, 1950, report of the campaign begun in Boston the night before. Billy Graham, *Just As I Am: The Autobiography of Billy Graham* (San Francisco: HarperCollins, 1997), 160. Up until that time, Graham had referred to his meetings as "campaigns," but shortly after that he began to designate them as "crusades" on the advice of Willis Haymaker, who thought the term "campaign" had been tarnished by association with older and more sensational styles of evangelism (ibid., 163).

4. Stanley High, *Billy Graham: The Personal Story of the Man, His Message, and His Mission* (New York: McGraw-Hill, 1956), 3.

5. Graham's term for those who respond to the invitation for commitment he makes at the end of every sermon. These include converts to Christianity, lapsed Christians who renew their faith, and practicing Christians who rededicate their lives to God.

6. Graham, *Just As I Am,* 722.

7. Ibid., 638.

8. Mark 4:41 KJV.

9. Graham, *Just As I Am,* 128-29.

10. Ibid., 186.

11. Ibid., 125-26.

12. William Martin, "Graham, William Franklin ('Billy')," in *Concise Encyclopedia of Preaching,* ed. William H. Willimon and Richard Lischer (Louisville: Westminster John Knox, 1995), 167. Martin is author of the recent biography, *A Prophet With Honor: The Billy Graham Story* (New York: William Morrow, 1991). This recency is important not only for its view of Graham's entire career, but also for perspective. By contrast, Marshall Frady, who ended his biography with Watergate, ends up with an understanding of Graham as an innocent on the order of Melville's Billy Budd (*Billy Graham: A Parable of American Righteousness* [Boston: Little, Brown, 1979], 11, 437-39, 483-84).

13. Graham, *Just As I Am,* xv.

14. A summary of ibid., 727-29.

15. Clyde E. Fant Jr. and William M. Pinson Jr., eds., *20 Centuries of Great Preaching: An Encyclopedia of Preaching* (Waco, Tex.: Word, 1971), 12:295. The whole treatment of Graham's preaching, pp. 294-302, is very good. Oddly enough, there are in the literature few analyses of his preaching as such. Some of the best observations on it are in High, *Billy Graham,* 49-100.

16. Martin, "Graham, William Franklin ('Billy')," 168.

17. Martin gives an example of that *ethos* when he tells of Graham's appearance for an interview at the National Press Club, where those accustomed to facing most of the world's newsmakers "seemed to acknowledge the sheer physical presence radiated by the world's most famous preacher" (Martin, *A Prophet With Honor,* 23).

18. Graham, *Just As I Am,* 139.

19. He is as frank to acknowledge the help he receives in writing it as he is to acknowledge any other assistance he receives (Graham, *Just As I Am,* 283). He does the same for the autobiography itself (ibid., 731-35).

20. One of Graham's sermons is a regular feature of *Decision* magazine.

21. Graham, *Just As I Am,* 433.

22. Jeffrey K. Hadden and Charles E. Swann, *Prime Time Preachers: The Rising Power of Televangelism* (Reading, Mass.: Addison-Wesley, 1981), 91. Their chapter "The Sermon from the Satellite" (85-102) is a good summary of the theology motivating TV evangelism, although it is not theologically nuanced. Hadden is a sociologist, and Swann is a cleric with a doctorate in religious communications who managed a PBS station at the time of writing. As good a treatment of televangelists as this is, it is primarily concerned with the threat of political power falling into the hands of these preachers. This is even truer of a later book on which Hadden collaborated with another sociologist, Anson Shupe, *Televangelism: Power and Politics on God's Frontier* (New York: Henry Holt, 1988).

23. At the time of this writing, one evangelist, Morris Cerullo, felt called to see that everyone in the world would have had an opportunity to repent before the year 2000 was over. While he has been active in this project for a number of years, I heard him talk about it on the Inspiration network on March 2, 2000.

24. "The 'millennium' is a prophesied thousand-year period of events on the earth surrounding the second coming of Jesus. Premillennialists believe Jesus will return before the millennium, to reign for a thousand years, finally defeat all the forces of evil, and claim the world for God. Postmillennialists believe that Jesus will come to reign after the thousand-year period of seeing the gospel finally conquer the world. Most TV preachers are premillennialists" (Hadden and Swann, *Prime Time Preachers,* 95).

25. This motivation for evangelism has been effective at least since James Hudson Taylor began his China Inland Mission in 1865.

26. A church service had already been aired by the U.S. Army Signal Corps on August 24, 1919, but that was an experimental program rather than a regular broadcast. This was also an Episcopal service, one from Trinity Church in Washington.

27. The history of religious broadcasting is given in a number of places. Hadden and Swann, *Prime Time Preachers* (17-45, 69-83), gives a good orientation. A more concise presentation occurs in William F. Fore, *Television and Religion: The Shaping of Faith, Values, and Culture* (Minneapolis: Augsburg, 1987), 77-85. Fore was assistant general secretary for communications of the National Council of Churches. The perspective of the televangelists themselves may be seen in *The Electric Church* (Nashville: Thomas Nelson, 1979), by the executive director of their National Religious Broadcasters, Ben Armstrong.

28. Hadden and Swann, *Prime Time Preachers,* 20-45.

29. The definition comes from Tim LaHaye, a member of the board of the Moral Majority. It is quoted in ibid., 85. Most of this summary of the theology of televangelism is based on ibid., 85-102. For a more concise statement, see Fore, *Television and Religion,* 85-86. For an effort to show that the teachings of some televangelists are not orthodox according to evangelical teaching, see *The Agony of Deceit: What Some TV Preachers Are Really Teaching,* ed. Michael Horton (Chicago: Moody, 1990).

30. Quentin J. Schulze has perceptively claimed a particular compatibility of the message and method of the evangelists with the medium of television in his article "Television and Preaching," in Willimon and Lischer, *Concise Encyclopedia of Preaching,* 469-76. He has also written a book on the subject, *Television and*

American Culture: The Business of Popular Religion (Grand Rapids, Mich.: Baker, 1991), which I have not seen.

31. Hadden and Swann acutely observe that "the tube makes up less than half of the technology that supports the new social movement of evangelism. The other half comes in the form of the ubiquitous computer" that enables the evangelists to keep track of individual donors and to personalize their mailings (*Prime Time Preachers*, 104).

32. For details of these and other scandals, see Hadden and Shupe, *Televangelism*, 1-19 passim, and Steve Bruce, *Pray TV: Televangelism in America* (London: Routledge), 1990), 198-212.

33. Bobby C. Alexander, *Televangelism Reconsidered: Ritual in the Search for Human Community*, American Academy of Religion Studies in Religion, no. 68 (Atlanta: Scholars Press, 1994), 21.

34. Bruce, *Pray TV*, 234.

35. See, for instance, the table in Mark A. Noll, *A History of Christianity in the United States and Canada* (Grand Rapids, Mich.: Eerdmans, 1992), 465. Some effort, however, will be necessary to move from his groupings to an overall figure for conservative Christians.

36. The largest of such groups, however, the Southern Baptists, do not belong to the NEA, but they do share the theology of most of those who do.

37. Alexander's thesis in *Televangelism Reconsidered* is that this religious broadcasting is, among other things, a "battle waged by televangelism's followers against mainstream American society for greater inclusion" (2). He calls televangelism "redressive ritual" to accomplish that goal, and analyzes different religious broadcasts in terms of what they accomplish in this way for their constituents. Thus Jerry Falwell's program furnishes legitimation, while Pat Robertson's *700 Club* offers adaptation, and Jimmy Swaggart's program offers evangelicals an opportunity to take the offensive against a culture that has ignored them.

38. The literature on the way the medium affects the message in television is too vast for citation here, but a short introduction can be gained from Schulze, "Television and Preaching," pp. 471-75. See also what was said in chapter 29 concerning Kathleen Hall Jamieson, *Eloquence in an Electronic Age: The Transformation of Political Speechmaking* (New York: Oxford University Press, 1988).

39. Lynne and Bill Hybels, *Rediscovering Church: The Story and Vision of Willow Creek Community Church* (Grand Rapids, Mich.: Zondervan, 1995). On the cover and title page, the title is followed by what looks like a dictionary entry for the word *church*: "*n* 1. A building for public, esp. Christian worship. 2. People who demonstrate their love for God by loving and serving others."

40. It is based secondarily on Saddleback Community Church in Orange County, California, founded by Rick Warren, which has an average weekend attendance of ten thousand. See Warren's book *The Purpose-Driven Church: Growth Without Compromising Your Message & Mission* (Grand Rapids, Mich.: Zondervan, 1995).

41. Millard J. Erickson, "Evangelicalism: USA," *The Blackwell Encyclopedia of Modern Christian Thought*, ed. Alister E. McGrath (Oxford: Basil Blackwell, 1993), 191.

42. This can be seen, for example, in the percentages of audience for televangelists in different regions. Hadden and Swann, *Televangelism*, 60-61.

43. Indications of this may be seen in the way two of the most important publishers of evangelical books, Eerdmans and Zondervan, come from this tradition, and a number of televangelists have Dutch names.

44. Hybels and Hybels, *Rediscovering Church*, 32.

45. Ibid., 29-30.

46. Ibid., 40.

47. Ibid., 57-59. Warren also used such a survey in starting Saddleback Church. *The Purpose-Driven Church*, 39-40.

48. Schulze, "Television and Preaching," 470.

49. One of the most attractive features of the way the Hybelses tell the story in *Rediscovering Church* is the "warts and all" portrait they give that does not hesitate to mention mistaken judgments, crises that occurred, and the way personal failings of themselves and others threatened at times to shipwreck the entire operation.

50. There are four other "teachers" who share weekend and midweek preaching duties with Hybels, two of whom are women. Disagreeing with many evangelicals, Hybels believes that "when the Bible is interpreted correctly and in its entirety, it teaches the full equality of men and women in status, giftedness, and opportunities for ministry" (ibid., 211-12).

51. Small groups are a key element in the strategy of Willow Creek, Saddleback, and all megachurches for much the same reason as John Wesley insisted that his converts become members of classes (see above, 439-40).

52. Hybels's advice to preachers at seeker services is to watch out for going overboard with "felt-need" and "helpful" messages; overprotecting seekers and new believers; the shadow side of team teaching; the sizzle of programming talents; and the temptation to make everything produced and slick (ibid., 185). Rick Warren's formula for preaching at seeker services is to follow the example of Jesus in attracting crowds by meeting people's needs and teaching in a practical, interesting way (Warren, *The Purpose-Driven Church*, 219-34; for his more detailed suggestions for preaching at seeker services, see 293-306).

53. Hybels and Hybels, *Rediscovering Church*, 176.

54. Warren, *The Purpose-Driven Church*, 294.

55. First Corinthians 12:28 refers to the gift, *kubernēsis*, rather than the person who has it, *kubernēsis*, from which are derived the Latin *gubernator* and our "governor." The root concept is of steering a ship. Older translations called the gift "administration," but newer ones call it "leadership."

56. Hybels and Hybels, *Rediscovering Church*, 150.

57. Ibid., 149.

58. Ibid., 168.

59. Ibid., 158.

60. The effort to use technology to spread the faith continues at Willow Creek. An e-mail News Brief from Episcopal News Service of July 12, 2001, says they are planning to open up satellite churches, where gatherings will feature live music and piped-in sermons on huge video screens for the sake of people who live farther than thirty minutes from the main church.

CHAPTER 32

A CRISIS IN COMMUNICATION[1]

THE CHANGED SITUATION

The previous four chapters have dealt with changes in American society during the last four decades of the twentieth century. Movements for civil, women's, student, and gay rights, and for peace and the environment were developing simultaneously with the sexual revolution, experimentation with drugs, changes in standards of acceptable speech and taste in popular music, growing ethnic and religious pluralism, and a marked increase in the number of retired people in the country. During the same period the American people, like those of other nations, were having their consciousness shaped by the intimate medium of television. Computers became pervasive in every aspect of daily living.

Along with the other changes occurring during this period was the disappearance of many of the common assumptions that made American life a culture. Trust was eroded on every hand. The Vietnam War, Watergate, and other evidences that national leaders had feet of clay undermined public confidence in government. The resistance met by the various rights movements that prevented their living up to their promises encouraged cynicism among those who had tasted hope. Meanwhile, church membership and participation were plummeting. Deep suspicion of the threat to human life posed by thermonuclear weapons, combined with the damage done to the environment through technology, replaced the awe and optimism with which the scientific enterprise had previously been regarded. This dethroning of the idol of science was abetted by a change in the understanding of its goal: from discovering laws of the universe, to merely devising models or paradigms that would enable a more effective prediction of performance. There was even a loss of confidence in the ability of language to describe reality or to convey univocal meaning. Eternal verities were vanishing right and left.

A result of this erosion of trust in public institutions and loss of consensus in beliefs and values was a growing individualism and loss of commitment. Marriages were postponed or forsaken altogether, and those who married did not rush to have children. Many sought to find the meaning of their lives in their careers, only to come to doubt the worth of what they were doing and the integrity of the corporations they worked for. Consumption became the measure of success, and the hollowness of its victory was reflected in a bumper sticker that read: "The one who dies with the most toys wins." People seemed to live as isolated individuals, yearning for but achieving little sense of personal fulfillment.

DISCONTENT WITH THE PAST

Consciousness had changed so radically in the 1970s and 1980s as to leave little sense of continuity with what it had been like to be human just a few decades before. In the anxious uncertainty that characterized this period, there was also widespread dis-ease among clergy about the effectiveness of preaching. At first there was a despair of preaching's capacity to make any difference in people's lives. Then followed a series of efforts to discover new ways of going about the task of Christian proclamation, ways that would have integrity and might elicit a hearing in the new world in which clergy found themselves.

These proposals, which have been referred to generally as "the New Homiletic," are bound together more by diagnosis than prescription. In this changed environment, the style of preaching that had reigned at least since John A. Broadus had published *On the Preparation and Delivery of Sermons* in 1870 no longer seemed adequate. There was, however, much less agreement about what should be done instead.

A deep distrust of words and a preference for action over speech had been expressed in the 1960s, an attitude not restricted to preaching but extended to all speech. That pessimism was captured in the first and one of the most important books espousing a New Homiletic, Fred Craddock's *As One Without Authority*.[2] Craddock opens his book by saying, "We are all aware that in countless courts of opinion the verdict on preaching has been rendered and the sentence passed." Yet, "all this slim volume asks is a stay of execution until one other witness is heard." This questioning of the value of preaching he relates to a crisis in language, "a general experience of the loss of the power of words."[3]

He relates this loss of the power of words to six factors, the first of which is that people are bombarded by so many words. The second is contempt for religious language in a scientific age, a contempt that has been extended to language in general. The effect of television on the human sensorium, through which the aural has been replaced by the visual, is another. The crisis of confidence in the power of the pulpit by those who occupy it is a fourth. Closely related to that is the fifth: Christian belief, which had been a part of Western consciousness since before the Middle Ages, is no longer reinforced by the society at large. And, finally, talking to people about the most serious issues of life always has been difficult and remains so.

Craddock and the others who were to join him in proposing a New Homiletic were deeply aware of all the changes in consciousness that had transpired since the 1950s, but their concentration on preaching caused them to begin by focusing on the sort of preaching that had been done before and criticizing its adequacy. *This attack on the previous homiletic rather than proposals for what should be done instead is what unifies these writers.* All believe that the old way is bad, but they have different ideas about what should replace it.

The traditional sermon form has long been described as "three points and a poem," although some of the New Homileticians take this more as an adequate description than as a satirical reduction. Craddock is closer to the point when he calls the traditional form deductive. He says:

> There are basically two directions in which thought moves: deductive and inductive. Simply stated, deductive movement is from the general truth to the particular application or experience, while induction is the reverse. Homiletically, deduction means stating the thesis, breaking it down into points or sub-theses, explaining and illustrating these points, and applying them to the particular situations of the hearers.[4]

Craddock diagrams what he means by deductive development with a form of outline that looks like this:

I.
   A.
      1.
         a.
         b.
      2.
         a.
         b.

The terms "deductive" and "inductive" are used in a special way here.[5] Strictly speaking, to deduce is to reason syllogistically from major premise and minor premise to a conclusion, and induction is "logical reasoning that a general law exists because particular cases that seem to be examples of it exist."[6] Yet, since Craddock defined the sense in which he uses the terms and he uses them that way consistently, no confusion should exist.[7]

Craddock's objection to traditional preaching was that it was deductive. Other New Homileticians have seen it falling short in a number of other respects as well. Don M. Wardlaw has provided a rather comprehensive list of the contrasts made between the old and new ways of preaching.[8] He writes of a "flight" of *continua* between the poles of the old and the new that "show shifts in homiletical theory in a number of categories."

The first of these *continua* is between deductive and inductive, and by that he means what Craddock means. Next, he sees a movement from static to tensive, from an analytical development concerned with timeless truth to a development that has movement. The third continuum is from the denotative to the connotative, from the explicit to the suggestive.

His continuum from left brain to right brain reflects studies of the activity of the brain hemispheres that find the left side to be the center of analysis, while the right side functions in a less linear and more imaginative and intuitive way. The continuum from points to moves reflects the work of David Buttrick, which will be considered below. The next movement is from facticity to the evocative. Wardlaw also says that preaching has moved from being authoritarian to being relational. And, finally, he says that it has become more collaborative and is done in less isolation, calling attention to sermon preparation groups and other ways of involving congregation members in the pastor's sermon preparation.

Needless to say, all these changes in performance reflect changes in value and emerging convictions about what it takes for preaching to be effective in a culture that has undergone so much change.[9]

"A MORE EXCELLENT WAY"

While the New Homileticians were in agreement about the inadequacy of traditional preaching to meet the needs of men and women today, their ideas of what sort of preaching is needed instead are by no means so uniform. It is not so much that they make contradictory recommendations as that they come at the question from different angles and make proposals that have not been integrated into a comprehensive system. Thus to look at the program of the New Homiletic, one must look at several components, proposals made by a number of individuals that are not necessarily interlocking.

Fred Craddock's Inductive Method

A good bit has already been said about Craddock's pioneering role, but now his constructive suggestions need to be looked at in detail. A little about the man himself helps to understand his work. Born in Humboldt, Tennessee, in 1928, Fred B. Craddock is an ordained minister of the Disciples of Christ. Trained as a New Testament scholar, he began his teaching career in 1965 with a joint appointment in New Testament and preaching at one of his denomination's seminaries, the Graduate Seminary of Phillips University in Enid, Oklahoma. From there he went to Candler School of Theology at Emory University, where he occupied the Bandy chair in preaching and New Testament until his retirement in 1993. Influences in the development of his thought include the existentialism of Søren Kirkegaard and the "New Hermeneutic" of Gerhard Ebeling. He is also an advocate of John Dewey's educational theories.

All these influences are apparent in the inductive method of preaching that he advocates. Dewey's influence is seen in Craddock's insistence that the sermon begin with concrete experiences rather than with conclusions. "On the basis of these concrete thoughts and events, by analogy and by the listener's identification with what he[10] hears, conclusions are reached, new perspectives are gained, decisions made" (61-62). As a good Disciple who believes in the priesthood of all believers, he goes on to say that inductive preaching involves a "movement of material that respects the hearer as not only capable of but deserving the right to participate in that movement and arrive at a conclusion that is his own, not just the speaker's" (62). A corollary of this second point is a third, which says that the listeners should be allowed to complete the sermon. They can see the implications of what has been said and are perfectly capable of applying it to their own lives.

Craddock agrees with Martin Heidegger that "the primary function of language" is "letting be what is through evocative images rather than conceptual structures" (77), because images are more basic to thought, and it is by changing images that a mind is changed. His rules for the selection of images are that they be: drawn from their hearers' world of experience; specific and concrete;[11] economical in their use of words—especially modifiers; uninterrupted by self-conscious insertions such as "we find" or "we see"; and in the preacher's own language (92-97).

Effective sermons preached in the inductive mode are characterized by conceptual unity: good biblical preaching is based on a single pericope in which there is only one such idea. Thus the plotting of a sermon begins after the preacher is able to express its "central germinal idea in one simple affirmative sentence" (105). By the same token, the sermon based on that pericope should not be allowed to break apart with one section focused on the text and another on the congregation.

> If the text wrestles with serious questions and if the reader does also, then the reader's own questions are not extraneous intrusions on a "pure understanding" of the text. (114)

Bringing such questions from the contemporary church to the text is not, however, a shortcut that eliminates the need for study; it rather gives point to the study.

According to Craddock, part of the difficulty of deductive preaching, which begins with a general principle and moves on to apply it, is that in the presentation of a sermonic insight, the mental processes by which the preacher has arrived at that insight are reversed:

> If . . . the first stage (exegesis) is like ascending a hill . . . the second (sermonizing) is like the descent on the other side. . . . The shift consists of a transition from inductive to deductive movement of thought. (123-24)

He recommends that instead, the preacher take the congregation over the exploratory path in the sermon that she herself traversed in discovering the insight to be communicated, ending with the insight as a conclusion rather than beginning with it as an assumption. The sermon, therefore, is designed as a process that leads from the present experience of the congregation to the conclusion, and the design begins with the identification of the conclusion to which they are to be led.

That insight should not be into the "human situation" in general, but into "the issues facing the particular congregation participating in the sermon experience" (129). Therefore, the preacher's preparation is listening to the dialogue between the scriptural passage that is the text and the situation of the local congregation. And when the sermon is preached, the thought of the text is to be expressed in the language of the congregation. In the construction of such inductive sermons, "the sole purpose is to engage the hearer in the pursuit of an issue or an idea so that he will think his own thoughts and experience his own feelings in the presence of Christ and in the light of the gospel" (157).

An example of such inductive preaching is a sermon that Craddock preached in chapel while he was still teaching at Phillips. His congregation was made up of seminarians in Oklahoma at the height of the civil rights movement. Most of them were student pastors, and they were probably accustomed to delivering fiery "prophetic" sermons[12] to their small rural congregations. The title of Craddock's sermon is "Praying Through Clenched Teeth."[13] (For the text of this sermon, see **Vol. 2, pp. 618-23.**) The scripture read was Galatians 1:11-24, in which Paul speaks of his conversion from persecuting Christians.

Craddock begins by saying that he wants to say a word and have his hearers associate a face and a name with it. The word is *bitter,* and he quickly sketches in concrete images of bitter people, a series of vignettes: a dustbowl farmer, a forty-seven-year-old widow at the cemetery, a small grocer watching a large supermarket going in across the street, a pregnant young woman whose soldier husband is being shipped overseas. These images are drawn from the lives of the students, because any one of the people described could belong to the churches they serve. The last of the images is even closer to home, because it is of a young pastor being given a cast-off TV by a parishioner who expects deep gratitude for the pittance.

Then he gives the image of bitterness from his text, the Pharisee Saul of Tarsus, who is bitter that Christian preachers would make salvation available to Gentiles, whose ancestors had not suffered generations for their faith. It is like a seventeen-year-old child suddenly being told by his parents that they are adopting a brother for him, of the same age, who will be a full coheir to the family business. The seventeen-year-old would do everything in his power to stop it, as Saul would try to stop the

Christians. Of course, Paul knew that God loves all creation, but "it's one thing to know something; it's another thing to *know* it" (51).

Craddock then asks his hearers if they know anyone like that who is bitter, and, if so, how do they respond. He hopes they do not do so with bitterness themselves. "A few years ago, many of us found ourselves more prejudiced against prejudiced people than the prejudiced people were prejudiced" (51).

Then he tells the story of a family out for a Sunday drive in the country. Along the way they see a homeless kitten beside the road, and the children beg the father to stop for it. He is reluctantly persuaded by his wife to go back for the kitten and gets out to pick it up. He is rewarded for his pains by being scratched. A few weeks later, after the kitten has been fed into health and sports a sleek coat, the man feels the kitten rubbing up against his leg. Craddock asks if it is the same cat and answers: "No. It's not the same as that frightened, hurt, hissing kitten on the side of the road. Of course not. And you know as well as I what makes the difference" (52).

He then closes quickly by saying:

> Not too long ago God reached out his hand to bless me and my family. When he did, I looked at his hand; it was covered with scratches. Such is the hand of love, extended to those who are bitter.

He began with concrete images, showed respect for his listeners' ability to arrive at their own conclusions, and did not state any conclusion explicitly. He never mentioned "prophetic" preaching that "dumped" on people whose lives gave them grounds for bitterness. But it is hard to imagine that any of his hearers were unaware of the one point he was making, a point that was the result of the dialogue he had overheard between the situation in the text and the situation in the congregation.

A postscript to this consideration of inductive preaching is to note how much it was a response to the cultural climate at the time Craddock wrote *As One Without Authority,* a climate in which there was deep distrust of any form of public speech, especially preaching. His Beecher lectures were his next book, *Overhearing the Gospel,*[14] which was published seven years later. It deals with a different crisis in preaching— not that of a secular distrust of religion but that of a Christian audience that has heard the gospel so often as to be unable to pay attention to it. His text for that book is a quotation from Kirkegaard: "There is no lack of information in a Christian land; something else is lacking, and this is a something which the one man cannot directly communicate to the other."[15] He recommends an indirect method of preaching by which people who hear the gospel can overhear[16] it. And that method has much in common with inductive preaching.

By the time Craddock got around to publishing a general homiletics textbook in 1985, the climate had changed even more. Thus he can say in the introduction to *Preaching*:[17]

> After a generation of walking alone, the object of general ridicule and preoccupied in self-flagellation, preaching is again making new friends among other disciplines and renewing old acquaintances with biblical studies, literary criticism, and communication theory. (13)

He is no longer so critical of traditional homiletics (14), and even suggests that some of its sermon forms are able to be used with profit today (176-77). Much can be said also for deriving the form of the sermon from the form of the biblical text. But often it will be good for the preacher to create a form for the particular sermon that grows out of its own particular demands. And, although it is not labeled as such, that sermon form has much in common with inductive preaching:

> Beginning at that intersection of message and hearer, the sermon begins to unfold, moving from where they are, through the text, using analogies, examples, images, perhaps even pleasant interruptions in the form of asides or hints of roads not now to be taken, until preacher and congregation know the message has been said. (188)

The Phenomenological Approach of David Buttrick

A proposal for what should be done to overcome the shortcomings of traditional homiletics comparable to Craddock's in its significance and influence is that of David Buttrick, who recently retired as professor of homiletics and liturgics at the Divinity School of Vanderbilt University. A son of the distinguished preacher George Buttrick,[18] he was ordained as a Presbyterian minister and later went over to the United Church of Christ on a principle of conscience. He served as a parish minister and taught in several seminaries, including St. Meinrad's, a Roman Catholic Benedictine theologate, before going to Vanderbilt.

The quality that most distinguishes Buttrick from his colleagues in homiletics[19] is the wideness of his intellectual horizons. He has made an effort to understand the universe in which he lives as fully as possible, using especially the tools of the phenomenological school of philosophy, which goes back to the early-twentieth-century work of Edmund Husserl in German universities. Further developed by European thinkers such as Remey Kwant, Maurice Merleau-Ponty, Martin Heidegger, Michel Foucault, and Paul Ricoeur, this movement has had much influence on theology. One of the theologians to show that influence is Edward Farley, with whom Buttrick served on the faculty of Pittsburgh Theological Seminary near the beginning of his teaching career, and at Vanderbilt at the end of it. During all this time, he and Buttrick have been close friends and partners in theological conversation.

The significance of phenomenology's influence on Buttrick's homiletic is spelled out in a contribution to his Festschrift by his closest and most able disciple, David Greenhaw.[20] He points out that phenomenology is a philosophical approach to understanding reality that seeks to do greater justice to the complexity of that process than is done by common sense. Common sense assumes that things exist objectively in the world, and the mind perceives them as doing so. Phenomenology points out that while the things exist in the external world, what they are understood as being is at least as much a function of the perceiving mind as it is of the thing itself. Pieces of wood can be joined together in such a way that they have a shape we recognize as that of a table, but it is the mind's recognition that the assembly of wood is a flat surface at which one can sit to eat or write or that otherwise functions in a tabular way that constitutes the thing as a table. Or, more precisely, it is the perceiver's intention to use or regard it as a table that makes it a table rather than just a configuration of lumber.

The mind, furthermore, does not necessarily perceive things as wholes. A complex reality may be experienced from a number of different perspectives before it dawns that the awareness is of a single reality. An analogy to this can be seen in a series of photographs a person takes of a house she is contemplating buying: someone to whom she shows the photos may take a while to realize that they are not of different houses but of the same one seen from different angles. It then becomes the intention of the viewer to see the collection as different aspects of the same house, which permits him to go on and imagine the house as a whole. But again, the fullness of the reality will not be experienced until the viewer says: "Oh, this is where you are going to live!" It is this purposive act that makes what is viewed a house in the fullest sense.

This forming of a whole out of a combination of perspectival aspects is what Buttrick means by consciousness.

> It is not simply that we passively perceive objects in the world or even just aspects of objects. It is rather that through an intentional act, the

perception is pulled together into a unitary experience, a lived experience, a formed consciousness.[21]

Therefore, "consciousness refers to lived experience, not simply an
idea or a thought, but the formation of a world out of the various worlds
that can be formed."[22] While the roof, walls, windows, and doors are all
there, the house itself and as a whole is "there only *in lived experience,*
not as a bundle of perceptions but *as a synthetic unity constituted by my
purposive presence.*"[23] The point is that reality does not exist objectively in the world but is formed when perceptions of what exists come
together with human intentionality in an act of consciousness.

It is this potentiality for the formation of a reality in consciousness that
makes preaching so important in Buttrick's understanding. The sort of
naming[24] that identified a series of photographs as a house could have
had various other outcomes: the building could have been named prison,
castle, ruin, or fortress. Everything can be named in a number of ways,
or, more accurately, everything can be given a number of names. Things
can be named mistakenly or accurately. And so Buttrick can say:
"Evangelism rests on the open option that anything may be renamed
gleefully into a consciousness of God."[25] "Preaching is to name God in
consciousness, and by naming God, to construct the world of the church
and the greater social order as a world in which we may live and love."[26]

The fundamental seriousness of the preaching enterprise should be recognized. What is at stake here is not just inspiration or even persuasion
that such and such a view of an aspect of reality is the correct one. The
formation of Christian consciousness in an individual or a congregation
is essentially transformative.[27] Although Urban T. Holmes III was using
the conceptual framework of Jungian psychology rather than that of phenomenology, his understanding of what preaching should accomplish is
as radical as that of Buttrick. Saying that the object of preaching is "the
inscape of existence, not the landscape," he insists that preaching is not
teaching, but rather "an act of evangelizing the deep memory."[28] And he
recognized that deep memory is a corporate as well as a personal
possession.

While others of the New Homileticians are as committed as Buttrick
to the view that the goal of preaching is transformation, his phenomenological approach may make his prescriptions for bringing that about
through preaching a little more nuanced than some of the others'. Before
looking at those prescriptions, however, it will be useful to notice what
Buttrick finds wrong with traditional homiletics. He thinks that for two-
thirds of the twentieth century American preaching was dominated by

two models, that of the biblical theology movement and that of what Philip Rieff calls "the triumph of the therapeutic," reflected in preaching in the tradition of Harry Emerson Fosdick.[29] The former is dominated by a view of revelation that treats God as existing "out there" independently of human perception. That God exists independently of us is not the issue because we do not know God as God is in the Divine Self. God is known to us only as God is revealed to our perception; all we know about God is what we have perceived. The phenomenological perspective applies even to God.

As biblical theology posited an "out there" God, so the therapeutic tradition posited an "in here" me, a focus on existential self-awareness that isolates the self from its social milieu. Buttrick calls the two tendencies represented in traditional homiletics the "objective/subjective split," and he regards it as a trap. "The first isolates revelation from contact with human understanding, and the second reduces divine revelation to a region of the human psyche."[30]

The presentation of such a detailed theoretical basis has been necessary to communicate the depth of Buttrick's homiletical project. Otherwise, his prescriptions could appear as just another set of "how-to" tips. When it is seen, however, that what he is concerned with is how truth forms in consciousness, the seriousness of his recommendations becomes clear. He recognizes that what he is proposing is a new partnership of preaching with rhetoric. Aware of the bad press rhetoric has received and of the reductionism with which it is often dismissed as "mere rhetoric," he nevertheless devotes himself to an analysis of the conditions under which language can be transformative, which is what rhetoric is really all about.

Granting the validity of that approach, we should still note that in his prescriptions he makes a lot of what appear to be apodictic judgments regarding what will or will not form in consciousness, down to such details as the number of sentences an introduction can incorporate. His text is peppered with many remarks such as "research shows," remarks that appear to give an empirical basis to the limits set. The book is so long, however, that a decision was made to publish it without notes,[31] so the warrant for those claims is not available for the reader's inspection. The reader's only recourse, then, is to decide if the cogency of Buttrick's arguments in the text implies that he is also reliable at times when he simply must be taken at his word.

His book, *Homiletic*, is essentially a preaching rhetoric. It deals with two questions, the way individual building blocks of a sermon are to be constructed (moves) and their position relative to one another in the whole (structures). "Sermons," Buttrick says, "involve an ordered sequence—they are not glossolalia. Sermons are a movement of language from one idea to another, each idea being shaped in a bundle of words."[32] Such bundles, "formed modules of language," he calls "moves," rejecting the traditional term "points" because it implies a more exclusively rational, objective, and static character than many such modules possess. A move is a module of language that forms in consciousness to pattern an understanding. The sequence in which such modules appear is not governed by strict logic, but by the many forms of association by which one statement follows another in a conversation.

Attention span today allows only about four minutes per move, and yet it is hard for an idea to form in communal consciousness in any less time. Thus a twenty-minute sermon can consist of only five or, at most, six moves. Each move needs to begin with a statement of the idea it is to communicate and should end with a restatement of that idea. In between come "internal development systems" (moves within a move), which enable the hearers to acknowledge the truth of the idea when it is restated at the end of the move. These systems may be information about the subject, evidence or arguments to deal with anticipated congregational resistance to the idea (which Buttrick calls "contrapuntals"), "phenomenal lived experience" (most of what traditional homiletics has called "illustrations" or "support material"), or theological concerns. The type chosen will depend on what the preacher is trying to do in the move. In any case, each move must be unified—must point in only one direction—so that the idea will not fragment, but will form in consciousness. And it should achieve closure in the idea's restatement at the end of the move. Introductions and conclusions are special kinds of moves that have their own problems and, therefore, their special set of rules.

When he comes to the structures in which moves are joined, Buttrick rejects the numbered points with transitions between them favored by traditional homiletics. Rather, he says, the sermon should be regarded as a sequence of ideas with its own connective logic. Hence one of the most important steps in sermon preparation is to write out the sequence of ideas, listing the move statements in the order in which the moves occur. These statements are not topics but the theses of the moves stated in conversational language. When the five or six move statements for the sermon are thus set down, the connective logic[33] of the whole can be tested. Adjustments can then be made so that the flow of thought is justified and unimpeded.

Buttrick uses the term "modes" to refer to the patterns in which the sequence of ideas, or structure, in a sermon may fall, and he considers there to be three that are legitimate. These he calls the Immediate Mode, the Reflective Mode, and the Mode of Praxis. Those in the Immediate Mode are based on narrative passages of scripture, including parables; those in the Reflective Mode are based on expository (nonnarrative) passages of scripture; and those in the Mode of Praxis do not begin with a text but with an issue before the congregation, moving on to theological questions and relevant biblical passages.

Buttrick believes that sermons on narrative passages should preserve the story's suspense, and thus should not separate telling the story and applying it. Sermons in the Mode of Reflection intend to form in consciousness a contemporary theological understanding produced by the structure of the text combined with contemporary images drawn from lived experience. While sermons on narrative passages have to follow the story sequence, in sermons on expository passages the preacher can replot the movement of thought into a basic sermon structure.

By sermons in the Mode of Praxis, Buttrick means legitimate forms of what traditional homiletics calls topical sermons. In these the preacher has the role of the resident theologian in the parish and takes people through a consideration of a problem that faces them or the community or society, sets it in theological perspective, and then rereads the situation in the light of revelation, story, and symbol. The outcome should be a new understanding if the issue was one of being, or a new course of action if it was one of doing.

The foregoing summary of a long and closely argued book is dangerously curtailed, but it is what is possible in the space available. Perhaps, though, it has been possible to suggest Buttrick's understanding of how a new partnership of preaching with rhetoric can enable the formation of Christian consciousness in individuals and congregations.

Narrative Proposals

A number of New Homileticians' suggestions about what should be done instead of preaching in the traditional mode have centered on some concept of story or narrative. All of a sudden in 1980, at least three proposals of this sort were made, suggesting that the time had come for the homiletical community to reappraise the role of narrative in sermons. First, a distinguished retired professor at Union, **Edmund A. Steimle,** published *Preaching the Story*[34] with two of his former graduate students, **Morris J. Niedenthal** and **Charles L. Rice.**[35] Their volume was intended to be a preaching textbook for seminary classes, and chapters in it were written not only by the three themselves, but by others as well. The introduction deals with the concept of preaching as shared story, while the major divisions of the book consider that theme from the perspectives of the preacher, the listeners, the congregation, and the message. There is also a final chapter on learning to preach in a new context in which women as well as men occupy pulpits.

The significance of this seminal volume lies in the way that it named and thus raised an issue and set others clamoring to answer it. By saying "story," the authors seemed to say the magic word. How they understood the term can be learned from three sorts of evidence: the way the book itself was written (for its style and way of presenting its content seems to be the one recommended for sermons), the sermons printed at the end of each of the four major sections, and Steimle's discussion of the "fabric" of the sermon. Of the sermons included as examples, it can be said that none were extended narratives in the strict sense, thus indicating what they did not mean by "preaching the story."

The four qualities of a sermon that functions as story listed by Steimle are "its secularity, its dialogical character, its dramatic story-form in the indicative mood, and its lean and spare style."[36] By "dramatic story-form in the indicative mood," he seems to mean that the sermon will eschew the imperatives of exhortation and display what John McClure refers to as the "delay of the arrival of the preacher's meaning."[37] Or, as Steimle says, "The end . . . is still in doubt."[38] The example he gives of how such a sermon may be constructed (see **Vol. 2, pp. 623-27**) does not take the form of a story proper but rather that of an unfolding sequence of images, thus raising the question of how the authors use their key term of "story."

It turns out that what Eslinger says of Rice applies to all three authors: they use "metaphor," "image," and "story" interchangeably.[39] In that original publication,[40] then, they were not sufficiently clear about what they meant by "story" to make it easy for others to construct sermons according to their formula. That in a way, however, shows how attuned they were to the spirit of the times, because, as will be seen, others began to develop models for correcting traditional preaching using the narratives and images Steimle, Niedenthal, and Rice had elided into one.

Before moving on to consider the proposed remedies of image-based preaching, it will be appropriate to see what has been recommended in the way of narrative preaching. The discussion to follow will take account of only two of those forms of narrative preaching, that which gives a narrative shape to nonstory sermons and that in which sermons consist of one long story.[41]

Narrative form is given to nonstory sermons to maintain suspense by delaying the preacher's meaning until the end of the sermon—that is, giving the sermon a dramatic plot. The main advocate of this kind of preaching is **Eugene L. Lowry,** William K. McElvaney Professor of Preaching at St. Paul School of Theology in Kansas City, Missouri.

His distinction between the sort of preaching he advocates and traditional preaching begins with his understanding of what is to be ordered in a sermon: experience, not ideas. Thus the task of preparing a sermon is shaping rather than organizing. The form of the sermon is to be thought of as a process rather than a structure. The focus of the sermon is not so much theme as events. Its principle is the resolution of ambiguity rather than the presentation of substance. The product of the work of preparation will be, therefore, a plot instead of an outline. The means used to put the sermon across will be ambiguity and suspense rather than logic and clarity. And the goal the sermon is to achieve is a happening rather than an understanding.[42]

All of this is to say that he thinks the sermon's meaning should be withheld to the end in the way of a literary plot. By that he does not mean that sermons should be fictional stories, but that the "experiences" presented should have the sequence of a plot.

> The stages are: 1) upsetting the equilibrium, 2) analyzing the discrepancy, 3) disclosing the clue to the resolution, 4) experiencing the gospel, and 5) anticipating the consequences. [His] students have found it helpful to remember these steps with the following abbreviations: 1) Oops; 2) Ugh; 3) Aha; 4) Whee; and 5) Yeah.[43]

Lowry thereby suggests that we begin our sermons by pointing out the inconsistency between the way we think life ought to be and the way it actually is. Next, he suggests that we go on to analyze this discrepancy. For him, this analysis is the most important stage in the sermon. It seeks to move from behavior to the motivation behind the behavior, wherein lies the real trouble. It is, then, a diagnosis of sin, and must be done accurately so that it can be matched accurately with the remedy of grace that is proposed by the text.

Yet, at this stage of diagnosis, the problem is still stated in the language of ordinary human wisdom rather than in theological language. The reason for this is that the third stage, the disclosure of the clue to resolution, can come not only as a revelation, but also as something of a surprise. A reversal occurs so that the situation is no longer seen from the perspective of human wisdom, but from the perspective of the gospel. This brings us to the next stage, that of experiencing the gospel. It is in this section that the most substantial positive presentation is made. Finally, the last stage is to anticipate the consequences, to apply the insight to future living.[44]

One of the first to advocate preaching in which the entire sermon is a story was **Richard A. Jensen,** who did not suggest this as the only valid sermon form, but saw it instead as a way of giving variety to preaching. Jensen was trained in systematic theology rather than homiletics, but his duties as speaker for the national Lutheran Vespers radio broadcast made him a popular conductor of preaching workshops for clergy. He also taught in doctor of ministry programs. His 1980 book, *Telling the Story: Variety and Imagination in Preaching,*[45] gives almost equal treatment to three sermon forms. The first he calls "didactic," by which he means traditional sermons of the sort that the New Homiletics understands itself over against. Although 90 percent of the preaching he had heard and done was of that sort, and it still has some legitimate use, he does not consider it to be very effective anymore. He considers it to be more like a physician's explaining what is wrong with one's body than giving the medicine one needs to recover.

He calls the second sort of preaching he considers, his default style, "proclamatory" preaching. While it has much in common with the preaching of the biblical theology movement discussed in chapter 26, it has its theological basis not so much in the thought of Barth as in that of Bultmann and of his disciples who developed the "New Hermeneutic." This sort of preaching announces and offers the help that people need, God's grace for healing sinners.

However, it is the third type of preaching Jensen discusses, story preaching, that is relevant to the present discussion. He was motivated to consider such preaching by a number of currents in the theological air, ranging from Frederick Buechner's thoughts about "preaching as fairy tale" through the growing importance of story in theology, to research about the division of labor between the hemispheres of the brain. He also found persuasive Amos Wilder's suggestion that if the biblical text makes its point in story form, then preachers should consider doing the same.[46]

What he has in mind as story sermons are not those in which stories illustrate points, but those in which the story itself is the preaching. The aim of such sermons is for the listeners to participate and become involved in the gospel story. For that to happen, it helps if the stories are open-ended. The hearers need to recognize themselves in the story and experience the "good turn"[47] the story takes because of God's grace.

Jensen gives some helpful hints to preachers who are considering story preaching. They need to work on their narrative skills before they attempt such sermons in the pulpit. The stories should be based on a biblical text, but not a simple retelling of a Bible story. To be persuasive, they should have characters who are recognizable as real people. For particular occasions the story can be autobiographical.[48] The story should function more like a parable than an allegory. Sometimes a visual prop can elicit interest in what lies ahead. People are more open to the message at times when they overhear it as if it were spoken to someone else than when they hear it as directly addressed to them.[49]

A simple way of beginning to preach story sermons is to tell stories that parallel the story in that day's Gospel closely enough for listeners to make the connection. It sometimes helps to provide a period of silence in which people can identify themselves with the story. People can be led to meditate on a biblical story in the light of stories they know from literature, theater, cinema, TV, music, or human life when the juxtaposition of the two suggests insights. And the final bit of advice is that the preachers who read the book should try the method.

The examples of story sermons from Jensen's own preaching are, not surprisingly, congruent with his suggestions. The first, for instance, is a modern story that parallels the parable of the prodigal son in a way that makes the older story seem more real. Another, in effect, tells the story of the lost sheep from the perspective of a sheep, which, Jensen admits, seems to contradict his principle that the stories should be about real people. He also offers a sermon that combines elements of proclamatory and story preaching as an intermediate step in introducing a congregation to story preaching.

Since the purpose of the present chapter is to list proposals of alternatives to traditional preaching made by New Homileticians rather than to trace the development of each of the proposals after they are made, much literature on narrative preaching cannot be considered here. For present purposes, it is enough to say that such literature exists.[50]

Image and Imagination in Preaching

The alternatives to traditional preaching proposed under this rubric are the most difficult to summarize, because they are the most diffuse. They seem to range from the general assumption that preaching would be better if it were more imaginative, to something as specific as the recommendation that a single image be used to tie a sermon together. The most influential writer in this field is one who clearly practices what he preaches. **Thomas Troeger,** a Presbyterian minister who has also received

Episcopal ordination and who occupies an endowed chair in preaching at Iliff Theological Seminary in Denver, has published a volume of hymns and another of his poetry, and is an accomplished flautist as well. Colleagues will never forget the 1985 meeting of the Academy of Homiletics, at which there was a celebration of the three-hundredth anniversary of the birth of Johann Sebastian Bach. For that program, Troeger both played some of Bach's music and gave voice to a sermon in which he claimed that Bach was the preacher.[51] (A form of this sermon is found in **Vol. 2, pp. 634-37.**)

In the first of his two books on the use of imagination in preaching, *Creating Fresh Images for Preaching: New Rungs for Jacob's Ladder,*[52] Troeger models the sort of preaching he recommends in the way he writes the book. His thesis is that "there are more cures for incoherence [in a sermon] than logic."[53] Instead of depending on logical connection, "a preacher can glue a sermon together through the being of an image or story. A repeated phrase or vision can hold the preacher's words together."[54] There are many such phrases and visions that recur through the length of this book. One is indicated in the subtitle, "new rungs for Jacob's ladder." Noting that the angels descend to earth before they ascend to heaven, Troeger says, "Don't start in heaven. Don't start with the sweeping generality. . . . Start on earth. Start with the particular, with what we see and hear and touch."[55] Other visions include members of a congregation who heard a particular sermon and elders of a Presbyterian church with whom Troeger began a workshop by asking them to identify their dominant relationship with God. These and other such visions reappear briefly throughout the book.

The book is a joy to read. It moves from image to image rather than from point to point. One recognizes along the way that complete sermons of the author have been woven into the text as illustrations of what can be done by the imaginative preacher. Some are stories in the mode of Jensen, so that it is difficult to tell where image leaves off and story begins. Or a sermon may be a secular love story, a scripture reading, and a prayer that renders the theological meaning of the story. There are other sections that model the way a passage of scripture can be brought to light by visualizing its images rather than looking for its point. The whole is connected by the recurring images in the way a musical composition is tied together by the reprise of motifs and themes.

Interspersed along the way are bits of instruction about how the reader can accomplish similar results, but they are hard to isolate and systematize. For the most part, the preaching student is expected to learn by example.[56] Perhaps not enough did, because Troeger's second book,

Imagining a Sermon, seems to go over much the same territory in a more linear way—although it, too, has stunning products of the author's creativity introduced every so often, causing the reader to gasp for breath. This work operates on Ricoeur's principle that imagination is a rule-governed activity. "The imaginative process can be compared to the art of sailing a boat: We cannot make the wind blow, but we can trim the sails and tend the helm."[57] This understanding "disallows any purely Romantic understanding"[58] of the creative process.

Some of the rules for this rule-governed activity are the chapter titles of *Imagining a Sermon.* Each chapter thus furnishes instruction on how to obey the particular rule and examples of what it looks like in action. The rules are:

1. Alert the eye to keener sight.
2. Feel the bodily weight of truth.
3. Listen to the music of speech.
4. Draw parables from life.
5. Understand the church's resistance to imagination.
6. Dream of new worlds.
7. Return to the Source.[59]

This work also includes sample sermons constructed according to the principles taught in the chapter, and they show what variety of sermon forms can be encompassed in the term "imaginative." While all of them use imagery, at least one is a continuous story—showing how slippery the distinction between narrative and imaginative preaching is.

A work that concentrates on a method of using a single image to connect a sermon is *Imagery for Preaching* by **Patricia Wilson-Kastner.**[60] The author, who died prematurely, was a former Roman Catholic nun who became an Episcopal priest. She taught Historical and Constructive Theology at United Theological Seminary of the Twin Cities before becoming Trinity Church Professor of Preaching at the General Theological Seminary. After that she served several parishes out of a desire to put into practice her understanding of ministry, especially preaching. She begins her book with a discussion, similar to that in the other works surveyed, of changes in the way human access to truth has been understood in philosophy, depth psychology, anthropology, history of science, and theology—changes that call for a more imaginative and less linear approach to communicating the gospel.

As a case in point in the study of the way that all thinking begins with images, she looks at the use of imagery in the Bible. After listing some of the primary images of the Old Testament, she gives five questions to be posed in assessing the helpfulness of such images:

1. What is the root of this image in common human experience?
2. How does this image portray God?
3. What does this image imply about God's relationship to human beings?
4. What response to God does this image evoke in the hearer?
5. How is this image complemented by other images? (pp. 48-61)

In preparing to preach a sermon bound together by an image, the preacher needs to note the congruence between the image and the spiritual reality to which it is related, what that image has in common with our world, the multidimensional quality of all powerful images (and sermons should not be based on any other sort), the appealing quality of the image to the congregation, and the open-endedness of the image.

A notable quality of Wilson-Kastner's work is her insistence that since preaching is a part of the liturgy, it is a form of prayer and, therefore, it is only appropriate that one pray in preparation for doing it. She recommends a particular form of prayer as suitable for this task, the Ignatian meditation.[61] This method of prayer, which is fundamental to the formation of members of the Jesuit order, begins by reconstructing imaginatively the scene in the biblical passage being prayed. Then the one who meditates asks God to be allowed to pray in that place. "After this one enters into the event, applying one's memory, mind, and will" (67). The prayer ends with a resolve to put the insight gained through the meditation into practice in one's own life.

While the passage on which the preacher has meditated is often narrative, the suggested method for constructing the sermon is imagistic rather than narrative. An example of the way such a sermon works is preached by the author on the parable of Dives (the rich man) and Lazarus (Luke 16:19-31). **(See Vol. 2, pp. 638.)** Instead of retelling the story of the two, she sets up the contrast between these two vivid figures "who see but do not encounter one another" (87). She sees a modern parallel in the contrast between a luxury hotel in Dallas, where she attended a meeting of a scholarly society, and the run-down neighborhood where she grew up in the same city, which she visited after the meeting. She then asks why the contrast is allowed to continue. After accounting for it in terms of human sin, Wilson-Kastner calls the church to both judgment and hope. Thus the sermon is based on a static rather than a kinetic use of the figures, an image rather than a story.[62]

Fitting the Form of the Sermon to the Form of the Text

The last proposal for what should be done instead of traditional preaching is not so much a separate way of creating sermons as it is an element of all the other proposals made. That element was already in place when Fred Craddock wrote *As One Without Authority*. He said: "If the minister feels lost at first with a body of ideas without a skeleton, he may adopt the form in which the biblical text is presented."[63] While all the authors surveyed have enunciated this principle in one way or the other, it has also been the subject of entire books. Two examples illustrate the emphasis on this principle, one a collection of essays by various authors edited by **Don M. Wardlaw**[64] and the other written by Thomas G. Long alone.

Preaching Biblically,[65] the Wardlaw volume, grew out of the work of a panel assembled by the editor.[66] After listing the inadequacies of traditional homiletics, the editor says that the contributors suggest ways in which the shape of the sermon can be determined by that of the biblical passage on which it is based. The aspects of the text identified by the contributors as offering such direction include: its language, its context, its claim on the readers, its interplay with a metaphor, its structure, the interaction of its shape with the preacher's individuality, and its encounter with the preacher. Wardlaw sorts these into three groups: those that "accent particularly the shaping of the sermon from the preacher's personal experience of the text"; those that "concentrate on the experience of the faith community embedded in the text and see possibilities of structuring the shape of the human drama that gave rise to the text"; and those that "see significant sermon shapes arising from the language of the text itself." He goes on to say, "No contributor dwells exclusively in any of these three categories" (23). It can also be said that the suggestions of contributors to this volume whose proposals of what to do in place of traditional preaching have already been considered in this chapter are consistent with those proposals. (For Wardlaw's sermon from this book, **see Vol. 2, pp. 642-46**.)

Thomas Long, who taught for a number of years at Princeton Theological Seminary, now occupies Fred Craddock's old chair at the Candler School of Theology of Emory University and is the author of a number of books. His *Preaching and the Literary Forms of the Bible*[67] is based upon "the relatively simple idea that the literary form and dynamics of a biblical text can and should be important factors in the preacher's navigation of the distance between text and sermon."[68] To help the preacher complete that voyage, he offers five questions to ask of the biblical passage on which the sermon is planned:

1. What is the genre of the biblical text?
2. What is the rhetorical function of this genre?
3. What literary devices does this genre employ to achieve its rhetorical effect?
4. How in particular does the text under consideration, in its own literary setting, embody the characteristics and dynamics described in the previous questions?
5. How may the sermon, in a new setting, say and do what the text says and does in its setting?[69]

Then, to help the reader see how to pose those questions to particular texts, he models the interrogatory process in chapters on such literary forms as psalms, proverbs, narratives, the parables of Jesus, and epistles. And, finally, he lists four broad types of "text-to-sermon bonds," which have been illustrated in his consideration of the literary forms. These are:

1. Allow the movement of the sermon to follow the movement of the text.
2. Allow the opposing forces in the text to become the opposing forces in the sermon.
3. Allow the central insight of the text to be the central insight of the sermon.
4. Allow the mood of the text to set the mood of the sermon.[70]

While such a bare-bones outline can only suggest the strategies that Long counsels, a careful study of his book should equip readers with the tools to create sermons shaped by the text on which they are based, rather than according to a points and subpoints outline growing out of abstract principles extrapolated from the text.

CODA

This concludes the list of the major alternatives proposed by the New Homileticians to the traditional homiletics, which continued the Puritan preachers' practice of distilling from biblical texts a set of abstract theological propositions—"doctrines"—that were to be applied to their congregations as "uses." Their proposals have included inductive preaching, forming ideas in consciousness, preaching narratively, using imagination, and allowing the shape of a sermon's text to govern the shape of the sermon itself. These are not mutually exclusive alternatives, but neither do they comprise a single, coherent homiletic. They share a rejection of traditional preaching and offer a number of alternatives to it, none of which have succeeded in establishing themselves as the ruling paradigm.

Completing the list brings this history of Christian preaching to an end, because it concludes the homiletical activity that is now history. Not that thought about how to preach has ended! Far from it! But the New Homiletic is the last stage that has been completed. Its practitioners represent the phase of homiletical thought that Lucy Rose calls "Transformational."[71] Already she and others are offering strategies to supersede those of the group studied in this chapter. But these new strategies are only emerging; they are not yet history.

FOR FURTHER READING

Buttrick, David. *Homiletic: Moves and Structures*. Philadelphia: Fortress, 1987.

Chatfield, Don. *Dinner with Jesus and Other Left-handed Story-sermons: Meeting God Through the Imagination*. Ministry Resources Library. Grand Rapids, Mich.: Zondervan, 1988.

Craddock, Fred. *As One Without Authority*. 3rd edition. Nashville: Abingdon, 1978.

Greenhaw, David. "The Formation of Consciousness." In *Preaching as a Theological Task: World, Gospel, Scripture: In Honor of David Buttrick*. Edited by Thomas G. Long and Edward Farley, 1-16. Louisville: Westminster John Knox, 1996.

Long, Thomas. *Preaching and the Literary Forms of the Bible*. Philadelphia: Fortress, 1989.

Lowry, Eugene L. *The Homiletical Plot: The Sermon as Narrative Form*. Atlanta: John Knox, 1980.

Steimle, Edmund A., Morris J. Niedenthal, and Charles L. Rice. *Preaching the Story*. Philadelphia: Fortress, 1980.

Troeger, Thomas H. *Imagining a Sermon*. Abingdon Preacher's Library. Nashville: Abingdon, 1990.

Wilson-Kastner, Patricia. *Imagery for Preaching*. Fortress Resources for Preaching. Minneapolis: Fortress, 1989.

Notes

1. I am grateful to Professors Don Wardlaw and David Schlafer for suggestions for this chapter, but I take full responsibility for the way it is developed. The subject

matter is treated in Richard L. Eslinger, *A New Hearing: Living Options in Homiletic Method* (Nashville: Abingdon, 1987); Lucy Atkinson Rose, *Sharing the Word: Preaching in the Roundtable Church* (Louisville: Westminster John Knox, 1997), 59-85; and Don Wardlaw, "Postmodern Homiletics: Which Language for What Consciousness?," in *Papers for the 1994 Annual Meeting of the Academy of Homiletics* (privately published).

2. Fred Craddock, *As One Without Authority*, 3rd ed. Originally published by Phillips University Press, Enid, Oklahoma, in 1971. The edition consulted was the 3rd, published by Abingdon Press, Nashville, Tennessee, in 1978.

3. Ibid., 6.

4. Ibid., 54.

5. Charles L. Campbell, "Inductive Preaching," in *Concise Encyclopedia of Preaching,* ed. William H. Willimon and Richard Lischer (Louisville: Westminster John Knox, 1995), 270.

6. *Oxford American Dictionary,* 1st ed., def. 3. According to Aristotle, for such reasoning to be valid, one would have to list all the particulars. About two thousand years later, Francis Bacon proposed the inductive method, by which it could be inferred that what is true of a part is true of the whole to which it belongs.

7. Something more likely to be misleading, an error several of the New Homileticians fall into, however, is the identification of the pattern of reasoning Craddock calls deductive as something that originated with Aristotle (Craddock, *As One Without Authority*, 54). What is confusing about the statement is that it is consistent with neither what Aristotle said in his *Logic* nor with what he said in his *Rhetoric*. The *Logic* is concerned with the rules of valid reasoning rather than outlines. As for rhetoric, Aristotle did not consider rigorously deductive reasoning to be the means of persuasion appropriate to oral presentation. Instead, he favored the *enthymeme*, "a 'syllogism' in which the premises are only generally true"—that is to say, not rigorously logical (Richard A. Lanham, *A Handlist of Rhetorical Terms*, 2nd ed. [Berkeley and Los Angeles: University of California Press, 1991], 65).

Aristotle taught that in speeches there are three means of persuasion *(pisteis)* that can be used: reason, the trustworthiness of the speaker, and emotion. The two forms rational persuasion may take are the enthymeme and the example (the rhetorical version of inductive reasoning). But even when reason was the means of persuasion to be used, no ancient rhetoricians recommended the sort of outline described by Craddock. They usually presented the outline of a speech in court as the norm.

Nor did Greek outlines enter Christian preaching through Augustine or another of the Fathers. As we have often noted above, none of the standard rhetorical outlines were appropriate for Christian preaching, especially the sort of exegetical homily preached by the Fathers, because none provided for an explication of a text. In *De doctrina christiana,* Augustine assumed that preachers would have been trained in rhetoric since that was almost the only sort of education there was at the time, but he did not get his sermon form from rhetoric.

This excursus has been longer than desirable, but it seemed necessary to point out that whatever the faults of the outline form Craddock describes, they cannot be blamed on either Greek logic or rhetoric or on the Fathers of the early church. Truthfully, I do not know when such outlining began; my guess is that it was during the Enlightenment. It has parallels with the preaching of Calvin and the Puritans and with that of the latitudinarians.

8. In a letter to me dated April 26, 2000. As he says, it overlaps some with a list drawn up by Eugene L. Lowry, "The Revolution of Sermonic Shape," in *Listening to the Word: Studies in Honor of Fred Craddock*, ed. Gail R. O'Day and Thomas G. Long (Nashville: Abingdon, 1993), 93-112, but I find that of Wardlaw more satisfactory.

9. To list the shortcomings with which New Homileticians charge traditional sermons is not the same as saying the sermons had all those faults. A review of collections of traditional sermons such as *The Protestant Pulpit: An Anthology of Master Sermons from the Reformation to Our Own Day*, ed. Andrew W. Blackwood (New York and Nashville: Abingdon-Cokesbury, 1947), and *The Twentieth-Century Pulpit*, ed. James W. Cox, 2 vols. (Nashville: Abingdon, 1978, 1981), does not reveal the sermons to be consistently in the pattern they are portrayed as having. Rather, the traditional sermon of the New Homileticians is a construct that enables them to account for the inability of previous preaching to meet the needs of their greatly changed cultural situation.

10. In his preface to the third edition of *As One Without Authority*, Craddock admits the "highly male-oriented language" he used in 1971, but he did not change it because he recognized that the great expense in doing so would be passed on to his readers (viii). Hereafter, references to *As One Without Authority* are page numbers inserted into the text parenthetically.

11. "If the sermon revives the memory of the odor of burped milk on a blouse, it evokes more meaning than the most thorough analysis of 'motherhood'" (ibid., 93).

12. For Craddock's evaluation of such "prophetic" preaching, see ibid., 19.

13. It is published in James Cox, *The Twentieth-Century Pulpit* (Nashville: Abingdon, 1981), 2:47-52 and is reprinted, with permission, in volume 2 of this book.

14. Fred Craddock, *Overhearing the Gospel* (Nashville: Abingdon, 1978).

15. Quoted in ibid., 9.

16. Overhearing is a practice Craddock advocates for preachers in their approach to scripture in *As One Without Authority*, 137.

17. Fred Craddock, *Preaching* (Nashville: Abingdon, 1985). Hereafter, references to this work are page numbers inserted into the text parenthetically.

18. George Buttrick was born in England, the son of a Primitive Methodist minister. He, however, was ordained in the Congregational Church before migrating to America. In time he was called to Madison Avenue Presbyterian Church in New York City, where he served from 1927 to 1954, becoming one of the most influential preachers in America. From there he went to Harvard as both minister to the university and professor of homiletics. Before and after his Harvard stint, he taught at Union. He later taught at Garrett and Louisville seminaries. He wrote fifteen books, was general editor of *The Interpreter's Bible* (Nashville: Abingdon, 1951–57) and *The Interpreter's Dictionary of the Bible* (Nashville: Abingdon, 1962), and was twice a Beecher lecturer.

19. Among whom I include myself.

20. David Greenhaw, "The Formation of Consciousness," in *Preaching as a*

Theological Task: World, Gospel, Scripture: In Honor of David Buttrick, ed. Thomas G. Long and Edward Farley (Louisville: Westminster John Knox, 1996), 1-16. Greenhaw is now president and professor of homiletics at Eden Theological Seminary. Another major study of the contribution of Buttrick is that of Eslinger in *A New Hearing*, 133-69, which is the more remarkable in that it was published before the appearance of Buttrick's *Homiletic: Moves and Structures* (Philadelphia: Fortress, 1987).

21. Greenhaw, "The Formation of Consciousness," 5.

22. Ibid., 5-6.

23. The words in quotation marks were quoted by Greenhaw, ibid., from Erazim Kodak.

24. Note that the intentional act that forms reality in consciousness occurs in language.

25. Buttrick, *Homiletics*, 8; quoted in Greenhaw, "The Formation of Consciousness," 6.

26. Ibid., 7.

27. Lucy Rose has characterized most of the practitioners of the New Homiletic as transformational (*Sharing the Word*, 59-85). She has called attention to the way practitioners depend on the power of language to effect change: "Discussions of language under the transformational umbrella tend not to focus on the unchanging reality behind the words, as in traditional or kerygmatic theories. The focus instead is on the change in the human situation created by words" (ibid., 67). While she discusses the contribution of Buttrick very little, she does distinguish between him and other transformational theorists by recognizing that the others concentrate on change within individuals, while Buttrick sees that "the goal of preaching is transformation of congregational consciousness" (ibid., 142).

28. Urban T. Holmes III, *Turning to Christ: A Theology of Renewal and Evangelization* (New York: Seabury, 1981), 216. Conversion is the process by which Christ becomes the dominant metaphor of the deep memory (74).

29. Philip Rieff, *The Triumph of the Therapeutic: Uses of Faith after Freud* (New York: Harper & Row, 1966).

30. Greenhaw, "The Function of Consciousness," 8.

31. Buttrick, *Homiletic*, xi. The book runs to 512 pages. His original plan was to treat "Worship and Preaching" and "Preaching and the Social World" as well. With these sections and documentation, the work would have been enormous.

32. Ibid., 23. The summary of Buttrick's thought about moves and structures will be too compressed to permit extensive citation of the pages on which ideas are expressed. Tracking down a particular statement, however, should not be difficult for anyone with a copy of the book who follows its table of contents.

33. This connective logic is not deductive, but is rather the conversational association mentioned above.

34. Edmund A. Steimle, Morris J. Niedenthal, and Charles L. Rice, *Preaching the Story* (Philadelphia: Fortress, 1980).

35. Niedenthal taught at the Lutheran School of Theology at Chicago and Rice at the Theological School of Drew University.

36. Steimle, Niedenthal, and Rice, *Preaching the Story*, 174.

37. John McClure, "Narrative and Preaching: Sorting It All Out," in *Journal for Preachers* 15 (Advent 1991): 24-25, quoted by Lowry, "The Revolution of Sermonic Shape," 99.

38. Steimle, Niedenthal, and Rice, *Preaching the Story,* 171.

39. Eslinger, *A New Hearing,* 30.

40. Rice especially went on to develop what he meant. See the list of his articles in the footnotes to Eslinger's treatment of his work, in ibid., 38.

41. John McClure (in "Narrative and Preaching," 24-27) has pointed out that preaching has been characterized as narrative in four different respects:

1. When the literary form of its biblical text has an impact on the shape of a sermon (narrative hermeneutics),
2. When the shape of the sermon itself is narrative (narrative semantics),
3. When there is an exploration of the use of culture and human experience that links narrative elements such as metaphor and image with current interest in imagination (narrative enculturation), and
4. When a theological worldview or faith story is cultivated through preaching (narrative worldview).

Only two forms of his second category will be considered here.

42. Eugene L. Lowry, *Doing Time in the Pulpit: The Relationship between Narrative and Preaching* (Nashville: Abingdon, 1985), 11-28. He gives a longer list in "The Revolution of Sermonic Shape," 100-112.

43. Eugene L. Lowry, *The Homiletical Plot: The Sermon as Narrative Form* (Atlanta: John Knox, 1980), 25.

44. Since the publication of *The Homiletical Plot,* Lowry has gone on to publish a number of books that continue to explore the basic theme of this first work from a number of angles. For instance, in *Doing Time in the Pulpit,* he gives the justification for his theory from the perspective of literary criticism. In *How to Preach a Parable: Designs for Narrative Sermons,* Abingdon Preacher's Library (Nashville: Abingdon, 1989), he analyzes several sermons preached by himself and others from the perspective of the homiletical plot. *The Sermon: Dancing the Edge of Mystery* (Nashville: Abingdon, 1997) is his textbook for preaching classes that correlates various narrative forms of the New Homiletic from the perspective of his own theory into a presentation of the various tasks of sermon preparation and delivery.

45. Richard A. Jensen, *Telling the Story: Variety and Imagination in Preaching* (Minneapolis: Augsburg, 1980).

46. Ibid., 128. The Wilder work referred to is *Early Christian Rhetoric: The Language of the Gospel* (Cambridge: Harvard University Press, 1971), a work that has influenced many of the narrative homileticians. It is not surprising that Wilder should have had a great appreciation of narrative, since his brother was the novelist and playwright Thornton Wilder. Most of the New Homileticians agree that the form of the biblical text on which it is based should influence the shape of a sermon, as will be seen below.

47. The literary term is "eucatastrophe," which is used by J. R. R. Tolkien to describe how he wishes his stories to work.

48. A point with which many homileticians would take issue.

49. This point is derived from Fred Craddock's book *Overhearing the Gospel*.

50. For example, Don Chatfield has published a volume of sermons that never leave the narrative mode of stories in *Dinner with Jesus and Other Left-handed Story-sermons: Meeting God Through the Imagination*, Ministry Resources Library (Grand Rapids, Mich.: Zondervan, 1988). A sermon from this book appears in Volume 2, pp. 627-34. Many who have advocated story sermons have been influenced by the work of the Roman Catholic priest John Shea through such books as *Stories of God: An Unauthorized Biography* (Chicago: Thomas More, 1978). The work of Henry Mitchell, discussed above in chapter 28 on recent African American preaching, is recognized as an important contribution to the thought of the New Homiletics about narrative preaching. Narrative concerns have also influenced the homiletical thought of conservative evangelicals, as may be seen in Bruce C. Salmon, *Storytelling in Preaching: A Guide to the Theory and Practice* (Nashville: Broadman, 1988); and Calvin Miller, *Spirit, Word, and Story: A Philosophy of Preaching* (Dallas: Word, 1989).

51. A form of that sermon is the concluding chapter to Troeger's *Imagining a Sermon*, Abingdon Preacher's Library (Nashville: Abingdon, 1990), 135-40. Troeger edits the Abingdon Preacher's Library.

52. Thomas Troeger, *Creating Fresh Images for Preaching: New Rungs for Jacob's Ladder* (Valley Forge, Pa.: Judson, 1982).

53. Ibid., 19.

54. Ibid.

55. Ibid., 30.

56. At the opposite end of the spectrum is Paul Scott Wilson's *Imagination of the Heart: New Understandings in Preaching* (Nashville: Abingdon, 1988), which gives a completely analytical approach to preaching with imagination. Drawing on his University of London dissertation on the understandings of imagination displayed in the literary criticism of Samuel Coleridge, Leigh Hunt, William Hazlitt, and Charles Lamb, he defines imagination as "the bringing together of two ideas that might not otherwise be connected and developing the creative energy they generate" (32) in the way that wires connected to the positive and negative poles of a generator will spark if they are brought close together. Thus the sermon preparation process he recommends is a series of steps in bringing two sets of poles together: the biblical text and our situation, law and gospel/judgment and grace, story and doctrine, and pastor and prophet.

57. Troeger, *Imagining a Sermon*, 14.

58. Ibid.

59. Ibid., 29-30.

60. Patricia Wilson-Kastner, *Imagery for Preaching*, Fortress Resources for Preaching (Minneapolis: Fortress, 1989). Hereafter, references to this work are page numbers inserted into the text parenthetically.

61. Although she cites a much fuller bibliography on Ignatian meditation, Wilson-Kastner particulary acknowledges the importance for her of Elizabeth Canham, *Praying the Bible* (Cambridge, Mass.: Cowley, 1987).

62. An important study on both narrative and imagistic preaching is Richard L.

Eslinger, *Narrative & Imagination: Preaching the Worlds That Shape Us* (Minneapolis: Fortress, 1995), particularly in its theoretical first half. Eslinger has a deeper understanding and acquaintance with the philosophical and literary studies behind contemporary approaches to narrative and imagery than most homileticians, and thus is able to argue the implications of those theories more cogently than most. An example is his warning against the experiential-expressive model of storytelling preaching in which Christian references are used to illustrate principles of some other system of thought that is assumed to be primary. Such an approach undercuts all biblical authority (see p. 17). His discussion of imagination, while too detailed to be summarized here, would provide much theoretical insight to anyone wishing to know how to use it effectively in preaching.

63. Craddock, *As One Without Authority*, 153.

64. Before his retirement, Wardlaw taught homiletics and worship for many years at McCormick Theological Seminary.

65. *Preaching Biblically*, ed. Don M. Wardlaw (Philadelphia: Westminster, 1983). The other writers are Ronald J. Allen; Thomas G. Long; Charles Rice; William J. Carl III; Gardner Taylor; and Thomas H. Troeger.

66. Wardlaw edited another book, one produced by an Academy of Homiletics study group, a textbook on the instruction of preaching from the perspective of the New Homiletics titled *Learning Preaching: Understanding and Participating in the Process* (Lincoln, Ill.: Lincoln Christian College and Seminary Press for the Academy of Homiletics, 1989). The other members of the writing team were Fred Baumer; Donald F. Chatfield; Joan Delaplane; O. C. Edwards Jr.; James A. Forbes Jr.; Edwina Hunter; and Thomas H. Troeger. Wardlaw, like most of the other New Homileticians considered in this chapter, has served as president of the Academy of Homiletics.

67. Thomas Long, *Preaching and the Literary Forms of the Bible* (Philadelphia: Fortress, 1989).

68. Ibid., 11.

69. Ibid., 24-34.

70. Ibid., 24.

71. Rose, *Sharing the Word*, 59-85.

CONCLUSION[1]

A t the end of this long survey, it is appropriate to ask what, if anything, has been learned about the nature of Christian preaching in this survey of its history. The answer begins with something that may be easily forgotten in preachers' daily preoccupation with their task: the importance of preaching. Most of the significant movements in the history of the church have involved preaching in their development and expansion.

That was true from the beginning, as may be seen in the way the gospel spread after Pentecost. In A.D. 49, just sixteen years after the classical date assigned to the crucifixion, the emperor Claudius ordered Jews out of Rome because of disturbances within their community resulting from the activity of Christian missionaries. In that short time, Christian preaching had moved from a backwater province of the empire to its very center, and was creating enough disturbance to come to the attention of the highest reaches of government. Fifteen years later, when the citizens of Rome believed the fire that had razed their city was set by the emperor Nero to inspire his poetic composition, he shifted the blame to the Christians, who in that short time had become the standard scapegoats on whom anything unpleasant could be blamed. Some very effective preaching must have been done to evangelize a Christian community in Rome large enough to have received so much public attention—even if it was largely negative.

It is certainly not coincidental that the period when Christianity finally displaced Greco-Roman religion as the official cult of the empire was a time when the church's greatest bishops and theologians had achieved success as sophists and teachers of rhetoric before ordination. Then, too, the church's response to the unchurched populations of the newly founded cities in the High Middle Ages was to create the mendicant orders of friars, itinerant preachers to be sent where the need was greatest. It belabors the obvious to mention the Reformation as a preaching movement.

These examples can be rounded off without being anywhere near exhausted by noting that the abolition movement in the nineteenth century and the civil rights movement in the twentieth century numbered preachers among their most effective leaders, and preaching was one of the major media through which they spread their message. Most of the great movements in church history have depended on preaching to accomplish their purposes.

This is not even to mention the importance of preaching in the ordinary life of the church. In a justly famous passage in *The Shape of the Liturgy,* Dom Gregory Dix listed the occasions on which the people of God have found making Eucharist to be their most appropriate activity.[2] A list of the times when preaching has seemed the natural thing to do would both overlap his to a considerable extent and, if anything, be even longer. And what Dix said about ordinary offerings of the Eucharist applies equally well to the preaching of sermons:

> Best of all, week by week and month by month, on a hundred thousand successive Sundays, faithfully, unfailingly, across all the parishes of Christendom, the pastors have done just this to *make* the *plebs sancta Dei*—the holy common people of God.[3]

That the same thing can be said of both the Eucharist and preaching should surprise no one because two of the main channels of grace in the church are Word and sacrament. Of the two, however, preaching has been the major means by which Christians have been converted and formed intellectually. As Paul said, "Faith comes from what is heard" (Rom. 10:17). Preaching thus gives specificity to the grace the Eucharist communicates sacramentally. Many historical examples could be given of the grace that has been communicated through preaching, but readers of this book probably do not need those because most can document that proposition from their own lives.

With such a reminder of the importance of preaching in the church's history, it is not surprising—though many would be surprised—that we have numerous examples of the sermons preached during most periods in church history. A case in point: For the years 1150 to 1350, a list of sermon manuscripts has been compiled that runs to nine volumes with a cumulative seventy-three hundred pages.[4] If the average number of sermons per page is consistent with a sample taken of forty-plus pages, more than eighty thousand sermons have been preserved in manuscript. Since this is one of the periods from which relatively few sermons could have been expected to survive, it can be taken as an indication of the number of sermons from the past that are still in existence.

It will amaze no one that most of the sermons that have come down from different periods of the Christian past are those of the homiletic equivalent of "the rich and famous," but we can assume that then as now ordinary preaching was very similar to that of the "tall steeple preachers" in form and content, since it would all reflect the consciousness of the church at the time. It cannot even be taken for granted that the sermons of the "giants of the pulpit" were necessarily more eloquent, profound, or filled with spiritual insight, because there have been too many excellent preachers whose reputation never reached beyond a small circle. By the same token, some proclaimers of the Word most esteemed in their own generation make a poor showing on the test of time.

Thus, while it can be said that ordinary preaching has been most important in the life of the church, it nevertheless remains true that for most Christian generations, we have to infer what that was like through sermons that have come down to us from the better-known preachers.

An example of what can be inferred about ordinary preachers from the ones whose sermons have not been lost is the qualities that have made all of them effective. A list of those qualities can begin with what F. Van der Meer said about his subject in *Augustine the Bishop:* "His real secret, which he shares with all orators who really succeed in fascinating us, is that he had such an enormous amount to say."[5] That recalls the old distinction between "sermons that have something to say and sermons that have to say something." There is no doubt about which sort is more memorable—or, perhaps more accurately, none about the sort from which one retains pleasant memories.

To break down the elements of having something to say, it can be noted that all truly effective preachers have at least three qualities in common. They all have a good mind, a rhetorical reflex, and personal holiness. Rhetorical reflex denotes a native sense of how to get one's point across when addressing a group; the meaning of the other two terms is obvious. It is likely that among the group of preachers respected in any given period there may be found all the possible ratios in which the relative strengths of these three elements may be combined. But preaching at its best requires each of these qualities in a high degree, because a lack of any one of the three will diminish the effect, and do so in a characteristic way.

In addition to the qualities of preachers, there must be considered as well the characteristics of the times in which they preached. There have been many different kinds of preaching in history, and they all were probably related to what was going on in the society in which they arose. More will be said of this later; the only point to be made right now is that these movements all draw on contemporary standards of what makes public speaking effective, and tastes in that have at times changed rapidly.

In most ages, a factor in the formation of taste in oratory has been Greco-Roman rhetoric. This is not surprising because that enterprise represents the best effort ever made to observe what does and does not work in public address, and to create a vocabulary with which to communicate that information.

Notice that the task of the discipline of rhetoric is value-free description. Rhetoric is often used in a pejorative sense in which it implies a lack of sincerity and a desire to manipulate an audience. It is to be understood instead as a body of observations that are value-neutral: These things seem to work and those do not. The choice to use what is more effective is up to the speaker, as are the speaker's motives in doing so. The issue has been stated by Augustine with utter clarity:

> Rhetoric, after all, being the art of persuading people to accept something, whether it is true or false, would anyone dare to maintain that truth should stand there without any weapons in the hands of its defenders against falsehood; that those speakers, that is to say, who are trying to convince their hearers of what is untrue, should know how to get them on their side, to gain their attention, and have them eating out their hands with their opening remarks, while those who are defending truth should not?[6]

Put that way, it becomes clear that rhetoric offers a speaker a set of tools, and all who have a message they want to get across, use the tools. Some do so by instinct and some because of training, but, as Cicero said, "when noble and elevated natural gifts are supplemented and shaped by the influence of theoretical knowledge, the result is then something truly remarkable and unique."[7] A case in point is Dr. Martin Luther King Jr., who developed his natural talent by analyzing the preaching of many clergy and by formally studying rhetoric.

In a pure form, however, the criteria of classical rhetoric have never served well as standards for Christian preaching. The reason is that none of the three classical *genera dicendi* (basic types of speech) provide for the explication of a text, and thus provide no place for the interpretation of passages from the Bible, which has been one of the most persistent elements in Christian preaching.

Incidentally, the method of choosing the text to be explicated has varied considerably over the centuries. Probably the use of a lectionary has been most common, but many preachers through the ages have seen virtue in preaching all the way through one biblical book before considering a passage from another *(lectio continua)*, even though this method is as fixed and artificial as following a lectionary. Other preachers have chosen the passage or verse that seemed to be the portion of the Bible most relevant to their congregation at the moment, the result being either expository or textual preaching, depending on the length of the passage chosen. And some have chosen a subject—a topic—to speak about, which they authorized scripturally by citations from various parts of the Bible.[8]

However the passage is chosen, it is nevertheless the case that the way text is explicated reflects the principles of biblical interpretation in vogue at the time. Or, more precisely, it reflects the hermeneutics of at least the community for which it was prepared, since at any given moment there is a variety of Christian communities, and each has its own characteristic method of discovering what a biblical passage means to and for them.

Within this overall variation, there nevertheless have been methods that have prevailed within large portions of the Christian community. Among these, the most dramatic shift has undoubtedly been from allegorical interpretation to use of the historical/critical method. Even that, however, has not made as much difference as one might think. While use of the two methods would produce very different understandings of the passage's original meaning, the way in which it is brought to bear on the life of the congregation would probably be very similar. The literal, grammatical, historical meaning of a biblical text is always the meaning it had for its first hearers or readers, and the relevance of the text to later congregations is necessarily always analogical.

That being so, it is disappointing that most Christians today can read few sermons of the past with much edification. (That probably is more a matter of different concerns preoccupying the churches than it is the result of changed methods of biblical interpretation.) In spite of this, it still can be seen that in every generation, the church has been able to turn to the Bible for necessary insight into its own situation. Somehow, through preaching, the Bible speaks to the condition of the local community of the people of God, whenever and wherever they are assembled. This capacity of the Scriptures to give needed insight into such an immense variety of situations is undoubtedly much of what is meant by calling them "inspired."

The rest of what is to be said about lessons to be learned from the history of preaching will be organized in terms of a speaker's five tasks, as recognized by Greco-Roman rhetoric: invention, disposition, elocution or style, memory, and delivery.

Invention consists of deciding what to say in a speech. Aristotle defined *rhetoric* as "an ability in each particular case to see the available means of persuasion."[9] Persuasion, as such, is not what we are trying to accomplish in all sermons, but preaching is motivated behavior—it is trying to accomplish something. A good list of the things we seek to do in preaching comes from Ronald E. Osborn:

> The skilful preacher attempts to catch the hearers' interest from the start and to sustain it throughout, engaging their problems and concerns, passing on the tradition, guiding understanding, correcting false impressions, answering objections, projecting a vision, undertaking to persuade, imparting grace.[10]

To have a chance of meeting these goals, preachers need to be strategic in their invention; they need to decide where they want their congregation to arrive, identify the obstacles that stand in the way of their getting there, and design a process to help them get by the roadblocks and arrive safely at their destination.

Part of all such processes is a demonstration that what is proposed is consistent with whatever is accepted as authoritative by members of the congregation. Most Christians have been willing to assume that the Bible is normative for their belief, but the way its authority has been brought to bear has varied enormously. Thus the preacher whose invention involves an appeal to the Bible has to make this appeal in accordance with the criteria acknowledged by those who will hear the sermon. While we all are probably familiar with some sort of proof-texting, that has by no means ever been the main way biblical warrant has been invoked for positions taken in sermons. Other appeals made in preaching have been to reason, emotion, and imagination.

The variety of possible combinations of these appeals can be seen in the sermons of five revivalists:

- **Jonathan Edwards** combined rigorous logic with acute psychological analysis to move people to love God's election of some to salvation and some to damnation.
- The published sermons of **John Wesley** seem to be instructions in Christian doctrine (modeled as they were on the Church of England's *Book of Homilies*), but in actual delivery, the calm voice of reason is not all that was heard. Horace Walpole, a litterateur and a pioneer in the Gothic Revival, has left an unsympathetic account of what it was like to hear Wesley preach: "He spoke his sermon, but so fast, and with so little accent, that I am sure he has often uttered it, for it was like a lesson; but towards the end he exalted his voice, and acted very ugly enthusiasm."[11]
- **George Whitefield,** on the other hand, preached in such a way that it was hard for people to remember afterward what he had said, but they did remember that it was enormously moving—as Benjamin Franklin testified in his autobiography. He went to hear Whitefield, intending to not give a penny to the orphanage in Georgia for which the preacher was trying to raise money, but he wound up emptying his pockets.
- **Charles Grandison Finney** had been trained in law rather than theology, and he argued to get a conviction, except that instead of trying to convince jurors that the defendant was guilty, he set out to make his hearers feel that they were.
- **Dwight L. Moody's** idea of a sermon, however, has been compared to the report of one businessman to another.

Since all these such different styles of preaching were for the single purpose of converting sinners to Christianity, we can see that sermon invention for all the many purposes of preaching must have varied enormously.

There has been equal variety in homiletical approaches to disposition. Greco-Roman rhetoric recognized three basic types of speech *(genera dicendi),* each with its characteristic outline. These were: (1) the forensic speech, the sort made in a law court, designed to persuade an audience about what happened in the past; (2) the deliberative, the type given in a legislative assembly to recommend what ought to be done in the future; and (3) the epideictic, made on public occasions to "point with pride" or to "view with alarm" some person or activity in the present life of the community—the sort of speech made on ceremonial occasions.

As noted earlier, sermons fit none of these three arrangements of a speech because none provide for the explication of a text. Nor was there one standard outline into which classical homilies fell.[12] A look through history reveals expository sermons with many different outlines:

- **Origen** would comment verse by verse as he went along, tossing out exegetical information and doing allegorical interpretation in which his application occurred, commenting on the biblical text the way a grammarian teaching in a secondary school at the time would comment on a classical text.
- Sometimes beginning with an introduction and sometimes not,[13] **Chrysostom** would do literal exegesis with no effort at application until he got to the last verse he had time to talk about. Even then, the moral lesson he found did not always come too obviously from the verse just exegeted.
- **Puritans** would go through three steps with each verse (or, sometimes, phrase): They would exegete it, state as a proposition the doctrine it taught (confirming that proposition from other passages in the Bible), and then find applications to the lives of the congregation or, as they called them, "uses."

Notice that this variety of disposition or outline occurs within a single basic type of sermon. How much greater the differences become when one considers the whole range of sermon forms can be imagined.

Incidentally, there seem to be more forms of preaching today than in all previous Christian centuries put together. That is probably because there are more Christians, more preachers, and consequently more sermons than ever before. This indicates how radically ad hoc all Christian preaching is. Just as at Pentecost all heard the good news in their own language, everyone always has to hear it not only in their own tongue, but in terms of the culture of which they are a part as well.

In classical rhetoric, the concept of *Elocutio* was not as inclusive as that of style today. It was generally limited to figures of sound and thought, that is, to figures of speech whose appeal lay in the way they struck the ear (such as alliteration or rhyme) and those that pleased the mind (metaphor, for example). It was recognized, however, that there were three levels of style, each with its characteristic use or abstention from figures: the plain style to teach, the middle to please, and the grand to move.

There has been a pendulum swing through the ages in the church's attitude toward the use of these figures. Some have thought that only plain style, which eschewed such ornamentation, was consistent with the gospel. Others have used great artistry to convey the Christian message. This alternation may be related to the dominance of the right brain or left brain in an individual or culture. It is certainly related to what Charles Williams has referred to as "the two chief approaches to God defined in Christian thought," the way of the rejection of images and that of the affirmation of them.[14]

It is a matter for reflection, for example, that Gregory the Great (ca. 540–604) was the first preacher in the history of the church to make much use of extended narratives to illustrate the points in his sermons, and his doing so was not widely imitated until the High Middle Ages when friars began using *exempla.*

I will combine memory and delivery in one of the few sweeping generalizations I can make about preaching through the ages, which is that, with rare exceptions, the most effective preachers have not preached from manuscripts. In not doing so they have to an extent honored the standard of the Greco-Roman rhetoricians, who either memorized their orations or spoke them extemporaneously.[15]

This generalization can be documented by noting that Augustine wanted never to impede his ability to gauge audience reactions to what he was saying. If he saw ready comprehension, he would move along, but if he saw uncertainty on his auditors' faces, he would go back over the point and offer analogies (*Doctr. chr.* 10.25). Bernard of Clairvaux did much the same. Indeed, the standard was so established that Archbishop William Laud apologized for using "papers" when he preached from the scaffold where he was beheaded. While Spurgeon would think all week about his sermon for the coming Sunday, he would wait until after Saturday afternoon tea to draw up the outline, which would be the only thing he took into the pulpit. Henry Ward Beecher would have several ideas for sermons going around in his mind at once and would decide on which to preach only Sunday morning after breakfast.

There are exceptions that prove this rule like any other, exceptions of the stature of Tillotson and Fosdick, but, nevertheless, the generalization that most of the greatest preachers spoke without a manuscript is the most sweeping I can make from the history of preaching.

With that, the only things left to be said are warnings voiced by far greater authorities than the present. Let us first hear from Dante:

> Christ did not say to his first company: "Go, and preach idle stories to the world," but he gave to them the true foundation; and that alone sounded in their mouths, so that to fight for kindling of the faith they made shield and lance of the Gospel. Now men go forth to preach with jests and with buffooneries, and so there be only a good laugh the cowl puffs up, and nothing more is asked.[16]

Or, to draw on an even more exalted authority, listen to the words of Paul:

> When I came to you, brothers and sisters, I did not come proclaiming the mystery of God to you in lofty words or wisdom. For I decided to know nothing among you except Jesus Christ, and him crucified. And I came to you in weakness and in fear and in much trembling. My speech and my proclamation were not with plausible words of wisdom, but with a demonstration of the Spirit and of power, so that your faith might rest not on human wisdom but on the power of God.
>
> Yet among the mature we do speak wisdom, though it is not a wisdom of this age or of the rulers of this age, who are doomed to perish. But we speak God's wisdom, secret and hidden, which God decreed before the ages for our glory. None of the rulers of this age understood this; for if they had, they would not have crucified the Lord of glory. But, as it is written,
> "What no eye has seen, nor ear heard,
>   nor the human heart conceived,
> what God has prepared for those who love him"—
> these things God has revealed to us through the Spirit; for the Spirit searches everything, even the depths of God. For what human being knows what is truly human except the human spirit that is within? So also no one comprehends what is truly God's except the Spirit of God. Now we have received not the spirit of the world, but the Spirit that is from God, so that we may understand the gifts bestowed on us by God. And we speak of these things in words not taught by human wisdom but taught by the Spirit, interpreting spiritual things to those who are spiritual. (1 Cor. 2:1-13)

This is as far as the history that began with Melito of Sardis and the author of *Second Clement* can go—for the time being.

Earlier, it seemed appropriate to apply to preaching what Dom Gregory Dix said about the occasions on which it had seemed appropriate to offer the Holy Eucharist. In the same spirit, then, the sacristy prayer after St. Basil's liturgy of the altar can be applied at this point to this effort to write a history of the liturgy of the proclaimed Word:

> The mystery of thy dispensation, O Christ, our God,
> Hath been accomplished as far as in us lies.
> We have seen the memory of thy death;
> We have seen the type of thy Resurrection;
> We have been filled with thine endless life;
> We have enjoyed thy heavenly delights, of which

we pray thee make us more worthy hereafter;
Through the grace of God the Father, and of thy holy,
good, and life-giving Spirit, let us depart in peace.
Amen.[17]

Notes

1. An earlier form of this chapter was presented to the Consortium of Episcopal Homileticians, meeting at St. Paul's College, Washington, D.C., May 27-29, 1999.

2. Dom Gregory Dix, *The Shape of the Liturgy* (London: Dacre, 1945), 744.

3. Ibid.

4. J. B. Schneyer, *Reportium der lateinischen Sermones des Mittelalters für die Zeit von 1150–1350,* Beiträge zur Geschichte der Philosophie und Theolgie des Mittelalters, Band 43, Heften 1-9 (Münster: Aschendorffsche Verlagsbuchhandlung, 1969–80).

5. F. van der Meer, *Augustine the Bishop: The Life and Work of a Father of a Church,* trans. Brian Battershaw and G. R. Lamb (London and New York: Sheed & Ward, 1961), 432.

6. St. Augustine, "Teaching Christianity: *De Doctrina Christiana,*" intro., trans., and notes, Edmund Hill, ed. John E. Rotelle, *The Works of Saint Augustine: A Translation for the 21st Century* (Hyde Park, N.Y.: New City Press, 1996), 201.

7. "In Defence of the Poet Aulus Licinius Archias" 7.15, *Selected Political Speeches of Cicero,* trans. with intro. Michael Grant (Harmondsworth: Penguin, 1969), 156.

8. In practice, however, these methods of choosing the text to be explicated do not automatically produce sermons of clearly different forms. Preachers following a lectionary, for instance, can do either expository or textual or even topical preaching.

9. *Rhet.* 1.2. The translation given is that of *Aristotle* On Rhetoric, *A Theory of Civic Discourse Newly translated with Introduction, Notes, and Appendixes by George A. Kennedy* (New York: Oxford University Press, 1991), 36. The translation given in the Loeb Classics edition is: "the faculty of discovering the possible means of persuasion in reference to any subject whatever."

10. Ronald E. Osborn, *A History of Christian Preaching, Vol. 1, Folly of God: The Rise of Christian Preaching* (St. Louis: Chalice, 1999), xiii.

11. Letter to John Chute of October 10, 1766.

12. To the extent that "homily" has a technical meaning, it refers to sermons following the pattern of verse-by-verse interpretation of a biblical passage—what is referred to today as "expository preaching."

13. When one was used, however, it was not an introduction in our sense, that is, it did not necessarily "lead into" the topic that was to be discussed. Often it was a discussion of a moral issue that happened to be on his mind and did not have to be related to the passage being interpreted. Sometimes, however, it would relate that sermon to the one that had preceded it.

14. Charles Williams, *The Figure of Beatrice: A Study in Dante* (1943; reprint, Cambridge: D. S. Brewer, 1994), 8.

15. Both traditions were highly honored. On the one hand, rhetoricians devised

elaborate methods of memorization that are still called on by anyone offering to help people improve their memories. On the other, itinerant sophists made glamorous careers of raising to an art form the schoolboy exercise of giving impromptu orations on topics set by their audience, speeches that observed all the rules of rhetoric, including periodic sentences, the figures, and frequent quotations from classical literature.

16. *Par.* 29: 109-17, *The Divine Comedy of Dante Alighieri,* trans. Charles Eliot Norton (Boston: Houghton Mifflin, 1902).

17. *The Priest's Book of Private Devotion,* compiled and arranged by J. Oldknow and A. D. Crake, revised by J. F. Briscoe, new ed. (London: Mowbray, 1952), 486 (noted as "From the Liturgy of St. Basil").

APPENDIX ON PIETISM

Although the seventeenth-century British movements listed in chapter 17 had great importance for the Evangelical Awakenings in the United Kingdom and America, the story line will be clearer if the influence of continental Pietism is considered.

The Thirty Years' War, which ended with the Peace of Westphalia in 1648, had begun as a religious tug-of-war between the some three hundred Catholic and Protestant petty states of the Holy Roman Empire, most of which were German-speaking, and ended as a less disguised struggle for political power. The military conflict was prompted by theological polemics that were at least as fierce. Among Lutherans, the result of this dogmatic warfare was the hardening of their theological system into what is known as Lutheran Scholasticism. This theology was reflected in a formalization of church life in which all that was expected of the faithful was that they receive the sacraments, hear the faith proclaimed in sermons that were virtuoso exercises in the splitting of theological hairs, and apparently earn salvation by the intellectual good work of having a correct understanding of the Lutheran confessions and their teaching of justification by faith alone. So the caricature goes.

This was the atmosphere in which **Philipp Jakob Spener** (1635–1705), the "Father of Pietism," exercised his ministry and became one of the most influential pastors in the German-speaking world.[1] Many things about him upset the stereotypical expectations of what such a person must have been like. To begin with, he was not a rabble-rouser; rather, he was the son of an official in one of the small state courts, and much of his ministry was carried out in close association with members of the nobility and in influential pastorates that were court appointments. Nor was he an anti-intellectual; he earned a doctorate and took parishes, reluctantly at first because he hoped to have an academic career. Perhaps most surprisingly, he had not even had a dramatic conversion experience to which he could point, nor did he show any expectation that others would have one.

The orthodoxy of his own Lutheranism was a matter of great concern to him. The main difference between his theology and that of the Reformer was in the place where they felt the problem lay. For Luther, it had to do with the assurance that he had been justified. For Spener, living after a century and a half of Lutheranism, it had to do with the effect of justification on the lives of the elect. Should being truly reborn not have its repercussions in the nature of the internal disposition of faith and the outward expression of faith? Certainly one could not merit salvation by good works, but if one were truly justified, would they not be inevitable? Obviously, the move from self-love to love of God could not be made on self-initiative, but if God had effected that change, shouldn't the difference be felt?

Spener's appointments were some of the most distinguished in his age's Lutheranism, and his influence was so great in his lifetime and ever afterward that it is common to see him referred to by a title such as "the second Luther." Much of that influence was exercised through his preaching. Tastes have changed enough in the centuries since that it is hard for people today to read his sermons and sense the effects they had on their first audience.

Something of Spener's appeal must be seen as the result of what else was available at the time. The preaching of Lutheran Scholasticism was not only polemical in its theology but also rhetorically complex. In the words of Yngve Brilioth, "the preference for pomposity, and for the curving and swelling forms of baroque architecture and poetry, also left its imprint on preaching."[2] While there actually was not only some good preaching but even some good homiletical theory at the time, there were obvious abuses.

Unfortunately, some of the worst abuses were at the hands of J. B. Carpzov the younger, a professor at the University of Leipzig. The university was in the Electorate of Saxony, and Spener had just become preacher at the Elector's Court in Dresden. In his previous ministerial appointment in Frankfurt am Main, Spener's Pietism had met with opposition, and it seemed even less likely to be popular in Saxony. Carpzov at first welcomed Spener, but later turned against him when he felt that his homiletic had been attacked.[3]

The offending passage had appeared in Spener's *De impedimentis studii theologici,* in which he had complained of the results of homiletical teaching he had seen in examining ministerial candidates in Dresden. These caused him to oppose professors who stopped for a whole month to explain one chapter of the Bible. Carpzov took that as a reference to himself, since he had treated the first chapter of Isaiah in great detail.[4] Carpzov was even more notorious for his role in the concentration of scholastic homiletics on the *exordium* as the chief place to introduce variety into preaching on the same lectionary pericopes year after year, having provided a hundred different ways to introduce a sermon on Psalm 14:7.[5]

Spener himself had definite ideas about the way a sermon should be preached. He was convinced, first and foremost, that preaching was for the edification of the congregation, not for arguing fine points of theology. He proposed as the sixth point of his *Pia Desideria* that "sermons be so prepared by all that their purpose (faith and its fruits) may be achieved by the hearers in the greatest possible degree."[6]

Thus he thought that basing sermons on Luther's lectionary of Gospel pericopes every Sunday was not ideal. To begin with, that meant many excellent texts were never preached upon. Furthermore, since the Epistles spoke more directly to issues of personal faith than did the Gospels, they made more useful sermons texts.[7]

He also had objections to the rhetorical ostentation of scholastic preaching.

> Many preachers are more concerned to have the introduction shape up well and transitions be effective, to have an outline that is artful and yet sufficiently concealed, and to have all the parts handled precisely according to the rules of oratory and suitably embellished, than they are concerned that the materials be chosen and by God's grace be developed in such a way that the hearers may profit from the sermon in life and death.[8]

It must be remembered, however, that all of this emphasis on edification did not mean that his preaching exhibited the hypersubjectivity or the emphasis on conversion of later revivalism in America. As noted above, he made no claim to having had a conversion experience himself.[9] He did not even follow his hero Arndt in stressing the mystical union *(unio mystica)* between the soul and God, with the accompanying states of emotion. His interest was ever in practical piety.[10] Therefore, he did not confuse faith with feeling. "Persons can be reassured that they stand within the new birth when they have the desire and make the effort to live according to the divine will."[11]

In order to achieve the results he believed preaching should have in changed lives, Spener did not think that he had to change the sermon form. All of his preaching was expository rather than topical, with an almost word-for-word analysis of the text. His sermons began with an introduction of what the text was about and then moved into the body, which involved four steps: (1) explanation of the truth in the passage, (2) refutation of misunderstandings of it, (3) application that made suggestions for the improvement of one's life, and (4) a concluding word of comfort.

He was, however, exceptional in the length of his sermons: the average at the time was about half an hour, and he often preached for as long as two hours. While he did avoid the contemporary fault of lengthy quotations in Greek and Latin, he did not lighten his tone with illustrations. He read from his manuscript in an unemotional way, appealing to the reason of the congregation rather than stirring them up. No one was more aware than he of the faults of his preaching. This humility undoubtedly contributed to the real reason for his popularity: his presence in the pulpit as one who believed implicitly in what he said, his "whole face reflecting a serene tranquility with kindness."[12]

While in some ways Spener's closest disciple was **August Hermann Francke** (1663–1727), it is also true that the entire nature of Pietism was changed with Francke. To begin with, Francke was aggressive, while there was a certain passivity in the character of Spener. This can be seen in the number of institutions for good works that Francke started when he was at the University of Halle; a list made in 1698 totals twenty-three.[13] Further, the students of Halle carried Francke's ideal around the world, and the university became the hub from which this work was coordinated. Further, unlike Spener, Francke did undergo a conversion experience after a crisis precipitated by an invitation to preach, and that experience became normative for him in his expectations of others.[14] Both of these differences from Spener had a great deal to do with the way Francke preached.

Francke expressed his understanding of what makes good preaching in a letter he wrote to a friend.[15] The purpose of the letter was to tell

> how a faithful minister, who earnestly desires to save and to edify the souls of his hearers, to gain sinners unto Christ, and to inflame their

hearts with a growing love to their Savior, may best adapt his preaching to these excellent purposes. (117)

He does this out of the conviction that "under-shepherds of the flock" (i.e., clergy, under the "great shepherd of the sheep") should "make it more designedly and zealously the purpose of their preaching to bring sinners" to Christ (122).

He begins by saying that the preacher should often list the differentia between the converted and unconverted so that members of the congregation will be able to recognize their own state. Later he says that preachers should often explain the renewing or change of mind involved in true religion. The distinction between mere morality and religion also needs to be made, and that between legal and evangelical religion is another such need. The necessity, nature, and progress of conversion should be delineated frequently.

The preacher needs to be filled with a zeal to win souls to Christ, and so the "excellency and glory of Christ's person" (123) ought to be a frequent topic, as should the love of Christ. The importance of prayer is to be stressed frequently. Indeed, "the whole faith and duty of a Christian" needs to be presented "in its most amiable and attractive light" (122). This includes calls to self-denial and warnings against worldliness. And parishioners should be encouraged both to read good evangelical books and to seek the counsel and prayers of more mature Christians.

Not much time in the sermon should be given to text explanation; only so much as is necessary to lead their hearers into "the true sense and meaning" (122). To preach in this way requires that the minister have a deep love for both Christ and the flock of Christ, a love that is expressed in deed as well as word. Thus the pastor needs to practice what is preached. The letter ends and is summarized in the prayer that

> none of (the clergy) vainly presume on their skill and ability to do any good by their preaching, and obtain any good success, but let them humbly wait upon you, and by fervent daily prayer let them seek for and obtain the aids of your grace, to enable them to dispense the word of life, and let your blessing render their preaching happily successful to the souls of those that hear them. (127)[16]

Pietistic preaching began to stress conversion and assumed a form that has characterized most evangelistic preaching since. But before Pietism was to exercise its influence on the Evangelical Awakening in the English-speaking world, it had to pass through another filter. That filter represents an alliance already noted between Pietism and the German nobility, but it also takes on its own unique hue. **Count Nikolaus Ludwig von Zinzendorf** (1700–1760), a godchild of Spener, began his higher education at Halle, but his family sent him to anti-Pietistic Wittenberg when they felt his "religious ideas" threatened the likelihood that he would perform the public and family duties his station required of him.

Zinzendorf dutifully served at the Saxon court until he felt free to devote himself to the Christian work to which he felt called. While that began in the characteristic institutional form of Halle, it soon took a turn when he became aware of the plight of the Bohemian[17] Brethren (the *Unitas Fratrum* or *Brüderunität*), a refugee remnant of the Hussite movement. He gave them a home on his estates, where they built their community, which they called *Herrnhut* ("the Lord's Watch").

In time, the count became more and more involved in the life of the community, eventually being ordained as a Lutheran pastor and then as a bishop by the Moravian Daniel Ernst Jablonski. The community experienced an awakening and began to send out missionaries to other parts of Europe and to the New World, especially Georgia and Pennsylvania. A particular sort of piety was cultivated at Herrnhut, one making much of bridal imagery and the blood of Christ, which has appeared sentimental and in bad taste to some other Christians. Nor did Zinzendorf place the emphasis on conversion that Francke did. Instead, he advocated a passive waiting upon the Lord, a "stillness" that had something in common with quietism.[18] His disciples, and later Zinzendorf himself, were to encounter a young Anglican missionary to Georgia and, through him, were to have great influence on the Awakenings in Britain and America.[19]

Notes

1. For this section on Pietism, I am grateful for the bibliographical suggestions of Prof. John Wyborg of North Park Theological Seminary.

2. Yngve Brilioth, *A Brief History of Preaching*, trans. Karl E. Mattson (Philadelphia: Fortress, 1965), 130.

3. Ibid., 133. "In Carpzov, technical homiletics not only reached its zenith but developed to the point of absurdity."

4. *De Impedimentis* appears in the volume of Spener's *Hauptschriften* edited by Paul Grünberg (Gotha, 1889), 184-231. Translations into English of Pietists' works are rare, but a selection from this treatise, which unfortunately does not include the passage under consideration, appears in *Pietists: Selected Writings*, ed. with intro. Peter C. Erb and pref. F. Ernest Stoeffler, Classics of Western Spirituality (New York: Paulist, 1983), 65-70. The only major biography of Spener in English is K. James Stein, *Philip Jakob Spener: Pietist Patriarch* (Chicago: Covenant, 1986). For the

Carpzov incident, see pp. 117-18. For more information on the incident, I am indebted to Professor Stein for his letter to me of June 2, 1992, and for his providing me with the relevant part of Hans Leube's article, *"Die Entscheidungsjahre der Reformbestrebungen Ph. J. Spener's," Neue Kirchliche Zeitschrift,* 35:155-74.

5. Brilioth, *A Brief History of Preaching,* 131.

6. This short work, which Spener wrote as a preface to a new edition of the *Postil* of Johann Arndt, is translated in Erb, *Pietists,* 31-49. The passage quoted appears on p. 47.

7. Stein, *Philip Jakob Spener,* 78-79. When Spener moved from Frankfurt to Dresden, he began preaching on the Gospels again (p. 112), but in Berlin he interrupted preaching from the lectionary to do series of sermons on topics such as new birth and its results (p. 128).

8. *Pia Desideria* in Erb, *Pietists,* 47.

9. Stein, *Philip Jakob Spener,* 157.

10. Ibid., 169.

11. Quoted in ibid., 175.

12. The quoted words come from a description of Spener's preaching by his contemporary, Gottfried Olearius, quoted ibid., 268. This paragraph is based on pp. 267-69. For a sample of one of Spener's sermons (admittedly shortened drastically), see Erb, *Pietists,* 83-96.

13. This list may be seen in Erb, *Pietists,* 163-64.

14. The portion of his autobiography recounting this experience is translated in Erb, *Pietists,* 99-107.

15. "A Letter to a Friend Concerning the Most Useful Way of Preaching" appears in a modernization of a 1754 translation in Erb, *Pietists,* pp. 117-27. Hereafter, references to this work will be given parenthetically in the text by page number alone.

16. Several of Francke's sermons appear in Erb, *Pietists,* 128-62.

17. Also called Moravians.

18. For the identification of the views of the Moravians with those of Madame Guyon, see Wesley's *Journal* for June 5, 1742.

19. Biographical sketches of Zinzendorf can be found in, among others, Kurt Aland, *A History of Christianity,* trans. James L. Schaaf (Philadelphia: Fortress, 1986), 2:255-59, and Erb, *Pietists,* 19-24. A selection of his writings, including his "Litany of the Life, Suffering, and Death of Jesus Christ" appears in ibid., 289-330. Zinzendorf's encounter with John Wesley is treated and documented in Outler, *John Wesley,* pp. 353-76.

SCRIPTURE INDEX

SUBJECT INDEX

Kennedy, George, 598
  on Chrysostom, 81, 82-83
  on Gregory Nazianzus, 61, 62, 63, 69n36
Kennedy, John F., 732, 733
Kennedy, Minnie, 575
Kenyon, Helen, 765
kephalaia, 13
kerygma, 6, 66
Kienzle, Beverly Mayne, 201
Kierkegaard, Søren, 680, 802, 805-6
King Philip's War, 477
King, Henry, 377
King, Martin Luther, Jr., 703-10, 715, 716, 718, 721, 724, 725, 731, 732, 736, 831
"Kingdom of God in the Parables of Jesus, The" (Rauschenbusch), 652-53
"Kingship of Christ, The" (Rauschenbusch), 653
Kingsley, Charles, 603, 610, 614, 616
Kinney, Anthony, 254
Kirkliche Dogmatik (Barth), 681
Kittel, Gerhard, 679
Klingshirn, William E., 135
Knights Templar, 186, 195, 369
knowledge
  of faith, 321-22
  sociology of, 192, 493
Knox, John, 353
Knox, Ronald, 439-40, 448
Koenker, Ernest B., 691
Koheleth, 274-75
konoi topoi, 708
Korean War, 736
Kwant, Remey, 807

"Labor and Capital" (Gladden), 651
Lafayette, Bernard, 704
Lainez, James, 333
Langton, Stephen, 207-8n91, 225
language
  abuse of, 766-67
  biblical, 184
  contempt for, 800
"Large Minutes" (Wesley), 445
LaRue, Cleophus J., 544, 552
"last of the Fathers," 373
Last Judgment, 165, 231
Last Supper, site of, 88
Latimer, Hugh, 354-55, 360-63, 368, 379, 444, 451
Latimer, Thomas, 264n43
Latin Vulgate, 43-44, 108

latitudinarianism, 353, 403-4, 405, 432, 591
Laud, William, 353, 377, 602, 836
Laudianism, 395
Lauds, 184
Lausanne, Henry of, 187
Lawless, Elaine J., 578-80, 762-64
Lawrence, Saint, 129
Lawrence, William B., 664-65
Lawson, James, 704
Lazarus, 295-96, 818
"Learned Discourse on Justification" (Hooker), 369
"Learned Sermon on the Nature of Pride" (Hooker), 369
Lebmeister, 245
Leclercq, Jean, 130, 185, 190, 192, 193, 197
lectio continua, 259, 279, 791-92, 832
lectio divina, 160, 184, 188, 189
lectures, sacred, 333
Lectures on the Doctrine of Justification (Newman), 604
Lectures and Essays on University Subjects (Newman), 604
Lectures to My Students (Spurgeon), 457, 459, 460
Lectures on Revivals of Religion (Finney), 511, 512, 520
Lectures to Young Men (Beecher), 635
lectures, grammarian's, 40
Lee, Ann, 563
Lee, Bernard, 704
Lee, Jarena, 565-66, 567
Lee, Robert E., 655
Lefèvre d'Étaples, Jacques, 309, 311
Legenda Aurea (Jacobus de Voraigne), 229
legislative speech. *See* deliberative speech
Leibniz, Gottfried, 410
Leipzig Disputation, 299
Leo the Great, 127-31, 148-49, 160
Leo X, 285
Leo XIII, 148, 603
Leonidas, 33
Les Ordonnances ecclésiastiques de l'Église de Genève, 312
Lesmeister, 245
Lessenich, Rolf, 400
Lessing, Gotthold, 594, 611
"Let our rabbi teach us," 10
Letter of Aristeas, 41
"Letter to a Young Clergyman Lately Entered into Holy Orders" (Swift), 416

At the beginning of every lesson of this course you will observe this motto:

"You can do it if you BELIEVE you can!"

This sentence is based upon a great *truth* which is practically the major premise of the entire Bible teaching. Observe the emphasis which is placed upon the word *BELIEVE.* Back of this word "believe" lies the power with which you can vitalize and give life to the suggestions that you pass on to your sub-conscious mind, through the principle of Auto-suggestion, with the aid of the law of the Master Mind. Do not miss this point. You cannot afford to miss it, as it is the very beginning, the middle and the end of all the power you will ever have.

All thought is creative! However, not all thought is constructive or positive. If you think *thoughts* of misery and poverty and see no way to avoid these conditions, then your *thoughts* will create those very conditions and curse you with them. But reverse the order, and think *thoughts* of a positive, expectant nature and your *thoughts* will create those conditions.

Thought magnetizes your entire personality and *attracts to you* the outward, physical things that harmonize with the nature of your *thoughts*. This has been made clear in practically every lesson preceding this one, yet it is repeated here, and will be repeated many times more in the lessons that follow. The reason for this constant repetition is that nearly all beginners in the study of mind operation overlook the importance of this fundamental and eternal *truth*.

When you plant a *definite chief aim* in your sub-conscious mind you must fertilize it with full *belief* that *infinite intelligence* will step in and mature that

FIRST acquire patience and perseverance, then make up your mind what else you want, and you will be almost sure to get it.

purpose into reality in exact accordance with the nature of the purpose. Anything short of such *belief*
will bring you disappointment.

When you suggest a *definite chief aim* which embodies some definite desire, in your sub-conscious
mind, you must accompany it with such *faith* and
belief in the ultimate realization of that purpose that
you can actually see yourself in possession of the
object of the purpose. Conduct yourself in the exact
manner in which you would if you were already in
possession of the object of your definite purpose, from
the moment you suggest it to your sub-conscious mind.

Do not question; do not wonder if the principles
of Auto-suggestion will work; do not *doubt,* but *believe!*

Surely this point has been sufficiently emphasized
to impress upon your mind its importance. *Positive
belief* in the attainment of your *definite purpose* is the
very germ with which you fertilize the "egg of your
thought" and if you fail to give it this fertilization,
you might as well expect an unfertilized hen-egg to
produce a chicken as to expect the attainment of the
object of your *definite chief aim.*

> You never can tell what a *thought* will do
>> In bringing you hate or love;
> For thoughts are things, and their airy wings
>> Are swifter than a carrier dove.
> They follow the law of the universe,—
>> Each thought creates its kind,
> And they speed o'er the track to bring you back
>> Whatever went out from your mind.

Thoughts are things! This is a great *truth* which

when you understand it, will bring you as close to the door of that secret passage-way to knowledge, previously mentioned, as is possible for another person to bring you. When you grasp this fundamental *truth* you will soon find that door and open it.

The power to *think* as you wish to *think* is the only power over which you have absolute control.

Please read and study the foregoing sentence until you grasp its meaning. If it is within your power to control your *thoughts* the responsibility then rests upon you as to whether your *thoughts* will be of the positive or the negative type, which brings to mind one of the world's most famous poems:

> Out of the night that covers me,
>   Black as the pit from pole to pole,
> I thank whatever gods may be
>   For my unconquerable soul.
>
> In the fell clutch of circumstance
>   I have not winced or cried aloud.
> Under the bludgeonings of chance
>   My head is bloody, but unbowed.
>
> Beyond this place of wrath and tears
>   Looms but the horror of the shade,
> And yet the menace of the years
>   Finds, and shall find, me unafraid.
>
> It matters not how strait the gate,
>   How charged with punishments the scroll,
> I am the master of my fate,
>   I am the captain of my soul.
>   —*Henley*

Henley did not write this poem until after he had discovered the door to that secret passage-way which I have mentioned.

You are the "master of your fate" and the "captain of your soul," by reason of the fact that you *control your own thoughts,* and, with the aid of your *thoughts,* you may create whatever you desire.

.   .   .   .

As we approach the close of this lesson, let us pull aside the curtain that hangs over the gateway called *death* and take a look into the Great Beyond. Behold a world peopled with beings who function without the aid of physical bodies. Look closely and, whether for weal or for woe, observe that you look at a world peopled with beings of your own creation, which correspond exactly to the nature of your own *thoughts* as you expressed them before *death.* There they are, the children of your own heart and mind, patterned after the image of your own *thoughts.*

Those which were born of your hatred and envy and jealousy and selfishness and injustice toward your fellow men will not make very desirable neighbors, but you must live with them just the same, for they are your children and you cannot turn them out.

You will be unfortunate, indeed, if you find there no children which were born of love, and justice, and truth, and kindness toward others.

In the light of this allegorical suggestion, the subject of *accurate thought* takes on a new and a much more important aspect, doesn't it?

If there is a possibility that every *thought* you release during this life will step out, in the form of a living being, to greet you after *death*, then you need no further reason for guarding all your *thoughts* more carefully than you would guard the food that you feed your physical body.

I refer to this suggestion as "allegorical" for a reason that you will understand only after you shall have passed through the door of that secret passage-way to knowledge that I have heretofore mentioned.

To ask me how I know these things, before you pass through that door, would be as useless as it would be for a man who has never seen with his physical eyes to ask me what the color red looks like.

I am not urging you to accept this viewpoint. I am not even arguing its soundness. I am merely fulfilling my duty and discharging my responsibility by giving you the suggestion. You must carry it out to a point at which you can accept or reject it, in your own way, and of your own volition.

The term "accurate thought" as used in this lesson refers to *thought* which is of your own creation. Thought that comes to you from others, through either suggestion or direct statement, is not *accurate thought* within the meaning and purpose of this lesson, although it may be thought that is based upon *facts*.

I have now carried you to the apex of the pyramid of this lesson on *accurate thought*. I can take you no further. However, you have not gone the entire distance; you have but *started*. From here on you must be your own guide, but, if you have not wholly missed the great *truth* upon which the lesson is founded, you will not have difficulty in finding your own way.

Let me caution you, however, not to become discouraged if the fundamental *truth* of this lesson does not dawn upon you at first reading. It may require weeks or even months of meditation for you to comprehend fully this *truth,* but it is worth working for.

The principles laid down in the beginning of this lesson you can easily understand and accept, because they are of the most elementary nature. However, as you began to follow the chain of *thought* along toward the close of the lesson, you perhaps found yourself being carried into waters too deep for you to fathom.

Perhaps I can throw one final ray of light on the subject by reminding you that the sound of every voice, and of every note of music, and of every other nature that is being released at the time you are reading these lines is floating through the ether right where you are. To hear these sounds you need but the aid of a modern radio outfit. Without this equipment as a supplement to your own sense of hearing you are powerless to hear these sounds.

Had this same statement been made twenty years ago, you would have believed the one who made it to be insane or a fool. But you now accept the statement without question, because you know it is true.

Thought is a much higher and more perfectly organized form of energy than is mere sound; therefore, it is not beyond the bounds of reason to suppose that every *thought* now being released and every *thought* that has ever been released is also in the ether (or somewhere else) and may be interpreted by those who have the equipment with which to do it.

And, what sort of equipment is necessary? you ask.

That will be answered when you shall have passed through the door that leads to the secret passage-way

SOME men die too soon from over-eating, others die from strong drink, while still others just wither up and die because they have nothing else to do.

to knowledge. It cannot be answered before. The passage-way can be reached only through the medium of *your own thoughts*. This is one reason why all the great philosophers of the past admonished man to know himself. "Know thyself" is and has been the cry of the ages. The life of Christ was one uninterrupted promise of hope and possibility based entirely upon the knowledge which all may discover who search within their own beings.

One of the unanswerable mysteries of God's work is the fact that this great discovery is always self-discovery. The *truth* for which man is eternally searching is wrapped up in his own being; therefore, it is fruitless to search far afield in the wilderness of life or in the hearts of other men to find it. To do so brings you no nearer that which you are seeking, but takes you further away from it.

And, it may be—who knows but *you?*—that even now, as you finish this lesson, you are nearer the door that leads to the secret passage-way to knowledge than you have ever been before.

With your mastery of this lesson will come a fuller understanding of the principle referred to in the Introductory Lesson as the "Master Mind." Surely you now understand the reason for friendly co-operative alliance between two or more people. This alliance "steps up" the minds of those who participate in it, and permits them to contact their thought-power with infinite intelligence.

With this statement the entire Introductory Lesson should have a new meaning for you. This lesson has familiarized you with the main reason why you should make use of the law of the Master Mind by showing you the height to which this law may be made to carry all who understand and use it.

By this time you should understand why a few men have risen to great heights of power and fortune, while others all around them remained in poverty and want. If you do not now understand the cause for this, you will by the time you master the remaining lessons of this course.

Do not become discouraged if complete understanding of these principles does not follow your first reading of this lesson. This is the one lesson of the entire course which cannot be fully assimilated by the beginner through one reading. It will give up its rich treasures of knowledge only through thought, reflection and meditation. For this reason you are instructed to read this lesson at least four times, at intervals of one week apart.

You are also instructed to read, again, the Introductory Lesson, that you may more accurately and definitely understand the law of the Master Mind and the relationship between this law and the subjects covered by this lesson on *accurate thought.*

The Master Mind is the principle through which you may become an accurate thinker!

Is not this statement both plain and significant?

FAILURE

An After-the-Lesson Visit With the Author

The Great Success Lessons That Can Be Learned From Reverses.

AN all-wise Providence has arranged the affairs of mankind so that every person who comes into the age of reason must bear the cross of FAILURE in one form or another.

You see, in the picture at the top of this page, the heaviest and most cruel of all the crosses, POVERTY!

Hundreds of millions of people living on this earth today find it necessary to struggle under the burden of this cross in order to enjoy the three bare necessities of life, a place to sleep, something to eat and clothes to wear.

Carrying the cross of POVERTY is no joke!

But, it seems significant that the greatest and most successful men and women who ever lived found it necessary to carry this cross before they "arrived."

.   .   .   .

FAILURE is generally accepted as a curse. But few people ever understand that failure is a curse only when it is accepted as such. But few ever learn the truth that FAILURE is seldom permanent.

Go back over your own experiences for a few years and you will see that your failures generally turned out to be blessings in disguise. Failure teaches men lessons which they would never learn without it. Moreover, it teaches in a language that is universal. Among the great lessons taught by failure is that of HUMILITY.

No man may become great without feeling himself humble and insignificant when compared to the world about him and the stars above him and the harmony with which Nature does her work.

For every rich man's son who becomes a useful, constructive worker in behalf of humanity, there are ninety-nine others rendering useful service who come up through POVERTY and misery. This seems more than a coincidence!

.   .   .   .

Most people who believe themselves to be failures are not failures at all. Most conditions which people look upon as failure are nothing more than temporary defeat.

If you pity yourself and feel that you are a failure, think how much worse off you would be if you had to change places with others who have real cause for complaint.

In the city of Chicago lives a beautiful young woman. Her eyes are a light blue. Her complexion is extremely fair. She has a sweet charming voice. She is educated and cultured. Three days after graduat-

ing in one of the colleges of the East she discovered
that she had negro blood in her veins.

The man to whom she was engaged refused to
marry her. The negroes do not want her and the
whites will not associate with her. During the remainder of her life she must bear the brand of permanent FAILURE.

Remember, this is PERMANENT failure!

As this essay is being written news comes of a beautiful girl baby who was born to an unwed girl and
taken into an orphanage, there to be brought up me-
chanically, without ever knowing the influence of a
mother's love. All through life this unfortunate child
must bear the brunt of another's mistake which can
never be corrected.

How fortunate are YOU, no matter what may be
your imaginary failures, that you are not this child.

If you have a strong body and a sound mind you
have much for which you ought to be thankful. Millions of people all about you have no such blessings.

.   .   .   .

Careful analysis of one hundred men and women
whom the world has accepted as being "great" shows
that they were compelled to undergo hardship and
temporary defeat and failure such as YOU probably
have never known and never will know.

Woodrow Wilson went to his grave altogether too
soon, the victim of cruel slander and disappointment,
believing, no doubt, that he was a FAILURE. TIME,
the great miracle worker that rights all wrongs and
turns failure into success, will place the name of

Woodrow Wilson at the top of the page of the really great.

Few now living have the vision to see that out of Wilson's "FAILURE" will come, eventually, such a powerful demand for universal peace that war will be an impossibility.

Lincoln died without knowing that his "FAILURE" gave sound foundation to the greatest nation on this earth.

Columbus died, a prisoner in chains, without ever knowing that his "FAILURE" meant the discovery of the great nation which Lincoln and Wilson helped to preserve, with their "FAILURES."

Do not use the word FAILURE carelessly.

Remember, carrying a burdensome cross temporarily is not FAILURE. If you have the real seed of success within you, a little adversity and temporary defeat will only serve to nuture that seed and cause it to burst forth into maturity.

When Divine Intelligence wants a great man or woman to render some needed service in the world, the fortunate one is tested out through some form of FAILURE. If you are undergoing what you believe to be failure, have patience; you may be passing through your testing time.

No capable executive would select, as his lieutenants, those whom he had not tested for reliability, loyalty, perseverance and other essential qualities.

Responsibility, and all that goes with it in the way of remuneration, always gravitates to the person who will not accept temporary defeat as permanent failure.

"The test of a man is the fight he makes,
  The grit that he daily shows;
The way he stands on his feet and takes
  Fate's numerous bumps and blows,
A coward can smile when there's naught to fear,
  When nothing his progress bars;
But it takes a man to stand up and cheer
  While some other fellow stars.

"It isn't the victory, after all,
  But the fight that a brother makes;
The man who, driven against the wall,
  Still stands up erect and takes
The blows of fate with his head held high:
  Bleeding, and bruised, and pale,
Is the man who'll win in the by and by,
  For he isn't afraid to fail.

"It's the bumps you get, and the jolts you get,
  And the shocks that your courage stands,
The hours of sorrow and vain regret,
  The prize that escapes your hands,
That test your mettle and prove your worth;
  It isn't the blows you deal,
But the blows you take on the good old earth,
  That show if your stuff is real."

Failure often places one in a position where unusual effort must be forthcoming. Many a man has wrung victory from defeat, fighting with his back to the wall, where he could not retreat.

Caesar had long wished to conquer the British. He quietly sailed his soldier-laden ships to the British island, unloaded his troops and supplies, then gave the order to burn all the ships. Calling his soldiers about him he said: "Now it is win or perish. We have no choice."

They won!   Men usually win when they make up their minds to do so.

Burn your bridges behind you and observe how well you work when you KNOW THAT YOU HAVE NO RETREAT.

A street car conductor got a leave of absence while he tried out a position in a great mercantile business. "If I do not succeed in holding my new position," he remarked to a friend, "I can always come back to the old job."

At the end of the month he was back, completely cured of all ambition to do anything except work on a street car. Had he resigned instead of asking for a leave of absence he might have made good in the new job.

.   .   .   .

The Thirteen Club movement, which is now spreading over the entire country, was born as the result of a shocking disappointment experienced by its founder. That shock was sufficient to open the mind to a broader and more comprehensive view of the needs of the age, and this discovery led to the creation of one of the most outstanding influences of this generation.

The Fifteen Laws of Success, upon which this course is based, grew out of twenty years of hardship and poverty and failure such as rarely come to one person in an entire lifetime.

Surely those of you who have followed this series of lessons from the beginning must have read between the lines and back of them a story of struggle which has meant self-discipline and self-discovery such as never would have been known without this hardship.

.   .   .   .

Study the roadway of life, in the picture at the beginning of this essay, and observe that everyone who
travels that road carries a cross.   Remember, as you
take inventory of your own burdens, that Nature's
richest gifts go to those who meet FAILURE without
flinching or whining.

Nature's ways are not easily understood.   If they
were, no one could be tested for great responsibility,
with FAILURE!

"When Nature wants to make a man,
And shake a man,
And wake a man;
When Nature wants to make a man
To do the Future's will;
When she tries with all her skill
And she yearns with all her soul
To create him large and whole . . .
With what cunning she prepares him!
How she goads and never spares him!
How she whets him, and she frets him,
And in poverty begets him. . . .
How she often disappoints
How she often anoints,
With what wisdom she will hide him,
Never minding what betide him
Though his genius sob with slighting
And his pride may not forget!
Bids him struggle harder yet.
Makes him lonely
So that only
God's high messages shall reach him,
So that she may surely teach him
What the Hierarchy planned.

Though he may not understand
Gives him passions to command.
How remorselessly she spurs him
With terrific ardor stirs' him
When she poignantly prefers him!

*   *   *

Lo, the crisis!   Lo, the shout
That must call the leader out.
When the people need salvation
Doth he come to lead the nation. . . .
Then doth Nature show her plan
When the world has found—A MAN!"

There is no FAILURE.   That which looks to be
failure is usually nothing but temporary defeat.   Make
sure that you do not accept it as PERMANENT!

Lesson Twelve

CONCENTRATION

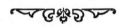

THERE is a sure way to avoid criticism: be nothing and do nothing. Get a job as street sweeper and kill off ambition. The remedy never fails.

"You Can Do It if You Believe You Can!"

 HIS lesson occupies a key-stone position in this course, for the reason that the psychological law upon which it is based is of vital importance to every other lesson of the course.

Let us define the word *concentration,* as it is here used, as follows:

"Concentration is the act of focusing the mind upon a given desire until ways and means for its realization have been worked out and successfully put into operation."

Two important laws enter into the act of *concentrating* the mind on a given *desire.* One is the law of *Auto-suggestion* and the other is the law of *habit.* The former having been fully described in a previous lesson of this course, we will now briefly describe the law of *habit.*

Habit grows out of environment—out of doing the same thing in the same way over and over again—out of repetition—out of thinking the same thoughts over and over—and, when once formed, it resembles a cement block that has hardened in the mold—in that it is hard to break.

Habit is the basis of all memory training, a fact which you may easily demonstrate in remembering the name of a person whom you have just met, by repeating that name over and over until you have fixed it permanently and plainly in your mind.

"The force of education is so great that we may mold the minds and manners of the young into whatever shape we please and give the impressions of such *habits* as shall ever afterwards remain."—Atterbury.

Except on rare occasions when the mind rises above environment, the human mind draws the material out of which *thought* is created, from the surrounding environment, and *habit* crystallizes this thought into a permanent fixture and stores it away in the subconscious mind where it becomes a vital part of our personality which silently influences our actions, forms our prejudices and our biases, and controls our opinions.

A great philosopher had in mind the power of *habit* when he said: "We first endure, then pity, and finally embrace," in speaking of the manner in which honest men come to indulge in crime.

Habit may be likened to the grooves on a phonograph record, while the mind may be likened to the needle point that fits into that groove. When any habit has been well formed (by repetition of thought or action) the mind attaches itself to and follows that habit as closely as the phonograph needle follows the groove in the wax record, no matter what may be the nature of that habit.

We begin to see, therefore, the importance of selecting our environment with the greatest of care, because environment is the mental feeding ground out of which the food that goes into our minds is extracted.

Environment very largely supplies the food and materials out of which we create *thought*, and *habit* crystallizes these into permanency. You of course understand that "environment" is the sum total of sources through which you are influenced by and through the aid of the five senses of seeing, hearing, smelling, tasting and feeling.

"Habit is force which is generally recognized by the average thinking person, but which is commonly viewed in its adverse aspect to the exclusion of its favorable phase. It has been well said that all men are 'the creatures of habit,' and that 'habit is a cable; we weave a thread of it each day and it becomes so strong that we cannot break it.'

"If it be true that habit becomes a cruel tyrant, ruling and compelling men against their will, desire, and inclination—and this is true in many cases—the question naturally arises in the thinking mind whether this mighty force cannot be harnessed and controlled in the service of men, just as have other forces of Nature. If this result can be accomplished, then man may master habit and set it to work, instead of being a slave to it and serving it faithfully though complaining. And the modern psychologists tell us in no uncertain tones that habit may certainly be thus mastered, harnessed and set to work, instead of being allowed to dominate one's actions and character. And thousands of people have applied this new knowledge and have turned the force of habit into new channels, and have compelled it to work their machinery of action, instead of being allowed to run to waste, or else permitted to sweep away the structures that men have erected with care and expense, or to destroy fertile mental fields.

"A habit is a 'mental path' over which our actions have traveled for some time, each passing making the path a little deeper and a little wider. If you have to walk over a field or through a forest, you know how natural it is for you to choose the clearest path in preference to the less worn ones, and greatly in preference to stepping out across the field or through the woods and making a new path. And the line of mental action is precisely the same. It is movement along the lines of least resistance—passage over the well-worn path. Habits are created by repetition and are formed in accordance to a natural law, observable in all animate things and some would say in inanimate things as well. As an instance of the latter, it is pointed out that a piece of paper once folded in a certain way will fold along the same lines the next time. And all users of sewing machines, or other delicate pieces of machinery, know that as a machine or instrument is once 'broken in' so will it tend to run thereafter. The same law is also observable in the case of musical instruments. Clothing or gloves form into creases according to the person using them, and these creases once formed will always be in effect, notwithstanding repeated pressings. Rivers and streams of water cut their courses through the land, and thereafter flow along the habit-course. The law is in operation everywhere.

"These illustrations will help you to form the idea

of the nature of habit, and will aid you in forming new mental paths—new mental creases. And—remember this always—the best (and one might say the only) way in which old habits may be removed is to form new habits to counteract and replace the undesirable ones. Form new mental paths over which to travel, and the old ones will soon become less distinct and in time will practically fill up from disuse. Every time you travel over the path of the desirable mental habit, you make the path deeper and wider, and make it so much easier to travel it thereafter. This mental path-making is a very important thing, and I cannot urge upon you too strongly the injunction to start to work making the desirable mental paths over which you wish to travel. Practice, practice, practice—be a good path-maker."

The following are the rules of procedure through which you may form the habits you desire:

First: At the beginning of the formation of a new habit put force and enthusiasm into your expression. Feel what you think. Remember that you are taking the first steps toward making the new mental path; that it is much harder at first than it will be afterwards. Make the path as clear and as deep as you can, at the beginning, so that you can readily see it the next time you wish to follow it.

Second: Keep your attention firmly *concentrated* on the new path-building, and keep your mind away from the old paths, lest you incline toward them. Forget all about the old paths, and concern yourself only with the new ones that you are building to order.

Third: Travel over your newly made paths as often as possible. Make opportunities for doing so,

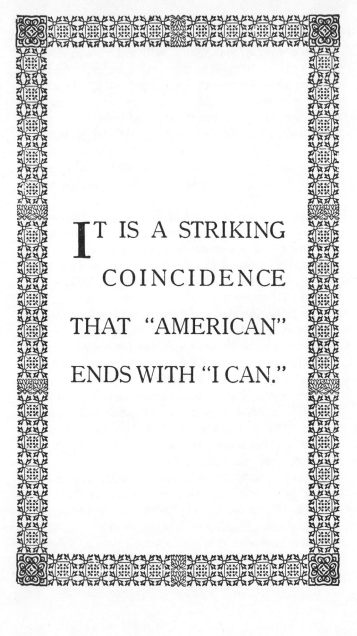

IT IS A STRIKING
COINCIDENCE
THAT "AMERICAN"
ENDS WITH "I CAN."

without waiting for them to arise through luck or chance. The oftener you go over the new paths the sooner will they become well worn and easily traveled. Create plans for passing over these new habit-paths, at the very start.

Fourth: Resist the temptation to travel over the older, easier paths that you have been using in the past. Every time you resist a temptation, the stronger do you become, and the easier will it be for you to do so the next time. But every time you yield to the temptation, the easier does it become to yield again, and the more difficult it becomes to resist the next time. You will have a fight on at the start, and this is the critical time. Prove your determination, persistency and will-power now, at the very beginning.

Fifth: Be sure that you have mapped out the right path, as your *definite chief aim,* and then go ahead without fear and without allowing yourself to doubt. "Place your hand upon the plow, and look not backward." Select your goal, then make good, deep, wide mental paths leading straight to it.

As you have already observed, there is a close relationship between *habit* and *Auto-suggestion* (self-suggestion). Through habit, an act repeatedly performed in the same manner has a tendency to become permanent, and eventually we come to perform the act automatically or unconsciously. In playing a piano, for example, the artist can play a familiar piece while his or her conscious mind is on some other subject.

Auto-suggestion is the tool with which we dig a mental path; Concentration is the hand that holds that tool; and Habit is the map or blueprint which the

mental path follows. An idea or desire, to be transformed into terms of action or physical reality, must
be held in the conscious mind *faithfully* and *persistently* until *habit* begins to give it permanent form.

Let us turn our attention, now, to *environment*.

As we have already seen, we absorb the material
for thought from our surrounding environment. The
term "environment" covers a very broad field. It
consists of the books we read, the people with whom
we associate, the community in which we live, the
nature of the work in which we are engaged, the
country or nation in which we reside, the clothes we
wear, the songs we sing, and, most important of all,
*the religious and intellectual training we receive prior
to the age of fourteen years.*

The purpose of analyzing the subject of *environment* is to show its direct relationship to the personality we are developing, and the importance of so
guarding it that its influence will give us the materials
out of which we may attain our *definite chief aim* in
life.

The mind feeds upon that which we supply it, or
that which is forced upon it, through our *environment;*
therefore, let us select our environment, as far as possible, with the object of supplying the mind with
suitable material out of which to carry on its work of
attaining our *definite chief aim.*

If *your* environment is not to your liking, change
it!

The first step is to create in your own mind an
exact, clear and well rounded out picture of the environment in which you believe you could best attain
your *definite chief aim,* and then *concentrate* your

mind upon this picture until you transform it into reality.

In Lesson Two, of this course, you learned that the first step you must take, in the accomplishment of any *desire,* is to create in your mind a clear, well defined picture of that which you intend to accomplish. This is the first principle to be observed in your plans for the achievement of *success,* and if you fail or neglect to observe it, you cannot succeed, except by chance.

Your daily associates constitute one of the most important and influential parts of your environment, and may work for your progress or your retrogression, according to the nature of those associates. As far as possible, you should select as your most *intimate* daily associates those who are in sympathy with your aims and ideals—especially those represented by your *definite chief aim*—and whose mental attitude inspires you with enthusiasm, self-confidence, determination and ambition.

Remember that every word spoken within your hearing, every sight that reaches your eyes, and every sense impression that you receive through any of the five senses, influences your thought as surely as the sun rises in the east and sets in the west. This being true, can you not see the importance of controlling, as far as possible, the environment in which you live and work? Can you not see the importance of reading books that deal with subjects which are directly related to your *definite chief aim?* Can you not see the importance of talking with people who are in sympathy with your aims, and, who will encourage you and spur you on toward their attainment?

We are living in what we call a "twentieth century

civilization." The leading scientists of the world are agreed that Nature has been millions of years in creating, through the process of evolution, our present civilized environment.

How many hundreds of centuries the so-called Indians had lived upon the North American continent, without any appreciable advance toward modern civilization, as we understand it, we have no way of ascertaining. Their environment was the wilderness, and they made no attempt whatsoever to change or improve that environment; the change took place only after new races from afar came over and *forced upon them the environment of progressive civilization in which we are living today.*

Observe what has happened within the short period of *three centuries.* Hunting grounds have been transformed into great cities, and the Indian has taken on education and culture, in many instances, that equal the accomplishment of his white brothers. (In Lesson Fifteen, we discuss the effects of environment from a worldwide viewpoint, and describe, in detail, the principle of *social heredity* which is the chief source through which the effects of environment may be imposed upon the minds of the young.)

The clothes you wear influence you; therefore, they constitute a part of your environment. Soiled or shabby clothes depress you and lower your self-confidence, while clean clothes, of an appropriate style, have just the opposite effect.

It is a well known fact that an observant person can accurately analyze a man by seeing his work-bench, desk or other place of employment. A well organized desk indicates a well organized brain. Show me the merchant's stock of goods and I will tell you whether he has an organized or disorganized brain, as there is a close relationship between one's mental attitude and one's physical environment.

The effects of environment so vitally influence those who work in factories, stores and offices, that employers are gradually realizing the importance of creating an environment that inspires and encourages the workers.

One unusually progressive laundryman, in the city of Chicago, has plainly outdone his competitors, by installing in his work-room a player-piano, in charge of a neatly dressed young woman who keeps it going during the working hours. His laundrywomen are dressed in white uniforms, and there is no evidence about the place that work is drudgery. Through the aid of this pleasant environment, this laundryman turns out more work, earns more profits, and pays better wages than his competitors can pay.

This brings us to an appropriate place at which to describe the method through which *you* may apply the principles directly and indirectly related to the subject of *concentration*.

Let us call this method the—

MAGIC KEY TO SUCCESS!

In presenting you with this "Magic Key" let me first explain that it is no invention or discovery of mine.

It is the same key that is used, in one form or another, by the followers of New Thought and all other sects which are founded upon the positive philosophy of optimism.

This Magic Key constitutes an irresistible power which all who will may use.

THE person who receives no pay for his services except that which comes in the pay envelope is underpaid, no matter how much money that envelope may contain.

It will unlock the door to riches!

It will unlock the door to fame!

And, in many instances, it will unlock the door to physical health.

It will unlock the door to education and let you into the storehouse of all your latent ability. It will act as a pass-key to any position in life for which you are fitted.

Through the aid of this Magic Key we have un‹ locked the secret doors to all of the world's great inventions.

Through its magic powers all of our great geniuses of the past have been developed.

Suppose you are a laborer, in a menial position, and desire a better place in life. The Magic Key will help you attain it! Through its use Carnegie, Rockefeller. Hill, Harriman, Morgan and scores of others of their type have accumulated vast fortunes of material wealth.

It will unlock prison doors and turn human derelicts into useful, trustworthy human beings. It will turn failure into success and misery into happiness.

You ask—"What is this Magic Key?"

And I answer with one word—*concentration!*

Now let me define *concentration* in the sense that it is here used. First, I wish it to be clearly understood that I have no reference to occultism, although I will admit that all the scientists of the world have failed to explain the strange phenomena produced through the aid of *concentration*.

Concentration, in the sense in which it is here used, means the ability, through fixed habit and practice, to keep your mind on one subject until you have thoroughly familiarized yourself with that subject and mastered it. It means the ability to *control your attention and focus it on a given problem until you have solved it.*

It means the ability to throw off the effects of habits which you wish to discard, and the power to build new habits that are more to your liking. It means complete *self-mastery.*

Stating it in another way, *concentration* is the ability to *think* as you wish to think; the ability to control your thoughts and direct them to a *definite* end; and the ability to organize your knowledge into a plan of action that is sound and workable.

You can readily see that in *concentrating* your mind upon your *definite chief aim* in life, you must cover many closely related subjects which blend into each other and complete the main subject upon which you are concentrating.

Ambition and *desire* are the chief factors which enter into the act of successful *concentration*. Without these factors the Magic Key is useless, and the main reason why so few people make use of this key is that most people lack *ambition,* and *desire nothing in particular.*

Desire whatever you may, and if your desire is within reason and if it is strong enough the Magic Key of *concentration* will help you attain it. There are learned men of science who would have us believe that the wonderful power of prayer operates through the principle of *concentration* on the attainment of a *deeply seated desire.*

Nothing was ever created by a human being which was not first created in the imagination, through *desire,* and then transformed into reality through *concentration*.

Now, let us put the Magic Key to a test, through the aid of a definite formula.

First, you must put your foot on the neck of skepticism and doubt! No unbeliever ever enjoyed the benefits of this Magic Key. You must believe in the test that you are about to make.

We will assume that you have thought something about becoming a successful writer, or a powerful public speaker, or a successful business executive, or an able financier. We will take public speaking as the subject of this test, but remember that you must follow instructions to the letter.

Take a plain sheet of paper, ordinary letter size, and write on it the following:

I am going to become a powerful public speaker because this will enable me to render the world useful service that is needed—and because it will yield me a financial return that will provide me with the necessary material things of life.

I will concentrate my mind upon this desire for ten minutes daily, just before retiring at night and just after arising in the morning, for the purpose of determining just how I shall proceed to transform it into reality.

I know that I can become a powerful and magnetic speaker, therefore I will permit nothing to interfere with my doing so.

(*Signed*)......................

Sign this pledge, then proceed to do as you have

pledged your word that you would do. Keep it up until the desired results have been realized.

Now, when you come to do your *concentrating,* this is the way to go about it: Look ahead one, three, five or even ten years, and see yourself as the most power-ful speaker of your time. See, in your imagination, an appropriate income. See yourself in your own home that you have purchased with the proceeds from your efforts as a speaker or lecturer. See yourself in pos-session of a nice bank account as a reserve for old age. See yourself as a person of influence, due to your great ability as a public speaker. See yourself engaged in a life-calling in which you will not fear the loss of your position.

Paint this picture clearly, through the powers of your imagination, and lo! it will soon become trans-formed into a beautiful picture of deeply seated *desire.* Use this *desire* as the chief object of your *concentra-tion* and observe what happens.

You now have the secret of the Magic Key!

Do not underestimate the power of the Magic Key because it did not come to you clothed in mysticism, or because it is described in language which all who will may understand. All great truths are simple in final analysis, and easily understood; if they are not they are not *great* truths.

Use this Magic Key with intelligence, and only for the attainment of worthy ends, and it will bring you enduring happiness and success. Forget the mistakes you have made and the failures you have experienced. Quit living in the past, for do you not know that your yesterdays never return? Start all over again, if your previous efforts have not turned out well, and make the next five or ten years tell a story of success that will satisfy your most lofty ambitions.

Make a name for yourself and render the world a great service, through *ambition, desire* and *concentrated effort!*

You can do it if you BELIEVE you can!

Thus endeth the Magic Key.

.   .   .   .

The presence of any idea or thought in your consciousness tends to produce an "associated" feeling and to urge you to appropriate or corresponding action. Hold a deeply seated *desire* in your consciousness, through the principle of *concentration,* and if you do it with full faith in its realization your act attracts to your aid powers which the entire scientific world has failed to understand or explain with a reasonable hypothesis.

When you become familiar with the powers of *concentration* you will then understand the reason for choosing a *definite chief aim* as the first step in the attainment of enduring success.

Concentrate your mind upon the attainment of the object of a deeply seated *desire* and very soon you will become a lode-stone that attracts, through the aid of forces which no man can explain, the necessary material counterparts of that *desire,* a statement of fact which paves the way for the description of a principle which constitutes the most important part of this lesson, if not, in fact, the most important part of the entire course, viz.:

When two or more people ally themselves, in a spirit of perfect harmony, for the purpose of attaining a

YOU have a tremen-
dous advantage over
the person who slanders
you or does you a wilful
injustice; you have it
within your power to
FORGIVE that person.

definite end, if that alliance is faithfully observed by
all of whom it is composed, the alliance brings, to each
of those of whom it is composed, power that is super-
human and seemingly irresistible in nature.

Back of the foregoing statement is a law, the nature
of which science has not yet determined, and it is this
law that I have had in mind in connection with my
repeated statements concerning the power of *organized*
effort which you will notice throughout this course.

In chemistry we learn that two or more elements
may be so compounded that the result is something
entirely different in nature, from any of the individual
elements.   For example, ordinary water, known in
chemistry under the formula of H_2O, is a compound
consisting of two atoms of hydrogen and one atom of
oxygen, *but water is neither hydrogen nor oxygen.*
This "marrying" of elements creates *an entirely dif-*
ferent substance from that of either of its component
parts.

The same law through which this transformation of
physical elements takes place may be responsible for
the seemingly superhuman powers resulting from the
alliance of two or more people, *in a perfect state of*
harmony and understanding, for the attainment of a
given end.

This world, and all matter of which the other planets
consist, is made up of electrons (an electron being the
smallest known analyzable unit of matter, and resembling, in nature, what we call electricity, or a form of
energy).   On the other hand, *thought,* and that which
we call the "mind," is also a form of energy; in fact it
is the highest form of energy known.   Thought, in

other words, is *organized energy,* and it is not improbable that *thought* is exactly the same sort of energy as that which we generate with an electric dynamo, although of a much more highly *organized* form.

Now, if all matter, in final analysis, consists of groups of electrons, which are nothing more than a form of energy which we call electricity, and if the mind is nothing but a form of highly organized electricity, do you not see how it is possible that the laws which affect matter may also govern the mind?

And if combining two or more elements of matter, in the proper proportion and under the right conditions, will produce something entirely different from those original elements (as in the case of H_2O), do you not see how it is possible so to combine the energy of two or more minds that the result will be a sort of composite mind that is totally different from the individual minds of which it consists?

You have undoubtedly noticed the manner in which you are influenced while in the presence of other people. Some people inspire you with optimism and enthusiasm. Their very presence seems to stimulate your own mind to greater action, and, this not only "seems" to be true, but it *is true.* You have noticed that the presence of others had a tendency to lower your vitality and depress you; a tendency which I can assure you was very *real!*

What, do you imagine, could be the cause of these changes that come over us when we come within a certain range of other people, unless it is the change resulting from the blending or combining of their minds with our own, through the operation of a law that is not very well understood, but resembles (if, in fact, it is not the same law) the law through which the combining of two atoms of hydrogen and one atom of oxygen produces water.

I have no scientific basis for this hypothesis, but I have given it many years of serious thought and always I come to the conclusion that it is at least a sound hypothesis, although I have no possible way, as yet, of reducing it to a provable hypothesis.

You need no proof, however, that the presence of some people inspires you, while the presence of others depresses you, as you know this to be a fact. Now it stands to reason that the person who inspires you and arouses your mind to a state of greater activity gives you more power to achieve, while the person whose presence depresses you and lowers your vitality, or causes you to *dissipate* it in useless, disorganized thought, has just the opposite effect on you. You can understand this much without the aid of a hypothesis and without further proof than that which you have experienced time after time.

Come back, now, to the original statement that:

"When two or more people ally themselves, *in a spirit of perfect harmony,* for the purpose of attaining a definite end, if that alliance is *faithfully observed by all of whom it is composed,* the alliance brings, to each of those of whom it is composed, power that is super-human and seemingly irresistible in nature."

Study, closely, the emphasized part of the foregoing statement, for there you will find the "mental formula" which, if not faithfully observed, destroys the effect of the whole.

One atom of hydrogen combined with one atom of

oxygen will not produce water, nor will an alliance in name only, that is not accompanied by *"a spirit of perfect harmony"* (between those forming the alliance), produce *"power that is superhuman and seemingly irresistible in nature."*

I have in mind a family of mountain-folk who, for more than six generations, have lived in the mountainous section of Kentucky. Generation after generation of this family came and went without any noticeable improvement of a mental nature, each generation following in the footsteps of its ancestors. They made their living from the soil, and as far as they knew, or cared, the universe consisted of a little spot of territory known as Letcher County. They married strictly in their own "set," and in their own community.

Finally, one of the members of this family strayed away from the flock, so to speak, and married a well educated and highly cultured woman from the neighbor-state of Virginia. This woman was one of those types of ambitious people who had learned that the universe extended beyond the border line of Letcher County, and covered, at least, the whole of the southern states. She had heard of chemistry, and of botany, and of biology, and of pathology, and of psychology, and of many other subjects that were of importance in the field of education. When her children began to come along to the age of understanding, she talked to them of these subjects; and they, in turn, began to show a keen interest in them.

One of her children is now the president of a great educational institution, where most of these subjects, and many others of equal importance, are taught. Another one of them is a prominent lawyer, while still another is a successful physician.

Her husband (thanks to the influence of her mind) is a well known dental surgeon, and the first of his family, for six generations, to break away from the traditions by which the family had been bound.

The blending of her mind with his *gave him the needed stimulus to spur him on and inspired him with ambition such as he would never have known without her influence.*

For many years I have been studying the biographies of those whom the world calls *great,* and it seems to me more than a mere coincidence that in every instance where the facts were available the person who was really responsible for the *greatness* was in the background, behind the scenes, and seldom heard of by the hero-worshiping public. Not infrequently is this "hidden power" a patient little wife who has inspired her husband and urged him on to great achievement, as was true in the case I have just described.

Henry Ford is one of the modern miracles of this age, and I doubt that this country, or any other, ever produced an industrial genius of his equal. If the *facts* were known (and perhaps they are known) they might trace the cause of Mr. Ford's phenomenal achievements to a woman of whom the public hears but little—*his wife!*

We read of Ford's achievements and of his enormous income and imagine him to be blessed with matchless ability; and he is—ability of which the world would never have heard had it not been for the modifying influence of his wife, who has co-operated with

DEFEAT, like a headache, warns us that something has gone wrong. If we are intelligent we look for the cause and profit by the experience.

him, during all the years of his struggle, *"in a spirit of perfect harmony, for the purpose of attaining a definite end."*

I have in mind another genius who is well known to the entire civilized world, Thomas A. Edison. His inventions are so well known that they need not be named. Every time you press a button and turn on an electric light, or hear a phonograph playing, you should think of Edison, for it was he who perfected both the incandescent light and the modern phonograph. Every time you see a moving picture you should think of Edison, for it was his genius, more than that of any other person, who made this great enterprise possible.

But, as in the case of Henry Ford, back of Mr. Edison stands one of the most remarkable women in America—his wife! No one outside of the Edison family, and perhaps a very few intimate personal friends of theirs, knows to what extent her influence has made Edison's achievements possible. Mrs. Edison once told me that Mr. Edison's outstanding quality, the one which, above all others, was his greatest asset, was that of—

Concentration!

When Mr. Edison starts a line of experiment or research or investigation; he never "lets go" until he either finds that for which he is looking or exhausts every possible effort to do so.

Back of Mr. Edison stand two great powers; one is *concentration* and the other is Mrs. Edison!

Night after night Mr. Edison has worked with such *enthusiasm* that he required but three or four hours of sleep. (Observe what was said about the sustaining effects of *enthusiasm* in Lesson Seven of this course.)

Plant a tiny apple seed in the right sort of soil, at the right time of the year, and gradually it will burst forth into a tiny sprig, and then it will expand and grow into an apple tree. That tree does not come from the soil, nor does it come from the elements of the air, but *from both of these sources,* and the man has not yet lived who could explain the law that attracts from the air and the soil the combination of cells of which that apple tree consists.

The tree does not come out of the tiny apple seed, but, *that seed is the beginning of the tree.*

When two or more people ally themselves, *"in a spirit of perfect harmony, for the purpose of attaining a definite end,"* the *end,* itself, or the *desire* back of that end, may be likened to the apple seed, and the blending of the forces of energy of the two or more minds may be likened to the air and the soil out of which come the elements that form the material objects of that *desire.*

The *power* back of the attraction and combination of these forces of the mind can no more be explained than can the power back of the combination of elements out of which an apple tree "grows."

But the all-important thing is that an apple tree will "grow" from a seed thus properly planted, and great *achievement* will follow the systematic blending of two or more minds with a definite object in view.

In Lesson Thirteen you will see this principle of allied effort carried to proportions which almost stagger the imagination of all who have not trained themselves to think in terms of *organized thought!*

This course, itself, is a very concrete illustration of

the principle underlying that which we have termed *organized effort,* but you will observe that it requires the entire sixteen lessons to complete the description of this principle.   Omit a single one of the sixteen lessons and the omission would affect the whole as the removal of one link would affect the whole of a chain.

As I have already stated in many different ways, and for the purpose of emphasis, I now repeat: there is a well founded hypothesis that when one concentrates one's mind upon a given subject, facts of a nature that is closely related to that subject will "pour" in from every conceivable source.   The theory is that a deeply seated *desire,* when once planted in the right sort of "mental soil," serves as a center of attraction or magnet that attracts to it everything that har-- monizes with the nature of the *desire.*

Dr. Elmer Gates, of Washington, D. C., is perhaps one of the most competent psychologists in the world. He is recognized both in the field of psychology and in other directly and indirectly related fields of science, throughout the world, as being a man of the highest scientific standing.

Come with me, for a moment, and study his methods!

After Dr. Gates has followed a line of investigation as far as possible through the usual channels of re-search, and has availed himself of all the recorded facts at his command, on a given subject, he then takes a pencil and a tablet and "sits" for further in-formation, by *concentrating his mind on that subject until thoughts related to it begin to FLOW IN UPON HIM.*   He writes down these thoughts, as they come

(from he knows not where). He told me that many
of his most important discoveries came through this
method. It was more than twenty years ago that I
first talked with Dr. Gates on this subject. Since that
time, through the discovery of the radio principle, we
have been provided with a reasonable hypothesis
through which to explain the results of these "sittings,"
viz.:

The ether, as we have discovered through the
modern radio apparatus, is in a constant state of
agitation. Sound waves are floating through the ether
at all times, but these waves cannot be detected, beyond a short distance from their source, except by the
aid of properly attuned instruments.

Now, it seems reasonable to suppose that *thought*,
being the most highly organized form of energy known,
is constantly sending waves through the ether, but
these waves, like those of sound, can only be detected
and correctly interpreted by a properly attuned mind.

There is no doubt that when Dr. Gates sat down in
a room and placed himself in a quiet, passive state of
mind, the dominating *thoughts* in his mind served as
a magnetic force that attracted the related or similar
thought waves of others as they passed through the
ether about him.

Taking the hypothesis just a step further, it has occurred to me many times since the discovery of the
modern radio principle, that *every thought that has
ever been released in organized form, from the mind
of any human being, is still in existence in the form of
a wave in the ether, and is constantly passing around
and around in a great endless circle: that the act of
concentrating* one's mind upon a given subject with

intensity sends out *thought waves* which reach and blend with those of a related or similar nature, thereby establishing a direct line of communication between the one doing the *concentrating* and the thoughts of a similar nature which have been previously set into motion.

Going still a step further, may it not be possible for one so to attune his mind and harmonize the rate of vibration of *thought* with the rate of vibration of the ether that all knowledge that has been accumulated through the *organized thoughts* of the past is available?

With these hypotheses in mind, go back to Lesson Two, of this course, and study Carnegie's description of the "master mind" through which he accumulated his great fortune.

When Carnegie formed an alliance between more than a score of carefully selected minds, he created, by that means of compounding mind power, one of the strongest industrial forces that the world has ever witnessed. With a few notable (and very disastrous) exceptions, the men constituting the "master mind" which Carnegie created thought and *acted* as *one!*

And, that "master mind" (composed of many individual minds) was *concentrated* upon a single purpose, the nature of which is familiar to everyone who knew Mr. Carnegie; *particularly those who were competing with him in the steel business.*

If you have followed Henry Ford's record, even slightly, you undoubtedly have observed that *concentrated effort* has been one of the outstanding features of his career. Nearly thirty years ago he adopted a policy of standardization as to the general type of

IS it not strange that the word "Boomerang" has been in the dictionary all these years without its having become generally known that a "Boomerang" is an instrument which comes back and may wound the hand that throws it?

automobile that he would build, and he consistently maintained that policy until the change in public demand forced him, in 1927, to change it.

A few years ago, I met the former chief engineer of the Ford plant, and he told me of an incident that happened during the early stages of Mr. Ford's automobile experience which very clearly points to *concentrated effort* as being one of his prominent fundamentals of economic philosophy.

On this occasion the engineers of the Ford plant had gathered in the engineering office for the purpose of discussing a proposed change in the design of the rear axle construction of the Ford automobile. Mr. Ford stood around and listened to the discussion until each man had had his "say," then he walked over to the table, tapped the drawing of the proposed axle with his finger, and said:

"Now listen! the axle we are using does the work for which it was intended, and does it well, and there's going to be no more change in that axle!"

He turned and walked away, and from that day until this the rear axle construction of the Ford automobile has remained substantially the same. It is not improbable that Mr. Ford's success in building and marketing automobiles has been due, very largely, to his policy of consistently *concentrating* his efforts back of one plan, with but one *definite purpose* in mind at a time.

A few years ago I read Edward Bok's book, The Man From Maine, which is the biography of his father-in-law, Mr. Cyrus H. K. Curtis, the owner of the Saturday Evening Post, the Ladies' Home Journal, and several other publications. All through the book

I noticed that the outstanding feature of Mr. Curtis' philosophy was that of *concentration* of effort back of a *definite purpose.*

During the early days of his ownership of the Saturday Evening Post, when he was pouring money into a losing venture by the hundreds of thousands of dollars, it required *concentrated effort* that was backed by courage such as but few men possess, to enable him to "carry on."

Read The Man From Maine. It is a splendid lesson on the subject of *concentration,* and supports, to the smallest detail, the fundamentals upon which this lesson is based.

The Saturday Evening Post is now one of the most profitable magazines in the world, but its name would have been long since forgotten had not Mr. Curtis *concentrated* his attention and his fortune on the one *definite purpose* of making it a great magazine.

.   .   .   .

We have seen what an important part *environment* and *habit* play in connection with the subject of *concentration.* We shall now discuss, briefly, a third subject which is no less related to the subject of *concentration* than are the other two, namely, *memory.*

The principles through which an accurate, unfaltering memory may be trained are few, and comparatively simple; viz.:

1. *Retention:* The receiving of a sense impression through one or more of the five senses, and the recording of this impression, in orderly fashion, in the mind. This process may be likened to the recording of a picture on the sensitized plate of a camera or kodak.

2. *Recall:*   The reviving or recalling into the conscious mind of those sense impressions which have been recorded in the sub-conscious mind. This process may be compared to the act of going through a card index and pulling out a card on which information had been previously recorded.

3. *Recognition:*   The ability to recognize a sense impression when it is called into the conscious mind, and to identify it as being a duplicate of the original impression, and to associate it with the original source from which it came when it was first recorded. This process enables us to distinguish between "memory" and "imagination."

These are the three principles that enter into the act of remembering. Now let us make application of these principles and determine how to use them effectively, which may be done as follows:

First: When you wish to be sure of your ability to recall a sense impression, such as a name, date or place, be sure to make the impression vivid by *concentrating your attention upon it* to the finest detail. An effective way to do this is to repeat, several times, that which you wish to remember. Just as a photographer must give an "exposure" proper time to record itself on the sensitized plate of the camera, so must we give the sub-conscious mind time to record properly and clearly any sense impression that we wish to be able to recall with readiness.

Second: Associate that which you wish to remember with some other object, name, place or date with which you are quite familiar, and which you can easily recall when you wish, as, for example, the name of your home town, your close friend, the date of your birth, etc., for your mind will then file away the sense impression that you wish to be able to recall, with the one that you can easily recall, so that when bringing forth one into the conscious mind it brings, also, the other one with it.

Third: Repeat that which you wish to remember, a number of times, at the same time *concentrating* your mind upon it, just as you would fix your mind on a certain hour at which you wished to arise in the morning, which, as you know, insures your awakening at that precise hour. The common failing of not being able to remember the names of other people, which most of us have, is due entirely to the fact that we do not properly record the name in the first place. When you are introduced to a person whose name you wish to be able to recall at will, repeat that name four or five times, first making sure that you understood the name correctly. If the name is similar to that of some person whom you know well, associate the two names together, thinking of both as you repeat the name of the one whose name you wish to be able to recall.

If someone gives you a letter to be mailed, look at the letter, then increase its size, in your imagination, and see it hanging over a letter-box. Fix in your mind a letter approximately the size of a door, and associate it with a letter box, and you will observe that the first letter box you pass on the street will cause you to recall that big, odd-looking letter, which you have in your pocket.

Suppose that you were introduced to a lady whose name was Elizabeth Shearer, and you wished to be able to recall her name at will. As you repeat her name associate with it a large pair of scissors, say ten feet in length, and Queen Elizabeth, and you will observe that the recalling of either the large pair of scissors or the name of Queen Elizabeth will help you recall, also, the name of Elizabeth Shearer.

If you wish to be able to remember the name of Lloyd Keith, just repeat the name several times and associate with it the name of Lloyd George and Keith's Theater, either of which you can easily recall at will.

The *law of association* is the most important feature of a well trained memory, yet it is a very simple law. All you have to do to make use of it is to record the name of that which you wish to remember with the name of that which you *can readily* remember, and the recalling of one brings with it the other.

Nearly ten years ago a friend gave me his residence telephone number, in Milwaukee, Wisconsin, and although I did not write it down I remember it today as well as I did the day he gave it to me. This is the way that I recorded it:

The number and exchange were Lakeview 2651.

At the time he gave me the number we were standing at the railroad station, in sight of Lake Michigan; therefore, I used the lake as an associated object with which to file the name of the telephone exchange. It so happened that the telephone number was made up of the age of my brother, who was 26, and my father, who was 51, therefore I associated their names with the number, thus insuring its recall. To recall the telephone exchange and number, therefore, I had only to think of Lake Michigan, my brother and my father.

An acquaintance of mine found himself to be suffering from what is ordinarily called a "wandering

D^O you see that "lucky" fellow over there who holds a "soft" position through "pull"? Let me whisper a secret in your ear—Fate is standing in wait for him just around the corner, with a a stuffed club, and it is not stuffed with cotton.

mind." He was becoming "absent-minded" and unable to remember. Let him tell you, in his own words which follow, how he overcame this handicap:

"I am fifty years old. For a decade I have been a department manager in a large factory. At first my duties were easy, then the firm had a rapid expansion of business which gave me added responsibilities. Several of the young men in my department developed unusual energy and ability—at least one of them had his eye on my job.

"I had reached the age in life when a man likes to be comfortable and, having been with the company a long time, I felt that I could safely settle back into an easy berth. The effect of this mental attitude was well nigh disastrous to my position.

"About two years ago I noticed that my power of *concentration* was weakening and my duties were becoming irksome. I neglected my correspondence until I looked with dread upon the formidable pile of letters; reports accumulated and subordinates were inconvenienced by the delay. I sat at my desk with my mind wandering elsewhere.

"Other circumstances showed plainly that my mind was not on my work; I forgot to attend an important meeting of the officers of the company. One of the clerks under me caught a bad mistake made in an estimate on a carload of goods, and, of course, saw to it that the manager learned of the incident.

"I was thoroughly alarmed at the situation! and asked for a week's vacation to think things over. I was determined to resign, or find the trouble and remedy it. A few days of earnest introspection at an out-of-the-way mountain resort convinced me that I was suffering from a plain case of mind wandering. I was lacking in *concentration;* my physical and mental activities at the desk had become desultory. I was careless and shiftless and neglectful—all because my mind was not *alertly* on the job. When I had diagnosed my case with satisfaction to myself I next sought the remedy. I needed a complete new set of *working habits,* and I made a resolve to acquire them.

"With paper and pencil I outlined a schedule to cover the working day: first, the morning mail; then, the orders to be filled; dictation; conference with subordinates and miscellaneous duties; ending with a clean desk before I left.

" *'How is habit formed?'* I asked myself mentally. 'By repetition,' came back the answer. 'But I have been doing these things over and over thousands of times,' the other fellow in me protested. 'True, but not in orderly *concentrated* fashion,' replied the echo.

"I returned to the office with mind in leash, but restless, and placed my new working schedule in force at once. I performed the same duties with the same zest and as nearly as possible at the same time every day. When my mind started to slip away I quickly brought it back.

"From a mental stimulus, created by will-power, I progressed in *habit building.* Day after day, I practiced *concentration* of thought. When I found *repetition* becoming comfortable, then I knew that I had won."

Your ability to train your memory, or to develop any desired habit, is a matter, solely, of being able to *fix your attention on a given subject until the outline of that subject has been thoroughly impressed upon the "sensitized plate" of your mind.*

Concentration, itself, is nothing but a matter of control of the *attention!*

You will observe that by reading a line of print with which you are not familiar, and which you have never seen before, and then closing your eyes, you can see that line as plainly as though you were looking at it on the printed page. In reality, you are "looking at it," not on the printed page, but on the sensitized plate of your own mind. If you try this experiment and it does not work the first time it is because you did not *concentrate your attention* on the line closely enough! Repeat the performance a few times and finally you will succeed.

If you wish to memorize poetry, for example, you can do so very quickly by training yourself to fix your *attention* on the lines so closely that you can shut your eyes and see them in your mind as plainly as you see them on the printed page.

So important is this subject of *control of attention* that I feel impelled to emphasize it in such a way that you will not pass it by lightly. I have reserved reference to this important subject until the last, as a climax to this lesson, for the reason that I consider it, by far, the most important part of the lesson.

The astounding results experienced by those who make a practice of "crystal-gazing" are due, entirely, to their ability to *fix attention* upon a given subject for an unbroken period far beyond the ordinary.

Crystal-gazing is nothing but *concentrated attention!*

I have already hinted at that which I will now state

as my belief, nameiy, that it is possible, through the aid of *concentrated attention,* for one so to attune one's mind to the vibration of the ether that all the secrets in the world of unfathomed and uncharted mental phenomena may become as open books which may be read at will.

What a thought this is to ponder over!

I am of the opinion, and not without substantial evidence to support me, that it is possible for one to develop the ability of *fixing the attention* so highly that one may "tune in" and understand that which is in the mind of any person. But this is not all, nor is it the most important part of a hypothesis at which I have arrived after many years of careful research, for I am satisfied that one may just as easily go a step further and "tune in" on the *universal mind* in which all knowledge is stored where it may be appropriated by all who master the art of coming after it.

To a highly orthodox mind these statements may seem very irrational; but, to the student (and, so far, there are but few people in the world who are more than mere students, of an elementary grade, of this subject) who has studied this subject with any appreciable degree of understanding, these hypotheses seem not only possible, but *absolutely probable.*

But put the hypothesis to a test of your own!

You can select no better subject upon which to try an experiment than that which you have selected as your *definite chief aim* in life.

Memorize your *definite chief aim* so you can repeat it without looking at the written page, then make a practice of *fixing your attention on it at least twice a day,* proceeding as follows:

Go into some quiet place where you will not be disturbed; sit down and completely relax your mind and your body; then close your eyes and place your fingers in your ears, thereby excluding the ordinary sound waves and all of the light waves. In that position repeat your *definite chief aim* in life, and as you do so see yourself, in your imagination, in full possession of the object of that aim. If a part of your aim is the accumulation of money, as it undoubtedly is, then see yourself in possession of that money. If a part of the object of your *definite aim* is the ownership of a home, then see a picture of that home, in your imagination, just as you expect to see it in reality. If a part of your *definite aim* is to become a powerful and influential public speaker, then see yourself before an enormous audience, and *feel* yourself playing upon the emotions of that audience as a great violinist would play upon the strings of the violin.

As you approach the end of this lesson, there are two things which you might do, viz.:

First: You might begin, now, to cultivate the ability to *fix attention*, at will, on a given subject, with a feeling that this ability, when fully developed, would bring you the object of your *definite chief aim* in life; or,

Second: You might tilt your nose in the air and with the smile of a cynic say to yourself—"Bosh" and thereby mark yourself a *fool!*

Take your choice!

This lesson was not written as an argument, nor as the subject of a debate. It is your privilege to accept it, in whole or in part, or reject it, just as you please.

Fish don't bite just for the
wishin',
    Keep a-pullin'!
Change your b a i t and
keep on fishin';
    Keep a-pullin'!
Luck ain't nailed, to any
spot;
Men you envy, like as not,
Envy you your job and
lot!
    Keep a-pullin'!

But at this place I wish to state, however, that this is not an age of cynicism or doubt. An age that has conquered the air above us and the sea beneath us, that has enabled us to harness the air and turn it into a messenger that will carry the sound of our voice half-way around the earth in the fractional part of a second, certainly is not an age that lends encouragement to the *"doubting Thomases"* or the *"I-don't-believe-it Joneses."*

The human family has passed through the "Stone Age" and the "Iron Age" and the "Steel Age," and unless I have greatly misinterpreted the trend of the times it is now entering the "Mind Power Age," which will eclipse, in stupendous achievement, all the other "ages" combined.

Learn to fix your attention on a given subject, at will, for whatever length of time you choose, and you will have learned the secret passage-way to power and plenty!

This is *concentration!*

You will understand, from this lesson, that the object of forming an alliance between two or more people, and thereby creating a "Master Mind," is to apply the Law of Concentration more effectively than it could be applied through the efforts of but one person.

The principle referred to as the "Master Mind" is nothing more nor less than group concentration of mind power upon the attainment of a definite object or end. Greater power comes through group mind concentration because of the "stepping up" process produced through the reaction of one mind upon another or others.

PERSUASION VS. FORCE

Success, as has been stated in dozens of different ways throughout this course, is very largely a matter of tactful and harmonious negotiation with other people. Generally speaking, the man who understands how to "get people to do things" he wants done may succeed in any calling.

As a fitting climax for this lesson, on the Law of Concentration, we shall describe the principles through which men are influenced; through which co-operation is gained; through which antagonism is eliminated and friendliness developed.

Force sometimes gets what appear to be satisfactory results, but force, alone, never has built and never can build enduring success.

The world war has done more than anything which has happened in the history of the world to show us the futility of force as a means of influencing the human mind. Without going into details or recounting the instances which could be cited, we all know that force was the foundation upon which German philosophy has been built during the past forty years. The doctrine that *might* makes *right* was given a world-wide trial and it failed.

The human body can be imprisoned or controlled by physical force, but it is not so with the human mind. No man on earth can control the mind of a normal, healthy person if that person chooses to exercise his God-given right to control his own mind. The majority of people do not exercise this right. They go through the world, thanks to our faulty educational system, without having discovered the strength which

lies dormant in their own minds. Now and then something happens, more in the nature of an accident than
anything else, which awakens a person and causes
him to discover where his real strength lies and how
to use it in the development of industry or one of the
professions. Result: a genius is born!

There is a given point at which the human mind
stops rising or exploring unless something out of the
daily routine happens to "push" it over this obstacle.
In some minds this point is very low and in others it
is very high. In still others it varies between low and
high. The individual who discovers a way to stimulate
his mind artificially, arouse it and cause it to go beyond this average stopping point frequently, is sure to
be rewarded with fame and fortune if his efforts are
of a constructive nature.

The educator who discovers a way to stimulate any
mind and cause it to rise above this average stopping
point without any bad reactionary effects, will confer
a blessing on the human race second to none in the
history of the world. We, of course, do not have
reference to physical stimulants or narcotics. These
will always arouse the mind for a time, but eventually
they ruin it entirely. We have reference to a purely
mental stimulant, such as that which comes through
intense interest, desire, enthusiasm, love, etc., the factors out of which a "Master Mind" may be developed.

The person who makes this discovery will do much
toward solving the crime problem. You can do almost
anything with a person when you learn how to influence his mind. The mind may be likened to a great
field. It is a very fertile field which always produces a crop after the kind of seed which is sown

in it. The problem, then, is to learn how to select the right sort of seed and how to sow that seed so that it takes root and grows quickly. We are sowing seed in our minds daily, hourly, nay, every second, but we are doing it promiscuously and more or less unconsciously. We must learn to do it after a carefully prepared *plan,* according to a well laid out design! Haphazardly sown seed in the human mind brings back a haphazard crop! There is no escape from this result.

History is full of notable cases of men who have been transformed from law-abiding, peaceful, constructive citizens to roving, vicious criminals. We also have thousands of cases wherein men of the low, vicious, so-called criminal type have been transformed into constructive, law-abiding citizens. In every one of these cases the transformation of the human being took place in the mind of the man. He created in his own mind, for one reason or another, a picture of what he desired and then proceeded to transform that picture into reality. As a matter of fact, if a picture of any environment, condition or thing be pictured in the human mind and if the mind be focused or concentrated on that picture long enough and persistently enough, and backed up with a *strong desire* for the thing pictured, it is but a short step from the picture to the realization of it in physical or mental form.

The world war brought out many startling tendencies of the human mind which corroborate the work which the psychologist has carried on in his research into the workings of the mind. The following account of a rough, uncouth, unschooled, undisciplined young mountaineer is an excellent case in point:

FOUGHT FOR HIS RELIGION; NOW GREAT WAR HERO

Rotarians Plan to Present Farm to Alvin York, Unlettered Tennessee Squirrel Hunter

By George W. Dixon

How Alvin Cullom York, an unlettered Tennessee squirrel hunter, became the foremost hero of the American Expeditionary Forces in France, forms a romantic chapter in the history of the world war.

York is a native of Fentress County. He was born and reared among the hardy mountaineers of the Tennessee woods. There is not even a railroad in Fentress County. During his earlier years he was reputed to be a desperate character. He was what was known as a gunman. He was a dead shot with a revolver, and his prowess with the rifle was known far and wide among the plain people of the Tennessee hills.

One day a religious organization pitched its tent in the community in which York and his parents lived. It was a strange sect that came to the mountains looking for converts, but the methods of the evangels of the new cult were full of fire and emotionalism. They denounced the sinner, the vile character and the man who took advantage of his neighbor. They pointed to the religion of the Master as an example that all should follow.

ALVIN GETS RELIGION

Alvin Cullom York startled his neighbors one night by flinging himself down at the mourners' bench. Old

THERE are twelve
good reasons for
Failure. The first one is
the avowed intention of
doing no more than one is
paid to do, and the per-
son who makes this
avowal may see the other
eleven by stepping before
a looking-glass.

men stirred in their seats and women craned their necks, as York wrestled with his sins in the shadows of the Tennessee mountains.

York became an ardent apostle of the new religion. He became an exhorter, a leader in the religious life of the community and, although his marksmanship was as deadly as ever, no one feared him who walked in the path of righteousness.

When the news of the war reached that remote section of Tennessee and the mountaineers were told that they were going to be "conscripted," York grew sullen and disagreeable. He didn't believe in killing human beings, even in war. His Bible taught him, "Thou shalt not kill." To his mind this was literal and final. He was branded as a "conscientious objector."

The draft officers anticipated trouble. They knew that his mind was made up, and they would have to reach him in some manner other than by threats of punishment.

WAR IN A HOLY CAUSE

They went to York with a Bible and showed him that the war was in a holy cause—the cause of liberty and human freedom. They pointed out that men like himself were called upon by the Higher Powers to make the world free; to protect innocent women and children from violation; to make life worth living for the poor and oppressed; to overcome the "beast" pictured in the Scriptures, and to make the world free for the development of Christian ideals and Christian manhood and womanhood. It was a fight between the hosts of righteousness and the hordes of Satan. The devil was trying to conquer the world through his chosen agents, the Kaiser and his generals.

York's eyes blazed with a fierce light. His big hands closed like a vise. His strong jaws snapped. "The Kaiser," he hissed between his teeth, "the beast! the destroyer of women and children! I'll show him where he belongs if I ever get within gunshot of him!"

He caressed his rifle, kissed his mother good-by and told her he would see her again when the Kaiser had been put out of business.

He went to the training camp and drilled with scrupulous care and strict obedience to orders.

His skill at target practice attracted attention. His comrades were puzzled at his high scores. They had not reckoned that a backwoods squirrel hunter would make fine material for a sniper in the front-line trenches.

York's part in the war is now history. General Pershing has designated him as the foremost individual hero of the war. He won every decoration, including the Congressional Medal, the Croix de Guerre, the Legion of Honor. He faced the Germans without fear of death. He was fighting to vindicate his religion, for the sanctity of the home; the love of women and children; the preservation of the ideals of Christianity and the liberties of the poor and oppressed. Fear was not in his code or his vocabulary. His cool daring electrified more than a million men and set the world to talking about this strange, unlettered hero from the hills of Tennessee.

Here we have a case of a young mountaineer who, had he been approached from just a slightly different angle, undoubtedly would have resisted conscription and, likely as not, would have become so embittered toward his country that he would have become an outlaw, looking for an opportunity to strike back at the first chance.

Those who approached him knew something of the principles through which the human mind works. They knew how to manage young York by first overcoming the resistance that he had worked up in his own mind. This is the very point at which thousands of men, through improper understanding of these principles, are arbitrarily classed as criminals and treated as dangerous, vicious people. Through suggestion these people could have been handled as effectively as young York was handled, and developed into useful, productive human beings.

In your search for ways and means of understanding and manipulating your own mind so you can persuade it to create that which you desire in life, let us remind you that, without a single exception, anything which irritates you and arouses you to anger, hatred, dislike, or cynicism, is destructive and very bad for you.

You can never get the maximum or even a fair average of constructive action out of your mind until you have learned to control it and keep it from becoming stimulated through anger or fear!

These two negatives, anger and fear, are positively destructive to your mind, and as long as you allow them to remain you can be sure of results which are unsatisfactory and away below what you are capable of producing.

In our discussion of environment and habit we learned that the individual mind is amenable to the suggestions of environment; that the minds of the individuals of a crowd blend with one another conforming to the suggestion of the prevailing influence of the leader or dominating figure. Mr. J. A. Fisk gives us an interesting account of the influence of mental suggestion in the revival meeting, which bears out the statement that the crowd mind blends into one, as follows:

MENTAL SUGGESTION IN THE REVIVAL

Modern psychology has firmly established the fact that the greater part of the phenomena of the religious "revival" are *psychical* rather than spiritual in their nature, and *abnormally psychical* at that. The leading authorities recognize the fact that the mental excitement attendant upon the emotional appeals of the "revivalist" must be classified with the phenomena of hypnotic suggestion rather than with that of true religious experience. And those who have made a close study of the subject believe that instead of such excitement tending to elevate the mind and exalt the spirit of the individual, it serves to weaken and degrade the mind and prostitute the spirit by dragging it in the mud of abnormal psychic frenzy and emotional excess. In fact, by some careful observers, familiar with the respective phenomena, the religious "revival" meeting is classed with the public hypnotic "entertainment" as a typical example of psychic intoxication and hysterical excess.

David Starr Jordan, chancellor emeritus of Leland Stanford University, says: "Whisky, cocaine and alcohol bring temporary insanity, and so does a revival of religion." The late Professor William James, of

Harvard University, the eminent psychologist, says:
"Religious revivalism is more dangerous to the life of
society than drunkenness."

It should be unnecessary to state that in this lesson
the term "revival" is used in the narrower significa-
tion indicating the typical religious emotional excitement known by the term in question, and is not
intended to apply to the older and respected religious
experience designated by the same term, which was so
highly revered among the Puritans, Lutherans and
others in the past. A standard reference work speaks
of the general subject of the "revival" as follows:

"Revivals occur in all religions. When one takes
place a large number of persons who have been comparatively dead or indifferent to spiritual considera·
tions simultaneously or in quick succession become
alive to their importance, alter spiritually and morally,
and act with exceeding zeal in converting others to
their views. A Mohammedan revival takes the form
of a return to the strict doctrines of the Koran, and
a desire to propagate them by the sword. A Christian
minority living in the place is in danger of being mas-
sacred by the revivalists. Pentecostal effusion of the
Holy Spirit produced a revival within the infant church,
followed by numerous conversions from outside. Revivals, though not called by that name, occurred at
intervals from apostolic times till the Reformation,
the revivalists being sometimes so unsympathetically
treated that they left the church and formed sects,
while, in other cases, and notably in those of the founders of the monastic orders, they were retained and
acted on the church as a whole. The spiritual impulse
which led to the Reformation, and the antagonistic one

NOTHING is so con-
tagious as enthu-
siasm. It is the real allegory of the tale of Or-
pheus. It moves stones,
it charms brutes. En-
thusiasm is the genius of
sincerity and truth ac-
complishes no victories
without it.

—*Bulwer.*

which produced or attended the rise of the Society
of Jesus, were both revivalist. It is, however, to
sudden increase of spiritual activity within the Protestant churches that the term 'revival' is chiefly confined.
The enterprise of the Wesleys and Whitefield in this
country and England from 1738 onward was thoroughly revivalist. . . . Since then, various revivals
have from time to time occurred, and nearly all denominations aim at their production. The means
adopted are prayer for the Holy Spirit, meetings continued night after night, often to a late hour, stirring
addresses, chiefly from revivalist laymen, and after-
meetings to deal with those impressed. Ultimately
it has been found that some of those apparently converted have been steadfast, others have fallen back,
while deadness proportioned to the previous excitement
temporarily prevails. Sometimes excitable persons at
revival meetings utter piercing cries, or even fall pros-
trate.

"These morbid manifestations are now discouraged,
and have in consequence become more rare."

In order to understand the principle of the operation of mental suggestion in the revival meeting, we
must first understand something of what is known as
the psychology of the crowd. Psychologists are aware
that the psychology of a crowd, considered as a whole,
differs materially from that of the separate individuals
composing that crowd. There is a crowd of separate
individuals, and a composite crowd in which the emotional natures of the units seem to blend and fuse.
The change from the first-named crowd to the second
arises from the influence of earnest attention, or deep
emotional appeals or common interest. When this

change occurs the crowd becomes a composite individual, the degree of whose intelligence and emotional control is but little above that of its weakest member. This fact, startling as it may appear to the average reader, is well known and is admitted by the leading psychologists of the day; and many important essays and books have been written thereupon. The predominant characteristics of this "composite-mindedness" of a crowd are the evidences of extreme suggestibility, response to appeals of emotion, vivid imagination, and action arising from imitation—all of which are mental traits universally manifested by primitive man. In short, the crowd manifests *atavism,* or reversion to early racial traits.

Diall, in his Psychology of the Aggregate Mind of an Audience, holds that the mind of an assemblage listening to a powerful speaker undergoes a curious process called "fusion," by which the individuals in the audience, losing their personal traits for the time being, to a greater or less degree, *are reduced, as it were, to a single individual, whose characteristics are those of an impulsive youth of twenty, imbued in general with high ideals, but lacking in reasoning power and will.* Tarde, the French psychologist, advances similar views.

Professor Joseph Jastrow, in his Fact and Fable in Psychology, says:

"In the production of this state of mind a factor as yet unmentioned plays a leading rôle, the power of mental contagion. Error, like truth, flourishes in crowds. At the heart of sympathy each finds a home. . . . No form of contagion is so insidious in its outset, so difficult to check in its advance, so certain to

leave germs that may at any moment reveal their
pernicious power, as a mental contagion—the contagion of fear, of panic, of fanaticism, of lawlessness,
of superstition, of error. . . . In brief, we must add to
the many factors which contribute to deception, the
recognized lowering of critical ability, of the power of
accurate observation, indeed, of rationality, which
merely being one of a crowd induces. The conjurer
finds it easy to perform to a large audience, because,
among other reasons, it is easier to arouse their admiration and sympathy, easier to make them forget themselves and enter into the uncritical spirit of wonderland.
It would seem that in some respects the critical tone
of an assembly, like the strength of a chain, is that of
its weakest member."

Professor Le Bon, in his The Crowd, says:

"The sentiments and ideas of all the persons in the
gathering take one and the same direction, and their
conscious personality vanishes. A collective mind is
formed, doubtless transitory, by presenting very
clearly marked characteristics. The gathering has
become what, in the absence of a better expression, I
will call an organized crowd, or, if the term be considered preferable, a psychological crowd. It forms
a single being, and is subjected to the law of the mental
unity of crowds. . . . The most striking peculiarity
presented by a psychological crowd is the following:
Whoever be the individuals that compose it, however
like or unlike be their mode of life, their occupation,
their character, or their intelligence, the fact that they
have been transformed into a crowd puts them in
possession of a sort of collective mind which makes
them feel, think and act in a manner quite different

from that in which each individual of them would feel,
think and act were he in a state of isolation. There
are certain ideas and feelings which do not come into
being, or do not transform themselves into acts, except
in the case of the individuals forming a crowd. . . .
In crowds it is stupidity and not mother wit that is
accumulated. In the collective mind the intellectual
aptitudes of the individuals, and in consequence their
individuality, is weakened. . . . The most careful observations seem to prove that an individual immerged
for some length of time in a crowd in action soon finds
himself in a special state, which most resembles the
state of fascination in which the hypnotized individual
finds himself. . . . The conscious personality has entirely vanished, will and discernment are lost. All
feelings and thoughts are bent in the direction determined by the hypnotizer. . . . Under the influence of
a suggestion he will undertake the accomplishment of
certain acts with irresistible impetuosity. This impetuosity is the more irresistible in the case of crowds,
from the fact that, the suggestion being the same for
all the individuals of the crowd, it gains in strength
by reciprocity. Moreover, by the mere fact that he
forms part of an organized crowd, a man descends
several rungs in the ladder of civilization. Isolated,
he may be a cultured individual; in a crowd, he is a
barbarian—that is, a creature acting by instinct. He
possesses the spontaneity, the violence, the ferocity,
and also the enthusiasm and heroism of primitive beings, whom he further tends to resemble by the facility
with which he allows himself to be induced to commit
acts contrary to his most obvious interests and his best
known habits. An individual in a crowd is a grain of

sand amid other grains of sand, which the wind stirs up at will."

Professor Davenport, in his Primitive Traits in Religious Revivals, says:

"The mind of the crowd is strangely like that of primitive man. Most of the people in it may be far from primitive in emotion, in thought, in character; nevertheless, the result tends always to be the same. Stimulation immediately begets action. Reason is in abeyance. The cool, rational speaker has little chance beside the skillful emotional orator. The crowd thinks in images, and speech must take this form to be accessible to it. The images are not connected by any natural bond, and they take each other's place like the slides of a magic lantern. It follows from this, of course, that appeals to the imagination have paramount influence. . . . The crowd is united and governed by emotion rather than by reason. Emotion is the natural bond, for men differ much less in this respect than in intellect. It is also true that in a crowd of a thousand men the amount of emotion actually generated and existing is far greater than the sum which might conceivably be obtained by adding together the emotions of the individuals taken by themselves. The explanation of this is that the attention of the crowd is always directed either by the circumstances of the occasion or by the speaker to certain common ideas—as 'salvation' in religious gatherings . . . and every individual in the gathering is stirred with emotion, not only because the idea or the shibboleth stirs him, but also because he is conscious that every other individual in the gathering believes in the idea or the shibboleth, and is stirred by it, too. And

SOME men are suc-cessful as long as someone else stands back of them and encourages them, and some men are successful in spite of Hell! Take your choice.

this enormously increases the volume of his own emotion and consequently the total volume of emotion in the crowd. As in the case of the primitive mind, imagination has unlocked the floodgates of emotion, which on occasion may become wild.enthusiasm or demoniac frenzy."

The student of suggestion will see that not only are the emotional members of a revival audience subject to the effect of the "composite-mindedness" arising from the "psychology of the crowd" and are thereby weakened in resistive power, but that they are also brought under the influence of two other very potent forms of mental suggestion. Added to the powerful suggestion of authority exercised by the revivalist, which is exerted to its fullest along lines very similar to that of the professional hypnotist, is the suggestion of imitation exerted upon each individual by the combined force of the balance of the crowd.

As Durkheim observed in his psychological investigations, the average individual is "intimidated by the mass" of the crowd around him, or before him, and experiences that peculiar psychological influence exerted by the mere number of people as against his individual self. Not only does the suggestible person find it easy to respond to the authoritative suggestions of the preacher and the exhortations of his helpers, but he is also brought under the direct fire of the imitative suggestions of those on all sides who are experiencing emotional activities and who are manifesting them outwardly. Not only does the voice of the shepherd urge forward, but the tinkle of the bell-wether's bell is also heard, and the imitative tendency of the flock, which causes one sheep to jump because one ahead of him does so (and so on until the last sheep has jumped), needs but the force of the example of a leader to start into motion the entire flock. This is not an exaggeration—human beings, in times of panic, fright, or deep emotion of any kind, manifest the imitative tendency of the sheep, and the tendency of cattle and horses to "stampede" under imitation.

To the student experienced in the experimental work of the psychological laboratory there is the very closest analogy observed in the respective phenomena of the revival and hypnotic suggestion. In both cases the attention and interest is attracted by the unusual procedure; the element of mystery and awe is induced by words and actions calculated to inspire them; the senses are tired by monotonous talk in an impressive and authoritative tone; and finally the suggestions are projected in a commanding, *suggestive* manner familiar to all students of hypnotic suggestion. The subjects in both cases are prepared for the final suggestions and commands, by previously given minor suggestions, such as: "Stand up," or "Look this way," etc., in the case of the hypnotist; and by: "All those who think so-and-so, stand up," and "All who are willing to become better, stand up," etc., in the case of the revivalist. The impressionable subjects *are thus accustomed to obedience to suggestion by easy stages.* And, finally, the commanding suggestion: "Come right up— *right up—this way—right up—come,* I say, come, *come,* COME!" etc., which takes the impressed ones right off their feet and rushes them to the front, are almost precisely the same in the hypnotic experiment or séance, on the one hand, and the sensational revival, on the other. Every good revivalist would make a good hypnotic operator, and every good hypnotic operator would make a good revivalist if his mind were turned in that direction.

In the revival, the person giving the suggestions has the advantage of breaking down the resistance of his audience by arousing their sentiments and emotions. Tales depicting the influence of mother, home and heaven; songs like "Tell Mother, I'll Be There"; and personal appeals to the revered associations of one's past and early life tend to reduce one to the state of emotional response, and render him most susceptible to strong, repeated suggestions along the same line. Young people and hysterical women are especially susceptible to this form of emotional suggestion. Their feelings are stirred, and the will is influenced by the preaching, the songs, and the personal appeals of the co-workers of the revivalist.

The most sacred sentimental memories are reawakened for the moment and old conditions of mind are reinduced. "Where Is My Wandering Boy Tonight?" brings forth tears to many a one to whom the memory of the mother is sacred, and the preaching that the mother is dwelling in a state of bliss beyond the skies, from which the unconverted child is cut off unless he professes faith, serves to move many to action for the time being. The element of fear is also invoked in the revival—not so much as formerly, it is true, but still to a considerable extent and more subtly. The fear of a sudden death in an unconverted condition is held over the audience, and, "Why not *now*—why not *tonight?*" is asked him, accompanied by the hymn; "Oh, Why Do You Wait, Dear Brother?" As Davenport says:

"It is well known that the employment of symbolic images immensely increases the emotion of an audience. The vocabulary of revivals abounds in them— the cross, the crown, the angel band, hell, heaven. Now vivid imagination and strong feeling and belief are states of mind favorable to suggestion as well as to impulsive action. It is also true that the influence of a crowd largely in sympathy with the ideas suggested is thoroughly coercive or intimidative upon the individual sinner. There is considerable professed conversion which results in the beginning from little more than this form of social pressure, and which may never develop beyond it. Finally, the inhibition of all extraneous ideas is encouraged in revival assemblies both by prayer and speech. There is, therefore, extreme sensitiveness to suggestion. When to these conditions of negative consciousness on the part of an audience there has been added a conductor of the meetings who has a high hypnotic potential, such as Wesley or Finney, or who is only a thoroughly persuasive and magnetic personality, such as Whitefield, there may easily be an influence exerted upon certain individuals of a crowd which closely approaches the abnormal or thoroughly hypnotic. When this point is not reached there is still a great amount of highly acute though normal suggestibility to be reckoned with."

The persons who show signs of being influenced are then "labored with" by either the revivalist or his co-workers. They are urged to surrender their will, and "Leave it all to the Lord." They are told to "Give yourself to God, now, right now, this minute"; or to "Only believe now, and you shall be saved"; or, "Won't you give yourself to Jesus?" etc. They are exhorted and prayed with; arms are placed around their shoulders, and every art of emotional persuasive suggestion is used to make the sinner "give up."

Starbuck in his The Psychology of Religion relates a number of instances of the experiences of converted persons at revivals. One person wrote as follows:

"My will seemed wholly at the mercy of others, particularly of the revivalist M———. There was absolutely no intellectual element. It was pure feeling. There followed a period of ecstasy. I was bent on doing good and was eloquent in appealing to others. The state of moral exaltation did not continue. It was followed by a complete relapse from orthodox religion."

Davenport has the following to say in reply to the claim that the old methods of influencing converts at a revival have passed away with the crude theology of the past:

"I lay particular stress upon this matter here, because, while the employment of irrational fear in revivals has largely passed away, the employment of the hypnotic method has not passed away. There has rather been a recrudescence and a conscious strengthening of it because the old prop of terror is gone. And it cannot be too vigorously emphasized that such a force is not a 'spiritual' force in any high and clear sense at all, but is rather uncanny and psychic and obscure. And the method itself needs to be greatly refined before it can ever be of any spiritual benefit whatever. It is thoroughly primitive and belongs with the animal and instinctive means of fascination. In this bald, crude form, the feline employs it upon the helpless bird and the Indian medicine-man upon the

YOU need have no fear of competition from the person who says, "I'm not paid to do this and I'll not do it." He will never be a dangerous competitor for your job. But watch out for the fellow who remains at his work until it is finished and performs a little more than is expected of him, for he may challenge you at the post and pass you at the grand-stand.

ghost-dance votary. When used, as it has often been, upon little children who are naturally highly suggestible, it has no justification whatever and is mentally and morally injurious in the highest degree. I do not see how violent emotional throes and the use of suggestion in its crude forms can be made serviceable even in the cases of hardened sinners, and certainly with large classes of the population the employment of this means is nothing but psychological malpractice. We guard with intelligent care against quackery in physiological obstetrics. It would be well if a sterner training and prohibition hedged about the spiritual obstetrician, whose function it is to guide the far more delicate process of the new birth."

Some who favor the methods of the revival, but who also recognize the fact that mental suggestion plays a most important part in the phenomena thereof, hold that the objections similar to those here advanced are not valid against the methods of the revival, inasmuch as mental suggestion, as is well known, *may be used for good purposes as well as bad* —for the benefit and uplifting of people as well as in the opposite direction. This being admitted, these good folks argue that mental suggestion in the revival is a legitimate method or "weapon of attack upon the stronghold of the devil." But this argument is found to be defective when examined in its effects and consequences. In the first place, it would seem to identify the emotional, neurotic and hysterical mental states induced by revival methods with the spiritual uplift and moral regeneration which is the accompaniment of true religious experience. It seeks to place the counterfeit on a par with the genuine—the baleful glare of the rays of the psychic moon with the invigorating and animating rays of the spiritual sun. It seeks to raise the hypnotic phase to that of the "spiritual-mindedness" of man. To those who are familiar with the two classes of phenomena, there is a difference as wide as that between the poles existing between them.

As a straw showing how the wind of the best modern religious thought is blowing, we submit the following, from the volume entitled Religion and Miracle, from the pen of Rev. Dr. George A. Gordon, pastor emeritus of the New Old South Church of Boston:

"For this end professional revivalism, with its organizations, its staff of reporters who make the figures suit the hopes of good men, the system of advertisements, and the exclusion or suppression of all sound critical comment, the appeals to emotion and the use of means which have no visible connection with grace and cannot by any possibility lead to glory, is utterly inadequate. The world waits for the vision, the passion, the simplicity and the stern truthfulness of the Hebrew prophet; it awaits the imperial breadth and moral energy of the Christian apostle to the nations; it awaits the teacher who, like Christ, shall carry his doctrine in a great mind and a great character."

While there have undoubtedly been many instances of persons attracted originally by the emotional excitement of the revival, and afterwards leading worthy religious lives in accordance with the higher spiritual nature, still in too many cases the revival has exerted but a temporary effect for good upon the persons yielding to the excitement, and after the stress has passed has resulted in creating an indifference and even an aversion for true religious feeling. The reaction is

often equal to the original action. The consequences
of "backsliding" are well known in all churches, after
a spirited revival. In others there is merely awakened
a susceptibility to emotional excitement, which causes
the individual to undergo repeated stages of "conversion" at each revival, and a subsequent "backsliding"
after the influence of the meeting is withdrawn.

Moreover, it is a fact known to psychologists that
persons who have given way to the emotional excitement and excesses of the typical revival are rendered
afterwards far more suggestible and open to "isms,"
fads and false religions than before. *The people
flocking to the support of the various pseudo-religious
adventurers and impostors of the age are generally
found to be the same people who were previously the
most ardent and excitable converts of the revival.*
The ranks of the "Messiahs," "Elijahs" and "Prophets
of the Dawn," who have appeared in great numbers
in this country and England during the past fifty years,
have been recruited almost exclusively from those who
have previously "experienced" the revival fervor in
the orthodox churches. It is the old story of the training of the hypnotic subject. Especially harmful is
this form of emotional intoxication among young
people and women. It must be remembered that the
period of adolescence is one in which the mental nature of the individual is undergoing great changes. It
is a period noted for peculiar development of the emotional nature, the sex nature, and the religious nature.
The existing conditions at this period render the psychic debauchery of the revival, séance or hypnotic
exhibition particularly harmful. Excessive emotional
excitement, coupled with mystery, fear and awe, at this

period of life, often results in morbid and abnormal conditions arising in after life. As Davenport well says: "It is no time for the shock of fear or the agony of remorse. The only result of such misguided religious zeal is likely to be a strengthening in many cases of those tendencies, especially in females, toward morbidity and hysteria, toward darkness and doubt."

There are other facts connected with the close relation existing between abnormal religious excitement and the undue arousing of the sexual nature, which are well known to all students of the subject, but which cannot be spoken of here. As a hint, however, the following, from Davenport, will serve its purpose: ". . . At the age of puberty there is an organic process at work which pushes into activity at nearly the same time the sexual and the spiritual. There is no proof, however, of the causation of the latter by the former. But it does appear to be true that the two are closely associated at the point in the physical process where they branch in different directions, *that at that critical period any radical excitation of the one has its influence upon the other.*" A careful consideration of this important statement will serve to explain many things that have sorely perplexed many good people in the past, in connection with revival excitement in a town, camp meetings, etc. This apparent influence of the devil, which so worried our forefathers, is seen to be but the operation of natural psychological and physiological laws. To understand it is to have the remedy at hand."

But what do the authorities say of the revival of the future—the new revival—the real revival? Let

Professor Davenport speak for the critics—he is well
adapted for the task. He says:

"There will be, I believe, far less use of the revival
meeting as a crass coercive instrument for overriding
the will and overwhelming the reason of the individual
man. The influence of public religious gatherings will
be more indirect, more unobtrusive. It will be recognized that hypnotization and forced choices weaken
the soul, and there will be no attempt to press to
decision in so great a matter under the spell of excitement and contagion and suggestion. . . . The converts
may be few. They may be many. They will be measured, not by the capacity of the preacher for administrative hypnotism, but rather by the capacity for
unselfish friendship of every Christian man and
woman. But of this I think we may be confident—
the days of religious effervescence and passional unre-
straint are dying. The days of intelligent, undemon-
strative and self-sacrificing piety are dawning. To do
justly, to love mercy, to walk humbly with God—
these remain the cardinal tests of the divine in man.
. . . Religious experience is an evolution. We go on
from the rudimentary and the primitive to the rational
and the spiritual. And, believe Paul, the mature fruit
of the Spirit is not the subliminal uprush, the lapse of
inhibition, but rational love, joy, peace, long-suffering,
kindness, goodness, faithfulness, meekness—self-
control."

. . . .

The Law of Concentration is one of the major principles which must be understood and applied intelligently by all who would successfully experiment with

UNTIL you have learned to be tolerant with those who do not always agree with you—until you have cultivated the habit of saying some kind word of those whom you do not admire—until you have formed the habit of looking for the good instead of the bad there is in others, you will be neither successful nor happy.

the principle described in this course as the "Master Mind."

The foregoing comments, by leading authorities of the world, will give you a better understanding of the Law of Concentration as it is often used by those who wish to "blend" or "fuse" the minds of a crowd so they will function as a single mind.

You are now ready for the lesson on Co-operation, which will take you further into the methods of applying the psychological laws upon which this phi· losophy of success is based.

IF you hesitate or turn backward while under fire, you're not a Fighter—you're a "Quitter"; and the Devil, himself, hates the person with a rubber backbone. He smells bad burning.

Lesson Thirteen

CO-OPERATION

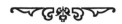

YOU have failed many times? How fortunate! You ought to know, by now, some of the things NOT to do.

THE LAW OF SUCCESS
Lesson Thirteen
CO-OPERATION

"You Can Do It if You Believe You Can!"

O-OPERATION is the beginning of all organized effort. As was stated in the second lesson of this course, Andrew Carnegie accumulated a gigantic fortune through the co-operative efforts of a small group of men numbering not more than a score.

You, too, can learn how to use this principle.

There are two forms of Co-operation to which your attention will be directed in this lesson; namely:

First, the Co-operation between people who group themselves together or form alliances for the purpose of attaining a given end, under the principles known as the Law of the Master Mind.

Second, the Co-operation between the conscious and the sub-conscious minds, which forms a reasonable hypothesis of man's ability to contact, communicate with and draw upon *infinite intelligence.*

To one who has not given serious thought to this subject, the foregoing hypothesis may seem unreasonable; but follow the evidence of its soundness, and study the facts upon which the hypothesis is based, and then draw your own conclusions.

Let us begin with a brief review of the physical construction of the body:

"We know that the whole body is traversed by a network of nerves which serve as the channels of communication between the indwelling spiritual ego, which we call mind, and the functions of the external organism.

"*This nervous system is dual.* One system, known as the Sympathetic, is the channel for all those activities which are not consciously directed by our volition, such as the operation of the digestive organs, the repair of the daily wear and tear of the tissues, and the like.

"The other system, known as the Voluntary or Cerebro-spinal system, is the channel through which we receive conscious perception from the physical senses and exercise control over the movements of the body. This system has its center in the brain, while the other has its center in the ganglionic mass at the back of the stomach known as the solar plexus, and sometimes spoken of as the abdominal brain. The cerebro-spinal system is the channel of our volitional or conscious mental action, and the sympathetic system is the channel of that mental action which unconsciously supports the vital functions of the body.

"Thus the cerebro-spinal system is the organ of the conscious mind and the sympathetic is that of the subconscious mind.

"But the interaction of conscious and sub-conscious minds requires a similar interaction between the corresponding systems of nerves, and one conspicuous connection by which this is provided is the "vagus" nerve. This nerve passes out of the cerebral region as a portion of the voluntary system, and through it we control the vocal organs; then it passes onward to the thorax, sending out branches to the heart and lungs; and finally, passing through the diaphragm, it loses the outer coating which distinguishes the nerves of the voluntary system and becomes identified with those of the sympathetic system, *so forming a connecting link* between the two and making the man physically a single entity.

"Similarly different areas of the brain indicate their connection with the objective and subjective activities of the mind respectively, and, speaking in a general way, we may assign the frontal portion of the brain to the former, and the posterior portion to the latter, while the intermediate portion partakes of the character of both.

"The intuitional faculty has its correspondence in the upper area of the brain, situated between the frontal and the posterior portions, and, physiologically speaking, it is here that intuitive ideas find entrance. These, at first, are more or less unformed and generalized in character, but are, nevertheless, perceived by the conscious mind; otherwise, we should not be aware of them at all. Then the effort of Nature is to bring these ideas into more definite and usable shape, so the conscious mind lays hold on them and induces a corresponding vibratory current in the voluntary system of nerves, and this in turn induces a similar current in the involuntary system, *thus handing the idea over to the subjective mind.* The vibratory current which had first descended from the apex of the brain to the frontal brain and thus through the voluntary system to the solar plexus is now reversed and ascends from the solar plexus through the sympathetic system to the posterior brain, this return current indicating the action of the subjective mind."

If we were to remove the surface portion of the apex of the brain we should find immediately below it the shining belt of brain substance called the "corpus callosum." *This is the point of union between the subjective and objective,* and, as the current returns from the solar plexus to this point, it is restored to the objective portion of the brain in a fresh form *which it has acquired by the silent alchemy of the subjective mind.* Thus the conception which was at first only vaguely recognized is restored to the objective mind in a definite and workable form, and then the objective mind, acting through the frontal brain —the area of comparison and analysis—proceeds to work upon a clearly perceived idea and to bring out the potentialities that are latent in it.*

The term "subjective mind" is the same as the term "sub-conscious mind," and the term "objective mind" is the same as the term "conscious mind."

Please understand these different terms.

By studying this *dual system* through which the body transmits energy, we discover the exact points at which the two systems are connected, and the manner in which we may transmit a *thought* from the conscious to the sub-conscious mind.

This Co-operative *dual nervous system* is the most

*Judge T. Troward, in The Edinburgh Lectures on Mental Science.

important form of co-operation known to man; for it is through the aid of this system that the principle of evolution carries on its work of developing *accurate thought,* as described in Lesson Eleven.

When you impress any idea on your sub-conscious mind, through the principle of Auto-suggestion, you do so with the aid of this *dual nervous system:* and when your sub-conscious mind works out a definite plan of any *desire* with which you impress it, the plan is delivered back to your conscious mind through this same *dual nervous system.*

This Co-operative system of nerves literally constitutes a direct line of communication between your ordinary conscious mind and *infinite intelligence.*

Knowing, from my own previous experience as a beginner in the study of this subject, how difficult it is to accept the hypothesis here described, I will illustrate the soundness of the hypothesis in a simple way that you can both understand and demonstrate for yourself.

Before going to sleep at night impress upon your mind the *desire* to arise the next morning at a given hour, say at four A.M., and if your impression is accompanied by a *positive determination* to arise at that hour, your sub-conscious mind will register the impression and awaken you at precisely that time.

Now the question might well be asked:

"If I can impress my sub-conscious mind with the *desire* to arise at a specified time and it will awaken me at that time, why do I not form the habit of impressing it with other and more important *desires?*"

If you will ask yourself this question, *and insist upon an answer,* you will find yourself very near, if not on

YOU can not scare a man who is at peace with God, his fellow men and himself. There is no room for fear in such a man's heart. When fear finds a welcome there is something that needs awakening.

the pathway that leads to the secret door to *knowl-edge,* as described in Lesson Eleven.

.   .   .   .

We will now take up the subject of Co-operation between men who unite, or group themselves together for the purpose of attaining a given end. In the second lesson of this course we referred to this sort of co-operation as *organized effort.*

This course touches some phase of co-operation in practically every lesson. This result was inevitable for the reason that the object of the course is to help the student develop *power,* and power is developed only through *organized effort.*

We are living in an age of co-operative effort. Nearly all successful businesses are conducted under some form of co-operation. The same is true in the field of industry and finance, as well as in the professional field.

Doctors and lawyers have their alliances for mutual aid and protection in the form of Bar Associations and Medical Associations.

The bankers have both local and national Associations for their mutual aid and advancement.

The retail merchants have their Associations for the same purpose.

The automobile owners have grouped themselves into Clubs and Associations.

The printers have their Associations; the plumbers have theirs and the coal dealers have theirs.

Co-operation is the object of all these Associations.

The laboring men have their unions and those who supply the working capital and superintend the efforts of laboring men have their alliances, under various names.

Nations have their co-operative alliances, although they do not appear to have yet discovered the full meaning of "co-operation." The attempt of the late President Wilson to perfect the League of Nations, followed by the efforts of the late President Harding to perfect the same idea under the name of the World Court, indicates the trend of the times in the direction of co-operation.

It is slowly becoming obvious to man that those who most efficiently apply the principle of co-operative effort survive longest, and, that this principle applies from the lowest form of animal life to the highest form of human endeavor.

Mr. Carnegie, and Mr. Rockefeller, and Mr. Ford have taught the business man the value of co-operative effort; that is, they have taught all who cared to observe, the principle through which they accumulated vast fortunes.

Co-operation is the very foundation of all successful leadership. Henry Ford's most tangible asset is the well organized agency force that he has established. This organization not only provides him with an outlet for all the automobiles he can manufacture, but, of greater importance still, it provides him with financial power sufficient to meet any emergency that may arise, a fact which he has already demonstrated on at least one occasion.

As a result of his understanding of the value of the co-operative principle Ford has removed himself from the usual position of dependence upon financial institutions and at the same time provided himself with more commercial power than he can possibly use.

The Federal Reserve Bank System is another example of co-operative effort which practically insures the United States against a money panic.

The chain-store systems constitute another form of commercial co-operation that provides advantage through both the purchasing and the distributing end of the business.

The modern department store, which is the equivalent of a group of small stores operating under one roof, one management and one overhead expense, is another illustration of the advantage of co-operative effort in the commercial field.

In Lesson Fifteen you will observe the possibilities of co-operative effort in its highest form and at the same time you will see the important part that it plays in the development of *power*.

As you have already learned, *power* is *organized effort*. The three most important factors that enter into the process of organizing effort are:

Concentration,
Co-operation and
Co-ordination.

HOW POWER IS DEVELOPED THROUGH CO-OPERATION

As we have already seen, power is organized effort or energy. Personal power is developed by developing, organizing and co-ordinating the faculties of the mind. This may be accomplished by mastering and applying the fifteen major principles upon which this course is founded. The necessary procedure through which these principles may be mastered is thoroughly described in the sixteenth lesson.

The development of personal power is but the first step to be taken in the development of the potential power that is available through the medium of allied effort, or *co-operation,* which may be called group power.

It is a well known fact that all men who have amassed large fortunes have been known as able "organizers." By this is meant that they possessed the ability to enlist the co-operative efforts of other men who supplied talent and ability which they, themselves, did not possess.

The chief object of this course is so to unfold the principles of *organized* and *co-operative* or allied effort that the student will comprehend their significance and make them the basis of his philosophy.

Take, as an example, any business or profession that you choose and you will observe, by analysis, that it is limited only by lack of application of *organized* and *co-operative* effort. As an illustration, consider the legal profession.

If a law firm consists of but one type of mind it will be greatly handicapped, even though it may be made up of a dozen able men of this particular type. The complicated legal system calls for a greater variety of talent than any one man could possibly provide.

It is evident, therefore, that mere organized effort is not sufficient to insure outstanding success; the organization must consist of individuals each of whom supplies some specialized talent which the other members of the organization do not possess.

A well organized law firm would include talent that

was specialized in the preparation of cases; men of vision and imagination who understood how to harmonize the law and the evidence of a case under a sound plan. Men who have such ability are not always possessed of the ability to try a case in court; therefore, men who are proficient in court procedure must be available. Carrying the analysis a step further, it will be seen that there are many different classes of cases which call for men of various types of specialized ability in both the preparation and the trial of these cases. A lawyer who had prepared himself as a specialist in corporation law might be wholly unprepared to handle a case in criminal procedure.

In forming a law partnership, the man who understood the principles of *organized, co-operative effort*, would surround himself with talent that was specialized in every branch of law and legal procedure in which he intended to practice. The man who had no conception of the potential power of these principles would probably select his associates by the usual "hit or miss" method, basing his selections more upon personality or acquaintanceship than consideration of the particular type of legal talent that each possessed.

The subject of *organized effort* has been covered in the preceding lessons of this course, but it is again brought up in connection with this lesson for the purpose of indicating the necessity of forming alliances or organizations consisting of individuals who supply *all of the necessary talent that may be needed for the attainment of the object in mind*.

In nearly all commercial undertakings, there is a need for at least three classes of talent; namely, buyers, salesmen and those who are familiar with finance.

A GOOD stock of self-confidence and a new suit of clothes will help you land a position without "pull," but remember that nothing will go so far toward helping you hold it as will push, enthusiasm and determination to do more than that for which you are paid.

It will be readily seen that when these three classes of men *organize* and *co-ordinate* their efforts they avail themselves, through this form of *co-operation,* of *power* which no single individual of the group possesses.

Many a business fails because all of the men back of it are salesmen, or financial men or buyers. By nature, the most able salesmen are optimistic, enthusiastic and emotional; while able financial men, as a rule, are unemotional, deliberate and conservative. Both classes are essential to the success of a commercial enterprise; but either class will prove too much of a load for any business, without the modifying influence of the other class.

It is generally conceded that James J. Hill was the most efficient railroad builder that America ever produced; but it is equally well known that he was not a civil engineer, nor a bridge builder, nor a locomotive engineer, nor a mechanical engineer, nor a chemist, although these highly specialized classes of talent are essential in railroad building. Mr. Hill understood the principles of *organized effort* and *co-operation;* therefore, he surrounded himself with men who possessed all this necessary ability which he lacked.

The modern department store is a splendid example of *organized, co-operative effort.*

Each merchandising department is under the management of one who understands the purchasing and marketing of the goods carried in that department.

Back of all these department managers is a general staff consisting of specialists in buying, selling, financing, and the management of units, or groups, of people. This form of *organized effort* places back of each department both *buying* and *selling* power such as that department could not afford if it were separated from the group and had to be operated under its own overhead, in a separate location.

The United States of America is one of the richest and most *powerful* nations of the world. Upon analysis, it will be seen that this enormous power has grown out of the *co-operative* efforts of the states of the Union.

It was for the purpose of saving this power that the immortal Lincoln made up his mind to erase the Mason and Dixon line. The saving of the Union was of far greater concern to him than was the freedom of the slaves of the South. Had this not been so, the present status of the United States as a power among the nations of the world would be far different from what it is.

It was this same principle of *co-operative* effort that Woodrow Wilson had in mind when he created his plan for a League of Nations. He foresaw the need of such a plan as a medium for preventing war between nations; just as Lincoln foresaw it as a medium for harmonizing the efforts of the people of the United States, thereby preserving the Union.

Thus it is seen that the principle of *organized, co-operative* effort through the aid of which the individual may develop personal power, is the selfsame principle that must be employed in developing group power.

Andrew Carnegie easily dominated the steel business during his active connection with that industry, for the reason that he took advantage of the principle of *organized, co-operative* effort by surrounding himself with highly specialized financial men, chemists, sales managers, buyers of raw materials, transportation experts and others whose services were essential to that industry. He organized this group of *"co-operators"* into what he called a "Master Mind."

Any great university affords an excellent example of the necessity of *organized, co-operative* effort. The professorate is made up of men and women of highly specialized, though vastly different, ability. One department is presided over by experts in literature; another department by expert mathematicians; another department by experts in chemistry; another department by experts in economic philosophy; another department by experts in medicine; another, by experts in law, etc. The university, as a whole, is the equivalent of a group of colleges each of which is directed by experts in its own line, whose efficiency is greatly increased through allied or *co-operative* effort that is directed by a single head.

Analyze *power*, no matter where, or in what form, it may be found, and you will find *organization* and *co-operation* as the chief factors back of it. You will find these two principles in evidence in the lowest form of vegetation no less than in the highest form of animal, which is man.

．　　．　　．　　．　　．　　．　　．

Off the coast of Norway is the most famous and irresistible maelstrom in the world. This great whirlpool of ceaseless motion has never been known to give up any victim who was caught in its circling embrace of foaming water.

No less sure of destruction are those unfortunate souls who are caught in the great maelstrom of life toward which all who do not understand the principle of *organized, co-operative* effort are traveling. We are living in a world in which the law of the survival of the fittest is everywhere in evidence. Those who are "fit" are those who have *power*, and power is *organized effort.*

Unfortunate is the person who either through ignorance, or because of egotism, imagines that he can sail this sea of life in the frail bark of independence. Such a person will discover that there are maelstroms more dangerous than any mere whirlpool of unfriendly waters. All natural laws and all of Nature's plans are based upon harmonious, *co-operative* effort, as all who have attained high places in the world have discovered.

Wherever people are engaged in unfriendly combat, no matter what may be its nature, or its cause, one may observe the nearness of one of these maelstroms that awaits the combatants.

Success in life cannot be attained except through peaceful, harmonious, *co-operative* effort. Nor can success be attained single-handed or independently. Even though a man live as a hermit in the wilderness, far from all signs of civilization, he is, nevertheless, *dependent* upon forces outside of himself for an existence. The more he becomes a part of civilization the more *dependent* upon *co-operative* effort he becomes.

Whether a man earns his living by days' work or from the interest on the fortune he has amassed, he will earn it with less opposition through friendly *co-operation* with others. Moreover, the man whose philosophy is based upon *co-operation* instead of *competition* will not only acquire the necessities and the luxuries of life with less effort, but he will enjoy an extra reward in *happiness* such as others will never feel.

Fortunes that are acquired through *co-operative* effort inflict no scars upon the hearts of their owners, which is more than can be said of fortunes that are acquired through conflict and competitive methods that border on extortion.

The accumulation of material wealth, whether the object is that of bare existence or luxury, consumes most of the time that we put into this earthly struggle. If we cannot change this materialistic tendency of human nature, we can, at least, change the method of pursuing it by adopting *co-operation* as the basis of the pursuit.

Co-operation offers the two-fold reward of providing one with both the necessities and the luxuries of life and the peace of mind which the covetous never know. The avaricious and covetous person may amass a great fortune in material wealth; there is no denying this fact; but he will have sold his soul for a mess of pottage in the bargain.

Let us keep in mind the fact that all success is based upon power, and power grows out of knowledge, that has been organized and expressed in terms of ACTION.

The world pays for but one kind of knowledge, and that is the kind which is expressed in terms of constructive service. In addressing the graduating class of a business college one of the best known bankers in America said:

"You ought to feel proud of your diplomas, because they are evidence that you have been preparing yourselves for *action* in the great field of business.

QUIBBLING" over salary "to start with" has lost many a man the big opportunity of a life-time. If the position you seek is one that you know you can throw your whole heart into, take it, even if you have to work for nothing until you deliver a good sample of your "goods." Thereafter you will receive pay in proportion to the quality and quantity of the work you perform.

"One of the advantages of a business college training is that it prepares you for *action!* Not to belittle other methods of education, but to exalt the modern business college method, I am reminded to say that there are some colleges in which the majority of the students are preparing for practically everything else except *action.*

"You came to this business college with but one object in view, and that object is to learn to render service and earn a living. The latest style of clothing has been of little interest to you because you have been preparing yourself for work in which clothes of the latest style will play no important part. You did not come here to learn how to pour tea at an afternoon party nor to become masters at affecting friendliness while inwardly feeling envy for those who wear finer gowns and drive costly motor cars—you came here to learn how to work!"

In the graduating class before which this man spoke were thirteen boys, all of whom were so poor that they had barely enough money with which to pay their way. Some of them were paying their own way by working before and after school hours.

That was twenty-five years ago. Last summer, I met the president of the business college which these boys attended and he gave me the history of each one of them, from the time that they graduated until the time when I talked to him. One of them is the president of one of the big wholesale drug companies, and a wealthy man; one is a successful lawyer; two own large business colleges of their own, one is a professor in the department of economics in one of the largest universities in America; one is the president of one of the large automobile manufacturing companies; two are presidents of banks, and wealthy men; one is the owner of a large department store; one is the vice-president of one of the great railway systems of the country; one is a well established Certified Public Accountant; one is dead; and the thirteenth is compiling this Reading Course on the Law of Success.

Eleven successes out of a class of thirteen boys is not a bad record, thanks to the spirit of *action* developed by that business college training.

It is not the schooling you have had that counts; it is the extent to which you express that which you learned from your schooling through well organized and intelligently directed *action*.

By no means would I belittle higher education, but I would offer hope and encouragement to those who have had no such education, provided they express that which they know, be it ever so little, in intensive *action*, along constructive lines.

One of the greatest Presidents who ever occupied the White House had but little schooling, but he did such a good job of expressing what knowledge he acquired by that little schooling, through properly directed *action*, that his name has been inseparably woven into the history of the United States.

Every city, town and hamlet has its population of those well known characters called "ne'er-do-wells," and if you will analyze these unfortunate people, you will observe that one of their outstanding features is *procrastination*.

Lack of *action* has caused them to slip backward until they got into a "rut," where they will remain unless, through accident, they are forced out into the open road of struggle where unusual *action* will become necessary.

Don't let yourself get into such a condition.

Every office, and every shop, and every bank, and every store, and every other place of employment has its outstanding victims of *procrastination* who are doing the goose-step down the dusty road of *failure* because they have not developed the habit of expressing themselves in *action*.

You can pick out these unfortunates all about you if you will begin to analyze those with whom you come in contact each day. If you will talk to them you will observe that they have built up a false philosophy somewhat of this nature:

"I am doing all I am paid to do, and I am getting by."

Yes, they are "getting by"—but that is all they are getting.

Some years ago, at a time when labor was scarce and wages unusually high, I observed scores of able-bodied men lying about in the parks of Chicago, doing nothing. I became curious to know what sort of an alibi they would offer for their conduct, so I went out one afternoon and interviewed seven of them.

With the aid of a generous supply of cigars and cigarettes and a little loose change I bought myself into the confidence of those whom I interviewed and thereby gained a rather intimate view of their philosophy. All gave exactly the same reason for being there, without employment. They said: "The world will not give me a chance!!!"

The exclamation points are my own.

Think of it—the world would not "give them a chance."

Of course the world wouldn't *give* them a chance. It never *gives* anyone a chance. A man who wants a chance may create it through *action,* but if he waits for someone to hand it to him on a silver platter he will meet with disappointment.

I fear that this excuse that the world does not *give* a man a chance is quite prevalent, and I strongly suspect that it is one of the commonest causes of poverty and failure.

The seventh man that I interviewed on that well-spent afternoon was an unusually fine looking specimen, physically. He was lying on the ground asleep, with a newspaper over his face. When I lifted the paper from his face, he reached up, took it out of my hands, put it back over his face and went right on sleeping.

Then I used a little strategy by removing the paper from his face and placing it behind me, where he could not get it. He then sat up on the ground and I interviewed him. That fellow was a graduate from two of the great universities of the east, with a master's degree from one, and a Ph.D. from the other.

His story was pathetic.

He had held job after job, but always his employer or his fellow employee "had it in for him." He hadn't been able to make them see the value of his college training. They wouldn't "give him a chance."

Here was a man who might have been at the head of some great business, or the outstanding figure in one of the professions had he not built his house upon the sands of *procrastination* and held to the false belief that the world should pay him for *what he knew!*

Luckily, most college graduates do not build upon such flimsy foundations, because no college on earth can crown with success the man who tries to collect for that which he knows instead of that which he *can do with what he knows.*

The man to whom I have referred was from one of the best known families of Virginia. He traced his ancestry back to the landing of the Mayflower. He threw back his shoulders, pounded himself on the breast with his fist and said: "Just think of it, sir! I am a son of one of the first families of old Virginia!"

My observations lead me to believe that being the son of a "first family" is not always fortunate for either the son or the family. Too often these sons of "first families" try to slide home from third base on their family names. This may be only a peculiar notion of mine, but I have observed that the men and women who are doing the world's work have but little time, and less inclination, to brag about their ancestry.

Not long ago I took a trip back to southwest Virginia, where I was born. It was the first time I had been there in over twenty years. It was a sad sight to compare the sons of some of those who were known as "first families" twenty years ago, with the sons of those who were but plain men who made it their business to express themselves in *action* of the most intensive nature.

The comparison reflected no credit upon the "first family" boys! It is with no feeling of exaltation that I express my gratitude for not having been brought into the world by parents who belonged to the "first family" class. That, of course, was not a matter of

HERE'S a good joke to play on your employer: Get to your work a little earlier and leave a little later than you are supposed to. Handle his tools as if they belonged to you. Go out of your way to say a kind word about him to your fellow-workers. When there is extra work that needs to be done, volunteer to do it. Do not show surprise when he "gets on to you" and offers you the head of the department or a partnership in the business, for this is the best part of the "joke."

choice with me, and if it had been perhaps I, too, would have selected parents of the "first family" type.

Not long ago I was invited to deliver an address in Boston, Mass. After my work was finished, a reception committee volunteered to show me the sights of the city, including a trip to Cambridge, where we visited Harvard University. While there, I observed many sons of "first families"—some of whom were equipped with Packards. Twenty years ago I would have felt proud to be a student at Harvard, with a Packard car, but the illuminating effect of my more mature years has led me to the conclusion that had I had the privilege of going to Harvard I might have done just as well without the aid of a Packard.

I noticed some Harvard boys who had no Packards. They were working as waiters in a restaurant where I ate, and as far as I could see they were missing nothing of value because they owned no Packards; nor did they seem to be suffering by comparison with those who could boast of the ownership of parents of the "first family" type.

All of which is no reflection upon Harvard University—one of the great universities of the world—nor upon the "first families" who send boys to Harvard. To the contrary, it is intended as a bit of encouragement to those unfortunates who, like myself, have but little and know but little, but express what little they know in terms of constructive, useful *action*.

The psychology of *inaction* is one of the chief reasons why some towns and cities are dying with the dry-rot!

Take the city of X, for example. You'll recognize the city by its description, if you are familiar with this part of the country. Sunday blue-laws have closed up all the restaurants on Sunday. Railroad trains must slow down to twelve miles an hour while passing through the city. "Keep off the grass" signs are prominently displayed in the parks. Unfavorable city ordinances of one sort or another have driven the best industries to other cities. On every hand one may see evidence of restraint. The people of the streets show signs of restraint in their faces, and in their manner, and in their walk.

The mass psychology of the city is negative.

The moment one gets off the train at the depot, this negative atmosphere becomes depressingly obvious and makes one want to take the next train out again. The place reminds one of a grave-yard and the people resemble walking ghosts.

They register no signs of *action!*

The bank statements of the banking institutions reflect this negative, *inactive* state of mind. The stores reflect it in their show windows and in the faces of their salespeople. I went into one of the stores to buy a pair of hose. A young woman with bobbed hair who would have been a "flapper" if she hadn't been too lazy, threw out a box of hose on the counter. When I picked up the box, looked the hose over and registered a look of disapproval on my face, she languidly yawned:

"They're the best you can get in this dump!"

"Dump!" She must have been a mind reader, for "dump" was the word that was in my mind before she spoke. The store reminded me of a rubbish dump; the city reminded me of the same. I felt the stuff getting into my own blood. The negative psychology

of the people was actually reaching out and gathering me in.

Maine is not the only state that is afflicted with a city such as the one I have described. I could name others, but I might wish to go into politics some day; therefore, I will leave it to you to do your own analyzing and comparing of cities that are alive with *action* and those that are slowly dying with the dry-rot of *inaction*.

I know of some business concerns that are in this same state of *inaction*, but I will omit their names. You probably know some, too.

Many years ago Frank A. Vanderlip, who is one of the best known and most capable bankers in America, went to work for the National City Bank, of New York City.

His salary was above the average from the start, for the reason that he was capable and had a record of successful achievement that made him a valuable man.

He was assigned to a private office that was equipped with a fine mahogany desk and an easy chair. On the top of the desk was an electric push button that led to a secretary's desk outside.

The first day went by without any work coming to his desk. The second, and third, and fourth days went by without any work. No one came in or said anything to him.

By the end of the week he began to feel uneasy (Men of *action* always feel uneasy when there is no work in sight.)

The following week Mr. Vanderlip went into the president's office and said, "Look here, you are paying me a big salary and giving me nothing to do and it is grating on my nerves!"

The president looked up with a lively twinkle in his keen eyes.

"Now I have been thinking," Mr. Vanderlip continued, "while sitting in there with nothing to do, of a plan for increasing the business of this bank."

The president assured him that both "thinking" and "plans" were valuable, and asked him to continue with his interview.

"I have thought of a plan," Mr. Vanderlip went on, "that will give the bank the benefit of my experience in the bond business. I propose to create a bond department for this bank and advertise it as a feature of our business."

"What! this bank advertise?" queried the president. "Why, we have never advertised since we began business. We have managed to get along without it."

"Well, this is where you are going to begin advertising," said Mr. Vanderlip, "and the first thing you are going to advertise is this new bond department that I have planned."

Mr. Vanderlip won! Men of *action* usually win— that is one of their distinctive features. The National City Bank also won, because that interview was the beginning of one of the most progressive and profitable advertising campaigns ever carried on by any bank, with the result that the National City Bank became one of the most powerful financial institutions of America.

There were other results, also, that are worth naming. Among them the result that Mr. Vanderlip grew with the bank, as men of *action* usually grow in whatever they help to build, until finally he became the president of that great banking house.

In the lesson on *Imagination* you learned how to recombine old ideas into new plans, but no matter how practical your plans may be they will be useless if they are not expressed in *action*. To dream dreams and see visions of the person you would like to be or the station in life you would like to obtain are admirable provided you transform your dreams and visions into reality through intensive *action*.

There are men who dream, but do nothing more. There are others who take the visions of the dreamers and translate them into stone, and marble, and music, and good books, and railroads, and steamships. There are still others who *both dream* and transform these dreams into reality. They are the dreamer-doer types.

There is a psychological as well as an economic reason why you should form the habit of intensive *action*. Your body is made up of billions of tiny cells that are highly sensitive and amenable to the influence of your mind. If your mind is of the lethargic, *inactive* type, the cells of your body become lazy and inactive also. Just as the stagnant water of an inactive pond becomes impure and unhealthful, so will the cells of an inactive body become diseased.

Laziness is nothing but the influence of an inactive mind on the cells of the body. If you doubt this, the next time you feel lazy take a Turkish bath and have yourself well rubbed down, thereby stimulating the cells of your body by artificial means, and see how quickly your laziness disappears. Or, a better way than this, turn your mind toward some game of which you are fond and notice how quickly the cells of your

EVERY failure will teach you a lesson that you need to learn if you will keep your eyes and ears open and be willing to be taught. Every adversity is usually a blessing in disguise. Without reverses and temporary defeat, you would never know the sort of metal of which you are made.

body will respond to your enthusiasm and your lazy feeling will disappear.

The cells of the body respond to the state of mind in exactly the same manner that the people of a city respond to the mass psychology that dominates the city. If a group of leaders engage in sufficient *action* to give a city the reputation of being a "live-wire" city this *action* influences all who live there. The same principle applies to the relationship between the mind and the body. An *active,* dynamic mind keeps the cells of which the physical portions of the body consist, in a constant state of activity.

The artificial conditions under which most inhabitants of our cities live have led to a physical condition known as auto-intoxication, which means self-poisoning through the inactive state of the intestines. Most headaches may be cured in an hour's time by simply cleansing the lower intestines with an enema.

Eight glasses of water a day and a reasonable amount of physical *action* popularly known as "exercise" will take the place of the enema. Try it for a week and then you will not have to be urged to keep it up, for you will feel like a new person, unless the nature of your work is such that you get plenty of physical exercise and drink plenty of water in the regular course of your duties.

On two pages of this book enough sound advice could be recorded to keep the average person healthy and ready for *action* during sixteen of the twenty-four hours of the day, but the advice would be so simple that most people would not follow it.

The amount of work that I perform every day and still keep in good physical condition is a source of wonderment and mystery to those who know me intimately, yet there is no mystery to it, and the system I follow does not cost anything.

Here it is, for your use if you want it:

First: I drink a cup of hot water when I first get up in the morning, before I have breakfast.

Second: My breakfast consists of rolls made of whole wheat and bran, breakfast cereal, fruit, soft-boiled eggs once in a while, and coffee. For luncheon I eat vegetables (most any kind), whole wheat bread and a glass of buttermilk. Supper, a well cooked steak once or twice a week, vegetables, especially lettuce, and coffee.

Third: I walk an average of ten miles a day: five miles into the country and five miles back, using this period for meditation and thought. Perhaps the thinking is as valuable, as a health builder, as the walk.

Fourth: I lie across a straight bottom chair, flat on my back, with most of my weight resting on the small of my back, with my head and arms relaxed completely, until they almost touch the floor. This gives the nervous energy of my body an opportunity to balance properly and distribute itself, and ten minutes in this position will completely relieve all signs of fatigue, no matter how tired I may be.

Fifth: I take an enema at least once every ten days, and more often if I feel the need of it, using water that is a little below blood temperature, with a tablespoonful of salt in it, chest and knee position.

Sixth: I take a hot shower bath, followed immediately by a cold shower, every day, usually in the morning when I first get up.

These simple things I do for myself. Mother Nature attends to everything else necessary for my health.

I cannot lay too much stress upon the importance of keeping the intestines clean, for it is a well known fact that the city dwellers of today are literally poisoning themselves to death by neglecting to cleanse their intestines with water. You should not wait until you are constipated to take an enema. When you get to the stage of constipation you are practically ill and immediate relief is absolutely essential, but if you will give yourself the proper attention regularly, just as you attend to keeping the outside of your body clean, you will never be bothered with the many troubles which constipation brings.

For more than fifteen years no single week ever passed without my having a headache. Usually I administered a dose of aspirin and got temporary relief. I was suffering with auto-intoxication and did not know it, for the reason that I was not constipated.

When I found out what my trouble was I did two things, both of which I recommend to you; namely, *I quit using aspirin* and I cut down my daily consumption of food nearly one half.

Just a word about aspirin—a word which those who profit by its sale will not like—it affords no permanent cure of headache. All it does might be compared to a lineman that cuts the telegraph wire while the operator is using that wire in a call for aid from the fire department to save the burning building in which he is located. Aspirin cuts or "deadens" the line of nerve communication that runs from the stomach or the intestinal region, where auto-intoxication is pouring poison into the blood, to the brain, where the effect of that poison is registering its call in the form of intense pain.

Cutting the telegraph line over which a call for the fire department is being sent does not put out the fire; nor does it remove the cause to deaden, with the aid of a dose of aspirin, the nerve line over which a headache is registering a call for help.

You cannot be a person of *action* if you permit yourself to go without proper physical attention until autointoxication takes your brain and kneads it into an inoperative mass that resembles a ball of putty. Neither can you be a person of *action* if you eat the usual devitalized concoction called "white bread" (which has had all the real food value removed from it) and twice as much meat as your system can digest and properly dispose of.

You cannot be a person of *action* if you run to the pill bottle every time you have, or *imagine* you have, an ache or a pain, or swallow an aspirin tablet every time your intestines call on your brain for a douche bag of water and a spoonful of salt for cleansing purposes.

You cannot be a person of *action* if you *overeat* and *under-exercise*.

You cannot be a person of *action* if you read the patent medicine booklets and begin to imagine yourself ailing with the symptoms described by the clever advertisement writer who has reached your pocket book through the power of *suggestion*.

I have not touched a drug for more than five years, and I have not been either sick or ailing during that time, in spite of the fact that I perform more work each day than most men of my profession. I have *enthusiasm, endurance* and *action* because I eat the sort of simple food that contains the body-building elements that I require, and look after the eliminative processes as carefully as I bathe my body.

If these simple and frank admissions appeal to you as being based upon common sense, take them and put them to the test, and if they serve you as well as they are serving me, both of us will have profited by the courage I had to summon to list them as a part of this lesson.

Usually, when anyone except a physician offers suggestions on the care of the body, he is immediately catalogued as a "long-haired crank," and I will admit that the analysis is often correct. In this instance, I make no stronger recommendations than this:

That you try an enema the next time you have a headache, and if any of the other suggestions appeal to you give them a trial until you are satisfied that they are either sound or unsound.

Before leaving the subject, perhaps I should explain that water which is barely luke-warm should be used for the enema for the reason that this causes the muscles of the intestines to contract, which, in turn, forces the poisonous matter out of the pores of the mucous linings. This exercises those muscles and eventually it will so develop them that they will do their work in the natural way, without the aid of the enema. A warm water enema is very detrimental for the reason that it relaxes the muscles of the intestines, which, in time, causes them to cease functioning altogether, producing what is ordinarily referred to as the "enema habit."

With due apologies to my friends, the physicians and

A N occasional mis-
fortune is a good
thing. It reminds us that
no one has absolute in-
dependence.

osteopaths and chiropractors and other health builders, I will now invite you back to that part of the
subject of this lesson over which there can be no conflict of opinion as to the soundness of my counsel.

. . . .

There is another enemy which you must conquer
before you can become a person of *action,* and that is
the *worry habit.*

Worry, and envy, and jealousy, and hatred, and
doubt, and fear are all states of mind which are fatal
to *action.*

Any of these states of mind will interfere with, and
in some instances destroy altogether, the digestive
process through which the food is assimilated and prepared for distribution through the body. This interference is purely physical, but the damage does not
stop here, because these negative states of mind destroy the most essential factor in the achievement of
success; namely, *desire* to achieve.

In the second lesson of this course you learned that
your *definite chief aim* in life should be supported by
a *burning desire* for its realization. You can have no
burning desire for achievement when you are in a negative state of mind, no matter what the cause of that
state of mind may be.

To keep myself in a positive frame of mind I have
discovered a very effective "gloom-chaser." That may
not be a very dignified way of expressing my meaning, but since the subject of this lesson is *action* and
not dignity I will make it serve. The "gloom-chaser"
to which I refer is a *hearty laugh.* When I feel "out
of sorts" or inclined to argue with somebody over

something that is not worthy of discussion, I know that I need my "gloom-chaser," and I proceed to get away where I will disturb no one and have a good hearty laugh. If I can find nothing really funny about which to laugh I simply have a forced laugh. The effect is the same in both cases.

Five minutes of this sort of mental and physical exercise—for it is both—will stimulate *action* that is free from negative tendencies.

Do not take my word for this—try it!

Not long ago I heard a phonograph record entitled, as I recall it, The Laughing Fool, which should be available to all whose dignity forbids them to indulge in a hearty laugh for their health's sake. This record was all that its name implies. It was made by a man and a woman; the man was trying to play a cornet and the woman was laughing at him. She laughed so effectively that she finally made the man laugh, and the suggestion was so pronounced that all who heard it usually joined in and had a good laugh, whether they felt like it or not.

"As a man thinketh in his heart, so is he."

You cannot think *fear* and act courageously. You cannot think hatred and act in a kindly manner toward those with whom you associate. The dominating thoughts of your mind—meaning by this, the strongest and deepest and most frequent of your thoughts—influence the physical *action* of your body.

Every thought put into action by your brain reaches and influences every cell in your body. When you think *fear* your mind telegraphs this thought down to the cells that form the muscles of your legs and tells those muscles to get into *action* and carry you away as rapidly as they can. A man who is afraid runs away because his legs carry him, and they carry him because the *fear* thought in his mind instructed them to do so, even though the instructions were given unconsciously.

In the first lesson of this course you learned how *thought* travels from one mind to another, through the principle of telepathy. In this lesson you should go a step further and learn that *your thoughts* not only register themselves in the minds of other people, through the principle of telepathy, but, *what is a million times more important to you to understand, they register themselves on the cells of your own body* and *affect those cells in a manner that harmonizes with the nature of the thoughts.*

To understand this principle is to understand the soundness of the statement: "As a man thinketh in his heart, so is he."

Action, in the sense that the term is used in this lesson, is of two forms. One is physical and the other is mental. You can be very active with your mind while your body is entirely inactive, except as to the involuntary action of the vital organs. Or you can be very active with both body and mind.

In speaking of men of *action,* either or both of two types may be referred to. One is the care-taker type and the other is the promoter or salesman type. Both of these types are essential in modern business, industry and finance. One is known as a "dynamo" while the other is often referred to as a "balance wheel."

Once in a great while you will find a man who is both a dynamo and a balance wheel, but such well

balanced personalities are rare. Most successful business organizations that assume great size are made up
of both of these types.

The "balance wheel" who does nothing but compile
facts and figures and statistics is just as much a man
of *action* as the man who goes upon the platform and
sells an idea to a thousand people by the sheer power
of his *active* personality. To determine whether a
man is a man of *action* or not it is necessary to analyze
both his mental and his physical habits.

In the first part of this lesson I said that "the world
pays you for what you do and not for what you know."
That statement might easily be misconstrued. What
the world really pays you for is *what you do* or *what
you can get others to do*.

A man who can induce others to co-operate and do
effective team-work, or inspire others so that they become more *active,* is no less a man of *action* than the
man who renders effective service in a more direct
manner.

In the field of industry and business there are men
who have the ability so to inspire and direct the efforts of others that all under their direction accomplish more than they could without this directing
influence. It is a well known fact that Carnegie so
ably directed the efforts of those who constituted his
personal staff that he made many wealthy men of
those who would never have become wealthy without
the directing genius of his brain. The same may be
said of practically all great leaders in the field of industry and business—the gain is not all on the side
of the leaders. Those under their direction often
profit most by their leadership.

It is a common practice for a certain type of man to berate his employers because of their opposite stations in a financial sense. It is usually true that such men would be infinitely worse off without these employers than they are with them.

In the first lesson of this course the value of allied effort was particularly emphasized for the reason that some men have the vision to plan while others have the ability to carry plans into *action* although they do not possess the *imagination* or the vision to create the plans they execute.

It was his understanding of this principle of allied effort that enabled Andrew Carnegie to surround himself with a group of men that was made up of those who could plan and those who could execute. Carnegie had in his group of assistants some of the most efficient salesmen in the world, but if his entire staff had been made up of men who could do nothing but sell he could never have accumulated the fortune that he did. If his entire staff had been made up of salesmen only he would have had *action* in abundance, but *action*, in the sense that it is used in this lesson, must be intelligently guided.

One of the best known law firms in America is made up of two lawyers, one of whom never appears in court. He prepares the firm's cases for trial and the other member of the firm goes to court and tries them. Both are men of intense *action*, but they express it in different ways.

There can be as much *action* in *preparation*, in most undertakings, as in *execution*.

In finding your own place in the world, you should analyze yourself and find out whether you are a "dy-

THOUSANDS of people walked over the great Calumet Copper Mine without discovering it. Just one lone man got busy with a pick and found it. You may be standing on your "Calumet Mine" right now, without knowing it, in whatever position you are filling. Dig down and see what is under the surface of your position.

namo" or a "balance wheel," and select a *definite chief aim* for yourself that harmonizes with your native ability. If you are in business with others, you should analyze them as well as yourself, and endeavor to see that each person takes the part for which his temperament and native ability best fit him.

Stating it another way, people may be classified under two headings: one is the promoter and the other is the care-taker. The promoter type makes an able salesman and organizer. The care-taker type makes an excellent conserver of assets after they have been accumulated.

Place the care-taker type in charge of a set of books and he is happy, but place him on the outside selling and he is unhappy and will be a failure at his job. Place the promoter in charge of a set of books and he will be miserable. His nature demands more intense *action*. Action of the passive type will not satisfy his ambitions, and if he is kept at work which does not give him the action his nature demands he will be a failure. It very frequently turns out that men who embezzle funds in their charge are of the promoter type and they would not have yielded to temptation had their efforts been confined to the work for which they are best fitted.

Give a man the sort of work that harmonizes with his nature and the best there is in him will exert itself. One of the outstanding tragedies of the world is the fact that most people never engage in the work for which they are best fitted by nature.

Too often the mistake is made, in the selection of a life-work, of engaging in the work which seems to be the most profitable from a monetary viewpoint, without consideration of native ability. If money alone brought success this procedure would be all right, but *success* in its highest and noblest form calls for peace of mind and enjoyment and happiness which come only to the man who has found the work that he likes best.

The main purpose of this course is to help you analyze yourself and determine what your native ability best fits you to do. You should make this analysis by carefully studying the chart that accompanies the Introductory Lesson before you select your *definite chief aim*.

We come, now, to the discussion of the principle through which *action* may be developed. To understand how to become *active* requires understanding of how not to *procrastinate*.

These suggestions will give you the necessary instructions:

First: Form the *habit* of doing each day the most distasteful tasks first. This procedure will be difficult at first, but after you have formed the *habit* you will take pride in pitching into the hardest and most undesirable part of your work first.

Second: Place this sign in front of you where you can see it in your daily work, and put a copy in your bedroom, where it will greet you as you retire and when you arise: *"Do not tell them what you can do; show them!"*

Third: Repeat the following words, aloud, twelve times each night just before you go to sleep: "Tomorrow I will do everything that should be done, when it should be done, and as it should be done. I will perform the most difficult tasks first because this will

destroy the habit of procrastination and develop the
habit of *action* in its place."

Fourth: Carry out these instructions with faith in
their soundness and with belief that they will develop
action, in body and in mind, sufficient to enable you
to realize your *definite chief aim*.

The outstanding feature of this course is the simplicity of the style in which it is written. All great
fundamental truths are simple, in final analysis, and
whether one is delivering an address or writing a
course of instruction, the purpose should be to convey
impressions and statements of fact in the clearest and
most concise manner possible.

Before closing this lesson, permit me to go back to
what was said about the value of a hearty laugh as
a healthful stimulant to *action,* and add the statement
that singing produces the same effect, and in some instances is far preferable to laughing.

Billy Sunday is one of the most dynamic and *active*
preachers in the world, yet it has been said that his
sermons would lose much of their effectiveness if it
were not for the psychological effect of his song
services.

It is a well known fact that the German army was
a winning army at the beginning, and long after the
beginning of the world war; and it has been said that
much of this was due to the fact that the German army
was a singing army. Then came the khaki-clad dough-
boys from America, and they, too, were singers. Back
of their singing was an enduring faith in the cause for
which they were fighting. Soon the Germans began
to quit singing, and as they did so the tide of war began to turn against them.

· If church attendance had nothing else to recommend it, except the psychological effect of the song service, that would be sufficient, for no one can join in the singing of a beautiful hymn without feeling better for it.

For many years I have observed that I could write more effectively after having participated in a song service. Prove my statement to your own satisfaction by going to church next Sunday morning and participating in the song service with all the enthusiasm at your command.

During the war I helped devise ways and means of speeding production in industrial plants that were engaged in manufacturing war supplies. By actual test, in a plant employing 3,000 men and women, the production was increased forty-five per cent in less than thirty days after we had organized the workers into singing groups and installed orchestras and bands that played at ten-minute intervals such stirring songs as "Over There," and "Dixie," and "There'll Be a Hot Time in the Old Town Tonight." The workers caught the rhythm of the music and speeded up their work accordingly.

Properly selected music would stimulate any class of workers to greater *action*, a fact which does not seem to be understood by all who direct the efforts of large numbers of people.

In all my travels I have found but one business firm whose managers made use of music as a stimulant for their workers. This was the Filene Department Store, in Boston, Mass. During the summer months this store provides an orchestra that plays the latest dance music for half an hour before opening time, in the morning. The salespeople use the aisles of the store for dancing and by the time the doors are thrown open they are in an *active* state of mind and body that carries them through the entire day.

Incidentally, I have never seen more courteous or efficient salespeople than those employed by the Filene store. One of the department managers told me that every person in his department performed more service and with less real effort, as a result of the morning music program.

A singing army is a winning army, whether on the field of battle, in warfare, or behind the counters in a department store. There is a book entitled Singing Through Life With God by George Wharton James, which I recommend to all who are interested in the psychology of song.

If I were the manager of an industrial plant in which the work was heavy and monotonous, I would install some sort of musical program that would supply every worker with music. On lower Broadway, in New York City, an ingenious Greek has discovered how to entertain his customers and at the same time speed up the work of his helpers by the use of a phonograph. Every boy in the place keeps time with the music as he draws the cloth across the shoes, and seems to get considerable fun out of his work in doing so. To speed up the work the proprietor has but to speed up the phonograph.

. . . . . .

Any form of group effort, where two or more people form a co-operative alliance for the purpose of accomplishing a definite purpose, becomes more powerful than mere individual effort.

I DO not know for sure, but I strongly suspect that the person who performs service that is greater in quantity and better in quality than that for which he is paid, is eventually paid for more than he performs.

A football team may win consistently and continuously, by well co-ordinated team-work, even though
the members of the team may be unfriendly and out
of harmony in many ways outside of their actual
work on the ball ground.

A group of men composing a board of directors may
disagree with one another; they may be unfriendly,
and in no way in sympathy with one another, and
still carry on a business which appears to be very
successful.

A man and his wife may live together, accumulate
a fair sized or even a great fortune, rear and educate
a family, without the bond of harmony which is essential for the development of a Master Mind.

But all of these alliances might be made more powerful and effective if based upon a foundation of
perfect harmony, thus permitting the development of
a supplemental power known as the Master Mind.

Plain co-operative effort produces power; there can
be no doubt about this; but co-operative effort that is
based upon complete harmony of purpose develops
super-power.

Let every member of any co-operative group set
his heart upon the achievement of the same definite
end, in a spirit of perfect harmony, and the way has
been paved for the development of a Master Mind,
providing all members of the group willingly subordinate their own personal interests for the attainment
of the objective for which the group is aiming.

The United States of America has become one of
the most powerful nations on earth, largely because
of the highly organized co-operative effort between the
states. It will be helpful to remember that these

United States were born as the result of one of the most powerful Master Minds ever created. The members of this Master Mind· were the signers of the Declaration of Independence.

The men who signed that document either consciously or unconsciously put into operation the power known as the "Master Mind," and that power was sufficient to enable them to defeat all the soldiers who were sent into the field against them. The men who fought to make the Declaration of Independence endure did not fight for money, alone; they fought for a principle—the principle of freedom, which is the highest known motivating force.

A great leader, whether in business, finance, industry or statesmanship, is one who understands how to create a motivating objective which will be accepted with enthusiasm by every member of his group of followers.

In politics a "live issue" is everything!

By "live issue" is meant some popular objective toward the attainment of which the majority of the voters can be rallied. These "issues" generally are broadcast in the form of snappy slogans, such as "Keep Cool with Coolidge," which suggested to the minds of the voters that to keep Coolidge was the equivalent of keeping prosperity. It worked!

During Lincoln's election campaign the cry was, "Stand back of Lincoln and preserve the Union." It worked.

Woodrow Wilson's campaign managers, during his second campaign, coined the slogan, "He kept us out of war," and it worked.

The degree of power created by the co-operative

effort of any group of people is measured, always, by the nature of the motive which the group is laboring to attain. This may be profitably borne in mind by all who organize group effort for any purpose whatsoever. Find a motive around which men may be induced to rally in a highly emotionalized, enthusiastic spirit of perfect harmony and you have found the starting point for the creation of a Master Mind.

It is a well known fact that men will work harder for the attainment of an ideal than they will for mere money. In searching for a "motive" as the basis for developing co-operative group effort it will be profitable to bear this fact in mind.

At the time of the writing of this lesson there is much adverse agitation and general criticism directed against the railroads of the country. Who is back of this agitation this author does not know, but he does know that the very fact that such agitation exists could and should be made the motivating force around which the railroad officials might rally the hundreds of thousands of railroad employees who earn their living by railroading, thereby creating a power that would effectively eliminate this adverse criticism.

The railroads are the very back-bone of the country. Tie up all railroad service and the people of the larger cities would starve before food could reach them. In this fact may be found a motive around which a large majority of the public could be caused to rally in support of any plan for self-protection which the railroad officials might wish to carry out.

The power represented by all of the railroad employees and a majority of the public who patronize the railroads is sufficient to protect the railroads against all manner of adverse legislation and other attempts to depreciate their properties, but the power is only potential until it is organized and placed definitely back of a specific motive.

.   .   .   .

Man is a queer animal. Give him a sufficiently vitalized motive and the man of but average ability, under ordinary circumstances, will suddenly develop superpower.

What man can and will accomplish to please the woman of his choice (providing the woman knows how to stimulate him to action) has ever been a source of wonderment to students of the human mind.

There are three major motivating forces to which man responds in practically all of his efforts. These are:

1. The motive of self-preservation
2. The motive of sexual contact
3. The motive of financial and social power.

Stated more briefly, the main motives which impel men to action are money, sex and self-preservation. Leaders who are seeking a motivating force out of which to secure action from a following may find it under one or more of these three classifications.

As you have observed, this lesson is very closely related to the Introductory Lesson and Lesson Two which cover the Law of the Master Mind. It is possible for groups to function co-operatively, without thereby creating a Master Mind, as, for example, where people co-operate merely out of necessity, without the spirit of harmony as the basis of their efforts. This sort of co-operation may produce considerable power, but nothing to compare with that which is possible when every person in an alliance subordinates his or her own individual interests and co-ordinates his or her efforts with those of all other members of the alliance, in perfect harmony.

The extent to which people may be induced to co-operate, in harmony, depends upon the motivating force which impels them to action. Perfect harmony such as is essential for creating a Master Mind can be obtained only when the motivating force of a group is sufficient to cause each member of the group completely to forget his or her own personal interests and work for the good of the group, or for the sake of attaining some idealistic, charitable or philanthropic objective.

The three major motivating forces of mankind have been here stated for the guidance of the Leader who wishes to create plans for securing co-operation from followers who will throw themselves into the carrying out of his plans in a spirit of unselfishness and perfect harmony.

Men will not rally to the support of a leader in such a spirit of harmony unless the motive that impels them to do so is one that will induce them to lay aside all thoughts of themselves.

We do well that which we love to do, and fortunate is the Leader who has the good judgment to bear this fact in mind and so lay his plans that all his followers are assigned parts that harmonize with this law.

The leader who gets all there is to be had from his followers does so because he has set up in the mind of each a sufficiently strong motive to get each to subordinate his own interests and work in a perfect spirit

YOUR position is nothing more than your opportunity to show what sort of ability you have. You will get out of it exactly what you put into it—no more and no less. A "big" position is but the sum total of numerous "little" positions well filled.

of harmony with all other members of the group.

Regardless of who you are, or what your *definite chief aim* may be, if you plan to attain the object of your *chief aim* through the co-operative efforts of others you must set up in the minds of those whose co-operation you seek a motive strong enough to insure their full, undivided, unselfish co-operation, for you will then be placing back of your plans the power of the Law of the Master Mind.

.   .   .   .

You are now ready to take up Lesson Fourteen, which will teach you how to make working capital out of all mistakes, errors and failures which you have experienced, and also how to profit by the mistakes and failures of others.

The president of one of the great railway systems of the United States said, after reading the next lesson, that "this lesson carries a suggestion which, if heeded and understood, will enable any person to become a master in his chosen life-work."

For reasons which will be plain after you have read the next lesson, it is the author's favorite lesson of this course.

YOUR STANDING ARMY
An After-the-Lesson Visit With the Author

(These fifteen soldiers are labeled: Definite Chief Aim, Self-Confidence, Habit of Saving, Imagination, Initiative and Leadership, Enthusiasm, Self-Control, Doing More Than Paid For, Pleasing Personality, Accurate Thought, Concentration, Co-operation, Failure, Tolerance, Golden Rule)

Power comes from organized effort. You see in the above picture the forces which enter into all organized effort. Master these fifteen forces and you may have whatever you want in life. Others will be helpless to defeat your plans. Make these fifteen forces your own and you will be an accurate thinker.

IN the picture at the top of this page you see the most powerful army on earth! Observe the emphasis on the word POWERFUL.

This army is standing at attention, ready to do the bidding of any person who will command it. It is YOUR army if you will take charge of it.

This army will give you POWER sufficient to mow

down all opposition with which you meet. Study the picture carefully, then take inventory of yourself and find out how many of these soldiers you need.

.   .   .   .

If you are a normal person you long for material success.

Success and POWER are always found together. You cannot be sure of success unless you have power. You cannot have power unless you develop it through fifteen essential qualities.

Each of these fifteen qualities may be likened to the commanding officer of a regiment of soldiers. Develop these qualities in your own mind and you will have POWER.

The most important of the fifteen commanding officers in this army is DEFINITE PURPOSE.

Without the aid of a definite purpose the remainder of the army would be useless to you. Find out, as early in life as possible, what your major purpose in life shall be. Until you do this you are nothing but a drifter, subject to control by every stray wind of circumstance that blows in your direction.

Millions of people go through life without knowing what it is they want.

All have a purpose, but only two out of every hundred have a DEFINITE purpose. Before you decide whether your purpose is DEFINITE or not, look up the meaning of the word in the dictionary.

NOTHING IS IMPOSSIBLE TO THE PERSON WHO KNOWS WHAT IT IS HE WANTS AND MAKES UP HIS MIND TO ACQUIRE IT!

Columbus had a DEFINITE PURPOSE and it be

came a reality. Lincoln's major DEFINITE PUR-
POSE was to free the black slaves of the South and he
turned that purpose into reality. Roosevelt's major
purpose, during his first term of office, was to build
the Panama Canal. He lived to see that purpose realized. Henry Ford's DEFINITE PURPOSE was to
build the best popular priced automobile on earth.
That purpose, backed persistently, has made him the
most powerful man on earth. Burbank's DEFINITE
PURPOSE was to improve plant life. Already that
purpose has made possible the raising of enough food
on ten square miles of land to feed the entire world.

.   .   .   .

Twenty years ago Edwin C. Barnes formed a DEF-
INITE PURPOSE in his mind. That purpose was to
become the business partner of Thomas A. Edison.
At the time his purpose was chosen Mr. Barnes had
no qualification entitling him to a partnership with
the world's greatest inventor. Despite this handicap
he became the partner of the great Edison. Five
years ago he retired from active business, with more
money than he needs or can use, wealth that he accumulated in partnership with Edison.

NOTHING IS IMPOSSIBLE TO THE MAN
WITH A DEFINITE PURPOSE!

Opportunity, capital, co-operation from other men
and all other essentials for success gravitate to the
man who knows what he wants!

Vitalize your mind with a DEFINITE PURPOSE
and immediately your mind becomes a magnet which
attracts everything that harmonizes with that purpose.

James J. Hill, the great railroad builder, was a poorly paid telegraph operator. Moreover, he had reached the age of forty and was still ticking away at the telegraph key without any outward appearances of success.

Then something of importance happened! Of importance to Hill and to the people of the United States. He formed the DEFINITE PURPOSE of building a railroad across the great waste desert of the West. Without reputation, without capital, without encouragement from others James J. Hill got the capital and built the greatest of all the railroad systems of the United States.

Woolworth was a poorly paid clerk in a general store. In his mind's eye he saw a chain of novelty stores specializing on five and ten cent sales. That chain of stores became his DEFINITE PURPOSE. He made that purpose come true, and with it more millions than he could use.

Cyrus H. K. Curtis selected, as his DEFINITE PURPOSE, the publishing of the world's greatest magazine. Starting with nothing but the name "Saturday Evening Post," and opposed by friends and advisers who said "It couldn't be done," he transformed that purpose into reality.

Martin W. Littleton is the most highly paid lawyer in the world. It is said that he will accept no retainer under $50,000.00. When he was twelve years old he had never been inside of a school house. He went to hear a lawyer defend a murderer. That speech so impressed him that he grabbed hold of his father's hand and said, "Some day I am going to be the best lawyer in the United States and make speeches like that man."

"Fine chance for an ignorant mountain youth to become a great lawyer," someone might say, but remember that NOTHING IS IMPOSSIBLE TO THE MAN WHO KNOWS WHAT HE WANTS AND MAKES UP HIS MIND TO GET IT.

.   .   .   .

Study each of the fifteen soldiers shown in command of the army in the picture at the beginning of this essay.

Remember, as you look at the picture, that no one of these soldiers alone is powerful enough to insure success. Remove a single one of them and the entire army would be weakened.

The powerful man is the man who has developed, in his own mind, the entire fifteen qualities represented by the fifteen commanding officers shown in the picture. Before you can have power you must have a DEFINITE PURPOSE; you must have SELF-CONFIDENCE with which to back up that purpose; you must have INITIATIVE and LEADERSHIP with which to exercise your self-confidence; you must have IMAGINATION in creating your definite purpose and in building the plans with which to transform that purpose into reality and put your plans into action. You must mix ENTHUSIASM with your action or it will be insipid and without "kick." You must exercise SELF-CONTROL. You must form the habit of DOING MORE THAN PAID FOR. You must cultivate a PLEASING PERSONALITY. You must acquire the HABIT OF SAVING.

You must become an ACCURATE THINKER, re-membering, as you develop this quality, that accurate thought is based upon FACTS and not upon hearsay evidence or mere information. You must form the habit of CONCENTRATION by giving your undi-vided attention to but one task at a time. You must acquire the habit of CO-OPERATION and practice it in all your plans. You must profit by FAILURE, your own and that of others. You must cultivate the habit of TOLERANCE. Last, but by no means the least important, you must make the GOLDEN RULE the foundation of all you do that affects other people.

Keep this picture where you can see it each day and, one by one, call these fifteen soldiers out of the line and study them. Make sure that the counterpart of each is developed in your own mind.

.   .   .   .

All efficient armies are well disciplined!

The army which you are building in your own mind must, also, be disciplined. It must obey your command at every step.

When you call out of the line the thirteenth sol-dier, "FAILURE," remember that nothing will go as far toward developing discipline as will failure and temporary defeat. While you are comparing your-self with this soldier determine whether or not you have been profiting by your own failures and tem-porary defeat.

FAILURE comes to all at one time or another. Make sure, when it comes your way, that you will learn something of value from its visit. Make sure, also, that it would not visit you if there was not room for it in your make-up.

To make progress in this world you must rely solely upon the forces within your own mind for your start. After this start has been made you may turn to others for aid, but the first step must be taken without outside aid.

After you have made this "start," it will surprise you to observe how many willing people you will encounter who will volunteer to assist you.

.   .   .   .

Success is made up of many facts and factors, chiefly of the fifteen qualities represented by these fifteen soldiers. To enjoy a well balanced and rounded out success one must appropriate as much or as little of each of these fifteen qualities as may be missing in one's own inherited ability.

When you came into this world you were endowed with certain inborn traits, the result of millions of years of evolutionary changes, through thousands of generations of ancestors.

Added to these inborn traits you acquired many other qualities, according to the nature of your environment and the teaching you received during your early childhood. You are the sum total of that which was born in you and that which you have picked up from your experiences, what you have thought and what you have been taught, since birth.

Through the law of chance one in a million people will receive, through inborn heredity and from knowledge acquired after birth, all of the fifteen qualities named in the picture above.

All who are not fortunate enough to have thus acquired the essentials for SUCCESS must develop them within themselves.

The first step in this "development" process is to realize what qualities are missing in your naturally acquired equipment. The second step is the strongly planted DESIRE to develop yourself where you are now deficient.

Prayer sometimes works, while at other times it does not work.

It always works when backed with unqualified FAITH. This is a truth which no one will deny, yet, it is a truth which no one can explain. All we know is that prayer works when we BELIEVE it will work. Prayer without FAITH is nothing but an empty collection of words.

A DEFINITE PURPOSE may be transformed into reality only when one BELIEVES it can be done. Perhaps the selfsame law that turns the prayer based upon FAITH into reality transforms, also, a DEFINITE PURPOSE that is founded upon belief into reality.

It can do no harm if you make your DEFINITE PURPOSE in life the object of your daily prayer. And, as you pray remember that prayer based upon FAITH always works.

Develop in your own mind all of the fifteen qualities, from a DEFINITE PURPOSE to the GOLDEN RULE, and you will find the application of FAITH is not difficult.

Take inventory of yourself. Find out how many of the fifteen qualities you now possess. Add to this inventory the missing qualities until you have, in your mind, the entire fifteen. You will then be ready to measure your success in whatever terms you DESIRE.

The qualities represented by the fifteen soldiers shown in this picture are the brick and the mortar and the building material with which you must build your Temple of Success. Master these fifteen qualities and you may play a perfect symphony of success in any undertaking, just as one who has mastered the fundamentals of music may play any piece at sight.

Make these fifteen qualities your own and you will be an EDUCATED person, because you will have the power to get whatever you want in life without violating the rights of others.

"All worlds are man's, to conquer and to rule
  This is the glory of his iife.
But this its iron law: first must he school
  Himself. Here 'gins at.d ends all strife."

Lesson Fourteen

FAILURE

Yesterday is but a dream,
Tomorrow is only a
vision.
But today well lived
makes
Every yesterday a dream
of happiness,
And every tomorrow a vi-
sion of hope.
Look well, therefore, to
this day.
—*From the Sanscrit.*

THE LAW OF SUCCESS

Lesson Fourteen

FAILURE

"You Can Do It if You Believe You Can!"

NDER ordinary circumstances the term "failure" is a negative term. In this lesson, the word will be given a new meaning, because the word has been a very much misused one; and, for that reason, it has brought unnecessary grief and hardship to millions of people.

In the outset, let us distinguish between "failure" and "temporary defeat." Let us see if that which is so often looked upon as "failure" is not, in reality, but "temporary defeat." Moreover, let us see if this temporary defeat is not usually a blessing in disguise, for the reason that it brings us up with a jerk and redirects our energies along different and more desirable lines.

In Lesson Nine of this course, we learned that strength grows out of resistance; and we shall learn, in this lesson, that sound character is usually the handiwork of reverses, and set-backs, and temporary defeat, which the uninformed part of the world calls "failure."

Neither temporary defeat nor adversity amounts to failure in the mind of the person who looks upon it as a teacher that will teach some needed lesson. As a matter of fact, there is a great and lasting lesson in every reverse, and in every defeat; and, usually, it is a lesson that could be learned in no other way than through defeat.

Defeat often talks to us in a "dumb language" that we do not understand. If this were not true, we would not make the same mistakes over and over again without profiting by the lessons that they might teach us. If it were not true, we would observe more closely the mistakes which other people make and profit by them.

The main object of this lesson is to help the student understand and profit by this "dumb language" in which defeat talks to us.

Perhaps I can best help you to interpret the meaning of defeat by taking you back over some of my own experiences covering a period of approximately thirty years. Within this period, I have come to the turning-point, which the uninformed call "failure," seven different times. At each of these seven turning-points I thought I had made a dismal failure; but now I know that what looked to be a failure was nothing more than a kindly, unseen hand, that halted me in my chosen course and with great wisdom forced me to redirect my efforts along more advantageous pathways.

I arrived at this decision, however, only after I had taken a retrospective view of my experiences and had analyzed them in the light of many years of sober and meditative thought.

FIRST TURNING-POINT

After finishing a course in a business college, I secured a position as stenographer and bookkeeper which I held for the ensuing five years. As a result of having practiced the habit of performing more work and better work than that for which I was paid, as described in Lesson Nine of this course, I advanced rapidly until I was assuming responsibilities and receiving a salary far out of proportion to my age. I saved my money; and my bank account amounted to several thousand dollars. My reputation spread rapidly and I found competitive bidders for my services.

To meet these offers from competitors my employer advanced me to the position of General Manager of the mines where I was employed. I was quickly getting on top of the world, and *I knew it!*

Ah! but that was the sad part of my fate—*I knew it!*

Then the kindly hand of Fate reached out and gave me a gentle nudge. My employer lost his fortune and I lost my position. This was my first real defeat; and, even though it came about as a result of causes beyond my control, I should have learned a lesson from it; which, of course, I did, but not until many years later.

SECOND TURNING-POINT

My next position was that of Sales Manager for a large lumber manufacturing concern in the South. I knew nothing about lumber, and but little about sales management; but I had learned that it was beneficial to render more service than that for which I was paid; and I had also learned that it paid to take the initiative and find out what ought to be done without someone telling me to do it. A good sized bank account, plus a record of steady advancement in my previous position, gave me all the self-confidence I needed, with some to spare, perhaps.

My advancement was rapid, my salary having been increased twice during the first year. I did so well in the management of sales that my employer took me into partnership with him. We began to make money and I began to see myself *on top of the world again!*

To stand "on top of the world" gives one a wonderful sensation; but it is a very dangerous place to stand, unless one stands very firmly, because the fall is so long and hard if one should stumble.

I was succeeding by leaps and bounds!

Up to that time it had never occurred to me that *success* could be measured in terms other than money and authority. Perhaps this was due to the fact that I had more money than I needed and more authority than I could manage safely at that age.

Not only was I "succeeding," from my viewpoint of success, but I knew I was engaged in the one and only business suited to my temperament. Nothing could have induced me to change into another line of endeavor. That is—nothing except that which happened, which *forced* me to change.

The unseen hand of Fate allowed me to strut around under the influence of my own vanity until I had commenced to feel my importance. In the light of my more sober years, I now wonder if the Unseen

Hand does not purposely permit us foolish human beings to parade ourselves before our own mirrors of vanity until we come to see how vulgarly we are acting and become ashamed of ourselves. At any rate, I seemed to have a clear track ahead of me; there was plenty of coal in the bunker; there was water in the tank; my hand was on the throttle—I opened it wide and sped along at a rapid pace.

Alas! Fate awaited me just around the corner, with a stuffed club that was not stuffed with cotton. Of course I did not see the impending crash until it came. Mine was a sad story, but not unlike that which many another might tell if he would be frank with himself.

Like a stroke of lightning out of a clear sky, the 1907 panic swept down upon me; and, overnight, it rendered me an enduring service by destroying my business and relieving me of every dollar that I possessed.

This was my first serious *defeat!* I mistook it, then, for failure; but it was not, and before I complete this lesson I will tell you why it was not.

THIRD TURNING-POINT

It required the 1907 panic, and the defeat that it brought me, to divert and redirect my efforts from the lumber business to the study of law. Nothing on earth, except defeat, could have brought about this result; thus, the third turning-point of my life was ushered in on the wings of that which most people would call "failure," which reminds me to state again that every defeat teaches a needed lesson to those who are ready and willing to be taught.

ONE of the greatest leaders who ever lived stated the secret of his leadership in six words, as follows: "Kindness is more powerful than compulsion."

When I entered law school, it was with the firm belief that I would emerge doubly prepared to catch up with the end of the rainbow and claim my pot of gold; for I still had no other conception of success except that of *money* and power.

I attended law school at night and worked as an automobile salesman during the day. My sales experience in the lumber business was turned to good advantage. I prospered rapidly, doing so well (still featuring the habit of performing more service and better service than that for which I was paid) that the opportunity came to enter the automobile manufacturing business. I saw the need for trained automobile mechanics, therefore I opened an educational department in the manufacturing plant and began to train ordinary machinists in automobile assembling and repair work. The school prospered, paying me over a thousand dollars a month in net profits.

Again I was beginning to near the end of the rainbow. Again I knew I had at last found my niche in the world's work; that nothing could swerve me from my course or divert my attention from the automobile business.

My banker knew that I was prospering, therefore he loaned me money with which to expand. A peculiar trait of bankers—a trait which may be more or less developed in the remainder of us also—is that they will loan us money without any hesitation when we are *prosperous!*

My banker loaned me money until I was hopelessly in his debt, then he took over my business as calmly as if it had belonged to him, which it did!

From the station of a man of affairs who enjoyed

an income of more than a thousand dollars a month, I was suddenly reduced to poverty.

Now, twenty years later, I thank the hand of Fate for this forced change; but at that time I looked upon the change as nothing but *failure*.

The rainbow's end had disappeared, and with it the proverbial pot of gold which is supposed to be found at its end. It was many years afterwards that I learned the truth that this temporary *defeat* was probably the greatest single blessing that ever came my way, because it forced me out of a business that in no way helped me to develop knowledge of self or of others, and directed my efforts into a channel which brought me a rich experience of which I was in need.

For the first time in life I began to ask myself if it were not possible for one to find something of value other than money and power at the rainbow's end. This temporary questioning attitude did not amount to open rebellion, mind you, nor did I follow it far enough to get the answer. It merely came as a fleeting thought, as do so many other thoughts to which we pay no attention, and passed out of my mind. Had I known as much then as I now know about the Law of Compensation, and had I been able to interpret experiences as I can now interpret them, I would have recognized that event as a gentle nudge from the hand of Fate.

After putting up the hardest fight of my life, up to that time, I accepted my temporary defeat as *failure* and thus was ushered in my next and fourth turning-point, which gave me an opportunity to put into use the knowledge of law that I had acquired.

FOURTH TURNING-POINT

Because I was my wife's husband and her people had influence I secured the appointment as assistant to the chief counsel for one of the largest coal companies in the world. My salary was greatly out of proportion to those uusally paid to beginners, and still further out of proportion to what I was worth; but pull was pull, and I was there just the same. It happened that what I lacked in legal skill I more than made up through the application of the principle of performing more service than that for which I was paid, and by taking the initiative and doing that which should have been done without being told to do it.

I was holding my position without difficulty. I practically had a soft berth for life had I cared to keep it.

Without consultation with my friends, and without warning, I resigned!

This was the first turning-point that was of my own selection. It was not forced upon me. I saw the old man Fate coming and beat him to the door. When pressed for a reason for resigning, I gave what seemed to me to be a very sound one, but I had trouble convincing the family circle that I had acted wisely.

I quit that position because the work was too easy and I was performing it with too little effort. I saw myself drifting into the habit of inertia. I felt myself becoming accustomed to taking life easily and I knew that the next step would be retrogression. I had so many friends at court that there was no particular impelling urge that made it necessary for me to keep moving. I was among friends and relatives, and I had a position that I could keep as long as

I wished it, without exerting myself. I received an income that provided me with all the necessities and some of the luxuries, including a motor car and enough gasoline to keep it running.

What more did I need?

"Nothing!" I was beginning to say to myself.

This was the attitude toward which I felt myself slipping. It was an attitude which, for some reason that is still unknown to me, startled me so sharply that I made what many believed to be an irrational move by resigning. However ignorant I might have been in other matters at the time, I have felt thankful ever since for having had sense enough to realize that strength and growth come only through continuous effort and *struggle,* that disuse brings atrophy and decay.

This move proved to be the next most important turning-point of my life, although it was followed by ten years of effort which brought almost every conceivable grief that the human heart can experience. I quit my job in the legal field, where I was getting along well, living among friends and relatives, where I had what they believed to be an unusually bright and promising future ahead of me. I am frank to admit that it has been an ever-increasing source of wonderment to me as to why and how I gathered the courage to make the move that I did. As far as I am able to interpret the event, I arrived at my decision to resign more because of a "hunch," or a sort of "prompting" which I then did not understand, than by logical reasoning.

I selected Chicago as my new field of endeavor. I did this because I believed Chicago to be a place where one might find out if one had those sterner qualities which are so essential for survival in a world of keen competition. I made up my mind that if I could gain recognition, in any honorable sort of work, in Chicago, it would prove that I had the sort of material in my make-up that might be developed into real ability. That was a queer process of reasoning; at least it was an unusual process for me to indulge in at that time, which reminds me to state that we human beings often take unto ourselves credit for intelligence to which we are not entitled. I fear we too often assume credit for wisdom and for results that accrue from causes over which we have absolutely no control.

While I do not mean to convey the impression that I believe all of our acts to be controlled by causes beyond our power to direct, yet I strongly urge you to study and correctly interpret those causes which mark the most vital turning-points of your life; the points at which your efforts are diverted—from the old into new channels—in spite of all that you can do. *At least refrain from accepting any defeat as failure until you shall have had time to analyze the final result.*

My first position in Chicago was that of advertising manager of a large correspondence school. I knew but little about advertising, but my previous experience as a salesman, plus the advantage gained by rendering more service than that for which I was paid, enabled me to make an unusual showing.

The first year I earned $5,200.00.

I was "coming back" by leaps and bounds. Gradually the rainbow's end began to circle around me, and I saw, once more, the shining pot of gold almost within

R EMEMBER this,
when things go
against you, that of all the
expressions you carry in
your face the light of joy
shines farthest out to sea.

my reach. History is full of evidence that a feast usually precedes a famine. I was enjoying a feast but did not anticipate the famine that was to follow. I was getting along so well that I thoroughly approved of myself.

Self-approval is a dangerous state of mind.

This is a great truth which many people do not learn until the softening hand of Time has rested upon their shoulders for the better part of a life-time. Some never do learn it, and those who do are those who finally begin to understand the "dumb language" of defeat.

I am convinced that one has but few, if any, more dangerous enemies to combat than that of self-approval. Personally I fear it more than defeat.

This brings me to my fifth turning-point, which was also of my own choice.

FIFTH TURNING-POINT

I had made such a good record as advertising manager of the correspondence school that the president of the school induced me to resign my position and go into the candy manufacturing business with him. We organized the Betsy Ross Candy Company and I became its first president, thus beginning the next most important turning-point of my life.

The business grew rapidly until we had a chain of stores in eighteen different cities. Again I saw my rainbow's end almost within my reach. I knew that I had at last found the business in which I wished to remain for life. The candy business was profitable and, because I looked upon money as being the only evidence of success, I naturally believed I was about to corner success.

Everything went smoothly until my business associate and a third man, whom we had taken into the business, took a notion to gain control of my interest in the business without paying for it.

Their plan was successful, in a way, but I balked more stiffly than they had anticipated I would; therefore, for the purpose of "gentle persuasion," they had me arrested on a false charge and then offered to withdraw the charge on condition that I turn over to them my interest in the business.

I had commenced to learn, for the first time, that there was much cruelty, and injustice, and dishonesty in the hearts of men.

When the time for a preliminary hearing came, the complaining witnesses were nowhere to be found. But I had them brought and forced them to go on the witness stand and tell their stories, which resulted in my vindication, and a damage suit against the perpetrators of the injustice.

This incident brought about an irreparable breach between my business associates and myself, which finally cost me my interest in the business, but that was but slight when compared to that which it cost my associates; for they are still paying, and no doubt will continue to pay as long as they live.

My damage suit was brought under what is known as a "tort" action, through which damages were claimed for malicious damage to character. In Illinois, where the action was brought, judgment under a tort action gives the one in favor of whom the judgment is rendered the right to have the person against whom it is obtained placed in jail until the amount of the judgment has been paid.

In due time I got a heavy judgment against my former business associates. *I could then have had both of them placed behind the bars.*

For the first time in my life I was brought face to face with the opportunity to strike back at my enemies in a manner that would hurt. I had in my possession a weapon with "teeth" in it—a weapon placed there by the enemies, themselves.

The feeling that swept over me was a queer one!

Would I have my enemies jailed, or would I take advantage of this opportunity to extend them mercy, thereby proving myself to be made of a different type of material.

Then and there was laid, in my heart, the foundation upon which the Sixteenth Lesson of this course is built, for I made up my mind to permit my enemies to go free—as free as they could be made by my having extended them mercy and forgiveness.

But long before my decision had been reached the hand of Fate had commenced to deal roughly with these misguided fellow men who had tried, in vain, to destroy me. Time, the master worker, to which we must all submit sooner or later, had already been at work on my former business associates, and it had dealt with them less mercifully than I had done. One of them was later sentenced to a long term in the penitentiary, for another crime that he had committed against some other person, and the other one had, meanwhile, been reduced to pauperism.

We can circumvent the laws which men place upon statute books, but the Law of Compensation never!

The judgment which I obtained against these men stands on the records of the Superior Court, of Chicago, as silent evidence of vindication of my character; but it serves me in a more important way than that— it serves as a reminder that I could forgive enemies who had tried to destroy me, and for this reason, instead of destroying my character, I suspect that the incident served to strengthen it.

Being arrested seemed, at the time, a terrible disgrace, even though the charge was false. I did not relish the experience, and I would not wish to go through a similar experience again, but I am bound to admit that it was worth all the grief it cost me, because it gave me the opportunity to find out that revenge was not a part of my make-up.

Here I would direct your attention to a close analysis of the events described in this lesson, for if you observe carefully you can see how this entire course of study has been evolved out of these experiences. Each temporary defeat left its mark upon my heart and provided some part of the material of which this course has been built.

We would cease to fear or to run away from trying experiences if we observed, from the biographies of men of destiny, that nearly every one of them was sorely tried and run through the mill of merciless experience before he "arrived." This leads me to wonder if the hand of Fate does not test "the metal of which we are made" in various and sundry ways before placing great responsibilities upon our shoulders.

Before approaching the next turning-point of my life, may I not call your attention to the significant fact that each turning-point carried me nearer and

nearer my rainbow's end, and brought me some useful knowledge which became, later, a permanent part
of my philosophy of life.

SIXTH TURNING-POINT

We come, now, to the turning-point which probably
brought me nearer the rainbow's end than any of the
others had, because it placed me in a position where
I found it necessary to bring into use all the knowledge I had acquired up to that time, concerning practically every subject with which I was acquainted, and
gave me opportunity for self-expression and development such as rarely comes to a man so early in life.
This turning-point came shortly after my dreams of
success in the candy business had been shattered,
when I turned my efforts to teaching Advertising and
Salesmanship as a department of one of the colleges
of the Middle West.

Some wise philosopher has said that we never learn
very much about a given subject until we commence
teaching it to others. My first experience as a teacher
proved this to be true. My school prospered from
the very beginning. I had a resident class and also
a correspondence school through which I was teaching
students in nearly every English-speaking country.
Despite the ravages of war, the school was growing
rapidly and I again saw the end of the rainbow within
sight.

Then came the second military draft which practically destroyed my school, as it caught most of those
who were enrolled as students. At one stroke I
charged off more than $75,000.00 in tuition fees and

IT is far better to be associated with a few who are right than with the mob which is wrong, because right is always the winner in the end.

at the same time contributed my own service to my country.

Once more I was penniless!

Unfortunate is the person who has never had the thrill of being penniless at one time or another; for, as Edward Bok has truthfully stated, poverty is the richest experience that can come to a man; an experience which, however, he advises one to get away from as quickly as possible.

Again I was forced to redirect my efforts, but, before I proceed to describe the next and last important turning-point, I wish to call your attention to the fact that no single event described up to this point is, within itself, of any practical significance. The six turning-points that I have briefly described meant nothing to me, taken singly, and they will mean nothing to you if analyzed singly. But take these events collectively and they form a very significant foundation for the next turning-point, and constitute reliable evidence that we human beings are constantly undergoing evolutionary changes as a result of the experiences of life with which we meet, even though no single experience may seem to convey a definite, usable lesson.

I feel impelled to dwell at length on the point which I am here trying to make clear, because I have now reached the point in my career at which men go down in permanent defeat or rise, with renewed energies, to heights of attainment of stupendous proportions, according to the manner in which they interpret their past experiences and use those experiences as the basis of working plans. If my story stopped here it would be of no value to you, but there is another and a more significant chapter yet to be written, covering the seventh and most important of all the turning-points of my life.

It must have been obvious to you, all through my description of the six turning-points already outlined, that I had not really found my place in the world. It must have been obvious to you that most, if not all, of my temporary defeats were due mainly to the fact that I had not yet discovered the work into which I could throw my heart and soul. Finding the work for which one is best fitted and which one likes best is very much like finding the one person whom one loves best; there is no rule by which to make the search, but when the right niche is contacted one immediately recognizes it.

SEVENTH TURNING-POINT

Before I finish I will describe the collective lessons that I learned from each of the seven turning-points of my life, but first let me describe the seventh and last of these turning-points. To do so, I must go back to that eventful day—*November Eleven, Nineteen Hundred and Eighteen!*

That was armistice day, as everyone knows. The war had left me without a penny, as I have already stated, but I was happy to know that the slaughter had ceased and reason was about to reclaim civilization once more.

As I stood in front of my office window and looked out at the howling mob that was celebrating the end of the war, my mind went back into my yesterdays, especially to that eventful day when that kind old gentleman laid his hand on my shoulder and told me that if I would acquire an education I could make my mark in the world. I had been acquiring that education without knowing it. Over a period of more than twenty years I had been going to school in the University of Hard Knocks, as you must have observed from my description of the various turning-points of my life. As I stood in front of that window my entire past, with its bitter and its sweet, its ups and its downs, passed before me in review.

The time had come for another turning-point!

I sat down to my typewriter and, to my astonishment, my hands began to play a regular tune upon the key-board. I had never written so rapidly or so easily before. I did not plan or think about that which I was writing—*I just wrote that which came into my mind!*

Unconsciously, I was laying the foundation for the most important turning-point of my life; for, when I had finished, I had prepared a document through which I financed a national magazine that gave me contact with people throughout the English-speaking world. So greatly did that document influence my own career, and the lives of tens of thousands of other people, that I believe it will be of interest to the students of this course; therefore, I am reproducing it, just as it appeared in Hill's Golden Rule magazine, where it was first published, as follows:

"A PERSONAL VISIT WITH YOUR EDITOR"

I am writing on Monday, November eleventh, 1918. Today will go down in history as the greatest holiday. On the street, just outside of my office window, the

surging crowds of people are celebrating the downfall
of an influence that has menaced civilization for the
past four years.

The war is over!

Soon our boys will be coming back home from the
battlefields of France.

The lord and master of Brute Force is nothing but
a shadowy ghost of the past!

Two thousand years ago the Son of man was an outcast, with no place of abode. Now the situation has
been reversed and the devil has no place to lay his
head.

Let each of us take unto himself the great lesson
that this world war has taught; namely, only that
which is based upon justice and mercy toward all—
the weak and the strong, the rich and the poor, alike—
can survive. All else must pass on.

Out of this war will come a new idealism—an idealism that will be based upon the Golden Rule philosophy; an idealism that will guide us, not to see how
much we can "do our fellow man for"; but how much
we can do for him that will ameliorate his hardships
and make him happier as he tarries by the wayside of
life.

Emerson embodied this idealism in his great essay,
the Law of Compensation. Another great Philosopher
embodied it in these words, "Whatsoever a man
soweth, that shall he also reap."

The time for practicing the Golden Rule philosophy
is upon us. In business as well as in social relationships he who neglects or refuses to use this philosophy
as the basis of his dealings will but hasten the time
of his failure.

And, while I am intoxicated with the glorious news of the war's ending, is it not fitting that I should attempt to do something to help preserve for the generations yet to come, one of the great lessons to be learned from William Hohenzollern's effort to rule the earth by *force?*

I can best do this by going back twenty-two years for my beginning. Come with me, won't you?

It was a bleak November morning, probably not far from the eleventh of the month, that I got my first job as a laborer in the coal mine regions of Virginia, at wages of a dollar a day.

A dollar a day was a big sum in those days; especially to a boy of my age. Of this, I paid fifty cents a day for my board and room.

Shortly after I began work, the miners became dissatisfied and commenced talking about striking. I listened eagerly to all that was said. I was especially interested in the organizer who had organized the union. He was one of the smoothest speakers I had ever heard, and his words fascinated me. He said one thing, in particular, that I have never forgotten; and, if I knew where to find him, I would look him up today and thank him warmly for saying it. The philosophy which I gathered from his words has had a most profound and enduring influence upon me.

Perhaps you will say that most labor agitators are not very sound philosophers; and I would agree with you if you said so. Maybe this one was not a sound philosopher, but surely the philosophy he expounded on this occasion was sound.

Standing on a dry goods box, in the corner of an old shop where he was holding a meeting, he said:

NO one is living aright
unless he so lives
that whoever meets him
goes away more confident
and joyous for the con-
tact.

—*Lilian Whiting.*

"Men, we are talking about striking. Before you vote I wish to call your attention to something that will benefit you if you will heed what I say.

"You want more money for your work; and I wish to see you get it, because I believe you deserve it.

"May I not tell you how to get more money and still retain the good-will of the owner of this mine?

"We can call a strike and probably force them to pay more money, but we cannot force them to do this and like it. Before we call a strike, let us be fair with the owner of the mine and with ourselves; let us go to the owner and ask him if he will divide the profits of his mine with us fairly.

"If he says 'yes,' as he probably will, then let us ask him how much he made last month and, if he will divide among us a fair proportion of any additional profits he may make if we all jump in and help him earn more next month.

"He, being human, like each of us, will no doubt say—'Why, certainly boys; go to it and I'll divide with you.' It is but natural that he would say that, boys.

"After he agrees to the plan, as I believe he will if we make him see that we are in earnest, I want every one of you to come to work with a smile on your face for the next thirty days. I want to hear you whistling a tune as you go into the mines. I want you to go at your work with the feeling that you are one of the partners in this business.

"Without hurting yourself you can do almost twice as much work as you are doing; and if you do more work, you are sure to help the owner of this mine make more money. And if he makes more money he will be glad to divide a part of it with you. He will do this for sound business reasons if not out of a spirit of fair play.

"He will retaliate as surely as there is a God above us. If he doesn't, I'll be personally responsible to you, and if you say so I'll help blow this mine into smithereens!

"That's how much I think of the plan, boys! Are you with me?"

They were, to the man!

Those words sank into my heart as though they had been burned there with a red-hot iron.

The following month every man in the mines received a bonus of twenty per cent of his month's earnings. Every month thereafter each man received a bright red envelope with his part of the extra earnings in it. On the outside of the envelope were these printed words:

Your part of the profits from the work which you did that you were not paid to do.

I have gone through some pretty tough experiences since those days of twenty-odd years ago, but I have always come out on top—a little wiser, a little happier, and a little better prepared to be of service to my fellow men, owing to my having applied the principle of performing more work than I was actually paid to perform.

It may be of interest to you to know that the last position I held in the coal business was that of Assistant to the Chief Counsel for one of the largest companies in the world. It is a considerable jump from the position of common laborer in the coal mines to that of Assistant to the Chief Counsel of one of the largest companies—a jump that I never could have made without the aid of this principle of performing more work than I was paid to perform.

I wish I had the space in which to tell you of the scores of times that this idea of performing more work than I was paid to perform has helped me over rough spots.

Many have been the times that I have placed an employer so deeply in my debt, through the aid of this principle, that I got whatever I asked for, without hesitation or quibbling; without complaint or hard feelings; and, what is more important, without the feeling that I was taking unfair advantage of my employer.

I believe most earnestly that anything a man acquires from his fellow man without the full consent of the one from whom it is acquired, will eventually burn a hole in his pocket, or blister the palms of his hands, to say nothing of gnawing at his conscience until his heart aches with regret.

As I said in the beginning, I am writing on the morning of the Eleventh of November, while the crowds are celebrating the great victory of *right* over *wrong!*

Therefore, it is but natural that I should turn to the silence of my heart for some thought to pass on to the world today—some thought that will help keep alive in the minds of Americans the spirit of idealism for which they have fought and in which they entered the world war.

I find nothing more appropriate than the philosophy which I have related, because I earnestly believe it was the arrogant disregard of this philosophy that brought Germany—the Kaiser and his people—to grief. To get this philosophy into the hearts of those who need it I shall publish a magazine to be called *Hill's Golden Rule.*

It takes money to publish national magazines, and I haven't very much of it at this writing; but before another month shall have passed, through the aid of the philosophy that I have tried to emphasize here, I shall find someone who will supply the necessary money and make it possible for me to pass on to the world the simple philosophy that lifted me out of the dirty coal mines and gave me a place where I can be of service to humanity. The philosophy which will raise you, my dear reader, whoever you may be and whatever you may be doing, into whatever position in life you may make up your mind to attain.

Every person has, or ought to have, the inherent desire to own something of monetary value. In at least a vague sort of way, every person who works for others (and this includes practically all of us) looks forward to the time when he will have some sort of a business or a profession of his own.

The best way to realize that ambition is to perform more work than one is paid to perform. You can get along with but little schooling; you can get along with but little capital; you can overcome almost any obstacle with which you are confronted, if you are honestly and earnestly willing to do the best work of which you are capable, regardless of the amount of money you receive for it. . . .

     .   .   .   .

(*Note:* It is the afternoon of November the twenty-first, just ten days since I wrote the foregoing editorial. I have just read it to George B. Williams, of Chicago, a man who came up from the bottom through the aid of the philosophy of which I have written, and he *has made the publication of Hill's Golden Rule magazine possible.*)

.   .   .   .

It was in this somewhat dramatic manner that a desire which had lain dormant in my mind for nearly twenty years became translated into reality. During all that time I had wanted to become the editor of a newspaper. Back more than thirty years ago, when I was a very small boy, I used to "kick" the press for my father when he was publishing a small weekly newspaper, and I grew to love the smell of printer's ink.

Perhaps this desire was subconsciously gaining momentum all those years of preparation, while I was going through the experiences outlined in the turning-points of my life, until it had finally to burst forth in terms of action; or it may be that there was another plan, over which I had no control, that urged me on and on, never giving me any rest in any other line of work, until I began the publication of my first magazine. That point can be passed for the moment. The important thing to which I would direct your attention is the fact that I found my proper niche in the world's work and I was very happy over it.

Strangely enough, I entered upon this work with never a thought of looking for either the end of the rainbow or the proverbial pot of gold which is supposed to be found at its end. For the first time in my life, I seemed to realize, beyond room for doubt, that

TO give pleasure to a single heart by a single kind act is better than a thousand head-bowings in prayer.

—*Saadi.*

there was something else to be sought in life that was worth more than gold; therefore, I went at my editorial work with but one main thought in mind—and I pause while you ponder over this thought—

And that thought was to render the world the best service of which I was capable, whether my efforts brought me a penny in return or not!

The publication of Hill's Golden Rule magazine brought me in contact with the thinking class of people all over the country. It gave me my big chance to be heard. The message of optimism and good-will among men that it carried became so popular that I was invited to go on a country-wide speaking tour during the early part of 1920, during which I had the privilege of meeting and talking with some of the most progressive thinkers of this generation. Contact with these people went a very long way toward giving me the courage to keep on doing the good work that I had started. This tour was a liberal education, within itself, because it brought me in exceedingly close contact with people in practically all walks of life, and gave me a chance to see that the United States of America was a pretty large country.

Comes, now, a description of the climax of the seventh turning-point of my life.

During my speaking tour I was sitting in a restaurant in Dallas, Texas, watching the hardest downpour of rain that I have ever seen. The water was pouring down over the plate-glass window in two great streams, and playing backward and forward from one of these streams to the other were little streams, making what resembled a great ladder of water.

As I looked at this unusual scene, the thought

"flashed into my mind" that I would have a splendid lecture if I organized all that I had learned from the seven turning-points of my life and all I had learned from studying the lives of successful men, and offered it under the title of the "Magic Ladder to Success."

On the back of an envelope I outlined the fifteen points out of which this lecture was built, and later I worked these points into a lecture that was literally built from the temporary defeats described in the seven turning-points of my life.

All that I lay claim to knowing that is of value is represented by these fifteen points; and the material out of which this knowledge was gathered is nothing more or less than the knowledge that was *forced* upon me through experiences which have undoubtedly been classed, by some, as *failures!*

The reading course, of which this lesson is a part, is but the sum total of that which I gathered through these "failures." If this course proves to be of value to you, as I hope it will, you may give the credit to those "failures" described in this lesson.

Perhaps you will wish to know what material, monetary benefits I have gained from these turning-points, for you probably realize that we are living in an age in which life is an irksome struggle for existence and none too pleasant for those who are cursed with poverty.

All right! I'll be frank with you.

To begin with, the estimated income from the sale of this course is all that I need, and this, despite the fact that I have insisted that my publishers apply the Ford philosophy and sell the course at a popular price that is within the reach of all who want it.

In addition to the income from the sale of the course

(which, please bear in mind, is but the sale of knowledge I have gathered through "failure"), I am now engaged in writing a series of illustrated editorials that is to be syndicated and published in the newspapers of the country. These editorials are based upon these same fifteen points as outlined in this course.

The estimated net income from the sale of the editorials is more than enough to care for my needs.

In addition to this I am now engaged in collaboration with a group of scientists, psychologists and business men, in writing a postgraduate course which will soon be available to all students who have mastered this more elementary course, covering not only the fifteen laws here outlined, from a more advanced viewpoint, but including still other laws which have but recently been discovered.

I have mentioned these facts only because I know what a common thing it is for all of us to measure success in terms of dollars, and to refuse, as unsound, all philosophy that does not foot up a good bank balance.

Practically all the past years of my life I have been poor—exceedingly poor—as far as bank balances were concerned. This condition has been, very largely, a matter of choice with me, because I have been putting the best of my time into the toilsome job of throwing off some of my ignorance and gathering in some of the knowledge of life of which I felt myself in need.

From the experiences described in these seven turning-points of my life, I have gathered a few golden threads of knowledge that I could have gained in no other way than through *defeat!*

My own experiences have led me to believe that the

"dumb language" of *defeat* is the plainest and most effective language in the world, once one begins to understand it. I am almost tempted to say that I believe it to be the universal language in which Nature cries out to us when we will listen to no other language.

I am glad that I have experienced much defeat!

It has had the effect of tempering me with the courage to undertake tasks that I would never have begun had I been surrounded by protecting influences.

Defeat is a destructive force only when it is accepted as failure! When accepted as teaching some needed lesson it is always a blessing.

I used to hate my enemies!

That was before I learned how well they were serving me by keeping me everlastingly on the alert lest some weak spot in my character provide an opening through which they might damage me.

In view of what I have learned of the value of enemies, if I had none I would feel it my duty to create a few. They would discover my defects and point them out to me, whereas my friends, if they saw my weaknesses at all, would say nothing about them.

Of all Joaquin Miller's poems none expressed a nobler thought than did this one:

"All honor to him who shall win a prize,"
  The world has cried for a thousand years;
But to him who tries, and who fails, and dies,
  I give great honor, and glory, and tears.

Give glory and honor and pitiful tears
  To all who fail in their deeds sublime;
Their ghosts are many in the van of years,
  They were born with Time, in advance of Time.

Oh, great is the hero who wins a name;
    But greater many, and many a time,
Some pale-faced fellow who dies in shame
    And lets God finish the thought sublime.

And great is the man with a sword undrawn,
    And good is the man who refrains from wine;
But the man who fails and yet still fights on,
    Lo, he is the twin-brother of mine.

There can be no failure for the man who "still fights on." A man has never failed until he accepts temporary defeat as failure. There is a wide difference between temporary defeat and failure; a difference I have tried to emphasize throughout this lesson.

In her poem entitled When Nature Wants a Man, Angela Morgan expressed a great truth in support of the theory set out in this lesson, that adversity and defeat are generally blessings in disguise.

When Nature wants to drill a man,
And thrill a man,
And skill a man.
When Nature wants to mold a man
To play the noblest part;
When she yearns with all her heart
To create so great and bold a man
That all the world shall praise—
Watch her method, watch her ways!
How she ruthlessly perfects
Whom she royally elects;
How she hammers him and hurts him,
And with mighty blows converts him

IF we could read the secret history of our enemies, we should find in each man's life sorrow and suffering enough to disarm all hostility.

—*Longfellow.*

Into trial shapes of clay which only Nature under-
    stands—
While his tortured heart is crying and he lifts be-
    seeching hands!—
How she bends, but never breaks,
When his good she undertakes. . . .
How she uses whom she chooses
And with every purpose fuses him,
By every art induces him
To try his splendor out—
Nature knows what she's about.

When Nature wants to take a man,
And shake a man,
And wake a man;
When Nature wants to make a man
To do the Future's will;
When she tries with all her skill
And she yearns with all her soul
To create him large and whole . . .
With what cunning she prepares him!
How she goads and never spares him,
How she whets him, and she frets him,
And in poverty begets him . . .
How she often disappoints
Whom she sacredly anoints,
With what wisdom she will hide him,
Never minding what betide him
Though his genius sob with slighting and his **pride**
    may not forget!
Bids him struggle harder yet.
Makes him lonely
So that only

God's high messages shall reach him,
So that she may surely teach him
What the Hierarchy planned.
Though he may not understand,
Gives him passions to command.
How remorselessly she spurs him
With terrific ardor stirs him
When she poignantly prefers him!

When Nature wants to name a man
And fame a man
And tame a man;
When Nature wants to shame a man
To do his heavenly best . . .
When she tries the highest test
That she reckoning may bring—
When she wants a god or king!
How she reins him and restrains him
So his body scarce contains him
While she fires him
And inspires him!
Keeps him yearning, ever burning for a tantalizing
    goal—
Lures and lacerates his soul.
Sets a challenge for his spirit,
Draws it higher when he's near it—
Makes a jungle, that he clear it;
Makes a desert that he fear it
And subdue it if he can—
So doth Nature make a man.
Then, to test his spirit's wrath
Hurls a mountain in his path—
Puts a bitter choice before him

And relentlessly stands o'er him.
"Climb, or perish!" so she says. . . .
Watch her purpose, watch her ways!

Nature's plan is wondrous kind
Could we understand her mind . . .
Fools are they who call her blind.
When his feet are torn and bleeding
Yet his spirit mounts unheeding,
All his higher powers speeding,
Blazing newer paths and fine;
When the force that is divine
Leaps to challenge every failure and his ardor still
    is sweet
And love and hope are burning in the presence of
    defeat . . .
Lo, the crisis! Lo, the shout
That must call the leader out.
When the people need salvation
Doth he come to lead the nation. . . .
Then doth Nature show her plan
When the world has found—a MAN! *

I am convinced that failure is Nature's plan through
which she hurdle-jumps men of destiny and prepares
them to do their work. Failure is Nature's great
crucible in which she burns the dross from the human
heart and so purifies the metal of the man that it can
stand the test of hard usage.

I have found evidence to support this theory in the
study of the records of scores of great men, from
Socrates and Christ on down the centuries to the well

* From "Forward, March!" The John Lane Company.

known men of achievement of our modern times. The success of each man seemed to be in almost exact ratio to the extent of the obstacles and difficulties he had to surmount.

No man ever arose from the knock-out blow of defeat without being stronger and wiser for the experience. Defeat talks to us in a language all its own; a language to which we must listen whether we like it or not.

Of course one must have considerable courage to look upon defeat as a blessing in disguise; but the attainment of any position in life, that is worth having requires a lot of "sand," which brings to mind a poem that harmonizes with the philosophy of this lesson.

I observed a locomotive in the railroad yards one day,
It was waiting in the roundhouse where the locomotives stay;
It was panting for the journey, it was coaled and fully manned,
And it had a box the fireman was filling full of sand.

It appears that locomotives cannot always get a grip
On their slender iron pavement, 'cause the wheels are apt to slip;
And when they reach a slippery spot, their tactics they command,
And to get a grip upon the rail, they sprinkle it with sand.

It's about the way with travel along life's slippery track—
If your load is rather heavy, you're always slipping back;

So, if a common locomotive you completely understand,
You'll provide yourself in starting with a good supply
  of sand.

If your track is steep and hilly and you have a heavy
  grade,
If those who've gone before you have the rails quite
  slippery made,
If you ever reach the summit of the upper tableland,
You'll find you'll have to do it with a liberal use of
  sand.

If you strike some frigid weather and discover to your
  cost,
That you're liable to slip upon a heavy coat of frost,
Then some prompt decided action will be called into
  demand,
And you'll slip 'way to the bottom if you haven't any
  sand.

You can get to any station that is on life's schedule
  seen,
If there's fire beneath the boiler of ambition's strong
  machine,
And you'll reach a place called Flushtown at a rate of
  speed that's grand,
If for all the slippery places you've a good supply of
  sand.

It can do you no harm if you memorize the poems
quoted in this lesson and make the philosophy upon
which they are based a part of your own.

'Tis the human touch in this
world that counts,
The touch of your hand and
mine,
Which means far more to
the fainting heart,
Than shelter and bread and
wine;
For shelter is gone when the
night is o'er,
And bread lasts only a day,
But the touch of the hand
and the sound of the
voice,
Sing on in the soul alway.
            —*Spencer M. Tree.*

As I near the end of this lesson on Failure, there comes to mind a bit of philosophy taken from the works of the great Shakespeare, which I wish to challenge because I believe it to be unsound. It is stated in the following quotation:

There is a tide in the affairs of men
Which, taken at the flood, leads on to fortune;
Omitted, all the voyage of their life
Is bound in shallows, and in miseries.
On such a full sea are we now afloat;
And we must take the current when it serves,
Or lose our ventures.

Fear and admission of failure are the ties which cause us to be "bound in shallows, and in miseries." We can break these ties and throw them off. Nay, we can turn them to advantage and make them serve as a tow-line with which to pull ourselves ashore if we observe and profit by the lessons they teach.

Who ne'er has suffered, he has lived but half,
    Who never failed, he never strove or sought,
Who never wept is stranger to a laugh,
    And he who never doubted never thought.

As I near the end of this, my favorite lesson of this course, I close my eyes for a moment and see before me a great army of men and women whose faces show the lines of care and despair.

Some are in rags, having reached the last stage of that long, long trail which men call *failure!*

Others are in better circumstances, but the fear of

starvation shows plainly on their faces; the smile of courage has left their lips; and they, too, seem to have given up the battle.

The scene shifts!

I look again and I am carried backward into the history of man's struggle for a place in the sun, and there I see, also, the "failures" of the past—failures that have meant more to the human race than all the so-called successes recorded in the history of the world.

I see the homely face of Socrates as he stood at the very end of that trail called failure, waiting, with upturned eyes, through those moments which must have seemed like an eternity, just before he drank the cup of hemlock that was forced upon him by his tormentors.

I see, also, Christopher Columbus, a prisoner in chains, which was the tribute paid him for his sacrifice in having set sail on an unknown and uncharted sea, to discover an unknown continent.

I see, also, the face of Thomas Paine, the man whom the English sought to capture and put to death as the real instigator of the American Revolution. I see him lying in a filthy prison, in France, as he waited calmly, under the shadow of the guillotine, for the death which he expected would be meted out to him for his part in behalf of humanity.

And I see, also, the face of the Man of Galilee, as he suffered on the cross of Calvary—the reward he received for his efforts in behalf of suffering humanity.

"Failures," all!

Oh, to be such a failure. Oh, to go down in history, as these men did, as one who was brave enough to place humanity above the *individual* and principle above pecuniary gain.

On such "failures" rest the hopes of the world.

Oh, men, who are labeled "failures"—up, rise up!
    again and do!
Somewhere in the world of action is room; there is
    room for you.
No failure was e'er recorded, in the annals of truthful
    men,
Except of the craven-hearted who fails, nor attempts
    again.
The glory is in the doing, and not in the trophy won;
The walls that are laid in darkness may laugh to the
    kiss of the sun.
Oh, weary and worn and stricken, oh, child of fate's
    cruel gales!
I sing—that it haply may cheer him—I sing to the
    man who fails.

Be thankful for the defeat which men call failure, because if you can survive it and keep on trying it gives you a chance to prove your ability to rise to the heights of achievement in your chosen field of endeavor.

No one has the right to brand you as a failure except yourself.

If, in a moment of despair, you should feel inclined to brand yourself as a failure, just remember those words of the wealthy philosopher, Croesus, who was advisor to Cyrus, king of the Persians:

"I am reminded, O king, and take this lesson to
heart, that there is a wheel on which the affairs

of men revolve and its mechanism is such that it prevents *any* man from being *always* fortunate."

What a wonderful lesson is wrapped up in those words—a lesson of hope and courage and promise.

Who of us has not seen "off" days, when everything seemed to go wrong? These are the days when we see only the flat side of the great wheel of life.

Let us remember that the wheel is always turning. If it brings us sorrow today, it will bring us joy tomorrow. Life is a cycle of varying events—fortunes and misfortunes.

We cannot stop this wheel of fate from turning, but we can modify the misfortune it brings us by remembering that good fortune will follow, just as surely as night follows day, if we but keep faith with ourselves and earnestly and honestly do our best.

In his greatest hours of trial the immortal Lincoln was heard, often, to say: *"And this, too, will soon pass."*

If you are smarting from the effects of some temporary defeat which you find it hard to forget, let me recommend this stimulating little poem, by Walter Malone.

OPPORTUNITY

They do me wrong who say I come no more
    When once I knock and fail to find you in;
For every day I stand outside your door,
    And bid you wake, and rise to fight and win.
Wail not for precious chances passed away;
    Weep not for golden ages on the wane;

Each night I burn the records of the day;
  At sunrise every soul is born again.
Laugh like a boy at splendors that have sped,
  To vanished joys be blind and deaf and dumb;
My judgments seal the dead past with its dead,
  But never bind a moment yet to come.

Though deep in mire wring not your hands and
      weep,
  I lend my arm to all who say, "I can!"
No shamefaced outcast ever sank so deep
  But yet might rise and be again a man!
Dost thou behold thy lost youth all aghast?
  Dost reel from righteous retribution's blow?
Then turn from blotted archives of the past
  And find the future's pages white as snow.
Art thou a mourner? Rouse thee from thy spell;
  Art thou a sinner? Sin may be forgiven;
Each morning gives thee wings to flee from hell,
  Each night a star to guide thy feet to heaven.

STRIVE not to banish
pain and doubt,
In pleasure's noisy din;
The peace thou seekest
from without,
Is only found within

—*Cary.*

Lesson Fifteen

TOLERANCE

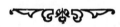

THERE are souls in this world which have the gift of finding joy everywhere, and of leaving it behind them everywhere they go.

—*Faber.*

THE LAW OF SUCCESS
Lesson Fifteen
TOLERANCE

HERE are two significant features about *intolerance,* and your attention is directed to these at the beginning of this lesson.

These features are:

First: Intolerance is a form of ignorance which must be mastered before any form of enduring success may be attained. It is the chief cause of all wars. It makes enemies in business and in the professions. It disintegrates the organized forces of society in a thousand forms, and stands, like a mighty giant, as a barrier to the abolition of war. It dethrones reason and substitutes mob psychology in its place.

Second: Intolerance is the chief disintegrating force in the organized religions of the world, where it plays havoc with the greatest power for good there is on this earth; by breaking up that power into small sects and denominations which spend as much effort opposing each other as they do in destroying the evils of the world.

But this indictment against *intolerance* is general.

55

Let's see how it affects you, the individual. It is, of course, obvious that anything which impedes the progress of civilization stands, also, as a barrier to each individual; and, stating it conversely, anything that beclouds the mind of the individual and retards his mental, moral and spiritual development, retards, also, the progress of civilization.

All of which is an abstract statement of a great truth; and, inasmuch as abstract statements are neither interesting nor highly informative, let us proceed to illustrate more concretely the damaging effects of *intolerance*.

I will begin this illustration by describing an incident which I have mentioned quite freely in practically every public address that I have delivered within the past five years; but, inasmuch as the cold printed page has a modifying effect which makes possible the misinterpretation of the incident here described, I believe it necessary to caution you not to read back of the lines a meaning which I had no intention of placing there. You will do yourself an injustice if you either neglect or intentionally refuse to study this illustration in the exact words and with the exact meaning which I have intended those words to convey—a meaning as clear as I know how to make the English language convey it.

As you read of this incident, place yourself in my position and see if you, also, have not had a parallel experience, and, if so, what lesson did it teach you?

One day I was introduced to a young man of unusually fine appearance. His clear eye, his warm handclasp, the tone of his voice and the splendid taste with which he was groomed marked him as a young man

of the highest intellectual type. He was of the typical
young American college student type, and as I ran
my eyes over him, hurriedly studying his personality,
as one will naturally do under such circumstances, I
observed a Knights of Columbus pin on his vest.

Instantly, I released his hand as if it were a piece
of ice!

This was done so quickly that it surprised both him
and me. As I excused myself and started to walk
away, I glanced down at the Masonic pin that I wore
on my own vest, then took another look at his Knights
of Columbus pin, and wondered why a couple of
trinkets such as these could dig such a deep chasm
between men who knew nothing of each other.

All the remainder of that day I kept thinking of the
incident, because it bothered me. I had always taken
considerable pride in the thought that I was tolerant
with all men; but here was a spontaneous outburst of
intolerance which proved that down in my sub-conscious mind existed a complex that was influencing me
toward narrow-mindedness.

This discovery so shocked me that I began a systematic process of psycho-analysis through which I
searched into the very depths of my soul for the cause
of my rudeness.

I asked myself over and over again:

*"Why did you abruptly release that young man's
hand and turn away from him, when you knew nothing
about him?"*

Of course the answer led me, always, back to that
Knights of Columbus pin that he wore. But that was
not a real answer and therefore it did not satisfy me

Then I began to do some research work in the field

of religion. I began to study both Catholicism and Protestantism until I had traced both back to their beginning, a line of procedure which I must confess brought me more understanding of the problems of life than I had gathered from all other sources. For one thing it disclosed the fact that Catholicism and Protestantism differ more in *form* than they do in *effect;* that both are founded on exactly the same *cause,* which is Christianity.

But this was by no means all, nor was it the most important of my discoveries, for my research led, of necessity, in many directions, and forced me into the field of biology where I learned much that I needed to know about life in general and the human being in particular. My research led, also, to the study of Darwin's hypothesis of evolution, as outlined in his Origin of Species, and this, in turn, led to a much wider analysis of the subject of psychology than that which I had previously made.

As I began to reach out in this direction and that, for knowledge, my mind began to unfold and broaden with such alarming rapidity that I practically found it necessary to—

Wipe the slate of what I believed to be my previously gathered knowledge, and to unlearn much that I had previously believed to be truth.

Comprehend the meaning of that which I have just stated!

Imagine yourself suddenly discovering that most of your philosophy of life had been built of bias and prejudice, making it necessary for you to acknowledge that, far from being a finished scholar, *you were barely qualified to become an intelligent student!*

That was exactly the position in which I found my-self, with respect to many of what I believed to be sound fundamentals of life; but of all the discoveries to which this research led, none was more important than that of the relative importance of *physical* and *social* heredity, for it was this discovery that disclosed the *cause* for my action when I turned away from a man whom I did not know, on the occasion that I have described.

It was this discovery that disclosed to me *how* and *where* I acquired my views of religion, of politics, of economics and many other equally important subjects, and I both regret and rejoice to state that *I found most of my views on these subjects without support by even a reasonable hypothesis,* much less sound *facts* or reason.

I then recalled a conversation between the late Sena-tor Robert L. Taylor and myself, in which we were discussing the subject of politics. It was a friendly discussion, as we were of the same political faith, but the Senator asked me a question for which I never forgave him until I began the research to which I have referred.

"I see that you are a very staunch Democrat," said he, "and I wonder if you know *why* you are?"

I thought of the question for a few seconds, then blurted out this reply:

"I am a Democrat because my father was one, of course!"

With a broad grin on his face the Senator then nailed me with this rejoinder:

"Just as I thought! Now wouldn't you be in a bad fix if your father had been a horse-thief?"

Hearts, like doors, can
ope with ease,
To very, very little keys;
And don't forget that they
are these:
"I thank you, sir," and
"If you please."

It was many years later, after I began the research work herein described, that I understood the real meaning of Senator Taylor's joke. Too often we hold opinions that are based upon no sounder foundation than that of what someone else believes.

.   .   .   .

That you may have a detailed illustration of the far-reaching effects of one of the important principles uncovered by the incident to which I have referred, and—

That you may learn how and where you acquired your philosophy of life, in general;

That you may trace your prejudices and your biases to their original source;

That you may discover, as I discovered, how largely you are the result of the training you received before you reached the age of fifteen years—

I will now quote the full text of a plan which I submitted to Mr. Edward Bok's Committee, The American Peace Award, for the abolition of war. This plan covers not only the most important of the principles to which I refer, but, as you will observe, it shows how the principle of *organized effort,* as outlined in Lesson Two of this course, may be applied to one of the most important of the world's problems, and at the same time gives you a more comprehensive idea of how to apply this principle in the *attainment* of your *definite chief aim.*

HOW TO ABOLISH WAR

The Background

Before offering this plan for the prevention of war, it seems necessary to sketch briefly a background that will clearly describe the principle which constitutes the warp and the woof of the plan.

The causes of war may be properly omitted for the reason that they have but little, if any, relation to the principle through which war may be prevented.

The beginning of this sketch deals with two important factors which constitute the chief controlling forces of civilization. One is *physical heredity* and the other is *social heredity*.

The size and form of the body, the texture of the skin, the color of the eyes, and the functioning power of the vital organs are all the result of physical heredity; they are static and fixed and cannot be changed, for they are the result of a million years of evolution; but by far the most important part of what we are is the result of social heredity, and came to us from the effects of our environment and early training.

Our conception of religion, politics, economics, philosophy and other subjects of a similar nature, including war, is entirely the result of those dominating forces of our environment and training.

The Catholic is a Catholic because of his early training, and the Protestant is a Protestant for the same reason; but this is hardly stating the truth with sufficient emphasis, for it might be properly said that the Catholic is a Catholic and the Protestant is a Protestant *because he cannot help it!* With but few exceptions the religion of the adult is the result of his religious training during the years between four and fourteen when his religion was *forced* upon him by his parents or those who had control of his schooling.

A prominent clergyman indicated how well he understood the principle of social heredity when he said: "Give me the control of the child until it is twelve years old and you can teach it any religion you may please after that time, for I will have planted my own religion so deeply in its mind that no power on earth could undo my work."

The outstanding and most prominent of man's beliefs are those which were forced upon him, or which he absorbed of his own volition, under *highly emotionalized* conditions, when his mind was receptive. Under such conditions the evangelist can plant the idea of religion more deeply and permanently during an hour's revival service than he could through years of training under ordinary conditions, when the mind was not in an emotionalized state.

The people of the United States have immortalized Washington and Lincoln because they were the leaders of the nation during times when the minds of the people were highly emotionalized, as the result of calamities which shook the very foundation of our country and vitally affected the interests of all the people. Through the principle of social heredity, operating through the schools (American history), and through other forms of impressive teaching, the immortality of Washington and Lincoln is planted in the minds of the young and in that way kept alive.

The three great *organized forces* through which social heredity operates are:

The *schools*, the *churches* and the *public press*.

Any ideal that has the active co-operation of these three forces may, *during the brief period of one generation, be forced upon the minds of the young so effectively that they cannot resist it.*

In 1914 the world awoke one morning to find itself aflame with warfare on a scale previously unheard of, and the outstanding feature of importance of that world-wide calamity was the highly organized German armies. For more than three years these armies gained ground so rapidly that world domination by Germany seemed certain. The German military machine operated with efficiency such as had never before been demonstrated in warfare. With "kultur" as her avowed ideal, modern Germany swept the opposing armies before her as though they were leaderless, despite the fact that the allied forces outnumbered her own on every front.

The capacity for sacrifice in the German soldiers, in support of the ideal of "kultur," was the outstanding surprise of the war; and that capacity was largely the result of the work of two men. Through the German educational system, which they controlled, the psychology which carried the world into war in 1914 was created in the definite form of "kultur." These men were Adalbert Falk, Prussian Minister of Education until 1879, and the German Emperor William II.

The agency through which these men produced this result was *social heredity:* the imposing of an ideal on the minds of the young, under highly emotionalized conditions.

"Kultur," as a national ideal, was fixed in the minds of the young of Germany, beginning first in the elementary schools and extending on up through the high schools and universities. *The teachers and professors were forced to implant the ideal of "kultur" in the minds of the students,* and out of this teaching, in a single generation, grew the capacity for sacrifice of the individual for the interest of the nation which surprised the modern world.

As Benjamin Kidd so well stated the case: "The aim of the state of Germany was everywhere to orientate public opinion through the heads of both its spiritual and temporal departments, through the bureaucracy, through the officers of the army, through the State direction of the press; and, last of all, through the State direction of the entire trade and industry of the nation, so as to bring the idealism of the whole people to a conception of and to a support of the national policy of modern Germany."

Germany controlled the press, the clergy and the schools; therefore, is it any wonder that she grew an army of soldiers, during one generation, which represented to a man her ideal of "kultur"? Is it any wonder that the German soldiers faced certain death with fearless impunity, when one stops to consider the fact that they had been taught, from early childhood, that this sacrifice was a rare privilege?

Turn, now, from this brief description of the modus operandi through which Germany prepared her people for war, to another strange phenomenon, Japan. No western nation, with the exception of Germany, has so clearly manifested its understanding of the far-reaching influence of social heredity, as has Japan. Within a single generation Japan has advanced from her standing as a fourth-rate nation to the ranks of nations that are the recognized powers of the civilized

IT takes but a second to administer a rebuke, but it may take a life-time for the one who has been rebuked to forget it.

world. Study Japan and you will find that she forces upon the minds of her young, through exactly the same agencies employed by Germany, the ideal of subordination of individual rights for the sake of accumulation of power by the nation.

In all of her controversies with China, competent observers have seen that back of the apparent causes of the controversies was Japan's stealthy attempt to control the minds of the young by controlling the schools. *If Japan could control the minds of the young of China, she could dominate that gigantic nation within one generation.*

If you would study the effect of social heredity as it is being used for the development of a national ideal by still another nation of the West, observe what has been going on in Russia since the ascendency to power of the soviet government of Russia which is now pat-terning the minds of the young to conform with a national ideal, *the nature of which it requires no master analyst to interpret.* That ideal, when fully developed during the maturity of the present generation, will represent exactly that which the soviet government wishes it to represent.

Of all the flood of propaganda concerning the soviet government of Russia that has been poured into this country through the tens of thousands of columns of newspaper space devoted to it since the close of the war, the following brief dispatch is by far the most significant:

"RUSS REDS ORDER BOOKS. Contracts being let in Germany for 20,000,000 volumes. Educational propaganda is aimed chiefly at children.

"(By GEORGE WITTS)

"Special Cable to the Chicago Daily News Foreign Service. Berlin, Germany, November 9th, 1920.

"Contracts for printing 20,000,000 books *in the Russian language,* chiefly for children, are being placed in Germany on behalf of the soviet government by Grschebin, a well known Petrograd publisher and a friend of Maxim Gorky. Grschebin first went to England, but was received with indifference when he broached the subject to the British government. *The Germans, however, not only welcomed him eagerly but submitted prices so low that they could not possibly be underbidden in any other country.* The Ullsteins, Berlin newspaper and book publishers, have agreed to print several million of the books at less than cost."

This shows what is going on over there.

Far from being shocked by this significant press dispatch, the majority of the newspapers of America did not publish it, and those that did give it space placed it in an obscure part of the paper, in small type. Its real significance will become more apparent some twenty-odd years from now, when the soviet government of Russia will have grown an army of soldiers who will support, to the man, *whatever national ideal the soviet government sets up.*

The possibility of war exists as a stern reality today solely because the principle of social heredity has not only been used as a sanctioning force in support of war, but it has actually been used as a chief agency through which the minds of men have been deliberately prepared for war. For evidence with which to support this statement, examine any national or world history and *observe how tactfully and effectively war has been*

*glorified and so described that it not only did not shock
the mind of the student, but it actually established a
plausible justification of war.*

Go into the public squares of our cities and observe
the monuments that have been erected to the leaders
of war. Observe the posture of these statues as they
stand as living symbols to glorify men who did nothing
more than lead armies on escapades of destruction.
Notice how well these statues of warriors, mounted on
charging steeds, serve as agencies through which to
stimulate the minds of the young and prepare them
for the acceptance of war, not only as a pardonable
act, but as a distinctly desirable source of attainment
of glory, fame and honor. At the time of this writing
some well meaning ladies are having the image of Confederate Soldiers carved in the deathless granite on the
face of Stone Mountain, in Georgia, in figures a hundred feet tall, thus seeking to perpetuate the memory
of a lost "cause" that never was a "cause" and therefore the sooner forgotten, the better.

If these references to far-away Russia, Japan and
Germany seem unimpressive and abstract, then let us
study the principle of social heredity as it is now
functioning on a highly developed scale here in the
United States; for it may be expecting too much of
the average of our race to suppose that they will be
interested in that which is taking place outside of the
spot of ground that is bounded on the north by Canada, on the east by the Atlantic, on the west by the
Pacific and on the south by Mexico.

We, too, are setting up in the minds of our young
a national ideal, and this ideal is being so effectively
developed, through the principle of social heredity,

that it has already become the dominating ideal of the nation.

This ideal is the desire for wealth!

The first question we ask about a new acquaintance is not, "Who are you?" but, "What have you?" And the next question we ask is, *"How can we get that which you have?"*

Our ideal is not measured in terms of warfare, but in terms of finance and industry and business. Our Patrick Henrys and our George Washingtons and our Abraham Lincolns of a few generations ago are now represented by the able leaders who manage our steel mills and our coal mines and our timber lands and our banking institutions and our railroads.

We may deny this indictment if we choose, but the facts do not support the denial.

The outstanding problem of the American people today is the spirit of unrest upon the part of the masses who find the struggle for existence becoming harder and harder because the most competent brains of the country are engaged in the highly competitive attempt to accumulate wealth and to control the wealth-producing machinery of the nation.

It is not necessary to dwell at length upon this description of our dominating ideal, or to offer evidence in support of its existence, for the reason that its existence is obvious and as well understood by the most ignorant as it is by those who make a pretense of thinking accurately.

So deeply seated has this mad desire for money become that we are perfectly willing for the other nations of the world to cut themselves to pieces in warfare so long as they do not interfere with our scramble for wealth; nor is this the saddest part of the indictment that we might render against ourselves, for we are not only *willing* for other nations to engage in warfare, but there is considerable reason to believe that those of us who profit by the sale of war supplies actually encourage this warfare among other nations.

THE PLAN

War grows out of the desire of the individual to gain advantage at the expense of his fellow men, and the smoldering embers of this desire are fanned into a flame through the grouping of these individuals who place the interests of the group above those of other groups.

War cannot be stopped suddenly!

It can be eliminated only by education, through the aid of the principle of subordination of the individual interests to the broader interests of the human race as a whole.

Man's tendencies and activities, as we have already stated, grow out of two great forces. One is *physical* heredity, and the other is *social* heredity. Through physical heredity, man inherits those early tendencies to destroy his fellow man out of self-protection. This practice is a hold-over from the age when the struggle for existence was so great that only the physically strong could survive.

Gradually men began to learn that the individual could survive under more favorable circumstances by allying himself with others, and out of that discovery grew our modern society, through which groups of people have formed states, and these groups, in turn,

UNFORTUNATE, indeed, is the man who becomes so used to evil that it no longer appears to be horrible.

have formed nations. There is but little tendency toward warfare between the individuals of a particular group or nation, for they have learned, through the principle of *social* heredity, that they can best survive by subordinating the interest of the individual to that of the group.

Now, the problem is to extend this principle of grouping so that *the nations of the world will subordinate their individual interests to those of the human race as a whole.*

This can be brought about only through the principle of *social* heredity. *By forcing upon the minds of the young of all races the fact that war is horrible and does not serve either the interest of the individual engaging in it or the group to which the individual belongs.*

The question then arises, "How can this be done?" Before we answer this question, let us again define the term *"social heredity"* and find out what its possibilities are.

Social heredity is the principle through which the young of the race absorb from their environment, and particularly from their earlier training by parents, teachers and religious leaders, *the beliefs and tendencies of the adults who dominate them.*

Any plan to abolish war, to be successful, depends upon the successful co-ordination of effort between *all the churches and schools of the world for the avowed purpose of so fertilizing the minds of the young with the idea of abolishing war that the very word "war" will strike terror in their hearts.*

THERE IS NO OTHER WAY OF ABOLISHING WAR!

The next question that arises, "How can the churches and schools of the world be organized with this high ideal as an objective?" The answer is that not all of them can be induced to enter into such an alliance, at one time; but a sufficient number of the more influential ones can be induced, and this, in time, will lead or *force* the remainder into the alliance, as rapidly as public opinion begins to *demand it*.

Then comes the question, "Who has sufficient influence to call a conference of the most powerful religious and educational leaders?" The answer is:

The President and Congress, of the United States.

Such an undertaking would *command* the support of the press on a scale heretofore unheard of, and through this source alone the propaganda would begin to reach and fertilize the minds of the people in every civilized country in the world, in preparation for the adoption of the plan in the churches and schools throughout the world.

The plan for the abolition of war might be likened to a great dramatic play, with these as the chief factors:

STAGE SETTING: At the Capitol of the United States.

STAR ACTORS: The President and members of Congress.

MINOR ACTORS: The leading clergymen of all denominations, and the leading educators, all on the stage by invitation and at the expense of the United States government.

PRESS ROOM: Representatives of the news-gathering agencies of the world.

STAGE EQUIPMENT: A radio broadcasting outfit

that would distribute the entire proceedings half-way round the earth.

TITLE OF THE PLAY: "Thou shalt not kill!"

OBJECT OF THE PLAY: The creation of a World Court, to be made up of representatives of all races, whose duty it would be to hear evidence and adjudicate the cases arising out of disagreement between nations.

Other factors would enter into this great world drama, but they would be of minor importance. The main issues and the most essential factors are here enumerated.

One other question remains, "Who will start the machinery of the United States government into action to call this conference?" and the answer is:

Public opinion, through the aid of an able organizer and leader, who will organize and direct the efforts of a Golden Rule Society, the object of which will be to move the President and Congress into action.

No League of Nations and no mere agreement between nations can abolish war as long as there is the slightest evidence of sanction of war in the hearts of the people. Universal peace between nations will grow out of a movement that will be begun and carried on, at first, by a comparatively small number of thinkers. Gradually this number will grow until it will be composed of the leading educators, clergymen and publicists of the world, and these, in turn, will so deeply and permanently establish *peace* as a world ideal that it will become a reality.

This desirable end may be attained in a single generation under the right sort of leadership; but, more likely, it will not be attained for many generations to come, for the reason that those who have the ability to assume this leadership are too busy in their pursuit of worldly wealth to make the necessary sacrifice for the good of generations yet unborn.

War can be eliminated, not by appeal to reason, but by appeal to the emotional side of humanity. This appeal must be made by *organizing and highly emotionalizing the people of the different nations of the world in support of a universal plan for peace, and this plan must be forced upon the minds of the oncoming generations with the same diligent care that we now force upon the minds of our young the ideal of our respective religions.*

It is not stating the possibilities too strongly to say that the churches of the world could establish universal peace as an international ideal within one generation if they would but *direct toward that end one-half of the effort which they now employ in opposing one another.*

We would still be within the bounds of conservatism if we stated that the Christian churches, alone, have sufficient influence to establish universal peace as a world-wide ideal, within three generations, if the various sects would combine their forces for the purpose.

That which the leading churches of all religions, the leading schools and the public press of the world could accomplish in forcing the ideal of universal peace upon *both the adult and the child mind of the world* within a single generation, staggers the imagination.

If the organized religions of the world, as they now exist, will not subordinate their individual interests and purposes to that of establishing universal peace, then the remedy lies in establishing a universal church of the world that will function through all races and whose creed will be based entirely upon the one purpose of implanting in the minds of the young the ideal of world-wide peace.

Such a church would gradually attract a following from the rank and file of all other churches.

And if the educational institutions of the world will not co-operate in fostering this high ideal of universal peace, then the remedy lies in the creation of an entirely new educational system that will implant in the minds of the young the ideal of universal peace.

And if the public press of the world will not co-operate in setting up the ideal of universal peace, then the remedy lies in the creation of an independent press that will utilize both the printed page and the forces of the air for the purpose of creating mass support of this high ideal.

In brief, if the present *organized forces* of the world will not lend their support to establishing universal peace, as an international ideal, then new organizations must be created which will do so.

The majority of the people of the world want peace, wherein lies the possibility of its attainment!

At first thought, it seems too much to expect that the organized churches of the world can be induced to pool their power and subordinate their individual interests to those of civilization as a whole.

But this seemingly insurmountable obstacle is, in reality, no obstacle at all, for the reason that whatever support this plan borrows from the churches it gives back to them, a thousandfold, through the increased power the church attains.

Let us see just what advantages the church realizes

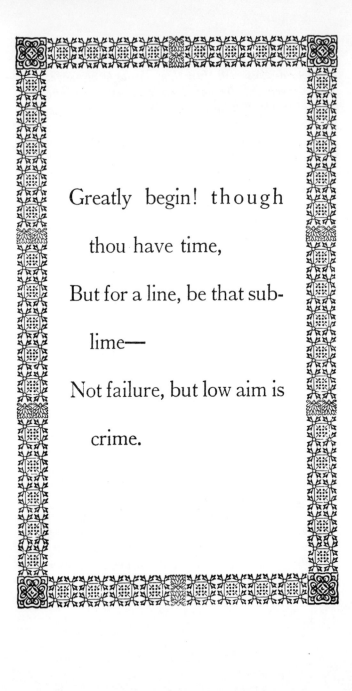

Greatly begin! though
thou have time,
But for a line, be that sublime—
Not failure, but low aim is
crime.

by participation in this plan to establish *universal peace* as a world ideal. First of all, it will be clearly seen that no individual church loses any of its advantages by allying itself with other denominations in establishing this world ideal. The alliance in no way changes or interferes with the creed of any church. Every church entering the alliance will come out of it with all the power and advantages that it possessed before it went in, plus the additional advantage of greater influence which the church, as a whole, will enjoy by reason of having served as the leading factor in forcing upon civilization the greatest single benefit it has enjoyed in the history of the world.

If the church gained no other advantages from the alliance, this one would be sufficient to compensate it. But *the important advantage that the church will have gained by this alliance is the discovery that it has sufficient power to force its ideals upon the world when it places its combined support back of the undertaking.*

By this alliance the church will have grasped the far-reaching significance of the principle of *organized effort* through the aid of which it might easily have dominated the world and imposed its ideals upon civilization.

The church is by far the greatest potential power in the world today, but its power is merely potential and will remain so until it makes use of the principle of allied or *organized* effort; that is to say, until *all denominations formulate a working agreement under which the combined strength of organized religion will be used as a means of forcing a higher ideal upon the minds of the young.*

The reason that the church is the greatest potential power in the world is the fact that its power grows out of man's emotions. *Emotion rules the world, and the church is the only organization which rests solely upon the power of emotion. The church is the only organized factor of society which has the power to harness and direct the emotional forces of civilization, for the reason that the emotions are controlled by FAITH and not by reason! And the church is the only great organized body in which faith of the world is centered.*

The church stands today as so many disconnected units of power, and it is not overstating the possibilities to say that when these units shall have been connected, *through allied effort,* the combined power of that alliance *will rule the world and there is no opposing power on earth that can defeat it!*

It is in no discouraging spirit that this statement is followed by another which may seem still more radical; namely:

The task of bringing about this alliance of the churches in support of the world ideal of universal peace must rest upon the female members of the church, for the reason that the abolition of war promises advantages that may be prolonged into the future and that may accrue only to the unborn generations.

In Schopenhauer's bitter arraignment of woman, he unconsciously stated a truth upon which the hope of civilization rests, when he declared that *the race is always to her more than the individual.* In terms that are uncompromising, Schopenhauer charges woman with being the natural enemy of man because of this

inborn trait *of placing the interests of the race above
those of the individual.*

It seems a reasonable prophecy to suggest that
civilization passed into a new era, beginning with the
world war, in which woman is destined to take into her
own hands the raising of the ethical standards of the
world. This is a hopeful sign, because it is woman's
nature to subordinate the interests of the present to
those of the future. It is woman's nature to implant,
in the mind of the young, ideals that will accrue to
the benefit of generations yet unborn, while man is
motivated generally by expediency of the present.

In Schopenhauer's vicious attack upon woman, he
has stated a great truth concerning her nature: a truth
which might well be utilized by all who engage in the
worthy work of establishing *universal peace as a world
ideal.*

The women's clubs of the world are destined to play
a part in world affairs other than that of gaining suffrage for women.

LET CIVILIZATION REMEMBER THIS!

Those who do not want peace are the ones who
profit by war. In numbers, this class constitutes but
a fragment of the power of the world, and could be
swept aside as though it did not exist, if the multitude
who do not want war were organized with the high
ideal of universal peace as their objective.

In closing, it seems appropriate to apologize for
the unfinished state of this essay, but it may be pardonable to suggest that the bricks and the mortar, and
the foundation stones, and all the other necessary materials for the construction of the *temple of universal
peace* have been here assembled, where they might be

re-arranged and transformed into this high ideal as a world reality.

.   .   .   .

Let us now proceed to apply the principle of *social heredity* to the subject of business economy, and ascertain whether or not it can be made of practical benefit in the attainment of material wealth.

If I were a banker I would procure a list of all the births in the families within a given distance of my place of business, and every child would receive an appropriate letter, congratulating it on its arrival in the world at such an opportune time, in such a favorable community; and from that time on it would receive from my bank a birthday reminder of an appropriate nature. When it arrived at the story-book age, it would receive from my bank an interesting story book in which the advantages of saving would be told in story form. If the child were a girl, it would receive doll "cut-out" books, with the name of my bank on the back of each doll, as a birthday gift. If it were a boy, it would receive baseball bats. One of the most important floors (or even a whole, near-by building) of my banking house would be set aside as a children's play-room; and it would be equipped with merry-go-rounds, sliding-boards, seesaws, scooters, games and sand piles, with a competent supervisor in charge to give the kiddies a good time. I would let that play-room become the popular habitat of the children of the community, where mothers might leave their youngsters in safety while shopping or visiting.

I would entertain those youngsters so royally that when they grew up and became bank depositors, whose accounts were worth while, they would be inseparably bound to my bank; and, meanwhile, I would, in no way, be lessening my chances of making depositors of the fathers and mothers of those children.

If I were the owner of a business school, I would begin cultivating the boys and girls of my community from the time they reached the fifth grade, on up through high school, so that by the time they were through high school and ready to choose a vocation, I would have the name of my business school well fixed in their minds.

If I were a grocer, or a department store owner, or a druggist, I would cultivate the children, thereby attracting both them and their parents to my place of business; for it is a well known fact that there is no shorter route to the heart of a parent than that which leads through interest manifested in the offspring. If I were a department store owner, and used whole pages of newspaper space, as most of them do, I would run a comic strip at the bottom of each page, illustrating it with scenes in my play-room, and in this way induce the children to read my advertisements.

If I were a preacher, I would equip the basement of my church with a children's play-room that would attract the children of the community every day in the week; and, if my study were near by, I would go into that play-room and enjoy the fun with the little fellows, thereby gaining the inspiration with which to preach better sermons while at the same time raising parishioners for tomorrow. I can think of no more effective method than this of rendering a service that would be in harmony with Christianity, and which would, at the same time, make my church a popular place of abode for the young folks.

SINGLENESS of pur-
pose is one of the
chief essentials for success
in life, no matter what
may be one's aim.

—*John D. Rockefeller, Jr.*

If I were a national advertiser, or the owner of a mail order house, I would find appropriate ways and means of establishing a point of contact with the children of the country; for, let me repeat, there is no better way of influencing the parent than that of "capturing" the child.

If I were a barber, I would have a room equipped exclusively for children, for this would bring me the patronage of both the children and their parents.

In the outskirts of every city there is an opportunity for a flourishing business for someone who will operate a restaurant and serve meals of the better "home-cooked" quality, and cater to families who wish to take the children and dine out occasionally. I would have the place equipped with well stocked fishing ponds, and ponies, and all sorts of animals and birds in which children are interested, if I were operating it, and induce the children to come out regularly and spend the entire day. Why speak of gold mines when opportunities such as this are abundant?

These are but a few of the ways in which the principle of *social heredity* might be used to advantage in business,

Attract the children and you attract the parents!

If nations can build soldiers of war to order, by bending the minds of their young in the direction of war, business men can build customers to order through the same principle.

. . . .

We come, now, to another important feature of this lesson through which we may see, from another angle, how power may be accumulated by co-operative, *organized effort.*

In the plan for the abolition of war, you observed how co-ordination of effort between three of the great organized powers of the world (the schools, churches and the public press) might serve to force universal peace.

We learned many lessons of value from the world war, outrageous and destructive as it was, but none of greater importance than that of the effect of *organized effort*. You will recall that the tide of war began to break in favor of the allied armies just after all armed forces were placed under the direction of General Foch, which brought about complete co-ordination of effort in the allied ranks.

Never before, in the history of the world, had so much power been concentrated in one group of men as that which was created through the *organized effort* of the allied armies. We come, now, to one of the most outstanding and significant facts to be found in the analysis of these allied armies, namely, that they were made up of the most cosmopolitan group of soldiers ever assembled on this earth.

Catholics and Protestants, Jews and Gentiles, blacks and whites, yellows and tans, and every race on earth were represented in those armies. If they had any differences on account of race or creed, they laid them aside and subordinated them to the *cause* for which they were fighting. Under the stress of war, that great mass of humanity was reduced to a common level where they fought shoulder to shoulder, side by side, without asking any questions as to each other's racial tendencies or religious beliefs.

If they could lay aside *intolerance* long enough to fight for their lives over there, why can we not do the same while we fight for a higher standard of ethics in business and finance and industry over here?

Is it only when civilized people are fighting for their lives that they have the foresight to lay aside *intolerance* and co-operate in the furtherance of a common end?

If it were advantageous to the allied armies to think and act as one thoroughly co-ordinated body, would it be less advantageous for the people of a city or a community or an industry to do so?

If all the churches and schools and newspapers and clubs and civic organizations of your city allied themselves for the furtherance of a common cause, do you not see how such an alliance would create sufficient power to insure the success of that cause?

Bring the illustration still nearer your own individual interests by an imaginary alliance between all of the employers and all of the employees of your city, for the purpose of reducing friction and misunderstandings, thereby enabling them to render better service at a lower cost to the public and greater profit to themselves.

We learned from the world war that we cannot destroy a part without weakening the whole; that when one nation or group of people is reduced to poverty and want, the remainder of the world suffers, also. Stated conversely, we learned from the world war that *co-operation* and *tolerance* are the very foundation of enduring success.

Surely the more thoughtful and observant individuals will not fail to profit (as individuals) by these great lessons which we learned from the world war.

I am not unmindful of the fact that *you* are probably studying this course for the purpose of profiting, in every way possible, from a purely personal viewpoint, by the principles upon which it is founded. For this very reason, I have endeavored to outline the application of these principles to as wide a scope of subjects as possible.

In this lesson, you have had opportunity to observe the application of the principles underlying the subjects of *organized effort, tolerance* and *social heredity* to an extent which must have given you much food for thought, and which must have given your *imagination* much room for profitable exercise.

I have endeavored to show you how these principles may be employed both in the furtherance of your own individual interests, in whatever calling you may be engaged, and for the benefit of civilization as a whole.

Whether your calling is that of preaching sermons, selling goods or personal services, practicing law, directing the efforts of others, or working as a day laborer, it seems not too much to hope that you will find in this lesson a stimulus to thought which may lead you to higher achievements. If, perchance, you are a writer of advertisements you will surely find in this lesson sufficient food for thought to add more power to your pen. If you have personal services for sale, it is not unreasonable to expect that this lesson will suggest ways and means of marketing those services to greater advantage.

In uncovering for you the source from which *intolerance* is usually developed, this lesson has led you, also, to the study of other thought-provoking subjects which might easily mark the most profitable turning-point of your life. Books and lessons, in themselves, are of but little value; their real value, if any, lies not in their printed pages, but *in the possible action which they may arouse in the reader.*

For example, when my proof-reader had finished reading the manuscript of this lesson, she informed me that it had so impressed her and her husband that they intended to go into the advertising business and supply banks with an advertising service that would reach the parents through the children. She believes the plan is worth $10,000.00 a year to her.

Frankly, her plan so appealed to me that I would estimate its value at a minimum of more than three times the amount she mentioned, and I doubt not that it could be made to yield five times that amount, if it were properly organized and marketed by an able salesman.

Nor is that all that this lesson has accomplished before passing from the manuscript stage. A prominent business college owner, to whom I showed the manuscript, has already begun to put into effect the suggestion which referred to the use of *social heredity* as a means of "cultivating" students; and he is sanguine enough to believe that a plan, similar to the one he intends using, could be sold to the majority of the 1500 business colleges in the United States and Canada, on a basis that would yield the promoter of the plan a yearly income greater than the salary received by the President of the United States.

And, as this lesson is being completed, I am in recepit of a letter from Dr. Charles F. Crouch, of Atlanta, Georgia, in which he informs me that a group of prominent business men in Atlanta have just crganized the Golden Rule Club, the main object of which is to put into operation, on a nation-wide scale, the plan for the abolition of war, as outlined in this lesson. (A copy of that portion of this lesson dealing with the subject of abolition of war was sent to Dr. Crouch several weeks before the completion of the lesson.)

These three events, happening one after the other, within a period of a few weeks, have strengthened my belief that this is the most important lesson of the entire sixteen, but its value to *you* will depend entirely upon the extent to which it stimulates you to *think* and to *act* as you would not have done without its influence.

The chief object of this course and, particularly, of this lesson is to *educate,* more than it is to *inform*— meaning by the word "educate" to educe, to draw out! to develop from within; *to cause you to use the power that lies sleeping within you, awaiting the awakening hand of some appropriate stimulus to arouse you to action.*

In conclusion, may I not leave with you my personal sentiments on tolerance, in the following essay which I wrote, in the hour of my most trying experience, when an enemy was trying to ruin my reputation and destroy the results of a life-time of honest effort to do some good in the world.

TOLERANCE!

When the dawn of Intelligence shall have spread its wings over the eastern horizon of progress, and Ignorance and Superstition shall have left their last footprints on the sands of Time, it will be recorded in the book of man's crimes and mistakes that his most grievous sin was that of Intolerance!

The bitterest Intolerance grows out of racial and religious differences of opinion, as the result of early childhood training. How long, O Master of Human Destinies, until we poor mortals will understand the folly of trying to destroy one another because of dogmas and creeds and other superficial matters over which we do not agree?

Our allotted time on this earth is but a fleeting moment, at most!

Like a candle, we are lighted, shine for a moment and flicker out! Why can we not so live during this short earthly sojourn that when the Great Caravan called Death draws up and announces this visit about finished we will be ready to fold our tents, and, like the Arabs of the Desert, silently follow the Caravan out into the Darkness of the Unknown without fear and trembling?

I am hoping that I will find no Jews or Gentiles, Catholics or Protestants, Germans or Englishmen, Frenchmen or Russians, Blacks or Whites, Reds or Yellows, when I shall have crossed the Bar to the Other Side.

I am hoping I will find there only human Souls, Brothers and Sisters all, unmarked by race, creed or color, for I shall want to be done with Intolerance so I may lie down and rest an æon or two, undisturbed by the strife, ignorance, superstition and petty misunderstandings which mark with chaos and grief this earthly existence.

IF a man has built a sound character it makes but little difference what people say about him, because he will win in the end.

—*Napoleon Hill, Sr.*

Lesson Sixteen

THE GOLDEN RULE

NO man could possibly read the Law of Success philosophy, even once, without becoming, thereby, better prepared to succeed in any calling.

—*Elbert H. Gary.*

THE LAW OF SUCCESS
Lesson Sixteen
THE GOLDEN RULE

"You Can Do It if You Believe You Can!"

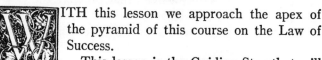ITH this lesson we approach the apex of the pyramid of this course on the Law of Success.

This lesson is the Guiding Star that will enable you to use profitably and *constructively* the knowledge assembled in the preceding lessons.

There is more power wrapped up in the preceding lessons of this course than most men could trust themselves with; therefore, this lesson is a governor that will, if observed and applied, enable you to steer your ship of knowledge over the rocks and reefs of failure that usually beset the pathway of all who come suddenly into possession of power.

For more than twenty-five years I have been observing the manner in which men behave themselves when in possession of power, and I have been forced to the conclusion that the man who attains it in any other than by the slow, step-by-step process, is constantly in danger of destroying himself and all whom he influences.

It must have become obvious to you, long before this, that this entire course leads to the attainment of *power* of proportions which may be made to perform the seemingly "impossible." Happily, it becomes apparent that this *power* can only be attained by the observance of many fundamental principles all of which converge in this lesson, which is based upon a law that both equals and transcends in importance every other law outlined in the preceding lessons.

Likewise, it becomes apparent to the thoughtful student that this *power* can endure only by faithful observance of the law upon which this lesson is based, wherein lies the "safety-valve" that protects the careless student from the dangers of his own follies; and protects, also, those whom he might endanger if he tried to circumvent the injunction laid down in this lesson.

To "prank" with the power that may be attained from the knowledge wrapped up in the preceding lessons of this course, without a full understanding and strict observance of the law laid down in this lesson, is the equivalent of "pranking" with a power which may destroy as well as create.

I am speaking, now, not of that which I suspect to be true, but, of that which *I KNOW TO BE TRUE!* The truth upon which this entire course, and this lesson in particular, is founded, is no invention of mine. I lay no claim to it except that of having observed its unvarying application in the every-day walks of life over a period of more than twenty-five years of struggle; and, of having appropriated as much of it as, in the light of my human frailties and weaknesses, I could make use of.

If you demand *positive* proof of the soundness of the laws upon which this course in general, and this lesson in particular, is founded, I must plead inability to offer it except through one witness, and that is *yourself*.

You may have *positive* proof only by testing and applying these laws for yourself.

If you demand more substantial and authoritative evidence than my own, then I am privileged to refer you to the teachings and philosophy of Christ, Plato, Socrates, Epictetus, Confucius, Emerson and two of the more modern philosophers, James and Münsterberg, from whose works I have appropriated all that constitutes the more important fundamentals of this lesson, with the exception of that which I have gathered from my own limited experience.

For more than four thousand years men have been preaching the Golden Rule as a suitable rule of conduct among men, but unfortunately the world has accepted the letter while totally missing the spirit of this Universal Injunction. We have accepted the Golden Rule philosophy merely as a sound rule of ethical conduct but we have failed to understand the law upon which it is based.

I have heard the Golden Rule quoted scores of times, but I do not recall having ever heard an explanation of the law upon which it is based, and not until recent years did I understand that law, from which I am led to believe that those who quoted it did not understand it.

The Golden Rule means, substantially, to do unto others as you would wish them to do unto you if your positions were reversed.

But why? What is the *real* reason for this kindly consideration of others?

The real reason is this:

There is an eternal law through the operation of which we reap that which we sow. When you select the rule of conduct by which you guide yourself in your transactions with others, you will be fair and just, very likely, if you know that you are setting into motion, by that selection, a *power* that will run its course for weal or woe in the lives of others, returning, finally, to help or to hinder you, according to its nature.

"Whatsoever a man soweth that shall he also reap"!

It is your privilege to deal unjustly with others, but, if you understand the law upon which the Golden Rule is based, you must know that your unjust dealings will "come home to roost."

If you fully understood the principles described in Lesson Eleven, on *accurate thought,* it will be quite easy for you to understand the law upon which the Golden Rule is based. You cannot pervert or change the course of this law, *but you can adapt yourself to its nature and thereby use it as an irresistible power that will carry you to heights of achievement which could not be attained without its aid.*

This law does not stop by merely flinging back upon you your *acts* of injustice and unkindness toward others; it goes further than this—much further—and returns to you the results of every *thought* that you release.

Therefore, not alone is it advisable to "do unto others as you wish them to do unto you," but tc avail yourself fully of the benefits of this great Universal Law you must "think of others as you wish them to think of you."

The law upon which the Golden Rule is based begins affecting you, either for good or evil, the moment you release a *thought*. It has amounted almost to a world-wide tragedy that people have not generally understood this law. Despite the simplicity of the law it is practically all there is to be learned that is of enduring value to man, for it is the medium through which we become the masters of our own destiny.

Understand this law and you understand *all* that the Bible has to unfold to you, for the Bible presents one unbroken chain of evidence in support of the fact that man is the maker of his own destiny; and, that his *thoughts* and *acts* are the tools with which he does the *making*.

During ages of less enlightenment and tolerance than that of the present, some of the greatest thinkers the world has ever produced have paid with their lives for daring to uncover this Universal Law so that it might be understood by all. In the light of the past history of the world, it is an encouraging bit of evidence, in support of the fact that men are gradually throwing off the veil of ignorance and intolerance, to note that I stand in no danger of bodily harm for writing that which would have cost me my life a few centuries ago.

.   .   .   .

While this course deals with the highest laws of the universe, which man is capable of interpreting, the aim, nevertheless, has been to show how these laws may

EVERY man takes care that his neighbor does not cheat him. But a day comes when he begins to care that he does not cheat his neighbor. Then all goes well. He has changed his market cart into a chariot of the sun.

be used in the practical affairs of life. With this object of practical application in mind, let us now proceed to analyze the effect of the Golden Rule through the following incident.

THE POWER OF PRAYER

"No," said the lawyer, "I shan't press your claim against that man; you can get someone else to take the case, or you can withdraw it; just as you please."

"Think there isn't any money in it?"

"There probably would be some little money in it, but it would come from the sale of the little house that the man occupies and calls his home! But I don't want to meddle with the matter, anyhow."

"Got frightened out of it, eh?"

"Not at all."

"I suppose likely the fellow begged hard to be let off?"

"Well, yes, he did."

"And you caved in, likely?"

"Yes."

"What in creation did you do?"

"I believe I shed a few tears."

"And the old fellow begged you hard, you say?"

"No, I didn't say so; he didn't speak a word to me."

"Well, may I respectfully inquire whom he did address in your hearing?"

"God Almighty."

"Ah, he took to praying, did he?"

"Not for my benefit, in the least. You see, I found the little house easily enough and knocked on the outer door, which stood ajar; but nobody heard me, so I stepped into the little hall and saw through the crack of a door a cozy sitting-room, and there on the bed, with her silver head high on the pillows, was an old lady who looked for all the world just like my mother did the last time I ever saw her on earth. Well, I was on the point of knocking, when she said: 'Come, father, now begin; I'm all ready.' And down on his knees by her side went an old, white-haired man, still older than his wife, I should judge, and I couldn't have knocked then, for the life of me. Well, he began. First, he reminded God they were still His submissive children, mother and he, and no matter what He saw fit to bring upon them they shouldn't rebel at His will. Of course 'twas going to be very hard for them to go out homeless in their old age, especially with poor mother so sick and helpless, and, oh! how different it all might have been if only one of the boys had been spared. Then his voice kind of broke, and a white hand stole from under the coverlid and moved softly over his snowy hair. Then he went on to repeat that nothing could be so sharp again as the parting with those three sons—unless mother and he should be separated.

"But, at last, he fell to comforting himself with the fact that the dear Lord knew that it was through no fault of his own that mother and he were threatened with the loss of their dear little home, which meant beggary and the alms-house—a place they prayed to be delivered from entering if it should be consistent with God's will. And then he quoted a multitude of promises concerning the safety of those who put their trust in the Lord. In fact, it was the most thrilling plea to which I ever listened. And at last, he prayed for God's blessing on those who were about to de-mand justice."

The lawyer then continued, more lowly than ever: "And I—believe—I'd rather go to the poor-house my-self tonight than to stain my heart and hands with the blood of such a prosecution as that."

"Little afraid to defeat the old man's prayer, eh?"

"Bless your soul, man, you couldn't defeat it!" said the lawyer. "I tell you he left it all subject to the will of God; but he claimed that we were told to make known our desires unto God; but of all the pleadings I ever heard that beat all. You see, I was taught that kind of thing myself in my childhood. Anyway, why was I sent to hear that prayer? I am sure I don't know, but I hand the case over."

"I wish," said the client, twisting uneasily, "you hadn't told me about the old man's prayer."

"Why so?"

"Well, because I want the money the place would bring; but I was taught the Bible straight enough when I was a youngster and I'd hate to run counter to what you tell about. I wish you hadn't heard a word about it, and, another time, I wouldn't listen to petitions not intended for my ears."

The lawyer smiled.

"My dear fellow," he said, "you're wrong again. It was intended for my ears, and yours, too; and God Almighty intended it. My old mother used to sing about God's moving in a mysterious way, as I re-member it."

"Well, my mother used to sing it, too," said the claimant, as he twisted the claim-papers in his fingers.

"You can call in the morning, if you like, and tell 'mother' and 'him' the claim has been met."

"In a mysterious way," added the lawyer, smiling.

.   .   .   .

Neither this lesson nor the course of which it is a part is based upon an appeal to maudlin sentiment, but there can be no escape from the truth that *success*, in its highest and noblest form, brings one, finally, to view all human relationships with a feeling of deep emotion such as that which this lawyer felt when he overheard the old man's prayer.

It may be an old-fashioned idea, but somehow I can't get away from the belief that *no man can attain success in its highest form without the aid of earnest prayer!*

Prayer is the key with which one may open the secret doorway referred to in Lesson Eleven. In this age of mundane affairs, when the uppermost thought of the majority of people is centered upon the accumulation of wealth, or the struggle for a mere existence, it is both easy and natural for us to overlook the power of earnest prayer.

I am not saying that you should resort to prayer as a means of solving your daily problems which press for immediate attention; no, I am not going that far in a course of instruction which will be studied largely by those who are seeking in it the road to *success* that is measured in dollars; but, may I not modestly suggest to *you* that you, at least, give *prayer* a trial after *everything else fails* to bring you a *satisfying success?*

Thirty men, red-eyed and disheveled, lined up before the judge of the San Francisco police court. It was the regular morning company of drunks and disorderlies. Some were old and hardened; others hung their heads in shame. Just as the momentary disorder attending the bringing in of the prisoners quieted down, a strange thing happened. A strong, clear voice from below began singing:

> "Last night I lay a-sleeping,
>   There came a dream so fair."

"Last night!" It had been for them all a nightmare or a drunken stupor. The song was such a contrast to the horrible fact that no one could fail of a sudden shock at the thought the song suggested.

> "I stood in old Jerusalem,
>   Beside the Temple there,"

the song went on. The judge had paused. He made a quiet inquiry. A former member of a famous opera company known all over the country was awaiting trial for forgery. It was he who was singing in his cell.

Meantime the song went on, and every man in the line showed emotion. One or two dropped on their knees; one boy at the end of the line, after a desperate effort at self-control, leaned against the wall, buried his face against his folded arms, and sobbed, "Oh, mother, mother."

The sobs, cutting to the very heart the men who heard, and the song, still welling its way through the court-room, blended in the hush. At length one man protested. "Judge," said he, "have we got to submit

A trifling kindness here

and there,

Is but a simple, small af-

fair;

Yet if your life has sown

this free,

Wide shall y o u r happy

harvest be.

to this? We're here to take our punishment, but this—" He, too, began to sob.

It was impossible to proceed with the business of the court; yet the court gave no order to stop the song. The police sergeant, after an effort to keep the men in line, stepped back and waited with the rest. The song moved on to its climax:

"Jerusalem, Jerusalem!
   Sing, for the night is o'er!
Hosanna, in the highest!
   Hosanna, for evermore!"

In an ecstasy of melody the last words rang out, and then there was silence. The judge looked into the faces of the men before him. There was not one who was not touched by the song; not one in whom some better impulse was not stirred. He did not call the cases singly—a kind word of advice, and he dismissed them all. No man was fined or sentenced to the work-house that morning. The song had done more good than *punishment* could possibly have accomplished.

You have read the story of a Golden Rule lawyer and a Golden Rule judge. In these two commonplace incidents of every-day life you have observed how the Golden Rule works when *applied*.

A passive attitude toward the Golden Rule will bring no results; it is not enough merely to *believe* in the philosophy, while, at the same time, failing to *apply* it in your relationships with others. If you want results you must take an *active* attitude toward the Golden Rule. A mere passive attitude, represented by belief in its soundness, will avail you nothing

Nor will it avail you anything to proclaim to the world your belief in the Golden Rule while your actions are not in harmony with your proclamation. Conversely stated, it will avail you nothing to appear to practice the Golden Rule, while, at heart, you are willing and eager to use this universal law of right conduct as a cloak to cover up a covetous and selfish nature. Murder will out. Even the most ignorant person will "sense" you for what you are.

"Human character does evermore publish itself. It will not be concealed. It hates darkness—it rushes into light. . . . I heard an experienced counselor say that he never feared the effect upon a jury of a lawyer who does not believe in his heart that his client ought to have a verdict. If he does not believe it, his unbelief will appear to the jury, despite all his protestations, and will become their unbelief. This is that law whereby a work of art, of whatever kind, sets us in the same state of mind wherein the artist was when he made it. That which we do not believe we cannot *adequately say,* though we may repeat the words ever so often. It was this conviction which Swedenborg expressed when he described a group of persons in the spiritual world endeavoring in vain to articulate a proposition which they did not believe; but they could not, though they twisted and folded their lips even to indignation.

"A man passes for what he is worth. What he is engraves itself on his face, on his form, on his fortunes, in letters of light which all men may read but himself. . . . If you would not be known to do anything, never do it. A man may play the fool in the drifts of

a desert, but every grain of sand shall seem to see."
—Emerson.

It is the law upon which the Golden Rule philosophy is based to which Emerson has reference in the foregoing quotation. It was this same law that he had in mind when he wrote the following:

"Every violation of truth is not only a sort of suicide in the liar, but is a stab at the health of human society. On the most profitable lie the course of events presently lays a destructive tax; whilst frankness proves to be the best tactics, for it invites frankness, puts the parties on a convenient footing and makes their business a friendship. Trust men and they will be true to you; treat them greatly and they will show themselves great, though they make an exception in your favor to all their rules of trade."

.   .   .   .   .   .

The Golden Rule philosophy is based upon a law which no man can circumvent. This law is the same law that is described in Lesson Eleven, on Accurate Thought, through the operation of which one's thoughts are transformed into reality corresponding exactly to the nature of the thoughts.

"Once grant the creative power of our thought and there is an end of struggling for our own way, and an end of gaining it *at some one else's expense;* for, since by the terms of the hypothesis we can create what we like, the simplest way of getting what we want is, not to snatch it from somebody else, but to make it for ourselves; and, since there is no limit to thought there can be no need for straining, and for everyone to have his own way in *this manner,* would be to banish all strife, want, sickness, and sorrow from the earth."

"Now, it is precisely on this assumption of the creative power of our thought that the whole Bible rests.
If not, what is the meaning of being saved by Faith?
Faith is essentially thought; and, therefore, every call
to have faith in God is a call to trust in the power of
our own thought about God. 'According to your faith
be it unto you,' says the Old Testament. The entire
book is nothing but one continuous statement of the
creative power of Thought.

"The Law of Man's Individuality is, therefore, the
Law of Liberty, and equally it is the Gospel of peace;
for when we truly understand the law of our own individuality, we see that the same law finds its expression in everyone else; and, consequently, we shall
reverence *the law in others* exactly in proportion as
we value it in ourselves. To do this is to follow the
Golden Rule of doing to others what we would they
should do unto us; and because we know that the
Law of Liberty in ourselves must include the free use
of our creative power, there is no longer any inducement to infringe the rights of others, for we can satisfy
all our desires by the exercise of our knowledge of the
law.

"As this comes to be understood, co-operation will
take the place of competition, with the result of removing all ground for enmity, whether between individuals, classes, or nations. . . ."

(The foregoing quotation is from Bible Mystery
and Bible Meaning by the late Judge T. Troward,
published by Robert McBride & Company, New York
City. Judge Troward was the author of several interesting volumes, among them The Edinburgh Lec-

tures, which is recommended to all students of this course.)

If you wish to know what happens to a man when he totally disregards the law upon which the Golden Rule philosophy is based, pick out any man in your community whom you know to live for the single dominating purpose of accumulating wealth, and who has no conscientious scruples as to how he accumulates that wealth. Study this man and you will observe that there is no warmth to his soul; there is no kindness to his words; there is no welcome to his face. He has become a slave to the desire for wealth; he is too busy to enjoy life and too selfish to wish to help others enjoy it. He walks, and talks, and breathes, but he is nothing but a human automaton. Yet there are many who envy such a man and wish that they might occupy his position, foolishly believing him to be a *success*.

There can never be *success* without happiness, and no man can be happy without dispensing happiness to others. Moreover, the dispensation must be voluntary and with no other object in view than that of spreading sunshine into the hearts of those whose hearts are heavy-laden with burdens.

George D. Herron had in mind the law upon which the Golden Rule philosophy is based when he said:

"We have talked much of the brotherhood to come; but brotherhood has always been the fact of our life, long before it became a modern and inspired sentiment. Only we have been brothers in slavery and torment, brothers in ignorance and its perdition, brothers in disease, and war, and want, brothers in prostitution and hypocrisy. What happens to one of

NO idle person is ever safe, whether he be rich or poor, white or black, educated or illiterate.

—*Booker T. Washington.*

us sooner or later happens to all; we have always been unescapably involved in common destiny. The world constantly tends to the level of the downmost man in it; and that downmost man is the world's real ruler, hugging it close to his bosom, dragging it down to his death. You do not think so, but it is true, and it ought to be true. For if there were some way by which some of us could get free, apart from others, if there were some way by which some of us could have heaven while others had hell, if there were some way by which part of the world could escape some form of the blight and peril and misery of disinherited labor, then indeed would our world be lost and damned; but since men have never been able to separate themselves from one another's woes and wrongs, since history is fairly stricken with the lesson that we cannot escape brotherhood of some kind, since the whole of life is teaching us that we are hourly choosing between brotherhood in suffering and brotherhood in good, it remains for us to choose the brotherhood of a co-operative world, with all its fruits thereof—the fruits of *love* and *liberty*."

The world war ushered us into an age of co-operative effort in which the law of "live and let live" stands out like a shining star to guide us in our relationships with each other. This great universal call for co-operative effort is taking on many forms, not the least important of which are the Rotary Clubs, the Kiwanis Clubs, the Lions Clubs and the many other luncheon clubs which bring men together in a spirit of friendly intercourse, for these clubs mark the beginning of an age of friendly competition in business. The next step will be a closer alliance of

all such clubs in an out-and-out spirit of friendly co-
operation.

The attempt by Woodrow Wilson and his contempo
raries to establish the League of Nations, followed by
the efforts of Warren G. Harding to give footing to
the same cause under the name of the World Court,
marked the first attempt in the history of the world
to make the Golden Rule effective as a common meeting ground for the nations of the world.

There is no escape from the fact that the world has
awakened to the truth in George D. Herron's statement
that "we are hourly choosing between brotherhood in
suffering and brotherhood in good." The world war
has taught us—nay, forced upon us—the truth that
a part of the world cannot suffer without injury to
the whole world. These facts are called to your attention, not in the nature of a preachment on morality, but for the purpose of directing your attention to
the underlying law through which these changes are
being brought about. For more than four thousand
years the world has been thinking about the Golden
Rule philosophy, and that *thought* is now becoming
transformed into realization of the benefits that accrue
to those who apply it.

Still mindful of the fact that the student of this
course is interested in a material success that can be
measured by bank balances, it seems appropriate to
suggest here that all who will may profit by shaping
their business philosophy to conform with this sweeping change toward co-operation which is taking place
all over the world.

If you can grasp the significance of the tremendous
change that has come over the world since the close of

the world war, and if you can interpret the meaning of all the luncheon clubs and other similar gatherings which bring men and women together in a spirit of friendly co-operation, surely your imagination will suggest to you the fact that this is an opportune time to profit by adopting this spirit of friendly co-operation as the basis of your own business or professional philosophy.

Stated conversely, it must be obvious to all who make any pretense of thinking accurately, that the time is at hand when failure to adopt the Golden Rule as the foundation of one's business or professional philosophy is the equivalent of economic suicide.

.   .   .   .

Perhaps you have wondered why the subject of *honesty* has not been mentioned in this course, as a prerequisite to *success,* and, if so, the answer will be found in this lesson. The Golden Rule philosophy, when rightly understood and applied, makes dishonesty impossible. It does more than this—it makes impossible all the other destructive qualities such as selfishness, greed, envy, bigotry, hatred and malice.

When you apply the Golden Rule, you become, at one and the same time, both the judge and the judged —the accused and the accuser. This places one in a position in which *honesty* begins in one's own heart, toward one's self, and extends to all others with equal effect. *Honesty* based upon the Golden Rule is not the brand of honesty which recognizes nothing but the question of expediency.

It is no credit to be honest, when honesty is obviously the most *profitable* policy, lest one lose a good

customer or a valuable client or be sent to jail for
trickery. But when honesty means either a temporary or a permanent material loss, then it becomes an
honor of the highest degree to all who practice it.
Such honesty has its appropriate reward in the accumulated power of character and reputation enjoyed
by all who deserve it.

Those who understand and apply the Golden Rule
philosophy are always scrupulously honest, not alone
out of their desire to be just with others, but because
of their desire to be just with themselves. They understand the eternal law upon which the Golden Rule
is based, and they know that through the operation of
this law *every thought they release and every act in
which they indulge has its counterpart in some fact or
circumstance with which they will later be confronted.*

Golden Rule philosophers are honest because they
understand the truth that honesty adds to their own
character that "vital something" which gives it life
and power. Those who understand the law through
which the Golden Rule operates would poison their
own drinking water as quickly as they would indulge
in acts of injustice to others, for they know that such
injustice starts a chain of causation that will not only
bring them physical suffering, but will destroy their
characters, stain for ill their reputations and render
impossible the attainment of enduring success.

The law through which the Golden Rule philosophy
operates is none other than the law through which
the principle of Auto-suggestion operates. This statement gives you a suggestion from which you should
be able to make a deduction of a far-reaching nature
and of inestimable value.

Test your progress in the mastery of this course by analyzing the foregoing statement and determining, before you read on, what suggestion it offers you.

Of what possible benefit could it be to you to know that when you do unto others as if you were the others, which is the sum and substance of the Golden Rule, you are putting into motion a chain of causation through the aid of a law which affects the others according to the nature of your act, *and at the same time planting in your character, through your sub conscious mind, the effects of that act?*

This question practically suggests its own answer, but as I am determined to cause you to think this vital subject out for yourself I will put the question in still another form, viz.:

If all your acts toward others, and even your thoughts of others, are registered in your sub-conscious mind, through the principle of Auto-suggestion, thereby building your own character in exact duplicate of your *thoughts* and *acts,* can you not see how important it is to guard those acts and thoughts?

We are now in the very heart of the real reason for doing unto others as we would have them do unto us, for it is obvious that whatever we do unto others we do unto ourselves.

Stated in another way, every *act* and every *thought* you release modifies your own character in exact conformity with the nature of the act or thought, and your character is a sort of center of magnetic attraction which attracts to you the people and conditions that harmonize with it.

You cannot indulge in an act toward another person without having first created the nature of that act in

THERE is no defeat except from w i t h i n. There is really no insurmountable barrier save your own inherent weakness of purpose.

—*Emerson.*

your own *thought, and you cannot release a thought without planting the sum and substance and nature of it in your own sub-conscious mind, there to become a part and parcel of your own character.*

Grasp this simple principle and you will understand why you cannot afford to hate or envy another person. You will also understand why you cannot afford to strike back, in kind, at those who do you an injustice. Likewise, you will understand the injunction, "Return good for evil."

Understand the law upon which the Golden Rule injunction is based and you will understand, also, the law that eternally binds all mankind in a single bond of fellowship and renders it impossible for you to injure another person, by *thought* or *deed*, without injuring yourself; and, likewise, adds to your own character the results of every kind *thought* and *deed* in which you indulge.

Understand this law and you will then know, beyond room for the slightest doubt, that you are constantly punishing yourself for every wrong you commit and rewarding yourself for every act of constructive conduct in which you indulge.

It seems almost an act of Providence that the greatest wrong and the most severe injustice ever done me by one of my fellow men was done just as I began this lesson. (Some of the students of this course will know what it is to which I refer.)

This injustice has worked a temporary hardship on me, but that is of little consequence compared to the advantage it has given me by providing a timely opportunity for me to test the soundness of the entire premise upon which this lesson is founded.

The injustice to which I refer left two courses of action open to me. I could have claimed relief by "striking back" at my antagonist, through both civil court action and criminal libel proceedings, or I could have stood upon my right to forgive him. One course of action would have brought me a substantial sum of money and whatever joy and satisfaction there may be in defeating and *punishing* an enemy. The other course of action would have brought me self-respect which is enjoyed by those who have successfully met the test and discovered that they have evolved to the point at which they can repeat the Lord's Prayer and *mean it!*

I chose the latter course. I did so, despite the recommendations of close personal friends to "strike back," and despite the offer of a prominent lawyer to do my "striking" for me *without cost.*

But the lawyer offered to do the impossible, for the reason that no man can "strike back" at another *without cost.* Not always is the cost of a monetary nature, for there are other things with which one may pay that are dearer than money.

It would be as hopeless to try to make one who was not familiar with the law upon which the Golden Rule is based understand why I refused to strike back at this enemy as it would to try to describe the law of gravitation to an ape. If you understand this law you understand, also, why I chose to *forgive* my enemy.

In the Lord's Prayer we are admonished to forgive our enemies, but that admonition will fall on deaf ears except where the listener understands the law upon which it is based. That law is none other than the law upon which the Golden Rule is based. It is the law that forms the foundation of this entire lesson, and through which we must inevitably reap that which we sow. There is no escape from the operation of this law, nor is there any cause to try to avoid its consequences if we refrain from putting into motion *thoughts* and *acts* that are destructive.

That we may more concretely describe the law upon which this lesson is based, let us embody the law in a code of ethics such as one who wishes to follow literally the injunction of the Golden Rule might appropriately adopt, as follows.

MY CODE OF ETHICS

I. I believe in the Golden Rule as the basis of all human conduct; therefore, I will never do to another person that which I would not be willing for that person to do to me if our positions were reversed.

II. I will be honest, even to the slightest detail, in all my transactions with others, not alone because of my desire to be fair with them, but because of my desire to impress the idea of honesty on my own subconscious mind, thereby weaving this essential quality into my own character.

III. I will forgive those who are unjust toward me, with no thought as to whether they deserve it or not because I understand the law through which forgiveness of others strengthens my own character and wipes out the effects of my own transgressions, in my sub-conscious mind.

IV. I will be just, generous and fair with others always, even though I know that these acts will go unnoticed and unrewarded, in the ordinary terms of reward, because I understand and intend to apply the law through the aid of which one's own character is but the sum total of one's own *acts* and *deeds*.

V. Whatever time I may have to devote to the discovery and exposure of the weaknesses and faults of others I will devote, more profitably, to the discovery and *correction* of my own.

VI. I will slander no person, no matter how much I may believe another person may deserve it, because I wish to plant no destructive suggestions in my own sub-conscious mind.

VII. I recognize the power of Thought as being an inlet leading into my brain from the universal ocean of life; therefore, I will set no destructive thoughts afloat upon that ocean lest they pollute the minds of others.

VIII. I will conquer the common human tendency toward hatred, and envy, and selfishness, and jealousy, and malice, and pessimism, and doubt, and fear; for I believe these to be the seed from which the world harvests most of its troubles.

IX. When my mind is not occupied with thoughts that tend toward the attainment of my *definite chief aim* in life, I will voluntarily keep it filled with thoughts of courage, and self-confidence, and good-will toward others, and faith, and kindness, and loyalty, and love for truth, and justice, for I believe these to be the seed from which the world reaps its harvest of progressive growth.

X. I understand that a mere passive belief in the soundness of the Golden Rule philosophy is of no value whatsoever, either to myself or to others; therefore, I will *actively* put into operation this universal rule for good in all my transactions with others.

XI. I understand the law through the operation of which my own character is developed from my own *acts* and *thoughts;* therefore, I will guard with care all that goes into its development.

XII. Realizing that enduring happiness comes only through helping others find it; that no act of kindness is without its reward, even though it may never be directly repaid, I will do my best to assist others when and where the opportunity appears.

You have noticed frequent reference to Emerson throughout this course. Every student of the course should own a copy of Emerson's Essays, and the essay on Compensation should be read and studied at least every three months. Observe, as you read this essay, that it deals with the same law as that upon which the Golden Rule is based.

.   .   .   .

There are people who believe that the Golden Rule philosophy is nothing more than a theory, and that it is in no way connected with an immutable law. They have arrived at this conclusion because of personal experience wherein they rendered service to others without enjoying the benefits of direct reciprocation.

How many are there who have not rendered service to others that was neither reciprocated nor appreciated? I am sure that I have had such an experience, not once, but many times, and I am equally sure that I will have similar experiences in the future, nor will I discontinue rendering service to others merely be-

Y OU have not fulfilled
every d u t y unless
you have fulfilled that of
being pleasant.

—*Charles Buxton.*

cause *they* neither reciprocate nor appreciate my efforts.

And here is the reason:

When I render service to another, or indulge in an act of kindness, I store away in my sub-conscious mind the effect of my efforts, which may be likened to the "charging" of an electric battery. By and by, if I indulge in a sufficient number of such acts I will have developed a positive, dynamic character that will *attract* to me people who harmonize with or resemble my own character.

Those whom I *attract* to me will reciprocate the acts of kindness and the service that I have rendered others, thus the Law of Compensation will have balanced the scales of justice for me, bringing back from one source the results of service that I rendered through an entirely different source.

You have often heard it said that a salesman's first sale should be to himself, which means that unless he first convinces himself of the merits of his wares he will not be able to convince others. Here, again, enters this same Law of Attraction, for it is a well known fact that *enthusiasm* is contagious, and when a salesman shows great *enthusiasm* over his wares he will arouse a corresponding interest in the minds of others.

You can comprehend this law quite easily by regarding yourself as a sort of human magnet that attracts those whose characters harmonize with your own. In thus regarding yourself as a magnet that attracts to you all who harmonize with your dominating characteristics and repels all who do not so harmonize, you should keep in mind, also, the fact that *you are the builder of that magnet;* also, that you may change its nature so that it will correspond to any ideal that you may wish to set up and follow.

And, most important of all, you should keep in mind the fact that this entire process of change takes place through *thought!*

Your character is but the sum total of your *thoughts* and *deeds!* This truth has been stated in many different ways throughout this course.

Because of this great truth it is impossible for you to render any useful service or indulge in any act of kindness toward others without benefiting thereby. Moreover, it is just as impossible for you to indulge in any destructive *act* or *thought* without paying the penalty in the loss of a corresponding amount of your own power.

.   .   .   .

Positive thought develops a dynamic personality. *Negative thought* develops a personality of an opposite nature. In many of the preceding lessons of this course, and in this one, definite instructions are given as to the exact method of developing personality through *positive thought*. These instructions are particularly detailed in Lesson Three, on *Self-confidence*. In that lesson you have a very definite formula to follow. All of the formulas provided in this course are for the purpose of helping you *consciously* to direct the power of *thought* in the development of a personality that will attract to you those who will be of help in the attainment of your *definite chief aim*.

You need no proof that your hostile or unkind *acts* toward others bring back the effects of retaliation. Moreover, this retaliation is usually definite and immediate. Likewise, you need no proof that you can accomplish more by dealing with others in such a way that they will want to co-operate with you. If you mastered the eighth lesson, on Self-control, you now understand how to induce others to act toward you as you wish them to act—*through your own attitude toward them.*

The law of "an eye for an eye and a tooth for a tooth" is based upon the selfsame law as that upon which the Golden Rule operates. This is nothing more than the law of retaliation with which all of us are familiar. Even the most selfish person will respond to this law, *because he cannot help it!* If I speak ill of you, even though I tell the truth, you will not think kindly of me. Furthermore, you will most likely retaliate in kind. But, if I speak of your virtues you will think kindly of me, and when the opportunity appears you will reciprocate in kind in the majority of instances.

Through the operation of this law of attraction the uninformed are constantly attracting trouble and grief and hatred and opposition from others by their *unguarded words* and *destructive acts.*

Do unto others as you would have them do unto you!

We have heard that injunction expressed thousands of times, yet how many of us understand the law upon which it is based? To make this injunction somewhat clearer it might be well to state it more in detail, about as follows:

Do unto others as you would have them do unto you, *bearing in mind the fact that human nature has a tendency to retaliate in kind.*

Confucius must have had in mind the law of retaliation when he stated the Golden Rule philosophy in about this way:

Do not unto others that which you would not have them do unto you.

And he might well have added an explanation to the effect that the reason for his injunction was based upon the common tendency of man to retaliate in kind.

Those who do not understand the law upon which the Golden Rule is based are inclined to argue that it will not work, for the reason that men are inclined toward the principle of exacting "an eye for an eye and a tooth for a tooth," which is nothing more nor less than the law of retaliation. If they would go a step further in their reasoning they would understand that they are looking at the *negative* effects of this law, and that the selfsame law is capable of producing *positive* effects as well.

In other words, if you would not have your own eye plucked out, then insure against this misfortune by refraining from plucking out the other fellow's eye. Go a step further and render the other fellow an act of kindly, helpful service, and *through the operation of this same law of retaliation* he will render you a similar service.

And, if he should fail to reciprocate your kindness —what then?

You have profited, nevertheless, because of the effect of your act on *your own sub-conscious mind!*

Thus by indulging in acts of kindness and applying, always, the Golden Rule philosophy, you are sure of benefit from one source and at the same time you have a pretty fair chance of profiting from another source.

It might happen that you would base all of your acts toward others on the Golden Rule without enjoying any direct reciprocation for a long period of time, and it might so happen that those to whom you rendered those acts of kindness would never reciprocate, but meantime you have been adding vitality to your own character and sooner or later this *positive character* which you have been building will begin to assert itself and you will discover that you have been receiving compound interest on compound interest in return for those acts of kindness which appeared to have been wasted on those who neither appreciated nor reciprocated them.

Remember that your *reputation* is made by others, but your *character* is made by *you!*

You want your reputation to be a favorable one, but you cannot be sure that it will be for the reason that it is something that exists outside of your own control, in the minds of others. It is what others believe you to be. With your character it is different. Your character is that which *you are,* as the results of your *thoughts* and *deeds.* You control it. You can make it weak, good or bad. When you are satisfied and know in your mind that your character is above reproach you need not worry about your reputation, for it is as impossible for your character to be destroyed or damaged by anyone except yourself as it is to destroy matter or energy.

It was this truth that Emerson had in mind when he said: "A political victory, a rise of rents, the recovery of your sick or the return of your absent friend, or some other quite external event raises your spirits.

and you think your days are prepared for you. *Do not believe it.* It can never be so. *Nothing can bring you peace but yourself. Nothing can bring you peace but the triumph of principles."*

One reason for being just toward others is the fact that such action may cause them to reciprocate, in kind, but a better reason is the fact that kindness and justice toward others develop *positive character* in all who indulge in these acts.

You may withhold from me the reward to which I am entitled for rendering you helpful service, but no one can deprive me of the benefit I will derive from the rendering of that service in so far as it adds to my own *character*.

.   .   .   .

We are living in a great industrial age. Everywhere we see the evolutionary forces working great changes in the method and manner of living, and rearranging the relationships 'between men, in the ordinary pursuit of life, liberty and a living.

This is an age of organized effort. On every hand we see evidence that organization is the basis of all financial success, and while other factors than that of organization enter into the attainment of success, this factor is still one of major importance.

This industrial age has created two comparatively new terms. One is called "capital" and the other "labor." Capital and labor constitute the main wheels in the machinery of organized effort. These two great forces enjoy success in exact ratio to the extent that both understand and apply the Golden Rule philosophy. Despite this fact, however, harmony between these two forces does not always prevail, thanks to the destroyers of confidence who make a living by sowing the seed of dissension and stirring up strife between employers and employees.

During the past fifteen years I have devoted considerable time to the study of the causes of disagreement between employers and employees. Also, I have gathered much information on this subject from other men who, likewise, have been studying this problem.

There is but one solution which will, if understood by all concerned, bring harmony out of chaos and establish a perfect working relationship between capital and labor. The remedy is no invention of mine. It is based upon a great universal law of Nature. This remedy has been well stated by one of the great men of this generation, in the following words:

"The question we propose to consider is exciting deep interest at the present time, but no more than its importance demands. It is one of the hopeful signs of the times that these subjects of vital interest to human happiness are constantly coming up for a hearing, are engaging the attention of the wisest men, and stirring the minds of all classes of people. The wide prevalence of this movement shows that a new life is beating in the heart of humanity, operating upon their faculties like the warm breath of spring upon the frozen ground and the dormant germs of the plant. It will make a great stir, it will break up many frozen and dead forms, it will produce great and, in some cases, it may be, destructive changes, but it announces the blossoming of new hopes, and the coming of new harvests for the supply of human wants and the means of greater happiness. There is great need of wisdom to guide the new forces coming into action. Every man is under the most solemn obligation to do his part in forming a correct public opinion and giving wise direction to popular will.

"The only solution for the problems of labor, of want, of abundance, of suffering and sorrow can only be found by regarding them from a moral and spiritual point of view. They must be seen and examined in a light that is not of themselves. *The true relations of labor and capital can never be discovered by human selfishness.* They must be viewed from a higher purpose than wages or the accumulation of wealth. They must be regarded from their bearing upon the purposes for which man was created. It is from this point of view I propose to consider the subject before us.

"Capital and labor are essential to each other. Their interests are so bound together that they cannot be separated. In civilized and enlightened communities they are mutually dependent. If there is any difference, capital is more dependent upon labor than labor upon capital. Life can be sustained without capital. Animals, with a few exceptions, have no property, and take no anxious thought for the morrow, and our Lord commends them to our notice as examples worthy of imitation. 'Behold the fowls of the air,' He says, 'for they sow not, neither do they reap nor gather into barns, yet your heavenly Father feedeth them.' The savages live without capital. Indeed, the great mass of human beings live by their labor from day to day, from hand to mouth. But no man can live upon his wealth. He cannot eat his gold and silver; he cannot clothe himself with deeds and certificates of stock. Capital can do nothing without labor, *and its only value consists in its power to purchase labor or its results.* It is itself the product of labor. It has no occasion, therefore, to assume an importance that does not belong to it. Absolutely dependent, however, as it is upon labor for its value, it is an essential factor in human progress.

"The moment man begins to rise from a savage and comparatively independent state to a civilized and dependent one, capital becomes necessary. Men come into more intimate relations with one another. Instead of each one doing everything, men begin to devote themselves to special employments, and to depend upon others to provide many things for them while they engage in some special occupation. In this way labor becomes diversified. One man works in iron, another in wood; one manufactures cloth, another makes it into garments; some raise food to feed those who build houses and manufacture implements of husbandry. This necessitates a system of exchanges, and to facilitate exchanges roads must be made, and men must be employed to make them. As population increases and necessities multiply, the business of exchange becomes enlarged, until we have immense manufactories, railroads girding the earth with iron bands, steamships plowing every sea, and a multitude of men who cannot raise bread or make a garment, or do anything directly for the supply of their own wants.

"Now, we can see how we become more dependent upon others as our wants are multiplied and civilization advances. Each one works in his special employment, does better work, because he can devote his whole thought and time to a form of use for which he is specially fitted, and contributes more largely to the public good. While he is working for others, all others are working for him. Every member of the community is working for the whole body, and the whole body for every member. This is the law of perfect life, a law which rules everywhere in the material body. Every man who is engaged in any employment useful to body or mind is a philanthropist, a public benefactor, whether he raises corn on the prairie, cotton in Texas or India, mines coal in the chambers of the earth, or feeds it to engines in the hold of a steamship. If selfishness did not pervert and blast human motives, all men and women would be fulfilling the law of charity while engaged in their daily employment.

"To carry on this vast system of exchanges, to place the forest and the farm, the factory and the mine side by side, and deliver the products of all climes at every door, requires immense capital. One man cannot work his farm or factory, and build a railroad or a line of steamships. As raindrops acting singly cannot drive a mill or supply steam for an engine, but, collected in a vast reservoir, become the resistless power of Niagara, or the force which drives the engine and steamship like mighty shuttles from mountain to seacoast and from shore to shore, so a few dollars in a multitude of pockets are powerless to provide the means for these vast operations, but combined they move the world.

"Capital is a friend of labor and essential to its economical exercise and just reward. It can be, and often is, a terrible enemy, when employed for selfish purposes alone; but the great mass of it is more friendly to human happiness than is generally supposed. It cannot be employed without in some way, either directly or indirectly, helping the laborer. We think of the evils we suffer, but allow the good we enjoy to pass unnoticed. We think of the evils that larger means would relieve and the comforts they would provide, but overlook the blessings we enjoy that would have been impossible without large accumulations of capital. It is the part of wisdom to form a just estimate of the good we receive as well as the evils we suffer.

"It is a common saying at the present time, that the rich are growing richer and the poor poorer; but when all man's possessions are taken into the account there are good reasons for doubting this assertion. It is true that the rich are growing richer. It is also true that the condition of the laborer is constantly improving. *The common laborer has conveniences and comforts which princes could not command a century ago.* He is better clothed, has a greater variety and abundance of food, lives in a more comfortable dwelling, and has many more conveniences for the conduct of domestic affairs and the prosecution of labor than money could purchase but a few years ago. An emperor could not travel with the ease, the comfort, and the swiftness that the common laborer can today. He may think that he stands alone, with no one to help. But, in truth, he has an immense retinue of servants constantly waiting upon him, ready and anxious to do his bidding. It requires a vast army of men and an immense outlay of capital to provide a common dinner, such as every man and woman, with few exceptions, has enjoyed today.

"Think of the vast combination of means and men and forces necessary to provide even a frugal meal. The Chinaman raises your tea, the Brazilian your coffee, the East Indian your spices, the Cuban your sugar, the farmer upon the western prairies your bread and possibly your beef, the gardener your vegetables, the dairyman your butter and milk; the miner has dug from the hills the coal with which your food was cooked and your house was warmed, the cabinet-maker has provided you with chairs and tables, the cutler with knives and forks, the potter with dishes, the Irishman has made your table-cloth, the butcher has dressed your meat, the miller your flour.

"But these various articles of food, and the means of preparing and serving them, were produced at immense distances from you and from one another. Oceans had to be traversed, hills leveled, valleys filled, and mountains tunneled, ships must be built, railways constructed, and a vast army of men instructed and employed in every mechanical art before the materials for your dinner could be prepared and served. There must also be men to collect these materials, to buy and sell and distribute them. Everyone stands in his own place and does his own work, and receives his wages. But he is none the less working for you, and serving you as truly and effectively as he would be if he were in your special employment and received his wages from your hand. In the light of these facts, which everyone must acknowledge, we may be able to see more clearly the truth, that every man and woman who does useful work is a public benefactor, and the thought of it and the purpose of it will ennoble the labor and the laborer. We are all bound together by common ties. The rich and the poor, the learned and the ignorant, the strong and the weak, are woven together in one social and civic web. Harm to one is harm to all; help to one is help to all.

"You see what a vast army of servants it requires to provide your dinner. Do you not see that it demands a corresponding amount of capital to provide and keep this complicated machinery in motion? And do you not see that every man, woman and child is enjoying the benefit of it? How could we get our coal, our meat, our flour, our tea and coffee, sugar and rice? The laborer cannot build ships and sail them and support himself while doing it. *The farmer cannot leave his farm and take his produce to the market. The miner cannot mine and transport his coal.* The farmer in Kansas may be burning corn today to cook his food and warm his dwelling, and the miner may be hungry for the bread which the corn would supply, because they cannot exchange the fruits of their labor. Every acre of land, every forest and mine has been increased in value by railways and steamboats, and the comforts of life and the means of social and intellectual culture have been carried to the most inaccessible places.

"But the benefits of capital are not limited to supplying present wants and comforts. It opens new avenues for labor. It diversifies it and gives a wider field to everyone to do the kind of work for which he is best fitted by natural taste and genius. The number of employments created by railways, steamships, telegraph, and manufactories by machinery can hardly be estimated. Capital is also largely invested in supplying the means of intellectual and spiritual culture

Books are multiplied at constantly diminishing prices, and the best thought of the world, by means of our great publishing houses, is made accessible to the humblest workman. There is no better example of the benefits the common laborer derives from capital than the daily newspaper. For two or three cents the history of the world for twenty-four hours is brought to every door. The laborer, while riding to or from his work in a comfortable car, can visit all parts of the known world and get a truer idea of the events of the day than he could if he were bodily present. A battle in China or Africa, an earthquake in Spain, a dynamite explosion in London, a debate in Congress, the movements of men in public and private life for the suppression of vice, for enlightening the ignorant, helping the needy, and improving the people generally,' are spread before him in a small compass, and bring him into contact and on equality, in regard to the world's history, with kings and queens, with saints and sages, and people in every condition in life. *Do you ever think,* while reading the morning paper, how many men have been running on your errands, collecting intelligence for you from all parts of the earth, and putting it into a form convenient for your use? It required the investment of millions of money and the employment of thousands of men to produce that paper and leave it at your door. And what did all this service cost you? A few cents.

"These are examples of the benefits which everyone derives from capital, benefits which could not be obtained without vast expenditures of money; benefits which come to us without our care and lay their blessings at our feet. Capital cannot be invested in any useful production without blessing a multitude of people. It sets the machinery of life in motion, it multiplies employment; it places the product of all climes at every door, it draws the people of all nations together; brings mind in contact with mind, and gives to every man and woman a large and valuable share of the product. These are facts which it would be well for everyone, however poor he may be, to consider.

"If capital is such a blessing to labor; if it can only be brought into use by labor, and derives all its value from it, how can there be any conflict between them? There could be none if both the capitalist and laborer acted from humane and Christian principles. But they do not. They are governed by inhuman and unchristian principles. Each party seeks to get the largest returns for the least service. Capital desires larger profits, labor higher wages. The interests of the capitalist and the laborer come into direct collision. In this warfare capital has great advantages, and has been prompt to take them. It has demanded and taken the lion's share of the profits. It has despised the servant that enriched it. It has regarded the laborer as a menial, a slave, whose rights and happiness it was not bound to respect. It influences legislators to enact laws in its favor, subsidizes governments and wields its power for its own advantage. Capital has been a lord and labor a servant. While the servant remained docile and obedient, content with such compensation as its lord chose to give, there was no conflict. But labor is rising from a servile, submissive, and hopeless condition. It has acquired strength and intelligence; has gained the idea that it has rights that ought to be respected, and begins to assert and combine to support them.

"Each party in this warfare regards the subject from its own selfish interests. The capitalist supposes that gain to labor is loss to him, and that he must look to his own interests first; that the cheaper the labor the larger his gains. Consequently it is for his interest to keep the price as low as possible. On the contrary, the laborer thinks that he loses what the capitalist gains, and, consequently, that it is for his interest to get as large wages as possible. From these opposite points of view their interests appear to be directly hostile. What one party gains the other loses; hence the conflict. Both are acting from selfish motives, and, consequently, must be wrong. Both parties see only half of the truth, and, mistaking that for the whole of it, they fall into a mistake ruinous to both. Each one stands on his own ground, and regards the subject wholly from his point of view and in the misleading light of his own selfishness. Passion inflames the mind and blinds the understanding; and when passion is aroused men will sacrifice their own interests to injure others, and both will suffer loss. They will wage continual warfare against each other; they will resort to all devices, and take advantage of every necessity to win a victory. Capital tries to starve the laborer into submission, like a beleaguered city; and hunger and want are most powerful weapons. Labor sullenly resists, and tries to destroy the value of capital by rendering it unproductive. If necessity or interest compels a truce, it is a sullen one, and maintained with the purpose of renewing hostilities as soon as there is any prospect of success. Thus laborers and capitalists confront each other like two armed hosts, ready at any time to renew the conflict. *It will be renewed, without doubt, and continued with varying success until both parties discover that they are mistaken, that their interests are mutual, and can only be secured to the fullest extent by co-operation and giving to each the reward it deserves.* The capitalist and the laborer must clasp hands across the bottomless pit into which so much wealth and work has been cast.

"How this reconciliation is to be effected is a question that is occupying the minds of many wise and good men on both sides at the present time. Wise and impartial legislation will, no doubt, be an important agent in restraining blind passion and protecting all classes from insatiable greed; and it is the duty of every man to use his best endeavors to secure such legislation both in state and national governments. Organizations of laborers for protecting their own rights and securing a better reward for their labor, will have a great influence. That influence will continue to increase as their temper becomes normal and firm, and their demands are based *on justice and humanity*. Violence and threats will effect no good. Dynamite, whether in the form of explosives or the more destructive force of fierce and reckless passion, will heal no wounds nor subdue any hostile feeling. Arbitration is, doubtless, the wisest and most practicable means now available to bring about amicable relations between these hostile parties and secure justice to both. Giving the laborer a share in the profits of the business has worked well in some cases, but it is attended with great practical difficulties which require more wisdom, self-control and genuine regard for the common interests of both parties than often can be found. Many devices may have a partial and temporary effect. But no permanent progress can be made in settling this conflict without restraining and finally removing its cause.

"Its real central cause is an inordinate love of self and the world, and that cause will continue to operate as long as it exists. It may be restrained and moderated, but it will assert itself when occasion offers. Every wise man must, therefore, seek to remove the cause, and as far as he can do it he will control effects. Purify the fountain, and you make the whole stream pure and wholesome.

"There is a principle of universal influence that must underlie and guide every successful effort to bring these two great factors of human good which now confront each other with hostile purpose, into harmony. It is no invention or discovery of mine. It embodies a higher than human wisdom. It is not difficult to understand or apply. The child can comprehend it and act according to it. It is universal in its application, and wholly useful in its effects. It will lighten the burdens of labor and increase its rewards. It will give security to capital and make it more productive. It is simply the Golden Rule, embodied in these words: *'Therefore all things whatsoever ye would that men should do to you, do ye even so to them: for this is the law and the prophets.'*

"Before proceeding to apply this principle to the case in hand, let me call your special attention to it. It is a very remarkable law of human life which seems to have been generally overlooked by statesmen, phi-

losophers and religious teachers. This rule embodies
the whole of religion; it comprises all the precepts,
commandments, and means of the future triumphs of
good over evil, of truth over error, and the peace and
happiness of men, foretold in the glorious visions of
the prophets. Mark the words. It does not merely
say that it is a wise rule; that it accords with the
principles of the Divine order revealed in the law and
the prophets. *It embodies them all; it 'IS the law
and the prophets.'* It comprises love to God. It says
we should regard Him as we desire to have Him regard us; that we should do to Him as we wish to have
Him do to us. If we desire to have Him love us with
all His heart, with all His soul, with all His mind, and
with all His strength, we must love Him in the same
manner. If we desire to have our neighbor love us as
he loves himself, we must love him as we love ourself.
Here, then, is the universal and Divine law of human
service and fellowship. It is not a precept of human
wisdom; it has its origin in the Divine nature, and its
embodiment in human nature. Now, let us apply it
to the conflict between labor and capital.

"You are a capitalist. Your money is invested in
manufactures, in land, in mines, in merchandise, railways, and ships, or you loan it to others on interest.
You employ, directly or indirectly, men to use your
capital. You cannot come to a just conclusion concerning your rights and duties and privileges by looking wholly at your own gains. The glitter of the silver
and gold will exercise so potent a spell over your mind
that it will blind you to everything else. You can see
no interest but your own. The laborer is not known
or regarded as a man who has any interests you are

bound to regard. You see him only as your slave, your tool, your means of adding to your wealth. In this light he is a friend so far as he serves you, an enemy so far as he does not. But change your point of view. Put yourself in his place; put him in your place. How would you like to have him treat you if you were in his place? Perhaps you have been there. In all probability you have, for the capitalist today was the laborer yesterday, and the laborer today will be the employer tomorrow. You know from lively and painful experience how you would like to be treated. Would you like to be regarded as a mere tool? As a means of enriching another? Would you like to have your wages kept down to the bare necessities of life? Would you like to be regarded with indifference and treated with brutality? Would you like to have your blood, your strength, your soul coined into dollars for the benefit of another? These questions are easy to answer. Everyone knows that he would rejoice to be treated kindly, to have his interests regarded, his rights recognized and protected. Everyone knows that such regard awakens a response in his own heart. Kindness begets kindness; respect awakens respect. Put yourself in his place. Imagine that you are dealing with yourself, and you will have no difficulty in deciding whether you should give the screw another turn, that you may wring a penny more from the muscles of the worker, or relax its pressure, and, if possible, add something to his wages, and give him respect for his service. Do to him as you would have him do to you in changed conditions.

"You are a laborer. You receive a certain sum for a day's work. Put yourself in the place of your employer. How would you like to have the men you employed work for you? Would you think it right that they should regard you as their enemy? Would you think it honest in them to slight their work, *to do as little and to get as much as possible?* If you had a large contract which must be completed at a fixed time or you would suffer great loss, would you like to have your workmen take advantage of your necessity to compel an increase of their wages? Would you think it right and wise in them to interfere with you in the management of your business? To dictate whom you should employ, and on what terms you should employ them? Would you not rather have them do honest work in a kind and good spirit? Would you not be much more disposed to look to their interests, to lighten their labor, to increase their wages when you could afford to do so, and look after the welfare of their families, when you found that they regarded yours? I know that it would be so. It is true that men are selfish, and that some men are so mean and contracted in spirit that they cannot see any interest but their own; whose hearts, not made of flesh but of silver and gold, are so hard that they are not touched by any human feeling, and care not how much others suffer if they can make a cent by it. But they are the exception, not the rule. We are influenced by the regard and devotion of others to our interests. The laborer who knows that his employer feels kindly toward him, desires to treat him justly and to regard his good, will do better work and more of it, and will be disposed to look to his employer's interests as well as his own.

"I am well aware that many will think this Divine

and humane law of doing to others as we would have them do to us, is impracticable in this selfish and worldly age. If both parties would be governed by it, everyone can see how happy would be the results. But, it will be said, they will not. The laborer will not work unless compelled by want. He will take advantage of every necessity. As soon as he gains a little independence of his employer he becomes proud, arrogant and hostile. The employer will seize upon every means to keep the workmen dependent upon him, and to make as much out of them as possible. Every inch of ground which labor yields capital will occupy and intrench itself in it, and from its vantage bring the laborer into greater dependence and more abject submission. But this is a mistake. The history of the world testifies that when the minds of men are not embittered by intense hostility and their feelings outraged by cruel wrongs, they are ready to listen to calm, disinterested and judicious counsel. A man who employed a large number of laborers in mining coal told me that he had never known an instance to fail of a calm and candid response when he had appealed to honorable motives, as a man to man, both of whom acknowledged a common humanity. There is a recent and most notable instance in this city of the happy effect of calm, disinterested and judicious counsel in settling difficulties between employers and workmen that were disastrous to both.

"When the mind is inflamed by passion men will not listen to reason. They become blind to their own interests and regardless of the interests of others. *Difficulties are never settled while passion rages. They are never settled by conflict. One party may be sub-*

dued by power; but the sense of wrong will remain; the fire of passion will slumber ready to break out again on the first occasion. But let the laborer or the capitalist feel assured that the other party has no wish to take any advantage, that there is a sincere desire and determination on both sides to be just and pay due regard to their common interests, and all the conflict between them would cease, as the wild waves of the ocean sink to calm when the winds are at rest. The laborer and the capitalist have a mutual and common interest. Neither can permanently prosper without the prosperity of the other. They are parts of one body. If labor is the arm, capital is the blood. Devitalize or waste the blood, and the arm loses its power. Destroy the arm, and the blood is useless. Let each care for the other, and both are benefited. *Let each take the Golden Rule as a guide,* and all cause of hostility will be removed, all conflict will cease, and they will go hand in hand to do their work and reap their just reward."

.   .   .   .

If you have mastered the fundamentals upon which this lesson is based, you understand why it is that no public speaker can move his audience or convince men of his argument unless he, himself, believes that which he is saying.

You also understand why no salesman can convince his prospective purchaser unless he has first convinced himself of the merits of his goods.

Throughout this entire course one particular principle has been emphasized for the purpose of illustrating the truth that every personality is the sum total of the individual's *thoughts* and *acts*—that we come to resemble the nature of our dominating *thoughts*.

Thought is the only power that can systematically organize, accumulate and assemble facts and materials according to a definite plan. A flowing river can assemble dirt and build land, and a storm can gather and assemble sticks into a shapeless mass of debris, but neither storms nor river can *think;* therefore, the materials which they assemble are not assembled in organized, definite form.

Man, alone, has the power to transform his *thoughts* into physical reality; man, alone, can dream and make his dreams come true.

Man has the power to create ideals and rise to their attainment.

How did it happen that man is the only creature on earth that knows how to use the power of *thought?* It "happened" because man is the apex of the pyramid of evolution, the product of millions of years of struggle during which man has risen above the other creatures of the earth *as the result of his own thoughts and their effects upon himself.*

Just when, where and how the first rays of *thought* began to flow into man's brain no one knows, but we all know that *thought* is the power which distinguishes man from all other creatures; likewise, we all know that *thought* is the power that has enabled man to lift himself above all other creatures.

No one knows the limitations of the power of *thought,* or whether or not it has any limitations. Whatever man *believes* he can do he eventually does. But a few generations back the more imaginative writers dared to write of the "horseless carriage," and lo!

it became a reality and is now a common vehicle. Through the evolutionary power of *thought* the hopes and ambitions of one generation become a reality in the next.

The power of *thought* has been given the dominating position throughout this course, for the reason that it belongs in that position. Man's dominating position in the world is the direct result of *thought*, and it must be this power that you, as an individual, will use in the attainment of *success*, no matter what may be your idea of what represents *success*.

You have now arrived at the point at which you should take inventory of yourself for the purpose of ascertaining what qualities you need to give you a well balanced and rounded out personality.

Fifteen major factors entered into the building of this course. Analyze yourself carefully, with the assistance of one or more other persons if you feel that you need it, for the purpose of ascertaining in which of the fifteen factors of this course you are the weakest, and then concentrate your efforts upon those particular lessons until you have fully developed those factors which they represent.

MASTERY of the Fifteen Laws of Success is the equivalent of an insurance policy against failure.

—*Samuel Gompers.*

INDECISION
An After-the-Lesson Visit With the Author

TIME!

Procrastination robs you of opportunity. It is a significant fact that no great leader was ever known to procrastinate. You are fortunate if AMBITION drives you into action, never permitting you to falter or turn back, once you have rendered a DECISION to go forward. Second by second, as the clock ticks off the distance TIME is running a race with YOU. Delay means defeat, because no man may ever make up a second of lost TIME. TIME is a master worker which heals the wounds of failure and disappointment and rights all wrongs and turns all mistakes into capital, but, it favors only those who kill off procrastination and remain in ACTION when decisions are to made.

Life is a great checker-board. The player opposite you is TIME.

If you hesitate you will be wiped off the board. If you keep moving you may win. The only real capital is TIME, but it is capital only when used.

You may be shocked if you keep accurate account of the TIME you waste in a single day. Take a look at the picture above if you wish to know the fate of all who play carelessly with TIME.

THE picture at top of previous page tells a true story of one of the chief causes of FAILURE!

One of the players is "TIME" and the other is Mr. Average Man; let us call him YOU.

Move by move Time has wiped off Mr. Average Man's men until he is finally cornered, where Time will get him, no matter which way he moves. IN-DECISION has driven him into the corner.

.   .   .   .   .   .

Ask any well informed salesman and he will tell you that indecision is the outstanding weakness of the majority of people. Every salesman is familiar with that time-worn alibi, "I will think it over," which is the last trench-line of defense of those who have not the courage to say either yes or no. Like the player in the picture above, they cannot decide which way to move. Meanwhile, Time forces them into a corner where they can't move.

The great leaders of the world were men and women of quick decision.

General Grant had but little to commend him as an able General except the quality of firm decision, but this was sufficient to offset all of his weaknesses. The whole story of his military success may be gathered from his reply to his critics when he said "We will fight it out along these lines if it takes all summer."

When Napoleon reached a decision to move his armies in a given direction, he permitted nothing to cause him to change that decision. If his line of march brought his soldiers to a ditch, dug by his opponents to stop him, he would give the order to charge the ditch until it had been filled with dead men and horses sufficient to bridge it.

The suspense of indecision drives millions of people to failure. A condemned man once said that the thought of his approaching execution was not so terrifying, once he had reached the decision in his own mind to accept the inevitable.

Lack of decision is the chief stumbling block of all revival meeting workers. Their entire work is to get men and women to reach a decision in their own minds to accept a given religious tenet. Billy Sunday once said, "Indecision is the devil's favorite tool."

.   .   .   .

Andrew Carnegie visualized a great steel industry, but that industry would not be what it is today had he not reached a decision in his own mind to transform his vision into reality.

James J. Hill saw, in his mind's eye, a great transcontinental railway system, but that railroad never would have become a reality had he not reached a decision to start the project.

Imagination, alone, is not enough to insure success.

Millions of people have imagination and build plans that would easily bring them both fame and fortune, but those plans never reach the DECISION stage.

Samuel Insul was an ordinary stenographer, in the employ of Thomas A. Edison. Through the aid of his imagination he saw the great commercial possibilities of electricity. But, he did more than see the possibilities—he reached a decision to transform the mere possibilities into realities, and today he is a multimillionaire electric light plant operator.

Demosthenes was a poor Greek lad who had a strong desire to be a great public speaker. Nothing unusual about that; others have "desired" this and similar ability without living to see their desires realized. But, Demosthenes added DECISION to DESIRE, and, despite the fact that he was a stammerer he mastered this handicap and made himself one of the great orators of the world.

Martin W. Littleton was a poor lad who never saw the inside of a school house until he was past twelve years of age. His father took him to hear a great lawyer defend a murderer, in one of the southern cities. The speech made such a profound impression on the lad's mind that he grabbed his father by the hand and said, "Father, one of these days I am going to become the ablest lawyer in America."

That was a DEFINITE DECISION!

Today Martin W. Littleton accepts no fee under $50,000.00, and it is said that he is kept busy all the time. He became an able lawyer because he reached a DECISION to do so.

Edwin C. Barnes reached a DECISION in his own mind to become the partner of Thomas A. Edison. Handicapped by lack of schooling, without money to pay his railroad fare, and with no influential friends to introduce him to Mr. Edison, young Barnes made his way to East Orange on a freight car and so thoroughly sold himself to Mr. Edison that he got his opportunity which led to a partnership. Today, just twenty years since that decision was reached, Mr.

Barnes lives at Bradenton, Florida, retired, with all
the money he needs.

Men of decision usually get all that they go after!

.   .   .   .

Well within the memory of this writer a little group
of men met at Westerville, Ohio, and organized what
they called the Anti-Saloon League.   Saloon men
treated them as a joke.   People, generally, made fun
of them.   But, they had reached a decision.

That decision was so pronounced that it finally
drove the powerful saloon men into the corner.

William Wrigley, Jr., reached a decision to devote
his entire business career to the manufacture and sale
of a five-cent package of chewing gum.   He has made
that decision bring him financial returns running into
millions of dollars a year.

Henry Ford reached a decision to manufacture and
sell a popular priced automobile that would be within
the means of all who wished to own it.   That decision
has made Ford the most powerful man on earth and
brought travel opportunity to millions of people.

All these men had two outstanding qualities: A
DEFINITE PURPOSE and a firm DECISION to
transform that purpose into reality.

.   .   .   .

The man of DECISION gets that which he goes
after, no matter how long it takes, or how difficult the
task.   An able salesman wanted to meet a Cleveland
banker.   The banker would not see him.   One morning this salesman waited near the banker's house until
he saw him get into his automobile and start down

town. Watching his opportunity, the salesman drove his own automobile into the banker's, causing slight damage to the automobile. Alighting from his own car, he handed the banker his card, expressed regret on account of the damage done, but promised the banker a new car exactly like the one that had been damaged. That afternoon a new car was delivered to the banker, and out of that transaction grew a friendship that terminated, finally, in a business partnership which still exists.

The man of DECISION cannot be stopped!

The man of INDECISION cannot be started! Take your own choice.

> "Behind him lay the gray Azores,
> Behind the Gates of Hercules;
> Before him not the ghosts of shores;
> Before him only shoreless seas.
> The good mate said: 'Now must we pray,
> For lo! the very stars are gone.
> Brave Adm'r'l, speak; what shall I say?'
> 'Why, say: "Sail on and on!" ' "

When Columbus began his famous voyage he made one of the most far-reaching DECISIONS in the history of mankind. Had he not remained firm on that decision the freedom of America, as we know it today, would never have been known.

Take notice of those about you and observe this significant fact—THAT THE SUCCESSFUL MEN AND WOMEN ARE THOSE WHO REACH DECISIONS QUICKLY AND THEN STAND FIRMLY BY THOSE DECISIONS AFTER THEY ARE MADE.

If you are one of those who make up their minds today and change them again tomorrow you are doomed to failure. If you are not sure which way to move it is better to shut your eyes and move in the dark than to remain still and make no move at all.

The world will forgive you if you make mistakes, but it will never forgive you if you make no DE-CISIONS, because it will never hear of you outside of the community in which you live.

No matter who you are or what may be your life-work, you are playing checkers with TIME! It is always your next move. Move with quick DECISION and Time will favor you. Stand still and Time will wipe you off the board.

You cannot always make the right move, but, if you make enough moves you may take advantage of the law of averages and pile up a creditable score before the great game of LIFE is ended.